Excel® 2013
IN DEPTH

Bill Jelen
MrExcel

que®

800 East 96th Street,
Indianapolis, Indiana 46240 USA

EXCEL® 2013 IN DEPTH

Copyright © 2013 by Que Publishing

ISBN-13: 978-0-7897-4857-7

ISBN-10: 0-7897-4857-6

Library of Congress Cataloging-in-Publication data is on file.

Printed in the United States of America

First Printing: January 2013

Trademarks

All terms mentioned in this book that are known to be trademarks or service marks have been appropriately capitalized. Que Publishing cannot attest to the accuracy of this information. Use of a term in this book should not be regarded as affecting the validity of any trademark or service mark.

Excel is a registered trademark of Microsoft Corporation.

Warning and Disclaimer

Every effort has been made to make this book as complete and as accurate as possible, but no warranty or fitness is implied. The information provided is on an "as is" basis. The author and the publisher shall have neither liability nor responsibility to any person or entity with respect to any loss or damages arising from the information contained in this book.

Bulk Sales

Que Publishing offers excellent discounts on this book when ordered in quantity for bulk purchases or special sales. For more information, please contact

U.S. Corporate and Government Sales

1-800-382-3419

corpsales@pearsontechgroup.com

For sales outside the United States, please contact

International Sales

international@pearsoned.com

Editor-in-Chief
Greg Wiegand

Executive Editor
Loretta Yates

Development Editor
Charlotte Kughen

Managing Editor
Sandra Schroeder

Senior Project Editor
Tonya Simpson

Copy Editor
Bart Reed

Indexer
Brad Herriman

Proofreader
Dan Knott

Technical Editor
Bob Umlas

Publishing Coordinator
Cindy Teeters

Book Designer
Anne Jones

Compositor
Bumpy Design

CONTENTS AT A GLANCE

TABLE OF CONTENTS

ABOUT THE AUTHOR

Bill Jelen, Excel MVP and the host of MrExcel.com, has been using spreadsheets since 1985, and he launched the MrExcel.com website in 1998. Bill was a regular guest on *Call for Help* with Leo Laporte and has produced more than 1,500 episodes of his daily video podcast, Learn Excel from MrExcel. He is the author of 36 books about Microsoft Excel, writes the monthly Excel column for *Strategic Finance* magazine, and his Excel tips appear regularly in the CFO Excel Pro Newsletter and *CFO* magazine. Before founding MrExcel.com, Bill Jelen spent 12 years in the trenches— working as a financial analyst for finance, marketing, accounting, and operations departments of a $500 million public company. He lives near Akron, Ohio with his wife, Mary Ellen.

Dedication

To Max Mahoney

Acknowledgments

Thanks to all the Excel project managers who were happy to take the time to discuss the how or why behind a feature. At various times, Keyur Patel, Chris Doan, Igor Peev, Nick Chiang, Michael Herman, Chad Rothschiller, Dan Battigan, Melissa MacBeth, Diego Oppenheimer, and Scott Ruble pitched in to help with a particular issue.

Kari Finn, Melissa Travers, Joe Camp, and Anneliese Wirth at the MVP team and Office Online team are true gems.

Other Excel MVPs often offered their take on a potential bug. I could send a group email over a weekend and someone like Kevin Jones, Zack Baresse, Ken Puls, Andy Pope, Mike Alexander, Tom Urtis, Debra Dalgleish, or Ingeborg Hawighorst would usually respond. I particularly loved launching a missive just after the Microsoft crew in Building 36 went home on Friday evening, knowing they would return on Monday morning with 40 or 50 responses to the conversation. Without any Excel project managers to temper the discussion, we would often have designed massive improvements that we would have liked to have implemented in Excel. Someone would show up on Monday and tell us why that could never be done.

I've learned that when writing a 1,100-page book, there is not much time for anything else. Thanks to Tracy Syrstad, Barb Jelen, and Scott Pierson for keeping MrExcel running while I wrote. As always, thanks to the hundreds of people answering 30,000 Excel questions a year at the MrExcel message board. Thanks to Wei Jiang and Jake Hildebrand for their programming-expertise.

At Pearson, Loretta Yates is an awesome acquisitions editor. If you have ever written a book for any other publisher, you are missing out by not working with Loretta Yates. Bob Umlas is the smartest Excel guy that I know, and I am thrilled to have him as the technical editor for this book. Thanks to Charlotte Kughen, Tonya Simpson, and Bart Reed for getting this book through the editing process.

Zeke Jelen asked me to mention that Zeke is awesome. He kept joking that he was going to randomly type that sentence somewhere in the book. I hope he didn't—or I hope the editors catch it. Mary Ellen Jelen plays the important role of brandishing the whip. If lunch time came around and I was not well on my way to the 22.3 pages I needed to write that day, she would jokingly, but pointedly, remind me to get to work.

WE WANT TO HEAR FROM YOU!

As the reader of this book, *you* are our most important critic and commentator. We value your opinion and want to know what we're doing right, what we could do better, what areas you'd like to see us publish in, and any other words of wisdom you're willing to pass our way.

We welcome your comments. You can email or write to let us know what you did or didn't like about this book—as well as what we can do to make our books better.

Please note that we cannot help you with technical problems related to the topic of this book.

When you write, please be sure to include this book's title and author as well as your name and email address. We will carefully review your comments and share them with the author and editors who worked on the book.

Email: feedback@quepublishing.com

Mail: Que Publishing
             ATTN: Reader Feedback
             800 East 96th Street
             Indianapolis, IN 46240 USA

Reader Services

Visit our website and register this book at quepublishing.com/register for convenient access to any updates, downloads, or errata that might be available for this book.

INTRODUCTION

The introduction is always written last. After updating 38 chapters, I reflect back on the things that simply knocked my socks off in this version of Excel.

For people who are new to Excel:

- The Flash Fill and Quick Analysis features will be huge timesavers. Read about those features in Chapter 2, "Introducing Flash Fill and Quick Analysis."

- The new JavaScript Excel App Store holds a lot of promise. A few good apps are there right now. Microsoft is currently training more people to write apps, so hopefully by the time you are reading this, there will be many more apps. Read about apps in Chapter 5, "Extending Excel with Excel Apps and Add-Ins."

For people who use Excel every day:

- After you create a chart, a paintbrush icon appears to the right of the chart. That icon offers 10 different ways to format the chart. They are all fabulous. This comes close to my favorite new feature in Excel 2013. It certainly wins the award for "the feature that I wasn't expecting to be amazing, but it was." Read about the charting changes in Chapter 32, "Graphing Data Using Excel Charts."

- The Recommended Pivot Table feature is good—using this feature can trim the six clicks it usually takes to create a pivot table down to four clicks. Pivot tables are covered in Chapter 23, "Using Pivot Tables to Analyze Data."

- PowerPivot evolves and becomes part of the core of Excel in this release. I gushed about it in Excel 2010. It actually gets a little harder to use in this release, but that's okay. For more information, read Chapter 25, "Mashing Up Data with PowerPivot."

- Power View enables you to take data stored in the PowerPivot model and do some amazing visualizations. Maps, pictures, tables, dashboards, and more are discussed in Chapter 26, "Creating Interactive Dashboards with Power View or GeoFlow."

- The most improved award for this version goes to the Excel Web App team. Excel Web Apps break new ground, enabling you to conduct surveys online, turn boring web pages into interactive gems, and more. Sometimes, I don't know what to tweet. Now that I can share my favorite spreadsheets to Twitter and LinkedIn via the Web App, I might be posting more to social media. Read about Excel Web Apps in Chapter 37, "Excel Web App and Other Ways to Share Workbooks."

For Excel gurus:

- The new `WEBSERVICE` and `FILTERXML` functions for returning data from a web service will be put to good use. Read about them in Chapter 12, "Using Powerful Functions: Logical, Lookup, Web, and Database Functions."

Microsoft marketing will be crowing a lot about the new Start screen (Chapter 1, "Staying Connected Using Excel 2013") and Timelines (Chapter 24, "Using Slicers and Filtering a Pivot Table"). I cover them both but also tell you how to live without them.

How This Book Is Organized

The book is organized into the following parts:

- **Part I, "Mastering the New User Interface"**—This first part of the book shows you the ribbon, Flash Fill, the Quick Analysis, the big grid, and the new Excel App Store.

- **Past II, "Calculating with Excel"**—This part covers what Excel does best, from formulas to functions to linking.

- **Part III, "Business Intelligence"**—Sorting, filtering, subtotals, pivot tables. These are the tools of the Excel data analyst. Learn about these tools and the new PowerPivot add-in in Part III. The chapter on VBA macros is also in this part of the book.

- **Part IV, "Visual Presentation"**—This part covers charting, SmartArt, data visualizations, and picture tools. After you get done analyzing the data, a few features from this part will make your reports look good.

- **Part V, "Sharing Information"**—This part discusses printing and sharing your Excel workbooks by creating PDFs or publishing to the Web.

Conventions Used in This Book

The special conventions used throughout this book are designed to help you get the most from the book as well as Excel 2013.

Text Conventions

Different typefaces are used to convey various things throughout the book. They include those shown in Table I.1.

Table I.1 Typeface Conventions

Typeface	Description
Monospace	Screen messages and Excel formulas appear in monospace.
Italic	New terminology appears in *italic*.
Bold	References to text you should type appear in **bold**.

Ribbon names, dialog names, and dialog elements are capitalized in this book (for example, Add Formatting Rule dialog, Home ribbon tab).

In this book, key combinations are represented with a plus sign. If the action you need to take is to press the Ctrl key and the T key simultaneously, the text tells you to press Ctrl+T.

There were not many changes from Excel 97 to Excel 2000 to Excel 2002 to Excel 2003. Most people upgrading to Excel 2013 will be coming from one of these versions of Excel. I collectively refer to these versions as "legacy versions of Excel."

Special Elements

Throughout this book, you'll find tips, notes, cautions, cross-references, case studies, Excel in Practice boxes, sidebars, and Troubleshooting Tip boxes. These elements provide a variety of information, ranging from warnings you shouldn't miss to ancillary information that will enrich your Excel experience but isn't required reading.

 Tip
Tips point out special features, quirks, or software tricks that will help you increase your productivity with Excel 2013.

 Note
Notes contain extra information or alternative techniques for performing tasks.

 Caution
Cautions call out potential gotchas.

 See Chapter 99 for more information is a cross-reference to another section or chapter in this book.

Case Study: Other Elements

Sections such as Case Study, Excel in Practice, and Troubleshooting Tips are set off in boxes such as this one:

- Case Studies walk you through the steps to complete a task.
- Excel in Practice boxes walk through real-life problems in Excel.
- Troubleshooting Tip boxes walk you through steps to avoid certain problems or explain how to react when certain problems occur.

Sidebars

Historical glimpses and other information that is not critical to your understanding appear as sidebars. I imagine that if the Cliff Clavin character from *Cheers* knew a lot about Excel, these would be the kinds of things he would write.

STAYING CONNECTED USING EXCEL 2013

The entire Excel installation and startup experience feels different in Office 2013. You might have purchased Office 2013 on a DVD at a store, but it is just as likely that you purchased Office online and were able to start using Excel while Office 2013 was still downloading. You might even be renting Office 365 on a month-to-month basis, where the Click-to-Run option will download a version of Office 2013 wherever you happen to sign in.

After Office installs, you are asked to sign in to a Windows Live account, which facilitates saving workbooks to the cloud. After that, you can connect Excel to many online accounts, such as Twitter, Flickr, YouTube, and more.

Every time you start Excel, you will be confronted with a colorful Start screen offering many built-in templates. But let's start with the best new feature—finally being able to use two monitors to show two different workbooks in the same instance of Excel.

Displaying Two Workbooks on Two Monitors

Having two monitors is common in the workplace today. Tens of millions of people have been trying to use Excel across a two-monitor setup—and it's never pretty. Finally, in Excel 2013, it is easy to put one workbook on the left monitor and another workbook on the right monitor. Each workbook has a ribbon, formula bar, status bar, and a set of Window controls (see Figure 1.1).

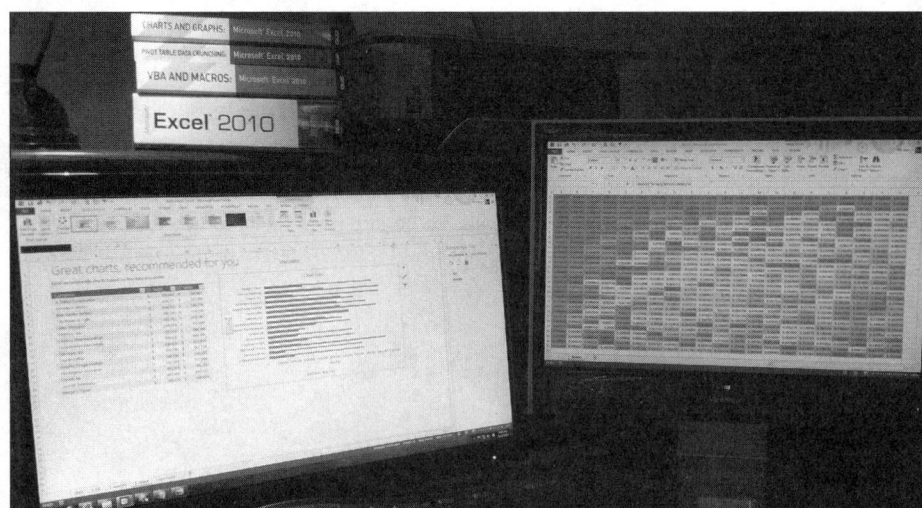

Figure 1.1
You can eas-
ily show two
workbooks on
two different
monitors.

Both workbooks will be running in a single instance of Excel. That means you can easily copy and paste between the two workbooks. You can switch between them with Ctrl+Tab. This is an improvement over Excel 2010, in which workbooks had to be running in separate instances of Excel in order to appear on different monitors.

The change is due to the transition from MDI (Multiple Document Interface) to SDI (Single Document Interface).

Understanding the Dark Side of SDI

Slowly, the Office applications have been transitioning from MDI to SDI. Word switched in Office 2007. PowerPivot switched in Office 2010. Now, Excel is transitioning in Office 2013. Although many people will love being able to display two screens on two monitors, there are a few instances where using Excel will become more difficult.

Several add-ins are available for Excel. An *add-in* is actually a hidden Excel workbook with some VBA macro code inside. Before, both the add-in and the data workbook shared the same Excel ribbon and window in Excel. The code in the add-in worked well. Now, the code in the add-in has to talk to another Excel window. There are ways to do this, but they aren't perfect. For example, consider this scenario:

1. You have Workbook A open.

2. You invoke a command from Add-In B.

3. Provided that Add-In B was properly rewritten for Excel 2013, it can successfully display a dialog on top of Workbook A.

4. Your phone rings, and you have to switch over to a browser or Word or any other program to answer a question.

5. When you reactivate Workbook A, the dialog from Add-In B is no longer visible. The Excel icon in the taskbar starts flashing to alert you that something is amiss. When you click the flashing Excel icon, you see the dialog from Add-In B.

This scenario happens to me all the time, and it is horribly frustrating. In fact, it happened when I tried to take a screenshot of the dialog from step 3, and I had to switch from Excel to the WinSnap screenshot-capture program. It might happen that you do not frequently switch to other applications while a dialog is displayed, so this might not be annoying to you. Time will tell.

The other frustration is trying to arrange many workbooks side by side. Back in Excel 2010, you could easily have 12 workbooks tiled under a single ribbon in a single window (see Figure 1.2). Some people love to tile many workbooks in a visible window. If you like to have multiple workbooks open, you will now find that you have a ribbon and Window controls for each workbook.

Figure 1.2
In Excel 2010, you could easily tile many workbooks in a single Excel application window.

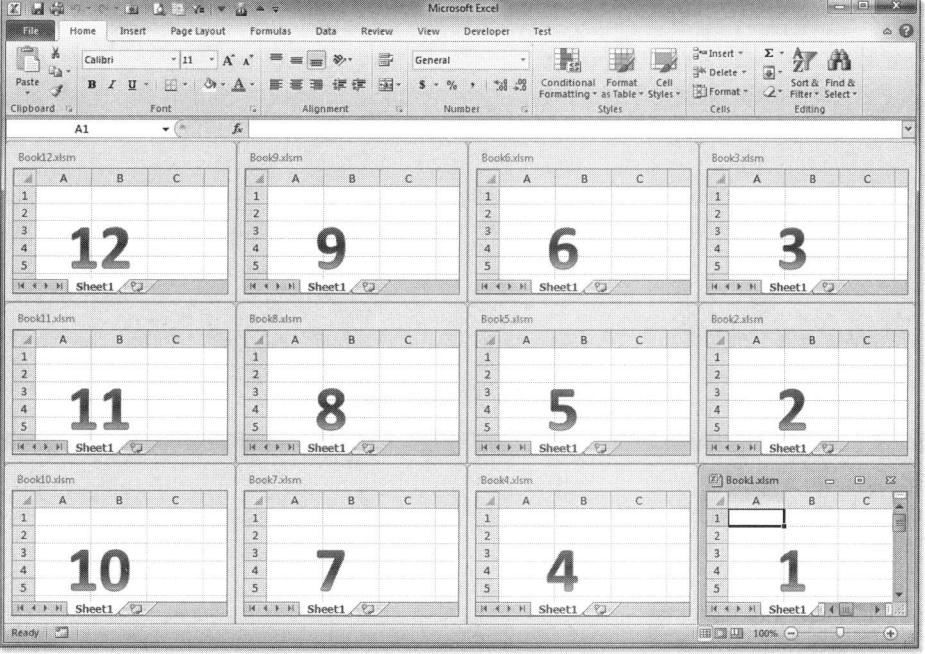

Figure 1.3 shows the same 12 workbooks in Excel 2013. You can see 12 status bars, 12 ribbons, and 12 title bars.

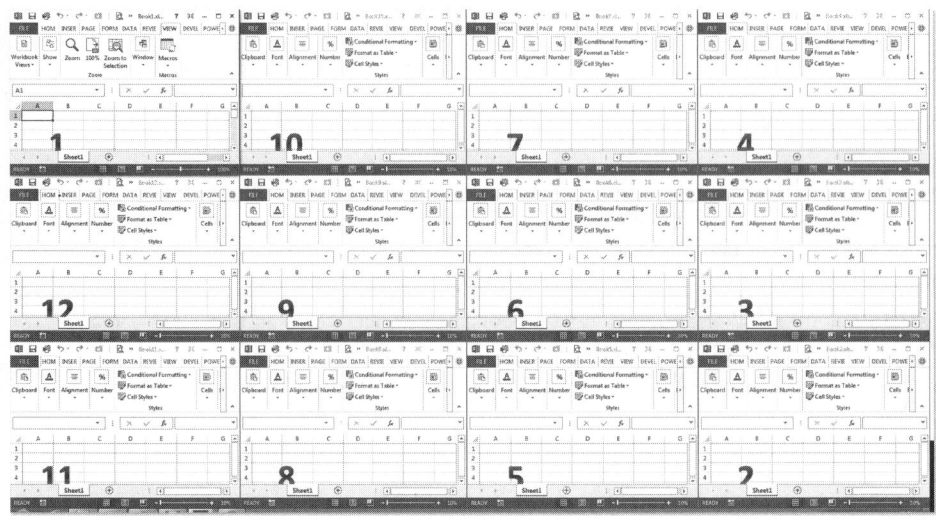

Figure 1.3
In Excel 2013, each workbook has a ribbon and other controls.

Even if you minimize the ribbon in each of the 12 workbooks in Figure 1.3, you still end up with six cells per workbook instead of the 15 cells per workbook in Excel 2010 (see Figure 1.4). There is no "fix" or workaround for this. You are simply out of luck. The number of people who wanted Excel on two monitors outnumbered the people who want 12 Excel workbooks in a single window. If you still want to tile workbooks like in Figure 1.2, you need to keep Excel 2010 on your machine.

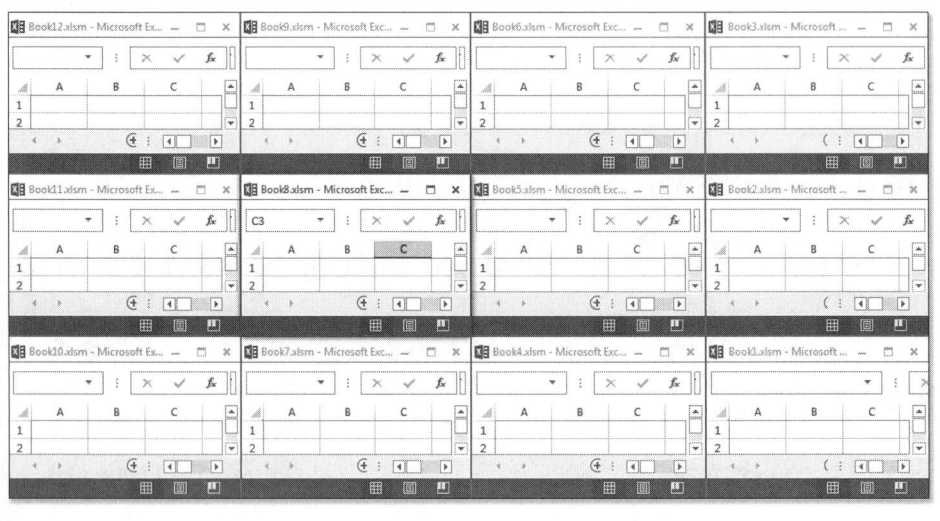

Figure 1.4
After clicking Minimize the Ribbon in each workbook, you still have more Excel controls visible than actual cells.

Forcing Excel to Open in a New Instance

There might be times when you want Excel to open in a separate instance. For example, you might have a macro in Workbook A that will run for an hour. You would like to continue to work in Workbook B while the macro is running in Workbook A.

To open a second instance of Excel 2013, go to the Start menu. Before you click the icon for Excel 2013, hold down the Alt key. As Excel starts to open, you get the message shown in Figure 1.5. Choose Yes to create a second instance of Excel.

Figure 1.5
Hold down Alt while opening Excel to force a separate instance of Excel.

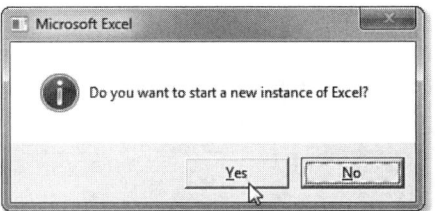

Signing In to Excel 2013

If you use Hotmail, SkyDrive, Xbox LIVE, or have a Windows Phone, you already have a Microsoft account. If you don't have an account, you will want to visit https://signup.live.com to get a free account before opening Excel the first time.

To get an account, you provide your name, birthdate, gender, an email address, and password. You can optionally fill out your profile, including a picture of yourself.

When you sign in to Office 2013 from any computer, your default settings transfer to the new computer.

Introducing the Excel 2013 Start Screen

For the last 28 years, Microsoft Excel opened to a big, empty grid. The Excel team decided that this was too intimidating for people new to Excel. Excel 2013 now opens to the Start screen, as shown in Figure 1.6.

Notice these elements of the start Screen:

- In the top right, you see your picture and Windows sign-in information. This lets you know that you are signed in as yourself.

- In the left panel, you see recent Excel files opened on this computer, or opened from SkyDrive or SharePoint 365 from any computer where you were signed in with the same account.

- In the bottom left, you have a link to display the File Open dialog to open a file that is not in the list.

Figure 1.6
When you
open Excel
2013, you
see the start
Screen.

- You have a large tile for a blank workbook.

- You have a tile for Take a Tour. This template includes information on Flash Fill, Quick Analysis, and Recommended Charts.

- Depending on your screen resolution, you have 20 or more very colorful tiles showing things you can do in Excel, such as keep inventory, track a budget, track wedding invitations, convert currency, and more.

- In the top of the panel, you see a search box where you can search for other templates online.

- You can switch from Featured templates to Personal templates in order to see any templates stored on your computer.

One member of the Excel team introduced the Start screen by saying he initially disliked it, but soon realized that he could predict where his mouse should be headed to open a certain recent workbook. I don't see this as a benefit. I rarely go back and process a workbook that I recently processed. I am always moving forward, needing to open another workbook in the folder. I think the Recent Places pane in Excel 2010 is superior to Recent Files. I find Excel 2013 now putting Recent Files in the forefront and making me spend several clicks to get to Recent Places.

Revealing the Fatal Flaw of the Start Screen

The Start screen is rarely useful to me. I never use any of the templates from Office Online. The Recent list along the left side is Recent Files instead of the more useful Recent Places. The only thing I do with the Start screen is to select Blank Workbook. (See Figure 1.7.)

Figure 1.7
This tile says "Blank Workbook," but it does not go through the same logic as pressing Ctrl+N.

Blank workbook

However, this Blank Workbook is not the same Blank Workbook you get when you open Excel 97 through Excel 2010. When you press Ctrl+N in Excel 2010, the program goes through a fairly complicated process. It searches the startup location and the alternate startup location for a file called Book.xltx, Book.xltm, or Book.xltb. If it finds one of these files in one of these locations, Excel 2010 opens that workbook and presents it as a blank workbook. This enables you to store your favorite settings in Book.xltx, and then every new book has those settings in the future.

The Blank Workbook tile in the Start screen does not follow this logic. It always opens a workbook with no default settings. After I realized that this Blank Workbook would not load my default settings, I gave up and abandoned the Start screen.

Note

I complained to the Excel team about this oversight of the Blank Workbook tile failing to load from Book.xltx. They responded that millions of people have used Excel 2007 and Excel 2010, and no one was complaining about the Blank Workbook tile on the New... panel. The root cause of the problem goes back even further. From Excel 1 through Excel 2003, there was an icon on the toolbar for "New." There was also a command on the File menu for "New...." Believe it or not, "New" and "New..." are very different things. "New" led to the logic that would load the default Book.xlt workbook, whereas "New..." led to a screen where you ended up with a workbook that did not contain your defaults. Back in Excel 2003, it was one click to select "New" and four clicks to go through File, New... Blank Workbook, OK. Therefore, most people used "New" and everything was fine.

Starting in Excel 2007, "New" was banished to the "Commands Not in the Ribbon" list of icons you could add to the Quick Access Toolbar and "New..." was pushed to the forefront. For people who understood the difference, they either switched to Ctrl+N or added "New" to the Quick Access Toolbar. Plus, just opening Excel 2007 or Excel 2010 automatically invoked the Ctrl+N version of "New" instead of "New...." Therefore, very few people ever encountered "New..." in Excel 2007 or Excel 2010. Hence, no one complained. Now, with the Start screen, people are going to encounter "New..." all the time, and they are going to be unhappy about it.

Dismissing the Start Screen with the Escape Key

The fastest way to kill the Start screen and to open a blank "New" workbook with your default settings is to simply press the Esc key when you see the Start Screen. This forces Excel into the Ctrl+N logic and your default Book.xltx file is opened.

Dismissing the Start Screen Permanently

If you decide that you never need to see the Start screen, open any workbook in Excel. Choose File, Options. The first category displayed is the General tab. At the bottom of the tab, unselect Show the Start screen When This Application Starts. (see Figure 1.8)

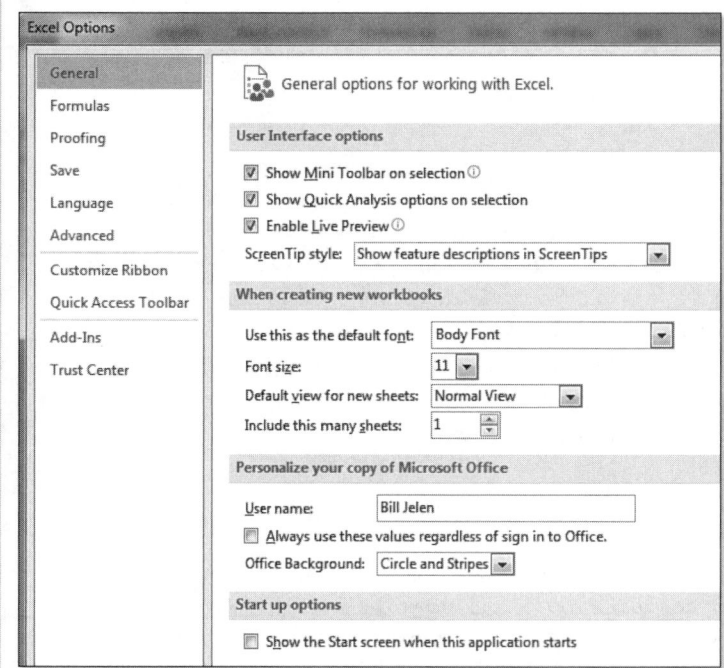

Figure 1.8
Turn off the Start screen.

Using the Cloud for Storage and More

With your Windows Live account, you automatically get access to an 8GB account on the SkyDrive. When you go to the File Open menu or File Save As menu, you first have to choose if you want to save to the SkyDrive, SharePoint, or your computer. After you make that first choice, you then can browse to the folders and select a file.

If you save to the SkyDrive from a work computer and then later open Excel 2013 on a home computer, the file saved to the SkyDrive appears in your Recent Files list on the other computer. There is no doubt that this is convenient and easier than carrying a flash drive back and forth. But are you ready to rely on the cloud for saving all of your Excel files?

Relying On the Cloud

When the notion of cloud computing first came up, I thought it was crazy. Why would anyone ever store files over the Internet? What if you had a big important meeting in a few minutes and the connection to the Internet goes down? It just seemed dangerous.

However, about a year ago, I began to rely on the cloud for email. I enjoy the freedom of check-ing email on my phone, tablet, home desktop, and office desktop. I don't do major emailing on the phone, but I can go through and delete emails so that I can get directly to work when I get to the desktop computer. Before making this switch, I would transfer a 1.5GB Outlook .OST file from a desktop to a laptop whenever I traveled. Now, I can sign in anywhere and get to my email. And, if the Internet connection goes down, I can switch to the phone or to the wireless access card to get to the email on the cloud. Bottom line: I would never go back to a client-based email program.

I am still not convinced about storing my Excel files on the cloud. Unlike email headers, which are tiny, Excel files can be huge. It takes a noticeable amount of time to save to and load from the cloud. I cannot picture ever editing Excel files on the phone, and the jury remains out on using Excel RT on the tablet. My primary storage is still on the computer. If I have to take a file home, then I save to the SkyDrive instead of copying to a USB flash drive.

Linking Excel to Various Accounts

Open Excel to a blank or any workbook, and then choose, File, Account. You see your Microsoft account at the top of the screen. You can use the Add a Service drop-down to connect Excel to vari-ous services. In Figure 1.9, you see that I connected to every possible service that I could.

Figure 1.9
Connect your Excel account to various services on the Account screen.

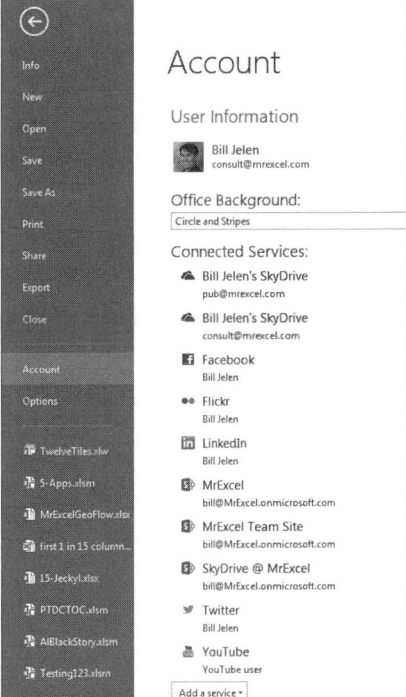

These services fall into three broad categories:

- **Saving to the cloud**—Use SkyDrive or SharePoint 365 accounts to enable saving to the cloud.

- **Sourcing images for your workbooks**—The new Insert, Online Pictures command shows you pictures from Flickr or from your SkyDrive (see Figure 1.10). Connecting to YouTube has no effect in Excel, but it provides functionality in PowerPoint when you use Insert Video.

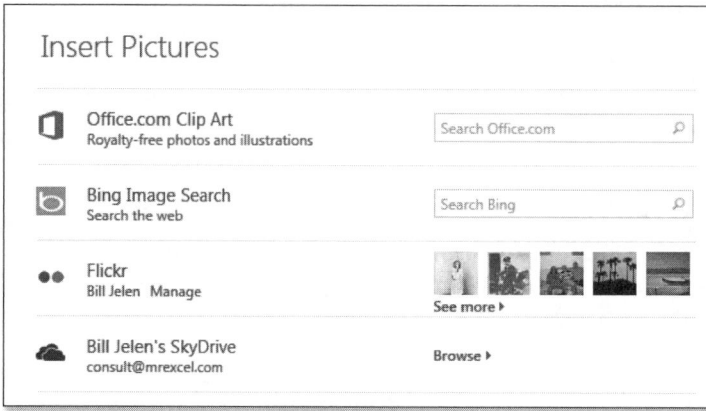

Figure 1.10
Connecting Excel to Flickr enables you to insert pictures from your Flickr account into Excel.

- **Publishing to social media**—After a workbook is saved to the SkyDrive, you can post workbooks to Facebook, LinkedIn, or Twitter using the File, Share, Post to Social Networks command (see Figure 1.11).

After you set up the link to the various accounts, you can forget about them.

Using the Open and Save As Panels

Excel 2013 took a giant leap backward with the Open and Save As processes. In Excel 2010, using the Recent Files icon in the Quick Access Toolbar would reveal a backstage view with a long list of recent workbooks and a long list of recent places. The places might be the last 25 folders where you accessed files. Think about the last 25 folders you've used. In my case, this represents three different book projects, a client directory, my desktop, the download folder, and the sample files folder from this past edition of this book. That list of 25 recent places covers 99% of the work that I could possibly do today.

Figure 1.11
Connecting
to Facebook,
Twitter, or
LinkedIn enables
you to share your
workbooks with
your social net-
working contacts.

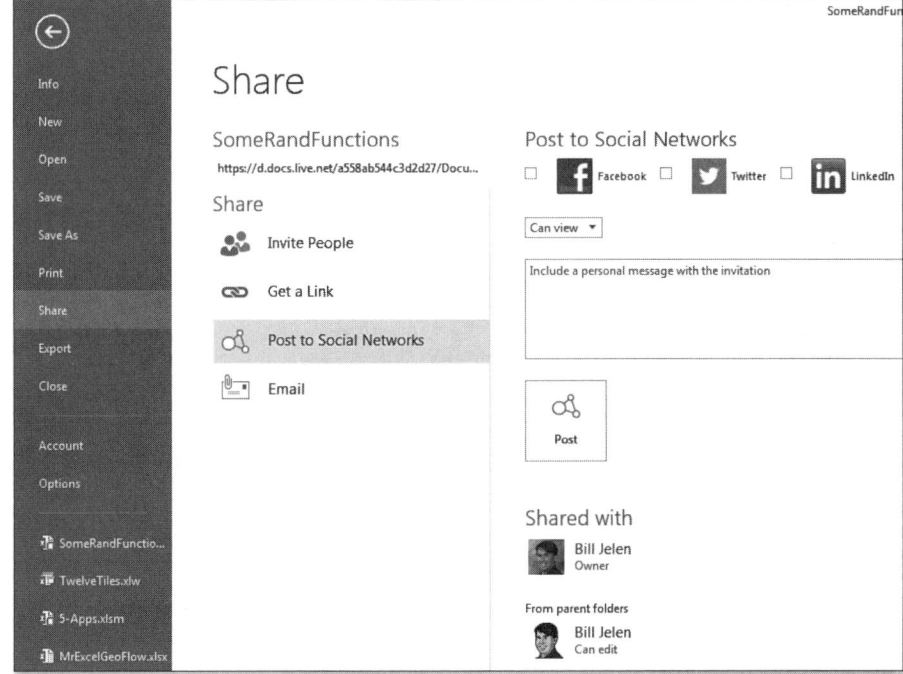

In Excel 2013, the Recent Places pane is gone and you start with Places and Recent Workbooks (see Figure 1.12). Unfortunately, Places is your SkyDrive, SharePoint, Computer, and Recent Workbooks. Because Recent Workbooks starts out selected, the right panel shows the last 25 workbooks you opened. As I like to say, I don't need to open the last 25 files that I finished. I need to open and work on other workbooks that are stored in the same folders as those files.

When you click Computer in the left panel, the right panel shows the last five Recent Folders. This is 80% worse than the Excel 2010 list of 25 recent folders (see Figure 1.13.)

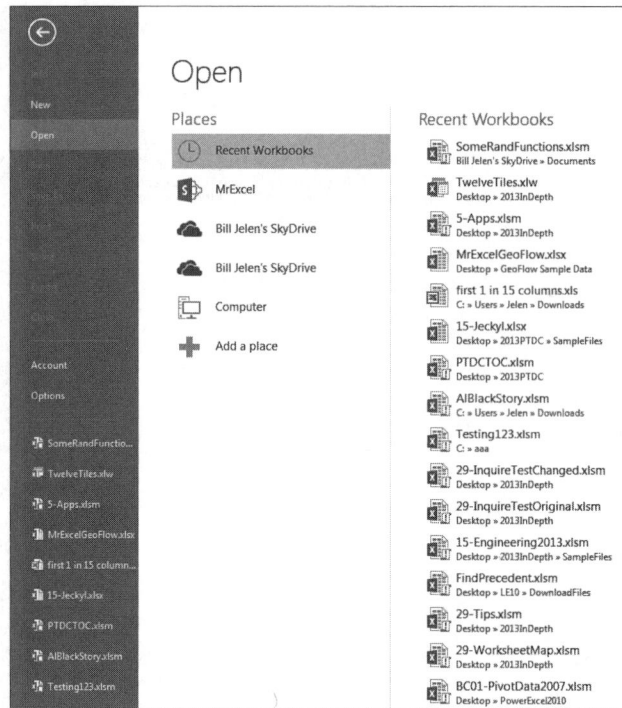

Figure 1.12
The fabulous Recent Folders pane in Excel 2010 is now the boring Places pane in Excel 2013.

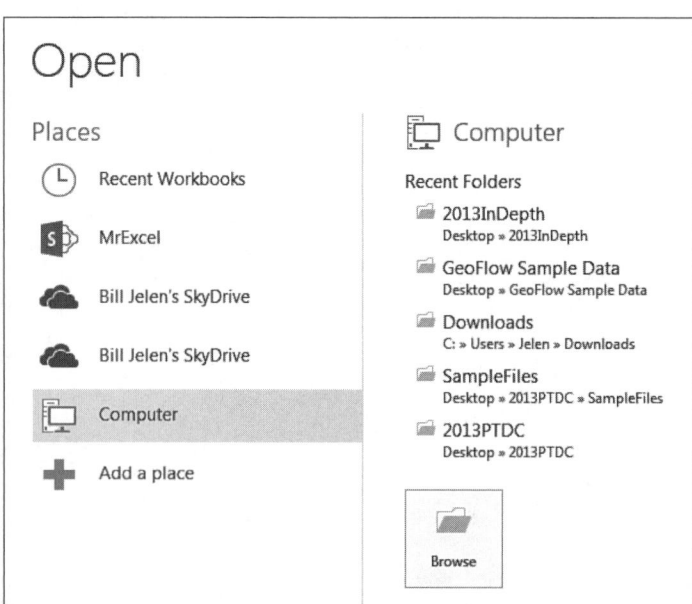

Figure 1.13
After an extra click on Computer in the left pane, you get this tiny list of recent folders.

If you click the Browse folder, you get to the traditional Open dialog shown in Figure 1.14.

The Save As command leads to the same irritating combination of places and a few recent folders (see Figure 1.15.)

Figure 1.14
If your folder is not listed in Recent Folders, click Browse to use the Open dialog.

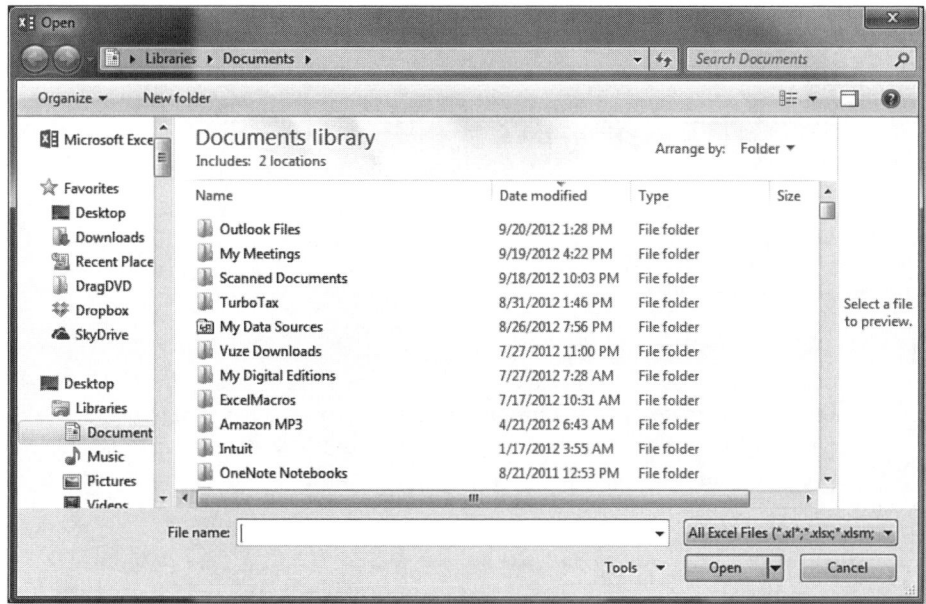

Figure 1.15
The Save As panel starts with Places on the left. Choose a place to see a too-short list of recent folders.

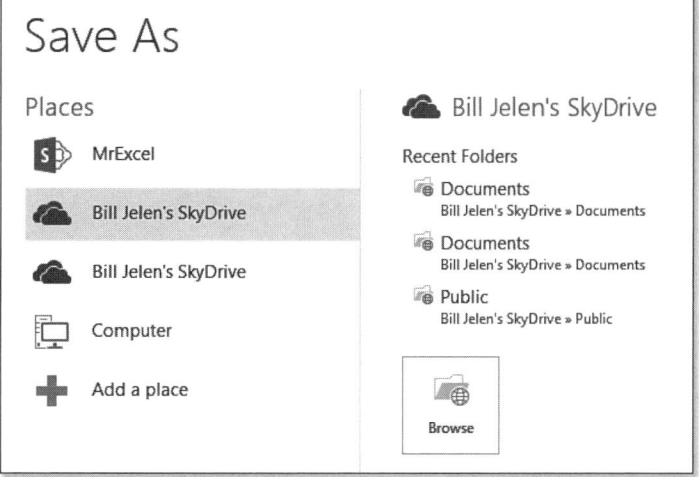

Note

Note that when you choose a place on the left, a set of bullet points at the bottom of the dialog tell you the benefits of the selected place. In Figure 1.16, the list shows that the SkyDrive is available on this device, offline, on other devices, and can be shared with others. When you choose Computer as the place, the options for Available on Other Devices and Can Be Shared with Others are grayed out.

About Bill Jelen's SkyDrive

* Available on this device
* Available offline
* Available on other devices
* Can be shared with others

Figure 1.16

An ad at the bottom of the screen sells you on the benefits of the SkyDrive.

You might wonder how a file saved to the SkyDrive can be available offline. To test this, I disconnected my computer from the Internet and tried to open a recent file from the SkyDrive. To my surprise, the file opened. However, a warning told me that I was viewing an "offline copy" that initially opened in read-only mode. (See Figure 1.17.)

| OFFLINE COPY | Workbook is in read-only mode. | Edit Workbook |

| B2 | ▾ | : | ✕ | ✓ | f_x | =RAND() |

▲	A	B	C	D	E	F	G
1							
2		0.72163	0.788622	0.945018	0.122824	0.625545	0.246732
3		0.14642	0.293007	0.544672	0.883071	0.362354	0.456443
4		0.176291	0.27961	0.130515	0.018909	0.851159	0.146298
5		0.694875	0.980173	0.488096	0.320628	0.944494	0.233082
6		0.730728	0.583878	0.948047	0.860364	0.300454	0.658712
7		0.638721	0.98875	0.720276	0.620892	0.981889	0.125876
8		0.176868	0.203973	0.190356	0.762046	0.938825	0.194737
9		0.68346	0.39664	0.367832	0.430739	0.614688	0.866269
10		0.252288	0.224298	0.195943	0.020802	0.084593	0.078204
11							

Figure 1.17

If you save the file to the SkyDrive from this computer, Excel creates a local copy for use if your Internet connection goes down.

The Info panel on the File menu tells the date and time of this cached copy of the data. It warns you that if someone edits the SkyDrive version from another computer, you won't have the latest changes. You can also click View Offline Files to see that the copy is stored in the Documents/SkyDrive folder (see Figure 1.18).

Figure 1.18
The Info pane provides a link to the folder where all cached SkyDrive workbooks are stored.

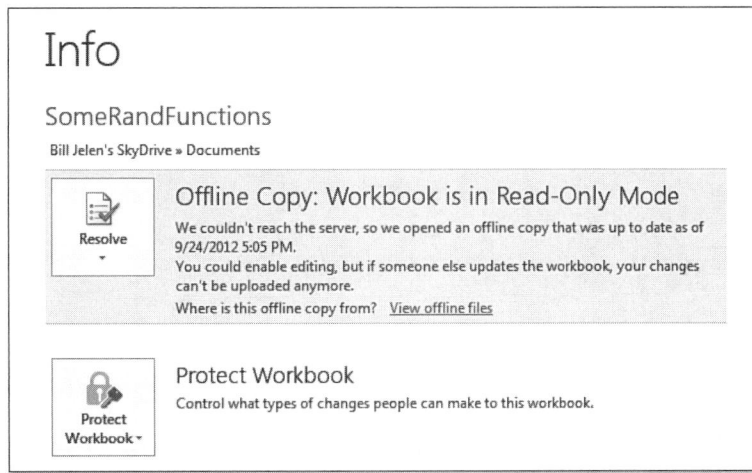

As shown in Figure 1.19, three options are available that might control how you interact with the SkyDrive. Go to File, Options, Save to access these new options:

- **Don't Show the Backstage When Opening or Saving Files**—This would take you immediately to the Open dialog when you press Ctrl+O or to the Save As dialog when you press Ctrl+S for an unsaved file.

- **Always Show "Sign In to SkyDrive" Location During Save**—If you are accessing your files from a public computer, you would want to force someone to re-enter the password for each save.

- **Save to Computer by Default**—When you use Ctrl+S, the Save dialog offers a folder on your computer instead of the SkyDrive.

Figure 1.19
New options deal with the SkyDrive.

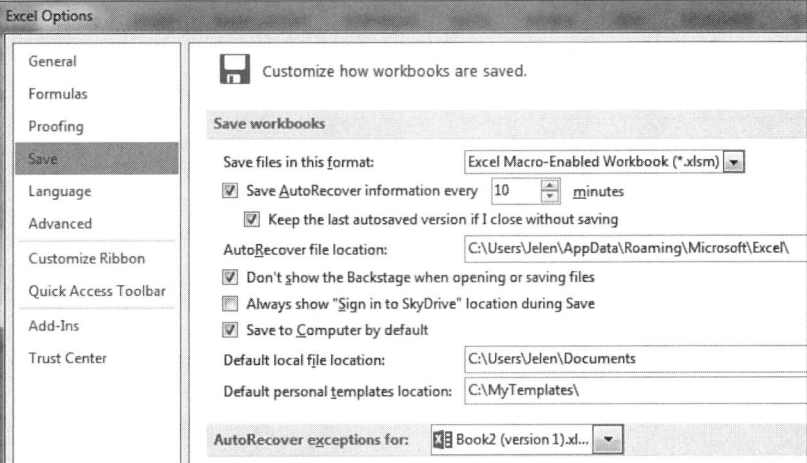

INTRODUCING FLASH FILL AND QUICK ANALYSIS

If you are overwhelmed by the many features in Excel, the new Quick Analysis provides an easy on-ramp to trying out formulas, charts, subtotals, and pivot tables. Many times, a person will ask how to do something in Excel. When he hears the answer is a pivot table, he shakes his head and says he was looking for something simpler. The Quick Analysis solves many problems without making you go through the steps to create a chart or a pivot table.

The Flash Fill feature saves you time when you are trying to reshape imperfect data. Many times, you get data from somewhere that isn't in the right format—the text is all caps, phone numbers appear without dashes, or a bunch of fields are jammed into a single column. By providing one or two examples of what you are trying to do, Flash Fill uses heuristics to make a correction of the data in an adjoining column.

Both of these features are new in Excel 2013.

Cleaning Data with Flash Fill

Say that you have data with first names in column A and last names in column B. The names are in uppercase. You would like to reshape the data so you have the full names in proper case.

If you have been using Excel for many years, you might instinctively think of the formula =PROPER(A2&" "&B2). Enter that formula in C2, copy down, copy, and paste values to solve the problem. Unfortunately, far too many people think that formula is too intimidating, and start simply typing the new data, as shown in Figure 2.1.

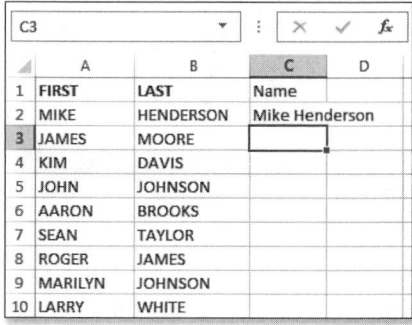

Figure 2.1
One solution to joining data is to start typing.

In Excel 2013, as soon as you type the first letter in the second cell, Excel springs into action and offers to fill the rest of the column for you (see Figure 2.2). Provided the preview looks right or even close, simply press Enter.

	A	B	C
1	FIRST	LAST	Name
2	MIKE	HENDERSON	Mike Henderso
3	JAMES	MOORE	James Moore
4	KIM	DAVIS	Kim Davis
5	JOHN	JOHNSON	John John
6	AARON	BROOKS	Aaron Bro
7	SEAN	TAYLOR	Sean Tayl
8	ROGER	JAMES	Roger Jam
9	MARILYN	JOHNSON	Marilyn Jo
10	LARRY	WHITE	Larry Whit
11	LORI	COLLINS	Lori Collin
12	CHRISTINE	LITTLE	Christine
13	DIANE	WILLIS	Diane Wil
14	STEVE	VASQUEZ	Steve Vas
15	DANIEL	RYAN	Daniel Rya
16	DIANA	CUNNINGHAM	Diana Cun
17	TAMMY	HICKS	Tammy Hi
18	GARY	ROMERO	Gary Rom
19	AMY	GARRETT	Amy Garre
20	LOUIS	GARRETT	Louis Garr
21	RANDY	WHEELER	Randy Wh
22	JAMES	HARRIS	James Har
23	GLORIA	BELL	Gloria Bel
24			

Figure 2.2
Type **J** in C3 and Excel offers to fill in the rest of the column.

In addition to filling the column, Excel provides two pieces of feedback. First, the status bar in the lower-left corner of the screen indicates that Flash Fill changed 21 cells (see Figure 2.3).

Figure 2.3
The status bar confirms that Flash Fill changed 21 cells.

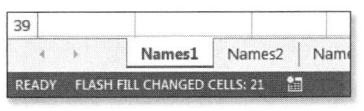

Second, a tiny on-grid Flash Fill drop-down icon appears next to the first changed cell (see Figure 2.4). Open the drop-down for choices such as Undo and Accept. You can also choose to select all changed cells or all unchanged cells. You find out more about unchanged cells in the next section.

Figure 2.4
The drop-down lets you undo or select the changed or unchanged cells.

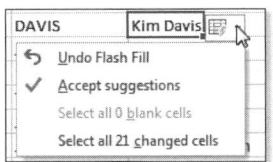

Excel easily recognizes all sorts of patterns. You could fill from "Mike", "Mike H.", or "HENDERSON, MIKE". Sometimes, Excel needs a bit more information. If you start with Mr. Mike Henderson in C2, nothing happens when you start to type **M** in C3. You have to type Mr. James Moore in C3. As soon as you type **M** in C4, Excel fills the column. However, Excel blindly uses Mr. for Marilyn, Lori, and Christine.

Coaching Flash Fill with a Second Example

That first Flash Fill example looks cool, right? In the world of imperfect data, things are not always so clear. In Figure 2.5, three people have been replaced by people with a single name. If your data includes Cher, Pele, or Sting, Excel doesn't know what to do.

Type **Mike H.** in C2, and then type **J** in C3. Excel sees that you are doing first name, last initial, and a period. The preview shows many names being filled in, as shown in Figure 2.5.

However, the status bar indicates "Flash Fill Blank Cells: 3 Flash Fill Changed Cells: 18." When there is missing data, such as no last name for Cher, Excel leaves column C blank (see Figure 2.6).

At this point, Excel is hoping you will provide a second example. Go to cell C5, type **Cher**, and press Enter. Excel now understands the rule for people without a last name. Excel fills in Sting in C10 and Pele in C15, as shown in Figure 2.7. The status bar indicates "Flash Fill Changed Cells: 2." Those two cells are automatically selected. You could change the font color to red and then sort or filter by color to inspect those changed cells.

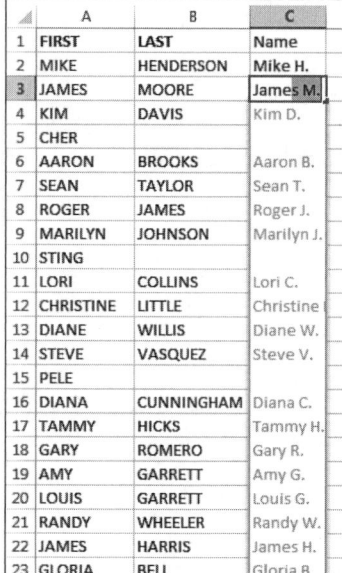

Figure 2.5
Excel understands the pattern and fills in many cells.

Figure 2.6
When Excel isn't sure, it leaves the cell blank.

Figure 2.7
Provide a second example for Flash Fill and it fills in the rows with missing data.

5	CHER		Cher
6	AARON	BROOKS	Aaron B.
7	SEAN	TAYLOR	Sean T.
8	ROGER	JAMES	Roger J.
9	MARILYN	JOHNSON	Marilyn J.
10	STING		Sting
11	LORI	COLLINS	Lori C.
12	CHRISTINE	LITTLE	Christine L.
13	DIANE	WILLIS	Diane W.
14	STEVE	VASQUEZ	Steve V.
15	PELE		Pele
16	DIANA	CUNNINGHAM	Diana C.
17	TAMMY	HICKS	Tammy H.
18	GARY	ROMERO	Gary R.
19	AMY	GARRETT	Amy G.
20	LOUIS	GARRETT	Louis G.
21	RANDY	WHEELER	Randy W.
22	JAMES	HARRIS	James H.
23	GLORIA	BELL	Gloria B.

Inserting New Characters in a Telephone Number

Flash Fill works great when you are formatting a telephone number. In Figure 2.8, the 10-digit phone numbers appear without parentheses or dashes in column B.

Insert a new column C. Type a heading in C1. Retype the first phone number in C2 as **(907) 555-2750**. As soon as you type the opening parenthesis in C3, Flash Fill offers to fill in the rest of the column (see Figure 2.8).

Figure 2.8
Excel inserts four new characters in a pattern in the phone number digits.

	A	B	C	D	E
1	NAME	PHONE	Telephone	LOCATION	DOB
2	KATHERINE BOWMAN	9075557250	(907) 555-7250	FAIRBANKS AK	19700305
3	CHARLES JONES	2055558215	(205) 555-8215	BIRMINGHAM AL	19501110
4	AMANDA FULLER	7025552947	(702) 555-2947	LAS VEGAS NV	19740327
5	LOUISE BAKER	3045557379	(304) 555-7379	WHEELING WV	19520623
6	CONNIE LANE	4845558146	(484) 555-8146	ALLENTOWN PA	19771102
7	DORIS CHAVEZ	8135553692	(813) 555-3692	TAMPA FL	19511106
8	JUDITH JOHNSON	6175552712	(617) 555-2712	BOSTON MA	19670913
9	VICTOR ARNOLD	8475555865	(847) 555-5865	NORTHBROOK IL	19821005
10	RAY MOORE	6025558659	(602) 555-8659	PHOENIX AZ	19640919
11	JEAN MURRAY	3145558149	(314) 555-8149	ST. LOUIS MO	19420312
12	JASON MOORE	8725554158	(872) 555-4158	CHICAGO IL	19621113
13	JOSEPHINE DANIELS	3305557448	(330) 555-7448	AKRON OH	19721104
14	RITA KNIGHT	6265555727	(626) 555-5727	PASADENA CA	19461203
15	PHYLLIS JOHNSON	2015559379	(201) 555-9379	HACKENSACK NJ	19421209
16	CAROL CHAPMAN	6825553875	(682) 555-3875	FORT WORTH TX	19481021
17	ALAN RODRIGUEZ	4025555209	(402) 555-5209	LINCOLN NE	19521003
18	ALBERT DANIELS	3055551928	(305) 555-1928	MARATHON FL	19520911
19	EVELYN TORRES	3215552157	(321) 555-2157	COCOA BEACH FL	19490817

Note that the new values are static values. They are not formulas. After Flash Fill works, you are free to delete the original column without having to worry about the new column changing to #REF errors.

Using Commas Helps Flash Fill

I have two versions of the data set shown in Figure 2.9. In the second version, a comma is used in column D to separate the city and state. When there is a comma, the Flash Fill in column F works perfectly to get the city every time.

D	E	F
LOCATION	DOB	City
FAIRBANKS AK	19700305	Fairbanks
BIRMINGHAM AL	19501110	Birmingham
LAS VEGAS NV	19740327	Las
WHEELING WV	19520623	Wheeling
ALLENTOWN PA	19771102	Allentown
TAMPA FL	19511106	Tampa
BOSTON MA	19670913	Boston
NORTHBROOK IL	19821005	Northbrook
PHOENIX AZ	19640919	Phoenix
ST. LOUIS MO	19420312	St
CHICAGO IL	19621113	Chicago
AKRON OH	19721104	Akron
PASADENA CA	19461203	Pasadena
HACKENSACK NJ	19421209	Hackensack
FORT WORTH TX	19481021	Fort
LINCOLN NE	19521003	Lincoln
MARATHON FL	19520911	Marathon
COCOA BEACH FL	19490817	Cocoa

Figure 2.9
Flash Fill gives you the first word from column D in column F.

But in real life, bad data isn't pretty. If someone has set out to personally annoy you by saving city and state in a single column, you can bet they aren't going to annoy you less by adding a comma for you.

In the example in Figure 2.9, Flash Fill isn't perfect the first time around. But with a simple correction from you, Flash Fill works correctly.

Let's say you want to isolate the city into its own column. Type **Fairbanks** in F2 and then type **B** from Birmingham in F3. Flash fill goes to work and fills in all of the cells for you.

This does not work for cities that have two words in the name. Las Vegas in row 4 becomes Las. St. Louis in row 11 is just St. Fort Worth in row 16 is Fort. Cocoa Beach in row 19 is Cocoa.

This problem is a bit more insidious. There aren't any blank cells to make you realize that it did not work. Luckily, the problems are showing up in the first part of the data, so you might notice the Las in F4. However, I can certainly foresee a situation where you have 9,000 records that say Henderson and only five records that say Las Vegas, and those latter records don't start until row 8642. In such a case, it would be really tough to realize that there is a problem.

Assuming you notice the problem, Excel can recover for you. Go to the first cell that is wrong in the Flash Fill results and type the correct value. Type **Las Vegas** in F4. Excel then fills in St. Louis, Fort Worth, and Cocoa Beach (see Figure 2.10).

Figure 2.10
Correct the first wrong cell, and Flash Fill makes the other corrections.

	D	E	F	G
	LOCATION	DOB	City	
	FAIRBANKS AK	19700305	Fairbanks	
	BIRMINGHAM AL	19501110	Birmingham	
	LAS VEGAS NV	19740327	Las Vegas	
	WHEELING WV	19520623	Wheeling	
	ALLENTOWN PA	19771102	Allentown	
	TAMPA FL	19511106	Tampa	
	BOSTON MA	19670913	Boston	
	NORTHBROOK IL	19821005	Northbrook	
	PHOENIX AZ	19640919	Phoenix	
	ST. LOUIS MO	19420312	St. Louis	
	CHICAGO IL	19621113	Chicago	
	AKRON OH	19721104	Akron	
	PASADENA CA	19461203	Pasadena	
	HACKENSACK NJ	19421209	Hackensack	
	FORT WORTH TX	19481021	Fort Worth	
	LINCOLN NE	19521003	Lincoln	
	MARATHON FL	19520911	Marathon	
	COCOA BEACH FL	19490817	Cocoa Beach	

If you can predict ahead of time that Flash Fill will have problems, you might want to wait until you've typed enough examples and then manually invoke Flash Fill using the icon on the Data tab. Here is an example of an alternative way to solve the city problem from Figure 2.10:

1. Type **City** in F1.

2. Type **Fairbanks** in F2.

3. Type **Birmingham** in F3. The entire time that you are typing Birmingha..., Excel shows you the Flash Fill preview. Ignore the preview and finish typing Birmingham. Press Enter, and Excel does not Flash Fill.

4. Type **Las Vegas** in F4.

5. Make sure that the active cell pointer is still in column F. Go to the Data tab and click the Flash Fill icon. Excel correctly fills all of the rows in column F.

When you get good at predicting which cells will cause a problem, you can shorten this process. These steps work:

1. Type **City** in F1.

2. Type **Las Vegas** in F4. Leave F2 and F3 blank.

3. Make sure that the active cell pointer is still in column F. Go to the Data tab and click Flash Fill. From the one Las Vegas example, Excel fills the city, even in F2 and F3.

Flash Fill Will Not Automatically Fill in Numbers

If you type a number in G2 and start to type another number in G3, Flash Fill will not automatically fill the column for you. With only 10 digits (as opposed to 26 letters), it is too likely that Excel could detect other patterns that are not the pattern you are intending.

It is possible for Flash Fill to work with numbers. Say that the original number is 477 and you type **77**. Excel could figure out that you want to strip off the leading digit. Press the Flash Fill icon to have Excel fill the other cells with this rule.

However, Flash Fill does not understand mathematical transformations. If the original number is 477 and you type **479** (add 2 to each cell) or **500** (round to the nearest hundred), Excel does not know how to Flash Fill the remaining cells.

Using Formatting with Dates

Dates are particularly troublesome. For example, in Figure 2.11, a date of birth appears in column E with the format of YYYYMMDD. If you type **3/5/1970** in G2 and then press the Flash Fill icon, Excel does not correctly recognize the pattern. You get 3/5/ and the first four digits from E in each row. This is an interesting result. You can sort of understand how Excel was tricked into seeing the wrong pattern.

	E	F	G	H
	DOB	City	Birthdate	
	19700305	Fairbanks	3/5/1970	
AL	19501110	Birmingham	3/5/1950	
	19740327	Las Vegas	3/5/1974	
	19520623	Wheeling	3/5/1952	
A	19771102	Allentown	3/5/1977	
	19511106	Tampa	3/5/1951	
	19670913	Boston	3/5/1967	
IL	19821005	Northbrook	3/5/1982	
	19640919	Phoenix	3/5/1964	
	19420312	St. Louis	3/5/1942	
	19621113	Chicago	3/5/1962	
	19721104	Akron	3/5/1972	
	19461203	Pasadena	3/5/1946	
J	19421209	Hackensack	3/5/1942	
X	19481021	Fort Worth	3/5/1948	
	19521003	Lincoln	3/5/1952	
	19520911	Marathon	3/5/1952	
FL	19490817	Cocoa Beach	3/5/1949	

Figure 2.11
The real problem is you are missing the leading zero.

You can solve the date problem by formatting the column to show MM/DD/YYYY first. Here's how:

1. Select column G.

2. Press Ctrl+1 to display the Format Cells dialog.

3. On the Number tab, choose the Date category.

4. Look for the date example of 03/14/2012. Ha, ha. There is no date example like that. All of the date examples have two-digit years. When the Y2K problem hit, they added a few examples with four-digit years, but none have two digits for month and day.

5. Click the Custom category instead of the Date category.

6. In the Type: box, type **MM/DD/YYYY**, and then click OK.

7. Now that the column is formatted to show the leading zeroes in the dates, type **3/5/1970** in G2. When you press Enter, Excel reformats the entry as 03/05/1970.

8. Go to cell G3 and type **11/10/1950**. Press Enter.

9. With the cell pointer in column G, click Flash Fill. Excel correctly fills the rest of the dates (see Figure 2.12).

10. You are now free to format column G with any date format, including M/D/YYYY, in order to leave off the leading zeroes.

Figure 2.12
With careful date formatting in advance, Flash Fill works with dates.

	E	F	G	H
	DOB	City	Birthdate	
	19700305	Fairbanks	03/05/1970	
L	19501110	Birmingham	11/10/1950	
	19740327	Las Vegas	03/27/1974	
	19520623	Wheeling	06/23/1952	
	19771102	Allentown	11/02/1977	
	19511106	Tampa	11/06/1951	
	19670913	Boston	09/13/1967	
L	19821005	Northbrook	10/05/1982	
	19640919	Phoenix	09/19/1964	
	19420312	St. Louis	03/12/1942	
	19621113	Chicago	11/13/1962	
	19721104	Akron	11/04/1972	
	19461203	Pasadena	12/03/1946	
J	19421209	Hackensack	12/09/1942	
X	19481021	Fort Worth	10/21/1948	
	19521003	Lincoln	10/03/1952	
	19520911	Marathon	09/11/1952	
FL	19490817	Cocoa Beach	08/17/1949	

Using Filter to Flash Fill a Subset of Records

Figure 2.13 shows a column with Movie Title (Year) Genre in each row. You would like to extract these into three fields. You would also like to sort by movie title, which means you want the word "The" to appear after the title.

▲	A	B	C	D
1	Movie List	Title	Year	Genre
2	2001: A Space Odyssey (1968) Sci-Fi			Sci-Fi
3	Airplane! (1980) Comedy			Comedy
4	Airport (1970) Disaster			Disaster
5	Armageddon (1998) Disaster			Disaster
6	Blade Runner (1982) Sci-Fi			Sci-Fi
7	Bringing Up Baby (1938) Comedy			Comedy
8	E.T. - The Extra-Terrestrial (1982) Sci-Fi			Sci-Fi
9	Forbidden Planet (1956) Sci-Fi			Sci-Fi
10	Monkey Business (1931) Comedy			Comedy
11	Star Wars (1977) Sci-Fi			Sci-Fi
12	The Full Monty (1997) Comedy			Comedy
13	The Pink Panther (1963) Comedy			Comedy
14	The Poseidon Adventure (1972) Disaster			Disaster
15	The Towering Inferno (1974) Disaster			Disaster
16	Twister (1996) Disaster			Disaster
17				

Figure 2.13
Because the headings are in B1 and C1, Flash Fill has no problem starting with Genre in D.

Fill in the headings of Title, Year, and Genre in row 1. Excel has no problem filling the Genre.

Type **1968** in C2 and start typing **1980** in C3, and Excel fills the year (see Figure 2.14).

Type the first title in B2. Start typing a title in B3. Excel fills all the titles. The problem is in rows 12:15, where you would like the titles to be in the format of "Pink Panther, The" (see Figure 2.15).

 Note

In this example, actually typing **2001: A Space Odyssey** is a challenge. I would copy A2 to B2, press F2 to edit the cell, and backspace through "(1968) Sci-Fi" to leave the movie title. After making that edit, stay in column B and click Flash Fill to manually invoke the command.

▲	A	B	C	D
1	Movie List	Title	Year	Genre
2	2001: A Space Odyssey (1968) Sci-Fi		1968	Sci-Fi
3	Airplane! (1980) Comedy		1980	Comedy
4	Airport (1970) Disaster		1970	Disaster
5	Armageddon (1998) Disaster		1998	Disaster
6	Blade Runner (1982) Sci-Fi		1982	Sci-Fi
7	Bringing Up Baby (1938) Comedy		1938	Comedy
8	E.T. - The Extra-Terrestrial (1982) Sci-Fi		1982	Sci-Fi
9	Forbidden Planet (1956) Sci-Fi		1956	Sci-Fi
10	Monkey Business (1931) Comedy		1931	Comedy
11	Star Wars (1977) Sci-Fi		1977	Sci-Fi
12	The Full Monty (1997) Comedy		1997	Comedy
13	The Pink Panther (1963) Comedy		1963	Comedy
14	The Poseidon Adventure (1972) Disaster		1972	Disaster
15	The Towering Inferno (1974) Disaster		1974	Disaster
16	Twister (1996) Disaster		1996	Disaster
17				

Figure 2.14
Extracting the year from inside the parentheses is easy.

Figure 2.15
Flash Fills gets the titles but does not understand the nuances of putting "The" after the title to allow for sorting.

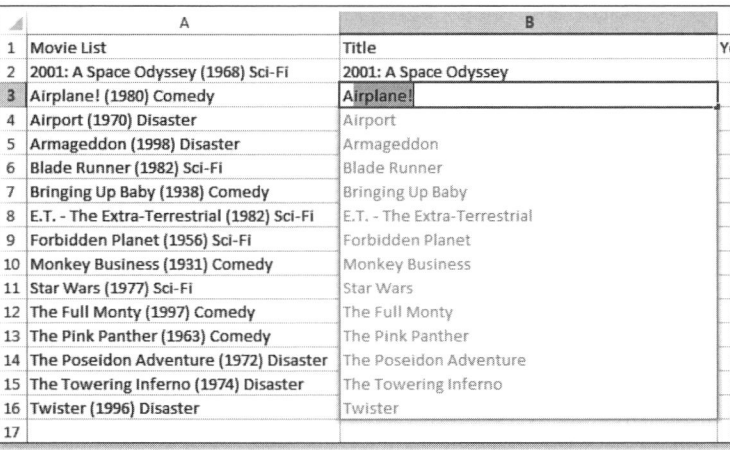

One solution is to filter to the records that need further adjustment. Follow these steps:

1. Choose one cell within the data set.

2. Click the Filter icon on the Data tab.

3. Open the filter drop-down in cell A1. Choose Text Filters, Begins With.

4. In the Custom AutoFilter dialog, choose Movie List Begins With. Type **The** and click OK (see Figure 2.16).

Figure 2.16
Filter to just the records that start with "The."

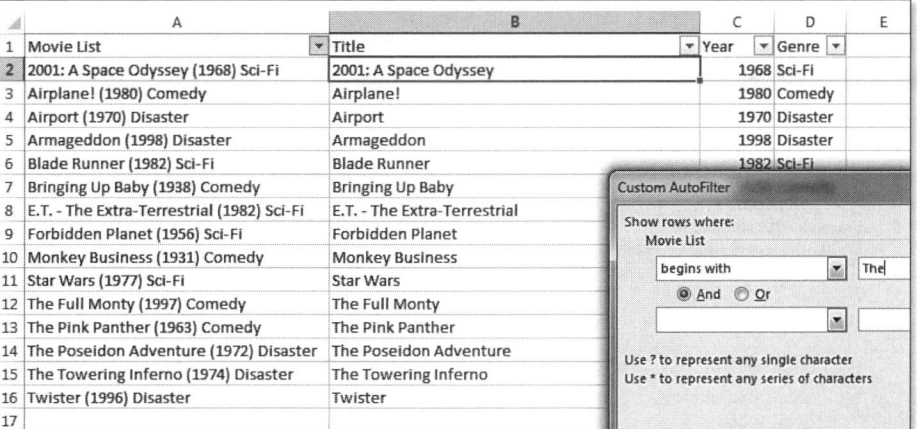

At this point, you see the headings in row 1 and then movie titles from rows 12–15. If you select cell B12, type **Full Monty, The,** and press Enter, then Flash Fill fixes the remaining three records (see Figure 2.17). The status bar indicates "4 of 15 Records Found. Flash Fill Changed Cells: 3."

	A	B
1	Movie List	Title
12	The Full Monty (1997) Comedy	Full Monty, The
13	The Pink Panther (1963) Comedy	Pink Panther, The
14	The Poseidon Adventure (1972) Disaster	Poseidon Adventure, The
15	The Towering Inferno (1974) Disaster	Towering Inferno, The
17		

Figure 2.17
Flash Fill only works on the visible rows if you've applied a filter.

You can now turn off the filter by clicking the Filter icon in the Data tab. You can now see all the movie information.

Troubleshooting Flash Fill

The following are some tips for making Flash Fill work correctly:

- There can be no blank columns. It is not necessary to be in the column immediately to the right of the data, but you can't have any completely blank columns between where you want to Flash Fill and the source data.
- For the automatic Flash Fill to work, you should type the first value and then immediately type the second value. Do not perform any other commands between the first and second value. Don't type **G2**, go to Sheet 3, and then come back and type **G3**. By then, Flash Fill has stopped watching for patterns. The only exception is sorting. You could type **G2**, sort, type **G3**, and Flash Fill will work.
- Type a heading in the column that you are filling to prevent Flash Fill from filling your heading. You could also bold the other headings. Flash Fill follows the same rules that the Sort dialog and the Ctrl+T Table dialog use to detect whether there are headings. If Ctrl+T opens with the My Data Has Headings box checked, then Flash Fill does not overwrite your headings. This matters more than you might think, because the headings don't usually follow the pattern of the data and confuse Flash Fill if it is trying to find a pattern.
- Pressing Esc makes the Flash Fill preview go away. More than once, I've pressed Esc by mistake and lost the Flash Fill. Don't worry. Type the first one or two cells and then use Ctrl+E or click the Flash Fill icon on the Data tab to force Excel to run Flash Fill again.
- Flash Fill only looks for patterns. Flash Fill does not understand that AZ is the abbreviation for Arizona. It does not understand that Jan 23 is another way to write 1-23. Flash Fill doesn't have any opinions. Writing "Awesome" next to Bruce Springsteen does not cue Flash Fill that you are trying to classify musical acts.

- Beware the ambiguous example. In Figure 2.18, you want to get the suffix from the part code. By random chance, the first example is ambiguous, with "IT" possibly representing the prefix or the suffix. In this case, skip B2 and type **ZA** in B3. Press Ctrl+Enter and then press Ctrl+E to fill the entire column (see Figure 2.19).

Figure 2.18
Skip the ambiguous example in row 2 and type an example in B3.

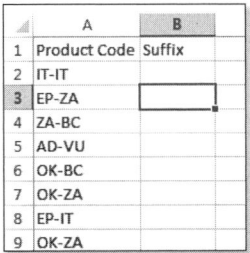

Figure 2.19
Use Ctrl+E to force Flash Fill to fill B2 as well.

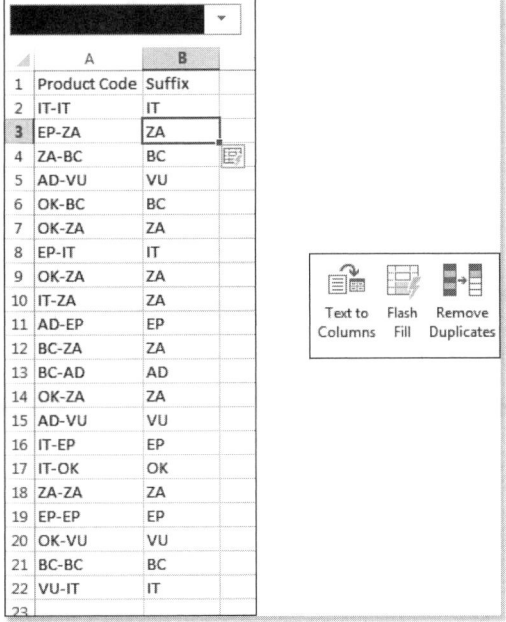

Flash Fill provides an easy way to solve many data problems. Even in the cases where an Excel pro knows a formula that can solve the problem, it is still easier to use Flash Fill.

Discovering Interesting Things in Your Data Using the Quick Analysis

You have some data in Excel. Now what? Print it out? Take it to your manager?

When I worked as a data analyst, I loved numbers and I loved Excel. But the people for whom I worked were not numbers people. If I handed them a page full of numbers, I could see their eyes glazing over. It was my goal to find something interesting in that sheet of numbers and call attention to that one bit of information.

Somehow, walking in to the VP of Sales's corner office with news like, "Wow, Walmart is up 20% over last year," gave him a talking point. Rather than just filing the report, he had a bit of news that might stick in his head and come up again in a later conversation. Of course, in my head, that later conversation would go something like, "You should see the analysis that our star employee Bill Jelen gave me today; Walmart is up 20%. We should give Bill a big bonus for discovering that!" In reality, the VP of Sales likely took credit for the discovery on the next sales conference call. But that's OK. He was the guy who kept me employed, and as long as I kept giving him a steady stream of sound bites, he would keep me off the RIF list.

Buried in Excel are many ways to find something interesting. It used to be intimidating to figure out where to start. Home, Conditional Formatting? Insert, PivotTable? Insert, Chart? Insert, Sparklines? Formulas, AutoSum? And after you get there, what do you do? I've written entire books about charts. I've written entire books about pivot tables. Others have written entire books about Excel formulas. The whole prospect is overwhelming.

How do you figure out where to start analyzing your data in Excel? You can use the Quick Analysis tool (see Figure 2.20).

The Quick Analysis tool, new in Excel 2013, is an on-ramp that lets you experiment with all those data tools without having to dive in and read an entire book. It is quick and easy to use, and it gives you a view of what you would get without actually doing anything with the data.

Follow these steps:

1. Select one cell in your data.

2. Press Ctrl+* to select all of the data.

3. Look for the Quick Analysis icon at the bottom right of your data (refer to Figure 2.20). If your data fills more than one screen, the icon appears near the last row or column that fits on your screen.

4. Click the icon and then start to click around.

The Quick Analysis appears, with five categories across the top: Formatting, Charts, Total, Tables, and Sparklines. When you select a category from the top, you see anywhere from four to ten icons in the Quick Analysis.

You can hover over any icon in the lens and Live Preview shows you what the results of using that tool would look like. The results appear either in a Live Preview in the data or in a thumbnail that appears above the Quick Analysis.

Figure 2.20
Customer,
sector, quar-
terly sales. So
what?

	A	B	C	D	E	F	G	H	I	J
1	Customer	Sector	Q1	Q2	Q3	Q4				
2	AT&T	Communications	42307	182303	152732	121595				
3	Bank of America	Financial	31376	111295	140688	122967				
4	CitiGroup	Financial	156704	89506	131185	236119				
5	Compaq	Electronics	0	9064	4380	25806				
6	Exxon	Energy	87167	150298	227772	239122				
7	Ford	Consumer Products	144954	178142	162705	136993				
8	General Electric	Energy	182426	135489	134246	116690				
9	General Motors	Consumer Products	214010	174295	174212	187646				
10	HP	Electronics	21015	4846	29390	0				
11	IBM	Electronics	124850	124728	102948	74823				
12	Kroger	Retail	0	19520	24659	2538				
13	Lucent	Communications	0	0	45554	17190				
14	Motorola	Communications	0	10807	17856	2358				
15	SBC Communications	Communications	14440	22140	0	36100				
16	State Farm	Financial	21730	18607	0	19544				
17	Texaco	Energy	30094	0	4270	0				
18	Verizon	Communications	88238	93207	82213	127320				
19	Wal-Mart	Retail	316189	162532	209181	181552				
20										
21										
22							**Quick Analysis**			
23							Use the Quick Analysis tool to			
24							quickly and easily analyze your data			
25							with some of Excel's most useful			
26							tools, such as charts, color-coding,			
27							and formulas.			
28										

Quick Analysis Icon

 Note

Everything you can do in the Quick Analysis can also be done the old way using commands on the ribbon tabs. The actual command in the ribbon often offers even more choices than the thumbnails offered in the Quick Analysis. If you want to discover more about any of the features in the Quick Analysis, see the last section of this chapter to find out where to learn more about the various features.

Color Coding Cells in the Data

The Formatting category in the Quick Analysis offers five different ways to color code cells in your data set.

Figure 2.21 shows a feature called Data Bars. For all of the numbers in your data set, Excel adds a swatch of color, almost like a little in-cell bar chart. The largest numbers get the largest amount of color and the smallest numbers get the smallest amount of color. This enables you to spot the largest numbers.

Figure 2.22 shows a color scale. The largest numbers are highlighted in dark green; the smallest numbers are in dark red. The numbers in the middle get varying shades of green or red.

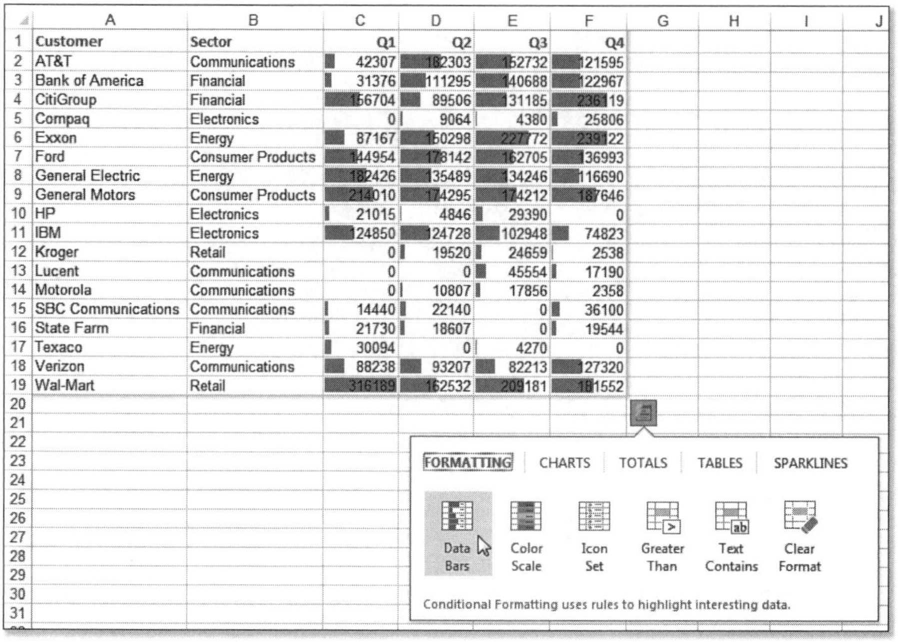

Figure 2.21
Data bars add more color to the larger numbers.

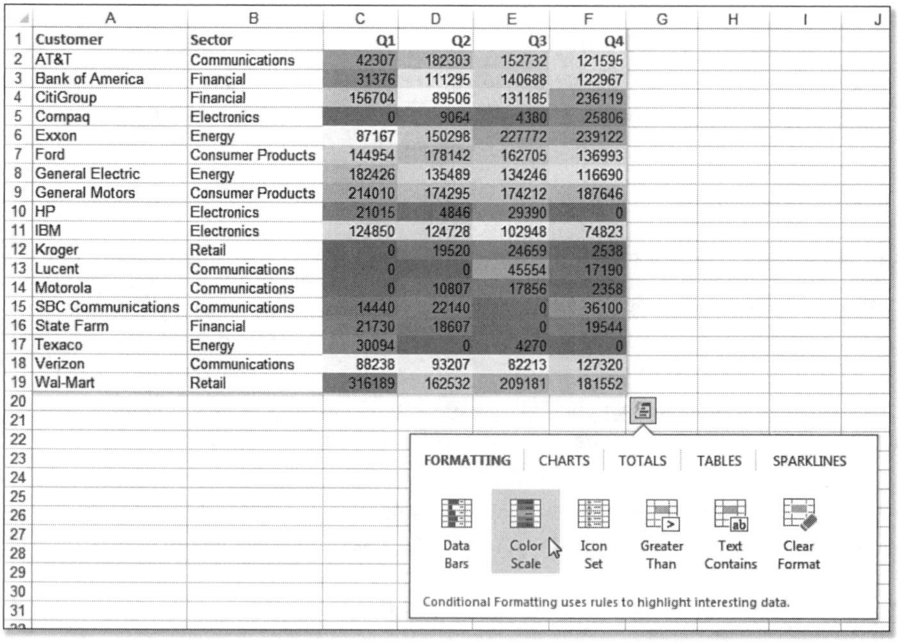

	A	B	C	D	E	F
1	Customer	Sector	Q1	Q2	Q3	Q4
2	AT&T	Communications	42307	182303	152732	121595
3	Bank of America	Financial	31376	111295	140688	122967
4	CitiGroup	Financial	156704	89506	131185	236119
5	Compaq	Electronics	0	9064	4380	25806
6	Exxon	Energy	87167	150298	227772	239122
7	Ford	Consumer Products	144954	178142	162705	136993
8	General Electric	Energy	182426	135489	134246	116690
9	General Motors	Consumer Products	214010	174295	174212	187646
10	HP	Electronics	21015	4846	29390	0
11	IBM	Electronics	124850	124728	102948	74823
12	Kroger	Retail	0	19520	24659	2538
13	Lucent	Communications	0	0	45554	17190
14	Motorola	Communications	0	10807	17856	2358
15	SBC Communications	Communications	14440	22140	0	36100
16	State Farm	Financial	21730	18607	0	19544
17	Texaco	Energy	30094	0	4270	0
18	Verizon	Communications	88238	93207	82213	127320
19	Wal-Mart	Retail	316189	162532	209181	181552

Figure 2.22
With a color scale, the largest numbers appear in green.

	A	B	C	D	E	F
1	Customer	Sector	Q1	Q2	Q3	Q4
2	AT&T	Communications	42307	182303	152732	121595
3	Bank of America	Financial	31376	111295	140688	122967
4	CitiGroup	Financial	156704	89506	131185	236119
5	Compaq	Electronics	0	9064	4380	25806
6	Exxon	Energy	87167	150298	227772	239122
7	Ford	Consumer Products	144954	178142	162705	136993
8	General Electric	Energy	182426	135489	134246	116690
9	General Motors	Consumer Products	214010	174295	174212	187646
10	HP	Electronics	21015	4846	29390	0
11	IBM	Electronics	124850	124728	102948	74823
12	Kroger	Retail	0	19520	24659	2538
13	Lucent	Communications	0	0	45554	17190
14	Motorola	Communications	0	10807	17856	2358
15	SBC Communications	Communications	14440	22140	0	36100
16	State Farm	Financial	21730	18607	0	19544
17	Texaco	Energy	30094	0	4270	0
18	Verizon	Communications	88238	93207	82213	127320
19	Wal-Mart	Retail	316189	162532	209181	181552

Figure 2.23 shows an icon set. Excel adds a green up-arrow icon to large numbers, a red down-arrow to the small numbers, and yellow arrows to the numbers in between.

Figure 2.23
Icon sets identify large, medium, and small numbers with different icons.

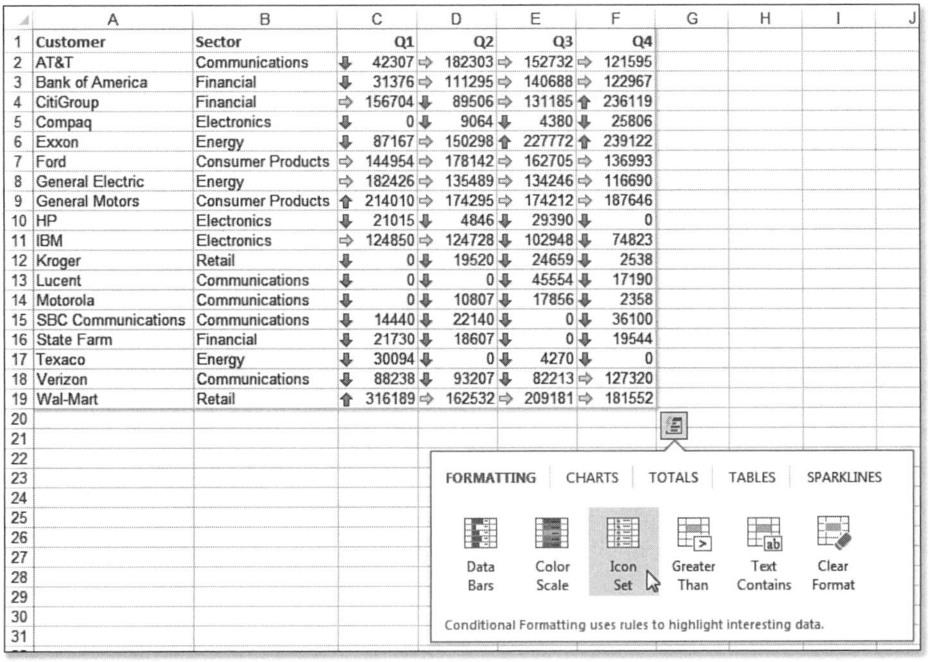

	A	B	C	D	E	F	G	H	I	J
1	Customer	Sector	Q1	Q2	Q3	Q4				
2	AT&T	Communications	42307	182303	152732	121595				
3	Bank of America	Financial	31376	111295	140688	122967				
4	CitiGroup	Financial	156704	89506	131185	236119				
5	Compaq	Electronics	0	9064	4380	25806				
6	Exxon	Energy	87167	150298	227772	239122				
7	Ford	Consumer Products	144954	178142	162705	136993				
8	General Electric	Energy	182426	135489	134246	116690				
9	General Motors	Consumer Products	214010	174295	174212	187646				
10	HP	Electronics	21015	4846	29390	0				
11	IBM	Electronics	124850	124728	102948	74823				
12	Kroger	Retail	0	19520	24659	2538				
13	Lucent	Communications	0	0	45554	17190				
14	Motorola	Communications	0	10807	17856	2358				
15	SBC Communications	Communications	14440	22140	0	36100				
16	State Farm	Financial	21730	18607	0	19544				
17	Texaco	Energy	30094	0	4270	0				
18	Verizon	Communications	88238	93207	82213	127320				
19	Wal-Mart	Retail	316189	162532	209181	181552				

FORMATTING	CHARTS	TOTALS	TABLES	SPARKLINES

Data Bars   Color Scale   Icon Set   Greater Than   Text Contains   Clear Format

Conditional Formatting uses rules to highlight interesting data.

The Greater Than icon highlights all the cells that are above a certain level. Figure 2.24 shows how the Live Preview highlights cells that are in the top 20%. After you click the command, you are allowed to specify the exact level.

I had never noticed this before, but Excel considers any text cell to be greater than any number. Thus, all of the text cells get highlighted by this icon.

If you have a column of text beyond the first column, the Quick Analysis offers a tool called Text Contains. It initially highlights the text value that appears more often than any other text. Figure 2.25 shows the Communications sector highlighted. After you actually click Text Contains, you can specify any particular text to highlight.

If you apply any of the formatting commands in the Quick Analysis and don't like the result, open the Quick Analysis again and choose Clear Format.

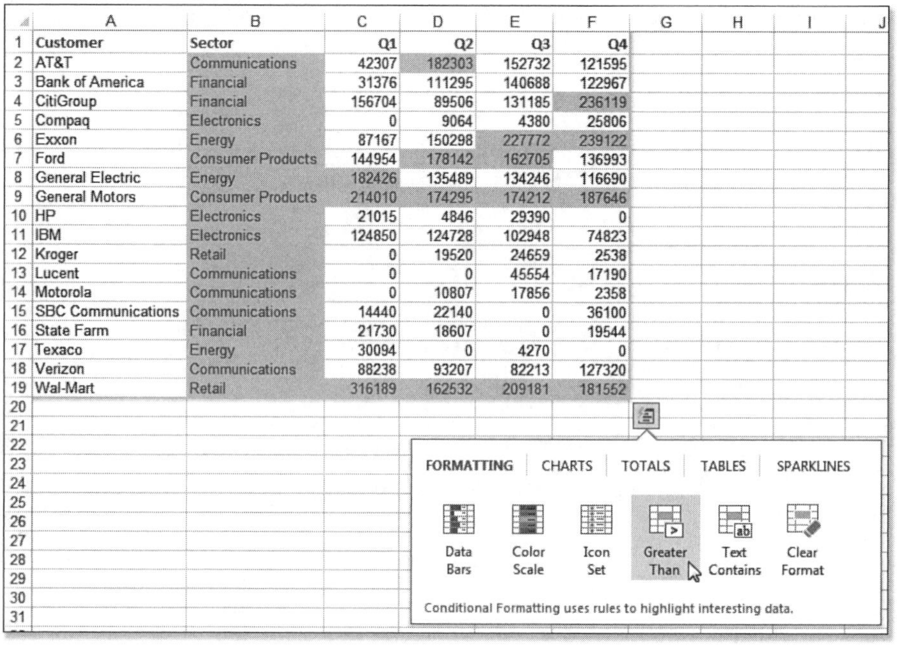

	A	B	C	D	E	F	G	H	I	J
1	Customer	Sector	Q1	Q2	Q3	Q4				
2	AT&T	Communications	42307	182303	152732	121595				
3	Bank of America	Financial	31376	111295	140688	122967				
4	CitiGroup	Financial	156704	89506	131185	236119				
5	Compaq	Electronics	0	9064	4380	25806				
6	Exxon	Energy	87167	150298	227772	239122				
7	Ford	Consumer Products	144954	178142	162705	136993				
8	General Electric	Energy	182426	135489	134246	116690				
9	General Motors	Consumer Products	214010	174295	174212	187646				
10	HP	Electronics	21015	4846	29390	0				
11	IBM	Electronics	124850	124728	102948	74823				
12	Kroger	Retail	0	19520	24659	2538				
13	Lucent	Communications	0	0	45554	17190				
14	Motorola	Communications	0	10807	17856	2358				
15	SBC Communications	Communications	14440	22140	0	36100				
16	State Farm	Financial	21730	18607	0	19544				
17	Texaco	Energy	30094	0	4270	0				
18	Verizon	Communications	88238	93207	82213	127320				
19	Wal-Mart	Retail	316189	162532	209181	181552				

FORMATTING   CHARTS   TOTALS   TABLES   SPARKLINES

Data Bars   Color Scale   Icon Set   Greater Than   Text Contains   Clear Format

Conditional Formatting uses rules to highlight interesting data.

Figure 2.24
Highlight numbers in the top 20% of values.

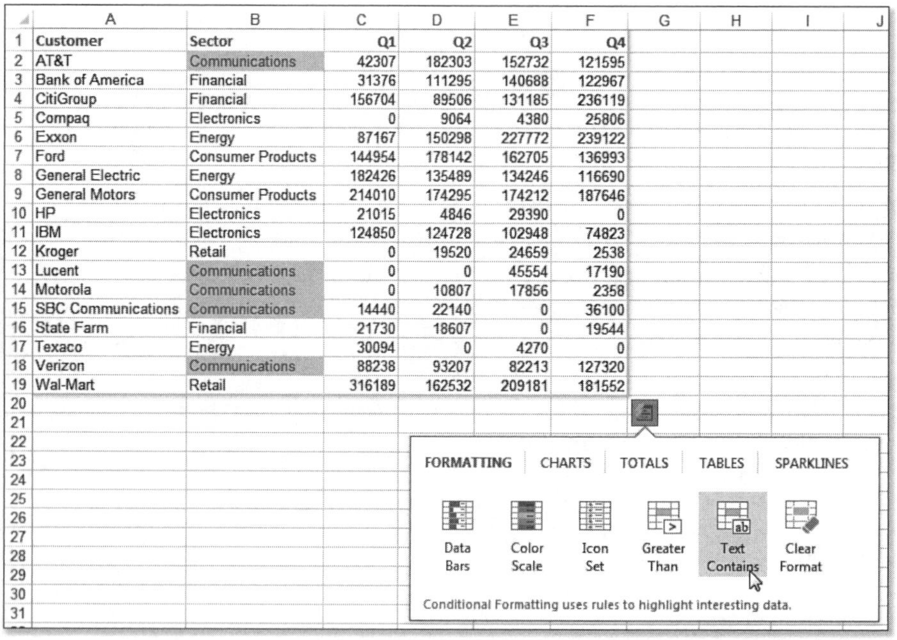

	A	B	C	D	E	F	G	H	I	J
1	Customer	Sector	Q1	Q2	Q3	Q4				
2	AT&T	Communications	42307	182303	152732	121595				
3	Bank of America	Financial	31376	111295	140688	122967				
4	CitiGroup	Financial	156704	89506	131185	236119				
5	Compaq	Electronics	0	9064	4380	25806				
6	Exxon	Energy	87167	150298	227772	239122				
7	Ford	Consumer Products	144954	178142	162705	136993				
8	General Electric	Energy	182426	135489	134246	116690				
9	General Motors	Consumer Products	214010	174295	174212	187646				
10	HP	Electronics	21015	4846	29390	0				
11	IBM	Electronics	124850	124728	102948	74823				
12	Kroger	Retail	0	19520	24659	2538				
13	Lucent	Communications	0	0	45554	17190				
14	Motorola	Communications	0	10807	17856	2358				
15	SBC Communications	Communications	14440	22140	0	36100				
16	State Farm	Financial	21730	18607	0	19544				
17	Texaco	Energy	30094	0	4270	0				
18	Verizon	Communications	88238	93207	82213	127320				
19	Wal-Mart	Retail	316189	162532	209181	181552				

FORMATTING   CHARTS   TOTALS   TABLES   SPARKLINES

Data Bars   Color Scale   Icon Set   Greater Than   Text Contains   Clear Format

Conditional Formatting uses rules to highlight interesting data.

Figure 2.25
Highlight cells that contain a certain value.

The Text Contains icon only appears if you have text in multiple columns. If your data has text in column A and the rest of the columns are numeric, the Text Contains icon changes to Top 10%. Excel calculates the difference between the Max and Min. Anything above 90% of that range is highlighted (see Figure 2.26).

Figure 2.26
When you have only one column of text, the Quick Analysis offers top 10%.

	A	B	C	D	E	F	G	H	I	J	K	L	M	N	O
1	Customer	Jan	Feb	Mar	Apr	May	Jun	Jul	Aug	Sep	Oct	Nov	Dec		
2	Wal-Mart	90K	115K	112K	67K	84K	11K	121K	23K	66K	76K	50K	56K		
3	General Motors	72K	80K	61K	84K	76K	14K	65K	44K	66K	22K	71K	94K		
4	Exxon	34K	41K	12K	42K	59K	49K	64K	105K	59K	96K	21K	122K		
5	Ford	23K	75K	47K	105K	51K	22K	60K	70K	32K	23K	41K	73K		
6	CitiGroup	69K	28K	59K	18K	32K	40K	22K	39K	70K	109K	92K	36K		
7	General Electric	61K	65K	55K	38K	55K	42K	56K	27K	51K	32K	55K	30K		
8	AT&T	14K	0K	28K	24K	122K	36K	35K	69K	48K	43K	29K	49K		
9	IBM	34K	46K	45K	20K	31K	74K	65K	20K	17K	40K	0K	35K		
10	Bank of America	0K	7K	24K	15K	57K	40K	25K	92K	23K	57K	21K	45K		
11	Verizon	24K	56K	9K	24K	23K	46K	28K	25K	29K	34K	49K	44K		
12															
13															
14															
15											FORMATTING	CHARTS	TOTALS	TABLES	SPARKLINES
16															
17															
18															
19											Data Bars	Color Scale	Icon Set	Greater Than	Top 10%	Clear Format
20															
21															
22											Conditional Formatting uses rules to highlight interesting data.				
23															

Charting Your Data

When you click the Quick Analysis and choose the Charting category, Excel offers five chart thumbnails. Hover over each thumbnail to preview the chart.

With the current data set, it is tough to predict which column is the most important. Will you want to chart Q1? Q2? The charts offered for this data set do not make a lot of sense. For example, in Figure 2.27, Excel is offering to roll the data up by sector, but then randomly chooses to show the revenue in Q2 (note the title, Sum of Q2 by Sector).

With a different data set, you see other charting choices. Figure 2.28 shows a chart illustrating the size of each customer. Each month is represented by a different color in the stacked bars.

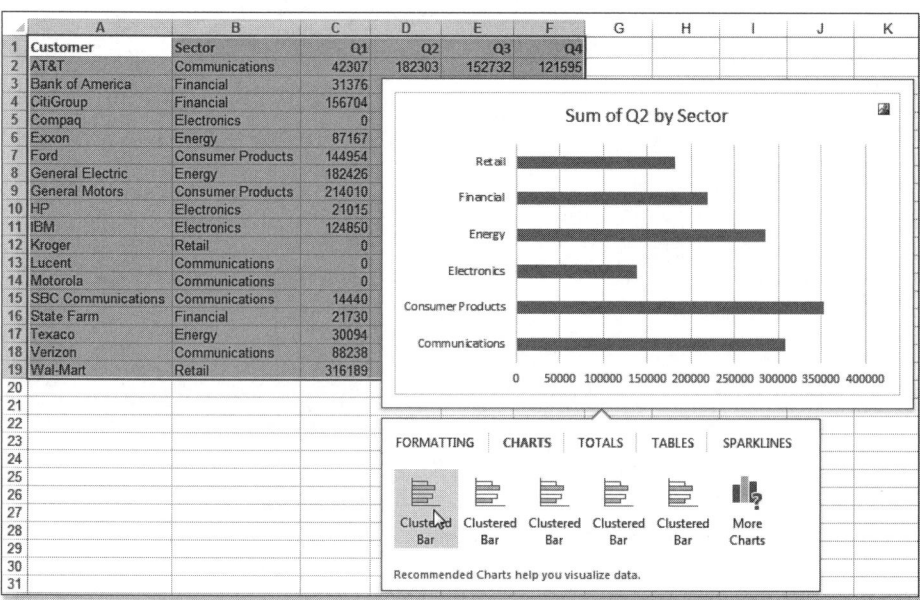

Figure 2.27
Rolling data up by sector is good, but why Q2?

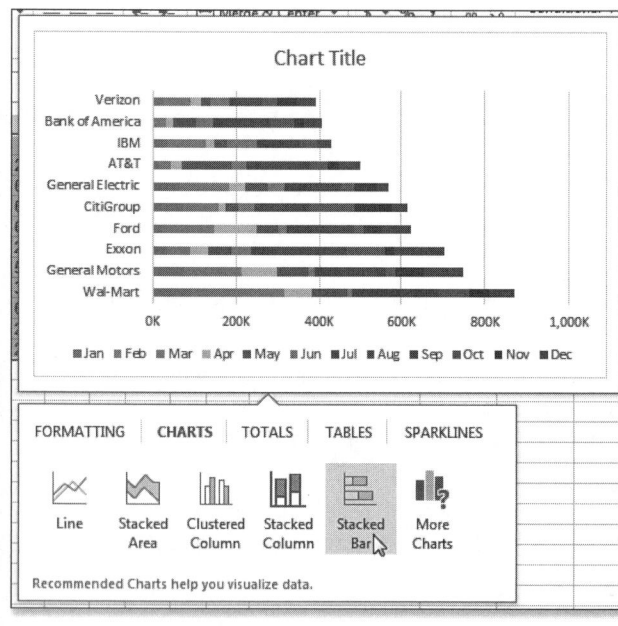

Figure 2.28
With a different data set, better charts are recommended.

Adding Statistics to the Bottom or Right Edge of Your Data

The Totals category contains 10 icons, and only the first five are visible. For me, the five that are scrolled off the right end of the Quick Analysis are much better than the five that are shown first. The first five icons add formulas to the bottom of your data set. If you click the right arrow at the right edge of the Quick Analysis, you can get to the five icons that add formulas to the right edge of your data.

Figure 2.29 shows the icons that add a new formula row to the bottom of your data set. The first icon adds a total to each column. Note that the total in cell B20 does not make a lot of sense in this context. The remaining icons add an average, count, % of row total, and running total across the bottom.

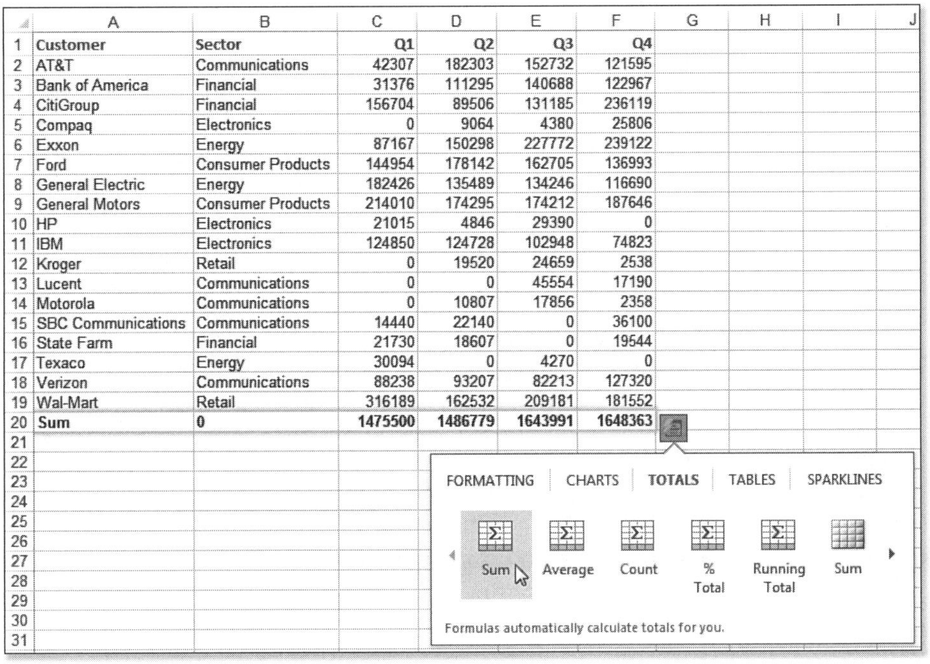

Figure 2.29
Add a total row
or an average
row below your
data.

	A	B	C	D	E	F	G	H	I	J
1	Customer	Sector	Q1	Q2	Q3	Q4				
2	AT&T	Communications	42307	182303	152732	121595				
3	Bank of America	Financial	31376	111295	140688	122967				
4	CitiGroup	Financial	156704	89506	131185	236119				
5	Compaq	Electronics	0	9064	4380	25806				
6	Exxon	Energy	87167	150298	227772	239122				
7	Ford	Consumer Products	144954	178142	162705	136993				
8	General Electric	Energy	182426	135489	134246	116690				
9	General Motors	Consumer Products	214010	174295	174212	187646				
10	HP	Electronics	21015	4846	29390	0				
11	IBM	Electronics	124850	124728	102948	74823				
12	Kroger	Retail	0	19520	24659	2538				
13	Lucent	Communications	0	0	45554	17190				
14	Motorola	Communications	0	10807	17856	2358				
15	SBC Communications	Communications	14440	22140	0	36100				
16	State Farm	Financial	21730	18607	0	19544				
17	Texaco	Energy	30094	0	4270	0				
18	Verizon	Communications	88238	93207	82213	127320				
19	Wal-Mart	Retail	316189	162532	209181	181552				
20	Sum	0	1475500	1486779	1643991	1648363				

Scroll to the right within the Total category to see five icons that add a new column of formulas to the right of your data. Figure 2.30 shows a SUM formula that totals the four columns.

Figure 2.31 shows the average column.

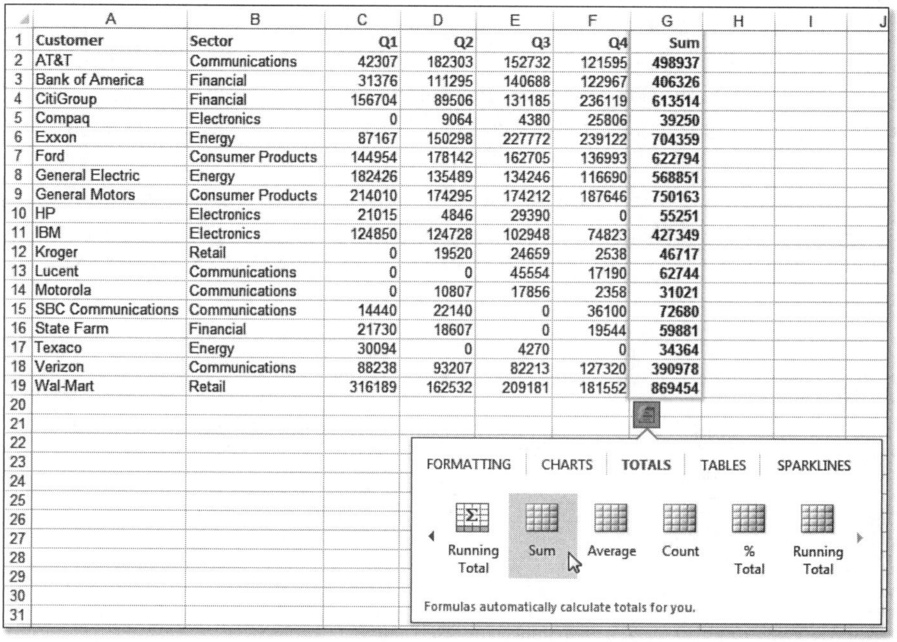

	A	B	C	D	E	F	G	H	I	J
1	Customer	Sector	Q1	Q2	Q3	Q4	Sum			
2	AT&T	Communications	42307	182303	152732	121595	498937			
3	Bank of America	Financial	31376	111295	140688	122967	406326			
4	CitiGroup	Financial	156704	89506	131185	236119	613514			
5	Compaq	Electronics	0	9064	4380	25806	39250			
6	Exxon	Energy	87167	150298	227772	239122	704359			
7	Ford	Consumer Products	144954	178142	162705	136993	622794			
8	General Electric	Energy	182426	135489	134246	116690	568851			
9	General Motors	Consumer Products	214010	174295	174212	187646	750163			
10	HP	Electronics	21015	4846	29390	0	55251			
11	IBM	Electronics	124850	124728	102948	74823	427349			
12	Kroger	Retail	0	19520	24659	2538	46717			
13	Lucent	Communications	0	0	45554	17190	62744			
14	Motorola	Communications	0	10807	17856	2358	31021			
15	SBC Communications	Communications	14440	22140	0	36100	72680			
16	State Farm	Financial	21730	18607	0	19544	59881			
17	Texaco	Energy	30094	0	4270	0	34364			
18	Verizon	Communications	88238	93207	82213	127320	390978			
19	Wal-Mart	Retail	316189	162532	209181	181552	869454			

FORMATTING   CHARTS   **TOTALS**   TABLES   SPARKLINES

Running Total   Sum   Average   Count   % Total   Running Total

Formulas automatically calculate totals for you.

Figure 2.30
Add a total column.

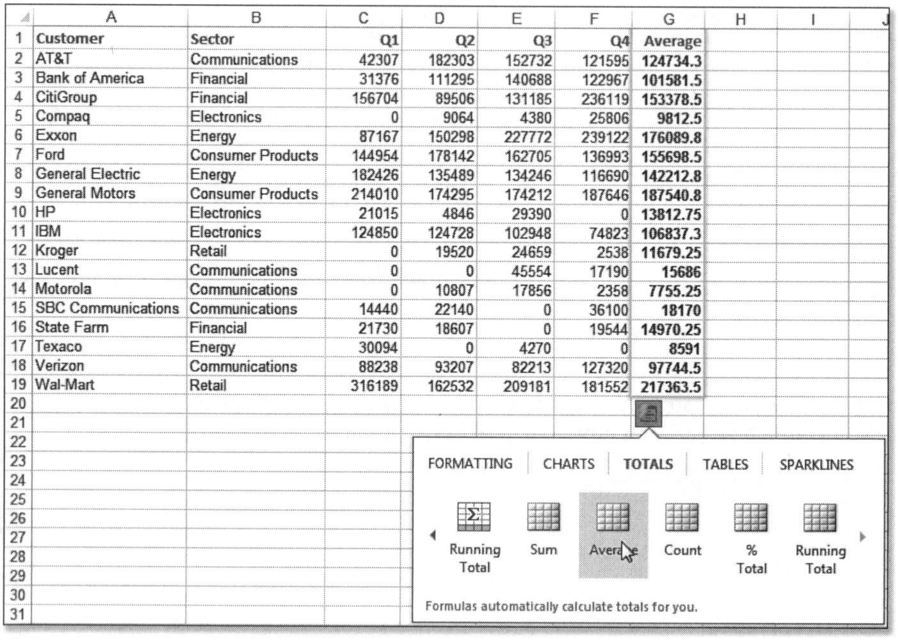

	A	B	C	D	E	F	G	H	I	J
1	Customer	Sector	Q1	Q2	Q3	Q4	Average			
2	AT&T	Communications	42307	182303	152732	121595	124734.3			
3	Bank of America	Financial	31376	111295	140688	122967	101581.5			
4	CitiGroup	Financial	156704	89506	131185	236119	153378.5			
5	Compaq	Electronics	0	9064	4380	25806	9812.5			
6	Exxon	Energy	87167	150298	227772	239122	176089.8			
7	Ford	Consumer Products	144954	178142	162705	136993	155698.5			
8	General Electric	Energy	182426	135489	134246	116690	142212.8			
9	General Motors	Consumer Products	214010	174295	174212	187646	187540.8			
10	HP	Electronics	21015	4846	29390	0	13812.75			
11	IBM	Electronics	124850	124728	102948	74823	106837.3			
12	Kroger	Retail	0	19520	24659	2538	11679.25			
13	Lucent	Communications	0	0	45554	17190	15686			
14	Motorola	Communications	0	10807	17856	2358	7755.25			
15	SBC Communications	Communications	14440	22140	0	36100	18170			
16	State Farm	Financial	21730	18607	0	19544	14970.25			
17	Texaco	Energy	30094	0	4270	0	8591			
18	Verizon	Communications	88238	93207	82213	127320	97744.5			
19	Wal-Mart	Retail	316189	162532	209181	181552	217363.5			

FORMATTING   CHARTS   **TOTALS**   TABLES   SPARKLINES

Running Total   Sum   Average   Count   % Total   Running Total

Formulas automatically calculate totals for you.

Figure 2.31
Add an average of the four quarters.

Figure 2.32 shows % Total. This one is very useful and generally hard to do. The result from this command is the moderately advanced formula =SUM(B2:F2)/SUM($B$2:$F$19). Figure 2.32 shows that Walmart is 13.90% of the total revenue. Note that the formula is ignoring column A in the totals but includes B in the totals, even though B is all text. If you ever had a sector called "7" and you stored the name as numeric, it would get added into the total.

Figure 2.32
Add a percentage of total.

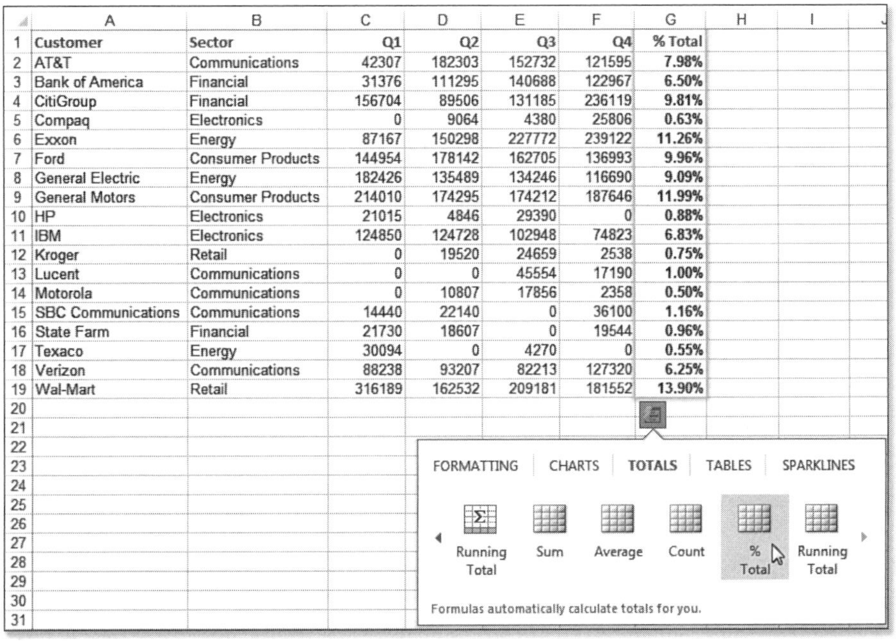

	A	B	C	D	E	F	G	H	I
1	Customer	Sector	Q1	Q2	Q3	Q4	% Total		
2	AT&T	Communications	42307	182303	152732	121595	7.98%		
3	Bank of America	Financial	31376	111295	140688	122967	6.50%		
4	CitiGroup	Financial	156704	89506	131185	236119	9.81%		
5	Compaq	Electronics	0	9064	4380	25806	0.63%		
6	Exxon	Energy	87167	150298	227772	239122	11.26%		
7	Ford	Consumer Products	144954	178142	162705	136993	9.96%		
8	General Electric	Energy	182426	135489	134246	116690	9.09%		
9	General Motors	Consumer Products	214010	174295	174212	187646	11.99%		
10	HP	Electronics	21015	4846	29390	0	0.88%		
11	IBM	Electronics	124850	124728	102948	74823	6.83%		
12	Kroger	Retail	0	19520	24659	2538	0.75%		
13	Lucent	Communications	0	0	45554	17190	1.00%		
14	Motorola	Communications	0	10807	17856	2358	0.50%		
15	SBC Communications	Communications	14440	22140	0	36100	1.16%		
16	State Farm	Financial	21730	18607	0	19544	0.96%		
17	Texaco	Energy	30094	0	4270	0	0.55%		
18	Verizon	Communications	88238	93207	82213	127320	6.25%		
19	Wal-Mart	Retail	316189	162532	209181	181552	13.90%		

FORMATTING   CHARTS   **TOTALS**   TABLES   SPARKLINES

Running Total   Sum   Average   Count   % Total   Running Total

Formulas automatically calculate totals for you.

Figure 2.33 shows a running total. This is particularly good when you have dates running down the first column and you want to show accumulated revenue.

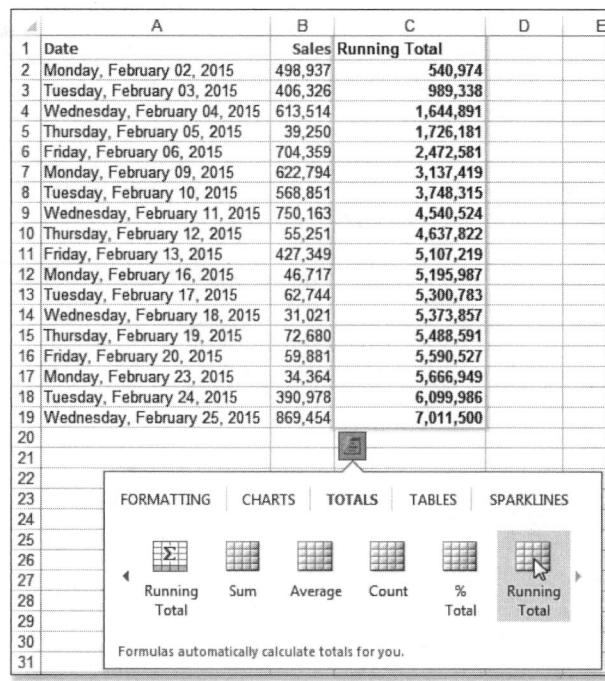

Figure 2.33
Calculate a running total.

Creating a Summary Report from Your Data

Many useful summary reports are available in the Table category of the Quick Analysis. Most of the commands in this category create a new summary report on a new worksheet to the left of the current worksheet. The first icon, called Table, is an exception.

The Table icon formats your report as a table. This allows for easy formatting using the Table Tools Design tab of the ribbon. You can apply banded-row formatting, add totals, filter, and more (see Figure 2.34).

The next several thumbnails offer up to four recommended pivot table reports. In Figure 2.35, data is summarized by sector with a total for Q1 sales.

Figure 2.34
Format the data with Table formatting. This is the same as pressing Ctrl+T.

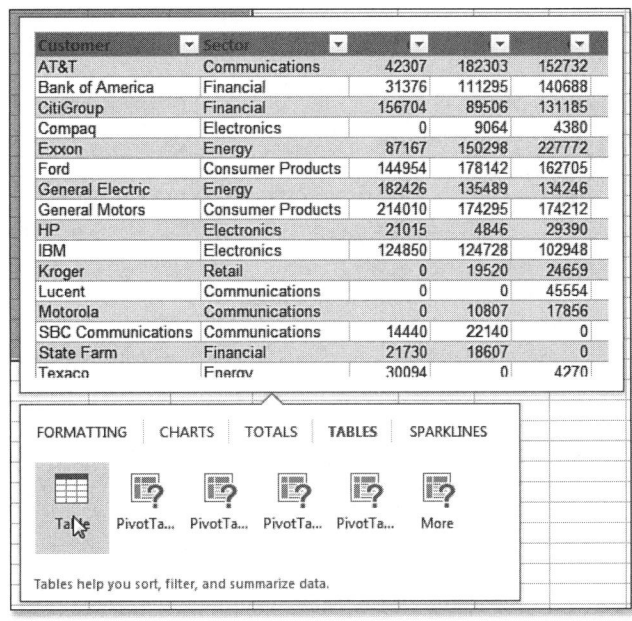

Customer	Sector			
AT&T	Communications	42307	182303	152732
Bank of America	Financial	31376	111295	140688
CitiGroup	Financial	156704	89506	131185
Compaq	Electronics	0	9064	4380
Exxon	Energy	87167	150298	227772
Ford	Consumer Products	144954	178142	162705
General Electric	Energy	182426	135489	134246
General Motors	Consumer Products	214010	174295	174212
HP	Electronics	21015	4846	29390
IBM	Electronics	124850	124728	102948
Kroger	Retail	0	19520	24659
Lucent	Communications	0	0	45554
Motorola	Communications	0	10807	17856
SBC Communications	Communications	14440	22140	0
State Farm	Financial	21730	18607	0
Texaco	Energy	30094	0	4270

FORMATTING | CHARTS | TOTALS | **TABLES** | SPARKLINES

Table   PivotTa...   PivotTa...   PivotTa...   PivotTa...   More

Tables help you sort, filter, and summarize data.

Figure 2.35
After you build this report, you could add Q2, Q3, and Q4 to the report.

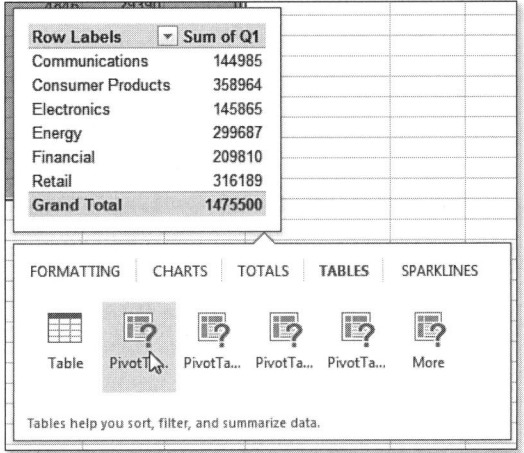

Row Labels	Sum of Q1
Communications	144985
Consumer Products	358964
Electronics	145865
Energy	299687
Financial	209810
Retail	316189
Grand Total	**1475500**

FORMATTING | CHARTS | TOTALS | **TABLES** | SPARKLINES

Table   PivotT...   PivotTa...   PivotTa...   PivotTa...   More

Tables help you sort, filter, and summarize data.

Figure 2.36 shows a fairly advanced pivot table summary report. It has sectors and the ability to drill down into each sector to see the customers within it.

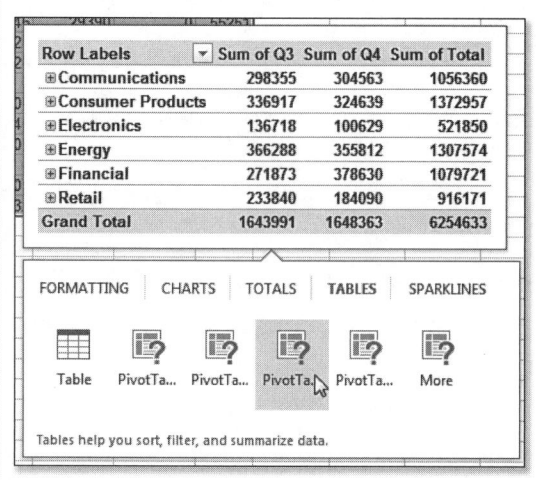

Figure 2.36
This pivot table offers drill-down buttons next to each sector.

Adding Tiny Charts to Each Row

Professor Edward Tufte started writing about tiny word-sized charts back in 2007. He dubbed these charts *sparklines*.

Excel 2010 offered support for these charts. The chart fills up the available space in a cell. After using sparklines for a while, I believe that they look better when they are bigger than the normal cell. Before creating the sparklines in the next two examples, I made column N wider and also made all of the rows in the data set taller.

Figure 2.37 shows a Line sparkline for each customer. You can see if the customer's purchases increased or decreased throughout the year.

Figure 2.38 shows a column chart for each customer. It is worthwhile to note that the scale for each chart is separate from the other charts.

The last sparkline, Win/Loss, is fairly specialized. I've never seen anyone have organic data that would make a good Win/Loss sparkline. You almost always have to add formulas to your data to get a proper sparkline. Win/Loss sparklines are discussed in detail in Chapter 33, "Using Sparklines."

Figure 2.37
A new in-cell chart is added for each row.

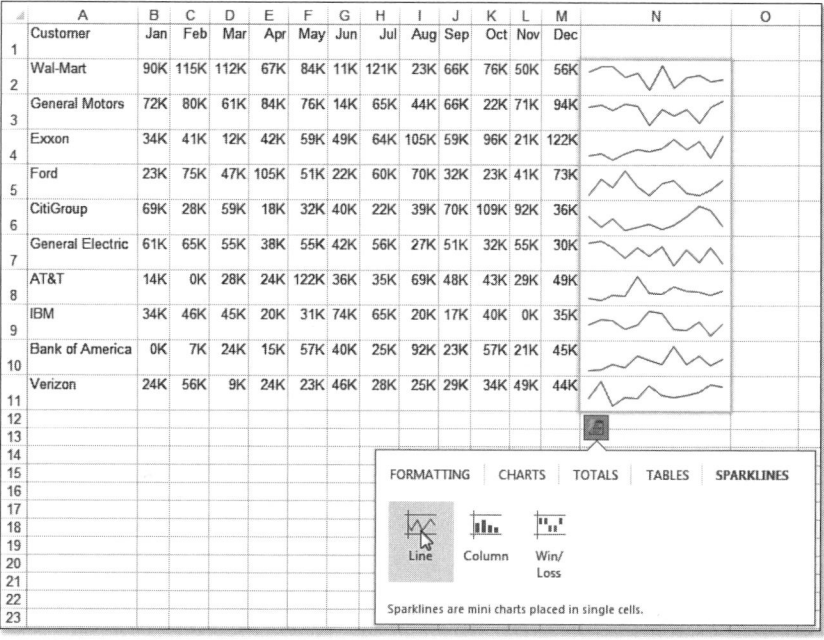

Figure 2.38
Column sparklines show the trend from month to month for each customer.

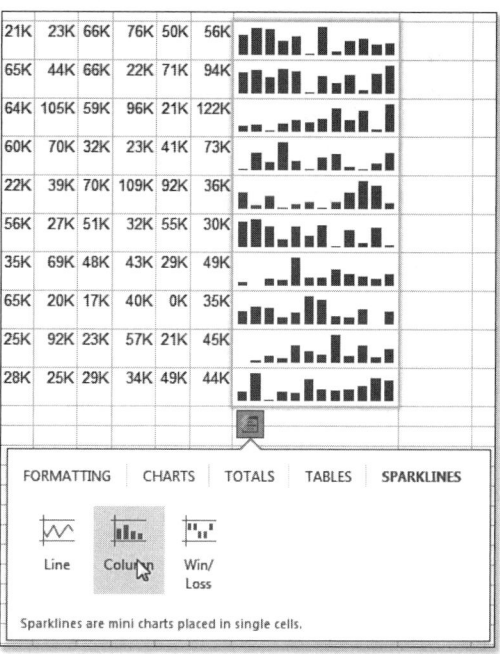

I've Used the Quick Analysis! Now What?

The Quick Analysis is cool because you can easily experiment with some powerful technologies. But the problem could be that you've added something to your data, and you might not fully understand how to control that data. This section guides you on how to further control what you added with the data lens.

Formatting Category

- All of the visualizations in this category come from Home, Conditional Formatting. In the ribbon drop-down, there are six times as many variations as in the Quick Analysis.

- You can change the defaults by visiting Home, Conditional Formatting, Manage Rules.

- To read more about these features, see Chapter 31, "Using Data Visualizations and Conditional Formatting."

Charts Category

- Charts are normally created by using Insert, Recommended Charts. The resulting dialog offers 10 suggested charts on the first tab and offers all charts on the second tab.

- After you have a chart, you can customize it. For information, see Chapter 32, "Graphing Data Using Excel Charts."

Totals Category

- You can replicate the Sum, Average, and Count formulas using the AutoSum button for totals or the AutoSum drop-down for Average and Count. The drop-down also offers Max and Min.

- The formulas for percentage of total are fine. The formula for running total is the slow method for calculating running totals. It does not matter with a 20-row data set. If you have 20,000 rows, however, you need to consider changing to a simple formula that adds the cell above to the cell to the left.

- Formulas are discussed in Chapter 8, "Understanding Formulas," and Chapter 9, "Controlling Formulas."

Tables Category

- The first icon in the Tables category is Format as a Table. This is discussed fully in Chapter 19, "Fabulous Table Intelligence."

- The remaining icons create pivot tables. These are discussed in Chapter 23, "Using Pivot Tables to Analyze Data."

Sparklines Category

- You can enhance sparklines by marking the high/low point or by controlling the axis. Chapter 33 discusses sparklines in depth.

3

USING THE EXCEL INTERFACE

The Excel interface has had a major makeover over the last decade. Excel 2007 introduced the ribbon and Quick Access Toolbar to replace the familiar command bar at the top of Excel. Excel 2010 brought the expanded File menu. Excel 2013 brings the Start menu, plus new Open and Save As panes. These were discussed in Chapter 1, "Staying Connected Using Excel 2013." This chapter reviews all of the remaining Excel interface elements.

Using the Ribbon

The ribbon is composed of seven permanent tabs labeled Home, Insert, Page Layout, Formulas, Data, Review, and View. Other permanent tabs appear if you install certain add-ins. For example, PowerPivot, Inquire, and Easy-XL are tabs that you see if you install certain add-ins. Other contextual ribbon tabs appear when you select a certain type of object, such as a chart, image, or pivot table.

Each tab is broken into rectangular groups of related commands. The group shown in Figure 3.1 is the Clipboard group on the Home tab.

The mantra of the ribbon is to use pictures and words. Many people have seen the little whisk broom icon in previous versions of Excel but never knew what it did. In Excel 2013, the same icon has the words "Format Painter" next to it. When you hover, the tooltip offers paragraphs explaining what the tool does. The tooltip also offers a little-known trick: You can double-click the Format Painter to copy the formatting to many places.

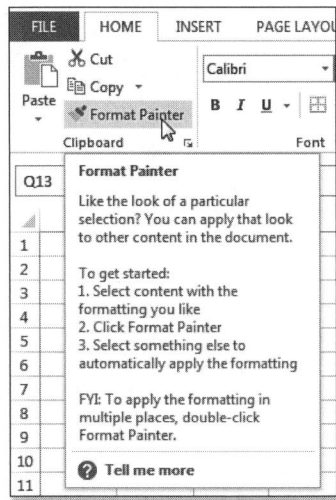

Figure 3.1
Detail of the Clipboard group of the Home tab of the ribbon.

Using Fly-out Menus and Galleries

The ribbon fits more commands in a smaller space by using new types of controls that were not available with the Excel 2003 menu bar and toolbars.

In Figure 3.1, the Cut icon is a pure command. You click the icon and Excel cuts the selection onto the Clipboard. In contrast, the Paste and Copy icons are a new type of element comprised of a button and a drop-down. If you click the top half of Paste or the left side of Copy, you invoke the command. But if you click the arrow in either icon, you get a fly-out menu with more choices.

Fly-out menus allow many choices from a single icon. For example, the Conditional Formatting icon on the Home tab takes up a 76×76 pixel area on the ribbon. Clicking Conditional Formatting leads to five new fly-out menus and three commands. In all, the fly-out menus lead to a total of 64 distinct commands, all driven from a single 76×76-pixel icon (see Figure 3.2).

Another new element in the ribbon is the gallery control. Galleries are used when there are dozens of options from which to choose. The gallery shows you a visual thumbnail of each choice. A gallery starts out showing a row or two of choices in the ribbon. The right side of the gallery offers icons for up, down, and open. If you click up or down, you scroll one row at a time through the choices (see Figure 3.3).

If you click the open control at the bottom-right side of the gallery, the gallery opens to reveal all choices at once (see Figure 3.4).

Figure 3.2
Fly-out menus offer dozens of choices from a single icon.

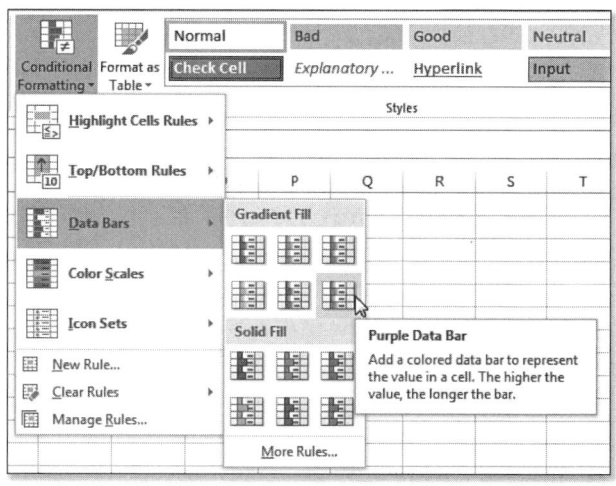

Figure 3.3
Use the up and down arrows on the right side of the gallery to move one row at a time through the choices.

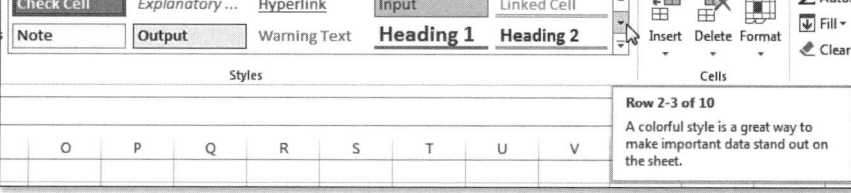

Figure 3.4
If you open the gallery control, you can see all of the choices at one time.

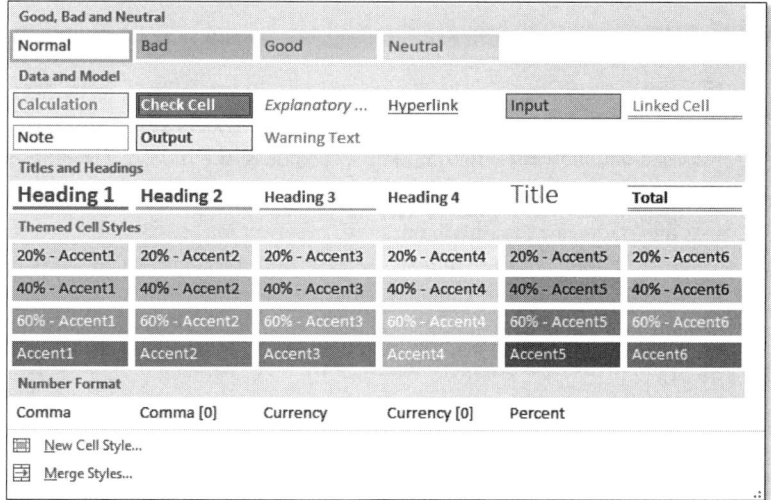

Rolling Through the Ribbon Tabs

With Excel as the active application, move the mouse anywhere over the ribbon and roll the scroll wheel on top of the mouse. Excel quickly flips from ribbon tab to ribbon tab. Scroll away from you to roll toward the Home tab on the left. Scroll toward you to move to the right.

Revealing More Commands Using Dialog Launchers, Task Panes, and "More" Commands

The ribbon holds perhaps 20% of the available commands. The set of commands and options available in the ribbon will be enough 80% of the time, but you will sometimes have to go beyond the commands in the ribbon. You can do this with dialog launchers, "More" commands, and the task pane.

A *dialog launcher* is a special symbol in the lower-right corner of many ribbon groups. Click the dialog launcher to open a related dialog with many more choices than those offered in the ribbon.

Figure 3.5 shows details of the Number group of the Home tab. In the lower-right corner is the dialog launcher. It looks like the top-left corner of a dialog, with an arrow pointing downward and to the right.

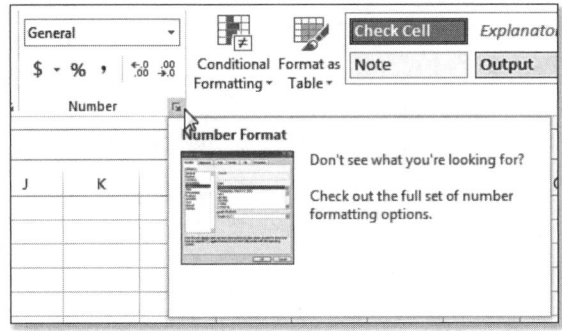

Figure 3.5
The dialog launcher takes you to additional options.

When you click the dialog launcher, you go to a dialog box that often offers many more choices than those available in the ribbon. In Figure 3.6, you see the Number tab of the Format Cells dialog.

Many menus in the ribbon end with an entry for "More *blank*..." or "*Blank* Options...". You will see menu options for More Rules..., Effects Options..., and so on. Look for these menu items as the last entry in many menus. Clicking a More item takes you to a dialog or task pane with far more choices than those available in the ribbon.

Figure 3.7 shows the More Rules menu item, which leads to the New Formatting Rule dialog.

Figure 3.6
After clicking the dialog launcher, you get access to far more choices.

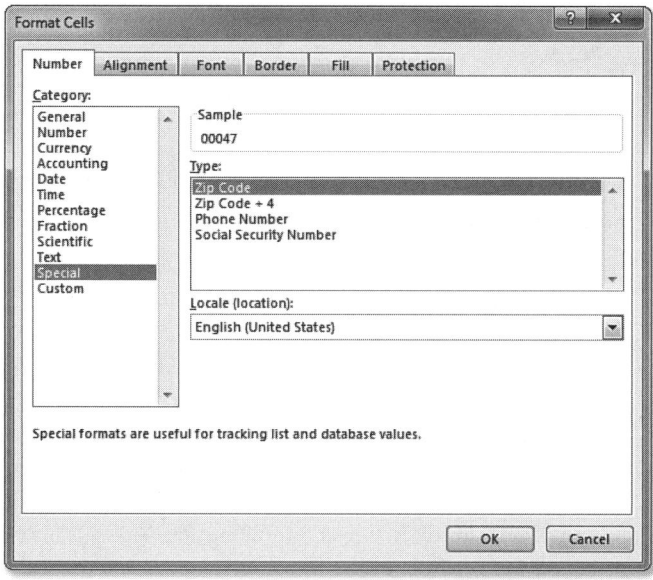

Figure 3.7
Choosing More Rules leads to a dialog with more choices.

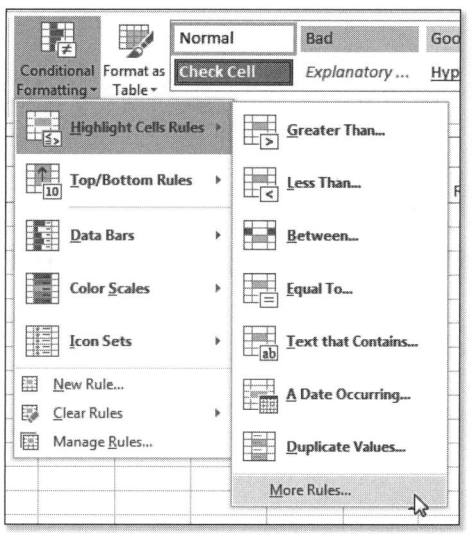

Charts in Excel 2013 show a plus icon to the right of the selected chart. This icon leads to fly-out menus that eventually lead to a "More…" menu item (see Figure 3.8). When you select More… from a chart, you go to a redesigned task pane. Task panes were popular in Excel 2003. They were nearly banished in Excel 2007 due to the edict that all commands must be at the top. However, they are back with a vengeance in Excel 2013.

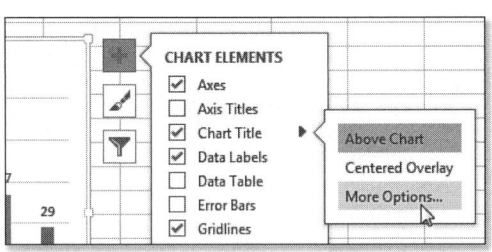

Figure 3.8
Choosing More... from the chart's plus icon leads to a task pane.

Task panes typically appear on the right side of the Excel window, although you can undock them and have them float above the worksheet. After a task pane appears, it typically stays visible until you close it by clicking the X button. Figure 3.9 shows a task pane for formatting the chart title. If you click a data label in the chart, the task pane changes to show options for chart labels. If you click a picture, SmartArt, or WordArt, the task pane changes to show options for the newly selected object.

 **Caution**

If you click away from an object and choose only a cell, the task pane stays visible with the choices for the last selected object. However, all of the choices are grayed out. This seems like a bug to me.

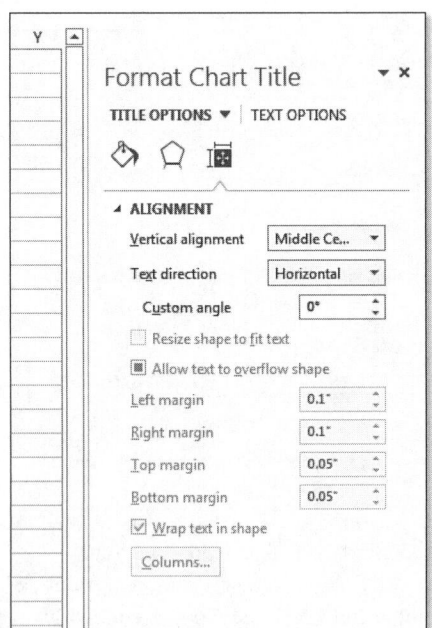

Figure 3.9
The Format dialog from Excel 2010 is now a task pane.

 **Tip**

To display the task pane for an object, press Ctrl+1. Although it is easy to display the task pane for a chart, it is not obvious how to display the task pane for an image or WordArt. However, as noted earlier, you can accidentally find your way to the Picture task pane by clicking a picture while the task pane is active. When you want to display a task pane but cannot figure out how to do it, try F1.

For charts, the task pane in Excel 2013 replaces the Format dialog from Excel 2010. It seems more confusing to use the task pane.

In Excel 2010, the Format dialog had a list of categories down the left side. These categories were arranged into groups with a horizontal separator between categories. For example, in Figure 3.10, the first group of categories is Fill, Border Color, and Border Styles. In a glance, you could see other categories such as Glow and Soft Edges, Properties, and Alt Text. I appreciated seeing a long list of words to choose from.

Figure 3.10
The Format dialog from Excel 2010 offered easy-to-understand words in the left navigation pane.

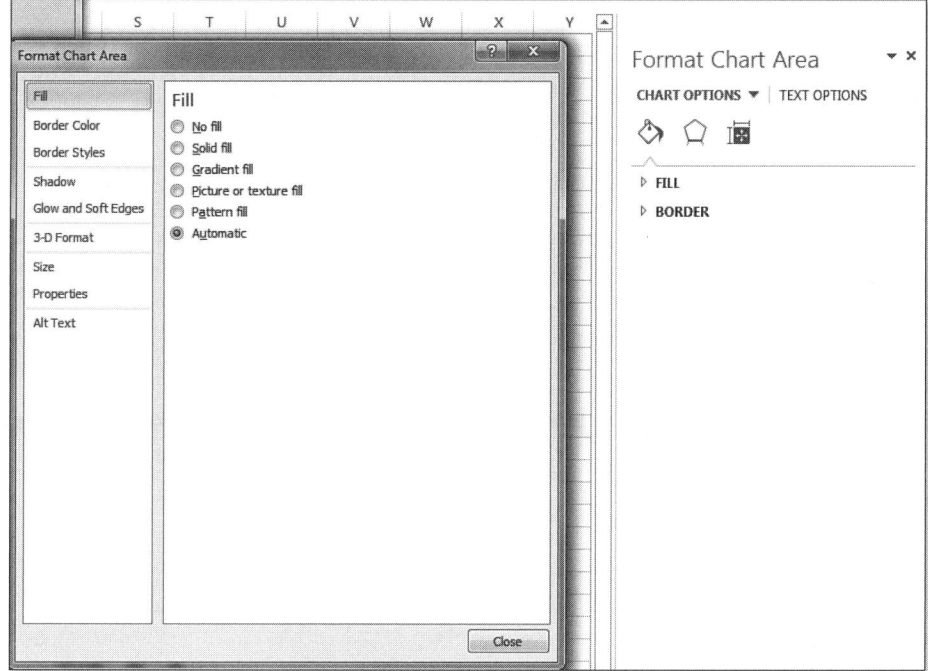

The Excel 2013 task pane offers a hierarchy of words, icons, and more words. In Figure 3.11, the equivalent task pane starts with two sets of words at the top: Chart Options and Text Options. It won't be obvious in the figure, but Chart Options is shown in green and is the currently selected choice. When Chart Options is selected, you have three icons: a paint bucket, a pentagon with a reflection, and a square that someone appears to be measuring. Again, it is not obvious from the figure, but the paint bucket is in green and selected. When the paint bucket is selected, two word choices appear in the task pane: Fill and Border. Click the triangle next to either word to show all of the choices for that word. Figure 3.12 shows the Border category after expanding.

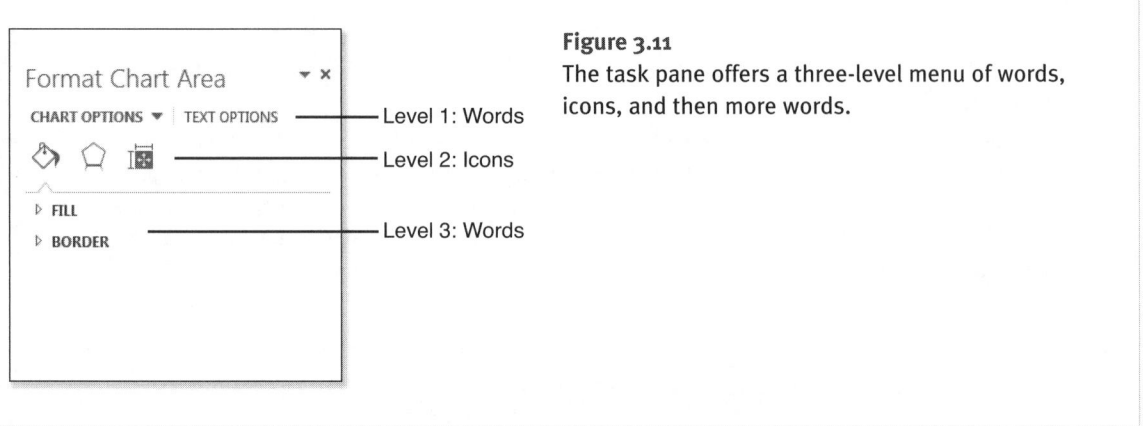

Figure 3.11
The task pane offers a three-level menu of words, icons, and then more words.

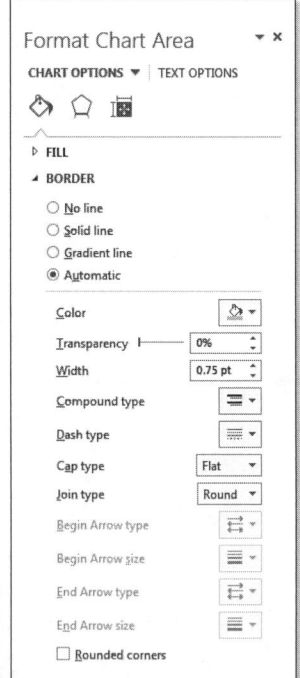

Figure 3.12
After choosing Chart Options, the paint bucket, and then Border, you get these options.

The task pane is confusing because you can't see all of the categories at one time. You will find yourself trying to guess which Level 1 word to choose and then clicking through each of the Level 2 icons trying to find the Level 3 category you want.

Figure 3.13 shows the name of each Level 2 icon and the types of categories you might find there.

Figure 3.13
Icons you might find in various task panes.

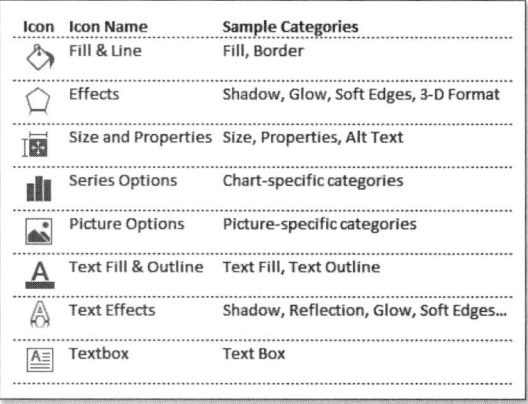

Icon	Icon Name	Sample Categories
	Fill & Line	Fill, Border
	Effects	Shadow, Glow, Soft Edges, 3-D Format
	Size and Properties	Size, Properties, Alt Text
	Series Options	Chart-specific categories
	Picture Options	Picture-specific categories
	Text Fill & Outline	Text Fill, Text Outline
	Text Effects	Shadow, Reflection, Glow, Soft Edges...
	Textbox	Text Box

Resizing Excel Changes the Ribbon

The ribbon appears different as the size of the Excel application window changes. You should be aware of this when you are coaching a co-worker over the phone. You might be looking at your screen and telling him to "look for the big Insert drop-down to the right of the orange word *Calculation.*" Although this makes perfect sense on your widescreen monitor, it might not make sense on his monitor. Figure 3.14 shows some detail of the Home tab on a widescreen monitor. The Cell Styles gallery shows 10 thumbnails, and Insert, Delete, and Format appear side-by-side.

Figure 3.14
On a wide-screen monitor, you see 10 choices in the Cell Styles gallery.

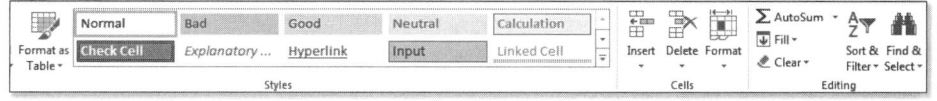

Figure 3.15 shows the typical view on a laptop. The Cell Styles gallery is collapsed to a single drop-down. The Insert, Delete, and Format icons are now arranged vertically.

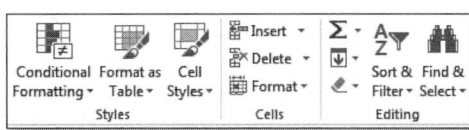

Figure 3.15
On a normal monitor, the cell styles gallery is collapsed.

As you resize the Excel screen, more items collapse. In Figure 3.16, the three icons for Insert, Delete, and Format are collapsed into a single drop-down called Cells.

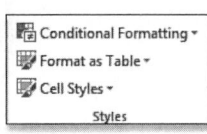

Figure 3.16
At small sizes, icons collapse into drop-downs.

New in Excel 2013, you can even coax a new right-arrow icon to scroll the ribbon right (see Figure 3.17).

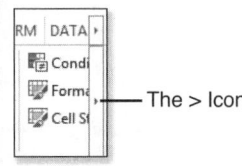

The > Icon

Figure 3.17
Click the right-arrow icon to scroll the ribbon to the right.

Eventually, the Excel ribbon gets too small, and Excel hides the ribbon completely (see Figure 3.18).

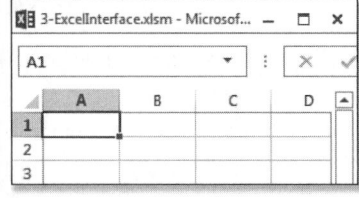

Figure 3.18
When the Excel windows gets too narrow, the ribbon is hidden.

Activating the Developer Tab

If you regularly record or write macros, you might be looking for the VBA tools in the ribbon. They are all located on the Developer tab, which is hidden by default. However, it is easy to make the Developer tab visible. Follow these steps:

1. Right-click the ribbon and choose Customize the Ribbon. Excel displays the Customize Ribbon category of the Excel Options dialog.

2. A long list box of ribbon tabs is shown on the right side of the screen. Every one of them is checked except for Developer. Check the box next to Developer.

3. Click OK. The Developer tab displays.

Activating Contextual Ribbon Tabs

The ribbon tabs you see all the time are called the *main tabs*. Another 18 tabs come and go, depending on what is selected in Excel.

For example, Excel offers a whole series of commands for dealing with photographs that you insert into your worksheet. However, 90% of people never bother to dress up their worksheets with clipart or pictures, so there's really no reason to show all the commands for working with photographs on the ribbon. However, after you insert a picture and the picture is selected, the Picture Tools, Format tab appears in the ribbon (see Figure 3.19).

Figure 3.19
Anywhere from one to three contextual ribbon tabs display when you activate certain objects.

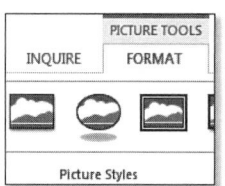

The 18 contextual tabs are identified in Figure 3.20.

Here is the frustrating thing: As soon as you click outside of the object (that is, the picture), it is no longer selected and the Picture Tools Format tab disappears.

If you need to format an object and you cannot find the icons for formatting it, try clicking the object to see if the contextual tabs appear.

Two other tabs occasionally appear, although Excel classifies them as main tabs instead of contextual tabs. If you add the Print Preview Full Screen icon to the interface, you arrive at a Print Preview tab. Also, from the Picture Tools Design tab, you can click Remove Background to end up at the Background Removal tab.

Contextual Tab Group	Analyze	Design	Format	Options	Pens	Displays When...
Chart Tools		●	●			Select a chart
Drawing Tools			●			Select a shape
Equation Tools			●			Insert, Equation
Header & Footer Tools			●			Page Layout View, Click in Header
Ink Tools					●	Insert, Ink
Picture Tools			●			Select a picture
PivotChart Tools	●	●	●			Select a pivot chart
PivotTable Tools	●	●				Cellpointer inside pivot table
Slicer Tools				●		Select a slicer
SmartArt Tools		●	●			Editing SmartArt
Sparkline Tools		●				Cellpointer in cell with sparkline
Table Tools		●				Cellpointer in a table
Timeline Tools				●		Select a timeline

Figure 3.20
This table shows which tabs appear and when.

Finding Lost Commands on the Ribbon

Often, the command you need is front and center on the Home tab and everything is fine. However, there are times when you simply cannot find an obscure command that you know used to be in Excel 2003. Here is my strategy for finding those commands:

1. Right-click the ribbon and select Customize Quick Access Toolbar. Excel displays the Quick Access Toolbar category of the Excel Options dialog.

2. Open the top-left drop-down and change Popular Commands to All Commands. You now have an alphabetical list of over 2,000 commands.

3. Scroll through this alphabetical list until you find the command you are trying to locate in the ribbon.

4. Hover over the command in the left list box. A tooltip appears, showing you where you can find the command. In Figure 3.21, the Justify command is located on the Home tab, in the Editing group, under the Fill drop-down.

Microsoft offers a free interactive ribbon guide that can help you locate an Excel 2003 menu command on the ribbon. Type **Interactive Ribbon Guide** in any search engine to find the latest incarnation of the ribbon guide. I've seen the guide and tried it out once, but given that the tooltips are built into the Customize Quick Access Toolbar panel of Excel Options, it seems pointless to go out to the Web when you can find the answer quickly using the steps just outlined.

 Note

Sometimes, a command truly is not in the ribbon. If you hover over a command in the Customize dialog and the tooltip indicates that this is a command that is not in the ribbon, you have to use Customize to add this command to the Quick Access Toolbar or to the ribbon.

Figure 3.21
This tooltip shows you where to find a command.

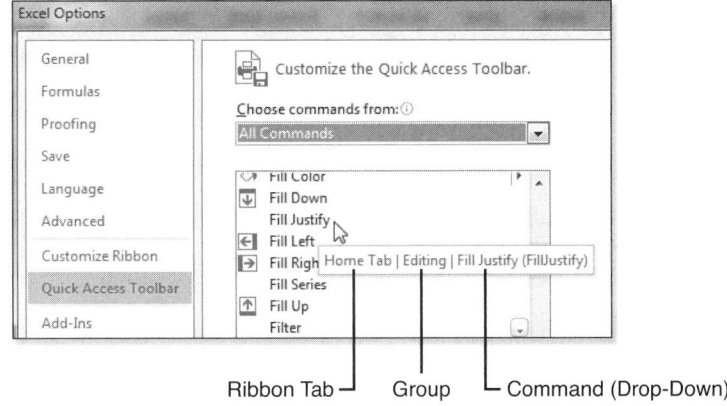

Ribbon Tab ⏋   Group   └ Command (Drop-Down)

Shrinking the Ribbon

The ribbon does take up four vertical rows of space. This won't be an issue on a big monitor, but it could be an issue on a tiny netbook.

Starting in Excel 2013, to shrink the ribbon, you can right-click the ribbon and choose Collapse the Ribbon. The ribbon collapses to show only the ribbon tabs. When you click a tab, the ribbon temporarily expands. To close the ribbon, choose a command or press Esc.

To permanently bring the ribbon back to full size, right-click a ribbon tab and uncheck Collapse the Ribbon.

Note that you can also minimize the ribbon using the carat (^) icon at the bottom right of the expanded ribbon. To expand the ribbon, click any tab and then click the pushpin icon in the lower-right corner of the ribbon.

> **Tip**
> Starting in Excel 2013, the ribbon often stays open after certain commands. For example, I frequently click the Increase Decimal icon three times in a row. When the ribbon is minimized, you can click Home and then click Increase Decimal three times without having the ribbon close.

Using the Quick Access Toolbar

A problem with the ribbon is that only one-seventh of the commands are visible at any given time. You will find yourself moving from one tab to another. The alternative is to use the Quick Access Toolbar (QAT) to store your favorite commands.

The QAT starts out as a tiny toolbar with Save, Undo, and Redo. It is initially located above the File tab in the ribbon.

If you start using the QAT frequently, you can right-click the toolbar and choose Show Quick Access Toolbar Below the Ribbon.

Adding Icons to the QAT

The drop-down at the right side of the QAT, shown on the right side in Figure 3.22, offers 12 popular commands you might choose to add to the Quick Access Toolbar. Choose a command from this list to add it to the QAT.

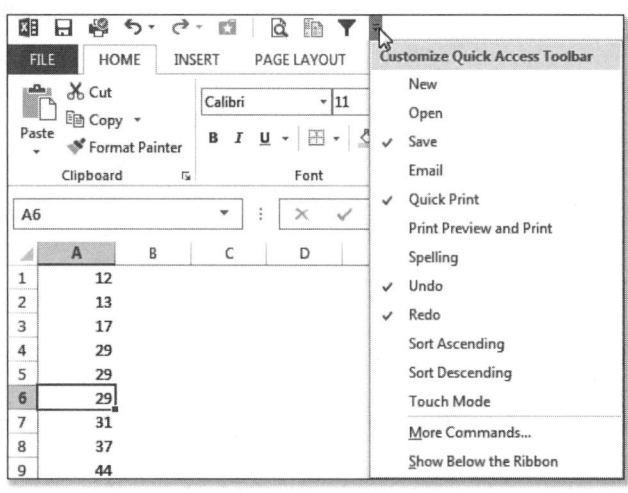

Figure 3.22
Use the drop-down at the right side of the QAT to add 12 popular commands.

Note that changes to the QAT made in Excel 2010 also appear in Excel 2013, and vice versa. The Open Recent File icon is no longer available in Excel 2013, but if you add it to the QAT in Excel 2010, it appears in Excel 2013. Unfortunately, the icon simply goes to the File, Open pane.

When you find a command in the ribbon you are likely to use often, you can easily add the command to the QAT. To do so, right-click any command in the ribbon and select Add to Quick Access Toolbar. Items added to the Quick Access Toolbar using the right-click method are added to the right side of the QAT.

The right-click method works for many commands, but not with individual items within commands. For example, you can put the Font Size drop-down on the QAT, but you cannot specifically put size 16 font in the QAT.

Removing Commands from the QAT

You can remove an icon from the QAT by right-clicking the icon and selecting Remove from Quick Access Toolbar.

Customizing the QAT

You can make minor changes to the QAT by using the context menus, but you can have far more control over the QAT if you use the Customize command. Right-click the QAT and select Customize Quick Access Toolbar to display the Quick Access Toolbar section of the Excel Options dialog, as shown in Figure 3.23.

Figure 3.23
You can cus-
tomize the QAT
using the Excel
Options dialog.

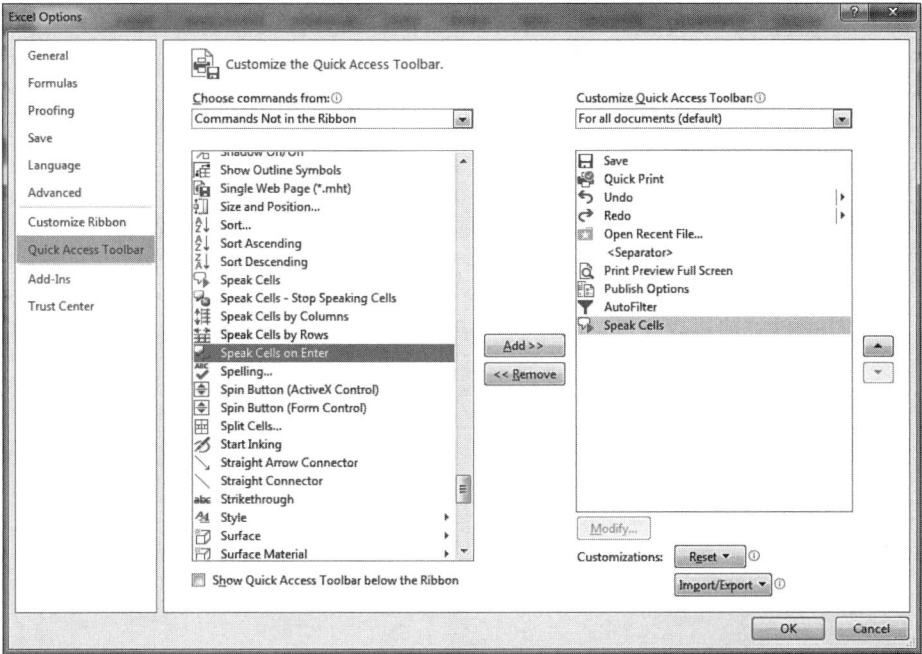

The Excel Options dialog offers many features for customizing the Quick Access Toolbar:

- You can choose to customize the QAT for all documents on your computer or just for the current workbook by using the top-right drop-down menu.

- You can add separators between icons to group the icons logically. A separator icon is available at the top of the left menu. Click the separator icon in the left list box and then click the Add>> icon in the center of the screen.

- You can resequence the order of the icons on the toolbar. Select an icon in the right list box and then click the up/down arrow icons on the right side of the dialog.

- You can access 2,000+ commands, including the commands from every tab and commands that are not available in the ribbon. Although the dialog starts with just 53 popular commands in the left list box, use the left drop-down to choose All Command or Commands Not in the Ribbon. When you find a command in the left list box, select the command and then click Add>> in the center of the dialog to add that command to the QAT.

- You can reset the QAT to its original default state using the Reset button in the lower right.

- You can export your custom QAT icons from your computer and import on another computer.

- You can move the QAT to appear above or below the ribbon using the check box in the lower right.

Assigning VBA Macros to Quick Access Toolbar Buttons

Typically, a VBA macro is assigned to a shortcut key. In legacy versions of Excel, it was easy to customize the menu system to add commands to invoke macros. Excel 2013 offers a weak interface for adding custom macros to the QAT. In the Excel Options dialog is a drop-down called Macros. If you select this group, you see all public macros in all open workbooks. You can select a macro and click Add to add that macro to the QAT.

Initially, every macro added to the Quick Access Toolbar gets an identical flowchart icon. However, you can select an icon in the Customize Quick Access Toolbar list box and click the Modify button. The Modify Button dialog that appears enables you to choose from 55 available icons for a macro as shown in Figure 3.24. Most of these buttons are similar to icons that are already popular. For example, the Print icon is fairly well known and has a meaning. In addition to choosing from the 55 icons, you can type any text for a display name. The display name does not appear next to the button. However, if you hover your mouse over the icon on the QAT, you can see the display name in a tooltip.

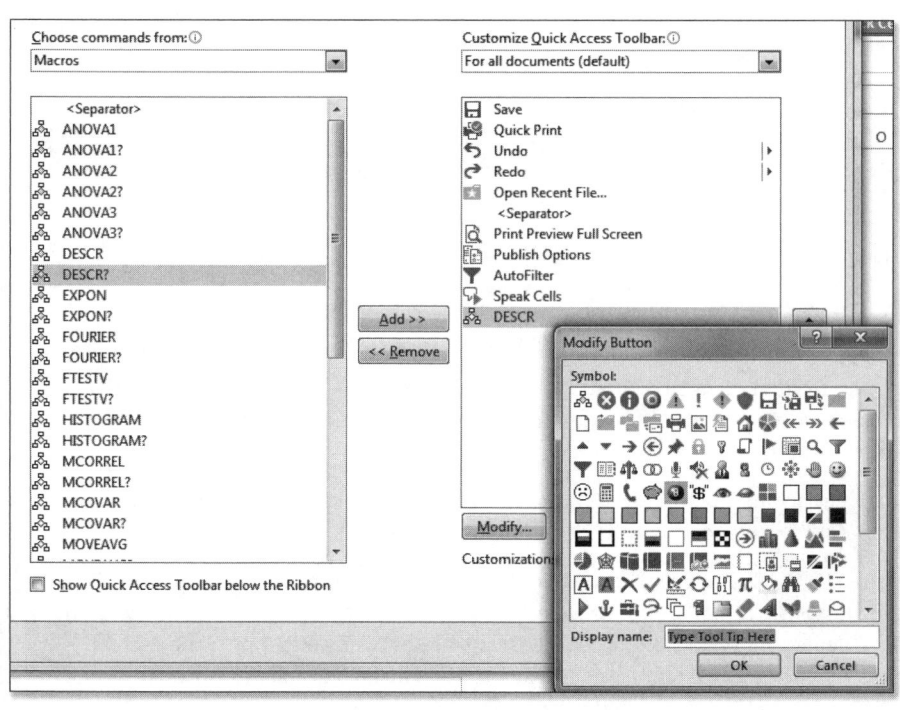

Figure 3.24
For macros, you can customize the button image and add a display name on the QAT.

Using the Full-Screen File Menu

Open the File menu in Excel 2013 and you might be shocked to see that it takes up 100% of your screen real estate. This panel is called the Backstage view and was introduced in Excel 2010. Here is the logic: When you are working on most ribbon tabs, you are working in your document. When you are about to change the font or something like that, you want to see the results of the change for the "in" commands. However, the Excel team feels that after you move to the File menu, you are done working in your document and you are about to do something with the whole document, such as send the workbook, print the workbook, post the workbook to Twitter, and so on. Microsoft calls these the "out" commands. The theory is that you don't need to see the worksheet for the "out" commands, so Microsoft fills the entire screen with the File menu.

To open the Backstage view, click the File menu. The Backstage view fills the screen, as shown in Figure 3.25. Backstage is split into three sections: the narrow left navigation panel and two wider sections that provide information.

Figure 3.25
The Backstage view
fills the entire screen.

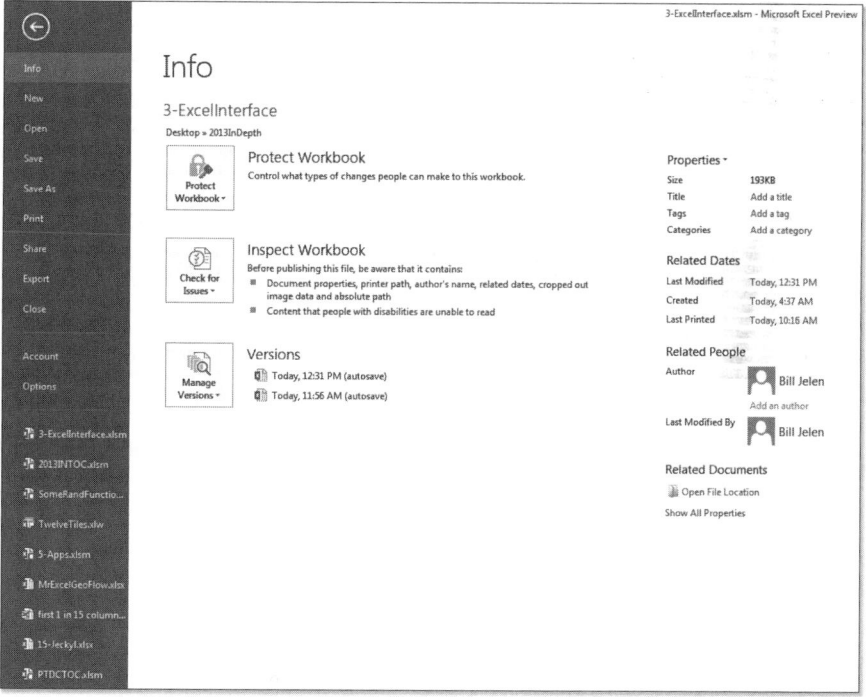

The left navigation panel includes these commands:

- **Info**—Provides information about the current workbook. This is discussed later in the "Getting Information About the Current Workbook" section.

- **New**—Used to create a new workbook or start from a template. Discussed in Chapter 1.

- **Open**—Used to access a file stored on your computer or the SkyDrive. Discussed in Chapter 1.

- **Save**—Saves the file in the same folder as it was previously stored. Note that Save is actually a command instead of a panel in Backstage.

- **Save As**—Stores the file on your computer or in the SkyDrive. Discussed in Chapter 1.

- **Print**—Used to choose print settings and print. Includes Print Preview. Discussed in Chapter 36, "Printing."

- **Share**—Used to post your workbook to Facebook, Twitter, or LinkedIn or to send it via email. Discussed in Chapter 36.

- **Export**—Used to create a PDF, control web publishing options, or change the file type. Discussed in Chapter 37, "Excel Web App and Other Ways to Share Workbooks."

- **Close**—Closes the current workbook. Like Save, this entry is a pure command.

- **Account**—Connects your copy of Excel to various social networking accounts. Discussed in Chapter 1.

- **Options**—Contains pages of Excel settings. See Chapter 4, "Customizing Excel," for details.

- **Recent File List**—This list appears only if you've changed a default setting in Excel Options. Visit File, Options, Advanced Display and choose Quickly Access This Number of Recent Workbooks.

Pressing the Esc Key to Close Backstage View

To get out of Backstage and return to your worksheet, you can either press the Esc key or click the back arrow in the top-left corner of Backstage.

Recovering Unsaved Workbooks

As in previous versions of Excel, the AutoSave feature can create copies of your workbook every n minutes. If an AutoSave version of your workbook exists, you can now access that file using the Recover Unsaved Workbooks icon at the bottom of the Recent Workbooks list. Note that you might have to scroll down to the bottom of the Recent Workbooks list to find the Recover Unsaved Workbooks icon (see Figure 3.26).

Do you ever get to the end of your workday, use Alt+F+X to close Excel, and then are greeted with a barrage of Do You Want to Save questions? I frequently forget that the nth workbook that I have open is not saved. I think that I had opened these workbooks to get information, that I had not made any significant changes, and will either start clicking Don't Save repeatedly or will hold down Shift and click Don't Save, which is equivalent to clicking the nonexistent Don't Save to All selection.

As I see that important file get closed, I realize that I just lost all my changes to that file and cringe. This is a common problem that happens to everyone sooner or later. Provided that the file was open long enough to experience an AutoSave, you might be able to get the file back.

Figure 3.26
If you set Excel to display more recent workbooks than will fit on the screen, you have to scroll down to find the Recover Unsaved Workbooks icon.

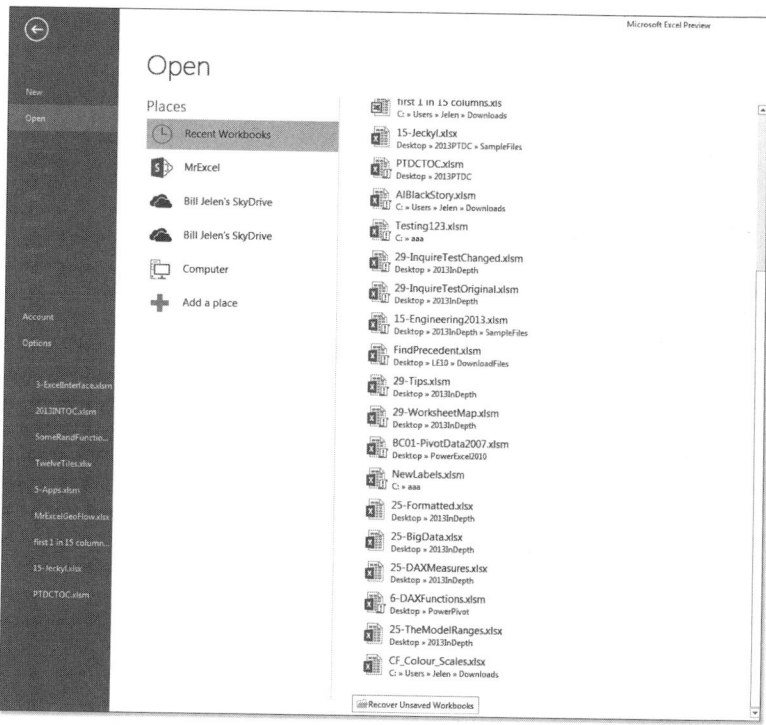

Go to Recover Unsaved Workbooks and find the date and time of the last AutoSave. It might be within 5 minutes of the last time you edited a cell in that document. When you find the file and open it, the Information Bar reports that this is a "recovered unsaved file" (see Figure 3.27). Click Save As to give the file a name.

Figure 3.27
Excel recovers the file. You need to use Save As to make the recovery permanent.

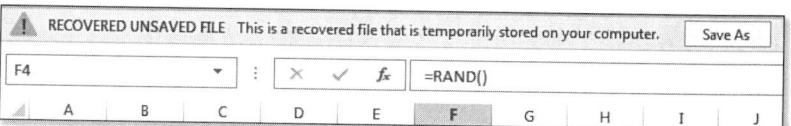

Clearing the Recent Workbooks List

If you need to clear out the Recent Workbooks list, you should visit File, Options, Advanced, Display. Set the Show This Number of Recent Documents list to zero. This is unlike the behavior in Excel 2003. In Excel 2003, to clear out the ninth item from the list, you had to reset only the number of files back to eight and Excel would forget about the ninth. In Excel 2013, if you switch from 50 files to one file, then back to 50 files, all 50 files will come back. The only way to clear the Recent Workbooks list is to set the value back to zero. You can then reset it to 50 and Excel will start collecting history again.

Getting Information About the Current Workbook

When a workbook is open and you go to the File menu, you start in the Info gallery for that workbook. As shown in Figure 3.28, the Info pane lists all sorts of information about the current workbook:

- The workbook path is shown at the top of the center panel.

- You can see the file size.

- You can see when the document was last modified and who modified it.

- If any special states exist, these will be reported at the top of the middle pane. Special states might include the following:

    - Macros not enabled

    - Links not updated

    - Checked out from SharePoint

Figure 3.28
The Info gallery includes all of the properties of the file.

- You can see if the file has been AutoSaved and recover those AutoSaved versions.

- You can mark the document as final, which will cause others opening the file to initially have a read-only version of the file.

- You can edit links to other documents.

- You can add tags or categories to the file.

- Using the Check for Issues drop-down, you can run a compatibility checker to see if the workbook is compatible with legacy versions of Excel. You can run an accessibility checker to see if any parts of the document will be difficult for people with disabilities. You can run a Document Inspector to see if any private information is hidden in the file.

Marking a Workbook as Final to Prevent Editing

Open the Protect Workbook icon in the Info gallery to access a setting called Mark as Final (see Figure 3.29). This marks the workbook as read-only. It prevents someone else from making changes to your final workbook.

Figure 3.29
Mark a document as read-only.

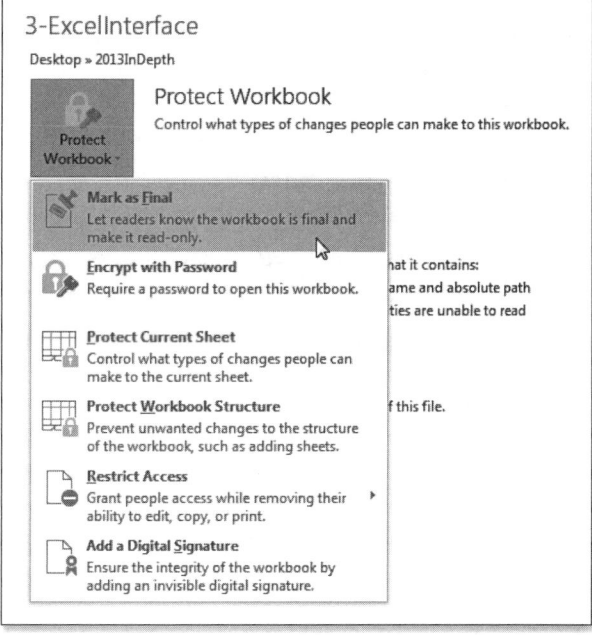

Of course, if the other person visits the Info gallery, that person can reenable editing. This feature is simply designed to warn the other people that you've marked it as final and no further changes should happen.

If you can convince everyone in your workgroup to sign up for a Windows Live ID, you can use the Restrict Permission by People setting. This layer of security enables you to define who can read, edit, and/or print the document.

Finding Hidden Content Using the Document Inspector

The Document Inspector can find a lot of hidden content, but it is not perfect. Still, finding 95% of the types of hidden content can protect you a lot of the time.

To run the Document Inspector, select File, Info, Check for Issues, Inspect Document, and click OK. The results of the Document Inspector will show that the document has personal information stored in the file properties (author's name) and perhaps a hidden worksheet.

 Caution

The Document Inspector is not foolproof. Do you frequently hide settings by changing the font color to white or by using the ;;; custom number format? This won't be found by the Document Inspector. The Document Inspector also won't note that you scrolled over outside the print area and jotted your after-work grocery list in column X.

Using Other Excel Interface Improvements

This is a recap of interface changes introduced in Excel 2007 through Excel 2013:

- **Slot-machining (2013)**—When you change an input cell, all of the calculated cells in view of the window animate as they change. This looks a lot like the spinning wheel in a slot machine.

- **Touch mode (2013)**—If you are using Excel on a touch screen or a tablet, you can put Excel in touch mode. A tiny bit of space appears around each icon, which hopefully gives you more of a chance to touch the correct icon.

- **Less chrome (2013)**—Microsoft really believes a lot of people will be using Excel on touch devices once Windows 8 begins to catch on. They tried to make the touch zones bigger by eliminating any decorations in the interface. Microsoft called these decorations the "chrome" in the interface. In addition to losing the chrome, you also lose some tiny icons that would be hard to use in touch mode. For example, the tiny icons in the edge of the scrollbars used to split a window are gone in Excel 2013. The set of four controls used to move between worksheets is reduced to two icons.

- **Paste options (2010)**—An expanded Paste Options menu introduces many popular shortcut key sequences to Excel.

- **Live preview (2007)**—You can preview formatting changes before you actually select the change.

- **Mini toolbar (2007)**—The mini toolbar appears whenever you select text. Although this might happen rarely when you edit cells in Excel, it does happen frequently when you work with charts, text boxes, and so on. The mini toolbar offers quick access to font, size, bold, italic, alignment, color, indenting, and bullets.

- **Formula bar (2007)**—The formula bar includes the capability to expand or contract itself at your whim instead of the whim of Excel.

- **Zoom slider (2007)**—The Zoom slider enables you to quickly change from seeing one page to hundreds of pages at a time.

- **Status bar (2007)**—The status bar appears at the bottom of your worksheet window. Although you probably never noticed it, the status bar in legacy versions of Excel reported the total of any selected cells. This information is now improved and expanded, offering multiple statistics at one time.

- **View control (2007)**—The View control gives you one-click access to Page Break Preview mode, Normal mode, and the Page Layout view introduced in Excel 2007.

- **New Sheet icon (2007/2013)**—The New Sheet icon enables you to add new worksheets to a workbook with a single click. In Excel 2013, the new sheet is added to the right of the active sheet.

Adding White Space Around Icons Using Touch Mode

If you are trying to use Excel on a tablet or a touch screen, you want to try touch mode. Follow these steps:

1. Go to the right side of the QAT and open the drop-down that appears there.

2. The twelfth command is called Touch Mode. The icon is a blue dot with a ring of white space and then dashed lines around the white space. Choose this command to add it to the QAT.

3. Click the icon on the QAT. You see white space added around all of the icons.

Figure 3.30 compares the first two groups of the Home tab in regular and touch mode.

 **Note**

As a public service to you, the reader, I went out and bought a Planar touch screen so I could try the touch gestures in Excel. Other than having some fun scribbling using the Ink tools, there really isn't any good reason to have a touch screen in Excel. However, one hot August day, I was writing this book and a house fly zoomed past me and landed on the touch screen. It landed with enough force to select cell C33, which I thought was pretty funny. Had it actually typed a VLOOKUP formula, it would definitely be the most proficient Excel house fly ever.

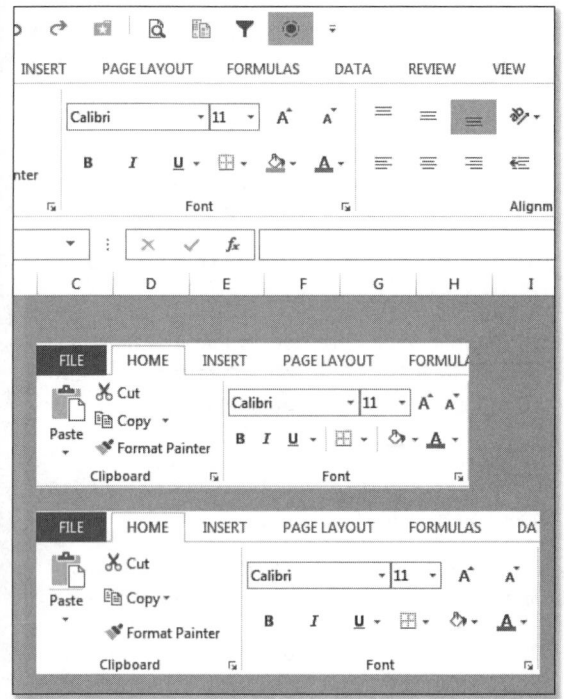

Figure 3.30
Touch mode adds white space around each icon, thus making the touch points larger.

Previewing Paste Using the Paste Options Gallery

Here's a quick survey: Have you ever opened a Notepad window, pasted your data to Notepad, copied from Notepad, and then pasted to your application? This is a great but tedious way to remove formatting from a selection. If you have discovered this painful workaround, you are going to love this feature that was added starting in Excel 2010: the Paste Options gallery.

Here is another survey: Suppose you have to copy a column of formulas and paste them as values. Do your fingers know how to do Ctrl+C, Alt+E+S+V+Enter? If so, you are going to love the new Ctrl+V, Ctrl, V keystrokes available in the Paste Options gallery. If you've ever done Ctrl+C, Alt+E+S+V+Enter, Alt+E+S+T+Enter, you will love the new Context+E keyboard shortcut.

As someone who uses both of those old keyboard shortcuts frequently, I love the Paste Options gallery. You can keep slicers, sparklines, even PowerPivot; the Paste Options gallery is going to be the one feature that makes a difference in my life every single hour of every single workday.

Microsoft discovered that Paste was the number-one command that was immediately followed by Undo. To improve the Paste command, Microsoft added the Paste Options gallery in three places in Excel 2010. These galleries support Live Preview and keyboard shortcuts. They should make mouse-centric as well as keyboard-centric people very happy.

You encounter the gallery when you have something on the Clipboard and one of these three events happens:

- You right-click a cell to access the context menu.

- You open the Paste drop-down from the Home tab.

- After you perform a typical Paste operation, the old Paste Repair menu icon appears with the tip that you can press Ctrl to access the gallery.

Accessing the Gallery After Performing a Paste Operation

Suppose that you copy a range with Ctrl+C and then paste with Ctrl+V. The icon for the old Paste Repair appears next to the paste, but this time it notes that you can open the menu by pressing Ctrl. When you press Ctrl, you are presented with a gallery of paste options.

The options available in the gallery are as follows:

- **Paste**—This is the standard paste that you would get using Ctrl+V.

- **Formulas**—Pastes only formulas, with no formatting. This is common when you are copying down from the first row of a table that has an outline border. To prevent the top border from copying, you can paste formulas. You then find that you have to reapply the number formatting.

- **Formulas & Number Formatting**—Copies formulas as previous formulas, along with the number formatting.

- **Keep Source Formatting**—This is particularly useful when copying from another application such as a web page. The formatting from the other application is pasted along with the values.

- **No Borders**—Pastes everything but the borders.

- **Column Widths**—Includes the column widths from the copied area.

- **Transpose**—Turns the data on its side. A 12-row-by-1-column copied range would paste as 1 row by 12 columns.

- **Values**—Converts formulas to values.

- **Values and Number Formatting**—Converts the formulas to values and includes the number formats from the copied data.

- **Values & Source Formatting**—Converts the formulas to values and includes all formatting such as cell styles, font color, number formatting, and borders.

- **Formats**—Does not bring any values, only the cell formatting. Similar to using the Format Painter but not as annoying.

- **Paste Link**—Creates formulas here that point back to the copied range.

- **Paste as Picture**—Pastes a picture of the original cells in this location.

- **Paste as Linked Picture**—Pastes a live picture of the original cell in this location. This is the elusive Camera tool from Excel 2003.

- **Open Paste Special**—Used to access the old Paste Special dialog. The Paste Special dialog still offers some choices not available in the Paste Options gallery: Comments, Validation, All using Source Theme, Add, Subtract, Multiply, Divide, and Skip Blanks.

Accessing the Paste Options Gallery from the Right-Click Menu

The Paste Options gallery appears in the right-click context menu and includes Live Preview. The top six options appear directly in the menu. A fly-out menu offers all 14 options.

As you start to hover over the various paste icons, Live Preview takes over. The rest of the context menu disappears so that you can see the worksheet. Hover over Transpose, and you get a preview of what Transpose actually does. Hover over Formatting and you see that the Formatting option copies only the cell formats and not the numbers. If you hover over Paste Special and then move out to the full gallery, all the context menu except the full gallery disappears, and Live Preview continues to work.

Why Keyboard-Centric People Like the Context Gallery

I am not a right-click person. I always use keyboard shortcuts instead of the mouse. I can press Alt+E+S+V+Enter before most people can even move their hand over to the mouse.

Take a close look at your keyboard. To the left of the spacebar, between the FN and Alt keys, do you have the Flying Windows key? I've memorized a few of its shortcuts, such as Win+E to open Windows Explorer. Now, look over to the right of the spacebar. What do you have between Alt and Ctrl there? I have a key that I had never used before today. This key looks like the right-click menu and is the Context Menu key. When I press that key in Excel, the right-click menu appears in the worksheet.

Those six icons in the Paste Options gallery in the right-click menu each have a keyboard accelerator:

P—Normal Paste

V—Paste Values

F—Formulas

T—Transpose

R—Formats

N—Paste Link

This means that there is an even faster keyboard method for converting formulas to values. Press Ctrl+C to copy, press the Context Menu key, and then press V to convert to values. You probably have to use two hands: Ctrl+C with the left hand, Context Menu key with the right hand, and V with the left hand. It takes a little practice until this is as fast as Ctrl+C, Ctrl+V, Ctrl, V, but it is worth a shot if you rely on keyboard shortcuts to speed your way through tasks.

Accessing the Paste Options Gallery from the Paste Drop-Down

The Paste Options gallery also appears when you open the Paste drop-down on the Home tab. Figure 3.31 shows the menu there.

Figure 3.31
The gallery replaces the old Paste drop-down in the Home tab.

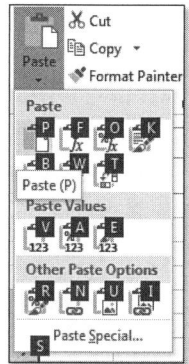

Using the New Sheet Icon to Add Worksheets

The Insert Worksheet icon looks different in Excel 2013 and behaves differently as well. The icon is a circle with a plus sign that appears to the right of the last sheet tab. It also looks like an aerial view of a Phillips-head machine screw.

When you click this icon, a new worksheet is added to the right of the active sheet. This is better than Excel 2010, where the new worksheet was added as the last worksheet in the workbook and then had to be dragged to the correct position.

Navigating Through Many Worksheets Using the Controls in the Lower Left

Previous versions of Excel had four controls for moving through the list of worksheet tabs. Due to the new "less chrome" mantra, the worksheet navigation icons are now a left and right arrowhead in the lower left (see Figure 3.32).

Figure 3.32
These worksheet navigation controls have been streamlined in Excel 2013.

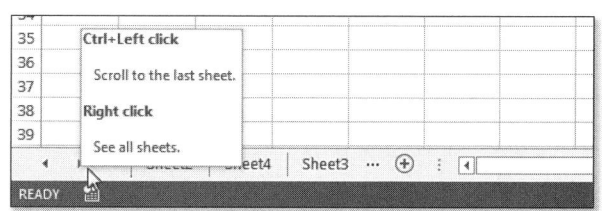

The controls are only active when you have more tabs than are visible across the bottom of the Excel window. Click the left or right icon to scroll the tabs one at a time. Ctrl+click either arrow to scroll to the last tab. Note that scrolling the tabs does not change the active sheet. It just brings more tabs into view so you can then click the selected tab.

Just as in prior versions of Excel, you can right-click the worksheet navigation arrows to see a complete list of worksheets. Click any item in the list to move to that worksheet.

In certain circumstances, an ellipsis (...) icon appears in the worksheet navigation area. This icon selects the worksheet to the left of the active sheet.

Using the Mini Toolbar to Format Selected Text

When you select some text in a chart title or within a cell, the mini toolbar appears above the selected text. If you move away from the mini toolbar, it fades away. However, if you move the mouse toward the mini toolbar, you see several text formatting options.

In your initial use of Excel 2013, you might not see the mini toolbar. Although you often select cells or ranges of cells, it is rare to select only a portion of a cell value in Cell Edit mode. However, as you begin using charts, SmartArt diagrams, and text boxes, you will have the mini toolbar appearing frequently.

To use the mini toolbar, follow these steps:

1. Select some text. If you select text in a cell, you must select a portion of the text in the cell by using Cell Edit mode. In a chart, SmartArt diagram, or text box, you can select any text. As soon as you release the mouse button, the mini toolbar appears above and to the right of the selection.

2. Move the mouse pointer toward the mini toolbar. The mini toolbar stays visible if your mouse is above it. If you move the mouse away from the mini toolbar, it fades away.

3. Make changes in the mini toolbar to affect the text you selected in step 1.

4. When you are done formatting the selected text, you can move the mouse away from the mini toolbar to dismiss it.

Getting the Mini Toolbar Back

The shyness of the mini toolbar might be the most frustrating part of using it. If you move the mouse away from the mini toolbar, it fades away. If you immediately move back toward the mini toolbar, it comes back. If you use the mouse for some other task, such as scrolling, the mini toolbar permanently goes away. In this case, you might have to reselect the text to get the mini toolbar to come back.

Disabling the Mini Toolbar

If you are annoyed by the mini toolbar, you can turn it off for all Excel workbooks. To do this, select File, Options. The first choice in Excel Options is a check box for Show Mini Toolbar on Selection. Clear this check box.

Expanding the Formula Bar

Formulas range from very simple to very complex. As people started writing longer and longer formulas in Excel, an annoying problem began to appear: If the formula for a selected cell was longer than the formula bar, the formula bar would wrap and extend over the worksheet (see Figure 3.33). In many cases, the formula would obscure the first few rows of the worksheet. This was frustrating, especially if the selected cell was in the top few rows of the spreadsheet.

Figure 3.33
In legacy versions of Excel, the formula bar could obscure cells on a worksheet.

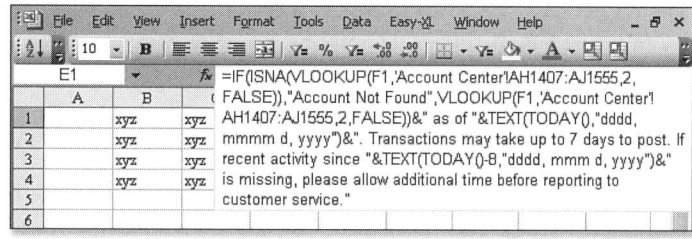

Excel 2013 includes a formula bar that prevents the formula from obscuring the spreadsheet. For example, in Figure 3.34, cell F1 contains a formula that is longer than the formula bar. Notice the down-arrow icon at the right end of the formula bar. This icon expands the formula bar.

Figure 3.34
Initially, Excel shows only the first row of the formula.

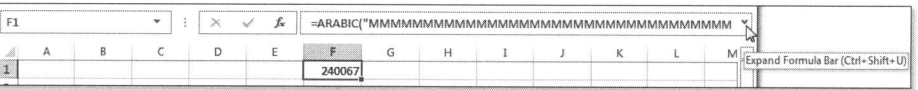

Press Ctrl+Shift+U or click the down arrow icon at the right side of the formula bar to expand the formula bar. The formula bar expands, but the entire worksheet moves down to accommodate the larger formula bar.

The formula in this example is too long for the default larger formula bar. You have to hover your mouse near the bottom of the formula bar until you see the up/down white arrow cursor. Click and drag down until you can see the entire formula (see Figure 3.35).

 Note

Excel MVP Bob Umlas keeps suggesting the formula bar should change color when you are not seeing the entire formula. That is a great suggestion that perhaps the Excel team will one day add to Excel.

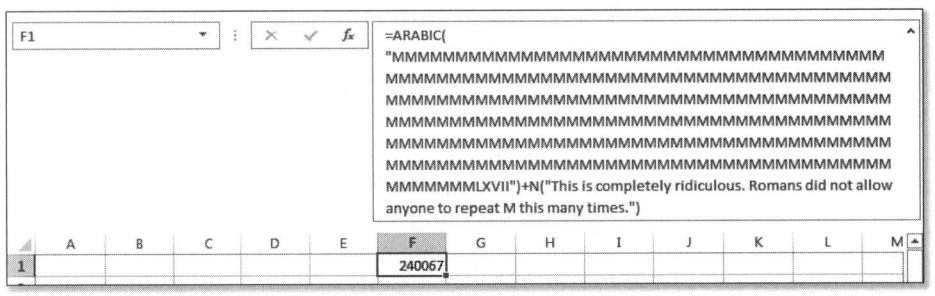

Figure 3.35
The worksheet moves down to accommodate the formula.

Zooming In and Out on a Worksheet

In the lower-right corner of the Excel window, a zoom slider enables you to zoom from 400% to 10% with lightning speed. You simply drag the slider to the right to zoom in and to the left to zoom out. The Zoom Out and Zoom In buttons on either end of the slider enable you to adjust the zoom in 10% increments.

Clicking the % indicator to the left of the zoom slider opens the legacy Zoom dialog.

Using the Status Bar to Add Numbers

If you select several cells that contain numeric data and then look at the status bar, at the bottom of the Excel window, you can see that the status bar reports the average, count, and sum of the selected cells (see Figure 3.36).

270	229	242	236
294	228	247	224
282	263	232	266
278	226	235	289
222	221	262	267
280	258	254	224
241	295	247	269
291	261	260	265
258	280	302	267

AVERAGE: 257.3611111   COUNT: 36   SUM: 9265

Figure 3.36
The status bar shows the sum, average, and count of the selected cells.

If you need to quickly add the contents of several cells, you can select the cells and look for the total in the status bar. This feature has been in Excel for a decade, yet very few people realized it was there. In legacy versions of Excel, only the sum would appear, but you could right-click the sum to see other values, such as the average, count, minimum, and maximum.

You can customize which statistics are shown in the status bar. Right-click the status bar and choose any or all of Min, Max, Numerical Count, Count, Sum, and Average.

Note that the panel might show values for items that you have recently unselected. These figures will be wrong if the selection has changed.

Switching Between Normal View, Page Break Preview, and Page Layout View Modes

Three shortcut icons to the left of the zoom slider enable you to quickly switch between three view modes:

- **Normal view**—This mode shows worksheet cells as normal.

- **Page Break preview**—This mode draws the page breaks in blue. You can actually drag the page breaks to new locations in Page Break preview. This mode has been available in several versions of Excel.

- **Page Layout view**—This view was introduced in Excel 2007. It combines the best of Page Break preview and Print Preview modes.

In Page Layout view mode, each page is shown, along with the margins, header, and footer. A ruler appears above the pages and to the left of the pages. You can make changes in this mode in the following ways:

- To change the margins, drag the gray boxes in the ruler.

- To change column widths, drag the borders of the column headers.

- To add a header, select Click to Add Header.

CUSTOMIZING EXCEL

The Excel Options dialog offers dozens of changes you can make in Excel. One of the primary changes available in Excel Options is customizing the ribbon and the Quick Access Toolbar. Back in Excel 2003, you could easily customize the menus and toolbars. In Excel 2007, customization was severely limited. Starting in Excel 2010, it was back, although not as flexible as in Excel 2003.

This chapter walks you through examples of customizing the ribbon and discusses some of the important option settings available in Excel.

Performing a Simple Ribbon Modification

Suppose that you generally like the ribbon, but there is one icon that seems to be misplaced. For me, that icon is the PivotTable command. I have no idea why this is on the Insert tab instead of on the Data tab where it belongs.

Take a look at the Data tab, as shown in Figure 4.1. It would make sense to have the PivotTable command right after the Sort & Filter group and before the Data Tools group.

Figure 4.1
Decide where the new command should go.

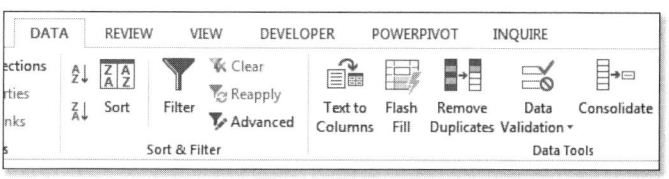

To add the pivot table command to the Data tab, follow these steps:

1. Right-click the ribbon and select Customize the Ribbon.

2. In the right list box, expand the Data tab by clicking the + sign next to Data.

3. Click the Sort & Filter entry in the right list box. The new group will go after this entry.

4. Click the New Group button at the bottom of the right list box. A New Group (Custom) item appears after Sort & Filter, as shown in Figure 4.2.

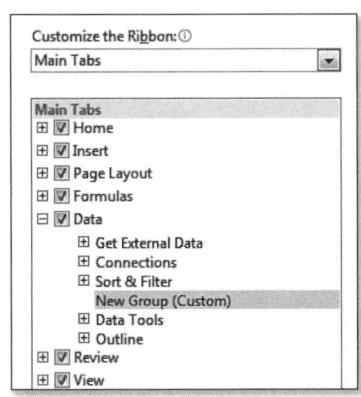

Figure 4.2
Commands have to be added to a new group.

5. While the New Group is selected, click the Rename button at the bottom of the list box. The Rename dialog appears.

6. The Rename dialog offers to let you choose an icon and specify a name for the group. The icon is only shown when the Excel window is too small to display the whole group. Choose any icon and type a display name of **Pivot**. Click OK.

7. The left list box shows the popular commands. You could change Popular Commands to All Commands and scroll through 2,400 commands. However, in this case, the commands you want are on the Insert tab. Choose All Tabs from the top-left drop-down. Expand the Insert tab and then Tables. Click PivotTable in the left list box. Click the Add>> button in the center of the dialog to add PivotTable to the new custom Pivot group on the ribbon. Excel automatically advances to the next icon of Recommended PivotTables. Click Add>> again.

8. In the drop-down above the left list box, select All Commands. The left list box changes to show an alphabetical list of all commands.

9. Scroll through the left list box until you find PivotTable and PivotChart Wizard. This is the obscure entry point to create Multiple Consolidation Range pivot tables. Select that item in the left list box. Click Add>>. At this point, the right side of the dialog should look like Figure 4.3

10. Click OK.

Figure 4.4 shows the new group in the Data tab of the ribbon.

Figure 4.3
Three new icons have been added to a new custom group on the Data tab.

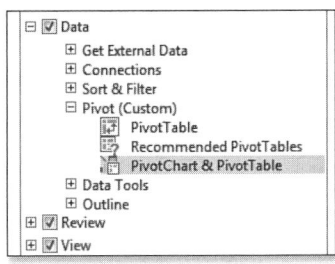

Figure 4.4
The results appear in the ribbon.

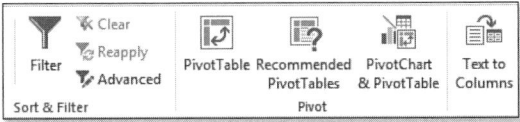

Adding a New Ribbon Tab

To add a new ribbon tab, follow these basic steps:

1. Right-click the ribbon and select Customize the Ribbon.

2. Click New Tab and Rename the tab.

3. Add New Group(s) to the new tab.

4. Add commands to the new groups.

As you go through the steps to add a new ribbon tab, you will discover how absolutely limiting the ribbon customizations are. You have no control over which items appear with large icons and which appear with small icons. This even applies to galleries. If you add the Cell Styles gallery to a group on the ribbon, it always appears as an icon instead of a gallery, even if it is the only thing on the entire ribbon tab (see the left icon in Figure 4.5). The workaround is to add an entire built-in group to the tab. In the right of Figure 4.5, the entire Styles group was added. The Cell Styles gallery is now allowed to appear as a gallery.

Figure 4.5
When added to a custom group, a gallery is reduced to a single icon with a drop-down.

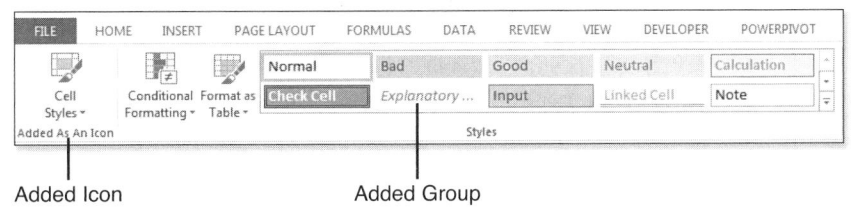

Added Icon   Added Group

Sharing Customizations with Others

If you have developed the perfect ribbon customization and you want everyone in your department to have the same customization, you can export all the ribbon customizations.

To export the changes, follow these steps:

1. Right-click the ribbon and select Customize the Ribbon.

2. Below the right list box, select Import/Export, Export All Customizations.

3. Browse to a folder and provide a name for the customization file. The file type will be .exportedUI. Click OK.

4. In Windows Explorer, find the exported .exportedUI file. Copy it to a co-worker's computer.

>  **Note**
>
> This is an all-or-nothing proposition. You cannot export your changes to one custom tab without exporting your changes to the Data and Home tabs.

5. On the co-worker's computer, repeat step 1. In step 2, select Import All Customizations. Find the file and click OK.

Questions About Ribbon Customization

Can the customizations apply to only a certain workbook?
No. The Customize the Ribbon command in Excel 2013 applies to all workbooks.

Can toolbars be docked to the side of the screen or floating as in Excel 97–2003?
No. The ribbon always must be at the top of the screen, in a horizontal position.

Can I reset my customizations and go back to the original Ribbon?
Right-click the ribbon and select Customize the Ribbon. Below the right list box, select Reset, Reset All Customizations.

Where is the Excel 2003 icon editor? Where is the list of 4,096 icons available back in Excel 2003?
Neither item is supported in Excel 2013.

How can I get complete control over the ribbon?
Learn RibbonX and write some VBA to build your own ribbon.

➡ *For more information on building your own ribbon,* **see** RibbonX: Customizing the Office 2007 Ribbon, *by Robert Martin, Ken Puls, and Teresa Hennig (Wiley, ISBN 0470191112).*

These ribbon customizations are really lacking. Is there another option that doesn't require me to write a program?
Yes, a number of third-party ribbon customization programs are available. For example, check out a free one from Excel MVP Andy Pope at www.andypope.info/vba/ribboneditor.htm.

Introducing the Excel Options Dialog

Open the File menu and select Options from the left navigation pane to open the Excel Options dialog. The dialog has categories for General, Formulas, Proofing, Save, Language, Advanced, Customize Ribbon, Quick Access Toolbar, Add-Ins, and Trust Center. The Trust Center leads to another 12 categories.

To the Excel team's credit, they tried to move the top options to the General category. Beyond those 15 settings, though, there are hundreds of settings spread throughout 21 different categories in Excel Options and Trust Center. Table 4.1 gives you a top-level view of where to start looking for settings.

Table 4.1   Excel Options Dialog Settings

Category	Types of Settings
General	The most commonly used settings, such as user interface settings, default font for new workbooks, number of sheets in a new workbook, customer name, and Start screen.
Formulas	All options for controlling calculation, error-checking rules, and formula settings. Note that options for multithreaded calculations are currently considered obscure enough to be on the Advanced tab rather than on the Formulas tab.
Proofing	Spell check options and a link to the AutoCorrect dialog.
Save	The default method for saving, AutoRecovery settings, legacy colors, and web server options.
Language	Choose the editing language, tooltip language, and Help language.
Advanced	All options that Microsoft considers arcane, spread among 13 headings.
Customize Ribbon	Icons to customize the ribbon.
Quick Access Toolbar	Icons to customize the Quick Access Toolbar.
Add-Ins	A list of available and installed add-ins. New add-ins can be installed from the button at the bottom of this category.
Trust Center	Links to the Microsoft Trust Center, with 12 additional categories.

Getting Help with a Setting

Many settings appear with a small *i* icon. If you hover the mouse near this icon, Excel displays a super tooltip for the setting. The tooltip explains what happens when you choose the setting. It also provides some tips about what you need to be aware of when you turn on the setting. For example, the tooltip in Figure 4.6 shows information about the calculation settings. It also explains that you should use the F9 key to invoke a manual calculation.

Help Icon

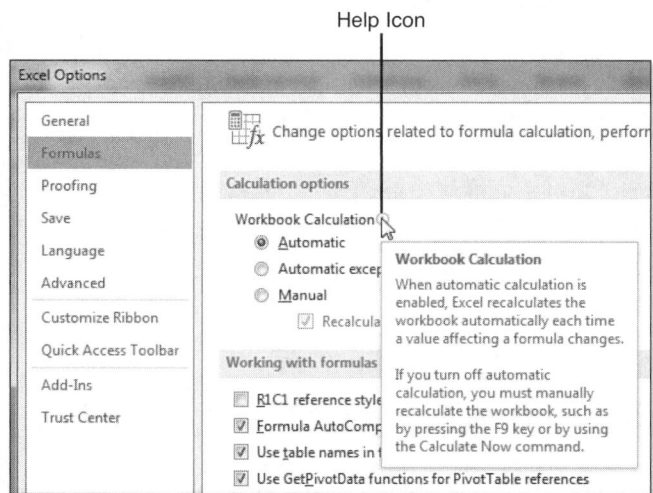

Figure 4.6
The *i* button offers an explanation of many settings.

New Options in Excel 2013

Excel 2013 offers 14 new settings, mostly allowing you to turn off new features introduced in this version. Here are some changes you might notice in Excel 2013 Options:

- Toggle Quick Analysis on Selection is found on the General tab. Use this to disable the Quick Analysis icon when you select a range of cells. A similar setting in the Editing section of the Advanced Category turns off Flash Fill.

- Always Use User Name Regardless of Sign-In to Office is new on the General tab. In the past, the user name entered in Excel options has been attached to each workbook you create. To keep this name instead of basing the name on your Windows account, choose this setting.

- Office now offers several background sketches that appear in the top-right corner of your Excel screen. If you are like me, you will change this setting every day for four days, then completely forget it is on the General tab.

- Show the Start Screen When This Application Starts is new on the General tab. Microsoft is pushing the new start screen as a great feature. If you do not agree, uncheck this setting on the General tab to open Excel to a blank workbook. You can also disable three settings on the Save tab. Choose Don't Show the Backstage View When Opening or Saving Files, uncheck Always Show "Sign in to SkyDrive" Location During Save, and choose Save to Computer by Default. These three settings should remove the slight delay as Excel tries to sign in to cloud storage.

- Inserting a screenshot was introduced in Excel 2010. Now, in Excel 2013, if you insert a screenshot of a browser, Excel offers to automatically create a hyperlink back to the web page. Excel offers to remember your choice. If you need to change that setting, it is on the Advanced category, in the Editing group. Note that hyperlinks don't happen with the more useful Screen Clipping feature.

- Excel 2013 offers new labeling options for charts. Two new options in the Chart group of the Advanced category cause a label to stick with a data point even if the point moves.

- Excel 2013 includes a new type of pivot table based on the PowerPivot engine. Excel calls this the Data Model. Options in the Data group of the Advanced category enable you to specify that all new pivot tables should automatically be based on the Data Model. You can also disable Undo for Data Model pivot tables over a certain size.

- The Trust Center provides a new category related to JavaScript apps. Also, check the Privacy option in the Trust Center to see if you can enable the Office Feedback tool. This feature debuted in the Excel 2007 beta as "Send a Smile." It has been in every Office beta since then, but never persists in the final product. It looks like Microsoft is giving you an option to turn this on in the regular version of Office 2013. When it is on, you can send a screenshot, description, and a smile or frown when you find something that you like or do not like in Excel. This is an opportunity to get your feedback directly to the project managers who will decide what happens in future versions of Office.

One option that debuted on the Excel 2010 File menu has moved to Excel Options. If you like seeing the last nine files that you opened at the bottom of the File menu, go to Excel Options, Advanced, Display. Choose Quickly Access This Number of Recent Workbooks.

Using AutoRecover Options

For many versions, Excel periodically saves a copy of your work every 10 minutes. If your computer crashes, the recovery pane offers to let you open the last AutoRecovered version of the file. This feature is sure to save you from retyping data that might have otherwise been lost.

Another painful situation occurs when you do not save changes and then close Excel. Yes, Excel asks if you want to save changes for each open document, but this question usually pops up at 5:00 p.m. when you are in a hurry to get out of the office. If you are thinking about what you need to do after work and not paying attention to which files are still open, you might click No to the first document and then click No again and again without noticing that the fifth open document was one that should have been saved.

Another scenario involves leaving an Excel file open overnight only to discover that Windows Update decided to restart the computer at 3:00 a.m. After being burned a dozen times, you can change the behavior of Windows Update to stop doing this. However, if Windows Update closed Excel without saving your documents, you can lose those AutoRecovered documents.

A setting introduced in Excel 2010 has Excel save the last AutoRecovered version of each open file when you close without saving. This setting is on the Save category of Excel Options and is called Keep the Last AutoSaved Version If I Close Without Saving. As soon as you realize that you saved without closing, visit the AutoRecover File Location (usually %AppData%\Roaming\Microsoft\Excel\) to see if your file is there. Copy it, rename it, and paste it back to a safe location.

Controlling Image Sizes

An Image Size & Quality section appears in the Advanced category. Most people add a photo to dress up the cover page of a document. However, you probably don't need an 8-megapixel image being saved in the workbook. By default, Excel compresses the image before saving the file. You can control the target output size using the drop-down in Excel options. Choices include 96 ppi, 150 ppi, and 220 ppi. The 96 ppi setting will look fine on your display. Use 220 ppi for images you will print. If you want to keep your images at the original size, you can select the new Do Not Compress Images in File setting.

You should also understand the Discard Editing Data check box. Say that you insert an image in your workbook and then crop out part of the photograph. If you do not enable Discard Editing Data, someone else can come along and uncrop your photo. This can be an embarrassing situation—just ask the former TechTV co-host who discovered certain bits of photographs were still hanging around after she cropped them out.

Working with Protected View for Files Originating from the Internet

Starting in Excel 2010, files from the Internet or Outlook initially open in protected mode. This mode gives you a chance to look at the workbook and formulas without having anything malicious happen. Unfortunately, you cannot actually view the macro code while the workbook is in protected view (see Figure 4.7).

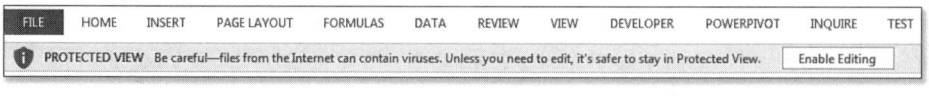

Figure 4.7 Protected view enables you to see your document before any warnings appear.

If you only want to view or print the workbook, protected mode works great. One statistic says that 40% of the time, people simply open a document and never make changes to it.

After you click Enable Editing, Excel will skip protected mode the next time you open the file.

Working with Trusted Document Settings

By default, Excel warns you about all sorts of things. If you open a workbook with macros, links, external data connections, or even the new WEBSERVICE function, a message bar appears above the worksheet to let you know that Excel disabled those "threats."

If you declare a folder on your hard drive to be a trusted folder, you can open those documents without Excel warning you about the items. Visit File, Options, Trust Center, Trust Center Settings, Trusted Locations to set up a trusted folder.

Starting in Excel 2010, if you open a file from your hard drive and enable the content, Excel will automatically enable that content the next time. The inherent problem here is that if you open a file and discover the macros are bad, you will not want those macros to open automatically the next time. There is no way to untrust a single document other than deleting, renaming, or moving it. Instead, you have to go to the Trusted Documents category of the Trust Center where you can choose to clear the entire list of trusted documents.

Ten Options to Consider

Although hundreds of Excel options exist, this section provides a quick review of just 10 options that might be helpful to you:

- Update your name in the General category. The name stored on this tab is used in cell comments and in the document properties.

- Save File in This Format in the Save category. If you regularly create macros, choose the Excel Macro-Enabled Workbook as the default format type.

- Update your Default File Location in the Save tab. Excel always wants to save new documents in your My Documents folder. However, if you always work in the C:\AccountingFiles\ folder, then update the default folder to match your preferred location.

- After Pressing Enter, Move Selection Direction is the first setting in the Advanced category. If you regularly perform data entry and prefer that the cell pointer move across the spreadsheet, change this setting from Down to Right.

- Show This Number of Recent Documents has been enhanced dramatically since Excel 2003. Whereas legacy versions of Excel showed up to nine recent documents at the bottom of the File menu, Excel 2013 allows you to see up to 50 recent documents in the Recent category of the File menu. You can change this setting by visiting the Display section of the Advanced category.

- Edit Custom Lists has been moved to the Display section of the Advanced category. Custom lists add functionality to the fill handle, allow custom sort orders, and control how fields are displayed in the label area of a pivot table. Type a list in the correct sequence in a worksheet. Edit Custom Lists and click Import. Excel can now automatically extend items from that list, the same as it can extend January into February, March, and so on.

- Make Excel look less like Excel by hiding interface elements in the three Display sections of the Advanced category. You can turn off the formula bar, scroll bars, sheet tabs, row and column headers, and gridlines. You can customize the ribbon to remove all main tabs except the File menu. The point is that if you design a model to be used by someone who never uses Excel, the person can open the model, plug in a few numbers, and get the result without having to see the entire Excel interface.

- Show Zero in Cells That Have Zero Value is in the Display Options for This Worksheet section of the Advanced category. Occasionally people want zeros to be displayed as blanks. Although a custom number format of 0;-0;; will do this, you can change the setting globally by clearing this option.

- Group Dates in the AutoFilter Menu is in the Display Options for This Workbook section of the Advanced category. Starting with Excel 2007, date columns show a hierarchical view of years, months, and days in the AutoFilter drop-down. If you like the old behavior of showing each individual date, turn off this setting.

- Add a folder on your local hard drive as a trusted location. Files stored in a trusted location automatically have macros enabled and external links updated. If you can trust that you will not write malicious code, then define a folder on your hard drive as a trusted location. From Excel Options, select the Trust Center category and then Trust Center Settings. In the Trust Center, select Trusted Locations, Add New Location.

Five Excel Oddities

You might rarely need any of the features presented in this section. However, in the right circumstance, they can be timesavers.

- Adjust the gridline color in the Display section of the Advanced category. If you are tired of gray gridlines, you can get a new outlook with bright red gridlines. I've met people who have changed the gridline color and can attest that nothing annoys an old accountant more than seeing bright red gridlines.

- Allow negative time by switching to the 1904 date system in the General section of the Advanced category. Excel never allows a time to return a negative time. However, if you are tracking comp time and you allow people to borrow against future comp time, it might be nice to allow negative time. In this case, switch to the 1904 date system to have up to 4 years of negative time. Use caution when changing this setting. All existing dates in the workbook will shift by approximately four years.

- Put an end to the green triangles on your account numbers stored as text. Most of the green triangle indicators are useful. However, if you have a column of text account numbers where most values are numbers, seeing thousands of green triangles can be annoying. In addition, the green triangles can hide other, more serious problems. Clear the Numbers Formatted as Text or Preceded by an Apostrophe in the Error Checking Rules check box in the Formulas category.

- Automatically Insert a Decimal Point replicates the antique adding machines that were office fixtures in the 1970s. When working with a manual adding machine, it was frustrating to type decimal points. You could type 123456 and the adding machine would interpret the entry as 1,234.56. If you find that you are doing massive data entry of numbers in dollars and cents, you can have Excel replicate the old adding machine functionality. After enabling this setting, you can indicate how many digits of the number should be interpreted as being after the decimal point. The only hassle is that you need to enter $5 as **500**. The old adding machines actually had a 00 key, but those are long since gone.

■ Change *Dwight* to *Diapers* using AutoCorrect Options. If you are a fan of the NBC sitcom *The Office*, you might remember the 2007 episode in which Jim allegedly put a macro on Dwight's computer that automatically changed the typed word *Dwight* to *Diapers*. However, this doesn't require a macro. From Excel Options, choose the Proofing Category and then click the AutoCorrect Options button. On the AutoCorrect tab, you can type new correction pairs. In this example, you would type **Dwight** into the Replace box and **Diapers** into the With box. The next time someone types *Dwight* and then a space, the word will automatically change to *Diapers*. You can also remove correction pairs by selecting the pairs and then pressing Delete. For example, if you hate that Microsoft converts (c) to ©, you can delete that entry from the list.

5

EXTENDING EXCEL WITH EXCEL APPS AND ADD-INS

Although Excel can do amazing things, it cannot do everything. Plenty of niche industries need more functions or more specialized operations than what are available in Excel.

Sometimes, someone recognizes a common need. After seeing dozens of questions in Excel newsgroups about converting uppercase to lowercase, for example, a developer might offer an add-in to make that task easier than the current five-step process.

Prior to Excel 2013, these add-ins would be written in Visual Basic for Applications (VBA) to create a regular add-in or in Visual Studio to create a COM add-in. Starting in Excel 2013, the Excel team debuts the Excel App. Found under Insert, Apps for Office, an Excel App is built in JavaScript or HTML5. Microsoft is hoping that many third-party developers begin writing apps for the Office Store that are free or inexpensive.

As I am writing this chapter, there are a small handful of apps in the App Store. This chapter walks you through installing an app and how to use some of the useful apps that were released early in the Excel 2013 cycle. By the time you are reading this, there will likely be hundreds of new apps available. The process for locating, installing, and using any app will be similar to the examples explained here.

Using Apps for Office

To start using Apps for Office, go to the Insert tab, open the Apps for Office drop-down, and choose See All.

Excel shows you a few featured apps, as shown in Figure 5.1. This is not the complete list of apps. You can click the icon in the lower-left corner of the Insert App dialog to browse more apps at the Office Store.

Figure 5.1
Browse for new apps using the Insert App dialog.

To learn more about an app, click the app. Your default web browser opens with information about the app. Figure 5.2 shows Keyur Patel's Geographic Heat Map displayed in Google's Chrome browser. The provider description explains that the current version enables you to plot values by state in the United States. By the way, Keyur Patel is a project manager on the Excel team and was an early adopter of developing apps.

To install the app, click the Add button. The next screen presents important information about how to activate the app in Excel, as shown in Figure 5.3. Don't skip over this information; the steps are actually required! Apps on the iPhone just work without these arcane steps. Perhaps Microsoft will improve the process over time.

 Caution

A big Add button appears in the center of the screen. This button works well in Internet Explorer but does not work in Google Chrome. By the time you are reading this, it is likely that Google and Microsoft will have corrected this problem, but it is also possible that they will not have sorted it out. In that case, copy the URL from the address bar in Chrome, open Internet Explorer, and paste the URL in the address bar. You might encounter similar problems in Opera or Firefox.

Figure 5.2
Get information about an app, including requirements and price.

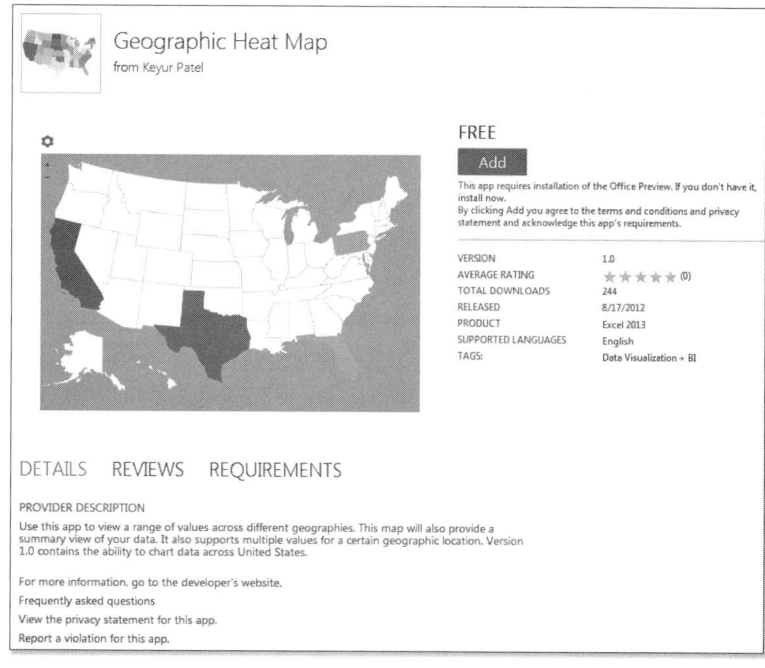

Figure 5.3
You've theoretically downloaded the app, but there are more steps to follow to make it available to use.

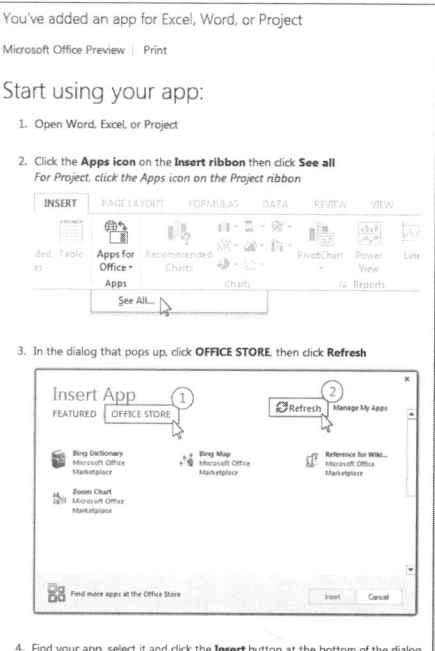

To enable the app, follow these steps:

1. Return to Microsoft Excel.

2. The Insert App dialog should still be open. If it is not, choose Insert, Apps for Office, See All.

3. At the top of the Insert App dialog, you see two choices: Featured and Office Store. Click Office Store. Nothing is shown.

4. Click the Refresh button in the top right of the dialog. This step actually adds the app you just downloaded. In Figure 5.4, the Geographic Heat Map icon appears along with Bing Maps, Bubbles, and Mini Calendar, which were previously installed on my machine.

5. To insert the app in your worksheet, click the icon and then Insert, as shown in Figure 5.5.

Figure 5.4
Choose Office Store and then Refresh to see the new app.

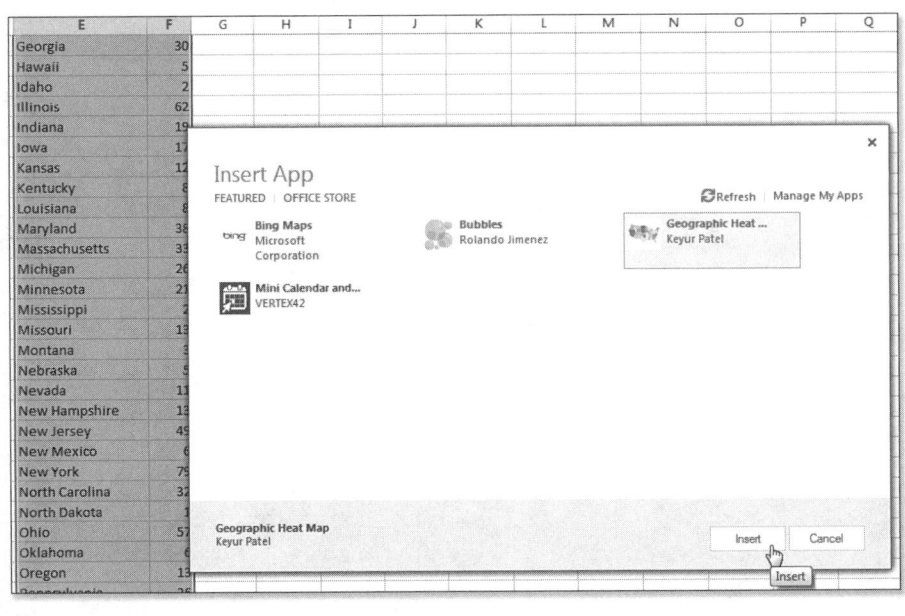

Figure 5.5
Choose an app and then click Insert.

6. The app appears in a floating object box roughly in the center of the worksheet. This box is just like the box that surrounds a chart. You can click the edge of the box and move it to a new location.

7. The app usually starts with a splash screen that provides some information on how to start. In this app, you should click the gear button to get started (see Figure 5.6).

Figure 5.6
The splash screen should tell you how to get started.

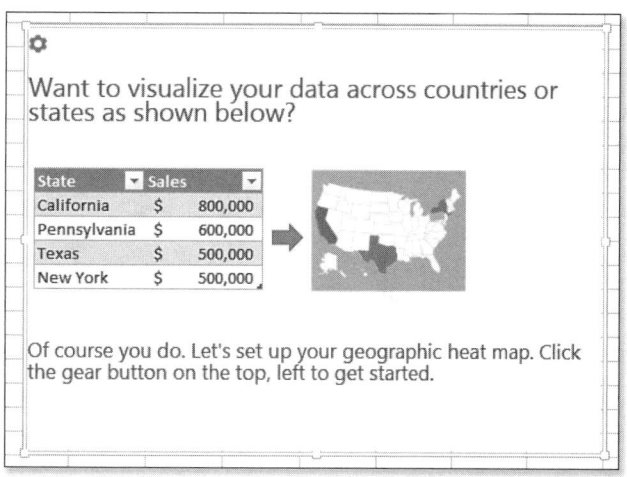

8. At this point, the app usually asks you to identify some data in your Excel worksheet. In the case of this example, the Geographic Heat Map then asks for additional settings, enabling you to identify which column contains states and which column contains number (see Figure 5.7).

Figure 5.7
Select the settings and then click Save.

9. The map is updated to reflect the data in the worksheet. If you change data in the worksheet, the map automatically updates (see Figure 5.8).

This app works great on your computer because you have the app installed. What if you need to distribute the map to others who might not have the app installed? Open the drop-down in the top right of the map and choose to save as an image.

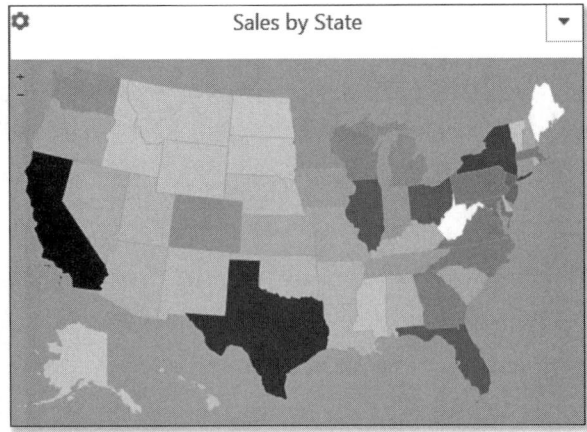

Figure 5.8
California and Texas have the highest values in the data set.

The one problem with the Geographic Heat Map is that you have to summarize your data by state. This takes a few minutes and a pivot table to produce the summary. What if you are not comfortable with a pivot table? You could turn to Chapter 23, "Using Pivot Tables to Analyze Data," for a quick introduction, or you can look for other apps.

In Figure 5.9, the Bubbles app took the unsummarized raw data, did the consolidation, and created an interesting bubble visualization. Click any bubble to have the values appear.

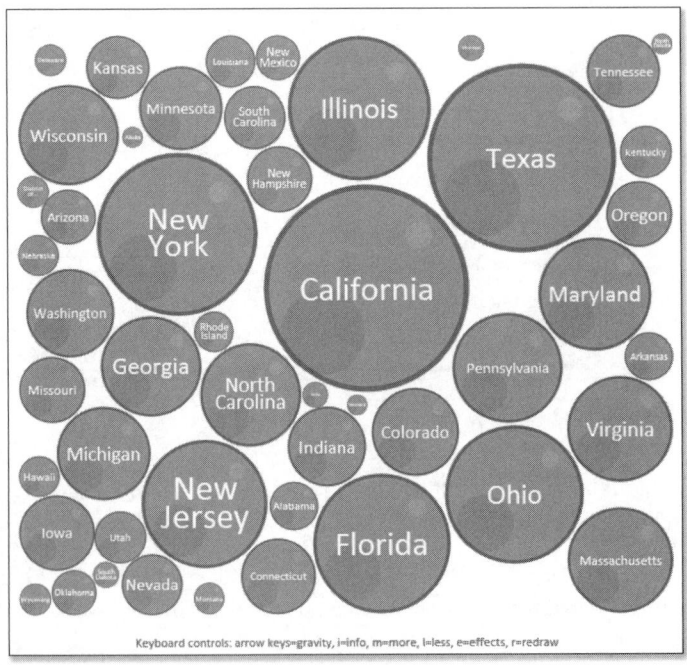

Figure 5.9
The Bubble app summarizes any data, not just states.

In Figure 5.10, the Bing Maps app read the City and State columns to produce data points on a regional map.

Figure 5.10
Bing Maps offers an app to show geographic data on a map.

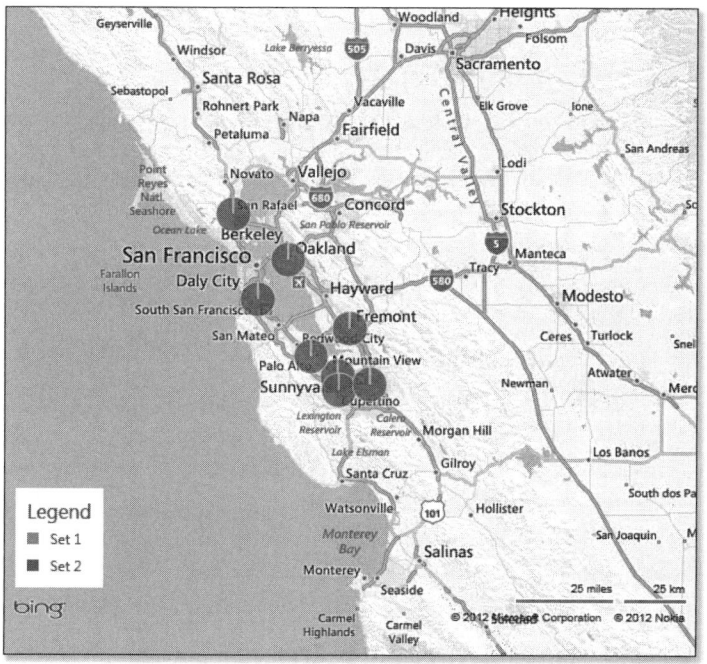

To delete an app from the worksheet, click the border of the app and press the Delete key.

After you have used an app one time, it is easier to use the app later. As soon as you open the Apps for Office drop-down on the Insert tab, you see the list of recently used apps, as shown in Figure 5.11.

Figure 5.11
After you begin using an app, it will appear in this list for easy use later.

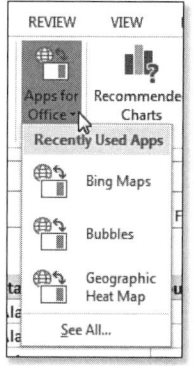

Using Traditional Add-Ins

Literally thousands of add-ins are available for Excel. This chapter by no means provides a comprehensive list of available add-ins, but it contains some of my favorites.

Charting Utilities from Jon Peltier

Jon Peltier's website has always listed bizarre techniques for coaxing unusual charts out of Excel. Jon now offers the PTS Chart Utilities add-ins that enable you to easily make the following types of charts illustrated in Figure 5.12:

 **Note**

You can read more about Jon's add-in at http://peltiertech.com/Utility/.

- Waterfall Charts

- Box and Whisker Charts

- Cluster-Stack Charts

- Marimekko (Mosaic) Charts

- Panel Charts

- Dot Plot Charts

- Cascade Charts

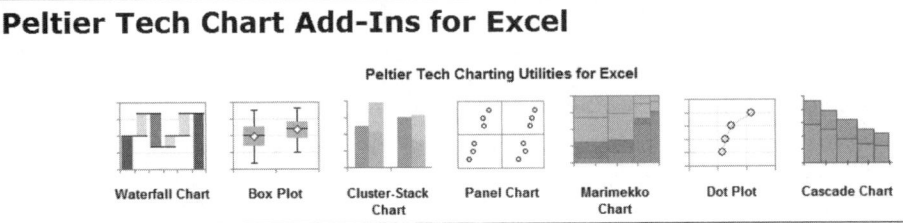

Peltier Tech Chart Add-Ins for Excel

Peltier Tech Charting Utilities for Excel

Waterfall Chart | Box Plot | Cluster-Stack Chart | Panel Chart | Marimekko Chart | Dot Plot | Cascade Chart

Figure 5.12
Jon Peltier simplifies the creation process for several unusual chart types.

Loading PDF Data to Excel by Using Able2Extract

People love sending data in PDF files. Now that Microsoft is providing a PDF-creation utility, more and more documents will be emailed via PDF.

 **Note**

You can download a free trial version of Able2Extract from www.investintech.com/able2extract.html.

The authors of PDF documents often use PDF format to ensure that the data cannot be altered. Other times, the authors want to make sure that someone who does not have Excel can still view the data. Although these are fine ideas, getting data back out of PDF and into Excel is very difficult.

Data copied and pasted from PDF to Excel usually loses its columnar format. Able2Extract solves this problem. You simply open a PDF file in Able2Extract, and you can convert the contained data to Excel with one click. If you need absolute control, you can specify regions so that, for example, titles and headers beyond page 1 are not imported.

In some PDF files, the entire document is a scanned image of the original file. The Professional version of Able2Extract can even deal with these.

Accessing More Functions by Using MoreFunc.dll

MVP Laurent Longre offers a free Excel add-in that has 66 new functions. Although some of the functions are specialized, there are great functions of use to many people using Excel. The following are just some of the new functions:

- **LastRow**—This function finds the last filled row in any column.

- **PageNum**—This function finds the page number of any cell.

- **SheetName**—This function finds the name of the current sheet.

- **WordCount**—This function finds the number of words in text.

- **NBText**—This function spells out a number as text in any of 13 languages.

- **CountIf.3D**—This function is the same as `Countif` but for 3-D references.

 Note

To merge all workbooks in a folder, Ron de Bruin offers many free add-ins at www.rondebruin.nl/addins.htm. One of the best is his RDBMerge add-in, which allows Excel to read all the workbooks in a folder and merge them into a single worksheet. This is great for doing budget roll-ups.

You can freely download MoreFunc.dll from http://xcell05.free.fr/.

General-Purpose Utility Suites

Many utilities add a new suite of commands to Excel. These utilities generally fall into one of two camps. The first set focuses on tasks for formatting worksheets. They might offer a way to format every *n*th row in a certain color or convert a range of uppercase data to proper case, and so on. The second set is designed to simplify data analysis. Here are the popular apps for formatting worksheets:

- ASAP Utilities offers a noncommercial, free version: www.asap-utilities.com.

- JMT Utilities offers a free version: www.andrewsexceltips.net/JMT%20Full%20List.htm.

- J-Walk's Power Utility Pack: http://spreadsheetpage.com/index.php/pupv6/home.

Utilities for Data Analysis Tasks

Two other utilities focus on data analysis tasks. The tagline for DigDB offers to let you do Access with Excel. When you have to match and merge massive amounts of data in Excel, these utilities simplify the process:

- DigDB offers a suite of 40 separate Excel add-ins that simplify data analysis. Download a trial from www.digdb.com.

- Easy-XL offers a similar integrated suite of data-processing commands, including support for macro recording. Download a trial from www.easy-xl.com.

You can also read more about the Easy-XL utility in Chapter 38, "Saving Time Using the Easy-XL Program."

6

KEYBOARD SHORTCUTS

If you do a lot of typing, being able to access commands from the keyboard is faster than moving your hand to the mouse. Excel 2013 still uses many of the old Alt keyboard shortcuts from Excel 2003. All the old Ctrl shortcut keys are still functional. For instance, Ctrl+C still copies a selection, Ctrl+X cuts a selection, and Ctrl+V pastes a selection.

This chapter points out which of the old Excel 2003 keyboard shortcuts still work, shows you some new shortcuts, and introduces you to the keyboard accelerators.

Learning the right ten shortcuts from this chapter can make you twice as fast in Excel.

Using New Keyboard Accelerators

The goal of the new Excel 2013 keyboard accelerators is to enable you to access every command by using only the keyboard. In legacy versions of Excel, many popular commands had keyboard accelerators, but other commands did not. Excel 2013 tries to ensure that every command can be invoked from the keyboard.

To access the new accelerators, press and release the Alt key. Notice that Excel places a KeyTip above each command. In addition, numeric KeyTips appear over each icon in the Quick Access Toolbar (see Figure 6.1). Press the F10 key to display or hide the KeyTips.

 Note

Although the Alt key always works, you might have an additional key that displays the KeyTips. It is possible that you turned on this setting in Excel 1995 and each successive upgrade of Excel has inherited the setting. Select File, Options, Advanced. Scroll to near the bottom for Lotus Compatibility. Just above Transition Navigation Keys is a setting for Microsoft Office Menu Key. I still have a slash (/) in that box, so when I type a slash in Excel, the KeyTips display.

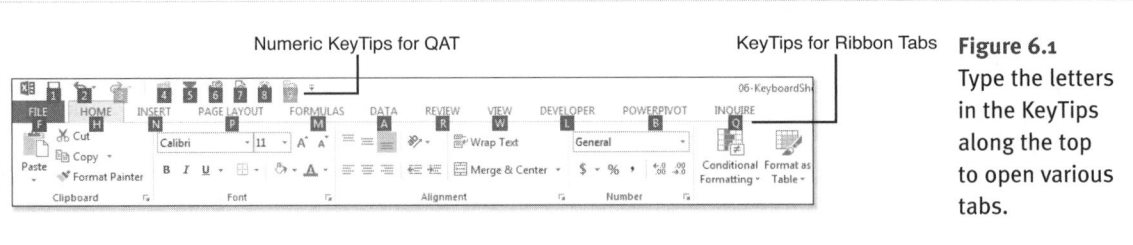

Numeric KeyTips for QAT   KeyTips for Ribbon Tabs

Figure 6.1
Type the letters in the KeyTips along the top to open various tabs.

It is possible to memorize the KeyTips for the ribbon tabs. Pressing Alt+F always accesses the File menu in all Office 2013 applications. Alt+H always accesses the Home tab in all Office 2013 applications. The accelerator definitions for each tab remain constant even if new ribbon tabs are displayed. When you activate a pivot table, the original KeyTip letters remain, and two new KeyTips appear for the contextual tabs: JT for PivotTable Tools Options and JY for PivotTable Tools Design (see Figure 6.2).

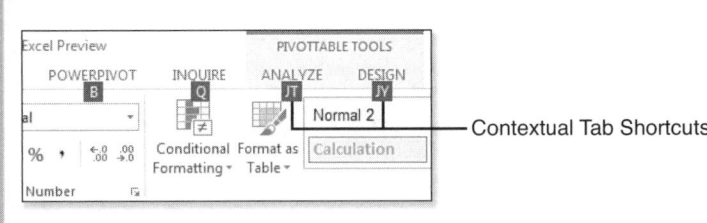

Contextual Tab Shortcuts

Figure 6.2
New ribbon tabs have new letters, so the old letters remain constant.

Unfortunately, the KeyTips for the Quick Access Toolbar change every time you add new buttons or rearrange buttons on the Quick Access Toolbar. If you want to memorize those KeyTips, you need to make sure you do not add a new Quick Access Toolbar icon at the beginning of the list.

Selecting Icons on the Ribbon

After you press the Alt key, you can press one of the KeyTip letters to bring up the appropriate tab. You now see that every icon on the ribbon has a KeyTip.

When you choose a ribbon tab, the KeyTips on the Quick Access Toolbar disappear, so Microsoft is free to use the letters A through Z and the numbers 0 through 9.

On very busy ribbon tabs, some commands require two keystrokes: for example, A+C for Align Center in the Alignments group of the Home tab, as shown in Figure 6.3. Note that after you press Alt to display the accelerators in the tooltips, you do not have to continue holding down the Alt key.

Some shortcut keys seem to make sense: AT for Align Top, AM for Align Middle, AB for Align Bottom, AL for Align Left, W for Wrap Text, and M for Merge. Other shortcut keys seem to be assigned at random. Some take a little pondering: FA for the dialog launcher in Figure 6.3 makes sense in that it opens the legacy Format dialog and moves to the Alignment tab. Others have a historical precedent. In Excel 2003, F was used for File, so O was used for Format. Similarly, in the

Home tab, O now opens the Format drop-down. However, because Microsoft no longer underlines the accelerator key in the menu name, O will never make sense to someone new to Excel. There might be some arcane, logical reason why 5 and 6 are used for increase and decrease indent, but it is unknown by most people.

Figure 6.3
After pressing the letter to switch to the ribbon, type the letter or letters to invoke a particular command.

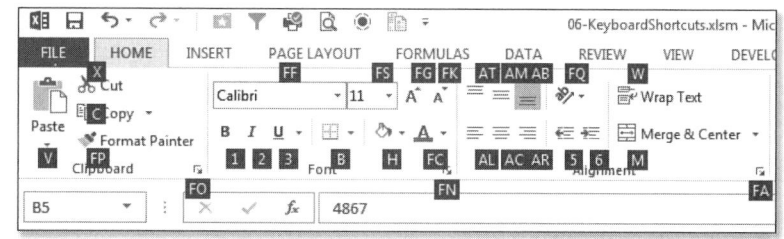

Selecting Options from a Gallery

Figure 6.4 shows the results of pressing Alt+H+J, which is the equivalent of selecting Home, Cell Styles. This opens the gallery of cell styles. As you can see in Figure 6.4, you can invoke the New Cell Style and Merge Styles commands at the bottom of the gallery by pressing N and M, respectively. However, there are no letters on the table style choices in the gallery.

Figure 6.4
After opening a gallery, you use the arrow keys to navigate through the gallery and press Enter to select a style.

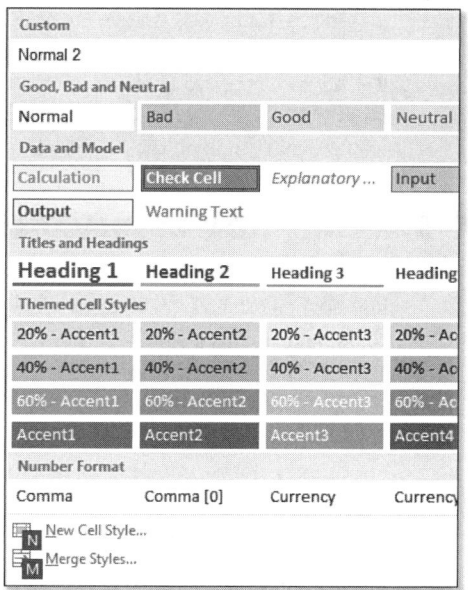

To select a cell style using the keyboard, use the arrow keys to move through the gallery. Because this gallery is two-dimensional, you can use the up arrow, down arrow, right arrow, left arrow, Page Down, Page Up, Home, and End keys to navigate through the gallery. When you have the desired table style highlighted, press the Enter key to select it.

Navigating Within Drop-Down Lists

If you press Alt+H+F+S, which is the equivalent of selecting Home, Font Size, the font size in the drop-down is selected. You can either type a font size and press Enter or press the down-arrow key to open the drop-down list. You can then use the down arrow, up arrow, Page Down, Page Up, Home, and End keys to navigate to a choice in the list. When you have the desired item highlighted, press Enter to select that item.

Backing Up One Level Through a Menu

Suppose you press Alt+H to access the Home tab and then realize you are in the wrong tab. You can press the Esc key to move back to display the tooltips for the main menu choices. If you want to clear the tooltips completely, press Alt again.

Dealing with Keyboard Accelerator Confusion

If you want to select something on the Home tab in Figure 6.2, you might be frustrated because you can see the menu choices but no tooltips appear for most commands. For icons in the top of the ribbon, it appears that the main KeyTips apply to the menu items. For example, you might think that the H KeyTip applies to Cut. Even though you are already on the Home tab, you need to press the H key to force Excel to show the tooltips for the individual menu items on the Home tab.

 Note

If you find the accelerator tooltips to be confusing and unwieldy, you must memorize them one at a time. Find a task that you use regularly, such as sorting the current data set ascending by the selected column. Press the Alt key. Press A for the Data tab. Notice that A sorts ascending and D sorts descending. This should be easy enough to remember: Alt+A+A for sort ascending, and Alt+A+D for sort descending.

Selecting from Legacy Dialog Boxes

Some commands lead to legacy dialog boxes like the ones in previous editions of Excel. These dialog boxes do not display the Excel 2013 KeyTips. However, most of the dialog boxes do use the convention of having one letter of each command underlined, which is called a *hotkey* in Microsoft parlance. In this case, you can press the underlined letter to select the command.

For example, press Alt+H+V+S instead of selecting Home, Paste, Paste Special. You are then presented with the Paste Special dialog box, as shown in Figure 6.5. To select Values and Transpose in this dialog, press V for Values and E for Transpose, because those are the letters underlined in the dialog. You can then press Enter instead of clicking the default OK button.

Figure 6.5
In a legacy dialog box, type the underlined letters to select options.

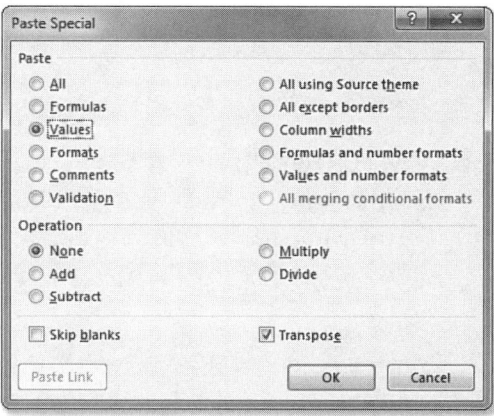

Using the Shortcut Keys

The following five tables provide what I believe to be a comprehensive list of shortcut keys. I have collected these over the many versions of Excel. For some reason, Excel Help no longer lists all the shortcut keys. I count 75 shortcut keys in the following tables that are no longer documented in Excel Help. I realize this is a mind-numbingly long list, but I want to include it here because the Excel team no longer provides a complete list.

If you decide to learn and start using one new shortcut key every week, you will quickly become very fast at using Excel. After Table 6.5, I identify my favorite shortcut keys from this list.

Excel 2013 automatically recognizes all the Ctrl shortcut keys that were used in legacy versions of Excel. In fact, many of these keys are consistent across all Windows applications. Table 6.1 lists the common Windows Ctrl shortcut keys.

Table 6.1   Windows Shortcut Keys

Key Combination	Action
Ctrl+C	Copy.
Ctrl+X	Cut.
Ctrl+V	Paste.
Ctrl+Alt+V	Paste Special.
Ctrl+Z	Undo.
Ctrl+Y or F4	Redo.
Ctrl+A or Ctrl+Shift+Spacebar	Select all. If the active cell contains data and is adjacent to other cells with data, Ctrl+A initially selects the current region. Pressing Ctrl+A again selects all.

Key Combination	Action
Ctrl+S	Save.
F12	Save As.
Ctrl+O	Open.
Ctrl+W or Ctrl+F4	Close workbook window.
Ctrl+N	New workbook.
Ctrl+P or Ctrl+F2	Display Print tab in File menu.
Ctrl+B	Bold.
Ctrl+U	Underline.
Ctrl+I	Italic.
Ctrl+F	Find.
Ctrl+H	Replace.
Ctrl+Shift+F or Ctrl+Shift+P	Font tab of Format Cells dialog.
Ctrl+G or F5	Go To dialog.
Ctrl+T or Ctrl+L	Format as Table.
Ctrl+E	Flash Fill.
Ctrl+Q	Quick Analysis options.

Table 6.2 illustrates the shortcut keys you use to navigate in Excel.

Table 6.2   Shortcut Keys for Navigation

Shortcut Key	Action
Ctrl+Home	Moves to cell A1 or the top-left unhidden cell in the worksheet.
Ctrl+End	Moves to the last cell in the used range of the worksheet. If the cursor is in the formula bar, it moves to the end of the formula text.
Page Down	Moves one screen down in the worksheet.
Page Up	Moves one screen up in the worksheet.
Alt+Page Down	Moves one screen right in the worksheet.
Alt+Page Up	Moves one screen left in the worksheet.
Ctrl+Page Up	Moves to the previous worksheet.
Ctrl+Page Down	Moves to the next worksheet.
Shift+F11	Inserts a new worksheet.
Alt+Tab	Switches to the next program.
Alt+Shift+Tab	Switches to the previous program.

Shortcut Key	Action
Ctrl+Esc	Displays the Windows Start menu.
Ctrl+F5	Restores the window size of the current workbook.
F6	Switches between the worksheet, ribbon, task pane, and zoom controls. If the workbook has been split, this also switches between panes.
Ctrl+F6	Switches to the next open workbook window when more than one workbook is open.
Ctrl+Shift+F6	Switches to the previous workbook window.
Ctrl+F9	Minimizes the window.
Ctrl+F10	Maximizes the window.
End	Toggles into End mode. Displays End Mode in the status bar. When in End mode, press an arrow key to move to the edge of the current region. If the active cell is already at the edge of a current region or is a blank cell, this jumps to next nonblank cell or to the edge of the worksheet.
End Home	Moves to the last used range in the worksheet. Similar to Ctrl+End.
Ctrl+arrow key or End followed by an arrow key	Moves to the edge of the current region. If the active cell is at the edge of a current region or is a blank cell, this jumps to the next nonblank cell or to the edge of the worksheet.
Home	Moves to the beginning of the row.
Ctrl+Backspace	Scrolls to display the active cell.
F5	Displays the Go To dialog.
Shift+F5	Display the Find dialog.
Shift+F4	Find Next.
Ctrl+. (period)	Moves to the next corner of the selected range.

Table 6.3 shows the shortcut keys you use to select data and cells.

Table 6.3 Shortcut Keys for Selecting Data and Cells

Shortcut Key	Action
Ctrl+Spacebar	When an object is selected, this selects all objects on the worksheet.
Ctrl+Spacebar	If used outside a table, this selects the entire column. If used inside a table, it toggles between selecting the data, data and headers, and the entire column.
Shift+Spacebar	Selects the entire row. If inside a table, this toggles between selecting the table row and the entire row.

Shortcut Key	Action
Ctrl+Shift+Spacebar or Ctrl+A	Selects the entire worksheet, unless the active cell is a region of two or more nonblank cells, in which case it selects the current region. Repeat the keystroke to select the entire worksheet. When the active cell is in a table, the first press selects the data rows of the table. The second press expands to include the headings and total row. The third press selects the entire worksheet.
Shift+Backspace	With multiple cells selected, this reverts the selection to only the active cell.
Ctrl+ *	Selects the current region. In a pivot table, this selects the entire table.
Ctrl+/	Selects the array containing the active cell.
Ctrl+Shift+O (letter O)	Selects all cells that contain comments.
Ctrl+\	In a selected row, this selects the cells that do not match the value in the active cell.
Ctrl+Shift+ |	In a selected column, this selects the cells that do not match the value in the active cell.
Ctrl+[(opening square bracket)	Selects all cells directly referenced by formulas in the selection.
Ctrl+Shift+{ (opening brace)	Selects all cells directly or indirectly referenced by formulas in the selection.
Ctrl+] (closing square bracket)	Selects cells that contain formulas that directly reference the active cell.
Ctrl+Shift+} (closing brace)	Selects cells that contain formulas that directly or indirectly reference the active cell.
Alt+; (semicolon)	Selects the visible cells in the current selection.
Ctrl+Shift+Page Down	Adds the next worksheet to the selected sheets and makes the next worksheet the active sheet. This puts the workbook in group mode if it is not already in group mode. Pressing Ctrl+Shift+Page Down three times puts the current sheet and the next three sheets in group mode. Any changes made to the visible sheet are also made to all sheets in group mode. To exit group mode, right-click a sheet tab and choose Ungroup Sheets.
Ctrl+Shift+Page Up	Adds the previous worksheet to the selected sheets. This puts the workbook in group mode if it was not already in group mode.

Table 6.4 shows the shortcut keys you use to extend a selection.

Table 6.4   Shortcut Keys for Extending Selections

Shortcut Key	Action
F8	Turns Extend mode on or off. In Extend mode, EXT appears in the status line and the arrow keys extend the selection.
Shift+F8	Adds another range of cells to the selection. You can use the arrow keys to move to the start of the range you want to add. Then press F8 and the arrow keys to select the next range.
Shift+arrow key	Extends the selection by one cell.
Ctrl+Shift+arrow key	Extends the selection to the last nonblank cell in the same column or row as the active cell.
Shift+Home	Extends the selection to the beginning of the row.
Ctrl+Shift+Home	Extends the selection to the beginning of the worksheet.
Ctrl+Shift+End	Extends the selection to the last used cell on the worksheet in the lower-right corner. If the cursor is in the formula bar, this selects to the end of the formula.
Shift+Page Down	Extends the selection down one screen.
Shift+Page Up	Extends the selection up one screen.
End Shift+arrow key	Extends the selection to the last nonblank cell in the same column or row as the active cell.
End+Shift+Home	Extends the selection to the last used cell on the worksheet in the lower-right corner.
End Shift+Enter	Extends the selection to the last cell in the current row.
Scroll Lock+Shift+Home	Extends the selection to the cell in the upper-left corner of the window.
Scroll Lock+Shift+End	Extends the selection to the cell in the lower-right corner of the window.

Table 6.5 shows the shortcut keys you use for entering, editing, formatting, and calculating data.

Table 6.5   Shortcut Keys for Data Entry, Formatting, and Calculating Data

Shortcut Key	Action
Enter	Completes a cell entry and selects the next cell. Often moves down one cell, but you can override this with File, Options, Advanced. In a data form, this moves to the first field in the next record. In a dialog box, this performs the action for the default button (often OK). After F10 is used to activate the menu bar, Enter selects the chosen menu item.
Alt+Enter	Starts a new line in the same cell.

Shortcut Key	Action
Ctrl+Enter	Fills the selected cell range with the current entry.
Shift+Enter	Completes a cell entry and selects the previous cell. Often the cell above, but you can override with File, Options Advanced. If the Move Selection Direction is set to *right*, then pressing Shift+Enter will move to the *left*.
Tab	Completes a cell entry and selects the next cell to the right. Moves between unlocked cells in a protected worksheet. Moves to the next option in a dialog box.
Shift+Tab	Completes a cell entry and selects the previous cell to the left. In a dialog box, this moves to the previous option.
Esc	Cancels a cell entry. Closes Full Screen mode. Closes an open menu dialog box or message window.
Arrow keys	Moves one cell up, down, left, or right. If in edit mode, this moves one character up, down, left, or right.
Home	Moves to the beginning of the line. Moves to the cell in the upper-left corner of the window when Scroll Lock is turned on. Selects the first command on the menu when a menu is visible.
F4 or Ctrl+Y	Repeats the last action. When a cell reference is selected in a formula, F4 toggles between the various combinations of relative and absolute references.
Ctrl+Shift+F3	Displays the Create Names From Selection dialog box to enable you to create names from row and column labels.
Ctrl+D	Fills down.
Ctrl+R	Fills to the right.
Ctrl+F3	Displays the Name Manager.
Ctrl+K	Inserts a hyperlink or enables you to edit the selected hyperlink.
Ctrl+; (semicolon)	Enters the date.
Ctrl+Shift+: (colon)	Enters the time.
Alt+down arrow	When a drop-down list is selected, this opens the drop-down list. Otherwise, it displays a drop-down list of the values in the current column of a range to enable you to select a cell value from the list.
Ctrl+Z or Alt+Backspace	Undoes the last action.
= (equal sign)	Starts a formula.
Backspace	In the formula bar or while you're editing a cell, this deletes one character to the left. When you're not in edit mode, this clears the contents of the current cell and puts the cell in edit mode.
Enter	Completes a cell entry from the cell or formula bar.
Ctrl+Shift+Enter	Enters a formula as an array formula.
Shift+F3	In a formula, this displays the Insert Function dialog box.

Shortcut Key	Action
Ctrl+A	When the insertion point is to the right of a function name in a formula, this displays the Function Arguments dialog box. See also Select All in Table 6.1.
Ctrl+Shift+A	When the insertion point is to the right of a function name in a formula, this inserts the argument names and parentheses.
F3	Pastes a defined name into a formula.
Alt+= (equal sign)	Inserts an AutoSum formula with the SUM function.
Ctrl+Shift+" (quotation mark)	Copies the value from the cell above the active cell into the cell or the formula bar.
Ctrl+' (apostrophe)	Copies a formula from the cell above the active cell into the cell or the formula bar and places the cell in edit mode. Note that the formula is an exact copy, any references are not moved down by a row.
Ctrl+` (backtick)	Alternates between displaying cell values and displaying formulas.
F9	Calculates all worksheets in all open workbooks. When a portion of a formula is selected, calculate the selected portion and then press Enter or Ctrl+Shift+Enter (for array formulas) to replace the selected portion with the calculated value.
Shift+F9	Calculates the active worksheet.
Ctrl+Alt+F9	Calculates all worksheets in all open workbooks, regardless of whether they have changed since the last calculation.
Ctrl+Alt+Shift+F9	Rechecks dependent formulas and then calculates all cells in all open workbooks, including cells not marked as needing to be calculated.
F1	Displays Help.
F2	Edits the active cell and positions the insertion point at the end of the cell contents. If in-cell editing is turned off, this moves the insertion point to the formula bar. When you're editing a formula or a reference in a dialog box, F2 toggles between Point and Enter mode. If pressing Backspace starts inserting cell references instead of moving back a character, press F2 and try again.
Delete	Removes cell contents (data and formulas) from selected cells without affecting cell formats or comments. In editing mode, this deletes the character to the right of the Insertion point or deletes the selection.
Ctrl+Delete	Deletes text to the end of the line.
F7	Displays the Spelling dialog box.
Shift+F2	Adds or edits a cell comment.
Ctrl+– (minus sign)	Displays the Delete dialog box.

Shortcut Key	Action
Ctrl+Shift++ (plus sign)	Displays the Insert dialog box to insert blank cells.
Alt+' (apostrophe)	Displays the Style dialog box.
Ctrl+1	Displays the Format Cells dialog box when cells are selected. When a chart element or object is selected, this displays the Format task pane for that object.
Ctrl+2 or Ctrl+B	Toggles bold formatting.
Ctrl+3 or Ctrl+I	Toggles italic formatting.
Ctrl+4 or Ctrl+U	Toggles underline formatting.
Ctrl+Shift+~	Applies the General number format.
Ctrl+Shift+$	Applies the Currency format with two decimal places (negative numbers in parentheses).
Ctrl+Shift+%	Applies the Percentage format with no decimal places.
Ctrl+Shift+^	Applies the Scientific number format with two decimal places.
Ctrl+Shift+#	Applies the Date format with the day, month, and year.
Ctrl+Shift+@	Applies the Time format with the hour and minute as well as AM or PM.
Ctrl+Shift+!	Applies the Number format with two decimal places, thousands separator, and minus sign (–) for negative values.
Ctrl+5	Applies or removes strikethrough.
Ctrl+9	Hides the selected rows.
Ctrl+Shift+((opening parenthesis)	Unhides any hidden rows within the selection.
Ctrl+0 (zero)	Hides the selected columns.
Ctrl+Shift+) (closing parenthesis)	Unhides any hidden columns within the selection. Although this shortcut key is shown as a tooltip in the Home tab, it has not worked since Excel 2010 and the Excel team has no immediate plans to fix it.
Ctrl+Shift+&	Applies the outline border to the selected cells.
Ctrl+Shift+_ (underscore)	Removes the outline border from the selected cells.
Ctrl+U	Toggles the formula bar between collapsed and expanded.
Ctrl+6	Toggles between hiding and displaying objects.
Ctrl+8	In group and outline mode, this toggles the display of outline symbols.
Ctrl+F1	Collapses or expands the ribbon.
Alt or F10	Displays KeyTips.
Shift+F10	Opens the right-click menu for the selection.

Shortcut Key	Action
Alt+Shift+F10	Displays the menu or message for an Error Checking button.
Alt+F11	Opens the Visual Basic for Applications Editor.
Alt+F8	Opens the Macros dialog.
Spacebar	In a dialog box, this selects or clears a check box or performs the action for a selected button.
Ctrl+Tab	In a dialog box, this switches to the next tab.
Ctrl+Shift+Tab	In a dialog box, this switches to the previous tab.
Arrow keys	In a dialog box or open menu, this moves between options in an open drop-down list or between options in a group of options.
End	When a menu is open, this selects the last item in the menu.
Alt+Shift+F1	Inserts a new worksheet to the left of the current worksheet.
F11	Creates a chart of the data in the current range in a new chart sheet.
Alt+F1	Creates a chart of the data in the current range in the current worksheet.
Alt+Spacebar	Opens the Control menu for the Excel window. The Control menu is attached to the XL logo in the top left of the window.
Ctrl+F4	Closes the selected workbook window.
Alt+F4	Closes Excel.
Ctrl+F10	Maximizes or restores the selected workbook window.
Ctrl+F7	When a workbook is not maximized, this moves the entire workbook window. Press Ctrl+F7. Use the arrow keys to move the window. Press Enter when you're finished or Esc to cancel.
Ctrl+F8	Performs the Size command when a workbook is not maximized. Press Ctrl+F8. Using the left or right arrow key expands the width of the window by moving the right edge of the window. Using the up or down arrow key moves the bottom edge of the window to shrink or stretch the window.
Shift+F6	Moves focus between the worksheet, ribbon, status bar, and task pane. For example, when focus is on the Status bar, you can use the arrows to move between the Record Macro, Normal, Page Layout, Page Break Preview, and Zoom icons.
Ctrl+F6	Moves between windows of a workbook. This would only apply if you used View, New Window.

Using My Favorite Shortcut Keys

The problem with a list of hundreds of shortcut keys is that it is overwhelming. You cannot possibly absorb 233 new shortcut keys and start using them. The following sections cover some of my favorite shortcut keys. Try to incorporate one new shortcut key every week into your Excel routine.

Quickly Move Between Worksheets

Ctrl+Page Down jumps to the next workbook. Ctrl+Page Up jumps to the previous workbook. Say that you have 12 worksheets named Jan, Feb, Mar, ..., Dec. If you are currently on the Jan worksheet, hold down Ctrl and press Page Down five times to move to Jun.

Jumping to the Bottom of Data with Ctrl+Arrow

Provided there are no blank cells in your data, press Ctrl+Down Arrow to move to the last row in the data set. Use Ctrl+Up Arrow to move to the first row in the data set.

Add the Shift key to select from the current cell to the bottom. If you have data in A2:J987654 and are in A2, you can hold down Ctrl+Shift while pressing the down arrow and then the right arrow to select all the data rows but exclude the headings in row 1.

Selecting the Current Region with Ctrl+*

Press Ctrl+* to select the current range. The current range is the whole dataset, in all directions from the current cell until Excel hits the edge of the worksheet or a completely blank row and column. On a desktop computer, pressing Ctrl and the asterisk on the numeric keypad does the trick.

Jumping to the Next Corner of a Selection

You've just selected A2:J987654 but you are staring at the bottom-right corner of your data. Press Ctrl+Period to move to the next corner of your data. Because you are at the bottom-right corner, it takes two presses of Ctrl+Period to move to the top-left corner. Although this moves the active cell, it does not undo your selection. Although I always use Ctrl+Period twice, I should probably learn Ctrl+Backspace to bring the active cell back into view. That will be my new trick for next week.

Pop Open the Right-Click Menu Using Shift+F10

When I do my seminars, people always ask why I don't use the right-click menus. I don't use them because my hand is not on the mouse! Pressing Shift+F10 opens the right-click menu. Use the up/down arrow keys to move to various menu choices and the right arrow key to open a fly-out menu. When you get to the item you want, press Enter to select it.

Crossing Tasks Off Your List with Ctrl+5

I love to make lists, and I love to cross stuff off my list. It makes me feel like I've gotten stuff done. Select a cell and press Ctrl+5 to apply strikethrough to the cell.

Date-Stamp or Time-Stamp Using Ctrl+; or Ctrl+:

Here is an easy way to remember this shortcut. What time is it right now? It is 11:21 here. There is a colon in the time. Press Ctrl+Colon to enter the current time in the active cell.

Need the current date? Same keystroke, minus the Shift key. Pressing Ctrl+Semicolon enters the current time.

Note that this is not the same as using =NOW( ) or =TODAY( ). Those functions change over time. These shortcuts mark the time or date that you pressed the key and the value does not change.

Repeating the Last Task with F4

Say that you just selected a cell and did Home, Delete, Delete Cells, Delete Entire Row, OK. You need to delete 24 more rows in various spots throughout your data set.

Select a cell in the next row to delete and press F4, which repeats the last command but on the currently selected cell.

Select a cell in the next row to delete and press F4. Before you know it, all the 24 rows are deleted without you having to click on Home, Delete, Delete Cells, Delete Entire Row, OK 24 times.

The F4 key works with 92% of the commands you will use. Try it. You'll love it. It'll be obvious when you try to use one of the unusual commands that cannot be redone with F4.

Adding Dollar Signs to a Reference with F4

That's right—two of my favorites in a row use F4. When you are entering a formula and you need to change A1 to $A$1, click F4 while the insertion point is touching A1. You can press F4 again to freeze only the row with A$1. Press F4 again to freeze the column with $A1. Press again to toggle back to A1.

Finding the One Thing That Takes You Too Much Time

The shortcuts in this section are the ones I learned over the course of 20 years. They were all for tasks that I had to do repeatedly. In your job, watch for any tasks you are doing over and over, especially things that take several mouse clicks. When you identify one, try to find a shortcut key that will save you time.

 **Tip**

When you perform commands with the mouse, do all the steps except the last one. Hover over the command until the tooltip appears. Many times, the tooltip tells you of the keyboard shortcut.

Using Excel 2003 Keyboard Accelerators

In legacy versions of Excel, most menu items included one underlined letter. In those versions, you could hold down the Alt key while pressing the underlined letter to invoke the menu item. In the Excel 2003 screen shown in Figure 6.6, you can display the Edit menu by pressing Alt+E, and you can select Edit, Fill, Justify by pressing Alt+E+I+J.

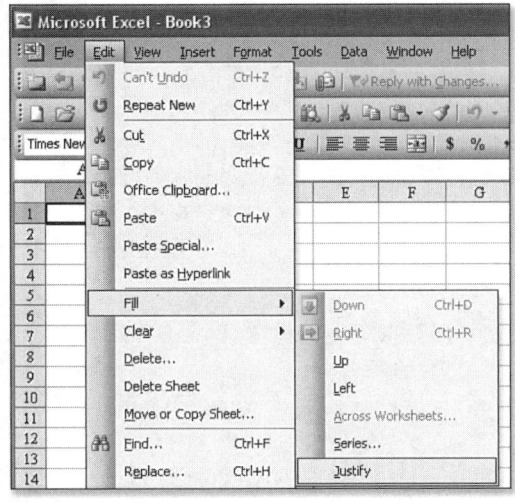

Figure 6.6
Pressing Alt+E+I+J performs Edit, Fill, Justify.

Instead of pressing Alt+E+I+J all at once, when the Edit menu is displayed, you can display the Fill fly-out menu by pressing I. Then you can perform the Justify command by pressing J.

If you are a power Excel user, you probably have a few of these commands memorized, such as Alt+E+I+J for Edit, Fill, Justify; Alt+E+S+V for Edit, Paste Special, Values; and Alt+D+L for Data Validation. If you have some of these commands memorized, when you hear that the ribbon has replaced the legacy menu, you might be worried that you have to relearn all the shortcut keys. However, there is good news for the power Excel gurus who have favorite Alt shortcut keys burned into their minds—most of them will continue to work as they did in Excel 2003.

If you are an intermediate Excel user who regularly uses the Excel 2003 keyboard accelerators but has to look at the screen to use them, you should start using the new keyboard accelerators discussed at the beginning of this chapter.

Invoking an Excel 2003 Alt Shortcut

In Excel 2003, the main menus are File, Edit, View, Insert, Format, Tools, Data, Window, and Help. The keyboard accelerator commands in Excel 2003 are Alt+F, Alt+E, Alt+V, Alt+I, Alt+O, Alt+T, Alt+D, Alt+W, and Alt+H.

If you are moving from Excel 2003 to Excel 2013, you will have the best success when trying to access commands on the Edit, View, Insert, Format, Tools, and Data menus. None of the keyboard accelerators associated with Window or Help work in Excel 2013. Alt+H takes you to the Home tab instead of the few commands on the Help menu, and Alt+W takes you to the View tab.

Some of the keyboard shortcuts associated with the File menu in Excel 2003 continue to work in Excel 2013. Pressing Alt+F opens the File menu. In Excel 2003, pressing Alt+F+O performs File, Open. It happens that O is the shortcut on the File menu for Open, so pressing Alt+F+O in Excel 2013 also performs File, Open.

For the shortcut keys Alt+E, Alt+V, Alt+I, Alt+O, Alt+T, and Alt+D, Excel switches into Office 2003 Access Key mode. In this mode, a tooltip appears over the ribbon, indicating which letters you have typed so far (see Figure 6.7). When you have entered enough letters, the command is invoked. If you have forgotten the sequence, you can press Esc to exit the Excel 2003 Access Key mode.

 Tip

You will have to train yourself to pause briefly after typing the first letter in the legacy shortcut key sequence. For example, press Alt+E, pause for a brief moment to allow Excel to display the Office Access Key window, and then press S, V for Edit, Paste Special, Values. If you do not pause, the second letter is lost because Excel displays the pop-up Office Key Sequence window.

Figure 6.7
The Office 2003 access key tooltip shows which keys you have used so far while entering a legacy shortcut.

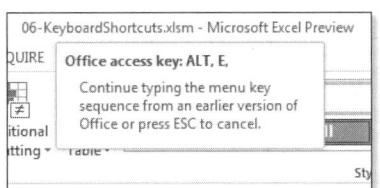

Determining Which Commands Work in Legacy Mode

If you try a command that no longer works in Excel 2013, nothing happens. Several commands don't make sense in the framework of Excel 2013, so they have been deprecated.

Table 6.6 lists the legacy keyboard commands and indicates which of them continue to work in Excel 2013.

Table 6.6 Excel Legacy Keyboard Commands

Works in Shortcut	Excel 2013?	Command
Alt+F+N	Yes	File, New
Alt+F+O	Yes	File, Open
Alt+F+C	Yes	File, Close
Alt+F+S	Yes	File, Save
Alt+F+A	Yes	File, Save As
Alt+F+G	No	File, Save as Web Page
Alt+F+W	No	File, Save Workspace
Alt+F+H	No	File, File Search
Alt+F+M	No	File, Permission

Works in Shortcut	Excel 2013?	Command
Alt+F+E	No	File, Check Out or Check In (toggle)
Alt+F+R	No	File, Version History
Alt+F+B	No	File, Web Page Preview
Alt+F+U	No	File, Page Setup
Alt+F+T+S	No	File, Print Area, Set Print Area
Alt+F+T+C	No	File, Print Area, Clear Print Area
Alt+F+V	No	File, Print Preview
Alt+F+P	Yes as Alt+F+P+P	File, Print
Alt+F+D+M	No	File, Send To, Mail Recipient
Alt+F+D+S	No	File, Send To, Original Sender
Alt+F+D+C	No	File, Send To, Mail Recipient (for Review)
Alt+F+D+A	No	File, Send To, Mail Recipient (as Attachment)
Alt+F+D+R	No	File, Send To, Routing Recipient
Alt+F+D+E	No	File, Send To, Exchange Folder
Alt+F+D+O	No	File, Send To, Online Meeting Participant
Alt+F+D+X	No	File, Send To, Recipient Using Internet Fax Service
Alt+F+I	No	File, Properties
Alt+F+1	Yes	File, 1
Alt+F+2	Yes	File, 2
Alt+F+3	Yes	File, 3
Alt+F+4	Yes	File, 4
Alt+F+5	Yes	File, 5
Alt+F+6	Yes	File, 6
Alt+F+7	Yes	File, 7
Alt+F+8	Yes	File, 8
Alt+F+9	Yes	File, 9
Alt+F+T	No	File, Sign Out
Alt+F+X	Yes	File, Exit
Alt+E+U	Yes	Edit, Undo
Alt+E+R	Yes	Edit, Repeat
Alt+E+T	Yes	Edit, Cut
Alt+E+C	Yes	Edit, Copy
Alt+E+B	Yes	Edit, Office Clipboard

Works in Shortcut	Excel 2013?	Command
Alt+E+P	Yes	Edit, Paste
Alt+E+S	Yes	Edit, Paste Special
Alt+E+H	No	Edit, Paste as Hyperlink
Alt+E+I+D	Yes	Edit, Fill, Down
Alt+E+I+R	Yes	Edit, Fill, Right
Alt+E+I+U	Yes	Edit, Fill, Up
Alt+E+I+L	Yes	Edit, Fill, Left
Alt+E+I+A	Yes	Edit, Fill, Across Worksheets
Alt+E+I+S	Yes	Edit, Fill, Series
Alt+E+I+J	Yes	Edit, Fill, Justify
Alt+E+A+A	Yes	Edit, Clear, All
Alt+E+A+F	Yes	Edit, Clear, Formats
Alt+E+A+C	Yes	Edit, Clear, Contents
Alt+E+A+M	Yes	Edit, Clear, Comments
Alt+E+D	Yes	Edit, Delete
Alt+E+L	Yes	Edit, Delete Sheet
Alt+E+M	Yes	Edit, Move or Copy Sheet
Alt+E+F	Yes	Edit, Find
Alt+E+E	Yes	Edit, Replace
Alt+E+G	Yes	Edit, Go To
Alt+E+K	Yes	Edit, Links
Alt+E+O	No	Edit, Object
Alt+E+O+V	No	Edit, Object, Convert
Alt+V+N	Yes	View, Normal
Alt+V+P	Yes	View, Page Break Preview
Alt+V+K	No	View, Task Pane
Alt+V+T+C	No	View, Toolbars, Customize
Alt+V+F	Yes	View, Formula Bar
Alt+V+S	No	View, Status Bar
Alt+V+H	Yes	View, Header and Footer
Alt+V+C	Yes	View, Comments
Alt+V+V	Yes	View, Custom Views
Alt+V+U	Yes	View, Full Screen (Caution: Use the maximize button to return.)

Works in Shortcut	Excel 2013?	Command
Alt+V+Z	Yes	View, Zoom
Alt+I+E	Yes	Insert, Cells
Alt+I+R	Yes	Insert, Rows
Alt+I+C	Yes	Insert, Columns
Alt+I+W	Yes	Insert, Worksheet
Alt+I+H	Yes	Insert, Chart
Alt+I+S	Yes	Insert, Symbol
Alt+I+B	Yes	Insert, Page Break
Alt+I+A	Yes	Insert, Reset All Page Breaks
Alt+I+F	Yes	Insert, Function
Alt+I+N+D	Yes	Insert, Name, Define
Alt+I+N+P	Yes	Insert, Name, Paste
Alt+I+N+C	Yes	Insert, Name, Create
Alt+I+N+A	Yes	Insert, Name, Apply
Alt+I+N+L	Yes	Insert, Name, Label
Alt+I+M	Yes	Insert, Comment
Alt+I+A	Yes	Insert, Ink Annotations
Alt+I+P+C	Yes	Insert, Picture, Clip Art
Alt+I+P+F	Yes	Insert, Picture, From File
Alt+I+P+S	Yes	Insert, Picture, From Scanner or Camera
Alt+I+P+D	Yes	Insert, Picture, Ink Drawing and Writing
Alt+I+P+A	No	Insert, Picture, AutoShapes
Alt+I+P+W	No	Insert, Picture, WordArt
Alt+I+P+O	No	Insert, Picture, Organization Chart
Alt+I+G	No	Insert, Diagram
Alt+I+O	Yes	Insert, Object
Alt+I+I	Yes	Insert, Hyperlink
Alt+O+E	Yes	Format, Cells
Alt+O+R+E	Yes	Format, Row, Height
Alt+O+R+A	Yes	Format, Row, AutoFit
Alt+O+R+H	Yes	Format, Row, Hide
Alt+O+R+U	Yes	Format, Row, Unhide
Alt+O+C+W	Yes	Format, Column, Width

Works in Shortcut	Excel 2013?	Command
Alt+O+C+A	Yes	Format, Column, AutoFit Selection
Alt+O+C+H	Yes	Format, Column, Hide
Alt+O+C+U	Yes	Format, Column, Unhide
Alt+O+C+S	Yes	Format, Column, Standard Width
Alt+O+H+R	Yes	Format, Sheet, Rename
Alt+O+H+H	Yes	Format, Sheet, Hide
Alt+O+H+U	Yes	Format, Sheet, Unhide
Alt+O+H+B	Yes	Format, Sheet, Background
Alt+O+H+T	Yes	Format, Sheet, Tab Color
Alt+O+A	No	Format, AutoFormat
Alt+O+D	Yes	Format, Conditional Formatting
Alt+O+S	Yes	Format, Style
Alt+T+S	Yes	Tools, Spelling
Alt+T+R	Yes	Tools, Research
Alt+T+K	Yes	Tools, Error Checking
Alt+T+H+H	No	Tools, Speech, Speech Recognition
Alt+T+H+T	No	Tools, Speech, Show Text to Speech Toolbar
Alt+T+D	Yes	Tools, Shared Workspace
Alt+T+B	Yes	Tools, Share Workbook
Alt+T+T+H	Yes	Tools, Track Changes, Highlight Changes
Alt+T+T+A	Yes	Tools, Track Changes, Accept or Reject Changes
Alt+T+W	Yes	Tools, Compare and Merge Workbooks
Alt+T+P+P	Yes	Tools, Protection, Protect Sheet
Alt+T+P+A	Yes	Tools, Protection, Allow Users to Edit Ranges
Alt+T+P+W	Yes	Tools, Protection, Protect Workbook
Alt+T+P+S	Yes	Tools, Protection, Protect and Share Workbook
Alt+T+N+M	Yes	Tools, Online Collaboration, Meet Now
Alt+T+N+S	Yes	Tools, Online Collaboration, Schedule Meeting
Alt+T+N+W	Yes	Tools, Online Collaboration, Web Discussions
Alt+T+N+N	Yes	Tools, Online Collaboration, End Review
Alt+T+G	Yes	Tools, Goal Seek
Alt+T+E	Yes	Tools, Scenarios
Alt+T+U+T	Yes	Tools, Formula Auditing, Trace Precedents

Works in Shortcut	Excel 2013?	Command
Alt+T+U+D	Yes	Tools, Formula Auditing, Trace Dependents
Alt+T+U+E	Yes	Tools, Formula Auditing, Trace Error
Alt+T+U+A	Yes	Tools, Formula Auditing, Remove All Arrows
Alt+T+U+F	Yes	Tools, Formula Auditing, Evaluate Formula
Alt+T+U+W	Yes	Tools, Formula Auditing, Show Watch Window
Alt+T+U+M	Yes	Tools, Formula Auditing, Formula Auditing Mode
Alt+T+U+S	No	Tools, Formula Auditing, Show Formula Auditing Toolbar
Alt+T+V	Yes	Tools, Solver
Alt+T+M+M	Yes	Tools, Macro, Macros
Alt+T+M+R	Yes	Tools, Macro, Record New Macro
Alt+T+M+S	Yes	Tools, Macro, Security
Alt+T+M+V	Yes	Tools, Macro, Visual Basic Editor
Alt+T+M+E	No	Tools, Macro, Microsoft Script Editor
Alt+T+I	Yes	Tools, Add-Ins
Alt+T+C	No	Tools, COM Add-Ins
Alt+T+A	Yes	Tools, AutoCorrect Options
Alt+T+C	No	Tools, Customize
Alt+T+O	No	Tools, Options
Alt+T+D	No	Tools, Data Analysis
Alt+D+S	Yes	Data, Sort
Alt+D+F+F	Yes	Data, Filter, AutoFilter
Alt+D+F+S	Yes	Data, Filter, Show All
Alt+D+F+A	Yes	Data, Filter, Advanced Filter
Alt+D+O	Yes	Data, Form
Alt+D+B	Yes	Data, Subtotals
Alt+D+L	Yes	Data, Validation
Alt+D+T	Yes	Data, Table
Alt+D+E	Yes	Data, Text to Columns
Alt+D+N	Yes	Data, Consolidate
Alt+D+G+H	Yes	Data, Group and Outline, Hide Detail
Alt+D+G+S	Yes	Data, Group and Outline, Show Detail
Alt+D+G+G	Yes	Data, Group and Outline, Group
Alt+D+G+U	Yes	Data, Group and Outline, Ungroup

Works in Shortcut	Excel 2013?	Command
Alt+D+G+A	Yes	Data, Group and Outline, Auto Outline
Alt+D+G+C	Yes	Data, Group and Outline, Clear Outline
Alt+D+G+E	Yes	Data, Group and Outline, Settings
Alt+D+P	Yes	Data, PivotTable and PivotChart Report
Alt+D+D+D	Yes	Data, Import External Data, Import Data
Alt+D+D+W	Yes	Data, Import External Data, New Web Query
Alt+D+D+N	Yes	Data, Import External Data, New Database Query
Alt+D+D+E	Yes	Data, Import External Data, List
Alt+D+I+D	No	Data, List, Discard Changes and Refresh
Alt+D+I+B	No	Data, List, Hide Border of Inactive Lists
Alt+D+X+I	Yes	Data, XML, Import
Alt+D+X+E	Yes	Data, XML, Export
Alt+D+X+R	Yes	Data, XML, Refresh XML Data
Alt+D+X+X	Yes	Data, XML, XML Source
Alt+D+X+P	Yes	Data, XML, XML Map Properties
Alt+D+X+Q	Yes	Data, XML, Edit Query
Alt+D+X+A	Yes	Data, XML, XML Expansion Packs Edit Query
Alt+D+D+A	Yes	Data, Import External Data, Data Range Properties
Alt+D+D+M	Yes	Data, Import External Data, Parameters
Alt+D+I+C	Yes	Data, List, Create List
Alt+D+I+R	Yes	Data, List, Resize List
Alt+D+I+T	Yes	Data, List, Total Row
Alt+D+I+V	Yes	Data, List, Convert to Range
Alt+D+I+P	Yes	Data, List, Publish List
Alt+D+I+L	No	Data, List, View List on Server
Alt+D+I+U	No	Data, List, Unlink List
Alt+D+I+Y	No	Data, List, Synchronize
Alt+D+R	Yes	Data, Refresh Data
Alt+W+N	No	Window, New Window
Alt+W+A	No	Window, Arrange
Alt+W+B	No	Window, Compare Side by Side with Filename
Alt+W+H	No	Window, Hide
Alt+W+U	No	Window, Unhide

Works in Shortcut	Excel 2013?	Command
Alt+W+S	No	Window, Split
Alt+W+F	No	Window, Freeze Panes
Alt+W+1	No	Window, 1
Alt+W+2	No	Window, 2
Alt+W+3	No	Window, 3
Alt+W+4	No	Window, 4
Alt+W+5	No	Window, 5
Alt+W+6	No	Window, 6
Alt+W+7	No	Window, 7
Alt+W+8	No	Window, 8
Alt+W+9	No	Window, 9
Alt+W+M	No	Window, More Windows
Alt+H+H	No	Help, Microsoft Excel Help
Alt+H+O	No	Help, Show the Office Assistant
Alt+H+M	No	Help, Microsoft Office Online
Alt+H+C	No	Help, Contact Us
Alt+H+L	No	Help, Lotus 1-2-3 Help
Alt+H+K	No	Help, Check for Updates
Alt+H+R	No	Help, Detect and Repair
Alt+H+V	No	Help, Activate Product
Alt+H+F	No	Help, Customer Feedback Options
Alt+H+A	No	Help, About Microsoft Office Excel

Some people liked using Alt+F+T+S in Excel 2003 for File, Print Area, Set Print Area. If you are one of those people, you will be unhappy to hear that your favorite shortcut key is not supported in Excel 2013. Instead, use Alt+P+R+S. However, most of the powerful and common shortcut keys are still available, so there is a good chance that your knowledge of past shortcut keys will help when you upgrade to Excel 2013.

THE BIG GRID AND FILE FORMATS

Word leaked out in 2004 that Microsoft would be increasing the number of rows in the 2007 version of Excel. Although at that time no one knew exactly how many rows, one thing was certain—the Excel file format would have to change. The old XLS file format was designed around cell addressing that would fit in a 2^{16} address space, hence the limit of 65,536 rows.

Excel Grid Limits

The new grid in Excel offers 1,048,576 rows—that is, 2^{20} rows—a sixteen-fold increase from 65,536 rows in Excel 2003. It offers 16,384 columns (that is, 2^{14} columns), an increase from 256 columns in Excel 2003. Overall, the new grid provides for 17.1 billion cells on each worksheet.

You can now analyze more complex data sets. For example, if you regularly analyze 2,000 items per month, you can analyze 2.5 years of monthly data in one Excel 2003 worksheet. In Excel 2013, you can analyze 10 years of weekly data or 43 years of monthly data. Columnwise, legacy versions of Excel could handle only 9 months of daily data going across the worksheet. Excel 2013 can handle 45 years of daily dates or 63 years of weekdays.

It is interesting to compare the size increase in the history of spreadsheets. You will see that the size increase is unprecedented. Here is a brief history of spreadsheets:

- In October 1979, VisiCalc debuted with 255 rows and 63 columns.

- In 1983, Lotus 1-2-3 debuted with 8,192 rows and 256 columns. The 2 million cells per worksheet in this version was a 13,000% increase over VisiCalc.

- In 1987, early versions of Excel offered 16,384 rows by 255 columns. This 4 million cells was double the amount offered in Lotus 1-2-3 release 2.2.

- In Excel 97, Microsoft increased Excel to offer 65,536 rows by 255 columns. This 16.7 million cells per spreadsheet was quadruple the previous limit.

- As of Excel 2007, the new grid size is 1,048,576 rows by 16,384 columns. This means 17.1 billion cells, which is a 102,300% increase over the previous limit.

Why Are There Only 65,536 Rows in My Excel 2013 Spreadsheet?

When you initially install Excel 2013 and open one of your large workbooks, you might be disappointed to find only 65,536 rows in the worksheet (see Figure 7.1). When this occurs, it means you are in Compatibility mode. Any time that you open an .xls format file, you are limited to the 65,536 rows that were available in legacy versions of Excel. If you see 65,536 rows, look in the title bar and you will see that you are in Compatibility mode.

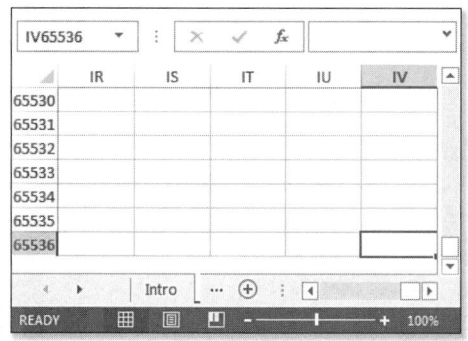

Figure 7.1
What is all the hype? There are still only 65,536 rows.

To leave Compatibility mode, select File and then select Convert, as shown in Figure 7.2. Excel tells you that the old file will be deleted and replaced by a new file. After the file conversion is done, Excel offers to close and reopen the file so that you are no longer in Compatibility mode.

With the bigger grid, it is far more likely that you will encounter larger files, formulas, and pivot tables. With a 102,300% increase in the file, many of the old limits in Excel 2003 no longer make sense. Because of the bigger grid, Microsoft has provided relaxed limits in many areas. Limits are discussed in the next section.

There is also an unusual quirk with the big grid. Previously, columns were labeled from A to IV. Now, columns are labeled from A to XFD. This means that many three-letter words are now valid column names. In legacy versions of Excel, range names such as ROI2011 and TAX2008 would have been legal names. Now that these are actual cell addresses, those names can no longer be used in

Figure 7.2
You select
Convert to leave
Compatibility
mode.

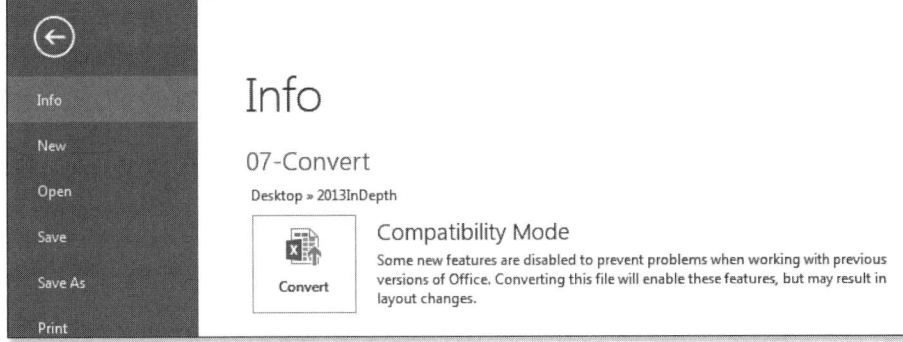

Excel 2013. Excel automatically changes such names during the conversion process. For example, a name such as YTD2012 changes to _YTD2012.

In addition, you don't have to worry about updating most formulas, because any formulas that reference the old name will change. However, if you have any VBA macros that refer to the old name, or any formulas that included the old name in double quotes in the INDIRECT function, you have to manually fix those.

Other Limits in Excel 2013

In addition to the grid size, a number of other aspects of Excel have new limits. Table 7.1 illustrates these new limits.

Table 7.1   Excel 2013 Limits

Item	Old Limit	New Limit
PC memory Excel can use	1GB	Max allowed by Windows
Number of unique colors in a single workbook	56	4.3 billion
Number of conditional format conditions on a cell	3	Limited by available memory
Number of levels of sorting	3	64
Number of items in the AutoFilter drop-down	1,000	10,000
Number of characters that can display in one cell	1,024	32,768
Number of characters in a cell that Excel can print	1,024	32,768
Number of unique cell styles in a workbook	4,096	65,536
Maximum length of formulas	1,024 characters	8,192 characters
Number of levels of nesting in formulas	7	64

Item	Old Limit	New Limit
Maximum number of arguments in a function	30	255
Number of characters that can be displayed	255	32K in a cell formatted as text
Number of items that can be found with Find All	65,536	~2 billion
Number of columns allowed in a pivot table	255	16,384
Number of unique items in a single pivot field	32,768	~1 million
Number of fields in a pivot table	255	16,384
Number of cells that can depend on a single area before Excel must perform full calculations instead of partial calculations (because it can no longer track the dependencies required to do partial calculations)	8,102	Limited by available memory
Number of different areas in a sheet that can have dependencies before Excel must perform full calculations instead of partial calculations (because it can no longer track the dependencies required to do partial calculations)	65,536	Limited by available memory
Number of array formulas in a worksheet that can refer to another (given) worksheet	65,536	Limited by available memory
Number of categories that custom functions can be grouped into	32	255
Number of characters that can be updated in a nonresident external workbook reference	255	32,768
Number of rows of a column or columns that can be referred to in an array formula (full-column references allowed)	65,335	Limitation removed

For people upgrading from Excel 2003, some of the new limits are excellent improvements. However, some of the new limits will allow people to build *worse* spreadsheets. Many people try to rely on nested IF functions when they should instead learn about VLOOKUP. Increasing from seven to 64 nested functions enables people to put off learning about VLOOKUP for even longer.

> *If you've been avoiding* VLOOKUP, *you can read about it in Chapter 12, "Using Powerful Functions: Logical, Lookup, Web, and Database Functions."*

With legacy versions of Excel, any pivot table that relied on daily dates almost always had to be built with the dates going down the side instead of across the rows. This was annoying, especially if you planned on rolling the dates up to months or quarters that would eventually fit in the 256 columns.

The number of Excel formats was a problem that was rarely encountered but caused horrible frustration when it was hit. Now the limit will be hit much less frequently.

Even with the current limits, some areas could still be improved. For example, there is still a limit of eight levels of indentation in outlining. However, for the most part, the new limits are incredible and allow much larger analyses to happen in Excel instead of elsewhere.

Tips for Navigating the Big Grid

The navigation tips described in the following sections are not new to Excel 2013. However, with 17 billion cells, there is a better chance that you don't want to be scrolling around with the Page Up and Page Down keys.

Using Shortcut Keys to Move Around

A variety of shortcuts enable you to move quickly around a worksheet:

Shortcut	What It Does
Ctrl+Home	Moves to cell A1
Home	Moves to column A of the current row
Ctrl+End	Moves to the last-used cell in a worksheet
Ctrl+any arrow key	Jumps to the end of a contiguous range
Ctrl+up arrow	Moves to the first row in the data if your data has no blank cells
Ctrl+down arrow	Moves to the last row in the data if your data has no blank cells

Using the End Key to Navigate

The End key is one of the six keys above the arrow keys on a standard U.S. keyboard. When you press the End key, an indicator lights up in the status bar of the Excel window. When Excel is in End mode, you can press an arrow key or the Home key. Pressing an arrow key takes you to the edge of a contiguous range of cells. Pressing Home while in End mode takes you to the last-used cell in the worksheet.

In Figure 7.3, pressing End and then the down arrow key causes the cell pointer to jump from C34 to C36. When the cell pointer is on the edge of a range, pressing End followed by the down arrow again causes Excel to jump over a range of blank cells and land on the starting edge of the next range. For example, pressing End+down arrow from C36 causes the cell pointer to jump to C39. Press End and then right arrow from C39 to jump the gap and land in F39.

If you press the End key to move right or down from the last cell that contains data, the cell pointer jumps to the last row or column in the spreadsheet. In a blank worksheet, you can press End+down arrow and End+right arrow to move to XFD1048576.

▲	A	B	C	D	E	F	G	H
31	6085999	999	279608			$6,086.0M	999	$280K
32	23683765	561	1465003			$23,684M	561	$1,465.0M
33	496250	635006	154527			$496K	$635K	$155K
34	8955611	820	29070652			$8,955.6M	820	$29,071M
35	653485	334702	941			$653K	$335K	941
36	221	10030144	801			221	$10,030M	801
37								
38								
39	780696	14217683	844883			$781K	$14,218M	$845K
40	17	878	669314			17	878	$669K
41	715	558812	25648			715	$559K	$26K
42	120194	28858528	751			$120K	$28,859M	751
43	505252	13753632	64939			$505K	$13,754M	$65K
44	928282	4072000	49851			$928K	$4,072.0M	$50K
45	491	502	812856			491	502	$813K

Figure 7.3
End+arrow key causes Excel to jump over a range of blank cells or a contiguous range of cells.

Using the Current Range to Navigate

If your data has many blank cells, using Ctrl+arrow keys or Ctrl+End key will lead to frustration.

You can press Ctrl+* to select the current region. A current region starts from the current nonblank cell and extends out in all directions until Excel encounters a completely blank row, a completely blank column, or the edge of the spreadsheet.

Then you can press Ctrl+. (that is, Ctrl plus the period key) to move the active cell to each corner of the selection. From the top-left cell of a region, you can press Ctrl+* and then press Ctrl+. twice to go to the last used cell in the current region.

Using Go To for Navigation

You can press the F5 key to display the Go To dialog. Then you can type a cell address and click OK to quickly jump to that cell.

You can also use the Name box the same way you use the Go To dialog. The Name box is the drop-down area immediately to the left of the formula bar. You click in the Name box, type a valid cell address, and press Enter. Excel then jumps to that cell.

Understanding the File Formats

Excel 2007 introduced three new file formats, which are discussed in this section. Later, the section on file compatibility discusses how you can continue to share files with people using legacy versions of Excel.

A Brief History of File Formats

Excel has traditionally stored workbooks in Binary Interchange File Format (BIFF). The BIFF specification has changed occasionally over time.

In 1993, when Excel expanded to 16,384 rows, Microsoft began using BIFF5 format. In 1993, most companies did not have corporate local area networks (LANs); a file format conversion therefore usually affected just one person on one computer. If you had upgraded from Excel 4 to Excel 5, as long as you had a way to convert your Excel 4 files to Excel's new BIFF5 format, everything was fine.

 Note

Although you will generally be saving files in one of the .XLSB, .XLSX, and .XLSM formats, there are other new file formats. The .XLAM format is used by developers to distribute add-ins. The .XLST is a template format.

In 1997, Microsoft introduced a major file change, BIFF8. This version of BIFF allowed 65,536 rows. The rise of the Internet and email meant that far more people were now sharing files. Excel 97 offered a way to save files in the old format in case you needed to share files with a person using a legacy version of Excel.

All BIFF versions are proprietary formats. Figure 7.4 shows an Excel 2003 spreadsheet as viewed in Notepad. You would certainly never be able to open a Notepad window and begin typing a new spreadsheet. Similarly, it would be very difficult for other applications to extract data from the BIFF format.

Figure 7.4
BIFF files are difficult for other applications to read.

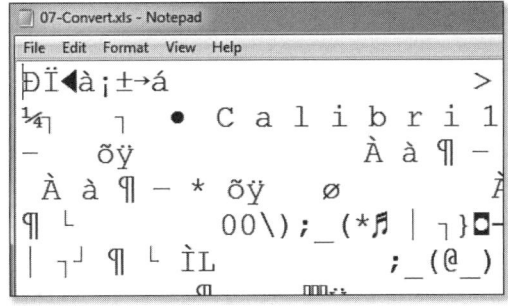

In Excel 2000, Microsoft flirted with a new HTML file format. By default, files were stored as XLS files in BIFF8 format. However, you could save a file as an HTML file and later open that HTML file in Excel 2000. With some limitations, most contents of the file and formatting could be successfully round-tripped from Excel to HTML and back to Excel.

This produced an interesting new paradigm: It would be possible for any program that could read or write text files to extract data from the Excel HTML file. A program other than Excel could easily read or produce this format.

Using HTML made sense in 1998 through 2000. The rise of the Internet made HTML a very popular format. However, although HTML is a great language for the display of information, it is not necessarily a smart language.

In 1998, the World Wide Web Consortium published the first 1.0 specification for a new language called Extensible Markup Language (XML), which presents data that any platform or application can read. Like HTML, XML is a simple text file that can be read or created with Notepad. Excel 2002 offered a way to export data in XML. Excel 2003 continued to use BIFF8 as the standard file format, but you could choose to save a workbook in XML format. When you later opened the XML file in Excel, all the formulas and formatting would be successfully round-tripped. XML in Excel 2003 did not support VBA or charts.

XML offers a number of advantages. Because an XML file is a simple text file, any program can easily read data from it. This file format is also less prone to corruption than BIFF. If you randomly wipe out several bytes of a BIFF file, it is likely that the file will be corrupt and no longer open in Excel. If you truncate or corrupt several bytes of an XML file, the rest of the data is still readable in Excel.

 Note

If you are extremely concerned with performance issues, you might want to use BIFF12 because a large BIFF12 file loads more quickly and saves more quickly than the new XML formats. However, if you are concerned with file size issues, the new XML file formats will win.

Excel 2013 offers three official file formats—BIFF12, XLSX, and XLSM—described in the following sections. In addition, Excel offers support for BIFF8 and even BIFF5, in case you have files floating around from Excel 95.

Using the New Binary File Format: BIFF12

With Excel 2007's increase in rows and columns, BIFF8 would no longer work. Excel 2013 can save files in a new binary file format known as BIFF12. Files stored in BIFF12 have an .xlsb file extension. The Save As dialog calls this type of file *Excel Binary Workbook*. For the first time, the binary workbook is not the default method for saving in Excel.

BIFF12 suffers from the same problems as all previous BIFF versions: It is difficult for other applications to read from or write to BIFF formats, and if parts of the BIFF12 file become corrupted or truncated, Excel has a difficult time successfully loading the file.

Using the New XML File Formats: XLSX and XLSM

XML in Excel 2003 was almost an ideal solution: Files could be round-tripped from Excel to XML and back to Excel, provided that the files did not include VBA macros, charts, or other embedded images.

Excel now offers complete 100% support for every feature in the new XML file formats. Workbooks can contain charts, tables, WordArt, SmartArt, shapes, and images. For security purposes, Excel supports XML file formats that are macro free and file formats that are macro enabled. Here are the two XML file formats that Excel 2013 supports:

- **XLSX**—Files stored with the .xlsx extension are the default file type in Excel 2013. This XML file format does not allow macros.

- **XLSM**—Files stored with the .xlsm extension are XML files that allow for the inclusion of VBA macros.

The new XLSX and XLSM file formats are actually Zip files, which makes it easy to look inside the file formats. Figure 7.5 shows a worksheet that has a number of elements. It has a pivot table in row 20, WordArt, SmartArt, sparklines, slicers, and a chart.

Figure 7.5
This workbook is saved in XLSM, one of the new XML formats.

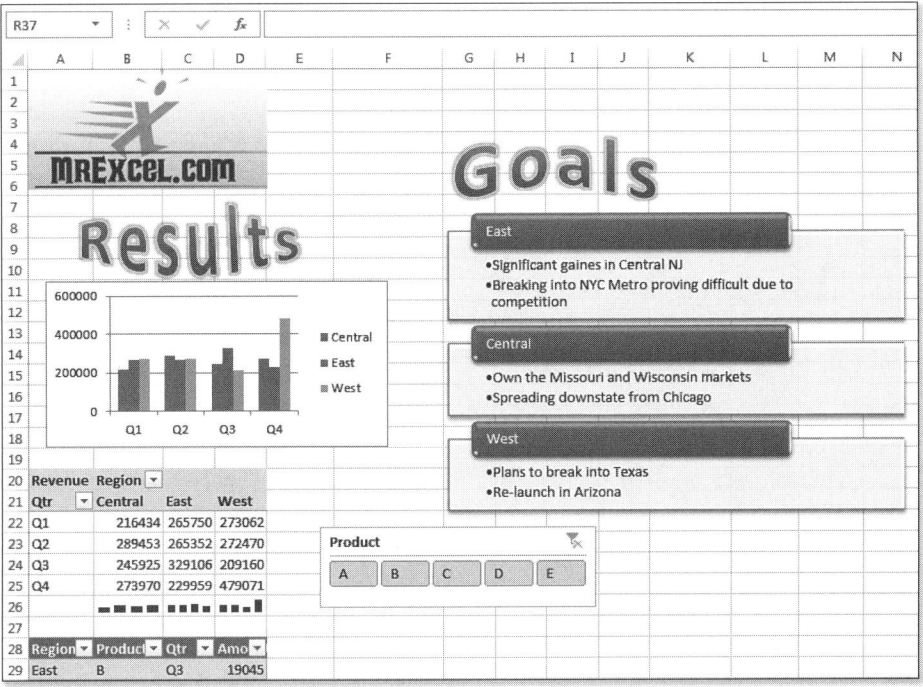

To look inside any Excel 2013 document, follow these steps:

1. In Windows Explorer, right-click the document name (which is in the format *filename*.xlsm) and select Rename.

2. Change the file extension to .zip. Windows warns you that if you change a file extension, the file may become unusable.

3. Click Yes to confirm the change.

4. Open the Zip file with WinZip or any other Zip utility.

As shown in Figure 7.6, inside the Zip file, you can see several XML components. The embedded image is included in the Zip file. All the settings and styles, drawings, and data are stored as separate XML files within the Zip file. Unzipped, these components would take up 115KB. However, because they are zipped files, only 40KB is needed to store the data.

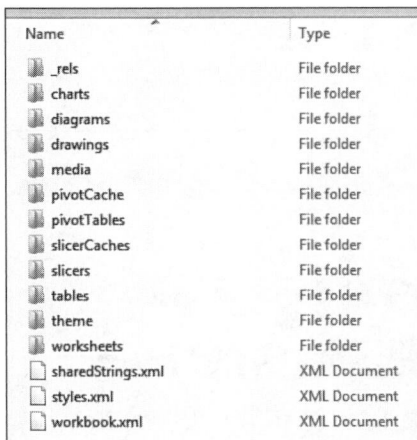

Name	Type
_rels	File folder
charts	File folder
diagrams	File folder
drawings	File folder
media	File folder
pivotCache	File folder
pivotTables	File folder
slicerCaches	File folder
slicers	File folder
tables	File folder
theme	File folder
worksheets	File folder
sharedStrings.xml	XML Document
styles.xml	XML Document
workbook.xml	XML Document

Figure 7.6
The components of the workbook are stored as XML files, zipped, and then renamed with an .xlsx or .xlsm extension.

Version Compatibility

With not just one new file format but three file formats in Excel 2013, you face a number of problems as you try to share files with people who use legacy versions of Excel.

If you are using Excel 2013 and want to open a file created in Excel 5 through Excel 2003, your copy of Excel gladly opens the file, but the file is in a special Compatibility mode. In this mode, you cannot use more than 65,536 rows, and you cannot use more than 256 columns. When you attempt to save the file, the Compatibility Checker tells you what functionality will be lost.

If you start with a new spreadsheet in Excel 2013 and want to share the file with someone using Excel 5, 95, 97, or 2000, you have to use the Compatibility Checker and save the file in a legacy version of Excel.

If you start with a new spreadsheet in Excel 2013 and want to share the file with someone using Excel 2002 or Excel 2003, you can encourage that person to download the Compatibility Pack for the Microsoft Office system. This converter allows Excel 2002 and Excel 2003 to open files stored in the new XLSB, XLSM, and XLSX formats.

However, before you send the file, you should run it through the Compatibility Checker. To do so, follow these steps:

1. With the file open, go to the File tab in the ribbon. Excel opens in Backstage view.

2. Along the left navigation, select Info.

3. In the middle of the center pane, open the Check for Issues drop-down.

4. Select Check Compatibility. Excel displays the Compatibility Checker, as shown in Figure 7.7.

Figure 7.7
The Compatibility Checker reports on any compatibility issues with legacy versions of Excel.

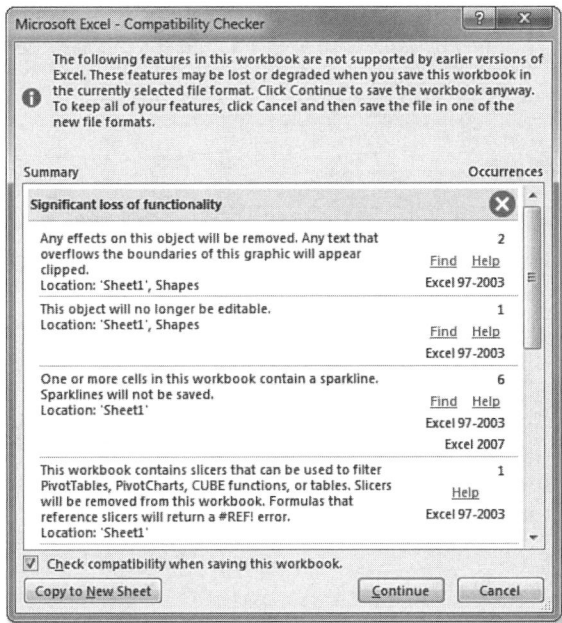

Although it is scrolled off the screen in Figure 7.7, the new Select Versions to Show button enables you to filter the list to problems that would affect Excel 2007 or problems that would affect only Excel 2002–2003.

If you know this is a workbook that will always be opened by someone using Excel 2002–2007, you can select the Check Compatibility When Saving This Workbook check box to make sure you have not introduced any incompatibilities.

You see two types of problems reported in the Compatibility Checker:

- **Minor loss of fidelity**—These issues involve formatting. If you used a color beyond the pallet of 56 colors, it is reported as a minor loss of fidelity. These types of issues are not considered serious. The person using Excel 2002, Excel 2003, or Excel 2007 is allowed to open the file, edit the file, and save the file.

- **Significant loss of functionality**—This means that you have used a feature in Excel 2013 that no longer functions in legacy versions of Excel. When you have these types of issues, the file opens in legacy versions of Excel, but it is forced into a read-only state.

When you have an issue reported as a significant loss of functionality, you can click the Find hyperlink. Excel closes the Compatibility Checker and takes you to the area of the worksheet that contains the problem. If you use this method, you constantly have to keep returning to the Compatibility Checker to test other problems.

If many problems exist, click the Copy to New Sheet button. Excel inserts a new Compatibility Report worksheet in the workbook. Each issue is listed, along with a count of the number of issues and hyperlinks to help you find the problem (see Figure 7.8).

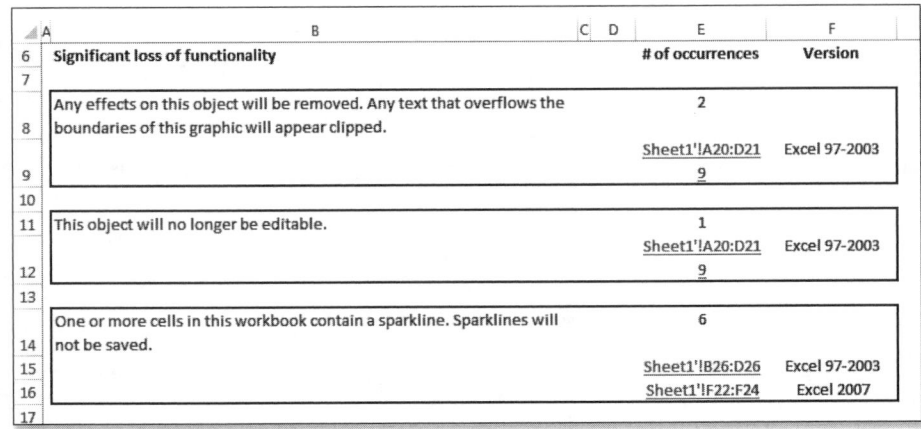

Figure 7.8
If you have many significant issues, it is easier to copy the contents of the Compatibility Checker to a new worksheet.

Opening Excel 2013 Files in Excel 2002 or 2003

If you attempt to open an Excel 2013 file in Excel 2002 or Excel 2003, you see a message that the file was created in a newer version of Excel. Excel allows you to download a converter so that you can open the file. The download process happens as part of the File Open process. It is quick. You have to do it only once per computer. Most people will not even remember downloading the utility.

After you install the Compatibility Pack, you can directly open XLSM, XLSX, and XLSB files in Excel 2003 or Excel 2002. You can also save your files back into the new format.

 Note

Keep in mind that you need to get the person to pay attention to the question that pops up when he first opens your file and chooses to download the converter. With the malware situation today, many people will automatically refuse to download anything. For this reason, a little hand-holding over the phone as the person opens your file for the first time might be appropriate.

Minor Loss of Fidelity

Suppose that you have a simple data worksheet in Excel 2013. You might have used a few custom colors or perhaps cell styles. When you open that file in Excel 2003, you receive a note that the custom color was converted to the closest color in the standard Excel 2003 pallet of 56 colors. Other than the formatting change, you can edit and then save the file back to an Excel 2013 format.

Significant Loss of Functionality

The Excel 2013 workbook shown previously in Figure 7.5 contains several elements that would report as a significant loss of functionality in Excel 2003.

When you attempt to open this workbook in Excel 2003, Excel warns you that there is significant loss of functionality. Because of the loss of functionality, Excel forces the document to be opened as read-only. You have to use File, Save As to save the file with a new name. This prevents the original document from losing the incompatible features.

Excel 2003 does its best to deal with the incompatible features. Figure 7.9 shows the file opened in Excel 2003. The WordArt changes to boring text. The SmartArt keeps the same basic look and feel, although it is now a static shape. The slicer and the icon sets are lost. Any cells using new functions such as SUMIFS calculate with a #NAME error. Any cells beyond row 65536 are lost.

Figure 7.9
Excel 2003 does its best to render certain features from Excel 2013.

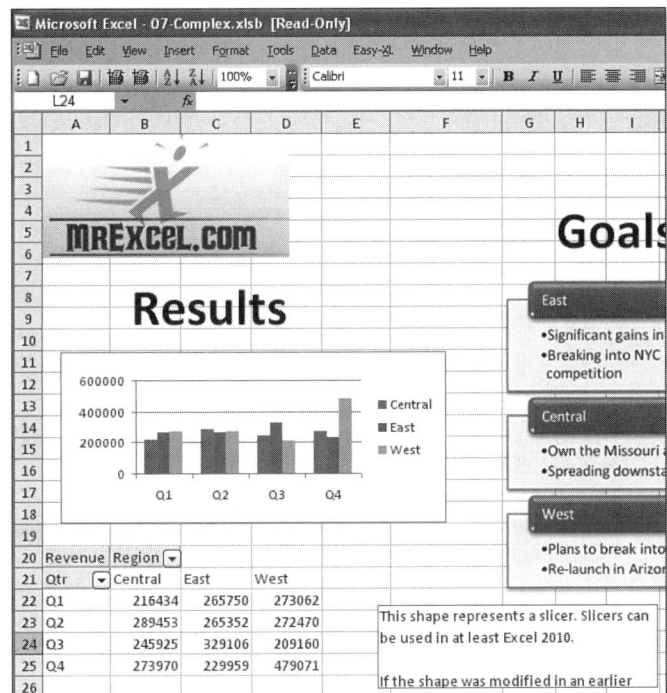

Creating Excel 2013 File Formats in Excel 2003

After you install the Office Compatibility Pack on a machine running Excel 2002 or Excel 2003, you can save files from Excel 2003 or Excel 2002 in one of the new Excel 2007–2013 file formats. The advantage is that when the file is later opened on a machine running Excel 2013, the file is not forced into the Compatibility mode.

After you have the Compatibility Pack installed, follow these steps to save files in an Excel 2007–2013 format:

1. Open or create a workbook in Excel 2002 or Excel 2003.

2. Select File, Save As. The Save As dialog appears.

3. Open the Save as Type drop-down and scroll to the bottom of the list. Choose one of the Excel "12" file types.

4. Type a filename.

5. Click Save. Excel runs a converter to convert the workbook to the chosen Excel 2013 format.

 Caution

Although Excel 2007 and 2013 seem fairly similar, Microsoft seems to have a freer attitude about the incompatibilities between Excel 2007 and Excel 2013. Because the files are not displaying warnings when opened in Excel 2007, there will probably be more serious problems with people unknowingly losing features when opening their Excel 2013 files on their home PC with Excel 2007.

Opening Excel 2013 Files in Excel 2007

Although Excel 2007 through Excel 2013 support the same file formats, some new Excel 2013 features do not work in Excel 2007.

Figure 7.10 shows the same workbook opened in Excel 2007. There is no warning that you have lost any functionality, and the workbook is not forced into Compatibility mode. However, the slicers are missing. The icon set happened to be using an Excel 2013 icon style, so the icons are missing. The new Chart Labels from the range are replaced with "[LABELRANGE]".

If you save that file in Excel 2007 and open it in Excel 2013, the icon set and the slicer are lost. The chart labels would come back. You have to refresh the pivot table to calculate it without the slicer.

Figure 7.10
You are not forced into read-only mode, but some features are lost in Excel 2007.

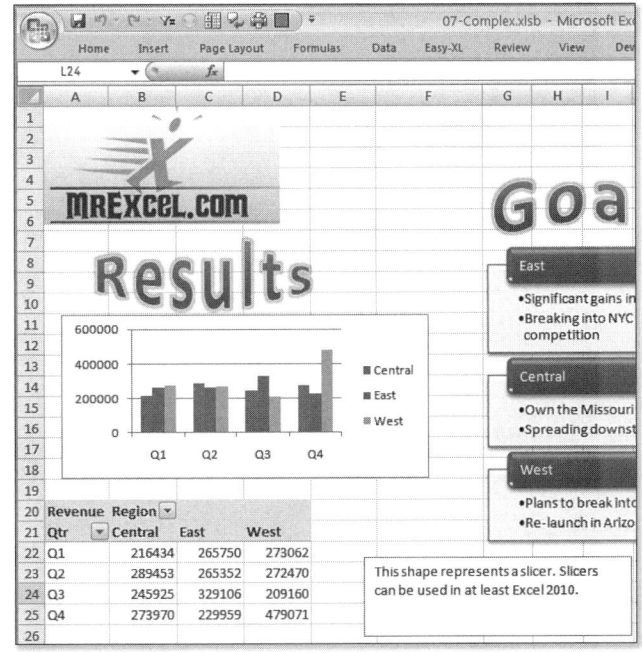

UNDERSTANDING FORMULAS

Excel's forté is performing calculations. When you use Excel, you typically use a combination of cells with numbers and cells with formulas. After you design a spreadsheet to calculate something, you can change the numbers used in the assumption cells and then watch Excel instantly calculate new results.

Getting the Most from This Chapter

Do not skip this entire chapter; one particular trick in this chapter can save you daily frustration.

I regularly entertain accountants and auditors with my Power Excel program. Although this program is a fun, laughter-filled tour through the inside tricks of Microsoft Excel, people always learn new things along the way.

I call them "gasp moments."

Imagine this setting: I am in front of 200 managerial accountants who have Excel open for 40 hours each week. You can generally figure that these folks are super-efficient with Excel. Any trick I show might already be in the arsenal of half to three-quarters of the room. A lot of the people nod their heads, while others look surprised. However, a few tricks I show will get a gasp from perhaps 90% of these managerial accountants because they didn't know these tricks before and now realize just how powerful they are. I thrive on the gasp moments.

Most people reading this book believe they know Excel formulas. To a certain extent, this chapter is a primer for the person who is new to Excel. However, even the most astute person using Excel should check out these sections of the chapter:

- Everyone should read the "Double-Click the Fill Handle to Copy a Formula" section. Somehow, most people have learned to drag the fill handle to copy a formula. This leads to horrible frustration on long data sets, as they go flying past the end of the data. This simple but powerful trick is the one that universally amazes attendees of my seminar.

- Honestly answer this question: Do you really understand the difference between cell H1 and cell $H$1? If you think the latter has anything to do with currency, you need to review the "Overriding Relative Behavior: Absolute Cell References" section thoroughly. This isn't a trick, but one of the fundamental building blocks to creating Excel worksheets. Roughly, 5% of the people in a Power Excel seminar do not understand this concept, and about 70% of the people in a community computer club presentation do not understand it. If you don't know when and why to use the dollar signs, you are in good company with 20 million other people using Excel. It is worth taking time to learn this essential technique.

- Finally, there are three ways to enter formulas, and I believe my preferred way is the best. I probably will not convince you to change, but when you understand my way, you can enter formulas far faster than the other two ways. To get a good understanding of the alternatives, read the "Three Methods of Entering Formulas" section later in this chapter.

>  **Tip**
>
> Designing a formula that can be written once and then copied to a rectangular range of data is a fantastic way to use Excel more efficiently.

Introduction to Formulas

When Microsoft overhauled Excel for the 2007 version, a number of formula limits were dramatically increased. For example, the number of characters in a formula increased from 1,024 to 8,192. The number of levels of nesting for IF functions increased from 7 to 64. Thanks to those improvements, you can calculate almost anything with a formula in Excel.

This chapter and Chapter 9, "Controlling Formulas," deal with formula basics. The chapters between Chapter 10, "Understanding Functions," and Chapter 15, "Using Trig, Matrix, and Engineering Functions," introduce adding functions to your formulas. Chapter 16, "Connecting Worksheets, Workbooks, and External Data," introduces formulas that calculate data found on other worksheets or in other workbooks. Chapter 17, "Using Super Formulas in Excel," provides interesting examples such as 3D formulas and the all-powerful array formulas.

Because of the record-oriented nature of spreadsheets, you can generally build a formula once and then copy that formula to hundreds or thousands of cells without changing anything in the formula.

Formulas Versus Values

When looking at an Excel grid, you cannot tell the difference between a cell with a formula and one that contains numbers. To see if a cell contains a number or a formula, select the cell. Look in the formula bar. If the formula bar contains a number, as shown in Figure 8.1, you know that it is a static value. If the formula bar contains a formula, you know that the number shown in the grid is the result of a formula calculation (see Figure 8.2). Keep in mind that formulas start with an equal sign.

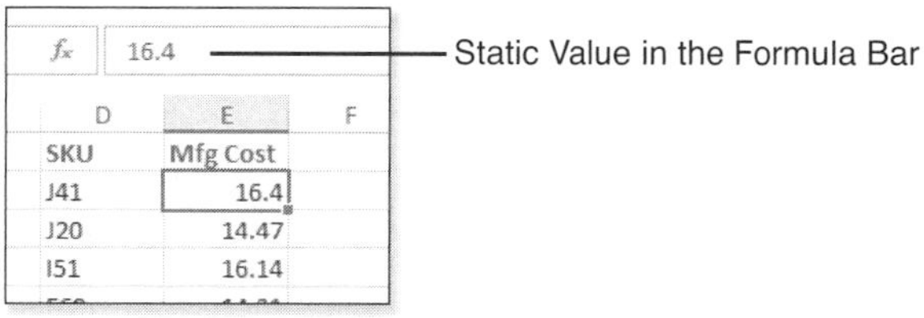

Figure 8.1
The formula bar reveals whether a value is a static number or a calculation. In this case, cell E2 contains a static number.

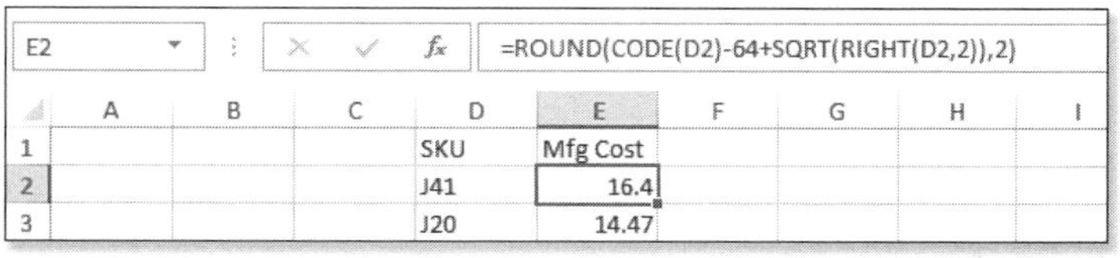

Static Value in the Formula Bar

Figure 8.2
In this case, cell E2 contains the result of a formula calculation. A formula starts with an equal sign.

Entering Your First Formula

Your first formula was probably a SUM function, entered with the Quick Analysis tool or the AutoSum button. However, this discussion is talking about a pure mathematical formula that uses a value in a cell that's added, subtracted, divided, or multiplied by a number or another cell.

Billions of variations of formulas can be used. Everyday life throws situations at you that can be solved with a formula. Keep these important points in mind as you start tinkering with your own formulas:

- Every formula starts with an equal sign.

- Entering formulas is just like typing an equation in a calculator with one exception (see the next point).

- If one of the terms in your formula is already stored in a cell in Excel, you can point to that cell's address instead of typing the number into that cell. Using this method enables you to change the value in one cell and then watch all the formulas recalculate. Excel 2013 adds a "slot machine" animation to show the cells in the visible window that are recalculating as the result of changing a cell.

To illustrate these points, see the steps to building a basic formula included in the following example.

Building a Formula

You want to enter a formula to calculate a target sales price, as shown in Figure 8.3. Cell D2 shows the product cost. In column E, you want to calculate the list price as two times the cost plus $3.

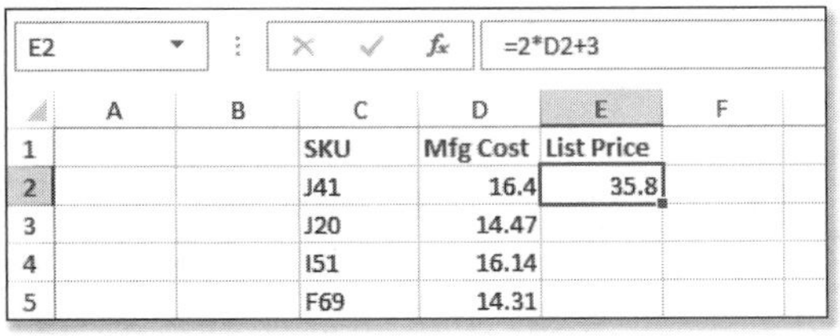

E2 | =2*D2+3

	A	B	C	D	E	F
1			SKU	Mfg Cost	List Price	
2			J41	16.4	35.8	
3			J20	14.47		
4			I51	16.14		
5			F69	14.31		

Figure 8.3
The formula in cell E2 recalculates if the value in cell D2 changes.

To enter a formula, follow these steps:

1. Select cell E2.
2. Type an equal sign. The equal sign tells Excel that you are starting a formula.
3. Type **2*D2** to indicate that you want to multiply two times the value in cell D2.
4. Type **+3** to add three to the result. There should be no spaces in the formula. If your formula reads `=2*D2+3`, proceed to step 5. Otherwise, use the backspace key to correct the formula.
5. Press Enter. Excel calculates the formula in cell E2.

By default, Excel usually moves the cell pointer down or to the right after you finish entering a formula. You should move the cell pointer back to cell E2 to inspect the formula, as shown in Figure 8.3. Note that Excel shows a number in the grid, but the formula bar reveals the formula behind the number.

The Relative Nature of Formulas

The formula `=2*D2+3` really says, "multiply two by the cell immediately to the left of me and then add three." If you need to put this formula in cells E3 to E999, you do not need to reenter the formula 997 times. Instead, copy the formula and paste it to all the cells. When you do, Excel copies the essence of the formula: "Multiply two by the cell to the left of me and add three." As you copy the formula to cell E3, the formula becomes `=2*D3+3`. Excel handles all this automatically. Figure 8.4 shows the formula after it is copied.

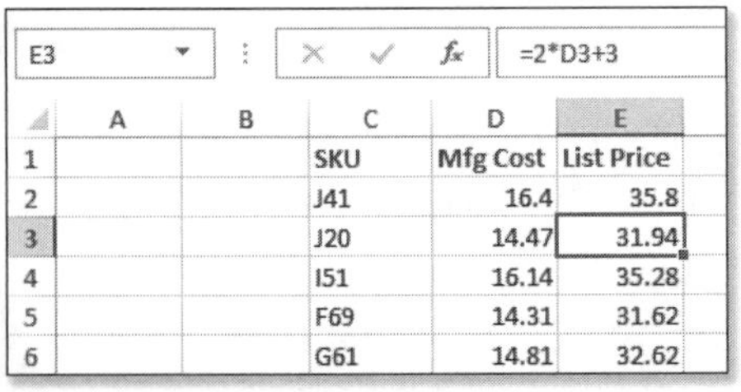

E3 | =2*D3+3

	A	B	C	D	E
1			SKU	Mfg Cost	List Price
2			J41	16.4	35.8
3			J20	14.47	31.94
4			I51	16.14	35.28
5			F69	14.31	31.62
6			G61	14.81	32.62

Figure 8.4
After you paste the formula, Excel automatically updates the cell reference to point to the current row.

Excel's capability to change D2 to D3 in the formula is called *relative referencing*. This is the default behavior of a reference. Sometimes, you do not want Excel to change a reference as the formula is copied, as explained in the next section.

Overriding Relative Behavior: Absolute Cell References

Relative referencing, which is Excel's ability to change a formula as it is copied, is what makes spreadsheets so useful. At times, however, you need part of a formula to always point at one particular cell. This happens a lot when you have a setting at the top of the worksheet such as a growth rate or a tax rate. It would be nice to change this cell once and have all the formulas use the new rate.

The following example sets up a sample worksheet that exhibits this problem and shows how to use an arcane notation style to solve the problem. When you see a reference with two dollar signs, such as $G$1, this indicates an absolute reference to G1. An absolute reference is a cell or range address where the row numbers and the column letters are locked and will not change during copying. Absolute references have a dollar sign before each column letter and each row number. Examples include $G$1 and $T$2:$W$99.

Suppose that you have a sales tax factor in a single cell at the top of a worksheet. After you enter the formula `=C2*G1`, it accurately calculates the tax in cell D2, as shown in Figure 8.5.

However, when you copy the same formula to cell D3, you get a zero as the result. As you can see in Figure 8.6, Excel correctly changed cell C2 to C3 in the copied formula. However, Excel also changed G1 to G2. Because there is nothing in G2, the formula calculates a zero.

Figure 8.5
This formula works fine in row 2.

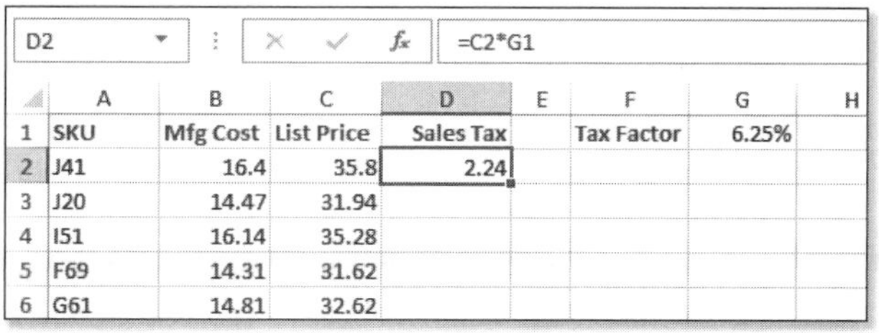

D2 =C2*G1

	A	B	C	D	E	F	G	H
1	SKU	Mfg Cost	List Price	Sales Tax		Tax Factor	6.25%	
2	J41	16.4	35.8	2.24				
3	J20	14.47	31.94					
4	I51	16.14	35.28					
5	F69	14.31	31.62					
6	G61	14.81	32.62					

Figure 8.6
This formula fails in row 3.

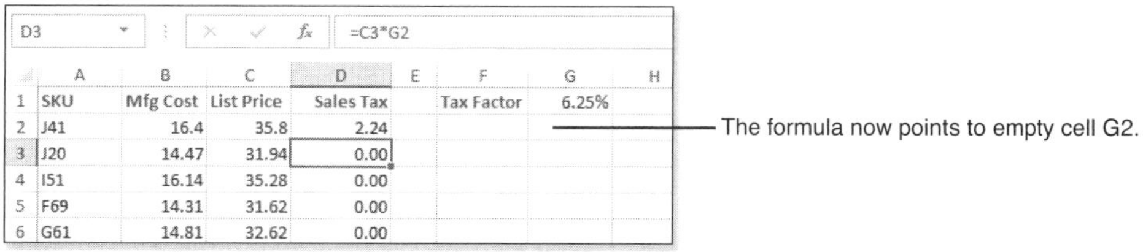

D3 =C3*G2

	A	B	C	D	E	F	G	H
1	SKU	Mfg Cost	List Price	Sales Tax		Tax Factor	6.25%	
2	J41	16.4	35.8	2.24				
3	J20	14.47	31.94	0.00				
4	I51	16.14	35.28	0.00				
5	F69	14.31	31.62	0.00				
6	G61	14.81	32.62	0.00				

The formula now points to empty cell G2.

Because the sales tax factor is only in G1, you want Excel to always point to G1. To make this happen, you need to build the original formula as =C2*$G$1. The two dollar signs tell Excel that you do not want to have the reference change as the formula is copied. The $ before the G freezes the reference to always point to column G. The $ before the 1 freezes the reference to always point to row 1. Now, when you copy this formula from cell D2 to other cells in column D, Excel changes the formula to =C3*$G$1, as shown in Figure 8.7.

To recap, a reference with two dollars signs is called an *absolute reference*.

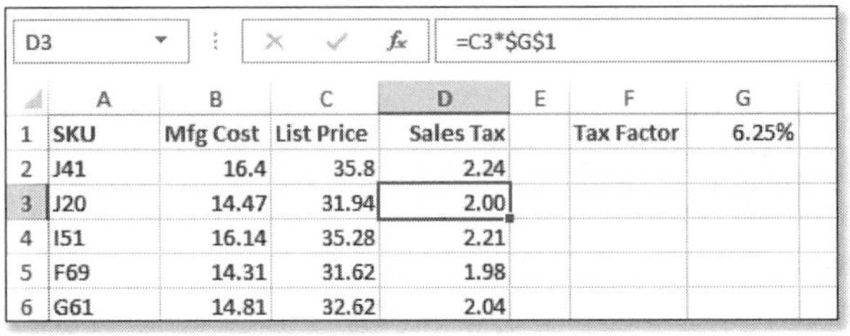

	A	B	C	D	E	F	G
1	SKU	Mfg Cost	List Price	Sales Tax		Tax Factor	6.25%
2	J41	16.4	35.8	2.24			
3	J20	14.47	31.94	2.00			
4	I51	16.14	35.28	2.21			
5	F69	14.31	31.62	1.98			
6	G61	14.81	32.62	2.04			

Figure 8.7
The dollar signs in the formula make sure that the copied formula always points to cell G1.

If you are never going to copy the formula to the left or right, you can safely use =C2*G$1. This formula freezes only the row number. Given the shape of the current data, it is likely that using a single dollar sign will be valid.

Using Mixed References to Combine Features of Relative and Absolute References

In a number of situations, you might want to build a reference that has only one dollar sign. For example, in Figure 8.8, you want to use the monthly bonus rate in row 3, but you want to allow the column to change. In this case, the formula for cell B13 would be =B6*B$3.

When you copy this formula, it always points to the bonus amount in row 3, but the remaining elements of the formula are relative. For example, the formula in E15 is =E8*E$3, which multiplies Dom's April sales by the April bonus rate.

There are two kinds of mixed references. One mixed reference freezes the row number and allows the column letter to change, as in A$1. The other mixed reference freezes the column letter but allows the row number to change, as in $A1. No one has thought up clever names to distinguish between these references, so they are simply called *mixed references*.

To illustrate the other kind of mixed reference, as shown in Figure 8.9, say you want a single formula to multiply the daily rate from column A by the number of days in row 4. This formula requires both kinds of mixed references.

In this case, you want the cell A6 reference to always point to column A, even when the formula is copied to the right. Therefore, the A6 portion of the formula should be entered as $A6. You also want the C5 portion of the formula to always point to row 5, even when the formula is copied down the rows. Therefore, the C5 portion of the formula should be entered as C$5.

Figure 8.8
By having the dollar sign before the 3 in C$3, you lock the reference to row 3 but allow the formula to point to columns D, E, and so on as you copy the formula.

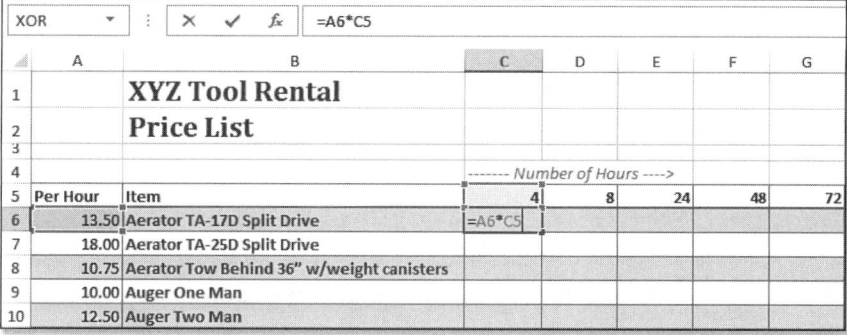

| B13 | ▼ | : | × | ✓ | *fx* | =B6*B$3 |

	A	B	C	D	E	F	G
1	**Widget Sales Bonus Calculation**						
2							
3	Bonus	3%	2%	0%	2%	3%	1%
4							
5	$ Sold	Jan	Feb	Mar	Apr	May	Jun
6	Zeke	6237	9009	5247	9207	7029	6435
7	Josh	7722	5544	6138	5445	9603	5544
8	Dom	8712	7524	6237	6336	8415	7623
9	Alec	5148	7524	9603	5049	5643	5445
10	Logan	5841	6534	8118	8910	9009	9405
11							
12	Bonus	Jan	Feb	Mar	Apr	May	Jun
13	Zeke	187.11	180.18	0.00	184.14	210.87	64.35
14	Josh	231.66	110.88	0.00	108.90	288.09	55.44
15	Dom	261.36	150.48	0.00	126.72	252.45	76.23
16	Alec	154.44	150.48	0.00	100.98	169.29	54.45
17	Logan	175.23	130.68	0.00	178.20	270.27	94.05

Figure 8.9
You can create a formula by using a combination of dollar signs to allow cell C6 to be copied to all cells in the table.

| XOR | ▼ | : | × | ✓ | *fx* | =A6*C5 |

	A	B	C	D	E	F	G
1		**XYZ Tool Rental**					
2		**Price List**					
3							
4			------- Number of Hours ---->				
5	Per Hour	Item	4	8	24	48	72
6	13.50	Aerator TA-17D Split Drive	=A6*C5				
7	18.00	Aerator TA-25D Split Drive					
8	10.75	Aerator Tow Behind 36" w/weight canisters					
9	10.00	Auger One Man					
10	12.50	Auger Two Man					

Using the F4 Key to Simplify Dollar Sign Entry

In the preceding section, you entered quite a few dollar signs in formulas. The good news is that you do not have to type the dollar signs! Instead, immediately after entering a reference, press the F4 key to toggle the reference from a relative reference to an absolute reference, which automatically has the dollar signs before the row and column. If you press F4 again, the reference toggles to a mixed reference with a dollar sign before the row number. When you press F4 once again, the reference toggles to a mixed reference with a dollar sign before the column letter. Pressing F4 one more time returns the reference to a relative reference. You might find it easier to choose the right reference by looking at the various reference options offered by the F4 key.

The following sequence shows how the F4 key works while you are entering a formula. This particular example was included because it requires two different types of mixed references.

The important concept is that you start pressing F4 after typing a cell reference but before you type a mathematical operator.

1. Type **=A6** (see Figure 8.10).

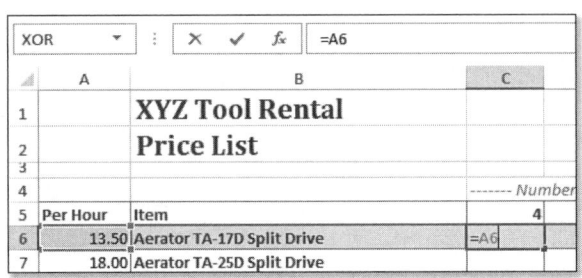

Figure 8.10
This is a relative reference: A6 without any dollar signs.

2. Before typing the asterisk to indicate multiplication, press the F4 key. On the first press of F4, the reference changes to =$A$6, as shown in Figure 8.11.

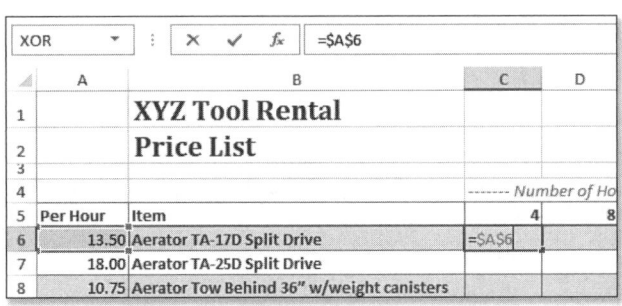

Figure 8.11
After you press F4 once, the reference changes to an absolute reference, with two dollar signs.

3. Press the F4 key again. The reference changes to A$6 to freeze the reference to row 6, as shown in Figure 8.12. This still isn't right because freezing the reference to row 6 will not help.

4. Press F4 one more time. Excel locks just the column, changing the reference to =$A6, as shown in Figure 8.13. This is the version of the reference you want. As you copy the formula across, the formula always points back to column A. As you copy the formula down, the row number in this reference is allowed to change to point to other rows.

Figure 8.12
Press F4 again to switch to a mixed reference with the row number locked.

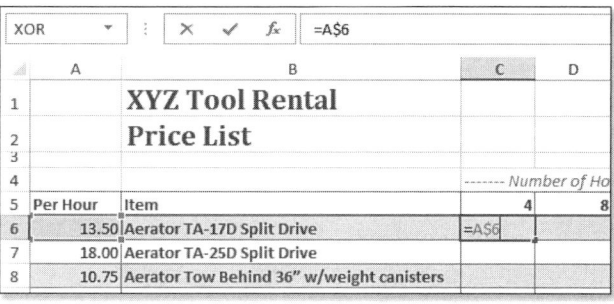

Figure 8.13
Press F4 again to switch to a mixed reference with the column letter locked.

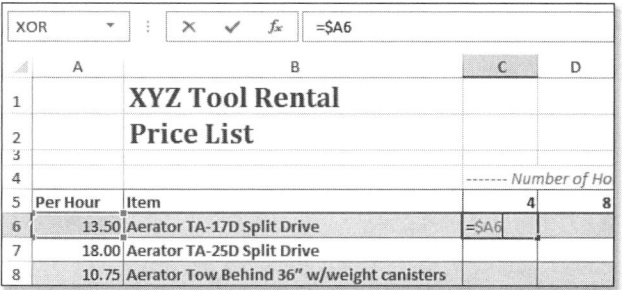

5. To continue the formula, type an asterisk to indicate multiplication and then click cell C5 with the mouse. At the point shown in Figure 8.14, you would press F4 twice to change C5 to a reference that locks only the row (that is, C$5).

6. Press Enter to accept the formula.

Figure 8.14
After clicking C5 with the mouse, press F4 twice to change this reference.

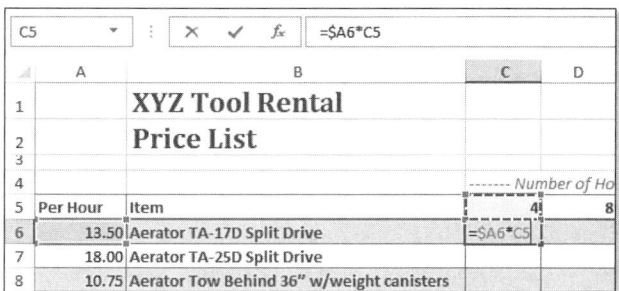

7. When you copy the formula from cell C6 to the range C6:G28, the formula automatically multiplies the rate in column A by the number of days in row 5. Figure 8.15 shows the copied formula in cell E9. The formula correctly multiplies the 10-dollar rate in cell A9 by the 24 hours figure in cell E5.

XOR ▼	:	× ✓ fx	=$A9*E$5					
	A	B	C	D	E	F	G	
1		**XYZ Tool Rental**						
2		**Price List**						
3								
4				------- Number of Hours ---->				
5	Per Hour	Item	4	8	24	48	72	
6	13.50	Aerator TA-17D Split Drive	$54.00	$108.00	$324.00	$648.00	$972.00	
7	18.00	Aerator TA-25D Split Drive	$72.00	$144.00	$432.00	$864.00	$1,296.00	
8	10.75	Aerator Tow Behind 36" w/weight canisters	$43.00	$86.00	$258.00	$516.00	$774.00	
9	10.00	Auger One Man	$40.00	$80.00	=$A9*E$5	$480.00	$720.00	
10	12.50	Auger Two Man	$50.00	$100.00	$300.00	$600.00	$900.00	

Figure 8.15
By using the correct combination of row and column mixed references, you can enter this formula once and successfully copy it to the entire rectangular range.

Using F4 After a Formula Is Entered

The F4 trick described in the preceding section works immediately after you enter a reference. If you try to change cell A6 after you type the asterisk, pressing the F4 key has no effect.

However, you can still use F4 by clicking somewhere in the formula bar adjacent to the characters A6. Pressing F4 now adds dollar signs to that reference.

Using F4 on a Rectangular Range

Some functions allow you to specify a rectangular range. For example, in Figure 8.16, you would like to enter a formula to calculate month-to-date sales. Although =SUM(B2:B29) works for cell C29, you cannot copy this formula to the other cells in the column. To copy this formula, you need to change the formula to =SUM(B$2:B29).

> 🔍 **Note**
>
> After you press F4 again, Excel returns the reference to the relative state A6. As you continue to press F4, Excel toggles between the four modes. It is fine to toggle between them all and then choose the correct one. If you accidentally toggle past the $A6 version, just keep pressing F4 until the correct mode comes up again.

At this point in the figure, you might be tempted to press the F4 key. This does not work. If you select B2:B29 with the mouse or arrow keys, pressing F4 now converts the reference to the fully absolute range $B$2:$B$29. Continuing to press F4 toggles to B$2:B$29, then $B2:$B29, and then B2:B29. Excel does not even attempt to go through the other 12 possible combinations of dollar signs to offer B$2:B29 eventually. If you typed B2:B29, pressing F4 adjusts only the B29 reference.

In this case, you need to click the insertion point just before, just after, or in the middle of the characters B2 in the formula. If you then press F4, toggle through the various dollar sign combinations on the B2 reference. Pressing F4 twice results in the proper combination, as shown in Figure 8.17.

Figure 8.16
Using F4 at this point never produces the desired result of B$2:B29.

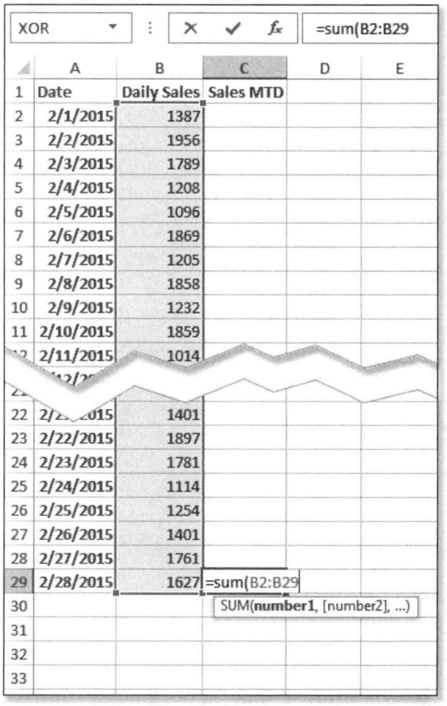

	A	B	C	D	E
					=sum(B2:B29
1	Date	Daily Sales	Sales MTD		
2	2/1/2015	1387			
3	2/2/2015	1956			
4	2/3/2015	1789			
5	2/4/2015	1208			
6	2/5/2015	1096			
7	2/6/2015	1869			
8	2/7/2015	1205			
9	2/8/2015	1858			
10	2/9/2015	1232			
11	2/10/2015	1859			
12	2/11/2015	1014			
22	2/21/2015	1401			
23	2/22/2015	1897			
24	2/23/2015	1781			
25	2/24/2015	1114			
26	2/25/2015	1254			
27	2/26/2015	1401			
28	2/27/2015	1761			
29	2/28/2015	1627	=sum(B2:B29		
30			SUM(**number1**, [number2], ...)		
31					
32					
33					

XOR ▼ : × ✓ *fx* =sum(B2:B29

Figure 8.17
Using F4 is tricky when your reference is a rectangular range—you must click into the formula.

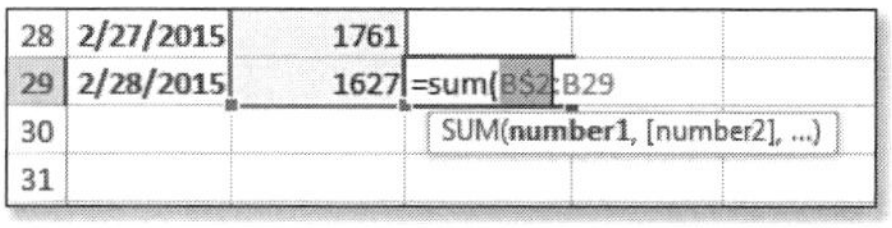

28	2/27/2015	1761	
29	2/28/2015	1627	=sum(B$2:B29
30			SUM(**number1**, [number2], ...)
31			

Three Methods of Entering Formulas

In the examples in the previous sections, you entered a formula by typing it. You generally need to start a formula by typing the equal sign (or the plus sign); after that point, you have three options:

- Type the complete formula as described in the previous sections.

- Type operator keys, but use the mouse to touch cell references. In this book, this is referred to as the *mouse method*.

- Type the operator keys and then use the arrow keys to specify the cell references by navigating to the cells. In this book, this method is referred to as the *arrow key method*.

Assume you would like to multiply the merchandise total in cell B2 by the sales tax rate in cell F1, as shown in Figure 8.18.

| XOR | ▼ | : | ✕ | ✓ | f_x | = |

◢	A	B	C	D	E	F
1	Invoice	Merch $	Tax		Rate	6.25%
2	1701	116.7	=			
3	1702	134.71				
4	1703	129.56				

Figure 8.18
You can use three methods to enter the formula
=B2*$F$1.

Enter Formulas Using the Mouse Method

If you started using computers in the last 20 years, it is likely that you use the mouse method for entering formulas. This method is intuitive, but it requires you to move your hand between the keyboard and the mouse several times, as in this example:

1. Type = or +.

2. Click in cell B2.

3. Type *.

4. Click in cell F1.

5. Press F4 to add the dollar signs.

6. Press Enter. This usually moves the cell pointer to cell F2.

This method requires only four keystrokes, but it requires you to move to the mouse twice. Moving to the mouse is the slowest part of entering formulas, but this method is easier than typing the entire formula if you are not a touch typist.

Entering Formulas Using the Arrow Key Method

The arrow key method is popular with people who started using spreadsheets in the days of Lotus 1-2-3 release 2.2. It is worthwhile to learn this method because it is incredibly fast. Almost all formula entry can be accomplished using keys on the right side of the keyboard. Here's how it works:

1. In cell C2, type +.

2. Press the left-arrow key to move the flashing cell border to cell B2. Note that the active cell, which is the one with a green solid border, is still cell C2. The flashing border is like a second cell pointer that you can use to point to the correct cell for the formula. As shown in Figure 8.19, the temporary formula in the formula bar reads +B2.

Tip

If you have a desktop keyboard, you can use the asterisk key on the numeric keypad to avoid pressing the Shift key.

Tip

If you use the mouse method to enter formulas, customize the Quick Access Toolbar (QAT) to icons for Equal Sign, Plus Sign, Minus Sign, Multiplication Sign, Division Sign, Exponentiation Sign, and Dollar Sign. You can then enter most formulas without reaching back to the keyboard. There isn't a QAT icon for the Enter key—use the green check mark to the left of the formula bar for Enter.

Figure 8.19
By using the arrow keys during formula entry, you create a flashing border that can be used to navigate to a cell reference.

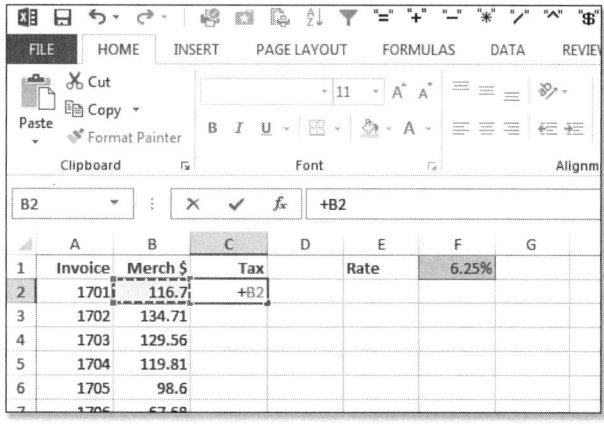

 Note
As you are moving the flashing cell border with the mouse, ignore the formula bar and watch just the flashing cell border.

3. To accept cell B2 as the correct reference in the formula, press either an operator key (for example, * or +), a parenthesis, or the Enter key. In this case, type *.

4. Note that the dashed cell pointer disappears, and the focus is now back to the original cell, C2.

5. Press the right-arrow key three times. The flashing cell border moves to D2, E2, and then F2. With each keypress, the temporary formula in the formula bar shows an incorrect formula (+B2*D2, +B2*E2, and +B2*F2). Figure 8.20 shows what the screen looks like after you press the right-arrow key three times.

 Tip
Even if you are mouse-centric, you should try this method for half a day. When you get the feel for navigating by using the arrow keys, you can enter formulas much faster by using this method.

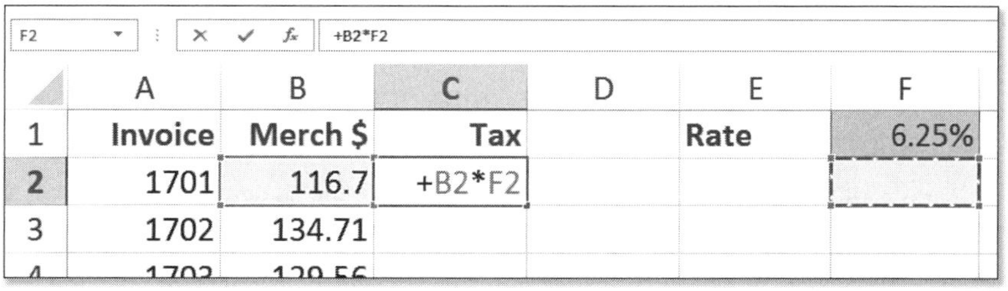

Figure 8.20
After step 4, the focus moves to the original cell. Thus, you only have to press the right-arrow key three times instead of four times to arrive at cell F2.

	A	B	C	D	E	F
1	Invoice	Merch $	Tax		Rate	6.25%
2	1701	116.7	+B2*F2			
3	1702	134.71				
4	1703	129.56				

F2   *fx*   +B2*F2

6. Press the up-arrow key to move the flashing cell border to the correct location, cell F1. The temporary formula in the formula bar now shows +B2*F1.

7. Press the F4 key to add dollar signs to the F1 reference.

8. Press Ctrl+Enter to accept the formula and keep the cell pointer in cell C2.

Using this method requires ten keystrokes, with no trips to the mouse. You can enter formulas that have no absolute references, mixed references, parentheses, or exponents by using just the arrow keys and the keys on the numeric keypad.

 Note

Officially, every formula must start with an equal sign. However, to make former Lotus 1-2-3 users comfortable, Excel allows you to start a formula with a plus sign. Power Excel users have discovered that using a plus sign enables them to start a formula by typing on the numeric keypad. Because I routinely start formulas with the plus sign, I am often asked why I start with =+ instead of just =. Even though the formulas appear that way onscreen, I don't actually enter the plus sign. When a formula starts with a plus sign, Excel adds an equal sign and does not remove the plus sign, so you end up with a formula that looks like =+B2*$F$1.

Entering the Same Formula in Many Cells

So far in this chapter, you have entered a formula in one cell and then copied and pasted to get the formula in many cells. To enter the same formula in many cells, you can use three alternatives:

- Preselect the entire range where the formulas need to go. Enter the formula for the first cell and press Ctrl+Enter to enter the formula in the entire selection simultaneously.

- Enter the formula in the first cell and then use the fill handle to copy the formula.

- Beginning with Excel 2007, the method is to define the range as a table. When you use this method, the new formulas are copied down a column automatically.

Copying a Formula by Using Ctrl+Enter

This strategy works when you are entering formulas for one or more screens that are full of data:

1. If you have just a few cells, select them before entering the formula.

2. Click in the first cell and drag down to the last cell, as shown in Figure 8.21. Notice from the name box that the active cell is the first cell.

3. Enter the formula by using any of the three methods described earlier in this chapter. Even if you use the arrow key method, Excel keeps the entire range selected. Figure 8.22 shows a formula after you press F4 to convert the F1 reference to $F$1.

Figure 8.21
Click in the first cell and drag down to the last cell to select a range with the first cell as the active cell.

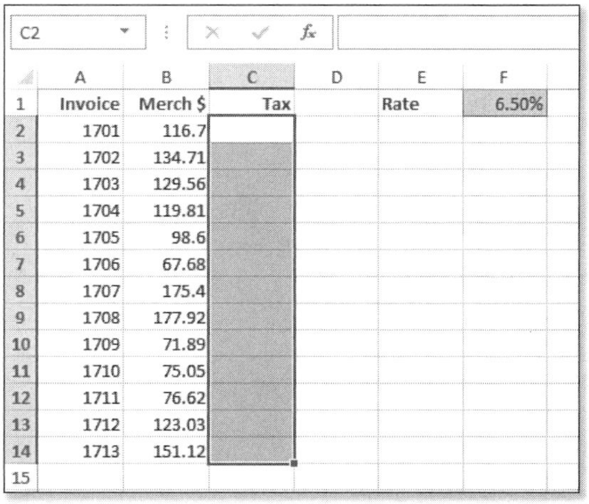

C2				fx			
	A	B	C	D	E	F
1	Invoice	Merch $	Tax		Rate	6.50%
2	1701	116.7				
3	1702	134.71				
4	1703	129.56				
5	1704	119.81				
6	1705	98.6				
7	1706	67.68				
8	1707	175.4				
9	1708	177.92				
10	1709	71.89				
11	1710	75.05				
12	1711	76.62				
13	1712	123.03				
14	1713	151.12				
15						

Figure 8.22
Even with a large range selected, the formula is built only in the active cell.

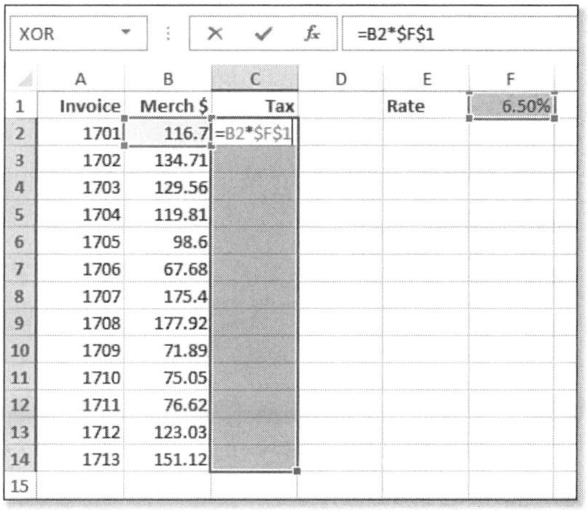

XOR				fx	=B2*$F$1		
	A	B	C	D	E	F
1	Invoice	Merch $	Tax		Rate	6.50%
2	1701	116.7	=B2*$F$1			
3	1702	134.71				
4	1703	129.56				
5	1704	119.81				
6	1705	98.6				
7	1706	67.68				
8	1707	175.4				
9	1708	177.92				
10	1709	71.89				
11	1710	75.05				
12	1711	76.62				
13	1712	123.03				
14	1713	151.12				
15						

4. At this point, you would normally press Enter to complete the formula. Instead, press Ctrl+Enter to enter this formula in the entire selected range. Note that Excel does not enter =B2*$F$1 in each cell. Instead, it converts the formula as if it were copied to each cell. Figure 8.23 shows the formula in cell C10.

Figure 8.23
Pressing Ctrl+Enter tells Excel to enter the formula in the active cell and to copy it to the rest of the selection.

C10 f_x =B10*$F$1

	A	B	C	D	E	F
1	Invoice	Merch $	Tax		Rate	6.50%
2	1701	116.7	7.5855			
3	1702	134.71	8.75615			
4	1703	129.56	8.4214			
5	1704	119.81	7.78765			
6	1705	98.6	6.409			
7	1706	67.68	4.3992			
8	1707	175.4	11.401			
9	1708	177.92	11.5648			
10	1709	71.89	4.67285			
11	1710	75.05	4.87825			
12	1711	76.62	4.9803			
13	1712	123.03	7.99695			
14	1713	151.12	9.8228			

Copying a Formula by Dragging the Fill Handle

If you want to enter a formula in one cell and then copy it to the other cells in a range, you can use the fill handle, which is the square dot in the lower-right corner of the cell pointer. There are two ways to use the fill handle:

- Drag the fill handle.

- Double-click the fill handle.

The dragging method works fine when you have less than one screen full of data:

1. Enter the formula in cell B2.

2. Press Ctrl+Enter to accept the formula and keep the cell pointer in cell B2.

3. Click the fill handle. You know that you are above the fill handle when the mouse pointer changes to a thick plus sign, as shown in Figure 8.24. Drag the mouse down to the last row of data, which in this case is cell C14.

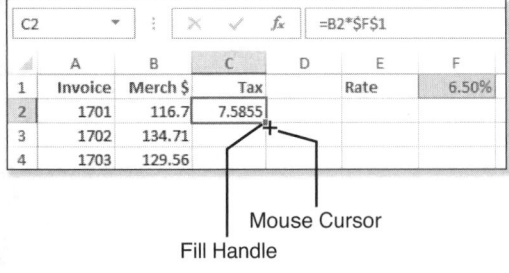

C2 f_x =B2*$F$1

	A	B	C	D	E	F
1	Invoice	Merch $	Tax		Rate	6.50%
2	1701	116.7	7.5855			
3	1702	134.71				
4	1703	129.56				

Mouse Cursor
Fill Handle

Figure 8.24
You can copy a formula by clicking and dragging the fill handle.

4. When you release the mouse button, the original cell is copied to all the cells in the selected range.

This method is fine for copying a formula to a few cells. However, if you have thousands or hundreds of thousands of cells, it is annoying to drag to the last row. In Excel 2003 and earlier, you would invariably end up flying past the last row. Note that Excel 2013 automatically slows down and briefly pauses at the last row. However, it is far easier to copy a formula by double-clicking the fill handle.

Double-Click the Fill Handle to Copy a Formula

In most data sets, double-clicking the fill handle is the fastest way to copy the formula. Although you will love this method, you need to understand a few shortcomings that can hamper the method when an adjacent column has blank cells among the data.

Figure 8.25 shows a table that has hundreds of rows of data. Suppose you want to copy the formula from cell C2 down to all the rows of data in column B.

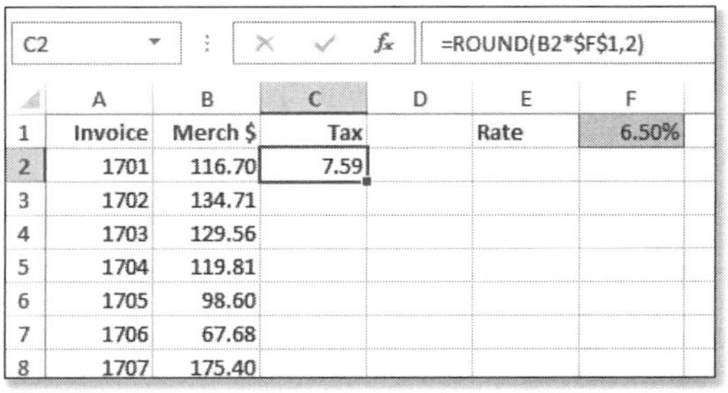

Figure 8.25
Dragging the fill handle is frustrating in a table that has hundreds of rows. The double-click method will end that frustration.

C2		:	×	✓	f_x	=ROUND(B2*$F$1,2)

	A	B	C	D	E	F
1	Invoice	Merch $	Tax		Rate	6.50%
2	1701	116.70	7.59			
3	1702	134.71				
4	1703	129.56				
5	1704	119.81				
6	1705	98.60				
7	1706	67.68				
8	1707	175.40				

In this particular case, cell B2 is nonblank, and column B contains a value in every row down to the end of the data. This is the perfect condition for using the technique of double-clicking the fill handle. Follow these steps:

1. Enter the formula in cell B2.

2. Press Ctrl+Enter to accept the formula and keep the cell pointer in cell B2.

3. Double-click the fill handle.

The active cell is copied down to the last row of your data, as shown in Figure 8.26.

The fill handle double-click method is fast. Excel 2013 follows any diagonal path of nonempty cells to figure out where the bottom of your data set is. You should always press End and then press the down arrow to make sure that the formula was copied far enough.

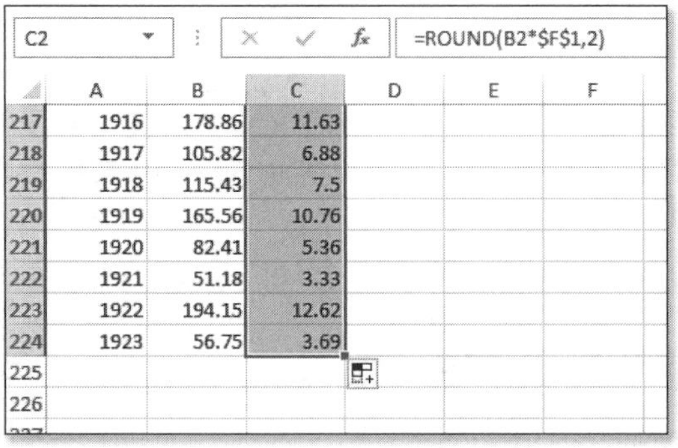

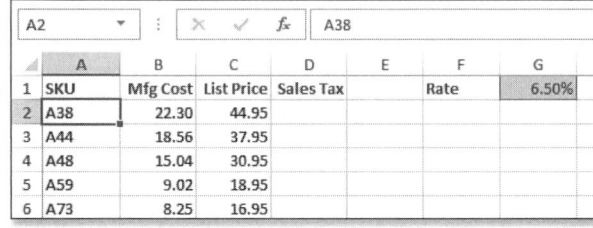

Figure 8.26
Double-click the fill handle to copy to the last row of your data.

Use the Table Tool to Copy a Formula

The table tool was improved dramatically in Excel 2007. When using this tool, if you tell Excel that your current data set is a table, Excel automatically copies new formulas down to the rest of the cells in the table.

Figure 8.27 shows an Excel worksheet that has headings at the top and many rows of data below the headings.

Figure 8.27
This is a typical worksheet in Excel.

To define a range as a table, select a cell within the data set and press Ctrl+T. Excel uses its IntelliSense to guess the edges of the table. If its guess is correct, click OK in the Create Table dialog, as shown in Figure 8.28.

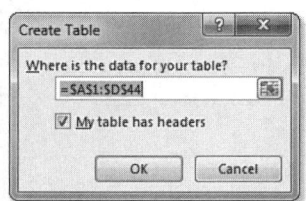

Figure 8.28
The Create Table dialog.

Ctrl+T is one of four entry points for creating a table. You can still use the Excel 2003 shortcut of Ctrl+L. You can choose Format as Table on the Home tab. You can choose the Table icon from the Insert tab.

As shown in Figure 8.29, after Excel recognizes the range as a table, several changes occur:

- The table is formatted with the default formatting. Depending on your preferences, this might include banded rows or columns.

- AutoFilter drop-downs are added to the headings.

- Any formulas you enter use the headings to refer to cells within the table.

Figure 8.29

Defining a range as a table provides formatting and powerful features such as autofilters and natural language formulas.

	SKU ▼	Mfg C ▼	List Pri ▼	Sales 1 ▼		Rate	6.50%
1							
2	A38	22.30	44.95	=[@[List Price]]*$G$1			
3	A44	18.56	37.95				
4	A48	15.04	30.95				
5	A59	9.02	18.95				
6	A73	8.25	16.95				

Now when you enter a formula in the table, Excel automatically copies that formula down to all rows of the table.

 Note

As shown in Figure 8.30, a lightning bolt drop-down appears to the right of cell D3. This drop-down offers you the opportunity to stop Excel from automatically copying the formula down.

Figure 8.30

Thanks to the Table tool in Excel, a new formula entered anywhere in column D is copied automatically to all the cells in column D.

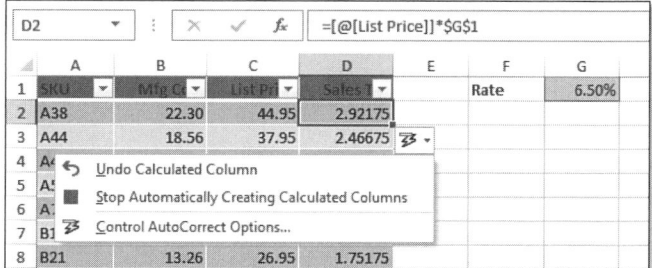

9

CONTROLLING FORMULAS

Although you can go a long way with simple formulas, it is also possible to build extremely powerful formulas. The topics in this chapter explain the finer points of formula operators, date math, and how Excel distinguishes between cutting and copying cells referenced in formulas.

Formula Operators

Excel offers the mathematical operators shown in Table 9.1.

Table 9.1   Mathematical Operators

Operator	Description
+	Addition
–	Subtraction
*	Multiplication
/	Division or fractions
^	Exponents
()	Overriding the order of operations
–	Unary minus (for negative numbers)
&	Joining text (concatenation)
>	Greater than
<	Less than
>=	Greater than or equal to
<=	Less than or equal to
<>	Not equal to
=	Equal to

Operator	Description
,	Union operator, as in SUM(A1,B2)
:	Range operator, as in SUM(A1:B2)
\<space\>	Intersection operator, as in SUM(A:J 2:4)

Order of Operations

When a formula contains many calculations, Excel evaluates the formula in a certain order. Rather than calculating from left to right as a calculator might, Excel performs certain types of calculations, such as multiplication, before calculations such as addition.

You can override the default order of operations with parentheses. If you do not use parentheses, Excel uses the following order of operations:

1. Unary minus is evaluated first.

2. Exponents are evaluated next.

3. Multiplication and division are handled next, in a left-to-right manner.

4. Addition and subtraction are handled next, in a left-to-right manner.

 **Note**

To see how Excel calculates the formulas you enter, first enter a formula in a cell. Next, from the Formulas tab, select Formulas, Formula Auditing, Evaluate Formula to open the Evaluate Formula dialog and watch the formula calculate in slow motion.

The following sections provide some examples of order of operations.

Unary Minus Example

The unary minus is always evaluated first. Think about when you use exponents to raise a number to a power. If you raise –2 to the second power, Excel calculates (–2) × (–2), which is +4. Therefore, the formula =-2^2 evaluates to 4.

If you raise –2 to the third power, Excel calculates (–2) × (–2) × (–2). Multiplying –2 by –2 results in +4, and multiplying +4 by –2 results in –8. Therefore, the simple formula =-2^3 generates –8.

You need to understand a subtle but important distinction. When Excel encounters the formula =-2^3, it evaluates the unary minus first. If you want the exponent to happen first and then have the unary minus applied, you have to write the formula as =-(2^3). However, in a formula such as =100-2^3, the minus sign is considered to be a subtraction operator and not a unary minus sign. In this case, 2^3 is evaluated as 8, and then 8 is subtracted from 100. To indicate a unary minus, use =100-(-2^3).

Figure 9.1 shows the results of four formulas involving raising –2 to various powers.

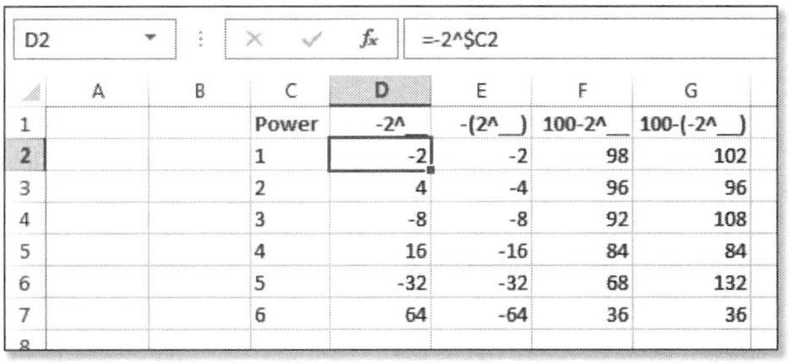

Figure 9.1
Beware of the unary minus. Four similar formulas have different results, depending on where the minus sign occurs.

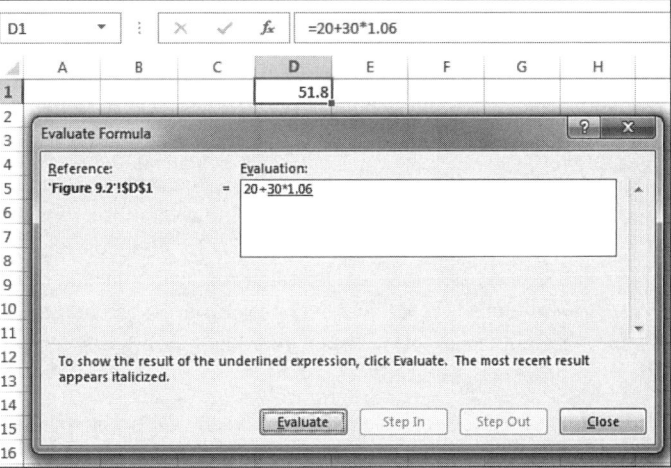

Addition and Multiplication Example

The order of operations is important when you are mixing addition/subtraction with multiplication/division. For example, if you want to add 20 to 30 and then multiply by 1.06 to calculate a total with tax, the following formula leads to the wrong result:

```
=20+30*1.06
```

The result you are looking for is 53. However, the Evaluate Formula dialog shows that Excel calculates the formula =20+30*1.06 like so (see Figure 9.2):

```
1.06 × 30 = 31.8
31.8 + 20 = 51.8
```

Excel's answer is $1.20 less than expected because the formula is not written with the default order of operations in mind.

Figure 9.2
The underline indicates that Excel does the multiplication first.

To force Excel to do the addition first, you need to enclose the addition in parentheses:

`=(20+30)*1.06`

Figure 9.3 shows the second step in the Evaluate Formula dialog for this formula. The addition in parentheses is done first, and then 50 is multiplied by 1.06 to get the correct answer of $53.

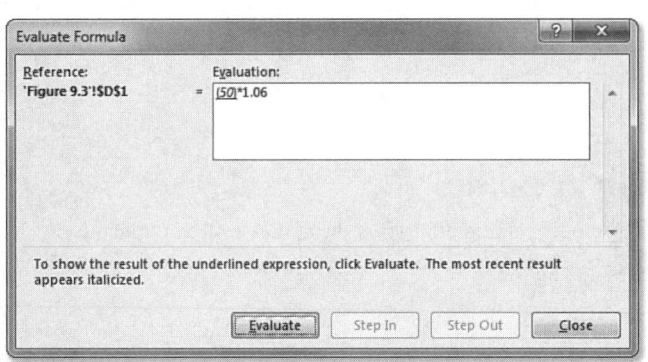

Figure 9.3
Excel evaluates the operation in parentheses first.

Stacking Multiple Parentheses

If you need to use multiple sets of parentheses when doing math by hand, you might write math formulas with square brackets and curly braces, like this:

`{3-[6*4*3-(3-6)+2]/27}*14`

In Excel, you use multiple sets of parentheses, as follows:

`=(3-(6*4*3-(3-6)+2)/27)*14`

Formulas with multiple parentheses in Excel are confusing. Excel does two things to try to improve this situation:

- As you type a formula, Excel colors the parentheses in a set order: black, red, purple, green, violet, topaz, aquamarine, blue. The colors then repeat starting with red. This is a subtle but important change in Excel 2013. By far, the most common problem is having one too few or one too many parentheses. By using red as the second color, the last parenthesis in most unbalanced equations is red. Excel only uses black for the first parenthesis and for the closing match to that parenthesis. This means if your last parenthesis in the formula is not black, you have the wrong number of parentheses.

- When you type a closing parenthesis, Excel shows the opening parenthesis in bold for a fraction of a second. This would be more helpful if Excel kept the opening parenthesis in bold for 5 seconds or 20 seconds. However, when it is displayed for only about half a second, it is nothing more than a frustrating reminder that your reflexes are not fast enough.

Understanding Error Messages in Formulas

Don't be frustrated when a formula returns an error result. This eventually happens to everyone. The key is to understand the difference between the various error values so that you can begin to troubleshoot the problem.

As you enter formulas, you might encounter a number of errors, including those listed next:

- **#VALUE!**—This error indicates that you are trying to do math with nonnumeric data. For example, the formula =4+"apple" returns a #VALUE! error. This error also occurs if you try to enter an array formula, but fail to use Ctrl+Shift+Enter, as described in Chapter 17, "Using Super Formulas in Excel."

- **#DIV/0!**—This error occurs when a number is divided by zero—that is, when a fraction's denominator evaluates to zero.

- **#REF!**—This error occurs when a cell reference is not valid. For example, this error can occur if one of the cells referenced in the formula has been deleted. It can also occur if you cut and paste another cell over a cell referenced in this formula. You may also get this error if you are using Dynamic Data Exchange (DDE) formulas to link to external systems and those systems are not running.

- **#N/A!**—This error occurs when a value is not available to a function or a formula. #N/A! errors most often occur because of key values not being found during lookup functions. They can occur as a result of HLOOKUP, LOOKUP, MATCH, or VLOOKUP. They can also result when an array formula has one argument that is not the same shape as the other arguments or when a function omits one or more required arguments. Interestingly, when an #N/A! error enters a range, all subsequent calculations that refer to the range have a value of #N/A!.

- **######**—This is not really an error. Instead, it means that the result is too wide to display in the current column width, so you need to make the column wider to see the actual result.

In Figure 9.4, cell E17 is a simple SUM function. It is returning an #N/A error because cell E11 contains the same error. Cell E11 contains the formula =D11*C11. The root cause of the problem is the VLOOKUP function in cell D11. Because Dill cannot be found in the product table in $G$7:$H$9, the VLOOKUP function returns #N/A.

Figure 9.4 shows only a small table, so it is relatively easy to find the earlier #N/A errors. However, if you were totaling 100,000 rows, it can be difficult to find the one offending cell. To track down errors, follow these steps:

> **Caution**
>
> Whereas ###### usually means the column is not wide enough, Excel also uses this symbol to indicate that you are subtracting a later date or time from an earlier date or time. If making the column wider does not clear the ###### signs, check the formula bar to see if your formula might be subtracting dates.

1. Select the cell that shows the final error. To the left of that cell, you should see an exclamation point in a yellow diamond.

2. Hover the cursor over the yellow diamond to reveal a drop-down arrow.

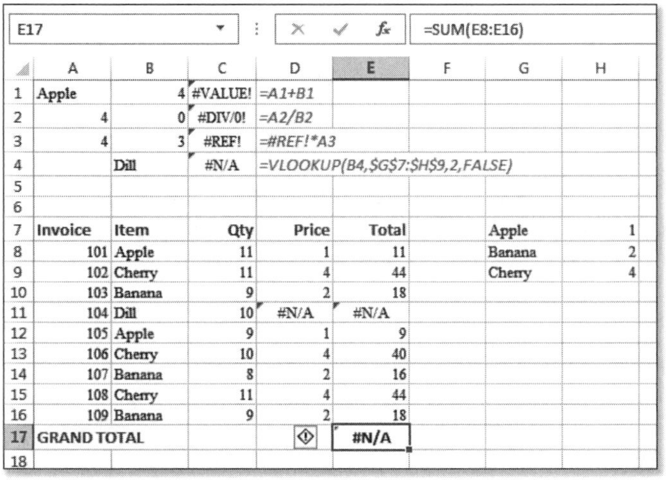

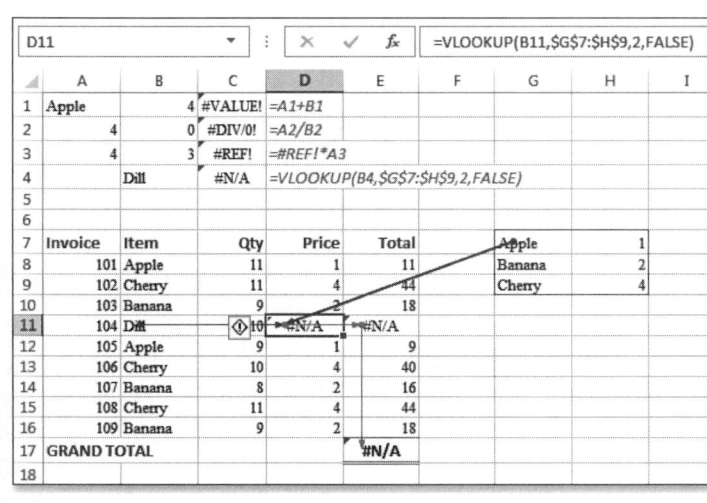

Figure 9.4
The error in E17 is actually caused by an error two calculations earlier.

3. From the drop-down menu, select Trace Error. Excel draws in red arrows pointing back to the source of the error, as shown in Figure 9.5. For example, from the original #N/A! error in cell D11, blue arrows demonstrate what cells were causing the error.

4. Repeat steps 1–3 for the cell causing the error to trace the original root cause of the problem.

Figure 9.5
Selecting Trace Error reveals the cells leading to the error.

Using Formulas to Join Text

The new Flash Fill feature discussed in Chapter 2, "Flash Fill and Quick Analysis," enables you to join text without using any formulas. By providing a few examples for Excel, you can replace a confusing combination of concatenations. However, Flash Fill creates a one-time snapshot. With formulas, the results change as the source columns change. You can also do some things with formulas that Flash Fill doesn't do.

You use the ampersand (&) operator when you need to join text. In Excel, the & operator is known as the concatenation operator.

For example, the formula =A2&B2 joins the text values shown in the two cells A2 and B2, as shown in Figure 9.6.

Figure 9.6
The & operator is used to join two text cells.

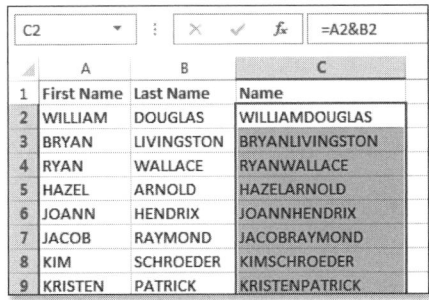

When using the & operator, you might want to include a space between the two items that are combined to improve the appearance of the output. For example, if the cells contain first name and last name, you might want to have a space between the names. To include a space between cells, you follow the & with a space enclosed in quotes, as in &" ". As shown in Figure 9.7, the formula =A2&" "&B2 generates a better-looking result than =A2&B2.

> ### 🔔 Caution
> When you enter the formula in Figure 9.7, you must hold down the Shift key to enter the quotation marks in " ". Many Excel users accidentally hold down the Shift key while pressing the spacebar. However, Shift+Spacebar is the Excel shortcut for selecting an entire row. If your formula changes to =A2&"A:A because you pressed Shift+Spacebar, you can press the Esc key and start over.

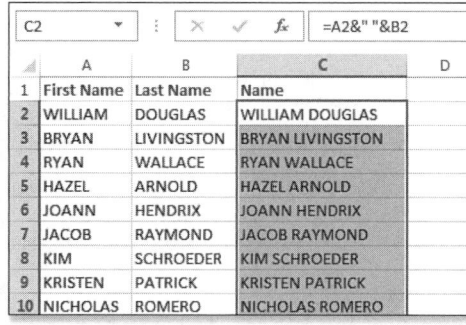

Figure 9.7
You can join cells with any text in quotation marks.

Joining Text and a Number

In many cases, you can use the & operator to join text with a number. In Figure 9.8, the formula in cell E2 joins the words "The price is $" with the result of the calculation in cell D2. Because cell B2 contains an integer with no special formatting, the answer appears correctly.

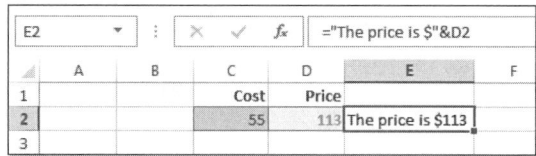

Figure 9.8
Joining text with a number works if the number is formatted with general formatting.

In Figure 9.9, cell D2 is formatted to display a currency symbol and two decimal places. When you join this value to text in cell E2, Excel ignores the formatting in cell D2 and shows the result with all the decimal places. A similar problem exists when you want to join text with a date. Excel ignores the fact that the text in cell D4 is formatted as a date and shows the underlying value in cell E4.

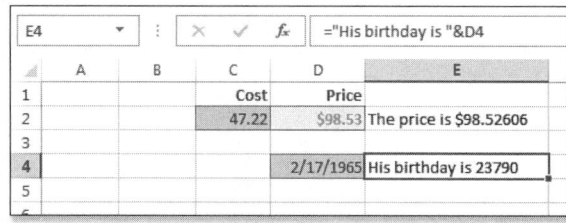

Figure 9.9
Joining text with a date or with formatted numbers rarely works well.

In this case, you need to discover the numeric formatting code associated with the original cell. To do so, follow these steps:

1. Select cell D2.

2. Press Ctrl+1 to display the Format Cells dialog.

3. On the Number tab, choose the Custom category. This reveals the actual formatting codes for the cell.

As shown in Figure 9.10, the actual formatting code for B2 is $#,##0.00. If you repeat these steps for cell D4, you learn that the actual formatting code is m/d/yyyy.

Figure 9.10
If you choose the Custom category, you learn the actual codes used to produce the numeric format.

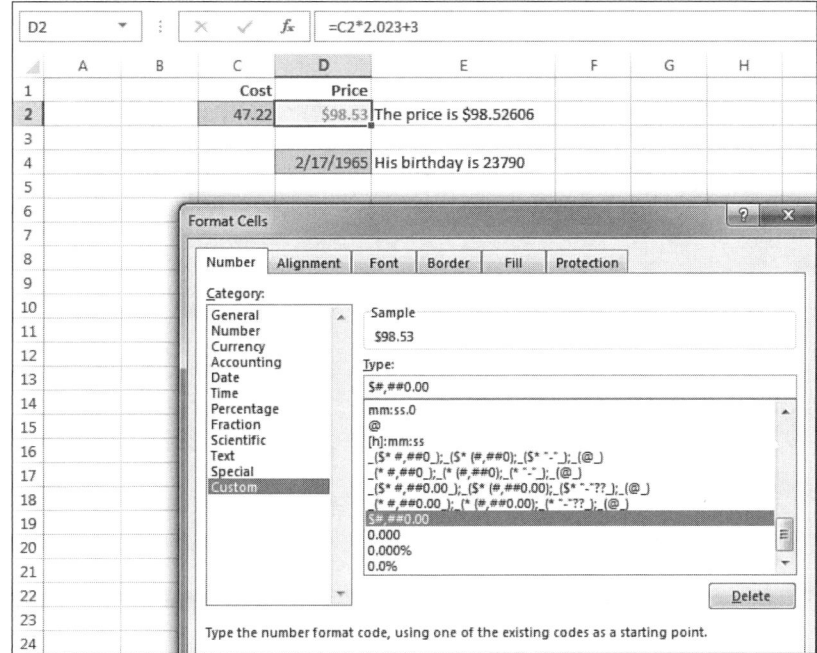

For a complete discussion of numeric formatting codes, **see** Chapter 30, "Formatting Worksheets."

When you know the numeric formatting codes, you can achieve the desired effect by using those codes, enclosed in quotation marks, as the second argument of the TEXT function. In Figure 9.11, the formula in cell E2 is ="The price is "&Text(D2, "$#,##0.00"). You can use your knowledge of custom numeric formatting codes to change the look of the joined value. In cell E4, the new formula is ="His birthday is "&TEXT(D4, "dddd mmmm d, yyyy").

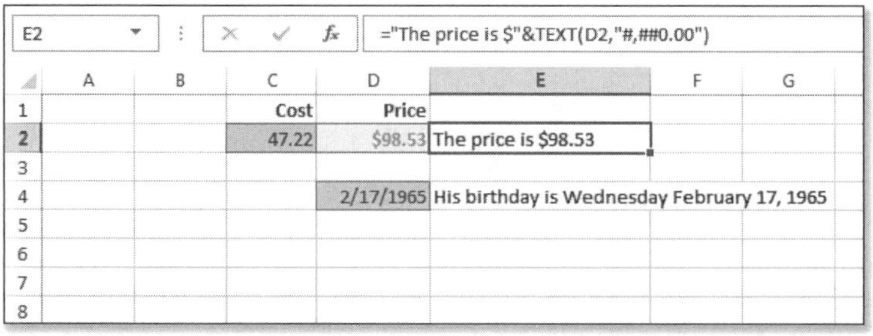

Figure 9.11
Use the TEXT function to replicate formatting, as in cell C2, or to change the formatting, as in cell C4.

Copying Versus Cutting a Formula

In Figure 9.12, the formula in cell C7 references A7+B7. Because there are no dollar signs within the formula, those are relative references.

➡ *To learn more about relative versus absolute references,* **see** *Chapter 10, "Understanding Functions."*

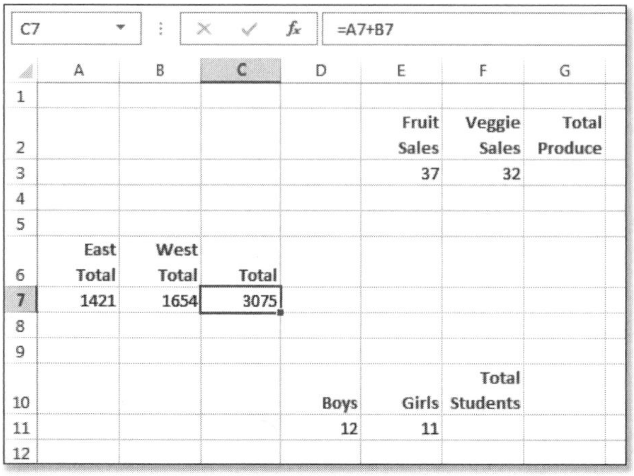

Figure 9.12
The formula in cell C7 adds the two numbers to the left of the formula.

If you copy cell C7 and paste it to cell G3, the formula works perfectly, as shown in Figure 9.13.

However, if you cut cell C7 and paste it to a new location, the formula continues to point to cells A7+B7, as shown in Figure 9.14. Whereas cutting and copying are relatively similar in applications such as Word, they are very different in Excel. It is important to understand the effect of cutting a formula in Excel in contrast to copying the formula.

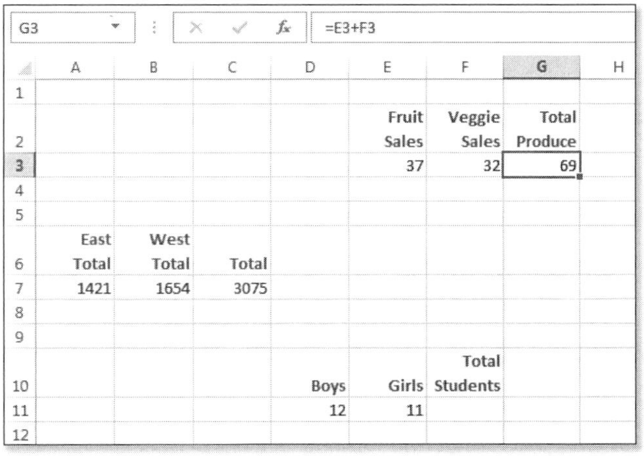

Figure 9.13
When cell C7 is copied to cell G3, the formula still adds the two numbers to the left of the formula.

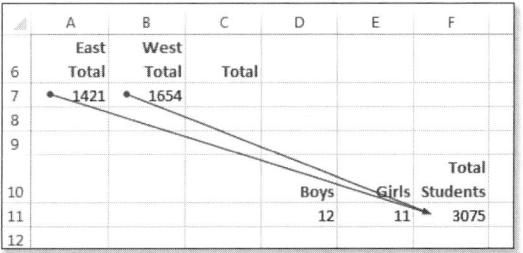

Figure 9.14
Using cut and paste on a formula forces the formula to continue to point to the original cells.

When you cut a formula, the formula continues to point to the original precedents, no matter where you paste it.

A similar rule applies to the references mentioned in a formula. For example, the formula in cell C7 points to A7 and B7. As long as you copy cell A7 and/or cell B7, you can paste them anywhere without changing the formula in C7. Figure 9.15 shows the result of copying A7:B7 for 20 rows: Nothing changes in the formula.

However, if you cut and paste A7:B7 to a new location, such as E5:F5, the formula in cell C7 changes. After the paste, the formula points to the new location of the pasted cells, as shown in Figure 9.16.

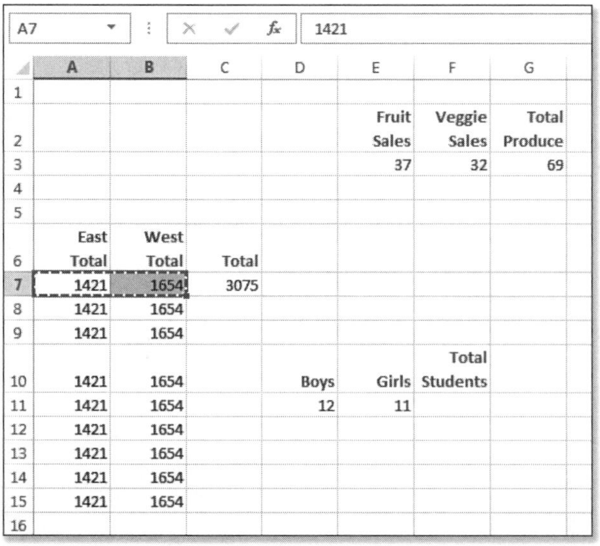

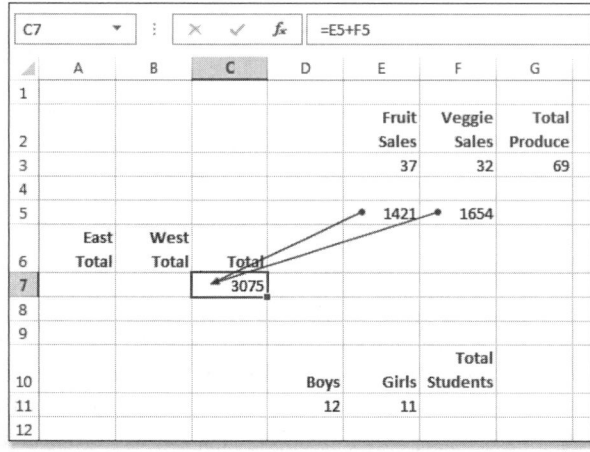

Figure 9.15
Copying the precedent cells from cell C7 does not have any effect on cell C7.

Figure 9.16
Cutting the precedent cells from cell C7 causes the formula in C7 to change to reflect the new location.

Automatically Formatting Formula Cells

The rules for formatting the result of a formula seem to be inconsistent. Suppose that you have $1.23 in cell A1. All cells in the worksheet have the general format except cell A1.

If you enter =A1+3 in another cell with general format, the result automatically inherits the currency format of cell A1, as shown in Figure 9.17.

Figure 9.17
No formatting is applied to B3. Instead, Excel copies the format from cell A1 automatically.

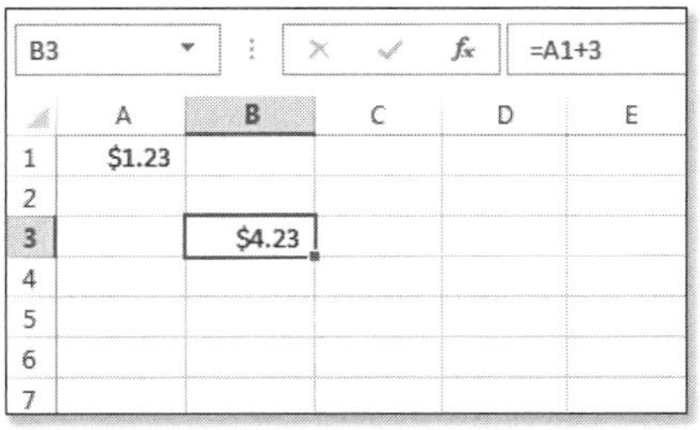

Note that the formatting is copied whether you use =A1+3 or =3+A1.

In Figure 9.17, cell B3 is formatted automatically to match the only cell mentioned in the formula. It becomes harder to predict the automatic format when your formula refers to several cells, each with a different format.

Furthermore, the result changes if you start your formula with a plus sign instead of an equal sign. Many people use the plus sign because it is easy to type on the numeric keypad. However, Microsoft probably considers using the plus sign as a Lotus transition issue and applies different rules.

In Figure 9.18, cell A1 is formatted as currency with two decimal places. Cell A3 is formatted as a number with three decimal places. Cell A5 is formatted as a percent with no decimal places. Cells in columns C and F all add the three original cells. Each formula specifies A1, A3, and A5 in a different sequence. Formulas in C were entered starting with a plus sign. Formulas in F were started with an equal sign.

Figure 9.18
When a formula refers to cells with different formats, the resulting cell's format varies depending on which cell was mentioned first or last.

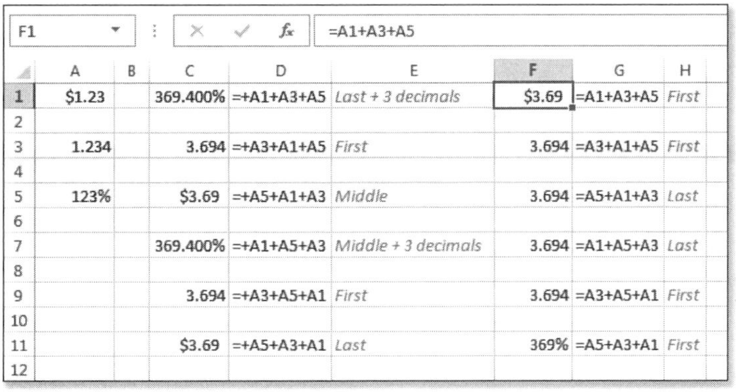

The resulting automatic format does not appear to follow any pattern. When you use an equal sign, either the format is copied from the first or the last cell referenced. When you use a plus sign, the format sometimes comes from the second, first, or last reference, and sometimes the format is a mix of two references.

If your formula is going to refer to multiple cells with different formatting, start the formula with an equal sign. Refer to the cell with the desired cell format first, but accept that you might have to explicitly format the resulting cell.

Using Date Math

Dates in Excel are stored as the number of days since January 1, 1900. For example, Excel stores the date Feb-17-2015 as 42052. In Figure 9.19, cell E1 contains the date. Cell E2 contains the formula =E1 and has been formatted to show a number.

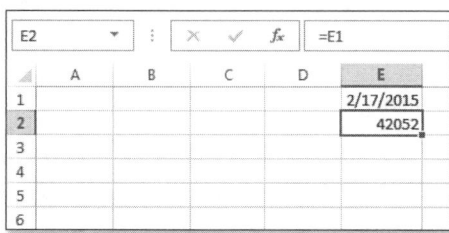

Figure 9.19
Although cell E1 is formatted as a date, Excel stores the date as the number of days since January 1, 1900.

This convenient system enables you to do some pretty simple math. For example, Figure 9.20 shows a range of invoice dates in column B. The terms for the invoice are in column D. You can calculate the due date by adding cells B2 and D2. Here is what actually happens in Excel's calculation engine:

1. The date in cell B2—2/1/2015—is stored as 42036.

2. Excel adds 10 to that number to get the answer 42046.

3. Excel formats this number as a date, to yield 2/11/2015.

	A	B	C	D	E
1	Invoice	Date	Amount	Terms	Due Date
2	2011	2/1/2015	107.60	10	2/11/2015
3	2012	2/1/2015	172.99	20	2/21/2015
4	2013	2/1/2015	170.66	20	2/21/2015
5	2014	2/2/2015	193.29	30	3/4/2015
6	2015	2/2/2015	220.87	30	3/4/2015
7	2016	2/3/2015	127.33	30	3/5/2015

E2   fx   =B2+D2

Figure 9.20
When the answer is formatted correctly, Excel's date math is very cool.

However, a frustrating problem can occur if the cell containing the formula has the wrong numeric format. For example, in Figure 9.21, the WORKDAY function in column D did not automatically convert the result to a date. It is important to recognize that dates in 2013–2016 fall in the range of 41,275 to 42,735. So, if you are expecting a date answer as the result of a formula and get a number in this range, the answer probably needs to have a date format applied.

Figure 9.21
The formula appears to give the wrong answer. However, this is a formatting problem.

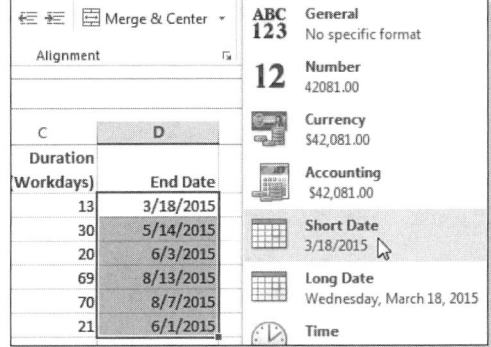

	A	B	C	D	E
1	Project	Start Date	Duration (Workdays)	End Date	
2	A	3/1/2015	13	42081	
3	B	4/2/2015	30	42138	
4	C	5/6/2015	20	42158	
5	D	5/8/2015	69	42229	
6	E	5/3/2015	70	42223	
7	F	5/2/2015	21	42156	

To apply a date format, on the Home tab use the Number drop-down to choose the Date format. The answer in column D now appears correctly, as shown in Figure 9.22.

Figure 9.22
After you apply the Date format, the answer is displayed correctly.

In general, most formulas that refer to a date cell are automatically formatted as a date. Most formulas that contain functions from the Date category are formatted as a date (the WORKDAY function is one annoying exception). However, sometimes you do not want the result formatted as a date.

For example, in Figure 9.23, you would like to count the number of days between two dates. The formula in C4 should calculate 16 days. However, because Excel automatically formatted the result as a date, the answer of 16 is shown as 1/16/1900. In this case, you need to apply a numeric format to the range containing the formula. When you select Number from the Number drop-down on the Home tab, the formula appears with the correct result (see Figure 9.24).

Any time you are doing math between two dates, you should plan to change the format of the result to be either Number or Date, depending on the situation.

> *To learn about many other useful date functions in Excel, **see** Chapter 11, "Using Everyday Functions: Math, Date and Time, and Text Functions."*

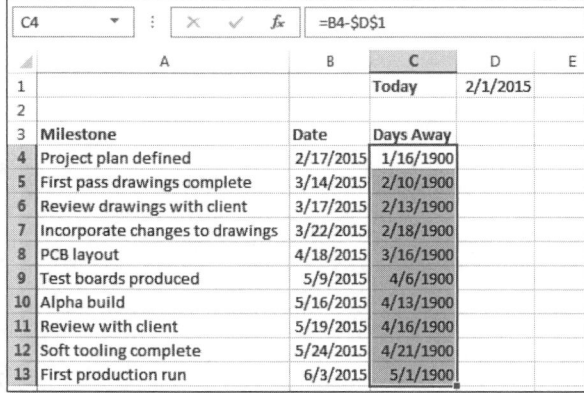

Figure 9.24
When you apply a numeric format, the answers are correct.

Troubleshooting Formulas

It is difficult to figure out worksheets that were set up by other people. When you receive a worksheet from a co-worker, use the information in the following sections to find and examine the formulas.

Highlighting All Formula Cells

The first technique to use when examining a new worksheet is to find all the cells that contain formulas. The following steps identify all the formula cells in the worksheet:

1. Ensure that you have a single cell selected.

2. Press F5 to display the Go To dialog.

3. In the lower-left corner of the Go To dialog, click the Special button to display the Go To Special dialog.

4. In the Go To Special dialog, select the Formulas option button, as shown in Figure 9.25. Click OK to select all formula cells.

Figure 9.25
The Go To Special dialog has many incredibly powerful features.

5. To highlight all the cells that contain formulas quickly, use the Paint Bucket icon in the Home tab to mark all the formula cells, as shown in Figure 9.26.

Figure 9.26
Immediately after selecting all formulas, select the Paint Bucket icon to color the formula cells.

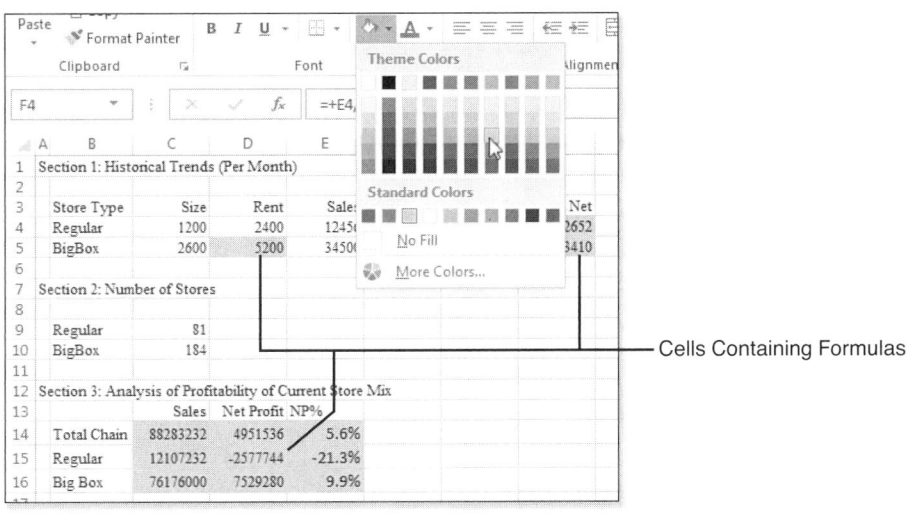

Cells Containing Formulas

Seeing All Formulas

For a long time, Excel has given users the ability to see all the formulas in a worksheet. The mode that provides this functionality is called *Show Formulas mode*.

To toggle into Show Formulas mode for a worksheet, select the Formulas tab, and then choose the Show Formulas icon in the Formula Auditing group. Alternatively, you can press Ctrl+` (the backtick) to toggle into this mode. On U.S. keyboards, the backtick is usually found just below the Esc key, on the same key with the tilde (~).

Figure 9.27 shows a worksheet with all formulas showing.

To hide the formulas and return to normal mode, choose the Show Formulas icon again.

12	Sect			
13			Sales	Net Profit	NP%
14	Total Chain	=C15+C16	=D15+D16	=D14/C14
15	Regular	=(C9*E4)*12	=(C9*H4)*12	=D15/C15
16	Big Box	=(C10*E5)*12	=(C10*H5)*12	=D16/C16
17				

Figure 9.27
Show Formulas mode reveals the formulas in the cells instead of the results. This is handy for quick formula auditing.

Editing a Single Formula to Show Direct Precedents

It is helpful to identify cells that are used to calculate a formula. These cells are called the *precedents* of the cell.

A cell can have several levels of precedents. In a formula such as =D5+D7, there are two direct precedents: D5 and D7. However, all the direct precedents of D5 and D7 are second-level precedents of the original formula.

If you are interested in visually examining the direct precedents of a cell, follow these steps:

1. Select a cell that has a formula.

2. Press F2 to put the cell in Edit mode. In this mode, each reference of the formula is displayed in a different color. For example, the formula in cell H5 in Figure 9.28 refers to three cells. The characters F5 in the formula appear in blue and correspond to the blue box around cell F5.

3. Visually check the formula to ensure that it is correct.

XOR	▼	:	✕ ✓ ƒx	=F5-G5-D5			

⊿	A	B	C	D	E	F	G	H
1		Section 1: Historical Trends (Per Month)						
2								
3		Store Type	Size	Rent	Sales	Profit	Labor	Net
4		Regular	1200	2400	12456	6228	6480	-2652
5		BigBox	26001	5200	345001	17250	8640	=F5-G5-D5
6								

Figure 9.28
Editing a single formula lights up the direct precedent cells.

Using Formula Auditing Arrows

If you have a complicated formula, you might want to identify direct precedents and then possibly second- or third-level precedents. You can have Excel draw arrows from the current cells to all cells that make up the precedents for the current cell. To have Excel draw arrows, follow these steps:

1. From the Formula Auditing group on the Formulas tab, click Trace Precedents. Excel draws arrows from the current cell to all the cells that are directly referenced in the formula. For example, in Figure 9.29, an arrow is drawn to a worksheet icon near cell B30. This indicates that at least one of the precedents for this cell is on another worksheet.

Figure 9.29
The results of Trace Precedents for cell D32.

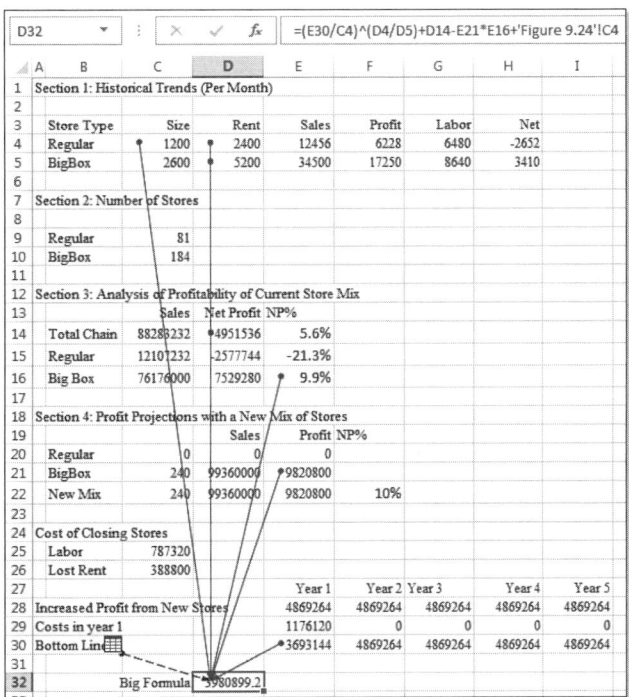

2. Click Trace Precedents again. Excel draws arrows from the precedent cells to the precedents of those cells. These are the second-level precedents of the original cell. Continue clicking Trace Precedents to see additional levels. In this case, practically every cell on the worksheet is a precedent of cell D32.

3. To remove the arrows, use the Remove Arrows icon in the Formula Auditing group.

Tracing Dependents

The Formula Auditing section provides another interesting option besides the ones discussed so far in this chapter. You can use the Formula Auditing section to trace dependents so you can find all the cells on the current worksheet that depend on the active cell. Before deleting a cell, consider clicking Trace Dependents to determine whether any cells on the current sheet refer to this cell. This prevents many #REF! errors from occurring.

 Caution

Even if tracing dependents does not show any cells that are dependent on the current cell, other cells on other worksheets or on other workbooks might rely on this cell.

Using the Watch Window

If you have a large spreadsheet, you might want to watch the results of some distant cells. You can use the Watch Window icon in the Formula Auditing section of the Formulas tab to open a floating box called the Watch Window screen. To use the Watch Window screen, follow these steps:

1. Click the Add Watch icon. The Add Watch dialog appears.

2. In the Add Watch dialog, specify a cell to watch, as shown in Figure 9.30. After you add several cells, the Watch Window screen floats above your worksheet, showing the current value of each cell that was added to it. The Watch Window screen identifies the current value and the current formula of each watched cell.

 Tip

To jump to a watched cell quickly, you can double-click the cell in the Watch Window screen. You can resize the watch window and resize the columns as necessary.

In theory, this feature can be used to watch a value in a far-off section of the worksheet.

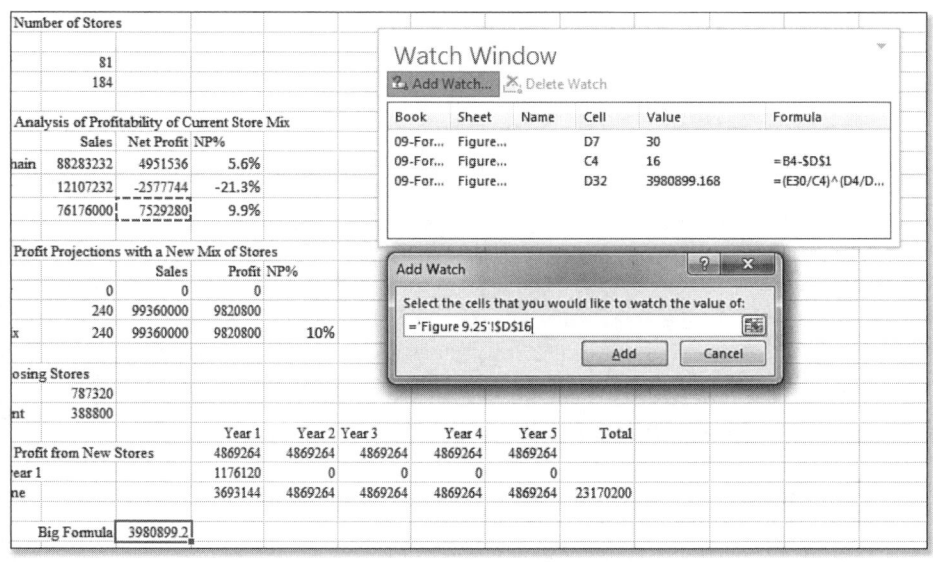

Figure 9.30
Adding a watch to the Watch Window screen.

Evaluate a Formula in Slow Motion

Most of the time, Excel calculates formulas in an instant. It can help your understanding of the formula to watch it being calculated in slow motion. If you need to see exactly how a formula is being calculated, follow these steps:

1. Select the cell that contains the formula in which you are interested.

2. On the Formulas tab, in the Formula Auditing group, select Evaluate Formula. The Evaluate Formula dialog appears, showing the formula. The following component of the formula is highlighted: It is the next section of the formula to be calculated.

3. If desired, click Evaluate to calculate the highlighted portion of the formula.

4. Click Step In to begin a new Evaluate section for the cell references in the underlined portion of the formula. Figure 9.31 shows the Evaluate Formula dialog after stepping in to the E30 portion of the formula.

Figure 9.31
The Evaluate Formula dialog enables you to calculate a formula in slow motion.

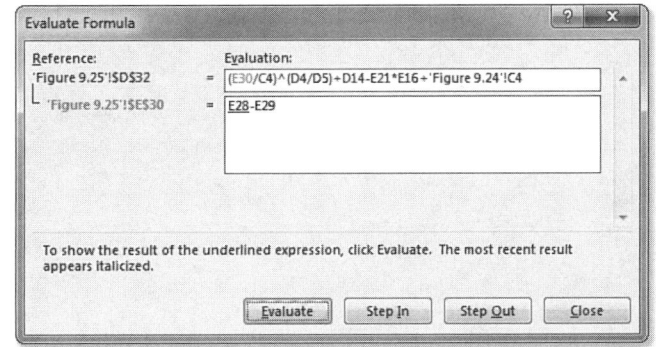

Evaluating Part of a Formula

When you do not need to evaluate an entire formula, use the Evaluate Formula feature. Follow these steps to evaluate part of a formula:

1. Use the mouse to select just the desired portion of the formula in the formula bar, as shown in Figure 9.32.

Figure 9.32
You can select a portion of the formula in the formula bar.

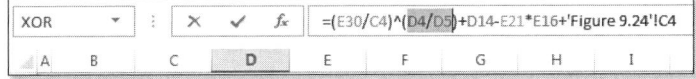

2. Press F9. Excel calculates just the highlighted portion of the formula, as shown in Figure 9.33.

| XOR | ▼ | ⋮ | × | ✓ | fx | =(E30/C4)^(0.461538461538462)+D14-E21*E16+'Figure 9.24'!C4 |

| ▲ | A | B | C | D | E | F | G | H | I | J |
| 1 | Section 1: Historical Trends (Per Month) | | | | | | | | | |

Figure 9.33
Press F9 to calculate just the highlighted portion of the formula.

Be sure to press the Esc key to exit the formula after you use this method. Instead, if you press Enter to accept the formula, that portion of the formula permanently stays in its calculated form, such as 0.407407.

Excel in Practice: Moving the Formula Tooltip

As you type a formula, Excel 2013 offers a tooltip to show the order of the arguments for a function. As shown in Figure 9.34, this tooltip can frequently get in the way by covering nearby cells.

A cool trick is to click the tooltip and drag it to a new location. As you continue entering the formula, the tooltip stays in the new, detached location (see Figure 9.35).

 **Tip**
If you click the function name in the tooltip, Excel opens the Help topic for that function.

| XOR | ▼ | ⋮ | × | ✓ | fx | =BASE(|

▲	A	B	C	D	E	F
1		Section 1: Historical Trends (Per Month)				
2						
3		Store Type	Size	Rent	Sales	Pro
4		Regular	1200	2400	12456	62
5		BigBox	2600	5200	34500	172
6						
7		Section 2: Number of Stores				
8		=BASE(				
9		R BASE(number, radix, [min_length])				
10		BigBox	184			
11						

Figure 9.34
The tooltip is covering adjacent cells.

7	Section 2: Number of Stores					
8	=BASE(					
9	Regular	81				
10	BigBox	184				
11						
12	Section 3: Analysis of Profitability of Current Store Mix					
13		Sales	Net Profit	NP%		
14	Total Chain	88283232	4951536	5.6%	BASE(number, radix, [min_length])	
15	Regular	12107232	-2577744	-21.3%		
16	Big Box	76176000	7529280	9.9%		

Figure 9.35
Drag the tooltip to an out-of-the way location.

UNDERSTANDING FUNCTIONS

Excel is used on 500 million desktops around the world. People in all career types use Excel, as do many home users who take advantage of Excel's powerful features to track their finances, investments, and more. Part of Excel's versatility is its wide range of built-in functions.

Excel 2013 offers 463 built-in calculation functions. This number grows with each new release. For example, 49 functions are new in Excel 2013. Some of these functions are invented by Microsoft. Some are added to keep Excel compliant with the Open Document Format standard.

Here are some interesting functions added in recent versions:

- Excel 2013 added the WEBSERVICE function to retrieve data from the Web. When it's combined with the ENCODEURL and FILTERXML functions, you can retrieve more data from the Internet from within your Excel functions. Read more about these functions in Chapter 12, "Using Powerful Functions: Logical, Lookup, Web, and Database Functions."

- Excel 2013 added the ISFORMULA and FORMULATEXT functions. The first function enables you to use conditional formatting to highlight formula cells and replaces an old Excel 4 Macro trick. FORMULATEXT is great for documenting worksheets and is used extensively in the creation of this book to display the formula next to a cell. Both are covered in Chapter 12.

- BASE and DECIMAL are flexible replacements for converting between binary, decimal, and hexadecimal. Unlike the BIN2DEC functions, BASE and DECIMAL can handle any number system, from Base 2 to Base 36. They are covered in Chapter 15, "Using Trig, Matrix, and Engineering Functions." In an ironic twist, the Open Document standard added ARABIC to convert back from roman numerals to decimal. Read about it in Chapter 11, "Using Everyday Functions: Math, Date and Time, and Text Functions."

- Excel 2013 now handles bit math with BITAND, BITOR, BITXOR, BITLSHIFT, and BITRSHIFT, as covered in Chapter 15. The XOR function for exclusive OR is new and is covered in Chapter 12.

- Trigonometry becomes a bit easier in Excel 2013. Trig fans might recall that 1/SIN is called a Cosecant. You won't have to divide by 1 anymore, as the Open Document standard now includes CSC (Cosecant), SEC (Secant), and COT (Cotangent). Of course, when you add trig functions, you also have to have their hyperbolic equivalent and their imaginary equivalent. In order to prevent you from using the "1/" in 1/SIN", you now have these new functions: ACOT, ACOTH, COT, COTH, CSC, CSCH, IMCOSH, IMCOT, IMCSC, IMCSCH, IMSEC, IMSECH, IMSINH, IMTAN, SEC, and SECH. Maybe it would have been easier to have just kept using the "1/". All of these are covered in Chapter 15.

- Excel 2010 added the AGGREGATE function, which is similar to SUBTOTALS but with 19 calculations instead of 11. This function can ignore other subtotals, error cells, and/or rows hidden manually. The arguments from 12 through 19 work as array formulas, allowing some flexibility. See Chapter 11.

- Excel 2007 added the IFERROR function to simplify handling of #N/A and #DIV/0 errors. See Chapter 12.

- Excel 2007 introduced plural SUMIFS, COUNTIFS, and AVERAGEIFS functions. The plural versions handle multiple conditions and are amazingly fast. If you've ever used SUMPRODUCT because SUMIF handles only one condition, you will love SUMIFS. See Chapter 11.

What are the other new functions? They include the following:

- New statistical functions, such as BINOM.DIST.RANGE, COMBIN, COMBINA, GAMMA, GAUSS, PERMUTATIONA, and PHI.

- The old CHAR and CODE are extended with UNICHAR and UNICODE to return extended characters beyond CHAR(255).

- New financial functions include PDURATION and RRI.

- New date functions are DAYS and ISOWEEKNUM, and NUMBERVALUE enables you to convert text to numbers, even text that has the "wrong" decimal character.

- SHEET and SHEETS tell you the worksheet number of a cell reference and how many sheets are in a 3D reference.

- MUNIT returns the correct Identity matrix, eliminating the chance of any floating-point errors creeping in when you use MMULT(Matrix,MINVERSE) to generate the identity matrix.

- The last two "new" functions are simply renamed functions: FLOOR.MATH and CEILING.MATH replace FLOOR.PRECISE and CEILING.PRECISE.

No matter what you are trying to do in Excel, there are functions for you. If you cannot find a built-in function, there's a good chance a third-party vendor sells an add-in program to Excel that adds new customized functions to assist in your particular industry. If not, you can pick up a book on programming VBA to learn how to write your own custom functions in Excel.

➥ *Refer to Chapter 14 of* VBA and Macros for Microsoft Excel 2013, *by Jelen and Syrstad (Que, ISBN 0789748614), to learn about 30 cool functions you can add to Excel.*

Working with Functions

To use functions successfully in a worksheet, you need to follow the function syntax. Keep in mind that a formula that makes use of a function needs to start with an equal sign. You type the function name, an opening parenthesis, function arguments (separated by commas), and the closing parenthesis.

The general syntax of a function looks like this:

```
=FunctionName(Argument1,Argument2,Argument3)
```

In general, there should be no spaces anywhere in a function. Specifically, you should never use a space between the function name and the opening parenthesis. Some people like to add a space after each comma in a function, like this:

```
=FunctionName(Argument1, Argument2, Argument3)
```

Although this is not required, it does increase the readability of the final function. For what it's worth, Excel correctly calculates a formula with or without these spaces, so it's a personal choice as to whether you include them.

Parentheses are needed with every function, including functions that require no arguments. For example, these functions still require the parentheses:

```
=NOW()
=DATE()
=TODAY()
=PI()
```

 Note

Chapters 11 through 15 cover all 463 functions. This chapter covers a number of the most commonly used functions.

The arguments for a function should be entered in the correct order, as specified in this book or Excel Help. For example, the PMT() function expects the arguments to have the interest rate first, followed by the number of periods, followed by the present value. If you attempt to send the arguments in the wrong order, Excel happily calculates the wrong result.

In many cases, you can enter arguments as numbers or as cell references. For example, all these formulas are valid:

```
=SUM(1,2,3^2,4/5,6*7)
=SUM(A1:A9,C1,D2,Sheet2!E3:M10)
=SUM(A1:A9,100,200,B3*5)
```

 Note

Excel functions can return a number of errors. This happens most frequently when one of the arguments passed to the function is outside the range of what the function expects. When you receive a #NUM!, #VALUE!, or #N/A error, you should look in Excel Help for the function. The Remarks section usually indicates exactly what problems can cause each type of error.

The Formulas Tab in Excel 2013

One way to find functions in Excel 2013 is on the Formulas tab. This tab offers the Insert Function, AutoSum, Recently Used, Financial, Logical, Text, Date & Time, Lookup & Reference, Math & Trig, and More Functions icons.

As shown in Figure 10.1, when you click the More Functions icon, a drop-down with six additional function groups—Statistical, Engineering, Cube, Information, Compatibility, and Web—appears.

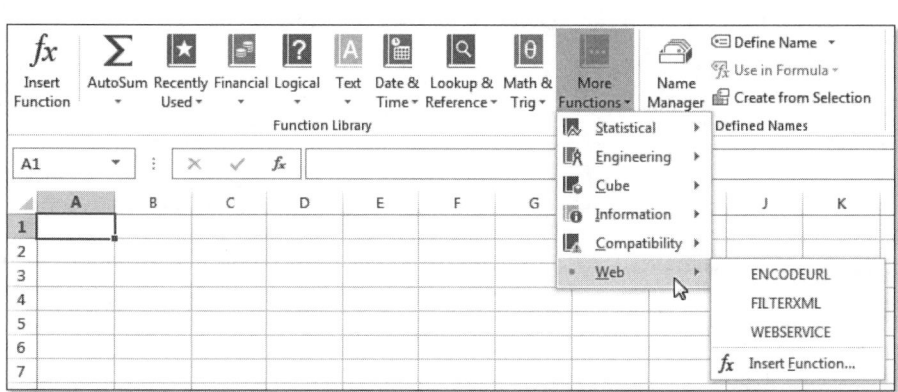

Figure 10.1
The Formulas tab contains icons for finding functions.

The Formulas tab is designed to make it easier to find the right function. You select an icon from the ribbon, and an alphabetical list of functions in that group appears. If you hover your mouse over a function in the list, Excel displays a description of what the function does, as shown in Figure 10.2.

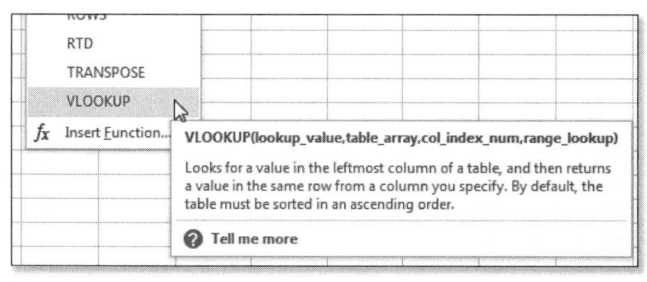

Figure 10.2
Hover over a function, and Excel displays a tip explaining what the function does.

Finding the Function You Need

The inherent problem with the Formulas tab is that you often have to guess where your desired function might be hiding. The function categories have been established in Excel for a decade, and in some cases, functions are tucked away in strange places.

For example, the SUM() function is a Math & Trig function. This makes sense because adding numbers is clearly a mathematical process. However, the AVERAGE() function is not available in the Math & Trig icon. (It is under More Functions, Statistical.) The COUNT() function could be math, reference, or information, but it is found under More Functions, Statistical.

By dividing the list of functions up into categories, Microsoft has made it rather difficult to find certain functions. Fortunately, as described in the following sections, you can use some tricks to make this process simpler.

Using AutoComplete to Find Functions

One feature in Excel 2013 is Formula AutoComplete. Sometimes you might remember the first letter of a function but not all the rest of the letters. For example, there are five varieties of the function you use to do averages, and they all start with A. Rather than trying to figure out whether the averaging function you need is in the Math or Statistical icon, you can just start typing **=AV** in a cell. Excel displays a pop-up window with all the functions that begin with AV, as shown in Figure 10.3.

To accept a function name from the list, you can either double-click the function name or select the name and press Tab.

 **Tip**

By the way, you can click the formula tooltip and drag it to a new location on the worksheet. This can be useful if the tooltip is covering cells that you need to click when building the function.

If you click the function name in the tooltip, Excel opens Help for that function.

Figure 10.3
Rather than use the icons on the Formulas tab, you can type **=AV** to display an alphabetical list of the AV functions.

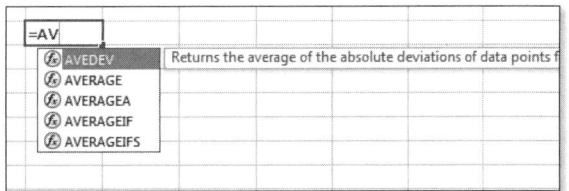

Using the Insert Function Dialog to Find Functions

At the bottom of every list of functions is an icon for Insert Function. To access the Insert Function dialog, you can also use the small fx button to the left of the formula bar, the More Functions option at the bottom of the AutoSum drop-down, or the large Function Wizard button on the Formulas tab. With 15 ways to access the Function Wizard, Microsoft is telling you that this is a good way to find functions.

Choosing any of these options to open the Function Wizard causes the Insert Function dialog to appear.

In the Excel 2003 version of the Function Wizard, Microsoft added a handy search utility. For example, if you typed Loan Payment and then clicked Go, Excel would suggest PMT (the correct function) as well as PPMT, ISPMT, RATE, and others. The search functionality was a fantastic addition to Excel 2003 and should be your first stop when trying to find a function in Excel 2013.

When you choose a function in the Insert Function dialog, the dialog displays the syntax for the function, as well as a one-sentence description of the function, as shown in Figure 10.4. If you need more details, you can click the Help on This Function hyperlink in the lower-left corner of the Insert Function dialog.

 **Tip**

If you type =FunctionName(in a cell, you can press Ctrl+A anytime after the opening parenthesis to display the Function Arguments dialog.

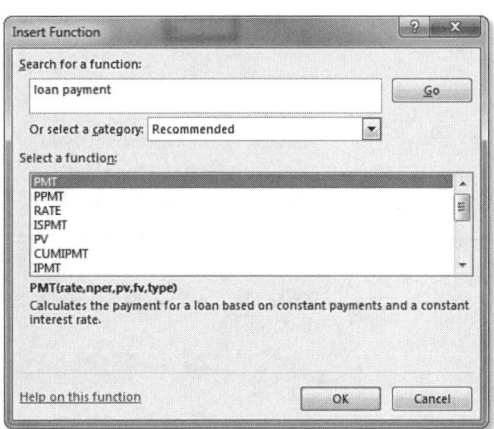

Figure 10.4
The Insert Function dialog enables you to browse the syntax and descriptions. The Help on This Function hyperlink leads to more help.

Getting Help with Excel Functions

Every Excel function has three levels of help:

- On-grid tooltip
- Function Arguments dialog
- Excel Help

The following sections discuss these levels of help. However, you are sure to find the Function Arguments dialog to be one of the best ways of getting help.

Using On-Grid Tooltips

In any cell, you can type an equal sign, a function name, and the opening parenthesis. Excel displays a tooltip that shows the expected arguments. In many cases, this tooltip is enough to guide you through the function. For example, I can usually remember that the function for figuring out a car loan payment is =PMT(), but I can never remember the order of the arguments. The tooltip, as shown in Figure 10.5, is enough to remind me that rate comes first, followed by number of periods, and then the principal amount or present value. Any function arguments displayed in square brackets are optional, so in the example shown in Figure 10.5, you know that you may not have to enter anything for fv or type.

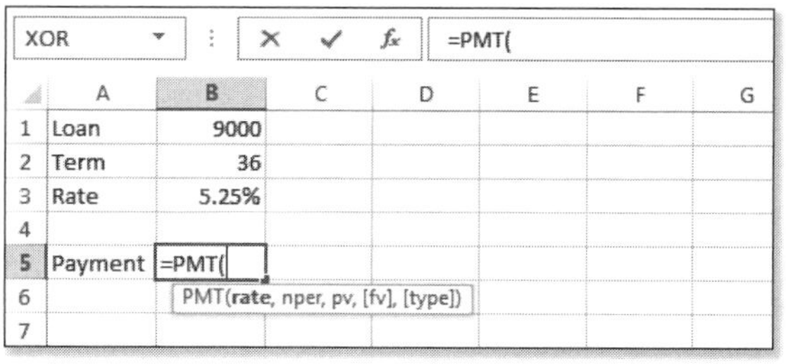

Figure 10.5
The tooltip assists you in remembering the proper order for the arguments.

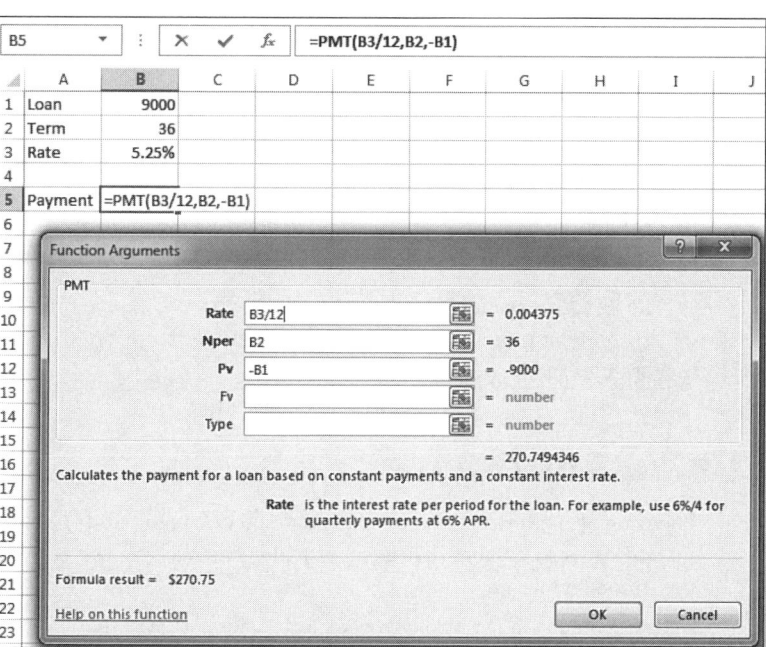

As you type each comma in the function, the next argument in the tooltip lights up in boldface. This way, you always know which argument you are entering.

Using the Function Arguments Dialog

When you access a function through the Function Wizard or a drop-down list, Excel displays the Function Arguments dialog. This dialog is one of the best features in Excel. If you've started to type the function and have typed the opening parenthesis, then pressing Ctrl+A or clicking the fx icon to the left of the toolbar displays the Function Arguments dialog.

As shown in Figure 10.6, the Function Arguments dialog has many elements:

Figure 10.6
The Function Arguments dialog helps you build a function, one step at a time.

- The one-sentence description of the function appears in the center of the dialog.

- As you tab into the text box for each argument, the description of the argument is shown in the dialog. This description guides you as to what Excel is expecting. For example, in the dialog shown in Figure 10.6, Excel reminds you that the interest rate needs to be divided by four for quarterly payments. This reminds you to divide the rate in cell B3 by 12 for monthly payments.

- To the right of each argument in the dialog is a reference button. You can click this button to collapse the dialog so you can point to the cells for that argument.

- To the right of each text box is a label that shows the result of the entry for that argument.

- Any arguments in bold are required. Arguments not in bold are optional.

- After you enter the required arguments, the dialog shows the preliminary result of the formula. This is on the right side, just below the last argument text box. It appears again in the lower-left corner, just above the Help on This Function hyperlink.

- A Help on This Function hyperlink to the Help topic for the function appears in the lower-left corner of the dialog.

Using Excel Help

The Excel Help topics for the functions are incredibly complete. Each function's Help topic includes the following sections:

- The function syntax appears at the top of the topic. This includes a description of each function that might be more complete than the description in the Function Arguments dialog.

- The Remarks section helps troubleshoot possible problems with the function. It discusses specific limits for each argument and describes the meaning of each possible error that could be returned from the function.

- Each function has an example section composed of an embedded Excel Web App worksheet. You can click the XL icon in the footer of the example to download the example to your computer.

- The See Also section at the bottom of a Help topic enables you to discover related functions. The logical groupings suggested by See Also are far more useful than the category groupings in the Formulas tab.

Using AutoSum

Microsoft realizes that the most common function is the SUM( ) function. It is so popular that Excel provides one-click access to the AutoSum feature.

The AutoSum icon is the large Greek letter sigma that is the second icon on the Formulas tab or a small icon on the right side of the Home tab. You can click this icon to use AutoSum, or you

 **Tip**
Pressing Alt+= is equivalent to clicking the AutoSum icon.

can use the drop-down at the bottom of the icon to access AutoSum versions of Average, Count Numbers, Max, and Min, as shown in Figure 10.7.

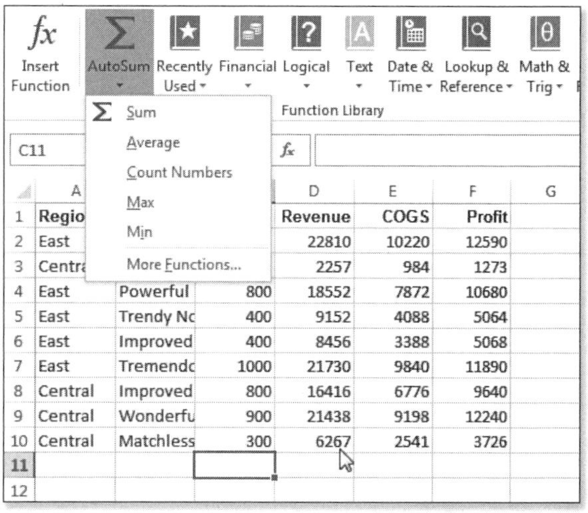

Figure 10.7
The AutoSum drop-down offers the capability to average and more.

When you click the AutoSum button, Excel seeks to add up the numbers that are above or to the left of the current cell. In general, when you click the AutoSum icon, Excel guesses which cells you are trying to sum. Excel automatically types the SUM( ) formula. You should review Excel's guess to make sure that Excel chose the correct range to sum. In Figure 10.8, for example, Excel correctly guesses that you want to sum the column of quantities above the cell.

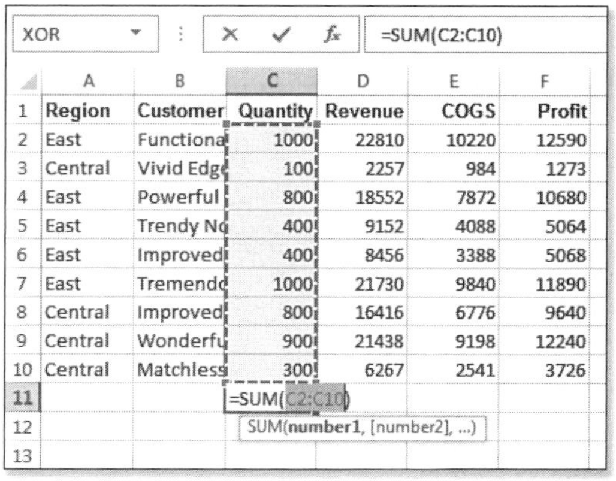

Figure 10.8
The AutoSum feature is proposing a formula to sum C2:C10.

Potential Problems with AutoSum

Although you should always check the range proposed by the AutoSum feature, in some cases you should be especially wary. If the headings above the data are numeric, for example, this will fool AutoSum. In Figure 10.9, the 2012 heading in C1 is numeric. This causes Excel to include the heading incorrectly in the total for column C.

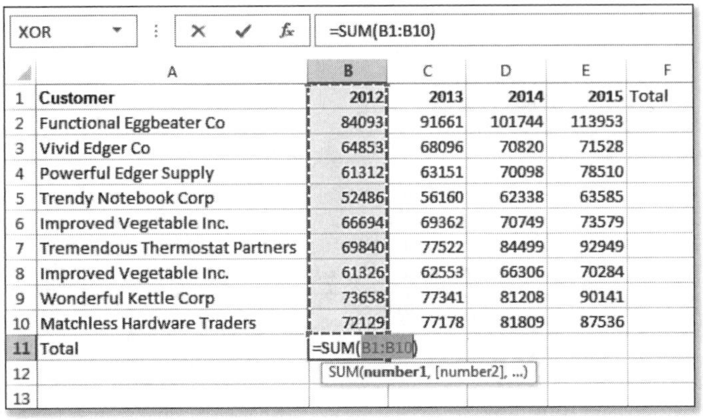

Figure 10.9
Numeric headings confuse AutoSum.

When Excel proposes the wrong range for a sum, you use your mouse to highlight the correct range before pressing Enter.

Excel avoids including other SUM( ) functions in an AutoSum range. If a range contains a SUM( ) function that references other cells, Excel prematurely stops just before the SUM( ) function. This problem happens only when the SUM( ) function references other cells. If the cell contained =7000+1878 or =H3+H4 or =SUM(7000,1878), AutoSum would include the cell.

Excel prefers to sum a column of numbers instead of a row of numbers. Figure 10.10 shows a strange anomaly. If you place the cell pointer in cell F2 and click AutoSum, Excel correctly guesses that you want to total B2:E2. Cell F3 works fine. However, when you get to cell F4, Excel has a choice. There are two numbers above F4 and four numbers to the left of F4. Because there are two numbers directly above, Excel tries to total those two numbers. This problem seems to happen only in the third row of the data set. After that, Excel sees that the three cells above are all summing across the rows, and AutoSum works perfectly in F5:F10.

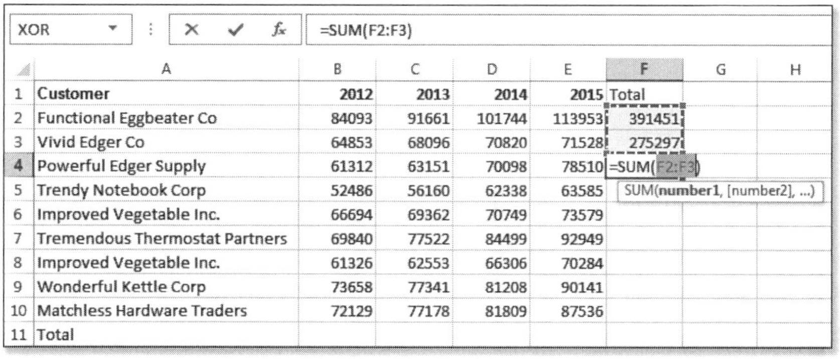

Figure 10.10
Excel can choose
between summing
two numbers above
or four numbers to
the left. Excel chooses
incorrectly.

	A	B	C	D	E	F	G	H
	XOR ▼ : × ✓ fx	=SUM(F2:F3)						
1	Customer	2012	2013	2014	2015	Total		
2	Functional Eggbeater Co	84093	91661	101744	113953	391451		
3	Vivid Edger Co	64853	68096	70820	71528	275297		
4	Powerful Edger Supply	61312	63151	70098	78510	=SUM(F2:F3)		
5	Trendy Notebook Corp	52486	56160	62338	63585	SUM(**number1**, [number2], ...)		
6	Improved Vegetable Inc.	66694	69362	70749	73579			
7	Tremendous Thermostat Partners	69840	77522	84499	92949			
8	Improved Vegetable Inc.	61326	62553	66306	70284			
9	Wonderful Kettle Corp	73658	77341	81208	90141			
10	Matchless Hardware Traders	72129	77178	81809	87536			
11	Total							

Special Tricks with AutoSum

There is an amazing trick you can use with AutoSum. If you select a range of cells before clicking the AutoSum button, Excel does a much better job of predicting what to sum.

In Figure 10.10, for example, you could select B11:E11 before clicking the AutoSum button, and Excel would know to sum each column. Be careful, though, because Excel does not preview its guess before entering the formula. You should always check a formula after using AutoSum to make sure the correct range was selected.

If your selection contains a mix of blank cells and nonblank cells, Excel adds the AutoSum to only the blank cells. In Figure 10.11, for example, you select the range B2:F11 before clicking the AutoSum button.

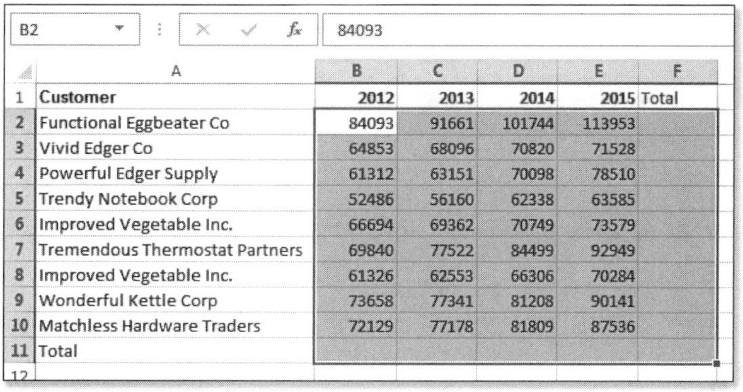

Figure 10.11
If your selection contains a mix of blank and nonblank cells, AutoSum writes only to the blank cells.

	A	B	C	D	E	F
	B2 ▼ : × ✓ fx	84093				
1	Customer	2012	2013	2014	2015	Total
2	Functional Eggbeater Co	84093	91661	101744	113953	
3	Vivid Edger Co	64853	68096	70820	71528	
4	Powerful Edger Supply	61312	63151	70098	78510	
5	Trendy Notebook Corp	52486	56160	62338	63585	
6	Improved Vegetable Inc.	66694	69362	70749	73579	
7	Tremendous Thermostat Partners	69840	77522	84499	92949	
8	Improved Vegetable Inc.	61326	62553	66306	70284	
9	Wonderful Kettle Corp	73658	77341	81208	90141	
10	Matchless Hardware Traders	72129	77178	81809	87536	
11	Total					
12						

After you click the AutoSum button, Excel correctly fills in totals for all the rows and columns, as shown in Figure 10.12.

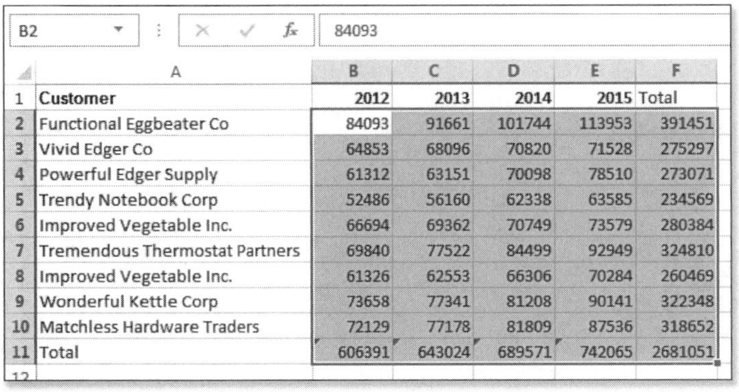

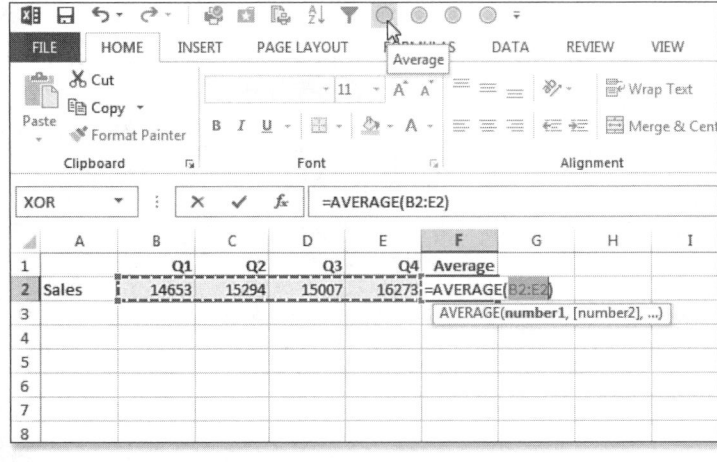

Figure 10.12
By using AutoSum, you can add 14 SUM( ) formulas with one click.

Using AutoAverage or AutoCount

The AutoSum button includes a drop-down arrow with choices for Average, Count, Max, and Min. If you find yourself frequently using the choices in this drop-down, you can add an icon to the Quick Access Toolbar that will AutoAverage, AutoCount, and so on. Open the AutoSum drop-down. Right-click Average and choose Add to Quick Access Toolbar to have one-click access to an icon that works similar to AutoSum, but uses the AVERAGE calculation instead (see Figure 10.13).

🔺 **Caution**

Microsoft uses the same green circle icon to represent Average, Count, Max, and Min. If you are going to add all four icons to the QAT, add them in alphabetical order to help you remember the sequence in which they appear.

Figure 10.13
Add icons to QAT to get one-click access to AutoAverage, AutoMin, AutoMax, and AutoCount.

Function Reference Chapters

Chapters 11 through 15 provide a fairly comprehensive reference for most of the 463 functions in Excel 2013. At the beginning of each of these chapters is an alphabetical list of the functions described, along with arguments and a short description of each function. Following the alphabetical list are examples of how to use the functions. These examples describe all the required arguments. The examples are designed to give you ideas of how to use the functions in real life.

Function coverage is broken out as follows:

- Chapter 11 describes functions that many people encounter in their everyday life: some of the math functions, date functions, and text functions.

- Chapter 12 describes functions that are a bit more difficult but that should be a part of your everyday arsenal. These include a series of functions for making decisions in a formula. They include the IF function and are known collectively as the *logical functions*. Chapter 12 also describes the information, lookup, and database functions.

- Chapter 13, "Using Financial Functions," describes the financial functions. The first section of the chapter includes functions that anyone can use to calculate a car loan or plan for retirement. The later sections of the chapter include functions for depreciation, business valuation, and bond investing.

- Chapter 14, "Using Statistical Functions," describes statistical functions. Many of these functions are functions that are useful everyday—for example, AVERAGE(), MAX(), MIN(), and RANK(). The chapter also describes many highly specialized functions that are useful to scientists and engineers.

- Chapter 15 describes trigonometry and engineering functions. The trigonometry functions are grouped along with the other math functions in the Math Functions icon, but they are described separately in this book because they are more specialized. The engineering functions are highly specialized.

USING EVERYDAY FUNCTIONS: MATH, DATE AND TIME, AND TEXT FUNCTIONS

Excel offers many functions for dealing with basic math, dates and times, and text. This chapter describes the functions found under the Text icon, the Date & Time icon, and the Math portion of the Math & Trig icon on the Formulas tab. Trig functions are covered in Chapter 15, "Using Trig, Matrix, and Engineering Functions."

A few of the new functions in Excel 2013 fall into this chapter:

- **NUMBERVALUE**—Converts text numbers to their number value, even when the text contains foreign punctuation. For example, your country might show numbers as $1,234.56. A text file from a foreign subsidiary might include that same number with punctuation of $1.234,56. The new NUMBERVALUE provides a formulaic way to convert the text to numbers. This might be useful if there was some reason you could not use Text to Columns.

- **ARABIC**—Converts Roman numerals stored as text back to numbers. This might be useful if you cannot figure out that Super Bowl XLIX is the 49th time the game has been played. Actually, =ROMAN(ARABIC(A1)+1) is a nice way to increment Roman numerals.

- **COMBIN** and **COMBINA**—These functions provide a way to calculate combinations and to calculate combinations where repeats are allowed, respectively. They join PERMUT and PERMUATIONA.

- **UNICHAR** and **UNICODE**—These functions extend the functionality of CHAR and CODE, respectively, beyond the 255 ASCII character set.

- **DAYS**—Calculates the number of days between two dates. This function works with dates stored as text in addition to regular dates, and it prevents you from having to use =IF(ISNUMBER(A2), A2,DATEVALUE(A2)) to convert a text date to a date.

- **ISOWEEKNUM**—Calculates the ISO week number. In the ISO system, a year is made up of either 52 or 53 full weeks (364 or 371 days). Weeks start on Monday. The week that contains the first Thursday of the year is numbered Week 1.

In addition, two functions have been renamed in Excel 2013. Microsoft had introduced CEILING.PRECISE and FLOOR.PRECISE in Excel 2010. These are now renamed as CEILING.MATH and FLOOR.MATH. How do these differ from CEILING and FLOOR? They are the same for positive numbers. For example, CEILING(1.23) will be 2. The difference is for negative numbers. When asked to calculate CEILING(-1.23), Excel would round away from 0 and provide –2 as the answer. Mathematicians point out that –1 is the integer "above" –1.23. CEILING.MATH(-1.23) will return –1 as a concession of this point to the mathematicians.

Table 11.1 provides an alphabetical list of all of Excel 2013's math functions. Detailed examples of these functions are provided later in this chapter.

Table 11.1 Alphabetical List of Math Functions

Function	Description
ABS(*number*)	Returns the absolute value of a number. The absolute value of a number is the number without its sign.
AGGREGATE(*function, options, array*, [k])	Performs one of 17 functions with the ability to ignore error values, other subtotals, and/or rows hidden by a filter.
ARABIC(*text*)	Converts a Roman numeral to Arabic.
CEILING(*number,significance*)	Returns the number rounded up, away from zero, to the nearest multiple of significance. For example, if you want to avoid using pennies in your prices and your product is priced at $4.42, you can use the formula =CEILING(4.42,0.05) to round the price up to the nearest nickel. Note that Excel calculates =CEILING(-2.1,-1) as –3, which is different than the ISO standard. See CEILING.MATH for an alternative.
CEILING.MATH(*number,[significance]*)	Rounds a number up to the nearest multiple of significance. Renamed in Excel 2013 from CEILING.PRECISE. Provides compatibility with the ISO standard for computing the ceiling of a negative number.
COMBIN(*number,number_chosen*)	Returns the number of combinations for a given number of items. You use COMBIN to determine the total possible number of groups for a given number of items.

Function	Description
COMBINA(*number*,*number_chosen*)	Returns the number of combinations with repetitions for a given number of items. New in Excel 2013.
COUNTIF(*range*,*criteria*)	Counts the number of cells within a range that meet the given criteria.
EVEN(*number*)	Returns number rounded up to the nearest even integer. You can use this function for processing items that come in twos. For example, suppose a packing crate accepts rows of one or two items. The crate is full when the number of items, rounded up to the nearest two, matches the crate's capacity.
EXP(*number*)	Returns e raised to the power of *number*. The constant e equals 2.71828182845904, the base of the natural logarithm.
FACT(*number*)	Returns the factorial of a number. The factorial of a number is equal to $1 \times 2 \times 3 \times ... \times number$.
FACTDOUBLE(*number*)	Returns the double factorial of a number.
FLOOR(*number*,*significance*)	Rounds the number toward zero, to the nearest multiple of significance.
FLOOR.MATH(*number*, *[significance]*)	Rounds the number down to the nearest multiple of significance. Added to Excel 2010 as FLOOR.PRECISE. Renamed in Excel 2013 to FLOOR.MATH. Differs from FLOOR when you have negative numbers. Whereas FLOOR(-1.2,-1) rounds toward zero to produce –1, the new FLOOR.MATH(-1.2) will round to the lower number, which is –2.
GCD(*number1*,*number2*,...)	Returns the greatest common divisor of two or more integers. The greatest common divisor is the largest integer that divides both *number1* and *number2* without a remainder.
INT(*number*)	Rounds a number down to the nearest integer.
LCM(*number1*,*number2*,...)	Returns the least common multiple of integers. The least common multiple is the smallest positive integer that is a multiple of all integer arguments *number1*, *number2*, and so on. You use LCM to add fractions that have different denominators.
MOD(*number*,*divisor*)	Returns the remainder after *number* is divided by *divisor*. The result has the same sign as *divisor*.
MROUND(*number*,*multiple*)	Returns a number rounded to the desired multiple.
MULTINOMIAL(*number1*,*number2*,...)	Returns the ratio of the factorial of a sum of values to the product of factorials.
ODD(*number*)	Returns a number rounded up to the nearest odd integer.

Function	Description
PI()	Returns the number 3.14159265358979, the mathematical constant pi, accurate to 15 digits.
POWER(*number*,*power*)	Returns the result of a number raised to a power.
PRODUCT(*number1*,*number2*,...)	Multiplies all the numbers given as arguments and returns the product.
QUOTIENT(*numerator*,*denominator*)	Returns the integer portion of a division operation. You use this function when you want to discard the remainder of a division.
RAND()	Returns an evenly distributed random number greater than or equal to 0 and less than 1. A new random number is returned every time the worksheet is calculated.
RANDBETWEEN(*bottom*,*top*)	Returns a random number between the numbers specified. A new random number is returned every time the worksheet is calculated.
ROMAN(*number*,*form*)	Converts an Arabic numeral to Roman, as text.
ROUND(*number*,*num_digits*)	Rounds a number to a specified number of digits.
ROUNDDOWN(*number*,*num_digits*)	Rounds a number down, toward zero.
ROUNDUP(*number*,*num_digits*)	Rounds a number up, away from zero.
SIGN(*number*)	Determines the sign of a number. Returns 1 if the number is positive, 0 if the number is 0, and –1 if the number is negative.
SQRT(*number*)	Returns a positive square root.
SQRTPI(*number*)	Returns the square root of (*number* × pi).
SUBTOTAL(*function_num*, *ref1*,*ref2*,...)	Returns a subtotal in a list or database. It is generally easier to create a list with subtotals by using the Subtotals command (from the Data menu). After the subtotal list is created, you can modify it by editing the SUBTOTAL function.
SUM(*number1*,*number2*,...)	Adds all the numbers in a range of cells.
SUMIF(*range*,*criteria*,*sum_range*)	Adds the cells specified by the given criteria.
SUMPRODUCT(*array1*,*array2*, *array3*,...)	Multiplies corresponding components in the given arrays and returns the sum of those products.
TRUNC(*number*,*num_digits*)	Truncates a number to an integer by removing the fractional part of the number.

Table 11.2 provides an alphabetical list of all of Excel 2013's date and time functions. Detailed examples of these functions are provided later in this chapter.

Table 11.2 Alphabetical List of Date and Time Functions

Function	Description
DATE (*year*,*month*,*day*)	Returns the serial number that represents a particular date.
DATEDIF (*start_date*,*end_date*,*unit*)	Calculates the number of days, months, or years between two dates. This function is provided for compatibility with Lotus 1-2-3.
DATEVALUE (*date_text*)	Returns the serial number of the date represented by *date_text*. You use DATEVALUE to convert a date represented by text to a serial number.
DAY (*serial_number*)	Returns the day of a date, represented by a serial number. The day is given as an integer ranging from 1 to 31.
DAYS (*end_date*, *start_date*)	Calculates the difference in days between two dates. Works even if one or both dates are stored as text instead of as a date.
DAYS360 (*start_date*,*end_date*,*method*)	Returns the number of days between two dates, based on a 360-day year (that is, twelve 30-day months), which is used in some accounting calculations. You use this function to help compute payments if your accounting system is based on twelve 30-day months.
EDATE (*start_date*,*months*)	Returns the serial number that represents the date that is the indicated number of months before or after a specified date (that is, the *start_date*). You use EDATE to calculate maturity dates or due dates that fall on the same day of the month as the date of issue.
EOMONTH (*start_date*,*months*)	Returns the serial number for the last day of the month that is the indicated number of months before or after *start_date*. You use EOMONTH to calculate maturity dates or due dates that fall on the last day of the month.
HOUR (*serial_number*)	Returns the hour of a time value. The hour is given as an integer, ranging from 0 (12:00 a.m.) to 23 (11:00 p.m.).
ISOWEEKNUM (*date*)	Returns the ISO week number of the given date. New in Excel 2013.
MINUTE (*serial_number*)	Returns the minutes of a time value. The minutes are given as an integer, ranging from 0 to 59.
MONTH (*serial_number*)	Returns the month of a date represented by a serial number. The month is given as an integer, ranging from 1 (for January) to 12 (for December).

Function	Description
NETWORKDAYS (*start_date*,*end_date*, *holidays*)	Returns the number of whole working days between *start_date* and *end_date*. Working days exclude weekends and any dates identified in holidays. You use NETWORKDAYS to calculate employee benefits that accrue based on the number of days worked during a specific term. Weekdays are defined as Saturday and Sunday. To handle other calendars, see NETWORKDAYS.INTL.
NETWORKDAYS.INTL (*start_date*,*end_date*, *weekend*, *holidays*)	Returns the number of whole working days between the start date and end date. Added in Excel 2010 to support calendars in which the weekend is a pair of days other than Saturday and Sunday.
NOW ()	Returns the serial number of the current date and time.
SECOND (*serial_number*)	Returns the seconds of a time value. The seconds are given as an integer in the range 0 to 59.
TIME (*hour*,*minute*,*second*)	Returns the decimal number for a particular time. The decimal number returned by TIME is a value ranging from 0 to 0.99999999, representing the times from 0:00:00 (12:00:00 a.m.) to 23:59:59 (11:59:59 p.m.).
TIMEVALUE (*time_text*)	Returns the decimal number of the time represented by a text string. The decimal number is a value ranging from 0 to 0.99999999, representing the times from 0:00:00 (12:00:00 a.m.) to 23:59:59 (11:59:59 p.m.).
TODAY ()	Returns the serial number of the current date. The serial number is the date/time code that Microsoft Excel uses for date and time calculations.
WEEKDAY (*serial_number*,*return_type*)	Returns the day of the week corresponding to a date. The day is given as an integer, ranging from 1 (for Sunday) to 7 (for Saturday), by default.
WEEKNUM (*serial_num*,*return_type*)	Returns a number that indicates where the week falls numerically within a year. See also ISOWEEKNUM.
WORKDAY (*start_date*,*days*,*holidays*)	Returns a number that represents a date that is the indicated number of working days before or after a date (the starting date). Working days exclude weekends and any dates identified as holidays. You use WORKDAY to exclude weekends and holidays when you calculate invoice due dates, expected delivery times, or the number of days of work performed. To view the number as a date, format the cell as a date. Weekends are defined as Saturday and Sunday. For alternative calendars, see WORKDAY.INTL.

Function	Description
WORKDAY.INTL (*start_date,days, weekend,holidays*)	Returns a number that represents a date that is the indicated number of working days before or after a starting date. Added to Excel 2010 to accommodate calendar systems where the weekend is a pair of days other than Saturday and Sunday.
YEAR (*serial_number*)	Returns the year corresponding to a date. The year is returned as an integer in the range 1900 through 9999.
YEARFRAC (*start_date,end_ date,basis*)	Calculates the fraction of the year represented by the number of whole days between two dates (*start_date* and *end_date*). You use the YEARFRAC worksheet function to identify the proportion of a whole year's benefits or obligations to assign to a specific term.

Table 11.3 provides an alphabetical list of all of Excel 2013's text functions. Detailed examples of these functions are provided later in this chapter.

Table 11.3 Alphabetical List of Text Functions

Function	Description
ASC (*text*)	Changes full-width (double-byte) English letters or katakana within a character string to half-width (single-byte) characters.
BAHTTEXT (*number*)	Converts a number to Thai text and adds the suffix Baht.
CHAR (*number*)	Returns the character specified by *number*. You use CHAR to translate code page numbers you might get from files on other types of computers into characters. See also UNICHAR.
CLEAN (*text*)	Removes all nonprintable characters from text. You use CLEAN on text imported from other applications that contains characters that might not print with your operating system. For example, you can use CLEAN to remove some low-level computer code that appears frequently at the beginning and end of data files and cannot be printed.
CODE (*text*)	Returns a numeric code for the first character in a text string. The returned code corresponds to the character set used by your computer. See also UNICODE.
CONCATENATE (*text1,text2,...*)	Joins several text strings into one text string.
DOLLAR (*number,decimals*)	Converts a number to text using currency format, with the decimals rounded to the specified place. The format used is $#,##0.00_);($#,##0.00).

Function	Description
EXACT (*text1,text2*)	Compares two text strings and returns TRUE if they are the same and FALSE otherwise. EXACT is case-sensitive but ignores formatting differences. You use EXACT to test text being entered into a document.
FIND (*find_text,within_text, start_num*)	Finds one text string (*find_text*) within another text string (*within_text*) and returns the number of the starting position of *find_text*, from the first character of *within_text*. You can also use SEARCH to find one text string within another, but unlike SEARCH, FIND is case-sensitive and doesn't allow wildcard characters.
FINDB (*find_text,within_ text,start_num*)	Finds one text string (*find_text*) within another text string (*within_text*) and returns the number of the starting position of *find_text*, based on the number of bytes each character uses, from the first character of *within_text*. You use FINDB with double-byte characters. You can also use SEARCHB to find one text string within another.
FIXED (*number,decimals,no_ commas*)	Rounds a number to the specified number of decimals, formats the number in decimal format using a period and commas, and returns the result as text.
JIS (*text*)	Changes half-width (single-byte) English letters or katakana within a character string to full-width (double-byte) characters.
LEFT (*text,num_chars*)	Returns the first character or characters in a text string, based on the number of characters specified.
LEFTB (*text,num_bytes*)	Returns the first character or characters in a text string, based on the number of bytes specified. You use LEFTB with double-byte characters.
LEN (*text*)	Returns the number of characters in a text string.
LENB (*text*)	Returns the number of bytes used to represent the characters in a text string. You use LENB with double-byte characters.
LOWER (*text*)	Converts all uppercase letters in a text string to lowercase.
MID (*text,start_num,num_chars*)	Returns a specific number of characters from a text string, starting at the position specified, based on the number of characters specified.
MIDB (*text,start_num,num_bytes*)	Returns a specific number of characters from a text string, starting at the position specified, based on the number of bytes specified. You use MIDB with double-byte characters.

Function	Description
NUMBERVALUE (*text*, *[decimal_ separator]*, *[group_separator]*)	Converts text to a number, allowing for different punctuation for thousands separators and decimal separators. New in Excel 2013.
PHONETIC (*reference*)	Extracts the phonetic (furigana) characters from a text string. Furigana are a Japanese reading aid. They consist of smaller kana printed next to a kanji to indicate its pronunciation.
PROPER (*text*)	Capitalizes the first letter in a text string and any other letters in text that follow any character other than a letter. Converts all other letters to lowercase.
REPLACE (*old_text*,*start_num*, *num_chars*,*new_text*)	Replaces part of a text string, based on the number of characters specified, with a different text string.
REPLACEB (*old_text*,*start_ num*,*num_bytes*,*new_text*)	Replaces part of a text string, based on the number of bytes specified, with a different text string. You use REPLACEB with double-byte characters.
REPT (*text*,*number_times*)	Repeats text a given number of times. You use REPT to fill a cell with a number of instances of a text string.
RIGHT (*text*,*num_chars*)	Returns the last character or characters in a text string, based on the number of characters specified.
RIGHTB (*text*,*num_bytes*)	Returns the last character or characters in a text string, based on the number of bytes specified. You use RIGHTB with double-byte characters.
SEARCH (*find_text*,*within_text*, *start_num*)	Returns the number of the character at which a specific character or text string is first found, beginning with *start_num*. You use SEARCH to determine the location of a character or text string within another text string so that you can use the MID or REPLACE function to change the text.
SEARCHB (*find_text*,*within_text*, *start_num*)	Finds one text string (*find_text*) within another text string (*within_text*) and returns the number of the starting position of *find_text*. The result is based on the number of bytes each character uses, beginning with *start_num*. You use SEARCHB with double-byte characters. You can also use FINDB to find one text string within another.
SUBSTITUTE (*text*,*old_text*,*new_ text*,*instance_num*)	Substitutes *new_text* for *old_text* in a text string. You use SUBSTITUTE when you want to replace specific text in a text string; you use REPLACE when you want to replace any text that occurs in a specific location in a text string.
T (*value*)	Returns the text referred to by *value*.
TEXT (*value*,*format_text*)	Converts a value to text in a specific number format.

Function	Description
TRIM (*text*)	Removes all spaces from text except for single spaces between words. You use TRIM on text that you have received from another application that might have irregular spacing.
UNICHAR(*number*)	Returns the Unicode character references by the given number. New in Excel 2013.
UNICODE(*text*)	Returns the number (code point) of the first character of the text. New in Excel 2013.
UPPER (*text*)	Converts text to uppercase.
VALUE (*text*)	Converts a text string that represents a number to a number.
YEN (*number,decimals*)	Converts a number to text, using the Japanese yen currency format, with the number rounded to a specified place.

Examples of Math Functions

The most common formula in Excel is a formula to add a column of numbers. In addition to SUM, Excel offers a variety of mathematical functions.

Using SUM to Add Numbers

The SUM function is by far the most commonly used function in Excel. This function can add numbers from one or more ranges of data.

Syntax:

=SUM(*number1,number2,...*)

The SUM function adds all the numbers in a range of cells. The arguments *number1, number2,...* are one to 255 arguments for which you want the total value or sum.

A typical use of this function is =SUM(B4:B12). It is also possible to use =SUM(1,2,3). In the latter example, you cannot specify more than 255 individual values. In the former example, you can specify up to 255 ranges, each of which can include thousands or millions of cells.

In Figure 11.1, cell B25 contains a formula to sum three individual cells: =SUM(B17,B19,B23).

It is unlikely that you will need more than 255 arguments in this function, but if you do, you can group arguments in parentheses. For example, =SUM((A10,A12),(A14,A16)) would count as only two of the 255 allowed arguments.

Figure 11.1

A variety of SUM formulas.

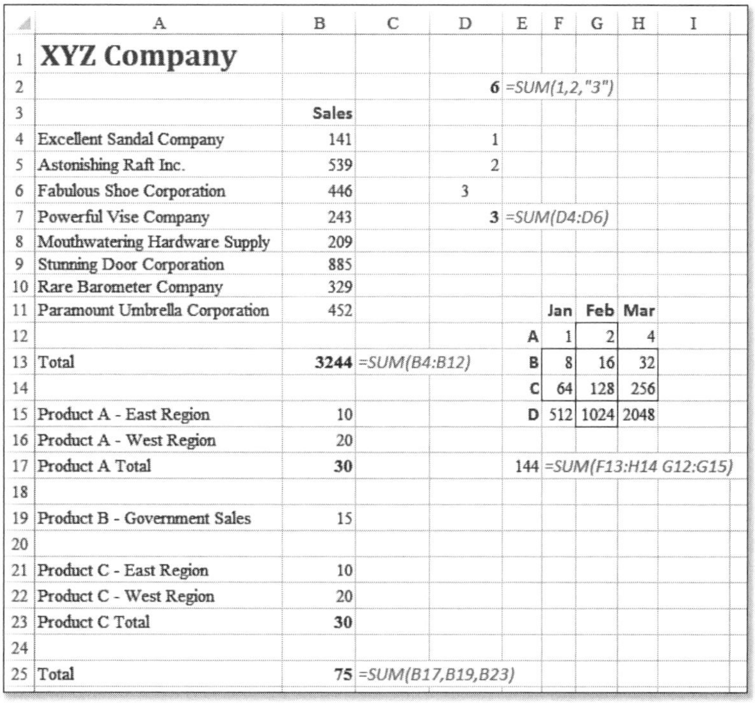

◢	A	B	C	D	E	F	G	H	I
1	**XYZ Company**								
2					6	=SUM(1,2,"3")			
3		**Sales**							
4	Excellent Sandal Company	141		1					
5	Astonishing Raft Inc.	539		2					
6	Fabulous Shoe Corporation	446		3					
7	Powerful Vise Company	243		3	=SUM(D4:D6)				
8	Mouthwatering Hardware Supply	209							
9	Stunning Door Corporation	885							
10	Rare Barometer Company	329							
11	Paramount Umbrella Corporation	452				**Jan**	**Feb**	**Mar**	
12					A	1	2	4	
13	Total	**3244**	=SUM(B4:B12)		B	8	16	32	
14					C	64	128	256	
15	Product A - East Region	10			D	512	1024	2048	
16	Product A - West Region	20							
17	Product A Total	**30**			144	=SUM(F13:H14 G12:G15)			
18									
19	Product B - Government Sales	15							
20									
21	Product C - East Region	10							
22	Product C - West Region	20							
23	Product C Total	**30**							
24									
25	Total	**75**	=SUM(B17,B19,B23)						

If a text value that looks like a number is included in a range, the text value is not included in the result of the sum. Strangely enough, if you specify the text value directly as an argument in the function, Excel adds it to the result. For example, =SUM(1,2,"3") will be 6, yet =SUM(D4:D6) in Figure 11.1 results in 3.

The comma is treated as a union operator. If you replace the comma with a space, Excel finds the cells that fall in the intersection of the selected ranges. In cell E17, the formula of =SUM(F13:H14 G12:G15) adds up the two cells that are in common between the two ranges.

If one cell in a referenced range contains an error, the result of the SUM function is an error. To add numbers while ignoring error cells, use the AGGREGATE function.

It is valid to create a spearing formula. This type of formula adds the identical cell from many worksheets. For example, =SUM(Jan:Dec!B20) adds cell B20 on all 12 sheets between Jan and Dec. If the sheet names contain spaces or other nonalphabetic characters, surround the sheet names with apostrophes: =SUM('Jan 2011:Dec 2011'!B20).

To quickly enter a SUM formula, you can press Alt+= or click the AutoSum icon on the Formulas tab. In Figure 11.2, clicking the AutoSum icon adds totals to the 13 selected blank cells all at once (see Figure 11.3).

AutoSum Button

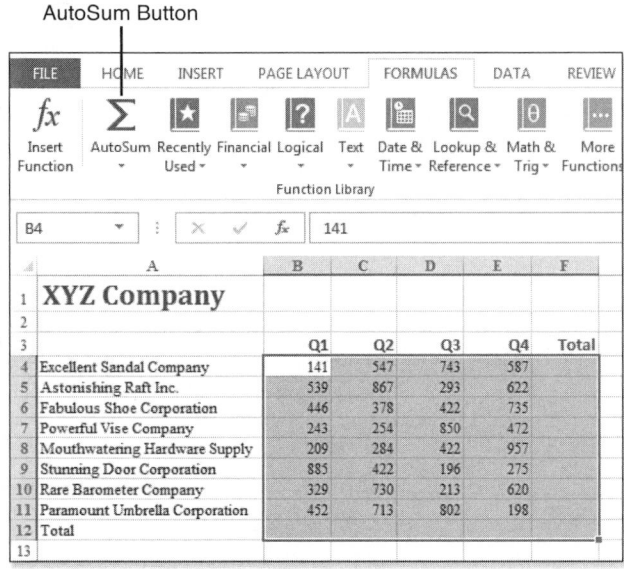

Figure 11.3
After you click AutoSum, the total formulas are automatically entered.

Using AGGREGATE to Ignore Error Cells or Filtered Rows

Added in Excel 2010, the AGGREGATE function lets you perform 17 functions on a range of data while selectively ignoring error cells and/or rows hidden by a filter.

Syntax:

=AGGREGATE(*function_num*, *options*, *array*, [*k*])

The *options* argument is the interesting feature of the new function. You can choose to ignore any, all, or none of these categories:

- Error values

- Hidden rows

- Other SUBTOTAL and AGGREGATE functions

On one hand, the capability to ignore filtered rows and other AGGREGATE functions is similar to the SUBTOTAL function. The capability of AGGREGATE to ignore error values solves a common Excel problem. For most Excel functions, a single #N/A error cell in a range causes most functions to return an #N/A error. The options in AGGREGATE enable you to ignore any error cells in the range.

The *options* argument controls which values are ignored. This is a simple binary system, as follows:

- To ignore other subtotals, add 0. To include subtotals, add 4.

- To ignore hidden rows, add 1.

- To ignore error values, add 2.

- Thus, to ignore other subtotals, hidden rows, and error values, you specify **3 (0+1+2)** as the *options* argument.

- To ignore error values but include other SUBTOTAL values, you specify **5 (1+4)** as the argument.

This calculation works out as shown in Table 11.4.

Table 11.4 Arguments for the AGGREGATE Function

Option	Meaning
0	Ignore other subtotals
1	Ignore hidden rows and subtotals
2	Ignore error cells and subtotals
3	Ignore all three
4	Ignore nothing
5	Ignore hidden rows
6	Ignore error cells
7	Ignore hidden rows and error cells

In Figure 11.4, the #N/A error in cell F13 causes the SUM function in F18 to also return an #N/A. If you use a 2, 3, 5, or 7 as the second argument of AGGREGATE, you can easily sum all the other numbers as in cell F1. You can also use other function numbers to calculate MIN, MAX, COUNT, MEDIAN, MODE, PERCENTILE, and QUARTILE values.

| B20 | ▼ | ⋮ | × | ✓ | f_x | {=AGGREGATE(14,6,(D9:D16)/((B9:B16="East")*(C9:C16="R1")),2)} |

◢	A	B	C	D	E	F	G	H	I	J
1	SUM Ignoring Errors:			255000		4530	=AGGREGATE(9,2,F9:F16)			
2	MIN Ignoring Errors:			1000		10	=AGGREGATE(5,2,F9:F16)			
3	3rd Smallest Ignoring Errors:			4000		80	=AGGREGATE(15,3,F9:F16,3)			
4	Value at 30th Percentile.exc:			4400		72	=AGGREGATE(16,3,F9:F16,0.3)			
5	Value at 30th Percentile.inc:			3400		56	=AGGREGATE(18,3,F9:F16,0.3)			
6	Value at 3rd Quartile:			40000		880	=AGGREGATE(17,3,F9:F16,3)			
7										
8	Customer	Region	Rep	Sales	Rate	Bonus				
9	Astonishing Raft Inc.	West	R3	16000	3%	480				
10	Excellent Sandal Company	East	R1	1000	1%	10				
11	Fabulous Shoe Corporation	East	R2	2000	2%	40				
12	Mouthwatering Hardware Supply	West	R4	64000	4%	2560				
13	Paramount Umbrella Corporation	West	R5	128000	#N/A	#N/A				
14	Powerful Vise Company	West	R4	32000	4%	1280				
15	Rare Barometer Company	East	R1	8000	1%	80				
16	Stunning Door Corporation	East	R2	4000	2%	80				
17										
18	SUM			255000		#N/A	=SUM(F9:F17)			
19										
20	2nd largest East R1 sale:	1000	{=AGGREGATE(14,6,(D9:D16)/((B9:B16="East")*(C9:C16="R1")),2)}							
21										

Figure 11.4
Using a 2 or 3 as the options argument for AGGREGATE allows the function to ignore error cells in a range.

You can also use the function to ignore cells hidden by a filter. Whereas the old SUBTOTAL function enabled you to do this for 11 calculation functions, the AGGREGATE function adds eight new functions to the list.

Table 11.5 shows the 19 functions available in the AGGREGATE function. This list mirrors the 11 functions available in SUBTOTAL (arranged alphabetically to match those in the SUBTOTAL function) and then eight new functions arranged in order of popularity.

Table 11.5   Functions Available in AGGREGATE

Fx #	Function
1	AVERAGE
2	COUNT
3	COUNTA
4	MAX
5	MIN
6	PRODUCT
7	STDDEV.S
8	STDDEV.P
9	SUM
10	VAR.S

Fx #	Function
11	VAR.P
12	MEDIAN
13	MODE.SNGL
14	LARGE
15	SMALL
16	PERCENTILE.INC
17	QUARTILE.INC
18	PERCENTILE.EXC
19	QUARTILE.EXC

The last six functions in this list require you to specify a value for k as the fourth argument. LARGE and SMALL typically return the *k*th largest or smallest value from a list. Use the fourth argument in AGGREGATE to specify the value for k. The last six functions allow for a calculated array instead of a range of cells.

In cell F3 of Figure 11.4, the final argument of 3 specifies that you want the third smallest number in the array. For LARGE, SMALL, and QUARTILE, you should specify an integer for k. For PERCENTILE, specify a decimal between 0 and 1.

When you are trying to return results from the visible rows of a filtered data set, you can use either SUBTOTAL or AGGREGATE. In Figure 11.5, the SUM function in D1 returns the sum of the visible and hidden rows. The SUBTOTAL function in D2 returns the sum of the visible rows, the same as the AGGREGATE function in D3. The advantage of AGGREGATE is that it can return MEDIAN, LARGE, SMALL, PERCENTILE, and QUARTILE on the visible rows as well.

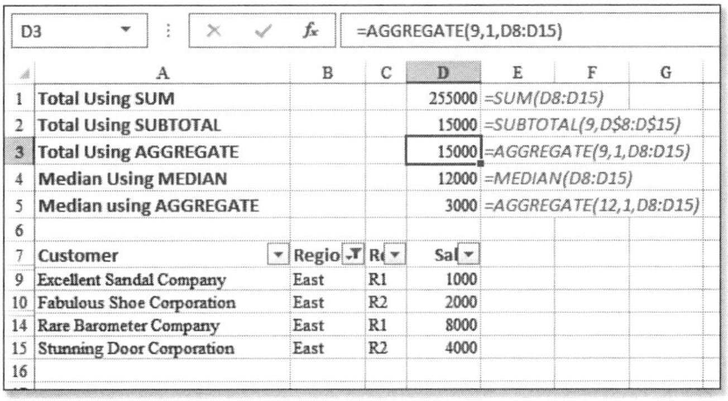

Figure 11.5
AGGREGATE performs calculations on the visible items of a filtered data set.

Tip

Simulating LARGEIFS, PERCENTILEIFS, and QUARTILEIFS

The function arguments of 13 through 19 allow the array to be calculated on the fly. The formula in B20 of Figure 11.4 is a wild, over-the-top formula that seems like it would have come from the *Excel Gurus Gone Wild* book I compiled in 2008.

The goal is to find records that match multiple criteria and then to apply the LARGE function to those matching records. The array argument starts out with the sales amounts in D9:D16. But then the sales amounts are divided by a Boolean expression.

(B9:B16="East") checks to see whether the record is in the East region. (C9:C16) checks to see whether the rep is R1. When you multiply these two conditions together, you get an array of ones and zeros. The 1 indicates both conditions are TRUE. In the figure, the result would be {0;1;0;0;0;0;1;0}.

When the formula evaluates the sales amounts divided by the array of ones and zeros, you either end up with the sales amount or a division-by-zero error. In the figure, the result of 16000 divided by 0 is #DIV/0!. The result of 1000 divided by 1 is 1000, and so on. The array contains mostly #DIV/0! errors and a few actual numbers. Because the AGGREGATE function has an option to ignore error values, the result is that the function simulates doing LARGE with multiple conditions.

Using COUNT or COUNTA to Count Numbers or Nonblank Cells

A number of functions process nonblank cells. =COUNT counts all the numeric or date cells in a range. =COUNTA counts all the non-blank cells in a range.

 **Caution**

You can find COUNT and COUNTA in the Statistical drop-down under the More Functions icon of the Formulas tab.

Syntax:

=COUNT(*value1*,*value2*,...)

The COUNT function counts the number of cells that contain numbers and also numbers within the list of arguments. You use COUNT to get the number of numeric entries in a range or array.

The arguments *value1*, *value2*,... are one to 255 arguments that can contain or refer to a variety of types of data, but only numbers are counted.

Note that whereas a single error cell in a range causes the SUM function to return an error, the same condition is ignored in the COUNT function.

=COUNT(1,2,"3") results in the text entry being counted. If you refer to a range that contains text that looks like a number, the text is not included in the count. To include text cells in the count, use COUNTA.

Syntax:

=COUNTA(*value1*,*value2*,...)

COUNTA counts the number of cells that are not empty and the values within the list of arguments. You use COUNTA to count the number of cells that contain data in a range or an array.

The arguments *value1*, *value2*,... are one to 255 arguments representing the values you want to count. In this case, a value is any type of information, including empty text (" ") but not including empty cells. If an argument is an array or a reference, empty cells within the array or reference are ignored. If you do not need to count logical values, text, or error values, you should use the COUNT function.

Note that error cells are included in the results from COUNTA.

Caution

Using more than 30 arguments in COUNT or COUNTA causes backward compatibility problems with Excel 2003 and earlier.

Choosing Between COUNT and COUNTA

The key to choosing between COUNT and COUNTA is to analyze the data you want to count. In Figure 11.6, someone has used the letter *X* in column B to indicate that training has been started. In this case, you would use COUNTA to get an accurate count. Column C contains dates (which are treated as numeric). In column C, either COUNT or COUNTA returns the correct result. Column D has a mix of text and numeric entries. If you want to count how many people took the test, use COUNTA. If you want to count how many people received a numeric score, use COUNT.

Figure 11.6
Whether you use COUNT or COUNTA depends on whether your data is numeric. COUNT counts only dates and numeric entries. COUNTA counts anything that is nonblank.

	A	B	C	D
				D18 ▾ : ✕ ✓ *fx* =COUNTA(D2:D15)

	A	B Training Started	C Training Completed	D Test Score
1	NAME			
2	TERRY LEBLANC			
3	LUIS CHRISTENSEN	X	3/1/2015	97
4	JENNIFER GALLOWAY	X		
5	ROSEMARY ATKINS	X	3/15/2011	85
6	GLORIA DUNLAP	X		
7	PATSY WARD			
8	CLAIRE RUSH	X	3/7/2015	Incomplete
9	MARIE HOFFMAN	X		
10	JEANNE CLEMONS			
11	MARJORIE LOPEZ	X	3/5/2015	92
12	JACOB INGRAM	X		
13	EDWARD HOOD			
14	MARTIN HAYES	X	3/9/2015	45
15	CHARLENE BURKE	X		
16				
17	COUNT:	0	5	4
18	COUNTA:	10	5	5
19				

Using ROUND, ROUNDDOWN, ROUNDUP, INT, TRUNC, FLOOR, FLOOR.MATH, CEILING, CEILING.MATH, EVEN, ODD, or MROUND to Remove Decimals or Round Numbers

You can use a variety of functions—including ROUND, ROUNDDOWN, ROUNDUP, INT, TRUNC, FLOOR, FLOOR.MATH, CEILING, CEILING.MATH, EVEN, ODD, and MROUND—to round a result or to remove decimals from a result.

Syntax:

=TRUNC(*number*)
=INT(*number*)
=EVEN(*number*)
=ODD(*number*)

The TRUNC, INT, EVEN, and ODD functions always change a number to an integer. The syntax in each case is similar: The function accepts a single number or a single cell containing a number.

To remove the decimals from a result, use the =TRUNC function. This truncates a number to the integer portion of the number. For example, =TRUNC(1.9) is 1, and =TRUNC(-1.9) is –1.

To remove the decimals from a result and always round down to the next lowest integer, use =INT. For positive numbers, TRUNC and INT return identical values. A subtle difference exists between TRUNC and INT. When you have a negative number, INT rounds away from zero to produce the next lowest integer. Thus, =INT(-1.1) is –2.

EVEN rounds a number away from zero to the next even integer. For example, =EVEN(3) is 4, and =EVEN(-3) is –4. If the number is already an even integer, no adjustment is made; for example, =EVEN(6) is 6. This function is ideal for ordering products packed two to a case.

ODD rounds a number away from zero to the next odd integer. For example, =ODD(1.1) is 3, and =ODD(-3.1) is –5. If the number is already an odd integer, no adjustment is made.

Figure 11.7 compares the results of TRUNC, INT, EVEN, and ODD.

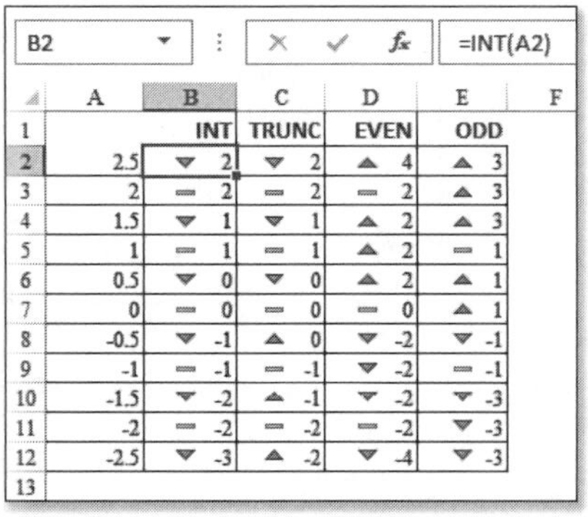

B2 =INT(A2)

	A	B	C	D	E
1		INT	TRUNC	EVEN	ODD
2	2.5	2	2	4	3
3	2	2	2	2	3
4	1.5	1	1	2	3
5	1	1	1	2	1
6	0.5	0	0	2	1
7	0	0	0	0	1
8	-0.5	-1	0	-2	-1
9	-1	-1	-1	-2	-1
10	-1.5	-2	-1	-2	-3
11	-2	-2	-2	-2	-3
12	-2.5	-3	-2	-4	-3
13					

Figure 11.7
TRUNC and INT are nearly identical, except when the numbers become negative.

Syntax:

```
=ROUND(number,num_digits)
=ROUNDUP(number,num_digits)
=ROUNDDOWN(number,num_digits)
```

Three more functions—ROUND, ROUNDUP, and ROUNDDOWN—round a number to a specified number of decimal places. They all take the following arguments:

- **number**—This is the number you want to round.

- **num_digits**—This specifies the number of digits to which you want to round *number*.

With ROUND, if the number of digits is zero, the number is rounded to the nearest integer, following these rules:

- Values up to 0.4999999 are rounded toward zero. For example, ROUND(1.49999,0) results in 1, and ROUND(-1.49999,0) results in –1.

- Values of 0.5 and above are rounded away from zero. For example, ROUND(1.5,0) results in 2, and ROUND(-1.5,0) results in –2.

If *num_digits* is positive, the number is rounded to have the specified number of decimal places. Use 2 for *num_digits* to round to dollars and cents. If the number of digits is negative, the number is rounded to the left of the decimal point. For example, ROUND(117,-1) is rounded to the nearest 10, or a value of 120.

To override the rounding rules, you can use ROUNDDOWN or ROUNDUP:

- The ROUNDDOWN function always rounds toward zero. For example, =ROUNDDOWN(1.999,0) rounds to 1, and =ROUNDDOWN(-19.999,0) rounds to –19. You might use this function when judging a contest in which if the entrant does not completely finish a task, he or she does not get credit for the unfinished portion of the task.

- The result of the ROUNDUP function always rounds away from zero. For example, =ROUNDUP(1.01,0) rounds up to 2, and =ROUNDUP(-1.01,0) rounds to –2. You might use this function when calculating prices because if the customer uses any fractional portion of a product, he or she is charged for the complete product.

Figure 11.8 compares ROUND, ROUNDUP, and ROUNDDOWN.

 **Note**

Using a negative number for the number of digits provides an interesting result. If you need to round a number to the nearest thousand, you can indicate that it should be rounded to –3 decimal places. For example, ROUND(1,234,567,-3) would be 1,235,000.

	A	B	C	D	E
1	Number	# Digits	Round	Round Up	Round Down
2	314159.265359	5	314159.265360	314159.265360	314159.265350
3	314159.265359	4	314159.265400	314159.265400	314159.265300
4	314159.265359	3	314159.265	314159.266	314159.265
5	314159.265359	2	314159.27	314159.27	314159.26
6	314159.265359	1	314159.3	314159.3	314159.2
7	314159.265359	0	314159	314160	314159
8	314159.265359	-1	314160	314160	314150
9	314159.265359	-2	314200	314200	314100
10	314159.265359	-3	314000	315000	314000
11	314159.265359	-4	310000	320000	310000
12	314159.265359	-5	300000	400000	300000
13	1.500000	0	2	2	1
14	-1.500000	0	-2	-2	-1
15	1.490000	0	1	2	1
16	-1.490000	0	-1	-2	-1
17					

Figure 11.8
These three functions always round to a power of 10.

 Caution

If you remember how they taught you to round in school, you know the rule that numbers ending in 0.5 should always round up. The Excel developers must have sat through the same curriculum as you and I did, because they implemented rounding in this manner.

However, if you have a large amount of data points that end in 0.5, you will introduce a fair amount of error in the data by using the method that we learned in school. In Figure 11.9, a million data points end with a single decimal place. Comparing the total of the points and the total of the ROUND of the data points shows a delta of nine hundredths of a percent. In this example, the rounded values total to $52,077 more than the original values.

A set of rules known as *Bankers' Rounding* or *ASTM E29 Rounding* prescribes that values ending in 0.5 should always be rounded to the nearest even integer. Thus, 1.5 would round up to 2 and 2.5 would round down to 2. Column D of Figure 11.9 contrasts the Bankers' Rounding method with the regular rounding method. This formula produces a result that is 91 times more accurate for this data set. The rounded values in column D are within 9.9 ten-thousandths of a percent for a total error of only $572 over the million rows of data.

| D6 | ▼ | : | ✕ | ✓ | *fx* | =IF(MOD(B6,1)=0.5,MROUND(B6,2),ROUND(B6,0)) |

	A	B	C	D	E	F	G
1	Total	57,639,716.20	57,691,794.00	57,639,144.00			
2	Difference		52077.8	-572.2			
3	Diff %		0.09035%	-0.00099%			
4							
5		Random		ROUND	Round to Even		
6			40.2	40	40		
7			40.6	41	41		
8			45.5	46	46		
9			89.5	90	90		
10			46.5	47	46		
11			89.5	90	90		
12			40.5	41	40		

Figure 11.9
ROUND skews your data.

Syntax:

=MROUND(*number*,*multiple*)
=CEILING(*number*,*significance*)
=CEILING.MATH(*number*,*[significance]*)
=FLOOR(*number*,*significance*)
=FLOOR.MATH(*number*,*[significance]*)

The last five functions in this group—MROUND, CEILING, CEILING.MATH, FLOOR, and FLOOR.MATH—round a number to a certain multiple. They require you to enter the number and the multiple to which to round. They all take the following arguments:

- ***number***—This is the number you want to round.
- ***multiple*** or ***significance***—This is the nearest multiple that you want to round toward. Note that if *number* is negative, *multiple* or *significance* must also be negative.

Suppose that you handle pricing for a line of products. Your general rule is to mark up the product cost, which results in a series of strange prices, such as $185.9375, as shown in Figure 11.10. To round each price to the nearest increment of $5, you use =MROUND(C2,5). You could also use MROUND to round to the nearest quarter: =MROUND(C2,0.25).

Figure 11.10
MROUND rounds a price to a certain multiple. Here, column D is the calculated prices rounded to the nearest $5.

D2 =MROUND(C2,5)

	A	B	C	D	E	F
1	SKU	COST	LIST	PRICE		
2	D194	87.81	185.9375	185		
3	A274	14.94	34.125	35		
4	B274	21.31	47.39583	45		
5	A164	12.75	29.5625	30		
6	F229	86.55	183.3125	185		
7	A150	24.14	53.29167	55		
8	A153	68.54	145.7917	145		
9	D298	77.5	164.4583	165		
10	F294	60.15	128.3125	130		
11	A159	85.24	180.5833	180		
12	F179	49.4	105.9167	105		
13	F307	18.74	42.04167	40		
14	C140	89.01	188.4375	190		

The *multiple* argument in MROUND is allowed to be negative.

In other situations, you might want to round a number up to a certain multiple. Figure 11.11 shows a requisition list. Column A shows the quantity needed, and column B shows the item. The purchasing agent discovered a vendor who offers a significant discount, but only if you buy in complete case quantities. Column C shows the size of the case for each product. To calculate the total number to order, you need to round a number in column A up to the nearest multiple of the case size found in column C. You use =CEILING(A4,C4) to achieve this effect.

CEILING rounds away from zero. If you use =CEILING(-9,-6), the function rounds –9 to –12.

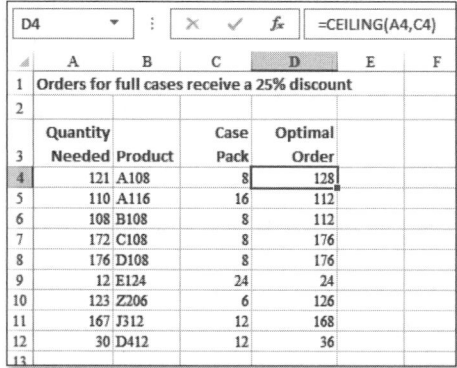

Figure 11.11
CEILING rounds a number up to the next multiple.

The ISO standard for calculating CEILING disagrees with Excel's calculation of CEILING for negative numbers. In Excel, CEILING(-2.5,-1) would round the –2.5 to a lower number of –3. The ISO standard says that CEILING should always round up. If you are at –2.5, the next higher value is actually –2.

Excel 2010 introduced the new CEILING.PRECISE function and Excel 2013 renamed this to CEILING.MATH. Here are the differences between CEILING and CEILING.MATH:

- The *significance* argument is optional in CEILING.MATH. When omitted, the significance is assumed to be 1.

- CEILING.MATH(-2.5) rounds up to –2 instead of –3.

- In Excel 2007, the *number* and *significance* had to have the same sign. Previously, =CEILING(-2,1) or =CEILING(2,-1) would have evaluated to a #NUM error. Starting in Excel 2010, either =CEILING.MATH(-2.5,1) or =CEILING.MATH(2.5,-1) calculates without a problem. Excel 2013 still calculates =CEILING(2.5,-1) as a #NUM! error. However, strangely, =CEILING(-2.5,1) no longer returns #NUM!. Excel 2013 returns –2, which is more like the CEILING.PRECISE result.

Caution

You should watch for one strange behavior with MROUND, FLOOR, and CEILING. If the number is negative, you must ensure that the second argument for the function is also negative. Certainly, in some situations you won't know in advance whether your numbers will be negative. If you think that your numbers might be a mix of positive and negative values, you should use =MROUND(C2,5*SIGN(C2)). This ensures that the second parameter matches the sign of the first parameter.

Figure 11.12 contrasts CEILING and CEILING.MATH.

The FLOOR function rounds a number to the next lowest multiple. Suppose that you employ several student workers who do piecework. They assemble products and then pack them six to a case. Your contract with the workers states that you pay only for complete cases. Column B in Figure 11.13 shows the total number of units assembled. You use =FLOOR(B6,6) to round this quantity down to the nearest multiple of six. Note that if the value is already a multiple of six, as in cell B10, FLOOR does not change the number.

Figure 11.12
For negative numbers, ISO.CEILING rounds toward zero.

C16 =CEILING.MATH(A16)

	A	B	C	D
1	**CEILING EXAMPLES**			
2				
3	Number	Sig.	Result	
4	2.5	1	3	*=CEILING(A4,B4)*
5	-2.5	-1	-3	*Rounds away from zero*
6	2.5	-1	#NUM!	*Invalid, signs don't match*
7	-2.5	1	-2	*Would have been #NUM! in 2007*
8				
9	**CEILING.MATH EXAMPLES**			
10				
11	Number	Sig.	Result	
12	2.5	1	3	*=CEILING.MATH(A12,B12)*
13	-2.5	-1	-2	*Rounds up*
14	2.5	-1	3	*Signs don't match, no problem*
15	-2.5	1	-2	*Signs don't match, no problem*
16	2.5		3	*=CEILING.MATH(A16)*
17	-2.5		-2	*Significance assumed to be 1*
18				

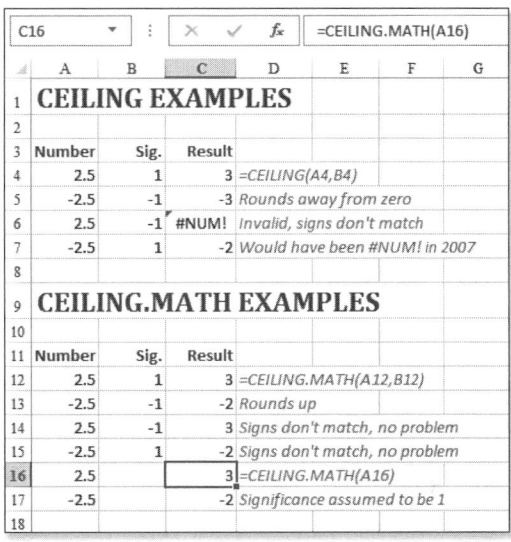

Figure 11.13
FLOOR rounds a number down to the next multiple.

D6 =FLOOR(B6,C6)

	A	B	C	D
1	**Piece Work Supply**			
2	**Productivity Report**			
3	**Workers are Paid for Complete Cases only**			
4				
5	NAME	Quantity Complete	Per Case	Complete Case Quantity
6	LAURIE	846	6	846
7	JOE	658	6	654
8	BRUCE	1186	6	1182
9	MELVIN	968	6	966
10	OLIVIA	942	6	942
11	RODNEY	782	6	780
12				
13				
14		-2	*=FLOOR(-2.5,-1)*	
15		-3	*=FLOOR.MATH(-2.5,1)*	
16				

Similar to the problems with CEILING, the scientific community does not agree that FLOOR should round toward zero for negative numbers. In cell B14 of Figure 11.13, the FLOOR of –2.5 actually rounds up to –2 instead of down to –3. You can use FLOOR.MATH to match the ISO standard. As shown in B15, the FLOOR.MATH of –2.5 is –3.

All the functions for rounding can be replaced with a clever combination of INT and ROUND functions. If you receive a spreadsheet from an old-time Lotus 1-2-3 user, you might see formulas like the ones in Figure 11.14:

- Cell B13 is equivalent to using MROUND with a multiple of 20. The formula divides 135 by 20, giving 6.75. ROUND rounds this to 7. Finally, outside the parentheses, the formula multiplies by 20 to arrive at the answer of 140.
- Cell C13 is equivalent to using FLOOR with a significance of 20. The formula divides 135 by 20, giving 6.75. The INT removes the decimal places, leaving the integer 6. The formula then multiplies this result by 20 to arrive at 120.
- Cell D13 is equivalent to using CEILING with a significance of 20. The formula divides 135 by 20, giving 6.75. Next, the formula adds just less than 0.5 to make sure that any value greater than 6 is rounded up to 7. Finally, the result is multiplied by 20 to arrive at 140.

D13 | =ROUND((A13/20)+0.49999,0)*20

	A	B	C	D	E	F	G	H	I	J
1		Nearest 20	Prev 20	Next 20						
2	348	340	340	360						
3	780	780	780	780						
4	82	80	80	100						
5	480	480	480	480						
6	644	640	640	660						
7	300	300	300	300						
8	630	640	620	640						
9	454	460	440	460						
10	658	660	640	660						
11	521	520	520	540						
12	87	80	80	100						
13	135	140	120	140						
14	**B13:**	=ROUND((A13/20),0)*20								
15		**C13:**	=INT(A13/20)*20							
16			**D13:**	=ROUND((A13/20)+0.49999,0)*20						

Figure 11.14
A combination of ROUND and INT can replace any of the eight other functions used for rounding.

In Excel 2003 and earlier, functions such as MROUND were not part of the core Excel. They were enabled when someone installed the Analysis Toolpack. Because new Excel users might never have installed the Analysis Toolpack, some people avoided using MROUND and instead wrote the formulas as shown in Figure 11.14. Now that Microsoft has elevated all the Analysis Toolpack functions to be part of the core Excel product, it is safe to use those functions.

Using SUBTOTAL Instead of SUM with Multiple Levels of Totals

Consider the data set shown in Figure 11.15. This report shows a list of invoices for each customer. Someone has manually inserted rows and used the SUM function to total each customer. Cells C5, C10, C15, and so on contain a SUM function.

Figure 11.15
Whoever manually summed these rows doesn't know about the Subtotal command on the Data tab.

	A	B	C	D
			C5 fx =SUM(C2:C4)	
1	Customer	Invoice	Revenue	
2	Amazing Flagpole Corporation	1158	114.93	
3	Amazing Flagpole Corporation	1127	622.12	
4	Amazing Flagpole Corporation	1118	736.38	
5	Amazing Flagpole Corporation	Total	1473.43	
6				
7	Brilliant Washer Partners	1139	430.33	
8	Brilliant Washer Partners	1129	614.59	
9	Brilliant Washer Partners	1146	346.09	
10	Brilliant Washer Partners	Total	1391.01	
11				

It would be very difficult to enter a grand total at the bottom of this data set. You might have to enter a long formula that points only at the summary rows. In this particular case, the formula to provide a grand total for 15 customers would be possible, as shown in Figure 11.16. If you had 500 customers, however, the formula would be nearly impossible to enter.

Figure 11.16
It is difficult to enter the grand total formula.

	A	B	C	D	E	F	G	H	I	J
	C77 fx =C5+C10+C15+C20+C25+C30+C35+C40+C45+C50+C55+C60+C65+C70+C75									
1	Customer	Invoice	Revenue							
70	Supreme Washer Supply	Total	1533.86							
71										
72	Well-Suited Utensil Corporation	1120	709.41							
73	Well-Suited Utensil Corporation	1153	224.07							
74	Well-Suited Utensil Corporation	1122	690.03							
75	Well-Suited Utensil Corporation	Total	1623.51							
76										
77	GRAND TOTAL		20598.01							
78										
79										

Many accountants can teach you the old accounting trick whereby you total the entire column and divide by two to get the grand total. This is based on the assumption that every dollar is in the column twice: once on the detail row and once on the summary row. As shown in Figure 11.17, this trick does work, but it is hard to explain to your manager why it works.

The solution is to use the SUBTOTAL function. This powerful function has been around since Excel 97.

 Tip

The best way to insert the SUBTOTAL function is to use the Subtotals icon on the Data tab. However, you can set up these functions manually.

➡ **See** Chapter 22, "Using Automatic Subtotals," for more information about working with subtotals.

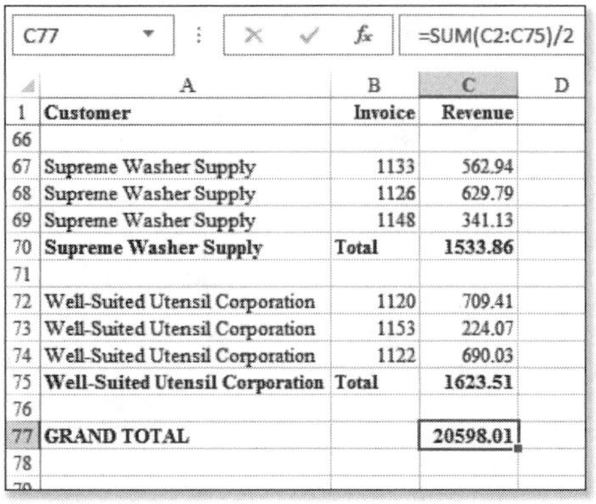

Figure 11.17
The old accounting trick of adding an entire column and dividing by two works but is hard to explain.

Syntax:

=SUBTOTAL(*function_num,ref1,ref2,...*)

In its default use, SUBTOTAL works just like the SUM function, except it throws out other instances of the SUBTOTAL function within the range being summed. The SUBTOTAL function takes the following arguments:

- **_function_num_**—This is a number from 1 to 11. The most common function number is the number 9, which (for no apparent logical reason) is used to sum. When Microsoft introduced the SUBTOTAL function, it offered 11 options: AVERAGE, COUNT, COUNTA, MAX, MIN, PRODUCT, STDEV, STDEVP, SUM, VAR, and VARP. It just happens that SUM is the ninth item in this list when these functions are arranged alphabetically in the English language, so 9 became the function number for SUM. Although SUBTOTAL always ignores rows hidden as the result of a filter, it does not automatically ignore rows hidden with the HIDE command. To ignore rows that have been manually hidden, add 100 to the *function_num*.

- **_ref1,ref2,..._**—These are up to 254 ranges or references that you want to subtotal. Unlike with SUM, the references in a SUBTOTAL function cannot be 3-D references.

Any other nested subtotals in the range are ignored to prevent double counting.

The SUBTOTAL function always ignores rows hidden as the result of a filter. This makes the SUBTOTAL function great in combination with filter, as you'll see later in this chapter, in Figure 11.19.

A feature added in Excel 2002 is that you can add 100 to the function number to prevent Excel from including rows hidden by using the Hide command. Note that this functionality works only with hidden rows. If you hide columns and attempt to subtotal in a horizontal fashion, the hidden columns are not ignored.

The arguments for SUBTOTAL are shown in Table 11.6.

Table 11.6   Function Arguments for SUBTOTAL

function_num (Includes Hidden Values)	function_num (Ignores Hidden Values)	Function
1	101	AVERAGE
2	102	COUNT
3	103	COUNTA
4	104	MAX
5	105	MIN
6	106	PRODUCT
7	107	STDEV
8	108	STDEVP
9	109	SUM
10	110	VAR
11	111	VARP

In Figure 11.18, the customer summary rows were built with the SUBTOTAL function, allowing the grand total row to be calculated with the simple formula =SUBTOTAL(9,C2:C76). In contrast, after someone has built manual subtotals using the SUM function, as shown previously in Figure 11.15, the SUBTOTAL function doesn't work. You must replace SUM(with SUBTOTAL(9, to convert the existing subtotal lines to the SUBTOTAL function.

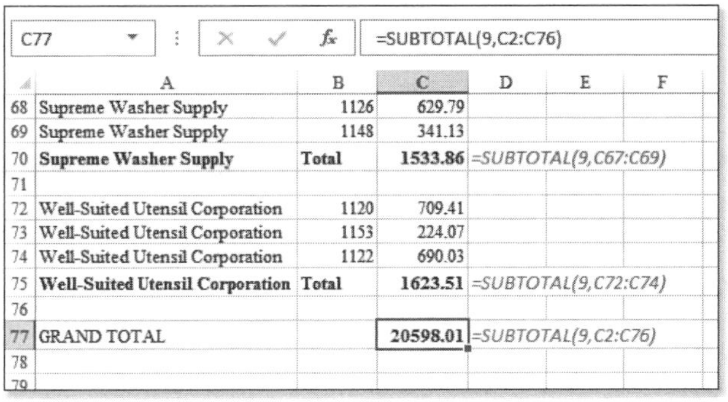

Figure 11.18
When you use SUBTOTAL instead of SUM for the customer totals, the problem of creating a grand total becomes simple.

Using SUBTOTAL Instead of SUM to Ignore Rows Hidden by a Filter

If you are using a filter to query a data set, you can use the SUBTOTAL function instead of the SUM function to show the total of the visible rows. In Figure 11.19, cell E1 contains a SUM function, which totals rows whether they are visible or not. Cell E2 contains a SUBTOTAL function. As you use the AutoFilter drop-downs to show just rows for sales of J730 by Jamie, the SUBTOTAL function updates to reflect the total of the visible rows. This makes the SUBTOTAL function a great tool for ad hoc reporting.

 Note

Although the function in Figure 11.19 uses the function number 109, the Subtotal command always ignores rows hidden as the result of a filter. =SUBTOTAL(9,E5:E5090) would return an identical result when the rows are hidden through a filter, as in this case. If you have rows hidden by the Hide command, you should use 109 to ignore the manually hidden rows.

| E2 | ▼ | ： | × | ✓ | fx | =SUBTOTAL(109,E5:E5090) |

⊿	A	B	C	D	E
1				Total:	1,050,884.39
2				Total Visible:	42,357.13
3					
4	Rep ▼	Produ ▼	Customer ▼	Da ▼	Revenue ▼
5	JAMIE	J730	Magnificent Notebook In	11/14/2015	191.09
61	JAMIE	J730	Stunning Glass Company	4/23/2015	306.50
62	JAMIE	J730	Magnificent Notebook In	8/7/2015	141.73
72	JAMIE	J730	New Vise Company	12/11/2015	155.46
141	JAMIE	J730	Wonderful Thermostat C	10/2/2015	100.31
186	JAMIE	J730	Wonderful Thermostat C	2/5/2015	137.85
230	JAMIE	J730	Magnificent Notebook In	8/17/2015	317.60

Figure 11.19
The SUBTOTAL function in cell E2 ignores rows hidden as the result of a filter.

Using RAND and RANDBETWEEN to Generate Random Numbers and Data

In a number of situations, you might want to generate random numbers. Excel offers two functions to assist with this process: RAND and RANDBETWEEN.

Syntax:

=RAND()

The RAND function returns an evenly distributed random number greater than or equal to 0 and less than 1. A new random number is returned every time the worksheet is calculated.

=RAND() generates a random decimal between 0 and 0.999988425925926. Whether you are a teacher trying to randomly assign the order for book report presentations, or the commissioner of a fantasy football league trying to figure out the draft sequence, =RAND() can help.

If you want to use RAND to generate a random number but don't want the numbers to change every time the cell is calculated, you can enter =RAND() in the formula bar and then press F9 to change the formula to a random number.

To generate a random number greater than or equal to 0 but less than 100, you can use RAND()*100.

To generate a random sequence for a list, you select a blank column next to your data and enter **=RAND()** in the column. Every time you press the F9 key, the column generates a new set of random numbers. You might want to agree up front with the draft participants that you will press F9 three times to randomize the list and then convert the formulas to values. To do so, follow these steps:

1. Enter the heading **Random** in row 1 next to your data.

2. Enter **=RAND()** in cell B2.

3. Move the cell pointer to cell B2 and double-click the fill handle.

4. Turn off automatic calculation by using Formulas, Calculation Options, Manual. This prevents the RAND() functions from recalculating after you sort in step 7.

5. Press the F9 key three times.

6. Choose one cell in column B.

7. From the Data tab, click the AZ button to sort ascending. The new sequence of items in column A is a random sequence (see Figure 11.20).

Figure 11.20
Harriet gets to draft first in this season's fantasy football league, thanks to the RAND function.

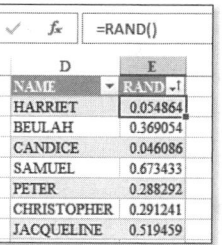

You can also use this technique to select a random subset from a data set. If your manager wants you to contact every 20th customer, you can select all the customers where =RAND() is 0.05 or less.

Syntax:

=RANDBETWEEN(*bottom*,*top*)

Whereas =RAND() returns a random decimal, =RANDBETWEEN generates an integer between two integers.

The RANDBETWEEN function returns a random integer between the numbers you specify. A new random number is returned every time the worksheet is calculated. This function takes the following arguments:

- **bottom**—This is the smallest integer RANDBETWEEN can return.

- **top**—This is the largest integer RANDBETWEEN can return.

To generate random numbers between 50 and 59, inclusive, you use =RANDBETWEEN(50,59). RANDBETWEEN is easier to use than =RAND to achieve random integers; with =RAND, you would have to use =INT(RAND()*10)+50 to generate this same range of data.

Even though RANDBETWEEN generates integers, you can use it to generate sales prices or even letters. =RANDBETWEEN(5000,9900)/100 generates random prices between $50.00 and $99.00.

The capital letter *A* is also known as character 65 in the ASCII character set. *B* is 66, *C* is 67, and so on up through *Z*, which is character 90. You can use =CHAR(RANDBETWEEN(65,90)) to generate random capital letters.

Many of the product SKUs in this book were generated using =CHAR(RANDBETWEEN(65,90))&RAND BETWEEN(101,199).

Figure 11.21 shows many examples of RANDBETWEEN.

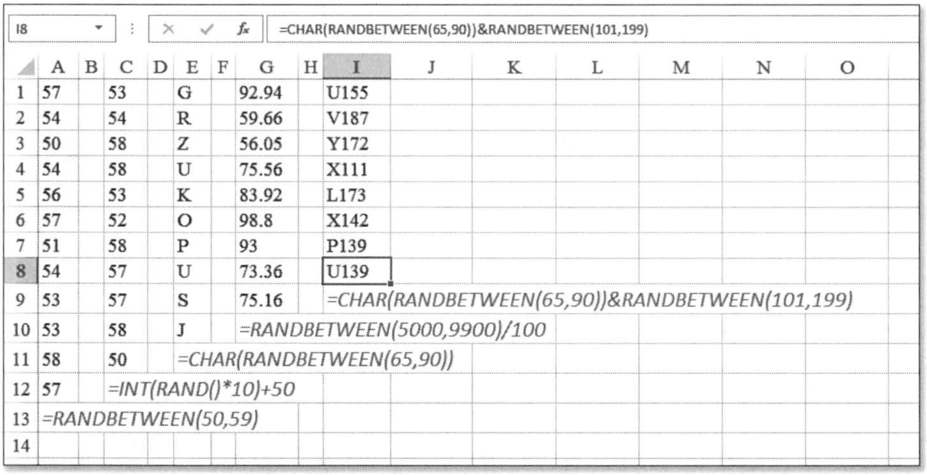

Figure 11.21
RANDBETWEEN can generate integers—and with a little creativity, even prices or letters.

Choosing a Random Item from a List

In Figure 11.22, you want to randomly assign employees to certain projects. The list of projects is in column A. The list of employees is in E2:E6. As shown in Figure 11.22, the function for B2:B11 is =INDEX($E$2:$E$6,RANDBETWEEN(1,5)).

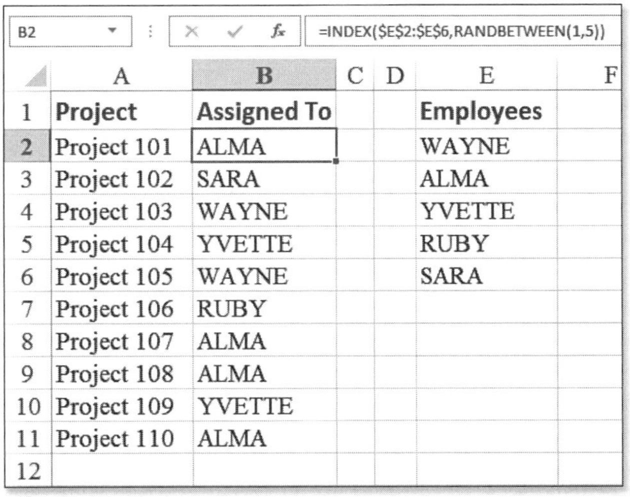

Figure 11.22
I wonder whether Dilbert's pointy-haired boss assigns projects this way.

B2		:	× ✓ *fx*	=INDEX($E$2:$E$6,RANDBETWEEN(1,5))	

	A	B	C	D	E	F
1	Project	Assigned To			Employees	
2	Project 101	ALMA			WAYNE	
3	Project 102	SARA			ALMA	
4	Project 103	WAYNE			YVETTE	
5	Project 104	YVETTE			RUBY	
6	Project 105	WAYNE			SARA	
7	Project 106	RUBY				
8	Project 107	ALMA				
9	Project 108	ALMA				
10	Project 109	YVETTE				
11	Project 110	ALMA				
12						

Using =ROMAN() to Finish Movie Credits and =ARABIC() to Convert Back to Digits

Excel can convert numbers to Roman numerals. If you stay in the theater after a movie until the end of movie credits, you see that the copyright date is always expressed in Roman numerals. If you are the next J.J. Abrams, you can use =ROMAN(2015) or =ROMAN(YEAR(Now())) to generate such a numeral.

Starting in Excel 2013, the =ARABIC() function can convert a Roman numeral back to a regular number. Whereas =ROMAN() only works with the numbers 1 through 3999, the ARABIC function deals with invalid Roman numerals from –255,000 through 255,000. *Leviculus!*

Syntax:

=ROMAN(*number*,*form*)

The ROMAN function converts an Arabic numeral to Roman, as text. The function works with the positive integers from 1 to 3999. This function takes the following arguments:

- *number*—This is the Arabic numeral you want converted.

- *form*—This is a number that specifies the type of Roman numeral you want. The Roman numeral style ranges from Classic to Simplified, becoming more concise as the value of *form* increases.

There are some arcane rules with Roman numerals. In classic Roman numbers, an I before a V is used to indicate the number 4. In classic Roman numbers, it is valid to use an I before a V or an X, but it is not valid to use an I before an L, a C, a D, or an M.

As shown in Figure 11.23, the form argument allows Excel to bend these rules progressively more:

- ROMAN(1999,0) results in MCMXCIX. The M is 1000, the CM is 900, the XC is 90, and the IX is 9; 1000 + 900 + 90 + 9 = 1999.

- ROMAN(1999,1) results in MLMVLIV. The M is 1000, the LM is 950, the VL is 45, and the IV is 4; 1000 + 950 + 45 + 4 = 1999.

- ROMAN(1999,2) results in MXMIX. The M is 1000, the XM is 990, and the IX is 9; 1000 + 990 + 9 = 1999.

- ROMAN(1999,3) results in MVMIV. The M is 1000, the VM is 995, and the IV is 4; 1000 + 995 + 4 = 1999.

- ROMAN(1999,4) results in MIM. The M is 1000 and the IM is 999; 1000 + 999 = 1999.

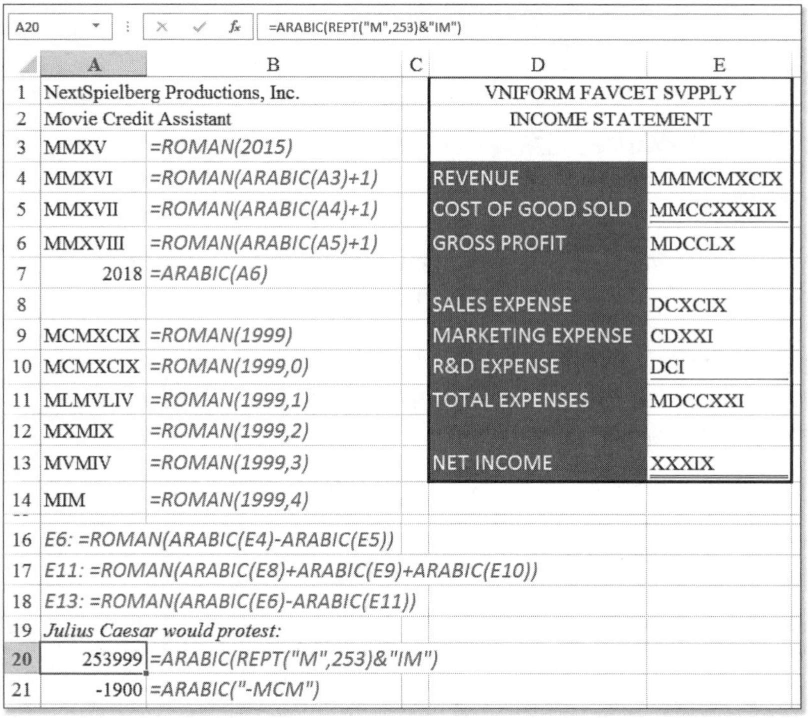

	A20 ▾ : ✕ ✓ *fx*	=ARABIC(REPT("M",253)&"IM")			
	A	B	C	D	E
1	NextSpielberg Productions, Inc.			VNIFORM FAVCET SVPPLY	
2	Movie Credit Assistant			INCOME STATEMENT	
3	MMXV	=ROMAN(2015)			
4	MMXVI	=ROMAN(ARABIC(A3)+1)		REVENUE	MMMCMXCIX
5	MMXVII	=ROMAN(ARABIC(A4)+1)		COST OF GOOD SOLD	MMCCXXXIX
6	MMXVIII	=ROMAN(ARABIC(A5)+1)		GROSS PROFIT	MDCCLX
7	2018	=ARABIC(A6)			
8				SALES EXPENSE	DCXCIX
9	MCMXCIX	=ROMAN(1999)		MARKETING EXPENSE	CDXXI
10	MCMXCIX	=ROMAN(1999,0)		R&D EXPENSE	DCI
11	MLMVLIV	=ROMAN(1999,1)		TOTAL EXPENSES	MDCCXXI
12	MXMIX	=ROMAN(1999,2)			
13	MVMIV	=ROMAN(1999,3)		NET INCOME	XXXIX
14	MIM	=ROMAN(1999,4)			
16	E6: =ROMAN(ARABIC(E4)-ARABIC(E5))				
17	E11: =ROMAN(ARABIC(E8)+ARABIC(E9)+ARABIC(E10))				
18	E13: =ROMAN(ARABIC(E6)-ARABIC(E11))				
19	Julius Caesar would protest:				
20	253999	=ARABIC(REPT("M",253)&"IM")			
21	-1900	=ARABIC("-MCM")			

Figure 11.23
You can create movie credit dates with cell A3 or present bad financial news with D1:E13. Compare the various forms of Roman numerals in A9:A14. Using ARABIC, you can actually do math with Roman numerals.

Syntax:

=ARABIC(*text*)

The ARABIC function converts text that represents a Roman numeral back to a regular number. This function takes one argument: *text* is up to 255 characters using letters I, V, X, L, C, M, and optionally a leading minus sign.

The text can be a Roman numeral in any of the formats in cells A9:A14. Even though you are not allowed to repeat M more than four times in a number, the ARABIC function attempts to convert the text to a number. Use ARABIC on a string of 255 M's and you get 255,000, even though this is against all the rules. Similarly, a minus sign and 254 M's will produce –254000.

 Note

Romans did have a way to represent 5000 and 10000, but the format cannot be typed on a modern keyboard; hence, the programmers behind ARABIC are apparently allowing nonsensical numbers like MMMMMIV.

Figure 11.23 shows various uses (and misuses) of ROMAN and ARABIC. Formulas in E6, E11, and E13 allow you to do math with Roman numerals.

Using ABS() to Figure Out the Magnitude of ERROR

Suppose that you work for a local TV station, and you want to prove that your forecaster is more accurate than those at the other stations in town. The forecaster at the rival station in town is horrible—some days he misses high, and other days he misses low. The rival station uses Figure 11.24 to say that his average forecast is 99% accurate. All those negative and positive errors cancel each other out in the average.

Figure 11.24
ABS measures the size of an error, ignoring the sign.

I4 f_x =ABS(G4-H4)

	A	B	C	D	E	F	G	H	I	J
1	Weather Forecast Accuracy - Action News					Weather Forecast Accuracy Using ABS()				
2										
3	Date	Forecast	Actual	Error		Date	Forecast	Actual	Error	
4	6/1/2015	87	67	20		6/1/2015	87	67	20	
5	6/2/2015	52	72	-20		6/2/2015	52	72	20	
6	6/3/2015	93	73	20		6/3/2015	93	73	20	
7	6/4/2015	55	75	-20		6/4/2015	55	75	20	
8	6/5/2015	94	74	20		6/5/2015	94	74	20	
9	6/6/2015	54	74	-20		6/6/2015	54	74	20	
10	6/7/2015	89	69	20		6/7/2015	89	69	20	
11	6/8/2015	49	69	-20		6/8/2015	49	69	20	
12	6/9/2015	93	73	20		6/9/2015	93	73	20	
13	6/10/2015	48	68	-20		6/10/2015	48	68	20	
14	6/11/2015	88	68	20		6/11/2015	88	68	20	
15	6/12/2015	53	73	-20		6/12/2015	53	73	20	
16	6/13/2015	98	78	20		6/13/2015	98	78	20	
17	6/14/2015	56	76	-20		6/14/2015	56	76	20	
18	6/15/2015	100	80	20		6/15/2015	100	80	20	
19	6/16/2015	62	82	-20		6/16/2015	62	82	20	
20	TOTAL	1171	1171	0		TOTAL	1171	1171	320	
21								=I20/G20	27.3%	
22	*Claim: Our forecast is 100% accurate!*					*Reality: The forecast averages 27% wrong*				
23										

The ABS function measures the size of the error. Positive errors are reported as positive, and negative errors are reported as positive as well. You can use =ABS(A2-B2) to demonstrate that the other station's forecaster is off by 20 degrees on average.

Syntax:

`=ABS(number)`

The ABS function returns the absolute value of a number—that is, the number without its sign. With this function, the argument *number* is the real number for which you want the absolute number.

Using PI to Calculate Cake or Pizza Pricing

How many more ingredients are in a 16-inch pizza than an 8-inch pizza? Be careful—it is not double!

The formula for the area of a circle is π × r2. The radius of a circle is half the diameter. The function =PI() returns the constant for pi. You use =PI()*(B7/2)^2 to calculate the number of square inches in a 16-inch pizza. As shown in Figure 11.25, the 16-inch size contains nearly four times the area of an 8-inch circle.

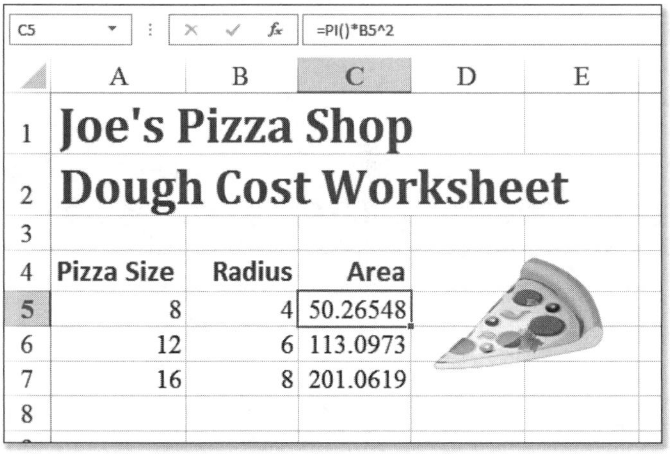

	A	B	C	D	E
1	Joe's Pizza Shop				
2	Dough Cost Worksheet				
3					
4	Pizza Size	Radius	Area		
5	8	4	50.26548		
6	12	6	113.0973		
7	16	8	201.0619		
8					

Figure 11.25
Most pizza shops don't have a dedicated cost accountant.

If your company makes anything round—drink coasters, drum heads, wedding cakes, pizzas, tires, or Frisbees—you want to use =PI() when calculating your product cost.

Syntax:

`=PI()`

The PI function returns the number 3.14159265358979, the mathematical constant, accurate to 15 digits.

Using =COMBIN to Figure Out Lottery Probability

Your office lottery pool might agree to bet $1 on the lottery each week but to double the bet when the jackpot is a higher payout than the odds against winning.

The COMBIN function can figure out the number of combinations for most lottery systems. If you have to correctly select six numbers out of a pool of 48 numbers, you can use =COMBIN(48,6) to find that there are 12.27 million combinations.

Figure 11.26 shows a variety of lottery odds.

> **See** Chapter 14, "Using Statistical Functions," for more information about working with the COMBIN function.

> **Note**
>
> The COMBIN function assumes that you don't care about the sequence of the numbers chosen. If you have to worry about the sequence, you should use =PERMUT. It also assumes that you cannot repe at a choice. Excel 2013 now offers COMBINA to calculate when an item can be selected multiple times.

Figure 11.26
The odds of winning the lottery in a 44-number game are twice as good as in a 50-number game.

	A	B	C	D	E
			fx =COMBIN(B3,A3)		
1	OurCo Lottery Pool (no repeats)				
2	Select	Out of...	Combinations		
3	6	40	3,838,380	:1	
4	6	44	7,059,052	:1	
5	6	46	9,366,819	:1	
6	6	47	10,737,573	:1	
7	6	48	12,271,512	:1	
8	6	50	15,890,700	:1	
9					
10	Combinations of 3 Scoops Ice Cream (repeats OK)				
11	Choc-Vanilla-Choc is the same as Choc-Choc-Vanilla				
12	# Flavors	# Scoops	COMBINA		
13	4	2	10		
14	5	3	35		
15	31	3	5456		

Using COMBINA to Calculate Triple-Dip Ice Cream Bowls

The traditional COMBIN function assumes that an item cannot be chosen twice. After a particular lottery number is drawn from the hopper, it cannot be drawn again in that drawing.

What if you are allowed to repeat a choice? Say that you are ordering three scoops of ice cream. You can choose chocolate, chocolate, chocolate. Or you can choose two chocolate and one peppermint. If you had to choose three scoops from five flavors of ice cream, you might think you have 5 × 5 × 5, or 125 combinations.

However, order does not matter in the ice cream bowl—chocolate, chocolate, peppermint is the same a chocolate, peppermint, chocolate. Microsoft added =COMBINA() to handle this scenario. As shown in C14 of Figure 11.26, there are really only 35 combinations of three scoops of ice cream.

Syntax:

=COMBIN(*number*, *number_chosen*)

Syntax:

=COMBINA(*number*, *number_chosen*)

These functions return the number of combinations for a given number of items. COMBIN assumes repeats are not allowed. COMBINA allows for repeats. These functions require two arguments:

- *number* is the total number of items.

- *number_chosen* is the number of items in each combination.

Using FACT to Calculate the Permutation of a Number

Suppose you have seven slides in a PowerPoint presentation. Furthermore, you want to find the number of unique sequences in which the slides can be arranged; this is called the factorial of seven. You calculated this by using 7 × 6 × 5 × 4 × 3 × 2 × 1. To find the factorial of any positive integer, you use the FACT function.

Syntax:

=FACT(*number*)

The FACT function returns the factorial of a number. The factorial of a number is equal to 1 × 2 × 3 × ... × *number*. *number* is the nonnegative number of which you want the factorial. If *number* is not an integer, it is truncated.

By definition, FACT(0) is 1. To figure out how many different ways you can arrange five people in a line, use =FACT(5).

There is a similar function called FACTDOUBLE. A double factorial multiplies every other number. For even numbers, this is a calculation such as FACTDOUBLE(8) = 8*6*4*2. For odd numbers, the calculation is FACTDOUBLE(9) = 9*7*5*3*1.

Various factorials are shown in Figure 11.27.

 Note

It is difficult to find real-world uses for FACTDOUBLE. MathWorld.com notes some interesting uses for FACTDOUBLE (N) where N is between –1 and –2, but Excel does not calculate FACTDOUBLE for negative numbers. Fans of the poker game Texas Hold 'Em will be delighted to know that FACTDOUBLE is useful in calculating Texas Hold 'Em probabilities. For complete details, look up Poker Probabilities (Texas Hold 'Em) in Wikipedia. Round-robin sporting tournaments can also use FACTDOUBLE.

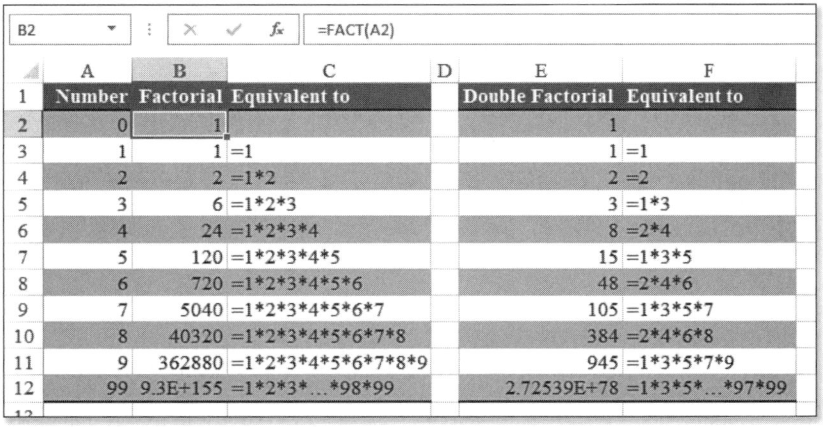

Figure 11.27
Excel calculates the FACT and FACTDOUBLE of various numbers.

B2	▼	:	✕	✓	*fx*	=FACT(A2)			

⊿	A	B	C	D	E	F
1	Number	Factorial	Equivalent to		Double Factorial	Equivalent to
2	0	1			1	
3	1	1	=1		1	=1
4	2	2	=1*2		2	=2
5	3	6	=1*2*3		3	=1*3
6	4	24	=1*2*3*4		8	=2*4
7	5	120	=1*2*3*4*5		15	=1*3*5
8	6	720	=1*2*3*4*5*6		48	=2*4*6
9	7	5040	=1*2*3*4*5*6*7		105	=1*3*5*7
10	8	40320	=1*2*3*4*5*6*7*8		384	=2*4*6*8
11	9	362880	=1*2*3*4*5*6*7*8*9		945	=1*3*5*7*9
12	99	9.3E+155	=1*2*3*...*98*99		2.72539E+78	=1*3*5*...*97*99

Using GCD and LCM to Perform Seventh-Grade Math

My seventh-grade math teacher, Mr. Irwin, taught me about greatest common denominators and least common multiples. For example, the least common multiple of 24 and 36 is 72. The greatest common denominator of 24 and 36 is 12. I have to admit that I never saw these concepts again until my son Josh was in seventh grade. This must be permanently part of the seventh-grade curriculum.

If you are in seventh grade or you are assisting a seventh grader with his or her math lesson, you will be happy to know that Excel can calculate these values for you.

Syntax:

=GCD(*number1*,*number2*,...)

The GCD function returns the greatest common divisor of two or more integers. The greatest common divisor is the largest integer that divides both *number1* and *number2* without a remainder.

The arguments *number1*, *number2*,... are one to 255 values. If any value is not an integer, it is truncated. If any argument is nonnumeric, GCD returns a #VALUE! error. If any argument is less than zero, GCD returns a #NUM! error. The number 1 divides any value evenly. A prime number has only itself and 1 as even divisors.

Syntax:

=LCM(*number1*,*number2*,...)

The LCM function returns the least common multiple of integers. The least common multiple is the smallest positive integer that is a multiple of all integer arguments—*number1*, *number2*, and so on. You use LCM to add fractions with different denominators.

The arguments *number1, number2,...* are one to 29 values for which you want the least common multiple. If the value is not an integer, it is truncated. If any argument is nonnumeric, LCM returns a #VALUE! error. If any argument is less than 1, LCM returns a #NUM! error.

Using MULTINOMIAL to Solve a Coin Problem

Although the multinomial distribution is a fairly complex mathematical concept, the following example illustrates a fun puzzle that can be solved with the function.

Syntax:

=MULTINOMIAL(*number1*,*number2*,...)

The MULTINOMIAL function returns the ratio of the factorial of a sum of values to the product of factorials. The arguments *number1, number2,...* are one to 255 values for which you want the multinomial. For example, MULTINOMIAL(a,b,c,d) is (a+b+c+d)! / a!×b!×c!×d!.

Suppose that you have a huge jar that contains hundreds of pennies, nickels, dimes, and quarters. You reach into the jar and pull out six coins. How many possible arrangements of the coins can there be? To picture this problem, you should sort the six types of coins from low to high. You can use three movable dividers to group the coins into denominations. In the left side of Figure 11.28, for example, you've arranged the dividers to indicate one penny, one nickel, three dimes, and one

Figure 11.28
Solving this problem with MULTINOMIAL will amuse Boy Scout groups and middle school math students.

quarter. It is possible to pull out none of a particular coin. In the image on the right in Figure 11.28, you've pulled out five pennies and one dime. In this case, the dividers are adjacent for nickels and pennies. In every case, the quarter divider must always be at the bottom, so how many ways are there to arrange the other three dividers among six coins?

Someone figured out that the answer to this problem is the factorial of (Dividers + Coins) / Factorial of Coins × Factorial of Dividers. In math terms, this is (3+6)! / 3!×6!. Remarkably, Excel has a function for solving the coin problem. =MULTINOMIAL(3,6) performs the calculation (3+6)! / 3!×6!.

Using MOD to Find the Remainder Portion of a Division Problem

The MOD function is one of the obscure math functions that I find myself using quite frequently. Have you ever been in a group activity where everyone in the group was to count off by sixes? This is a great way to break up a group into six subgroups. It makes sure that friends who were sitting together get put into disparate groups.

Using the MOD function is a great way to perform this concept with records in a database. Perhaps for auditing, you need to check every eighth invoice. Or you need to break up a list of employees into four groups. You can solve these types of problems by using the MOD function.

Think back to when you were first learning division. If you had to divide 43 by 4, you would have written that the answer was 10 with a remainder of 3. If you divide 40 by 4, the answer is 10 with a remainder of 0.

The MOD function divides one number by another and reports back just the remainder portion of the result. You end up with an even distribution of remainders. If you convert the formulas into values and sort, your data is broken into similar-size groups.

Syntax:

=MOD(*number*,*divisor*)

The MOD function returns the remainder after *number* is divided by *divisor*. The result has the same sign as *divisor*. This function takes the following arguments:

- ■ *number*—This is the number for which you want to find the remainder.

- ■ *divisor*—This is the number by which you want to divide *number*. If *divisor* is 0, MOD returns a #DIV/0! error.

> **Note**
>
> MOD is short for *modulo*, the mathematical term for this operation. You would normally say that 17 modulo 3 is 2.

The MOD function is good for classifying records that follow a certain order. For example, the SmartArt gallery contains 84 icons arranged with four icons per row. To find the column for the 38th icon, use =MOD(38,4).

The example in Figure 11.29 assigns all employees to one of four groups.

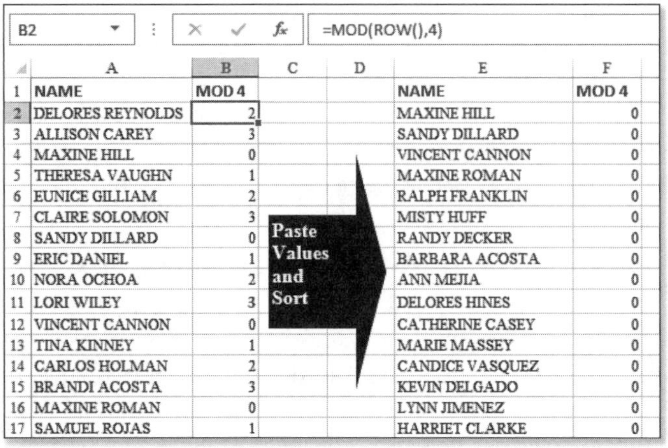

Figure 11.29
To organize these employees into four groups, use =MOD(ROW(),4). Then paste the values and sort by the remainders.

Using QUOTIENT to Isolate the Integer Portion in a Division Problem

As you just learned, the MOD function isolates the remainder portion in a division problem. The QUOTIENT function isolates the integer portion in a division problem.

If you divide 43 by 4, the answer is 10 with a remainder of 3. The QUOTIENT function returns just the whole number 10 and ignores the remainder.

This function is great for calculating full cases of products. Suppose you pay a worker for assembling products. You pay the worker for each complete case of four items produced. If he produces 43 items in his shift, this is 10 complete cases. =QUOTIENT(43,4) would provide an answer of 10.

Syntax:

=QUOTIENT(*numerator,denominator*)

The QUOTIENT function returns the integer portion in a division problem. You use this function when you want to discard the remainder in a division problem. This function takes the following arguments:

- *numerator*—This is the dividend.

- *denominator*—This is the divisor.

If either argument is nonnumeric, QUOTIENT returns a #VALUE! error.

Many people simulate the QUOTIENT function by using the INT function. To keep the integer portion of a division, you could use =INT(43/4). However, QUOTIENT and INT differ when the result is negative. Whereas QUOTIENT(5,-4) returns –1, INT(5/-4) actually goes down to –2. Thus, using

QUOTIENT is more accurate than using INT if the results might be negative. If you are a fan of using INT to simulate the QUOTIENT, consider using TRUNC() or CEILING.MATH() instead. Figure 11.30 shows the differences between QUOTIENT, INT, TRUNC, and CEILING.MATH.

Figure 11.30
QUOTIENT is more accurate than INT when the result is negative.

	A	B	C	D	E	F
				fx	=QUOTIENT(A9,B9)	
1	Number	Divisor	Quotient	INT(a/b)	TRUNC(a/b)	CEILING.MATH(a/b)
2	1	4	0	0	0	1
3	2	4	0	0	0	1
4	3	4	0	0	0	1
5	4	4	1	1	1	1
6	5	4	1	1	1	2
7	6	4	1	1	1	2
8	7	4	1	1	1	2
9	8	4	2	2	2	2
10	9	4	2	2	2	3
11	10	4	2	2	2	3
12	11	4	2	2	2	3
13	12	4	3	3	3	3
14	1	-4	0	-1	0	0
15	2	-4	0	-1	0	0
16	3	-4	0	-1	0	0
17	4	-4	-1	-1	-1	-1
18	5	-4	-1	-2	-1	-1
19	6	-4	-1	-2	-1	-1
20	7	-4	-1	-2	-1	-1
21	8	-4	-2	-2	-2	-2
22	9	-4	-2	-3	-2	-2
23	10	-4	-2	-3	-2	-2
24	11	-4	-2	-3	-2	-2
25	12	-4	-3	-3	-3	-3
26						

Using PRODUCT to Multiply Numbers

The PRODUCT function multiplies a range of numbers by each other. Although you could calculate =PRODUCT(2,2), the PRODUCT function is designed to multiply all numbers in a range, such as =PRODUCT(A2:A50).

Syntax:

=PRODUCT(number1,number2,...)

The PRODUCT function multiplies all the numbers given as arguments and returns the product. The arguments number1, number2,... are one to 255 numbers that you want to multiply. If you pass a single-cell argument that contains a text representation of a number, it is used in the multiplication. However, if one of the arguments is a multicell range, any text entry in that range is ignored.

In Figure 11.31, an array formula in B16 finds all the steps matching a particular book and multiplies the completion flags together. If 100% of the steps for a book are marked with a 1 to indicate complete, the product will also be 1. If any step is incomplete, the product will be 0. Note that the formula in B16 needs to be completed by holding down Ctrl+Shift while pressing Enter.

B16	▼	:	×	✓	fx	{=PRODUCT(IF($A$2:$A$13=A16,$C$2:$C$13,""))}

◢	A	B	C	D	E	F	G	H	I	J
1	Book	Step	Complete							
2	In Depth	Cover	1							
3	In Depth	Text	1							
4	In Depth	Layout	0							
5	In Depth	Bar Code	0							
6	PTDC	Cover	1							
7	PTDC	Text	1							
8	PTDC	Layout	1							
9	PTDC	Bar Code	1							
10	VBA	Cover	0							
11	VBA	Text	1							
12	VBA	Layout	1							
13	VBA	Bar Code	1							
14										
15		100% Done								
16	In Depth		0	{=PRODUCT(IF($A$2:$A$13=A16,$C$2:$C$13,""))}						
17	PTDC		1	{=PRODUCT(IF($A$2:$A$13=A17,$C$2:$C$13,""))}						
18	VBA		0	{=PRODUCT(IF($A$2:$A$13=A18,$C$2:$C$13,""))}						
19										

Figure 11.31
PRODUCT can check to see whether all steps are nonzero.

Using SQRT and POWER to Calculate Square Roots and Exponents

Most calculators offer a square root button, so it seems natural that Excel would offer a SQRT function to do the same thing. To square a number, you multiply the number by itself, ending up with a square. For example, 5 × 5 = 25.

A square root is a number that, when multiplied by itself, leads to a square. For example, the square root of 25 is 5, and the square root of 49 is 7. Some square roots are more difficult to calculate. The square root of 8 is a number between 2 and 3—somewhere close to 2.828. You can calculate the number with =SQRT(8).

A related function is the POWER function. If you want to write the shorthand for 6 × 6 × 6 × 6 × 6, you would say "six to the fifth power," or 65. Excel can calculate this with =POWER(6,5).

 Note

SQRTPI is a specialized version of SQRT. This function is handy for converting square shapes to equivalent-sized round shapes.

Syntax:

=SQRT(*number*)

The SQRT function returns a positive square root. The argument number is the number for which you want the square root. If *number* is negative, SQRT returns a #NUM! error.

Syntax:

=POWER(*number*,*power*)

The POWER function returns the result of a number raised to a power. This function takes the following arguments:

- *number*—This is the base number. It can be any real number.

- *power*—This is the exponent to which the base number is raised.

The POWER function works with all sorts of irrational numbers, such as 98.2 raised to the 3.4 power.

Figuring Out Other Roots and Powers

The SQRT function is provided because some math people expect it to be there. There are no equivalent functions to figure out other roots.

If you multiply 5 × 5 × 5 to get 125, then the third root of 125 is 5. The fourth root of 625 is 5. Even a $30 calculator offers a key to generate various roots beyond a square root. Excel does not offer a cube root function. In reality, even the POWER and the SQRT functions are not necessary.

- =6^3 is 6 raised to the third power, which is 6 × 6 × 6, or 216.

- =2^8 is 2 to the eighth power, which is 2 × 2 × 2 × 2 × 2 × 2 × 2 × 2, or 256.

For roots, you can raise a number to a fractional power:

- =256^(1/8) is the eighth root of 256. This is 2.

- =125^(1/3) is the third root of 125. This is 5.

> To review information on how the carat operator is used to calculate powers and roots, **see** Chapter 8, "Understanding Formulas."

Thus, instead of using =SQRT(25), you could just as easily use =25^(1/2). However, people reading your worksheets are more likely to understand =SQRT(25) than =25^(1/2).

> **See** Chapter 15, "Using Trig, Matrix, and Engineering Functions," to read more about the SQRT and SQRTPI functions.

Using SIGN to Determine the Sign of a Number

Although the SIGN function belongs with the information functions, Microsoft groups it with the math functions. You can see it used in the MROUND function example shown previously in this chapter to prevent an error. Simply, =SIGN(*number*) reports whether *number* is negative, zero, or positive.

Syntax:

=SIGN(*number*)

SIGN determines the sign of a number. It returns 1 if the number is positive, 0 if the number is 0, and −1 if the number is negative. The argument *number* is any real number.

Using COUNTIF, AVERAGEIF, and SUMIF to Conditionally Count, Average, or Sum Data

The COUNTIF and SUMIF functions are young and popular. In contrast to most functions that have been around since the 1980s, these functions were added in Excel 97. The AVERAGEIF function is even newer, having been added in Excel 2007. Math purists might point out that you could perform equivalent calculations by using DSUM, SUMPRODUCT, or even an array formula long before Microsoft added these functions. However, it is far easier to grasp doing calculations with COUNTIF, AVERAGEIF, and SUMIF.

Figure 11.32 shows a database that contains thousands of records. Your goal is to find out how many records came from each region. One way to write the formula for the East region is =COUNTIF($C$11:$C$5011,"East"). However, it is far more interesting to write the formula as shown in cell B2:

=COUNTIF($C$11:$C$5011,A2)

After you enter this formula, you can build a table of the unique regions in column A, copy the formula down column B, and quickly have a summary table built with the help of COUNTIF.

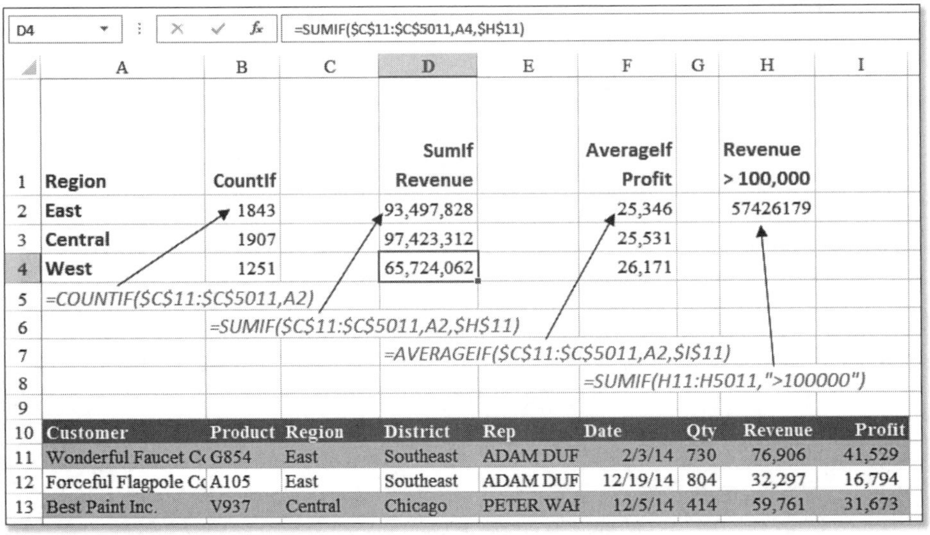

Figure 11.32
COUNTIF and SUMIF are simpler to use than DSUM, SUMPRODUCT, or array formulas.

Syntax:

=COUNTIF(range,criteria)

The COUNTIF function counts the number of cells within a range that meet the given criteria. This function takes the following arguments:

- *range*—This is the range of cells from which you want to count cells.

- *criteria*—This is the criteria in the form of a number, an expression, or text that defines which cells will be counted. For example, `criteria` can be expressed as 32, "32", ">32"", or "apples". Any criteria that contains text or a mathematical operator must be enclosed in quotes. For numeric criteria, the quotes are not required.

- You can use the wildcard characters question mark (?) and asterisk (*) in `criteria`. A question mark matches any single character; an asterisk matches any sequence of characters. If you want to find an actual question mark or asterisk, you need to type a tilde (~) before the character.

After you have mastered COUNTIF, it is easy to master SUMIF and AVERAGEIF. In most cases, the SUMIF function adds one new argument. Whereas COUNTIF would ask for a range of data and then the value to look for in that range, SUMIF usually needs three arguments: SUMIF asks for a range of data, the value to look for in that range, and then another range of data to be summed when a match is found.

In Figure 11.32, B11:B5011 contains the range to search. Cell A2 contains the value for which to search. When Excel finds a matching value in column B, you want Excel to return the corresponding cell from the Revenue column in H11:H5011. Most people would write =SUMIF($C$11:$C$5011,A2,$H$11:$H$5011) to do this. It turns out that Excel forces the third argument to have the same shape as the first argument. If you happen to accidentally specify H11:H4011, Excel ignores your range and uses H11:H5011 because it is the same shape as the first argument. Thus, it is sufficient to write the formula as =SUMIF($C$11:$C$5011,A2,$H$11).

Mastering the SUMIF and COUNTIF functions invariably leads to more questions about doing more powerful versions. If you need to sum based on more than one condition, you can use DSUM, SUMPRODUCT, or SUMIFS. The SUMIFS function is discussed in the next section.

 Note

An interesting variation on the SUMIF, AVERAGEIF, and COUNTIF functions is worth mentioning. It is possible to build the criteria argument on the fly. To count records that are above average, you can use =COUNTIF(H11:H5011,">"& AVERAGE(H11:H5011)).

Syntax:

=SUMIF(*range,criteria,sum_range*)

Syntax:

=AVERAGEIF(*range,criteria,average_range*)

The SUMIF function adds the cells specified by a given criteria. The AVERAGEIF function averages the cells specified by a given criteria. Occasionally, the range you want to search is also the range to sum. For example, perhaps your criteria is to look for rows where the revenue is greater than 100,000. In this case, because your range to add is the same as your range to search, you can leave off the third argument, as shown in cell H2 of Figure 11.32.

The SUMIF function takes the following arguments:

- **range**—This is the range of cells you want evaluated.

- **criteria**—This is the criteria in the form of a number, an expression, or text that defines which cells will be counted. For example, criteria can be expressed as 32, "32", ">32", or "apples".

- **sum_range**—This is the range of cells to sum. The cells in *sum_range* are summed only if their corresponding cells in *range* match the criteria. If *sum_range* is omitted, the cells in *range* are summed.

- **average_range**—If cells in the *average_range* are empty or contain text or TRUE/FALSE, they are ignored in the calculation of average.

> ➡ **See** *Chapter 12, "Using Powerful Functions: Logical, Lookup, and Database Functions," to learn more about using the* DSUM *function. To learn more about the* SUMPRODUCT *function, see Chapter 15, "Using Trig, Matrix, and Engineering Functions."*

Using Conditional Formulas with Multiple Conditions: SUMIFS(), AVERAGEIFS(), and COUNTIFS()

When someone sees how easy using SUMIF() is, they invariably want the function to do more. One of the most frequent questions at the MrExcel message board is along the lines of this: "I am using SUMIF() to get a total by region. How can I put two conditions in there to only get the total for a certain region and product?" In legacy versions of Excel, there were ways to do this, but they were difficult. You had to use either SUMPRODUCT(), DSUM(), or an array formula. There is a lot of complexity in going from a simple SUMIF() to the intricate Boolean logic required to understand SUMPRODUCT().

Thankfully, Excel 2007 added plural versions of SUMIF(), COUNTIF(), and AVERAGEIF() that can handle not just two conditions, but up to 127 conditions. The three new functions add the letter S to the end of the function name (that is, SUMIFS(), COUNTIFS(), and AVERAGEIFS()) to signify that multiple IFs are being considered. With SUMIFS() and AVERAGEIFS(), you first specify the range to be summed or averaged. You then specify pairs of arguments. In each pair, you first specify the range to check and then the value to match in that range. The following sections describe these three functions.

 **Tip**

The order of the arguments differs between SUMIF and SUMIFS. The *sum_range* is the first argument in SUMIFS but the third argument in SUMIF. It seems pretty common that you would be editing a SUMIF function to add additional conditions. Remember to move the *sum_range* to be the first argument when you are moving from SUMIF to SUMIFS.

Syntax:

SUMIFS(*sum_range*,*criteria_range1*,*criteria1*[,*criteria_range2*, *criteria2*...])

The SUMIFS() function adds the cells in a range that meet multiple criteria.

Note the following in this syntax:

- *sum_range* is the range to sum.
- *criteria_range1*, *criteria_range2*, ... are one or more ranges in which to evaluate the associated criteria.
- *criteria1*, *criteria2*, ... are one or more criteria in the form of a number, an expression, a cell reference, or text that define which cells will be added. For example, they can be expressed as 32, "32", ">32", "apples", or B4.
- Each cell in *sum_range* is summed only if all the corresponding criteria specified are true for that cell.
- Cells in *sum_range* that contain TRUE evaluate to 1; cells in *sum_range* that contain FALSE evaluate to 0.
- You can use the wildcard characters question mark (?) and asterisk (*) in *criteria*. A question mark matches any single character; an asterisk matches any sequence of characters. If you want to find an actual question mark or asterisk, you need to type a tilde (~) before the character.
- Unlike the range and criteria arguments in SUMIF, the size and shape of each *criteria_range* and *sum_range* must be the same.

In Figure 11.33, you want to build a table that shows the total by region and product. *sum_range* is the revenue in H11:H5011. The first criteria pair consists of the regions in $C$11:$C$5011 being compared to the word *East* in B$1. The second criteria pair consists of the divisions in $B$11:$B$5011 being compared to G854 in $A2. The formula in B2 is `=SUMIFS($H$11:$H$5011,$C$11:$C$5011,B$1,$B$11:$B$5011,$A2)`. You can copy this formula to B2:D6.

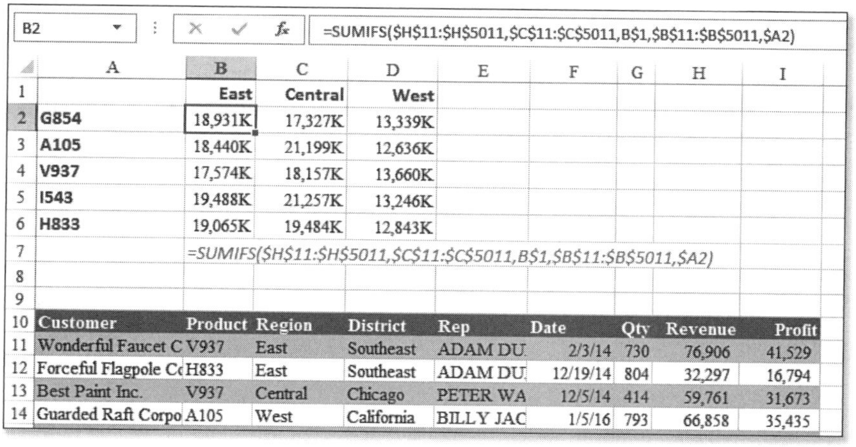

B2 =SUMIFS($H$11:$H$5011,$C$11:$C$5011,B$1,$B$11:$B$5011,$A2)

	A	B	C	D	E	F	G	H	I
1		East	Central	West					
2	G854	18,931K	17,327K	13,339K					
3	A105	18,440K	21,199K	12,636K					
4	V937	17,574K	18,157K	13,660K					
5	I543	19,488K	21,257K	13,246K					
6	H833	19,065K	19,484K	12,843K					
7		=SUMIFS($H$11:$H$5011,$C$11:$C$5011,B$1,$B$11:$B$5011,$A2)							
8									
9									
10	Customer	Product	Region	District	Rep	Date	Qty	Revenue	Profit
11	Wonderful Faucet C	V937	East	Southeast	ADAM DU	2/3/14	730	76,906	41,529
12	Forceful Flagpole Co	H833	East	Southeast	ADAM DU	12/19/14	804	32,297	16,794
13	Best Paint Inc.	V937	Central	Chicago	PETER WA	12/5/14	414	59,761	31,673
14	Guarded Raft Corpo	A105	West	California	BILLY JAC	1/5/16	793	66,858	35,435

Figure 11.33
The new SUMIFS() function is used to create this summary by region and product.

Syntax:

AVERAGEIFS(*average_range,criteria_range1,criteria1*[,*criteria_range2,criteria2...*])

The AVERAGEIFS() function is similar to SUMIFS(). It returns the average (arithmetic mean) of all cells that meet multiple criteria. The arguments are the same as for SUMIFS().

Syntax:

COUNTIFS(*range1,criteria1*[,*range2, criteria2...*])

COUNTIFS() counts the number of cells in a range that meet multiple criteria. The COUNTIFS() syntax is a bit different from the syntax of the other functions. With COUNTIFS(), there is no need to specify *sum_range*. The arguments in COUNTIFS() consist of pairs specifying criteria. The first argument in each pair specifies a criteria region. The second argument in each pair specifies the criteria value to match.

Dates and Times in Excel

Date calculations can drive people crazy in Excel. If you gain a certain confidence with dates in Excel, you will be able to quickly resolve formatting issues that come up.

Here is why dates are a problem. First, Excel stores dates as the number of days since January 1, 1900. For example, June 30, 2015 is 42185 days after 1/1/1900. When you enter 6/30/2015 in a cell, Excel secretly converts this entry to 42185 and formats the cell to display a date instead of the value. So far, so good. The problem arises when you try to calculate something based on the date.

When you try to perform a calculation on two cells when the first cell is formatted as currency and the second cell is formatted as fixed numeric with three decimals, Excel has to decide if the new cell inherits the currency format or the fixed with three decimals format. These rules are hard to figure out. In any given instance, you might get the currency format or the fixed with three decimals format, or you might get the format previously assigned to the cell with the new formula. With numbers, a result of $80.52 or 80.521 looks about the same. You can probably understand either format.

However, imagine that one of the cells is formatted as a date. Another cell contains the number 30. If you add the 30 to the date, which format does Excel use? If the cell containing the new formula happened to be previously assigned a numeric format, the answer suddenly switches from a date format to the numeric equivalent. This is frustrating. It is confusing. You start with June 30, 2015, add 30 days, and get an answer of 42215. This makes no sense to an Excel novice. It forces many people to give up on dates and start storing dates as text that looks like dates. This is unfortunate because you can't easily do calculations on text cells that look like dates.

Here is a general guideline to remember: If you work with dates in the range of the years 2000 to 2020, those numeric equivalents are from 36,526 through 44,196. If you do some date math and get a strange answer in the 35,000–45,000 range, Excel probably has the right answer, but the numeric format of the answer cell is wrong. You need to select Date from the Number drop-down on the Home tab to correct the format.

The Excel method for storing dates is simple when you understand it. If you have a date cell and need to add 15 days to it, you add the number 15 to the cell. Every day is equivalent to the number 1, and every week is equivalent to the number 7. This is very simple to understand.

When you see 42185 instead of June 30, 2015, Excel calls the 42185 a *serial number*. Some of the Excel functions discussed here convert from a serial number to text that looks like a date, or vice versa.

For time, Excel adds a decimal to the serial number. There are 24 hours in a day. The serial number for 6:00 a.m. is 0.25. The serial number for noon is 0.5. The serial number for 6:00 p.m. is 0.75. The serial number for 3:00 p.m. on June 30, 2015 is 42185.625. To see how this works, try this out:

1. Open a blank Excel workbook.

2. In any cell, enter a number in the range of 35,000 to 45,000.

3. Add a decimal point and any random digits after the decimal.

4. Select that cell.

5. From the Home tab, select the dialog launcher in the lower-right corner of the Number group.

6. In the Date category, scroll down and select the format 3/14/01 1:30 PM. Excel displays your random number as a date and time. If the decimal portion of your number is greater than 0.5, the result will be in the p.m. portion of the day.

7. Go to another cell and enter the date you were born, using a four-digit year. (This doesn't work if you are older than 113.)

8. Again select the cell and format it as a number. Excel converts it to show how many days after the start of the last century you were born. This is great trivia but not necessarily useful.

The point is that Excel dates are nothing to be afraid of. You need to understand that behind the scenes, Excel is storing your dates as serial numbers and your times as decimal serial numbers. Occasionally, circumstances cause a date to be displayed as a serial number. Although this freaks some people out, it is easy to fix using the Format Cells dialog. Other times, when you want the serial number (for example, to calculate elapsed days between two dates), Excel converts the serial number to a date, indicating, for example, that an invoice is past due by "February 15 1900" days. When you get these types of non sequiturs, you can visit the Format Cells dialog.

 Caution

Although most Excel date issues can be resolved with formatting, you should be aware of some real date problems:

On a Macintosh, Excel dates are stored since January 1, 1904. If you are using a Mac, your serial number for a date in 2015 will be different from that on a Windows PC. Excel handles this conversion when files are moved from one platform to another:

- Excel dates cannot handle dates in the 1800s or before. This really hacks off all my friends who do genealogy. If your Great-Great-Great Uncle Silas was born on February 17, 1895, you are going to have to store that as text.

- Excel dates from January 1, 1900 through March 1, 1900 are generally wrong. See Figure 11.34 and the following sidebar for more details.

- Around Y2K, someone decided that 1930 is the dividing line for two-digit years. If you enter a date with a two-digit year, the result is in the range of 1930 through 2029. If you enter 12/31/29, this will be interpreted as 2029. If you enter 1/1/30, it will be interpreted as 1930. If you need to enter a mortgage ending date of 2040, for example, be sure to use the four-digit year, 6/15/2040.

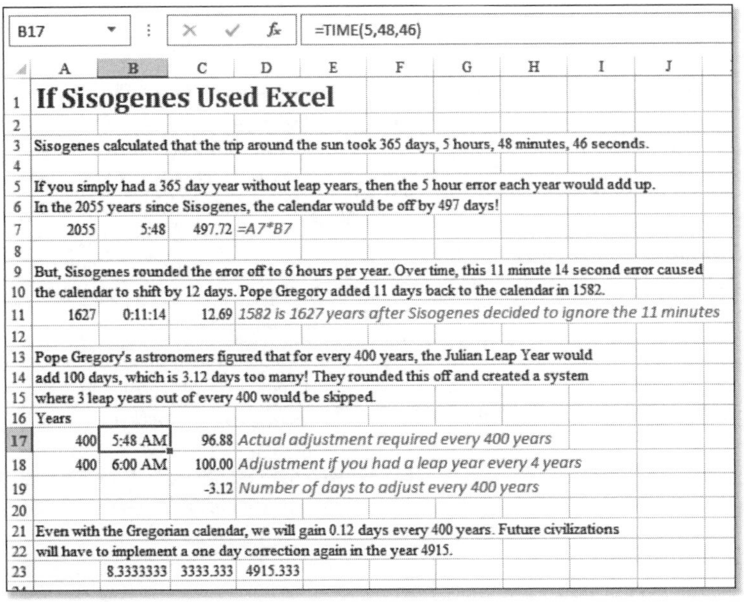

B17 =TIME(5,48,46)

	A	B	C	D	E	F	G	H	I	J
1	If Sisogenes Used Excel									
2										
3	Sisogenes calculated that the trip around the sun took 365 days, 5 hours, 48 minutes, 46 seconds.									
4										
5	If you simply had a 365 day year without leap years, then the 5 hour error each year would add up.									
6	In the 2055 years since Sisogenes, the calendar would be off by 497 days!									
7	2055	5:48	497.72	=A7*B7						
8										
9	But, Sisogenes rounded the error off to 6 hours per year. Over time, this 11 minute 14 second error caused									
10	the calendar to shift by 12 days. Pope Gregory added 11 days back to the calendar in 1582.									
11	1627	0:11:14	12.69	1582 is 1627 years after Sisogenes decided to ignore the 11 minutes						
12										
13	Pope Gregory's astronomers figured that for every 400 years, the Julian Leap Year would									
14	add 100 days, which is 3.12 days too many! They rounded this off and created a system									
15	where 3 leap years out of every 400 would be skipped.									
16	Years									
17	400	5:48 AM	96.88	Actual adjustment required every 400 years						
18	400	6:00 AM	100.00	Adjustment if you had a leap year every 4 years						
19			-3.12	Number of days to adjust every 400 years						
20										
21	Even with the Gregorian calendar, we will gain 0.12 days every 400 years. Future civilizations									
22	will have to implement a one day correction again in the year 4915.									
23		8.3333333	3333.333	4915.333						

Figure 11.34
A team of astronomers probably worked for hours to calculate what now takes seconds in Excel.

Understanding Excel Date and Time Formats

It is worthwhile to learn the various Excel custom codes for date and time formats. Figure 11.35 shows a table of how March 5 would be displayed in various numeric formats. The codes in A4:A17 are the possible codes for displaying just date, month, or year. Most people know the classic `mm/dd/yyyy` format, but far more formats are available. You can cause Excel to spell out the month and weekday by using codes such as `dddd, mmmm d, yyyy`. Here are the possibilities:

mm—Displays the month with two digits. Months before October are displayed with a leading zero (for example, January is 01).

m—Displays the month with one or two digits, as necessary.

mmm—Displays a three-letter abbreviation for the month (for example, Jan, Feb).

mmmm—Spells out the month (for example, January, February).

mmmmm—First letter of the month, useful for creating "JFMAMJJASOND" chart labels.

dd—Displays the day of the month with two digits. Dates earlier than the 10th of the month are displayed with a leading zero (for example, the 1st is 01).

d—Displays the day of the month with one or two digits, as needed.

ddd—Displays a three-letter abbreviation for the name of the weekday (for example, Mon, Tue).

dddd—Spells out the name of the weekday (for example, Monday, Tuesday).

yy or y—Uses two digits for the year (for example, 15).

yyyy or yyy—Uses four digits for the year (for example, 2015).

Blame It on Sisogenes

The programmer who designed Lotus 1-2-3 was not a date fanatic.

Back in 45 BC, an astronomer named Sisogenes calculated that the earth took 365 days, 5 hours, 48 minutes, and 46 seconds to travel around the sun. He advised Julius Caesar that this was "close enough" to 365.25 days, and the leap year was born.

This worked through Caesar's lifetime. But those missing 11 minutes and 14 seconds began to add up. By 1582, things were out of whack by about 11 days. The spring equinox was falling on March 10 instead of March 21.

Pope Gregory mandated that the calendar jump by 11 days. In Catholic countries, they went from October 4, 1582 to October 15, 1582. Other countries, though, resisted the change. England finally added the 11 days in 1752. Russia added them in 1918. Historians note that there was rioting over the change (possibly from all the people who lost out on their birthday cake?).

To prevent further rioting, Gregory proposed that we skip three leap years out of every 400 years. This led to some arcane rules for leap years:

- Leap years happen in years divisible by 4.
- Leap years are skipped if the year is divisible by 100.
- Leap years are not skipped if the year is divisible by 400.

The date February 29, 2000 was actually an exception to an exception to an exception to an exception. But everyone thought it was just another leap year.

The problem is that there was no leap year in 1900. The programmer working on Lotus 1-2-3 in Mitch Kapor's Cambridge basement didn't know this rule and programmed a 2/29/1900 into Lotus 1-2-3.

By the late 1980s, there were millions of Lotus spreadsheets created that had dates in them. Any competitor to Lotus had to ensure that its program would come up with the exact same result as the industry-standard Lotus 1-2-3. This forced Excel, Quattro, and others to program the same error into their packages. Now, billions of spreadsheets exist with dates in them. If Microsoft ever corrects this problem, there will again be rioting in the streets.

The odds of this problem actually affecting you are slim. You would need to be calculating a date span from before February 28, 1900 to after March 1, 1900. Because Excel can handle dates going back only to January 1, 1900, only 49 possible starting dates can cause problems.

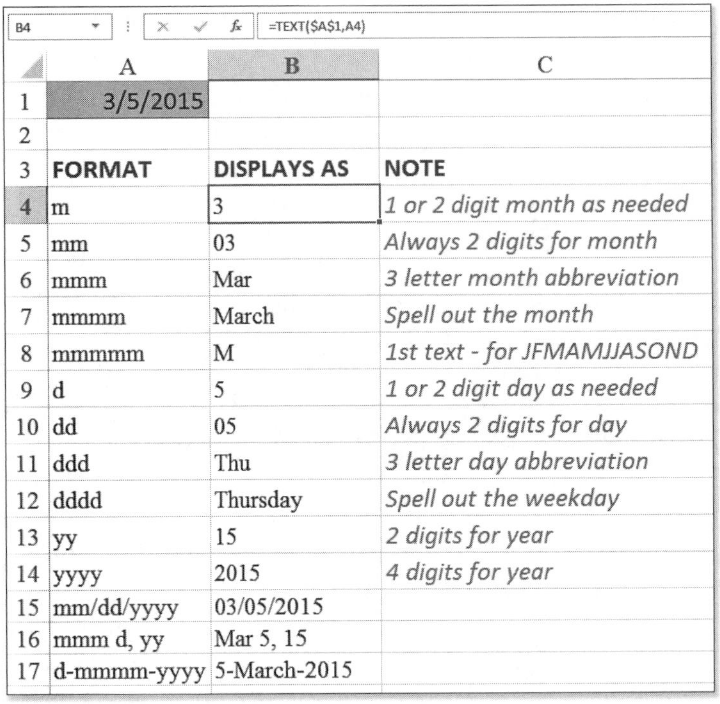

B4	▼	:	×	✓	fx	=TEXT($A$1,A4)

	A	B	C
1	3/5/2015		
2			
3	**FORMAT**	**DISPLAYS AS**	**NOTE**
4	m	3	*1 or 2 digit month as needed*
5	mm	03	*Always 2 digits for month*
6	mmm	Mar	*3 letter month abbreviation*
7	mmmm	March	*Spell out the month*
8	mmmmm	M	*1st text - for JFMAMJJASOND*
9	d	5	*1 or 2 digit day as needed*
10	dd	05	*Always 2 digits for day*
11	ddd	Thu	*3 letter day abbreviation*
12	dddd	Thursday	*Spell out the weekday*
13	yy	15	*2 digits for year*
14	yyyy	2015	*4 digits for year*
15	mm/dd/yyyy	03/05/2015	
16	mmm d, yy	Mar 5, 15	
17	d-mmmm-yyyy	5-March-2015	

Figure 11.35
Any of these custom date format codes can be typed in the Custom Numeric Format box.

You are allowed to string together any combination of these codes with a space, comma, slash, or dash. It is valid to repeat a portion of the date format. For example, the format dddd, mmmm d, yyyy shows the day portion twice in the date and would display as Thursday, March 5, 2015.

Although the date formats are mostly intuitive, several difficulties exist in the time formats. The first problem is the M code. Excel has already used M to mean month. In a time format, you cannot use M alone to mean minutes. The M code must either be preceded or followed by a colon.

There is another difficulty: When you are dealing with years, months, and days, it is often perfectly valid to mention only one of the portions of the date without the other two. It is common to hear any of these statements:

- "I was born in 1965."
- "I am going on vacation in July."
- "I will be back on the 27th."

If you have a date such as March 5, 2015 and use the proper formatting code, Excel happily tells you that this date is March or 2015 or the 5th. Technically, Excel is leaving out some really important information—the 5th of what? As humans, we can often figure out that this probably means the 5th of the next month. Thus, we aren't shocked that Excel is leaving off the fact that it is March 2015.

Imagine how strange it would be if Excel did this with regular numbers. Suppose you have the number 352. Would Excel ever offer a numeric format that would display just the tens portion of the number? If you put 352 in a cell, would Excel display 5 or 50? It would make no sense.

Excel treats time as an extension of dates and is happy to show you only a portion of the time. This can cause great confusion. To Excel, 40 hours really means 1 day and 16 hours. If you create a timesheet in Excel and format the total hours for the week as H:MM, Excel thinks that you are purposefully leaving off the day portion of the format! Excel presents 45 hours as just 21 hours because it assumes you can figure out there is 1 day from the context. But our brains don't work that way; 21 hours means 21 hours, not 1 day and 21 hours.

To overcome this problem in Excel, you use square brackets. Surrounding any time element with square brackets tells Excel to include all greater time/date elements in that one element, as in the following examples:

■ 5 days and 10 hours in [H] format would be 130.

■ 5 days and 10 hours in [M] format would be 7,800, to represent that many minutes.

■ 5 days and 10 hours in [S] format would be 468,000, to represent that many seconds.

As shown in Figure 11.36, the time formatting codes include various combinations of h, hh, s, ss, :mm, and mm:, all of which can be modified with square brackets.

To display date and time, you enter the custom date format code, a space, and then the time format code.

Tip

Custom number formats are entered in the Format Cells dialog. There are three ways to display this dialog:

■ Press Ctrl+1.

■ From the Home tab, in the Number group, select the drop-down and select More from the bottom of the drop-down.

■ Click the expand icon in the lower-right corner of the Number group on the Home tab.

When the Format Cells dialog is displayed, you select the Number tab. In the Category list, you select Custom. In the Type box, you enter your custom format. The Sample box displays the active cell with the format applied.

| B4 | : | × | ✓ | fx | =TEXT($A$1,A4) | | | |

	A	B	C	D	E
1	20:05:07				
2					
3	**FORMAT**	**DISPLAYS AS**	**NOTE**		
4	h	20	*1 or 2 digit hour as needed*		
5	hh	20	*Always 2 digits for hour*		
6	h:mm	20:05	*1 or 2 digit hour as needed*		
7	hh:mm	20:05	*Always 2 digits for hour*		
8	h:mm:ss	20:05:07	*Hours, minutes, seconds in military time*		
9	h:m:s	20:5:7	*Strange looking, but a valid code*		
10	s	7	*Seconds, using 1 or 2 digits*		
11	ss	07	*Seconds, using 2 digits*		
12	h:mm AM/PM	8:05 PM	*Hours and minutes with AM or PM*		
13	[h]:mm	44:05	*Include any full days as hours*		
14	[m]	2645	*Include any hours or days as minutes*		
15	[s]	158707	*Include any days, hours or minutes as seconds*		
16	mm.ss.00	05.07.00	*Show decimal portions of seconds*		
17					

Figure 11.36
Custom time format codes.

Examples of Date and Time Functions

In all the examples in the following sections, you should use care to ensure that the resulting cell is formatted using the proper format, as discussed in the preceding section.

Using NOW and TODAY to Calculate the Current Date and Time or Current Date

There are a couple keyboard shortcuts for entering date and time. Pressing Ctrl+; enters the current date in a cell. Pressing Ctrl+: enters the current time in a cell. However, both of these hotkeys create a static value; that is, the date or time reflects the instant that you typed the hotkey, and it never changes in the future.

Excel offers two functions for calculating the current date: NOW and TODAY. These functions are excellent for figuring out the number of days until a deadline or how late an open receivable might be.

 Caution

It would be nice if NOW( ) would function like a real-time clock, constantly updating in Excel. However, the result is calculated when the file is opened, with each press of the F9 key, and when an entry is made elsewhere in the worksheet.

Syntax:

```
=NOW()
=TODAY()
```

NOW returns the serial number of the current date and time. TODAY returns the serial number of the current date. The TODAY function returns today's date, without any time attached. The NOW function returns the current date and time.

Both of these functions can be made to display the current date, but there is an important distinction when you are performing calculations with the functions. In Figure 11.37, column A contains NOW functions, and column C contains TODAY functions. Row 2 is formatted as a date and time. Row 3 is formatted as a date. Row 4 is formatted as numeric. Cell A3 and C3 look the same. If you need to display the date without using it in a calculation, then NOW or TODAY work fine.

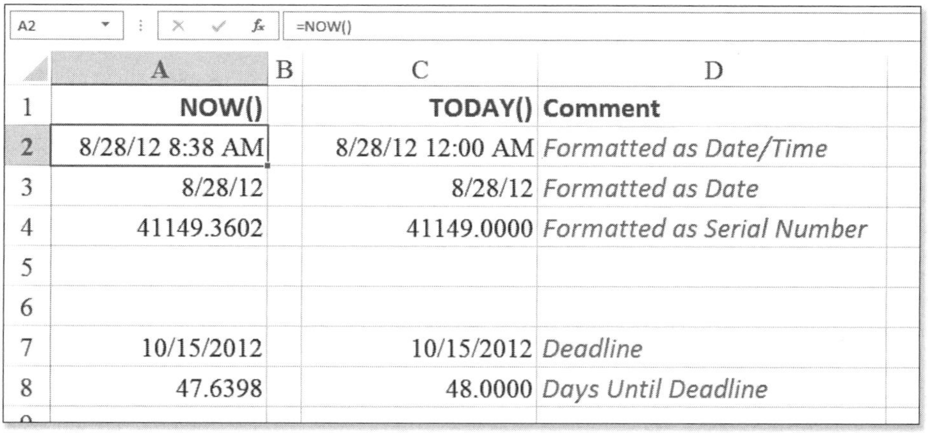

Figure 11.37
NOW and TODAY can be made to look alike, but you need to choose the proper one if you are going to be using the result in a later calculation.

A2	▾	:	×	✓	fx	=NOW()		

	A	B	C	D
1	**NOW()**		**TODAY()**	**Comment**
2	8/28/12 8:38 AM		8/28/12 12:00 AM	*Formatted as Date/Time*
3	8/28/12		8/28/12	*Formatted as Date*
4	41149.3602		41149.0000	*Formatted as Serial Number*
5				
6				
7	10/15/2012		10/15/2012	*Deadline*
8	47.6398		48.0000	*Days Until Deadline*

Row 8 calculates the number of days until a deadline approaches. Although most people would say that tomorrow is one day away, the formula in A8 would tend to say that the deadline is 0.6969 days away. This can be deceiving. If you are going to use the result of NOW or TODAY in a date calculation, you should use TODAY to prevent Excel from reporting fractional days. The formula in A8 is =A7-A3, formatted as numeric instead of a date.

Using YEAR, MONTH, DAY, HOUR, MINUTE, and SECOND to Break a Date/Time Apart

If you have a column of dates from the month of July 2015, you can easily make them all look the same by using the MMM-YY format. However, the dates in the actual cells are still different. The July 2015 records are not sorted as if they were a tie. Excel offers six functions that you can use to extract a single portion of the date: YEAR, MONTH, DAY, HOUR, MINUTE, and SECOND.

In Figure 11.38, cell A1 contains a date and time. Functions in A3 through A8 break out the date into components:

- =YEAR(*date*) returns the year portion as a four-digit year.

- =MONTH(*date*) returns the month number, from 1 through 12.

- =DAY(*date*) returns the day of the month, from 1 through 31.

- =HOUR(*date*) returns the hour, from 0 to 23.

- =MINUTE(*date*) returns the minute, from 0 to 59.

- =SECOND(*date*) returns the second, from 0 to 59.

In each case, *date* must contain a valid Excel serial number for a date. The cell containing the date serial number may be formatted as a date or as a number.

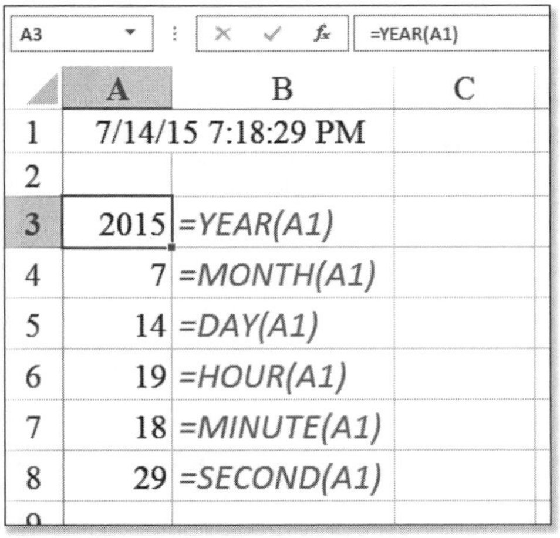

Figure 11.38
These six functions allow you to isolate any portion of a date or time.

Using DATE to Calculate a Date from Year, Month, and Day

The DATE function is one of the most amazing functions in Excel. Microsoft's implementation of this function is excellent, allowing you to do amazing date calculations.

Syntax:

=DATE(*year*,*month*,*day*)

The DATE function returns the serial number that represents a particular date. This function takes the following arguments:

- *year*—This argument can be one to four digits. If *year* is between 0 and 1899 (inclusive), Excel adds that value to 1900 to calculate the year. For example, =DATE(100,1,2) returns January 2, 2000 (1900+100). If year is between 1900 and 9999 (inclusive), Excel uses that value as the year. For example, =DATE(2000,1,2) returns January 2, 2000. If *year* is less than 0 or is 10000 or greater, Excel returns a #NUM! error.

- *month*—This is a number representing the month of the year. If month is greater than 12, month adds that number of months to the first month in the year specified. For example, =DATE(1998,14,2) returns the serial number representing February 2, 1999.

- *day*—This is a number representing the day of the month. If *day* is greater than the number of days in the month specified, it adds that number of days to the first day in the month. For example, =DATE(1998,1,35) returns the serial number representing February 4, 1998. In a trivial example, =DATE(2011,3,5) returns March 5, 2011.

The true power in the DATE function occurs when one or more of the year, month, or day are calculated values. Here are some examples:

- If cell A2 contains an invoice date and you want to calculate the day one month later, you use =DATE(Year(A2),Month(A2)+1,Day(A2)).

- To calculate the beginning of the month, you use =DATE(Year(A2),Month(A2),1).

- To calculate the end of the month, you use =DATE(Year(A2),Month(A2)+1,1)-1.

The DATE function is amazing because it enables Excel to deal perfectly with invalid dates. If your calculations for month cause it to exceed 12, this is no problem. For example, if you ask Excel to calculate =DATE(2010,16,45), Excel considers the 16th month of 2010 to be April 2011. To find the 45th day of April 2011, Excel moves ahead to May 15, 2011.

Figure 11.39 shows various results of the DATE and TIME functions.

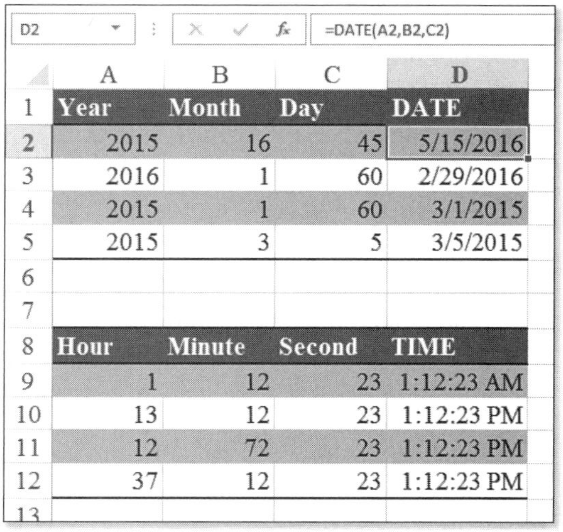

Figure 11.39
The formulas in column D use DATE or TIME functions to calculate an Excel serial number from three arguments.

	A	B	C	D
				=DATE(A2,B2,C2)
1	Year	Month	Day	DATE
2	2015	16	45	5/15/2016
3	2016	1	60	2/29/2016
4	2015	1	60	3/1/2015
5	2015	3	5	3/5/2015
6				
7				
8	Hour	Minute	Second	TIME
9	1	12	23	1:12:23 AM
10	13	12	23	1:12:23 PM
11	12	72	23	1:12:23 PM
12	37	12	23	1:12:23 PM
13				

Using TIME to Calculate a Time

The TIME function is similar to the DATE function. It calculates a time serial number given a specific hour, minute, and second.

Syntax:

=TIME(*hour*,*minute*,*second*)

The TIME function returns the decimal number for a particular time. The decimal number returned by TIME is a value ranging from 0 to 0. 999988425925926, representing the times from 0:00:00 (12:00:00 a.m.) to 23:59:59 (11:59:59 p.m.). This function takes the following arguments:

- *hour*—This is a number from 0 to 23, representing the hour.

- *minute*—This is a number from 0 to 59, representing the minute.

- *second*—This is a number from 0 to 59, representing the second.

As with the DATE function, Excel can handle situations in which the minute or second argument calculates to more than 60. For example, =TIME(12,72,120) evaluates to 1:14 PM.

Additional examples of TIME are shown in the bottom half of Figure 11.39.

Using DATEVALUE to Convert Text Dates to Real Dates

It is easy to end up with a worksheet full of text dates. Sometimes this is due to importing data from another system. Sometimes it is caused by someone not understanding how dates work.

If your dates are in many conceivable formats, you can use the DATEVALUE function to convert the text dates to serial numbers, which can then be formatted as dates.

Syntax:

=DATEVALUE(*date_text*)

The DATEVALUE function returns the serial number of the date represented by *date_text*. You use DATEVALUE to convert a date represented by text to a serial number. The argument *date_text* is text that represents a date in an Excel date format. For example, "1/30/1998" and "30-Jan-1998" are text strings within quotation marks that represent dates. Using the default date system in Excel for Windows, *date_text* must represent a date from January 1, 1900 to December 31, 9999. DATEVALUE returns a #VALUE! error if *date_text* is out of this range. If the year portion of *date_text* is omitted, DATEVALUE uses the current year from your computer's built-in clock. Time information in *date_text* is ignored.

 Caution

The DATEVALUE function must be used with text dates. If you have a column of values in which some values are text and some are actual dates, using DATEVALUE on the actual dates causes a #VALUE error. You could use =IF(ISNUMBER(A1),A1,DATEVALUE(A1)). Also consider the new =DAYS(End,Start) function, which deals with either text dates or real dates.

Any of the text values in column A of Figure 11.40 are successfully translated to a date serial number. In this instance, Excel should have been smart enough to automatically format the resulting cells as dates. By default, the cells are formatted as numeric. This leads many people to believe that DATEVALUE doesn't work. You have to apply a date format to achieve the desired result.

Figure 11.40
The formulas in column B use DATEVALUE to convert the text entries in column A to date serial numbers.

	A	B
1	**TEXT**	**DATEVALUE**
2	3/5/2011	40607
3	03/05/2011	40607
4	3/5/2011	40607
5	5-Mar-11	40607
6	Mar 5, 2011	40607
7	March 05, 2011	40607
8	03-05-2011	40607
9	3-5-2011	40607
10		

B2 ▼ : × ✓ fx =DATEVALUE(A2)

Using TIMEVALUE to Convert Text Times to Real Times

It is easy to end up with a column of text values that look like times. Similar to using DATEVALUE, you can use the TIMEVALUE function to convert these to real times.

Syntax:

=TIMEVALUE(*time_text*)

The TIMEVALUE function returns the decimal number of the time represented by a text string. The decimal number is a value ranging from 0 to 0. 999988425925926, representing the times from 0:00:00 (12:00:00 a.m.) to 23:59:59 (11:59:59 p.m.). The argument *time_text* is a text string that represents a time in any one of the Microsoft Excel time formats. For example, "6:45 PM" and "18:45" are text strings within quotation marks that represent time. Date information in *time_text* is ignored.

> **⚡ Caution**
> There are a few examples of text that DATEVALUE cannot recognize. One common example is when there is no space after the comma. For example, "January 21,2011" returns an error. To solve this particular problem, use Replace to change a comma to a comma space.

The TIMEVALUE function is difficult to use because it is easy for a person to enter the wrong formats. In Figure 11.41, many people would interpret cell A8 as meaning 45 minutes and 30 seconds. Excel, however, treats this as 45 hours and 30 minutes. This misinterpretation makes TIMEVALUE almost useless for a column of cells that contain a text representation of minute and seconds.

Caution

There are a few examples of text that TIMEVALUE cannot recognize. One common example is when there is no space before the AM or PM. For example, "11:00PM" returns an error. To solve this particular problem, use Replace to change "PM" to " PM" and to change "AM" to " AM".

➡ *The "Excel Troubleshooting" section later in this chapter discusses how to solve the problem of misinterpreting the* TIMEVALUE *function.*

Frustratingly, Excel does not automatically format the results of this function as a time. Column B shows the result as Excel presents it. Column C shows the same result after a time format has been applied.

	A	B	C
	B2 ▼ : × ✓ ƒx =TIMEVALUE(A2)		
1	**TEXT**	**TIMEVALUE**	**FORMATTED**
2	1:10	0.048611111	1:10:00 AM
3	1:10 AM	0.048611111	1:10:00 AM
4	1:10 PM	0.548611111	1:10:00 PM
5	13:10	0.548611111	1:10:00 PM
6	1:10:30	0.048958333	1:10:30 AM
7	1:45:30	0.073263889	1:45:30 AM
8	45:30	0.895833333	9:30:00 PM
9	0:45:30	0.031597222	12:45:30 AM

Figure 11.41
The formulas in column B use TIMEVALUE to convert the text entries in column A to times. If there is no leading zero before entries with minutes and seconds, the formula produces an unexpected result.

Using WEEKDAY to Group Dates by Day of the Week

The WEEKDAY function would not be so intimidating if people could just agree how to number the days. This one function can give eight different results, just for Monday.

Syntax:

=WEEKDAY(*serial_number*,*return_type*)

The WEEKDAY function returns the day of the week corresponding to a date. The day is given as an integer, ranging from 1 (Sunday) to 7 (Saturday), by default. This function takes the following arguments:

- ***serial_number***—This is a sequential number that represents the date of the day you are trying to find. Dates may be entered as text strings within quotation marks (for example, `"1/30/1998"`, `"1998/01/30"`), as serial numbers (for example, 35825, which represents January 30, 1998), or as results of other formulas or functions (for example, `DATEVALUE("1/30/1998")`).
- ***return_type***—This is a number that determines the type of return value:
    - If *return_type* is 1 or omitted, WEEKDAY works like the calendar on your wall. Typically, calendars are printed with Sunday on the left and Saturday on the right. The default version of WEEKDAY numbers these columns from 1 through 7.
    - If *return_type* is 2, you are using the biblical version of WEEKDAY. In the biblical version, Sunday is the seventh day. Working backward, Monday must occupy the 1 position.
    - If *return_type* is 3, you are using the accounting version of WEEKDAY. In this version, Monday is assigned a value of 0, followed by 1 for Tuesday, and so on. This version makes it very easy to group records by week. If cell A2 contains a date, then `A2-WEEKDAY(A2,3)` converts the date to the Monday that starts the week.
    - *return_types* of 11 through 17 were added in Excel 2010. 11 returns Monday as 1 and Sunday as 7 (the same as using 2). 12 returns Tuesday as 1, 13 returns Wednesday as 1, and so on, up to 17 returning Sunday as 1.

Figure 11.42 shows the results of WEEKDAY for all 10 return types.

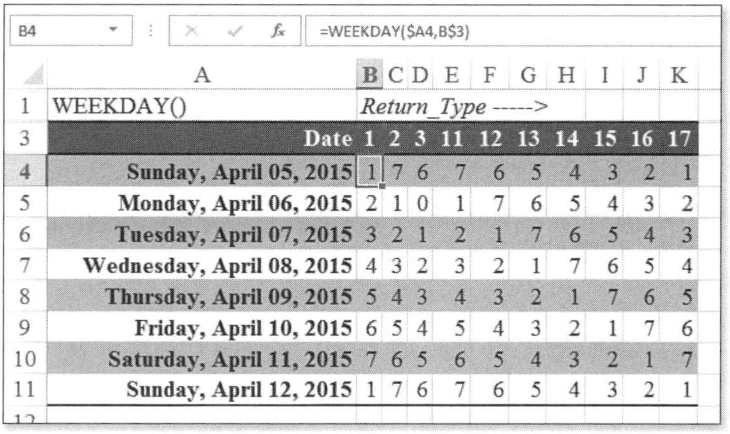

	A	B	C	D	E	F	G	H	I	J	K
1	WEEKDAY()	*Return_Type ----->*									
3	Date	1	2	3	11	12	13	14	15	16	17
4	Sunday, April 05, 2015	1	7	6	7	6	5	4	3	2	1
5	Monday, April 06, 2015	2	1	0	1	7	6	5	4	3	2
6	Tuesday, April 07, 2015	3	2	1	2	1	7	6	5	4	3
7	Wednesday, April 08, 2015	4	3	2	3	2	1	7	6	5	4
8	Thursday, April 09, 2015	5	4	3	4	3	2	1	7	6	5
9	Friday, April 10, 2015	6	5	4	5	4	3	2	1	7	6
10	Saturday, April 11, 2015	7	6	5	6	5	4	3	2	1	7
11	Sunday, April 12, 2015	1	7	6	7	6	5	4	3	2	1

Figure 11.42
Columns B, C, and D compare the WEEKDAY function for the three different `return_type` values shown in row 3.

Using WEEKNUM or ISOWEEKNUM to Group Dates into Weeks

WEEKNUM offers new options in Excel 2013. One of the new options is also promoted to a new function: ISOWEEKNUM.

For many versions, Excel did not calculate weeks to match the ANSI standard. The new *return_type* of 21 or the ISOWEEKNUM function returns the week number to match the ANSI standard. In this system, weeks always start on Monday. The first week of the year must have four days that fall into this year. Another way to say this is that the week containing the first Thursday of the month is numbered as Week 1.

In the ANSI system, you might have Week 1 actually starting as early as December 29 or as late as January 4. The last week of the year is numbered 52 in most years, but is 53 every fourth year. This system ensures that a year is made up of whole seven-day weeks. This is better than the old results of WEEKNUM.

In the old system with WEEKNUM, the week containing the first of the year was always labeled as Week 1. If the first fell on a Sunday, and your weeks started on Monday, then Sunday January 1 is Week 1 and Monday January 2 is Week 2. The possibility of having weeks that last for one day made it difficult to compare one week to the next. Nonetheless, the Excel team added new *return_types* for this system as well. In the past, 1 meant weeks started on Sunday and 2 meant weeks started on Monday. Now, you can specify weeks should start on Monday (11), Tuesday (12), and so on, up to Sunday (17).

Syntax:

=WEEKNUM(*serial_num*,[*return_type*])

The WEEKNUM function returns a number that indicates where the week falls numerically within a year. This function takes the following arguments:

- *serial_num*—This is a date within the week.

- *return_type*—This is a number that determines on what day the week begins. The default is 1. If *return_type* is 1 or omitted, the week begins on Sunday. If *return_type* is 2, the week begins on Monday. *return_types* of 11 through 17 are new in Excel 2013 and specify that the week should start on Monday (11) through Sunday (17). The new *return_type* of 21 ensures that every week has exactly 7 days. Weeks always start on Monday, but the first Thursday of the year is the middle of Week 1.

Syntax:

=ISOWEEKNUM(*serial_num*)

The ISOWEEKNUM function is the same as using a *return_type* of 21 in the WEEKNUM function. ISOWEEKNUM is new in Excel 2013. It returns a #NAME? error in previous versions of Excel.

Figure 11.43 compares ISOWEEKNUM to WEEKNUM. Notice that the outlined Week 1 in columns B:E is always 7 days in duration.

Figure 11.43
Excel 2013 offers better ways to calculate week numbers.

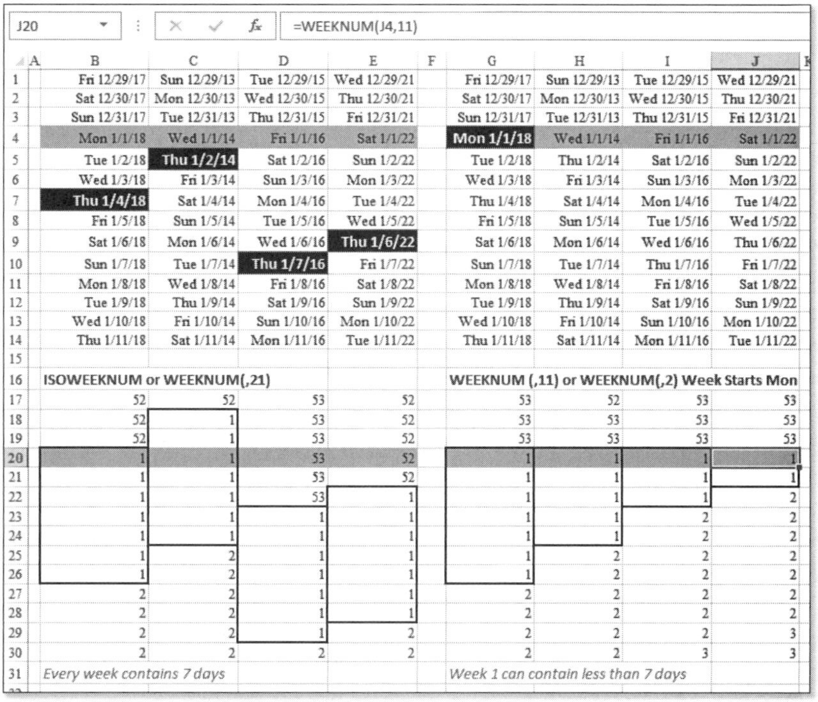

J20	▼	:	×	✓	fx	=WEEKNUM(J4,11)			
⊿ A	B	C	D	E	F	G	H	I	J
1	Fri 12/29/17	Sun 12/29/13	Tue 12/29/15	Wed 12/29/21		Fri 12/29/17	Sun 12/29/13	Tue 12/29/15	Wed 12/29/21
2	Sat 12/30/17	Mon 12/30/13	Wed 12/30/15	Thu 12/30/21		Sat 12/30/17	Mon 12/30/13	Wed 12/30/15	Thu 12/30/21
3	Sun 12/31/17	Tue 12/31/13	Thu 12/31/15	Fri 12/31/21		Sun 12/31/17	Tue 12/31/13	Thu 12/31/15	Fri 12/31/21
4	Mon 1/1/18	Wed 1/1/14	Fri 1/1/16	Sat 1/1/22		Mon 1/1/18	Wed 1/1/14	Fri 1/1/16	Sat 1/1/22
5	Tue 1/2/18	Thu 1/2/14	Sat 1/2/16	Sun 1/2/22		Tue 1/2/18	Thu 1/2/14	Sat 1/2/16	Sun 1/2/22
6	Wed 1/3/18	Fri 1/3/14	Sun 1/3/16	Mon 1/3/22		Wed 1/3/18	Fri 1/3/14	Sun 1/3/16	Mon 1/3/22
7	Thu 1/4/18	Sat 1/4/14	Mon 1/4/16	Tue 1/4/22		Thu 1/4/18	Sat 1/4/14	Mon 1/4/16	Tue 1/4/22
8	Fri 1/5/18	Sun 1/5/14	Tue 1/5/16	Wed 1/5/22		Fri 1/5/18	Sun 1/5/14	Tue 1/5/16	Wed 1/5/22
9	Sat 1/6/18	Mon 1/6/14	Wed 1/6/16	Thu 1/6/22		Sat 1/6/18	Mon 1/6/14	Wed 1/6/16	Thu 1/6/22
10	Sun 1/7/18	Tue 1/7/14	Thu 1/7/16	Fri 1/7/22		Sun 1/7/18	Tue 1/7/14	Thu 1/7/16	Fri 1/7/22
11	Mon 1/8/18	Wed 1/8/14	Fri 1/8/16	Sat 1/8/22		Mon 1/8/18	Wed 1/8/14	Fri 1/8/16	Sat 1/8/22
12	Tue 1/9/18	Thu 1/9/14	Sat 1/9/16	Sun 1/9/22		Tue 1/9/18	Thu 1/9/14	Sat 1/9/16	Sun 1/9/22
13	Wed 1/10/18	Fri 1/10/14	Sun 1/10/16	Mon 1/10/22		Wed 1/10/18	Fri 1/10/14	Sun 1/10/16	Mon 1/10/22
14	Thu 1/11/18	Sat 1/11/14	Mon 1/11/16	Tue 1/11/22		Thu 1/11/18	Sat 1/11/14	Mon 1/11/16	Tue 1/11/22
15									
16	ISOWEEKNUM or WEEKNUM(,21)					WEEKNUM (,11) or WEEKNUM(,2) Week Starts Mon			
17	52	52	53	52		53	52	53	53
18	52	1	53	52		53	53	53	53
19	52	1	53	52		53	53	53	53
20	1	1	53	52		1	1	1	1
21	1	1	53	52		1	1	1	1
22	1	1	53	1		1	1	1	2
23	1	1	1	1		1	1	2	2
24	1	1	1	1		1	1	2	2
25	1	2	1	1		1	2	2	2
26	1	2	1	1		1	2	2	2
27	2	2	1	1		2	2	2	2
28	2	2	1	1		2	2	2	2
29	2	2	1	2		2	2	2	3
30	2	2	2	2		2	2	3	3
31	Every week contains 7 days					Week 1 can contain less than 7 days			

Alternative Calendar Systems and DAYS360

You might have to work with many alternative calendar systems in Excel. Here are some examples:

- Manufacturers often redefine a quarter as being composed of 13 workweeks, with the first 4 weeks being called Month 1, the next 4 weeks being Month 2, and the final 5 weeks being Month 3. This is known as a 4-4-5 calendar.

- Retailers use a special retail calendar composed of 52 seven-day weeks. Each week ends on a Sunday. If you compare Week 7, Day 6 of one year to Week 7, Day 6 of another year, you are assured that you are comparing a Saturday to a Saturday and can have a like comparison.

- Some accounting systems use a 360-day calendar. In this type of system, the year is divided into 12 months of 30 days. There is special handling for months with 31 days. Unfortunately, U.S. and European accounting boards disagree on the special handling, so there are two sets of rules.

Out of these three alternative calendar systems, Excel handles only the 360-day calendar. Excel provides the DAYS360 function and the YEARFRAC function to deal with the date system.

Syntax:

=DAYS360(*start_date*,*end_date*,*method*)

The DAYS360 function returns the number of days between two dates, based on a 360-day year (twelve 30-day months), which is used in some accounting calculations. You use this function to help compute payments if your accounting system is based on twelve 30-day months. This function takes the following arguments:

- *start_date* and *end_date*—These are the two dates between which you want to know the number of days. If *start_date* occurs after *end_date*, DAYS360 returns a negative number. Dates may be entered as text strings within quotation marks (for example, "1/30/2015", "2015/01/30"), as serial numbers (for example, 42034, which represents January 30, 2015, if you're using the 1900 date system), or as results of other formulas or functions (for example, DATEVALUE("1/30/2015")).

- *method*—This is a logical value that specifies whether to use the U.S. or European method in the calculation:

  - FALSE or omitted is a U.S. (National Association of Securities Dealers) method. If the starting date is the 31st of a month, it becomes equal to the 30th of the same month. If the ending date is the 31st of a month and the starting date is earlier than the 30th of a month, the ending date becomes equal to the 1st of the next month; otherwise, the ending date becomes equal to the 30th of the same month.

  - TRUE is a European method. Starting dates or ending dates that occur on the 31st of a month become equal to the 30th of the same month.

Using YEARFRAC, DATEDIF, or DAYS to Calculate Elapsed Time

If you work in a human resources department, you might be concerned with years of service in order to calculate a certain benefit. Excel provides one function, YEARFRAC, that can calculate decimal years of service in five different ways. An old function, DATEDIF, has been hanging around since Lotus 1-2-3; it can calculate the difference between two dates in complete years, months, or days. Excel 2013 adds the DAYS function, which can calculate elapsed days even if one or both of the values are text dates.

Syntax:

=YEARFRAC(*start_date*,*end_date*,*basis*)

The YEARFRAC function calculates the fraction of the year represented by the number of whole days between two dates (*start_date* and *end_date*). You use the YEARFRAC worksheet function to identify the proportion of a whole year's benefits or obligations to assign to a specific term.

This function takes the following arguments:

- **_start_date_**—This is a date that represents the start date. Dates may be entered as text strings within quotation marks (for example, `"1/30/1998"`, `"1998/01/30"`), as serial numbers (for example, 35825, which represents January 30, 1998, if you're using the 1900 date system), or as results of other formulas or functions (for example, `DATEVALUE("1/30/1998")`).

- **_end_date_**—This is a date that represents the end date.

- **_basis_**—This is the type of day count basis to use. Figure 11.44 compares the five types of _basis_ available:

    - If _basis_ is 0 or omitted, Excel uses a 30/360 plan, modified for American use. In this plan, the employee earns 1/360 of a year's credit on most days. The employee earns no service on the day after any 31st of the month. In a leap year, the employee earns 2/360 of a year for showing up on March 1. In a non-leap year, the employee earns 3/360 of a year for showing up on March 1.

    - If _basis_ is 1, the actual number of elapsed days is divided by the actual number of days in the year. This method works well and ensures that the year fraction ends up being 1 on the anniversary date, whether it is a leap year.

    - If _basis_ is 2, the actual number of elapsed days is divided by 360. If someone would show up and work for 30 years straight for one employer, this method would give that person an extra 0.43 years of credit. Sisogenes would be spinning in his grave.

    - If _basis_ is 3, the actual number of elapsed days is divided by 365. This works great for three out of every four years. It is slightly wrong in leap years.

    - If _basis_ is 4, Excel uses a 30/360 plan, modified for European use. This is similar to the default _basis_ of 0. In this plan, the employee gets no credit for working any 31st of the month. The employee still gets triple credit for working March 1 (to make up for the 29th and 30th of February). In a leap year, March 1 is worth only double credit.

Syntax:

`=DATEDIF(start_date,end_date,unit)`

In contrast to `YEARFRAC`, the `DATEDIF` function calculates complete years, months, or days. This function calculates the number of days, months, or years between two dates. It is provided for compatibility with Lotus 1-2-3. This function takes the following arguments:

- **_start_date_**—This is a date that represents the first, or starting, date of the period. Dates may be entered as text strings within quotation marks (for example, `"2001/1/30"`), as serial numbers, or as the results of other formulas or functions (for example, `DATEVALUE("2001/1/30")`).

- **_end_date_**—This is a date that represents the last, or ending, date of the period.

- **_unit_**—This is the type of information you want returned. The various values for _unit_ are shown in Table 11.7.

Table 11.7   Unit Values Used by the DATEDIF Function

Unit Value	Description
Y	The number of complete years in the period. A complete year is earned on the anniversary date of the employee's start date.
M	The number of complete months in the period. This number is incremented on the anniversary date. If the employee was hired on January 18, that person has earned 1 month of service on the 18th of February. If an employee is hired on January 31, then she earns credit for the month when she shows up for work on the 1st after any month with fewer than 31 days.
D	The number of days in the period. This could be figured out by simply subtracting the two dates.
MD	The number of days, ignoring months and years. You could use a combination of two DATEDIF functions—one using M and one using MD—to calculate days.
YM	The number of months, ignoring years. You could use a combination of two DATEDIF functions—one using Y and one using YM—to calculate months.
YD	The number of days, ignoring complete years.

Figure 11.44 compares the five types of *basis* of YEARFRAC with the six unit values of DATEDIF. Each cell uses $A$1 as the start date and that row's column A as the end date.

 Caution

DATEDIF has been in Excel forever, but it was only documented in Excel 2000. Why doesn't Microsoft reveal DATEDIF in Help? Probably because of the strange anomaly when you try to calculate the gap from the 31st of January to the 1st of March in a non-leap year.

The "D" version of DATEDIF reports this as 29 days. This is correct.

The "M" version of DATEDIF reports this as one full month. This has to be correct because the dates span the entire month of February.

The "MD" version of DATEDIF reports this as a negative 2 days in excess of a full month. See cell D9 in Figure 11.45. This is simply the downside of trying to express a measurement in months, when the length of a month is not constant. Negative values for this version of DATEDIF happen only when the end date is March 1 or March 2.

Despite this problem, for 363 days a year, DATEDIF remains an effective way to express a date delta as a certain number of years, months, and days.

Syntax:

=DAYS(*end_date*, *start_date*,)

The DAYS function always calculates elapsed days between two dates. Introduced in Excel 2013, the function offers one new trick: It will work with text dates as well as real dates. This function takes the following arguments:

- *end_date, start_date*—The two dates between which you want to know the number of days. If either argument is text, that argument is passed through DATEVALUE() to return a date.

Figure 11.44
If your benefits package includes information about complete months, then YEARFRAC with a basis value of 0 works best. Otherwise, a basis value of 1 is the most accurate.

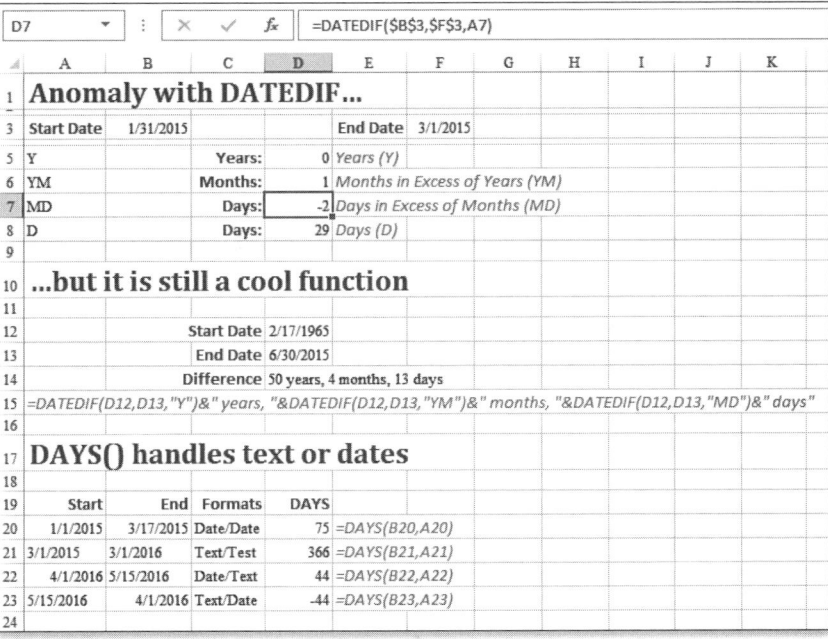

| J372 | ▼ | : | × | ✓ | fx | =DATEDIF($A$6,$A372,J$5) |

	A	B	C	D	E	F	G	H	I	J	K	L	M
1	1/1/15	Basis - for YEARFRAC ---->						Unit - for DATEDIF ---->					
2		30/360	/Actual	/360	/365	30/360		Y	M	D	D²	M³	D⁴
3		(Amer.)				(Euro)							
5	DATE	0	1	2	3	4		Y	M	D	MD	YM	YD
366	12/27/15	0.989	0.986	1.	0.986	0.989		0	11	360	26	11	360
367	12/28/15	0.992	0.989	1.003	0.989	0.992		0	11	361	27	11	361
368	12/29/15	0.994	0.992	1.006	0.992	0.994		0	11	362	28	11	362
369	12/30/15	0.997	0.995	1.008	0.995	0.997		0	11	363	29	11	363
370	12/31/15	1.	0.997	1.011	0.997	0.997		0	11	364	30	11	364
371	1/1/16	1.	1.	1.014	1.	1.		1	12	365	0	0	0
372	1/2/16	1.003	1.001	1.017	1.003	1.003		1	12	366	1	0	1
373													
374		D^2 = days in excess of months											
375		M^3 = months in excess of full years											
376		D^4 = days in excess of full years											
377													

Figure 11.45
In rare cases, DATEDIF will report 1 month and –2 days.

| D7 | ▼ | : | × | ✓ | fx | =DATEDIF($B$3,$F$3,A7) |

	A	B	C	D	E	F	G	H	I	J	K
1	**Anomaly with DATEDIF...**										
3	Start Date	1/31/2015			End Date	3/1/2015					
5	Y		Years:	0	*Years (Y)*						
6	YM		Months:	1	*Months in Excess of Years (YM)*						
7	MD		Days:	-2	*Days in Excess of Months (MD)*						
8	D		Days:	29	*Days (D)*						
9											
10	**...but it is still a cool function**										
11											
12			Start Date	2/17/1965							
13			End Date	6/30/2015							
14			Difference	50 years, 4 months, 13 days							
15	=DATEDIF(D12,D13,"Y")&" years, "&DATEDIF(D12,D13,"YM")&" months, "&DATEDIF(D12,D13,"MD")&" days"										
16											
17	**DAYS() handles text or dates**										
18											
19	Start	End	Formats	DAYS							
20	1/1/2015	3/17/2015	Date/Date	75	=DAYS(B20,A20)						
21	3/1/2015	3/1/2016	Text/Test	366	=DAYS(B21,A21)						
22	4/1/2016	5/15/2016	Date/Text	44	=DAYS(B22,A22)						
23	5/15/2016	4/1/2016	Text/Date	-44	=DAYS(B23,A23)						
24											

Using EDATE to Calculate Loan or Investment Maturity Dates

If someone invests in a 6-month CD on the 17th of the month, the maturity date is on the 17th of another month. This would be a fairly straightforward calculation if no one invested on the 31st of a month.

The maturity rules work such that if you invest on the 31st of a month, and the CD would be scheduled to mature on the 31st of June, the CD maturity actually happens on the last day of June, which is June 30.

If a CD is to mature on the 31st, 30th, or 29th day of February, the CD matures on the last day of February.

Syntax:

=EDATE(*start_date*,*months*)

The EDATE function returns the serial number that represents the date that is the indicated number of months before or after a specified date (that is, *start_date*). You use EDATE to calculate maturity dates or due dates that fall on the same day of the month as the date of issue. This function takes the following arguments:

- *start_date*—This is a date that represents the start date. Dates may be entered as text strings within quotation marks (for example, "1/30/2015", "2015/01/30"), as serial numbers (for example, 42034, which represents January 30, 2015, if you're using the 1900 date system), or as results of other formulas or functions (for example, DATEVALUE("1/30/2015")). If the *start_date* is not valid, EDATE returns a #NUM! error.

- *months*—This is the number of months before or after *start_date*. A positive value for *months* yields a future date; a negative value yields a past date. If months is not an integer, it is truncated.

Figure 11.46 shows several examples of EDATE. Note that in column B, the function is a no-brainer. You could easily calculate it by using the DATE function. The only interesting cases occur on the 29th, 30th, and 31st of the month.

Note that EDATE can be used to back into an investment date from a maturity date. For example, the records in rows 11 through 16 pass a negative number for the *months* parameter.

Using EOMONTH to Calculate the End of the Month

Before Excel 2007, about 89 functions were available only in the Analysis Toolpack. Some companies had rules that you were not allowed to build spreadsheets using the functions in the Analysis Toolpack. This rule was probably created by some corporate executive who didn't know how to turn on the Analysis Toolpack!

Figure 11.46
You can use EDATE to calculate the maturity date for a security.

| E9 | ▼ | : | × | ✓ | f_x | =EDATE(E$3,$A9) |

⁴	A	B	C	D	E	F
1	**MATURITY DATES**					
2						
3	**Months**	1/1/15	1/29/15	1/30/15	1/31/15	
4	6	7/1/15	7/29/15	7/30/15	7/31/15	
5	5	6/1/15	6/29/15	6/30/15	6/30/15	
6	4	5/1/15	5/29/15	5/30/15	5/31/15	
7	3	4/1/15	4/29/15	4/30/15	4/30/15	
8	2	3/1/15	3/29/15	3/30/15	3/31/15	
9	1	2/1/15	2/28/15	2/28/15	2/28/15	
10	0	1/1/15	1/29/15	1/30/15	1/31/15	
11	-1	12/1/14	12/29/14	12/30/14	12/31/14	
12	-2	11/1/14	11/29/14	11/30/14	11/30/14	
13	-3	10/1/14	10/29/14	10/30/14	10/31/14	
14	-4	9/1/14	9/29/14	9/30/14	9/30/14	
15	-5	8/1/14	8/29/14	8/30/14	8/31/14	
16	-6	7/1/14	7/29/14	7/30/14	7/31/14	
17						

One of my favorite puzzles at MrExcel.com came from someone who worked at such a company. How can you calculate the end of the month without using EOMONTH? This is a hard question; the end of the month is the 31st if the month number is 1, 3, 5, 7, 8, 10, or 12. It is the 30th if the month number is 4, 6, 9, or 11. If the month number is 2, then you have to look at the year to figure out if it is a leap year for 29 days or not a leap year for 28 days. The formula to solve this was horrible:

```
=DATE(YEAR(A2),MONTH(A2),CHOOSE(MONTH(A2),31,28,31,30,31,30,31,31,30,31,30,31)
    +IF(MOD(YEAR(A2),4)=0,1,0))
```

Well-known Excel guru Aladin Akyurek weighed in with the great answer and ended the entire discussion. Aladin suggested using the DATE function to move up to the first of the next month and then simply subtract 1 day, using this formula:

```
=DATE(YEAR(A2),MONTH(A2)+1,1)-1
```

The sheer simplicity of this is beautiful. However, the whole question becomes immaterial now that EOMONTH has been promoted to be part of the actual Excel function set.

Syntax:

```
=EOMONTH(start_date,months)
```

The EOMONTH function returns the serial number for the last day of the month that is the indicated number of months before or after *start_date*. You use EOMONTH to calculate maturity dates or due dates that fall on the last day of the month. This function takes the following arguments:

 **Caution**

You must format the result of the EOMONTH formula to be a date to see the expected results.

- **start_date**—This is a date that represents the starting date. Dates may be entered as text strings within quotation marks (for example, "1/30/2015", "2015/01/30"), as serial numbers, or as results of other formulas or functions (for example, DATEVALUE("1/30/2015")). If *start_date* is not a valid date, EOMONTH returns a #NUM! error.

> **⚷ Caution**
>
> You must format the result of the EDATE formula to be a date to see the expected results.

- **months**—This is the number of months before or after *start_date*. A positive value for *months* yields a future date; a negative value yields a past date. If *months* is not an integer, it is truncated. If *start_date* plus *months* yields an invalid date, EOMONTH returns a #NUM! error.

=EOMONTH(A2,0) converts any date to the end of the month.

Using WORKDAY or NETWORKDAYS or Their International Equivalents to Calculate Workdays

The functions WORKDAY and NETWORKDAYS are pretty cool. They calculate days by excluding weekends and holidays. Weekends can be any two-day period, such as Saturday/Sunday or Thursday/Friday, or any one day, such as only Sunday.

These functions are great for calculating shipping days when you ship with FedEx or UPS. They are great for making sure your result doesn't fall on a bank holiday. Here's how you do it:

1. In an out-of-the-way section of a spreadsheet, enter any holidays that will fall during the work-week. This might be federal holidays, floating holidays, company holidays, and so on. The list of holidays can either be entered down a column or across a row. In the top portion of Figure 11.47, the holidays are in E2:E11.

2. Enter a starting date in a cell, such as B1.

3. In another cell, enter the number of workdays that the project is expected to take, such as B2.

4. Enter the ending date formula as **=WORKDAY(B1,B2,E2:E7)**.

The NETWORKDAYS function takes two dates and figures out the number of workdays between them. For example, you might have a project that is due on June 17, 2015. If today is April 14, 2015, NETWORKDAYS can calculate the number of workdays until the project is due.

Syntax:

=WORKDAY(*start_date,days,holidays*)

Syntax:

=NETWORKDAYS(*start_date,end_date,holidays*)

The NETWORKDAYS function returns the number of whole workdays between *start_date* and *end_date*. Workdays exclude weekends and any dates identified in holidays. You use NETWORKDAYS to calculate employee benefits that accrue based on the number of days worked during a specific term. This function takes the following arguments:

- ■ *start_date*—This is a date that represents the start date. Dates may be entered as text strings within quotation marks (for example, "1/30/1998", "1998/01/30"), as serial numbers, or as results of other formulas or functions (for example, DATEVALUE("1/30/1998")).

- ■ *end_date*—This is a date that represents the end date.

- ■ *holidays*—This is an optional range of one or more dates to exclude from the working calendar, such as state and federal holidays and floating holidays. The list can be either a range of cells that contain the dates or an array constant of the serial numbers that represent the dates. If any argument is not a valid date, NETWORKDAYS returns a #NUM! error.

Both of the functions described in this section assume that Saturday and Sunday are weekends and are not workdays. If you have any other weekend system, you can use WORKDAY.INTL or NETWORKDAYS.INTL, as described in the next section.

In Figure 11.47, the current date is entered in cell B6. The project due date is entered in cell B7. The holidays range is in E2:E7, as in the previous example. The formula in cell B8 to calculate workdays is =NETWORKDAYS(B6,B7,E2:E7).

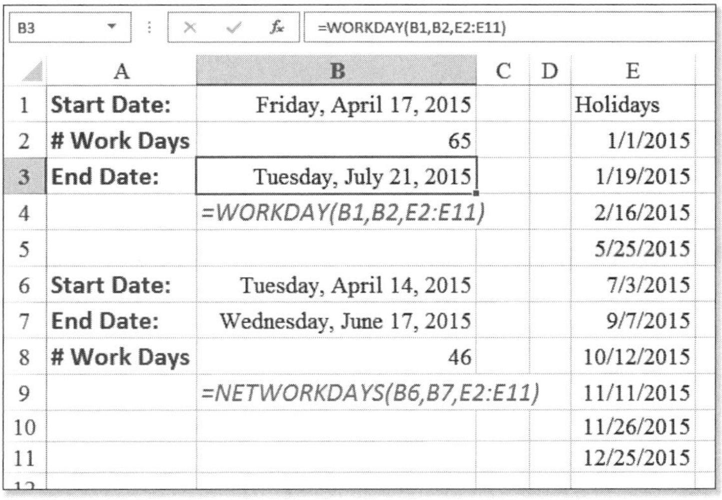

Figure 11.47
WORKDAY and NETWORKDAY can calculate the number of Monday-through-Friday days, exclusive of a range of holidays.

	A	B	C	D	E
B3		=WORKDAY(B1,B2,E2:E11)			
1	Start Date:	Friday, April 17, 2015			Holidays
2	# Work Days	65			1/1/2015
3	End Date:	Tuesday, July 21, 2015			1/19/2015
4		=WORKDAY(B1,B2,E2:E11)			2/16/2015
5					5/25/2015
6	Start Date:	Tuesday, April 14, 2015			7/3/2015
7	End Date:	Wednesday, June 17, 2015			9/7/2015
8	# Work Days	46			10/12/2015
9		=NETWORKDAYS(B6,B7,E2:E11)			11/11/2015
10					11/26/2015
11					12/25/2015

Excel in Practice: Converting a Holiday Range to an Array

The problem with putting the list of holidays in a range on a worksheet is that someone might accidentally overwrite or change the range of holidays.

The syntax for the workdays functions mentions that you can convert the holiday range to an array of serial numbers. To embed the holidays inside a function, you follow these steps:

1. In Figure 11.47, select cell B3.

2. In the formula bar, use the mouse to select the characters E2:E11.

3. Press the F9 key. Excel replaces the selected characters with the calculated version of those characters. In this case, the calculation is the array {42005;42023;42051,...}, as shown in Figure 11.48.

4. Press Enter to accept the new formula.

5. You can now delete the holidays in column E.

	A	B	C	D	E	F	G	H
B3		=WORKDAY(B1,B2,{42005;42023;42051;42149;42188;42254;42289;42319;42334;42363})						
1	Start Date:	Friday, April 17, 2015			Holidays			
2	# Work Days	65			1/1/2015			
3	End Date:	Tuesday, July 21, 2015			1/19/2015			
4	=WORKDAY(B1,B2,{42005;42023;420				2/16/2015			
5	51;42149;42188;42254;42289;4231				5/25/2015			
6	9;42334;42363})				7/3/2015			
7					9/7/2015			
8					10/12/2015			
9					11/11/2015			
10					11/26/2015			
11					12/25/2015			
12								

Figure 11.48
You can remove the holiday cells from the worksheet after embedding the array in the formula.

Using International Versions of WORKDAY or NETWORKDAYS

Two functions introduced in Excel 2010 expand the WORKDAY and NETWORKDAYS functions for situations where the work week is not Monday through Friday. The most common example is a weekend on Friday and Saturday, which has become popular in Qatar, Bahrain, Kuwait, United Arab Emirates, and Algeria. It also handles the situation where a manufacturing plant is working six days and the weekend is only Sunday.

Syntax:

=WORKDAY.INTL(*start_date*,*days*,*weekend*,*holidays*)

Syntax:

`=NETWORKDAYS.INTL(`*start_date*`,`*end_date*`,`*weekend*`,`*holidays*`)`

Both of these functions work as their noninternational equivalents, with the addition of having the weekend specified as two specific consecutive days of the week.

Here are the values for the *weekend* argument:

- **1**—Weekend on Saturday and Sunday
- **2**—Weekend on Sunday and Monday
- **3**—Weekend on Monday and Tuesday
- **4**—Weekend on Tuesday and Wednesday
- **5**—Weekend on Wednesday and Thursday
- **6**—Weekend on Thursday and Friday
- **7**—Weekend on Friday and Saturday
- **11**—Sunday only
- **12**—Monday only
- **13**—Tuesday only
- **14**—Wednesday only
- **15**—Thursday only
- **16**—Friday only
- **17**—Saturday only

Examples of Text Functions

When they think of Excel, most people think of numbers. Excel is great at dealing with numbers, and it lets you write formulas to produce new numbers. Excel offers a whole cadre of formulas for dealing with text.

You might sometimes be frustrated because you receive data from other users, and the text is not in the format you need. Or the mainframe might send customer names in uppercase, or the employee in the next department might put a whole address into a single cell. Excel provides text functions to deal with all these situations and more.

Joining Text with the Ampersand (&) Operator

Chapter 8 mentions the ampersand (&) operator, but it is worth mentioning again here because it is the most important tool for dealing with text. The & operator enables you to join text.

Suppose you have a worksheet with first name in column A and last name in column B, as shown in Figure 11.49. You need to put these names together in a single cell. If you use the formula =A2&B2 in cell C2, Excel smashes the names together (for example, STEVENWOODWARD). Instead, you must join three elements. In between A2 and B2, you must join a single space in double quotes. The formula to do this is =A2&" "&B2.

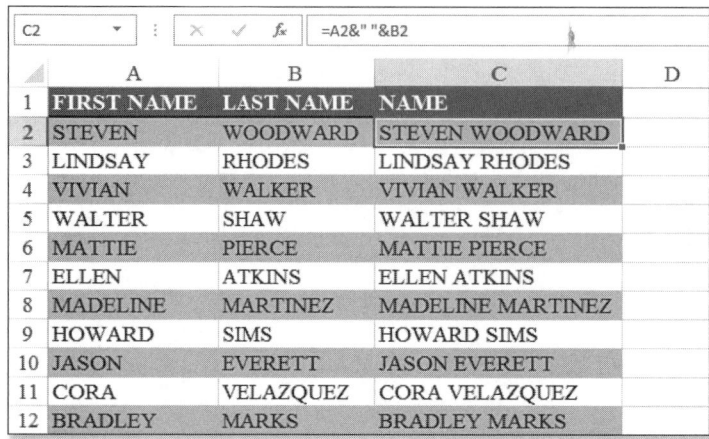

Figure 11.49
You can use the & character to join text in cells or text enclosed in quotes.

Some people prefer to use the CONCATENATE function instead of the &. This function does not perform the way that I want it to perform, and I generally avoid it, but it is described in the following section.

> **Note**
> The new Flash Fill feature can simplify this process, although the results do not update if values in A and B later change. To read about Flash Fill, see Chapter 2, "Introducing Flash Fill and Quick Analysis."

Syntax:

=CONCATENATE (*text1*,*text2*,...)

The CONCATENATE function joins several text strings into one text string. The arguments *text1*, *text2*, ... are one to 255 text items to be joined into a single text item. The text items can be text strings, numbers, or single-cell references.

The problem with this function is that it can select only single-cell references. An attempt to use =CONCATENATE(A2:B2) returns a #VALUE! error. If you have to enter =CONCATENATE(A2," ",B2), it is easier to use =A2&" "&B2.

Using LOWER, UPPER, or PROPER to Convert Text Case

Three functions—LOWER, UPPER, and PROPER—convert text to or from capital letters. In Figure 11.50, the products in column A were entered in a haphazard fashion. Some products used lowercase, and some products used uppercase. Column B uses =UPPER(A2) to make all the products a uniform uppercase.

> **Note**
> If you want to keep the data only in column C, you have to convert the formulas to values before deleting columns A and B. To do this, select the data in column C and then press Ctrl+C to copy. Then select Home, Paste, Paste Values to convert the formulas to values.

In cell E13, text was entered by someone who never turns off Caps Lock. You can convert this uppercase to lowercase with =LOWER(E13).

In column E, you see a range of names in uppercase. You can use =PROPER(E2) to convert the name to proper case, which capitalizes just the first letter of each word. The PROPER function is mostly fantastic, but there are a few cells that you have to manually correct. PROPER correctly capitalizes names with apostrophes, such as O'Rasi in cell F3. It does not, however, correctly capitalize the interior *c* in McCartney in cell F4. The function is also notorious for creating company names such as Ibm, 3m, and Aep.

Syntax:

=LOWER(*text*)

The LOWER function converts all uppercase letters in a text string to lowercase. The argument *text* is the text you want to convert to lowercase. LOWER does not change characters in *text* that are not letters.

Figure 11.50
UPPER, LOWER, and PROPER can convert text to and from capital letters.

F2	▼	:	×	✓	*fx*	=PROPER(E2)	

	A	B	C	D	E	F	G
1	Quantity	Product	Upper		NAME	Proper	
2	2	q754	Q754		ERIN RICHMOND	Erin Richmond	
3	1	g644	G644		JACK O'RASI	Jack O'Rasi	
4	5	G644	G644		KEITH MCCARTNEY	Keith Mccartney	
5	4	q754	Q754		ERNEST CURTIS	Ernest Curtis	
6	7	Q754	Q754		LEAH HARRISON	Leah Harrison	
7	7	d350	D350		ALLISON BRIGGS	Allison Briggs	
8	1	Q754	Q754		STEVEN CARR	Steven Carr	
9	1	g644	G644		TERRI HARDY	Terri Hardy	
10	3	G644	G644		KYLE SANCHEZ	Kyle Sanchez	
11	2	n870	N870		RYAN PITTS	Ryan Pitts	
12	3	q754	Q754				
13	4	d350	D350		MY MANAGER TYPES IN ALL CAPITALS		
14	8	q754	Q754		my manager types in all capitals		
15	5	I175	I175				
16	2	i175	I175				
17	3	i175	I175				
18							
19	C2: =UPPER(B2)						
20	E14: =LOWER(E13)						

Syntax:

=PROPER(*text*)

The PROPER function capitalizes the first letter in a text string and any other letters in text that follow any character other than a letter. It converts all other letters to lowercase letters.

The argument *text* is text enclosed in quotation marks, a formula that returns text, or a reference to a cell containing the text you want to partially capitalize.

Syntax:

=UPPER(*text*)

The UPPER function converts text to uppercase. The argument *text* is the text you want converted to uppercase. *text* can be a reference or text string.

Using TRIM to Remove Trailing Spaces

If you frequently import data, you might be plagued with a couple of annoying situations. This section and the next one deal with those situations.

You may have trailing spaces at the end of text cells. Although " ABC" and "ABC " might look alike when viewed in Excel, they cause functions such as MATCH and VLOOKUP to fail. TRIM removes leading and trailing spaces.

In Figure 11.51, you can see a simple VLOOKUP in column B. The formula in cell B2 is =VLOOKUP(A2,$F$2:$G$5,2,FALSE). Even though you can clearly see that M40498 is in the lookup table, VLOOKUP returns an #N/A! error, indicating that the product ID is missing from the lookup table.

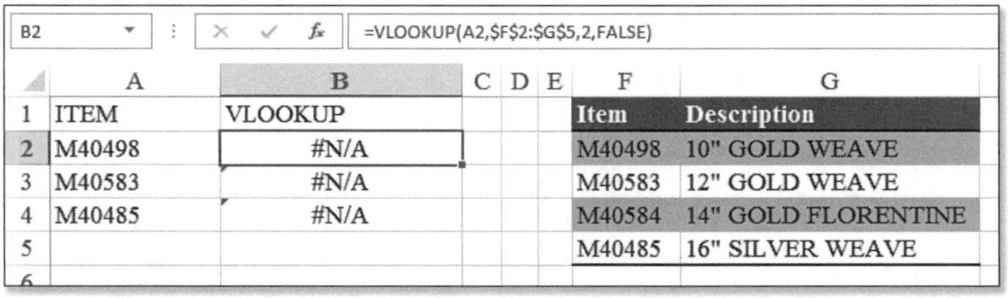

| B2 | ▼ | : | × | ✓ | *fx* | =VLOOKUP(A2,$F$2:$G$5,2,FALSE) |

	A	B	C	D	E	F	G
1	ITEM	VLOOKUP				Item	Description
2	M40498	#N/A				M40498	10" GOLD WEAVE
3	M40583	#N/A				M40583	12" GOLD WEAVE
4	M40485	#N/A				M40584	14" GOLD FLORENTINE
5						M40485	16" SILVER WEAVE
6							

Figure 11.51
This VLOOKUP should work, but in this instance, it fails.

To diagnose and correct this problem, follow these steps:

1. Select one of the data cells in column F. Press the F2 key to put the cell in Edit mode. A flashing insertion character appears at the end of the cell. Check to see if the flashing cursor is immediately after the last character.

2. Select one of the data cells in column A. Press the F2 key to put the cell in Edit mode. Note whether the flashing insertion character is immediately after the last character. Figure 11.52 shows that the products in column A have several trailing spaces after them. The products in the lookup table do not have any trailing spaces.

Figure 11.52
Spaces are padding the right side of the products in column A.

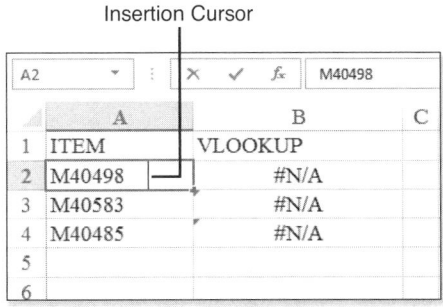

3. If the problem is occurring in the values being looked up, you could modify the formula in cell B2 to use the TRIM function. The new formula would be =VLOOKUP(TRIM(A2),$F$2:$G$5,2, FALSE). Figure 11.53 shows how this solves the problem.

Figure 11.53
Using TRIM to remove leading spaces allows VLOOKUP to work.

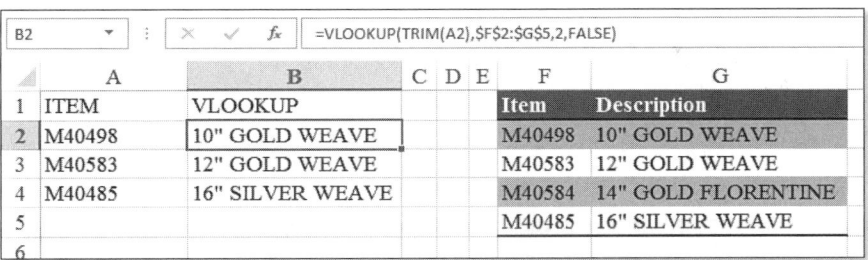

4. If the problem is occurring in the first column of the lookup table, insert a new temporary column. Enter the function **=TRIM(F2)** in the temporary column. Copy this formula down to all rows of the lookup table. Copy the new formulas. Select A2. Select Home, Paste, Values to paste the new values. Although the old and new values look the same, the TRIM function has removed the trailing spaces, and now the products match.

 **Note**

It is not necessarily efficient to calculate, but you can solve the trailing spaces in column F by using =VLOOKUP(A2, TRIM(F$2:G$5),2,FALSE) if you press Ctrl+Shift+Enter to accept the formula.

Syntax:

=TRIM(*text*)

The TRIM function removes all spaces from text except for single spaces between words. You use TRIM on text that you have received from another application that might have irregular spacing. The argument *text* is the text from which you want spaces removed.

In Figure 11.54, cell C1 contains six letters: ABC DEF. You might assume that the cell is set to be centered. However, the formula in cell C2 appends an asterisk to each end of the value in cell C1. This formula shows that there are several leading and trailing spaces in the value.

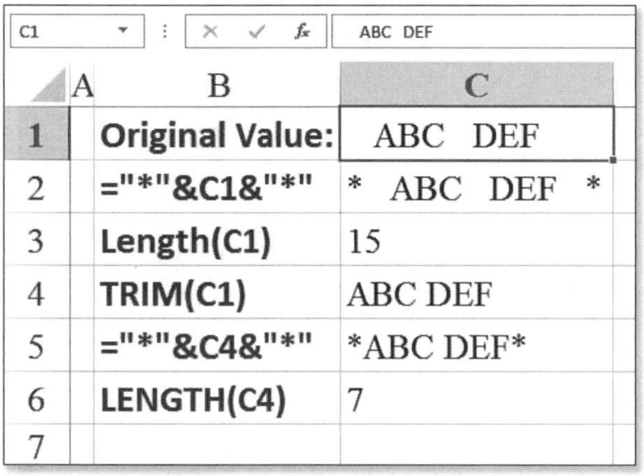

	A	B	C
1		Original Value:	ABC DEF
2		="*"&C1&"*"	* ABC DEF *
3		Length(C1)	15
4		TRIM(C1)	ABC DEF
5		="*"&C4&"*"	*ABC DEF*
6		LENGTH(C4)	7
7			

Figure 11.54
TRIM removes leading spaces and extra interior spaces.

Using =LEN(C1) shows that the text actually contains 15 characters instead of six characters. The TRIM(C1) formula removes any leading spaces, any trailing spaces, and any extra interior spaces. The function still leaves one space between ABC and DEF because you want to continue to have words separated by a single space.

The formulas in cells C5 and C6 confirm that the leading and trailing spaces are removed and that the length of the new value is only seven characters.

Using CLEAN to Remove Nonprintable Characters from Text

Although TRIM works great, the CLEAN function no longer works as advertised. CLEAN is designed to remove nonprintable characters from text.

Besides extra spaces, another annoying problem with data from other systems is that it might contain nonprintable characters. Excel offers a function that is supposed to remove nonprintable characters, but Microsoft's definition of a nonprintable character is far too narrow. The function was clearly written before the proliferation of web queries, Oracle, and SAP.

Syntax:

`=CLEAN(text)`

The CLEAN function removes 35 nonprintable characters from text. You use CLEAN on text imported from other applications that contains characters that might not print with your operating system. For example, you can use CLEAN to remove some low-level computer code that is frequently at the beginning and end of data files and cannot be printed.

The argument *text* is any worksheet information from which you want to remove nonprintable characters.

Figure 11.55 shows which characters are removed by CLEAN.

Figure 11.55
CLEAN removes a short list of nonprintable characters. Unfortunately, today's data is littered with a new crop of nonprintable characters.

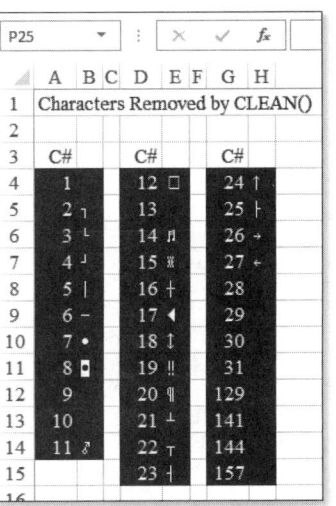

Using the CHAR or UNICHAR Function to Generate Any Character

Early computers used a character set of 128 ASCII characters. Any computer that you've had in your home offered at least an 8-bit processor and could easily display 255 characters. Thus, computers sold in the United States offered the original 128 ASCII characters and an extended 128 characters with accented characters needed for German, French, and some other European languages. The CHAR( ) function makes it possible to display any of these 255 characters.

Today, the Unicode character set includes 110,000 characters, covering most written languages used on Earth. Unicode includes glyphs used in languages from Aboriginal to Yijing. You will find glyphs from Braille, Burmese, Cherokee, Greek, Old Persian, and many languages that you have not heard of. There are also map symbols, playing card symbols, emoticons, dice, domino, and mahjong markings. Unfortunately, the Unicode organization officially rejected including Klingon in 2001. Also, although the Calibri font will render chess, dice, and playing card symbols, it does not support domino or mahjong.

All versions of Excel supported CHAR() to generate symbols 0 through 255. Excel 2013 adds support for UNICHAR() to render the 100,000+ symbols defined by Unicode.

You might have ventured into Start, All Programs, Accessories, System Tools, Character Map to find a particular character in the Wingdings character set. Also, if you have a favorite symbol, you might have memorized that you can insert the symbol by using a hotkey. For example, if you hold down Alt, type 0169 on the numeric keypad, and then release Alt, an Office program inserts the copyright symbol (©).

 **Tip**

Although I know a few characters off the top of my head, I usually take a look at all characters in a set by entering =**CHAR(ROW())** in cells A1:A255. This returns character 65 in row 65, and so on. In Excel 2013, you can use =UNICHAR(ROW()) in column A1:A1048576 to browse for symbols. To find something in particular, check out http://www.alanwood.net/unicode/menu.html.

Syntax:

=CHAR(*number*)

The CHAR function returns the character specified by a number. You use CHAR to translate code page numbers you might get from files on other types of computers into characters.

The argument *number* is a number between 1 and 255 that specifies which character you want. The character is from the character set used by your computer.

Syntax:

=UNICHAR(*number*)

The UNICHAR function returns the Unicode character specified by a number.

Figure 11.56 shows some symbols available from CHAR and UNICHAR.

If you see a strange character in your data, you can learn the character number by using the CODE or UNICODE function, as described in the following section.

Using the CODE or UNICODE Function to Learn the Character Number for Any Character

If you can't remember that a capital *A* is character code 65, you can use the CODE function to learn the code associated with the character. The function returns the ASCII code for the first character in text. =CODE("A") returns 65.

Figure 11.56
This figure shows examples of
CHAR and UNICHAR results.

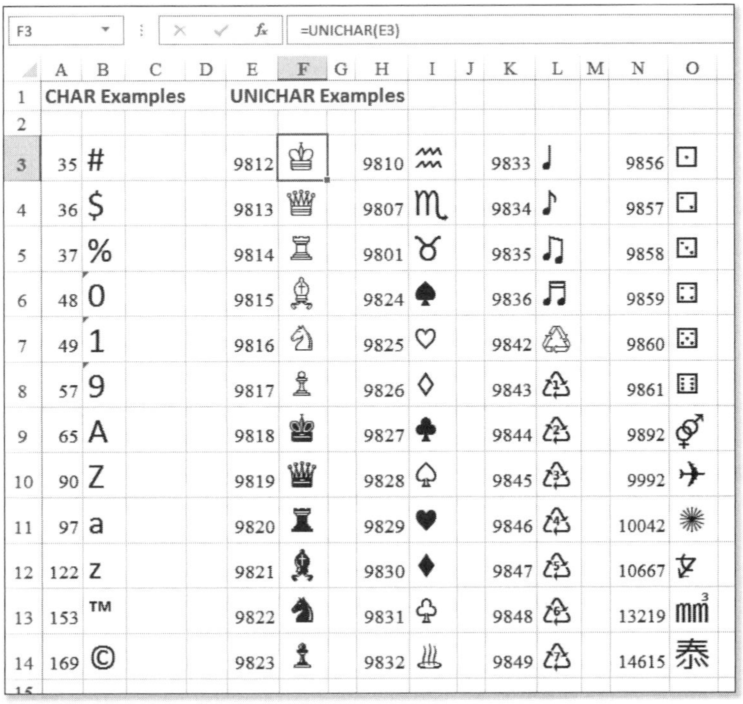

The old CHAR function did not work with characters beyond the first 255 characters. Starting in Excel 2013, the Excel team added the UNICODE function to return the Unicode character number for a character.

Syntax:

```
=CODE(text)
=UNICODE(text)
```

The CODE function returns a numeric code for the first character in a text string. The returned code corresponds to the character set used by your computer. The argument *text* is the text for which you want the code of the first character. This is an important distinction. CODE returns the code for only the first character in a cell. =CODE("A") and =CODE("ABC") return only 65 to indicate the capital letter *A*.

The UNICODE function returns the character code for the 100,000+ characters currently defined.

A new problem began happening in Excel in the past few years. People started encountering values with which TRIM would not remove the spaces from the text. For example, Figure 11.57 shows a value in cell A2 that very clearly contains a space between the letters *A* and *B*.

Figure 11.57
CODE is instrumental in learning why the TRIM function won't work on the data in column A.

	A	B	C	D	E	F
1	What code is the space not removed by TRIM?					
2	A B	160	=CODE(MID($A$2,2,1))			
3						
4	What is the character code for these symbols?					
5	J	74	=CODE(A5)			
6	♫	14	=CODE(A6)			
7	¼	188	=CODE(A7)			
8						
9	What is the Unicode for the symbols?					
10	↬	8620	=UNICODE(A10)			
11	⁞	10255	=UNICODE(A11)			
12	Ⓩ	9423	=UNICODE(A12)			
13	◕	9685	=UNICODE(A13)			
14						

The formula in B2 shows the character number for the second character in A2. The space is a character 160 instead of a typical space—character 32.

If you've ever created a small web page, you might have learned that browsers ignore consecutive spaces. If you really want to keep two words separated by four spaces, you need to use *Word 1*   *Word2*. I learned this trick somewhere on the Web and never really thought about what   means. It turns out that it is a nonbreaking space. And, you guessed it, a nonbreaking space occupies character position 160, so it looks just like a space. Web designers use it all the time to format web pages. Consequently, it is ending up in data that people paste into Excel from the Web, and it is making it appear that TRIM does not always work.

 Note

Excel pros know that they can remove the extra interior spaces by using =TRIM(A2). But TRIM still doesn't remove nonbreaking spaces.

Using LEFT, MID, or RIGHT to Split Text

One of the newer rules in information processing is that each field in a database should contain exactly one piece of information. Throughout the history of computers, there have been millions of examples of people trying to cram many pieces of information into a single field. Although this works great for humans, it is pretty difficult to have Excel sort a column by everything in the second half of a cell.

Column A in Figure 11.58 contains part numbers. As you might guess, the Part Number field contains two pieces of information: a three-character vendor code, a dash, and a five-digit part number.

Figure 11.58
LEFT makes quick work of extracting the vendor code. Several varieties of MID or RIGHT extract the part number.

D2		▼	:	×	✓	*fx*	=LEFT(A2,3)				

	A	B	C	D	E	F	G	H	I	J
1	PART NUMBER	OH	OO	LEFT	MID					
2	RPM-104020	1	2	RPM	104020		Alternate choices for MID			
3	BOR-21862	1	0	BOR	21862		=MID(A2,5,100)			
4	LUK-04-158	3	1	LUK	04-158		=TRIM(MID(A2,5,100))			
5	BOR-10294E	1	0	BOR	10294E		=MID(A2,5,LEN(A2)-5)			
6	BOR-10643	3	2	BOR	10643		=RIGHT(A2,LEN(A2)-FIND("-",A2))			
7	BOR-10625B	1	2	BOR	10625B					
8	BOR-10635	1	0	BOR	10635		If the Vendor code was not always 3 letters:			
9	BOR-22816	3	1	BOR	22816		=LEFT(A2,FIND("-",A2)-1)			
10	BWW-BC42TF	0	0	BWW	BC42TF					
11	BOR-21764	0	1	BOR	21764					

When a customer comes in to buy a part, he probably doesn't care about the vendor. So the real question is, "Do you have anything in stock that can fix my problem?"

Excel offers three functions—LEFT, MID, and RIGHT—that allow you to isolate just the first or just the last characters, or even just the middle characters, from a column.

Syntax:

=LEFT(*text*,*num_chars*)

The LEFT function returns the first character or characters in a text string, based on the number of characters specified. This function takes the following arguments:

- ■ **text**—This is the text string that contains the characters you want to extract.

- ■ **num_chars**—This specifies the number of characters you want LEFT to extract. *num_chars* must be greater than or equal to zero. If *num_chars* is greater than the length of text, LEFT returns all of *text*. If *num_chars* is omitted, it is assumed to be 1.

Syntax:

=RIGHT(*text*,*num_chars*)

The RIGHT function returns the last character or characters in a text string, based on the number of characters specified. This function takes the following arguments:

- ■ **text**—This is the text string that contains the characters you want to extract.

- ■ **num_chars**—This specifies the number of characters you want RIGHT to extract. *num_chars* must be greater than or equal to zero. If *num_chars* is greater than the length of text, RIGHT returns all of *text*. If *num_chars* is omitted, it is assumed to be 1.

Syntax:

`=MID(text,start_num,num_chars)`

MID returns a specific number of characters from a text string, starting at the position specified, based on the number of characters specified. This function takes the following arguments:

- **text**—This is the text string that contains the characters you want to extract.

- **start_num**—This is the position of the first character you want to extract in text. The first character in text has *start_num 1*, and so on. If *start_num* is greater than the length of text, MID returns "" (that is, empty text). If *start_num* is less than the length of text, but *start_num* plus *num_chars* exceeds the length of text, MID returns the characters up to the end of text. If *start_num* is less than 1, MID returns a #VALUE! error.

- **num_chars**—This specifies the number of characters you want MID to return from text. If *num_chars* is negative, MID returns a #VALUE! error.

In Figure 11.58, it is easy to extract the three-digit vendor code by using `=LEFT(A2,3)`. It is a bit more difficult to extract the part number. As you scan through the values in column A, it is clear that the vendor code is consistently three letters. With the dash in the fourth character of the text, it means that the part number starts in the fifth position. If you are using MID, you therefore use 5 as the *start_num* argument.

However, there are a few thousand part numbers in the data set. Right up front, in cell A4, is a part number that breaks the rule. LUK-04-158 contains six characters after the first dash. This might seem to be an isolated incident, but in row 10, BWW-BC42TW also contains six characters after the dash. Because this type of thing happens in real life, two errors in the first nine records are enough to warrant a little extra attention. The four possible strategies for extracting the part number are listed in G2:G6. They are as follows:

- Ask MID to start at the fifth character and return a large enough number of characters to handle any possible length (that is, `=MID(A2,5,100)`).

- Ask MID to start at the fifth character but use TRIM around the whole function to prevent any trailing spaces from being included (that is, `=TRIM(MID(A2,5,100))`).

- Ask MID to start at the fifth character, but calculate the exact number of characters by using the LEN function (that is, `=MID(A2,5,LEN(A2)-4)`).

- Skip MID altogether and ask RIGHT to return all the characters after the first dash. This requires you to use the FIND function to locate the first dash—that is, `=RIGHT(A2,LEN(A2)-FIND("-",A2))`.

Using LEN to Find the Number of Characters in a Text Cell

It seems pretty obscure, but you will find the LEN function amazingly useful. The LEN function determines the length of characters in a cell, including any leading or trailing spaces.

Syntax:

`=LEN(text)`

The LEN function returns the number of characters in a text string. The argument `text` is the text whose length you want to find. Spaces count as characters.

There are instances in which you can use LEN along with LEFT, MID, or RIGHT to isolate a portion of text.

➡ *To review information on this topic, refer to the example in the previous section.*

You can also use LEN to find records that are longer than a certain limit. Suppose you are about to order nameplates for company employees. Each nameplate can accommodate 15 characters. In Figure 11.59, you add the LEN function next to the names and sort by the length, in descending order. Any problem names appear at the top of the list.

Figure 11.59
LEN identifies the number of characters in a cell.

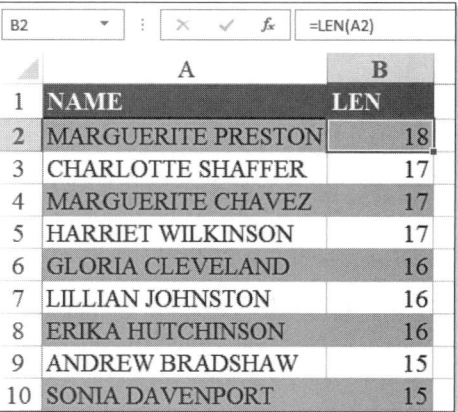

Using SEARCH or FIND to Locate Characters in a Particular Cell

Two nearly identical functions can scan through a text cell, looking for a particular character or word. Many times, you just want to know if the word appears in the text. These functions go further than telling you if the character exists in the text; they tell you at exactly which character position the character or word is found. The character position can be useful in subsequent formulas with LEFT, RIGHT, or REPLACE.

First, let's look at an example of using FIND to determine whether a word exists in another cell. Figure 11.60 shows a database of customers. The database was created by someone who doesn't know Excel and jammed every field into a single cell.

| A2 | ▾ | : | ✕ | ✓ | *fx* | Kayla Zimmerman, 265 Hickory Street, Rochester, IN 40154 |

	A
1	**Name & Address**
2	Kayla Zimmerman, 265 Hickory Street, Rochester, IN 40154
3	Joshua Moreno, 1469 Hickory Street, Mill Valley, CA 41204
4	Cynthia Kemp, 264 Ash Lane, Naperville, MS 81585
5	Jacqueline Bradshaw, 561 Forest Road, St Joseph, CT 65131
6	Bobby Salazar, 1774 Laurel Street, Bloomingdale, VI 73546
7	Henry Thomas, 153 Ridge Highway, Bainbridge, OR 91072
8	Christina Preston, 1311 Broadway Blvd., City, NY 12363
9	Leah Manning, 1639 Sunset Road, Mill Valley, MS 35862

Figure 11.60
When the manager asked an employee to type this in Excel, she didn't realize that the employee had never used Excel before.

 Note

Like all the other data sets in this book, these names and addresses are randomly generated from lists of the most popular first name, last name, street name, and city names. Don't try to send Christmas cards to these people, because none of the addresses exist. And don't think that the ZIP Codes are real; everything here is completely random.

Here is how to make this work properly:

1. To find all the customers in California, in cell B2, enter `=FIND(", CA",A2)`. When you enter the formula, you get a #VALUE! error. This is okay. In fact, it is useful information: It tells you that CA is not found in the first record.

2. Copy the formula down to all rows.

3. Sort low to high by column B. You'll see that 98% of the records have a #VALUE! error and sort to the bottom of the list. The few California records have a valid result for the formula in column B and sort to the top of the list, as shown in Figure 11.61.

FIND and SEARCH are similar to one another. The FIND function does not distinguish between uppercase and lowercase letters. FIND identifies CA, ca, Ca, and cA as matches for CA. If you need to find a cell with exactly AbCdEf, you need to use the SEARCH command instead of FIND. Also, SEARCH allows for wildcard characters in *find_text*. A question mark (?) finds a single character, and an asterisk (*) finds any number of characters.

 Caution

The trick with this application of FIND is to look for something that is likely to be found only in California records. If you had customers in Cairo, Illinois, they would have also been found by the FIND command you just used. The theory with this sort of search is that you can quickly check through the few matching records to find false positives.

Figure 11.61
You don't care where FIND found the text; you simply want to divide the list into records with valid values versus errors.

| B2 | ▼ | : | × | ✓ | *fx* | =FIND(", CA",A2) |

	A	B
1	**Name & Address**	**California?**
2	Marilyn Atkins, 1581 Twelfth Avenue, Oak Grove, CA 69942	47
3	Joshua Moreno, 1469 Hickory Street, Mill Valley, CA 41204	48
4	Kayla Zimmerman, 265 Hickory Street, Rochester, IN 40154	#VALUE!
5	Cynthia Kemp, 264 Ash Lane, Naperville, MS 81585	#VALUE!
6	Jacqueline Bradshaw, 561 Forest Road, St Joseph, CT 65131	#VALUE!
7	Bobby Salazar, 1774 Laurel Street, Bloomingdale, VI 73546	#VALUE!
8	Henry Thomas, 153 Ridge Highway, Bainbridge, OR 91072	#VALUE!
9	Christina Preston, 1311 Broadway Blvd., City, NY 12363	#VALUE!
10	Leah Manning, 1639 Sunset Road, Mill Valley, MS 35862	#VALUE!
11	Timothy Talley, 190 East Avenue, Mount Pleasant, VT 77296	#VALUE!

The FIND function makes it easy to find the first instance of a particular character in a cell. However, if your text values contain two instances of a character, your task is a bit more difficult. In Figure 11.62, the part numbers in column A really contain three segments, each separated by a dash:

1. To find the first dash, enter **=FIND("-",A2)** in column B.

2. To find the second dash, use the optional *start_num* parameter to the FIND function. The *start_num* parameter is a character position. You want the function to start looking after the first instance of a dash. This can be calculated as the result of the first FIND in column B plus one. Thus, the formula in cell C2 is =FIND("-",A2,B2+1).

3. After you find the character positions of the dashes, isolate the various portions of the part number. In column D, for the first part of the number, enter **=LEFT(A2,B2-1)**. This basically asks for the left characters from the part number, stopping at one fewer than the first dash.

Figure 11.62
Formulaically isolating data between the first and second dashes can be done, but it helps to break each number down into small parts.

| C2 | ▼ | : | × | ✓ | *fx* | =FIND("-",A2,B2+1) |

	A	B	C	D	E	F	G	H
		First	Second	First	2nd	3rd		
1	**Part Number**	**Dash**	**Dash**	**Part**	**Part**	**Part**		*Formulas:*
2	37767-33-385568	6	9	37767	33	385568		*B2: =FIND("-",A2)*
3	632-6-43	4	6	632	6	43		*C2: =FIND("-",A2,B2+1)*
4	10-13-5656	3	6	10	13	5656		*D2: =LEFT(A2,B2-1)*
5	9-671672-119067	2	9	9	671672	119067		*E2: =MID(A2,B2+1,C2-B2-1)*
6	41-50555-51	3	9	41	50555	51		*F2: =RIGHT(A2,LEN(A2)-C2)*
7	568-536-177914	4	8	568	536	177914		

4. In column E, for the middle part of the number, enter **=MID(A2,B2+1,C2-B2-1)**. This asks Excel to start at the character position one after the first dash and then continue for a length that is one fewer than the first dash subtracted from the second dash.

5. In Column F, for the final part of the number, enter **=RIGHT(A2,LEN(A2)-C2)**. This calculates the total length of the part number, subtracts the position of the second dash, and returns those right characters.

Syntax:

=FIND(*find_text*,*within_text*,*start_num*)

FIND finds one text string (*find_text*) within another text string (*within_text*) and returns the number of the starting position of *find_text* from the first character of *within_text*. You can also use SEARCH to find one text string within another, but unlike SEARCH, FIND is case-sensitive and doesn't allow wildcard characters.

The FIND function takes the following arguments:

- *find_text*—This is the text you want to find. If *find_text* is " " (that is, empty text), FIND matches the first character in the search string (that is, the character numbered *start_num* or 1). *find_text* cannot contain any wildcard characters.

- *within_text*—This is the text that contains the text you want to find.

- *start_num*—This specifies the character at which to start the search. The first character in *within_text* is character number 1. If you omit *start_num*, it is assumed to be 1.

Syntax:

=SEARCH(*find_text*,*within_text*,*start_num*)

SEARCH returns the number of the character at which a specific character or text string is first found, beginning with *start_num*. You use SEARCH to determine the location of a character or text string within another text string so that you can use the MID or REPLACE function to change the text.

The SEARCH function takes the following arguments:

- *find_text*—This is the text you want to find. You can use the wildcard characters question mark (?) and asterisk (*) in *find_text*. A question mark matches any single character; an asterisk matches any sequence of characters. If you want to find an actual question mark or asterisk, you type a tilde (~) before the character. If you want to find a tilde, you type two tildes. If *find_text* is not found, a #VALUE! error is returned.

- *within_text*—This is the text in which you want to search for *find_text*.

 Caution

If *find_text* does not appear in *within_text*, FIND returns a #VALUE! error. If *start_num* is not greater than zero, FIND returns a #VALUE! error. If *start_num* is greater than the length of *within_text*, FIND returns a #VALUE! error.

- *start_num*—This is the character number in *within_text* at which you want to start searching. If *start_num* is omitted, it is assumed to be 1. If *start_num* is not greater than zero or is greater than the length of *within_text*, a #VALUE! error is returned.

Using SUBSTITUTE and REPLACE to Replace Characters

When you have the ability to find text, you might want to replace text. Excel offers two functions for this: SUBSTITUTE and REPLACE. The SUBSTITUTE function is easier to use and should be your first approach.

Syntax:

=SUBSTITUTE(*text*,*old_text*,*new_text*,*instance_num*)

The SUBSTITUTE function substitutes *new_text* for *old_text* in a text string. You use SUBSTITUTE when you want to replace specific text in a text string; you use REPLACE when you want to replace any text that occurs in a specific location in a text string.

The SUBSTITUTE function takes the following arguments:

- *text*—This is the text or the reference to a cell that contains text for which you want to substitute characters.

- *old_text*—This is the text you want to replace.

- *new_text*—This is the text you want to replace *old_text* with.

- *instance_num*—This specifies which occurrence of *old_text* you want to replace with *new_text*. If you specify *instance_num*, only that instance of *old_text* is replaced. Otherwise, every occurrence of *old_text* in text is changed to *new_text*.

For example, =SUBSTITUTE("Sales Data","Sales","Cost") would generate "Cost Data".

The SUBSTITUTE function works similarly to a traditional find-and-replace command. Compared to the SUBSTITUTE function, the REPLACE function is difficult enough to make even an old programmer's head spin.

Syntax:

=REPLACE(*old_text*,*start_num*,*num_chars*,*new_text*)

REPLACE replaces part of a text string, based on the number of characters specified, with a different text string. This function takes the following arguments:

- *old_text*—This is text in which you want to replace some characters.

 **Tip**

To successfully use REPLACE, you must use functions to determine the location and number of characters to replace. In most circumstances, SUBSTITUTE is easier to use.

- **start_num**—This is the position of the character in *old_text* that you want to replace with *new_text*.

- **num_chars**—This is the number of characters in *old_text* that you want REPLACE to replace with *new_text*.

- **new_text**—This is the text that will replace characters in *old_text*.

Using REPT to Repeat Text Multiple Times

The REPT function repeats a character or some text a certain number of times.

Syntax:

=REPT(*text*,*number_times*)

The REPT function repeats text a given number of times. You use REPT to fill a cell with a number of instances of a text string. This function takes the following arguments:

- **text**—This is the text you want to repeat.

- **number_times**—This is a positive number that specifies the number of times to repeat text. If *number_times* is 0, REPT returns "" (that is, empty text). If *number_times* is not an integer, it is truncated. The result of the REPT function cannot be longer than 32,767 characters.

In Microsoft Word, it is easy to create a row of periods between text and a page number. In Excel, you have to resort to clever use of the REPT function to do this.

In Figure 11.63, column A contains a page number. Column B contains a chapter title. The goal in column C is to join enough periods between columns B and A to make all the page numbers line up.

The number of periods to print is the total desired length, less the length of columns A and B. The formula for cell C2 is =B2&REPT(".",45-(LEN(A2)+LEN(B2)))&A2.

 Note

To make this work, you must change the font in column C to be a fixed-width font, such as Courier New.

	A	B	C
			=B2&REPT(".",45-(LEN(A2)+LEN(B2)))&A2
1	Page	Title	
2	7	Chapter 1 - Backstage View	Chapter 1 - Backstage View.................7
3	23	Chapter 2 - The Ribbon	Chapter 2 - The Ribbon...................23
4	39	Chapter 3 - Other Excel Improvements	Chapter 3 - Other Excel Improvements.......39
5	47	Chapter 4 - Customizing the Ribbon	Chapter 4 - Customizing the Ribbon........47
6	105	Chapter 5 - Keyboard Shortcuts	Chapter 5 - Keyboard Shortcuts...........105
7			
8		Hello Hello Hello	
9		=REPT("Hello ",3)	

C2 ▾ : × ✓ *fx* =B2&REPT(".",45-(LEN(A2)+LEN(B2)))&A2

Figure 11.63
The REPT function can be used to calculate a certain number of repeated entries.

 **Tip**

An alternative solution is to format column A with the custom format of "@*.". This shows the text in the cell and follows it with a series of periods, enough to fill the current width of the column.

Using EXACT to Test Case

For the most part, Excel isn't concerned about case. To Excel, ABC and abc are the same thing. In Figure 11.64, cells A1 and B1 contain the same letters, but the capitalization is different.

Figure 11.64
Excel usually overlooks differences in capitalization when deciding whether two values are equal. You can use EXACT to find out whether they are equal and the same case.

C1		:	×	✓	f_x	=A1=B1	
	A	B	C		D		
1	AbC	ABC	TRUE		=A1=B1		
2	AbC	ABC	FALSE		=EXACT(A2,B2)		
3							

The formula in cell C1 tests whether these values are equal. In the rules of Excel, AbC and ABC are equivalent. The formula in cell C1 indicates that the values are equal. To some people, these two text cells might not be equivalent. If you work in a store that sells the big plastic letters that go on theater marquees, your order for 20 letter *a* figures should not be filled with 20 letter *A* figures.

Excel forces you to use the EXACT function to compare these two cells to learn that they are not exactly the same.

Syntax:

=EXACT(*text1*,*text2*)

The EXACT function compares two text strings and returns TRUE if they are exactly the same and FALSE otherwise. EXACT is case-sensitive but ignores formatting differences. You use EXACT to test text being entered into a document. This function takes the following arguments:

- **text1**—This is the first text string.
- **text2**—This is the second text string

Using TEXT, DOLLAR, and FIXED to Format a Number as Text

Excel is great at numbers. Put a number in a cell, and you can format it in a variety of ways. However, when you join a cell containing text with a cell containing a number or a date, Excel falls apart.

Consider Figure 11.65. Cell A11 contains a date and is formatted as a date. When you join the name in cell B11 with the date in cell A11, Excel automatically converts the date back to a numeric serial number. This is frustrating.

B1	▼ : ✕ ✓ *fx*	=DOLLAR(A1)						
	A	B	C	D	E	F	G	H
1	1234.56	$1,234.56	=DOLLAR(A1)					
2	1234.56	$1,235	=DOLLAR(A2,0)					
3	1234.56	$1,234.56	=DOLLAR(A3,2)					
4								
5	1234.56	1,234.56	=FIXED(A5)					
6	1234.56	1,235	=FIXED(A6,0)					
7	1234.56	1235	=FIXED(A7,0,TRUE)					
8								
9	3/5/2015	Thursday, March 5, 2015						
10								
11	12/1/1989	Joe	Joe was born on 32843	=B11&" was born on "&A11				
12	12/1/1989	Joe	Joe was born on 12/1/89	=B12&" was born on "&TEXT(A12,"m/d/y")				

Figure 11.65
TEXT, DOLLAR, and FIXED can be used to format a number as text.

Today, the TEXT function is the most versatile solution to this problem. If you understand the basics of custom numeric formatting codes, you can easily use TEXT to format a date or a number in any conceivable format. For example, the formula in cell C12 uses =TEXT(A12, "m/d/y") to force the date to display as a date.

The TEXT function gives you a lot of versatility. To learn the custom formatting codes for a cell, you can select the cell, display the Format Cells dialog (by pressing Ctrl+1), and select the Custom category on the Number tab. Excel shows you the codes used to create that format.

If you don't care to learn the number formatting codes, you can use either the DOLLAR or FIXED function to return a number as text, with a few choices regarding number of decimals and whether Excel should use the thousands separator. The formulas shown in C1:C7 in Figure 11.65 return the formatted text values shown in column B.

Syntax:

=TEXT(*value*,*format_text*)

The TEXT function converts a value to text in a specific number format. Formatting a cell with an option on the Number tab of the Format Cells dialog changes only the format, not the value. Using the TEXT function converts a value to formatted text, and the result is no longer calculated as a number.

The TEXT function takes the following arguments:

- *value*—This is a numeric value, a formula that evaluates to a numeric value, or a reference to a cell that contains a numeric value.

- *format_text*—This is a number format in text form from the Category box on the Number tab in the Format Cells dialog. *format_text* cannot contain an asterisk (*) and cannot be the general number format.

Syntax:

=DOLLAR(*number*,*decimals*)

The DOLLAR function converts a number to text using currency format, with the decimals rounded to the specified place. The format used is $#,##0.00_);($#,##0.00). The major difference between formatting a cell that contains a number with the Format Cells dialog and formatting a number directly with the DOLLAR function is that DOLLAR converts its result to text. A number formatted with the Cells command is still a number. You can continue to use numbers formatted with DOLLAR in formulas because Microsoft Excel converts numbers entered as text values to numbers when it calculates.

The DOLLAR function takes the following arguments:

- *number*—This is a number, a reference to a cell that contains a number, or a formula that evaluates to a number.

- *decimals*—This is the number of digits to the right of the decimal point. If *decimals* is negative, *number* is rounded to the left of the decimal point. If you omit *decimals*, it is assumed to be 2.

Syntax:

=FIXED(*number*,[*decimals*],[*no_commas*])

The FIXED function rounds a number to the specified number of decimals, formats the number in decimal format using a period and commas, and returns the result as text. The major difference between formatting a cell that contains a number with the Format Cells dialog and formatting a number directly with the FIXED function is that FIXED converts its result to text. A number formatted with the Format Cells dialog is still a number. This function takes the following arguments:

- *number*—This is the number you want to round and convert to text.

- *decimals*—This is the number of digits to the right of the decimal point. Numbers in Microsoft Excel can never have more than 15 significant digits, but *decimals* can be as large as 127. If *decimals* is negative, *number* is rounded to the left of the decimal point. If you omit *decimals*, it is assumed to be 2.

- *no_commas*—This is a logical value that, if TRUE, prevents FIXED from including commas in the returned text. If *no_commas* is FALSE or omitted, the returned text includes commas as usual.

Converting Number Punctuation Using the NUMBERVALUE Functions

The NUMBERVALUE function is new in Excel 2013. You might receive a data file from a foreign subsidiary where they use commas for the decimal separator and periods for the thousands separator. These values never import to Excel as numbers—they end up as text.

You can use NUMBERVALUE to convert them to numbers. Specify the text, the character used as the decimal separator, and the character used as the thousands separator. Excel extracts the digits and gets the decimals in the correct place.

Syntax:

`=NUMBERVALUE(text, [decimal_separator],[group_separator])`

Converts text to a number, independent of locale. This function takes the following arguments:

- ***text***—The text to convert to a number.
- ***decimal_separator***—The character used to separate the integer and fractional part of the result.
- ***group_separator***—The character used to separate groupings of numbers, such as thousands from hundreds.

Empty spaces in the *text* argument are ignored, even in the middle of the text. For example "2 000" is returned as 2000. If the text ends in one or more percent signs, they are used and are treated as additive. "9%%" returns 0.0009.

Figure 11.66 illustrates the NUMBERVALUE function.

B3 =NUMBERVALUE(A3,",",".")

	A	B	C	D	E
1	Converting Numbers With Opposite Punctuation				
2					
3	407.699,23	407,699.23	=NUMBERVALUE(A3,",",".")		
4	767.817,48	767,817.48			
5	965.236,58	965,236.58			
6	821.195,26	821,195.26			
7	380.323,25	380,323.25			
8	981.487,61	981,487.61			
9	573.736,96	573,736.96			
10	187.345,47	187,345.47			
11	216.463,27	216,463.27			
12	950.498,28	950,498.28			
13	247.129,20	247,129.20			
14	722.135,58	722,135.58			
15	137.970,30	137,970.30			
16	739.576,77	739,576.77			
17	830.244,92	830,244.92			
18	955.545,86	955,545.86			
19	121.683,97	121,683.97			
20	618.489,44	618,489.44			
21					

Figure 11.66
Numbers in column A used the wrong punctuation for the U.S. version of Excel.

Using the T and VALUE Functions

The T and VALUE functions are left over from Lotus days.

=T("text") returns the original text. If cell B1 contains the number 123, =T(B1) would return empty text. Basically, T() returns the value in the cell only if it is text.

=VALUE() converts text that looks like a number or a date to the number or the date.

 Note

The following functions are beyond the scope of this edition: ASC, BAHTTEXT, FINDB, JIS, LEFTB, MIDB, PHONETIC, REPLACEB, RIGHTB, SEARCHB, and YEN. Even so, these functions are described earlier in this chapter in Table 11.3.

Using Functions for Non-English Character Sets

Eleven more functions have not been covered in this section. These functions deal with text in character systems where each character takes up more than 1 byte. This is true in many Asian languages.

 ## Text Times Entered as M:SS Instead of H:MM:SS

In Figure 11.67, column B contains a series of time trial results. When you total the column in cell B12, you realize that all the times were entered as text.

Figure 11.67
You can use the LEFT and RIGHT text functions to provide the arguments for the TIME function.

| D2 | ▼ | : | × | ✓ | fx | =TIME(0,LEFT(B2,1),RIGHT(B2,2)) |

	A	B	C	D	E
1	NAME	TIME	TIMEVALUE	TIME2	TIMEVALUE-2
2	CHARLOTTE	2:50	2:50:00	0:02:50	0:02:50
3	HARRIET	1:38	1:38:00	0:01:38	0:01:38
4	JUAN	1:25	1:25:00	0:01:25	0:01:25
5	KARLA	1:23	1:23:00	0:01:23	0:01:23
6	JERRY	2:44	2:44:00	0:02:44	0:02:44
7	ROSEMARY	2:39	2:39:00	0:02:39	0:02:39
8	TERRI	1:42	1:42:00	0:01:42	0:01:42
9	FRED	1:17	1:17:00	0:01:17	0:01:17
10	JESSE	1:10	1:10:00	0:01:10	0:01:10
11	ADA	1:34	1:34:00	0:01:34	0:01:34
12	TOTAL	0:00:00	18:22:00	0:18:22	0:18:22

The formulas in column C use =TIMEVALUE(B2). However, a time such as 2 minutes 50 seconds is converted in the function to 2 hours 50 minutes. In this case, TIMEVALUE does not work.

There are two alternative strategies:

- One solution is to use the TIME function. In column D, the text times are converted to real times by using the TIME function. In each case, the hours should be zero. The minutes are =LEFT(B2,1). The seconds are =RIGHT(B2,2). The formula in cell D2 is =TIME(0,LEFT(B2,1), RIGHT(B2,2)). You copy this formula down and format the range as a time.

- The other solution is to use the concatenation operator to pad the left of column B with 0:0. This allows the text to work in the TIMEVALUE function. The formula in cell E2 is =TIMEVALUE("0:0"&B2). Again, you need to copy this formula down and format the range as a time.

USING POWERFUL FUNCTIONS: LOGICAL, LOOKUP, WEB, AND DATABASE FUNCTIONS

This chapter covers five groups of workhorse functions. If you process spreadsheets of medium complexity, you will turn to logical and lookup functions regularly.

- The logical functions, including the ubiquitous IF function, help make decisions. Excel 2013 adds the XOR function (for eXclusive OR) and the IFNA function.

- The information functions might be less important than they once were, now that Microsoft has added the IFERROR function, but INFO, CELL, and TYPE still come in handy. New in Excel 2013 are the SHEET, SHEETS, and ISFORMULA functions.

- The lookup functions include the powerful VLOOKUP, MATCH, and INDIRECT functions. These functions are invaluable, particularly when you are doing something in Excel when it would be better to use Access. In addition, let's face it: With 1.1 million rows in Excel 2013, we will all do more things in Excel that should be done in Access. Excel 2013 adds the FORMULATEXT function.

- Excel 2013 adds the Web category, with RNCODEURL, FILTERXML, and WEBSERVICE functions.

- Finally, the database functions provide the DSUM functions. Even though these functions fell out of favor with the introduction of pivot tables, they are a powerful set of functions that are worthwhile to master.

Table 12.1 provides an alphabetical list of all Excel 2013's logical functions. Detailed examples of these functions are provided later in this chapter.

Table 12.1   Alphabetical List of Logical Functions

Function	Description
AND(*logical1,logical2,...*)	Returns TRUE if all its arguments are TRUE; returns FALSE if one or more arguments are FALSE.
FALSE()	Returns the logical value FALSE.
IF(*logical_test,value_if_true, value_if_false*)	Returns one value if a condition specified evaluates to TRUE and another value if it evaluates to FALSE.
IFERROR(*value,value_if_error*)	Returns *value_if_error* if the expression is an error and the value itself otherwise.
IFNA(*value,value_if_na*)	Returns value_if_na if the expression resolves to #N/A; otherwise, returns the result of the expression.
NOT(*logical*)	Reverses the value of its argument. You use NOT when you want to make sure a value is not equal to another particular value.
OR(*logical1,logical2,...*)	Returns TRUE if any argument is TRUE; returns FALSE if all arguments are FALSE.
TRUE()	Returns the logical value TRUE.

Table 12.2 provides an alphabetical list of all of Excel 2013's information functions. Detailed examples of these functions are provided in the remainder of the chapter.

Table 12.2   Alphabetical List of Information Functions

Function	Description
CELL(*info_type,reference*)	Returns information about the formatting, location, or contents of the upper-left cell in a reference.
ERROR.TYPE(*error_val*)	Returns a number corresponding to one of the error values in Microsoft Excel or returns an #N/A error if no error exists. You can use ERROR.TYPE in an IF function to test for an error value and return a text string, such as a message, instead of the error value.
INFO(*type_text*)	Returns information about the current operating environment.
ISBLANK(*value*)	Returns TRUE if *value* refers to an empty cell.

Function	Description
ISERROR(*value*)	Returns TRUE if *value* refers to any error value (that is, #N/A, #VALUE!, #REF!, #DIV/0!, #NUM!, #NAME?, or #NULL!).
ISERR(*value*)	Returns TRUE if *value* refers to any error value except #N/A.
ISEVEN(*number*)	Returns TRUE if *number* is even and FALSE if *number* is odd.
ISFORMULA(*reference*)	Checks whether a reference is to a cell containing a formula and returns TRUE or FALSE. New in Excel 2013.
ISLOGICAL(*value*)	Returns TRUE if *value* refers to a logical value.
ISNA(*value*)	Returns TRUE if *value* refers to the #N/A (value not available) error value.
ISNONTEXT(*value*)	Returns TRUE if *value* refers to any item that is not text. (Note that this function returns TRUE if *value* refers to a blank cell.)
ISNUMBER(*value*)	Returns TRUE if *value* refers to a number.
ISODD(*number*)	Returns TRUE if *number* is odd and FALSE if *number* is even.
ISREF(*value*)	Returns TRUE if *value* refers to a reference.
ISTEXT(*value*)	Returns TRUE if *value* refers to text.
N(*value*)	Returns a *value* converted to a number.
NA()	Returns the error value #N/A, which means "no value is available." You use NA to mark empty cells or cells that are missing information to avoid the problem of unintentionally including empty cells in your calculations. When a formula refers to a cell containing #N/A, the formula returns the #N/A error value.
SHEET([*value*])	Returns the sheet number of the referenced sheet. New in Excel 2013.
SHEETS([*reference*]	Returns the number of sheets in a reference. New in Excel 2013
TYPE(*value*)	Returns the type of *value*. You use TYPE when the behavior of another function depends on the type of value in a particular cell.

Table 12.3 provides an alphabetical list of all of Excel 2013's lookup functions. Detailed examples of these functions are provided later in this chapter.

Table 12.3   Alphabetical List of Lookup Functions

Function	Description
ADDRESS(*row_num*,*column_num*, *abs_num*,a1,*sheet_text*)	Creates a cell address as text, given specified row and column numbers.
AREAS(*reference*)	Returns the number of areas in a reference. An area is a range of contiguous cells or a single cell.
CHOOSE(*index_num*,*value1*, *value 2*, ...)	Uses *index_num* to return a value from the list of *value* arguments. You use CHOOSE to select one of up to 254 values, based on the index number. For example, if *value1* through *value7* are the days of the week, CHOOSE returns one of the days when a number between 1 and 7 is used as *index_num*.
COLUMN(*reference*)	Returns the column number of the given reference.
COLUMNS(*array*)	Returns the number of columns in an array or a reference.
FORMULATEXT(*reference*)	Returns a formula as a reference. New in Excel 2013.
GETPIVOTDATA(*data_field*, *pivot_ table*,[*field1*],[*item1*],...)	Returns data stored in a pivot table report. You can use GETPIVOTDATA to retrieve summary data from a pivot table report, if the summary data is visible in the report.
HLOOKUP(*lookup_value*, *table_array*, *row_index_num*, *range_lookup*)	Searches for a value in the top row of a table or an array of values, and then returns a value in the same column from a row you specify in the table or array. You use HLOOKUP when your comparison values are located in a row across the top of a table of data and you want to look down a specified number of rows. You use VLOOKUP when your comparison values are located in a column to the left of the data you want to find.
HYPERLINK(*link_location*, *friendly_name*)	Creates a shortcut or jump that opens a document stored on a network server, an intranet, or the Internet. When you click the cell that contains the HYPERLINK function, Excel opens the file stored at *link_location*.
INDEX(*array*, *row_num*, *column_num*)	Returns the value of a specified cell or array of cells within *array*.
INDEX(*reference*, *row_num*, *column_num*, *area_num*)	Returns a reference to a specified cell or cells within *reference*.
INDIRECT(*ref_text*, a1)	Returns the reference specified by a text string. References are evaluated immediately to display their contents. You use INDIRECT when you want to change the reference to a cell within a formula without changing the formula itself.

Function	Description
LOOKUP(*lookup_value*, *lookup_vector*, *result_vector*)	Returns a value from either a one-row or one-column range. This vector form of LOOKUP looks in a one-row or one-column range, known as a *vector*, for a value and returns a value from the same position in a second one-row or one-column range. This function is included for compatibility with other worksheets. You should use VLOOKUP instead.
LOOKUP(*lookup_value*, *array*)	Returns a value from an array. The array form of LOOKUP looks in the first row or column of an array for the specified value and returns a value from the same position in the last row or column of the array. This function is included for compatibility with other spreadsheet programs. You should use VLOOKUP instead. However, unlike VLOOKUP, the LOOKUP function can process an array of *lookup_values*.
MATCH(*lookup_value*, *lookup_array*, *match_type*)	Returns the relative position of an item in an array that matches a specified value in a specified order. You use MATCH instead of one of the LOOKUP functions when you need the position of an item in a range instead of the item itself.
OFFSET(*reference*, *rows*, *cols*, *height*, *width*)	Returns a reference to a range that is a specified number of rows and columns away from a cell or range of cells. The reference that is returned can be a single cell or a range of cells. You can specify the number of rows and the number of columns to be returned.
ROW(*reference*)	Returns the row number of a reference.
ROWS(*array*)	Returns the number of rows in a reference or an array.
RTD(*progid*, *server*, *topic*,[*topic2*],...)	Retrieves real-time data from a program that supports COM automation. This function was new in Excel XP.
TRANSPOSE(*array*)	Returns a vertical range of cells as a horizontal range, or vice versa. TRANSPOSE must be entered as an array formula in a range that has the same number of rows and columns, respectively, because *array* has columns and rows. You use TRANSPOSE to shift the vertical and horizontal orientation of an array on a worksheet. For example, some functions, such as LINEST, return horizontal arrays. LINEST returns a horizontal array of the slope and y-intercept for a line. Use TRANSPOSE to convert the LINEST result to a vertical array.
VLOOKUP(*lookup_value*, *table_array*, *col_index_num*, *range_lookup*)	Searches for a value in the leftmost column of a table and then returns a value in the same row from a column you specify in the table. You use VLOOKUP instead of HLOOKUP when your comparison values are located in a column to the left of the data you want to find.

Table 12.4 provides an alphabetical list of all of Excel 2013's web functions. Detailed examples of these functions are provided later in this chapter.

Table 12.4 Alphabetical List of Web Functions

Function	Description
ENCODEURL(*text*)	Returns a URL-encoded string
FILTERXML(*xml*, *xpath*)	Returns specific data from the XML content by using the xpath
WEBSERVICE(*url*)	Returns data from a web service

Table 12.5 provides an alphabetical list of all of Excel 2013's database functions. Detailed examples of these functions are provided later in this chapter.

Table 12.5 Alphabetical List of Database Functions

Function	Description
DAVERAGE(*database*, *field*, *criteria*)	Averages the values in a column in a list or database that match the conditions specified
DCOUNT(*database*, *field*, *criteria*)	Counts the cells that contain numbers in a column in a list or database that match the conditions specified
DCOUNTA(*database*, *field*, *criteria*)	Counts all the nonblank cells in a column in a list or database that match the conditions specified
DGET(*database*, *field*, *criteria*)	Extracts a single value from a column in a list or database that matches the conditions specified
DMAX(*database*, *field*, *criteria*)	Returns the largest number in a column in a list or database that matches the conditions specified
DMIN(*database*, *field*, *criteria*)	Returns the smallest number in a column in a list or database that matches the conditions specified
DPRODUCT(*database*, *field*, *criteria*)	Multiplies the values in a column in a list or database that match the conditions specified
DSTDEV(*database*, *field*, *criteria*)	Estimates the standard deviation of a population based on a sample, using the numbers in a column in a list or database that match the conditions specified
DSTDEVP(*database*, *field*, *criteria*)	Calculates the standard deviation of a population based on the entire population, using the numbers in a column in a list or database that match the conditions specified

Function	Description
DSUM(*database*, *field*, *criteria*)	Adds the numbers in a column in a list or database that match the conditions specified
DVAR(*database*, *field*, *criteria*)	Estimates the variance of a population based on a sample, using the numbers in a column in a list or database that match the conditions specified
DVARP(*database*, *field*, *criteria*)	Calculates the variance of a population based on the entire population, using the numbers in a column in a list or database that match the conditions specified

Examples of Logical Functions

With only eight functions, the logical function group is one of the smallest in Excel. The IF function is easy to understand, and it enables you to solve a variety of problems.

Using the IF Function to Make a Decision

Many calculations in our lives are not straightforward. Suppose that a manager offers a bonus program if her team meets its goals. Or perhaps a commission plan offers a bonus if a certain profit goal is met. You can solve these types of calculations by using the IF function.

Syntax:

IF(*logical_test*,*value_if_true*,*value_if_false*)

There are three arguments in the IF function. The first argument is any logical test that results in a TRUE or FALSE. For example, you might have logical tests such as these:

A2>100
B5="West"
C99<=D99

All logical tests involve one of the comparison operators shown in Table 12.6.

Table 12.6   Comparison Operators

Comparison Operator	Meaning	Example
=	Equal to	C1=D1
>	Greater than	A1>B1
<	Less than	A1<B1

Comparison Operator	Meaning	Example
>=	Greater than or equal to	A1>=0
<=	Less than or equal to	A1<=99
<>	Not equal to	A2<>B2

The remaining two arguments are the formula or value to use if the logical test is `true` and the formula or value to use if the logical test is `false`.

When you read an IF function, you should think of the first comma as the word *then* and the second comma as the word *otherwise*. For example, =IF(A2>10,25,0) would be read as "If A2>10, then 25; otherwise, 0."

Figure 12.1 calculates a sales commission. The commission rate is 1.5 percent of revenue. However, if the gross profit percentage is 50% or higher, the commission rate is 2.5 percent of revenue.

In this case, the logical test is H2>=50%. The formula for whether that test is true is 0.025*F2. Otherwise, the formula is 0.015*F2. You could build the formula as =IF(H2>=50%,0.025*F2,0.015*F2).

 **Note**

Mathematicians would correctly note that in both the second and third arguments of the formula =IF(H2>=50%,0.025*F2, 0.015*F2), you are multiplying by F2. Therefore, you could simplify the formula by using =IF (H2>=50%,0.025,0.015) *F2.

I2   ▼   :   ×   ✓   fx   =IF(H2>=50%,0.025*F2,0.015*F2)

▲	D	E	F	G	H	I	J
1	Associate	Qty	Revenue	Cost	GP%	Commission	
2	GERALD	400	15456	8400	45.7%	231.84	1.5%
3	JOSEPH	700	53928	25200	53.3%	1348.2	2.5%
4	SHELLY	100	4784	2600	45.7%	71.76	1.5%
5	JOY	1000	67680	36000	46.8%	1015.2	1.5%
6	JOY	300	20088	9300	53.7%	502.2	2.5%
7	FANNIE	600	32760	15600	52.4%	819	2.5%
8	JOSEPH	400	34768	16400	52.8%	869.2	2.5%
9	JOY	100	7704	3600	53.3%	192.6	2.5%

Figure 12.1
In rows 2, 4, and 5, the commission is 1.5%. In rows 3 and 6 through 9 the commission is 2.5%.

Using the AND Function to Check for Two or More Conditions

The previous example had one simple condition: If the value in column H was greater than or equal to 50%, the commission rate changed.

However, in many cases you might need to test for two or more conditions. For example, suppose that a retail store manager offers a $25 bonus for every leather jacket sold on Fridays this month. In this case, the logical test requires you to determine whether both conditions are true. You can do this with the AND function.

Syntax:

```
AND(logical1,logical2,...)
```

The arguments *logical1,logical2,...* are from one to 255 expressions that evaluate to either TRUE or FALSE. The function returns TRUE only if all arguments are TRUE.

In Figure 12.2, the function in cell F2 checks whether cell E2 is a jacket and whether the date in cell D2 falls on a Friday:

```
=AND(E2="Jacket",WEEKDAY(D2,2)=5)
```

Figure 12.2
The AND function is TRUE only when every condition is met.

	A	B	C	D	E	F	G	H
	Store	Cust	Associate	Date	Item	Bonus?		
2	S18	C422	Jenny	Tue 4/14/2015	Handbag	FALSE		
3	S5	C244	Bill	Fri 4/10/2015	Jacket	TRUE		
4	S13	C668	Diana	Mon 4/27/2015	Hat	FALSE		
5	S19	C825	Bill	Tue 4/14/2015	Jacket	FALSE		
6	S15	C590	Bill	Fri 4/24/2015	Coaster	FALSE		
7	S5	C857	Bill	Fri 4/10/2015	Handbag	FALSE		

F2   fx   =AND(E2="Jacket",WEEKDAY(D2,2)=5)

Using the AND Function to Compare Two Lists

The AND function can handle up to 255 expressions. Each expression can contain a range that might contain many instances of TRUE or FALSE.

A common issue is figuring out whether two worksheets are identical. In Figure 12.3, columns A:E contain the original worksheet. After this worksheet was passed among several co-workers, it ended back at your desk. Follow these steps to compare the two worksheets:

   1. Leave three blank columns—columns F, G, and H—to the right of your original data.

Figure 12.3
AND can test whether a large range of logical tests are all TRUE.

G6   fx   =AND(A6=I6,B6=J6,C6=K6,D6=L6,E6=M6)

	A	B	C	D	E	F	G	H	I	J	K	L	M	N
1			Woodlawn - 1	Woodlawn - 1	Woodlawn - 2		All Match				Woodlawn -	Woodlawn -	Woodlawn - 2	
2			8AM-9:30AM	10AM-11:30AM	8AM-9:30AM		FALSE				8AM-9:30AM	AM-11:30AM	AM-9:30AM	
3														
4														
5							Match?							
6	25-Apr	Saturday	**Black**	Blue	Green		TRUE		25-Apr	Saturday	**Black**	Blue	Green	
7	28-Apr	Tuesday	N/A	N/A	N/A		TRUE		28-Apr	Tuesday	N/A	N/A	N/A	
8	29-Apr	Wednesday	N/A	N/A	N/A		TRUE		29-Apr	Wednesda	N/A	N/A	N/A	
9	30-Apr	Thursday	N/A	N/A	N/A		TRUE		30-Apr	Thursday	N/A	N/A	N/A	
10	2-May	Saturday	Open	**Black**	Blue		TRUE		2-May	Saturday	Open	**Black**	Blue	
11	5-May	Tuesday	N/A	N/A	N/A		FALSE		5-May	Tuesday	Red at Gray	N/A	N/A	
12	6-May	Wednesday	N/A	N/A	N/A		TRUE		6-May	Wednesda	N/A	N/A	N/A	
13	7-May	Thursday	N/A	N/A	N/A		TRUE		7-May	Thursday	N/A	N/A	N/A	
14	9-May	Saturday	**Black** at Blue	**Green** at Orange	**Red** at Purple		TRUE		9-May	Saturday	ack at Blue	n at Ora	d at Purple	
15	12-May	Tuesday	N/A	N/A	N/A		TRUE		12-May	Tuesday	N/A	N/A	N/A	

2. Copy the data range of the returned worksheet. Paste this copy, starting in column I of the original worksheet.

3. Add the heading **All Match?** in column G.

4. Add a formula in column G to compare whether each of the cells in the original data set matches the cells in the returned data set. Add the formula =AND(A6=I6,B6=J6,C6=K6,D6=L6,E6=M6) in cell G6 to compare all five cells in the data set.

5. Copy the formula down column G from cell G6 to match the number of rows in the data set.

6. In cell G2, enter an AND formula to test whether all the formulas in column G are TRUE. Even though this range contains more than 255 cells, it is still valid to use it as one of the expressions in the AND function. The formula in G2 is =AND(G6:G999). This is a quick way to find out whether every row is identical without having to scroll through pages of data, looking for a single FALSE result. If cell G2 returns TRUE, you know that the original and returned worksheets are identical. If cell G2 returns FALSE, you know that one or more of the rows were changed.

7. Select G6:G999. From the Home tab, select Find & Select, Find. The Find and Replace dialog appears.

8. In the Find and Replace dialog, type **FALSE** into the Find What box. You must click the Options button and change the Look In drop-down from Formulas to Values to find formulas that result in a value of FALSE.

 **Tip**

Instead of using the AND function, you can multiply the conditions. =(A6=I6)*(B6=J6)*(C6=K6)*(D6*L6)* (E6=M6) will return 1 if all the conditions are true and 0 if any one of the conditions is false. Alternatively, you can type =AND(A6:E6=I6:M6) and press Ctrl+Shift+Enter to have AND evaluate the array of comparisons.

Using OR or XOR to Check Whether One or More Conditions Are Met

In the earlier examples, all the conditions had to be met for the IF function to be true. In other cases, you might need to identify when exactly one condition is true, or when one or more conditions are true.

For example, a sales manager may want to reward big orders and orders from new customers. The manager may offer a commission bonus if the order is more than $50,000 or if the customer is a new customer this year. The bonus is awarded if either condition is true. But only one bonus is paid; you do not give two bonuses if a customer is both new and the order is large. In this case, you would use the OR function with logical tests to check whether the customer is new or if the order is large.

To test whether a particular sale meets either condition, use the OR function. The OR function returns TRUE if any condition is TRUE and returns FALSE if none of the conditions are TRUE.

In another example, a crating bill of lading is correct if the crate contains one dog or one cat. If the crate is empty, or if the crate contains both a dog and a cat, the crate is invalid. In this case, you would use XOR to test for an Exclusive Or function.

To test whether a particular record matches exactly one condition, use the XOR function.

Syntax:

OR(*logical1*,*logical2*,...)

The OR function checks whether any of the arguments are TRUE. It returns a FALSE only if all the arguments are FALSE. If any argument is TRUE, the function returns TRUE.

The arguments *logical1*,*logical2*,... are one to 255 conditions that can evaluate to TRUE or FALSE.

Syntax:

XOR(*logical1*,*logical2*,...)

The XOR function checks whether an odd number of the arguments are TRUE.

The arguments *logical1*,*logical2*,... are one to 254 conditions you want to test that can either be TRUE or FALSE. They can be logical values, arrays, or references.

In Figure 12.4, the OR function in column E is contrasted with the XOR function in column F.

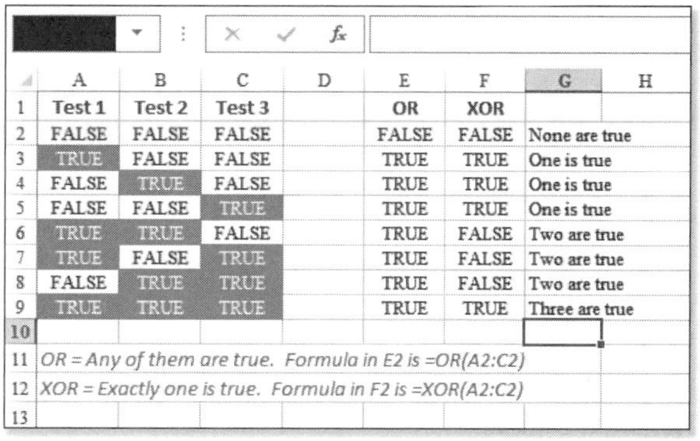

Figure 12.4
OR checks whether a record meets at least one of several criteria. XOR checks to see if an odd number of criteria is true.

	A	B	C	D	E	F	G	H
1	Test 1	Test 2	Test 3		OR	XOR		
2	FALSE	FALSE	FALSE		FALSE	FALSE	None are true	
3	TRUE	FALSE	FALSE		TRUE	TRUE	One is true	
4	FALSE	TRUE	FALSE		TRUE	TRUE	One is true	
5	FALSE	FALSE	TRUE		TRUE	TRUE	One is true	
6	TRUE	TRUE	FALSE		TRUE	FALSE	Two are true	
7	TRUE	FALSE	TRUE		TRUE	FALSE	Two are true	
8	FALSE	TRUE	TRUE		TRUE	FALSE	Two are true	
9	TRUE	TRUE	TRUE		TRUE	TRUE	Three are true	
10								
11	OR = Any of them are true. Formula in E2 is =OR(A2:C2)							
12	XOR = Exactly one is true. Formula in F2 is =XOR(A2:C2)							
13								

Caution

The TRUE in F9 of Figure 12.4 seems surprising. With all three arguments TRUE, the Exclusive Or function is returning a TRUE. This answer is based on the actual results of XOR gates such as the 74LVC1G386 microchip. This chip first does an XOR of the first two arguments. This results in the top Venn diagram shown in Figure 12.5. The chip then cascades that resulting Venn diagram into an XOR with the third argument. The result is that the scribbled FALSE area of the top Venn diagram when XOR'd with the TRUE third argument returns a TRUE. Electrical engineers call this a *parity generator* or a *modulo-2 adder*. Although it would be difficult to continue the Venn diagram showing the intersection of 4, 5, or 254 circles, you can imagine how the intersection area flips to FALSE for an even number of circles and then back to TRUE for an odd number of circles.

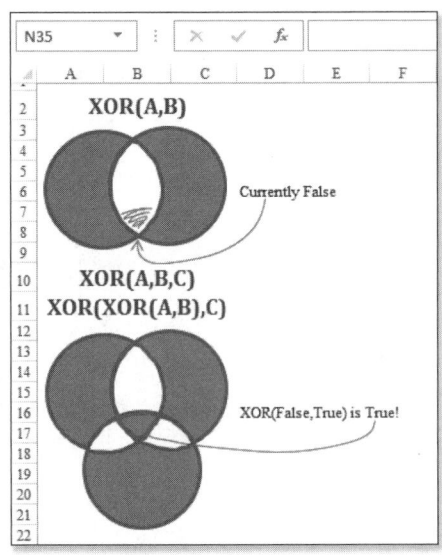

Figure 12.5
XOR(TRUE,TRUE,TRUE) surprisingly returns TRUE.

Nesting IF Functions

The IF function offers only two possible formulas. Either the logical test is TRUE and the first formula is used, or the logical test is FALSE and the second formula is used.

Many situations have a series of choices. For example, in a human resources department, annual merit raises might be given based on the employee's numeric rating in an annual review, in which employees are ranked on a 5-point scale. The rules for setting the raise are as follows:

- 4.5 or higher: 5% raise

- 4 or higher: 4.5% raise

- 3.25 or higher: 3% raise

- 2.5 or higher: 1% raise

- Under 2.5: no raise

You can build the IF statement by following these steps:

1. Test for the highest condition first. Excel stops testing when the first condition is met. If the first test checks to see whether an employee had a rating of higher than 2.5, then anyone from 2.5 to 5 receives a 1% raise. In this case, you want to give a 5% raise to anyone with a rating of 4.5 or greater. Therefore, the formula starts out as =IF(D2>=4.5,5%,.

2. There is only one argument left in the current IF function—the argument for *value_if_false*. Instead of using a value as the third argument, start a second IF function to be used if the first test is FALSE. This IF function starts out IF(D2>=4,4.5%,. Combine this start of an IF function with the first IF function: =IF(D2>=4.5,5%,IF(D2>=4,4.5%,.

3. There are still three possible raise levels and only one argument left in the second IF function. Start a third IF function to be used as the *value_if_false* argument for the second IF function: IF(D2>=3.25,3%,. At this point, if the employee did not rank above 3.25, only two possibilities are left. The employee is either 2.5 and above for a 1% raise, or he or she gets no raise.

4. Create the fourth IF function: IF(D2>=2.5,1%,0).

5. With the four IF functions, be careful to provide four closing parentheses at the end of the function: =IF(D2>=4.5,5%,IF(D 2>=4,4.5%,IF(D2>=3.25,3%,IF(D2>=2.5,1%,0%)))) (see Figure 12.6).

> ## ⚠ Caution
>
> These IF formulas are hard to read. There is a temptation to use them for situations with very long lists of conditions. Whereas Excel 2003 prevented you from nesting more than seven levels of IF functions, Excel 2007 and later allow you to nest up to 64 IF statements. Before you start nesting that many IF statements, you should consider using VLOOKUP, which is explained later in this chapter.

Figure 12.6
This formula contains four nested IF functions.

	C	D	E	F	G	H
	\=IF(D2>=4.5,5%,IF(D2>=4,4.5%,IF(D2>=3.25,3%,IF(D2>=2.5,1%,0%))))					
	EMPLOYEE	RANK	RAISE			
	JIMMY CAMPBELL	1.6	0.00%			
	DENNIS PENA	3.4	3.00%			
	MARK LANCASTER	4.8	5.00%			
	KEITH AGUIRRE	4.3	4.50%			
	MARIAN SUAREZ	3.8	3.00%			
	SAMUEL WOODWARD	3	1.00%			
	PHILLIP MULLINS	2.4	0.00%			
	JOHNNY KNOX	1.3	0.00%			
	SEAN HAYES	2.3	0.00%			
	ROGER COTTON	5	5.00%			
	TERESA ROJAS	4.3	4.50%			

Using the TRUE and FALSE Functions

There are two remaining functions in the logical group, but you should not need to use either of them. If you encounter a function with either the TRUE or FALSE function, you can replace the function with the value TRUE or FALSE. Microsoft added TRUE and FALSE to provide compatibility with other vendors' spreadsheet programs.

A formula such as =IF(OR(A2>5,B2=0),TRUE(),FALSE()) can be rewritten as =IF(OR(A2>5, B2=0),TRUE,FALSE). If you are trying to return TRUE or FALSE, you can simply use the Boolean expression: =OR(A2>5,B2=0).

Using the NOT Function to Simplify the Use of AND and OR

In the language of Boolean logic, there are typically NAND, NOR, and XOR functions, which stand for Not And, Not Or, and Exclusive Or. To simplify matters, Excel offers the NOT function.

Syntax:

`NOT(logical)`

Quite simply, NOT reverses a logical value. TRUE becomes FALSE, and FALSE becomes TRUE when processed through a NOT function.

For example, suppose you need to find all flights landing outside Oklahoma. You can build a massive OR statement to find every airport code in the United States. Alternatively, you can build an OR function to find Tulsa and Oklahoma City and then use a NOT function to reverse the result: =NOT(OR(A2 ="Tulsa",A2="Oklahoma City")).

Using the IFERROR or IFNA Function to Simplify Error Checking

The IFERROR function, which was introduced in Excel 2007, was added at the request of many customers. To better understand the IFERROR function, you need to understand how error checking was performed during the 22 years before Excel 2007 was released.

Figure 12.7 shows a typical spreadsheet that calculates a ratio of sales to hours. Even though this formula works most of the time, in occasional records, the divisor is zero, and the formula returns a #DIV/0 error.

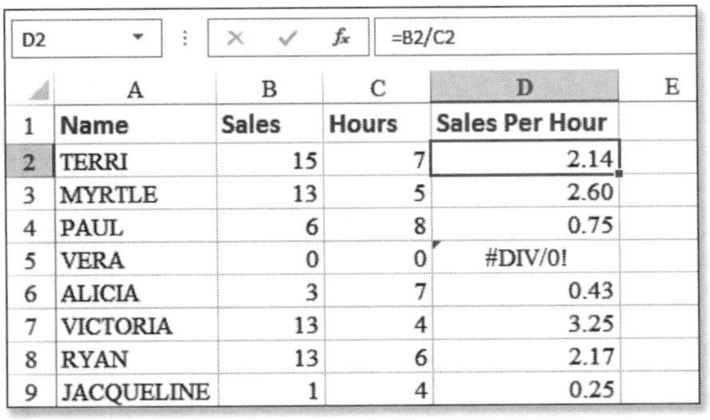
D2 =B2/C2

	A	B	C	D	E
1	Name	Sales	Hours	Sales Per Hour	
2	TERRI	15	7	2.14	
3	MYRTLE	13	5	2.60	
4	PAUL	6	8	0.75	
5	VERA	0	0	#DIV/0!	
6	ALICIA	3	7	0.43	
7	VICTORIA	13	4	3.25	
8	RYAN	13	6	2.17	
9	JACQUELINE	1	4	0.25	

Figure 12.7
The zero in the divisor in row 5 causes a division-by-zero error.

The typical way to deal with this in legacy versions of Excel was to set up an IF function to check whether the divisor was zero: =IF(C5=0,0,B5/C5). If the divisor was zero, the formula returned a zero as the result. Otherwise, the formula performed the calculation.

In legacy versions of Excel, it was typical to use this type of IF formula on thousands of rows of data. The formula is more complex and takes longer to calculate than the new IFERROR function. However, this particular formula is tame compared to some of the formulas needed to check for errors.

A common error occurs when you use the VLOOKUP function to retrieve a value from a lookup table. In Figure 12.8, the VLOOKUP function in cell D2 asks Excel to look for the rep number S07 from cell B2 and find the corresponding name in the lookup table of F2:G9. This works great, returning JESSE from the table. However, a problem arises when the sales rep is not found in the table. In row 7, rep S09 is new and has not yet been added to the table, so Excel returns the #N/A result.

Figure 12.8
An #N/A error means that the value is not in the lookup table.

| D2 | ▼ | : | ✕ | ✓ | *fx* | =VLOOKUP(B2,$F$2:$G$9,2,FALSE) |

	A	B	C	D	E	F	G
1	Invoice	Rep	Amount	Name		Rep	Name
2	15100	S07	128.59	JESSE		S01	GRACE
3	15101	S06	144.67	ERIN		S02	JULIE
4	15102	S05	121	JEREMY		S03	CHRISTY
5	15103	S04	169.47	THELMA		S04	THELMA
6	15104	S04	169.62	THELMA		S05	JEREMY
7	15105	S09	172.55	#N/A		S06	ERIN
8	15106	S08	112.68	MARION		S07	JESSE
9	15107	S02	145.44	JULIE		S08	MARION
10	15108	S01	101.05	GRACE			
11	15109	S05	197.68	JEREMY			
12	15110	S09	140.55	#N/A			
13	15111	S07	190.37	JESSE			
14	15112	S08	135.51	MARION			
15	15113	S09	177.18	#N/A			
16	15114	S01	122.07	GRACE			

If you want to avoid #N/A errors, the generally accepted workaround in legacy versions of Excel was to write this horrible formula:

```
=IF(ISNA(VLOOKUP(B7,$F$2:$G$9,2,FALSE)),"New Rep", VLOOKUP(B7,$F$2:$G$9,2,FALSE))
```

In English, this formula says to first find the rep name in the lookup table. If the rep is not found and returns the #N/A error, then use some other text, which in this case is the words *New Rep*. If the rep is found, then perform the lookup again and use that result.

Because VLOOKUP was one of the most time-intensive functions, it was horrible to have Excel perform every VLOOKUP twice in this formula. In a data set with 50,000 records, it could take minutes for the VLOOKUP to complete. Microsoft wisely added the new IFERROR function to handle all these error-checking situations.

Starting in Excel 2013, Microsoft has added the `IFNA` function. It works just like the `IFERROR` function, but the second argument is only used when the first argument results in an #N/A error. You might be able to imagine a situation where you want to replace the #N/A errors but allow other errors to appear.

Syntax:

`IFERROR(`*value,value_if_error*`)`

The advantage of the `IFERROR` function is that the calculation is evaluated only once. If the calculation results in any type of an error value, such as #N/A, #VALUE!, #REF!, #DIV/0!, #NUM!, #NAME?, or #NULL!, Excel returns the alternative value. If the calculation results in any other valid value, whether it is numeric, logical, or text, Excel returns the calculated value.

Syntax:

`IFNA(`*value,value_if_na*`)`

If the expression evaluates to a value of #N/A, then `IFNA` returns *value_if_na* instead of the expression. Added in Excel 2013, this function only replaces #N/A errors and allows other errors to appear as the result.

The formula from the preceding section can be rewritten as `=IFERROR(VLOOKUP(B7,` `$F$2:$G$9,2,FALSE),"New Rep")` or as `=IFNA(VLOOKUP(B7, $F$2:$G$9,2,FALSE),"New Rep")` (see Figure 12.9). Although `IFNA` is a bit shorter than `IFERROR`, the new `IFNA` function fails for anyone using Excel 2010 or earlier. This makes `IFERROR` a safer function to use for the next several years. Either `IFERROR` or `IFNA` calculates much more quickly than putting two VLOOKUPs in an IF function.

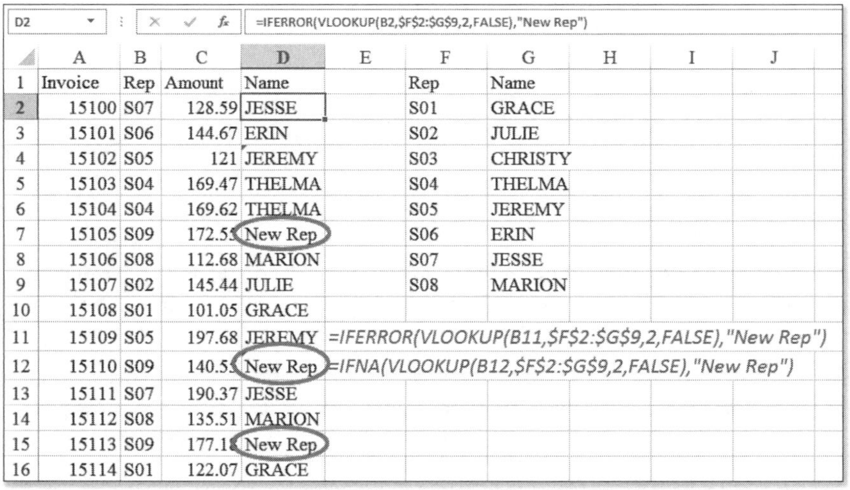

Figure 12.9
IFERROR or IFNA will replace the #N/A errors.

Examples of Information Functions

Found under the More Function icon, the 20 information functions return eclectic information about any cell. Eleven of the 20 functions are called the IS functions because they test for various conditions.

Using the IS Functions to Test for Errors

Figure 12.10 shows the results of the following four functions for testing error values:

- **ISERROR**—This function evaluates whether a calculation or value results in any type of error. If people using only Excel 2007 or later will use your workbooks, you should use the IFERROR function instead of ISERROR. However, if you need to share your workbook with people using legacy versions of Excel, you should use ISERROR, which is usually combined with an IF function. Here is an example: =IF(ISERROR(A2),"Unknown",A2).

- **ISERR**—This function is similar to ISERROR, except it does not report #N/A errors.

- **ISNA**—This function specifically tests whether a result returns an #N/A error.

- **ERROR.TYPE**—This function lets you know specifically what error is being returned. This function returns a value from 1 through 7 to indicate #NULL!, #DIV/0!, #VALUE!, #REF!, #NAME?, #NUM!, and #N/A, respectively. It is possible to write a lengthy formula such as the following to decode these values and provide a friendlier error message:

```
=IF(NOT(ISERROR(A2)),A2,CHOOSE(ERROR.TYPE(A2),"Null Value Found",
"Division by Zero","Invalid Value","Missing Reference","Undefined Name",
"Numeric Error","Value Not Available"))
```

Figure 12.10
The results of IS functions for detecting errors.

| B2 | ▼ | : | × | ✓ | fx | =ERROR.TYPE(A2) |

◢	A	B	C	D	E
1	Value	Error.Type	IsErr	IsError	IsNA
2	#NULL!	1	TRUE	TRUE	FALSE
3	#DIV/0!	2	TRUE	TRUE	FALSE
4	#VALUE!	3	TRUE	TRUE	FALSE
5	#REF!	4	TRUE	TRUE	FALSE
6	#NAME?	5	TRUE	TRUE	FALSE
7	#NUM!	6	TRUE	TRUE	FALSE
8	#N/A	7	FALSE	TRUE	TRUE

Using the ISFORMULA Function with Conditional Formatting to Mark Formula Cells

The Excel team introduced the ISFORMULA function in Excel 2013 to identify whether or not a cell contains a formula. A hack had been floating around for years to mark formula cells using an old XL4 Macro Language function. Being able to use ISFORMULA is a great improvement.

Syntax:

ISFORMULA(*reference*)

Checks whether *reference* contains a formula. Returns TRUE or FALSE.

Figure 12.11 shows a worksheet where all the cells have a conditional formatting formula that uses =ISFORMULA. Any cells that contain a formula are shown in white text on black fill.

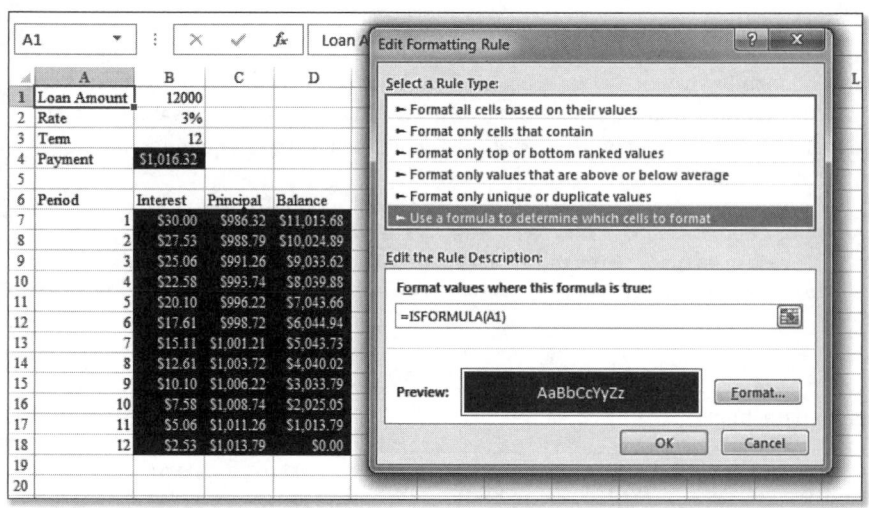

Figure 12.11
Use the new ISFORMULA function with conditional formatting to mark all of the formula cells.

Using IS Functions to Test for Types of Values

Figure 12.12 shows the results for the seven remaining IS functions. Each of these functions reveals whether a cell contains a particular type of value:

- **ISBLANK**—This function returns TRUE only if a cell is completely empty. A cell that contains several spaces is not considered blank. Even a cell that contains a single apostrophe and no spaces is not considered blank by the ISBLANK function. It would have been more appropriate if the folks at Lotus 1-2-3 would have called this the @IsEmpty function, but you are stuck with the bad name now that it has been in use forever.

Figure 12.12
The results of
IS functions
for detecting
certain types of
values.

L20	▼	:	× ✓ *fx*					
	A	B	C	D	E	F	G	H
1	Value	IsBlank	IsEven	IsOdd	IsLogical	IsText	IsNonText	IsNumber
2	1	FALSE	FALSE	TRUE	FALSE	FALSE	TRUE	TRUE
3	2	FALSE	TRUE	FALSE	FALSE	FALSE	TRUE	TRUE
4	TRUE	FALSE	#VALUE!	#VALUE!	TRUE	FALSE	TRUE	FALSE
5	FALSE	FALSE	#VALUE!	#VALUE!	TRUE	FALSE	TRUE	FALSE
6	7/1/2015	FALSE	TRUE	FALSE	FALSE	FALSE	TRUE	TRUE
7	ABC	FALSE	#VALUE!	#VALUE!	FALSE	TRUE	FALSE	FALSE
8		TRUE	TRUE	FALSE	FALSE	FALSE	TRUE	FALSE
9	#N/A	FALSE	#N/A	#N/A	FALSE	FALSE	TRUE	FALSE
10								

- **ISEVEN**—This function indicates whether a number is evenly divisible by 2. Note that cell A8 is an empty cell, which is considered zero and reports as even. Using a date as the value in ISEVEN returns a value, but that value does not make sense. Using text or logical values in the ISEVEN function causes a #VALUE! error.

- **ISODD**—This function indicates whether a number is not evenly divisible by 2. An empty cell is considered zero and returns FALSE to ISODD. The same limitations listed for ISEVEN apply to ISODD. In addition, if your value contains decimal places, they are ignored by both the ISEVEN and ISODD functions. Numbers such as 1.02, 1.2, 1.5, 1.9, and 1.99999999 all return TRUE for the ISODD function.

 Note

Mathematicians in the audience might suggest that you could just as easily use =MOD(A2,2)=0 to figure out whether a number is even. However, unless you are a mathematician, it is far easier to remember =ISEVEN().

- **ISLOGICAL**—This function indicates whether the value is TRUE, FALSE, or an expression that results in TRUE or FALSE.

- **ISTEXT**—This function returns TRUE if the value contains text. This is good for finding values such as ABC in cell A16 and for finding cells that look like numbers but are actually stored as text.

- **ISNONTEXT**—This returns TRUE for anything that is nontext. Numbers, logicals, dates, empty cells, and even error cells return TRUE for ISNONTEXT.

- **ISNUMBER**—This function returns TRUE for numeric cells and dates. Note that although the empty cell A8 can be calculated as even in cell C8, it returns FALSE to ISNUMBER in cell H8.

The functions in this section are nearly always used with an IF function. For example, ZIP Codes in the United States should always be five digits. This causes problems when someone keys in a ZIP Code for certain Eastern cities that start with a zero. For example, in cell C6 of Figure 12.13, the proper way to key a ZIP Code for Portland, Maine is to type an apostrophe and then **04123**. Most people forget the apostrophe, and Excel drops the leading zero, as shown in cell C5.

| D5 | ▾ | : | × | ✓ | fx | =IF(ISNONTEXT(C5),RIGHT("0000"&C5,5),C5) |

	A	B	C	D	E	F
1	City	ST	Zip Code	Zip Fixed		
2	Salem	OH	44460	44460		
3	Uniontown	OH	44685	44685		
4	Merritt Island	FL	32953	32953		
5	Portland	ME	4123	04123		
6	Portland	ME	04123	04123		
7	St Thomas	VI	801	00801		
8	St Thomas	VI	00801	00801		
9						

Figure 12.13
The formula in column D detects nontext ZIP Codes and converts to text with five digits.

The formula in column D, =IF(ISNONTEXT(C5),RIGHT("0000"&C5,5),C5), fixes errant ZIP Codes in column C. If the value in column C is nontext, the program pads the left side of the ZIP Code with zeros and then takes the five rightmost digits.

Using the SHEETS and SHEET Functions to Dynamically Build a 3-D Reference

Both the SHEETS and SHEET functions are new in Excel 2013. It will be fascinating to see how Excel gurus put these to use. SHEETS tells you how many worksheets are in a workbook or reference. SHEET tells you the position of one worksheet within the workbook.

Syntax:

SHEETS()

SHEETS returns the number of worksheets in the workbook in which the function is entered. It includes worksheets that are hidden or very hidden.

Syntax:

SHEETS([3-D Reference])

SHEETS returns the number of worksheets included in a 3-D reference. For example, if you have 12 worksheets from Jan through Dec, =SHEETS(Apr:Jun!A1) indicates that there are three worksheets included in the group.

Syntax:

SHEET(Sheet_Name)

SHEET returns the position of the worksheet named Sheet_Name.

Syntax:

SHEET(*Reference*)

SHEET returns the position of the worksheet that contains *reference*.

Syntax:

SHEET()

SHEET returns the position of the worksheet that contains the SHEET() function.

In Figure 12.14, the workbook contains five worksheets labeled Jan, Feb, Mar, Apr, and May. The Apr worksheet is the current worksheet. Theoretically, a new worksheet will be added for each month as data becomes available.

Figure 12.14
Using SHEET and SHEETS lets you figure out the position of the current worksheet.

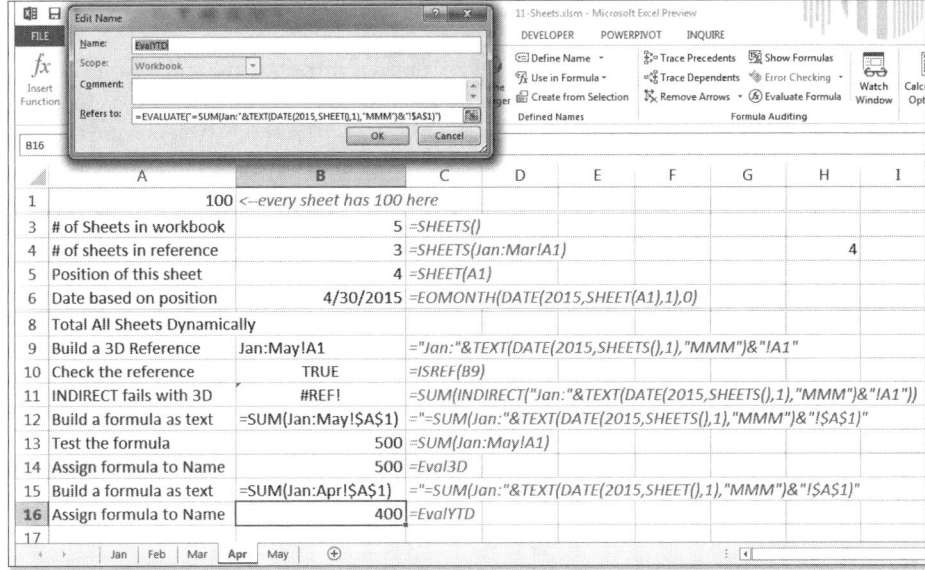

In cell B3, =SHEETS() tells you that there are currently five sheets in the workbook. This formula seems far more useful than the syntax in cell B4, which indicates how many worksheets are included in a 3-D reference. =SHEETS(Jan:Mar!A1) returns 3 to indicate that the reference contains three worksheets.

In cell B5, a formula of =SHEET() or =SHEET(A1) indicates that this worksheet is the fourth worksheet in the workbook. Certainly in this case, you would want to use =SHEET(). However, the figure shows the other syntax in case you would want to get the sheet number of another worksheet, such as =SHEET(Feb!A1).

You might wonder how this information could be useful. Who cares that this is worksheet 4 of 5? Well, if you set up the worksheets and can assume that the structure of the worksheets will remain constant, you can ascertain information based on the position. For example, in cell B6, the sheet number is used in conjunction with EOMONTH and DATE functions to get the ending date for the current worksheet.

It would be useful to build a formula that sums all worksheets or sums all worksheets up to the current worksheet. Formulas in B9, B12, and B15 show how to build a text reference or a text formula that would work. Unfortunately, the INDIRECT function fails when you pass it a 3-D reference, as in B11.

The workaround is to use an ancient XL4 Macro Language function called EVALUATE. This function is not a worksheet function. You won't be able to enter =EVALUATE in a worksheet cell and have it calculate correctly. However, these old XL4 Macro functions may be entered in defined names and will calculate correctly. Define a name such as Eval3D and use =EVALUATE("=SUM(Jan:"&TEXT (DATE(2015,SHEETS(),1),"MMM")&"!$A$1)") as the Refers To. This formula builds a SUM function on the fly. The EVALUATE function returns the result of the formula. You can then enter =Eval3D as shown in cell B14. Because each worksheet contains 100 in cell A1, the formula is returning the correct total of 500 from the five worksheets.

A similar approach is used in B16. This formula returns the total from January to the current worksheet, hence the 400 to total January through April. Here, the name refers to =EVALUATE("=SUM (Jan:"&TEXT(DATE(2015,SHEET(),1),"MMM")&"!$A$1)"). The one subtle difference is the use of SHEET() instead of SHEETS() to return the current worksheet.

Using the ISREF Function to Check a Reference

The ISREF function tests whether a value is a reference.

Syntax:

ISREF(*value*)

ISREF returns TRUE if the value is a valid reference. Initially, this function might seem to be useless. After all, inherently you know that A2 is a valid reference, so you would not have to use a function to test it.

The following formulas return TRUE: =ISREF(A2), =ISREF(XFD1048576), and =ISREF(A2:Z99). The following formulas return FALSE: =ISREF("A2"), =ISREF(99), and =ISREF(2+2).

ISREF is useful in one special circumstance. For example, suppose you have designed a spreadsheet with the named range ExpenseTotal. If you are worried that someone might have deleted this particular row, you can check whether ExpenseTotal is still a valid name by using =ISREF(ExpenseTotal). Here's an example:

```
=IF(ISREF(ExpenseTotal),ExpenseTotal*2,"Named Range Has Been Deleted")
```

Using the N Function to Add a Comment to a Formula

You can call Excel's N function a creative use for an obsolete function. Lotus 1-2-3 used to offer an N() function that converted a value as follows:

- N(*any number*) returned that number.

- N(*a date*) returned the serial number of the date.

- N(True) returned 1.

- N(False) returned 0.

- N(*any error*) returned the error.

- N(*any text*) returned 0.

None of these functions is terribly interesting. You can replicate just about any of them by referring to the value and changing the cell format.

An interesting unintended use of the function is that N(*any text*) always returns zero. A useful trick is to insert a comment about a formula by adding the N function to the end of the formula. However, make sure that your comment contains text. Because N(*text*) is zero, the outcome of the function does not change. When you come back to the formula several months later, you can see the comment in the formula bar (see Figure 12.15).

Figure 12.15
Because N of text is zero, you can store a comment in the N function.

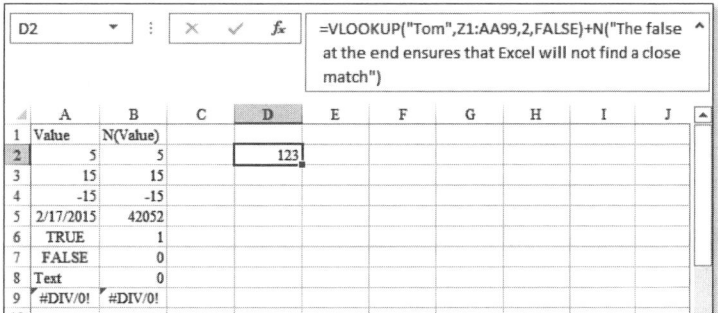

Using the NA Function to Force Charts to Not Plot Missing Data

Suppose that you are in charge of a school's annual fund drive. Each day, you mark the fundraising total on a worksheet by following these steps:

1. In column A, you enter the results of each day's collection through nine days of the fund drive (see Figure 12.16).

2. You enter a formula in column C to keep track of the total collected throughout the fund drive.

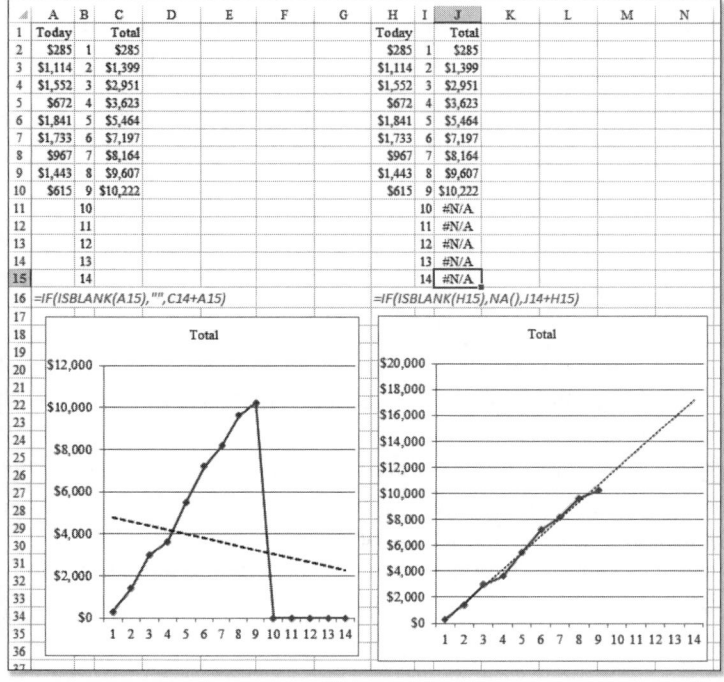

Figure 12.16
Using NA in the chart on the right allows the trendline to ignore future missing data points and project a reasonable ending result.

3. To avoid making it look like the fund drive collected nothing in days 10 through 14, you enter a formula in column C to check whether column A is blank. If it is, then the IF function inserts a null cell in column C. For example, the formula in cell C15 is =IF(ISBLANK(A15),"",A15+C14).

4. You build a line chart based on B1:C15. You then add a trendline to the chart to predict future fundraising totals.

5. As shown in columns A:C of Figure 12.16, this technique fails. Even though the totals for days 10 through 14 are blank, Excel charts those days as zero. The linear trendline predicts that your fundraising will go down, with a projected total of just over $2,000.

6. You try the same chart again, but this time you use the NA function instead of " " in the IF statement in step 3. The formula is shown in cell H16, and the results are in cell J15. Excel understands that NA values should not be plotted. The trendline is calculated based on only the data points available and projects a total just under $18,000.

In many cases, you are trying to avoid #N/A! errors. However, in the case of charting a calculated column, you might want to have #N/A! produce the correct look to the chart.

Using the INFO Function to Print Information About a Computer

The remaining information functions tell you some piece of information about a particular cell or about the computer. The INFO function is left over from Lotus 1-2-3. Some of the information it provides was useful only in Lotus. However, a few of the options may be useful to display in an Excel spreadsheet.

Syntax:

=INFO(*type_text*)

The INFO function returns information about the current operating environment. The following are valid values for the *type_text* argument:

- **Directory**—Returns the folder where the current workbook is saved. If the file is not yet saved, Directory returns #N/A.

- **NumFile**—Returns the number of open files. This is not just open workbooks, but all files open on the system.

- **MemAvail**—Returns the available memory. This appears to be some old DOS version of the memory available. Although the worksheet is running on a computer with 8GB of memory, the function never reports more than 1MB available.

- **MemUsed**—Specifies the memory in use by Excel. Clearly wrong. The Processes tab of the Task Manager shows that Excel is using almost 100 times the memory reported by this function.

- **TotMem**—Returns the total of the previous two results.

- **Origin**—Returns the text "$A:" and the absolute cell address of the upper-left cell visible in the current window. The "$A:" prefix is a notation used by Lotus 1-2-3 release 3.0. You might think there could be uses for this result. For example, = INDIRECT(TRIM(MID(INFO("Origin"),2,50))) returns the value shown in the upper-left corner of the visible window. However, note that beginning with Excel 2007, you can use the scrollbars to change the upper-left cell, and Excel does not recalculate, leaving the Origin result incorrect until you change a cell in Excel.

- **OSVersion**—Returns the version number of your operating system.

- **Recalc**—Returns either Manual or Automatic to indicate the current recalculation status. You might provide a hint to the spreadsheet reader with =IF(INFO("Recalc")="Manual","Press F9 to calculate","").

- **Release**—Specifies the release number of Excel. For Excel 2013, this is 15.0. Excel 2010 was 14.0. Excel 2007 was 12.0. Yes, Microsoft skipped Excel version 13.0 for superstitious reasons. When I asked if they would actually name this version Excel 2013, the new project manager for Excel scoffed at the idea that they would avoid Excel 2013 for superstitious reasons.

- **System**—Returns either mac or pcdos to indicate Macintosh or Windows.

Figure 12.17 shows the results of several variations of the INFO function.

D6 =INFO(C6)

	C	D	E	F	G
5	Type_text	=INFO(Type_Text)	Comment		
6	Directory	C:\Users\Jelen\Desktop\2013	Folder where current file is stored		
7	NumFile	9	Number of workbooks open		
8	MemAvail	1,048,576	Available Memory		
9	MemUsed	2,650,220	Used Memory		
10	TotMem	3,698,796	Total Memory		
11	Origin	$A:$C$5	Top-left visible cell in this window		
12	OSVersion	Windows (64-bit) NT 6.01	Operating System Version		
13	Recalc	Automatic	Is Recalc turned on?		
14	Release	15.0	Version of Excel		
15	System	pcdos	Windows or Mac?		
16					

Figure 12.17
A few of the argument values for `INFO()` still return useful results.

Using the `CELL` Function

The `CELL` function can tell you specific information about a specific cell, or it can tell you specific information about the last cell changed in the worksheet.

Again, some of the types of information are a bit dated. For example, the `Color` argument was written in the day when a cell was either black or possibly red if the value was negative. The `Prefix` argument is based on when cells could be left-aligned, centered, or right-aligned. Even though Excel has offered several levels of indenting for a decade, the `Prefix` version of the `CELL` function does not reveal anything about the indentation level.

Syntax:

```
CELL(info_type,reference)
```

To use the `CELL` function, you specify the type of information and optionally a cell reference. If you specify a cell reference, Excel provides information about the cell in the reference. If you leave off the reference, Excel returns information about the last cell changed in the workbook.

The argument *`info_type`* is a text value that specifies what type of cell information you want. The following are the possible values of *`info_type`* and the corresponding results:

- **`contents`**—Returns the value in the upper-left cell in *`reference`*.
- **`address`**—Returns the address of the first cell in *`reference`*, as text. As shown in cell B5 of Figure 12.18, this is always returned in absolute reference style.
- **`row`**—Returns the row number of the cell in *`reference`*.
- **`col`**—Returns the column number of the cell in *`reference`*.

Figure 12.18
The CELL function returns information about a specific cell—in this case, cell A1.

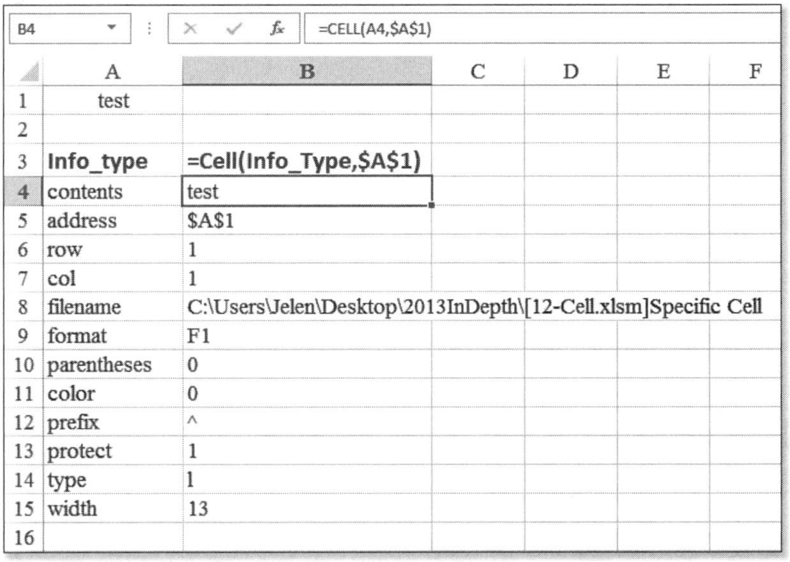

B4	▼	:	×	✓	*fx*	=CELL(A4,$A$1)				

◢	A	B	C	D	E	F
1	test					
2						
3	**Info_type**	**=Cell(Info_Type,$A$1)**				
4	contents	test				
5	address	$A$1				
6	row	1				
7	col	1				
8	filename	C:\Users\Jelen\Desktop\2013InDepth\[12-Cell.xlsm]Specific Cell				
9	format	F1				
10	parentheses	0				
11	color	0				
12	prefix	^				
13	protect	1				
14	type	l				
15	width	13				
16						

- **filename**—Returns the filename as text, including the full path of the file that contains *reference*. If the worksheet that contains reference has not yet been saved, empty text (" ") is returned. Interestingly, this argument now also returns the worksheet name if the workbook contains multiple worksheets.

- **format**—Returns the text value corresponding to the number format of the cell. Returns - at the end of the text value if the cell is formatted in color for negative values. If the cell is formatted with parentheses for positive or all values, ( ) is returned at the end of the text value. The values reported as a *format* reflect old Lotus 1-2-3 codes. When you format, Excel attempts to convert the current numeric format to an old-style Lotus 1-2-3 formatting code. Table 12.7 shows some examples.

- **parentheses**—Returns 1 if the cell is formatted with parentheses for positive or all values; otherwise, returns 0.

Table 12.7 Custom Codes in Excel and Lotus 1-2-3

Excel Format	Excel Custom Code	Lotus Format Code
General	General	G
Numeric, no decimal	0	F0
Numeric, 2 decimals	0	F2
Comma, 2 decimals	#,##0.00	,2

Excel Format	Excel Custom Code	Lotus Format Code
Currency, 2 decimals	$#,##0.00_)	C2
Percent, 1 decimal	0.00%	P1
Scientific notation	0.00E+00	S2
Fractions	# ?/?	G
Date	m/d/yy	D4
Date	d-mmm-y	D1
Date	d-mmm	D2
Date	mmm-yy	D3
Time	H:mm AM/PM	D7

- **color**—Returns 1 if the cell is formatted in color for negative values; otherwise, returns 0.

- **prefix**—Returns the text value corresponding to the "label prefix" of the cell, as follows:

  - Returns a single quotation mark (') if the cell contains left-aligned text.

  - Returns a double quotation mark (") if the cell contains right-aligned text.

  - Returns a caret (^) if the cell contains centered text.

  - Returns a backslash (\) if the cell contains fill-aligned text.

  - Returns an empty text (" ") if the cell contains anything else.

- **protect**—Returns 0 if the cell is not locked and 1 if the cell is locked. Remember that, by default, all Excel cells start with their locked property set to TRUE. The locked property is taken into account only if protection is enabled. This argument for the CELL function reports a 1 even if protection is not turned on.

- **type**—Returns the text value corresponding to the type of data in the cell, as follows:

  - Returns b for blank if the cell is empty.

  - Returns l for label if the cell contains a text constant.

  - Returns v for value if the cell contains anything else.

- **width**—Returns the column width of the cell, rounded to an integer. Each unit of column width is equal to the width of one character in the default font size.

- **reference**—Is an optional cell reference. If reference is omitted, CELL returns the information about the last changed cell.

Refer to Figure 12.18, which shows every CELL option for a specific cell: cell A1.

> **Caution**
>
> Be careful with this: It is now possible to change column widths without causing Excel to calculate. You might have to press F9 to have the result of this formula change.

Using CELL to Track the Last Cell Changed

If you leave off the second argument of the CELL function, Excel returns the information about the last cell changed in the workbook.

Follow these steps to create an interesting watch window of the last cells changed:

1. In an out-of-the-way spot, enter the formula =CELL("*address*").

2. Just below this formula, enter the formula =CELL("*Contents*").

3. Just below that formula, enter the formula =CELL("*filename*").

4. Select all three of these cells.

5. From the Formulas tab, select the Watch Window icon. The Watch Window dialog appears.

6. Click the Add Watch button in the Watch Window dialog.

7. Because initially, the default file widths are not wide enough to show the complete value, drag the vertical bars between the headings in the Watch Window so that you can see the complete Value and Formula columns. The other columns for Book, Sheet, and Cell can be made smaller.

The result, as shown in Figure 12.19, is a floating window that always reveals the last changed cell address and contents.

Figure 12.19
The Watch Window always shows the last cell changed and the value of that cell. Note that as in this case, the last changed cell might be on another worksheet.

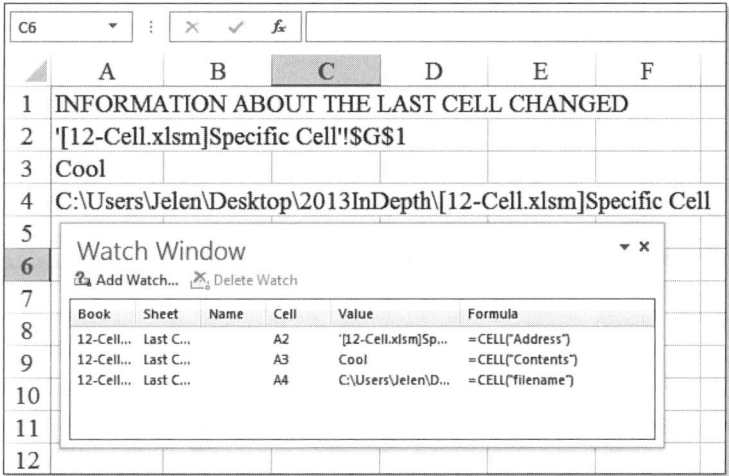

Using TYPE to Determine the Type of Cell Value

The final information function is the TYPE function. You use =TYPE(*value*) to determine whether a value is a number, text, logical, an error value, or an array. Note that dates are treated as numbers.

Syntax:

=TYPE(*value*)

The TYPE function returns a numeric code that tells you about the type of value.

The TYPE function returns the following values:

- **1**—For a numeric or date type
- **2**—For a text type
- **4**—For a logical type
- **16**—For an error type
- **64**—An array type

Figure 12.20 shows the results for various values in the TYPE function.

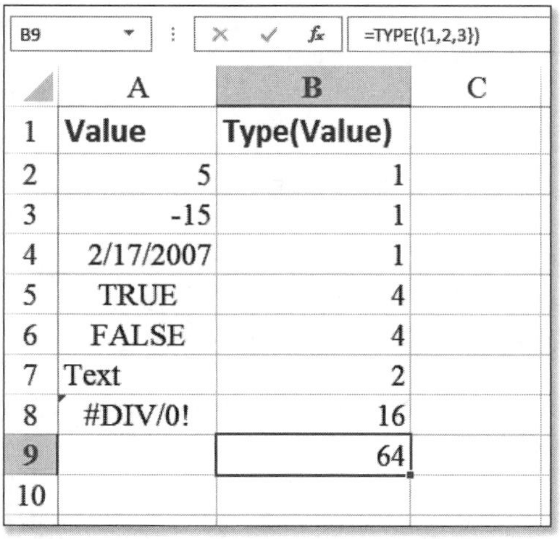

B9 =TYPE({1,2,3})

	A	B	C
1	Value	Type(Value)	
2	5	1	
3	-15	1	
4	2/17/2007	1	
5	TRUE	4	
6	FALSE	4	
7	Text	2	
8	#DIV/0!	16	
9		64	
10			

Figure 12.20
The TYPE function returns what type of value is specified as an argument.

Examples of Lookup and Reference Functions

The Lookup & Reference icon contains 18 functions. The all-star of this group is the venerable VLOOKUP function, which is one of the most powerful and most used functions in Excel. As database people point out, a lot of work done in Excel should probably be done in Access. The VLOOKUP function enables you to perform the equivalent of a join operation in a database.

This lookup and reference group also includes several functions that seem useless when considered alone. However, when combined, they allow for some very powerful manipulations of data. The examples in the following sections reveal details on how to use the lookup functions and how to combine them to create powerful results.

Using the CHOOSE Function for Simple Lookups

Most lookup functions require you to set up a lookup table in a range on the worksheet. However, the CHOOSE function enables you to specify up to 254 choices right in the syntax of the function. The formula that requires the lookup should be able to calculate an integer from 1 to 254 in order to use the CHOOSE function.

Syntax:

CHOOSE(*index_num*,*value1*,*value2*,...)

The CHOOSE function chooses a value from a list of values, based on an index number. The CHOOSE function takes the following arguments:

- ***index_num***—This specifies which value argument is selected. *index_num* must be a number between 1 and 254 or a formula or reference to a cell containing a number between 1 and 254:

  - If *index_num* is 1, CHOOSE returns *value1*; if it is 2, CHOOSE returns *value2*; and so on.

  - If *index_num* is a decimal, it is rounded down to the next lowest integer before being used.

  - If *index_num* is less than 1 or greater than the number of the last value in the list, CHOOSE returns a #VALUE! error.

- ***value1*,*value2*,...**—These are one to 254 value arguments from which CHOOSE selects a value or an action to perform based on *index_num*. The arguments can be numbers, cell references, defined names, formulas, functions, or text.

The example in Figure 12.21 shows survey data from a number of respondents. Columns B:F indicate their responses on five measures of your service. Column G calculates an average that ranges from 1 to 5. Say that you want to add words to column H to characterize the overall rating from the respondent. The following formula is used in cell H4:

=CHOOSE(G4,"Strongly Disagree","Disagree","Neutral","Agree","Strongly Agree")

Figure 12.21
CHOOSE is great for simple choices where the index number is between 1 and 254.

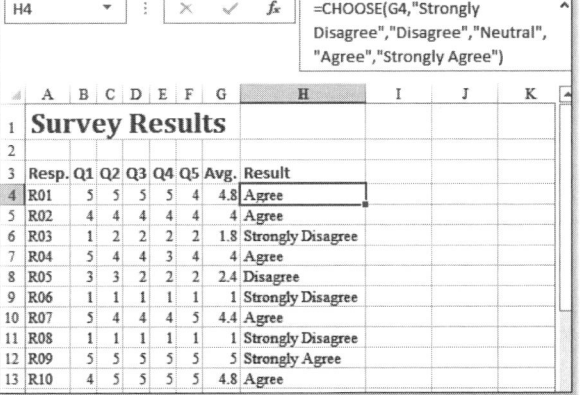

Using VLOOKUP with TRUE to Find a Value Based on a Range

VLOOKUP stands for *vertical lookup.* This function behaves differently, depending on the fourth parameter. This section describes using VLOOKUP where you need to choose a value based on a table that contains ranges.

Suppose that you have a list of students and their scores on a test. The school grading scale is based on these ranges:

- 92–100 is an A.
- 85–91 is a B.
- 70–84 is a C.
- 65–69 is a D.
- Below 65 is an F.

Follow these steps to set up a VLOOKUP for this scenario:

1. Because in this version of VLOOKUP you do not have to list every possible grade, build a table showing the scores where the grading scale changes from one grade to the next.
2. Although the published grading scale starts with the higher values, your lookup table must be sorted in ascending sequence. This requires a bit of translation as you set up the table. Although the grading scale says below 65 is an F, you need to set up the table to show that an F corresponds to any grade at 0 or higher. Therefore, in cell E2 enter **0**, and in cell F2, enter **F** (see Figure 12.22).

C2 =VLOOKUP(B2,$E$2:$F$6,2,TRUE)

	A	B	C	D	E	F
1	Student	Score	Grade			
2	CECILIA ALBERT	96	A		0	F
3	KRISTEN FOREMAN	88	B		65	D
4	DOROTHY MARTINEZ	76	C		70	C
5	LUIS FISCHER	93	A		85	B
6	TERRY SKINNER	89	B		92	A
7	SHELLEY OSBORN	69	D			
8	MARVIN SCHULTZ	77	C			
9	JOE TRUJILLO	93	A			

Figure 12.22
The VLOOKUP formula in column C finds the correct grade from the table in columns E and F.

3. Continue building the grading scale in successive rows of columns E and F. Anything above a 65 is given a D. Anything above 70 is given a C. Note that this is somewhat counterintuitive because it is the opposite order that you would use if you were building a grading scale using nested IF functions.

4. Ensure that the numeric values are the leftmost column in your lookup table. In Figure 12.22, the lookup table range is E2:F6. When you use VLOOKUP, Excel searches the first column of the lookup table for the appropriate score.

5. When using this version of VLOOKUP with ranges, sort the list in ascending order. If you are not sure of the proper order, use the Sort command from the Home tab to sort the table.

6. Because the first argument in the VLOOKUP function is the student's score, in cell C2, enter **=VLOOKUP(B2,**.

7. Because the next argument is the range of the lookup table, be sure to press the F4 key after entering E2:F6 to change to an absolute reference of $E$2:$F$6.

8. Ensure that the third argument specifies which column of the lookup table should be returned. Because the letter grade is in the second column of E2:F6, use 2 for the third argument.

9. Ensure that the final argument is either TRUE or simply omitted. This tells Excel that you are using the sorted range variety of lookup.

10. After you enter the formula in cell C2, again select cell C2 and double-click the fill handle to copy the formula down to all students.

Using VLOOKUP with FALSE to Find an Exact Value

In some situations, you do not want VLOOKUP to return a value based on a close match. Instead, you want Excel to find the exact match in the lookup table.

Figure 12.23 shows a table of sales. The original table had just columns A through C: Rep, Date, and Sale Amount. Although a data analyst might have all the rep numbers memorized, the manager who is going to see the report prefers to have the rep names on the report.

Figure 12.23
In this case, VLOOKUP needs to find the exact rep number from the table in columns E and F.

	D2	▼	:	×	✓	fx		=VLOOKUP(A2,$F$2:$G$7,2,FALSE)		

◢	A	B	C	D	E	F	G
1	Rep	Date	Sale Amt	Rep Name			
2	R5	2/17/2006	119.78	Manny		R4	Amar
3	R7	2/17/2006	113.84	Michael		R8	Jerry
4	R5	2/17/2006	137.44	Manny		R6	Linda
5	R3	2/17/2006	126.17	Marc		R5	Manny
6	R6	2/18/2006	131.26	Linda		R3	Marc
7	R3	2/18/2006	178.16	Marc		R7	Michael
8	R8	2/18/2006	171.48	Jerry			
9	R8	2/18/2006	126.84	Jerry			
10	R2	2/19/2006	171.21	#N/A			
11	R3	2/19/2006	152.55	Marc			

To fill in the rep names from a lookup table, you follow these steps:

1. In columns F and G, enter a table of rep numbers and rep names. Note that it is not important that this table be sorted by the rep number field. It is fine that the table is sorted alphabetically by name.

2. Use FALSE as the fourth parameter in VLOOKUP. You need to do this because close matches are not acceptable here. If something was sold by a new rep with number R9, you do not want to give credit to the name associated with R8 just because it is a close match. Either Excel finds an exact match and returns the result, or Excel does not give you a result.

3. For cell D2, you want Excel to use the rep number in A2, so in cell D2, enter **=VLOOKUP(A2,**.

4. The lookup table is in F2:G7, so enter **F2:G7** and then press the F4 key to make the reference absolute. This enables you to copy the formula in step 7. After pressing F4, type a comma.

5. In the lookup table, the rep name is in column 2 of the table, so type **2** to specify that you want to return the second column of the lookup table.

6. Finish the function with **FALSE)**. Press Ctrl+Enter to accept the formula and keep the cursor in cell D2.

7. Double-click the fill handle to copy the formula down to all the rows.

8. VLOOKUP is a very time-intensive calculation. Having thousands of VLOOKUP formulas significantly affects your recalculation times. In this particular case, you have successfully added rep names. It would be appropriate to convert these live formulas to their current values. Therefore, press Ctrl+C to copy. Then, from the Home tab, select Paste, Paste Values to convert the formulas to values.

9. Look through the results. If a sale was credited to a new rep who is not in the table, the name appears as #N/A. Manually fix these records, if needed.

> **Note**
>
> If your lookup table is arranged with the key field in row 1, you should use HLOOKUP, which is discussed later in this chapter. If your data is vertical but the key field is not the leftmost column, you can use a combination of INDEX and MATCH, also explained later in this chapter.

To recap, the two versions of the VLOOKUP formula behave very differently. VLOOKUP with FALSE as the fourth parameter looks for an exact match, whereas VLOOKUP with TRUE as the fourth parameter looks for the closest (lower) match. In the TRUE version, the lookup table must be sorted. In the FALSE version, the table can be in any sequence. In every case, the key field must be in the left column of the lookup table.

Syntax:

VLOOKUP(*lookup_value*,*table_array*,*col_index_num*,*range_lookup*)

VLOOKUP searches for a value in the leftmost column of a table and then returns a value in the same row from a column you specify in the table. The VLOOKUP function takes the following arguments:

- *lookup_value*—This is the value to be found in the first column of the table. *lookup_value* can be a value, reference, or text string.

- *table_array*—This is the table of information in which data is looked up. You can use a reference to a range such as E2:F9 or a range name such as RepTable.

- *col_index_num*—This is the column number in *table_array* from which the matching value must be returned. A *col_index_num* value of 1 returns the value in the first column in *table_array*; a *col_index_num* value of 2 returns the value in the second column in *table_array*, and so on. If *col_index_num* is less than 1, VLOOKUP returns the #VALUE! error value; if *col_index_num* is greater than the number of columns in *table_array*, VLOOKUP returns the #REF! error value.

- *range_lookup*—This is a logical value that specifies whether VLOOKUP should find an exact match or an approximate match. If it is TRUE or omitted, an approximate match is returned. In other words, if an exact match is not found, the next largest value that is less than *lookup_value* is returned. If it is FALSE, VLOOKUP finds an exact match. If one is not found, the error value #N/A is returned. If VLOOKUP cannot find *lookup_value* and if *range_lookup* is TRUE, it uses the largest value that is less than or equal to *lookup_value*. If *lookup_value* is smaller than the smallest value in the first column of *table_array*, VLOOKUP returns an #N/A error. If VLOOKUP cannot find *lookup_value*, and *range_lookup* is FALSE, VLOOKUP returns an #N/A error.

Using VLOOKUP to Match Two Lists

If Excel is used throughout your company, you undoubtedly have many lists in Excel. People use Excel to track everything. How many times are you faced with a situation in which you have two versions of a list and you need to match them up?

In Figure 12.24, the worksheet has two simple lists. Column A shows last week's version of who was coming to an event. Column C shows this week's version of who is coming to an event. Follow these steps if you want to find out quickly if anyone is new:

1. Add the heading **There?** to cell D2.

2. Because the formula in cell D3 should look at the value in cell C3 to see whether that person is in the original list in column A, start the formula with **=VLOOKUP(C3,$A$3:$A$15,**.

3. Because your only choice for the column number is to return the first column from the original list, finish the function with **1,FALSE)**. Then press Ctrl+Enter to accept the formula and stay in cell D3.

4. Double-click the fill handle to copy the formula down to all rows.

For any cells where column D contains a name, it means that the person was on the RSVP list from last week. If the result of the VLOOKUP is #N/A, you know that this person is new since the previous week.

| D3 | ▼ | : | × | ✓ | fx | =VLOOKUP(C3,$A$3:$A$15,1,FALSE) |

◢	A	B	C	D
1	RSVP's LAST WEEK		RSVP's THIS WEEK	
2				There?
3	VERONICA HAHN		ARTHUR FLETCHER	ARTHUR FLETCHER
4	ELLEN LINDSAY		BARBARA BERGER	BARBARA BERGER
5	CECILIA HARMON		CANDICE GLENN	CANDICE GLENN
6	DONALD TYLER		CECILIA HARMON	CECILIA HARMON
7	NICOLE KELLY		CHRIS PAGE	CHRIS PAGE
8	MARCIA ERICKSON		CHRISTOPHER DONOVAN	#N/A
9	BARBARA BERGER		JOANN BROOKS	#N/A
10	CHRIS PAGE		ELLEN LINDSAY	ELLEN LINDSAY
11	CANDICE GLENN		JACOB MCINTYRE	#N/A
12	STACY DUNLAP		JOHN GARRISON	JOHN GARRISON
13	ARTHUR FLETCHER		KATHLEEN RICHARD	KATHLEEN RICHARD
14	KATHLEEN RICHARD		MARCIA ERICKSON	MARCIA ERICKSON
15	JOHN GARRISON		MYRTLE MOON	#N/A
16			NICOLE KELLY	NICOLE KELLY
17			STACY DUNLAP	STACY DUNLAP
18			VERONICA HAHN	VERONICA HAHN
19				

Figure 12.24
An #N/A error as the result of VLOOKUP tells you that the person is new to the list.

Tip

If you study the data in Figure 12.24, you will see that three more names are in the column C list than in the column A list, yet four people were reported as being new this week. This means that one of the people from last week has dropped off the list. To quickly find who dropped off the list, use the formula =VLOOKUP(A3,$C$3:$C$18,1, FALSE) in B3:B15 to find that Donald Tyler has dropped off the list.

Note that you can also use MATCH to solve this problem.

Using COLUMN to Assist with VLOOKUP When Filling a Wide Table

This section discusses some special considerations to keep in mind when you have to retrieve many columns from a table. If you think carefully about the first formula, you can quickly copy it to the entire table.

Figure 12.25 shows a table of several hundred SKUs, starting in row 21. For each SKU, the table contains the inventory of that product on hand in the 12 regional warehouses. Range A6:B13 contains a customer order for various SKUs. You want to build a table to help visualize which warehouse has most of the items in stock. If you find one warehouse that has all the inventory, you can minimize order shipping costs by shipping the entire order from that particular warehouse.

To solve this problem, follow these steps:

1. Copy the range of warehouse names from B20:M20 to C5:N5.

Figure 12.25
The COLUMN function in row 4 ensures that you can enter the VLOOKUP formula once and copy it to the entire rectangular range.

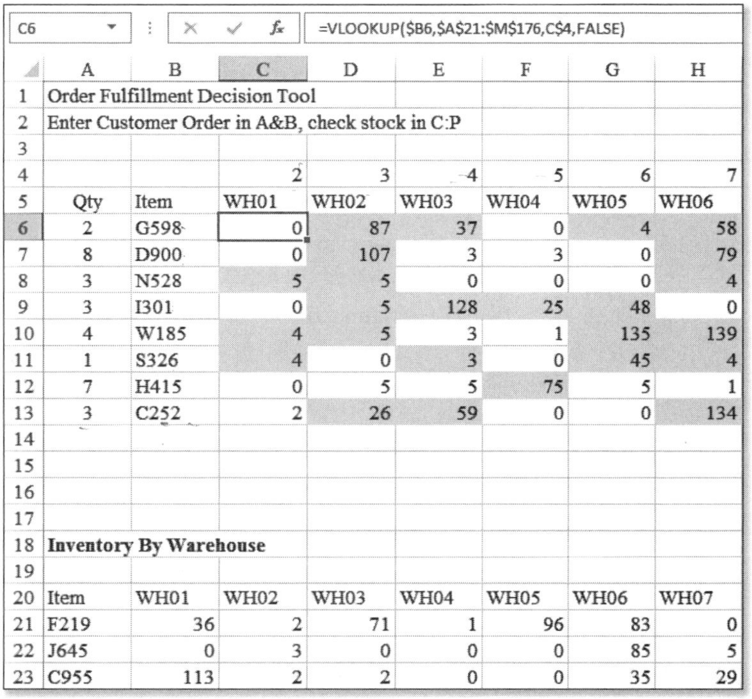

C6		:	×	✓	f_x	=VLOOKUP($B6,$A$21:$M$176,C$4,FALSE)		

◢	A	B	C	D	E	F	G	H
1	Order Fulfillment Decision Tool							
2	Enter Customer Order in A&B, check stock in C:P							
3								
4			2	3	4	5	6	7
5	Qty	Item	WH01	WH02	WH03	WH04	WH05	WH06
6	2	G598	0	87	37	0	4	58
7	8	D900	0	107	3	3	0	79
8	3	N528	5	5	0	0	0	4
9	3	I301	0	5	128	25	48	0
10	4	W185	4	5	3	1	135	139
11	1	S326	4	0	3	0	45	4
12	7	H415	0	5	5	75	5	1
13	3	C252	2	26	59	0	0	134
14								
15								
16								
17								
18	Inventory By Warehouse							
19								
20	Item	WH01	WH02	WH03	WH04	WH05	WH06	WH07
21	F219	36	2	71	1	96	83	0
22	J645	0	3	0	0	0	85	5
23	C955	113	2	2	0	0	35	29

2. Think about the third argument in the VLOOKUP function. For the formula in column C, you want to return the second column from the table. For the formula in column D, you want to return the third column. If you actually enter the **2** in the formula in column C, then after copying the formula over to D:N, you have to edit the third argument repeatedly.

3. Create a range above your table, perhaps in row 4, that contains the numbers 2 through 13. You can then use cells in this row when building the third argument in the formula. In cell C4, enter the function **=COLUMN(B2)**. Because column B is the second column, this formula returns 2.

4. Select cell C4. Drag the fill handle to the right to copy the formula through column N. The cell B2 reference is relative, resulting in the formula returning the numbers 2, 3, 4, and so on.

5. In cell C6, enter **=VLOOKUP(B6**. When you later copy this formula, you always want the formula to point to column B, but you want to allow the formula to point to rows 7, 8, and so on. If you press the F4 key three times, the reference changes to $B6. Type a comma.

6. Type **A21:M176**. Press F4 to change this reference to **$A$21:$M$176**. Type a comma.

7. For the third argument, you want to point to the number 2 in cell C4. You always want this part of the formula to point to row 4, and you want to allow the column letter to change as the formula is copied to the right. Press the F4 key twice to change the reference to C$4.

8. Finish the formula with **,FALSE)**. Press Ctrl+Enter to accept the formula and stay in cell C4.

9. Optionally, add a conditional format to cell C4 to highlight the cell if this formula is true: =C6>=$A6.

10. Double-click the fill handle to copy the formula to C4:C13.

11. Drag the fill handle from the corner of C13 to the right until you have filled in the formula in the range of C:N.

The result is a table that shows the current inventory for each item, by warehouse. If you added the conditional formatting in step 9, you can quickly see which warehouses can fulfill most of the order.

Although having the COLUMN function in row 4 enables you to visually understand the example better, you can eliminate row 4 and rewrite the formula in cell C6 as =VLOOKUP($B6,$A$21:$M$176, COLUMN(B1),FALSE).

Syntax:

COLUMN(*reference*)

The COLUMN function returns the column number of a given reference. This function takes the argument *reference*, which is the cell or range of cells for which you want the column number. If *reference* is omitted, it is assumed to be the reference of the cell in which the COLUMN function appears.

If *reference* is a range of cells, and if COLUMN is entered as a horizontal array, COLUMN returns the column numbers of *reference* as a horizontal array. In this case, *reference* cannot refer to multiple areas.

Using HLOOKUP for Horizontal Lookup Tables

HLOOKUP stands for *horizontal lookup*. This function is similar to VLOOKUP.

HLOOKUP operates in two distinct manners, based on the fourth parameter. If the fourth parameter is the value FALSE, then HLOOKUP is looking for an exact match in the top row of the table. This is fine when you are looking up product codes, customer numbers, or any other discrete bits of information.

However, if the fourth parameter is the value TRUE or is omitted, HLOOKUP is treating the first row of the table as a sorted range of values. Excel looks for the closest lower value than the one you specified. This is fine when you are trying to determine in which range a value belongs.

Syntax:

HLOOKUP(*lookup_value*,*table_array*,*row_index_num*,*range_lookup*)

The HLOOKUP function searches for a value in the top row of a table. When the value is found, HLOOKUP returns a value from a particular row in the column. This function takes the following arguments:

- ***lookup_value***—This is a value to be found in the first row of the table. *lookup_value* can be a value, a reference, or a text string.
- ***table_array***—This is a table of information in which data is looked up. You use a reference to a range or a range name. The values in the first row of *table_array* can be text, numbers, or logical values. If *range_lookup* is TRUE, the values in the first row of *table_array* must be placed in ascending order, such as ..., –2, –1, 0, 1, 2,...; A–Z; or FALSE, TRUE. Otherwise, HLOOKUP might not give the correct value. If *range_lookup* is FALSE, *table_array* does not need to be sorted. The search is not case-sensitive: Both uppercase and lowercase text are equivalent.
- ***row_index_num***—This is the row number in *table_array* from which the matching value is returned. A *row_index_num* of 1 returns the first row value in *table_array*, a *row_index_num* of 2 returns the second row value in *table_array*, and so on. If *row_index_num* is less than 1, HLOOKUP returns a #VALUE! error; if *row_index_num* is greater than the number of rows in *table_array*, HLOOKUP returns a #REF! error.
- ***range_lookup***—This is a logical value that specifies whether you want HLOOKUP to find an exact match or an approximate match. If it is TRUE or omitted, an approximate match is returned. In other words, if an exact match is not found, the next largest value that is less than *lookup_value* is returned. If it is FALSE, HLOOKUP finds an exact match. If one is not found, the error #N/A is returned.

Even though you are probably familiar with sorting a list from top to bottom, most people rarely sort a list from left to right. If you are using the TRUE version of HLOOKUP, make sure that your table is sorted from left to right by the top row. To sort data from left to right, follow these steps:

1. Select your range of data. In Figure 12.26, this is G3:L8. Do not include column F because it should not be sorted.

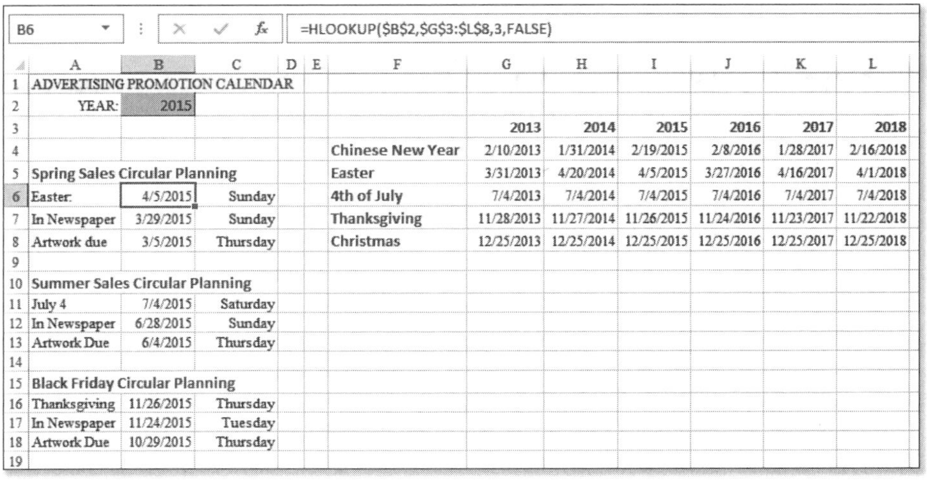
B6 =HLOOKUP($B$2,$G$3:$L$8,3,FALSE)

	A	B	C	D	E	F	G	H	I	J	K	L
1	ADVERTISING PROMOTION CALENDAR											
2	YEAR:	2015										
3							2013	2014	2015	2016	2017	2018
4						Chinese New Year	2/10/2013	1/31/2014	2/19/2015	2/8/2016	1/28/2017	2/16/2018
5	Spring Sales Circular Planning					Easter	3/31/2013	4/20/2014	4/5/2015	3/27/2016	4/16/2017	4/1/2018
6	Easter	4/5/2015	Sunday			4th of July	7/4/2013	7/4/2014	7/4/2015	7/4/2016	7/4/2017	7/4/2018
7	In Newspaper	3/29/2015	Sunday			Thanksgiving	11/28/2013	11/27/2014	11/26/2015	11/24/2016	11/23/2017	11/22/2018
8	Artwork due	3/5/2015	Thursday			Christmas	12/25/2013	12/25/2014	12/25/2015	12/25/2016	12/25/2017	12/25/2018
9												
10	Summer Sales Circular Planning											
11	July 4	7/4/2015	Saturday									
12	In Newspaper	6/28/2015	Sunday									
13	Artwork Due	6/4/2015	Thursday									
14												
15	Black Friday Circular Planning											
16	Thanksgiving	11/26/2015	Thursday									
17	In Newspaper	11/24/2015	Tuesday									
18	Artwork Due	10/29/2015	Thursday									
19												

Figure 12.26 The table in F:L is horizontal, so you use the HLOOKUP function.

2. From the Home tab, select the Sort & Filter drop-down. The Sort dialog appears.

3. In the Sort dialog, click the Options button. The Sort Options dialog appears.

4. In the Sort Options dialog, select Sort Left to Right. Click OK to close the Sort Options dialog.

5. In the Sort dialog, choose to sort by row 3. Click OK to sort.

Figure 12.26 shows a tool used by the advertising department of a retail store. The store runs annual promotions for certain holidays. The table in F3:L8 tells the days for holidays in each of several years.

The advertising manager knows that the store wants to run a sale circular the Sunday before the holiday and that the art department needs the material 24 days before the ad is to run. By changing the year in cell B2, the advertising manager can create a new schedule for each year. To help the advertising manager, follow these steps:

1. Ensure that the formula for each holiday starts as =HLOOKUP($B$2,. This tells Excel to use the year found in cell B2 as the value to look up.

2. Ensure that the lookup table is in $G$3:$L$8. Excel looks through the first row of this table to find the matching year.

3. When the matching column is found, you want Excel to return the date for Easter. Although this is in row 5 of the worksheet, it is in the third row of the table, so ensure that the third parameter for the function is 3.

4. Your years are already sorted left to right, but if you use a value of TRUE for the fourth parameter, this causes problems in the year 2014, so make the fourth parameter FALSE. Ensure that the formula in cell B6 is =HLOOKUP($B$2,$G$3:$L$8,3,FALSE).

5. Copy this formula to cell B11 and edit the formula to change the third parameter from 3 to 4 because the Fourth of July is the fourth row of the table.

Using the MATCH Function to Locate the Position of a Matching Value

At first glance, MATCH seems like a function that would rarely be useful. MATCH returns the relative position of an item in a range that matches a specified value in a specified order. You use MATCH instead of one of the lookup functions when you need the position of an item in a range instead of the item itself.

Suppose that your manager asks, "Can you tell me on which row I would find this value?" The manager wants to know the value or some piece of data on that record. However, the manager rarely wants to know that XYZ is found on the 111th relative row within the range A99:A11432.

MATCH comes in handy in several instances. In the first instance, consider a situation in which you are using VLOOKUP to find whether an item is in a list. In this case, you do not care what value is returned. You are either interested in seeing if a valid value is returned, meaning that the entry is in the old list, or if an #N/A is returned, meaning that the entry is new. In this case, using MATCH is a slightly faster way to achieve the same result.

Another handy way to use MATCH is with the INDEX function. MATCH has two features that make it more versatile than VLOOKUP. MATCH allows for wildcard matches. MATCH also allows for a search based on an exact match, based on the number just below the value, or based on a value greater than or equal to the lookup value. This third option is not available in the VLOOKUP or HLOOKUP functions.

Syntax:

MATCH(*lookup_value*,*lookup_array*,*match_type*)

The MATCH function returns the relative position of an item in a column of values. It is useful for determining if a certain value exists in a list.

The MATCH function takes the following arguments:

- *lookup_value*—This is the value you use to find the value you want in a table. *lookup_value* can be a value, which is a number, text, or logical value or a cell reference to a number, text, or logical value.

- *lookup_array*—This is a contiguous range of cells that contains possible lookup values. *lookup_array* can be an array or an array reference.

- *match_type*—This is the number –1, 0, or 1. Note that you can use TRUE instead of 1 and FALSE instead of 0. *match_type* specifies how Microsoft Excel matches *lookup_value* with values in *lookup_array*. If *match_type* is 1, MATCH finds the largest value that is less than or equal to *lookup_value*. *lookup_array* must be placed in ascending order, such as ... –2, –1, 0, 1, 2,...; A–Z; or FALSE, TRUE. If *match_type* is 0, MATCH finds the first value that is exactly equal to *lookup_value*. *lookup_array* can be in any order. If *match_type* is –1, MATCH finds the smallest value that is greater than or equal to *lookup_value*. *lookup_array* must be placed in descending order, such as TRUE, FALSE; Z–A; or ...2, 1, 0, –1, –2,.... If *match_type* is omitted, it is assumed to be 1.

MATCH returns the position of the matched value within *lookup_array*, not the value itself. For example, MATCH("b",{"a","b","c"},0) returns 2, the relative position of b within the array {"a","b","c"}.

MATCH does not distinguish between uppercase and lowercase letters when matching text values. If MATCH is unsuccessful in finding a match, it returns an #N/A error.

If *match_type* is 0 and *lookup_value* is text, *lookup_value* can contain the wildcard characters asterisk (*) and question mark (?). An asterisk matches any sequence of characters; a question mark matches any single character.

Using MATCH to Compare Two Lists

You might face situations in which you have two versions of a list, and you need to match them up.

In Figure 12.27, the worksheet has two simple lists. Column A shows last week's list. Column C shows this week's version of the list. You want to find out quickly which items are new. Here's how you do it:

1. Add the heading **There?** to cell D2.

D3	▼ : × ✓ fx	=MATCH(C3,$A$3:$A$11,0)	
	A	B	C	D
1	ENTRIES LAST WEEK		ENTRIES THIS WEEK	
2				There?
3	PILGRIM		COLUMBIA	2
4	COLUMBIA		CONSTELLATION	8
5	MAYFLOWER		COURAGEOUS	#N/A
6	VOLUNTEER		DEFENDER	5
7	DEFENDER		FREEDOM	#N/A
8	RELIANCE		INTREPID	9
9	RANGER		MAYFLOWER	3
10	CONSTELLATION		PILGRIM	1
11	INTREPID		RANGER	7
12			RELIANCE	6
13			STARS AND STRIPES	#N/A
14			VOLUNTEER	4
15			WEATHERLY	#N/A
16			YOUNG AMERICA	#N/A
17				

Figure 12.27
MATCH operates slightly more quickly than VLOOKUP and achieves the same result in this special case where you are trying to figure out whether a value is in another list.

2. Because the formula in cell D3 looks at the value in cell C3 to see if that value is in the original list in column A, start the formula with `=MATCH(C3,$A$3:$A$11,`.

3. Because you want an exact match, use **0** as the third parameter. Finish the function with a `)`. Press Ctrl+Enter to accept the formula and stay in cell C3.

4. Double-click the fill handle to copy the formula down to all rows.

For any cells where column D contains a number, it means that the entry was on the original list from last week. If the result of MATCH is #N/A, you know that this item is new since the previous week.

Using INDEX and MATCH for a Left Lookup

INDEX is another function that does not immediately seem to have many great uses. In its basic form, INDEX returns the value from a particular row and column of a rectangular range. It returns a value from a particular position of a vertical or horizontal vector.

Typically, you specify a rectangular range and then indicate the row number and column number of the value that you want to return. In Figure 12.28, the formula in C3 returns the third row and second column of B5:D9. Certainly, this is a needlessly complicated way to point to cell C7.

INDEX becomes interesting when you have a formula calculating the position argument. Still in Figure 12.28, a list of people is in M1:M7. You can randomly select from the list by using INDEX and RANDBETWEEN(1,7), as shown in C4.

Figure 12.28
INDEX can be used in a variety of situations without the MATCH function.

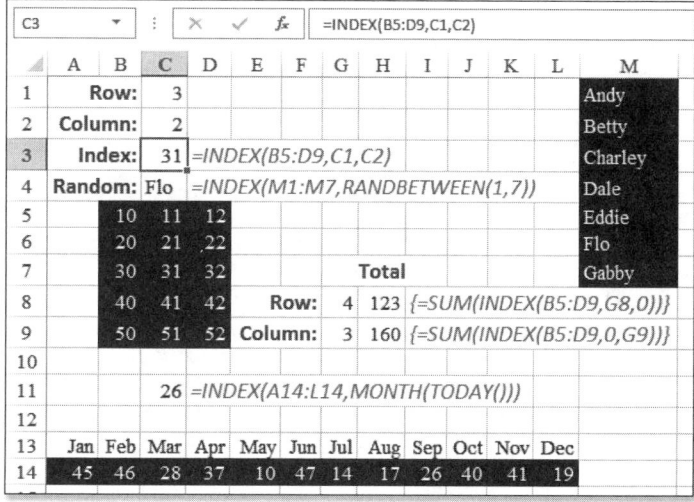

If you specify zero as the row or column argument, INDEX returns the entire row or column. The INDEX in H8 is returning all three values from row 4 of the table, so you have to wrap the index function in a SUM or COUNT or AVERAGE function.

The data in row 14 illustrates an undocumented feature of INDEX. When the reference contains data in a single row, you can specify the column number as the second argument. To get the data for September, you can use the correct =INDEX(A14:L14,0,9) or the shortened =INDEX(A14:L14,9). In Figure 12.28, the formula in C11 returns the value from the current month by using =MONTH(TODAY()) to return a 9 as the second argument of the INDEX function. (This was written in September, hence the 9).

You've reached Excel guru status when you start combining INDEX and MATCH. On its own, neither INDEX nor MATCH seems particularly useful. Used together, though, they become a powerful combination that is more flexible than VLOOKUP and often faster to calculate than VLOOKUP.

In Figure 12.29, a customer number is entered in cell A1. The customer lookup table appears in columns F, G, and H. The main problem is that the customer table does not have the customer number on the left side.

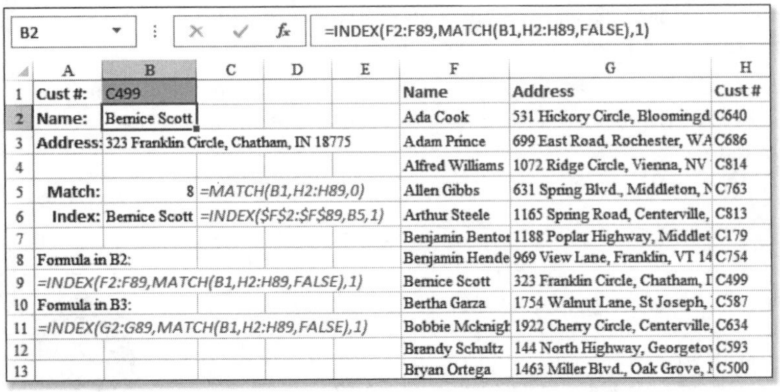

Figure 12.29
This combination of INDEX and MATCH enables you to look up data that is to the left of a key field.

In many cases, you would copy column H to column E and use column E as the key of the table. However, the table in F:H is likely to be repopulated every day from a web query or an OLAP query. Therefore, it might become monotonous to move the data after every refresh. The solution is to use a combination of INDEX and MATCH. Here's what you do:

1. Use the formula =MATCH(B1,H2:H89,0) to search through column H to find the row with the customer number that matches the one in cell B1. In this case, C499 is in row 9, which is the eighth row of the table.

2. Be sure to use exactly the same shape range as the first argument in the INDEX function: =INDEX (F2:F89,*WhichRow*,*WhichColumn*) searches through the customer names in column F.

3. For the second parameter of the INDEX function, specify the relative row number. This information was provided by the MATCH function in step 1.

4. Ensure that the third parameter of the INDEX function is the relative column number. Because the range F2:F89 has only one column, this is either 1 or can simply be omitted.

5. Putting the formula together, the formula in cell B2 is =INDEX(F2:F89,MATCH(B1,H2:H89, 0),1).

Syntax:

```
INDEX(array,row_num,[column_num])
INDEX(reference,row_num,[column_num],[area_num])
```

The INDEX function returns the value at the intersection of a particular row and column within a range. This function takes the following arguments:

- *array*—This is a range of cells or an array constant. If *array* contains only one row or column, the corresponding *row_num* or *column_num* argument is optional. If *array* has more than one row and more than one column, and if only *row_num* or *column_num* is used, INDEX returns an array of the entire row or column in array.

- **row_num**—This selects the row in *array* from which to return a value. If *row_num* is omitted, then *column_num* is required.

- **column_num**—This selects the column in *array* from which to return a value. If *column_num* is omitted, then *row_num* is required.

If both the *row_num* and *column_num* arguments are used, INDEX returns the value in the cell at the intersection of *row_num* and *column_num*.

If you set *row_num* or *column_num* to 0, INDEX returns the array of values for the entire column or row, respectively. To use values returned as an array, you use the INDEX function as an array formula in a horizontal range of cells for a row and in a vertical range of cells for a column. To enter an array formula, you press Ctrl+Shift+Enter.

row_num and *column_num* must point to a cell within array; otherwise, INDEX returns a #REF! error.

Using MATCH and INDEX to Fill a Wide Table

The lookup functions VLOOKUP, HLOOKUP, and MATCH can be very processor-intensive when the lookup table contains hundreds of thousands of rows.

Back in Figure 12.25, Excel had to do 96 VLOOKUP functions. However, after Excel figured out the position of item G598 in the lookup table for cell C6, it had to go back through exactly the same steps for cell D6, E6, F6, G6, and so on. You made Excel find exactly the same item 12 times, which is a very slow process.

If the recalculation times are taking too long, you should consider using one MATCH per row to find the relative row number and then using 12 speedy INDEX functions to fill in the values in that row. Figure 12.30 illustrates a problem where you can use this trick. In this case, the list of inventory items is 14,000 rows. Here's what you do:

1. Copy the range of warehouse names from B16:M16 to D4:O4.

2. In cell C5, enter **=MATCH(B5,$A$17:$A$14056,0)**. This formula finds an exact match for C529. The answer 8005 means that product C529 is on the 8,005th relative row of the lookup table.

3. Copy the formula in cell C5 down to C12. Each of these eight MATCH functions will take just about as long as the equivalent VLOOKUP function would take.

4. As you build the INDEX function in D5, be careful that the array range encompasses the same rows used in the MATCH function. Use dollar signs before the row numbers, but not before the column letters. Start the formula in cell D6 as **=INDEX(B$17:B$14056**.

5. Make the next argument the relative row number within the lookup range. This is the value from column C, so use $C5. If you type **C6** and then press the F4 key three times, Excel adds the dollar sign before the C in C5. The formula =INDEX(B$17:B$14056,$C5) contains a brilliant combination of mixed references. The $17 and $14056 ensure that you are always retrieving values from rows 17:14056. The lack of a dollar sign before both B's allows the formula to retrieve from columns C, D, E, ... as the formula gets copied across. In the second argument, the $C makes sure that the INDEX always uses the row number from column C. The lack of a dollar sign before the 5 in $C5 allows the formula to grab the row number from C6, C7, C8, ... as the formula gets copied down.

INDEX Function

MATCH Function

D5	▼	:	×	✓	fx	=INDEX(B$17:B$14056,$C5)					

⊿	A	B	C	D	E	F	G	H	I	J	K	L	M
1	Order Fulfillment Decision Tool												
2	Enter Customer Order in A&B, check stock in D:O												
3													
4	Qty	Item	Match	WH1	WH2	WH3	WH4	WH5	WH6	WH7	WH8	WH9	WH10
5	2	C529	8005	0	5	0	81	96	5	5	0	2	0
6	10	F708	3635	1	2	0	88	1	0	53	2	0	0
7	9	X291	452	0	80	0	0	0	50	29	33	0	87
8	1	E890	6335	2	87	0	1	2	0	5	0	95	4
9	5	C299	12192	0	2	4	0	48	0	2	0	89	66
10	4	S323	7450	4	5	3	69	5	0	4	102	97	0
11	1	V600	9038	131	48	129	1	0	1	0	105	67	117
12	9	P765	8596	3	0	70	2	1	3	0	0	0	0
13			C12: =MATCH(B12,$A$17:$A$14056,0)				H12: =INDEX(F$17:F$14056,$C12)						
14	Inventory By Warehouse												
15													
16	Item	WH1	WH2	WH3	WH4	WH5	WH6	WH7	WH8	WH9	WH10	WH11	WH12
17	G245	36	2	71	1	96	83	0	34	81	59	0	0
18	J535	0	3	0	0	0	85	5	137	0	32	0	5
19	X286	113	2	2	0	0	35	29	0	58	4	0	1
20	M562	4	72	0	58	5	0	110	133	0	3	0	136

Figure 12.30
This performs eight relatively slow MATCH functions and then 96 relatively fast INDEX functions.

6. Optionally, add a conditional format to cell D5 to highlight the cell if this formula evaluates to TRUE: =D5>=$A5.

7. Copy the formula from cell D5 to D5:O12.

The eight MATCH functions in column C take a similar amount of calculation time as eight VLOOKUP functions would take for Warehouse 1. The advantage of this method is that the 96 INDEX functions are much faster calculating than 88 VLOOKUP functions. Even though this method uses 104 formulas instead of the 96 formulas back in Figure 12.25, this method calculates in one-eighth the time.

Performing Many Lookups with LOOKUP

Even Excel Help tells you to avoid the old LOOKUP function. However, LOOKUP can do one useful trick that VLOOKUP and HLOOKUP cannot do—it can process many lookups in one single array formula. LOOKUP can also deal with a lookup range that is vertical and a return range that is horizontal, or vice versa.

The next section looks at the common use of LOOKUP and how it contrasts with VLOOKUP and HLOOKUP.

Syntax:

LOOKUP(*lookup_value*, *array*)

In this case, LOOKUP is acting similar to VLOOKUP or HLOOKUP. Excel examines the height and width of the array. If the array has more rows than columns, Excel assumes you are doing a VLOOKUP and looks through the first column of the array for the lookup value. If the array has more columns than rows, Excel assumes you are doing an HLOOKUP and looks through the first row of the array for the lookup value. If the array has the same number of rows as columns, it does a VLOOKUP.

In this syntax of LOOKUP, Excel always returns the value from the last column or row of the array. In Figure 12.31, the formula in C2 is returning a value from cell G3. Because the array is described as E2:G5, Excel automatically returns a value from the final column of E2:G5. Because the array is four rows and three columns, Excel assumes you want the equivalent to VLOOKUP instead of HLOOKUP. In cell C3, the lookup array is E8:H9. Because this array is wider than it is tall, cell C3 does the equivalent of an HLOOKUP.

In addition, LOOKUP always performs a range lookup, similar to leaving off the FALSE as the fourth parameter of VLOOKUP or HLOOKUP. For this reason, your lookup array must always be sorted.

If you do not want to return a value from the last column of the array, you can specify two vectors in the alternative form of the syntax discussed in the next section.

Syntax:

```
LOOKUP(lookup_value, lookup_vector, result_vector)
```

In this version of the LOOKUP function, you specify vectors that are either one row tall or one column wide. This version enables you to do a lookup similar to VLOOKUP where the result field is to the left of the key field. It also enables you to perform the mythical *VHLOOKUP*, where you look up a value in a vertical vector and get the result from a horizontal vector. In cell C4 of Figure 12.31, the result vector E7:H7 is horizontal whereas the lookup vector E2:E5 is vertical.

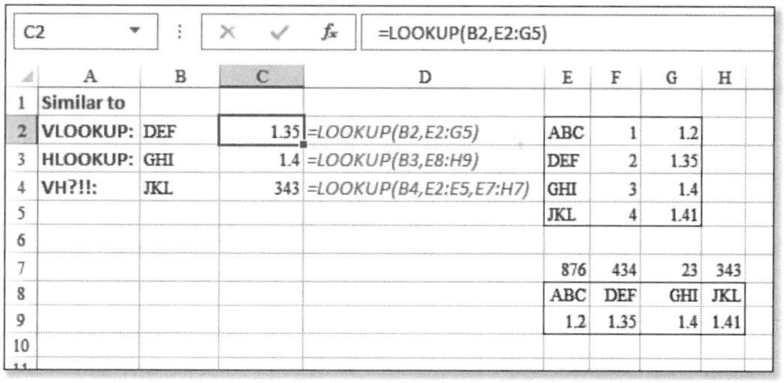

C2 =LOOKUP(B2,E2:G5)

	A	B	C	D	E	F	G	H
1	Similar to							
2	VLOOKUP:	DEF	1.35	=LOOKUP(B2,E2:G5)	ABC	1	1.2	
3	HLOOKUP:	GHI	1.4	=LOOKUP(B3,E8:H9)	DEF	2	1.35	
4	VH?!!:	JKL	343	=LOOKUP(B4,E2:E5,E7:H7)	GHI	3	1.4	
5					JKL	4	1.41	
6								
7					876	434	23	343
8					ABC	DEF	GHI	JKL
9					1.2	1.35	1.4	1.41
10								

Figure 12.31
The quirky LOOKUP function decided to do a VLOOKUP or HLOOKUP, depending on the shape of the lookup array.

One additional super-power of the old LOOKUP function is the ability to look up several values at once. You have to use Ctrl+Shift+Enter to accept the formula, and because LOOKUP will be returning an array of answers, you should enclose the LOOKUP in a wrapper function such as SUM to add all the results from the function.

In Figure 12.32, a series of invoices appear in rows 4 through 17. A GP% (gross profit percentage) is associated with each invoice. The sales rep will earn a bonus depending on the GP% of each invoice, as shown in E6:F10. Instead of calculating a bonus for each row, you can calculate a bonus for all the rows at once. The formula in B1 of Figure 12.32 specifies an array of B4:B17 as the lookup value. This causes Excel to perform the LOOKUP 14 times, once for each value in the range B4:B17. The formula wraps the LOOKUP results in a SUM function to add up all the bonus results. To calculate correctly, you must hold down Ctrl+Shift while pressing Enter after typing this formula. When you press Ctrl+Shift+Enter, Excel adds the curly braces around the formula. You do not type the curly braces manually. Typing the curly braces will not work.

B1	▼ : × ✓ *fx* {=SUM(LOOKUP(B4:B17,E6:F10))}							

▲	A	B	C	D	E	F	G	H	I	J
1	Bonus Total:	236	{=SUM(LOOKUP(B4:B17,E6:F10))}							
2										
3	Invoice	GP%								
4	1001	51%								
5	1002	51%			GP%	Bonus				
6	1003	56%			0%	$0				
7	1004	43%			45%	$2				
8	1005	49%			50%	$10				
9	1006	50%			55%	$20				
10	1007	43%			60%	$50				
11	1008	63%								
12	1009	63%								
13	1010	57%								
14	1011	47%								
15	1012	61%								
16	1013	50%								
17	1014	48%								

Figure 12.32
Unlike VLOOKUP and HLOOKUP, the aging LOOKUP function can process many lookups in a single array formula.

Using FORMULATEXT to Document a Worksheet

Quiz: Which Excel function is used the most in this book? It is FORMULATEXT. The FORMULATEXT function is brand new in Excel 2013. If you ask for the =FORMULATEXT(A1), Excel will show the formula that is in cell A1 as text. All the formulas shown in this book (such as cell C1 in Figure 12.32) are generated with the FORMULATEXT function.

You can use FORMULATEXT to document the formulas used in your worksheet. Normally, you can either print your worksheet with formulas showing or with the results from the formulas. By using FORMULATEXT, you can show both the formula and the result.

In Figure 12.33, the text of the formula shown in C3 comes from a FORMULATEXT function.

Syntax:

FORMULATEXT(*reference*)

This function returns a formula as text.

Figure 12.33
A FORMULATEXT function in C3 shows the formula used in B3.

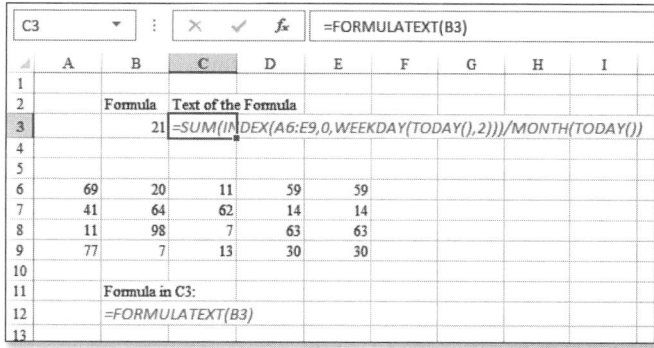

Using Functions to Describe the Shape of a Contiguous Reference

Four functions can be used to identify the location and shape of a contiguous range:

- **COLUMN(*reference*)**—This returns the column number of the upper-left corner of a reference, using numbers from 1 to 16,384. If *reference* is omitted, the function returns the column number of the cell where the formula is entered.

- **ROW(*reference*)**—This returns the row number of the upper-left corner of the reference, using numbers from 1 to 1,048,576. If *reference* is omitted, the function returns the row number of the cell where the formula is entered.

- **COLUMNS(*reference*)**—This returns the number of columns in a reference. In this case, *reference* must be a single contiguous range.

- **ROWS(*reference*)**—This returns the number of rows in a reference. Again, *reference* must be a single contiguous range.

Figure 12.34 displays the ROW, COLUMN, ROWS, and COLUMNS functions of a named range. The range occupies the black cells in B7:D11.

Figure 12.34
These functions describe the location and shape of a range.

	A	B	C	D	E
1	Column	2	=COLUMN(MyRange)		
2	Row	7	=ROW(MyRange)		
3	Columns	3	=COLUMNS(MyRange)		
4	Rows	5	=ROWS(MyRange)		
5	Areas	1	=AREAS(MyRange)		
6					
7		1	2	4	
8		8	16	32	
9		64	128	256	
10		512	1024	2048	
11		4096	8192	16384	
12					

B1 — fx =COLUMN(MyRange)

Using AREAS and INDEX to Describe a Range with More Than One Area

All the functions listed in the preceding section fail if the *reference* describes a noncontiguous range. However, you can check for that condition by using the AREAS function.

Syntax:

AREAS(*reference*)

This function returns the number of contiguous ranges in a reference. The argument *reference* usually refers to a named range.

In Figure 12.35, MyAreas is a defined name that describes the cells in black. In rows 1 through 4, all the traditional functions fail with #REF! errors because the reference contains more than one contiguous range.

B16	▼	:	×	✓	*fx*	=COLUMN(INDEX(MyAreas,,,B$15))			
◢	A	B	C	D	E	F	G	H	I
1	Column	#REF!	=COLUMN(MyAreas)						
2	Row	#REF!	=ROW(MyAreas)						
3	Columns	#REF!	=COLUMNS(MyAreas)						
4	Rows	#REF!	=ROWS(MyAreas)						
5	Areas	4	=AREAS(MyAreas)						
7		1	2	4					
9			8	16	32				
11		64	128	256					
13	512	1024	2048						
15	**Area:**	**1**	**2**	**3**	**4**	*Formulas in B:*			
16	**Column**	2	3	2	1	*=COLUMN(INDEX(MyAreas,,,B$15))*			
17	**Row**	7	9	11	13	*=ROW(INDEX(MyAreas,,,B$15))*			
18	**Columns**	3	3	3	3	*=COLUMNS(INDEX(MyAreas,,,B$15))*			
19	**Rows**	1	1	1	1	*=ROWS(INDEX(MyAreas,,,B$15))*			
20	**Areas**	1	1	1	1	*=AREAS(INDEX(MyAreas,,,B$15))*			
21									

Figure 12.35
To describe a reference with multiple contiguous ranges, you must use the reference form of the INDEX function.

Syntax:

INDEX(*reference*,*row_num*,*column_num*,*area_num*)

If you need to determine the location and shape of each contiguous range, do so one area at a time. A second syntax for the INDEX function returns a reference to one specific area of a reference. This syntax includes the following arguments:

- *reference*—Reference to one or more cell ranges. If you are entering a nonadjacent range for the reference, enclose *reference* in parentheses. If each area in *reference* contains only one row or column, the *row_num* or *column_num* argument, respectively, is optional. For example, for a single row reference, you use INDEX(*reference,column_num*).

- *row_num*—The number of the row in *reference* from which to return a reference.

- *column_num*—The number of the column in *reference* from which to return a reference.

- *area_num*—Selects a range in *reference* from which to return the intersection of *row_num* and *column_num*. The first area selected or entered is numbered 1, the second is 2, and so on. If *area_num* is omitted, INDEX uses area 1. For example, if *reference* describes the cells (A1:B4,D1:E4,G1:H4), then *area_num* 1 is the range A1:B4, *area_num* 2 is the range D1:E4, and *area_num* 3 is the range G1:H4.

After *reference* and *area_num* have selected a particular range, *row_num* and *column_num* select a particular cell: *row_num* 1 is the first row in the range, *column_num* 1 is the first column, and so on. The reference returned by INDEX is the intersection of *row_num* and *column_num*.

If you set *row_num* or *column_num* to 0, INDEX returns the reference for the entire column or row, respectively.

row_num, *column_num*, and *area_num* must point to a cell within *reference*; otherwise, INDEX returns a #REF! error. If *row_num* and *column_num* are omitted, INDEX returns the area in *reference* specified by *area_num*.

The result of the INDEX function is a reference, and it is interpreted as such by other formulas. Depending on the formula, the return value of INDEX may be used as a reference or as a value. For example, the formula CELL("width",INDEX(A1:B2,1,2)) is equivalent to CELL("width",B1). The CELL function uses the return value of INDEX as a cell reference. On the other hand, a formula such as 2*INDEX(A1:B2,1,2) translates the return value of INDEX into the number in cell B1.

Using this version of INDEX, you can build formulas that work on one particular area in a named range. Here's how you do it:

1. In B15:E15, enter the numbers 1 through 4. These correspond to the four areas in MyAreas.

2. When you build the INDEX function, you want Excel to return a reference to all the rows and columns of the first area of the range, so use =INDEX(MyAreas,,,1) to return such a reference.

3. Instead of using 1 for the *areas* argument of INDEX, use =INDEX(MyAreas,,,B$15).

4. Enter the formula **=COLUMN(INDEX(MyAreas,,,B$15))** in cell B16 to define the starting column of area 1 of MyAreas.

5. Copy the formula from step 4 to B17:B20. Edit each function to change COLUMN to ROW, COLUMNS, ROWS, and AREAS.

6. Copy B17:B20 to columns C, D, and E.

The result, as shown in Figure 12.35, includes four sets of formulas in B16:E20 that completely describe the four areas of the named range MyAreas.

Using Numbers with OFFSET to Describe a Range

The language of Excel is numbers. There are functions that count the number of entries in a range. There are functions that can tell you the numeric position of a looked-up value. You might know that a particular value is found in row 20, but what if you want to perform calculations on other cells in row 20?

The OFFSET function handles this very situation. You can use OFFSET to describe a range using mostly numbers. OFFSET is flexible: It can describe a single cell, or it can describe a rectangular range.

Although INDEX can return a single cell, row, or column from a rectangular range, it has limitations. If you specify C5:Z99 as the range for an INDEX function, you can select only cells below and/or to the right of C5. The OFFSET function can move up and down or left and right from the starting cell, which is C5.

Syntax:

OFFSET(*reference*,*rows*,*cols*,*height*,*width*)

The OFFSET function returns a reference to a range that is a given number of rows and columns from a given reference. This function takes the following arguments:

- *reference*—This is the reference from which you want to base the offset. *reference* must be a reference to a cell or range of adjacent cells; otherwise, OFFSET returns a #VALUE! error.

- *rows*—This is the number of rows, up or down, that you want the upper-left cell to refer to. Using 5 as the *rows* argument, for example, specifies that the upper-left cell in the reference is five rows below *reference*. *rows* can be positive, which means below the starting reference, or negative, which means above the starting reference.

- *cols*—This is the number of columns to the left or right that you want the upper-left cell of the result to refer to. For example, using 5 as the *cols* argument specifies that the upper-left cell in the reference is five columns to the right of *reference*. *cols* can be positive, which means to the right of the starting reference, or negative, which means to the left of the starting reference. If *rows* and *cols* offset *reference* over the edge of the worksheet, OFFSET returns a #REF! error. Figure 12.36 demonstrates various combinations of *rows* and *cols* from a starting cell of cell C5.

- *height*—This is the height, in number of rows, that you want the returned reference to be. *height* must be a positive number.

- *width*—This is the width, in number of columns, that you want the returned reference to be. *width* must be a positive number. If *height* or *width* is omitted, Excel assumes it is the same height or width as *reference*.

OFFSET enables you to specify a reference. It does not move any cell. It does not change the selection. It is just a numeric way to describe a reference. OFFSET can be used in any function that is expecting a reference argument.

Figure 12.36
These OFFSET functions return a single cell that is a certain number of rows and columns away from cell C5.

C10	▼	:	✕	✓	*fx*	=OFFSET($C$5,A10,B10,1,1)

	A	B	C	D	E	F
1	Examples of 1-cell ranges returned by Offset					
2						
3	1	2	4	8	16	
4	32	64	128	256	512	
5	1024	2048	4096	8192	16384	
6	32768	65536	131072	262144	524288	
7	1048576	2097152	4194304	8388608	16777216	
8						
9	Row	Column	Offset			
10	-2	0	4	=OFFSET($C$5,A10,B10,1,1)		
11	0	-2	1024	=OFFSET($C$5,A11,B11,1,1)		
12	0	2	16384	=OFFSET($C$5,A12,B12,1,1)		
13	2	0	4194304	=OFFSET($C$5,A13,B13,1,1)		
14	-2	-2	1	=OFFSET($C$5,A14,B14,1,1)		
15	2	2	16777216	=OFFSET($C$5,A15,B15,1,1)		
16						

Excel Help provides a trivial example of =SUM(OFFSET(C2,1,2,3,1)), which sums E3:E5. However, this example is silly because no one would ever write such a formula! If you were to write such a formula, you would just write =SUM(E3:E5) instead. The power of OFFSET comes when at least one of the four numeric arguments is calculated by the COUNT function or a lookup function.

In Figure 12.37, you can use COUNT(A5:A99) to count how many entries are in column A. If you assume that there are no blanks in the range of data, you can use the COUNT result as the *height* argument in OFFSET to describe the range of numbers. Here's what you do:

1. There is nothing magic about the reference, so write it as **=OFFSET(A5,**.

2. Do not move the starting position any rows or columns from cell A5. The starting position is A5, so you always use 0 and 0 for rows and columns. Therefore, the formula is now **=OFFSET(A5,0,0,**.

3. If you want to include only the number of entries in the list, use COUNT(A5:A999) as the height of the range. The formula is now **=OFFSET(A5,0,0,COUNT(A5:A999),**.

4. The width is one column, so make the function **=OFFSET(A5,0,0,COUNT(A5:A999),1)**.

5. Use your OFFSET function anywhere you would normally specify a reference. You can use =SUM(OFFSET(A5,0,0,COUNT(A5:A999),1)) or specify that formula as the series in a chart. This creates a dynamic chart that grows or shrinks as the number of entries changes.

A3	▼	:	×	✓	*fx*	=SUM(OFFSET(A5,0,0,COUNT(A5:A999),1))

	A	B	C	D	E	F	G	H	I	J	K
1	Example of Dynamic Range Generated by Offset										
2	=SUM(OFFSET(A5,0,0,COUNT(A5:A999),1))										
3	3			15		31		63	255		1023
4											
5	1		1		1		1		1		1
6	2		2		2		2		2		2
7			4		4		4		4		4
8			8		8		8		8		8
9					16		16		16		16
10							32		32		32
11									64		64
12									128		128
13											256
14											512

Figure 12.37
Every argument except
`height` is hard-coded
in these functions.
The `height` argument
comes from a COUNT
function to allow the
range to expand as
more entries are added.

For a more complex example of OFFSET, examine Figure 12.38, which shows several yearly tables starting in cell C8. Each month of the table contains from one to five entries. The person using this spreadsheet will select a year and a month from cells E1 and E2. The goal is to find information about the entries for that particular month and year. Here's how you do it:

1. Have the formula in cell I1 find the starting row for the particular year, using the MATCH function shown in cell J1.

2. Have the formula in cell I2 find the column for the chosen month, using the MATCH function shown in cell J2.

3. Build the OFFSET function to describe the range for that month and year. You know that it starts in the *row* in I1 and the *column* in I2. If you make the *reference* cell A1, then row 15 is 14 rows below A1. Therefore, use **=OFFSET(A1,I1-1,**.

4. The starting column is in cell I2. Column 8 is seven columns to the right of A1. Therefore, you now use **=OFFSET(A1,I1-1,I2-1**.

5. The structure of the worksheet allows for up to five entries per month, arranged down a row. Thus, *height* is 5 and *width* is 1. Use the following formula to describe the possible range for the month: **=OFFSET(A1,I1-1,I2-1,5,1)**. This is good enough to use for MIN, MAX, SUM, and so on.

6. To chart the data, figure out the exact height. Use the **=COUNT(OFFSET(A1,I1-1,I2-1,5,1))** formula in cell I3 to count the number of entries for the month.

Figure 12.38
Even with
a poorly
designed data-
base spread-
sheet, various
combinations
of OFFSET can
locate and total
cells for a spe-
cific month.

	C	D	E	F	G	H	I	J	K	L	M	N	O
								=MIN(OFFSET(A1,I1-1,I2-1,I$3,1))					
1	Select a Year:		2014		Row for Year:		9	=MATCH(E1,C1:C96,0)					
2	Select a month:		May		Column for Month:		8	=MATCH(E2,$A$8:$O$8,0)					
3					# of Entries:		4	=COUNT(OFFSET(A1,I1-1,I2-1,5,1))					
4					Min Entry:		2165	=MIN(OFFSET(A1,I1-1,I2-1,I$3,1))					
5					Max Entry:		4817	=MAX(OFFSET(A1,I1-1,I2-1,I$3,1))					
6					Sum for Month:		13843	=SUM(OFFSET(A1,I1-1,I2-1,I$3,1))					
7													
8			Jan	Feb	Mar	Apr	May	Jun	Jul	Aug	Sep	Oct	Nov	Dec
9	2014	2050	2820	1485	1576	4647	3451	1361	1066	2078	3565	3455	1359
10		1160		1633		2165		3135		2750		3679	3884
11		1864				2214				4437		3122	
12		1217				4817						4166	
13												3950	
14			Jan	Feb	Mar	Apr	May	Jun	Jul	Aug	Sep	Oct	Nov	Dec
15	2015	2422	2292	1641	1270	4110	1012	3071	3783	4400	3966	2629	3077
16		1248		1031		2708		2830		3290		4307	3666
17		1313				2590		1095		1134		1399	
18		2531				3575						1956	
19						4524							
20			Jan	Feb	Mar	Apr	May	Jun	Jul	Aug	Sep	Oct	Nov	Dec
21	2016	1011	1902	1567	3474	2184	4663	3841	1087	3229	4640	4353	1420
22		1963	3230		2894	3662	4167	2821		1824		4293	3935
23		1245	2379			4964		4049		1718		1150	
24						4078						1986	
25												1024	

7. Use the formula `=OFFSET(A1,I1-1,I2-1,I3,1)` to describe the exact month. Add additional formulas in I4:I6 to figure out the minimum, maximum, and sum of those cells.

The OFFSET function initially seems intimidating, especially in light of the example you just walked through. Remember that for useful results from OFFSET, you usually replace one or more of the final four arguments with a calculation.

Using ADDRESS to Find the Address for Any Cell

If someone asks you for the cell address for the cell in row 5, column 5, you could probably come up with E5 quickly. What if someone asks you for the cell address of the cell in row 26, column 26? This is Z26. Again, you should come up with this if you know there are 26 letters in the alphabet.

If someone asks you to calculate the address of row 2 and column 30, you have to divide 30 by 26 to learn that the result is 1 with a remainder of 4. This could lead you to conclude the cell address is the first letter of the alphabet (A) and the fourth letter of the alphabet (D) to come up with AD2.

This type of calculation becomes far more complex with 16,384 columns. For example, how would you calculate the address for row 2 of column 14123?

Fortunately, Excel provides the ADDRESS function to convert any intersection of row and column number to an address. =ADDRESS(2,14123) returns the text of $TWE$2.

Syntax:

ADDRESS(*row_num*,*column_num*,*abs_num*,*a1*,*sheet_text*)

The default version of ADDRESS returns the cell address as an absolute address with both dollar signs. There are optional parameters to control this behavior:

- **_row_num_**—This is the row number to use in the cell reference.

- **_column_num_**—This is the column number to use in the cell reference.

- **_abs_num_**—This specifies the type of reference to return. If it is 1 or omitted, the returned address has both dollar signs and is absolute. If it is 2, the row is held absolute, but the column is relative. If it is 3, the row is relative and the column is absolute. If it is 4, the address is relative, with no dollar signs.

- **_a1_**—This is a logical value that specifies the A1 or R1C1 reference style. If *a1* is TRUE or omitted, ADDRESS returns an A1-style reference; if it is FALSE, ADDRESS returns an R1C1-style reference.

- **_sheet_text_**—This is text that specifies the name of the worksheet to be used as the external reference. If *sheet_text* is omitted, no sheet name is used.

> **Tip**
>
> To find the value of a cell described by ADDRESS, use the INDIRECT function.

Figure 12.39 shows eight ways to describe one cell, depending on the various combinations of absolute and A1 arguments.

	A	B	C	D	E	F	G	H
			fx		=ADDRESS(A2,B2,C2,D2)			
1	Row	Column	Abs	A1 vs R1C1	Result			
2	123	28	1	TRUE	$AB$123	=ADDRESS(A2,B2,C2,D2)		
3	123	28	2	TRUE	AB$123	=ADDRESS(A3,B3,C3,D3)		
4	123	28	3	TRUE	$AB123	=ADDRESS(A4,B4,C4,D4)		
5	123	28	4	TRUE	AB123	=ADDRESS(A5,B5,C5,D5)		
6	123	28	1	FALSE	R123C28	=ADDRESS(A6,B6,C6,D6)		
7	123	28	2	FALSE	R123C[28]	=ADDRESS(A7,B7,C7,D7)		
8	123	28	3	FALSE	R[123]C28	=ADDRESS(A8,B8,C8,D8)		
9	123	28	4	FALSE	R[123]C[28]	=ADDRESS(A9,B9,C9,D9)		
10								
11		'[C:\JanIncome.xls]Income Statement'!A1						
12		=ADDRESS(1,1,4,TRUE,"[C:\JanIncome.xls]Income Statement")						

(Cell reference box: E2 ... =ADDRESS(A2,B2,C2,D2))

Figure 12.39
ADDRESS can return a cell address in A1 or R1C1 style.

The *sheet_text* argument is interesting. It is difficult to remember the arcane rules for when to use apostrophes and where the exclamation point needs to go in an address. If you specify *sheet_text* as the name of a worksheet or use the style [*book_name*]*SheetName*, Excel builds the proper reference. Cell B11 in Figure 12.39 shows the result from an ADDRESS function that builds a reference to another workbook.

Using INDIRECT to Build and Evaluate Cell References on the Fly

The INDIRECT function is deceivingly powerful. Consider this trivial example: In cell A1, enter the text **B2**. In cell B2, enter a number. In cell C3, enter the formula **=INDIRECT(A1)**. Excel returns the number that you entered in cell B2 in cell C3. The INDIRECT function looks in cell A1 and expects to find something that is a valid cell or range reference. It then looks in that address to return the answer for the function.

The reference text can be any text that you can string together using various text functions. This enables you to create complex references that dynamically point to other sheets or to other open workbooks.

The reference text can also be a range name. You could have a validation list box where someone selects a value from a list. If you have predefined a named range that corresponds to each possible entry on the list, INDIRECT can point to the various named ranges on the fly.

When you use traditional formulas, even absolute formulas, there is a chance that someone might insert rows or columns that will move the reference. If you need a formula to always point to cell J10, no matter how someone rearranges the worksheet, you can use =INDIRECT("J10") to handle this.

Syntax:

INDIRECT(*ref_text*,*a1*)

The INDIRECT function returns the reference specified by a text string. This function takes the following arguments:

- **ref_text**—This is a reference to a cell that contains an A1-style reference, an R1C1-style reference, a name defined as a reference, or a reference to a cell as a text string. If *ref_text* is not a valid cell reference, INDIRECT returns a #REF! error. If *ref_text* refers to an external workbook, the other workbook must be open. If the source workbook is not open, INDIRECT returns a #REF! error.

- **a1**—This is a logical value that specifies what type of reference is contained in the cell *ref_text*. If *a1* is TRUE or omitted, *ref_text* is interpreted as an A1-style reference. If a1 is FALSE, *ref_text* is interpreted as an R1C1-style reference.

Figure 12.40 is a monthly worksheet in a workbook that has 12 similar sheets. In each worksheet, the data headings are in row 6, and the invoices appear for some number of rows, starting in row 7. Each worksheet has a total for the month in cell D2.

| D3 | ▼ | : | × | ✓ | ƒx | =INDIRECT(TEXT(DATE(YEAR(A1),MONTH(A1)-1,1),"mmm")&"!D3")+D2 |

▲	A	B	C	D	E	F	G	H	I	J
1	March, 2015									
2			Total This Month:	3088						
3			Total Year to Date:	10173						
4										
5	Database of sales for this month:									
6	Date	Invoice	Customer	Amount						
7	3/15/15	1001	Innovative Briefcase Inc.	274						
8	3/17/15	1002	New Opener Company	120						
9	3/1/15	1003	Ideal Gadget Corporation	223						
10	3/13/15	1004	Ideal Treadmill Company	231						
11	3/10/15	1005	Bright Bottle Inc.	153						
12	3/9/15	1006	Fully Patio Company	115						
13	3/4/15	1007	First-Rate Aerobic Supply	221						
14	3/20/15	1008	Innovative Luggage Corpora	126						
15	3/3/15	1009	Cool Opener Inc.	145						
16	3/23/15	1010	Secure Sprayer Company	144						
17	3/5/15	1011	Matchless Toothpick Compa	158						
18	3/8/15	1012	Trouble-Free Gadget Compa	123						
19	3/1/15	1013	Bright Aquarium Corporatio	190						
20	3/9/15	1014	Trendy Meter Traders	163						
21	3/8/15	1015	Supreme Flagpole Corporatic	147						
22	3/24/15	1016	Amazing Tripod Inc.	150						
23	3/29/15	1017	Steadfast Quilt Inc.	122						
24	3/31/15	1018	Enhanced Flagpole Corporat	283						
25										

Figure 12.40
Cell D4 dynamically builds a text formula to reference the previous sheet, and then INDIRECT evaluates the formula.

In this example, you want to add a year-to-date total in cell D3 on each worksheet. This is fairly difficult to do without VBA. Many VBA books include a user-defined function to describe the previous sheet in a workbook. However, this function fails if you send the workbook to someone who disables macros on her computer. Instead, you can solve this problem with the clever use of text functions and the INDIRECT function. To do so, follow these steps:

1. Select the Jan worksheet.

2. Shift+click the Dec worksheet to put all 12 sheets in Group mode.

3. In cell A1, enter the formula =**A7**. This adds the first date as a title for the worksheet.

4. Format cell A1 with the custom format mmmm, yyyy. This causes the date to appear as January, 2015.

5. Right-click the Jan tab name and select Ungroup Sheets.

6. Enter =**D2** as the year-to-date formula in cell D3 of the Jan tab.

7. On the Feb worksheet, build a text formula that returns the name of the previous month. The quest becomes how to build a formula that looks like =Jan!D3.

8. Jan is a three-letter abbreviation for any date in the month of January. Therefore, enter a January date in a cell and format the cell with the custom number format mmm, so that the result is the word Jan.

9. The TEXT function takes a number or date and displays it using a specific custom number format, so on the February sheet, use =TEXT(A1,"mmm"), which results in the value Feb. This is close. If you can find a way to get the name of the previous month, the problem will be solved.

10. The value in cell A1 is a live date. You can use date math to calculate a different date, such as the date one month earlier. Use the DATE(*year*,*month*,*day*) function to return a date in the previous month. For the *year* parameter, use YEAR(A1). For the *month* parameter, use MONTH(A1)–1. For the *day* parameter, use DAY(A1). The formula =DATE(YEAR(A1),MONTH(A1)–1,1) returns a date that is the first of the previous month.

11. Combining steps 9 and 10 into a single formula, use =TEXT(DATE(YEAR(A1),MONTH(A1)–1,1),"MMM") to return the value of Jan on the Feb worksheet, Feb on the Mar worksheet, and so on.

12. Use the generic formula =TEXT(DATE(YEAR(A1),MONTH(A1)–1,1),"MMM")&"!D3" to build the reference.

13. Select the Feb worksheet. Shift+click the Dec worksheet to place these 11 worksheets in Group mode. In cell D3, enter this formula: =INDIRECT(TEXT(DATE(YEAR(A1),MONTH(A1)–1,1),"mmm")&"!D3")+D2.

14. Right-click any sheet tab and select Ungroup to take the workbook out of Group mode.

The result, as shown in Figure 12.40, is a formula on the last 11 worksheets that automatically pulls the year-to-date total from the previous worksheet and adds it to the current worksheet total.

Using the HYPERLINK Function to Quickly Add Hyperlinks

Excel enables you to add a hyperlink by using the Excel interface. On the Insert tab, select the Hyperlink icon. Next, you specify text to appear in the cell and the underlying address. Building links in this way is easy, but it is tedious to build them one at a time. If you have hundreds of links to add, you can add them quickly by using the HYPERLINK function.

Syntax:

HYPERLINK(*link_location*,*friendly_name*)

The HYPERLINK function creates a shortcut that opens a document stored on your hard drive, a network server, or on the Internet. This function takes the following arguments:

- **link_location**—This is the URL address on the Internet. It could also be a path, filename, and location in another file. For example, you could link to "[C:\files\Jan2015.xls]!Sheet1!A15". Note that *link_location* can be a text string enclosed in quotes or a cell that contains the link.

 Note

Note that Excel does not check whether the link location is valid at the time you created the link. If the link is not valid when someone clicks it, the person encounters an error.

- *friendly_name*—This is the underlined text or numeric value that is displayed in the cell. *friendly_name* is displayed in blue and is underlined. If *friendly_name* is omitted, the cell displays the *link_location* value as the jump text. *friendly_name* can be a value, a text string, a name, or a cell that contains the jump text or value. If *friendly_name* returns an error (for example, #VALUE!), the cell displays the error instead of the jump text.

 **Tip**

It is difficult to select a cell that contains a HYPERLINK function. If you click the cell, Excel attempts to follow the hyperlink. Instead, click the cell and hold the mouse button until the pointer changes from a hand to a plus.

Figure 12.41 shows a list of web pages in column A. Column B contains the titles of those web pages. To quickly build a table of hyperlinks, you use =HYPERLINK(A2,B2) in cell C2 and copy the formula down the column. Unfortunately, you must keep columns A and B intact for the hyperlink to keep working. You can hide those columns, but there is no Paste Special option to convert the formula to values that will keep the hyperlink.

C2	▼	:	✕	✓	fx	=HYPERLINK(A2,B2)

	A	B	C	D	E	F	G
1	Web Page	Title	Hyperlink				
2	http://www.mrexcel.com/tip035.shtml	5 Tips to Eliminate Redundant Data	5 Tips to Eliminate Redundant Data				
3	http://www.mrexcel.com/tip048.shtml	Absolute Reference Uses	Absolute Reference Uses				
4	http://www.mrexcel.com/td0132.html	Add a Certain Number to All Numbe	Add a Certain Number to All Numbers in a Range Using Paste Special Add				
5	http://www.mrexcel.com/td0072.html	Add a percentage to all cells in a ran	Add a percentage to all cells in a range				
6	http://www.mrexcel.com/tip067.shtml	Add a Trendline with 3 clicks	Add a Trendline with 3 clicks				
7	http://www.mrexcel.com/tip062.shtml	Add Median to Pivot Tables with Di	Add Median to Pivot Tables with DigDB's One-Step-Summary				
8	http://www.mrexcel.com/td0028.html	Add Row while copying and manipu	Add Row while copying and manipulating data				
9	http://www.mrexcel.com/tip055.shtml	Add the Path to your Worksheet Fo	Add the Path to your Worksheet Footer when Printing				
10	http://www.mrexcel.com/td0019.html	Add today's entries to the next empt	Add today's entries to the next empty row on a master sheet				
11	http://www.mrexcel.com/td0066.html	Adding every other cell in a column	Adding every other cell in a column with =SUM(MOD...				
12	http://www.mrexcel.com/tip015.shtml	Advanced Pivot Table Tips	Advanced Pivot Table Tips				
13	http://www.mrexcel.com/tip083.shtml	Array-CSE Entering using Condition	Array-CSE Entering using Conditional Sum Wizard				
14	http://www.mrexcel.com/tip031.shtml	Array-CSE Further Uses	Array-CSE Further Uses				

Figure 12.41
The formulas in column C enable you to create hundreds of hyperlinks in seconds.

To keep only the hyperlinks, copy column C and paste to a blank Word document. Open a new workbook. Copy from Word and paste back to the new Excel document.

Alternatively, use ="#HYPERLINK("""&A2&""""&", "&""""&B2&""""&")" in C2. Copy down and paste Special Values. Use Find and Replace to change # to =.

Using the TRANSPOSE Function to Formulaically Turn Data

With many people using Excel in a company, there are bound to be different usage styles from person to person. Some people build their worksheets horizontally, and other people build their worksheets vertically. For example, in Figure 12.42, the monthly totals stretch horizontally across row 80. However, for some reason, you need these figures to be arranged going vertically down from cell B84.

The typical method is to copy C80:N80 and then use Home, Paste, Transpose. This copies a snapshot of the totals in row 80 to a column of data.

Figure 12.42
One TRANSPOSE function
occupies 12 cells, from
B84:B95.

| ▼ | : | ✕ | ✓ | f_x | {=TRANSPOSE(C80:N80)} |

◢	A	B	C	D	E	F	G	H	I	J	K	L	M	N
1			Jan	Feb	Mar	Apr	May	Jun	Jul	Aug	Sep	Oct	Nov	Dec
80		Total	98592	87432	66091	83809	89668	77451	90330	91691	90209	63349	71840	82001
81														
82														
83		Sales												
84	Jan	98592												
85	Feb	87432												
86	Mar	66091												
87	Apr	83809												
88	May	89668												
89	Jun	77451												
90	Jul	90330												
91	Aug	91691												
92	Sep	90209												
93	Oct	63349												
94	Nov	71840												
95	Dec	82001												
96														

This is fine if you only need a snapshot of the totals. However, what if you want to see the totals continually updated in column B? Excel provides the TRANSPOSE function for such situations.

Because the function returns several answers, you need to use special care when entering the formula. Here's how:

1. Note that C80:N80 contains 12 cells.

2. Select an identical number of cells starting in B84. Select B84:B95.

3. Even though you have 12 cells selected, type the formula **=TRANSPOSE(C80:N80)** as if you had only one cell selected.

4. To tell Excel that this is a special type of formula called an *array formula,* hold down Ctrl+Shift while you press Enter.

Excel shows the formula surrounded by curly braces in the formula bar. This is one single formula entered in 12 cells. Therefore, you cannot delete or change one cell in the range. If you want to change the formula, you need to delete all 12 cells in B84:B95 in a single command.

Figure 12.42 shows a TRANSPOSE function that occupies 12 cells.

Syntax:

TRANSPOSE(*array*)

The TRANSPOSE function transposes a vertical range into a horizontal array, or vice versa.

> 🔍 **Note**
> You can also use TRANSPOSE to turn a vertical range into a horizontal range.

The argument *array* is an array or a range of cells on a worksheet that you want to transpose. The transposition of an array is accomplished by using the first row of the array as the first column of the new array, the second row of the array as the second column of the new array, and so on.

Using the RTD Function and COM Add-ins to Retrieve Real-time Data

Third-party applications are available to send streaming real-time data to an Excel spreadsheet. They became very popular with stock day traders in the late 1990s. If you have one of these COM add-ins installed on your system, you can set up a formula to retrieve real-time data from the COM add-in by using the RTD function. If you have such a COM add-in installed, the vendor of the add-in should provide sample workbooks with RTD functions already in place.

Syntax:

RTD(*progid,server,topic1,[topic2],..*])

The RTD function returns real-time data from a program that supports COM automation. This function takes the following arguments:

- *progid*—This is the name of the program ID of a registered COM automation add-in that has been installed on the local computer. You need to enclose the name in quotation marks.

- *server*—This is the name of the server where the add-in should be run. If there is no server and the program is run locally, leave this argument blank.

- *topic1, topic2,...*—These are one to 253 parameters that together represent a unique piece of real-time data.

Using GETPIVOTDATA to Retrieve One Cell from a Pivot Table

You might turn to this book to find out how to use most of the Excel functions. However, for the GETPIVOTDATA function, you are likely to turn to this book to find out why the function is being automatically generated for you.

Suppose that you have a pivot table on a worksheet. You should click outside the pivot table. Next, you type an equal sign and then with the mouse, click one of the cells in the data area of the pivot table. Although you might expect this to generate a formula such as =E9, instead, Excel puts in the formula =GETPIVOTDATA("Sales",$B$5,"Customer","Astonishing Glass Company","Region","West"), as shown in Figure 12.43.

This function is annoying. As you copy the formula down to more rows, the function keeps retrieving sales to Astonishing Glass in the West region. By default, Excel is generating this function instead of a simple formula such as =E9. This happens whether you use the mouse or the arrow keys to specify the cell in the formula.

To avoid this behavior, you can enter the entire formula by manually typing it on the keyboard. Typing **=E9** in a cell forces Excel to create a relative reference to cell E9. You are then free to copy the formula to other cells.

Figure 12.43
Excel inserts this strange function in the worksheet.

| H9 | ▼ | : | × | ✓ | *fx* | =GETPIVOTDATA("Sales",$B$5,"Customer","Astonishing Glass Company","Region","West") |

◢	B	C	D	E	F	G	H	I
5	**Sum of Sales**	**Region** ▼						
6	**Customer**	▼ **East**	**Central**	**West**	**Grand Total**			
7	Alluring Ink Company	0	170	0	170			
8	Alluring Quilt Company	289	0	0	289			
9	Astonishing Glass Company	0	0	314	314		314	
10	Astonishing Shovel Inc.	190	0	0	190			
11	Bright Shoe Company	0	246	0	246			
12	Brilliant Luggage Inc.	0	307	0	307			
13	Different Belt Corporation	0	0	249	249			

There is also a way to turn off this behavior permanently:

1. Select a cell inside an active pivot table.

2. The Pivot Table Tools tabs displays. Select the Analyze tab. From the PivotTable group, select the Options drop-down and then select the Generate GetPivotData icon. The behavior turns off.

3. Enter formulas by using the mouse, arrow keys, or keyboard without generating the GETPIVOTDATA function.

Microsoft made GETPIVOTDATA the default behavior because the function is pretty cool. Now that you have learned how to turn off the behavior, you might want to understand exactly how it works in case you ever need to use the function.

Syntax:

GETPIVOTDATA(*data_field*,*pivot_table*,*field1*,*item1*,*field2*,*item2*,...)

The GETPIVOTDATA function returns data stored in a pivot table report. You can use GETPIVOTDATA to retrieve summary data from a pivot table report, provided that the summary data is visible in the report. This function takes the following arguments:

- ***data_field***—This is the name, enclosed in quotation marks, for the data field that contains the data you want to retrieve.

- ***pivot_table***—This is a reference to any cell, range of cells, or named range of cells in a pivot table report. This information is used to determine which pivot table report contains the data you want to retrieve.

- ***field1, item1, field2, item2,...***—These are one to 126 pairs of field names and item names that describe the data you want to retrieve. The pairs can be in any order. Field names and names for items other than dates and numbers are enclosed in quotation marks. For OLAP pivot table reports, items can contain the source name of the dimension as well as the source name of the item.

Calculated fields or items and custom calculations are included in GETPIVOTDATA calculations.

If *pivot_table* is a range that includes two or more pivot table reports, data is retrieved from whichever report was created in the range most recently.

If the *field* and *item* arguments describe a single cell, the value of that cell is returned, regardless of whether it is a string, a number, an error, and so on.

If an item contains a date, the value must be expressed as a serial number or populated by using the DATE function so that the value is retained if the spreadsheet is opened in a different locale. For example, an item referring to the date March 5, 2015 could be entered as 42068 or DATE(2015,3,5). Times can be entered as decimal values or by using the TIME function.

If *pivot_table* is not a range in which a pivot table report is found, GETPIVOTDATA returns #REF!. If the arguments do not describe a visible field, or if they include a page field that is not displayed, GETPIVOTDATA returns #REF!.

Cube Functions Introduced in Excel 2007

If you are creating pivot tables from OLAP data or from PowerPivot, Excel offers a Convert to Formulas command. Excel uses a series of cube functions to retrieve the data cells from the data source. The following functions were introduced in Excel 2007.

Syntax:

CUBEMEMBER(*connection*,*member_expression*[,*caption*])

The CUBEMEMBER() function returns a member or tuple in a cube hierarchy. You can use it to validate that the member or tuple exists in the cube.

Syntax:

CUBEMEMBERPROPERTY(*connection*,*member_expression*,*property*)

The CUBEMEMBERPROPERTY() function returns the value of a member property in the cube. You can use it to validate that a member name exists within the cube and to return the specified property for that member.

Syntax:

CUBERANKEDMEMBER(*connection*,*set_expression*,*rank*[,*caption*])

The CUBERANKEDMEMBER() function returns the *n*th, or ranked, member in a set. You can use it to return one or more elements in a set, such as the top sales performer or top 10 students.

Syntax:

CUBESET(*connection*,*set_expression*[,*caption*][,*sort_order*][,*sort_by*])

The CUBESET() function defines a calculated set of members or tuples by sending a set expression to the cube on the server, which creates the set. The function then returns that set to Excel. You can use CUBESET() to build dynamic reports that aggregate and filter data by using the return value as a slicer in the CUBEVALUE() function, the CUBERANKEDMEMBER() function to choose specific members from the calculated set, and the CUBESETCOUNT() function to control the size of the set.

Syntax:

CUBESETCOUNT(*set*)

The CUBESETCOUNT() function returns the number of items in a set.

Syntax:

CUBEVALUE(*connection*,*member_expression1*[,*member_expression2*...])

The CUBEVALUE() function returns an aggregated value from a cube.

Syntax:

CUBEKPIMEMBER(*connection*,*kpi_name*,*kpi_property*[,*caption*])

The CUBEKPIMEMBER() function returns a key performance indicator (KPI) name, property, and measure, and it displays the name and property in the cell. A KPI is a quantifiable measurement, such as monthly gross profit or quarterly employee turnover, used to monitor an organization's performance.

 **Note**

To use this function, you must have SQL Server Analysis Services 2005 or later.

Examples of Web Functions

Excel 2013 introduces the WEBSERVICE function and two helper functions. The ENCODEURL changes reserved characters in a URL string to their percent-encoded equivalents. FILTERXML helps you to parse out the results from the WEBSERVICE function. FILTERXML uses the XPath language to retrieve data from an XML data set.

To get started, you need to find a free web service that returns results in ATOM or JSON. From there, be prepared to do some experimenting before things begin going smoothly.

The examples in this section are from the Twitter Application Programming Interface. The documentation at https://dev.twitter.com/docs/using-search is quite helpful. It tells you how to build a successful URL at the regular Twitter search page and how to convert that URL to an API URL.

For example, to find the last 15 tweets about VLOOKUP, you would end up at the URL of https://twitter.com/#!/search/vlookup. The Twitter API documentation says that you want to convert this to http://search.twitter.com/search.atom?lang=en&q=vlookup.

Using ENCODEURL to Replace Reserved Characters

Certain characters cause problems in URLs. In particular, many occurrences of !#$&'()*+,/:;=?@ [] need to be encoded. For example, instead of an exclamation point, you need to use %21. Unless you have memorized the complete list, it is easier to use ENCODEURL to encode those characters. Figure 12.44 shows the complete set of reserved characters and the result of using ENCODEURL to convert them.

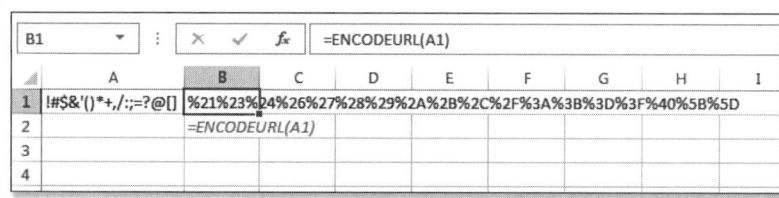

Figure 12.44
If necessary, encode the arguments for your web service URL.

Syntax:

ENCODEURL(*text*)

The ENCODEURL function URL encodes the argument text. Note that you will rarely pass the entire URL to the function. This would encode characters such as http:// into http%3A%2F%2F. This is not necessary and will not work.

Instead, you usually pass just the arguments to ENCODEURL, as in this example:

=WEBSERVICE("http://xml.weather.yahoo.com/forecastrss/"&ENCODEURL(B2)&"_f.xml")

Note that you should experiment by using WEBSERVICE with and without ENCODEURL. The weather.yahoo.com example works better with ENCODEURL, but the Twitter API in the next section does not require ENCODEURL.

Returning XML or JSON Using the WEBSERVICE Function

The WEBSERVICE function is new in Excel 2013. You pass a URL to the function. Excel goes out to the Web and instead of returning the data to a browser, it returns the entire web page to one cell in Excel.

Syntax:

WEBSERVICE(*url*)

Returns data from a web service on the Internet or an intranet. *url* must be 2,048 characters or less. The data returned from the web service must be less than 32,767 characters that fit in a cell. WEBSERVICE does not work with ftp:// or file:// protocols. If the arguments are invalid and cannot return data, WEBSERVICE returns the #VALUE! error.

Here is an example of how to build the WEBSERVICE function and how to interpret the results (see Figure 12.45):

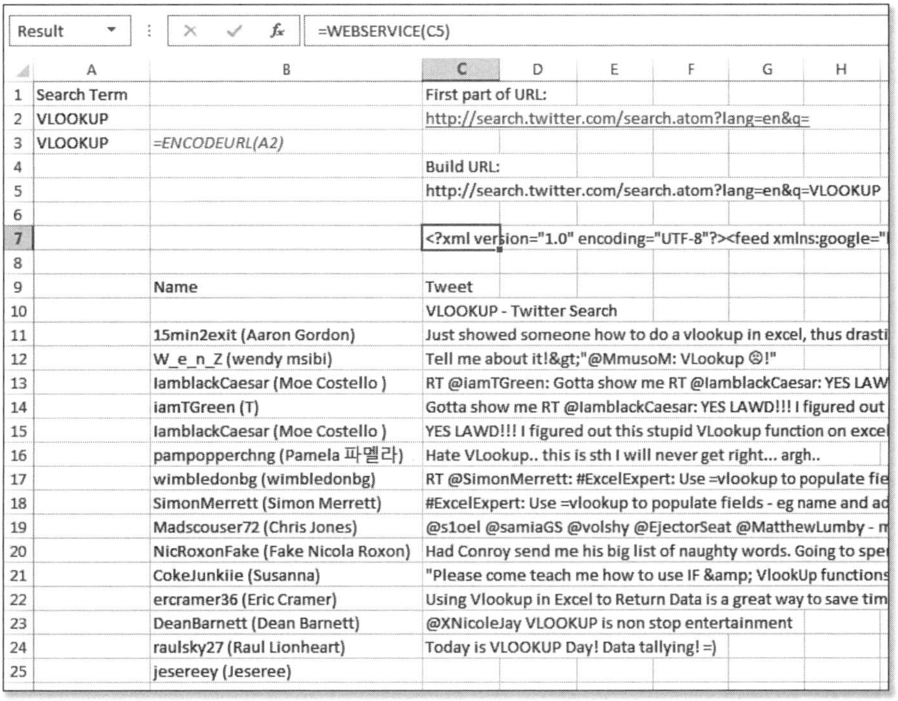

Figure 12.45
If necessary, encode the arguments for your web service URL.

1. Enter the search term in cell A2.

2. A formula in A3 encodes the argument with =ENCODEURL(A2).

3. Cell C2 holds the first part of the URL.

4. A formula in C5 concatenates the URL with =C2&A3.

5. The formula in C7 is =WEBSERVICE(C5). This function takes several seconds to calculate.

6. The results in cell C7 encompass 17,038 characters. It is impossible to view this many characters in a cell. If you keep scrolling to the right, Excel finally gives up displaying characters, as shown in Figure 12.46.

Figure 12.46
Excel does not display the complete set of results.

7. To get a full view of what you are dealing with, copy cell C7. Open Notepad and paste the text into Notepad. You can now see the complete result of the query (see Figure 12.47). In this figure, you can make out elements of the results. A field called "Name" indicates that the author was pampopperchng. A field called "Published" indicates 2012-09-04 with a time. A field called "Title" has the actual tweet, which in this case is "RT @SimonMerrett: #ExcelExpert: Use =vlookup to populate fields—eg name and address by using customer number."

Figure 12.47
After copying to Notepad, you can look for field names.

This web service is returning data in XML. Excel provides the FILTERXML function that enables you to deal with XML. Other web services might return JSON instead of XML. In this case, you have to parse the return string, looking for instances of field names and using MID to extract data. This will be more difficult. Read on to learn how to parse XML using FILTERXML.

 **Tip**

By design, the WEBSERVICE function is not volatile. Excel does not run back out to the Web on every recalc to pull in new data. First, this would slow down the workbook dramatically. Second, the owner of the API where you are pulling data has likely published limits of how many requests you can do per hour. If you exceed these limits, the query starts returning an error message until the top of the next hour. In the example in Figure 12.46, the WEBSERVICE calculates when you open the workbook, when you change the search term, or when you go to the cell with the WEBSERVICE function and press F2 followed by Enter. If you want the WEBSERVICE to calculate more frequently, append &REPT(" ",RAND()*0) to the formula. This forces the formula to update every time any cell is updated.

 Caution

There are two throttles on the WEBSERVICE function. First, the owner of the API limits how many times you can call the API per hour. Second, Microsoft has imposed throttling limits to prevent you from using Excel in a Denial of Service attack.

Parsing XML from the WEBSERVICE Function Using the FILTERXML Function

The XPath query language lets you query XML results such as the data shown in Figure 12.47. If you Bing "XPath tutorial," you find several websites that help you get up to speed with XPath. The following examples also help.

Syntax:

FILTERXML(*xml*,*xpath*)

Returns specific data from the XML content by using the specified XPath. This function requires two arguments:

- *xml*—A string in valid XML format. If *xml* is not valid, FILTERXML returns the #VALUE! error. If *xml* contains a namespace with a prefix that is not valid, FILTERXML returns the #VALUE! error.

- *xpath*—A string in standard XPath format.

In the example in Figure 12.46, the web service is returning the first 15 results. A single piece of XML can contain several children nodes. The Name and Title fields appear 15 times each in the results in C7. To break out the 15 results, follow these steps:

1. To simplify the formulas, name the cell containing the XML. Select cell C7. Click in the Name box to the left of the formula bar. Type **Result** and press Enter.

2. Select a single column of cells that is 15 cells tall.

3. Type the formula `=FILTERXML(Result, "//title")`.
   Instead of pressing Enter, hold down Ctrl and Shift while
   pressing Enter. Excel parses out the 15 tweets.

4. Select an adjacent range of one column by 15 rows. With this
   web service, this range should start one row below the range
   in step 2. Type the formula `=FILTERXML(Result,"//name")`.
   Press Ctrl+Shift+Enter. Excel returns the author of the 15 tweets.

Caution
Actually, the results show a page title and then 14 tweets.

You should always verify the results. By checking Twitter for recent tweets by Twitter user
15min2exit, I was able to figure out that the value in C10 is a page title and that the second Title
field was associated with the first Name field.

Figure 12.48 shows the last 15 VLOOKUP tweets and their authors.

B11	▼	:	×	✓	fx	{=FILTERXML(Result, "//name")}									
⊿	A		B		C	D	E	F	G	H	I	J	K	L	M	N
7					<?xml version="1.0" encoding="UTF-8"?><feed xmlns:google="http://base.google.com/ns/1.0" xml:lang="en-US" xmlns:ope
8					
9			Name		Tweet
10					VLOOKUP - Twitter Search
11			15min2exit (Aaron Gordon)		Just showed someone how to do a vlookup in excel, thus drastically increasing his quality of life.
12			W_e_n_Z (wendy msibi)		Tell me about it!>" @MmusoM: VLookUp ☺!"
13			IamblackCaesar (Moe Costello)		RT @iamTGreen: Gotta show me RT @IamblackCaesar: YES LAWD!!! I figured out this stupid VLookup function on excel !!!
14			iamTGreen (T)		Gotta show me RT @IamblackCaesar: YES LAWD!!! I figured out this stupid VLookup function on excel !!!
15			IamblackCaesar (Moe Costello)		YES LAWD!!! I figured out this stupid VLookup function on excel !!!
16			pampopperchng (Pamela 파멜라)		Hate VLookup.. this is sth I will never get right... argh..
17			wimbledonbg (wimbledonbg)		RT @SimonMerrett: #ExcelExpert: Use =vlookup to populate fields - eg name and address by using customer number
18			SimonMerrett (Simon Merrett)		#ExcelExpert: Use =vlookup to populate fields - eg name and address by using customer number
19			Madscouser72 (Chris Jones)		@s1oel @samiaGS @volshy @EjectorSeat @MatthewLumby - macro's are good, but you need funky formulaes such as vlooku
20			NicRoxonFake (Fake Nicola Roxon)		Had Conroy send me his big list of naughty words. Going to spend the night learning how to do a vlookup. #dataretention
21			CokeJunkiie (Susanna)		"Please come teach me how to use IF & VlookUp functions basically teach me Excel, i don't understand." #resnetissues
22			ercramer36 (Eric Cramer)		Using Vlookup in Excel to Return Data is a great way to save time and energy. #Microsoft Office #Accountant #Admin #IT http:
23			DeanBarnett (Dean Barnett)		@XNicoleJay VLOOKUP is non stop entertainment
24			raulsky27 (Raul Lionheart)		Today is VLOOKUP Day! Data tallying! =)
25			jesereey (Jeseree)		

Figure 12.48
Use FILTERXML
entered as an
array to return
results from the
WEBSERVICE
function.

If you check out Excel Help for WEBSERVICE, there is a tiny workbook you can download that retrieves data from weather.yahoo.
com. This workbook provides a good example that you can follow
and also shows how you can extend the results.

Caution
The next time you open this
workbook, Excel warns you that
the WEBSERVICE does not automatically update. This ensures
that you can see the previous
results even if the Internet is
down.

The example returns weather data for a ZIP Code. You can see
that they are building a URL such as http://xml.weather.yahoo.
com/forecastrss/44685_f.xml to return data for ZIP Code 44685.

The existing formulas in the workbook use FILTERXML to return
city and region from yweather:location. Other formulas return
temp and text from yweather:condition. An array formula returns
a column of day names from yweather:forecast/@day. Another array formula returns a column of
forecast text from yweather:forecast/@text.

After exploring these formulas, paste the results from cell A2 into Notepad. Find the
yweather:forecast tag. You see there are fields called day, date, low, high, text, and code. I have
no idea what the code means, but the other fields are self-explanatory (see Figure 12.49).

Figure 12.49
Find the
yweather:
Forecast tag to
see what fields
are available.

```
High: 80 Low: 62<br />Sat - Showers. High: 69 Low: 60<br /><br
/><a
href=""http://us.rd.yahoo.com/dailynews/rss/weather/Uniontown_
_OH/*http://weather.yahoo.com/forecast/USOH0970_f.html"">Full
Forecast at Yahoo! Weather</a><BR/><BR/>(provided by <a
href=""http://www.weather.com"" >The Weather Channel</a>)
<br/>]]></description><yweather:forecast day=""Tue"" date=""4
Sep 2012"" low=""68"" high=""78"" text=""Thunderstorms Early""
code=""47"" /><yweather:forecast day=""Wed"" date=""5 Sep
2012"" low=""67"" high=""86"" text=""Partly Cloudy""
code=""30"" /><yweather:forecast day=""Thu"" date=""6 Sep
2012"" low=""62"" high=""83"" text=""PM Thunderstorms""
code=""38"" /><yweather:forecast day=""Fri"" date=""7 Sep
2012"" low=""62"" high=""80"" text=""Partly Cloudy""
code=""30"" /><yweather:forecast day=""Sat"" date=""8 Sep
2012"" low=""60"" high=""69"" text=""Showers"" code=""11"" />
```

— yweather:Forecast Record

From this information, you can surmise that you can build a column of high temperatures using
=FILTERXML(A2,"//yweather:forecast/@high"). Select five cells, type the formula, and press
Ctrl+Shift+Enter. Excel returns the high temperatures (see Figure 12.50).

Figure 12.50
After you
see working
examples, it
is easy to add
new FILTERXML
formulas.

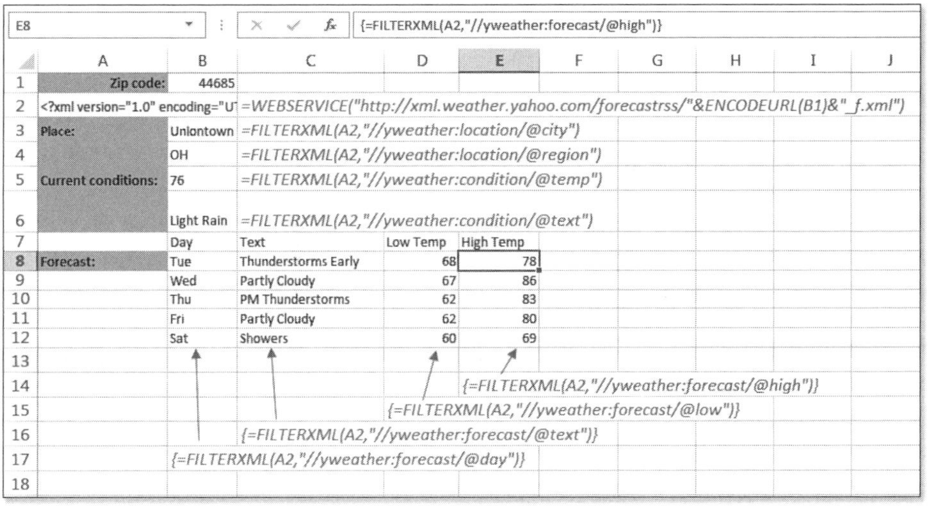

| E8 | ▼ | : | × | ✓ | *fx* | {=FILTERXML(A2,"//yweather:forecast/@high")} |

	A	B	C	D	E	F	G	H	I	J
1		Zip code:	44685							
2	<?xml version="1.0" encoding="U	=WEBSERVICE("http://xml.weather.yahoo.com/forecastrss/"&ENCODEURL(B1)&"_f.xml")							
3	Place:	Uniontown	=FILTERXML(A2,"//yweather:location/@city")							
4		OH	=FILTERXML(A2,"//yweather:location/@region")							
5	Current conditions:	76	=FILTERXML(A2,"//yweather:condition/@temp")							
6		Light Rain	=FILTERXML(A2,"//yweather:condition/@text")							
7		Day	Text	Low Temp	High Temp					
8	Forecast:	Tue	Thunderstorms Early	68	78					
9		Wed	Partly Cloudy	67	86					
10		Thu	PM Thunderstorms	62	83					
11		Fri	Partly Cloudy	62	80					
12		Sat	Showers	60	69					
13										
14					{=FILTERXML(A2,"//yweather:forecast/@high")}					
15				{=FILTERXML(A2,"//yweather:forecast/@low")}						
16			{=FILTERXML(A2,"//yweather:forecast/@text")}							
17		{=FILTERXML(A2,"//yweather:forecast/@day")}								
18										

Examples of Database Functions

If you were a serious data analyst in the 1980s and the early 1990s, you would have been enamored
with the database functions. I personally used @DSUM every hour of my work life for many years. It
was one of the most powerful weapons in any spreadsheet arsenal. Combined with a data table, the
DSUM, DMIN, DMAX, and DAVERAGE functions got a serious workout when users performed data analysis in a spreadsheet.

Then, in 1993, Microsoft Excel added the pivot table to the Data menu in Excel. Pivot tables changed everything. Those powerful database functions seemed tired and worn out. Since that day in 1993, I had never used DSUM again until I created the example described in the following section. As far as I knew, the database functions had been living in a cave in South Carolina.

Maybe it is like the nostalgia of finding a box of photos of an old girlfriend, but I realized that the database functions are still pretty powerful. Customers whined enough to have Microsoft add AVERAGEIF to the COUNTIF and SUMIF arsenal. This was unnecessary: Customers could have done this easily by setting up a small criteria range and using DAVERAGE.

Eleven of the 12 database functions are similar. DSUM, DAVERAGE, DCOUNT, DCOUNTA, DMAX, DMIN, DPRODUCT, DSTDEV, DSTDEVP, DVAR, and DVARP all perform the equivalent operation of their non-D equivalents, but they allow for complex criteria to include records that meet certain criteria. See examples of each of these in Figure 12.51.

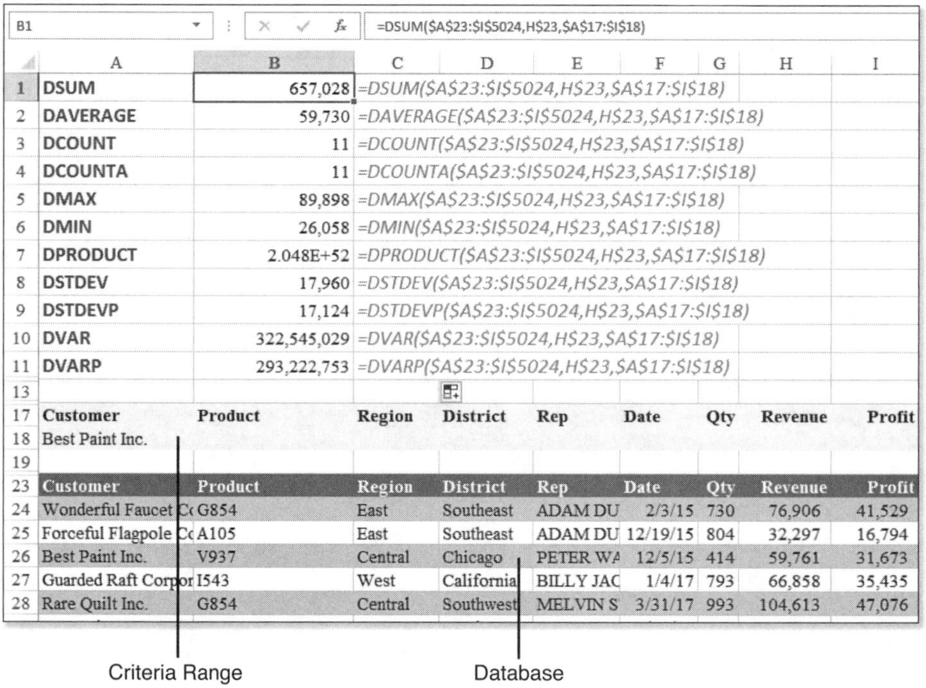

Figure 12.51
A simple criteria range specifies to limit DSUM to only records for Best Paint Inc. as a customer.

To save you the hassle of looking up the confusing few, DCOUNT counts numeric cells, and DCOUNTA counts nonblank cells. DSTDEV and DVAR calculate the standard deviation and variance of a sample of a population, respectively. DSTDEVP and DVARP calculate the standard deviation and variance of the entire population, respectively. The 12th database function, DGET, has the same arguments, but it acts a bit differently, as explained later in this chapter.

Using DSUM to Conditionally Sum Records from a Database

There are three arguments to every database function. It is very easy to get your first DSUM working. The *criteria* argument is the one that offers vast flexibility. The following section explains the syntax for DSUM. The syntax for the other 11 database functions is identical to this.

Syntax:

DSUM(*database*,*field*,*criteria*)

The DSUM function adds records from one field in a data set, provided that the records meet some criteria that you specify. The DSUM function takes the following arguments:

- ■ ***database***—This is the range of cells that make up the list or database, including the heading row. A *database* is a list of related data in which rows of related information are records and columns of data are fields. In Figure 12.51, the database is the 5,001 rows of data located at A23:I5024.

- ■ ***field***—This indicates which column is used in the function. You have three options when specifying a field:

  - ■ You can point to the cell with the field name, such as H23 for Revenue.

  - ■ You can include the word Revenue as the *field* argument.

  - ■ You can use the number 8 to indicate that Revenue is the eighth field in the database.

> **Note**
>
> To conserve space, the remaining examples in the following sections show only the DSUM result. You can compare the various results to the $657,028 of revenue for the current example.

- ■ ***criteria***—This is the range of cells that contains the conditions specified. You can use any range for the *criteria* argument. The criteria range typically includes at least one column label and at least one cell below the column label for specifying a condition for the column. You can also use the computed criteria discussed in "Using the Miracle Version of the Criteria Range," later in this chapter. Learning how to create powerful criteria ranges enables you to unlock the powerful potential of the database functions. Several examples are provided in the following sections.

Creating a Simple Criteria Range for Database Functions

Although a criteria range needs only one field heading from the database, it is just as easy to copy the entire set of headings to a blank section of the worksheet. In Figure 12.51, for example, the headings in A17:I17, along with at least one additional row, create a criteria range.

In Figure 12.51, you see results of the 11 database functions for a simple criteria where the customer is Best Paint Inc. Each formula specifies a database of $A$23:$I$5024. The field is H23, which is the heading for Revenue. The criteria range is A17:I18. In this example, the criteria range could have easily been A17:A18, but the A17:I18 form enables you to enter future criteria without specifying the criteria range again.

Using a Blank Criteria Range to Return All Records

This is a trivial example, but if the second row of the criteria range is completely blank, the database function returns the total of all rows in the data set. As shown in Figure 12.52, this is $256.6 million. This is equivalent to using the SUM function.

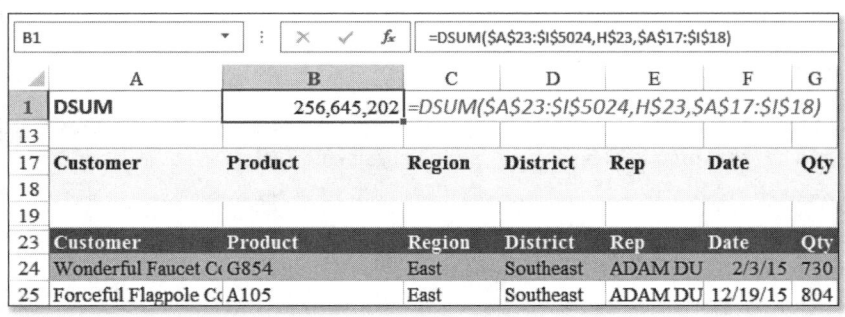

Figure 12.52
If the second row of the criteria is blank, the result reflects all rows.

Using AND to Join Criteria

Many people using SUMIF in Excel 2003 and earlier are likely to want to know how to conditionally sum based on two conditions. This is simple to do with DSUM. If two criteria are placed on the same row of the criteria range, they are joined by an AND. In Figure 12.53, for example, the $123,275 is the sum of records where the customer is Best Paint Inc. and the product is V937.

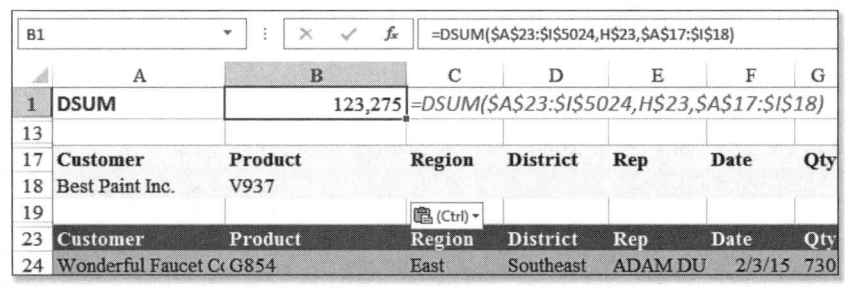

Figure 12.53
When two criteria are on the same line, they are joined by an AND function; rows must meet both criteria to be included in the DSUM.

Using OR to Join Criteria

When two criteria are placed on separate rows of the criteria range, they are joined by an OR function. In Figure 12.54, the $2.1 million represents records for either Improved Radio Traders or Best Paint Inc.

You can use OR to join criteria from different fields. The criteria range in Figure 12.55 shows a Region value of West joined by an OR with a District value of Texas. This pulls a superset of all the West records plus just the Texas records, which happen to fall in the Central region.

Figure 12.54
When two criteria are on different rows, they are joined by an OR function; rows can meet either criteria to be included in the DSUM.

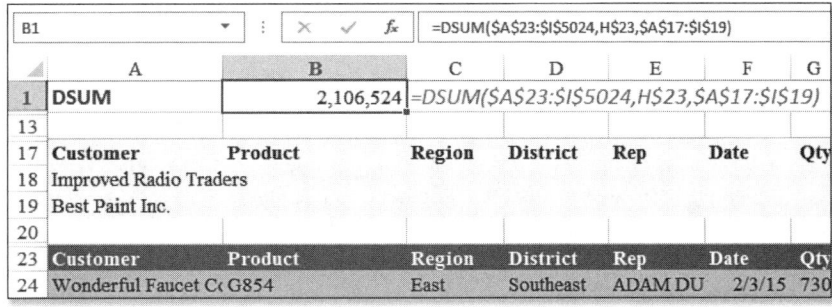

	A	B	C	D	E	F	G
1	DSUM	2,106,524	=DSUM($A$23:$I$5024,H$23,$A$17:$I$19)				
13							
17	Customer	Product	Region	District	Rep	Date	Qty
18	Improved Radio Traders						
19	Best Paint Inc.						
20							
23	Customer	Product	Region	District	Rep	Date	Qty
24	Wonderful Faucet C(G854		East	Southeast	ADAM DU	2/3/15	730

B1 =DSUM($A$23:$I$5024,H$23,$A$17:$I$19)

Figure 12.55
The criteria to be joined with OR can be in separate columns.

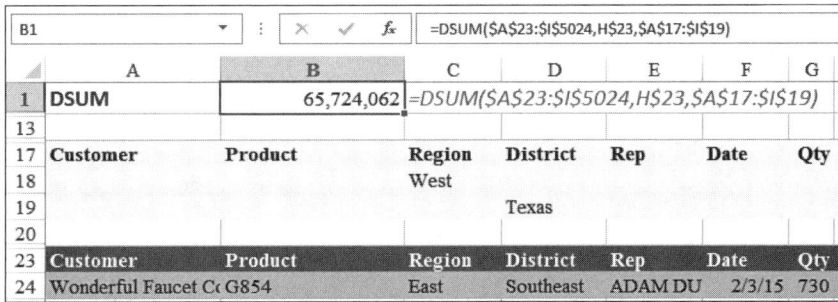

	A	B	C	D	E	F	G
1	DSUM	65,724,062	=DSUM($A$23:$I$5024,H$23,$A$17:$I$19)				
13							
17	Customer	Product	Region	District	Rep	Date	Qty
18			West				
19				Texas			
20							
23	Customer	Product	Region	District	Rep	Date	Qty
24	Wonderful Faucet C(G854		East	Southeast	ADAM DU	2/3/15	730

B1 =DSUM($A$23:$I$5024,H$23,$A$17:$I$19)

Using Dates or Numbers as Criteria

The example in Figure 12.56 finds records with a date after 2017 and with revenue under $50,000. The criteria in F18 for the date could have used any of these formats:

```
>12/31/2017
>=1/1/2018
>31-Dec-2017
```

Figure 12.56
Using dates or numbers in criteria.

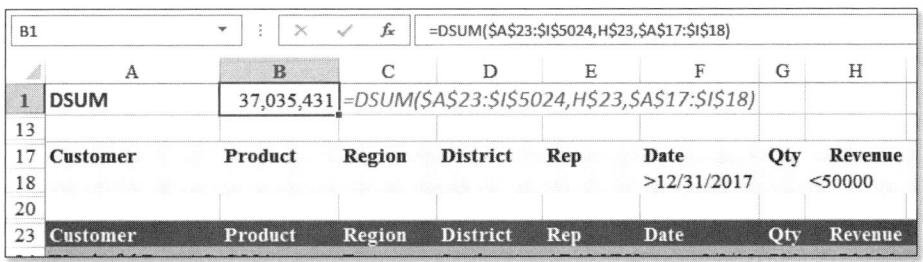

	A	B	C	D	E	F	G	H
1	DSUM	37,035,431	=DSUM($A$23:$I$5024,H$23,$A$17:$I$18)					
13								
17	Customer	Product	Region	District	Rep	Date	Qty	Revenue
18						>12/31/2017		<50000
20								
23	Customer	Product	Region	District	Rep	Date	Qty	Revenue

B1 =DSUM($A$23:$I$5024,H$23,$A$17:$I$18)

Using the Miracle Version of a Criteria Range

Using the criteria ranges in the preceding examples, you could easily build any complex criteria with multiple AND or OR operators.

However, this could get complex. Imagine if you wanted to pull all the records for five specific customers and five specific products. You would have to build a criteria range that is 26 rows tall. Basically, the first row is the headings for customer and product. The second row indicates that you want to see records for Customer1 and Product1. The third row indicates that you want to see records for Customer1 and Product2. The fourth row indicates that you want to see records for Customer1 and Product3. The seventh row indicates Customer2 and Product1. The 26th row indicates Customer5 and Product5.

If you need to pull the records for seven customers and seven products from five districts, your criteria range would grow to 246 rows tall and will probably never finish calculating.

There is a miraculous version of the criteria range that completely avoids this problem. Here's how it works:

- The criteria range consists of a range that is two cells tall and one or more cells wide.

- Contrary to instructions in Excel help, the top cell of the criteria range cannot contain a field heading. The top cell must be blank or contain anything that does not match the database header row. For example, you could put a heading of "Computed Criteria."

- The second row in the criteria range can contain any formula that evaluates to TRUE or FALSE. This formula must point to cells in the first data row of the database. The formula can be as complex as you want provided the formula returns TRUE or FALSE. You can combine AND, OR, VLOOKUP, NOT, MATCH, and any other functions.

For a simple example, suppose you want to find records that match one of 15 customers. You copy the customers to K24:K38. In the second row of the criteria field, write the formula =NOT(ISNA (MATCH(A24,$K$24:$K$38,0))). This formula does a MATCH on the first customer in the database to see if it is in the list in K. The ISNA and NOT functions make sure that the criteria cell returns a TRUE when the customer is one of the 15 customers.

Very quickly and without complaint, Excel compares the 5,000 rows of your database with this complex formula, and the DSUM produces the correct value, as shown in Figure 12.57.

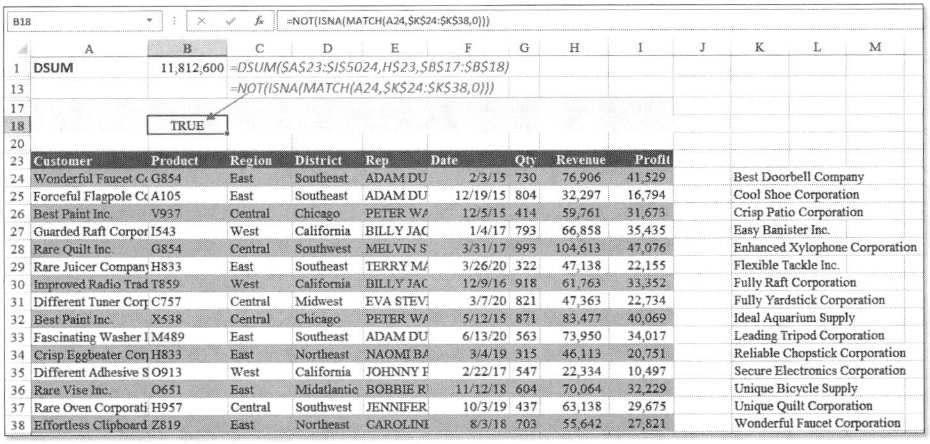

Figure 12.57
The formula version of the criteria range is rare but incredibly powerful.

Using the DGET Function

The DGET function returns a single cell from a database. The problem is that this function is picky. If your criteria range matches zero records, DGET returns a #VALUE error. If your criteria range returns more than one row, DGET returns a #NUM! error.

To have DGET work, you need to write a criteria record that causes one and only one row to be evaluated as TRUE.

Syntax:

DGET(*database*,*field*,*criteria*)

The DGET function returns a single cell matching criteria from a data set. This function takes the following arguments:

- *database*—This is the range of cells that make up the list or database. A *database* is a list of related data in which rows of related information are records and columns of data are fields. The first row of the list contains labels for each column.

- *field*—This indicates which column is used in the function. *field* can be given as text, with the column label enclosed between double quotation marks, such as "Age" or "Yield", or as a number that represents the position of the column within the list (for example, 1 for the first column, 2 for the second column, and so on).

- *criteria*—This is the range of cells that contains the conditions you specify. You can use any range for the *criteria* argument, as long as it includes at least one column label and at least one cell below the column label for specifying a condition for the column.

Excel in Practice: Using DSUM with a Data Table

If you do not want to use a pivot table, you can do a crosstab analysis by using a combination of the DSUM function and the Data Table command. The Data Table command works best when a problem is set up with two variables. In the DSUM function, you might have two variables defined in the criteria range.

To set up a two-variable table using the DSUM function, follow these steps:

1. Ensure that the upper-left corner of the table is a formula that relies on at least two variables. In Figure 12.58, cell B1 contains a DSUM that relies on the criteria ranges in A17:I18.

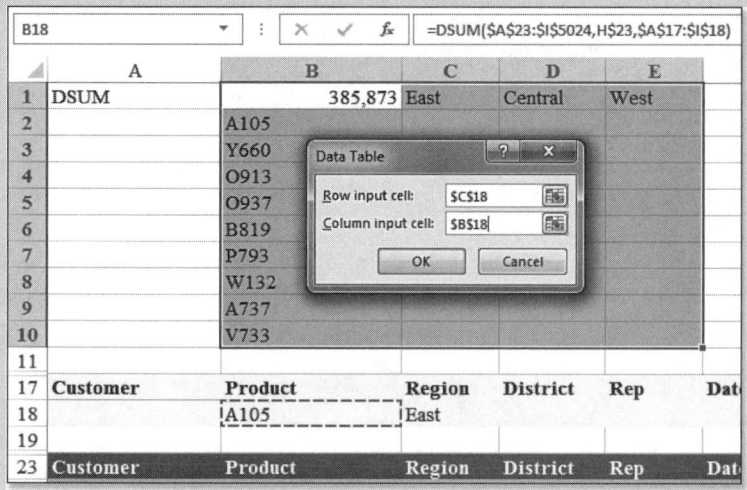

Figure 12.58
The Data Table dialog requires two cells.

2. Down the left side of the table, arrange a list of values that should be substituted for one variable. In this example, the column contains a list of products that will eventually be substituted into cell B18.

3. Across the top row of the table, arrange a list of values that should be substituted for the other variable. In this example, the row contains a list of regions that will eventually be substituted into cell C18.

4. Select the range for the table. This selection should include the formula as the upper-left corner cell. It should also include the column and row of headings.

5. From the Data tab, select What-if Analysis, Data Table. The Data Table dialog appears, asking for two cells.

6. For the row input cell, enter the cell where the regions should be substituted. In this case, it is cell C18 in the criteria range.

7. For the Column input cell, enter the cell where the values down the left column will be substituted. In this case, it is cell B18 in the criteria range. The complete dialog should look as shown in Figure 12.58.

The result shown in Figure 12.59 is a crosstab analysis that shows the DSUM for every com-bination of product and region. Excel actually creates a TABLE array function to produce the answers. This is a live formula: If you change the product names or regions, the cells inside the table recalculate.

Figure 12.59
The resulting table provides a crosstab analysis similar to that in a pivot table.

	A	B	C	D	E
C2			{=TABLE(C18,B18)}		
1	DSUM	385,873	East	Central	West
2		A105	385,873	601,184	259,097
3		Y660	1,152,227	1,422,736	1,111,337
4		O913	533,199	420,141	250,002
5		O937	1,562,404	1,498,932	1,146,197
6		B819	939,941	887,263	744,571
7		P793	553,087	690,740	146,925
8		W132	831,363	612,993	409,939
9		A737	1,609,888	952,950	919,978
10		V733	781,398	1,034,379	617,554
11					
17	**Customer**	**Product**	**Region**	**District**	**Rep**	**Dat**
18		A105	East			
19						
23	Customer	Product	Region	District	Rep	Dat

USING FINANCIAL FUNCTIONS

Although the bulk of Excel's financial functions are for professional financiers and investors, a few functions are useful for anyone planning to use a loan to purchase a car or house. The examples in this chapter represent a small subset of the calculations possible with Excel's financial functions.

Excel 2013 adds two new financial functions:

- **PDURATION**—Calculates how many periods it will take for an investment to reach a certain value given a specific interest rate.

- **RRI**—Calculates the equivalent rate for the growth of an investment. You can enter the beginning value, the value now, and how many years have gone by, and the function will calculate the average annual interest rate you earned.

 Note

Eight other functions began using "new algorithms" starting in Excel 2010. This means that a worksheet in Excel 2007 might return different answers from a worksheet in Excel 2013. These improved algorithms often affect only fringe cases of the functions. For normal usage, the results are usually the same. However, if Excel 2013 returns a different result, it is more accurate than the Excel 2007 result. Here are the functions affected:

CUMIPMT—Cumulative interest paid on a loan

CUMPRINC—Cumulative principal paid on a loan

IPMT—Interest payment for an investment

IRR—Internal rate of return for a series of cash flows

PMT—Payment for a loan

PPMT—Payment on principal for an investment

XIRR—Internal rate of return for a schedule of cash flows

Table 13.1 provides an alphabetical list of all of Excel 2013's financial functions. Detailed examples of the functions are provided in the remainder of the chapter.

Table 13.1   Alphabetical List of Financial Functions

Function	Description
ACCRINT (*issue*, *first_ interest*, *settlement*, *rate*, *par*, *frequency*, *basis*)	Returns the accrued interest for a security settlement that pays periodic interest.
ACCRINTM (*issue*, *settlement*, *rate*, *par*, *basis*)	Returns the accrued interest for a security that pays interest at maturity.
AMORDEGRC (*cost*, *date_purchased*, *first_ period*, *salvage*, *period*, *rate*, *basis*)	Returns the depreciation for each accounting period. This function is provided for the French accounting system. If an asset is purchased in the middle of the accounting period, the prorated depreciation is taken into account. The function is similar to AMORLINC, except that a depreciation coefficient is applied in the calculation, depending on the life of the assets.
AMORLINC (*cost*, *date_purchased*, *first_ period*, *salvage*, *period*, *rate*, *basis*)	Returns the depreciation for each accounting period. This function is provided for the French accounting system. If an asset is purchased in the middle of the accounting period, the prorated depreciation is taken into account.
COUPDAYBS (*settlement*, *maturity*, *frequency*, *basis*)	Returns the number of days from the beginning of the coupon period to the settlement date.
COUPDAYS (*settlement*, *maturity*, *frequency*, *basis*)	Returns the number of days in the coupon period that contains the settlement date.
COUPDAYSNC (*settlement*, *maturity*, *frequency*, *basis*)	Returns the number of days from the settlement date to the next coupon date.
COUPNCD (*settlement*, *maturity*, *frequency*, *basis*)	Returns a number that represents the next coupon date after the settlement date. To view the number as a date, you select Date in the Number Format drop-down on the Home tab.
COUPNUM (*settlement*, *maturity*, *frequency*, *basis*)	Returns the number of coupons payable between the settlement date and maturity date, rounded up to the nearest whole coupon.
COUPPCD (*settlement*, *maturity*, *frequency*, *basis*)	Returns a number that represents the previous coupon date before the settlement date. To view the number as a date, choose a date from the Number Format drop-down on the home tab.
CUMIPMT (*rate*, *nper*, *pv*, *start_period*, *end_ period*, *type*)	Returns the cumulative interest paid on a loan between *start_period* and *end_period*.
CUMPRINC (*rate*, *nper*, *pv*, *start_period*, *end_ period*, *type*)	Returns the cumulative principal paid on a loan between *start_period* and *end_period*.
DB (*cost*, *salvage*, *life*, *period*, *month*)	Returns the depreciation of an asset for a specified period, using the fixed-declining balance method.

Function	Description
DDB (*cost*, *salvage*, *life*, *period*, *factor*)	Returns the depreciation of an asset for a specified period using the double-declining-balance method or some other specified method.
DISC (*settlement*, *maturity*, *pr*, *redemption*, *basis*)	Returns the discount rate for a security.
DOLLARDE (*fractional_ dollar*, *fraction*)	Converts a dollar price expressed as a fraction into a dollar price expressed as a decimal number. Use DOLLARDE to convert fractional dollar numbers, such as securities prices, to decimal numbers.
DOLLARFR (*decimal_ dollar*, *fraction*)	Converts a dollar price expressed as a decimal number into a dollar price expressed as a fraction. Use DOLLARFR to convert decimal numbers to fractional dollar numbers, such as securities prices.
DURATION (*settlement*, *maturity*, *coupon yld*, *frequency*, *basis*)	Returns the Macaulay duration for an assumed par value of $100. The duration is defined as the weighted average of the present value of the cash flows and is used as a measure of a bond price's response to changes in yield.
EFFECT (*nominal_rate*, *npery*)	Returns the effective annual interest rate, given the nominal annual interest rate and the number of compounding periods per year.
FV (*rate*, *nper*, *pmt*, *pv*, *type*)	Returns the future value of an investment, based on periodic, constant payments and a constant interest rate.
FVSCHEDULE (*principal*, *schedule*)	Returns the future value of an initial principal after applying a series of compound interest rates. Use FVSCHEDULE to calculate future value of an investment with a variable or adjustable rate.
INTRATE (*settlement*, *maturity*, *investment*, *redemption*, *basis*)	Returns the interest rate for a fully invested security.
IPMT (*rate*, *per*, *nper*, *pv*, *fv*, *type*)	Returns the interest payment for a given period for an investment, based on periodic, constant payments and a constant interest rate. For a more complete description of the arguments in IPMT and for more information about annuity functions, see PV.
IRR (*values*, *guess*)	Returns the internal rate of return for a series of cash flows represented by the numbers in values. These cash flows do not have to be even, as they would be for an annuity. However, the cash flows must occur at regular intervals, such as monthly or annually. The internal rate of return is the interest rate received for an investment consisting of payments (negative values) and income (positive values) that occur at regular periods.
ISPMT (*rate*, *per*, *nper*, *pv*)	Calculates the interest paid during a specific period of an investment. This function is provided for compatibility with Lotus 1-2-3.
MDURATION (*settlement*, *maturity*, *coupon*, *yld*, *frequency*, *basis*)	Returns the modified duration for a security coupon with an assumed par value of $100.

Function	Description
MIRR (*values*, *finance_rate*, *reinvest_rate*)	Returns the modified internal rate of return for a series of periodic cash flows. MIRR considers both the cost of the investment and the interest received on reinvestment of cash.
NOMINAL (*effect_rate*, *npery*)	Returns the nominal annual interest rate, given the effective rate and the number of compounding periods per year.
NPER (*rate*, *pmt*, *pv*, *fv*, *type*)	Returns the number of periods for an investment, based on periodic, constant payments and a constant interest rate.
NPV (*rate*, *value1*, *value2*, ...)	Calculates the net present value of an investment by using a discount rate and a series of future payments (negative values) and income (positive values).
ODDFPRICE (*settlement*, *maturity*, *issue*, *first_coupon*, *rate*, *yld*, *redemption*, *frequency*, *basis*)	Returns the price per $100 face value of a security having an odd (short or long) first period.
ODDFYIELD (*settlement*, *maturity*, *issue*, *first_coupon*, *rate*, *pr*, *redemption*, *frequency*, *basis*)	Returns the yield of a security that has an odd (short or long) first period.
ODDLPRICE (*settlement*, *maturity*, *last_interest*, *rate*, *yld*, *redemption*, *frequency*, *basis*)	Returns the price per $100 face value of a security having an odd (short or long) last coupon period.
ODDLYIELD (*settlement*, *maturity*, *last_interest*, *rate*, *pr*, *redemption*, *frequency*, *basis*)	Returns the yield of a security that has an odd (short or long) last period.
PDURATION (*rate*, *pv*, *fv*)	Returns the number of periods required by an investment to reach a specified value.
PMT (*rate*, *nper*, *pv*, *fv*, *type*)	Calculates the payment for a loan based on constant payments and a constant interest rate.
PPMT (*rate*, *per*, *nper*, *pv*, *fv*, *type*)	Returns the payment on the principal for a given period for an investment based on periodic, constant payments and a constant interest rate.
PRICE (*settlement*, *maturity*, *rate*, *yld*, *redemption*, *frequency*, *basis*)	Returns the price per $100 face value of a security that pays periodic interest.
PRICEDISC (*settlement*, *maturity*, *discount*, *redemption*, *basis*)	Returns the price per $100 face value of a discounted security.

Function	Description
PRICEMAT (*settlement*, *maturity*, *issue*, *rate*, *yld*, *basis*)	Returns the price per $100 face value of an issue security that pays interest at maturity.
PV (*rate*, *nper*, *pmt*, fv, *type*)	Returns the present value of an investment. The *present value* is the total amount that a series of future payments is worth now. For example, when you borrow money, the loan amount is the present value to the lender.
RATE (*nper*, *pmt*, *pv*, fv, *type*, *guess*)	Returns the interest rate per period of an annuity. RATE is calculated by iteration and can have zero or more solutions. If the successive results of RATE do not converge to within 0.0000001 after 20 iterations, RATE returns a NUM! error.
RECEIVED (*settlement*, *maturity*, *investment*, *discount*, *basis*)	Returns the amount received at maturity for a fully invested security.
RRI (*nper*, *pv*, fv)	Returns an equivalent interest rate for the growth of an investment.
SLN (*cost*, *salvage*, *life*)	Returns the straight-line depreciation of an asset for one period.
SYD (*cost*, *salvage*, *life*, *per*)	Returns the sum-of-years'-digits depreciation of an asset for a specified period.
TBILLEQ (*settlement*, *maturity*, *discount*)	Returns the bond-equivalent yield for a Treasury bill (T-bill).
TBILLPRICE (*settlement*, *maturity*, *discount*)	Returns the price per $100 face value for a T-bill.
TBILLYIELD (*settlement*, *maturity*, *pr*)	Returns the yield for a T-bill.
VDB (*cost*, *salvage*, *life*, *start_period*, *end_period*, *factor*, *no_switch*)	Returns the depreciation of an asset for any specified period, including partial periods, using the double-declining-balance method or some other specified method. VDB stands for *variable declining balance*.
XIRR (*values*, *dates*, *guess*)	Returns the internal rate of return for a schedule of cash flows that is not necessarily periodic. To calculate the internal rate of return for a series of periodic cash flows, use the IRR function.
XNPV (*rate*, *values*, *dates*)	Returns the net present value for a schedule of cash flows that is not necessarily periodic. To calculate the net present value for a series of cash flows that is periodic, use the NPV function.
YIELD (*settlement*, *maturity*, *rate*, *pr*, *redemption*, *frequency*, *basis*)	Returns the yield on a security that pays periodic interest. You use YIELD to calculate bond yield.

Function	Description
YIELDDISC (*settlement*, *maturity*, *pr*, *redemption*, *basis*)	Returns the annual yield for a discounted security.
YIELDMAT (*settlement*, *maturity*, *issue*, *rate*, *pr*, *basis*)	Returns the annual yield of a security that pays interest at maturity.

Examples of Common Household Loan and Investment Functions

Although Excel is popular with banking and investment professionals, it is handy for just about anyone who deals with financial transactions. This first section of the chapter applies to anyone who is planning to buy a car or a house. With a little preplanning with Excel, you can build simple worksheets that enable you to calculate various monthly payments for various loan amounts.

You need to keep in mind two universal rules when dealing with all financial functions:

- Make sure your time units are consistent. If you calculate a monthly loan payment, the interest rate argument should be expressed as a monthly figure. Most interest rates are quoted as an annual figure, such as 4%. To convert to a monthly figure, divide 4% by 12.

- When money changes hands, consider the direction in which money flows. In any transaction, some cash flows toward you (positive), and some cash flows away from you (negative). If you try to enter all terms as positive, you end up with a result that is not meaningful. For example, if you do not make the payment or pv negative, you are saying that you want a car loan where the bank gives $20,000 at the beginning and then gives you another $377 per month. NPER(5%/12,377,20000) would come up with an incorrect result for your problem because one of the cash flows needs to be negative. If you consider the loan from the point of view of the customer, the formula would be NPER(5%/12,-377,20000). If you consider the loan from the point of view of the bank, the formula would be NPER(5%/12,377,-20000).

Using RRI to Calculate the Investment Return After Many Years

You left your starter job a decade ago and rolled your 401K into a rollover IRA. How well has that IRA performed? The new RRI function calculates an average interest rate.

Enter the number of years the money was in the IRA, the starting amount, and the ending amount. RRI calculates the result.

 **Caution**

RRI is new in Excel 2013. This function returns a #NAME? error if you open the workbook in Excel 2010 or earlier.

Syntax:

RRI(*nper*,*pv*,*fv*)

The RRI function calculates the equivalent interest rate for the growth of an investment. This function takes the following arguments:

- *nper*—This is the number of years that the money was invested.

- *pv*—This is the original amount invested.

- *fv*—This is the ending value of the investment account.

Figure 13.1 shows an example. If $150,000 grew to $175,000 in 12 years, the return was essentially 1.29% per year.

Figure 13.1
RRI calculates an equivalent return of an investment.

B11	▾	:	×	✓	*fx*	=PDURATION(B9,B7,B8)				
	A			B		C	D	E		F
1	**Original Amount**			150000		*Money I put into the rollover IRA*				
2	**Amount Today**			175000		*Value today*				
3	**Years Invested**			12		*Years*				
4										
5	**Average Return**			**1.29%**		=RRI(B3,B1,B2)				
6										
7	**Value Today**			175000		*What I have today*				
8	**Goal at Retirement**			1000000		*What I need to retire on*				
9	**Assumed Rate**			1.29%		*Historical average*				
10										
11	**Years Until Retirement**			**135.7**		=PDURATION(B9,B7,B8)				
12										

Using PDURATION to Calculate How Long It Will Take Before You Are a Millionaire

You have some money in a rollover IRA. How long will it take before that IRA grows to a million dollars? The new PDURATION function calculates how many years it will take. You have to specify the current value, the goal value, and the assumed annual interest rate.

 **Caution**

PDURATION is new in Excel 2013. This function returns a #NAME? error if you open the workbook in Excel 2010 or earlier.

Syntax:

PDURATION(*rate,pv,fv*)

The PDURATION function calculates the number of periods for an investment to reach a certain value given an interest rate. This function takes the following arguments:

- *rate*—This is the assumed annual interest rate that the investment will earn.

- *pv*—This is the current value of the investment.

- *fv*—This is the target ending value of the investment account.

Refer to Figure 13.1 for an example. An IRA with $175,000 earning 1.29% interest will require 135.7 years to reach $1,000,000 in value.

Using PMT to Calculate the Monthly Payment on an Automobile Loan

Buying a car is one of the most exciting purchases. Whether the car is brand new or just new to you, nothing attracts attention in your neighborhood like a new car pulling into the driveway.

Before shopping for a car, you should take a 5-minute spin through Excel to calculate potential car payments. Knowing the price that will get you to the desired car payment will enable you to haggle with the sales rep from a position of knowledge.

Syntax:

`PMT(rate,nper,pv,fv,type)`

The PMT function calculates the payment for a loan based on constant payments and a constant interest rate. This function takes the following arguments:

- **rate**—This is the interest rate for the loan. Note that interest rate is often expressed as an annual rate. To calculate a monthly payment, you have to divide that rate by 12.

- **nper**—This is the term, or the total number of payments for the loan.

- **pv**—This is the present value, or the loan amount; it is also known as the *principal*.

- **fv**—This is an optional future value, or a cash balance you want to attain after the last payment is made. For a car payment calculation, this should be 0. If *fv* is omitted, it is assumed to be 0; that is, the future value of a loan is zero.

- **type**—This is the number 0 or 1 and indicates when payments are due. The default value of 0 assumes that the first payment is due after a month has elapsed. If you have to make the first payment on the day the loan is issued, you should set this value to 1.

For a reality check, try multiplying the calculated payment by *nper*. This way, you can calculate the total of all payments over the life of the loan. In Figure 13.2, you see that a $29,000 car actually costs $32,044.75 in principal and interest.

 Note

The payment returned by PMT includes principal and interest but not taxes, insurance, escrow, or fees sometimes associated with loans.

Using RATE to Determine an Interest Rate

The PMT function is useful when you are considering a new loan. If you are analyzing a loan that you have been paying for a while, you might know the monthly payment but forget the interest rate. The RATE function can help you determine the rate.

 Caution

The algorithm behind the PMT function is new and more accurate in Excel 2013. Although this will not affect basic loan payment calculations like the one shown here, be aware that Excel 2007 and Excel 2013 might produce different results for some uses of PMT.

Figure 13.2
PMT calculates
a monthly loan
payment.

	A	B	C	D	E	F	G
			=PMT(B2/12,B3,B1)				
1	**Loan Amount**	-29000	*Negative, as the money is leaving the bank*				
2	**Rate**	4%	*Annual rate; divide by 12 in the function*				
3	**Term**	60	*Months*				
4							
5	**PMT**	**$534.08**	*=PMT(B2/12,B3,B1)*				
6							
7	**Total Paid**	$32,044.75	*=B3*B5*				
8							

Syntax:

RATE(nper,pmt,pv,fv,type,guess)

The RATE function returns the interest rate per period of an annuity. RATE is calculated by iteration and can have zero or more solutions. If the successive results of RATE do not converge to within 0.0000001 after 20 iterations, RATE returns a #NUM! error. This function takes the following arguments:

- *nper*—This is the total number of payment periods in an annuity.

- *pmt*—This is the payment made each period and cannot change over the life of the annuity. Typically, *pmt* includes principal and interest but no other fees or taxes. If *pmt* is omitted, you must include the *fv* argument.

- *pv*—This is the present value—the total amount that a series of future payments is worth now.

- *fv*—This is the future value, or a cash balance you want to attain after the last payment is made. If *fv* is omitted, it is assumed to be 0, which means the future value of a loan is zero.

- *type*—This is the number 0 or 1 to indicate when payments are due. The default value of 0 assumes that payments are due at the end of the period. A value of 1 means the payments are due at the beginning of each period.

- *guess*—This is your guess for what the rate will be. If you omit *guess*, the rate is assumed to be 10%. If RATE does not converge, you can try different values for *guess*. RATE usually converges if *guess* is between 0 and 1.

Make sure you are consistent about the units you use for specifying *guess* and *nper*. If you make monthly payments on a 4-year loan at 12% annual interest, you use 12% / 12 for *guess* and 4 × 12 for *nper*. If you make annual payments on the same loan, you use 12% for *guess* and 4 for *nper*.

Figure 13.3 shows how to calculate an interest rate.

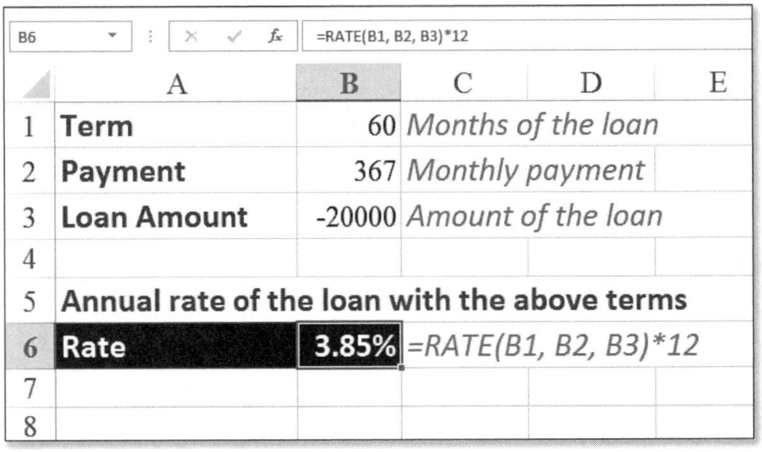

Figure 13.3
Given the other terms for a loan, you can back into the interest rate with RATE.

Using PV to Figure Out How Much House You Can Afford

If you are looking for a monthly house payment of $1,500 with a 15-year loan at 3.2% annual interest rate, you can back into the loan amount by using the PV function.

Syntax:

PV(rate,nper,pmt,fv,type)

The PV function returns the present value of an investment. The present value is the total amount that a series of future payments is worth now. For example, when you borrow money, the loan amount is the present value to the lender. This function takes the following arguments:

- **rate**—This is the interest rate per period. For example, if you obtain an automobile loan at a 10% annual interest rate and make monthly payments, your interest rate per month is 10% / 12, or 0.008333. Therefore, you would enter **10%** / **12**, or **0.8333%**, or **0.00833** into the formula as rate.

- **nper**—This is the total number of payment periods in an annuity. For example, if you get a 4-year car loan and make monthly payments, your loan has 4 × 12 (or 48) periods. You would enter **48** into the formula for *nper*.

- **pmt**—This is the payment made each period and cannot change over the life of the annuity. Typically, *pmt* includes principal and interest but no other fees or taxes. For example, the monthly payments on a $10,000, 4-year car loan at 12% are $263.33. You would enter **-263.33** into the formula for *pmt*. If *pmt* is omitted, you must include the *fv* argument.

- **fv**—This is the future value, or a cash balance you want to attain after the last payment is made. If *fv* is omitted, it is assumed to be **0**, which means the future value of a loan is zero. For example, if you want to save $50,000 to pay for a special project in 18 years, then $50,000 is the future value. You could then make a conservative guess at an interest rate and determine how much you must save each month. If *fv* is omitted, you must include the *pmt* argument.

- **type**—This is either 0 or 1 to indicate when payments are due. The default value of 0 assumes that payments are due at the end of the period. A value of 1 means the payments are due at the beginning of each period.

In Figure 13.4, cell B5 calculates the loan principal amount that would result in the desired payment, including principal and interest. You also need to budget for monthly insurance, taxes, and fees that might be a part of your monthly payment to the bank.

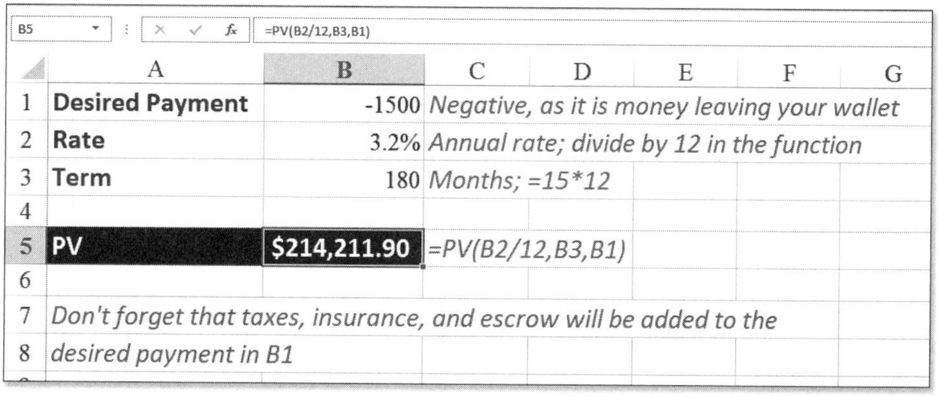

Figure 13.4
Use PV to calculate how much you can borrow to meet a monthly payment budget.

B5	▼	:	×	✓	*fx*	=PV(B2/12,B3,B1)

	A	B	C	D	E	F	G
1	**Desired Payment**	-1500	*Negative, as it is money leaving your wallet*				
2	**Rate**	3.2%	*Annual rate; divide by 12 in the function*				
3	**Term**	180	*Months; =15*12*				
4							
5	PV	$214,211.90	*=PV(B2/12,B3,B1)*				
6							
7	*Don't forget that taxes, insurance, and escrow will be added to the*						
8	*desired payment in B1*						

Using NPER to Estimate How Long a Nest Egg Will Last

NPER stands for number of periods. If you have a 401K retirement account and are trying to calculate how long you can withdraw fixed monthly payments from the account, use NPER.

Syntax:

NPER(*rate, pmt, pv, fv, type*)

The NPER function returns the number of periods for an investment, based on periodic, constant payments and a constant interest rate. This function takes the following arguments:

- **rate**—This is the interest rate per period.

- **pmt**—This is the payment made each period; it cannot change over the life of the annuity. Typically, *pmt* contains principal and interest but no other fees or taxes.

- **pv**—This is the present value, or the lump-sum amount that a series of future payments is worth right now.

- *fv*—This is the future value, or a cash balance you want to attain after the last payment is made. If *fv* is omitted, it is assumed to be 0, which means the future value of a loan is zero. If you want to leave an inheritance to your kids, you use that amount as *fv*.

- *type*—This is either 0 or 1 to indicate when payments are due. The default value of 0 assumes that payments are due at the end of the period. A value of 1 means the payments are due at the beginning of each period.

In Figure 13.5, the NPER function in cell B5 estimates how many months you can withdraw the amount in cell B2. Note that the monthly withdrawal is negative from the point of view of the retirement account.

B5	▾	:	✕	✓	*fx*	=NPER(B3/12,B2,B1)

	A	B	C
1	**Nest Egg Today**	457124	*Value of retirement account*
2	**Monthly Withdrawal**	-2800	*Desired monthly withdrawal*
3	**Interest Rate**	2.5%	*Assumed interest rate*
4			
5	Months	199.74	=NPER(B3/12,B2,B1)
6	Years	16.6	=B5/12
7			

Figure 13.5
Use NPER to figure out how long an annuity can pay out before it ends in a zero balance.

Using FV to Estimate the Future Value of a Regular Savings Plan

The future value calculation assumes that you will make regular monthly payments to a savings plan every month. It also assumes that the interest rate does not change throughout the life of the savings plan. If you are young, it is likely that you can save more as your income grows later. However, using the savings calculator in Figure 13.6 helps you to realize the value of regular savings.

Syntax:

FV(*rate*,*nper*,*pmt*,*pv*,*type*)

The FV function returns the future value of an investment, based on periodic, constant payments and a constant interest rate. This function takes the following arguments:

- *rate*—This is the interest rate per period.

- *nper*—This is the total number of payment periods in an annuity.

Figure 13.6
You can estimate the future value of a regular savings plan.

B8	▾	⋮	✕	✓	ƒx	=FV(B5/12,B3,-B4,-B6)

◢	A	B	C
1	**Age Now**	25	
2	**Retirement Age**	65	
3	**Number of Months**	480	*=(B2-B1)*12*
4	**Monthly Savings**	125	
5	**Interest Rate**	4%	
6	**Savings Balance Now**	542	
7			
8	**Future Value**	**$150,422.58**	*=FV(B5/12,B3,-B4,-B6)*
9			

- **pmt**—This is the payment made each period; it cannot change over the life of the annuity. Typically, *pmt* contains principal and interest but no other fees or taxes. If *pmt* is omitted, you must include the *pv* argument.

- **pv**—This is the present value, or the lump-sum amount that a series of future payments is worth right now. If *pv* is omitted, it is assumed to be 0, and you must include the *pmt* argument.

- **type**—This is either 0 or 1 to indicate when payments are due. The default value of 0 assumes that payments are due at the end of the period. A value of 1 means the payments are due at the beginning of each period.

For all the arguments, the cash you pay out, such as deposits to savings, is represented by negative numbers; the cash you receive, such as dividend checks, is represented by positive numbers.

Figure 13.6 shows how to use FV for a simple savings calculator. The formula in cell B8 assumes that you continue making the deposit each month from cell B4 until you retire and that interest rates remain constant. If you already have some amount in savings, you enter that in cell B6.

 Note

Note that the FV formula uses a negative version of cells B4 and B6. This occurs because these are amounts that leave your wallet and go to the bank or mutual fund.

Examples of Functions for Financial Professionals

Whereas a typical consumer is interested in the amount of his or her monthly car payment, a loan maker is interested in the month-by-month breakdown of principal and interest. Excel offers a complete cadre of functions to perform these calculations.

Using PPMT to Calculate the Principal Payment for Any Month

After a bank writes a car loan, the consumer makes monthly payments. To calculate the principal portion of the payment for any period in the loan, you use PPMT. Of course, you can use a range of these formulas—one for each month—to build an amortization table.

Syntax:

PPMT(*rate*,*per*,*nper*,*pv*,*fv*,*type*)

The PPMT function returns the payment on the principal for a given period for an investment, based on periodic, constant payments and a constant interest rate. This function takes the following arguments:

- *rate*—This is the interest rate per period.

- *per*—This specifies for which period the principal payment will be returned. It must be in the range 1 to *nper*.

- *nper*—This is the total number of payment periods in an annuity.

- *pv*—This is the present value—the total amount that a series of future payments is worth now.

- *fv*—This is the future value, or a cash balance you want to attain after the last payment is made. If *fv* is omitted, it is assumed to be 0, which means the future value of a loan is zero.

- *type*—This is either 0 or 1 to indicate when payments are due. The default value of 0 assumes that payments are due at the end of the period. A value of 1 means the payments are due at the beginning of each period.

In Figure 13.7, cell B9 calculates the principal payment for Period 1. The Per argument comes from the month number in column A. Copying the formula down for all months produces an amortization table.

Using IPMT to Calculate the Interest Portion of a Loan Payment for Any Month

Whereas the PPMT function calculates the principal payment for any month of a loan, the IPMT function calculates the interest portion of the payment. The results of IPMT are shown in column C of Figure 13.7.

 Note

In this example, the interest component could be calculated with either PMT–PPMT or using the IPMT function. IPMT is discussed in the next section.

Figure 13.7
Similar PPMT functions in B9:B56 calculate the monthly principal portion of the loan payment.

| B9 | ▼ | : | × | ✓ | *fx* | =PPMT($B$2/12,A9,$B$3,$B$1) |

	A	B	C	D	E
1	**Loan Amt**	-22000			
2	**Rate**	3.5%			
3	**Term**	48			
4	**PMT**	491.83202			
5	**A9:**	=ROW(1:1)			
6	**B9:**	=PPMT($B$2/12,A9,$B$3,$B$1)			
7	**C9:**	=IPMT($B$2/12,A9,$B$3,$B$1)			
8	**Month**	**Principal**	**Interest**		
9	1	$427.67	$64.17		
10	2	$428.91	$62.92		
11	3	$430.16	$61.67		

Syntax:

IPMT(*rate*,*per*,*nper*,*pv*,*fv*,*type*)

The IPMT function returns the interest payment for a given period for an investment, based on periodic, constant payments and a constant interest rate. This function takes the following arguments:

- **rate**—This is the interest rate per period.

- **per**—This is the period for which you want to find the interest and must be in the range 1 to *nper*.

- **nper**—This is the total number of payment periods in an annuity.

- **pv**—This is the present value, or the lump-sum amount that a series of future payments is worth right now.

- **fv**—This is the future value, or a cash balance you want to attain after the last payment is made.

- **type**—This is either 0 or 1 to indicate when payments are due. The default value of 0 assumes that payments are due at the end of the period. A value of 1 means the payments are due at the beginning of each period.

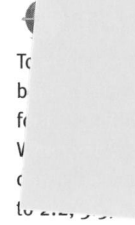

Tc
b
f
v
c
to ...., , ...
fast way to generate a column of sequential numbers using a single formula. Alternatively, use =ROW(A1) for the same result.

 Note

You may encounter an old worksheet that uses ISPMT, which is the Lotus 1-2-3 version of IPMT. For details on ISPMT, see Excel Help. For new worksheets, you should use IPMT instead of ISPMT.

The IPMT function is similar to the PPMT function. Combined, they can create a simple amortization table (refer to Figure 13.7).

Using CUMIPMT to Calculate Total Interest Payments During a Time Frame

The CUMIPMT function is great for figuring out your yearly tax deduction for your mortgage interest. After specifying the typical components of a loan, such as the rate, term, and amount, you need to specify that you want to calculate the interest for particular periods, such as Periods 6 through 18.

Syntax:

CUMIPMT(*rate*,*nper*,*pv*,*start_period*,*end_period*,*type*)

The CUMIPMT function returns the cumulative interest paid on a loan between *start_period* and *end_period*. This function takes the following arguments:

- **rate**—This is the interest rate.

- **nper**—This is the total number of payment periods.

- **pv**—This is the present value.

- **start_period**—This is the first period in the calculation. Payment periods are numbered beginning with 1.

- **end_period**—This is the last period in the calculation.

- **type**—This is either 0 or 1 to indicate when payments are due. The default value of 0 assumes that payments are due at the end of the period. A value of 1 means the payments are due at the beginning of each period.

The *nper*, *start_period*, *end_period*, and *type* arguments are truncated to integers. If *rate* is less than or equal to 0, *nper* is less than or equal to 0, or *pv* is less than or equal to 0, CUMIPMT returns a #NUM! error. If *start_period* is less than 1, *end_period* is less than 1, or *start_period* is greater than *end_period*, CUMIPMT returns a #NUM! error. If *type* is any number other than 0 or 1, CUMIPMT returns a #NUM! error.

Figure 13.8 calculates the total interest paid during each year of the loan. The mildly difficult portion of the sample spreadsheet is that the number of months in the first year will likely be less than 12. Cell D12 uses =13-MONTH(B5). Cell C13 uses =D12+1. Cell D13 uses =C12+11 to calculate the last period for each year.

Column F of this spreadsheet uses CUMPRINC, which is discussed in the next section.

Caution
The algorithm behind the IPMT function is new and more accurate in Excel 2013. Be aware that Excel 2007 and Excel 2013 might produce different results for some uses of IPMT.

Caution
The algorithm behind the CUMIPMT function is new and more accurate in Excel 2013. Be aware that Excel 2007 and Excel 2013 might produce different results for some uses of CUMIPMT.

Figure 13.8
Use column E
to plan your tax
deductions by
year.

| E12 | ▼ | : | × | ✓ | fx | =CUMIPMT($B$2/12,$B$3,$B$1,$C12,$D12,0) |

◢	A	B	C	D	E	F	G
1	**Mortage Amt.**	225,000					
2	**Rate**	4%					
3	**Term**	180					
4	**PMT**	-1,664.30	*Not necessary for the calculation, here FYI*				
5	**First Payment**	Aug-05	*Cell D12 uses this in =13-MONTH(B5)*				
6							
7			**E12:**	*=CUMIPMT($B$2/12,$B$3,$B$1,$C12,$D12,0)*			
8			**F12:**	*=CUMPRINC($B$2/12,$B$3,$B$1,$C12,$D12,0)*			
9				**Payment Numbers**			
11		**Year**	**From**	**Through**	**Interest**	**Principal**	
12		2005	1	5	-3,719.42	-4,602.07	
13		2006	6	17	-8,609.11	-11,362.47	
14		2007	18	29	-8,146.18	-11,825.39	

Using CUMPRINC to Calculate Total Principal Paid in Any Range of Periods

The corollary to CUMIPMT is CUMPRINC, a function to calculate the total principal paid during any range of periods of a loan.

Syntax:

CUMPRINC(*rate*,*nper*,*pv*,*start_period*,*end_period*,*type*)

The CUMPRINC function returns the cumulative principal paid on a loan between *start_period* and *end_period*. This function takes the following arguments:

- *rate*—This is the interest rate.

- *nper*—This is the total number of payment periods.

- *pv*—This is the present value.

- *start_period*—This is the first period in the calculation. Payment periods are numbered beginning with 1.

- *end_period*—This is the last period in the calculation.

- *type*—This is either 0 or 1 to indicate when payments are due. The default value of 0 assumes that payments are due at the end of the period. A value of 1 means the payments are due at the beginning of each period.

The *nper*, *start_period*, *end_period*, and *type* arguments are truncated to integers. If *rate* is less than or equal to 0, *nper* is less than or equal to 0, or *pv* is less than or equal to 0, CUMPRINC returns a #NUM! error. If *start_period* is less than 1, *end_period* is less than 1, or *start_period* is greater than *end_period*, CUMPRINC returns a #NUM! error. If *type* is any number other than 0 or 1, CUMPRINC returns a #NUM! error.

Refer to Figure 13.8 for an example of CUMPRINC.

>  **Caution**
>
> The algorithm behind the CUMPRINC function is new and more accurate in Excel 2013. Be aware that Excel 2007 and Excel 2013 might produce different results for some uses of CUMPRINC.

Using EFFECT to Calculate the Effect of Compounding Period on Interest Rates

Does it really matter if your bank compounds interest daily, monthly, or quarterly? If the numbers are big enough, it can matter. The EFFECT function converts an interest rate to an effective rate, depending on how frequently the bank compounds the interest.

Syntax:

EFFECT(*nominal_rate*,*npery*)

The EFFECT function returns the effective annual interest rate, given the nominal annual interest rate and the number of compounding periods per year. This function takes the following arguments:

- **nominal_rate**—This is the nominal interest rate.

- **npery**—This is the number of compounding periods per year. npery is truncated to an integer.

If either argument is nonnumeric, EFFECT returns a #VALUE! error. If *nominal_rate* is less than or equal to 0 or if *npery* is less than 1, EFFECT returns a #NUM! error.

In Figure 13.9, the nominal interest rate is 4%. If the bank compounds interest once per year, the effective interest rate is still 4%, as shown in cell A5. If interest is compounded monthly, the effective rate increases to 4.07%. Row 9 compares the monthly mortgage payment at the various effective rates. Daily compounding adds about $10 per month to a typical mortgage payment.

Using NOMINAL to Convert the Effective Interest Rate to a Nominal Rate

If you need to compare two investments, one quoting a nominal rate and one quoting an effective rate, you can convert the effective rate to a nominal rate by using NOMINAL.

Syntax:

NOMINAL(*effect_rate*,*npery*)

Figure 13.9
Row 5 shows the effective interest rates for various compounding periods. Row 9 shows the monthly payment difference.

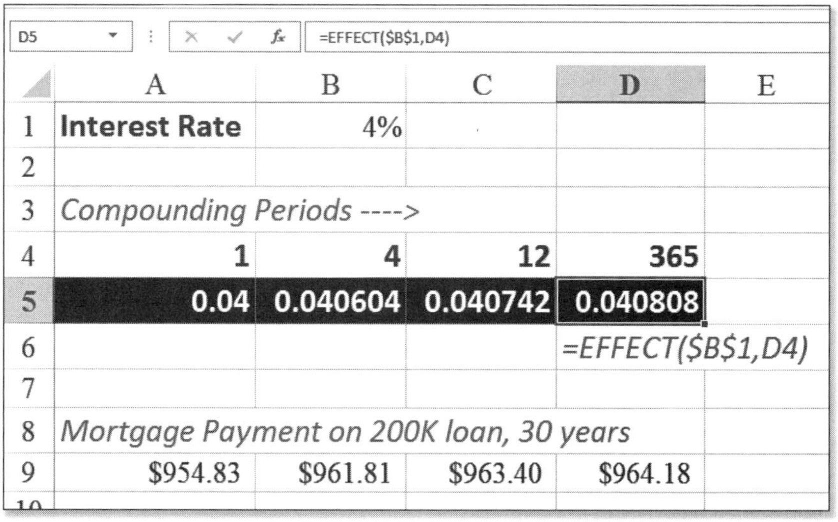

D5	▾	:	✕	✓	*fx*	=EFFECT($B$1,D4)		
◢	A		B		C	D		E
1	**Interest Rate**		4%					
2								
3	*Compounding Periods ---->*							
4		**1**		**4**		**12**	**365**		
5		**0.04**		**0.040604**		**0.040742**	**0.040808**		
6							*=EFFECT($B$1,D4)*		
7									
8	*Mortgage Payment on 200K loan, 30 years*							
9		$954.83		$961.81		$963.40	$964.18		
10									

The NOMINAL function returns the nominal annual interest rate, given the effective rate and the number of compounding periods per year. This function takes the following arguments:

- *effect_rate*—This is the effective interest rate.

- *npery*—This is the number of compounding periods per year.

The *npery* argument is truncated to an integer. If either argument is nonnumeric, NOMINAL returns a #VALUE! error. If *effect_rate* is less than or equal to 0 or if *npery* is less than 1, NOMINAL returns a #NUM! error.

Examples of Depreciation Functions

When a company buys a large asset such as a piece of machinery, accounting rules specify how the asset should be expensed each year. This is called *depreciation*. Excel offers four common methods for calculating depreciation: straight-line, declining-balance, double-declining-balance, and sum-of-years'-digits methods.

The following terms are common to all the depreciation methods:

- **Cost**—This is the initial cost of the asset. For example, the machinery might cost $120,000.

- **Useful life**—This is how long you expect to use the asset. If you think you will use the machinery for 10 years before replacing it, the life is 10 years.

- **Salvage value**—This is the value of the asset at the end of the useful life. Perhaps after 10 years, you can sell the machine to a scrap dealer for $1,000 or to a trade school for $5,000. This is the salvage value.

Figure 13.10 compares the four depreciation methods.

D6	▾	:	×	✓	fₓ	=DDB($B$1,$B$2,$B$3,A6)		

◢	A	B	C	D	E
1	Cost	120000			
2	Salvage Value	20000			
3	Useful Life	10 *years*			
4					
5	Year	Straight Line	Declining Balance	Double Declining	Sum of Years Digits
6	1	$10,000.00	$19,680.00	$24,000.00	$18,181.82
7	2	$10,000.00	$16,452.48	$19,200.00	$16,363.64
8	3	$10,000.00	$13,754.27	$15,360.00	$14,545.45
9	4	$10,000.00	$11,498.57	$12,288.00	$12,727.27
10	5	$10,000.00	$9,612.81	$9,830.40	$10,909.09
11	6	$10,000.00	$8,036.31	$7,864.32	$9,090.91
12	7	$10,000.00	$6,718.35	$6,291.46	$7,272.73
13	8	$10,000.00	$5,616.54	$5,033.16	$5,454.55
14	9	$10,000.00	$4,695.43	$132.66	$3,636.36
15	10	$10,000.00	$3,925.38	$0.00	$1,818.18
16					
17	**B6:** =SLN($B$1,$B$2,$B$3)				
18	**C6:** =DB($B$1,$B$2,$B$3,A6)				
19	**D6:** =DDB($B$1,$B$2,$B$3,A6)				
20	**E6:** =SYD($B$1,$B$2,$B$3,A6)				

Figure 13.10
Columns B through E compare four methods of depreciation.

Using SLN to Calculate Straight-Line Depreciation

The straight-line method is the simplest depreciation method. Using this method, the value of the asset is depreciated evenly over the asset's useful life. At the end of the useful life, the item is depreciated on the company's books to the salvage value level.

Syntax:

SLN(*cost*,*salvage*,*life*)

The SLN function returns the straight-line depreciation of an asset for one period. This function takes the following arguments:

- *cost*—This is the initial cost of the asset.

- *salvage*—This is the asset's value at the end of the depreciation period. Sometimes this is called the *salvage value* of the asset.

- *life*—This is the number of periods over which the asset is being depreciated. Sometimes this is called the *useful life* of the asset.

Using DB to Calculate Declining-Balance Depreciation

In the declining-balance method, depreciation happens at a constant rate. The advantage of this method is that more depreciation happens in the earlier years, providing a better tax benefit in early years.

> **Note**
>
> See Excel Help for this function for details on special handling of Year 1 and the last year, as well as the algebra behind the rate formula.

Let's look at a simple example. Suppose that a $100,000 asset is depreciated 20% in Year 1. This results in a $20,000 depreciation expense. After Year 1, the asset would have a value of $80,000 on the books. In Year 2, the remaining balance of $80,000 is multiplied by the same 20% rate to yield a depreciation of $16,000. The depreciation in Year 3 is 20% of the remaining $64,000, or $12,800.

The trick to this method is figuring out the correct percentage to use for each year. This involves fractional exponents and a little algebra. If you use the DB function, however, you do not have to worry about any of that. Excel calculates this rate, rounded to three decimal places, as the first step in the process. This rounding to three decimal places causes the calculation to be off by a few dollars at the end of the useful life.

Syntax:

DB(*cost*,*salvage*,*life*,*period*,*month*)

The DB function returns the depreciation of an asset for a specified period, using the fixed-declining-balance method. This function takes the following arguments:

- *cost*—This is the initial cost of the asset.

- *salvage*—This is the value at the end of the depreciation period. Sometimes this is called the *salvage value* of the asset.

- *life*—This is the number of periods over which the asset is being depreciated. Sometimes this is called the *useful life* of the asset.

- *period*—This is the period for which you want to calculate the depreciation. *period* must use the same units as *life*.

- *month*—This is the number of months in the first year. If *month* is omitted, it is assumed to be 12.

Using DDB to Calculate Double-Declining-Balance Depreciation

The double-declining-balance method is an aggressive (and legal) method for calculating depreciation. Suppose you purchase a computer. In the first year, the item might be state-of-the-art. By Year 2, it is worth far less because technology would have passed the computer by.

The name of this method reflects the fact that the depreciation rate is double the normal rate but also that the depreciation rate is applied to the declining balance of the asset's value.

If the asset is depreciated over five years, the normal straight-line rate would be 20%. In the double-declining-balance method, you get to use 40% in each year. For example, the first year, depreciation on a $100,000 asset would be 40%. But in Year 2, the 40% is multiplied by the remaining asset value of $60,000. This method generates much higher depreciation in the first few years of the asset life than the other methods.

 Note

In many depreciation systems, you are allowed to switch from double-declining-balance to the straight-line method when the straight-line method produces a higher depreciation. To do this, use the VDB function, which is described later in this chapter.

Although the name of this method contains the world *double*, Microsoft covered the possibility of other multipliers. There is a 150DB method that multiplies the rate by 1.5 instead of 2. To calculate 150DB, you use 1.5 as the fifth argument. If no fifth argument is supplied, the fifth argument is assumed to be 2, resulting in DDB.

Syntax:

DDB(*cost*,*salvage*,*life*,*period*,*factor*)

The DDB function returns the depreciation of an asset for a specified period using the double-declining-balance method or some other specified method. This function takes the following arguments:

- *cost*—This is the initial cost of the asset.

- *salvage*—This is the value at the end of the depreciation period.

- *life*—This is the number of periods over which the asset is being depreciated.

- *period*—This is the period for which you want to calculate the depreciation. The *period* must use the same units as *life*.

- *factor*—This is the rate at which the balance declines. If *factor* is omitted, it is assumed to be 2, which is the double-declining-balance method.

 **Tip**

Keep in mind that all five of the arguments listed must be positive numbers.

To allow DDB to work, you need to abandon the method at some point and switch to a straight-line method for the remaining asset value. If you attempt to use DDB for the entire life of the asset, you will not write off enough of the value.

Figure 13.11 illustrates how DDB fails to accumulate $500,000 of depreciation. You might want to use the newer VDB method, which automatically switches for you. Column D in Figure 13.11 shows this method.

Figure 13.11
The DDB method fails to accumulate enough depreciation.

| D12 | ▼ | : | × | ✓ | *fx* | =VDB($B$1,$B$2,$B$3,$A12-1,$A12,2,FALSE) |

⬜	A	B	C	D	E	F
1	Cost	500000	*Note that saying False to NoSwitch is a*			
2	Salvage Value	0	*double negative. You are saying that you*			
3	Useful Life	10	*do want to switch to SLN...*			
4						
5	Year	Straight Line	Double Declining	VDB NoSwitch= FALSE	VDB NoSwitch= TRUE	
6	1	$50,000.00	$100,000.00	$100,000.00	$100,000.00	
7	2	$50,000.00	$80,000.00	$80,000.00	$80,000.00	
8	3	$50,000.00	$64,000.00	$64,000.00	$64,000.00	
9	4	$50,000.00	$51,200.00	$51,200.00	$51,200.00	
10	5	$50,000.00	$40,960.00	$40,960.00	$40,960.00	
11	6	$50,000.00	$32,768.00	$32,768.00	$32,768.00	
12	7	$50,000.00	$26,214.40	**$32,768.00**	$26,214.40	
13	8	$50,000.00	$20,971.52	$32,768.00	$20,971.52	
14	9	$50,000.00	$16,777.22	$32,768.00	$16,777.22	
15	10	$50,000.00	$13,421.77	$32,768.00	$13,421.77	
16	TOTAL	$500,000.00	$446,312.91	$500,000.00	$446,312.91	
17						
18	**B6:**	*=SLN($B$1,$B$2,$B$3)*				
19	**C6:**	*=DDB($B$1,$B$2,$B$3,A6)*				
20	**C6 Alt:**	*=VDB($B$1,$B$2,$B$3,$A6-1,$A6)*				
21	**D6:**	*=VDB($B$1,$B$2,$B$3,$A6-1,$A6,2,FALSE)*				
22	**E6:**	*=VDB($B$1,$B$2,$B$3,$A6-1,$A6,2,TRUE)*				

To overcome this problem with DDB, you can use the VDB method. The VDB function is a far more powerful function. Using VDB to calculate a double-declining-balance problem correctly is somewhat like using a sledgehammer to push in a thumbtack. VDB is covered in detail later in this chapter, but you can follow these steps to solve the current problem:

1. Change the function name from DDB to VDB.

2. Because both DDB and VDB take the same first three arguments—*cost*, *salvage*, and *life*— leave those three arguments alone.

3. Change the period number in DDB to the start period and end period for VDB. Cell C6 specifies A6 as the period number. Change this argument to A6-1,A6. This is a bit strange because you are asking VDB to calculate the depreciation from the end of Year 0 to the end of Year 1.

4. Determine whether the DDB function is done. factor, which is usually left off the function, is assumed to be 2. If DDB has no fifth argument, then VDB does not need a fifth argument.

5. To allow VDB to switch to the straight-line method, ensure that the sixth argument is FALSE. The name of this argument is no_switch. By specifying FALSE, you are invoking a double negative to ask VDB to switch to the straight-line method when appropriate. Because FALSE is the default, you can often leave off the fifth and sixth arguments with VDB.

➡ *Complete details on the more powerful uses of VDB are provided later in this chapter.*

Using SYD to Calculate Sum-of-Years'-Digits Depreciation

The sum-of-years'-digits method is another accelerated depreciation system. It ensures that the value of the asset drops more in the earlier years of the asset's life than in later years.

Suppose you have an asset with a useful life of seven years. You need to add all the years from seven to one: 7 + 6 + 5 + 4 + 3 + 2 + 1 = 28. In the first year, you can write off 7 / 28 of the value. In the next year, you can write off 6 / 28. In successive years, you can write off 5 / 28, 4 / 28, 3 / 28, 2 / 28, and 1 / 28, respectively, of the depreciable value.

Syntax:

SYD(*cost*,*salvage*,*life*,*per*)

The SYD function returns the sum-of-years'-digits depreciation of an asset for a specified period. This function takes the following arguments:

- *cost*—This is the initial cost of the asset.

- *salvage*—This is the value at the end of the depreciation period. Sometimes this is called the *salvage value* of the asset.

- *life*—This is the number of periods over which the asset is being depreciated. Sometimes this is called the *useful life* of the asset.

- *per*—This is the period and must use the same units as *life*.

Using VDB to Calculate Depreciation for Any Period

As mentioned in the discussion of the DDB function, the VDB function is newer and far more powerful than the other depreciation functions.

It is interesting for tax purposes to know the annual depreciation amounts. However, if you work for a public company, you have to report depreciation at least quarterly. Figure 13.12 shows an example that calculates the exact depreciation to be booked each quarter.

Syntax:

VDB(*cost*,*salvage*,*life*,*start_period*,*end_period*,*factor*,*no_switch*)

The VDB function returns the depreciation of an asset for any specified period, including partial periods, using the double-declining-balance method or some other specified method. VDB stands for *variable declining balance*.

The VDB function takes the following arguments:

- *cost*—This is the initial cost of the asset.

- *salvage*—This is the value at the end of the depreciation period.

Figure 13.12
VDB enables
you to calculate
depreciation
for each month
or quarter.

| C7 | ▼ | : | × | ✓ | f_x | =VDB($B$1,$B$2,$B$3*365,$A7-$B$4,$B7-$B$4,2,FALSE) |

◢	A	B	C	D	E	F
2	**Salvage Value**	5000				
3	**Useful Life**	7				
4	**Start Date**	5/1/2015				
5						
6	**Start Date**	**End Date**	**VDB**			
7	5/1/2015	6/30/2015	**$2,294.92**			
8	7/1/2015	9/30/2015	$3,278.63			
9	10/1/2015	12/31/2015	$3,050.74			
10	1/1/2016	3/31/2016	$2,808.57			
11	4/1/2016	6/30/2016	$2,615.40			
12	7/1/2016	9/30/2016	$2,461.61			
13						
14	**A7:**	=B4				
15	**C7:**	=VDB($B$1,$B$2,$B$3*365,$A7-$B$4,$B7-$B$4,2,FALSE)				
16	**A8:**	=+B7+1				
17	**C8:**	=VDB($B$1,$B$2,$B$3*365,$A8-$B$4,$B8-$B$4,2,FALSE)				

- ***life***—This is the number of periods over which the asset is being depreciated. To calculate depreciation for periods smaller than a year, multiply the number of years by 12, or even 365.

- ***start_period***—This is the starting period for which you want to calculate the depreciation. *start_period* must use the same units as *life*.

- ***end_period***—This is the ending period for which you want to calculate the depreciation. *end_period* must use the same units as *life*.

- ***factor***—This is the rate at which the balance declines. If *factor* is omitted, it is assumed to be 2, which is the double-declining-balance method. You change *factor* if you do not want to use the double-declining-balance method.

- ***no_switch***—This is a logical value that specifies whether to switch to straight-line depreciation when depreciation is greater than with the declining-balance calculation. If this is FALSE or omitted, Excel switches to the straight-line method when it becomes more beneficial to do so. If this value is TRUE, Excel holds on to the DDB method until the end of *life*.

 **Tip**

Keep in mind that all the arguments listed, except *no_switch*, must be positive numbers.

To set up a schedule that shows depreciation for each quarter, you follow these steps:

1. Enter the cost, salvage value, and useful life at the top of the worksheet.

2. Enter the date on which the equipment is placed in service in cell B4.

3. Enter dates for the first quarter in cells A7 and B7. The value in cell A7 is the date the unit is placed in service. Manually figure out the last date of the quarter for cell B7.

4. Ensure that the formula for columns A and B in each subsequent row is the same. In cell A8, enter **=B7+1**. In cell B8, enter **=EOMONTH(A8,2)**. The EOMONTH function reports the end of the month that falls two months after what is shown in cell A8. Copy these formulas down as far as necessary.

5. To build the VDB function, use the normal values for cost and salvage value. Instead of 7 for life, use 7 × 365 to have the function calculate a daily depreciation rate.

6. For *start_period*, use the date in column A minus the date in service.

7. For *end_period*, use the date in column B minus the date in service.

8. If you are using the double-declining-balance method, omit the fifth and sixth arguments.

9. Copy the VDB function down to all your rows.

The table in Figure 13.12 shows the depreciation to be booked each quarter for this particular piece of machinery.

Functions for Investment Analysis

The invention of the computer spreadsheet in 1979 enabled the rapid growth of the mergers and acquisitions business in the 1980s. Business plans can be modeled in Excel, with the resulting series of net income values discounted to determine the current value of a business. Excel offers a wide array of functions that you can use to analyze a business investment.

Using the NPV Function to Determine Net Present Value

Suppose that you have a pile of cash. You have the opportunity to invest that cash in a long-term CD that earns 2% interest. You also have the opportunity to use that cash to buy a business. The 2% is called the *hurdle rate*. If the business cannot return more than the 2% hurdle rate, you should probably look for another business.

You have analyzed the business plan and projected that the business will generate a certain series of net income over each of the next 5 years. You can analyze the net present value of the investment by using the NPV function.

> **Note**
>
> If you happen to work for a French-owned company, keep in mind special considerations when calculating depreciation. Read the Help topics for AMORDEGRC and AMORLINC to understand these methods that have been added to Excel to accommodate the French accounting rules.

Syntax:

NPV(*rate*,*value1*,*value2*,...)

The NPV function calculates the net present value of an investment by using a discount rate and a series of future payments (negative values) and income (positive values). This function takes the following arguments:

- **rate**—This is the rate of discount over the length of one period.

- **value1, value2, ...**—These are 1 to 254 arguments representing the payments and income. Instead, you can refer to a range of values. *value1, value2, ...* must be equally spaced in time and occur at the end of each period. The function uses the order of *value1, value2, ...* to interpret the order of cash flows. You need to be sure to enter your payment and income values in the correct sequence.

The NPV investment begins one period before the date of the *value1* cash flow and ends with the last cash flow in the list.

Arguments of *value1, value2, ...* are cash flows at the end of Year 1, Year 2, and so on.

In this example, if you buy a business for $50,000, this amount should not be entered as a value in the function. Instead, you should subtract the $50,000 from the result of NPV.

NPV is similar to the PV function. The primary difference between PV and NPV is that PV allows cash flows to begin either at the end or at the beginning of the period. Unlike the variable NPV cash flow values, PV cash flows must be constant throughout the investment.

NPV is also related to the IRR function. IRR is the rate for which NPV equals zero: NPV(IRR(...), ...) = 0.

In Figure 13.13, the business will cost $50,000. The business will lose $5,000 in Year 1 and then generate $61,000 over the next 4 years. Based on these cash flows, NPV is positive, which means that the investment will do better than a CD at 2% interest.

> **Note**
>
> NPV requires the cash flows to occur at a regular rate. If you instead have a series of projected cash flows on varying dates, you should use XNPV instead. See the section "Using XNPV to Calculate the Net Present Value When the Payments Are Not Periodic," later in this chapter.

Using IRR to Calculate the Return of a Series of Cash Flows

In the previous section, you used the NPV function to determine whether a business investment met or did not meet a certain desired rate of return. In Figure 13.13, NPV is positive, indicating that the business was able to beat a 2% return after 5 years. If you want to figure out the internal rate of return, use the IRR function.

One critical difference exists between IRR and NPV: In the NPV function, the initial investment in the business is *not* included in

> **Note**
>
> IRR fails to take into account that the money earned in Year 1 could start generating interest if invested in a CD. To calculate a rate of return including the reinvestment of profits, use MIRR, which is described in the following section.

| C14 | ▾ | : | × | ✓ | fx | =FORMULATEXT(B14) |

▲	A	B	C	D
1	**Discount Rate**	2%		
2	**Cost of Business:**	-50,000		
3	**Return from year 1:**	-5,000		
4	**Return from year 2:**	5,000		
5	**Return from year 3:**	12,000		
6	**Return from year 4:**	19,000		
7	**Return from year 5:**	25,000		
8				
9	**NPV**	**1,408**	=NPV(B1,B3:B7)+B2	
10				
13	**Internal Rates of Return:**			
14	**After 2 years:**	-72.98%	=IRR(B$2:B4,-0.5)	
15	**After 3 years:**	-35.93%	=IRR(B$2:B5,0.01)	
16	**After 4 years:**	-11.97%	=IRR(B$2:B6)	
17	**After 5 years:**	**2.66%**	=IRR(B$2:B7)	

Figure 13.13
NPV can analyze a periodic series of cash flows.

the list of arguments. In the IRR function, the initial investment in the business needs to be included as the first cash flow. Because this is money paid for the business, it should be negative.

Syntax:

`IRR(values,guess)`

The IRR function returns the internal rate of return for a series of cash flows, represented by the numbers in *values*. These cash flows do not have to be even, as they would be for an annuity. However, the cash flows must occur at regular intervals, such as monthly or annually. The internal rate of return is the interest rate received for an investment, consisting of payments (negative values) and income (positive values) that occur at regular periods.

The IRR function takes the following arguments:

- ■ *values*—This is an array or a reference to cells that contain numbers for which you want to calculate the internal rate of return. *values* must contain at least one positive value and one negative value to calculate the internal rate of return. IRR uses the order of *values* to interpret

 Caution
The algorithm behind the IRR function is new and more accurate in Excel 2013. Be aware that Excel 2007 and Excel 2013 might produce different results for some uses of IRR.

the order of cash flows. You need to be sure to enter your payment and income values in the sequence you want. If an array or a reference argument contains text, logical values, or empty cells, those values are ignored.

- *guess*—This is a number that you guess is close to the result of IRR. Microsoft Excel uses an iterative technique for calculating IRR. Starting with *guess*, IRR cycles through the calculation until the result is accurate within 0.00001%. If IRR cannot find a result that works after 20 tries, a #NUM! error is returned. In most cases, you do not need to provide *guess* for the IRR calculation. If *guess* is omitted, it is assumed to be 0.1, which is 10%. If IRR gives a #NUM! error, or if the result is not close to what you expected, you can try again with a different value for *guess*.

IRR is closely related to NPV, the net present value function. The rate of return calculated by IRR is the interest rate corresponding to a net present value of zero. The following formula demonstrates how NPV and IRR are related: Enter = **NPV(IRR(B1:B6),B1:B6)** in a cell, which equals 3.60E-08. Within the accuracy of the IRR calculation, the value 3.60E-08 is effectively zero.

In Figure 13.13, the formula in cell B17 shows that the business investment would generate a rate of return of 2.66% if analyzed over a 5-year period. The arguments for this function include the initial $50,000 investment in the business as well as the net incomes from the next 5 years.

Similar formulas in cells B14 and B15 return a #NUM! error. The formulas were edited to add a *guess* value. Based on the –12% return through 4 years, *guess* for 3 years was –10%.

Using MIRR to Calculate Internal Rate of Return, Including Interest Rates

MIRR calculates a modified internal rate of return. This function assumes that cash flows from the business are reinvested at some interest rate. It also offers an argument to specify the initial interest rate of the business loan used to purchase the business.

Syntax:

MIRR(*values*,*finance_rate*,*reinvest_rate*)

The MIRR function returns the modified internal rate of return for a series of periodic cash flows. MIRR considers both the cost of the investment and the interest received on reinvestment of cash. This function takes the following arguments:

- *values*—This is an array or a reference to cells that contain numbers. These numbers represent a series of payments (negative values) and income (positive values) occurring at regular periods. *values* must contain at least one positive value and one negative value to calculate the modified internal rate of return. Otherwise, MIRR returns a #DIV/0! error. If an array or a reference argument contains text, logical values, or empty cells, those values are ignored; however, cells with the value 0 are included.

- *finance_rate*—This is the interest rate you pay on the money used in the cash flows.

- *reinvest_rate*—This is the interest rate you receive on the cash flows as you reinvest them.

MIRR uses the order of values to interpret the order of cash flows. You need to be sure to enter your payment and income values in the sequence you want and with the correct signs. In other words, enter positive values for cash received and negative values for cash paid.

In Figure 13.14, you are analyzing a business that was started 5 years ago with a $120,000 loan. The business has generated profits of $17,000, $34,000, $38,000, $5,000, and $32,000. The original loan had an interest rate of 4%, and the profits were reinvested at 0.10%. The MIRR in cell B10 is 1.0%. For comparison, the IRR of the same cash flows would be 1.64%.

	A	B	C
	B10 ▾ : ✕ ✓ *fx* =MIRR(B1:B6,B7,B8)		
1	**Cost of Business:**	($120,000)	
2	**Return first year**	17,000	
3	**Return second year**	34,000	
4	**Return third year**	38,000	
5	**Return fourth year**	5,000	
6	**Return fifth year**	32,000	
7	**Int. rate for $120K Loan**	4.00%	
8	**Int. rate for reinvested profits**	0.10%	
9			
10	**MIRR**	**1.0%** =MIRR(B1:B6,B7,B8)	
11			

Figure 13.14
You can determine a modified rate of return, figuring in a financing rate and the interest rate for reinvested profits.

Using XNPV to Calculate the Net Present Value When the Payments Are Not Periodic

The previous examples assume that everything happens on the last day of each year. In reality, the business purchase date and the business sales date might occur on other days. In such a case, you use XNPV.

Syntax:

XNPV(*rate*,*values*,*dates*)

The XNPV function returns the net present value for a schedule of cash flows that is not necessarily periodic. To calculate the net present value for a series of cash flows that is periodic, you use the NPV function. The XNPV function takes the following arguments:

- **rate**—This is the discount rate to apply to the cash flows.

- **values**—This is a series of cash flows that corresponds to a schedule of payments in dates. The first payment is optional and corresponds to a cost or payment that occurs at the beginning of the investment. If the first value is a cost or payment, it must be a negative value. All succeeding payments are discounted based on a 365-day year. The series of values must contain at least one positive value and one negative value.

- **dates**—This is a schedule of payment dates that corresponds to the cash flow payments. The first payment date indicates the beginning of the schedule of payments. All other dates must be later than this date, but they may occur in any order. Only dates are considered; any times appended to the dates are truncated.

If any argument is nonnumeric, XNPV returns a #VALUE! error. If any number in dates is not a valid date, XNPV returns a #NUM! error. If any number in dates precedes the starting date, XNPV returns a #NUM! error. If *values* and *dates* contain different numbers of values, XNPV returns a #NUM! error.

In Figure 13.15, the company was purchased on March 15, 2010. The company posted no net profit in 2010. The company was sold in February 2015. The *XNPV* function in row 9 shows that this deal clearly beat the 3% hurdle rate.

Figure 13.15
XNPV takes into account a series of cash flows on a series of dates. The dates do not have to have identical periods, as in NPV.

	A	B	C	D	E
	B9 ▼ : × ✓ *fx* =XNPV(B1,B2:B7,A2:A7)				
1	**Discount Rate**	3%			
2	3/15/2010	-50,000	*Buy the business*		
3	12/31/2010	-5,000	*Loss in year 1*		
4	12/30/2012	5,000	*profit in year 3*		
5	12/31/2013	12,000	*more profit in year 4*		
6	12/31/2014	19,000	*profit in year 5*		
7	2/17/2015	242,000	*sell the business*		
8					
9	XNPV	186,106	=XNPV(B1,B2:B7,A2:A7)		
10					
11	XIRR	40.71%	=XIRR(B2:B7,A2:A7)		
12					

Using XIRR to Calculate a Return Rate When Cash Flow Dates Are Not Periodic

As in the XNPV example, you can calculate an internal rate of return for a business deal where the dates do not necessarily fall on the last day of the year. To do so, use XIRR, as shown in the example at the bottom of Figure 13.15.

Syntax:

XIRR(*values*,*dates*,*guess*)

The XIRR function returns the internal rate of return for a schedule of cash flows that is not necessarily periodic. To calculate the internal rate of return for a series of periodic cash flows, use the IRR function. This function takes the following arguments:

- *values*—This is a series of cash flows that corresponds to a schedule of payments in *dates*. The first payment is optional and corresponds to a cost or payment that occurs at the beginning of the investment. If the first value is a cost or payment, it must be a negative value. All succeeding payments are discounted based on a 365-day year. The series of values must contain at least one positive and one negative value.

- *dates*—This is a schedule of payment dates that corresponds to the cash flow payments. The first payment date indicates the beginning of the schedule of payments. All other dates must be later than this date, but they may occur in any order.

- *guess*—This is a number that you guess is close to the result of XIRR.

Numbers in *dates* are truncated to integers. XIRR expects at least one positive cash flow and one negative cash flow; otherwise, XIRR returns a #NUM! error. If any number in *dates* is not a valid date, XIRR returns a #NUM! error. If any number in *dates* precedes the starting date, XIRR returns a #NUM! error. If *values* and *dates* contain different numbers of values, XIRR returns a #NUM! error. In most cases, you do not need to provide *guess* for the XIRR calculation. If it is omitted, *guess* is assumed to be 0.1, which is 10%.

Caution

The algorithm behind the XIRR function is new and more accurate in Excel 2013. Be aware that Excel 2007 and Excel 2013 might produce different results for some uses of XIRR.

XIRR is closely related to XNPV, the net present value function.
The rate of return calculated by XIRR is the interest rate corresponding to XNPV = 0.

Examples of Functions for Bond Investors

A bond is an I.O.U. in which you lend an amount to the issuer. The issuer pays you periodic interest payments and at the maturity date of the bond returns your money. Various governments issue many bonds. Bond maturities can extend anywhere from 1 day to 30 years. Many concepts and terms apply to the bond functions.

For the following discussion, let's assume that a city issues a 30-year municipal bond. The bond is issued on July 1, 2015. The bond's maturity date is June 30, 2044. The city agrees to pay 3% interest semiannually.

Here is what makes bonds interesting: They can be bought and sold after the issue date. Suppose that 14 months have gone past. Interest rates have now risen. The bond is going to keep paying 3% interest for the next 30 years. If interest rates have moved above 3%, a potential buyer of the bond will not want to pay $1,000 for the bond. Instead, the buyer might pay $950. Thus, there is a price paid for the bond, and there is a value of the bond at maturity.

Many bond functions ask for these arguments:

- **settlement**—This is the day that the buyer purchases the bond. It might be the issue date but is usually after the issue date. In the preceding example, the settlement date is September 1, 2015.

- **maturity**—This is the day that the issuer will pay the face value of the bond. In the preceding example, the maturity date is June 30, 2044.

- **rate**—This is the published coupon rate for the bond. In the preceding example, it is 3%.

- **pr**—This is the price that the current buyer paid for the bond. If the bond was purchased on the issue date, the price matches the face value of the bond. If it was purchased on a later date, the price is higher or lower than the face value, depending on whether interest rates go up or down. For example, if interest rates go up, bond prices go down. If interest rates go down, bond prices go up. The *pr* is expressed as the price per $100 of face value. If you buy a $1,000 face-value bond for $950, the price is $95 per $100, so you enter 95 for the *pr* argument.

- **redemption**—This is the value of the bond on the maturity date. It is the amount the issuer will pay back to the holder of the bond. The price is expressed as the price per $100 of face value. If you buy a $1,000 face-value bond that will pay $1,000 at maturity, you enter 100 for the *redemption* argument.

- **frequency**—This is the number of interest payments per year. For semiannual interest payments, enter 2. For quarterly payments, enter 4. For annual payments, enter 1. In Excel, these are the only three *frequency* values allowed.

- **basis**—This is a code used to identify the number of days in a year. The values are the same as those available in the YEARFRAC function. For most U.S. bonds, *basis* is 0 to indicate a 30/360 NASD calendar. For European bonds, consult Excel Help for the YIELD function.

> For more information on basis, **see** *"Using* YEARFRAC, DATEDIF *or* DAYS *to Calculate Elapsed Time,"* **p. 262.**

Using YIELD to Calculate a Bond's Yield

A $1,000 bond might promise to pay 3% interest. However, if you buy the bond on the secondary market for $95, the actual yield will not be 3%. As you are trying to compare various investments, comparing the yield is one way to decide between multiple investment opportunities. To do this, you can use Excel's YIELD function.

Syntax:

YIELD(*settlement*,*maturity*,*rate*,*pr*,*redemption*,*frequency*,*basis*)

The YIELD function returns the yield on a security that pays periodic interest. You use YIELD to calculate bond yield. This function takes the following arguments:

- ■ *settlement*—This is the security's settlement date. The security settlement date is the date after the issue date when the security is traded to the buyer. Dates may be entered as the following:

  - ■ Text strings within quotation marks, such as "9/1/2015" and "2015/09/01"

  - ■ Serial numbers such as 42248, which represents September 1, 2015

  - ■ Results of other formulas or functions, such as DATE(2015,9,1)

- ■ *maturity*—This is the security's maturity date. The maturity date is the date when the security expires.

- ■ *rate*—This is the security's annual coupon rate.

- ■ *pr*—This is the security's price per $100 face value.

- ■ *redemption*—This is the security's redemption value per $100 face value.

- ■ *frequency*—This is the number of coupon payments per year. For annual payments, *frequency* is 1; for semiannual, *frequency* is 2; and for quarterly, *frequency* is 4.

- ■ *basis*—This is the type of day count basis to use. It defaults to 0, which is appropriate for U.S. bonds.

The *settlement*, *maturity*, *frequency*, and *basis* arguments are truncated to integers. If *settlement* or *maturity* is not a valid date, YIELD returns a #NUM! error. If *rate* is less than 0, YIELD returns a #NUM! error. If *pr* is less than or equal to 0 or if *redemption* is less than or equal to 0, YIELD returns a #NUM! error. If *frequency* is any number other than 1, 2, or 4, YIELD returns a #NUM! error. If *basis* is less than 0 or if *basis* is greater than 4, YIELD returns a #NUM! error. If *settlement* is greater than or equal to *maturity*, YIELD returns a #NUM! error.

Figure 13.16 shows an example of YIELD.

Figure 13.16
Use YIELD to calculate
the yield rate for a
bond. In these exam-
ples, the price in row 4
changes.

	A	B	C	D
	B9 f_x =YIELD(B1,B2,B3,B4,B5,B6,B7)			
1	Settlement date	1-Sep-15	1-Sep-15	1-Sep-15
2	Maturity date	30-Jun-44	30-Jun-44	30-Jun-44
3	Percent coupon	3.00%	3.00%	3.00%
4	Price	$95	$93	$105
5	Redemption value	$100	$100	$100
6	Frequency	2	2	2
7	30/360 basis	0	0	0
8				
9	Yield	3.27%	3.38%	2.75%
10		=YIELD(B1,B2,B3,B4,B5,B6,B7)		

Using PRICE to Back into a Bond Price

If you know the yield for a bond, you can use PRICE to calculate the price per $100 of face value.

Syntax:

PRICE(*settlement*,*maturity*,*rate*,*yld*,*redemption*,*frequency*,*basis*)

The PRICE function returns the price per $100 face value of a security that pays periodic interest. This function takes the following arguments:

- *settlement*—This is the security's settlement date, which is the date on which you purchased the bond.

- *maturity*—This is the security's maturity date, which is the date when the security expires.

- *rate*—This is the security's annual coupon rate.

- *yld*—This is the security's annual yield.

- *redemption*—This is the security's redemption value per $100 face value.

- *frequency*—This is the number of coupon payments per year. For example, use 2 for semiannual.

- *basis*—This is the type of day count basis to use. For example, use 0 for U.S. bonds.

The *settlement*, *maturity*, *frequency*, and *basis* arguments are truncated to integers. If *settlement* or *maturity* is not a valid date, PRICE returns a #NUM! error. If *yld* is less than 0 or if *rate* is less than 0, PRICE returns a #NUM! error. If *redemption* is less than or equal to 0, PRICE returns a #NUM! error. If *frequency* is any number other than 1, 2, or 4, PRICE returns a #NUM! error. If *basis* is less than 0 or if *basis* is greater than 4, PRICE returns a #NUM! error. If *settlement* is greater than or equal to *maturity*, PRICE returns a #NUM! error.

In Figure 13.17, the yield for the bond exceeds the coupon rate. This indicates that the price will be less than $100.

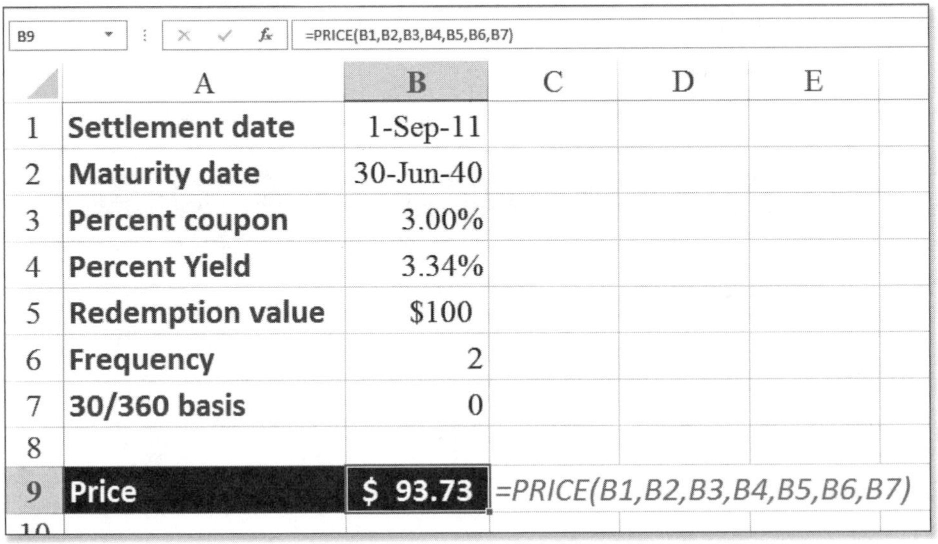

B9 =PRICE(B1,B2,B3,B4,B5,B6,B7)

	A	B	C	D	E
1	Settlement date	1-Sep-11			
2	Maturity date	30-Jun-40			
3	Percent coupon	3.00%			
4	Percent Yield	3.34%			
5	Redemption value	$100			
6	Frequency	2			
7	30/360 basis	0			
8					
9	Price	$ 93.73	=PRICE(B1,B2,B3,B4,B5,B6,B7)		
10					

Figure 13.17 If you know the yield, you can back into the price by using the PRICE function.

When a bond is sold on the secondary market, it is often sold in between interest payments. Each interest payment date is called a *coupon date*. You analyze days until the next coupon date by using the COUP functions.

A whole series of COUP functions analyze the coupon period. The functions can tell you the previous coupon date, the next coupon date, how many days since the previous coupon date, and how many days until the next coupon date:

- **COUPDAYS**—This returns the number of days in this coupon period.
- **COUPDAYBS**—This returns the number of days from the beginning of the coupon period until the settlement date. The BS in the function name stands for *from beginning to settlement*.
- **COUPDAYSNC**—This returns the number of days from the settlement until the next coupon date. NC stands for *next coupon*.
- **COUPPCD**—This returns the date of the previous coupon date.

- **COUPNCD**—This returns the date of the next coupon date.

- **COUPNUM**—This returns the number of coupon dates left until maturity.

All the COUP functions require the same four arguments: *settlement*, *maturity*, *frequency*, and *basis*. For an explanation of these arguments, see the sections on YIELD and PRICE.

Figure 13.18 shows these coupon functions for a particular security.

Figure 13.18
You can analyze what portion of a coupon period has gone past at the settlement date for the bond.

B5	fx	=COUPDAYS(B$1,B$2,B$3)		
	A		B	C
1	Settlement date		15-Jan-15	
2	Maturity date		30-Jun-44	
3	Frequency		4	
4				
5	# days in this coupon period		90	=COUPDAYS(B$1,B$2,B$3)
6	# days from beginning to settlement		15	=COUPDAYBS(B$1,B$2,B$3)
7	# days from settlement to next coupon		75	=COUPDAYSNC(B$1,B$2,B$3)
8	Previous coupon date		12/31/14	=COUPPCD(B$1,B$2,B$3)
9	Next coupon date		3/31/15	=COUPNCD(B$1,B$2,B$3)
10	Number of coupon dates remaining		118	=COUPNUM(B$1,B$2,B$3)

Using RECEIVED to Calculate Total Cash Generated from a Bond Investment

When you buy a bond, your settlement date is probably between two coupon dates. Unless you are buying the bond on the issue date, you receive less than the complete number of interest payments. To calculate the total future cash flows from a bond from the day you buy it until the maturity date, you use the RECEIVED function.

Syntax:

RECEIVED(*settlement*,*maturity*,*investment*,*discount*,*basis*)

The RECEIVED function returns the amount received at maturity for a fully invested security. This function takes the following arguments:

- **settlement**—This is the security's settlement date, which is the date on which you purchased the security.

- **maturity**—This is the security's maturity date, which is the date when the security expires.

- **investment**—This is the amount invested in the security.

- *discount*—This is the security's discount rate.

- *basis*—This is the type of day count basis to use. For example, use 0 for U.S. bonds.

The *settlement*, *maturity*, and *basis* arguments are truncated to integers. If *settlement* or *maturity* is not a valid date, RECEIVED returns a #NUM! error. If *investment* is less than or equal to 0 or if *discount* is less than or equal to 0, RECEIVED returns a #NUM! error. If *basis* is less than 0 or if *basis* is greater than or equal to 4, RECEIVED returns a #NUM! error. If *settlement* is greater than or equal to *maturity*, RECEIVED returns a #NUM! error.

In Figure 13.19, columns B, C, and D show the total received for a bond purchased on various dates. The function takes into account the days to the next coupon date.

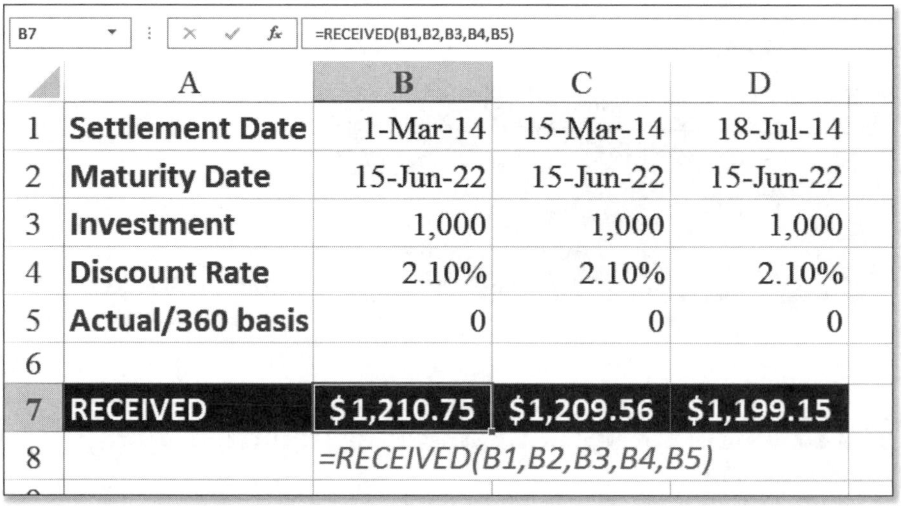

B7	▾	:	× ✓ *fx*	=RECEIVED(B1,B2,B3,B4,B5)		
	A		B	C	D	
1	Settlement Date		1-Mar-14	15-Mar-14	18-Jul-14	
2	Maturity Date		15-Jun-22	15-Jun-22	15-Jun-22	
3	Investment		1,000	1,000	1,000	
4	Discount Rate		2.10%	2.10%	2.10%	
5	Actual/360 basis		0	0	0	
6						
7	RECEIVED		$1,210.75	$1,209.56	$1,199.15	
8			=RECEIVED(B1,B2,B3,B4,B5)			

Figure 13.19
In the 15 days between cells B1 and C1, you lose $1.19 in interest.

Using INTRATE to Back into the Coupon Interest Rate

If you have a fully invested bond and know what it will pay on maturity, you can use Excel's INTRATE function to back into the interest rate.

Syntax:

INTRATE(*settlement,maturity,investment,redemption,basis*)

The INTRATE function returns the interest rate for a fully invested security. This function takes the following arguments:

- *settlement*—This is the security's settlement date.

- *maturity*—This is the security's maturity date.

- *investment*—This is the amount invested in the security.

- *redemption*—This is the amount to be received at maturity.

- *basis*—This is the type of day count basis to use. You use 0 for U.S. bonds.

The *settlement*, *maturity*, and *basis* arguments are truncated to integers. If *settlement* or *maturity* is not a valid date, INTRATE returns a #NUM! error. If *investment* is less than or equal to 0 or if *redemption* is less than or equal to 0, INTRATE returns a #NUM! error. If *basis* is less than 0 or if *basis* is greater than 4, INTRATE returns a #NUM! error. If *settlement* is greater than or equal to *maturity*, INTRATE returns a #NUM! error.

INTRATE calculates

(Redemption value – Investment) / Investment

and multiplies this by

(Number of days in year / Days from *settlement* to maturity).

In Figure 13.20, Excel uses INTRATE to back into the interest rate that the bond is paying.

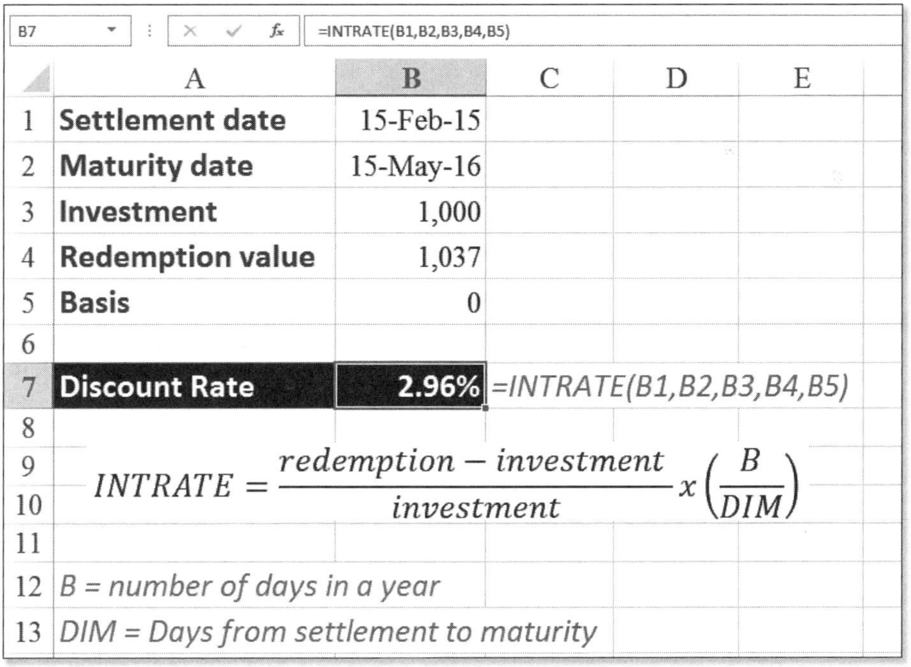

Figure 13.20
You can use the INTRATE function to derive the underlying interest rate for the bond.

B7		:	×	✓	*fx*	=INTRATE(B1,B2,B3,B4,B5)

	A	B	C	D	E
1	**Settlement date**	15-Feb-15			
2	**Maturity date**	15-May-16			
3	**Investment**	1,000			
4	**Redemption value**	1,037			
5	**Basis**	0			
6					
7	**Discount Rate**	**2.96%**	=INTRATE(B1,B2,B3,B4,B5)		
8					

$$INTRATE = \frac{redemption - investment}{investment} x \left(\frac{B}{DIM}\right)$$

B = number of days in a year

DIM = Days from settlement to maturity

Using DISC to Back into the Discount Rate

If you have a security and know the price, you can back into the discount rate by using DISC.

Syntax:

DISC(*settlement*,*maturity*,*pr*,*redemption*,*basis*)

The DISC function returns the discount rate for a security. It takes the following arguments:

- **settlement**—This is the security's settlement date.

- **maturity**—This is the security's maturity date. The maturity date is the date when the security expires.

- **pr**—This is the security's price per $100 face value.

- **redemption**—This is the security's redemption value per $100 face value.

- **basis**—This is the day count basis. You use 0 for U.S. bonds.

The *settlement*, *maturity*, and *basis* arguments are truncated to integers. If *settlement* or *maturity* is not a valid date, DISC returns a #NUM! error. If *pr* is less than or equal to 0 or if *redemption* is less than or equal to 0, DISC returns a #NUM! error. If *basis* is less than 0 or if *basis* is greater than 4, DISC returns a #NUM! error. If *settlement* is greater than or equal to *maturity*, DISC returns a #NUM! error.

DISC calculates

(Redemption value – Par value) / Par value

and multiplies this by

(Number of days in year / Days from settlement to *maturity*)

In Figure 13.21, Excel uses DISC to back into the discount rate.

Handling Bonds with an Odd Number of Days in the First or Last Period

Excel provides four functions—ODDFPRICE, ODDFYIELD, ODDLPRICE, and ODDLYIELD—to handle the special case in which a bond has a short or long first or last period. This period has more or fewer days than all the other periods and is called an *odd period*.

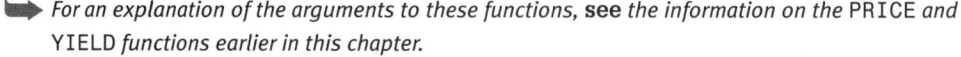 *For an explanation of the arguments to these functions,* **see** *the information on the* PRICE *and* YIELD *functions earlier in this chapter.*

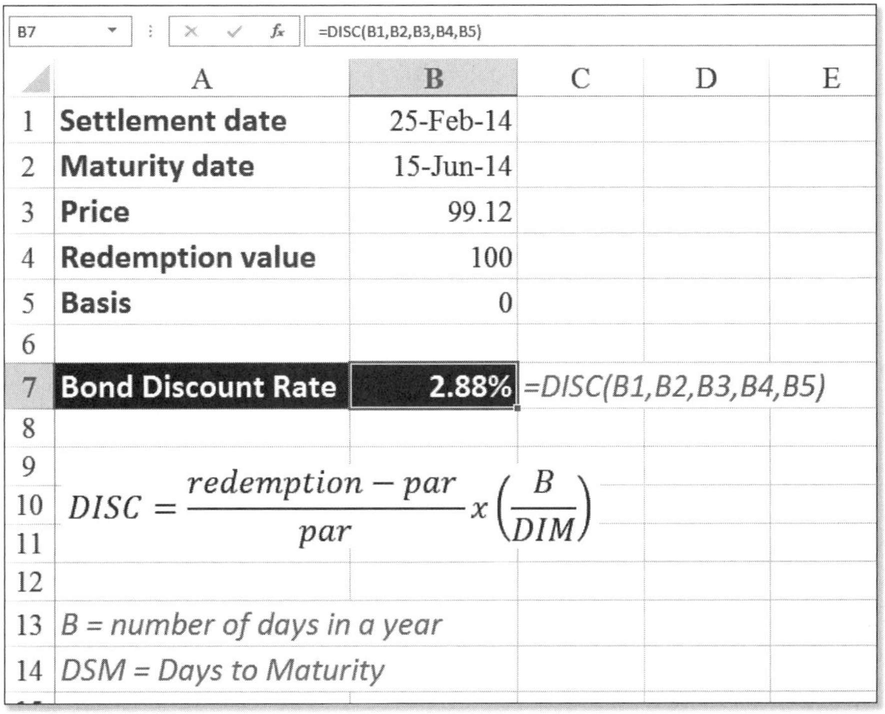

Figure 13.21
You can use the
DISC function to
derive the underly-
ing discount rate
for a bond.

		B7 ▾ : × ✓ fx	=DISC(B1,B2,B3,B4,B5)			
		A	B	C	D	E
	1	**Settlement date**	25-Feb-14			
	2	**Maturity date**	15-Jun-14			
	3	**Price**	99.12			
	4	**Redemption value**	100			
	5	**Basis**	0			
	6					
	7	**Bond Discount Rate**	**2.88%**	=DISC(B1,B2,B3,B4,B5)		
	8					
	9					
	10	$DISC = \dfrac{redemption - par}{par} \ x \left(\dfrac{B}{DIM}\right)$				
	11					
	12					
	13	*B = number of days in a year*				
	14	*DSM = Days to Maturity*				

Syntax:

```
ODDFPRICE(settlement,maturity,issue,first_coupon,rate,yld,redemption,frequency,
↪basis)
ODDFYIELD (settlement,maturity,issue,first_coupon,rate,pr,redemption,frequency,
↪basis)
```

The ODDF functions handle cases in which the first period has an odd number of days. These are
ODDFPRICE and ODDFYIELD. Each function has the extra argument *first_coupon*, which specifies
the date for the odd first period.

Syntax:

```
ODDLPRICE(settlement,maturity,last_interest,rate,yld,redemption,frequency,basis)
ODDLYIELD(settlement,maturity,last_interest,rate,pr,redemption,frequency,basis)
```

The ODDL functions handle cases in which the last period has an odd number of days. These are
ODDLPRICE and ODDLYIELD. These functions have the extra argument *last_interest*, which is the
date of the final interest payment before maturity. Using this date, Excel can determine the length of
the time for the last period.

Using PRICEMAT and YIELDMAT to Calculate Price and Yield for Zero-Coupon Bonds

A zero-coupon bond does not pay interest on the coupon dates. All interest is paid at maturity. Excel provides PRICEMAT and YIELDMAT to calculate price and yield for these securities. Figure 13.22 illustrates both of these functions.

	A	B	C	D	E	F
1	Settlement date	15-Feb-15				
2	Maturity date	13-Apr-15				
3	Issue date	11-Nov-14				
4	Percent semiannual coupon	3.10%				
5	Percent yield	3.10%				
6	30/360 basis	0				
7						
8	PRICEMAT	99.995977	=PRICEMAT(B1,B2,B3,B4,B5,B6)			
9						
10	Settlement date	15-Feb-15				
11	Maturity date	13-Apr-15				
12	Issue date	11-Nov-14				
13	Percent semiannual coupon	3.10%				
14	Price	100.0123				
15	30/360 basis	0				
16						
17	YIELDMAT	3.00%	=YIELDMAT(B10,B11,B12,B13,B14,B15)			

Cell B8 formula bar: =PRICEMAT(B1,B2,B3,B4,B5,B6)

Figure 13.22
YIELDMAT and PRICEMAT calculate bonds for which the interest is not paid until maturity.

Syntax:

PRICEMAT(*settlement_date*,*maturity_date*,*issue_date*,*rate_at_date_of_issue*,
➡*annual_yield*,*day_basis*)

The PRICEMAT function returns the price per $100 face value of a security that pays interest at maturity.

Syntax:

YIELDMAT(*settlement_date*,*maturity_date*,*issue_date*,*rate_at_date_of_issue*,
➡*price_per_$100_of_face_value*,*day_basis*)

The YIELDMAT function returns the annual yield of a security that pays interest at maturity.

Using PRICEDISC and YIELDDISC to Calculate Discount Bonds

Excel provides PRICEDISC and YIELDDISC for calculating discounted bonds. Figure 13.23 illustrates these functions.

Figure 13.23
YIELDDISC and PRICEDISC calculate discounted bonds.

	A	B	C
	B8 ▾ : ✕ ✓ *fx*	=PRICEDISC(B2,B3,B4,B5,B6)	
1	**Description**	**Data**	
2	**Settlement date**	16-Feb-15	
3	**Maturity date**	1-Mar-15	
4	**Percent discount rate**	2.25%	
5	**Redemption value**	$100	
6	**Day Basis**	0	
7			
8	**Bond Price**	**99.90625**	*=PRICEDISC(B2,B3,B4,B5,B6)*
9			
10	**Settlement date**	16-Feb-15	
11	**Maturity date**	1-Mar-15	
12	**Price**	99.90625	
13	**Redemption value**	$100	
14	**Actual/360 basis**	0	
15			
16	**YIELDDISC**	**2.25%**	*=YIELDDISC(B10,B11,B12,B13,B14)*

Syntax:

PRICEDISC(*settlement_date*,*maturity_date*,*discount_rate*,*redemption_value_per_$100*,
➥*day_basis*)

The PRICEDISC function returns the price per $100 face value of a discounted security.

Syntax:

YIELDDISC(*settlement_date*,*maturity_date*,*price_per_$100_face_value*,
➥*redemption_value_per_$100_of_face_value*,*day_basis*)

The YIELDDISC function returns the annual yield for a discounted security.

Calculating T-Bills

Treasury bills, which are also referred to as *T-bills*, are a popular short-term investment. Backed by the U.S. government, T-bills are considered one of the safest investments, although they offer a slightly lower interest rate than other types of investments.

The Federal Reserve uses a strange method for advertising the yield on T-bills: The Fed compares the total interest to the final value paid on maturity. This is backward from every other bond yield.

For example, suppose that you pay $98.70 for a T-bill that will pay $100 on maturity 13 weeks later. The Fed expresses the yield by comparing the $1.30 in interest to the $100 final value. Every other bond yield compares the $1.30 in interest to the $98.70 invested.

The Excel TBILL functions enable you to compare T-bills and regular bonds. Figure 13.24 illustrates the three T-bill functions.

B5	▾	:	× ✓ ƒx	=TBILLEQ(B1,B2,B3)	
	A		B	C	
1	**Settlement date**		31-Mar-15		
2	**Maturity date**		1-Jun-15		
3	**Percent discount rate**		2.375%		
4					
5	**Bond Equivalent Yield**		**2.418%**	*=TBILLEQ(B1,B2,B3)*	
6					
7	**Settlement date**		31-Mar-15		
8	**Maturity date**		1-Jun-15		
9	**Percent discount rate**		2.375%		
10					
11	**T-Bill Price**		**99.590972**	*=TBILLPRICE(B7,B8,B9)*	
12					
13	**Settlement date**		31-Mar-15		
14	**Maturity date**		1-Jun-15		
15	**Price per $100 face value**		99.42		
16					
17	**T-Bill Yield**		**3.39%**	*=TBILLYIELD(B13,B14,B15)*	

Figure 13.24
TBILLEQ and the other TBILL functions deal with the irregularities of T-bill investing.

Syntax:

TBILLEQ(*settlement_date*,*maturity_date*,*discount_rate*)

The TBILLEQ function returns the bond-equivalent yield for a T-bill.

Syntax:

TBILLPRICE(*settlement_date,maturity_date,discount_rate*)

The TBILLPRICE function returns the price per $100 face value for a T-bill.

Syntax:

TBILLYIELD(*settlement_date,maturity_date,price_per_$100_face_value*)

The TBILLYIELD function returns the yield for a T-bill.

Using ACCRINT or ACCINTM to Calculate Accrued Interest

If you are the original buyer of a bond and you buy that bond after the issue date, the bond will have earned some accrued interest during that gap. As the original buyer of the bond, you generally pay this interest back to the issuer when you take possession of the bond. This basically simplifies accounting for the issuer, which can issue identical payments at the next coupon date without having to worry about dozens of different settlement dates.

The ACCRINT function calculates this accrued interest.

Syntax:

ACCRINT(*issue,first_interest,settlement,rate,par,frequency,basis*)

The ACCRINT function returns the accrued interest for a security that pays periodic interest. This function takes the following arguments:

- *issue*—This is the security's issue date.

- *first_interest*—This is the security's first interest date.

- *settlement*—This is the security's settlement date. The security settlement date is the date after the issue date when the security is traded to the buyer. The ACCRINT function calculates the interest that would have been earned between the issue date and the settlement date.

- *rate*—This is the security's annual coupon rate.

- *par*—This is the security's par value. If you omit par, ACCRINT uses $1,000.

- *frequency*—This is the number of coupon payments per year.

- *basis*—This is the type of day count basis to use. You use 0 for U.S. bonds.

If *issue* is greater than or equal to *settlement*, ACCRINT returns a #NUM! error.

 Note

The ACCRINTM function calculates accrued interest for zero-coupon bonds, as shown in row 18 in Figure 13.25.

Figure 13.25 demonstrates how the accrued interest changes when the gap between the issue date and settlement date extends.

	A	B	C	D	E	F
		B9 ▾ : ✕ ✓ *fx* =ACCRINT(B1,B2,B3,B4,B5,B6,B7)				
1	Issue date	1-Apr-15	1-Apr-15	1-Apr-15	1-Apr-15	1-Apr-15
2	First interest date	31-Aug-15	31-Aug-15	31-Aug-15	31-Aug-15	31-Aug-15
3	Settlement date	1-Jun-15	7-Apr-15	14-Apr-15	1-May-15	15-May-15
4	Coupon rate	3.00%	3.00%	3.00%	3.00%	3.00%
5	Par value	1,000	1,000	1,000	1,000	1,000
6	Frequency	2	2	2	2	2
7	30/360 basis	0	0	0	0	0
8						
9	Accrued Interest	5.00	0.50	1.08	2.50	3.67
10		=ACCRINT(B1,B2,B3,B4,B5,B6,B7)				
11						
12	Issue date	1-Apr-15				
13	Maturity date	15-Jun-15				
14	Percent coupon	3.00%				
15	Par value	$1,000				
16	30/360 basis	0				
17						
18	Accrued Interest	6.16667	=ACCRINTM(B12,B13,B14,B15,B16)			

Figure 13.25
As the original buyer of the bond, you owe the accrued interest to the issuer.

Using DURATION to Understand Price Volatility

Duration is a measurement, in years, of how long it takes for the price of a bond to be repaid by its cash flows. This measurement is not relevant for zero-coupon bonds because with a zero-coupon bond, the duration is simultaneous with the maturity date.

Suppose that you have a 20-year bond with a 9% yield that pays interest twice a year. It might take about 6 years of interest payments before you earn back the original purchase price of the bond.

Duration is constantly changing. Immediately after a coupon date, the duration goes up slightly because the interest payment is no longer counted as a future cash flow. However, over the life of the bond, the duration gets progressively shorter, until the duration date corresponds with the maturity date. Duration is important because the higher the duration, the higher the price volatility for the security.

When Excel uses the DURATION function to calculate a duration, it uses the method designed by Frederick Macaulay in the 1930s. This method multiplies the present value of each cash flow by the time it is received. Those values are summed and divided by the total price for the security.

Excel also has a modified duration function, MDURATION. This function calculates the duration if the yield would increase by 1 percentage point. In Figure 13.26, the duration for the 5% yield is 6.879 years. The MDURATION return is 6.712 years. This is the duration if the yield would change from 5% to 6%. The difference between the duration and modified duration is an indicator of a bond price's volatility.

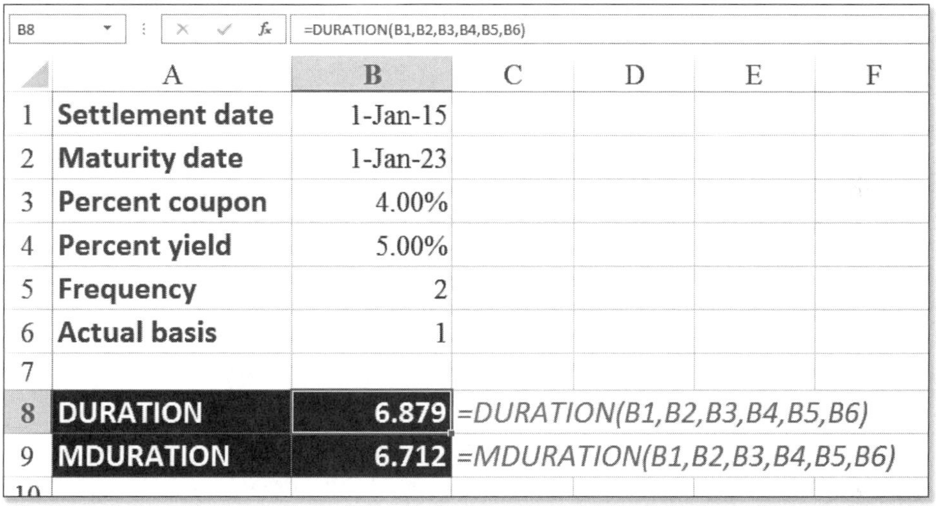

Figure 13.26
DURATION indicates how many years it will take to earn back the security's purchase price. MDURATION shows the change in duration if the yield were to increase by 1%.

| B8 | ▾ | : | × | ✓ | fx | =DURATION(B1,B2,B3,B4,B5,B6) |

◢	A	B	C	D	E	F
1	Settlement date	1-Jan-15				
2	Maturity date	1-Jan-23				
3	Percent coupon	4.00%				
4	Percent yield	5.00%				
5	Frequency	2				
6	Actual basis	1				
7						
8	DURATION	6.879	=DURATION(B1,B2,B3,B4,B5,B6)			
9	MDURATION	6.712	=MDURATION(B1,B2,B3,B4,B5,B6)			
10						

Syntax:

DURATION(*settlement_date,maturity_date,coupon_rate,yield_rate,frequency,basis*)

The DURATION function returns the Macaulay duration for an assumed par value of $100. Duration is defined as the weighted average of the present value of the cash flows and is used as a measure of a bond price's response to changes in yield.

Syntax:

MDURATION(*settlement_date,maturity_date,coupon_rate,yield_rate,frequency,basis*)

The MDURATION function returns the modified duration for a security with an assumed par value of $100.

Examples of Miscellaneous Financial Functions

Excel offers a few other financial functions that may be useful if you are dealing with ancient historical data. On April 9, 2001, all U.S. stock markets were forced to start trading securities in dollars and cents instead of dollars and fractions. The United States was the last nation using the fractional system, which was an eighteenth-century system.

In the fractional system, a stock price may have been reported in the newspaper as 5 5/8, which is roughly equivalent to $5.63. However, a common system in brokerage houses was to record this as 5.5, with the .5 indicating 5/8. In an alternative system, prices were recorded in 16ths, with, for example, 1.03 meaning 3/16.

Using DOLLARDE and DOLLARFR to Convert Between Decimals and Fractions

If you encounter an old worksheet that uses fractional prices, you can convert them to decimals by using DOLLARDE. You must specify the price in the nomenclature of the system and specify whether the number after the decimal point is in 8ths, 16ths, or 32nds.

Syntax:

DOLLARDE(*fractional_dollar,fraction*)

The DOLLARDE function converts a dollar price expressed as a fraction into a dollar price expressed as a decimal number. You use DOLLARDE to convert fractional dollar numbers, such as securities prices, to decimal numbers. This function takes the following arguments:

- *fractional_dollar*—This is a number expressed as a fraction.
- *fraction*—This is the integer to use in the denominator of the fraction.

Syntax:

DOLLARFR(*decimal_dollar,fraction*)

The DOLLARFR function converts a dollar price expressed as a decimal number into a dollar price expressed as a fraction.

Using FVSCHEDULE to Calculate the Future Value for a Variable Scheduled Interest Rate

The FV function discussed at the beginning of this chapter assumes a constant interest rate. If you have a loan agreement that specifies a variable interest rate for future years, you can calculate the future value based on the scheduled interest rate. To do so, you use the FVSCHEDULE function.

Syntax:

FVSCHEDULE(*principal*,*schedule*)

The FVSCHEDULE function returns the future value of an initial principal after applying a series of compound interest rates. Use FVSCHEDULE to calculate the future value of an investment with a variable or adjustable rate. This function takes the following arguments:

- **principal**—This is the present value.

- **schedule**—This is an array of interest rates to apply.

The values in *schedule* can be numbers or blank cells; any other value produces a #VALUE! error for FVSCHEDULE. Blank cells are assumed to be zeros, which means no interest.

Figure 13.27 shows three examples of variable interest rates.

Figure 13.27
Calculating a future value for a series of scheduled future interest rates by using FVSCHEDULE.

B5	▾	:	✕	✓	fx	=FVSCHEDULE(1000,B1:B3)

	A	B	C	D	E
1	**Year 1**	9%	9%	11%	
2	**Year 2**	11%	9%	10%	
3	**Year 3**	10%	9%	9%	
4					
5	**FVSCHEDULE**	**1331**	**1295**	**1331**	
6		*=FVSCHEDULE(1000,B1:B3)*			
7					
8					

14

USING STATISTICAL FUNCTIONS

Statistics in Excel fall into three broad categories:

- **Descriptive statistics that describe a data set**—These include measures of central tendency and dispersion.

- **Regression tools**—These allow you to predict future values based on past values.

- **Inferential statistics**—This type of statistic allows you to predict the likelihood of an event happening, based on a sample of a population.

Table 14.1 provides an alphabetical list of all the Excel 2013 statistical functions. Detailed examples of the functions are provided in the remainder of the chapter.

Table 14.1   Alphabetical List of Statistical Functions

Function	Description
AVEDEV(*number1*,*number2*,...)	Returns the average of the absolute deviations of data points from their mean. AVEDEV is a measure of the variability in a data set.
AVERAGE(*number1*,*number2*,...)	Returns the average (arithmetic mean) of the arguments.
AVERAGEA(*value1*,*value2*,...)	Calculates the average (arithmetic mean) of the values in the list of arguments. In addition to numbers, text and logical values, such as TRUE and FALSE, are included in the calculation.
BETA.DIST (*x*,*alpha*,*beta*,*cumulative*,*A*,*B*)	Returns the cumulative beta probability density function. The cumulative beta probability density function is commonly used to study variation in the percentage of something across samples, such as the fraction of the day people spend watching television.

Function	Description
BETA.INV (*probability*,*alpha*,*beta*,*A*,*B*)	Returns the inverse of the cumulative beta probability density function. That is, if probability is equal to BETADIST(x,...), then BETA.INV(*probability*,...) is equal to x. You can use the cumulative beta distribution in project planning to model probable completion times, given an expected completion time and variability.
BINOM.DIST (*number_s*,*trials*,*probability_s*, *cumulative*)	Returns the individual term binomial distribution probability. You use BINOM.DIST in problems with a fixed number of tests or trials, when the outcomes of any trial are only success or failure, when trials are independent, and when the probability of success is constant throughout the experiment. For example, BINOM.DIST can calculate the probability that two of the next three babies born will be male.
BINOM.DIST.RANGE(*trials*, *probability_s*,*number_s*, [*number_s2*])	Returns the probability of a trial result using a binomial distribution.
BINOM.INV(*trials*,*probability_s*, *alpha*)	Returns the smallest value for which the cumulative binomial distribution is greater than or equal to a criterion value. You use this function for quality assurance applications. For example, you can use BINOM.INV to determine the greatest number of defective parts that are allowed to come off an assembly line run without having to reject the entire lot.
CHISQ.DIST(*x*,*degrees_freedom*, *cumulative*)	Returns the one-tailed probability of the chi-squared distribution. The chi-squared distribution is associated with a chi-squared test. You use the chi-squared test to compare observed and expected values. For example, in a genetic experiment, you might hypothesize that the next generation of plants will exhibit a certain set of colors. By comparing the observed results with the expected ones, you can decide whether your original hypothesis is valid.
CHISQ.DIST.RT(*x*,*degrees_freedom*)	Returns the right-tailed probability of the chi-squared distribution.
CHISQ.INV(*probability*, *degrees_freedom*)	Returns the inverse of the one-tailed probability of the chi-squared distribution. If probability is equal to CHISQ.DIST(x,...), then CHISQ.INV(*probability*,...) is x. You use this function to compare observed results with expected ones to decide whether your original hypothesis is valid.
CHISQ.INV.RT (*probability*,*degrees_freedom*)	Returns the inverse of the right-tailed probability of the chi-squared distribution.

Function	Description
CHISQ.TEST (*actual_range*,*expected_range*)	Returns the test for independence. CHISQ.TEST returns the value from the chi-squared distribution for the statistic and the appropriate degrees of freedom. You can use chi-squared tests to determine whether hypothesized results are verified by an experiment.
CONFIDENCE.NORM (*alpha*,*standard_dev*,*size*)	Returns the confidence interval for a population mean. The confidence interval is a range on either side of a sample mean. For example, if you order a product through the mail, you can determine, with a particular level of confidence, the earliest and latest the product will arrive. Uses standard normal distribution.
CONFIDENCE.T (*alpha*,*standard_dev*,*size*)	Returns the confidence interval based on the Student's *t*-distribution.
CORREL(*array1*,*array2*)	Returns the correlation coefficient of the *array1* and *array2* cell ranges. You use the correlation coefficient to determine the relationship between two properties. For example, you can examine the relationship between a location's average temperature and the use of air conditioners.
COVARIANCE.P(*array1*,*array2*)	Returns covariance, the average of the products of deviations for each data point pair. You use covariance to determine the relationship between two data sets. For example, you can examine whether greater income accompanies greater levels of education. Based on a population.
COVARIANCE.S(*array1*,*array2*)	Returns covariance, the average of the products of deviations for each data point pair. You use covariance to determine the relationship between two data sets. For example, you can examine whether greater income accompanies greater levels of education. Based on a sample.
DEVSQ(*number1*,*number2*,...)	Returns the sum of squares of deviations of data points from their sample mean.
EXPON.DIST(*x*,*lambda*,*cumulative*)	Returns the exponential distribution. You use EXPON.DIST to model the time between events, such as how long a bank's automated teller machine takes to deliver cash. For example, you can use EXPON.DIST to determine the probability that the process takes, at most, 1 minute.

Function	Description
F.DIST(*x*,*degrees_freedom1*, *degrees_freedom2*,*cumulative*)	Returns the *F* probability distribution. You can use this function to determine whether two data sets have different degrees of diversity. For example, you can examine test scores given to men and women entering high school and determine whether the variability in the females is different from that found in the males.
F.DIST.RT(*x*,*degrees_freedom1*, *degrees_freedom2*)	Returns the right-tailed *F* probability distribution.
F.INV(*probability*,*degrees_ freedom1*,*degrees_freedom2*)	Returns the inverse of the *F* probability distribution. If *probability* is equal to F.DIST(*x*,...), then F.INV(*probability*,...) is equal to *x*.
F.INV.RT(*probability*,*degrees_ freedom1*,*degrees_freedom2*)	Returns the inverse of the right-tailed *F* probability distribution.
F.TEST(*array1*,*array2*)	Returns the result of an *F*-test. An *F*-test returns the one-tailed probability that the variances in *array1* and *array2* are not significantly different. You use this function to determine whether two samples have different variances. For example, given test scores from public and private schools, you can test whether those schools have different levels of diversity.
FISHER(*x*)	Returns the Fisher transformation at *x*. This transformation produces a function that is approximately normally distributed rather than skewed. You use this function to perform hypothesis testing on the correlation coefficient.
FISHERINV(*y*)	Returns the inverse of the Fisher transformation. You use this transformation when analyzing correlations between ranges or arrays of data. If *y* is equal to FISHER(*x*), then FISHERINV(*y*) is equal to *x*.
FORECAST(*x*,*known_y's*,*known_x's*)	Calculates, or predicts, a future value by using existing values. The predicted value is a y value for a given x value. The known values are existing x values and y values, and the new value is predicted by using linear regression. You can use this function to predict future sales, inventory requirements, or consumer trends.
FREQUENCY(*data_array*,*bins_array*)	Calculates how often values occur within a range of values and returns a vertical array of numbers. For example, you can use FREQUENCY to count the number of test scores that fall within ranges of scores. Because FREQUENCY returns an array, it must be entered as an array formula.
GAMMA(*x*)	Returns the gamma function value.

Function	Description
GAMMA.DIST(*x*,*alpha*,*beta*, *cumulative*)	Returns the gamma distribution. You can use this function to study variables that might have a skewed distribution. The gamma distribution is commonly used in queuing analysis.
GAMMA.INV(*probability*,*alpha*,*beta*)	Returns the inverse of the gamma cumulative distribution. If *probability* is equal to GAMMA.DIST(*x*,...), then GAMMA.INV (*probability*,...) is equal to *x*.
GAMMALN(*x*)	Returns the natural logarithm of the gamma function.
GAUSS(*x*)	Returns 0.5 less than the standard normal curve distribution.
GEOMEAN(*number1*,*number2*,...)	Returns the geometric mean of an array or a range of positive data. For example, you can use GEOMEAN to calculate average growth rate given compound interest with variable rates.
GROWTH(*known_y's*,*known_x's*, *new_x's*,*const*)	Calculates predicted exponential growth by using existing data. GROWTH returns the y values for a series of new x values that you specify by using existing x values and y values. You can also use the GROWTH worksheet function to fit an exponential curve to existing x values and y values.
HARMEAN(*number1*,*number2*,...)	Returns the harmonic mean of a data set. The harmonic mean is the reciprocal of the arithmetic mean of reciprocals.
HYPGEOM.DIST(*sample_s*, *number_sample*,*population_s*, *number_population*)	Returns the hypergeometric distribution. HYPGEOM.DIST returns the probability of a given number of sample successes, given the sample size, population successes, and population size. You use HYPGEOM.DIST for problems with a finite population, where each observation is either a success or a failure, and where each subset of a given size is chosen with equal likelihood.
INTERCEPT(*known_y's*,*known_x's*)	Calculates the point at which a line will intersect the y-axis by using existing x values and y values. The intercept point is based on a best-fit regression line plotted through the known x values and known y values. You use the intercept when you want to determine the value of the dependent variable when the independent variable is 0. For example, you can use the INTERCEPT function to predict a metal's electrical resistance at 0 degrees Celsius when your data points were taken at room temperature or higher.

Function	Description
KURT(*number1*,*number2*,...)	Returns the kurtosis of a data set. *Kurtosis* characterizes the relative peakedness or flatness of a distribution compared with the normal distribution. Positive kurtosis indicates a relatively peaked distribution. Negative kurtosis indicates a relatively flat distribution.
LARGE(*array*,*k*)	Returns the *k*th largest value in a data set. You can use this function to select a value based on its relative standing. For example, you can use LARGE to return a highest, runner-up, or third-place score.
LINEST(*known_y's*,*known_x's*, *const*,*stats*)	Calculates the statistics for a line by using the least-squares method to calculate a straight line that best fits the data and returns an array that describes the line. Because this function returns an array of values, it must be entered as an array formula.
LOGEST(*known_y's*,*known_x's*, *const*,*stats*)	In regression analysis, calculates an exponential curve that fits the data and returns an array of values that describes the curve. Because this function returns an array of values, it must be entered as an array formula.
LOGNORM.DIST(*x*,*mean*, *standard_dev*,*cumulative*)	Returns the cumulative lognormal distribution of *x*, where LN(*x*) is normally distributed with the parameters *mean* and *standard_dev*. You use this function to analyze data that has been logarithmically transformed.
LOGNORM.INV(*probability*,*mean*, *standard_dev*)	Returns the inverse of the lognormal cumulative distribution function of *x*, where LN(*x*) is normally distributed with the parameters *mean* and *standard_dev*. If *probability* is equal to LOGNORM.DIST(*x*,...), LOGNORM.INV(*probability*,...) is equal to *x*.
MAX(*number1*,*number2*,...)	Returns the largest value in a set of values.
MAXA(*value1*,*value2*,...)	Returns the largest value in a list of arguments. Text and logical values such as TRUE and FALSE are compared, as are numbers.
MEDIAN(*number1*,*number2*,...)	Returns the median of the given numbers. The median is the number in the middle of a set of numbers; that is, half the numbers have values that are greater than the median and half have values that are less.
MIN(*number1*,*number2*,...)	Returns the smallest number in a set of values.
MINA(*value1*,*value2*,...)	Returns the smallest value in a list of arguments. Text and logical values such as TRUE and FALSE are compared, as are numbers.

Function	Description
MODE.MULT(*number1*,*number2*,...)	Returns a vertical array of the most frequently occurring, or repetitive, values in an array or a range of data. MODE.MULT was new in Excel 2010 and handles the specific case when there are two or more values that are tied for the most frequently occurring value. Whereas MODE.SNGL returns only the first mode value, MODE.MULT returns all the mode values.
MODE.SNGL(*number1*,*number2*,...)	Returns the most frequently occurring, or repetitive, value in an array or a range of data. Like MEDIAN, MODE.SNGL is a location measure. If there are two values that are tied for the most frequently occurring value, only the first one will be returned by MODE.SNGL. If you need to return all of the tied values, use the new MODE.MULT.
NEGBINOM.DIST(*number_f*,*number_s*, *probability_s*,*cumulative*)	Returns the negative binomial distribution. NEGBINOM.DIST returns the probability that there will be *number_f* failures before the *number_s*th success, when the constant probability of a success is *probability_s*. This function is similar to the binomial distribution function, except that the number of successes is fixed and the number of trials is variable. As with the binomial distribution function, trials are assumed to be independent.
NORM.DIST(*x*,*mean*, *standard_dev*,*cumulative*)	Returns the normal cumulative distribution for the specified mean and standard deviation. This function has a very wide range of applications in statistics, including hypothesis testing.
NORM.INV (*probability*,*mean*,*standard_dev*)	Returns the inverse of the normal cumulative distribution for the specified mean and standard deviation.
NORM.S.DIST(*z*)	Returns the standard normal cumulative distribution function. The distribution has a mean of zero and a standard deviation of one. You use this function in place of a table of standard normal curve areas.
NORM.S.INV(*probability*)	Returns the inverse of the standard normal cumulative distribution. The distribution has a mean of zero and a standard deviation of one.
PEARSON(*array1*,*array2*)	Returns the Pearson product–moment correlation coefficient, r, a dimensionless index that ranges from −1.0 to 1.0, inclusive, and reflects the extent of a linear relationship between two data sets.
PERCENTILE.EXC(*array*,*k*)	Returns the kth percentile of values in a range. You can use this function to establish a threshold of acceptance. For example, you can decide to examine candidates who score above the 90th percentile. PERCENTILE.EXC assumes the percentile is between 0 and 1, exclusive.

Function	Description
PERCENTILE.INC(*array*,*k*)	Returns the *k*th percentile of values in a range. PERCENTILE.INC assumes the percentile is between 0 and 1, inclusive.
PERCENTRANK.EXC(*array*,*x*, *significance*)	Returns the rank of a value in a data set as a percentage of the data set. You can use this function to evaluate the relative standing of a value within a data set. PERCENTRANK.EXC is renamed from PERCENTRANK. It assumes the percentile is between 0 and 1, exclusive.
PERCENTRANK.INC(*array*,*x*, *significance*)	Returns the rank of a value in a data set as a percentage of the data set. You can use this function to evaluate the relative standing of a value within a data set. For example, you can use PERCENTRANK.INC to evaluate the standing of an aptitude test score among all scores for the test. PERCENTRANK.INC assumes percentiles from 0 to 1, inclusive.
PERMUT(*number*,*number_chosen*)	Returns the number of permutations for a given number of objects that can be selected from number objects. A permutation is any set or subset of objects or events where internal order is significant. Permutations are different from combinations, for which the internal order is not significant. You use this function for lottery-style probability calculations.
PERMUTATIONA(*number*, *number_chosen*)	Returns the number of permutations for a given number of objects (with repetitions) that can be selected from the total objects.
PHI(*x*)	Returns the value of the density function for a standard normal distribution. New in Excel 2013.
POISSON.DIST(*x*,*mean*,*cumulative*)	Returns the Poisson distribution. A common application of the Poisson distribution is predicting the number of events over a specific time, such as the number of cars arriving at a toll plaza in 1 minute.
PROB(*x_range*,*prob_range*, *lower_limit*,*upper_limit*)	Returns the probability that values in a range are between two limits. If *upper_limit* is not supplied, returns the probability that values in *x_range* are equal to *lower_limit*.
QUARTILE.EXC(*array*,*quart*)	Returns the quartile of a data set. Quartiles are often used in sales and survey data to divide populations into groups. For example, you can use QUARTILE.EXC to find the top 25% of incomes in a population. This function assumes percentiles run from 0 to 1, exclusive.

Function	Description
QUARTILE.INC(*array*,*quart*)	Returns the quartile of a data set. Quartiles are often used in sales and survey data to divide populations into groups. This function assumes percentiles run from 0 to 1, inclusive.
RANK.AVG(*number*,*ref*,*order*)	Returns the rank of a number in a list of numbers. The rank of a number is its size relative to other values in a list. (If you were to sort the list, the rank of the number would be its position.) When two or more items are tied, RANK.AVG averages their ranks.
RANK.EQ(*number*,*ref*,*order*)	Returns the rank of a number in a list of numbers. When two or more items are tied, RANK.EQ assigns the lower rank to all items in the tie. Renamed from RANK in Excel 2010.
RSQ(*known_y's*,*known_x's*)	Returns the square of the Pearson product–moment correlation coefficient through data points in *known_y's* and *known_x's*. The *r*-squared value can be interpreted as the proportion of the variance in *y* attributable to the variance in *x*.
SKEW(*number1*,*number2*,...)	Returns the skewness of a distribution. *Skewness* characterizes the degree of asymmetry of a distribution around its mean. Positive skewness indicates a distribution with an asymmetric tail extending toward more positive values. Negative skewness indicates a distribution with an asymmetric tail extending toward more negative values.
SKEW.P(*number1*,*number2*,...)	Returns the skewness of a distribution based on a population. Skewness characterizes the degree of asymmetry of a distribution around its mean. Positive skewness indicates a distribution with an asymmetric tail extending toward more positive values. Negative skewness indicates a distribution with an asymmetric tail extending toward more negative values. New in Excel 2013.
SLOPE(*known_y's*,*known_x's*)	Returns the slope of the linear regression line through data points in *known_y's* and *known_x's*. The *slope* is the vertical distance divided by the horizontal distance between any two points on the line, which is the rate of change along the regression line.
SMALL(*array*,*k*)	Returns the *k*th smallest value in a data set. You use this function to return values with a particular relative standing in a data set.
STANDARDIZE(*x*,*mean*,*standard_dev*)	Returns a normalized value from a distribution characterized by *mean* and *standard_dev*.

Function	Description
STDEV.P(*number1*,*number2*,...)	Calculates standard deviation based on the entire population given as arguments. The standard deviation is a measure of how widely values are dispersed from the average value (that is, the mean).
STDEV.S(*number1*,*number2*,...)	Estimates standard deviation based on a sample. The *standard deviation* is a measure of how widely values are dispersed from the average value (that is, the mean).
STDEVA(*value1*,*value2*,...)	Estimates standard deviation based on a sample. The standard deviation is a measure of how widely values are dispersed from the average value (that is, the mean). Text and logical values such as TRUE and FALSE are included in the calculation.
STDEVPA(*value1*,*value2*,...)	Calculates standard deviation based on the entire population given as arguments, including text and logical values. The standard deviation is a measure of how widely values are dispersed from the average value (that is, the mean).
STEYX(*known_y's*,*known_x's*)	Returns the standard error of the predicted y value for each x in the regression. The standard error is a measure of the amount of error in the prediction of y for an individual x.
SUMSQ(*number1*,*number2*, ...)	Returns the sum of the squares of the arguments.
SUMX2MY2(*array_x*,*array_y*)	Returns the sum of the difference of squares of corresponding values in two arrays.
SUMX2PY2(*array_x*,*array_y*)	Returns the sum of the sum of squares of corresponding values in two arrays. The *sum of the sum of squares* is a common term in many statistical calculations.
SUMXMY2(*array_x*,*array_y*)	Returns the sum of squares of differences of corresponding values in two arrays.
T.DIST(*x*,*degrees_freedom*, *tails*,*cumulative*)	Returns the percentage points (that is, probability) for the Student t-distribution, where a numeric value (x) is a calculated value of t for which percentage points are to be computed. The t-distribution is used in the hypothesis testing of small sample data sets. You use this function in place of a table of critical values for the t-distribution.
T.DIST.2T(*x*,*degrees_freedom*)	Returns the two-tailed probability for the Student t-distribution.
T.DIST.RT(*x*,*degrees_freedom*)	Returns the right-tailed probability for the Student t-distribution.

Function	Description
T.INV(*probability*, *degrees_freedom*)	Returns the *t*-value of the Student's *t*-distribution as a function of the probability and the degrees of freedom.
T.INV.2T(*probability*, *degrees_freedom*)	Returns the right-tailed *t*-value of the Student's *t*-distribution as a function of the probability and the degrees of freedom.
T.TEST(*array1*,*array2*,*tails*,*type*)	Returns the probability associated with a Student's *t*-test. You use T.TEST to determine whether two samples are likely to have come from the same two underlying populations that have the same mean.
TREND(*known_y's*,*known_x's*, *new_x's*,*const*)	Returns values along a linear trend. Fits a straight line (using the method of least squares) to the arrays *known_y's* and *known_x's*. Returns the *y* values along that line for the array of *new_x's* that you specify.
TRIMMEAN(*array*,*percent*)	Returns the mean of the interior of a data set. TRIMMEAN calculates the mean taken by excluding a percentage of data points from the top and bottom tails of a data set. You can use this function when you want to exclude outlying data from your analysis.
VAR.P(*number1*,*number2*,...)	Calculates variance based on the entire population.
VAR.S(*number1*,*number2*,...)	Estimates variance based on a sample.
VARA(*value1*,*value2*,...)	Estimates variance based on a sample. In addition to numbers, text and logical values such as TRUE and FALSE are included in the calculation.
VARPA(*value1*,*value2*,...)	Calculates variance based on the entire population. In addition to numbers, text and logical values such as TRUE and FALSE are included in the calculation.
WEIBULL.DIST.DIST(*x*,*alpha*, *beta*, *cumulative*)	Returns the Weibull distribution. You use this distribution in reliability analysis, such as to calculate a device's mean time to failure.
Z.TEST(*array*,*x*,*sigma*)	Returns the two-tailed *p* value of a z-test. The z-test generates a standard score for *x* with respect to the data set, *array*, and returns the two-tailed probability for the normal distribution. You can use this function to assess the likelihood that a particular observation is drawn from a particular population.

Functions That Have Been Renamed

Before Excel 2010, the statistical functions had been poorly named. Depending on the distribution that you were using, the naming conventions varied. For the Chi Squared distribution, the inverse function was called CHIINV. For the Binomial distribution, the inverse function was called CRITBINOM.

Starting in Excel 2010, the existing statistical functions have been renamed. Watch for these suffixes:

- .DIST is used for the probability density function and for the left-tailed cumulative distribution function. An argument explains whether the function is the PDF (point distribution function) or the CDF (cumulative distribution function).

- .INV is used for the inverse cumulative distribution function.

- .RT is used for right-tailed.

- .LT is used for left-tailed.

- .TEST is used for hypothesis-testing functions.

- .P is used for functions based on a population.

- .S is used for functions based on a sample.

Table 14.2 shows a list of all the distribution function names.

Table 14.2   New Distribution Function Names

Distribution	PDF/CDF	Right-tailed CDF	Inverse Left-Tailed CDF	Inverse Right-Tailed CDF
Beta	BETA.DIST		BETA.INV	
Binomial	BINOM.DIST		BINOM.INV	
Chi-Squared	CHISQ.DIST	CHISQ.DIST.RT	CHISQ.INV	CHISQ.INV.RT
Exponential	EXPON.DIST			
F	F.DIST	F.DIST.RT	F.INV	F.INV.RT
Gamma	GAMMA.DIST		GAMMA.INV	
Hypergeometric	HYPGEOM.DIST			
Lognormal	LOGNORM.DIST		LOGNORM.INV	
Negative Binomial	NEGBINOM.DIST			
Normal	NORM.DIST		NORM.INV	
Standard Normal	NORM.S.DIST		NORM.S.INV	

Distribution	PDF/CDF	Right-tailed CDF	Inverse Left-Tailed CDF	Inverse Right-Tailed CDF
Poisson	POISSON.DIST			
Student's t	T.DIST	T.DIST.RT	T.INV	
Student's t (two-tailed)		T-DIST.2T		T.INV.2T
Weibull	WEIBULL.DIST			

For hypothesis testing, the functions are F.TEST, T.TEST, and Z.TEST. Confidence tests are CONFIDENCE.NORM for the normal distribution and CONFIDENCE.T for the Student's t-distribution.

Variance and standard deviation have always been available as functions for a sample (VAR and STDEV) and a population (VARP and STDEVP). Microsoft renamed these to be VAR.S, STDEV.S, VAR.P, STDEV.P. Microsoft also formalized the fact that the old COVAR function is based on a population by renaming it to COVARIANCE.P, and it added a sample version named COVARIANCE.S.

Using Worksheets with Legacy Function Names

With the new naming scheme, many functions are in Excel 2013 twice. The new VAR.P function works, but Microsoft has to support the old VAR function because millions of legacy spreadsheets exist that have been using VAR.

Furthermore, if you are creating a new workbook in Excel 2013 and that workbook will be shared with people who are using Excel 2007 or earlier, you pretty much have to keep using the old naming convention.

Still, Microsoft is hopeful that people will start using the new naming scheme. In the Statistical function drop-down, the new names appear. The old names have been moved to the Compatibility drop-down.

As you start to type a function name, the formula AutoComplete always lists the new names first. The old names are listed at the end with a symbol to indicate that it is here for compatibility only.

Table 14.3 compares the old and new function names.

Table 14.3   Comparison of Old and New Function Names

2007	2010 and 2013
BETADIST	BETA.DIST
BETAINV	BETA.INV
BINOMDIST	BINOM.DIST
CHIDIST	CHISQ.DIST
CHIINV	CHISQ.INV
CHITEST	CHISQ.TEST

2007	2010 and 2013
CONFIDENCE	CONFIDENCE.NORM
COVAR	COVARIANCE.P
CRITBINOM	BINOM.INV
EXPONDIST	EXPON.DIST
FDIST	F.DIST
FINV	F.INV
FTEST	F.TEST
GAMMADIST	GAMMA.DIST
GAMMAINV	GAMMA.INV
HYPGEOMDIST	HYPGEOM.DIST
LOGINV	LOGNORM.INV
LOGNORMDIST	LOGNORM.DIST
MODE	MODE.SNGL
NEGBINOMDIST	NEGBINOM.DIST
NORMDIST	NORM.DIST
NORMINV	NORM.INV
NORMSDIST	NORM.S.DIST
NORMSINV	NORM.S.INV
PERCENTILE	PERCENTILE.INC
PERCENTRANK	PERCENTRANK.INC
POISSON	POISSON.DIST
QUARTILE	QUARTILE.INC
RANK	RANK.EQ
STDEV	STDEV.S
STDEVP	STDEV.P
TDIST	T.DIST
TINV	T.INV
TTEST	T.TEST
VAR	VAR.S
VARP	VAR.P
WEIBULL	WEIBULL.DIST
ZTEST	Z.TEST

Examples of Functions for Descriptive Statistics

Descriptive statistics help describe a population of data. What is the largest? The smallest? The average? Are data points grouped to the left of the average or to the right of the average? How wide is the range of expected values? Do many members of the population have values in the middle, or are they evenly spread throughout the range? All these are measures of descriptive statistics.

Many situations in a business environment involve finding basic information about a data set, such as the largest or smallest value or the rank within a data set.

Using MIN or MAX to Find the Smallest or Largest Numeric Value

If you have a large data set and want to find the smallest or largest value in a column, rather than sort the data set, you can use a function to find the value. To find the smallest numeric value, you use MIN. To find the largest numeric value, you use MAX.

Figure 14.1 shows a list of open receivables, by customer, for 59 customers. Even though the function references say that you can find the MIN for only 255 numbers, a single rectangular reference counts as one of the 255 arguments for the function. To find the smallest value in the range, you use =MIN(B2:B60). To find the largest value in the range, you use =MAX(B2:B60).

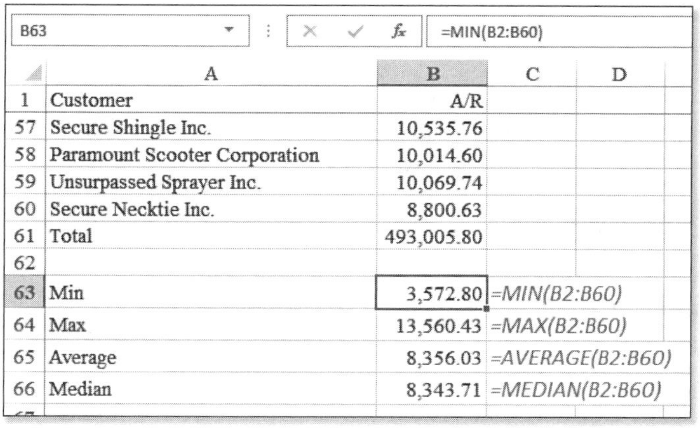

Figure 14.1
You use MIN and MAX to find the smallest or largest receivables.

	A	B	C	D
			B63	=MIN(B2:B60)
1	Customer	A/R		
57	Secure Shingle Inc.	10,535.76		
58	Paramount Scooter Corporation	10,014.60		
59	Unsurpassed Sprayer Inc.	10,069.74		
60	Secure Necktie Inc.	8,800.63		
61	Total	493,005.80		
62				
63	Min	3,572.80	=MIN(B2:B60)	
64	Max	13,560.43	=MAX(B2:B60)	
65	Average	8,356.03	=AVERAGE(B2:B60)	
66	Median	8,343.71	=MEDIAN(B2:B60)	

Syntax:

```
=MIN(number1,number2,...)
```

The MIN function returns the smallest number in a set of values. The arguments *number1*, *number2*, ... are one to 255 numbers for which you want to find the minimum value. You can specify arguments that are numbers, empty cells, logical values, or text representations of numbers. Arguments that are error values or text that cannot be translated into numbers cause errors. If an argument is an array or a reference, only numbers in that array or reference are used. Empty cells, logical values, and text in the array or reference are ignored. If logical values and text should not be ignored, you should use MINA instead. If the arguments contain no numbers, MIN returns 0.

Syntax:

=MAX(*number1*,*number2*,...)

The MAX function returns the largest value in a set of values. The arguments *number1*, *number2*, ... are one to 255 numbers for which you want to find the maximum value. The remaining rules are similar to those for MIN, described in the preceding section.

Finding a Minimum Text Value

If you read the descriptions for MINA and MAXA, you might think that the functions can be used to find the smallest text value in a range. However, here is the Excel Help description for MAXA:

MAXA(*value1*,*value2*) returns the largest value in a list of arguments. Text and logical values such as TRUE and FALSE are compared as well as numbers.

The problem, however, is that text values are treated as the number o in the compare operation. It is a struggle to imagine a scenario where this would be mildly useful. If you have a series of positive numbers and want to know if any of them are text, you can use =MINA(A1:A99). If the result is o, then you know that there is a text value in the range.

Similarly, if you have a range of negative numbers in A1:A99, you could use =MAXA(A1:A99). If any of the values are text, the result returns o instead of a negative number.

MINA and MAXA could be used to evaluate a series of TRUE/FALSE values. FALSE values are treated as o. TRUE values are treated as 1.

Using LARGE to Find the Top *N* Values in a List of Values

The MAX function discussed in the preceding section finds the single largest value in a list. Sometimes it is interesting to find the top 10 values in a list. Say that with a list of customer receivables, someone in accounts receivable might want to call the top 10 receivables in an attempt to collect the accounts. The LARGE function can find the first, second, third, and so on largest values in a list.

Syntax:

=LARGE(*array*,*k*)

The LARGE function returns the *k*th largest value in a data set. You can use this function to select a value based on its relative standing. For example, you can use LARGE to return a highest, runner-up, or third-place score. This function takes the following arguments:

- ■ *array*—This is the array or range of data for which you want to determine the *k*th largest value. If *array* is empty, LARGE returns a #NUM! error.

- ■ *k*—This is the position (from the largest) in the array or cell range of data to return. If *k* is less than or equal to 0, or if *k* is greater than the number of data points, LARGE returns a #NUM! error.

Follow these steps to build a table of the five largest customer receivables:

1. Make the second argument of the function the numbers 1 through 5. Starting from the data set shown in Figure 14.1, insert a new column A to hold the values 1 through 5.

2. In A66:A70, enter the numbers **1** through **5**, as shown in Figure 14.2.

Figure 14.2
The LARGE function in column C allows this dynamic table to be built to show the five largest values.

| C66 | | ▼ | : | × | ✓ | *fx* | =LARGE($C$2:$C$60,A66) |

◢	A	B	C	D	E	F
1		Customer	A/R			
58		Paramount Scooter Corporation	10,014.60			
59		Unsurpassed Sprayer Inc.	10,069.74			
60		Secure Necktie Inc.	8,800.63			
61		Total	493,005.80			
62						
63		Largest	13,560.43	=MAX(C2:C60)		
64						
65		Largest Receivables				
66	1	Fully Toothpick Company	13,560.43	=LARGE($C$2:$C$60,A66)		
67	2	Savory Calculator Company	12,493.41	=LARGE($C$2:$C$60,A67)		
68	3	Inventive Clipboard Corporation	11,604.13	=LARGE($C$2:$C$60,A68)		
69	4	Best Raft Company	11,582.61	=LARGE($C$2:$C$60,A69)		
70	5	Magnificent Electronics Partners	11,087.71	=LARGE($C$2:$C$60,A70)		
71						
72		B66: =INDEX($B$2:$B$60,MATCH(C66,$C$2:$C$60,0))				
73						

3. In the column letters above the grid, grab the line between columns A and B. Drag to the left to make this column narrower. It should be just wide enough to display the numbers in column A.

4. In cell C66, enter **=LARGE(**. Use the mouse or arrow keys to highlight the range of data. After highlighting the data, press the F4 key to add dollar signs to the reference. This allows you to copy the reference to the next several rows while always pointing at the same range.

5. For the second argument, point to the 1 in cell A66. Leave this reference as relative (that is, no dollar signs) so that it will change to A67, A68, and so on when copied. The first formula in cell C66 indicates that the largest value is 13,560.43. So far, you've done a lot of work just to find out the same thing that the MAX function could have told you. However, the power comes in the next step.

6. Select cell C66. Click the fill handle and drag down to cell C70. You now have a list of the top five open receivables.

7. At this point, you know the amounts of the top receivables, but this immediately brings up the question of which customers have those receivables. Using lookup functions discussed in Chapter 12, "Using Powerful Functions: Logical, Lookup, Web, and Database Functions," you can retrieve the name associated with each receivable amount. Note that this method assumes that no two customers in the top five have exactly the same receivable.

8. Enter the following intermediate formula in cell B66: **=MATCH(C66,$C$2:$C$60,0)**. This formula tells Excel to take the receivable value in cell C66 and to find it in the list of open receivables. The MATCH function returns the row number within C2:C60 that has the matching value. For example, 13,560.43 is found in cell C9. This is the eighth row in the range of C2:C60, so MATCH returns the number 8.

9. The largest receivable in the eighth row of a range is not useful to a person trying to collect accounts receivables, so to return the name, ask for the eighth value in the range of B2:B66. You can use the INDEX function to do this. =INDEX($B$2:$B$66,8) returns the customer with the largest receivable.

10. Combine the formulas from step 8 and step 9 into a single formula in cell B66: =INDEX($B$2:$B$60,MATCH(C66,$C$2:$C$60,0)).

11. Copy the formula in cell B66 down through cell B70.

As shown in Figure 14.2, the result is a table in A66:A70 that shows the five largest customers. After receiving checks today, you can update the receivable amounts in C2:C60. If Best Raft sent in a check for $10,000, the formulas would automatically move Magnificent Electronics up to the fourth position and move the sixth customer up to the fifth spot.

Rather than entering the numbers 1 through 5 in A66:A70, you could use the ROW() function to return the values of 1 to 5. In cell C66, use =LARGE($C$2:$C$60,ROW(A1)). Because the row number of cell A1 is 1, the row function returns a 1 as the second argument to the LARGE function. This method has the advantage that as you drag the formula down, it switches to ROW(A2) for 2, ROW(A3) for 3, and so on.

Using SMALL to Sequence a List in Date Sequence

The MIN function finds the smallest value in a data set. The SMALL function can find the kth smallest value. This can be great for finding not just the smallest value but the second-smallest, third-smallest, and so on. If n is the number of data points in an array, SMALL($array,1$) equals the smallest value, and SMALL($array,n$) equals the largest value.

Syntax:

=SMALL($array,k$)

The SMALL function returns the *k*th smallest value in a data set. You use this function to return values with a particular relative standing in a data set. *array* is an array or a range of numeric data for which you want to determine the *k*th smallest value. If *array* is empty, SMALL returns a #NUM! error. *k* is the position (from the smallest) in the array or range of data to return. If *k* is less than or equal to 0 or if *k* exceeds the number of data points, SMALL returns a #NUM! error.

In Figure 14.3, range A2:B19 contains a list of book titles and their publication dates. To find the earliest dates for the books, you use =SMALL().

Figure 14.3
The SMALL function in column D finds the earliest years in the list.

	A	B	C	D	E
1	**Titles in Wisdom's Light Sculpture**	**Date**		*Sorted with SMALL function*	
2	The Marines Of Autumn	2000		1615	Don Quixote
3	Notes On The State Of Virginia	1781		1781	Notes On The State Of Virginia
4	Swiss Family Robinson	1812		1812	Swiss Family Robinson
5	To Kill A Mockingbird	1959		1885	Adventures Of Huckleberry Finn
6	Adventures Of Huckleberry Finn	1885		1902	The Wings Of The Dove
7	The Old Man And The Boy	1953		1924	A Passage To India
8	The Lord Of The Rings	1955		1936	Gone With The Wind
9	A Passage To India	1924		1939	The Grapes Of Wrath
10	The Wings Of The Dove	1902		1945	Malabar Farm
11	Gone With The Wind	1936		1948	My Road To Rotary
12	Don Quixote	1615		1950	A Town Like Alice
13	My Road To Rotary	1948		1953	The Old Man And The Boy
14	Malabar Farm	1945		1955	The Lord Of The Rings
15	The Grapes Of Wrath	1939		1959	To Kill A Mockingbird
16	Green Eggs And Ham	1960		1960	Green Eggs And Ham
17	A Town Like Alice	1950		1998	Harry Potter & The Sorcerer's Stone
18	Harry Potter & The Sorcerer's Stone	1998		2000	The Marines Of Autumn
19	VBA & Macros for Microsoft Excel	2004		2004	VBA & Macros for Microsoft Excel
20			D2:	=SMALL($B$2:$B$19,ROW(A1))	
21			E2:	=INDEX($A$2:$A$19,MATCH(D2,$B$2:$B$19,0))	

This example contains a twist that makes the formula easier than in the example for LARGE. In the initial formula in cell D2, the argument for *k* was generated using ROW(A1). This function returns the number 1. As the formula is copied from cell D2 down to the remaining rows, the reference changes to ROW(A2) and so on. This allows each row in column D to show a successively larger value from *array*.

The formula in cell D2 is =SMALL($B$2:$B$19,ROW(A1)). After you have found the year in column D, the formula in cell E2 to return the title is =INDEX($A$2:$A$19,MATCH(D2,$B$2:$B$19,0)). This assumes there are no duplicates in column B.

Using MEDIAN, MODE.SNGL, MODE.MULT, and AVERAGE to Find the Central Tendency of a Data Set

You can use three popular measures when trying to find the middle scores in a range:

- **Mean**—The mean of a data set is the mathematical average. It is calculated by adding all the values in the range and dividing by the number of values in the set. To calculate a mean in Excel, use the AVERAGE function.

- **Median**—The median of a data set is the value in the middle when the set is arranged from high to low. In the data set, half the values are higher than the median and half the numbers are lower than the median. To calculate a median in Excel, use the MEDIAN function. When there is an even number of items, the median is the average of the two middle numbers.

- **Mode**—The mode of a data set is the value that happens most often. To calculate a mode in Excel 2013, use the MODE.SNGL and MODE.MULT functions.

> **Caution**
>
> When averaging cells, keep in mind the difference between empty cells and those that contain the value 0. This can be particularly troubling if you have cleared the Show a Zero in Cells That Have a Zero Value check box. You find this setting by selecting File, Options, Advanced, Display Options for This Worksheet.

Syntax:

=AVERAGE(*number1*,*number2*,...)

The AVERAGE function returns the average (that is, arithmetic mean) of the arguments. The arguments *number1*, *number2*, ... are one to 255 numeric arguments for which you want the average. The arguments must be either numbers or names, arrays, or references that contain numbers. If an array or a reference argument contains text, logical values, or empty cells, those values are ignored; however, cells containing the value 0 are included.

If you have a range of True/False values and you want to see what percentage of people answered True, you can use =AVERAGEA() of the range. The AVERAGEA function treats True values as 1 and False values as 0.

Syntax:

=MEDIAN(*number1*,*number2*,...)

The MEDIAN function returns the median of the given numbers. The median is the number in the middle of a set of numbers; that is, half the numbers have values that are greater than the median and half have values that are less. If there is an even number of numbers in the set, MEDIAN calculates the average of the two numbers in the middle.

The arguments *number1*, *number2*, ... are one to 255 numbers for which you want the median. The arguments should be either numbers or names, arrays, or references that contain numbers. Microsoft Excel examines all the numbers in each reference or array argument. If an array or a reference argument contains text, logical values, or empty cells, those values are ignored; however, cells that contain the value 0 are included.

Syntax:

=MODE.SNGL(*number1*,*number2*,...)

The MODE.SNGL function returns the most frequently occurring, or repetitive, value in an array or a range of data. Like MEDIAN, MODE.SNGL is a location measure. In a set of values, the mode is the most frequently occurring value; the median is the middle value; and the mean is the average value. No single measure of central tendency provides a complete picture of the data. Suppose data is clustered in three areas, half around a single low value and half around two large values. Both `AVERAGE` and `MEDIAN` may return a value in the relatively empty middle, and `MODE.SNGL` may return the dominant low value.

The arguments *`number1, number2, ...`* are one to 255 arguments for which you want to calculate the mode. You can also use a single array or a reference to an array instead of arguments separated by commas. The arguments should be numbers, names, arrays, or references that contain numbers. If an array or reference argument contains text, logical values, or empty cells, those values are ignored; however, cells that contain the value 0 are included. If the data set contains no duplicate data points, `MODE` returns an `#N/A` error.

It is possible to have multiple values that tie as the mode. In the `MODE.SNGL` calculation, when two values tie as the mode, only the first mode value appears as the result. In Figure 14.4, the `MODE.SNGL` in E4 is reported as 88, even though both 88 and 82 appear most frequently in the data set. Microsoft added `MODE.MULT` to Excel 2010 to handle the situation where multiple values tie as the mode.

Figure 14.4 `AVERAGE`, `MEDIAN`, and `MODE.SNGL` all describe the central tendencies of a data set.

E6 =IF(COUNT(MODE.MULT(B2:B19))>2,INDEX(MODE.MULT(B2:B19),3),"")

	A	B	C	D	E	F
1	STUDENT	SCORE				
2	ALFRED	84		Mean	81.4444	=AVERAGE(B2:B19)
3	BRADLEY	75		Median	82.5	=MEDIAN(B2:B19)
4	CARLOS	83		Mode	88	=MODE.SNGL(B2:B19)
5	CHARLOTTE	91		Mode (Tie)	82	=IF(COUNT(MODE.MULT(B2:B19))>1,INDEX(MODE.MULT(B2:B19),2),"")
6	CLARA	73		Mode (Tie)		=IF(COUNT(MODE.MULT(B2:B19))>2,INDEX(MODE.MULT(B2:B19),3),"")
7	CLARENCE	83				
8	DENNIS	88				
9	EVA	82				
10	JUSTIN	88				
11	LOLA	79				
12	LUIS	87				
13	LYNN	82				
14	NORMAN	88				
15	REGINA	61				
16	RYAN	86				
17	SHELLEY	82				
18	VICTOR	78				
19	WHITNEY	76				

Figure 14.4 shows examples of `AVERAGE`, `MEAN`, and `MODE.SNGL`. Cell E2 calculates the arithmetic mean of the test scores in column B: 81.4444. The median in cell E3 is higher: 82.5. This means that half the students scored above 82.5 and half scored below 82.5. The mode in cell E4 as reported by `MODE.SNGL` is 88. A formula in E5 indicates that 82 is also tied as a mode. This is because 82 and 88 each appeared three times in the data set.

The range in Figure 14.4 demonstrates two anomalies with the median and mode. In this case, there are an even number of entries—18. It is impossible to figure out a median in this case, so Excel takes the average of the two values in the middle—82 and 83—to produce 82.5. This is the only situation in which the median is not a value from the table.

There are also two modes in the table. Both 88 and 82 appear three times. MODE.SNGL reports 88 as the mode because it encounters the 88 in B8 before it encounters the 82 in B9. This is rather arbitrary, and MODE.SNGL would change if the data were sorted in ascending sequence.

Read on to see how MODE.MULT can report all the mode values.

Syntax:

=MODE.MULT(*number1*,*number2*,...)

The MODE.MULT function returns a vertical array of the most frequently occurring, or repetitive, value in an array or a range of data. MODE.MULT was introduced in Excel 2010 to specifically address the situations where two or more values tie as the mode. The MODE.MULT function returns a vertical array of values as the answer.

Because MODE.MULT can return multiple values, you might think that you should enter the function in several cells and use Ctrl+Shift+Enter to enter the formula. Although this works, the unpredictability of the number of values returned by MODE.MULT makes this a dicey proposition.

In Figure 14.5, you see four different cases with MODE.MULT:

- In column B, five values each occur twice, creating a five-way tie for the MODE. Select cells C3:C7, type **=MODE.MULT(B3:B12)**, and hold down Ctrl+Shift while pressing Enter. This enters one formula in those five cells. This works out great; five values are returned, and they fill the five cells where the formula is entered.

- The first case has been copied to columns E:F. Cell E12 is changed from 5 to 6. This creates a four-way tie for the MODE.MULT. Because the formula is entered in five cells, you get the four-way tie as the first four cells and then #N/A as the fifth cell. This makes sense. There are a number of ways to deal with the #N/A value.

- In column H, all 10 values appear exactly once. Excel help warns that if no value appears two or more times, the answer for mode is #N/A. The results are all #N/A because there is officially no mode.

- In column K, the "normal" case of having one mode causes all sorts of problems. Because MODE.MULT returns a one-cell answer, the array formula assumes that you must want to expand that one-cell answer over the entire range where the formula is entered, so you get five 9s as the answer.

In row 14 of Figure 14.5, a nonarray formula counts how many results the MODE.MULT function will return. Using =COUNT(MODE.MULT(B3:B12)) is probably the best way to go.

To return the first mode, you can use

=MODE.SNGL(*range*)

To see whether there is a two-way tie, use

=IF(COUNT(MODE.MULT(*range*))>1,INDEX(MODE.MULT(*range*),2),"")

Figure 14.5
MODE.MULT is challenging to use.

B14				:	×	✓	*fx*	=COUNT(MODE.MULT(B3:B12))				

	A	B	C	D	E	F	G	H	I	J	K	L	M	N
1		5-way tie			4-way tie			No mode			1 mode			
2		Array	MM		Array	MM		Array	MM		Array	MM		
3		1	1		1	1		1	#N/A		1	9		
4		1	2		1	2		2	#N/A		2	9		
5		2	3		2	3		3	#N/A		3	9		
6		2	4		2	4		4	#N/A		4	9		
7		3	5		3	#N/A		5	#N/A		5	9		
8		3			3			6			6			
9		4			4			7			7			
10		4			4			8			8			
11		5			5			9			9			
12		5			6			10			9			
13														
14	Count:	5			4			0			1			
15		=COUNT(MODE.MULT(B3:B12))												

To see whether there is a three-way tie, use

```
=IF(COUNT(MODE.MULT(range))>2,INDEX(MODE.MULT(range),3),"")
```

You can continue this pattern for as many possible modes as you might expect. In an *N*-row data set, there might be as many as *N*/2 possible modes!

Using TRIMMEAN to Exclude Outliers from the Mean

Sometimes a data set includes a few outliers that radically skew the average. For example, suppose you have a list of gross margin percentages. Most percentages fall in the 45% to 50% range, but there was one deal where for customer satisfaction reasons, the product was given away at a loss. This one data point would skew the average unusually low.

The TRIMMEAN function takes the mean of data points but excludes the *n*% highest and lowest values. You have to use some care in expressing the *n*%.

Syntax:

```
=TRIMMEAN(array,percent)
```

The TRIMMEAN function returns the mean of the interior of a data set. TRIMMEAN calculates the mean taken by excluding a percentage of data points from the top and bottom tails of a data set. You can use this function when you want to exclude outlying data from your analysis. This function takes the following arguments:

- *array*—This is the array or range of values to trim and average.

- *percent*—This is the fractional number of data points to exclude from the calculation. For example, if *percent* is 0.2, 4 points are trimmed from a data set of 20 points (that is, 20 × 0.2): 2 from the top and 2 from the bottom of the set.

If *percent* is less than 0 or greater than 1, TRIMMEAN returns a #NUM! error. TRIMMEAN rounds the number of excluded data points down to the nearest multiple of 2. If *percent* equals 0.1, 10% of 30 data points equals 3 points. For symmetry, TRIMMEAN excludes a single value from the top and bottom of the data set.

Using GEOMEAN to Calculate Average Growth Rate

Suppose that your 401(k) plan is invested in a stock market index fund. The stock market goes up 5%, 40%, and 15% in three successive years. Taking the average of these numbers might lead someone to believe that the average increase was 20% per year. This is not correct. The growth rates are all multiplied together to find an ending value of your investment. To find the average growth rate, you need to find a number that, when multiplied together three times, yields the same result as 105% × 140% − 115%. You can calculate this by using GEOMEAN.

To find the geometric mean of 10 numbers, you multiply the 10 numbers together and raise the sum to the 1/10 power. Excel lets you do this quickly with GEOMEAN.

 Caution

The arguments must be either numbers or names, arrays, or references that contain numbers. If an array or a reference argument contains text, logical values, or empty cells, those values are ignored. However, cells that contain the value 0 are included. If any data point is less than or equal to 0, GEOMEAN returns a #NUM! error.

Syntax:

```
=GEOMEAN(number1, number2,...)
```

The GEOMEAN function returns the geometric mean of an array or a range of positive data. For example, you can use GEOMEAN to calculate average growth rate, given compound interest with variable rates.

The arguments *number1*, *number2*, ... are one to 255 arguments for which you want to calculate the mean. You can also use a single array or a reference to an array instead of arguments separated by commas.

Using HARMEAN to Find Average Speeds

The typical averaging function fails when you are measuring speeds over a period of time. Suppose that your exercise regimen is 5 minutes of walking at 2 mph, 25 minutes of running at 5 mph, and then 10 minutes of jogging at 3 mph. If you took the average of (2, 5, 5, 5, 5, 5, 3, 3), you would assume that you averaged 4.125 miles per hour.

The actual calculation for average speed would be to take the reciprocals of each speed, average those values, and then take the reciprocal of the result. In the exercise example, you would average (1/2, 1/5, 1/5, 1/5, 1/5, 1/5, 1/3, 1/3) to obtain 13/48. Then you would take the reciprocal, 48/13, to find the actual average speed of 3.69 mph.

Syntax:

=HARMEAN(*number1*,*number2*,...)

The HARMEAN function returns the harmonic mean of a data set. The harmonic mean is the reciprocal of the arithmetic mean of reciprocals. The arguments *number1*, *number2*, ... are one to 255 arguments for which you want to calculate the mean. You can also use a single array or a reference to an array instead of arguments separated by commas.

The arguments must be either numbers or names, arrays, or references that contain numbers. If an array or a reference argument contains text, logical values, or empty cells, those values are ignored; however, cells that contain the value 0 are included. If any data point is less than or equal to 0, HARMEAN returns a #NUM! error. The harmonic mean is always less than the geometric mean, which is always less than the arithmetic mean.

Using AVERAGEIF or AVERAGEIFS

Excel 2007 included two new conditional calculation functions: AVERAGEIF and AVERAGEIFS. These functions find the mean of records that match one or more criteria.

Syntax:

AVERAGEIF(*range*,*criteria*,*average_range*)

AVERAGEIF returns the arithmetic mean of all the cells in a range that meet a given criteria.

- *range*—One or more cells to average, including numbers or names, arrays, or references that contain numbers.

- *criteria*—The criteria in the form of a number, expression, cell reference, or text that defines which cells are averaged. For example, criteria can be expressed as 32, "32", ">32", "apples", or B4.

- *average_range*—The actual set of cells to average. If omitted, *range* is used.

Syntax:

AVERAGEIFS(*average_range*,*criteria_range1*, *criteria1*,*criteria_range2*,*criteria2*...)

AVERAGEIFS returns the arithmetic mean of all cells that meet multiple criteria.

- *average_range*—One or more cells to average, including numbers or names, arrays, or references that contain numbers.

- *criteria_range1*, *criteria_range2*, ...—One to 127 ranges in which to evaluate the associated criteria.

- *criteria1, criteria2, ...*—One to 127 criteria in the form of a number, expression, cell reference, or text that defines which cells will be averaged. For example, criteria can be expressed as 32, "32", ">32", "apples", or B4.

Using RANK to Calculate the Position Within a List

At times you need to determine the order of values, but you are not allowed to sort the data. The RANK function helps with this task.

Suppose five bowlers scored 187, 185, 185, 170, and 160. The traditional way to rank the players is that two players would have a rank of 2, and the next player would have a rank of 4. No one would be ranked number 3. Although this is technically correct, it can cause problems if you have lookup values expecting to find a person ranked number 3. The example at the end of this section explains how to overcome such a situation. The clever Excellers who hoped to use RANK to sort a list using formulas really want RANK to return one of every rank.

As of Excel 2010, Microsoft renamed the old RANK as RANK.EQ. It added a new rank called RANK.AVG. In the same situation with the five bowlers, both of the scores of 185 would get a rank of 2.5. A rank of 2.5 is the average of the ranks of 2 and 3.

 Note

Excel gurus have been complaining about an anomaly with the RANK function. Apparently, a bunch of scientists have also been complaining about RANK. Microsoft fixed the RANK function in Excel 2010. But they listened to the complaints of the scientists instead of the gurus. So, now there are two rank functions and neither one is going to make the Excel pros happy.

Syntax:

```
=RANK.EQ(number,ref,order)
=RANK.AVG(number,ref,order)
```

Neither RANK.EQ nor RANK.AVG calculates in Excel 2007 or earlier. In legacy versions of Excel, use the RANK function to calculate RANK.EQ. There was no equivalent of RANK.AVG in versions of Excel before 2010.

The RANK functions return the rank of a number in a list of numbers. The rank of a number is its size relative to other values in a list. If you were to sort the list, the rank of the number would be its position. This function takes the following arguments:

- *number*—This is the number whose rank you want to find.

- *ref*—This is an array of, or a reference to, a list of numbers. Nonnumeric values in *ref* are ignored.

- *order*—This is a number that specifies how to rank *number*. For a value of 0 or if this argument is omitted, Excel ranks *number* as if *ref* were a list sorted in descending order. If *order* is any nonzero value, Excel ranks *number* as if *ref* were a list sorted in ascending order.

RANK.EQ gives duplicate numbers the same lower rank. However, the presence of duplicate numbers affects the ranks of subsequent numbers. For example, in a list of integers, if the number 10 appears twice and has a rank of 5, then 11 would have a rank of 7. (No number would have a rank of 6.)

RANK.AVG gives duplicate numbers the same rank by averaging the ranks of the next two positions. In the same example, if the number 10 appears twice and would hold the number 5 and 6 positions, both of the 10s would receive an average rank of 5.5.

In Figure 14.6, column B contains a list of scores. The formula for cell C2 is =RANK. EQ(B2,$B$2:$B$13). Notice that the third argument is omitted, so the highest score is ranked as number 1. Also notice that the second argument is marked as absolute so that the formula can be copied, and it always points to the same ref range.

Figure 14.6
In this case, RANK.EQ and RANK.AVG return different values when a tie occurs.

	B7			▼	:	×	✓	f_x	117			
▲	A	B	C	D	E	F	G	H				
1	NAME	COMPLETED	RANK.EQ	RANK.AVG								
2	YOLANDA HILL	83	8	8	C2: =RANK.EQ(B2,$B$2:$B$13)							
3	LEE DOUGLAS	80	9	9	D2: =RANK.AVG(B2,$B$2:$B$13)							
4	GREGORY BOWEN	135	2	2								
5	LOUIS MOLINA	85	7	7								
6	ANDREW HALL	69	12	12								
7	RANDY TRUJILLO	117	4	4								
8	MARTHA PHELPS	70	10	10.5								
9	CRAIG VAUGHAN	70	10	10.5								
10	SHARON COMPTON	146	1	1								
11	DOUGLAS BYERS	104	5	5								
12	LAURIE MEYER	133	3	3								
13	SONIA TRUJILLO	93	6	6								

Column D uses the new RANK.AVG to rank the scores. Note the differences in rows 8 and 9. The tied values both receive a lower rank of 10 with RANK.EQ and a value of 10.5 with RANK.AVG. None of the records are ranked 11.

If you need the lowest value to be ranked as number 1, add a third argument of 1 to indicate that the lowest number is the best—for example, =RANK(B2,$B$2:$B$13,1).

A common Excel trick is to use the ranking function combined with VLOOKUP or MATCH to sort a range with a formula. You might assign ranks and then use VLOOKUP to find the people who are ranked first, second, and third.

The VLOOKUP function certainly is not expecting two people to be ranked at number 2 as RANK.EQ would do. It definitely would never expect the duplicate 2.5 values that RANK.AVG would return. The generally accepted solution is to use RANK.EQ and then add a COUNTIF function that checks to see how many rows above this row have the identical value.

In Figure 14.7, examine the formula in cell C7. COUNTIF asks how many times the value in cell B7 was found in B$2:B6. This final reference is an interesting reference. It tells Excel to count always from row 2 down to the row above the current row. It is easier to build this formula in the final cell of the column and then copy it upward.

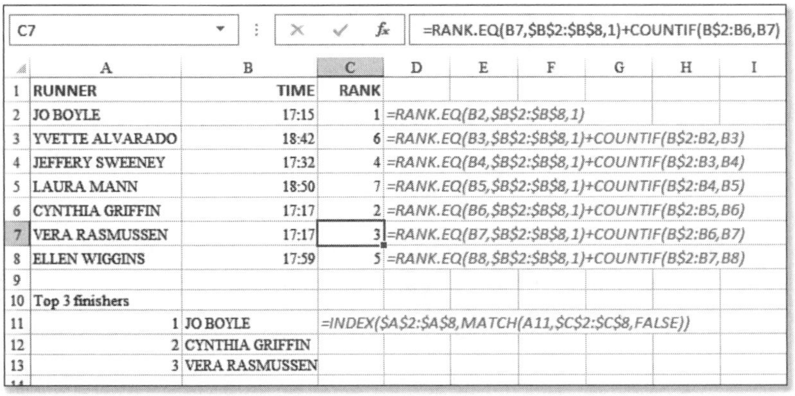

C7 =RANK.EQ(B7,$B$2:$B$8,1)+COUNTIF(B$2:B6,B7)

	A	B	C	D
1	RUNNER	TIME	RANK	
2	JO BOYLE	17:15	1	=RANK.EQ(B2,$B$2:$B$8,1)
3	YVETTE ALVARADO	18:42	6	=RANK.EQ(B3,$B$2:$B$8,1)+COUNTIF(B$2:B2,B3)
4	JEFFERY SWEENEY	17:32	4	=RANK.EQ(B4,$B$2:$B$8,1)+COUNTIF(B$2:B3,B4)
5	LAURA MANN	18:50	7	=RANK.EQ(B5,$B$2:$B$8,1)+COUNTIF(B$2:B4,B5)
6	CYNTHIA GRIFFIN	17:17	2	=RANK.EQ(B6,$B$2:$B$8,1)+COUNTIF(B$2:B5,B6)
7	VERA RASMUSSEN	17:17	3	=RANK.EQ(B7,$B$2:$B$8,1)+COUNTIF(B$2:B6,B7)
8	ELLEN WIGGINS	17:59	5	=RANK.EQ(B8,$B$2:$B$8,1)+COUNTIF(B$2:B7,B8)
9				
10	Top 3 finishers			
11	1	JO BOYLE	=INDEX($A$2:$A$8,MATCH(A11,$C$2:$C$8,FALSE))	
12	2	CYNTHIA GRIFFIN		
13	3	VERA RASMUSSEN		

Figure 14.7
You use a `COUNTIF` to break ties.

More Than You Ever Wanted to Know About the Controversy of Percentiles and Quartiles

A huge argument is raging over the best way to calculate percentiles and quartiles. Suppose that you have 11 scores. You ask Excel to tell you the score at the 15th percentile. Typically, Excel assigns the smallest value to the 0th percentile and the largest value to the 100th percentile. Because there are 10 steps between the smallest and largest value, the 10th percentile will be the second-smallest number, and the 20th percentile will be the third-smallest number. What number is at the 15th percentile? How about at the 17th percentile? Excel divides the gap between the second and third values into 10 equal parts and uses that interpolation to calculate the number at the 11th percentile and so on.

In 1996, two scholars named Hyndman and Fan published a paper detailing 12 different methods for calculating percentiles and quartiles. Legacy versions of Excel used method #7, which was defined by Gumbull. Other software such as MiniTab and SPSS used method #6, which was defined by Weibull. People who care a lot about percentiles and quartiles talk about "Hyndman and Fan Method #X."

In Excel, the Hyndman and Fan method #7 is still available as `QUARTILE.INC`, `PERCENTILE.INC`, and `PERCENTRANK.INC`. Excel 2010 introduced support for Hyndman and Fan method #6 as `QUARTILE.EXC`, `PERCENTILE.EXC`, and `PERCENTRANK.EXC`.

Here is what you have to know about the controversy: With a data set of 100 numbers or more, the difference between `.EXC` and `.INC` versions are small—less than one-half of 1%. However, in small data sets of n=4 to n=7, the values at the first quartile can swing by 40%. For example, in the data set of {10,22,33,40}, Weibull calculates the first quartile at 13 and Gumbull calculates the first quartile at 19. The delta between 19 and 13 is 6, which is 46% of 13.

Also, in the `.EXC` version, there is no 0th percentile and no 100th percentile. The `.EXC` stands for percentiles from 0% to 100%, exclusive. The `.INC` stands for percentiles from 0% to 100% inclusive.

> ▶ *If you want to read all the details about the Hyndman and Fan Method #X, check out www.daheiser.info/excel/notes/NOTE% 20N.pdf for a comparison of the methods.*

Using QUARTILE.INC to Break a Data Set into Quarters

Use QUARTILE.INC to divide populations into groups.

Syntax:

=QUARTILE.INC(*array*,*quart*)
=QUARTILE.EXC(*array*,*quart*)

 Note

MIN, MEDIAN, and MAX return the same value as QUARTILE.INC when *quart* is equal to 0, 2, and 4, respectively.

The old QUARTILE function is included in Excel for compatibility only. QUARTILE.INC is the renamed version of QUARTILE. The QUARTILE.INC function returns the quartile of a data set. Quartiles are often used in sales and survey data to divide populations into groups. For example, you can use QUARTILE.INC to find the top 25% of incomes in a population. These functions take the following arguments:

- **array**—This is the array or cell range of numeric values for which you want the quartile value. If array is empty, QUARTILE returns a #NUM! error.

- **quart**—This indicates which value to return. You use 0 for the minimum value, 1 for the first quartile (25th percentile), 2 for the median value (50th percentile), 3 for the third quartile (75th percentile), and 4 for the maximum value. If *quart* is not an integer, it is truncated. If *quart* is less than 0 or greater than 4, QUARTILE returns a #NUM! error.

In Figure 14.8, the formulas in B20:C23 break out the limits for each quartile. The formula in cell B20 is =QUARTILE.INC($B$2:$B$17,0) to find the minimum value. The formula in cells C20 and B21 is =QUARTILE.INC($B$2:$B$17,1) to define the end of the first quartile and the start of the second quartile.

After the QUARTILE.INC functions build the table in B20:C23, the VLOOKUP function returns the text in C2:C17. The formula in cell C2 is =VLOOKUP(B2,$B$20:$D$23,3,TRUE).

B20 | =QUARTILE.INC($B$2:$B$17,0)

	A	B	C	D	E	F	G	H
1	Customer	Revenue	Where					
2	New Toothpick Inc.	100	First Quartile		=VLOOKUP(B2,$B$20:$D$23,3,TRUE)			
3	Easy Furnace Supply	300	First Quartile					
4	Distinctive Marble Supply	600	First Quartile					
5	Bright Linen Inc.	600	First Quartile					
6	Tasty Chopstick Corporation	1000	Second Quartile					
7	Agile Freezer Corporation	3000	Second Quartile					
8	Powerful Shingle Corporation	6000	Second Quartile					
9	Wonderful Luggage Inc.	7000	Second Quartile					
10	Trendy Shovel Inc.	10000	Third Quartile					
11	Trouble-Free Toothpick Company	10000	Third Quartile					
12	Easy Quilt Company	10000	Third Quartile					
13	Stunning Vise Inc.	40000	Fourth Quartile					
14	Astonishing Bottle Corporation	40000	Fourth Quartile					
15	First-Rate Marble Inc.	70000	Fourth Quartile					
16	Unique Tuner Corporation	90000	Fourth Quartile					
17	Refined Marble Inc.	100000	Fourth Quartile					
18								
19		From	Thru					
20	First Quartile	100	900	First Quartile				
21	Second Quartile	900	8500	Second Quartile				
22	Third Quartile	8500	40000	Third Quartile				
23	Fourth Quartile	40000	100000	Fourth Quartile				
24								

Figure 14.8
The `QUARTILE.INC` function can break up a data set into four equal pieces.

Using `PERCENTILE.INC` to Calculate Percentile

The `QUARTILE.INC` function is fine if you are trying to find every record that is in the top 25% of a range. Sometimes, however, you need to find some other percentile. For example, all employees ranked above the 81st percentile might be eligible for a bonus this year. You can use the `PERCENTILE.INC` function to determine the threshold for any percentile.

Syntax:

```
=PERCENTILE.INC(array,k)
=PERCENTILE.EXC(array,k)
```

The Excel 2007 `PERCENTILE` function is included in Excel 2013 for compatibility with older versions. In Excel 2013, the `PERCENTILE.INC` function is equivalent to `PERCENTILE`. The new `PERCENTILE.EXC` function made its debut in Excel 2010.

The `PERCENTILE.INC` function returns the *k*th percentile of values in a range. You can use this function to establish a threshold of acceptance. For example, you can decide to examine candidates who score above the 90th percentile. This function takes the following arguments:

- ***array***—This is the array or range of data that defines relative standing. If *array* is empty, `PERCENTILE.INC` returns a `#NUM!` error.
- ***k***—This is the percentile value in the range 0–1, inclusive. If *k* is nonnumeric, `PERCENTILE.INC` returns a `#VALUE!` error. If *k* is less than 0 or greater than 1, `PERCENTILE.INC` returns a `#NUM!`

error. If *k* is not a multiple of 1 / (n – 1), `PERCENTILE.INC` interpolates to determine the value at the *k*th percentile. In this case, n is the number of items in the array.

In Figure 14.9, 33 employees are in column A. Their ratings on an annual review are shown in column B. The formula in cell F3, `=PERCENTILE.INC(B2:B34,F2)`, calculates the level of the 81st percentile. After you determine the particular percentile, you can mark all the qualifying employees by using the formula `=B2>=$F$3` in cells C2:C33.

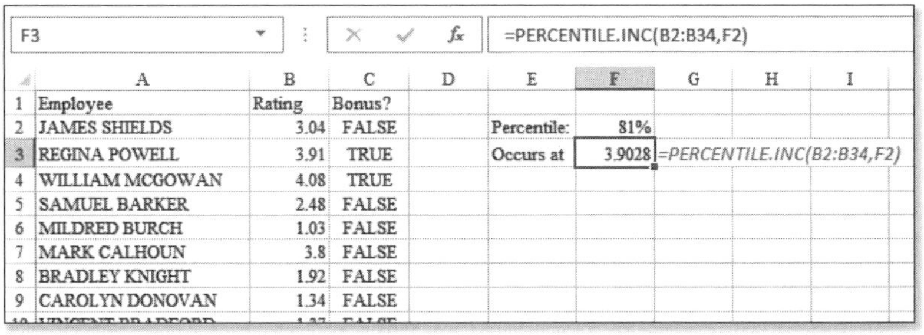

F3 =PERCENTILE.INC(B2:B34,F2)

	A	B	C	D	E	F	G	H	I
1	Employee	Rating	Bonus?						
2	JAMES SHIELDS	3.04	FALSE		Percentile:	81%			
3	REGINA POWELL	3.91	TRUE		Occurs at	3.9028	=PERCENTILE.INC(B2:B34,F2)		
4	WILLIAM MCGOWAN	4.08	TRUE						
5	SAMUEL BARKER	2.48	FALSE						
6	MILDRED BURCH	1.03	FALSE						
7	MARK CALHOUN	3.8	FALSE						
8	BRADLEY KNIGHT	1.92	FALSE						
9	CAROLYN DONOVAN	1.34	FALSE						

Figure 14.9
Unlike `QUARTILE.INC`, the `PERCENTILE.INC` function can determine the breaking point for any particular percentile.

Using `PERCENTRANK.INC` to Assign a Percentile to Every Record

Suppose you have a database of students in a graduating class. Each student has a certain grade point average. To determine each student's standing in the class, you use the `PERCENTRANK.INC` function.

Syntax:

```
=PERCENTRANK.INC(array,x,significance)
=PERCENTRANK.EXC(array,x,significance)
```

The Excel 2007 `PERCENTRANK` function is being replaced by `PERCENTRANK.INC`. The `PERCENTRANK.EXC` function made its debut in Excel 2010.

The `PERCENTRANK.INC` function returns the rank of a value in a data set as a percentage of the data set. You can use this function to evaluate the relative standing of a value within a data set. For example, you can use `PERCENTRANK.INC` to evaluate the standing of an aptitude test score among all scores for the test. This function takes the following arguments:

- ***array***—This is the array or range of data with numeric values that defines relative standing. If *array* is empty, `PERCENTRANK.INC` returns a `#NUM!` error.
- ***x***—This is the value for which you want to know the rank. If *x* does not match one of the values in *array*, `PERCENTRANK.INC` interpolates to return the correct percentage rank.
- ***significance***—This is an optional value that identifies the number of significant digits for the returned percentage value. If it is omitted, `PERCENTRANK.INC` uses three digits (that is, 0.xxx). If *significance* is less than 1, `PERCENTRANK.INC` returns a `#NUM!` error.

This function is slightly different from RANK, so use caution. Typically, RANK and other functions would ask for *x* as the first argument and *array* as the second argument. If you use this function and everyone is assigned to the 100% level, you might have reversed the arguments. The Excel Help is a bit misleading with regard to significance. The Help topic indicates that a significance of 3 generates a value accurate to 0.xxx%. In fact, a significance of 3 returns xx.x%.

In Figure 14.10, the students' GPAs are in B3:B302. The rank for the first student is `=PERCENTRANK.INC($B$3:$B$302,B3,3)`. Note that PERCENTRANK.INC always starts with the lowest score at the lowest percentile.

D302 | =PERCENTRANK.EXC($B$3:$B$302,B302,3)

	A	B	C	D	E	F	G	H	I	J
1			PERCENTRANK							
2	Student	GPA	.INC	.EXC						
3	TRAVIS COMPTON	4.00	99.6%	99.3%		C3: =PERCENTRANK.INC($B$3:$B$302,B3,3)				
4	VICTOR REID	4.00	99.6%	99.3%		D3: =PERCENTRANK.EXC($B$3:$B$302,B3,3)				
5	ERIN COLE	3.99	98.6%	98.3%						
6	CANDICE MATTHEWS	3.99	98.6%	98.3%						
7	KEITH RATLIFF	3.99	98.6%	98.3%		Significance				
8	RONALD GAMBLE	3.98	98.3%	98.0%		1	0.9			
9	PHILLIP BLEVINS	3.97	97.9%	97.6%		2	0.99			
10	JANICE LEWIS	3.96	97.6%	97.3%		3	0.996			
11	JAMIE TURNER	3.95	97.3%	97.0%		4	0.9966			
12	MAXINE HENDRIX	3.93	96.9%	96.6%		5	0.99665			
13	LYNN POTTS	3.92	96.6%	96.3%						
298	ANDREW NOEL	1.83	1.3%	1.6%						
299	RYAN BRADLEY	1.82	0.6%	0.9%						
300	KRISTINE DAY	1.82	0.6%	0.9%						
301	TIFFANY BOOTH	1.81	0.3%	0.6%						
302	CHRISTOPHER MOON	1.80	0.0%	0.3%						
303										

Figure 14.10
The PERCENTRANK.INC function assigns percentile values to an array of values.

The table in F7:G12 shows the actual behavior of the *significance* argument. The values in column G show the PERCENTRANK.INC of cell B2 to the significance in column F. You can see that the student ranked at the 99.6th percentile is in the 90th percentile when the significance is 1. A significance of 1 would assign 30 records to be at the 90th percentile.

Figure 14.10 also shows the difference between PERCENTRANK.INC and PERCENTRANK.EXC. Although Christopher Moon is at the 0.0th percentile in cell C302 using PERCENTRANK.INC, the .EXC version never assigns a value to the 0.0 percentile. Cell D302 shows a percentile of 0.3% for the lowest score in a 300 row data set.

Using AVEDEV, DEVSQ, VAR.S, and STDEV.S to Calculate Dispersion

Functions such as AVERAGE tell you about the center of a range of data. Seeing the center is not always the entire picture. The other key element of descriptive statistics is dispersion. If you have a population, the average height might be *x*. If you look at dispersion, you can find out if every member of the population is tightly grouped around the average or if there is wide variability.

Here are several measures of dispersion:

- Average deviation is calculated by measuring the absolute difference of each data point from the mean and then averaging these values. Suppose the values in a population are 12, 14, 16, 18, and 20. The mean is 16. Average deviation adds up 4, 2, 0, 2, and 4 and divides the total by 5 to yield 2.4. Excel offers AVEDEV to calculate this.

- Average deviation is not perfect. Suppose you have another population of 11, 15, 16, 17, and 21. Again, the mean is 16. The average deviation averages 5, 1, 0, 1, and 5 to yield an average deviation of 2.4. If you want to measure how far from the mean the points range, you can add up the squares of each deviation. In this case, the square of 5 is 25, and it indicates more dispersion than the square of 4. Excel offers DEVSQ to calculate the squares of each deviation.

- Variance is a common measurement of dispersion. It averages the square deviations to come up with the variance of a data set. Here is the one odd thing about variance: Suppose you have 20 measurements, and they represent the entire population (for example, the 20 fish in an aquarium). In this case, you divide DEVSQ by 20 to calculate the variance. You use VAR.P in Excel to do this. However, if your 20 values are a random sample, then variance is calculated by dividing DEVSQ by 20 − 1, or 19. You use VAR.S in Excel to calculate this.

- The measurement for variance is a square, right? You took all the deviations, squared them, and then averaged (or nearly averaged) them. The final popular measure of dispersion is calculated by taking the square root of the variance. This number is called *standard deviation*. Excel offers two functions for standard deviation. You use STDEV.P if your data set represents the entire population, and you use STDEV.S if your data set represents only a sample of the population.

Theories About Standard Deviation

There are many theories about standard deviation. One general rule states that 95% of a population is located within two standard deviations of the mean. If you extend your range to within three standard deviations of the mean, that range should encompass 99.7% of the population.

Figure 14.11 shows the lengths of fish. Column A contains the lengths of all 20 fish in one particular tank at a science museum. Column E contains the lengths of 20 random fish observed while snorkeling at a coral reef. Both groups have a mean value of 18.58 inches, as shown in cells C4 and G4.

The fish in the museum tank have an average deviation of 1.45 inches from the mean. Cells C6, C8, and C10 walk through the calculation of squares of deviation, variance, and standard deviation. The theory about standard deviation says that of the fish in the tank, 95% occur between 15.08 inches and 22.07 inches.

The fish at the coral reef have an average deviation of 6.7 inches from the mean. Cells G6, G7, and G9 walk through the calculation of squares of deviation, variance, and standard deviation. The theory about standard deviation says that of the fish at the coral reef, 95% will be between 0.78 inches and 36.37 inches long.

Comparing these two results helps you to picture the likely populations of both locations. Although both have the same mean size, the variety of fish (that is, the measure of dispersion) at the coral reef is much higher than that at the aquarium.

G9			:	×	✓	*fx*	=STDEV.S(E4:E23)	
▲	A	B	C	D	E	F	G	H
1	**Length of Fish**							
2								
3	Aquarium				Coral Reef			
4	15.6	Mean	18.58		2	Mean	18.58	
5	15.8	AveDev	1.45		8	AveDev	6.774	
6	16.6	DevSq	57.992		9.7	DevSq	1503.452	
7	16.7	VAR.S	3.052211		10.3	VAR.S	79.12905	
8	16.8	VAR.P	2.8996		12	VAR.P	75.1726	
9	17.4	StDev.S	1.747058		14	StDev.S	8.89545	
10	17.7	StDev.P	1.702821		14.3	StDev.P	8.670213	
11	18.2				16.2			
12	18.2	95% of population:			16.7	95% of population:		
13	18.3	From:	15.08588		16.9	From:	0.789098	
14	18.6	Thru:	22.07412		17.7	Thru:	36.3709	
15	18.7				18			

Figure 14.11
Although the averages are the same, the dispersion measurements paint a different picture of these populations.

Syntax:

=AVEDEV(*number1*,*number2*,...)

The AVEDEV function returns the average of the absolute deviations of data points from their mean. AVEDEV is a measure of the variability in a data set. AVEDEV is influenced by the unit of measurement in the input data.

Syntax:

=DEVSQ(*number1*,*number2*,...)

The DEVSQ function returns the sum of squares of deviations of data points from their sample mean.

Syntax:

=VAR.S(*number1*,*number2*,...)

The VAR.S function estimates variance based on a sample.

Syntax:

=VAR.P(*number1*,*number2*,...)

The VAR.P function calculates variance based on the entire population.

 Caution

Logical values (TRUE/FALSE) are ignored in the STDEV.S and STDEV.P calculations. For some statistics, you need to figure out how many people answered TRUE to a question. To count TRUE values as 1 and FALSE values as 0, you use VARA, VARPA, STDEVA, and STDEVPA versions of those four functions.

Syntax:

```
=STDEV.S(number1,number2,...)
```

The STDEV.S function estimates standard deviation based on a sample. The standard deviation is a measure of how widely values are dispersed from the average value (that is, the mean). The standard deviation is calculated using the "nonbiased" or "n − 1" method.

Syntax:

```
=STDEV.p(number1,number2,...)
```

The STDEV.P function calculates standard deviation based on the entire population, given as arguments. The standard deviation is a measure of how widely values are dispersed from the average value (that is, the mean). STDEV.P assumes that its arguments are the entire population. If your data represents a sample of the population, you can compute the standard deviation by using STDEV.S. For large sample sizes, STDEV.S and STDEV.P return approximately equal values. The standard deviation is calculated using the "biased" or "n" method.

Prior to Excel 2007, VAR.S was simply known as VAR. VAR.P was known as VARP. STDEV.S was STDEV. STDEV.P was STDEVP. If you are going to be sharing your workbook with people using Excel 2003 or earlier, use the old names instead of the new names.

The arguments *number1, number2, ...* are one to 255 arguments for which you want the average of the absolute deviations. You can also use a single array or a reference to an array instead of arguments separated by commas. The arguments must be either numbers or names, arrays, or references that contain numbers. If an array or a reference argument contains text, logical values, or empty cells, those values are ignored; however, cells that contain the value 0 are included.

Examples of Functions for Regression and Forecasting

Regression analysis allows you to predict the future, based on past events. Suppose you have observed total sales for the past several years. Regression analysis finds a line that best fits the past data points. You can then use the description of that line to predict results for the future data points.

Regression works by finding a line that can best be drawn through existing data points. In real-life data, the data points aren't arranged exactly in a line. Any line that the computer draws will have errors at any data point. Regression finds the line that minimizes the errors at each data point.

Consider the error in a regression line. The actual data point in Year 1 might be higher than the regression line by 2. In Year 2, the data might be lower by 1, and in Year 3 it might be lower by 1. If you added up these three errors, you would have an error of 0. This is a bad method. If you used this method to judge a line with errors of +400, −300, −100, it would also add up to an error of 0.

Instead, the regression engine sums the square of each error. In this case, the first line would have an error of $2^2 + {-1}^2 + {-1}^2$ or $4 + 1 + 1$, or 6. The second line would have an error of $400^2 + {-300}^2 + {-100}^2$ or $160{,}000 + 90{,}000 + 10{,}000$, or 260,000. With this method, the error for the first line is clearly better than the error for the second line. This method is called the *least-squares method*.

You might wonder why regression doesn't add the absolute value of each error. Ideally, the errors around the regression line should be narrow. A line with errors of −4, +4, −4, +4 would result in a sum of squares of 64. A line with errors of −7, 1, 7, −1 would result in a sum of squares of 100. The sum of squares method would deem the earlier line to be better, whereas using absolute values would call them equal.

Considerations When Using Regression Analysis

You need to consider one question before doing regression analysis: Is the data series growing linearly or exponentially? Sales for a company might grow linearly. The number of bacteria cells in a Petri dish might grow exponentially. You use LINEST and TREND to predict sales that are growing linearly. You use LOGEST and GROWTH to predict bacteria that are growing exponentially.

In Figure 14.12, the chart on the left shows sales over time. These sales are growing linearly and could probably be predicted fairly well by a straight line. The dotted line in the chart is the straight-line regression for the data set. Although each data point is either above or below the regression line, the error at any given data point is fairly small.

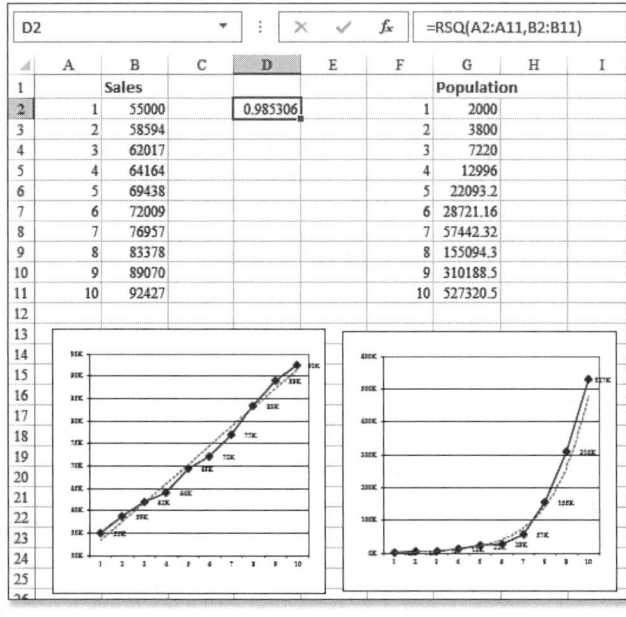

Figure 14.12
These two data sets can be accurately predicted using regression.

The chart on the right shows an exponential growth curve. In this chart, the dotted line shows the regression line plotted using LOGEST. Again, although the dotted line does not correlate exactly with the actual data points, it is fairly close.

Here is the problem: Regression always finds a line to fit your data set. In Figure 14.13, no apparent correlation exists between sales and time. Each year, the sales fluctuate wildly up or down. If you asked Excel to use regression, it would gladly predict the dotted line shown in the graph. The problem is that this line has no predictive ability. If you base your future sales on this line, you will get results that will vary greatly from the prediction.

Figure 14.13
This data set has no correlation to time. LINEST happily predicts a line, but it is severely wrong most of the time.

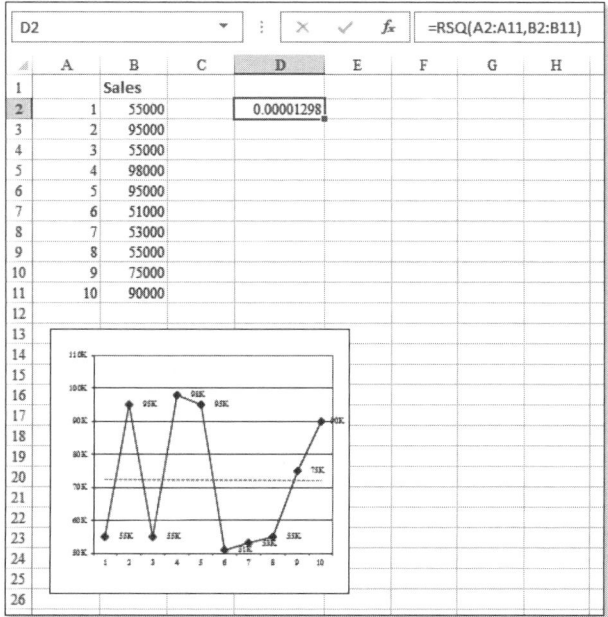

Part of the results of regression analysis are statistics that tell how well the regression line fits the actual data. You should always check statistics such as *r*-squared or the standard error to see if the past data shows a relationship between the variables. The *r*-squared value is a value between 0 and 1. The closer that *r*-squared is to 1, the better the regression line. The *r*-squared for the left chart in Figure 14.12 is 0.985. The *r*-squared for the chart in Figure 14.13 is 0.000001, indicating that no correlation exists.

When you have data like the data in Figure 14.13, it does not mean that you cannot use regression analysis. It means that you need to think about the data to see if other factors could help describe the data. Suppose that the data represents sales of squares of roofing shingles in Florida. If you add data to the chart that describes the number of category 3+ hurricanes making landfall each year, the sales numbers begin to make sense. The *r*-squared for predicting sales based on year is nearly 0. The *r*-squared for predicting sales based on hurricanes is 0.987. Because an *r*-squared of 1 means almost perfect correlation, you could base prediction of sales on a forecast of hurricanes.

Regression Function Arguments

For all the following regression functions, the arguments list generally includes these two arguments (for brevity, they are described here once):

- **_known_y_'s**—This is an array or a cell range of numeric dependent data points. This is the range of data that you want to predict. It might be the actual sales for the past several years or the population of bacteria for the past several hours.

- **_known_x_'s**—This is the set of independent data points. These are the values that you think will lead to a prediction of the y values. For a simple time series, this might be a list of year numbers. It might be a list of other independent data points, such as the number of hurricanes making landfall each year.

The arguments must be numbers or names, arrays, or references that contain numbers. If an array or a reference argument contains text, logical values, or empty cells, those values are ignored; however, cells that contain the value 0 are included. If _known_y_'s and _known_x_'s are empty or have a different number of data points, the function returns an #N/A error.

Functions for Simple Straight-Line Regression: SLOPE and INTERCEPT

With many things in Excel, there is a right way to do something. However, sometimes the powers-that-be decide that the right way is too difficult for Excel customers, so they offer alternative, easier ways to solve problems.

The LINEST function is powerful, and using it is the right way to calculate straight-line regression. However, because the LINEST function returns an array of values, it seemed too difficult, so Microsoft also offers the SLOPE and INTERCEPT functions to retrieve the key results from LINEST.

In mathematical terms, a line is described as $y = mx + b$:

- **y**—This is the value you are trying to predict. It could be sales for a given year.

- **b**—This is called the y-intercept. This is the base level of sales that you can count on year after year.

- **m**—This is the slope of the line. If your sales are going up by 1,000 per year, the slope is 1,000. If your sales are going up by 100,000 per year, the slope is 100,000.

- **x**—This is a point along the x-axis. In a problem where you are measuring sales over a span of several years, you can assign year numbers 1, 2, 3, and so on to each year. x then corresponds to a year number.

If you have a series of year numbers and sales for each year, you need to calculate both the SLOPE and INTERCEPT to describe the line.

Syntax:

=SLOPE(*known_y's*,*known_x's*)

The SLOPE function returns the slope of the linear regression line through data points in *known_y's* and *known_x's*. The slope is the vertical distance divided by the horizontal distance between any two points on the line; in other words, it is the rate of change along the regression line.

Syntax:

=INTERCEPT(*known_y's*,*known_x's*)

The INTERCEPT function calculates the point at which a line intersects the y-axis by using existing x values and y values. The intercept point is based on a best-fit regression line plotted through the known x values and known y values. You use the intercept when you want to determine the value of the dependent variable when the independent variable is 0.

In Figure 14.14, the sales in B2:B11 are the dependent variables. In the language of Excel, these are the *known_y's*. You are predicting that sales are increasing linearly over time. The year numbers in A2:A11 are the independent variables. In the language of Excel, these are the *known_x's*.

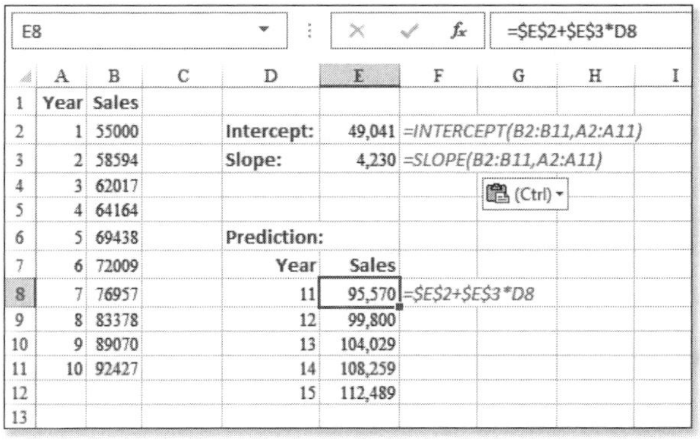

E8 =$E$2+$E$3*D8

	A	B	C	D	E	F	G	H	I
1	Year	Sales							
2	1	55000		Intercept:	49,041	=INTERCEPT(B2:B11,A2:A11)			
3	2	58594		Slope:	4,230	=SLOPE(B2:B11,A2:A11)			
4	3	62017					(Ctrl)		
5	4	64164							
6	5	69438		Prediction:					
7	6	72009		Year	Sales				
8	7	76957		11	95,570	=$E$2+$E$3*D8			
9	8	83378		12	99,800				
10	9	89070		13	104,029				
11	10	92427		14	108,259				
12				15	112,489				
13									

Figure 14.14
Using the SLOPE and INTERCEPT functions is a simple way to calculate a linear regression line.

The formula in cell E2 calculates the intercept for the line by using =INTERCEPT(B2:B11,A2:A11). The answer of 49,041 means that the model predicts that your sales in a hypothetical Year 0 would have been 49,041.

The formula in cell E3 calculates the slope of the line by using =SLOPE(B2:B11,A2:A11). The answer of 4,230 means that the model predicts that your sales are increasing by about 4,230 each year.

When you have the slope and y-intercept, you can build a new table to predict future sales. You enter year numbers 11 through 15 in D8:D12. The formula in cell E8 needs to multiply the year number by the slope and add the intercept. That formula is =$E$2+$E$3*D8.

The values in cells E8 through E12 are one prediction of future sales. This assumes that the past trends continue to work over the next 5 years.

Using LINEST to Calculate Straight-Line Regression with Complete Statistics

Although SLOPE and INTERCEPT would do the job, the more powerful function is LINEST. Here is the difficulty: LINEST returns both the slope and the intercept. In addition, it returns a whole series of statistics. Anytime a function returns several values, you must enter the function by using Ctrl+Shift+Enter. You should also select a large enough range in advance before entering the formula. Figuring out the size of the range in advance is difficult because it varies, depending on the shape of the independent variables and also if you ask for statistics.

However, LINEST is far more powerful than SLOPE and INTERCEPT. Additional arguments available in LINEST are not available in the easier functions.

 Note

Note that y, x, and m can be vectors. The array that LINEST returns is backward from what you would expect. The slope for the last independent variable appears first: {mn,mn-1, ...,m1,b}. LINEST can also return additional regression statistics.

Syntax:

=LINEST(*known_y's*,*known_x's*,*const*,*stats*)

The LINEST function calculates the statistics for a line by using the least-squares method to calculate a straight line that best fits the data, and it returns an array that describes the line. Because this function returns an array of values, you must enter it as an array formula with Ctrl+Shift+Enter. The equation for the line is y = mx + b or y = m1x1 + m2x2 + ... + b (if there are multiple ranges of x values) where the dependent y value is a function of the independent x values. The m values are coefficients corresponding to each x value, and b is a constant value.

The LINEST function takes the following arguments:

- ***known_y's***—This is the set of y values you already know in the relationship y = mx + b. If the array *known_y's* is in a single column, each column of *known_x's* is interpreted as a separate variable. If the array *known_y's* is in a single row, each row of *known_x's* is interpreted as a separate variable.

- ***known_x's***—This is an optional set of x values that you might already know in the relationship y = mx + b. The array *known_x's* can include one or more sets of variables. If only one variable is used, *known_y's* and *known_x's* can be ranges of any shape, as long as they have equal dimensions. If more than one variable is used, *known_y's* must be a vector (that is, a range with a height of one row or a width of one column). If *known_x's* is omitted, it is assumed to be the array {1,2,3,...} that is the same size as *known_y's*.

- ***const***—This is a logical value that specifies whether to force the constant b to equal 0. If *const* is TRUE or omitted, b is calculated normally. If *const* is FALSE, b is set equal to 0, and the m values are adjusted to fit y = mx.

■ *stats*—This is a logical value that specifies whether to return additional regression statistics. If *stats* is TRUE, LINEST returns the additional regression statistics, so the returned array is {mn,mn-1,...,m1,b;sen,sen1,...,se1,seb;r2,sey;F,df;ssreg,ssresid}. If *stats* is FALSE or omitted, LINEST returns only the m coefficients and the constant b. If you specify TRUE for *stats*, the additional regression statistics shown in Table 14.4 are possible return values.

Table 14.4 Additional Regression Statistics for LINEST

Statistic	Description
se1,se2,...,sen	The standard errors for the coefficients m1,m2,...,mn.
seb	The standard error for the constant b (seb = #N/A when *const* is FALSE).
r2	The coefficient of determination. You compare estimated and actual y values and ranges in value from 0 to 1. If it is 1, there is a perfect correlation in the sample—that is, no difference exists between the estimated y value and the actual y value. At the other extreme, if the coefficient of determination is 0, the regression equation is not helpful in predicting a y value.
Sey	The standard error for the y estimate.
F	The *F* statistic, or the *F* observed value. You use the *F* statistic to determine whether the observed relationship between the dependent and independent variables occurs by chance.
df	The degrees of freedom. You use the degrees of freedom to help you find *F* critical values in a statistical table. You compare the values you find in the table to the *F* statistic returned by LINEST to determine a confidence level for the model.
ssreg	The regression sum of squares.
ssresid	The residual sum of squares.

Figure 14.16, later in this chapter, shows a visual map of the statistics being returned.

The accuracy of the line calculated by LINEST depends on the degree of scatter in the data. The more linear the data, the more accurate the LINEST model. LINEST uses the method of least squares for determining the best fit for the data.

The line- and curve-fitting functions LINEST and LOGEST can calculate the best straight line or exponential curve that fits the data. However, you have to decide which of the two results best fits the data. You can calculate TREND(*known_y's,known_x's*) for a straight line or GROWTH(*known_y's, known_x's*) for an exponential curve. These functions, without the *known_x's* argument, return an array of y values predicted along that line or curve at your actual data points. You can then compare the predicted values with the actual values. You might want to chart them both for a visual comparison.

In regression analysis, Microsoft Excel calculates for each point the squared difference between the y value estimated for that point and its actual y value. The sum of these squared differences is called the residual sum of squares. Microsoft Excel then calculates the sum of the squared differences between the actual y values and the average of the y values, which is called the total sum of squares (that is regression sum of squares + residual sum of squares). The smaller the residual sum of squares compared with the total sum of squares, the larger the value of the coefficient of determination, *r*-squared, which is an indicator of how well the equation resulting from the regression analysis explains the relationship among the variables.

Case Study: Application of Regression Analysis

Suppose that you rent a snow-cone cart at a local amusement park. You create a table showing total snow cones sold for each day of last summer. In Figure 14.15, column E shows the total snow cones sold by day. As you can see, the sales rise and fall sharply from day to day.

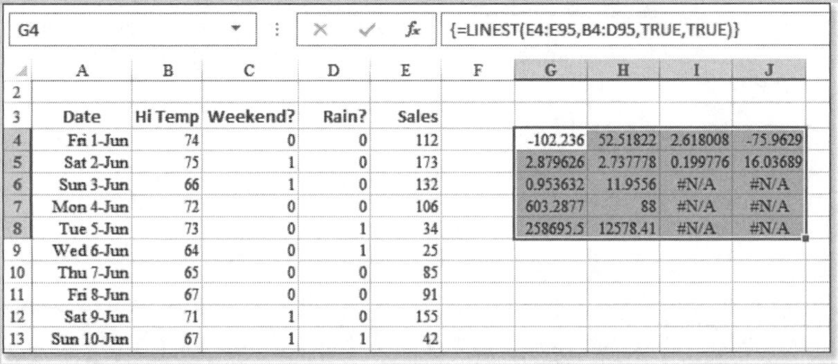

	A	B	C	D	E	F	G	H	I	J
2										
3	Date	Hi Temp	Weekend?	Rain?	Sales					
4	Fri 1-Jun	74	0	0	112		-102.236	52.51822	2.618008	-75.9629
5	Sat 2-Jun	75	1	0	173		2.879626	2.737778	0.199776	16.03689
6	Sun 3-Jun	66	1	0	132		0.953632	11.9556	#N/A	#N/A
7	Mon 4-Jun	72	0	0	106		603.2877	88	#N/A	#N/A
8	Tue 5-Jun	73	0	1	34		258695.5	12578.41	#N/A	#N/A
9	Wed 6-Jun	64	0	1	25					
10	Thu 7-Jun	65	0	0	85					
11	Fri 8-Jun	67	0	0	91					
12	Sat 9-Jun	71	1	0	155					
13	Sun 10-Jun	67	1	1	42					

Figure 14.15
The results of the LINEST function in G4:J8 are seemingly meaningless.

The previous manager of the cart had noticed certain trends in the data. Sales were better on the weekends than on weekdays. Sales were horrible when it rained. Sales improved as the weather became hotter in July and August.

Columns B:D in Figure 14.15 contain data related to temperature, weekends, and rain. Note that in column C, the weekend data is binary data—either 0 or 1. In column D, the manager could have kept information about the amount of rainfall each day but instead kept this as binary data as well. If the day was predominantly rainy, the manager recorded a 1 to indicate a rainout. If the day had just a spot of rain, the manager recorded it as a nonrainy day.

To perform regression on this data, follow these steps:

1. Total the number of independent variables and add one. This is the number of columns the results of the regression will occupy. In the snow cone cart example, that is four columns.
2. Figure out how many rows the result of the regression will occupy. Because you plan to ask for statistics in the snow cone example, this is five rows. LINEST returns one row of results and four rows of statistics, as shown in Figure 14.16.

Figure 14.16
When you have
the LINEST
results, you can
perform many
more tests and
charts that
test how good
the regression
model is.

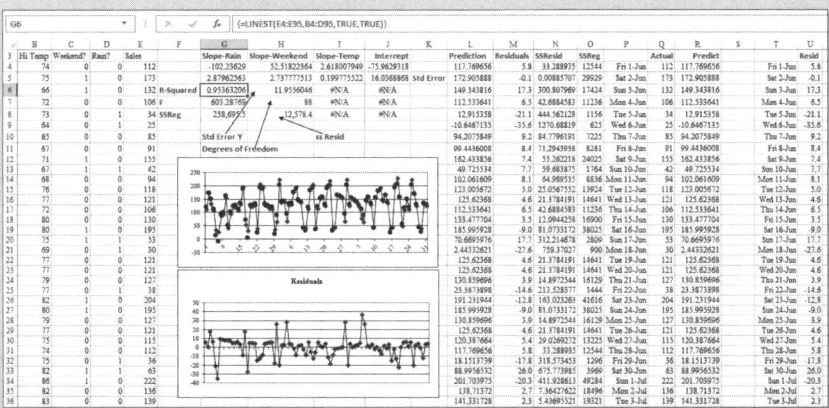

3. Off to the side of the data, select a range that is four columns wide by five columns tall. This size is determined by the results of the first two steps.

4. Start to type the formula **=LINEST(**.

5. For the *known_y's*, use the sales data in column E; this is E4:E95.

6. For the *known_x's*, use the values for temperature, weekend, and rain. This is B4:D95. Note that the dates in column A are not being used as an independent variable. The amusement park is an established park, and there is nothing to indicate that attendance rises over the course of the season.

7. Use TRUE for the next argument, which asks whether the intercept should be forced to be 0. This is not a requirement in the current situation. You want to allow the intercept to be calculated normally.

8. Use 1 or TRUE for the *stats* argument.

9. Although you have now typed the complete formula, **=LINEST(E4:E95,B4:D95, TRUE,TRUE)**, do not press the Enter key. This is one formula that returns many results. You have to tell Excel to interpret the formula as an array formula. To do this, hold down Ctrl+Shift while pressing Enter. The function returns a seemingly meaningless range of numbers, as shown in Figure 14.15.

10. Start labeling the regression results in the upper-right corner. The value in the upper-right corner is the y-intercept. This is equivalent to the result of the INTERCEPT function.

11. Working in the top row from right to left, look at the slopes of the independent variables. These appear backward from how you originally specified them. Your independent variables were temperature, weekend, and rain. The slope for the last independent variable is in the top-left corner of the results. In Figure 14.16, cell G4 is the slope associated with rain. Cell H4 is the slope associated with weekend. Cell H5 is the slope associated with temperature.

12. Take a look at these numbers for a second to see if they make sense. The intercept says you are going to sell –75 snow cones each day. This initially seems wrong. However, the value in column I says that you will sell 2.6 snow cones for every degree of temperature. Because the lowest minimum high temperature for the summer would be about 60 degrees, the result suggests that you would sell a minimum of (60 × 2.6), or about 156 snow cones, due to temperature. Adding the –75 and 156 gets you to a minimum of 80 snow cones on a sunny day. Cell H4 suggests that you would sell about 52 extra snow cones on a weekend. Cell G4 suggests that you would sell 102 fewer snow cones on a rainy day.

13. Fill in the rest of the labels for statistics. The second row of the results shows the standard error for the number above it. The first column of the third row returns the all-important *r*-squared value. If this value is close to 1, your model is doing a good job of predicting the data. The value of 0.95 shows that this model is fairly good. Row 3, column 2 shows the standard error of Y. It is normal to have #N/A in any additional columns of row 3. Row 4 contains the *F* statistic and degrees of freedom. Row 5 contains the sum of squares of the regression and the residual sum of squares. This is the number that Excel is trying to minimize when it fits the line using least squares.

14. In column L, build a formula to predict sales with the results of the regression. This formula would be Intercept + Slope temp × Temp + Slope weekend × Weekend + Slope rain × Rain. The formula in cell L4 is therefore =$J$4+$I$4*B4+$H$4*C4+$G$4*D4.

15. To visually compare the data, plot the actuals in column E and the prediction in column L on a chart. The chart in rows 12:22 shows that the prediction is tracking fairly well with the actual. There was a cold, rainy weekday near the beginning where the model predicted –10 sales versus an actual of 25.

16. For another interesting test, calculate the residual or error for each day. The data in column M is the difference between L and E. Plot this data. You should see many small positive and negative values. (Notice that the scale of this chart is smaller than the original chart.) The values should swing from positive to negative frequently. The amount of scatter should not vary over time. You should not see many clusters of points that are either positive or negative. The chart in rows 24:34 shows that there are many positive residuals early in the summer, and fewer later in the summer. This might mean that the model is less successful at lower June temperatures than at higher August temperatures. Perhaps only real snow cone fans buy the product at temperatures of 60 to 80. Above 80 degrees, more people might buy the product.

Troubleshooting LINEST

Remember that LINEST returns an array of values. In addition, you need to select a large enough range before entering the function, and you need to use Ctrl+Shift+Enter to enter the formula.

If you forget to use Ctrl+Shift+Enter, Excel returns just the top-left cell from the result set. In the data set in Figure 14.15, this would be the slope for the final independent variable (−102.236). If you enter LINEST and receive just one value, you should follow these steps:

1. Select a range starting with the LINEST formula in the upper-left corner. The range should be five rows tall. It should be at least two columns wide for models with one *known_x* column. Add additional columns for additional *known_x* series.

2. Press the F2 key to edit the current LINEST formula.

3. Hold down Ctrl+Shift+Enter to reenter the formula as an array.

Alternatively, you can use the INDEX function to pluck one particular value out of the LINEST function. For example, if you want to retrieve the *F* statistic from row 4, column 1, you could use =INDEX(LINEST(E4:E95,B4:D95,TRUE,TRUE),4,1).

In the simpler situation when you have only one independent x variable, you can obtain the slope and y-intercept values directly by using the following formula for slope:

INDEX(LINEST(*known_y's,known_x's*),1)

Use the following formula for the y-intercept:

INDEX(LINEST(*known_y's,known_x's*),2)

Using FORECAST to Calculate Prediction for Any One Data Point

When you understand straight-line regression, you can use the FORECAST function to return a prediction for any point in the future.

Syntax:

=FORECAST(*x,known_y's,known_x's*)

The FORECAST function calculates, or predicts, a future value by using existing values. The predicted value is a y value for a given x value. The known values are existing x values and y values, and the new value is predicted by using linear regression. You can use this function to predict future sales, inventory requirements, or consumer trends.

 Note

Note that FORECAST works only for straight-line regression. It also does not offer the capability to force the intercept to be 0. If you need this capability, you must use LINEST and then build a prediction formula as in step 14 of the previous section or the TREND function, as discussed in the next section.

The FORECAST function takes the following arguments:

- **x**—This is the data point for which you want to predict a value. If *x* is nonnumeric, FORECAST returns a #VALUE! error.
- ***known_y's***—This is the dependent array or range of data.
- ***known_x's***—This is the independent array or range of data.

If *known_y's* and *known_x's* are empty or contain a different number of data points, FORECAST returns an #N/A error. If the variance of *known_x's* equals 0, then FORECAST returns a #DIV/0! error.

Figure 14.17 shows actual sales data for the past decade. Years are in column A, and sales are in column C. The sales data in C2:C12 is the range of *known_y's*. The years in A2:A12 comprise the range of *known_x's*.

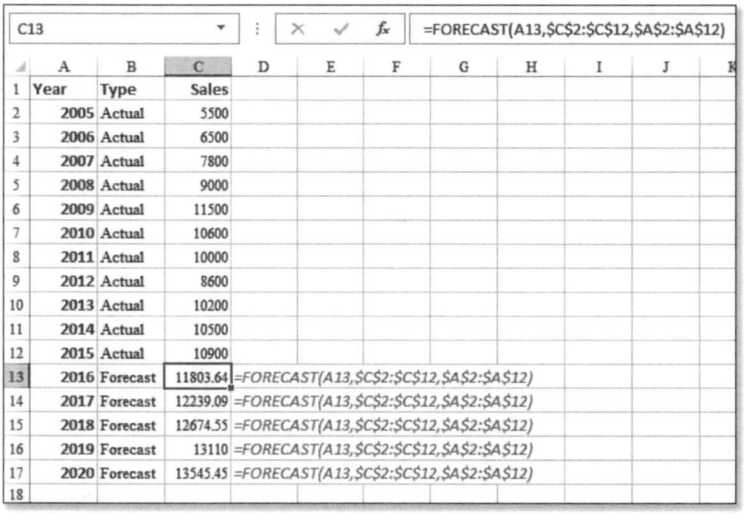
C13 =FORECAST(A13,$C$2:$C$12,$A$2:$A$12)

	A	B	C	D
1	Year	Type	Sales	
2	2005	Actual	5500	
3	2006	Actual	6500	
4	2007	Actual	7800	
5	2008	Actual	9000	
6	2009	Actual	11500	
7	2010	Actual	10600	
8	2011	Actual	10000	
9	2012	Actual	8600	
10	2013	Actual	10200	
11	2014	Actual	10500	
12	2015	Actual	10900	
13	2016	Forecast	11803.64	=FORECAST(A13,$C$2:$C$12,$A$2:$A$12)
14	2017	Forecast	12239.09	=FORECAST(A13,$C$2:$C$12,$A$2:$A$12)
15	2018	Forecast	12674.55	=FORECAST(A13,$C$2:$C$12,$A$2:$A$12)
16	2019	Forecast	13110	=FORECAST(A13,$C$2:$C$12,$A$2:$A$12)
17	2020	Forecast	13545.45	=FORECAST(A13,$C$2:$C$12,$A$2:$A$12)
18				

Figure 14.17
You use the FORECAST function to find the data point for one future time period.

To predict sales for future periods, follow these steps:

1. Enter future years in A13:A17.
2. In column B, enter **Actual** or **Forecast** for each row so that the person reading the table understands that the new values are a forecast.
3. To predict sales for 2016, enter this formula in cell C13: =FORECAST(A13,$C$2:$C$12,$A$2:$A$12).
4. Copy the formula from cell C13 down to C14:C17.

Using TREND to Calculate Many Future Data Points at Once

The TREND function is another array function. This means that it can return many values from a single formula. If you think about the previous use of FORECAST in Figure 14.17, you realize that Excel really had to perform the linear regression multiple times—once for each of the cells in C13:C17. It would be better if you could perform the regression once and have Excel calculate all the values from that regression. The TREND function helps you do this.

Syntax:

=TREND(*known_y's*,*known_x's*,*new_x's*,*const*)

The TREND function returns values along a linear trend. It fits a straight line (using the least-squares method) to the arrays *known_y's* and *known_x's*. It returns the y values along that line for the array of *new_x's* that you specify.

The TREND function takes the following arguments:

- ***known_y's***—This is the set of y values you already know in the relationship y = mx + b. If the array *known_y's* is in a single column, each column of *known_x's* is interpreted as a separate variable. If the array *known_y's* is in a single row, each row of *known_x's* is interpreted as a separate variable.

- ***known_x's***—This is an optional set of x values that you might already know in the relationship y = mx + b. The array *known_x's* can include one or more sets of variables. If only one variable is used, *known_y's* and *known_x's* can be ranges of any shape, as long as they have equal dimensions. If more than one variable is used, *known_y's* must be a vector (that is, a range with a height of one row or a width of one column). If *known_x's* is omitted, it is assumed to be the array {1,2,3,...} that is the same size as *known_y's*.

- ***new_x's***—These are new x values for which you want TREND to return corresponding y values. *new_x's* must include a column (or row) for each independent variable, just as *known_x's* does. So, if *known_y's* is in a single column, *known_x's* and *new_x's* must have the same number of columns. If *known_y's* is in a single row, *known_x's* and *new_x's* must have the same number of rows. If you omit *new_x's*, it is assumed to be the same as *known_x's*. If you omit both *known_x's* and *new_x's*, they are assumed to be the array {1,2,3,...} that is the same size as *known_y's*.

- ***const***—This is a logical value that specifies whether to force the constant b to equal 0. If *const* is TRUE or omitted, b is calculated normally. If *const* is FALSE, b is set equal to 0 and the m values are adjusted so that y = mx.

The result is shown in D26:D33. The TREND function predicts that you will need a base level of 115,000 in 2010 with no hurricanes. With two hurricanes in 2010, demand would rise to 174,000.

Case Study: Forecasting Using Regression Analysis

Suppose that you are responsible for forecasting the material needs for a company that supplies roofing material. You have historical trends of usage by year. You've included past hurricane and recession data because those events caused extraordinary demand. Your job is not only to predict how much roofing material you will sell, assuming that there are no hurricanes, but how much you might want to have lined up in case there are one, two, or three hurricanes. Here's what you do:

1. As in the worksheet shown in Figure 14.18, enter the actual data in A4:D26. The sales in column D are the *known_y's*.

| D29 | | | | ▼ | : | × | ✓ | f_x | {=TREND(D5:D26,A5:C26,A29:C36)} |

	A	B	C	D	E	F	G	H	I	J
1	Demand for Roofing Materials in Florida									
3	Actual Demand									
4	Year	Recession	Hurricanes	Sales						
5	1991	1	0	51000						
6	1992	0	1	81650						
7	1993	0	0	61800						
8	1994	0	0	63050						
9	1995	0	0	67900						
10	1996	0	0	72750						
11	1997	0	0	78400						
12	1998	0	0	85850						
13	1999	0	0	92700						
14	2000	0	0	96900						
15	2001	1	0	95000						
16	2002	0	0	107100						
17	2003	0	0	107800						
18	2004	0	2	168450						
19	2005	0	2	170000						
20	2006	0	0	108000						
21	2007	0	0	109000						
22	2008	1	0	104030						
23	2009	2	0	99456						
24	2010	2	0	101245						
25	2011	1	0	103654						
26	2012	1	0	102456						
28	Forecast Demand									
29	2013	1	0	120,551						
30	2013	1	1	151,552						
31	2013	1	2	182,553						
32	2013	1	3	213,553						
33	2014	0	0	135,028						
34	2014	0	1	166,028						
35	2014	0	2	197,029						
36	2014	0	3	228,030						
37										

Figure 14.18
The TREND function is an array formula that can do one regression and return many future data points.

2. The years, recession, and hurricane data in columns A:C are the *known_x's*.

3. Enter a new table in A29:C36. You want to find the forecasted requirements for 2013 and 2014 for the possibility that there are zero, one, two, or three hurricanes. The year, recession, and hurricane columns must be in the same format as the *known_x's* in step 2.

4. Keep in mind that because the TREND function is an array function, it can return several answers from one formula. Select the range D26:D33. With that range selected, start to type the formula **=TREND(**.

5. Enter **D5:D23** for *known_y's*, which are past sales. Enter **A5:C23** for *known_x's*. The new x values are the data in A26:C33.

6. Ensure that your formula is now =TREND(D5:D23,A5:C23,A26:C33). To finish the formula, hold down Ctrl+Shift while pressing Enter.

Using LOGEST to Perform Exponential Regression

Some patterns in business follow a linear regression. However, other items are not linear at all. If you are a scientist monitoring the growth of bacteria in a Petri dish, you see exponential growth in the generations.

If you try to fit an exponential growth to a straight line, you have a large error. If the *r*-squared from linear regression is too low, you can try using exponential regression to see if the pattern of data matches exponential regression better. For exponential regression, you use the LOGEST function, which is similar to the LINEST function.

Syntax:

=LOGEST(*known_y's*,*known_x's*,*const*,*stats*)

In regression analysis, the LOGEST function calculates an exponential curve that fits the data and returns an array of values that describes the curve. Because this function returns an array of values, it must be entered as an array formula. The equation for the curve is y = b*m^x or y = (b*(m1^x1)*(m2^x2)*_) (if there are multiple x values), where the dependent y value is a function of the independent x values. The m values are bases that correspond to each exponent x value, and b is a constant value.

The LOGEST function takes the following arguments:

- ***known_y's***—This is the set of y values you already know in the relationship y = b × m^x. If the array *known_y's* is in a single column, each column of *known_x's* is interpreted as a separate variable. If the array *known_y's* is in a single row, each row of *known_x's* is interpreted as a separate variable.

- ***known_x's***—This is an optional set of x values you might already know in the relationship y = b × m^x. The array *known_x's* can include one or more sets of variables. If only one variable is used, *known_y's* and *known_x's* can be ranges of any shape, as long as they have equal dimensions. If more than one variable is used, *known_y's* must be a range of cells with a height of one row or a width of one column (which is also known as a vector). If *known_x's* is omitted, it is assumed to be the array {1,2,3,...} that is the same size as *known_y's*.

- ***const***—This is a logical value that specifies whether to force the constant b to equal 1. If *const* is TRUE or omitted, b is calculated normally. If *const* is FALSE, b is set equal to 1, and the m values are fitted to y = m^x.

- ***stats***—This is a logical value that specifies whether to return additional regression statistics. If *stats* is TRUE, LOGEST returns the additional regression statistics (refer to Figure 14.16), so the returned array is {mn,mn-1,...,m1,b;sen,sen-1,...,se1,seb;r2,sey; F,df;ssreg,ssresid}. If *stats* is FALSE or omitted, LOGEST returns only the m coefficients and the constant b.

The more a plot of data resembles an exponential curve, the better the calculated line fits the data. Like LINEST, LOGEST returns an array of values that describes a relationship among the values, but LINEST fits a straight line to the data; LOGEST fits an exponential curve.

Performing an Exponential Regression

Figure 14.19 shows an estimated population in column B and the generation in column A. To perform an exponential regression, follow these steps:

1. Because there is one independent variable, the results from the regression occupy two columns, so find a blank range of the spreadsheet and select a range that is two columns wide by five rows tall, such as E2:F6.

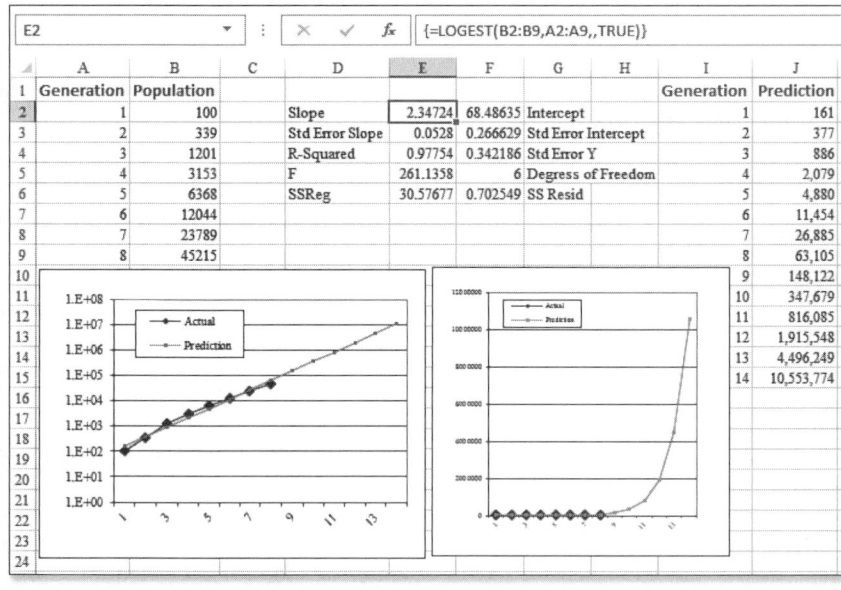

Figure 14.19
When data is growing at an exponential rate, you use LOGEST to perform a regression analysis.

2. Enter the beginning of the formula: **=LOGEST(**. Enter the *known_y's* as **B2:B9** and the *known_x's* as **A2:A9**. Leave the *const* value blank. Specify TRUE for *stats*. The formula should be =LOGEST(B2:B9,A2:A9,,TRUE).

3. Do not press Enter for the formula. Instead, hold down Ctrl+Shift while pressing Enter to tell Excel to interpret the result as an array formula and to return a table of values from LOGEST.

4. Add some labels to help interpret the statistics. The labels shown in columns D and G are examples.

5. To use the results of the regression in a prediction calculation, enter a different formula than with LINEST. The formula is Intercept × Slope^X. In Figure 14.19, to predict population values for a given generation in cell I2, use =$F$2*$E$2^I2. Alternatively, you can use the GROWTH function, discussed in the next section.

Using GROWTH to Predict Many Data Points from an Exponential Regression

As the TREND function is able to extrapolate points from a linear regression, the GROWTH function is able to extrapolate points from an exponential regression.

Syntax:

=GROWTH(*known_y's,known_x's,new_x's,const*)

The GROWTH function calculates predicted exponential growth by using existing data. GROWTH returns the y values for a series of new x values that you specify by using existing x values and y values. You can also use the GROWTH worksheet function to fit an exponential curve to existing x values and y values. This function takes the following arguments:

- **known_y's**—This is the set of y values you already know in the relationship $y = b \times m^x$. If the array *known_y's* is in a single column, each column of *known_x's* is interpreted as a separate variable. If the array *known_y's* is in a single row, each row of *known_x's* is interpreted as a separate variable. If any of the numbers in *known_y's* is 0 or negative, GROWTH returns a #NUM! error.

- **known_x's**—This is an optional set of x values that you may already know in the relationship $y = b \times m^x$. The array *known_x's* can include one or more sets of variables. If only one variable is used, *known_y's* and *known_x's* can be ranges of any shape, as long as they have equal dimensions. If more than one variable is used, *known_y's* must be a vector (that is, a range with a height of one row or a width of one column). If *known_x's* is omitted, it is assumed to be the array {1,2,3,...} that is the same size as *known_y's*.

 Tip

When you have formulas that return arrays, you must enter them as array formulas after selecting the correct number of cells. To specify an array formula, you hold down Ctrl+Shift while pressing Enter.

- **new_x's**—These are new x values for which you want GROWTH to return corresponding y values. *new_x's* must include a column (or row) for each independent variable, just as *known_x's* does. So, if *known_y's* is in a single column, *known_x's* and *new_x's* must have the same number of columns. If *known_y's* is in a single row, *known_x's* and *new_x's* must have the same number of rows. If *new_x's* is omitted, it is assumed to be the same as *known_x's*. If both *known_x's* and *new_x's* are omitted, they are assumed to be the array {1,2,3,...} that is the same size as *known_y's*.

- **const**—This is a logical value that specifies whether to force the constant b to equal 1. If *const* is TRUE or omitted, b is calculated normally. If *const* is FALSE, b is set equal to 1, and the m values are adjusted so that $y = m^x$.

In Figure 14.20, the original data is the population for the first 10 generations in A2:B11.

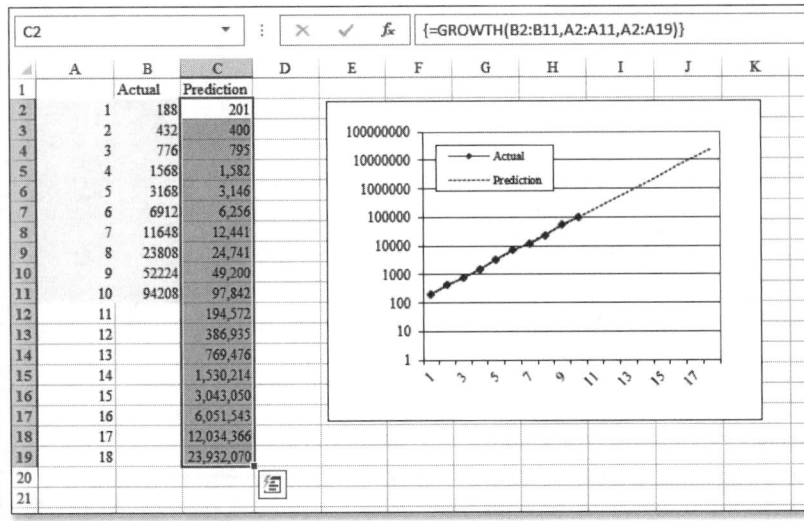

Figure 14.20

GROWTH performs an exponential regression and extrapolates the results in one step.

Exponential Regression Used to Predict Future Generations

It would be interesting to run an exponential regression and see the prediction for future generations but also for the known generations. This would enable you to see how well the prediction tracks with current values. To do this, follow these steps:

1. Add new generation numbers in A12:A19. The GROWTH function uses these numbers and returns an array of values.

2. Select the entire range C2:C19 for the results before entering the formula.

3. Put the *known_y's* in B2:B11. The *known_x's* are in A2:A11. Put the *new_x's* in A2:A19. The formula is =GROWTH(B2:B11,A2:A11,A2:A19).

4. After typing the formula, hold down Ctrl+Shift while pressing Enter. This should cause the formula to return values in each cell in C2:C19.

5. To visualize the original data and the prediction, plot A1:C19 on a line chart. Numbers at the end of the progression (24 million) make the scale of the chart so large that you cannot see the detail of the first 12 generations.

6. Right-click the numbers along the y-axis and select Format Axis. On the Scale tab, select Logarithmic Scale. The resulting chart enables you to examine both the smaller and larger numbers in the chart.

Using PEARSON to Determine Whether a Linear Relationship Exists

Remember that Excel blindly fits a regression line to any data set. The fact that Excel returns a regression line does not mean that you should use it to make any predictions. The initial question to ask yourself is, "Does a linear relationship exist in this data?"

The Pearson product–moment correlation coefficient, named after Karl Pearson, returns a value from −1.0 to +1.0. The calculation could make your head spin, but the important thing to know is that a PEARSON value closer to 1 or −1 means that a linear relationship exists. A value of 0 indicates no correlation between the independent and dependent variables.

> **Note**
>
> I am somewhat jealous that Microsoft has named an obscure function after fellow Excel consultant Chip Pearson. I am lobbying Microsoft for the inclusion of a JELEN function, possibly used to measure the degree of laid-backness caused by the gel in your shoe insoles. Seriously, Chip Pearson's website is one of the best established sources of articles on the Web about Excel. To peruse the articles, visit www.cpearson.com.

Syntax:

`=PEARSON(array1,array2)`

The PEARSON function returns the Pearson product–moment correlation coefficient, r, a dimensionless index that ranges from −1.0 to 1.0, inclusive, and reflects the extent of a linear relationship between two data sets.

The PEARSON function takes the following arguments:

- *array1*—This is a set of independent values.

- *array2*—This is a set of dependent values.

The arguments must be either numbers or names, array constants, or references that contain numbers. If an array or a reference argument contains text, logical values, or empty cells, those values are ignored; however, cells that contain the value 0 are included. If *array1* and *array2* are empty or have a different number of data points, PEARSON returns an #N/A error.

The result of PEARSON is also sometimes known as r. Multiplying PEARSON by itself leads to the more famous r-squared test.

Using RSQ to Determine the Strength of a Linear Relationship

r-squared is a popular measure of how well a regression line explains the variability in the y values. It is popular because the values range from 0 to 1. Numbers close to 1 mean that the regression line does a great job of predicting the values. Numbers close to 0 mean that the regression result can't predict the values at all.

r-squared is the statistic in the third row, first column of a LINEST function. It is also the square of the PEARSON function. You could use `=INDEX(LINEST(),3,1)` or `=PEARSON()^2`. But instead, Excel provides the easy-to-remember RSQ function.

Syntax:

=RSQ(*known_y's*,*known_x's*)

The RSQ function returns the square of the Pearson product–moment correlation coefficient through data points in *known_y's* and *known_x's*. The *r*-squared value can be interpreted as the proportion of the variance in *y* that is attributable to the variance in *x*.

> For more information on the Pearson coefficient, **see** *"Using* PEARSON *to Determine Whether a Linear Relationship Exists,"* **p. 477.**

The RSQ function takes the following arguments:

- **known_y's**—This is an array or a range of data points.

- **known_x's**—This is an array or a range of data points.

The arguments must be either numbers or names, arrays, or references that contain numbers. If an array or a reference argument contains text, logical values, or empty cells, those values are ignored; however, cells that contain the value 0 are included. If *known_y's* and *known_x's* are empty or have a different number of data points, RSQ returns an #N/A error.

Figure 14.21 shows four data sets and their associated *r*-squared values:

- The chart in the top-left corner has an *r*-squared near 0. There is little predictive ability in this regression line. In fact, the regression line is practically a horizontal line drawn through the mean of the data points.

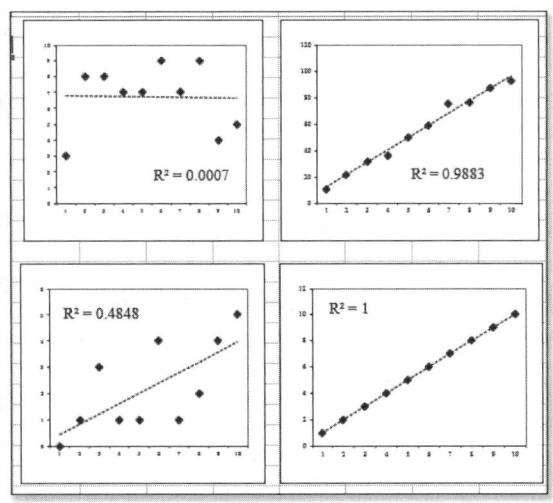

Figure 14.21
As r-squared approaches 1.0, the predictive ability of the regression line improves.

- The chart in the lower-left corner has an *r*-squared of 0.48. There is a lot of variability in the dots, but they do seem to trend up. There are huge relative errors on certain data points (for example, the value of y equals 1 when x equals 7).

- The chart in the upper-right corner shows a nearly perfect correlation. The *r*-squared is appropriately high, at 0.988. This means that most of the variability in y is explained by x. There are some tiny minor variations above or below the line, but the regression is doing a great job.

- The final chart, in the lower right, illustrates a perfect correlation and an *r*-squared of 1.0. Every occurrence of y falls exactly on the regression line.

Using STEYX to Calculate Standard Regression Error

Standard error is a measure of the quality of a regression line. In rough terms, the standard error is the size of an error that you might encounter for any particular point on the line. Smaller errors are better, and larger errors are worse. Standard error can also be used to calculate a confidence interval for any point.

Syntax:

=STEYX(*known_y's*,*known_x's*)

The STEYX function returns the standard error of the predicted y value for each x in the regression. The standard error is a measure of the amount of error in the prediction of y for an individual x.

The STEYX function takes the following arguments:

- *known_y's*—This is an array or a range of dependent data points.

- *known_x's*—This is an array or a range of independent data points.

The arguments must be either numbers or names, arrays, or references that contain numbers. If an array or a reference argument contains text, logical values, or empty cells, those values are ignored; however, cells that contain the value 0 are included. If *known_y's* and *known_x's* are empty or have a different number of data points, STEYX returns an #N/A error.

To calculate standard error, you square all the residuals and add them together. Then you divide by the number of points, excluding the starting and ending points. Finally, you take the square root of that result to calculate standard error.

In general, a lower standard error is better than a higher one. A standard error of 2,000 when you are trying to predict the price of a $30,000 car isn't too bad. A standard error of 2,000 when you are trying to predict the price of a $3 jar of pickles is horrible. You need to compare the standard error to the size of the value you are predicting.

In Figure 14.22, two regressions attempt to predict the price of a car based on either mileage or age. The standard error for the mileage method is a little less than the standard error for the age method.

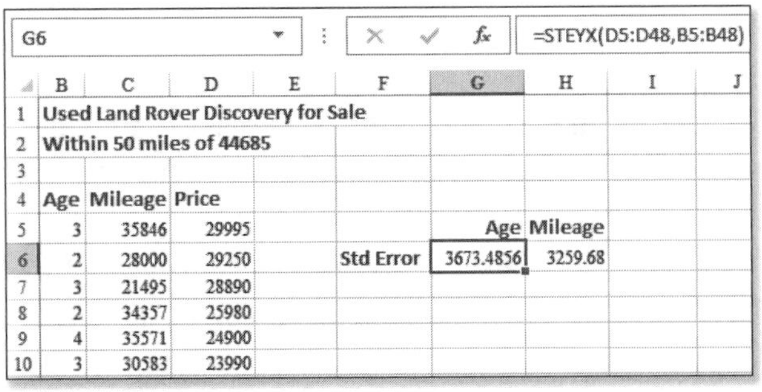

G6 =STEYX(D5:D48,B5:B48)

	B	C	D	E	F	G	H	I	J
1	Used Land Rover Discovery for Sale								
2	Within 50 miles of 44685								
3									
4	Age	Mileage	Price						
5	3	35846	29995			Age	Mileage		
6	2	28000	29250		Std Error	3673.4856	3259.68		
7	3	21495	28890						
8	2	34357	25980						
9	4	35571	24900						
10	3	30583	23990						

Figure 14.22
Standard error is another measure of the quality of a regression line.

Using COVARIANCE.P to Determine Whether Two Variables Vary Together

Covariance is a measure of how greatly two variables vary together. If the value is 0, the variables do not appear to be related. For positive values, covariance indicates that as *x* increases, *y* also increases. For negative values, covariance indicates that as *x* increases, *y* decreases.

Syntax:

```
=COVARIANCE.P(array1,array2)
=COVARIANCE.S(array1,array2)
```

The COVARIANCE.P function returns covariance, the average of the products of deviations for each data point pair. You use covariance to determine the relationship between two data sets. For example, you can examine whether greater income accompanies greater levels of education. COVARIANCE.P assumes that the arrays represent an entire population. If the arrays are a sample of the population, use the COVARIANCE.S function.

The COVARIANCE.P and COVARIANCE.S functions take the following arguments:

- ***array1***—This is the first cell range of integers.
- ***array2***—This is the second cell range of integers.

The arguments must be either numbers or names, arrays, or references that contain numbers. If an array or a reference argument contains text, logical values, or empty cells, those values are ignored; however, cells that contain the value 0 are included. If *array1* and *array2* have different numbers of data points, COVARIANCE.P returns an #N/A error. If either *array1* or *array2* is empty, COVARIANCE.P returns a #DIV/0! error.

Covariances can become incredibly large. The unit of measurement is on the order of x times y. For a dimensionless measurement of correlation, you use CORREL instead of COVARIANCE.P.

In Figure 14.23, the CORREL function measures the covariance between mileage and price. As mileage increases, price decreases.

Using CORREL to Calculate Positive or Negative Correlation

Instead of using covariance, you can calculate a correlation coefficient for two arrays. Let's use the mileage and price comparison from Figure 14.23. The two values would have a strong positive correlation if price went up as mileage went up. A perfect positive correlation would result in a correlation coefficient of 1.0.

Figure 14.23
COVARIANCE.P shows that price and mileage are inversely correlated.

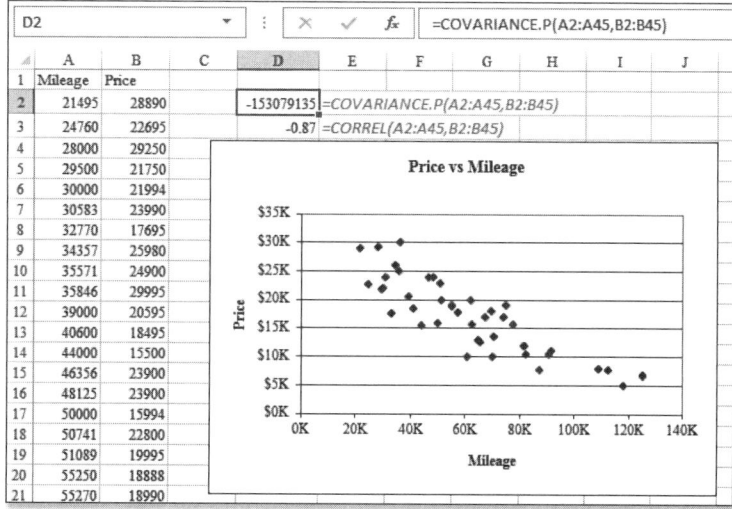

It is also possible (as in the mileage–price comparison case) for values to have an inverse correlation. As mileage increases, the price tends to decrease. If mileage were the only factor in the price of a car, the correlation coefficient would be −1.0 to indicate a perfect inverse correlation.

A correlation coefficient of 0 indicates that there is no correlation between the values.

Syntax:

=CORREL(*array1*,*array2*)

The CORREL function returns the correlation coefficient of the *array1* and *array2* cell ranges. You use the correlation coefficient to determine the relationship between two properties. For example, you can examine the relationship between a location's average temperature and the use of air conditioners.

The CORREL function takes the following arguments:

- *array1*—This is a cell range of values.

- *array2*—This is a second cell range of values.

The arguments must be numbers or names, arrays, or references that contain numbers. If an array or reference argument contains text, logical values, or empty cells, those values are ignored; however, cells that contain the value 0 are included. If *array1* and *array2* have a different number of data points, CORREL returns an #N/A error. If either *array1* or *array2* is empty, or if the standard deviation of their values equals 0, CORREL returns a #DIV/0! error.

In Figure 14.24, price and mileage have a correlation coefficient of −0.87. This indicates a fairly strong inverse correlation. As mileage increases, price decreases. The bottom-left chart shows two series with no correlation at all; the correlation coefficient is very close to 0. The bottom-right chart shows two series with perfect positive correlation of 1.0.

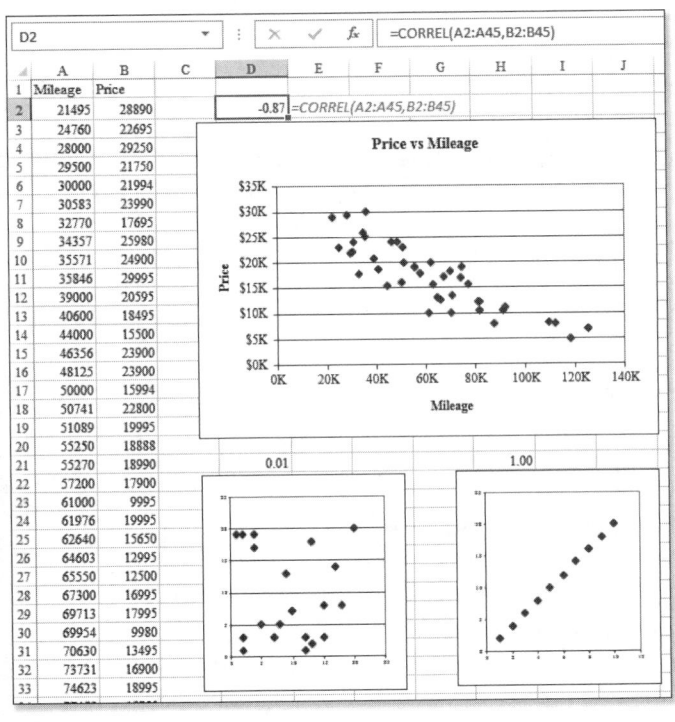

Figure 14.24
The CORREL function returns values from −1.0 to 1.0. Values near 0 indicate no correlation.

Using FISHER to Perform Hypothesis Testing on Correlations

The Pearson value does not have a normal distribution. The graph of expected *r* values skews heavily toward 1. A statistician named Fisher found a formula that would transform the skewed *r* value into a normal distribution. You use the FISHER function to convert an *r* value. To take a FISHER value and return it to an *r* value, you use FISHERINV.

Syntax:

`=FISHER(x)`

The `FISHER` function returns the Fisher transformation at *x*. This transformation produces a function that is approximately normally distributed rather than skewed. You use this function to perform hypothesis testing on the correlation coefficient.

The argument *x* is a numeric value for which you want the transformation. If *x* is nonnumeric, `FISHER` returns a `#VALUE!` error. If *x* is less than or equal to −1 or if *x* is greater than or equal to 1, `FISHER` returns a `#NUM!` error.

Syntax:

`=FISHERINV(y)`

The `FISHERINV` function returns the inverse of the Fisher transformation. You use this transformation when analyzing correlations between ranges or arrays of data. If *y* is equal to `FISHER(x)`, then `FISHERINV(y)` is equal to *x*.

The argument *y* is the value for which you want to perform the inverse of the transformation. If *y* is nonnumeric, `FISHERINV` returns a `#VALUE!` error.

Using SKEW, SKEW.P, and KURTOSIS

Three final statistics are used to describe a population:

- **Skew**—*Skew* is an indicator of symmetry. Actually, it is a measure of lack of symmetry. A skew value of 0 indicates that the population is perfectly symmetrical around the mean. Negative values indicate that the data is skewed to the left of the mean. Positive values indicate that the data is skewed to the right of the mean. If you are measuring skew of an entire population, use the `SKEW.P` function. If you are measuring skew of a sample, use the `SKEW` function. Note that `SKEW.P` is new in Excel 2013.

- **Kurtosis**—*Kurtosis* indicates whether the distribution contains a spiky peak or is relatively flat. This measure compares a population to the standard normal distribution. If the kurtosis is less than 0, the population is flatter than the normal distribution. If the kurtosis is greater than 0, the population is spikier than the normal distribution. You use Excel's `KURT` function to calculate kurtosis.

In Figure 14.25, there are two populations illustrated by two frequency distribution charts. The population in column A contains one large spike of 19 data points in the 2.1–2.7 range and a single data point at 60.25 inches. You can think of this as a tank with one shark and 19 goldfish. The average size is 5.25 inches. The tail of the distribution is a very long tail to the right of the 5.25 inches mean, indicating a positive skew. The 19 goldfish cause a very spiky data point, causing a high kurtosis.

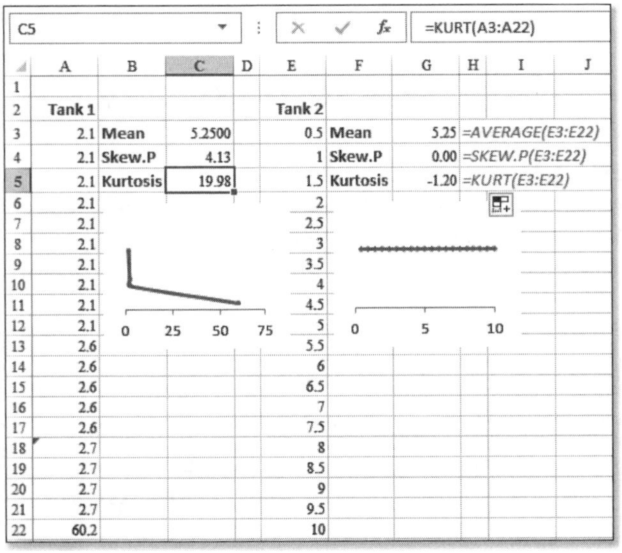

	A	B	C	D	E	F	G	H
1								
2	Tank 1				Tank 2			
3	2.1	Mean	5.2500		0.5	Mean	5.25	=AVERAGE(E3:E22)
4	2.1	Skew.P	4.13		1	Skew.P	0.00	=SKEW.P(E3:E22)
5	2.1	Kurtosis	19.98		1.5	Kurtosis	-1.20	=KURT(E3:E22)
6	2.1				2			
7	2.1				2.5			
8	2.1				3			
9	2.1				3.5			
10	2.1				4			
11	2.1				4.5			
12	2.1				5			
13	2.6				5.5			
14	2.6				6			
15	2.6				6.5			
16	2.6				7			
17	2.6				7.5			
18	2.7				8			
19	2.7				8.5			
20	2.7				9			
21	2.7				9.5			
22	60.2				10			

Figure 14.25
Skew and kurtosis return information about the symmetry and spikiness of a data set.

In column E, the data points are uniformly distributed around the mean. The data is perfectly symmetrical, leading to a skew of 0.00. No data point has more than one member, causing the data to be extremely flat, with a negative kurtosis.

Syntax:

```
=SKEW(number1,number2,...)
=SKEW.P(number1,number2,...)
```

The SKEW function returns the skewness of a sample. Skewness characterizes the degree of asymmetry of a distribution around its mean. Positive skewness indicates a distribution with an asymmetric tail extending toward more positive values. Negative skewness indicates a distribution with an asymmetric tail extending toward more negative values. SKEW.P is new in Excel 2013 and measures the skewness of a population.

The arguments *number1*, *number2*, ... are one to 255 arguments for which you want to calculate skewness. You can also use a single array or a reference to an array instead of arguments separated by commas. The arguments must be either numbers or names, arrays, or references that contain numbers. If an array or a reference argument contains text, logical values, or empty cells, those values are ignored; however, cells that contain the value 0 are included. If there are fewer than three data points, or if the sample standard deviation is 0, SKEW returns a #DIV/0! error.

Syntax:

```
=KURT(number1,number2,...)
```

The KURT function returns the kurtosis of a data set. Kurtosis characterizes the relative peakedness or flatness of a distribution compared with the normal distribution. Positive kurtosis indicates a relatively peaked distribution. Negative kurtosis indicates a relatively flat distribution.

The arguments *number1, number2, ...* are one to 255 arguments for which you want to calculate kurtosis. You can also use a single array or a reference to an array instead of arguments separated by commas. The arguments must be either numbers or names, arrays, or references that contain numbers. If an array or a reference argument contains text, logical values, or empty cells, those values are ignored; however, cells that contain the value 0 are included. If there are fewer than four data points, or if the standard deviation of the sample equals zero, KURT returns a #DIV/0! error.

Examples of Functions for Inferential Statistics

Inferential statistics is the powerful side of statistics. With descriptive statistics, you can describe a data set. Describing a data set might allow you to understand the data set better. With regression, you use past trends to predict future results. With inferential statistics, you extrapolate information about a sample of the population to make predictions about the entire population.

Understanding the Language of Inferential Statistics

Excel 2013 offers functions for 14 different types of probability distributions. Each distribution predicts a different shape of the population. The following sections cover the various distributions, but for now, consider the distribution in Figure 14.26.

Figure 14.26
The Point Density Function describes the probability that a member of a population has one specific value.

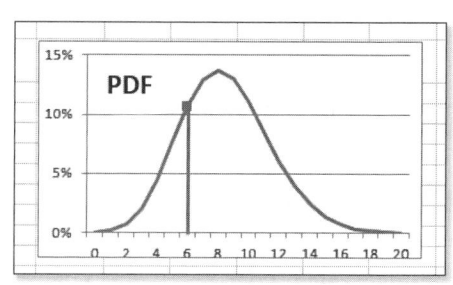

If you are asked to predict the likelihood that a member of a population has a value of 6, you can look at Figure 14.26 and see that the probability is just over 10%. This value is called the Point Density Function, or PDF.

A different question would be to estimate what percentage of the population has a value of 6 or less. This is known as the Cumulative Density Function (CDF). Figure 14.27 graphs the CDF. To calculate the CDF without Excel, you would have to use a little Calculus to integrate from 0 to 6 over the distribution function. Thankfully, with Excel, you do not have to use Calculus!

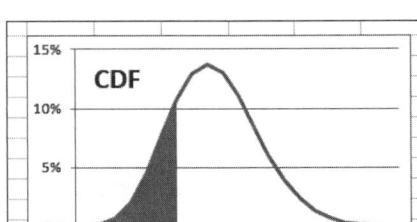

Figure 14.27
The Cumulative Density Function describes the probability that a member of a population is less than one specific value.

All 14 distribution functions in Excel calculate both the PDF and CDF. Look for an argument in each function called *cumulative*. If you specify True for *cumulative*, you are getting the CDF function from Figure 14.27. If you specify False, you are getting the PDF function from Figure 14.26.

When you see a function that includes .DIST, this function is used to calculate either the PDF or the CDF, depending on whether you specify *cumulative* equals False or *cumulative* equals True.

Here is a simple math quiz: If the .DIST function predicts that there is a 30% chance the value is 6 or less, what is the prediction that the value is more than 6? Although you would have needed Calculus to figure out the 30% answer, after you know the 30% answer, you don't even need a calculator to know that the probability of the answer being more than 6 is 70%.

If the area in Figure 14.27 is 30%, the area in Figure 14.28 is going to be 100% − 30%, or 70%. That is called the right-tailed CDF. You can calculate the right-tailed CDF by subtracting the left-tailed CDF from 100%. But, for a matter of convenience, Excel offers .RT versions of Chi-Squared, *F*, and *t*-distributions.

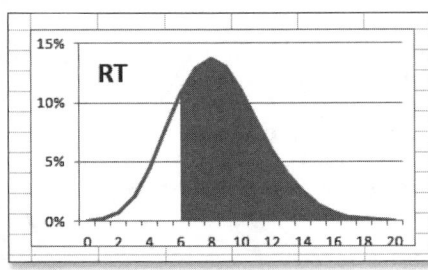

Figure 14.28
Three distributions in Excel include a function to calculate the right-tailed CDF.

Some distributions are symmetric around a mean. With these distributions, you might ask about the probability of a member of the population being within x% of the mean. The opposite question is to find the probability that a member will fall outside of that area. This is known as a two-tailed CDF and is shown in the bottom chart in Figure 14.29. Excel offers a 2T version of the Student's *t*-distribution.

Figure 14.29
The area shown in the lower chart is a two-tailed CDF. T.DIST.2T is the only function to calculate two-tailed probability.

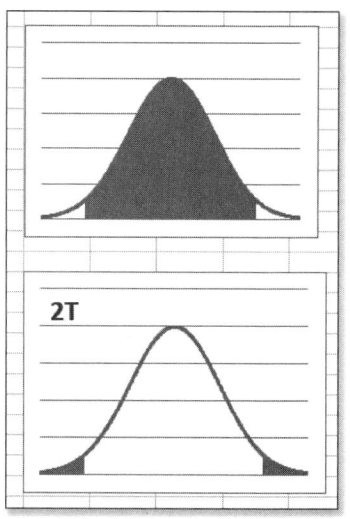

The real-life applications of inferential statistics usually involve a different type of question. The manager of a bank wants to make sure that the staffing levels allow there to be no wait 80% of the time. Whereas the DIST function can tell you the probability for a certain value, the INV function does the opposite. It tells you the value at a certain probability. The INV functions are always cumulative.

Of the 14 types of distributions, nine of them offer an inverse function.

To recap, when you see an inferential statistics function in Excel, it will start with the name of the distribution and be followed by one or more suffixes:

- .DIST indicates that you can calculate the PDF or CDF.

- .RT indicates it calculates the right-tailed CDF.

- .2T indicates it calculates the two-tailed CDF.

- .INV indicates that it finds the value at which the CDF meets a certain probability.

Figure 14.30 shows a matrix of the distribution functions in Excel 2013.

 Caution

One hundred percent of the function names in Figure 14.30 were new as of Excel 2010. None of those function names are backward compatible with Excel 2007 or earlier. To find the Excel 2007 name, go to a cell, type the equal sign, and the first few letters of the function name. The functions displayed at the bottom of the list, with a yellow triangle icon, are the Excel 2007 equivalents.

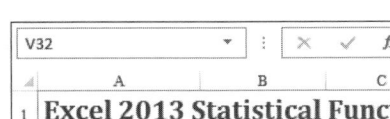

Figure 14.30
Functions for inferential statistics in Excel 2013.

Excel 2013 Statistical Functions

Distribution	PDF/CDF	Right-tailed CDF	Inverse left-tail CDF	Inverse right-tailed
Beta	BETA.DIST		BETA.INV	
Binomial	BINOM.DIST		BINOM.INV	
Chi-squared	CHISQ.DIST	CHISQ.DIST.RT	CHISQ.INV	CHISQ.INV.RT
Exponential	EXPON.DIST			
F	F.DIST	F.DIST.RT	F.INV	F.INV.RT
Gamma	GAMMA.DIST		GAMMA.INV	
Hypergeometric	HYPGEOM.DIST			
Lognormal	LOGNORM.DIST		LOGNORM.INV	
Negative Binomial	NEGBINOM.DIST			
Normal	NORM.DIST		NORM.INV	
Standard Normal	NORM.S.DIST		NORM.S.INV	
Poisson	POISSON.DIST			
Student's t	T.DIST	T.DIST.RT	T.INV	
Student's t (2 tailed)		T.DIST.2T		T.INV.2T
Weibull	WEIBULL.DIST			

Using `BINOM.DIST` to Determine Probability

A *binomial test* is a situation in which there are only two possible outcomes: Either an event happens or it does not happen.

For example, suppose you have determined that on several nights of the week, someone has been sneaking in and eating leftovers from the department fridge. You don't know if it is the night security guard or the cleaning crew or even just Charley, who works later than everyone else. After tracking this behavior for a month, you determine that food has been missing 27% of the time. How many days next week will food be missing? The `BINOM.DIST` function can answer this question.

Syntax:

`=BINOM.DIST(number_s,trials, probability_s,cumulative)`

The `BINOM.DIST` function returns the individual term binomial distribution probability. You use `BINOM.DIST` in problems with a fixed number of tests or trials, when the outcome of any trial is only success or failure, when trials are independent, and when the probability of success is constant throughout the experiment. For example, `BINOM.DIST` can calculate the probability that two of the next three babies born will be male.

The `BINOM.DIST` function takes the following arguments:

- *number_s*—This is the number of successes in trials.

- *trials*—This is the number of independent trials.

- *probability_s*—This is the probability of success on each trial.

- *cumulative*—This is a logical value that determines the form of the function. If *cumulative* is TRUE, then BINOM.DIST returns the cumulative distribution function, which is the probability that there are at most *number_s* successes; if *cumulative* is FALSE, BINOM.DIST returns the probability mass function, which is the probability that there are *number_s* successes.

number_s and *trials* are truncated to integers. If *number_s*, *trials*, or *probability_s* is nonnumeric, BINOM.DIST returns a #VALUE! error. If *number_s* is less than 0 or *number_s* is greater than *trials*, BINOMDIST returns a #NUM! error. If *probability_s* is less than 0 or *probability_s* is greater than 1, BINOM.DIST returns a #NUM! error.

In Figure 14.31, range B5:B10 calculates the probability that food will be missing *x* days next week. In each case, *trials* is 5 because there are five workdays next week. The *probability_s* is the mean of 0.27 entered in cell B2.

Cell B15 calculates the cumulative probability that zero or one success will be encountered next week.

 Tip

The BINOM.DIST always calculates the probability starting from the left side of the curve. If you wanted to calculate the probability of three or more successes next week, you could use one minus the probability of two or fewer successes, as shown in cell B22 above, or you could use the newly introduced BINOM.DIST.RANGE function, asking for the probability from three to five successes.

Figure 14.31

For tests that are either TRUE or FALSE, the BINOM.DIST function can calculate the probability of events.

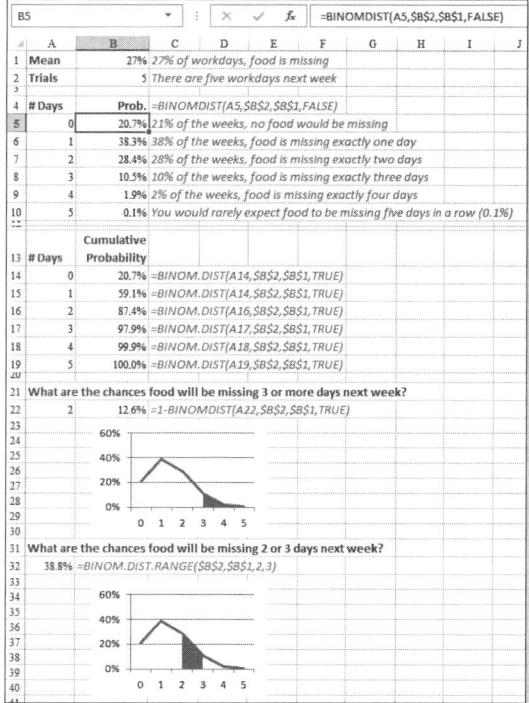

Using BINOM.DIST.RANGE to Calculate the Probability of *N* to *N* Binomial Events

In cell B22 of Figure 14.31, a formula calculates the probability of three or more successes by subtracting the probability of zero to two successes from one. What if you want to calculate the probability of two, three, or four successes? Excel 2013 introduces the BINOM.DIST.RANGE function. You can specify a range of values, such as =BINOM.DIST.RANGE(Trials,Probability,2,4) to return the probability of two to four successes.

Syntax:

=BINOM.DIST.RANGE(*trials,probability_s,number_s1,[number_s2]*)

The BINOM.DIST.RANGE function returns the probability of a range of results using the binomial distribution. You can specify a range using both *number_s1* and *number_s2*. For example, use **,2,5)** to find the probability of two, three, four, or five successes. Although Excel Help says that *number_s2* is optional, specifying only *number_s1* is equivalent to using BINOMDIST with a final argument of FALSE.

The BINOM.DIST.RANGE function takes the following arguments:

- *trials*—This is the number of Bernoulli trials.

- *probability_s*—This is the probability of a success on each trial.

- *number_s1*—This is the lower limit of the number of successes range.

- *number_s2*—This is the upper limit of the number of successes range. If provided, the function returns the probability that the number of successful tries lies between *number_s1* and *number_s2*, inclusive.

In Figure 14.31, the formula in A32 measures the probability of two to three successes.

Using BINOM.INV to Cover Most of the Possible Binomial Events

Many tests are binomial, as described in the preceding sections. Suppose you are exhibiting at a trade show. You expect 2,000 attendees at the trade show. Based on data from past trade shows, you predict that there is a 17% chance that an attendee will visit your booth and take a catalog. Your goal is to have enough catalogs so that you will be 95% sure to have enough catalogs for everyone. You can use the BINOM.INV function to predict how many catalogs you need.

Syntax:

=BINOM.INV(*trials,probability_s,alpha*)

The BINOM.INV function returns the smallest value for which the cumulative binomial distribution is greater than or equal to a criterion value. You use this function for quality assurance applications.

For example, you can use BINOM.INV to determine the greatest number of defective parts you can allow to come off an assembly line run without needing to reject the entire lot.

The BINOM.INV function takes the following arguments:

- **trials**—This is the number of Bernoulli trials.

- **probability_s**—This is the probability of a success on each trial.

- **alpha**—This is the criterion value.

If any argument is nonnumeric, BINOM.INV returns a #VALUE! error. If *trials* is not an integer, it is truncated. If *trials* is less than 0, BINOM.INV returns a #NUM! error. If *probability_s* is less than 0 or greater than 1, BINOM.INV returns a #NUM! error. If *alpha* is less than 0 or greater than 1, BINOM.INV returns a #NUM! error.

In the trade show example, the number of trials is 2,000: Each attendee has a chance of picking up a catalog. The *probability_s* is 17%, and *alpha* is 0.95, although it would be interesting to see how many catalogs could be required at each level. Using this information, you follow these steps to determine how many catalogs you need:

1. Build a range with different values for alpha in column A.

2. End the formula =BINOM.INV($B$2,$B$1,A8) in cell B8.

3. Copy the formula from cell B8 to the other cells in column B.

As shown in Figure 14.32, you need to have 368 catalogs for the trade show.

 **Note**

In legacy versions of Excel, BINOM.INV was called CRITBINOM.

Figure 14.32
Based on response rates at last year's trade show, you can use BINOM.INV to predict how many catalogs to print.

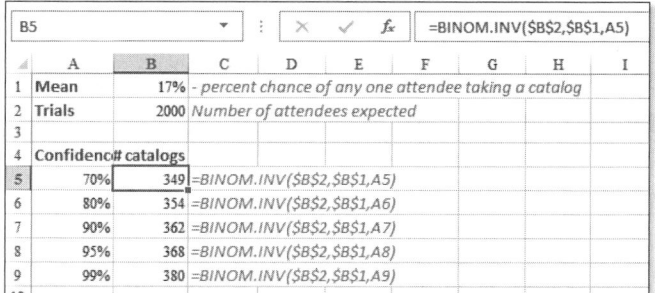

	A	B	C	D	E	F	G	H	I
1	Mean	17%	- percent chance of any one attendee taking a catalog						
2	Trials	2000	Number of attendees expected						
3									
4	Confidenc# catalogs								
5	70%	349	=BINOM.INV($B$2,$B$1,A5)						
6	80%	354	=BINOM.INV($B$2,$B$1,A6)						
7	90%	362	=BINOM.INV($B$2,$B$1,A7)						
8	95%	368	=BINOM.INV($B$2,$B$1,A8)						
9	99%	380	=BINOM.INV($B$2,$B$1,A9)						

B5 | =BINOM.INV($B$2,$B$1,A5)

Using NEGBINOM.DIST to Calculate Probability

It is a fact that Kobe Bryant has a career free-throw percentage of 0.838. What are the odds that Bryant would miss three free throws before he makes one free throw? You can use Excel's NEGBINOM.DIST function to figure this out.

Syntax:

```
=NEGBINOM.DIST(number_f,number_s,probability_s)
```

The NEGBINOM.DIST function returns the negative binomial distribution. It returns the probability that there will be *number_f* failures before the *number_s*th success, when the constant probability of a success is *probability_s*.

This function is similar to the binomial distribution function, except that the number of successes is fixed, and the number of trials is variable. As with the binomial distribution function, trials are assumed to be independent. For example, you need to find 10 people who have excellent reflexes, and you know the probability that a candidate has these qualifications is 0.3. NEGBINOM.DIST calculates the probability that you will interview a certain number of unqualified candidates before finding all 10 qualified candidates.

The NEGBINOM.DIST function takes the following arguments:

- *number_f*—This is the number of failures.

- *number_s*—This is the threshold number of successes.

- *probability_s*—This is the probability of a success.

number_f and *number_s* are truncated to integers. If any argument is nonnumeric, NEGBINOM.DIST returns a #VALUE! error. If *probability_s* is less than 0 or greater than 1, NEGBINOM.DIST returns a #NUM! error. If (*number_f* + *number_s* — 1) is less than or equal to 0, NEGBINOM.DIST returns a #NUM! error.

To solve the Kobe Bryant problem, you use =NEGBINOM.DIST(3,1,0.838,0). The answer is a 0.36% probability.

Using POISSON.DIST to Predict a Number of Discrete Events Over Time

Suppose you have to predict the number of discrete events that will happen over a certain period of time. This might be the number of customers who walk into a bank in an hour. It might be the number of lightning strikes on the John Hancock Building in a year. (It can also be discrete events that occur in a certain distance or area or any other measurement.)

Unlike the binomial distribution, in which an event either happens or does not happen, the Poisson distribution can be zero, one, two, three, and so on events in the period. The nature of the Poisson distribution is that before the third customer can walk into the bank, the second customer has to walk into the bank. In theory, if you had a run on the bank, the upper limit would be the number of total account holders, but in practice, there is probably some logical upper limit to how many customers walk in, such as the number that walk in during a Friday payday lunch hour.

If you measure the average number of customers per hour over the several weeks, you can use this number to predict the likelihood that a particular number of customers will enter the bank in any hour by using the POISSON.DIST function.

Syntax:

=POISSON.DIST(*x*,*mean*,*cumulative*)

The POISSON.DIST function returns the Poisson distribution. A common application of the Poisson distribution is predicting the number of events over a specific time, such as the number of cars arriving at a toll plaza in 1 minute. This function takes the following arguments:

- *x*—This is the number of events.

- *mean*—This is the expected numeric value.

- *cumulative*—This is a logical value that determines the form of the probability distribution returned.

If *x* is not an integer, it is truncated. If *x* or *mean* is nonnumeric, POISSON.DIST returns a #VALUE! error. If *x* is less than or equal to 0, POISSON.DIST returns a #NUM! error. If *mean* is less than 0, POISSON.DIST returns a #NUM! error. If cumulative is TRUE, POISSON.DIST returns the cumulative Poisson probability that the number of random events occurring will be between 0 and *x*, inclusive; if *cumulative* is FALSE, it returns the Poisson probability mass function that the number of events occurring will be exactly *x*.

To solve the bank customer example, follow these steps:

1. Calculate the mean number of customers entering the bank per hour over several weeks. Enter this in cell B1 of the worksheet.

2. In A4:A24, enter the numbers from **0** to **20**.

3. In column B, calculate the probability that exactly *n* customers will enter the bank. In cell B4, enter the formula **=POISSON.DIST($A4,$B$1,FALSE)**.

4. In column C, calculate the probability that 0 to n customers will enter the bank. In cell C4, enter the formula **=POISSON.DIST($A4,$B$1,TRUE)**.

In Figure 14.33, you can see that 84% of the time, your number of customers is expected to be between zero and 11 customers per hour. If you staff up to handle 11 customers per hour, you should be covered 85% of the time.

B4		▾	:	×	✓	fx	=POISSON.DIST($A4,$B$1,FALSE)		

⊿	A	B	C	D	E	F	G	H	I	J
1	Mean	8.5	Average number of customers per hour at the bank							
2										
3		Individual Probability	CDF							
4	0	0.02%	0.02%	B2: =POISSON.DIST($A4,$B$1,FALSE)						
5	1	0.17%	0.19%	C2: =POISSON.DIST($A4,$B$1,TRUE)						
6	2	0.74%	0.93%							
7	3	2.08%	3.01%							
8	4	4.43%	7.44%							
9	5	7.52%	14.96%							
10	6	10.66%	25.62%							
11	7	12.94%	38.56%							
12	8	13.75%	52.31%							
13	9	12.99%	65.30%							
14	10	11.04%	76.34%							
15	11	8.53%	84.87%							
16	12	6.04%	90.91%							
17	13	3.95%	94.86%							
18	14	2.40%	97.26%							
19	15	1.36%	98.62%							
20	16	0.72%	99.34%							
21	17	0.36%	99.70%							
22	18	0.17%	99.87%							
23	19	0.08%	99.95%							
24	20	0.03%	99.98%							

Figure 14.33
You can figure the number of customers per hour by using POISSON.DIST.

Using FREQUENCY to Categorize Continuous Data

The past few examples count whole numbers. It would be fairly difficult to have 0.3 persons walk into a bank. The outcome from the Poisson distribution would therefore have to be a whole number.

Other measurements are continuous. The speed of a car passing a checkpoint is an example. Depending on the accuracy of the radar unit, a car could be determined to be going 55.1, 55.2, 55.3, 55.4 and so on miles per hour. It would not make sense to try to predict how many cars will be going exactly 55.0123 miles per hour. If you did, you would be lucky to have a height of 2 for any point along the continuous scale. Typically, the prediction question would be, "What percentage of cars are likely to be going between 65 and 70 miles per hour?"

When you are working with a continuous range of measurements, the normal procedure is to group the measurements into ranges. Statisticians call each range a *bin*.

In Figure 14.34, the left chart shows the frequency curve for the speed of 2,000 cars passing a highway checkpoint. The recording unit measured speeds to the accuracy of 0.1 mile. The curve is incredibly noisy, with intense variation from point to point.

The middle chart shows the frequency curve after the data has been fit into bins of 1 mph each. There is still some noise in the distribution. For some reason, fewer people happened to be going 56 mph.

Figure 14.34
With continuous variables, you can group the observed values into bins to see the underlying distribution curve emerge.

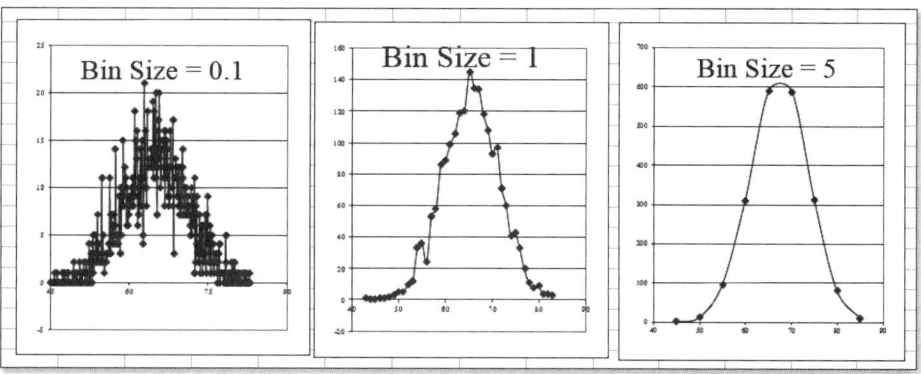

The right chart shows the frequency curve after the data has been fit into bins of 5 mph each. This curve is very smooth and shows that the data points seem to follow the normal bell curve.

The process of grouping data into bins is handled with another array function: the FREQUENCY function.

Syntax:

=FREQUENCY(*data_array*,*bins_array*)

The FREQUENCY function calculates how often values occur within a range of values, and it returns a vertical array of numbers. For example, you can use FREQUENCY to count the number of test scores that fall within ranges of scores. Because FREQUENCY returns an array, you must enter it as an array formula.

The FREQUENCY function takes the following arguments:

- *data_array*—This is an array of or a reference to a set of values for which you want to count frequencies. If *data_array* contains no values, FREQUENCY returns an array of zeros.

- *bins_array*—This is an array of or a reference to intervals into which you want to group the values in *data_array*. If *bins_array* contains no values, FREQUENCY returns the number of elements in *data_array*.

You enter FREQUENCY as an array formula after you select a range of adjacent cells into which you want the returned distribution to appear.

The number of elements in the returned array is one more than the number of elements in *bins_array*. The extra element in the returned array returns the count of any values above the highest interval. For example, when counting three ranges of values (intervals) that are entered into three cells, you need to be sure to enter FREQUENCY into four cells for the results. The extra cell returns the number of values in *data_array* that are greater than the third interval value. FREQUENCY ignores blank cells and text.

To use the FREQUENCY function, follow these steps:

1. Figure out the expected range of values in the original data set. You can do this by sorting the data set or by using the MIN and MAX functions.

2. Decide on your bin sizes. Each bin should be roughly the same size. Use enough bins to get an accurate picture, but not so many bins that the data becomes spiky and noisy. In Figure 14.35, the goal was bins of 5 mph each.

3. Enter the bins. This process is a bit tricky. If you want a bin for 40–45 mph, enter the number **45**. For the bin of 45–50 mph, enter the number **50**. In C2–C10, the numbers represent bins starting with 40–45 and ending with 80–85.

4. Select the range where the values will be returned. (The FREQUENCY function returns several values at once.) In Figure 14.35, select cells D2:D11. Notice that this selection is one cell larger than your range of bins. The function returns one extra value in case there are any speeds faster than your top bin speed.

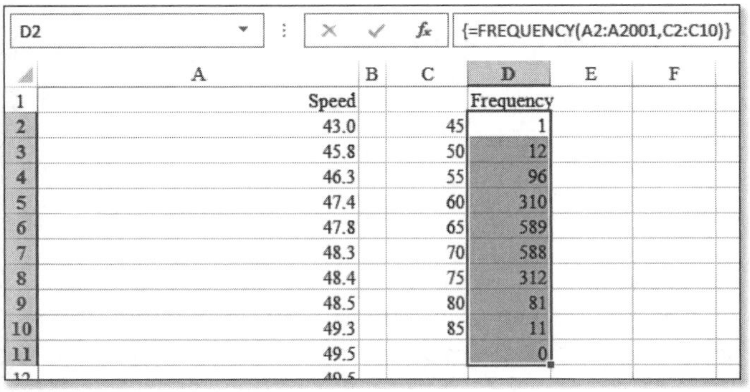

Figure 14.35
The tedious process of grouping values into ranges is handled easily with the FREQUENCY function.

5. With D2:D11 selected, type the formula **=FREQUENCY(A2:A2001,C2:C10)**. Do not press Enter at the end. You must tell Excel to evaluate the formula as an array formula, so hold down Ctrl+Shift and then press Enter. Excel automatically groups the 2,000 individual data points into the 10 bins. You can then chart or analyze this range.

Using NORM.DIST to Calculate the Probability in a Normal Distribution

In Figure 14.36, the observed speeds along a highway seem to be following a normal distribution. A normal distribution is sometimes referred to as a *bell curve*. When you have a normal distribution, the curve can be described mathematically using only the average and standard deviation of the data.

Figure 14.36
If your data is normally distributed, you can predict the future by using NORM.DIST.

F4			⁝	×	✓	f_x	=NORM.DIST(75,$D$1,$D$2,TRUE)			

▲	A	B	C	D	E	F	G	H	I	J
1	Speed		Mean	65.0	=AVERAGE(A2:A2001)					
2	43.0		Std Dev	5.979512	=STDEV.S(A2:A2001)					
3	45.8									
4	46.3		Probability car going 75 or less:			95.3%	=NORM.DIST(75,$D$1,$D$2,TRUE)			
5	47.4		Probability car going 65 or less:			50.2%	=NORM.DIST(65,$D$1,$D$2,TRUE)			
6	47.8	Probability car going between 65 and 75:				45.1%	=F4-F5			
7	48.3									
8	48.4									

The NORM.DIST function has a strange twist: It always returns the probability that a car will be going less than or equal to a value *x*. If you want to know the probability that the next car will be traveling between 65 and 75 mph, you have to figure out the cumulative probability of the car going less than 75 miles per hour and then subtract the cumulative probability of the car going less than 65 miles per hour. This requires two calls to the NORM.DIST function.

Syntax:

=NORM.DIST(*x*,*mean*,*standard_dev*,*cumulative*)

The NORM.DIST function returns the normal cumulative distribution for the specified mean and standard deviation. This function has a very wide range of applications in statistics, including hypothesis testing. This function takes the following arguments:

- *x*—This is the value for which you want the distribution.

- *mean*—This is the arithmetic mean of the distribution.

- *standard_dev*—This is the standard deviation of the distribution.

- *cumulative*—This is a logical value that determines the form of the function. If *cumulative* is TRUE, NORM.DIST returns the cumulative distribution function; if cumulative is FALSE, NORM.DIST returns the probability mass function.

If *mean* or *standard_dev* is nonnumeric, NORM.DIST returns a #VALUE! error. If *standard_dev* is less than or equal to 0, NORM.DIST returns a #NUM! error. If *mean* is 0 and *standard_dev* is 1, NORM.DIST returns the standard normal distribution.

In Figure 14.36, the range of observed values is in A2:A2001. Formulas in cells D1 and D2 calculate the average and standard deviation of the data set. The goal is to find the probability of any car going between 65 and 75 mph. The formula in cell F4 is =NORM.DIST(75,$D$1,$D$2,TRUE); it predicts the likelihood of a car going 75 mph or less at 95.3%. The formula in cell F5 is =NORM.DIST(65,$D$1,$D$2,TRUE). This predicts the probability of a car going 65 mph or less at 50.2%.

 **Note**

In Excel 2007, this function was called NORMDIST.

You can back into the probability that the car will be going between 65 and 75 mph by subtracting 50.2% from 95.3%. The answer to your problem is 45.1% that the next car passing the checkpoint will be going between 65 and 75 mph.

Using NORM.INV to Calculate the Value for a Certain Probability

In the preceding section, you used NORM.DIST to find the probability that a car was going less than 75 mph. Sometimes, you might want to find the speed associated with a certain probability. For example, say you need to design a billboard that can be read by 80% of the drivers. If you know the mean and standard deviation of the speeds on the highway, you can use the NORM.INV function to ask Excel to tell you that 80% of the drivers will be driving at X miles per hour or less.

Syntax:

=NORM.INV(*probability*,*mean*,*standard_dev*)

The NORM.INV function returns the inverse of the normal cumulative distribution for the specified mean and standard deviation. This function takes the following arguments:

- ***probability***—This is a probability corresponding to the normal distribution.
- ***mean***—This is the arithmetic mean of the distribution.
- ***standard_dev***—This is the standard deviation of the distribution.

If any argument is nonnumeric, NORM.INV returns a #VALUE! error. If *probability* is less than 0 or if *probability* is greater than 1, NORM.INV returns a #NUM! error. If *standard_dev* is less than or equal to 0, NORM.INV returns a #NUM! error.

NORM.INV uses an iterative technique for calculating the function. Given a probability value, NORM.INV iterates until the result is accurate to within ± 3 × 10^−7. If NORM.INV does not converge after 100 iterations, the function returns an #N/A error.

In Figure 14.37, a sample of speeds is listed in column A. The formulas in cells D1 and D2 calculate the mean and standard deviation. If you assume that the speeds follow a normal distribution, then 80% of the cars will be traveling 70 mph or less along this stretch of highway. The formula in cell E6 is =NORM.INV(D6,D$1,D$2).

E6 =NORM.INV(D6,D$1,D$2)

	A	B	C	D	E	F	G	H	I
1	Speed		Mean	65.0	=AVERAGE(A2:A2001)				
2	43.0		Std Dev	5.978017	=STDEV.P(A2:A2001)				
3	45.8								
4	46.3								
5	47.4			Probability	Speed				
6	47.8			80%	70.00	=NORM.INV(D6,D$1,D$2)			
7	48.3			85%	71.16	=NORM.INV(D7,D$1,D$2)			
8	48.4			90%	72.63	=NORM.INV(D8,D$1,D$2)			
9	48.5			95%	74.80	=NORM.INV(D9,D$1,D$2)			
10	49.3								

Figure 14.37
Rather than use Goal Seek with the NORM.DIST function, you can let Excel handle the iterations to back into an answer using NORM.INV.

Functions for the Standard Normal Distribution

The standard normal distribution is a normal distribution with a mean of 0 and a standard deviation of 1.

Before spreadsheets made it possible to calculate probabilities with NORM.DIST, you would have to find a statistics textbook and turn to the appendix. There, you would find pages and pages of probability tables for the standard normal distribution.

The convoluted process would work like this: Say that you had a population with a mean of 70 and a standard deviation of 9. You want to find the probability that any member of the population is at 82 or less. 82 is 12 above the mean, and 12 is 12/9 of a standard deviation or 1.333 standard deviations above the mean. You could then take the 1.333 and flip to the appendix of a textbook to find the cumulative probability for +1.333 is 90.9%.

Using NORM.S.DIST to Return Cumulative Probabilities

Starting in Excel 2010, the NORM.S.DIST function offered both cumulative and noncumulative calculations for the standard normal distribution. (Remember that this is the special population with a mean of 0 and a standard deviation of 1.)

The first argument, z, indicates the number of standard deviations from the mean. If you specify TRUE for the *cumulative* argument, you would return probabilities just like the appendix in the back of old statistics textbooks. NORM.S.DIST replaced the Excel 2007 function of NORMSDIST.

Figure 14.38 shows four charts with four different regions highlighted.

Figure 14.38
Combinations of NORM.S.DIST calculate the probability of each shaded area.

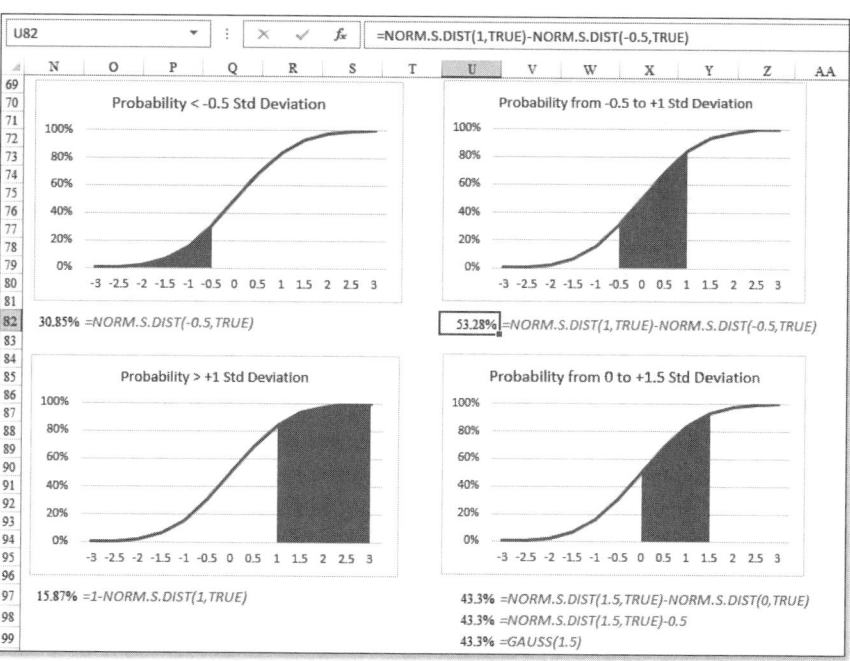

Say that you wanted to calculate the probability that any member of a population will be smaller than one-half of a standard deviation below the mean. Look at the top-left chart in Figure 14.38 to visualize this area. You can simply calculate =NORM.S.DIST(-0.5,True) to learn that 30.85% of the population will be smaller than this size.

Fascinating, right?

Except, how often in real life will anyone only be interested in the small members of the population? In real life, you will be interested in all sorts of different ranges. The top-right chart in Figure 14.38 illustrates one such range. What is the probability of falling between −0.5 and +1 standard deviations from the mean?

There is not a NORM.S.DIST.RANGE function yet, so you are forced to use two functions in the formula. Use NORM.S.DIST(1,True) to calculate the probability of being below +1 standard deviation. Then, subtract NORM.S.DIST(-0.5,True) to eliminate the 30.85% of the population who will be below −0.5 standard deviations from the mean. Cell U82 shows that 53.28% of the population will fall in this range.

In my list of things to complain about, the fact that I have to use two NORM.S.DIST functions to calculate a range does not really bother me at all.

Stick with me here. In the bottom-left chart, you want to measure how many members of the population will be larger than +1 standard deviation from the mean. One way, as shown in cell N97, is to subtract NORM.S.DIST(1,True) from 100%. NORM.S.DIST(1,True) tells you that about 84% of the people are smaller than +1 standard deviation from the mean. Subtracting this from 100% means that 15.87% of the population will be larger than +1 standard deviation from the mean. Alternatively, you could flip the chart and measure =NORM.S.DIST(-1,True) and get the same result.

These are all just little tricks of the trade. Yes, it might be slightly painful to enter NORM.S.DIST twice in a formula, but it sure is easier than using the printed tables in the back of a dusty statistics book.

And, yes, if you do =SUM(N82,U82,N97), the result is exactly 100%, so the checks and balances are all working fine.

Syntax:

=NORM.S.DIST(*z,cumulative*)

The NORM.S.DIST function returns the standard normal distribution function. The distribution has a mean of 0 and a standard deviation of 1. You use this function in place of a table of standard normal curve areas.

The argument *z* is the value for which you want the distribution. If *z* is nonnumeric, NORM.S.DIST returns a #VALUE! error.

Using GAUSS in Excel 2013 to Measure Probability Above the Mean

Check out the bottom-right chart in Figure 14.38. In this special case, you want to measure the probability of falling between the mean and +1.5 standard deviations from the mean.

If you've understood the examples in the previous section, you could easily use =NORM.S.DIST(1.5,True)-NORM.S.DIST(0,True) to calculate the probability of 43.3%.

If you are a bit quicker than the rest of the class, you might realize that the probability of being below the mean is 50%, so you could shorten the preceding formula to =NORM.S.DIST(1.5,True)-50%. Or, even save the percent sign and use =NORM.S.DIST(1,5.True)-.5.

The fine folks who maintain the OpenDocument Spreadsheet standard decided that all of the formulas are too hard and introduced the GAUSS function to calculate the probability shown in the bottom-right chart of Figure 14.38.

The Excel team had to add GAUSS to Excel 2013, even if they believe it is a bit pointless. The explanation in Excel 2013 Help for GAUSS is lackluster—the Help topic says that it returns 0.5 less than the standard normal cumulative distribution function.

Syntax:

=GAUSS(x)

The GAUSS function measures the cumulative probability from the mean to x standard deviations from the mean. This function is new in Excel 2013. It's mathematically equivalent to subtracting 0.5 from NORM.S.DIST(x,True).

Using PHI to Plot a Standard Normal Curve

As mentioned earlier, Excel 2010 introduced the noncumulative version of NORM.S.DIST. =NORM.S.DIST(z,False) gives you the height of the bell curve for a specific z value. For compliance with the Open Document Format, Excel 2013 replicates this exact same calculation using the new PHI function.

Recall that the standard normal distribution has a mean of 0 and a standard deviation of 1. If you calculated the discrete values of =NORM.S.DIST(z,False) where z is the range of whole numbers from −6 to +6, you get a probability of 100%.

The best use of PHI or NORM.S.DIST(z,False) is to plot a nice-looking standard normal curve. Fill A2:A62 with −3, −2.9, and so on down to +3. In column B, use =PHI(A2) and copy down. Use a heading of Standard Normal Distribution in B1. Plot A1:B62 as a line chart, and you have the bell curve shown in the bottom of Figure 14.38.

Syntax:

=PHI(*z*)

The PHI function returns the probability density function for a standard normal distribution. The argument *z* is the number of standard deviations away from the mean.

Using NORM.S.INV to Calculate a *z* Score for a Given Probability

To calculate a *z* score for a given probability, you use the NORM.S.INV function. In Figure 14.39, the *z* score for 15% is −1.036. This means that in a normally distributed population, 15% of the population exists at the value of the mean minus 1.036 standard deviations.

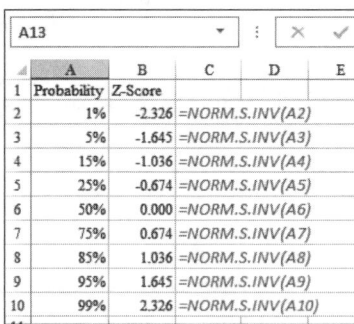

Figure 14.39
You can back into a z score from a probability by using NORM.S.INV. You can then take the z score multiplied by a standard deviation to figure out the distance that your value lies from the mean.

Syntax:

=NORM.S.INV(*probability*)

The NORM.S.INV function returns the inverse of the standard normal cumulative distribution. The distribution has a mean of 0 and a standard deviation of 1.

The argument *probability* is a probability that corresponds to the normal distribution. If *probability* is nonnumeric, NORMSINV returns a #VALUE! error. If *probability* is less than 0 or if *probability* is greater than 1, NORM.S.INV returns a #NUM! error.

NORM.S.INV uses an iterative technique for calculating the function. Given a probability value, NORM.S.INV iterates until the result is accurate to within $\pm\ 3 \times 10^{-7}$. If NORM.S.INV does not converge after 100 iterations, the function returns an #N/A error.

The *z* score refers to a number of standard deviations away from the mean. If the *z* score is negative, the value lies to the left of the mean. If the *z* score is positive, the value lies to the right of the mean.

Using STANDARDIZE to Calculate the Distance from the Mean

To calculate the distance from a mean, use the STANDARDIZE function. This function returns the positive or negative distance from the mean, expressed as the number of standard deviations.

Syntax:

```
=STANDARDIZE(x,mean,standard_dev)
```

The STANDARDIZE function returns a normalized value from a distribution characterized by *mean* and *standard_dev*. This function takes the following arguments:

- ***x***—This is the value you want to normalize.
- ***mean***—This is the arithmetic mean of the distribution.
- ***standard_dev***—This is the standard deviation of the distribution.

If *standard_dev* is less than or equal to 0, STANDARDIZE returns a #NUM! error. In Figure 14.40, a population has a mean of 65 and a standard deviation of 5. The normalized value of 50 is -3, indicating that 50 is 3 standard deviations below from the mean of 65.

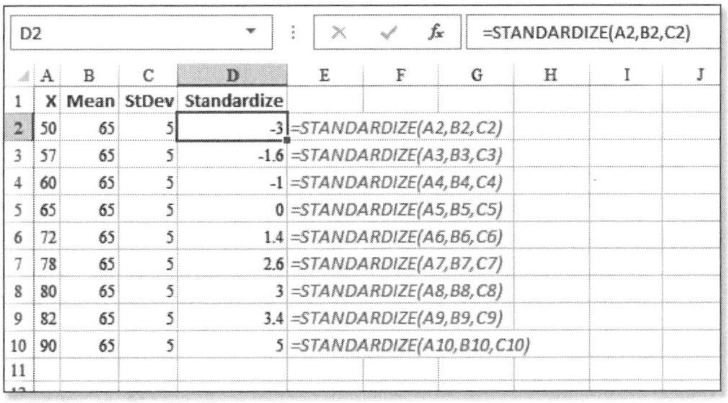

D2 =STANDARDIZE(A2,B2,C2)

	A	B	C	D	E
1	X	Mean	StDev	Standardize	
2	50	65	5	-3	=STANDARDIZE(A2,B2,C2)
3	57	65	5	-1.6	=STANDARDIZE(A3,B3,C3)
4	60	65	5	-1	=STANDARDIZE(A4,B4,C4)
5	65	65	5	0	=STANDARDIZE(A5,B5,C5)
6	72	65	5	1.4	=STANDARDIZE(A6,B6,C6)
7	78	65	5	2.6	=STANDARDIZE(A7,B7,C7)
8	80	65	5	3	=STANDARDIZE(A8,B8,C8)
9	82	65	5	3.4	=STANDARDIZE(A9,B9,C9)
10	90	65	5	5	=STANDARDIZE(A10,B10,C10)

Figure 14.40
STANDARDIZE does the basic math to calculate the distance from the mean, expressed as a number of standard deviations.

Using Student's *t*-Distribution for Small Sample Sizes

All the previous examples using a normal distribution assume that the sample size is 30 or more. If you are using a small sample size—even as small as three members—you should use the Student's *t*-distribution.

An important concept in the Student's *t*-distribution is the degrees of freedom. If you know the mean of the sample but not the standard deviation of the population, the degrees of freedom is the sample size minus 1. When the degrees of freedom is 29 or greater, the Student's *t*-distribution is nearly identical with the normal distribution. However, as the degrees of freedom drops, the distribution becomes flatter and wider.

Changes to the TDIST Function Starting in Excel 2010

Microsoft added several functions to Excel 2010. In legacy versions of Excel, the TDIST function required three arguments: *x*, *degrees_freedom*, and *#_tails*. In Excel 2010, Microsoft moved the # of tails to the function name.

In Excel 2007, the two-tailed TDIST function was as follows:

```
=TDIST(2.5,10,2)
```

This is now equivalent to Excel 2013's T.DIST.2T function:

```
=T.DIST.2T(2.5,10)
```

In Excel 2007, the one-tailed TDIST function was as follows:

```
=TDIST(2.5,10,1)
```

This is now equivalent to the T.DIST.RT function:

```
=T.DIST.RT(2.5,10)
```

Excel 2013 offers a new T.DIST function with arguments for *x*, *degrees_freedom*, and *cumulative*.

Syntax:

```
=T.DIST(x,degrees_freedom,cumulative)
=T.DIST.2T(x,degrees_freedom)
=T.DIST.RT(x,degrees_freedom)
```

The T.DIST.2T function returns the percentage points (that is, probability) for the Student's *t*-distribution, where a numeric value (*x*) is a calculated value of *t* for which the percentage points are to be computed. The *t*-distribution is used in the hypothesis testing of small sample data sets. You use this function in place of a table of critical values for the *t*-distribution.

The T.DIST.2T function takes the following arguments:

- *x*—This is the numeric value at which to evaluate the distribution.

- *degrees_freedom*—This is an integer that indicates the number of degrees of freedom.

If any argument is nonnumeric, T.DIST returns a #VALUE! error. If *degrees_freedom* is less than 1, T.DIST returns a #NUM! error. The *degrees_freedom* argument is truncated to integers.

Syntax:

```
=T.INV.2T(probability,degrees_freedom)
```

The T.INV.2T function returns the *t*-value of the Student's *t*-distribution as a function of the probability and the degrees of freedom. This function takes the following arguments:

- ■ *probability*—This is the probability associated with the two-tailed Student's *t*-distribution.

- ■ *degrees_freedom*—This is the number of degrees of freedom to characterize the distribution.

If either argument is nonnumeric, T.INV.2T returns a #VALUE! error. If *probability* is less than 0 or if *probability* is greater than 1, T.INV.2T returns a #NUM! error. If *degrees_freedom* is not an integer, it is truncated. If *degrees_freedom* is less than 1, T.INV.2T returns a #NUM! error. T.INV.2T is calculated as T.INV.2T = p(t<X), where X is a random variable that follows the *t*-distribution.

T.INV.2T uses an iterative technique for calculating the function. Given a probability value, T.INV.2T iterates until the result is accurate to within $\pm 3 \times 10^{-7}$. If T.INV.2T does not converge after 100 iterations, the function returns an #N/A error.

Syntax:

=T.TEST(*array1*,*array2*,*tails*,*type*)

Excel can also calculate the *t*-test to predict whether two samples come from populations with the same mean. For this, you use the T.TEST function. The T.TEST function returns the probability associated with a Student's *t*-test. You use T.TEST to determine whether two samples are likely to have come from the same two underlying populations that have the same mean.

The T.TEST function takes the following arguments:

- ■ *array1*—This is the first data set.

- ■ *array2*—This is the second data set.

- ■ *tails*—This specifies the number of distribution tails. If *tails* is 1, T.TEST uses the one-tailed distribution. If *tails* is 2, T.TEST uses the two-tailed distribution.

- ■ *type*—This is the kind of *t*-test to perform. See Table 14.5 for more information.

Table 14.5 Types of *t*-Tests Available with the T.TEST Function

If Type Equals	This Test Is Performed
1	Paired
2	Two-sample equal variance (homoscedastic)
3	Two-sample unequal variance (heteroscedastic)

If *array1* and *array2* have a different number of data points, and if *type* is 1 (paired), T.TEST returns an #N/A error. The *tails* and *type* arguments are truncated to integers. If *tails* or *type* is nonnumeric, T.TEST returns a #VALUE! error. If *tails* is any value other than 1 or 2, T.TEST returns a #NUM! error.

In Figure 14.41, the means of the two samples are different: 11.15 versus 13.5. However, in cell F2, T.TEST returns 0.1577. Because this is greater than the typical alpha of 0.05, the difference in means might not be statistically significant. It is possible that these two samples were taken from the same population.

F2				▾	:	×	✓	*fx*		=T.TEST($A$2:$A$14,$B$2:$B$14,F$1,$G2)

⊿	A	B	C	D	E	F	G	H
1	Sample 1	Sample 2			1	2		
2	9.962434	14.73364		1 - Paired Samples	0.07887199	0.15774397	1	
3	10.98365	15.23975		2 - Two-sample equal variance	0.03895041	0.07790082	2	
4	15.2866	7.784814		3 - Two-sample unequal variance	0.03968814	0.07937628	3	
5	13.02461	8.080393						
6	8.806905	15.30991		t-Test: Paired Two Sample for Means				
7	10.15532	12.99917						
8	16.14824	8.154726			*Variable 1*	*Variable 2*		
9	10.23477	14.61543		Mean	11.1500653	13.5482847		
10	8.594735	17.13872		Variance	7.22510765	14.8168691		
11	12.7652	18.02172		Observations	13	13		
12	7.527358	17.2393		Pearson Correlation	-0.52637247			
13	12.93556	17.29219		Hypothesized Mean Difference	0			
14	8.525473	9.51795		df	12			
15				t Stat	-1.50673146			
16				P(T<=t) one-tail	0.07887199			
17				t Critical one-tail	1.78228755			
18				P(T<=t) two-tail	0.15774397	◂		
19				t Critical two-tail	2.17881283			
20								

Figure 14.41
T.TEST helps you determine whether two samples came from the same population.

Later in this chapter, you find out how the Analysis ToolPak offers several varieties of *t*-Test reports. Using the T.TEST function is a formulaic way to return the *t*-Test values. In Figure 14.41, the report in D6:F19 is generated by the Analysis ToolPak.

Using CHISQ.TEST to Perform Goodness-of-Fit Testing

A Chi-Squared test compares expected frequencies with observed frequencies. The CHISQ.TEST function performs the Chi-Squared test for independence.

CHISQ.INV.RT is used to find the critical Chi value for a certain probability and degrees of freedom. CHISQ.DIST.RT is used to determine the probability for a Chi value and certain degrees of freedom.

Syntax:

=CHISQ.TEST(*actual_range*,*expected_range*)

The CHISQ.TEST function returns the test for independence. CHISQ.TEST returns the value from the Chi-Squared distribution for the statistic and the appropriate degrees of freedom. You can use Chi-Squared tests to determine whether hypothesized results are verified by an experiment.

The CHISQ.TEST function takes the following arguments:

- *actual_range*—This is the range of data that contains observations to test against expected values.

- *expected_range*—This is the range of data that contains the ratio of the product of row totals and column totals to the grand total.

If *actual_range* and *expected_range* have different numbers of data points, CHISQ.TEST returns an #N/A error.

The Chi-Squared test first calculates a Chi-Squared statistic and then sums the differences of actual values from the expected values. CHISQ.TEST returns the probability for a Chi-Squared statistic and degrees of freedom (df), where df = (r - 1)(c - 1).

Syntax:

=CHISQ.DIST.RT(*x*,*degrees_freedom*)

The CHISQ.DIST.RT function returns the one-tailed probability of the Chi-Squared distribution. The Chi-Squared distribution is associated with a Chi-Squared test. You use the Chi-Squared test to compare observed and expected values. For example, a genetic experiment might hypothesize that the next generation of plants will exhibit a certain set of colors. By comparing the observed results with the expected ones, you can decide whether your original hypothesis is valid.

The CHISQ.DIST.RT function takes the following arguments:

- *x*—This is the value at which you want to evaluate the distribution.

- *degrees_freedom*—This is the number of degrees of freedom.

If either argument is nonnumeric, CHISQ.DIST.RT returns a #VALUE! error. If *x* is negative, CHISQ.DIST.RT returns a #NUM! error. If *degrees_freedom* is not an integer, it is truncated. If *degrees_freedom* is less than 1 or if *degrees_freedom* is greater than or equal to 10^{10}, CHISQ.DIST.RT returns a #NUM! error.

Syntax:

=CHISQ.INV.RT(*probability*,*degrees_freedom*)

The CHISQ.INV.RT function returns the inverse of the one-tailed probability of the Chi-Squared distribution. If *probability* equals CHISQ.DIST.RT(*x*,...), CHISQ.INV.RT(*probability*,...) equals *x*. You use the CHISQ.INV.RT function to compare observed results with expected ones to decide whether your original hypothesis is valid.

The CHISQ.INV.RT function takes the following arguments:

- *probability*—This is a probability associated with the Chi-Squared distribution.

- *degrees_freedom*—This is the number of degrees of freedom.

If either argument is nonnumeric, `CHISQ.INV.RT` returns a `#VALUE!` error. If *`probability`* is less than 0 or *`probability`* is greater than 1, `CHISQ.INV.RT` returns a `#NUM!` error. If *`degrees_freedom`* is not an integer, it is truncated. If *`degrees_freedom`* is less than 1 or if *`degrees_freedom`* is greater than or equal to 10^10, `CHISQ.INV.RT` returns a `#NUM!` error.

`CHISQ.INV.RT` uses an iterative technique for calculating the function. Given a *`probability`* value, `CHISQ.INV.RT` iterates until the result is accurate to within ±3 × 10^−7. If `CHISQ.INV` does not converge after 100 iterations, the function returns an `#N/A` error.

Figure 14.42 shows `CHITEST` and `CHISQ.INV.RT` functions.

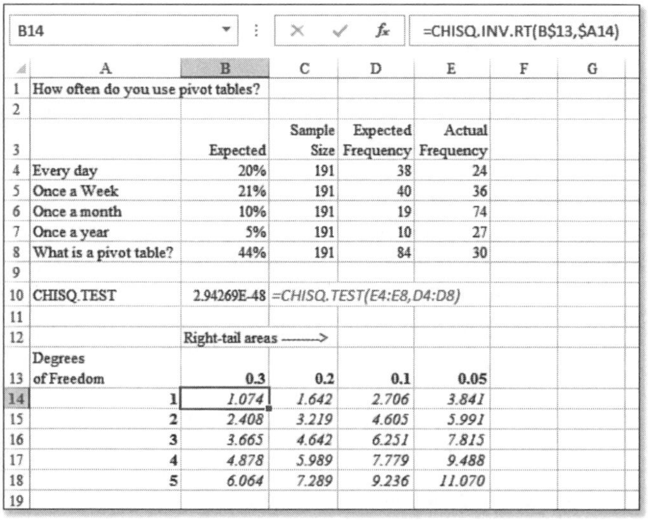

	A	B	C	D	E
1	How often do you use pivot tables?				
2					
3		Expected	Sample Size	Expected Frequency	Actual Frequency
4	Every day	20%	191	38	24
5	Once a Week	21%	191	40	36
6	Once a month	10%	191	19	74
7	Once a year	5%	191	10	27
8	What is a pivot table?	44%	191	84	30
9					
10	CHISQ.TEST	2.94269E-48	=CHISQ.TEST(E4:E8,D4:D8)		
11					
12		Right-tail areas ------->			
13	Degrees of Freedom	0.3	0.2	0.1	0.05
14	1	1.074	1.642	2.706	3.841
15	2	2.408	3.219	4.605	5.991
16	3	3.665	4.642	6.251	7.815
17	4	4.878	5.989	7.779	9.488
18	5	6.064	7.289	9.236	11.070
19					

Figure 14.42
You can calculate Chi-Squared testing with `CHISQ.TEST`.

The Sum of Squares Functions

Excel offers four functions with confusingly similar names. The hardest part of using these functions is figuring out which function does what. The first three functions require two identically sized arrays, named `x` and `y`. These are Excel's four sum of squares functions:

- **SumX2MY2**—For each pair of `x` and `y`, Excel calculates `x^2 - y^2` and then sums these values. In this case, the `M` in the function name indicates *minus*.

- **SumX2PY2**—For each pair of `x` and `y`, Excel calculates `x^2 + y^2` and then sums these values. In this case, the `P` in the function name indicates *plus*.

- **SumXMY2**—For each pair of `x` and `y`, Excel calculates `(x - y)^2` and then sums these values. Again, the `M` indicates *minus*, and the lack of a 2 after the `X` indicates that it is the difference that is squared.

- **SumSQ**—Returns the sum of the squares of the arguments.

In Figure 14.43, the x array is in A2:A5, and the y array is in B2:B5. The formulas in D2:D5 calculate x - y for each pair. The formulas in E2:E5 square that difference for each pair. The formula in cell E6 totals the sum of the squares. You could replace the five formulas in column E with a single formula in cell D6: =SUMSQ(D2:D5). Alternatively, you could replace all the formulas in columns D and E with a single use of SumXMY2 in cell B9.

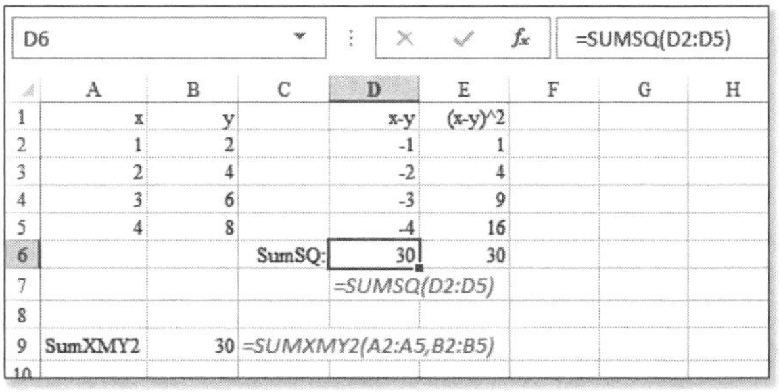

D6 =SUMSQ(D2:D5)

	A	B	C	D	E	F	G	H
1	x	y		x-y	(x-y)^2			
2	1	2		-1	1			
3	2	4		-2	4			
4	3	6		-3	9			
5	4	8		-4	16			
6			SumSQ:	30	30			
7				=SUMSQ(D2:D5)				
8								
9	SumXMY2	30	=SUMXMY2(A2:A5,B2:B5)					
10								

Figure 14.43
Without doing any regression, you use SUMXMY2 to calculate the sum of the squares of the difference of two arrays.

Sum of the Sum of the Squares

Some statistical processes ask you to calculate the sum of the sum of the squares. However, a casual survey of several mathematicians could not find one concrete example of when this would be useful. In fact, the formula for SUMX2PY2(A2:A5,B2:B5) is mathematically equivalent to SUMSQ(A2:B5). Furthermore, the formula for SUMX2MY2(A2:A5,B2:B5) is the same as SUMSQ(A2:A5)-SUMSQ(B2:B5). My theory on this is that some early spreadsheets included these functions in an effort to claim that they had more functions than a competitor did. All future spreadsheets have included the functions just because some other competitor included them.

Syntax:

=SUMSQ(*number1*,*number2*,...)

The SUMSQ function returns the sum of the squares of the arguments. The arguments *number1*, *number2*, ... are one to 255 arguments for which you want the sum of the squares. You can also use a single array or a reference to an array instead of arguments separated by commas.

Syntax:

=SUMXMY2(*array_x*,*array_y*)

The SUMXMY2 function returns the sum of squares of differences of corresponding values in two arrays. It takes the following arguments:

- ***array_x***—This is the first array or range of values.
- ***array_y***—This is the second array or range of values.

The arguments should be either numbers or names, arrays, or references that contain numbers. If an array or reference argument contains text, logical values, or empty cells, those values are ignored; however, cells that contain the value 0 are included. If *array_x* and *array_y* have a different number of values, SUMXMY2 returns an #N/A error.

Syntax:

=SUMX2MY2(*array_x*,*array_y*)

The SUMX2MY2 function returns the sum of the difference of squares of corresponding values in two arrays. This function takes the following arguments:

- *array_x*—This is the first array or range of values.

- *array_y*—This is the second array or range of values.

The arguments should be either numbers or names, arrays, or references that contain numbers. If an array or a reference argument contains text, logical values, or empty cells, those values are ignored; however, cells that contain the value 0 are included. If *array_x* and *array_y* have a different number of values, SUMX2MY2 returns an #N/A error.

Syntax:

=SUMX2PY2(*array_x*,*array_y*)

The SUMX2PY2 function returns the sum of the sum of squares of corresponding values in two arrays. The *sum of the sum of squares* is a common term in many statistical calculations. This function takes the following arguments:

- *array_x*—This is the first array or range of values.

- *array_y*—This is the second array or range of values.

The arguments should be either numbers or names, arrays, or references that contain numbers. If an array or reference argument contains text, logical values, or empty cells, those values are ignored; however, cells that contain the value 0 are included. If *array_x* and *array_y* have a different number of values, SUMX2PY2 returns an #N/A error.

In Figure 14.44, the one SUMX2PY2 formula in cell B9 is much simpler than the five formulas in column D, but if you really want to do this calculation, you could use SUMSQ, as shown in cell B12.

Testing Probability on Logarithmic Distributions

In the life sciences, a number of populations have logarithmic distributions. In the population shown in Figure 14.45, the values in the sample range from less than two to more than 38,000. The data clearly does not follow a normal distribution.

B9 =SUMX2PY2(A2:A5,B2:B5)

	A	B	C	D	E
1	x	y		(x^2+y^2)	(x^2-y^2)
2	1	2		5	-3
3	2	4		20	-12
4	3	6		45	-27
5	4	8		80	-48
6			Total	150	-90
7					
8					
9	SumX2pY2	150	=SUMX2PY2(A2:A5,B2:B5)		
10	SumX2mY2	-90	=SUMX2MY2(A2:A5,B2:B5)		
11					
12	SumSQ	150	=SUMSQ(A2:B5)		
13	SumSQ	-90	=SUMSQ(A2:A5)-SUMSQ(B2:B5)		

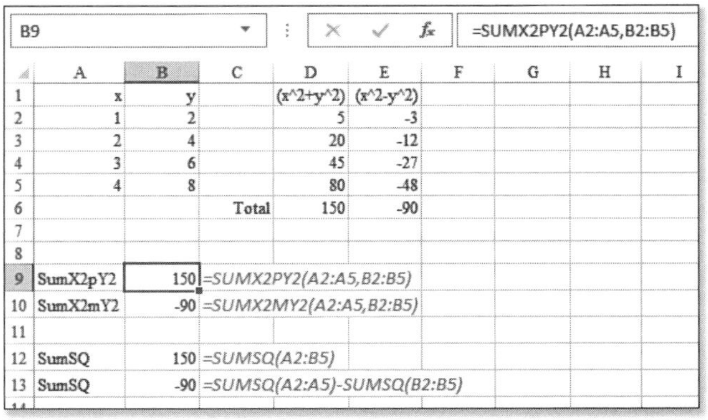

Figure 14.44
Microsoft won't say that these two functions are useful in statistics. I don't think they are useful anywhere.

S	T	
20	15.8%	=LOGNORM.DIST(S51,5,2,1)
50	29.3%	
150	50.2%	
500	72.8%	
1500	87.6%	
5000	96.1%	
25000	99.5%	
80%	798.9	=LOGNORM.INV(S59,5,2)
85%	1179.5	
95%	3982.7	

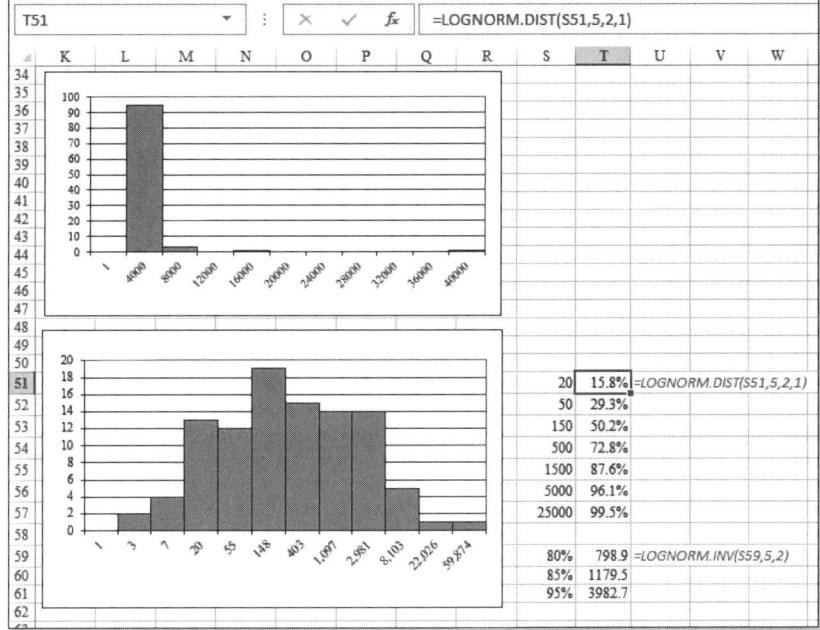

Figure 14.45
The LOGNORM.DIST and LOGNORM.INV functions can make sense of a population where the natural logarithm of the population is normally distributed.

However, if you took the natural logarithm of each data point, the LN(x) of the members does follow a normal distribution. The mean of the natural logarithms is 5, with a standard deviation of 2.

Populations where the natural logarithm is normally distributed are called *lognormal distributions*. An example of a population with a lognormal distribution is the length of time that bacteria live in a disinfectant.

In the example where the mean of the natural logarithm values is 5 and the standard deviation is 2, take a look at what this really means: You use EXP(5) to see that the mean of 5 translates to 148. You would expect 65% of the population to be within 1 standard deviation of the mean. This range from EXP(3) to EXP(7) is from 20 to 1,096. The range for 2 standard deviations from the mean is EXP(1) and EXP(9), or 2.7 and 8,103.

Given a lognormal distribution where the mean of the natural logarithm of the population is 5 and the standard deviation is 2, you can predict what percentage of the population will be at a number (*x*) or below by using LOGNORM.DIST. To find the value of *x* associated with a certain probability, you use LOGNORM.INV.

Syntax:

=LOGNORM.DIST(*x*,*mean*,*standard_dev*,*cumulative*)

The LOGNORM.DIST function returns the cumulative lognormal distribution of *x*, where the natural logarithm is normally distributed with the parameters *mean* and *standard_dev*. You use this function to analyze data that has been logarithmically transformed. This function takes the following arguments:

- *x*—This is the value at which to evaluate the function.

- *mean*—This is the mean of the natural logarithm.

- *standard_dev*—This is the standard deviation of the natural logarithm.

- *cumulative*—Use 1 or True to calculate the CDF. Use 0 or False to calculate the PDF.

If any argument is nonnumeric, LOGNORM.DIST returns a #VALUE! error. If *x* is less than or equal to 0 or if *standard_dev* is less than or equal to 0, LOGNORM.DIST returns a #NUM! error.

Syntax:

=LOGNORM.INV(*probability*,*mean*,*standard_dev*)

The LOGNORM.INV function returns the inverse of the lognormal cumulative distribution function of *x*, where the natural logarithm is normally distributed with the parameters *mean* and *standard_dev*. If *probability* is equal to LOGNORM.DIST(*x*,...), LOGNORM.INV(*probability*,...) is equal to *x*. You use the lognormal distribution to analyze logarithmically transformed data.

The LOGNORM.INV function takes the following arguments:

- *probability*—This is a probability associated with the lognormal distribution.

- *mean*—This is the mean of the natural logarithm.

- *standard_dev*—This is the standard deviation of the natural logarithm.

If any argument is nonnumeric, LOGNORM.INV returns a #VALUE! error. If *probability* is less than 0 or if *probability* is greater than 1, LOGNORM.INV returns a #NUM! error. If *standard_dev* is less than or equal to 0, LOGNORM.INV returns a #NUM! error.

In Figure 14.45, the population varies from 1.7 to 38,577, but the LOGNORM.DIST function predicts that 72.8% of the population is less than 500, 87.6% is less than 1,500, and 96.1% is less than 5,000.

In cell T61, the LOGNORM.INV function reveals that 95% of the population should be less than 3,983.

 Note

In Excel 2007, the NORMDIST function always calculated the CDF. When you switch to the LOGNORM.DIST function, you need to add a fourth argument of 1 or True to calculate the equivalent function.

Using GAMMA.DIST and GAMMA.INV to Analyze Queuing Times

Earlier in this chapter, we discussed how to use a Poisson distribution to analyze how many customers might walk into a bank during any given hour. However, if the time between customers is relevant, you need to use the gamma distribution. The gamma distribution is described by two variables—*alpha* for shape and *beta* for rate. For a gamma distribution described by *alpha* and *beta*, you can find the probability that a value of *x* or less will occur with GAMMA.DIST. To find the value of *x* for a certain probability, you use GAMMA.INV. The other remaining gamma-related functions are GAMMALN and GAMMA.

Syntax:

=GAMMA.DIST(*x*,*alpha*,*beta*,*cumulative*)

The GAMMA.DIST function returns the gamma distribution. You can use this function to study variables that might have a skewed distribution. The gamma distribution is commonly used in queuing analysis. This function takes the following arguments:

- **x**—This is the value at which you want to evaluate the distribution.

- **alpha**—This is a parameter to the distribution.

- **beta**—This is a parameter to the distribution.

- **cumulative**—This is a logical value that determines the form of the function. If *cumulative* is TRUE, GAMMA.DIST returns the cumulative distribution function; if *cumulative* is FALSE, GAMMA.DIST returns the probability mass function.

If *beta* is 1, GAMMA.DIST returns the standard gamma distribution. If *x*, *alpha*, or *beta* is nonnumeric, GAMMA.DIST returns a #VALUE! error. If *x* is less than 0, GAMMA.DIST returns a #NUM! error. If *alpha* is less than or equal to 0 or if *beta* is less than or equal to 0, GAMMA.DIST returns a #NUM! error. When *alpha* is a positive integer, GAMMA.DIST is also known as the Erlang distribution.

Syntax:

`=GAMMA.INV(probability,alpha,beta)`

The `GAMMA.INV` function returns the inverse of the gamma cumulative distribution. If *probability* is equal to `GAMMA.DIST(x,...)`, then `GAMMA.INV(probability,...)` is equal to *x*. You can use this function to study a variable whose distribution might be skewed. This function takes the following arguments:

- *probability*—This is the probability associated with the gamma distribution.

- *alpha*—This is a parameter to the distribution.

- *beta*—This is a parameter to the distribution. If *beta* is 1, `GAMMA.INV` returns the standard gamma distribution.

If any argument is nonnumeric, `GAMMA.INV` returns a #VALUE! error. If *probability* is less than 0 or *probability* is greater than 1, `GAMMA.INV` returns a #NUM! error. If *alpha* is less than or equal to 0 or if *beta* is less than or equal to 0, `GAMMA.INV` returns the #NUM! error. If *beta* is less than or equal to 0, `GAMMA.INV` returns a #NUM! error.

`GAMMA.INV` uses an iterative technique to do its calculation. Given a *probability* value, `GAMMA.INV` iterates until the result is accurate to within $\pm 3 \times 10^{-7}$. If `GAMMA.INV` does not converge after 100 iterations, the function returns an #N/A error.

Syntax:

`=GAMMALN(x)`

The `GAMMALN` function returns the natural logarithm of the gamma function, $G(x)$. The argument *x* is the value for which you want to calculate `GAMMALN`.

If *x* is nonnumeric, `GAMMALN` returns a #VALUE! error. If *x* is less than or equal to 0, `GAMMALN` returns a #NUM! error. The number *e* raised to the `GAMMALN(i)` power, where *i* is an integer, returns the same result as $(i - 1)!$.

Syntax:

`=GAMMA(x)`

The `GAMMA` function returns the Gamma value of *x*. This function is new in Excel 2013 for compatibility with the Open Document Spreadsheet format.

Calculating Probability of Beta Distributions

A *beta distribution* is used to describe the variability of the percentage of something across samples, such as the percentage of the day people spend sleeping.

A beta distribution curve is described by two parameters: *alpha* and *beta*. For any given distribution, you can predict the likelihood that a value will be less than or equal to *x* by using BETA.DIST. To find the value of *x* associated with a certain probability, you use BETA.INV.

Syntax:

=BETA.DIST(*x*,*alpha*,*beta*,*cumulative*,*A*,*B*)

The BETA.DIST function returns the cumulative beta probability density function, which is commonly used to study variation in the percentage of something across samples, such as the fraction of the day people spend watching television. This function takes the following arguments:

- ▪ *x*—This is the value between *a* and *b* at which to evaluate the function.

- ▪ *alpha*—This is a parameter to the distribution.

- ▪ *beta*—This is a parameter to the distribution.

- ▪ *cumulative*—True or 1 for the CDF; False or 0 for the PDF.

- ▪ *A*—This is an optional lower bound to the interval of *x*.

- ▪ *B*—This is an optional upper bound to the interval of *x*.

If any argument is nonnumeric, BETA.DIST returns a #VALUE! error. If *alpha* is less than or equal to 0 or *beta* is less than or equal to 0, BETA.DIST returns a #NUM! error. If *x* is less than *A*, *x* is greater than *B*, or *A* equals *B*, BETA.DIST returns a #NUM! error. If you omit values for *A* and *B*, BETA.DIST uses the standard cumulative beta distribution, so that *A* equals 0 and *B* equals 1.

 Note

BETA.DIST in Excel 2013 is similar to BETADIST in legacy versions of Excel. BETADIST always calculated the CDF. To switch from BETADIST to BETA.DIST, add a 1 as the third argument to indicate that the function should be cumulative.

Syntax:

=BETA.INV(*probability*,*alpha*,*beta*,*A*,*B*)

The BETA.INV function returns the inverse of the cumulative beta probability density function. That is, if *probability* is equal to BETADIST(*x*,...), then BETA.INV(*probability*,...) is equal to *x*. The cumulative beta distribution can be used in project planning to model probable completion times, given an expected completion time and variability.

The BETA.INV function takes the following arguments:

- ▪ *probability*—This is a probability associated with the beta distribution.

- ▪ *alpha*—This is a parameter to the distribution.

- ▪ *beta*—This is a parameter to the distribution.

- ▪ *A*—This is an optional lower bound to the interval of *x*.

- ▪ *B*—This is an optional upper bound to the interval of *x*.

If any argument is nonnumeric, BETA.INV returns a #VALUE! error. If *alpha* is less than or equal to 0 or if *beta* is less than or equal to 0, BETA.INV returns a #NUM! error. If *probability* is less than or equal to 0 or *probability* is greater than 1, BETA.INV returns a #NUM! error. If you omit values for *A* and *B*, BETA.INV uses the standard cumulative beta distribution, so that *A* equals 0 and *B* equals 1.

BETA.INV uses an iterative technique for calculating the function. Given a probability value, BETA.INV iterates until the result is accurate to within $\pm 3 \times 10 - 7$. If BETA.INV does not converge after 100 iterations, the function returns an #N/A error.

Using F.TEST to Measure Differences in Variability

There are three functions for measuring variability among two populations. Suppose you need to compare test results from males and test results from females. To determine whether one population has more variability than the other, you use F.TEST. The F.DIST function determines the probability that a value will be less than or equal to x. The F.INV function returns the x value associated with a certain probability.

> **Note**
> An F.TEST in Excel 2013 (or 2010) is equivalent to FTEST in legacy versions of Excel.

Syntax:

`=F.TEST(array1,array2)`

The F.TEST function returns the result of an *F*-test. An *F*-test returns the one-tailed probability that the variances in *array1* and *array2* are not significantly different. You use this function to determine whether two samples have different variances. For example, given test scores from public and private schools, you can test whether these schools have different levels of diversity.

The F.TEST function takes the following arguments:

- *array1*—This is the first array or range of data.
- *array2*—This is the second array or range of data.

The arguments must be numbers or names, arrays, or references that contain numbers. If an array or a reference argument contains text, logical values, or empty cells, those values are ignored. However, cells that contain the value 0 are included. If the number of data points in *array1* or *array2* is less than 2, or if the variance of *array1* or *array2* is 0, F.TEST returns a #DIV/0! error.

Syntax:

`=F.DIST.RT(x,degrees_freedom1,degrees_freedom2)`

The F.DIST.RT function returns the *F* probability distribution. You can use this function to determine whether two data sets have different degrees of diversity. For example, you can examine test scores given to men and women entering high school and determine whether the variability in the females is different from that found in the males.

The F.DIST.RT function takes the following arguments:

- **x**—This is the value at which to evaluate the function.

- **degrees_freedom1**—This is the numerator degrees of freedom.

- **degrees_freedom2**—This is the denominator degrees of freedom.

If any argument is nonnumeric, F.DIST.RT returns a #VALUE! error. If x is negative, F.DIST.RT returns a #NUM! error. If *degrees_freedom1* or *degrees_freedom2* is not an integer, it is truncated. If *degrees_freedom1* is less than 1 or *degrees_freedom1* is greater than or equal to $10^{\wedge}10$, F.DIST.RT returns a #NUM! error. If *degrees_freedom2* is less than 1 or *degrees_freedom2* is greater than or equal to $10^{\wedge}10$, F.DIST.RT returns a #NUM! error. F.DIST.RT is calculated as F.DIST.RT=P(F<x), where F is a random variable that has an F distribution.

 Note

F.DIST.RT in Excel 2013 (or 2010) is equivalent to FDIST in legacy versions of Excel. As of Excel 2010, F.DIST was a new function to return the PDF or CDF of the F distribution.

Syntax:

=F.INV.RT(*probability*, *degrees_freedom1*,*degrees_freedom2*)

The F.INV.RT function returns the inverse of the F probability distribution. If *probability* is equal to F.DIST.RT(*x*,...), then F.INV.RT(*probability*,...) is equal to *x*. The F distribution can be used in an F-test that compares the degree of variability in two data sets. For example, you can analyze income distributions in the United States and Canada to determine whether the two countries have a similar degree of diversity.

This function takes the following arguments:

 Note

F.INV.RT is the Excel 2010 and 2013 equivalent of FINV in legacy versions of Excel. The Excel 2013 function of F.INV returns the inverse of the F distribution.

- **probability**—This is a probability associated with the F cumulative distribution.

- **degrees_freedom1**—This is the numerator degrees of freedom.

- **degrees_freedom2**—This is the denominator degrees of freedom.

If any argument is nonnumeric, F.INV.RT returns a #VALUE! error. If *probability* is less than 0 or *probability* is greater than 1, F.INV.RT returns a #NUM! error. If *degrees_freedom1* or *degrees_freedom2* is not an integer, it is truncated. If *degrees_freedom1* is less than 1 or *degrees_freedom1* is greater than or equal to $10^{\wedge}10$, F.INV.RT returns a #NUM! error. If *degrees_freedom2* is less than 1 or *degrees_freedom2* is greater than or equal to $10^{\wedge}10$, F.INV.RT returns a #NUM! error.

F.INV.RT can be used to return critical values from the F distribution. For example, the output of an ANOVA calculation often includes data for the F statistic, F probability, and F critical value

Note

HYPGEOM.DIST in Excel 2010 and 2013 is similar to HYPGEOMDIST in legacy versions of Excel. To convert to HYPGEOMDIST, add a 1 as the *cumulative* argument for HYPGEOMDIST.

at the 0.05 significance level. To return the critical value of *F*, you use the significance level as the probability argument to F.INV.RT.

F.INV.RT uses an iterative technique for calculating the function. Given a probability value, F.INV.RT iterates until the result is accurate to within $\pm 3 \times 10^{-7}$. If F.INV.RT does not converge after 100 iterations, the function returns an #N/A error.

Other Distributions: Exponential, Hypergeometric, and Weibull

A few remaining probability distributions are available in Excel: exponential, hypergeometric, and Weibull.

Syntax:

=EXPON.DIST(*x*,*lambda*,*cumulative*)

> **Note**
>
> EXPON.DIST in Excel 2010 and 2013 is equivalent to the EXPONDIST in legacy versions of Excel.

The EXPON.DIST function returns the exponential distribution.

You use EXPON.DIST to model the time between events, such as how long a bank's automated teller machine takes to deliver cash. For example, you can use EXPON.DIST to determine the probability that the process takes, at most, 1 minute.

The EXPON.DIST function takes the following arguments:

- *x*—This is the value of the function.

- *lambda*—This is the parameter value.

- *cumulative*—This is a logical value that indicates which form of the exponential function to provide. If *cumulative* is TRUE, EXPON.DIST returns the cumulative distribution function; if *cumulative* is FALSE, EXPON.DIST returns the probability density function.

If *x* or *lambda* is nonnumeric, EXPON.DIST returns a #VALUE! error. If *x* is less than 0, EXPON.DIST returns a #NUM! error. If *lambda* is less than or equal to 0, EXPON.DIST returns a #NUM! error.

Syntax:

=HYPGEOM.DIST(*sample_s*,*number_sample*,*population_s*,*number_population*,*cumulative*)

The HYPGEOM.DIST function returns the hypergeometric distribution. HYPGEOM.DIST returns the probability of a given number of sample successes, given the sample size, population successes, and population size. You use HYPGEOM.DIST for a problem that has a finite population, where each observation is either a success or a failure, and where each subset of a given size is chosen with equal likelihood.

The HYPGEOM.DIST function takes the following arguments:

- *sample_s*—This is the number of successes in the sample.

- *number_sample*—This is the size of the sample.

- *population_s*—This is the number of successes in the population.

- *number_population*—This is the population size.

- *cumulative*—1 or True for CDF. False or 0 for PDF.

All arguments are truncated to integers. If any argument is nonnumeric, HYPGEOM.DIST returns a #VALUE! error. If *sample_s* is less than 0 or *sample_s* is greater than the lesser of *number_sample* and *population_s*, HYPGEOM.DIST returns a #NUM! error. If *sample_s* is less than the larger of 0 or (*number_sample - number_population + population_s*), HYPGEOM.DIST returns a #NUM! error. If *number_sample* is less than 0 or *number_sample* is greater than *number_population*, HYPGEOM.DIST returns a #NUM! error. If *population_s* is less than 0 or *population_s* is greater than *number_population*, HYPGEOM.DIST returns a #NUM! error. If *number_population* is less than 0, HYPGEOM.DIST returns a #NUM! error. HYPGEOM.DIST is used in sampling without replacement from a finite population.

Syntax:

=WEIBULL.DIST(*x,alpha,beta,cumulative*)

The WEIBULL.DIST function returns the Weibull distribution. You use this distribution in reliability analysis, such as for calculating a device's mean time to failure. This function takes the following arguments:

- *x*—This is the value at which to evaluate the function.

- *alpha*—This is a parameter to the distribution.

- *beta*—This is a parameter to the distribution.

- *cumulative*—This determines the form of the function.

If *x*, *alpha*, or *beta* is nonnumeric, WEIBULL.DIST returns a #VALUE! error. If *x* is less than 0, WEIBULL.DIST returns a #NUM! error. If *alpha* is less than or equal to 0 or if *beta* is less than or equal to 0, WEIBULL.DIST returns a #NUM! error.

Using PROB to Calculate Probability for a Population That Fits No Distribution Curve

In some cases, you might have a data set that does not appear to follow any standard probability distribution curve. However, you may have sufficient past data to figure the probability of each outcome. In such a case, you can build a table of the possible outcomes and the probability of each outcome. You use the PROB function to figure out the chances that a value *x* will fall between an upper and a lower limit.

Syntax:

```
=PROB(x_range,prob_range,lower_limit,upper_limit)
```

The PROB function returns the probability that values in a range are between two limits. If *upper_limit* is not supplied, PROB returns the probability that values in *x_range* are equal to *lower_limit*. This function takes the following arguments:

- **x_range**—This is the range of numeric values of *x* with which there are associated probabilities.

- **prob_range**—This is a set of probabilities associated with values in *x_range*.

- **lower_limit**—This is the lower bound on the value for which you want a probability.

- **upper_limit**—This is the optional upper bound on the value for which you want a probability.

If any value in *prob_range* is less than or equal to 0, or if any value in *prob_range* is greater than 1, PROB returns a #NUM! error. If the sum of the values in *prob_range* is greater than 1, PROB returns a #NUM! error. If *upper_limit* is omitted, PROB returns the probability of being equal to *lower_limit*. If *x_range* and *prob_range* contain a different number of data points, PROB returns an #N/A error.

In Figure 14.46, the table in A2:B9 shows the probability of achieving a particular score on a seven-point quiz. The range of possible scores in A2:A9 is used as the first argument. The range of probabilities in B2:B9 is used as the second argument. Various formulas in column G find the probability of any given test falling between two values.

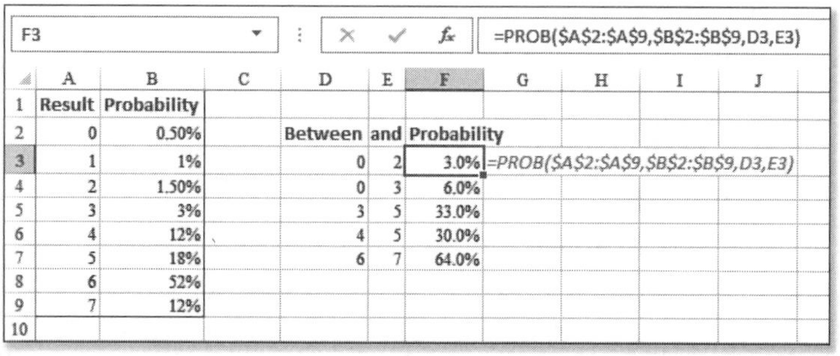

	F3				▼	:	×	✓	*fx*	=PROB($A$2:$A$9,$B$2:$B$9,D3,E3)	

◢	A	B	C	D	E	F	G	H	I	J
1	Result	Probability								
2	0	0.50%		Between	and	Probability				
3	1	1%		0	2	3.0%	=PROB($A$2:$A$9,$B$2:$B$9,D3,E3)			
4	2	1.50%		0	3	6.0%				
5	3	3%		3	5	33.0%				
6	4	12%		4	5	30.0%				
7	5	18%		6	7	64.0%				
8	6	52%								
9	7	12%								
10										

Figure 14.46
This might not fall into any known distribution curve, but the PROB function can calculate probabilities, nonetheless.

Using Z.TEST, CONFIDENCE.NORM, and CONFIDENCE.T to Calculate Confidence Intervals

Confidence testing is one of the most confusing topics in statistics. Suppose that you have a very large population, such as the 500 million people who use Microsoft Excel. You would like to find out how many minutes per month people use pivot tables. It would be difficult to survey the 500 million people.

Instead, you find a way to survey 30 people. The mean of those 30 answers is 155 minutes per month. Think about the standard deviation of the entire population. There has to be wide variability because more than half the people using Excel never use pivot tables, and their answer would be zero. Somehow, you miraculously figure out that the standard deviation of the entire population is 220.

You can use the CONFIDENCE.NORM function to ask for the 90% confidence interval about this statistic. The formula =CONFIDENCE(0.10,220,30) returns a confidence interval of 66. This means that for any sample of 30 people using Excel, the mean of that sample will be within 66 of the true population mean 90% of the time.

In Figure 14.47, a confidence interval is drawn around the sample mean of 11 samples. The 90% confidence level is saying that in 90% of the samples, the confidence level drawn on the chart includes the true mean of the population.

 Caution

It is tempting to interpret the CONFIDENCE.NORM result to say that 90% of the population is within the error bars. This is wrong. Reread the last paragraph: If you use the sample mean plus or minus the confidence interval, you include the true mean nine out of 10 times.

Figure 14.47
The CONFIDENCE. NORM function does not give me a lot of confidence that I can predict the activities of 500 million people using Excel based on a survey of 10 people.

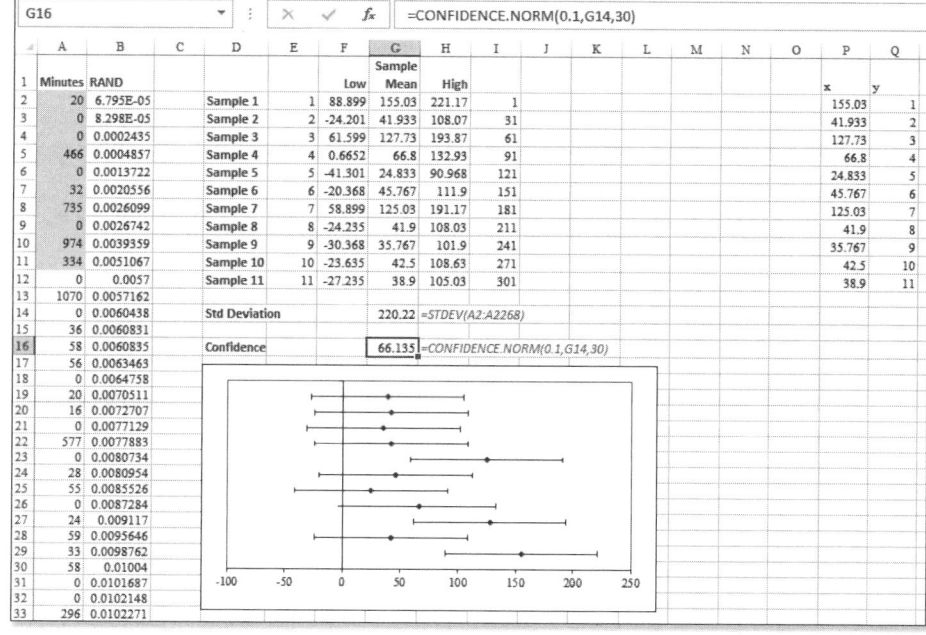

Although the data in Figure 14.47 is fictitious, the actual mean of that entire population is 78. Of the 11 series drawn on the chart, 10 of the 11 happen to encompass the true mean of 78. Note, however, that the first sample mean of 155 is the one that does not include the true mean.

Syntax:

`=CONFIDENCE.NORM(alpha,standard_dev,size)`

The `CONFIDENCE.NORM` function returns the confidence interval for a population mean. The confidence interval is a range on either side of a sample mean. For example, if you order a product through the mail, you can determine, with a particular level of confidence, the earliest and latest the product will arrive. This function takes the following arguments:

- **alpha**—This is the significance level used to compute the confidence level. The confidence level equals $100 \times (1 - alpha)\%$. In other words, an alpha of 0.05 indicates a 95% confidence level.

- **standard_dev**—This is the population standard deviation for the data range and is assumed to be known.

- **size**—This is the sample size.

 Caution

A slight problem with the confidence interval function is that the `CONFIDENCE.NORM` function expects that you know with certainty the standard deviation of the entire population. In real life, if you don't know the mean of the 500 million people using Excel, how would you ever calculate the standard deviation? In reality, when you don't know the population standard deviation, you often substitute the sample standard deviation, but this causes you to have to use the t-distribution instead of `CONFIDENCE.NORM`. Microsoft added `CONFIDENCE.T` to Excel 2010 to handle this situation.

If any argument is nonnumeric, `CONFIDENCE.NORM` returns a `#VALUE!` error. If *alpha* is less than or equal to 0 or *alpha* is greater than or equal to 1, `CONFIDENCE.NORM` returns a `#NUM!` error. If *standard_dev* is less than or equal to 0, `CONFIDENCE.NORM` returns a `#NUM!` error. If *size* is not an integer, it is truncated. If *size* is less than 1, `CONFIDENCE.NORM` returns a `#NUM!` error.

Using Z.TEST to Accept or Reject an Hypothesis

You use the Z.TEST function for hypothesis testing. Suppose that I make a claim that you will be more confident using pivot tables after attending one of my Power Excel seminars. One month after one of my seminars, I randomly select 30 students from the class and ask them how many minutes during the month they used pivot tables. The sample mean comes back at 156 minutes. This mean is higher than most sample means. But is it high enough to be statistically valid? Could I have achieved a sample mean of 156 just randomly?

Syntax:

`=Z.TEST(array,x,sigma)`

The Z.TEST function returns the two-tailed p value of a z-test. The z-test generates a standard score for x with respect to the data set and array, and it returns the two-tailed probability for the normal distribution. You can use this function to assess the likelihood that a particular observation is drawn from a particular population. This function takes the following arguments:

- **array**—This is the array or range of data against which to test x.

- *x*—This is the value to test.

- *sigma*—This is the population (known) standard deviation. If this argument is omitted, the sample standard deviation is used.

If *array* is empty, Z.TEST returns an #N/A error.

Using PERMUT to Calculate the Number of Possible Arrangements

Suppose your company has 40 products in its catalog. You must choose four items to be featured in an upcoming SkyMall issue. The sequence in which the products appear in the ad is relevant. You would like to test the possible ads with a test audience. How many different possible ads could you generate? You use the PERMUT function to solve this problem.

Syntax:

=PERMUT(*number*,*number_chosen*)

The PERMUT function returns the number of permutations for a given number of objects that can be selected from *number* objects. A *permutation* is any set or subset of objects or events in which internal order is significant. Permutations are different from combinations, for which the internal order is not significant. You use this function for lottery-style probability calculations.

The PERMUT function takes the following arguments:

- *number*—This is an integer that describes the number of objects.

- *number_chosen*—This is an integer that describes the number of objects in each permutation.

Both arguments are truncated to integers. If *number* or *number_chosen* is nonnumeric, PERMUT returns a #VALUE! error. If *number* is less than or equal to 0 or if *number_chosen* is less than 0, PERMUT returns a #NUM! error. If *number* is less than *number_chosen*, PERMUT returns a #NUM! error.

The formula to solve the SkyMall problem is =PERMUT(40,4). The result is that there are 2,193,360 possible permutations of products to appear in a one-page ad in the catalog. That is a lot of possibilities!

Using PERMUTATIONA to Calculate the Number of Possible Arrangements When Repeats Are Allowed

The previous example assumed that you would never advertise the same product on the same page twice. Thus, the calculation was 40 choices for the first slot, 39 choices for the second slot, 38 choices for the third slot, and 37 choices for the last slot. =40*39*38*37 is 2,193,360.

What if you had a situation where you were allowed to repeat a product on the page? In that case, you would have 40*40*40*40 choices, or 2,560,000. This calculation is actually trivial, it can be expressed as *number*^(*number_chosen*). In this case, =40^4 provides the correct answer of 2,560,000 permutations.

Rather than believe that people could figure out *=number^(number_chosen)*, the fine folks on the Open Document Spreadsheet board decided that you needed the PERMUTATIONA function. Because Microsoft supports the .ODS file type, they were forced to add this function.

Syntax:

=PERMUTATIONA(*number,number_chosen*)

The PERMUTATIONA function raises *number* to the *number_chosen* power. This represents the number of permutations when repeats are allowed.

Using the Analysis ToolPak to Perform Statistical Analysis

The functions discussed in this chapter are wonderful for doing statistical analysis. If you can use a function to perform some analysis, the function offers a live result. You can change some assumptions, and the results automatically update.

However, many statisticians instead rely on the data tools available in the Analysis ToolPak. The Analysis ToolPak can provide beautiful snapshot-type reports that analyze a data set. Although these reports provide more information than a typical function, they have the downside that they do not automatically recalculate. If you change one of the assumptions in the data set, you have to rerun the analysis.

 Note

The Data Analysis tools in the Analysis ToolPak vary greatly. Some of them are poorly implemented and provide such narrow functionality that it is usually better to use your own functions rather than those tools.

Excel offers many options for performing statistical analysis. Using functions in Excel provides real-time, live results of the data.

On the other hand, some of the tools, such as Regression, provide additional statistics that run circles around the equivalent functions in Excel. In this case, it would be advantageous to use the Analysis ToolPak.

Remember, however, that when you use the Data Analysis tools from the Analysis ToolPak, they create static snapshots of the results. If you change the underlying data, you have to rerun the analysis.

Installing the Analysis ToolPak in Excel 2013

In legacy versions of Excel, many people would install the Analysis ToolPak because they needed it to enable the 89 functions it contained. When you enabled the Analysis ToolPak to access the additional functions, Excel silently added a new Data Analysis item to the Tools menu.

However, in Excel 2013, those 89 functions are already part of the core Excel product. Therefore, it is much less likely that you already have the Analysis ToolPak installed. To install it, follow these steps:

1. In Excel, press Alt+T followed by the letter I. Excel displays the Add-Ins dialog.

2. In the Add-Ins dialog, select the Analysis ToolPak check box. Click OK. It appears that nothing happened.

If this process is successful, you have a Data Analysis icon in the Analysis group near the right side of the Data tab (see Figure 14.48). You must click Data Analysis to invoke the Data Analysis dialog.

Figure 14.48
After you successfully install the Analysis ToolPak, a new group on the Data tab offers access to the Data Analysis dialog.

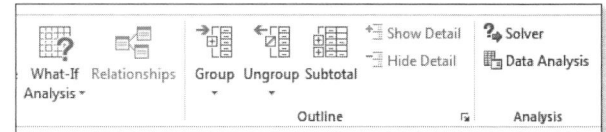

 Caution

Recall that Excel 2013 switched from a Multiple Document Interface to a Single Document Interface. This means that each Excel workbook has its own ribbon. Although this is wonderful for people trying to show two workbooks on two different monitors, it creates new challenges for the developers who use VBA to control Excel. It is particularly challenging for WorkbookA to display a dialog in front of WorkbookB. The Analysis ToolPak is really an Excel workbook with a lot of VBA code. As you work with the Analysis ToolPak, do not be alarmed if a dialog seemingly disappears without reason. Look in the Windows task bar to see whether the XL icon is flashing. Click the flashing icon to return focus to the dialog. Although this is frustrating behavior, it is simply a numbers game; 250 million people wanted to display two workbooks on two different monitors and only 100,000 people ever venture into the Analysis ToolPak, so the Excel team figures it's okay to inconvenience a few for the betterment of many.

Generating Random Numbers Based on Various Distributions

Whereas the RAND and RANDBETWEEN functions generate random numbers, the Random Number Generation choice in the Data Analysis dialog enables you to create more sophisticated random-number populations. Here's how you use it:

1. Make sure the Analysis ToolPak is installed.

2. From the Data tab, select Data Analysis.

3. Scroll down and select Random Number Generation and click OK. The Random Number Generation dialog appears (see Figure 14.49).

4. In the Random Number Generation dialog, choose the number of columns that you would like to fill with random numbers. If you want five columns of random numbers, enter **5** in the Number of Variables text box.

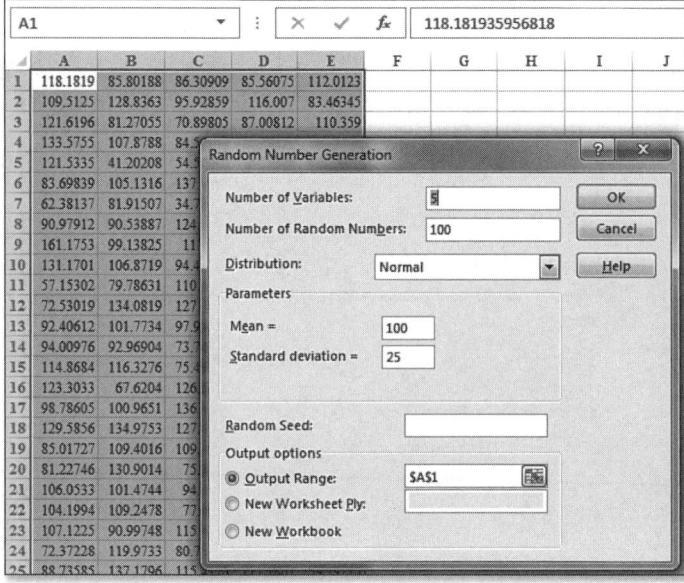

Figure 14.49
You can generate random numbers by using the Random Number Generation dialog.

5. Choose the number of rows that you would like to fill with random numbers. If you want 100 rows of random numbers, fill in **100** in the Number of Random Numbers text box.

6. Select one of the seven options in the Distribution drop-down. The questions in the Parameters frame change for each distribution option:

   ■ For a uniform distribution, you choose upper and lower limits in the Parameters frame. This functionality is similar to using the RAND worksheet function.

   ■ For a normal distribution, you choose a mean and standard deviation. This functionality is very cool and is not available through the normal Excel functions.

 Note
There is nothing random about a patterned distribution method. You are simply creating numbers that follow a certain pattern.

   ■ For a Bernoulli distribution, you choose a probability of success on each trial. Bernoulli random variables have a value of 0 or 1. If you want to model Kobe Bryant's ability to make free throws, you use a Bernoulli distribution with a probability of success of 83.87%.

   ■ For a binomial distribution, you specify a *p* value and the number of trials. For example, you can generate number-of-trials Bernoulli random variables, the sum of which is a binomial random variable.

   ■ For a Poisson distribution, you specify a value, *lambda*, that is equal to 1 / Mean. Poisson distributions are often used to characterize the number of events that occur per unit of time (for example, the average rate at which cars arrive at a toll plaza).

- For a patterned distribution, you specify five parameters. You specify a lower and upper limit in steps of a certain value. You can also specify that each number repeats *n* times and that the whole sequence repeats *y* times.

- For a discrete distribution, you specify a range of values and their probabilities. In this case, you might have a list of 40 products in A2:A41 and then their probabilities of being selected in B2:B41. Note that the sum of the values in the probability column must add to 100%.

7. In the Random Seed text box, enter any numeric seed. This concept is a little bizarre. In a computer, random numbers are not really random. Scientists call them *pseudo-random*. If you leave the Random Seed text box empty, Excel uses some strange number (perhaps the number of seconds since 1900 or perhaps the free memory in the stack) as a seed. This ensures that you get different random numbers every time. However, if you enter your own seed, such as 123, and then come back a month later with the same seed, Excel generates exactly the same list of random numbers.

8. For the Output Range field, you can choose an output range, a new worksheet, or a new workbook. For some unknown reason, this dialog refers to a new worksheet as "New Worksheet Ply."

Generating a Histogram

Consider a set of 100 observations. If the possible values are from a continuous series, it is likely that you won't have any two values that are exactly the same. The chart of this data will show a lot of noise, as shown in Figure 14.50.

Figure 14.50
Plotting the individual points of a sample does not tell you a lot about the sample.

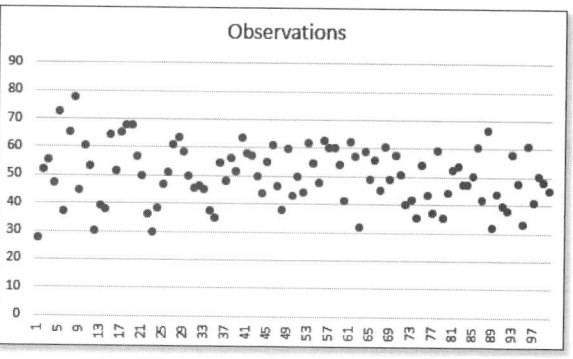

Statisticians instead prefer to group those values into similar categories. Perhaps logical categories for this data set are 24–34, 35–44, 45–54, and so on. The technical term for these groups is *bins*.

The Histogram tool takes a set of observations and groups them into bins, similarly to the way that the FREQUENCY function normally does. However, the histogram function goes further, offering the cumulative percentage of each bin. Then it re-sorts the bins into a Pareto analysis. Excel also offers to create a chart based on the output.

To use the Histogram tool, follow these steps:

1. Make sure the Analysis ToolPak is installed.

2. Think about some groupings for your data and enter these in a new column in the worksheet. The first bin should be less than the minimum value in your data set. If your bin range contains 25, 35, 45, the first bin includes from 25 up through values just less than 35.

3. From the Data tab, select Data Analysis. Then select Histogram and click OK. The Histogram dialog appears.

4. In the Histogram dialog, specify the range that contains your observations as the input range. This range does not need to be sorted. You might include a one-cell heading as part of the range. If you do, you must also include a one-cell heading for the bin range and also check the Labels option in step 6.

5. Specify your range from step 2 as the bin range.

6. If your input and bin ranges contain one-cell headings, select the Labels check box.

7. For the output, specify the upper-left corner of a blank spot on the current worksheet, or specify a new worksheet or a new workbook.

8. Select the Pareto check box. Excel produces the histogram and then produces a second histogram. In the second histogram, the most popular bin is sorted to the top of the list.

9. Select the Cumulative check box. Excel reports the cumulative percentage accounted for by values from the bottom of the list through the current bin.

10. Select the Chart Output check box to ask for a chart. Note that this default chart is fairly plain looking and needs some customization to be acceptable.

11. Click OK to create the histogram.

Figure 14.51 shows the Histogram dialog, along with the results of the histogram and a chart created from the histogram.

Figure 14.51
Using an input area of column A and the bins in column C, Excel produces a histogram in E:J. This is significantly easier than using the FREQUENCY array formula.

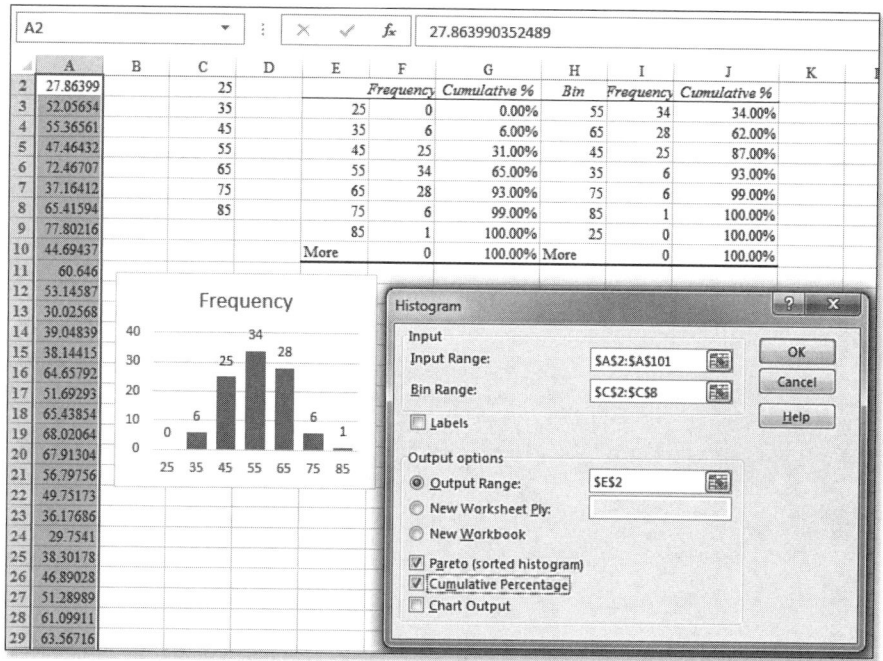

Generating Descriptive Statistics of a Population

Excel provides a large number of functions to describe data sets. Earlier in this chapter, you learned about functions to calculate the mean, median, mode, skew, and so on of your data. By using the Data Analysis tools, you can generate all these statistics in a single command. To do so, follow these steps:

1. Make sure the Analysis ToolPak is installed.

2. From the Data tab, select Data Analysis. Then select Descriptive Statistics and click OK. The Descriptive Statistics dialog appears.

3. In the Descriptive Statistics dialog, choose the input range for your data set.

4. If the range in step 3 contains a heading in the first row, select the Labels check box.

5. Set the output as a new range, a new worksheet, or a new workbook.

6. Select Summary Statistics. Excel provides values for mean, standard error (of the mean), median, mode, standard deviation, variance, kurtosis, skewness, range, minimum, maximum, sum, count, largest (#), smallest (#), and confidence level.

7. Select the Confidence Level for Mean check box and specify the confidence level you want to use. For example, a confidence level of 95% calculates the confidence level of the mean at a significance of 5%.

8. If you would like row(s) in the output for the *k*th largest and/or smallest values, select the appropriate check boxes and fill in the value for *k*. For example, if you ask for the *k*th largest with a value of 3, Excel reports the third-largest value in the data set.

9. Click OK. Results similar to those shown in Figure 14.52 are generated.

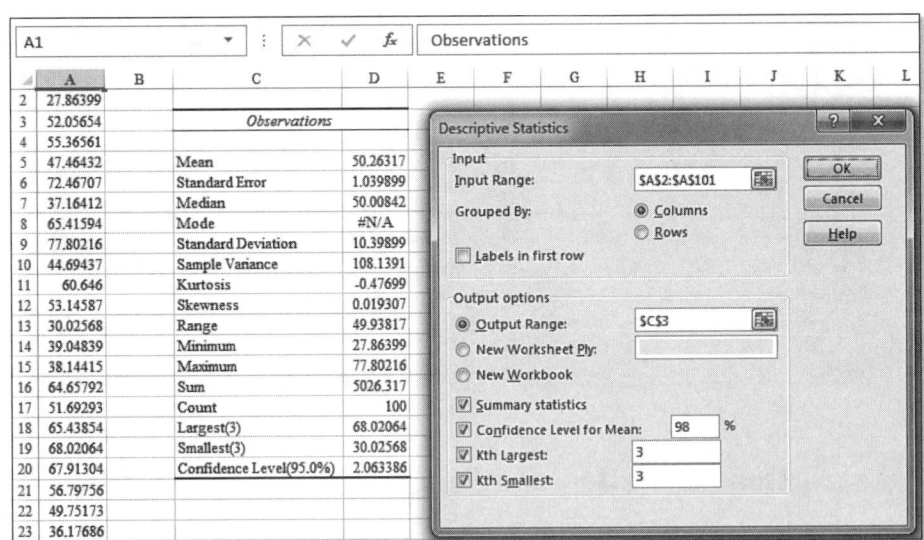

Figure 14.52
Excel can generate every descriptive statistic for a data set with a single command. The output range in C3:D20 is generated from the dialog shown.

Ranking Results

The Excel RANK function has an inherent problem when two results in the data set are tied. Whereas the RANK.AVG function provides a workaround for this problem, the Rank and Percentile feature cannot overcome this limitation. If you are worried about the possibility of a tie in your data set, you should use the RANK.AVG function instead of this command.

To assign a rank and percentage to a data set, follow these steps:

1. Make sure the Analysis ToolPak is installed. Then scroll down and select Rank and Percentile and click OK. The Rank and Percentile dialog appears.

2. From the Data tab, select Data Analysis.

3. In the Rank and Percentile dialog, choose the input range for your data set. The input range may contain a single-cell heading at the top of the data, but it may not contain any other nonnumeric data. In Figure 14.53, it would be nice if Excel could accept the names associated with each data point, but it cannot. You have to add them back later.

Figure 14.53
The Rank and Percentile function sorts the data and calculates a rank and a percentile function. It cannot resolve ties, however.

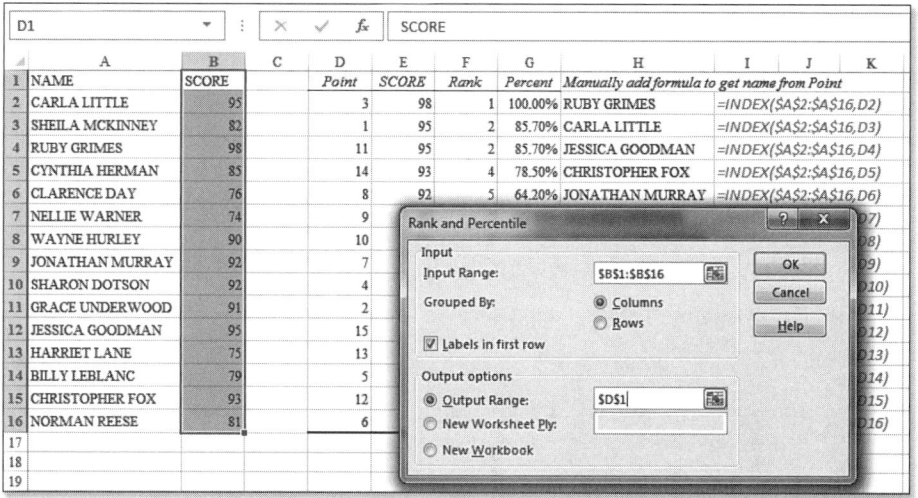

4. If your input range has a heading in the first row, select the Labels in First Row check box.

5. Choose an output range for the data set. Excel returns the statistics shown in D1:G16 in Figure 14.53. Notice that the scores have been sorted in high-to-low sequence. In column D, Excel refers to each cell as being at Point 1, Point 2, Point 3, and so on.

In Figure 14.53, column H was added after the fact, using the formula =INDEX($A$2:$A$16,D2). Cell D2 contains the point number for this row. Basically, this function asks for the third value in A2:A16.

Notice that Carla and Jessica are in a tie for second place. No one in this data set is ranked third because of this tie. If you used the RANK function as described earlier in this chapter, you could break the ties by using a COUNTIF function.

Using Regression to Predict Future Results

The Regression tool available in the Analysis ToolPak runs circles around the LINEST function in Excel. As described previously, LINEST returns a bizarre unlabeled set of results for a regression. The Regression tool, on the other hand, provides myriad well-labeled statistics, analyses, and charts as the output.

To perform a regression analysis using the Regression tool, you follow these steps:

1. Make sure the Analysis ToolPak is installed.

2. Ensure that your data includes one independent variable, such as sales per day. It can also contain one or more dependent variables—items that might explain the variability in sales. (In this example, dependent variables include outside temperature, if it rained, and if it was a weekend.)

3. From the Data tab, select Data Analysis. Then scroll down, select Regression, and click OK. The Regression dialog appears.

4. In the Regression dialog, the Input Y range must be a single column of data. In this example, it is the range containing sales for each day. Be sure to include a cell at the top of the column that describes the data.

5. In the Input X Range text box, use a range that is the same height as the Y range. The X range can contain one column for each independent variable. In this example, the X range contains columns for temperature, rain, and weekend. For best results, include a cell at the top of each column, with the name of the variable.

6. If your ranges in steps 4 and 5 include headings, select the Labels check box.

7. If you want to force the y-intercept to be 0, select the Constant Is Zero check box.

8. The Confidence Level box is interesting. The program always gives statistics for a 95% confidence level. If you enter a different percentage in this box, you get two confidence levels: one for the default 95%, and one for the other value you enter.

9. Specify the output range as the top-left cell of a range. In this example, the regression output occupies from G2 to O119, so make sure that you have a really large area set aside for the results.

10. Fill in the remaining options in the Regression dialog to add sections to the report:

   ▪ **Residuals**—Select this to include residuals in the residuals output table.

   ▪ **Standardized Residuals**—Select this to include standardized residuals in the residuals output table.

   ▪ **Residual Plots**—Select this to generate a chart for each independent variable versus the residual.

   ▪ **Line Fit Plots**—Select this to generate a chart for predicted values versus the observed values.

   ▪ **Normal Probability Plots**—Select this to generate a chart that plots normal probability.

When you are done, the dialog should look roughly as shown in Figure 14.54.

After you run the regression, Excel provides the following sections of the report (see Figure 14.55):

   ▪ Regression statistics such as r-squared are provided in the top section.

   ▪ An ANOVA analysis is provided.

   ▪ The actual regression results are provided in column 2 of the third section. In this example, the prediction for sales comes from H18:H21. The formula would be that sales for any day will be $-76 + 2.6 \times$ High temperature $+ 52$ if it is a weekend. If it is raining, you subtract 102 from this prediction. Remaining columns in this section return the standard error, t statistic, p value, and confidence limits for each variable.

Figure 14.54
The hardest part of specifying a regression is remembering that the Y range is the value you are trying to predict.

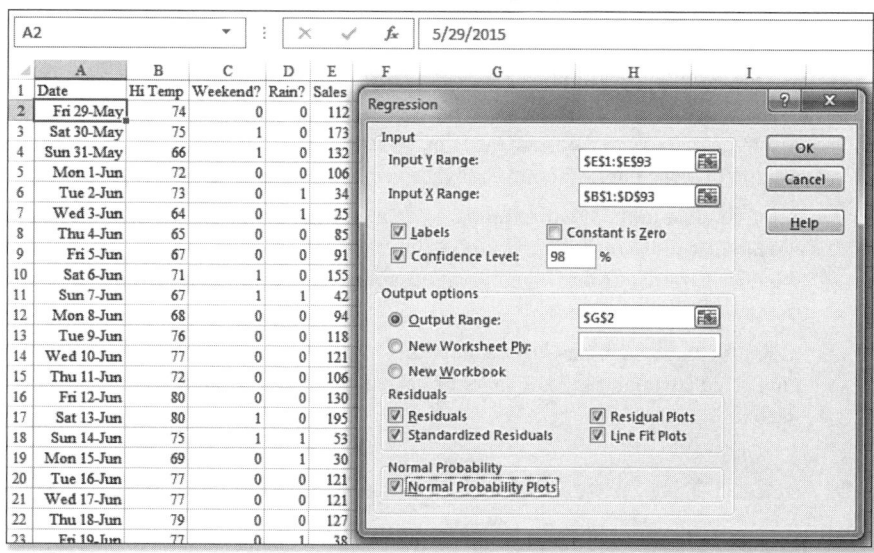

Figure 14.55
The regression report from the Analysis ToolPak is fantastic. It provides a more comprehensive view than the LINEST function.

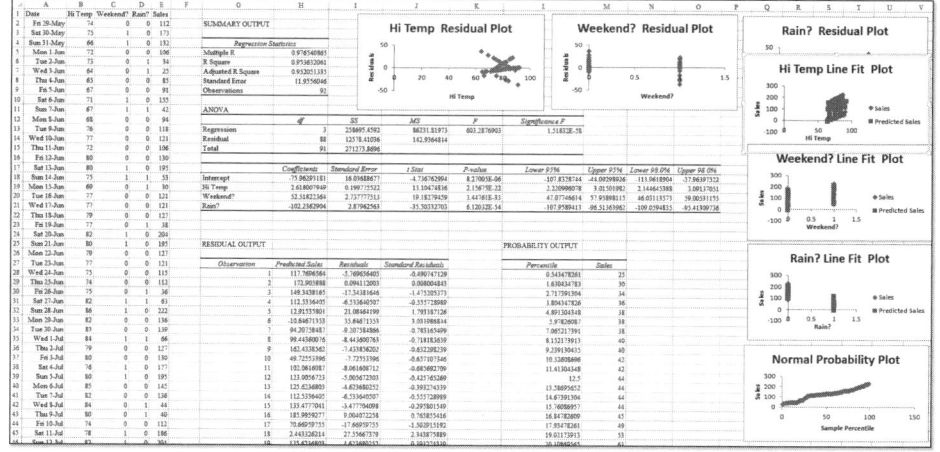

- The next section goes far beyond the LINEST function. Excel uses the regression results to predict sales for each day in the data set. The predicted sales are in column 2 of the data set, which is column H in the figure. The comparison of predicted sales to actual sales is shown in the Residuals column.

- Finally, Excel provides a probability table. The table explains that on the worst 12.5% of days, you might sell $44 or less.

Using a Moving Average to Forecast Sales

The Moving Average command in the Data Analysis tools is disappointing. The technique of using a moving average to produce future forecasts is based on the concept that variability in the month-to-month actuals is lessened if you always average three months.

After choosing Data Analysis, Moving Average, you can specify an input range that contains one column of sales data. The interval value of 3 produces a three-month moving average.

After you use the Moving Average command, Excel adds one column with a series of simple =AVERAGE() formulas. Each formula averages the sales from the previous month, this month, and the next month. In theory, you would then use this column as input to the forecasting methods to produce a future forecast.

In Figure 14.56, column C is the new moving average column. Column D is the standard error column. This command is really a lot of hassle when you could easily add your own =AVERAGE formula in column C.

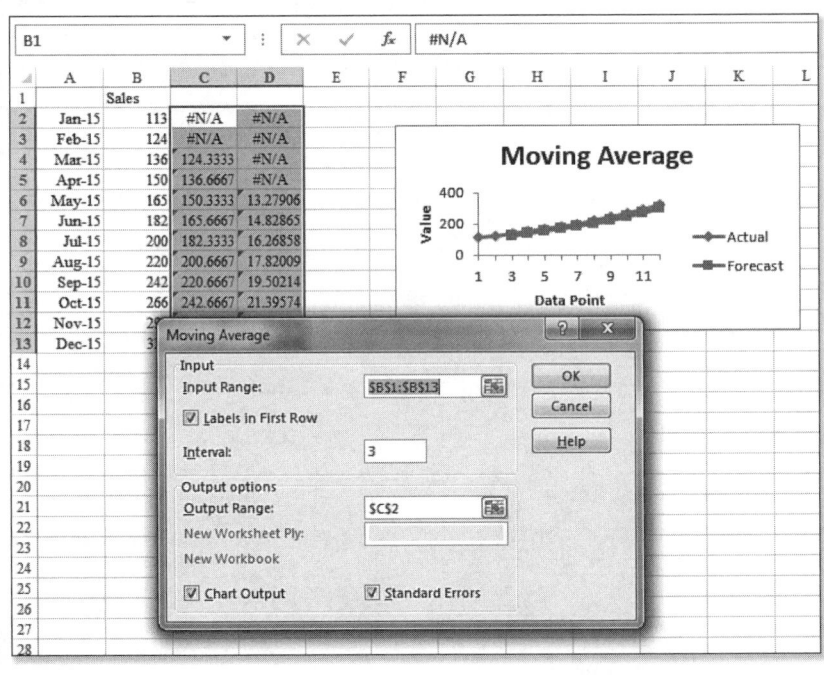

Figure 14.56
The Moving Average feature of the Data Analysis tools is a long route to adding a simple formula.

Using Exponential Smoothing to Forecast Sales

The Exponential Smoothing feature in the Data Analysis tools enables you to set up a forecasting formula that uses exponential smoothing.

This method of forecasting requires only two points: the forecast for the previous month and the actual for the current month. The forecast for the next month is created by adding 75% of the most recent actuals and 25% of the prior forecast.

In this example, the 25% is called a *damping factor*. You can assign any damping factor that you want, but values in the 20% to 30% range are recommended.

To set up an exponential smoothing forecast, follow these steps:

1. Make sure the Analysis ToolPak is installed.

2. Ensure that your data includes one column of sales data, such as sales per month.

3. From the Data tab, select Data Analysis. Then select Exponential Smoothing and click OK. The Exponential Smoothing dialog appears.

4. In the Exponential Smoothing dialog, the Input range should be your single column of sales data. If you include a heading cell, select the Labels check box.

5. Ensure that the damping factor is between 0.20 and 0.30. With a damping factor of 0.30, the current forecast is based 70% on the most recent actuals and 30% on all the past forecasts.

6. Limit the output range to a cell on the current worksheet. Ideally, this range starts in the same row as your input range, in an adjacent column.

7. To create a chart comparing forecast and actuals, select the Chart Output check box.

8. Select the Standard Errors check box. The output contains a second column with a standard error calculation. This calculation analyzes the current period and last three periods. In D6, enter the standard error formula =**SQRT(SUMXMY2(B3:B5,C2:C4)/3)**. This formula subtracts the forecast from the actual for the last three months, squares the differences, adds them, divides to find an average, and then takes the square root of the average.

9. Click OK to produce the analysis.

Figure 14.57 shows the Exponential Smoothing dialog and the subsequent results of the analysis.

Because the standard error column must analyze four months of forecasts and actuals, the first three data points in the standard error column are always #N/A!.

 Note

A bug prevents Excel from entering the label Sales Forecast in the top row of the output. You have to manually change the headings Excel generates.

PART

II

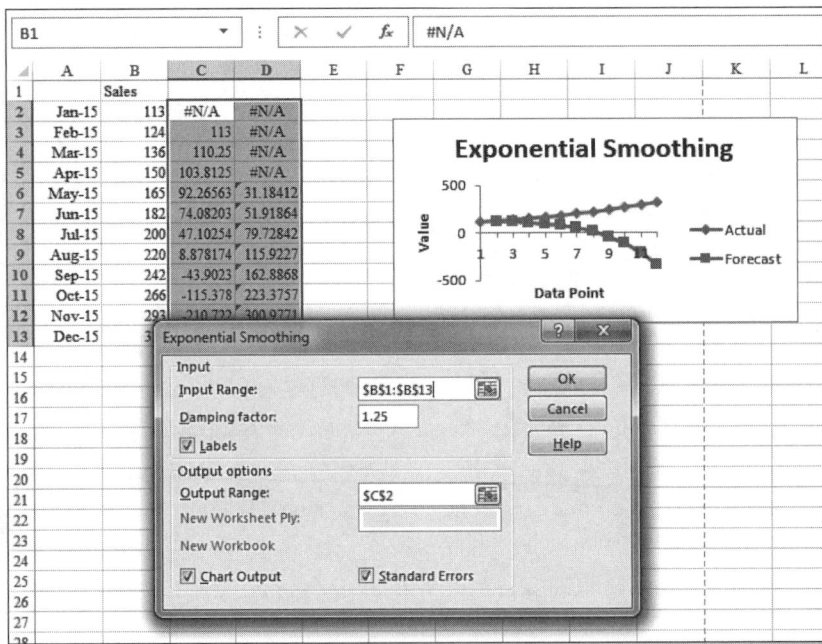

Figure 14.57
Exponential smoothing provides a forecast that is heavily weighted toward recent actuals.

Using Correlation or Covariance to Calculate the Relationship Between Many Variables

Both covariance and correlation are measures of the extent to which two measurement variables vary together. I prefer the correlation coefficient because it is independent of the units involved.

Say that you are comparing height in inches or centimeters to weight in pounds or kilograms. The correlation coefficient returns a value from 1 to −1. Correlation coefficient values close to 0 indicate little or no correlation between the measures. A value close to 1 indicates a strong positive correlation: As one variable increases, the other is likely to increase. A value close to −1 indicates a strong negative correlation: The value of one variable is likely to decrease as the value of the other variable increases.

You could calculate these values manually by using the CORREL or PEARSON functions in Excel, but the Data Analysis version is particularly well suited to data sets that have many measurements for each member of a population. In this case, the Correlation tool generates a correlation coefficient for every possible combination of the measurement statistics.

Figure 14.58 shows a database of body statistics for a sample of 125 people. For each person, the clinician measured 13 key measurements, such as height, weight, and so on. It would be interesting to see if height is a good predictor of weight or if some other measurement is appropriate.

Figure 14.58
In a collection of key measurement stats for 125 members of a population, which measurements are most related?

	A	B	C	D	E	F	G	H	I	J	K	L	M	N
	B2			▾	:	×	✓	f_x	160.5					
1	ID	Weight	Age	Height	Abdomen	Ankle	Biceps	Chest	Forearm	Hip	Knee	Neck	Thigh	Wrist
2	101	160.5	29	71.5	84.7	21.7	30.3	93.7	26.6	100.8	39	37.5	58.7	18.1
3	102	198.25	54	72.25	100	22	35.9	107.6	30.2	99.6	38	39.9	57.2	18.9
4	103	158.5	47	72.5	86.9	22.6	26.2	90.4	26	98.5	37.4	35.1	52.8	17.5
5	104	188	35	69.75	96.4	23.1	36.1	101.3	30.5	100.1	39	40.5	69	18.2
6	105	203.25	50	67.25	108.3	24.9	34.3	115	31.2	102.7	41.3	40.4	61.5	18.5
7	106	177.25	46	70.25	95.6	22.5	29.1	99.7	27.7	102.2	38.2	37.2	58.3	17.7
8	107	205.25	44	29.75	104.5	23.9	33.8	106.2	28.9	115.7	42.7	36.8	70.8	17.6
9	108	217.25	48	70.25	111.2	25	36.7	113.3	29.8	114.1	40.9	37.3	67.7	18.4
10	109	177.25	43	69.5	98.8	22.2	30.3	104.2	27.4	99.7	36.3	39.8	59.7	17.9

To build a matrix of correlation coefficients (or covariances), you follow these steps:

1. Make sure the Analysis ToolPak is installed.

2. Ensure that your data includes several columns of measurements for a population. Each row should represent another member of the population. Try to avoid missing values. If one measurement is missing for a population member, that member is thrown out of the entire calculation.

3. From the Data tab, select Data Analysis. Then select Correlation (or Covariance) and click OK. The Correlation dialog appears.

4. In the Correlation dialog, ensure that the input range includes your row of headings and all the measurements. If you have an ID field, do not include it in the input range.

5. If your data has labels as the first row or column of the input range, select the Labels check box.

6. Select the upper-left corner of the output range. If your input range has n columns, the size of the output range will be $(n + 1) \times (n + 1)$.

7. Click OK to create the correlation matrix.

Figure 14.59 shows the Correlation dialog and the resulting correlation matrix. In this particular example, height and weight have a weak correlation coefficient of 0.21. You can compare this to the correlation coefficient for hip and weight, which has a positive correlation of 0.93.

The covariance feature works the same as the correlation feature, except the output table is not scaled to provide answers between −1 and 1.

P	Q	R	S	T	U	V	W	X	Y	Z	AA	AB	AC
	Weight	Age	Height	Abdomen	Ankle	Biceps	Chest	Forearm	Hip	Knee	Neck	Thigh	Wrist
Weight	1												
Age	-0.04385	1											
Height	0.212495	-0.10121	1										
Abdomen	0.875	0.199683	0.017032	1									
Ankle	0.551508	-0.09416	0.178332	0.389644	1								
Biceps	0.783243	-0.0635	0.138199	0.665566	0.430837	1							
Chest	0.894235	0.093076	0.093197	0.906529	0.434664	0.724031	1						
Forearm	0.696212	-0.11284	0.214936	0.542617	0.392694	0.71767	0.668817	1					
Hip	0.932978	-0.08046	0.03459	0.869817	0.488254	0.720737	0.831917	0.582675	1				
Knee	0.846664	-0.0283	0.116215	0.747254	0.529144	0.69455	0.730452	0.631785	0.819955	1			
Neck	0.811978	0.084627	0.223508	0.723415	0.416404	0.690761	0.762351	0.667752	0.708693	0.65764	1		
Thigh	0.85348	-0.22601	-0.02171	0.766655	0.443509	0.753886	0.749784	0.636531	0.894339	0.803796	0.686064	1	
Wrist	0.725927	0.196743	0.305715	0.603123	0.485761	0.625066	0.653793	0.718965	0.595863	0.632301	0.749882	0.531882	1

Correlation

Input

Input Range: `$B$1:$N$126`

Grouped By:
- ◉ Columns
- ○ Rows

☑ Labels in first row

Output options
- ◉ Output Range: `$P$1`
- ○ New Worksheet Ply:
- ○ New Workbook

OK
Cancel
Help

Figure 14.59
The correlation coefficient matrix produces results from −1 to 1. Values further away from 0 indicate a strong correlation between the measurement variables.

Using Sampling to Create Random Samples

Earlier in this chapter, in the section on the RAND function, you learned about a way to collect a random sample. You can also allow the Data Analysis tools to produce a random sample for you.

The Random Sampling feature offers two interesting ways to collect a sample. Excel can either randomly select *n* members of the population, or you can specify that Excel should select every *k*th member of the population.

You follow these steps to select a random sample:

1. Make sure the Analysis ToolPak is installed.

2. Ensure that your data is completely numeric. This feature works best on a single column of data, so ensure that you are selecting just a single column. If you have multiple columns of data, Excel randomly selects cells from the entire range; for example, the random sample might include cells B2, A5, C7, D10, B2. Ensure that you do not include column headings if your data spans multiple columns.

3. From the Data tab, select Data Analysis. Then scroll down, select Sampling, and click OK. The Sampling dialog appears.

4. In the Sampling dialog, ensure that the input range includes your data range. If your data includes a single column, and you have headings in the first cell, select the Labels check box.

 Tip

In step 4, do not include labels if your population spans multiple columns.

5. For random sampling, ask for a specific number of samples. The other option is to specify periodic sampling, which provides every *n*th value in the data set.

6. Specify either the top-left cell of the output range or the entire output range and click OK.

In Figure 14.60, Excel has produced a random sample of 10 from a rectangular range of data.

Figure 14.60
A random sample from the Sampling dialog might include duplicates.

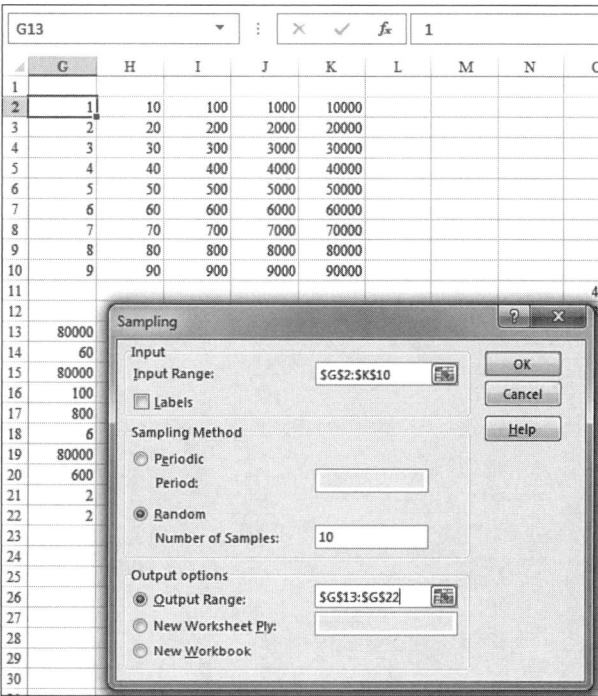

The Random Sampling feature allows for duplicates within the same sample. If you need to make sure that any given sample contains no duplicates, you should use the RAND function instead.

If you ask for a periodic sample, Excel traverses each column from left to right. Selecting every fourth value from G2:K10 in Figure 14.60 would select 4, 8 from the first column, and then 30, 70 from the second column. From 70, Excel would skip the next three values of 80, 90, and 100, and it would return 200 as the next periodic member of the sample.

Using ANOVA to Perform Analysis of Variance Testing

ANOVA stands for analysis of variance. The Data Analysis tools offer three forms of ANOVA testing:

- **Single-factor ANOVA**—This is for measuring variance for two or more samples with a single variable. For example, suppose that you have 18 farm fields. All are planted with the same variety of wheat. Six are treated with Nutrient A, six are treated with Nutrient B, and six are treated with Nutrient C. Single-variable ANOVA would analyze whether the variances in the populations were random or due to the fertilizers.

- **Two-factor ANOVA without replication**—This is for use when your data can be classified along two different dimensions. For example, suppose that half of the farm fields are downwind from an interstate highway that is heavily traveled by diesel trucks. You could analyze the variance caused by the fertilizer versus the variance caused by the carbon monoxide from the highway.

- **Two-factor ANOVA with replication**—If you have enough samples so that every combination of {fertilizer, highway} has multiple samples, you can perform two-factor ANOVA with replication. Otherwise, you use two-factor ANOVA without replication.

Follow these steps to perform a one-way ANOVA test:

1. If your data is set up as records with data for each field, arrange the data in columns for each variable. In Figure 14.61, this means taking the data from column B and arranging it in three columns, E, F, and G, with a heading above each column.

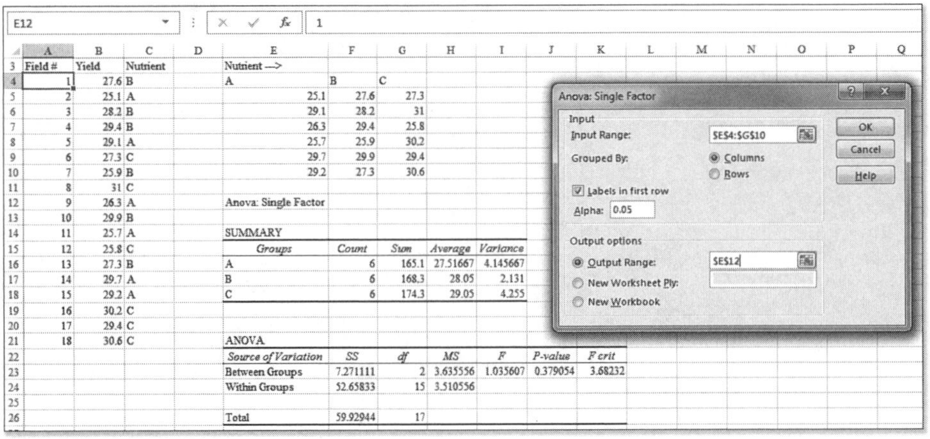

Figure 14.61
The difference in the sample means it is statistically significant.

2. Choose a null hypothesis. For example, your null hypothesis might be that all the nutrients produce a similar mean. If you can reject the null hypothesis, then your hypothesis is that the selection nutrient has an impact on yield.

3. Choose a significance level, alpha, of 0.05. If the statistics from the ANOVA output show a p value greater than the alpha, you can reject the null hypothesis and assume that the nutrient has an impact on yield.

4. Make sure the Analysis ToolPak is installed.

5. From the Data tab, select Data Analysis. Then select ANOVA: Single Factor and click OK. The ANOVA: Single Factor dialog appears.

6. In the ANOVA: Single Factor dialog, ensure that the input range includes your columns of means.

7. If your input range includes a heading above each column, select the Labels in First Row check box.

8. In the Alpha box, enter the level at which you want to evaluate critical values for the F statistic. The alpha level is a significance level related to the probability of having a type I error (that is, rejecting a true hypothesis).

9. Select the top-left corner for the output range.

10. Click OK to produce the result.

In Figure 14.61, the important statistic is the p value in cell J23. Because this number is larger than alpha, you can reject the null hypothesis and assume that the nutrients had an effect on the yield.

Follow these steps to perform a two-way ANOVA test with replication:

1. Arrange your data so that one dimension is spread across the columns. (This can be tricky.)

2. Ensure that you have equal numbers of samples along the second dimension. In Figure 14.62, there were three rows of yields from fields downwind from a highway. These rows must be arranged together. For convenience, have a row label in cell G7 to identify this block of data.

3. Because you had three rows of sample yields for fields adjacent to highways, you also have to find three rows of sample yields for fields away from highways. This block of three rows must immediately follow the other data.

>  **Tip**
>
> Again, for convenience, in step 3 make sure there is a heading in the first column and first row of this block to identify the value along the second dimension.

Figure 14.62
Setting up the input range in equal size rows is the key to successful use of Two-Factor ANOVA analysis.

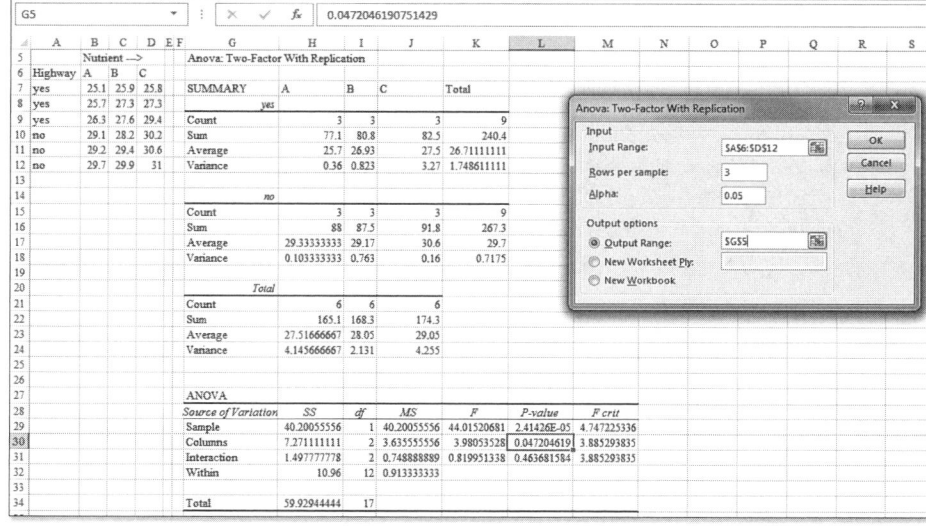

4. Make sure the Analysis ToolPak is installed.

5. From the Data tab, select Data Analysis. Then select ANOVA: Two-Factor with Replication and click OK. The ANOVA: Two-Factor with Replication dialog appears.

6. In the ANOVA: Two-Factor with Replication dialog, ensure that the input range includes sample values as well as an additional row above to identify the first-dimension variables and an additional column to the left to identify the second-dimension variable.

7. In the Rows per Sample text box, enter the number of rows in each block of data. In this present example, there are three rows of yields for highway fields and three rows for non-highway fields, so enter **3**.

8. In the Alpha box, enter the level at which you want to evaluate critical values for the F statistic. The alpha level is a significance level related to the probability of having a type I error (that is, rejecting a true hypothesis).

9. For the output range, select the top-left corner of a large blank area. The ANOVA results will take up 30 rows by seven columns.

10. Click OK to perform the analysis.

Evaluating the Results

In the results from this analysis, watch for the values in italic in the first column of the output range. The first block of data in the output range describes the first block of three rows in the input range, with a value of "yes" to the highway question.

The final block of the analysis shows the p values for each dimension and the two dimensions combined. In this particular analysis, it appears that much of the variability is due to highway proximity and does not necessarily have that much to do with the nutrients. The p value of 0.047 for the columns is not enough to reject the null hypothesis that the variability due to nutrients could be random.

In some cases, you may have two factors for the ANOVA testing, but you may not have multiple samples for every combination of {*dimension1*, *dimension2*}. In this case, you can run two-factor ANOVA testing without replication. The results from this test contain less analysis than do the results from the test with replication. In this test, Excel does not predict whether factors beyond the two dimensions are causing variability.

To perform a two-factor ANOVA without replication, follow these steps:

1. Arrange your data in a crosstab fashion. Have values from Dimension 1 going across the top row of the data. Have values from Dimension 2 going down the left column of the data. Enter the sample value in each intersection.

2. Make sure the Analysis ToolPak is installed.

3. From the Data tab, select Data Analysis. Then select ANOVA: Two-Factor Without Replication and click OK. The ANOVA: Two-Factor Without Replication dialog appears.

4. In the ANOVA: Two-Factor Without Replication dialog, ensure that the input range includes sample values, as well as an additional row above to identify the first-dimension variables and an additional column to the left to identify the second-dimension variables.

5. Select the Labels check box so Excel can get the headings for the Dimension 1 and Dimension 2 values from the worksheet.

6. In the Alpha box, enter the level at which you want to evaluate critical values for the F statistic. The alpha level is a significance level related to the probability of having a type I error (that is, rejecting a true hypothesis).

7. Click OK to run the analysis.

Excel analyzes the variance based on the rows and columns, as shown in Figure 14.63.

Figure 14.63
In this particular sample, the column drives variability more than the rows.

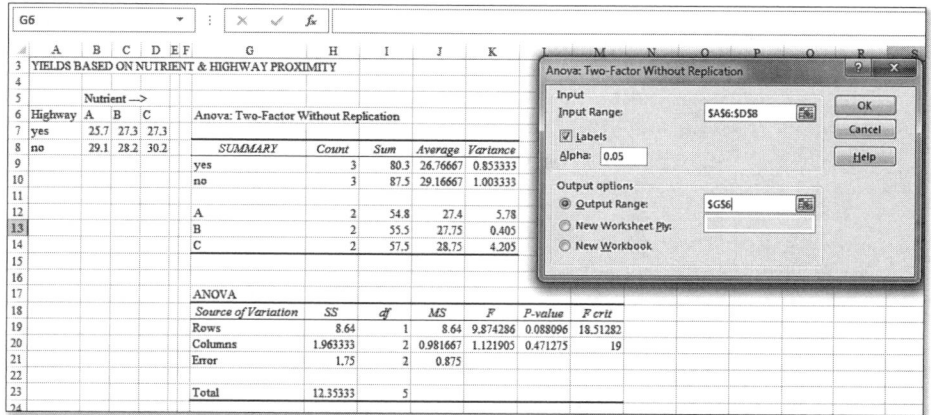

Using the *F*-Test to Measure Variability Between Methods

If you want to compare two methods, it is helpful to know if the variances in the two methods are roughly the same. The F-test was designed by statistician R. A. Fisher. (The F here stands for Fisher and nothing intuitive.) The F-test compares two variances, V1 / V2, to produce an F statistic. Values close to 1 indicate that the variances are similar.

To run an F-test, follow these steps:

1. Set up two ranges with samples from each population. These samples do not have to have the same number of members.

2. Make sure the Analysis ToolPak is installed.

3. From the Data tab, select Data Analysis. Then select F-Test Two-Sample for Variances. The F-Test Two Sample for Variances dialog appears.

4. In the F-Test Two Sample for Variances dialog, choose the range for both of your sample ranges.

5. In the Alpha box, enter the level at which you want to evaluate critical values for the F statistic. The alpha level is a significance level related to the probability of having a type I error (that is, rejecting a true hypothesis).

6. Select the top-left cell of an output range.

7. Click OK to produce the analysis.

The F-Test tool provides the result of a test of the null hypothesis that these two samples come from distributions with equal variances against the alternative that the variances are not equal in the underlying distributions.

The F-Test tool calculates the value of an F statistic. A value of F close to 1 provides evidence that the underlying population variances are equal.

There is a tricky element to the output table. If the F value is less than 1, you need to look to the next row, which has the label "P(F <= f) one-tail." It gives the probability of observing a value of the F statistic less than f when population variances are equal. The next row, labeled "F Critical one-tail," gives the critical value less than 1 for the chosen significance level, alpha.

If the F statistic is greater than 1, the meanings of these rows are reversed. The row labeled "P(F <= f) one-tail" gives the probability of observing a value of the F statistic greater than f when population variances are equal, and "F Critical one-tail" gives the critical value greater than 1 for alpha.

In Figure 14.64, the F statistic of 0.88 is less than 1. This means that the null hypothesis is that the variances are unequal. The F critical value is 0.35, meaning that you can reject the null hypothesis.

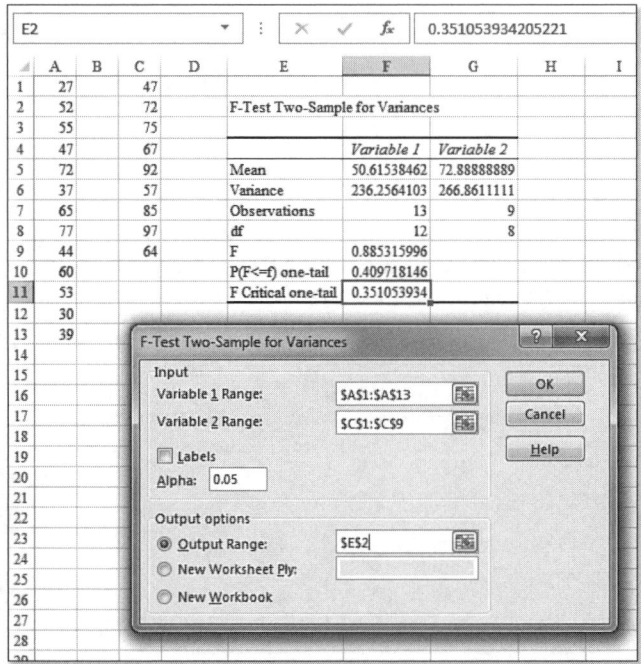

Figure 14.64
The F-test indicates whether two populations have an equal variance.

Performing a *z*-Test to Determine Whether Two Samples Have Equal Means

You use the Z-Test tool to test the null hypothesis that there is no difference between two population means against either one-sided or two-sided alternative hypotheses. *z*-tests are appropriate when the sample sizes are greater than 30. For sample sizes smaller than 30, you use *t*-tests, as described in the following section.

Note

If variances are not known, the worksheet function Z.TEST should be used instead.

To run a *z*-test, follow these steps:

1. Set up two ranges with data from each sample. Calculate the standard deviation of each population.

2. Make sure the Analysis ToolPak is installed.

3. From the Data tab, select Data Analysis. Then scroll down and select z-Test: Two-Sample for Means. The z-Test: Two Sample for Means dialog appears.

4. For Variable 1 Range, select the range of data for your first sample.

Tip

In step 4, if you choose a heading cell in this range, be sure to also choose a heading cell in step 5.

5. For Variable 2 Range, select the range of data for your second sample.

6. For Hypothesized Mean Difference, if you have a reason to believe that there is a shift from one population to the other caused by an external event, note it here. For example, if you measured the height of every kid in the classroom, and the next day you measured the height of every kid while they were standing on a 6-inch bench, the 6 inches would be an explainable shift in the means.

7. For the variances, enter the standard deviations for both populations. As mentioned previously, if you don't know these, you should use the Z.TEST worksheet function instead of this tool.

8. In the Alpha box, enter the confidence level for the test. This value must be in the range 0–1. The alpha level is a significance level related to the probability of having a type I error (that is, rejecting a true hypothesis).

9. Select the top-left cell of an output range.

10. Click OK to produce the analysis.

The results of a *z*-test are shown in Figure 14.65.

When analyzing the results, you should be careful to understand the output:

- "P(Z <= z) one-tail" is really P(Z >= ABS(z)), the probability of a z value further from 0 in the same direction as the observed z value when there is no difference between the population means.

- "P(Z <= z) two-tail" is really P(Z >= ABS(z) or Z <= -ABS(z)), the probability of a z value further from 0 in either direction than the observed z value when there is no difference between the population means. The two-tailed result is just the one-tailed result multiplied by 2.

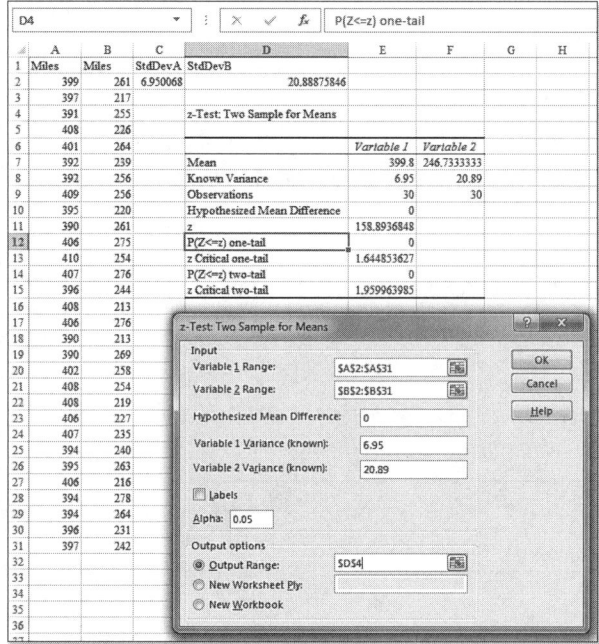

Figure 14.65
This z-test indicates that the samples came from different populations.

Performing Student's *t*-Testing to Test Population Means

The two-sample T-Test tool tests for equality of the population means underlying each sample. There are three varieties of this test, based on assumptions:

- **t-Test: Paired Two Sample for Means**—If the two samples came from the same population, one before a treatment and one after the treatment, you use this test.

- **t-Test: Two-Sample Assuming Equal Variances**—If you believe that the variances of each population are equal, you use this test.

- **t-Test: Two Sample Assuming Unequal Variances**—If you believe that the variances of the two populations are unequal, you use this test.

All three varieties produce a *t* statistic. The *t* statistic can be negative or nonnegative. Under the assumption of equal underlying population means, if *t* is less than 0, "P(T <= t) one-tail" gives the probability that a value of the *t* statistic would be observed that is more negative than *t*. If *t* is greater than or equal to 0, "P(T <= t) one-tail" gives the probability that a value of the *t* statistic would be observed that is more positive than *t*. "t Critical one-tail" gives the cutoff value so that the probability of observing a value of the *t* statistic greater than or equal to "t Critical one-tail" is alpha.

"P(T <= t) two-tail" gives the probability that a value of the *t* statistic would be observed that is larger in absolute value than *t*. "P Critical two-tail" gives the cutoff value so that the probability of an observed *t* statistic larger in absolute value than "P Critical two-tail" is alpha.

To perform a *t*-test, follow these steps:

1. Set up two ranges with data from each sample.

2. Make sure the Analysis ToolPak is installed.

3. From the Data tab, select Data Analysis. Then scroll down and select t-Test: Two-Sample Assuming Equal Variance. The t-Test dialog appears.

4. For Variable 1 Range, select the range of data for your first sample.

5. For Variable 2 Range, select the range of data for your second sample.

6. For Hypothesized Mean Difference, if you have a reason to believe that there is a shift from one population to the other caused by an external event, note it here.

7. In the Alpha box, enter the confidence level for the test. This value must be in the range 0–1. The alpha level is a significance level related to the probability of having a type I error (that is, rejecting a true hypothesis).

8. Select the top-left cell of an output range.

9. Click OK to produce the analysis.

The results of a *t*-test are shown in Figure 14.66.

Figure 14.66
Based on a *t* statistic close to 0, you cannot assume that these came from different populations.

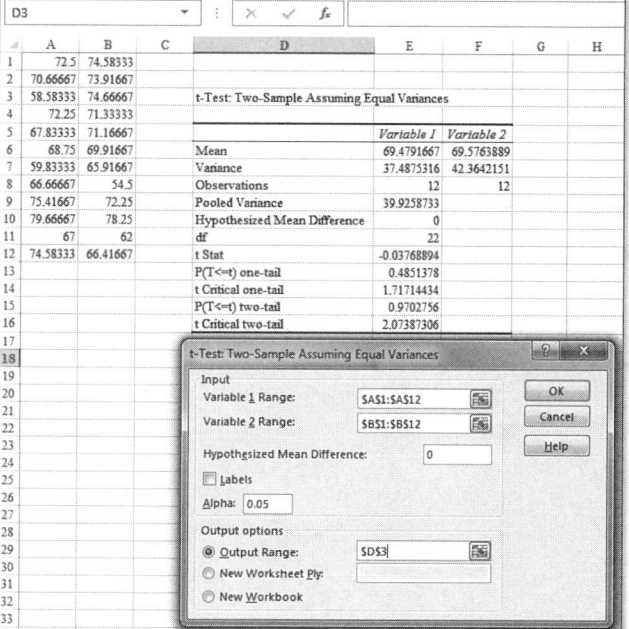

Using Functions Versus the Analysis ToolPak Tools

Excel offers many options for performing statistical analysis. Using functions in Excel provides real-time, live results of the data.

The Data Analysis tools in the Analysis ToolPak vary greatly. Some of them are poorly implemented and provide such narrow functionality that it is usually better to use your own functions rather than those tools.

On the other hand, some of the tools, such as Regression, provide additional statistics that run circles around the equivalent functions in Excel. In this case, it would be advantageous to use the Analysis ToolPak.

Remember, however, that when you use the Data Analysis tools from the Analysis ToolPak, they create static snapshots of the results. If you change the underlying data, you have to rerun the analysis.

USING TRIG, MATRIX, AND ENGINEERING FUNCTIONS

Scientists, mathematicians, and engineers, as well as high school mathematics students, will get the broadest use out of the functions in this chapter. Even though many of the trigonometry functions might seem intimidating, this chapter includes practical household examples for many of the functions. Anyone who has to lean a ladder against a house can find a use for the trig functions.

The imaginary number functions might be useful only to electrical engineers, but any business analyst can make use of the techniques for solving linear equations.

Excel 2013 debuts 24 new functions in this chapter:

- **Trig**—Functions for cotangent, cosecant, secant, arccotangent, and hyperbolic versions of each.

- **Matrix**—A new MUNIT function to return the unit matrix.

- **Engineering**—Eight new imaginary functions, five new binary functions, and BASE / DECIMAL for converting to various number systems.

Table 15.1 provides an alphabetical list of all of Excel 2013's trig functions. Detailed examples of the functions are provided later in the chapter.

Table 15.1 Alphabetical List of Trig Functions

Function	Description
ACOS(*number*)	Returns the arccosine of a number. The arccosine is the angle whose cosine is *number*. The returned angle is given in radians in the range 0 to π.
ACOSH(*number*)	Returns the inverse hyperbolic cosine of a *number*, which must be greater than or equal to 1. The inverse hyperbolic cosine is the value whose hyperbolic cosine is *number*, so ACOSH(COSH(*number*)) equals number.
ACOT(*number*)	Returns the arccotangent of a number in radians, in the range of 0 to π. New in Excel 2013.
ACOTH(*number*)	Returns the inverse hyperbolic cotangent of a number. New in Excel 2013.
ASIN(*number*)	Returns the arcsine of a number. The arcsine is the angle whose sine is *number*. The returned angle is given in radians in the Range −π / 2 to π/ 2.
ASINH(*number*)	Returns the inverse hyperbolic sine of a number. The inverse hyperbolic sine is the value whose hyperbolic sine is *number*, so ASINH(SINH(*number*)) equals *number*.
ATAN(*number*)	Returns the arctangent of a number. The arctangent is the angle whose tangent is *number*. The returned angle is given in radians in the range −π/2 to π/2.
ATAN2(*x_num,y_num*)	Returns the arctangent of the specified x- and y-coordinates. The arctangent is the angle from the x-axis to a line containing the origin (0, 0) and a point with coordinates (*x_num, y_num*). The angle is given in radians between −π and π, excluding −π.
ATANH(*number*)	Returns the inverse hyperbolic tangent of a number. *number* must be between −1 and 1 (excluding −1 and 1). The inverse hyperbolic tangent is the value whose hyperbolic tangent is *number*, so ATANH(TANH(*number*)) *equals* number.
COS(*number*)	Returns the cosine of the given angle.
COSH(*number*)	Returns the hyperbolic cosine of a number.
COT(*number*)	Returns the cotangent of an angle. New in Excel 2013.
COTH(*number*)	Returns the hyperbolic cotangent of a number. New in Excel 2013.
CSC(*number*)	Returns the cosecant of a number. New in Excel 2013.
CSCH(*number*)	Returns the hyperbolic cosecant of a number. New in Excel 2013.
DEGREES(*angle*)	Converts radians into degrees.
LN(*number*)	Returns the natural logarithm of *number*. Natural logarithms are based on the constant e (2.71828182845904).
LOG(*number,base*)	Returns the logarithm of *number* to the specified base.
LOG10(*number*)	Returns the base-10 logarithm of *number*.

Function	Description
RADIANS(*angle*)	Converts degrees to radians.
SEC(*number*)	Returns the secant of an angle. New in Excel 2013.
SECH(*number*)	Returns the hyperbolic secant of an angle. New in Excel 2013.
SIN(*number*)	Returns the sine of the given angle.
SINH(*number*)	Returns the hyperbolic sine of *number*.
TAN(*number*)	Returns the tangent of the given angle.
TANH(*number*)	Returns the hyperbolic tangent of *number*.

Table 15.2 provides an alphabetical list of all Excel 2013's matrix functions. Detailed examples of the functions are provided later in the chapter.

Table 15.2 Alphabetical List of Matrix Functions

Function	Description
MDETERM(*array*)	Returns the matrix determinant of an array.
MINVERSE(*array*)	Returns the inverse matrix for the matrix stored in an array.
MMULT(*array1*,*array2*)	Returns the matrix product of two arrays. The result is an array with the same number of rows as *array1* and the same number of columns as *array2*.
MUNIT(*dimension*)	Returns the unit matrix for the specified dimension. New in Excel 2013.
SERIESSUM(*x*,*n*,*m*,*coefficients*)	Returns the sum of a power series based on the formula $SERIES(x,n,m,a) \approx a_1xn + a_2x^{(n+m)} + a_3x^{(n+2m)} + \ldots + a_ix^{(n+(i-1)m)}$
SUMPRODUCT(*array1*,*array2*,*array3* ,...)	Multiplies corresponding components in the given arrays and returns the sum of those products.

Table 15.3 provides an alphabetical list of all Excel 2013's engineering functions. Detailed examples of the functions are provided later in the chapter.

Table 15.3 Alphabetical List of Engineering Functions

Function	Description
BASE(*number, radix, min_length*)	Converts a number into a text representation with the given radix (base). New in Excel 2013.
BESSELI(*x*,*n*)	Returns the modified Bessel function, which is equivalent to the BESSELJ function evaluated for purely imaginary arguments.

Function	Description
BESSELJ(*x*,*n*)	Returns the Bessel function of the first kind.
BESSELK(*x*,*n*)	Returns the modified Bessel function of the second kind, which is equivalent to the BESSELY functions evaluated for purely imaginary arguments.
BESSELY(*x*,*n*)	Returns the Bessel function of the second kind. This is the most commonly used form of the Bessel functions. This function provides solutions of the Bessel differential equation and are infinite at x=0. This function is sometimes called the Neumann function.
BIN2DEC(*number*)	Converts a binary number to decimal.
BIN2HEX(*number*,*places*)	Converts a binary number to hexadecimal.
BIN2OCT(*number*,*places*)	Converts a binary number to octal.
BITAND(*number1*, *number2*)	Returns a bitwise AND of two numbers. New in Excel 2013.
BITLSHIFT(*number*, *shift_amount*)	Returns a number shifted left by *shift_amount* bits. New in Excel 2013.
BITOR(*number1*, *number2*)	Returns a bitwise OR of two numbers. New in Excel 2013.
BITRSHIFT(*number*, *shift_amount*)	Returns a number shifted right by *shift_amount* bits. New in Excel 2013.
BITXOR(*number1*, *number2*)	Returns a bitwise Exclusive OR of two numbers. New in Excel 2013.
COMPLEX(*real_num*,*i_num*,*suffix*)	Converts real and imaginary coefficients into a complex number in the form x + yi or x + yj. Use *suffix* to control whether "i" or "j" is used.
CONVERT(*number*,*from_unit*,*to_unit*)	Converts a number from one measurement system to another. For example, CONVERT can translate a table of distances in miles to a table of distances in kilometers.
DEC2BIN(*number*,*places*)	Converts a decimal number to binary.
DEC2HEX(*number*,*places*)	Converts a decimal number to hexadecimal.
DEC2OCT(*number*,*places*)	Converts a decimal number to octal.
DECIMAL(*number*, *radix*)	Converts a text representation of a number with a given base into a decimal number. New in Excel 2013.
DELTA(*number1*,*number2*)	Tests whether two values are equal. Returns 1 if *number1* = *number2*; returns 0 otherwise. You use this function to filter a set of values. For example, by summing several DELTA functions, you can calculate the count of equal pairs. This function is also known as the Kronecker Delta function.

Function	Description
ERF(*lower_limit,upper_limit*)	Returns the ERROR function integrated between *lower_limit* and *upper_limit*.
ERFC(*x*)	Returns the complementary ERF function integrated between x and infinity.
GESTEP(*number,step*)	Returns 1 if *number* is greater than or equal to *step*; otherwise, returns 0. You use this function to filter a set of values. For example, by summing several GESTEP functions, you can calculate the count of values that exceed a threshold.
HEX2BIN(*number,places*)	Converts a hexadecimal number to binary.
HEX2DEC(*number*)	Converts a hexadecimal number to decimal.
HEX2OCT(*number,places*)	Converts a hexadecimal number to octal.
IMABS(*inumber*)	Returns the absolute value (modulus) of a complex number in x + yi or x + yj text format.
IMAGINARY(*inumber*)	Returns the imaginary coefficient of a complex number in x + yi or x + yj text format.
IMARGUMENT(*inumber*)	Returns the argument Θ (theta), an angle expressed in radians.
IMCONJUGATE(*inumber*)	Returns the complex conjugate of a complex number in x + yi or x + yj text format.
IMCOS(*inumber*)	Returns the cosine of a complex number in x + yi or x + yj text format.
IMCOSH(*inumber*)	Returns the hyperbolic cosine of a complex number. New in Excel 2013.
IMCOT(*inumber*)	Returns the cotangent of a complex number. New in Excel 2013.
IMCSC(*inumber*)	Returns the cosecant of a complex number. New in Excel 2013.
IMCSCH(*inumber*)	Returns the hyperbolic cosecant of a complex number. New in Excel 2013.
IMDIV(*inumber1,inumber2*)	Returns the quotient of two complex numbers in x + yi or x + yj text format.
IMEXP(*inumber*)	Returns the exponential of a complex number in x + yi or x + yj text format.
IMLN(*inumber*)	Returns the natural logarithm of a complex number in x + yi or x + yj text format.
IMLOG10(*inumber*)	Returns the common logarithm (base-10) of a complex number in x + yi or x + yj text format.
IMLOG2(*inumber*)	Returns the base-2 logarithm of a complex number in x + yi or x + yj text format.

Function	Description
IMPOWER(*inumber,number*)	Returns a complex number in x + yi or x + yj text format raised to a power.
IMPRODUCT(*inumber1,inumber2, ...*)	Returns the product of 2 to 255 complex numbers in x + yi or x + yj text format.
IMREAL(*inumber*)	Returns the real coefficient of a complex number in x + yi or x + yj text format.
IMSEC(*inumber*)	Returns the secant of a complex number. New in Excel 2013.
IMSECH(*inumber*)	Returns the hyperbolic secant of a complex number. New in Excel 2013.
IMSIN(*inumber*)	Returns the sine of a complex number in x + yi or x + yj text format.
IMSINH(*inumber*)	Returns the hyperbolic sin of a complex number. New in Excel 2013.
IMSQRT(*inumber*)	Returns the square root of a complex number in x + yi or x + yj text format.
IMSUB(*inumber1,inumber2*)	Returns the difference of two complex numbers in x + yi or x + yj text format.
IMSUM(*inumber1,inumber2,...*)	Returns the sum of two or more complex numbers in x + yi or x + yj text format.
IMTAN(*inumber*)	Returns the tangent of a complex number. New in Excel 2013.
OCT2BIN(*number,places*)	Converts an octal number to binary.
OCT2DEC(*number*)	Converts an octal number to decimal.
OCT2HEX(*number,places*)	Converts an octal number to hexadecimal.

A Brief Review of Trigonometry Basics

Numerous real-life situations offer you an opportunity to use trigonometry. In case trigonometry is just a distant nightmare for you, the following sections review some of the basics.

Radians Versus Degrees

Nonmathematicians discuss angles in terms of *degrees*. Most corners of a room are at a 90-degree angle. Mathematicians discuss angles in a different measurement called *radians*.

Although a circle is composed of 360 degrees, it is also composed of about 6.28 radians. Each radian is equal to about 57.3 degrees. The exact relationship of degrees to radians requires you to use the mathematical constant pi (π), which is about 3.14159. There are two π radians in a circle.

Because the trig functions were written with mathematicians in mind, they always expect the arguments to be expressed in radians.

The formula to convert degrees to radians is to multiply the degrees by PI() and divide by 180. To use this method, you need to write formulas as shown in cell C16 of Figure 15.1. Fortunately, Excel provides the functions RADIANS and DEGREES to convert from one measurement to another.

Figure 15.1
The trig functions in Excel expect degrees to be in radians. These two functions convert back and forth from radians to degrees.

C17	▾	:	✕ ✓ *fx*	=FORMULATEXT(B17)

◢	A	B	C	D
1	**Degrees**	**Radians**		
2	30	0.523599	*=RADIANS(A2)*	
3	45	0.785398		
4	60	1.047198		
5	90	1.570796		
6	120	2.094395		
7	135	2.356194		
8	150	2.617994		
9	180	3.141593		
10				
11	**Radians**	**Degrees**		
12	1.570796	90	*=DEGREES(A12)*	
13	1.047198	60		
14	0.785398	45		
15				
16		0.866025	*=SIN(60*PI()/180)*	
17		0.866025	*=SIN(RADIANS(60))*	
18				

Syntax:

DEGREES(*angle*)

The DEGREES function converts radians into degrees. The argument *angle* is the angle, in radians, that you want to convert.

Syntax:

RADIANS(*angle*)

The RADIANS function converts degrees to radians. The argument *angle* is an angle, in degrees, that you want to convert.

In Figure 15.1, B2:B9 converts degrees to radians. The range B12:B14 converts radians back to degrees. The formulas in rows 16 and 17 contrast using `PI()` / `180` with the `RADIANS` function.

Pythagoras and Right Triangles

Trigonometry relies on triangles. Figure 15.2 shows a right triangle, which is a triangle that has one 90-degree angle. In a right triangle, the side opposite the right angle is known as the *hypotenuse*. In a right triangle, the square of the hypotenuse is equal to the sum of the squares of the two other sides. This is frequently expressed as c^2 = a^2 + b^2.

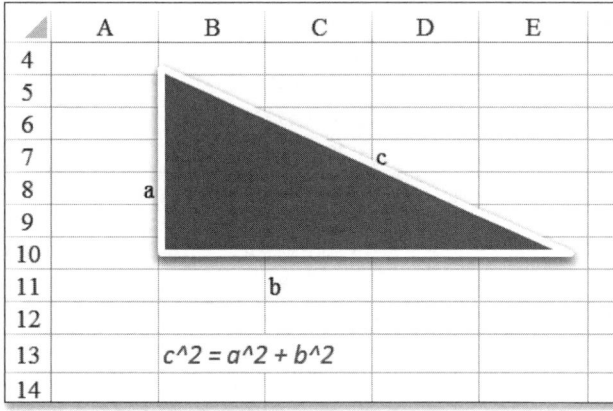

Figure 15.2
The Pythagorean theorem enables you to figure out the length of one leg of a right triangle if you know the length of the other two legs.

If you know that the two shorter legs of a right triangle measure 3 feet and 4 feet, then you know the following:

```
c^2 = 3^2 + 4^2
c^2 = 9 + 16
c^2 = 25
c = SQRT(25)
c = 5
```

Although this formula was discovered a thousand years before Pythagoras was alive, he certainly popularized this formula, which is known as the *Pythagorean theorem*.

One Side + One Angle = Trigonometry

The three classic functions in trigonometry are sine, cosine, and tangent. These functions describe the ratio of two sides of a triangle when you know the angles of the triangle.

Consider Figure 15.3. One angle is a right angle, which is 90 degrees. If you can figure out one of the other angles and the length of one leg of the triangle, you can figure out the length of all three sides of the triangle by using Excel.

Figure 15.3
If you know one angle and the length of one side of a right triangle, you can calculate all the sides of the triangle by using trigonometry.

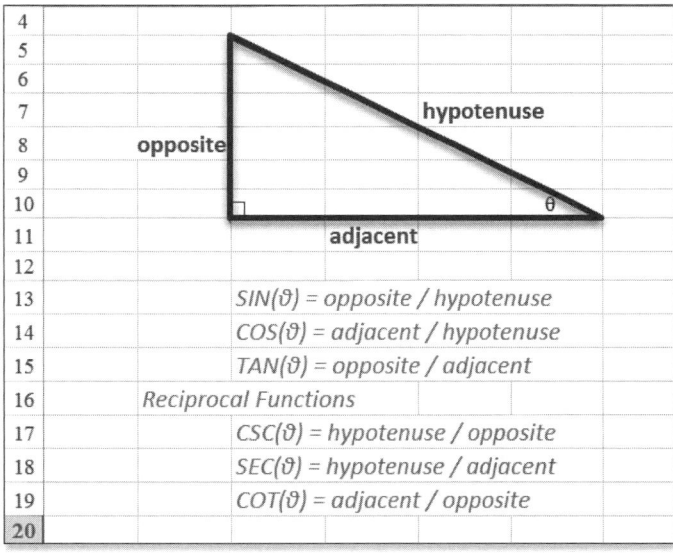

In Figure 15.3, one angle is marked Θ (theta). The side across from Θ is known as the *opposite* side. The side that is not the hypotenuse and is part of the angle Θ is the *adjacent* side. Five classic functions describe the ratio of any two sides, as detailed in Table 15.4.

Table 15.4 Guide to Trig Functions

SIN(Θ)	= Opposite / Hypotenuse
COS(Θ)	= Adjacent / Hypotenuse
TAN(Θ)	= Opposite / Adjacent
CSC(Θ)	= Hypotenuse / Opposite
SEC(Θ)	= Hypotenuse / Adjacent
COT(Θ)	= Adjacent / Opposite

Excel offers trig functions that enable you to find various angles or lengths of a right triangle when you know various combinations of the other angles and/or sides. Excel 2013 adds the reciprocal functions of cosecant, secant, and cotangent. The examples in this section provide some real-world examples of using trigonometry.

Using TAN to Find the Height of a Tall Building from the Ground

Suppose you want to measure the height of a tall building from the ground. The tangent function can find the height of a right triangle if you know the length of the base and the angle to the top of the triangle. To calculate the height of a building, follow these steps:

1. Starting from the building, measure out 35 feet along level ground. Sight to the top of the building and determine the angle from that point on the ground to the top of the building (for example, 69 degrees). The 35-feet figure is the length of the adjacent side of the triangle. You want to solve for the opposite side of the triangle. The TAN function describes the ratio of the opposite side to the adjacent side.

2. In a cell in Excel, enter **=TAN(RADIANS(69))**. This tells you that the ratio of the height of the building to the 35 feet is 2.605.

3. Because 2.605 = Opposite / Adjacent, plug in 35 for the adjacent side, to get 2.605 = Opposite / 35.

4. To solve this equation, multiply both sides by 35. The answer, as shown in cell E8 in Figure 15.4, is that the building is more than 91 feet tall.

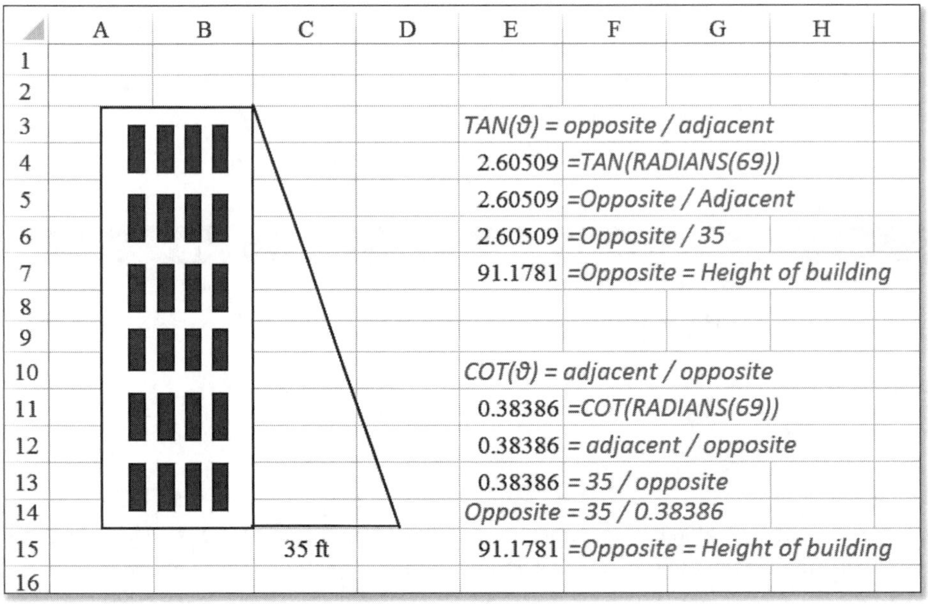

Figure 15.4
You can use the TAN function to find the height of this building.

Starting in Excel 2013, Microsoft offers the COT function to calculate the cotangent. The cotangent is the reciprocal of the tangent—it is Adjacent / Opposite. As shown in rows 10–15 of Figure 15.4, you could use =35/COT(RADIANS(69)) to calculate the height of the building.

Syntax:

TAN(*number*)

The TAN function returns the tangent of the given angle. The argument *number* is the angle, in radians, for which you want the tangent. If your argument is in degrees, you convert it to radians by using RADIANS(degrees) or multiply it by PI() / 180.

Syntax:

COT(*number*)

The COT function returns the cotangent of the given angle. The argument *number* is the angle, in radians, for which you want the tangent. This function is new in Excel 2013.

Using SIN to Find the Height of a Kite in a Tree

Suppose your children are flying a kite. They have let out all 150 feet of string. The kite is caught at the top of a faraway tree, as shown in Figure 15.5.

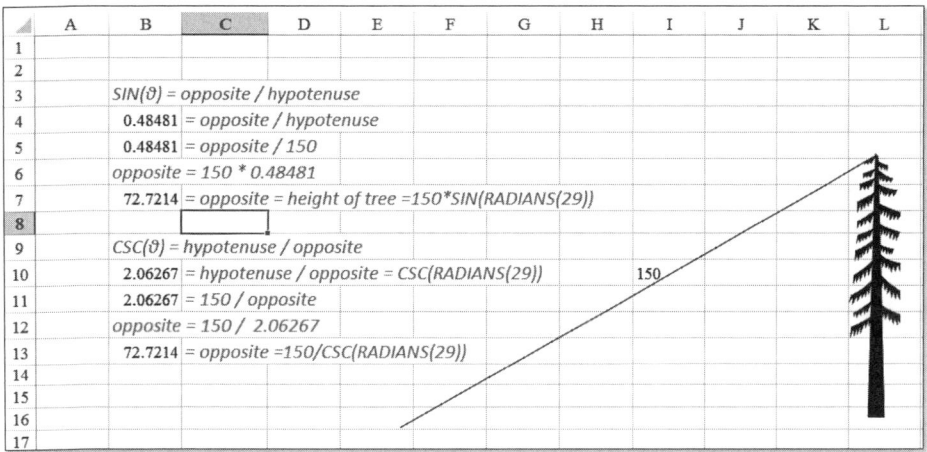

Figure 15.5
The SIN function can find the height of this tree when you know the length of the string.

To find the height of this tree, follow these steps:

1. Sight the angle from the end of the string to the top of the tree. It measures 29 degrees.

2. Refer to Table 15.4 earlier in this chapter. Because you know the hypotenuse and want to find the opposite side, use the SIN function.

3. In a cell in Excel, enter =SIN(RADIANS(29)). The result is 0.484.

4. Because the sine is the ratio of the opposite side to the hypotenuse, create the formula 0.484 = Opposite / 150.

5. To solve for the opposite side, multiply both sides of the equation by 150. You find that the tree is over 72 feet tall.

6. Assess your tree-climbing skills. If you do not currently work for Davey Tree Experts, perhaps you should decide to buy the kids a new kite.

Starting in Excel 2013, Microsoft offers the CSC function to calculate cosecant. The cosecant is the reciprocal of sine, or Hypotenuse / Opposite. As shown in rows 9–13 of Figure 15.5, you could calculate the height of the tree with 150/CSC(RADIANS(29)).

Syntax:

SIN(*number*)

The SIN function returns the sine of the given angle. The argument *number* is the angle, in radians, for which you want the sine. If your argument is in degrees, you multiply it by PI() / 180 to convert it to radians.

Syntax:

CSC(*number*)

The CSC function returns the cosecant of the given angle. The argument *number* is the angle, in radians, for which you want the cosecant. CSC is the reciprocal of SIN. Whereas previous versions of Excel assumed you could use 1/SIN() to calculate the cosecant, Excel 2013 explicitly adds CSC as a function.

Using COS to Figure Out a Ladder's Length

Every year, my wife, Mary Ellen, hires Kevin the landscaper to hang a huge holiday wreath on the second story of our house. The holidays come and go, and I find that Kevin is wintering in Florida. The ladder that I own is not long enough to reach the wreath. Much to the humor of my neighbors, I stand next to the house, with my too-short ladder, and assess the situation. Figure 15.6 shows that I am 10 feet from the house, and the angle to the wreath hanger is 55 degrees. How long of a ladder do I need to borrow from the neighbors?

Table 15.4, earlier in this chapter, shows that the COS function determines the relationship between the adjacent side and the hypotenuse. To find the length of the ladder, follow these steps:

1. In Excel, enter **=COS(RADIANS(55))**. The result is 0.574.

2. Create the equation Adjacent / Hypotenuse = 0.574.

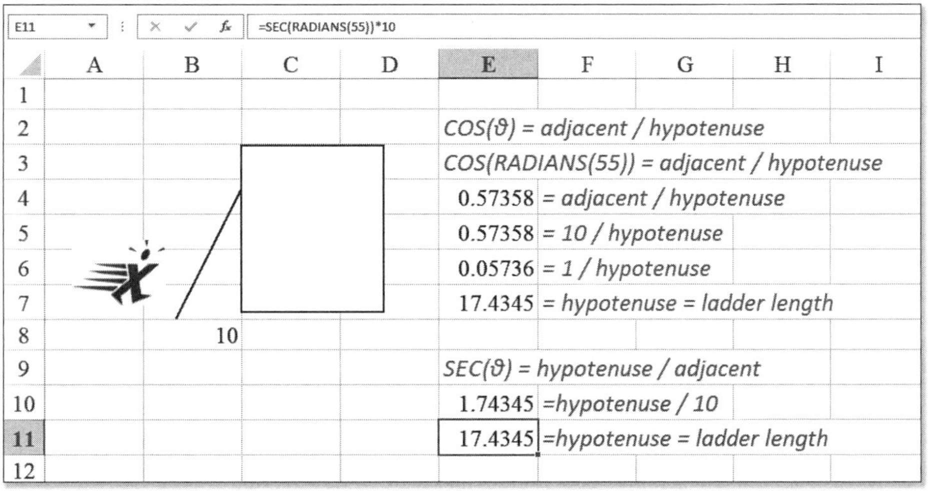

Figure 15.6
The COS function can find the length of the ladder needed to reach the objective.

E11	▼	:	×	✓	*fx*	=SEC(RADIANS(55))*10				
	A	B	C	D	E	F	G	H	I
1									
2					*COS(ϑ) = adjacent / hypotenuse*				
3					*COS(RADIANS(55)) = adjacent / hypotenuse*				
4					*0.57358 = adjacent / hypotenuse*				
5					*0.57358 = 10 / hypotenuse*				
6					*0.05736 = 1 / hypotenuse*				
7					*17.4345 = hypotenuse = ladder length*				
8		10							
9					*SEC(ϑ) = hypotenuse / adjacent*				
10					*1.74345 =hypotenuse / 10*				
11					*17.4345* =hypotenuse = ladder length				
12									

3. Divide both sides of the equation by 10. This tells you that the 1 / Hypotenuse is 17.43.

4. Divide both sides of the equation into 1. The result tells you that the hypotenuse is almost 17.5 feet.

It looks like I had better visit Dick, the neighbor with the 18-foot ladder.

Excel 2013 adds the SEC function, which is the reciprocal of the cosine function. In cell E11 of Figure 15.6, the secant is used to calculate the ladder length using =SEC(RADIANS(55))*10.

Syntax:

COS(*number*)

The COS function returns the cosine of the given angle. The argument *number* is the angle, in radians, for which you want the cosine. If the angle is in degrees, you multiply it by PI() / 180 to convert it to radians.

Syntax:

SEC(*number*)

The SEC function returns the secant of the given angle. The argument *number* is the angle, in radians, for which you want the cosine. This function was added in Excel 2013.

Excel in Practice: Measuring the Distance Across a Canyon

Have you ever seen a pair of surveyors working in your neighborhood? One of the pair is holding a tall pole, and the other person is looking through a sighting device. The surveyor can use trigonometry to measure distances or the angle of decline of a piece of land.

To try your surveying skills, you can measure the distance across a canyon. You start by standing on one side of the canyon with a sighting tool. Have your friend stand on the other side of the canyon, holding a 6-foot pole. The angle from the sighting device to the bottom of the 6-foot pole will be ridiculously small, but measurable. You find that the angle comes out to 0.006 degrees. If you know the height of the opposite side is 6 feet and the angle is 0.006 degrees, you can find the distance across that portion of the canyon by using trigonometry.

Table 15.4 defines the tangent as the length of Opposite / Adjacent. Now that you have this information, you can follow these steps to find the distance across the canyon:

1. To convert 0.006 degrees to a tangent, use `=TAN(RADIANS(0.006))`. The result, 0.000105, is 6 / Adjacent.

2. Multiply both sides of the equation by Adjacent. Divide both sides of the equation by 0.000105.

3. In cell F16 in Figure 15.7, the formula `=6/0.000105` indicates that the canyon is 57,142 feet across.

4. In cell F17, divide F16 by 5,280 to find that the canyon is 10.82 miles across at that point. Even if you are Evel Knievel, you probably do not want to attempt to jump across in your rocket-powered motorcycle.

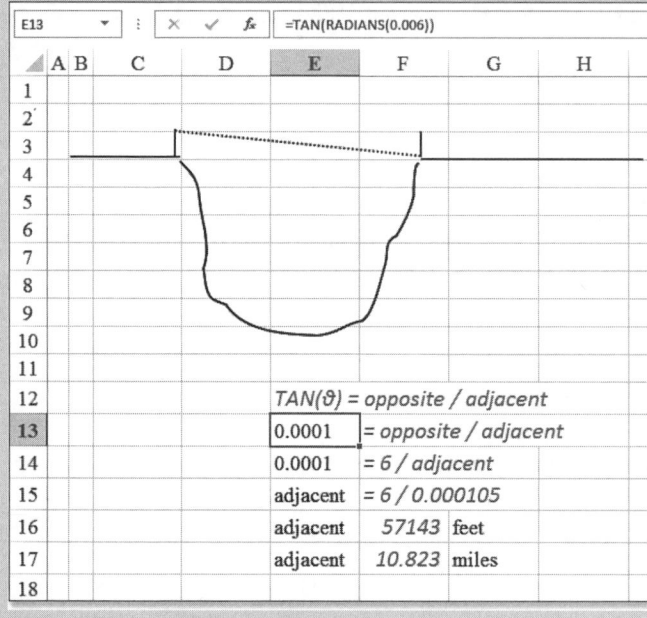

Figure 15.7
You can calculate distances across a lake or canyon by using trigonometry.

Using the "Arc" Functions to Find the Measure of an Angle

If you know the lengths of two sides of a right triangle, you can determine the angles of the triangle by using trigonometry.

The "arc" functions convert a sine value to an angle, in radians. Suppose that you know the opposite side of a triangle has a length of 3 and the hypotenuse has a length of 5. The sine value is Opposite / Hypotenuse, or 0.6. You use =ASIN(0.6) to convert the sine back to the measure of the angle.

Excel provides functions to reverse all three of the basic trig functions. You use ACOS to reverse COS, ASIN to reverse SIN, and ATAN to reverse TAN. Excel 2013 adds ACOT to reverse COT. Strangely, there is neither an arccosecant nor arcsecant function.

Figure 15.8 demonstrates how to use ACOS, ASIN, and ATAN to find the angle size of a right triangle. Keep in mind that the three angles in a triangle always add up to 180. Because you know that the right angle is 90 degrees, and Figure 15.8 calculates the second angle as 37 degrees, the third angle must be 53 degrees.

 Note

The result of ASIN(0.6) produces the size of the angle, in radians. To convert from radians to degrees, you use =DEGREES(ASIN(0.6)).

Figure 15.8
The ARC functions find an angle from the ratio of two sides of the triangle.

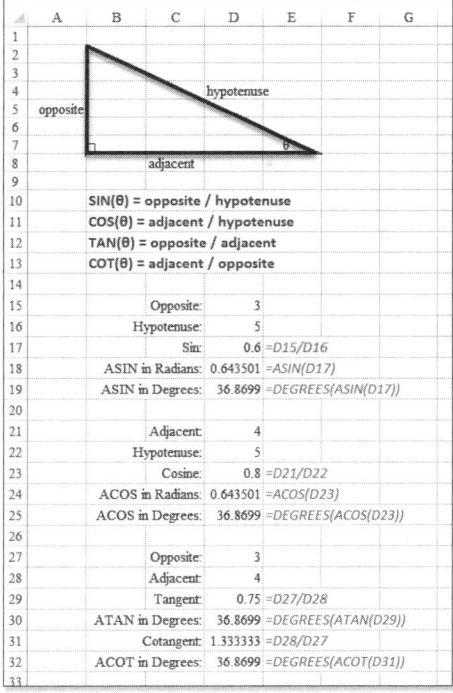

Syntax:

ACOS(*number*)

The ACOS function returns the arccosine of a number. The arccosine is the angle whose cosine is *number*. The returned angle is given in radians, in the range 0 to π. The argument *number* is the cosine of the angle you want and must be from −1 to 1. If you want to convert the result from radians to degrees, multiply it by 180 / PI() or use the DEGREES function.

Syntax:

ASIN(*number*)

The ASIN function returns the arcsine of a number. The arcsine is the angle whose sine is *number*. The returned angle is given in radians, in the range −π / 2 to π /2. The argument *number* is the sine of the angle you want and must be from −1 to 1. To express the arcsine in degrees, multiply the result by 180 / PI().

Syntax:

ATAN(*number*)

The ATAN function returns the arctangent of a number. The arctangent is the angle whose tangent is *number*. The returned angle is given in radians, in the range −π / 2 to π / 2. The argument *number* is the tangent of the angle you want. To express the arctangent in degrees, you multiply the result by 180 / PI().

Syntax:

ACOT(*number*)

The ACOT function returns the arccotangent of a number. The arccotangent is the angle whose cotangent is *number*. The returned angle is given in radians, in the range −π / 2 to π / 2. The argument *number* is the cotangent of the angle you want. To express the arccotangent in degrees, you multiply the result by 180 / PI().

Using ATAN2 to Calculate Angles in a Circle

Figure 15.9 shows a unit circle. This is a circle with a radius of 1, plotted on a Cartesian grid. The point on the right side of the circle has a value of x = 1 and y = 0. This is defined as the *angle at zero degrees*.

The point at the top of the circle has a value of y = 1 and x = 0. This is defined as the *angle at 90 degrees*.

Given the coordinates of any two points on the circle, or of any two points anywhere, you can calculate the angle by using the ATAN2 function.

Figure 15.9
You use ATAN2 to find the angle from the x-axis to any point in Cartesian coordinates.

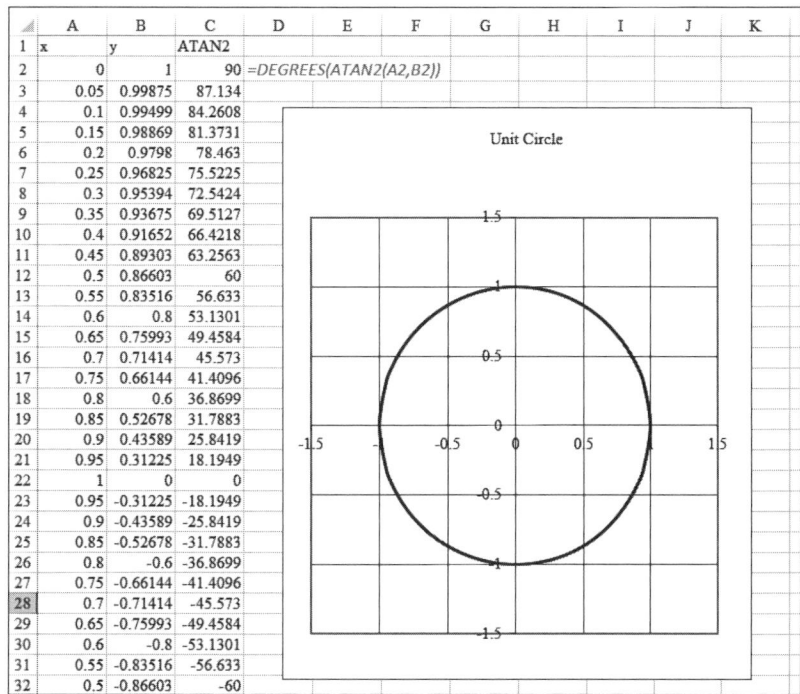

	A	B	C	D	E	F	G	H	I	J	K
1	x	y	ATAN2								
2	0	1	90	=DEGREES(ATAN2(A2,B2))							
3	0.05	0.99875	87.134								
4	0.1	0.99499	84.2608								
5	0.15	0.98869	81.3731								
6	0.2	0.9798	78.463								
7	0.25	0.96825	75.5225								
8	0.3	0.95394	72.5424								
9	0.35	0.93675	69.5127								
10	0.4	0.91652	66.4218								
11	0.45	0.89303	63.2563								
12	0.5	0.86603	60								
13	0.55	0.83516	56.633								
14	0.6	0.8	53.1301								
15	0.65	0.75993	49.4584								
16	0.7	0.71414	45.573								
17	0.75	0.66144	41.4096								
18	0.8	0.6	36.8699								
19	0.85	0.52678	31.7883								
20	0.9	0.43589	25.8419								
21	0.95	0.31225	18.1949								
22	1	0	0								
23	0.95	-0.31225	-18.1949								
24	0.9	-0.43589	-25.8419								
25	0.85	-0.52678	-31.7883								
26	0.8	-0.6	-36.8699								
27	0.75	-0.66144	-41.4096								
28	0.7	-0.71414	-45.573								
29	0.65	-0.75993	-49.4584								
30	0.6	-0.8	-53.1301								
31	0.55	-0.83516	-56.633								
32	0.5	-0.86603	-60								

Syntax:

ATAN2(x_num,y_num)

The ATAN2 function returns the arctangent of the specified x- and y-coordinates. The arctangent is the angle from the x-axis to a line containing the origin (0, 0) and a point with coordinates (x_num, y_num). The angle is given in radians, between −π and π, excluding −π. A positive result represents a counterclockwise angle from the x-axis; a negative result represents a clockwise angle.

This function takes the following arguments:

- **x_num**—This is the x-coordinate of the point.

- **y_num**—This is the y-coordinate of the point.

ATAN2(a,b) equals ATAN(b/a), except that a can equal 0 in ATAN2.

If both x_num and y_num are 0, ATAN2 returns a #DIV/0! error. To express the arctangent in degrees, you multiply the result by 180 / PI() or use the DEGREES function.

The formulas in column C of Figure 15.9 find the ATAN2 of the points in columns A and B. The result must be converted to degrees by using =DEGREES(ATAN2(A2,B2)).

Emulating Gravity Using Hyperbolic Trigonometry Functions

You can apply the trigonometry functions shown so far in this chapter to solve problems in your environment. The hyperbolic trigonometry functions, which are covered next, are far more complex. As shown in Figure 15.10, the hyperbolic cosine function, COSH, is effective at graphing the arc of a rope hung between two points.

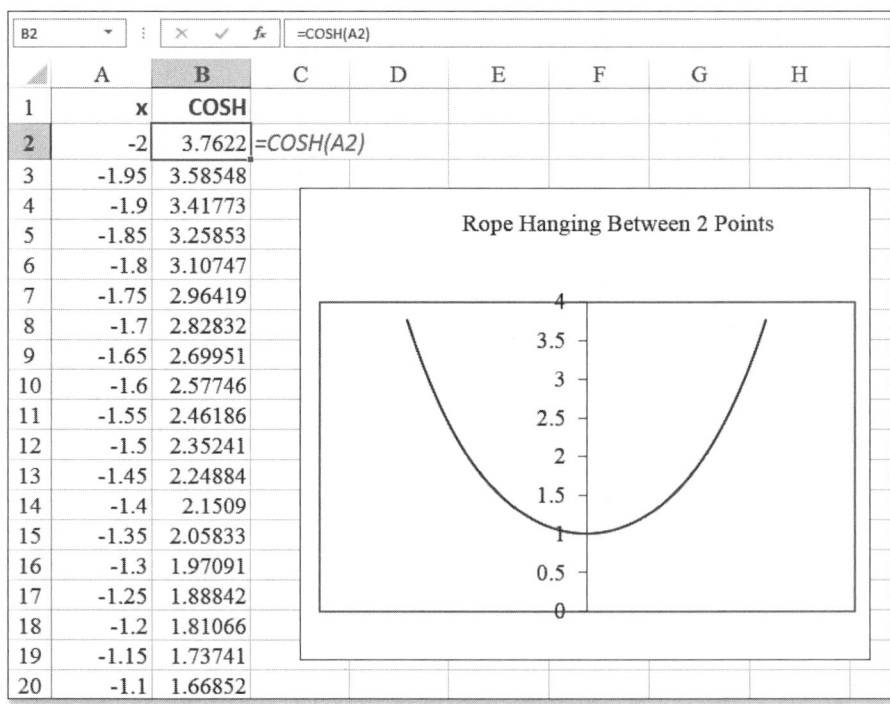

Figure 15.10
This shape defined by COSH is also known as a catenary.

According to MathWorld.com, other uses for hyperbolic trigonometry include the following:

- Calculating the gravitational potential of a cylinder

- Calculating the rapidity of special relativity

- Calculating the profile of a laminar jet

- Calculating the Schwarzschild metric, using external isotropic Kruskal coordinates

- Emulating a uniform gravity field by a uniform acceleration, in general relativity

These are complex tasks and I won't fill you in on the details here. However, if you need to calculate the profile of a laminar jet, head to MathWorld.com for details.

Excel offers the hyperbolic functions SINH, COSH, and TANH, as well as the reverse functions ASINH, ACOSH, and ATANH. Excel 2013 adds the reciprocal functions ACOTH, COTH, CSCH, and SECH.

Syntax:

SINH(*number*)

The SINH function returns the hyperbolic sine of a number. The argument *number* is any real number.

Syntax:

CSCH(*number*)

The CSCH function returns the hyperbolic cosecant of a number. The argument *number* is the angle in radians for which you want the hyperbolic cosecant. The absolute value of *number* must be less than 2^27. CSCH is new in Excel 2013. It is the reciprocal of the SINH function. In versions before Excel 2013, you could use =1/SINH(number) to calculate the hyperbolic cosecant.

Syntax:

COSH(*number*)

The COSH function returns the hyperbolic cosine of a number. The argument *number* is any real number for which you want to find the hyperbolic cosine.

In Figure 15.10, the COSH function is used in column B to calculate the path of a rope hanging between two points.

Syntax:

SECH(*number*)

The SECH function returns the hyperbolic secant of a number. The argument *number* is the angle in radians. The absolute value of *number* must be less than 2^27. Microsoft introduced SECH in Excel 2013. Prior to Excel 2013, you would use =1/COSH(number) to calculate the hyperbolic secant.

Syntax:

TANH(*number*)

The TANH function returns the hyperbolic tangent of a number. The argument *number* is any real number.

Syntax:

COTH(*number*)

The COTH function returns the hyperbolic cotangent of a hyperbolic angle. The argument *number* is an angle in radians. The absolute value must be less than 2^27. Microsoft introduced COTH in Excel 2013.

Syntax:

ASINH(*number*)

The ASINH function returns the inverse hyperbolic sine of a number. The inverse hyperbolic sine is the value whose hyperbolic sine is *number*, so ASINH(SINH(number)) equals *number*. The argument *number* is any real number.

Syntax:

ACOSH(*number*)

The ACOSH function returns the inverse hyperbolic cosine of a number. *number* must be greater than or equal to 1. The inverse hyperbolic cosine is the value whose hyperbolic cosine is *number*, so ACOSH(COSH(number)) equals *number*. The argument *number* is any real number equal to or greater than 1.

Syntax:

ATANH(*number*)

The ATANH function returns the inverse hyperbolic tangent of a number. *number* must be between −1 and 1, excluding −1 and 1. The inverse hyperbolic tangent is the value whose hyperbolic tangent is *number*, so ATANH(TANH(number)) equals *number*. The argument *number* is any real number between 1 and −1.

Syntax:

ACOTH(*number*)

The ACOTH function returns the inverse hyperbolic cotangent of a number. The absolute value of *number* must be greater than 1. Microsoft added this function in Excel 2013.

Examples of Logarithm Functions

If you have read many of my books, you know that I used to have a day job involving forecasting and operations planning. I was constantly battling with the sales force to provide accurate sales forecasts. At the end of each month, we produced a chart to show the forecasted demand and the actual demand. If the forecast and actual were within 15% of each other, this was considered a tolerable error, and no discussion was necessary. However, for any points outside the 15% tolerance, a team would figure out why we missed the forecast and how to prevent a similar miss in future months.

The initial charts looked horrible. There were 20 products being forecasted, and the monthly demand fell by anywhere from 50 units a month to 10,000 units a month. There were only a few products above the 5,000-unit level, but those few products made it impossible to see any detail for the 17 smaller products, as shown in Figure 15.11.

Rather than produce several different charts, our solution involved giving the y-axis of the chart a logarithmic scale.

Figure 15.11
No one can make out any detail for the smaller values on this chart. The scale of the two or three large products ruins the view of the smaller products.

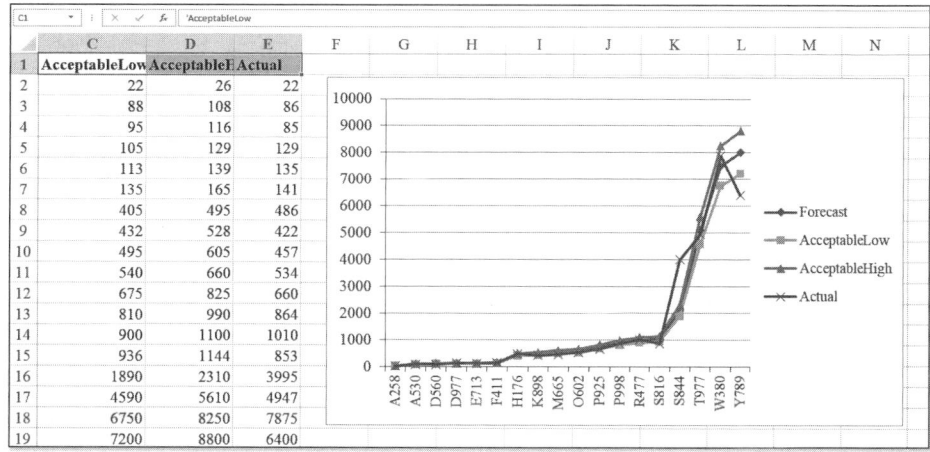

Common Logarithms on a Base-10 Scale

In a logarithmic scale, the distance from 1 to 10 on the scale is the same as the distance from 10 to 100 and the same as the distance from 100 to 1,000, and the same as the distance from 1,000 to 10,000. Each gridline basically appears at 10^1, 10^2, 10^3, 10^4, and so on.

The resulting chart enables you to see detail for the items selling 100 units as well as the items selling 8,000 units. Figure 15.12 shows the result of converting the chart in Figure 15.11 to a chart with a logarithmic y-axis.

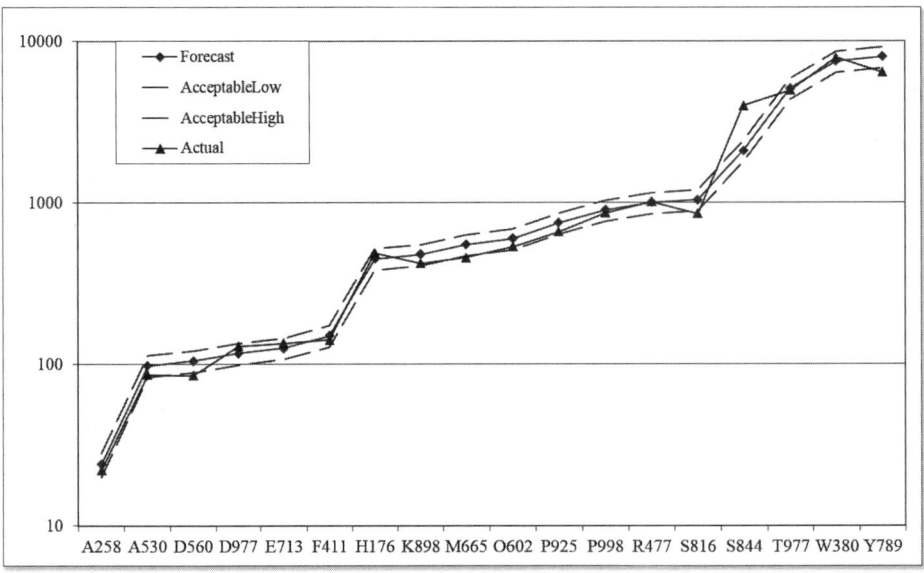

Figure 15.12
You can change the y-axis to show a logarithmic scale, and the detail of the smaller quantities becomes clear.

Basically, a logarithm raises a number—the base—to a certain power. In the case of the chart in Figure 15.12, each plot on the chart is located at a certain power of 10. In Figure 15.13, columns B:E show the original numbers for the table. Columns G:J show the base-10 logarithm for the number.

	A	B	C	D	E	F	G	H	I	J
			Acceptable	Acceptable						
1	Product	Forecast	Low	High	Actual		LOG10	LOG10	LOG10	LOG10
2	A258	24	20	28	22		1.38021	1.30103	1.44716	1.34242
3	A530	98	83	113	86		1.99123	1.91908	2.05308	1.9345
4	D560	105	89	121	85		2.02119	1.94939	2.08279	1.92942
5	D977	117	99	135	129		2.06819	1.99564	2.13033	2.11059
6	E713	126	107	145	135		2.10037	2.02938	2.16137	2.13033
7	F411	150	128	173	141		2.17609	2.10721	2.23805	2.14922
8	H176	450	383	518	486		2.65321	2.5832	2.71433	2.68664
9	K898	480	408	552	422		2.68124	2.61066	2.74194	2.62531
10	M665	550	468	633	457		2.74036	2.67025	2.8014	2.65992
11	O602	600	510	690	534		2.77815	2.70757	2.83885	2.72754
12	P925	750	638	863	660		2.87506	2.80482	2.93601	2.81954
13	P998	900	765	1035	864		2.95424	2.88366	3.01494	2.93651
14	R477	1000	850	1150	1010		3	2.92942	3.0607	3.00432
15	S816	1040	884	1196	853		3.01703	2.94645	3.07773	2.93095
16	S844	2100	1785	2415	3995		3.32222	3.25164	3.38292	3.60152
17	T977	5100	4335	5865	4947		3.70757	3.63699	3.76827	3.69434
18	W380	7500	6375	8625	7875		3.87506	3.80448	3.93576	3.89625
19	Y789	8000	6800	9200	6400		3.90309	3.83251	3.96379	3.80618
20										

fx =LOG10(B2)

Figure 15.13
The table in G:J is the base-10 logarithm of the numbers in B:E.

10^1 is 10. 10^2 is 100. The number in cell B3 is 98. This logarithm is going to be between 1 and 2, and probably much closer to 2. The formula in cell G3 reveals that if 10 is raised to the 1.99126th power, you get 98.

As another example, 10^2 is 100, and 10^3 is 1,000. Cell B17 contains 5,100. The logarithm for 5,100 is somewhere between 2 and 3. The formula in cell G17, =LOG10(B17), shows that 10^3.708 results in 5,100.

Excel offers four functions for dealing with logarithms. LOG10 calculates the logarithms based on raising 10 to a certain power. LOG can calculate the logarithm for any base. LN and EXP deal with a special logarithm.

Syntax:

LOG10(*number*)

The LOG10 function returns the base-10 logarithm of a number. The argument *number* is the positive real number for which you want the base-10 logarithm.

Using LOG to Calculate Logarithms for Any Base

Excel makes it simple to calculate the logarithm for any base, using the LOG function. Cell B2 of Figure 15.14 contains the formula =LOG(A2,2) to express the number in column A as a base-2 logarithm. Cell E2 contains the formula =LOG(D2,5) to express the number in column E as a base-5 logarithm.

Figure 15.14
The LOG function can calculate a logarithm with any base.

	A	B	C	D	E	F	G	H	I	J	K	L
	K2	▾	:	×	✓	*fx*	=LOG($J$1,J2)					
1	**Number**	=LOG(A2,2)		**Number**	=LOG(D2,5)		**Number**	=LOG(G2,12)		123456	=LOG($J$1,J2)	
2	2	1		5	1		12	1		2	16.9136	
3	4	2		25	2		144	2		3	10.6713	
4	8	3		125	3		1728	3		4	8.45682	
5	16	4		625	4		20736	4		5	7.28431	
6	32	5		3125	5		248832	5		6	6.54309	
7	64	6		15625	6					7	6.02476	
8	128	7		15630	6.0002					8	5.63788	
9	256	8		1250	4.43068					9	5.33566	
10	512	9		15630	6.0002					10	5.09151	
11	1024	10		3750	5.11328					11	4.88914	
12	2048	11		15750	6.00495					12	4.71794	
13	4096	12										
14	2080	11.02237										
15												

Syntax:

LOG(*number*,*base*)

The LOG function returns the logarithm of a number to the specified base. It takes the following arguments:

- *number*—This is the positive real number for which you want the logarithm.

- *base*—This is the base of the logarithm. If *base* is omitted, it is assumed to be 10.

Little TwelveToes

Here is a simple test to see whether you attended the same Saturday morning school that I did. Fill in this phrase: "Conjunction Junction, _____ _____ _____?"

If you instinctively sang, "What's Your Function?" then you are a fellow alumnus of the school of Tom Yohe and David McCall. From 1973 until 1985, ABC snuck in educational cartoons in the middle of its other Saturday morning fare. Known collectively as *School House Rock*, these segments taught children multiplication tables, grammar, science facts, and American history.

Perhaps the most ambitious segment was the "Multiplication Rock" segment, about an alien planet where everyone had 12 toes. In this system, there are new digits after 9: "dek, el, do." In addition, the 12—do—is written 1-0. Get it?" This little 60-second cartoon and jingle introduced a generation of children to the concept of a base-12 numbering system in a way that made perfect sense.

Column H of Figure 15.14 uses =LOG(x,12) to express logarithms in a base-12 system.

Using LN and EXP to Calculate Natural Logarithms

Only two logarithms are used frequently in science. The first is the base-10 logarithm that was discussed previously. The second is a natural logarithm where numbers are expressed as a power of the number e. e is a special number. You can calculate e by adding up all the numbers in the series of $1 + [1 / (1!)] + [1 / (2!)] + [1 / (3!)] + [1 / (4!)] + [1 / (5!)] + [1 / (6!)] + [1 / (7!)] + [1 / (8!)] + [1 / (9!)] + [1 / (10!)] + \ldots$.

Luckily, 10! is 3.7 million, so 1 / (10!) is a very small number: 0.000000275573. After about 1 / (17!), the numbers are small enough that they are beyond Excel's 15-digit precision.

This infinite series converges toward a number around 2.718281. This number is known as the *transcendental number*, which is abbreviated as e. Logarithms for base e are known as natural logarithms. You can calculate e in Excel by using a range such as the one shown in A4:C22 in Figure 15.15, or you can use =EXP(1), as shown in cell C24.

Figure 15.15
The calculation of e is fairly complex, as shown in A4:C22. Instead, you can use =EXP(1).

| C24 | ▼ | : | × | ✓ | f_x | =EXP(1) |

	A	B	C
1	$e = 1 + (1/1!) + (1/2!) + (1/3!) + (1/4!) + (1/5!) + ...$		
2			
3	**x**	**FACT(x)**	**1/Fact(x)**
4	0	1	1.00000000000000000000
5	1	1	1.00000000000000000000
6	2	2	0.50000000000000000000
7	3	6	0.16666666666666700000
8	4	24	0.04166666666666670000
9	5	120	0.00833333333333333000
10	6	720	0.00138888888888889000
11	7	5040	0.00019841269841269800
12	8	40320	0.00002480158730158730
13	9	362880	0.00000275573192239859
14	10	3628800	0.00000027557319223986
15	11	39916800	0.00000002505210838544
16	12	479001600	0.00000000208767569879
17	13	6227020800	0.00000000016059043837
18	14	87178291200	0.00000000001147074560
19	15	1,307,674,368,000	0.00000000000076471637
20	16	20,922,789,888,000	0.00000000000004779477
21	17	355,687,428,096,000	0.00000000000000281146
22		Total:	2.71828182845905000000
23			
24		=EXP(1)	2.71828182845905000000

Natural logarithms are very popular in science because anything with a constant rate of growth follows a curve described by natural logarithms. Radioactive isotopes, for example, decay along a curve described by natural logarithms.

Whereas common logarithms with base 10 are called *logs*, natural logarithms with base e are written as *ln*, which is often pronounced *lon*. You calculate natural logarithms by using the LN function.

Syntax:

LN(*number*)

The LN function returns the natural logarithm of a number. Natural logarithms are based on the constant e, which is 2.71828182845905. The argument *number* is the positive real number for which you want a natural logarithm.

With common logarithms, you can convert the logarithm back to the original number by using =10^x. However, it is fairly difficult to write 2.71828182845905^x. Therefore, Excel provides the function EXP to raise e to any power.

Syntax:

EXP(*number*)

The EXP function returns e raised to the power of *number*. The constant e equals 2.71828182845905, the base of the natural logarithm. The argument *number* is the exponent applied to the base e.

To calculate powers of other bases, you use the exponentiation operator (^). EXP is the inverse of LN, the natural logarithm of *number*.

To convert the logarithms in column B in Figure 15.16, use EXP(B2), as shown in column C.

G6	▼	:	×	✓	fx	=EXP(F6)			
◢	A	B	C	D	E	F	G	H	
1	x	LN(x)	EXP(b)						
2	2	0.69315	2		Question: What is 4.215 * 7.643?				
3	4	1.38629	4		**Number**	LN			
4	5	1.60944	5		4.215	1.43865	=LN(E4)		
5	8	2.07944	8		7.643	2.03379	=LN(E5)		
6	9	2.19722	9		Total	3.47244	32.2152	=EXP(F6)	
7	10	2.30259	10						
8	13	2.56495	13		4.215	7.643	32.2152	=F8*E8	
9	14	2.63906	14						
10	19	2.94444	19		Question: What is 27.453 / 4.873?				
11					**Number**	LN			
12		9			27.453	3.31248	=LN(E12)		
13		2.19722	=LOG(B12,EXP(1))		4.873	1.58371	=LN(E13)		
14		2.19722	=LN(B12)		**Difference**	1.72877	=F12-F13		
15		9	=EXP(1)^B14		**EXP(F14)**	5.6337	=EXP(F14)		
16									
17						27.453			
18						4.873			
19					Check	5.6337	=F17/F18		
20									

Figure 15.16
To reverse the LN function, you use EXP.

The decay of radioactive isotopes follows a natural logarithmic curve. The basic formula is as follows:

Number of atoms after time T = Original number of atoms × e^(T × *Constant*).

For Radium 226, the constant is −0.000436. The table in Figure 15.17 shows how to raise e to a certain power by using a table of years. You can see that about half the original sample will have decayed after 1,500 years!

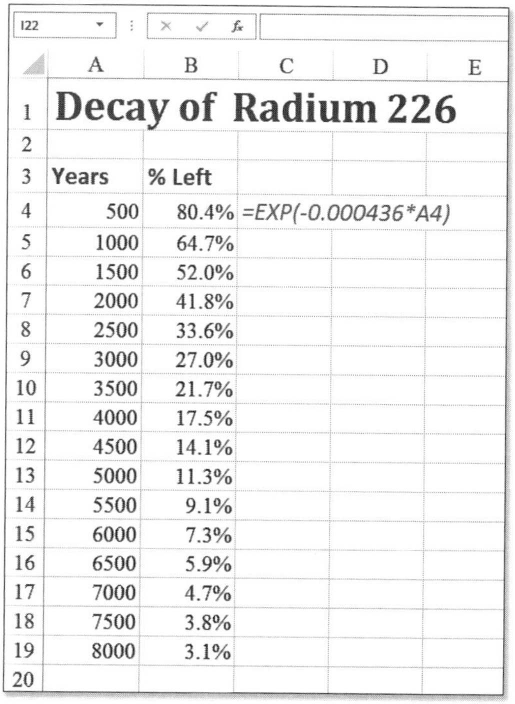

Figure 15.17
For constant growth or decay problems, you can use EXP to raise e to a power.

	A	B	C	D	E
1	**Decay of Radium 226**				
2					
3	**Years**	**% Left**			
4	500	80.4%	=EXP(-0.000436*A4)		
5	1000	64.7%			
6	1500	52.0%			
7	2000	41.8%			
8	2500	33.6%			
9	3000	27.0%			
10	3500	21.7%			
11	4000	17.5%			
12	4500	14.1%			
13	5000	11.3%			
14	5500	9.1%			
15	6000	7.3%			
16	6500	5.9%			
17	7000	4.7%			
18	7500	3.8%			
19	8000	3.1%			
20					

Multiplying and Dividing by Adding and Subtracting

Think about the problem $3\char94 4 \times 3\char94 7$. In this problem, both of the base numbers are the same. The result is $3\char94(7+4)$, or $3\char94 11$.

Similarly, if you want to divide $7\char94 21$ by $7\char94 5$, you can find the solution by subtracting: $7\char94(21 - 5)$, or $7\char94 16$.

In Figure 15.16, E2:H8 walks through a long-winding way of multiplying using only LN and addition. To multiply 4.215 by 7.643, you take the LN of each number in cells F4 and F5. You can then add these numbers in cell F6. The formula in cell G6 uses EXP to find the actual answer of 32.2152. Now, I realize that this all seems ridiculous because if you are doing this, you obviously have Excel and can just do the multiplication directly, as shown in cell G8. However, this is an interesting property of logarithms.

Working with Imaginary Numbers

Multiply the number 2 by itself: =2^2 is 4. The square root of 4 is 2. Multiply the number –2 by itself: =-2^2 is also 4. Excel says =SQRT(4) is 2, but clearly it can also be –2 as well.

So, what is the square root of –4? There is no real number that produces –4 when multiplied by itself. Excel says that =SQRT(-4) is #NUM!.

To deal with theoretical numbers where the square root is a negative number, mathematicians invented the concept of the imaginary number, i. This number is the square root of –1. At first, no one was sure if this was relevant, so these numbers were given the name *imaginary numbers*. Since their invention, imaginary numbers have been discovered to have real-world applications. They are used extensively in the physics of electrical circuits. The name *imaginary* continues to stick.

In the parlance of imaginary numbers, the square root of –4 is 2i.

Often, the answer to a problem appears as an expression such as $a + b \times i$. In this case, a and b are both real numbers. This expression is a complex number. You can plot complex numbers on a coordinate graph, plotting a along the x-axis and b along the y-axis, and then do trigonometry with imaginary numbers.

Excel offers 17 functions that deal with imaginary, or complex, numbers: COMPLEX, IMREAL, IMAGINARY, IMSUM, IMPRODUCT, IMDIV, IMABS, IMARGUMENT, IMCONJUGATE, IMCOSH, IMCOT, IMCSC, IMCSCH, IMSEC, IMSECH, IMSINH, and IMTAN.

Using COMPLEX to Convert a and b into a Complex Number

It is hard to deal with complex numbers in Excel because they are basically text. Think about how you can store 5 + 2*i* in a cell; it will be difficult to do.

You can create a large range of complex numbers in the form $a + bi$ if you have ranges of values for a and b. In Figure 15.18, pairs of a and b values are stored in the first two columns of a worksheet. The COMPLEX function in column C converts these numbers to complex numbers.

Syntax:

COMPLEX(*real_num*,*i_num*,*suffix*)

The COMPLEX function converts real and imaginary coefficients into a complex number in the form $x + yi$ or $x + yj$. This function takes the following arguments:

- *real_num*—This is the real coefficient of the complex number.

- *i_num*—This is the imaginary coefficient of the complex number.

- *suffix*—This is the suffix for the imaginary component of the complex number. If omitted, the suffix is assumed to be i.

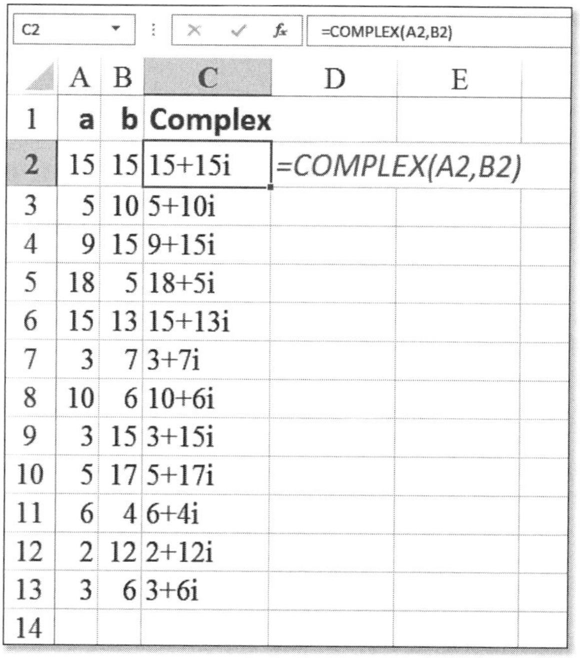

Figure 15.18
The COMPLEX function builds text results in column C. The eight IM functions can do math on these text values.

▲	A	B	C	D	E
1	a	b	Complex		
2	15	15	15+15i	=COMPLEX(A2,B2)	
3	5	10	5+10i		
4	9	15	9+15i		
5	18	5	18+5i		
6	15	13	15+13i		
7	3	7	3+7i		
8	10	6	10+6i		
9	3	15	3+15i		
10	5	17	5+17i		
11	6	4	6+4i		
12	2	12	2+12i		
13	3	6	3+6i		
14					

C2 ▾ : × ✓ f_x =COMPLEX(A2,B2)

If *real_num* is nonnumeric, COMPLEX returns a #VALUE! error. If *i_num* is nonnumeric, COMPLEX returns a #VALUE! error. If *suffix* is neither *i* nor *j*, COMPLEX returns a #VALUE! error.

Using IMREAL and IMAGINARY to Break Apart Complex Numbers

Complex numbers are in the form $a + bi$, where i is the imaginary square root of -1. Excel stores all complex numbers as text. If you use any of the IM functions to generate new complex numbers, you can extract the numbers a and b by using IMREAL and IMAGINARY.

In Figure 15.19, column A contains a range of complex numbers. The formulas in column B extract the real number portion of the complex number. The formulas in column C extract the value that is multiplied by i in the complex number.

Syntax:

IMREAL(*inumber*)

The IMREAL function returns the real coefficient of a complex number in $x + yi$ or $x + yj$ text format. The argument *inumber* is a complex number for which you want the real coefficient.

If *inumber* is not in the form $x + yi$ or $x + yj$, IMREAL returns a #NUM! error.

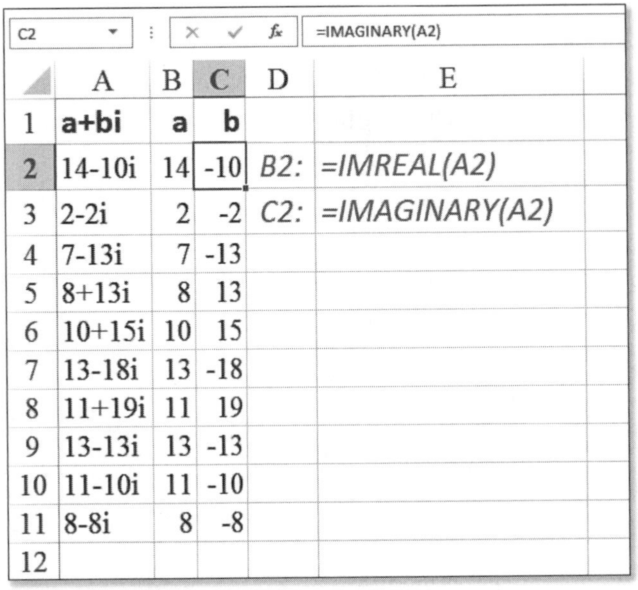

▲	A	B	C	D	E
1	**a+bi**	**a**	**b**		
2	14-10i	14	-10	B2:	=IMREAL(A2)
3	2-2i	2	-2	C2:	=IMAGINARY(A2)
4	7-13i	7	-13		
5	8+13i	8	13		
6	10+15i	10	15		
7	13-18i	13	-18		
8	11+19i	11	19		
9	13-13i	13	-13		
10	11-10i	11	-10		
11	8-8i	8	-8		
12					

C2 | ▼ | : | × ✓ f_x | =IMAGINARY(A2)

Figure 15.19
IMREAL and IMAGINARY break a complex number expression in the form a + bi into the numbers for a and b.

Syntax:

IMAGINARY(*inumber*)

The IMAGINARY function returns the imaginary coefficient of a complex number in $x + yi$ or $x + yj$ text format. The argument *inumber* is a complex number for which you want the imaginary coefficient.

If *inumber* is not in the form $x + yi$ or $x + yj$, IMAGINARY returns a #NUM! error.

Using IMSUM to Add Complex Numbers

Figure 15.20 shows two columns of complex numbers. A complex number is in the form $a + bi$. Both a and b are real numbers. The letter i is the imaginary square root of -1. Note that all of the "numbers" stored in columns A and B are stored as text.

To add $(a + bi) + (c + di)$, you use the formula $(a + b) + (c + d)\,i$. You use IMSUM to calculate this.

Syntax:

IMSUM(*inumber1*,*inumber2*,...)

The IMSUM function returns the sum of two or more complex numbers in $x + yi$ or $x + yj$ text format. The arguments *inumber1*,*inumber2*,... are 1 to 255 complex numbers to add.

If any argument is not in the form $x + yi$ or $x + yj$, IMSUM returns a #NUM! error.

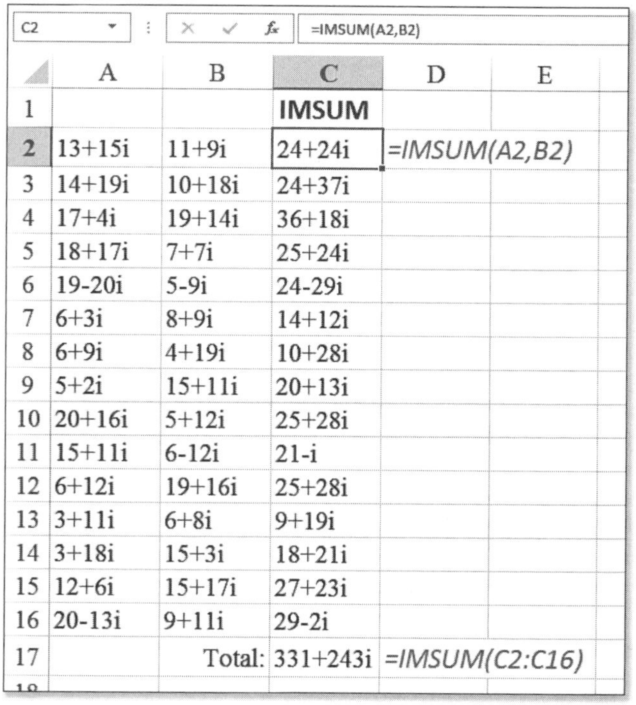

Figure 15.20
Even though all the complex numbers in columns A and B are text, the IMSUM function adds them with ease.

	A	B	C	D	E
				=IMSUM(A2,B2)	
1			**IMSUM**		
2	13+15i	11+9i	24+24i	=IMSUM(A2,B2)	
3	14+19i	10+18i	24+37i		
4	17+4i	19+14i	36+18i		
5	18+17i	7+7i	25+24i		
6	19-20i	5-9i	24-29i		
7	6+3i	8+9i	14+12i		
8	6+9i	4+19i	10+28i		
9	5+2i	15+11i	20+13i		
10	20+16i	5+12i	25+28i		
11	15+11i	6-12i	21-i		
12	6+12i	19+16i	25+28i		
13	3+11i	6+8i	9+19i		
14	3+18i	15+3i	18+21i		
15	12+6i	15+17i	27+23i		
16	20-13i	9+11i	29-2i		
17		Total:	331+243i	=IMSUM(C2:C16)	

Using IMSUB, IMPRODUCT, and IMDIV to Perform Basic Math on Complex Numbers

As with the IMSUM function, similar rules exist for subtracting, multiplying, and dividing complex numbers. These are numbers stored as text in the form $a + bi$, where the constant i is an imaginary number representing the square root of −1. These are the rules for the IMSUB, IMPRODUCT, and IMDIV functions:

- To subtract complex numbers, you use IMSUB. The formula for $(a + bi) − (c + di)$ is $(a − c) + (b − d)\,i$.

- To multiply complex numbers, you use IMPRODUCT. The formula for $(a + bi) \times (c + di)$ is $(ac − bd) + (ad + bc)\,i$.

- To divide complex numbers, you use IMDIV. The formula for $(a + bi) / (c + di)$ is $[(ac + bd) + (bc − ad)\,i] / (c^2 + d^2)$.

Figure 15.21 shows the results of the basic math functions for complex numbers.

D2 =IMPRODUCT(A2,B2)

	A	B	C	D	E
1			IMSUB	IMPRODUCT	IMDIV
2	19-18i	12+11i	7-29i	426-7i	0.113207547169811-1.60377358490566i
3	9+2i	17+5i	-8-3i	143+79i	0.519108280254777-0.035031847133758i
4	5-15i	5-9i	-6i	-110-120i	1.50943396226415-0.283018867924528i
5	14+20i	13-13i	1+33i	442+78i	-0.230769230769231+1.30769230769231i
6	17+4i	2+3i	15+i	22+59i	3.53846153846154-3.30769230769231i
7	18-18i	17+16i	1-34i	594-18i	0.0330275229357798-1.08990825688073i
8	13+1i	19+5i	-6-4i	242+84i	0.652849740932643-0.119170984455959i
9	20-9i	18+5i	2-14i	405-62i	0.902578796561605-0.750716332378223i
10	18+7i	11+7i	7	149+203i	1.45294117647059-0.288235294117647i
11	20+8i	12+10i	8-2i	160+296i	1.31147540983607-0.426229508196721i
12					

Figure 15.21
You can perform basic math with complex numbers.

Syntax:

`IMSUB(`*`inumber1`*`,`*`inumber2`*`)`

The `IMSUB` function returns the difference between two complex numbers in $x + yi$ or $x + yj$ text format. This function takes the following arguments:

- ***`inumber1`***—This is the complex number from which to subtract *`inumber2`*.
- ***`inumber2`***—This is the complex number to subtract from *`inumber1`*.

If either number is not in the form $x + yi$ or $x + yj$, `IMSUB` returns a `#NUM!` error.

Syntax:

`IMPRODUCT(`*`inumber1`*`,`*`inumber2`*`,...)`

The `IMPRODUCT` function returns the product of 2 to 255 complex numbers in $x + yi$ or $x + yj$ text format. The arguments *`inumber1, inumber2,...`* are 1 to 255 complex numbers to multiply.

If *`inumber1`* or *`inumber2`* is not in the form $x + yi$ or $x + yj$, `IMPRODUCT` returns a `#NUM!` error.

Syntax:

`IMDIV(`*`inumber1`*`,`*`inumber2`*`)`

The `IMDIV` function returns the quotient of two complex numbers in $x + yi$ or $x + yj$ text format. This function takes the following arguments:

- ***`inumber1`***—This is the complex numerator or dividend.
- ***`inumber2`***—This is the complex denominator or divisor.

If *`inumber1`* or *`inumber2`* is not in the form $x + yi$ or $x + yj$, `IMDIV` returns a `#NUM!` error.

Using IMABS to Find the Distance from the Origin to a Complex Number

A complex number is in the form $a + bi$, where i is an imaginary number representing the square root of -1. To plot complex numbers on a Cartesian grid, you use a for the x-axis and b for the y-axis.

The IMABS function calculates the distance from the (0, 0) origin in the grid. If you have a complex number in the form $a + bi$, the formula for an absolute value is =SQRT(a^2+b^2). This results in a real number.

Syntax:

IMABS(*inumber*)

The IMABS function returns the absolute value, or modulus, of a complex number in $x + yi$ or $x + yj$ text format. The argument *inumber* is a complex number for which you want the absolute value.

If *inumber* is not in the form $x + yi$ or $x + yj$, IMABS returns a #NUM! error.

Figure 15.22 shows IMABS functions for several complex numbers. Note that the result of IMABS(a+bi) is equal to IMABS(b+ai).

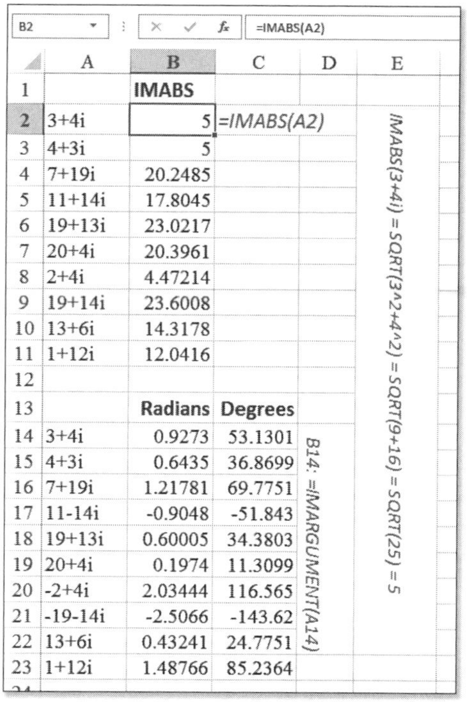

Figure 15.22
Taking the absolute value of a complex number results in a real number.

	A	B	C	D	E
	B2	▼ : × ✓ *fx* =IMABS(A2)			
1		**IMABS**			
2	3+4i	5	=IMABS(A2)		
3	4+3i	5			
4	7+19i	20.2485			
5	11+14i	17.8045			
6	19+13i	23.0217			
7	20+4i	20.3961			
8	2+4i	4.47214			
9	19+14i	23.6008			
10	13+6i	14.3178			
11	1+12i	12.0416			
12					
13		**Radians**	**Degrees**		
14	3+4i	0.9273	53.1301		
15	4+3i	0.6435	36.8699		
16	7+19i	1.21781	69.7751		
17	11-14i	-0.9048	-51.843		
18	19+13i	0.60005	34.3803		
19	20+4i	0.1974	11.3099		
20	-2+4i	2.03444	116.565		
21	-19-14i	-2.5066	-143.62		
22	13+6i	0.43241	24.7751		
23	1+12i	1.48766	85.2364		

IMABS(3+4i) = SQRT(3^2+4^2) = SQRT(9+16) = SQRT(25) = 5

B14: =IMARGUMENT(A14)

Using IMARGUMENT to Calculate the Angle to a Complex Number

A complex number is in the form $a + bi$, where i is an imaginary number representing the square root of -1. To plot complex numbers on a Cartesian grid, you use a for the x-axis and b for the y-axis.

The angle to a complex number assumes that the x-axis is 0 and rotates counterclockwise. To find the angle, in radians, to any complex number plotted on a grid, you use IMARGUMENT.

B14:B23 in Figure 15.22 shows the angle for several complex numbers.

Syntax:

IMARGUMENT(*inumber*)

The IMARGUMENT function returns the angle (Θ) for an imaginary number. *inumber* is a complex number for which you want to calculate theta.

If *inumber* is not in the form $x + yi$ or $x + yj$, IMARGUMENT returns a #NUM! error.

Using IMCONJUGATE to Reverse the Sign of an Imaginary Component

A complex number is in the form $a + bi$, where i is an imaginary number representing the square root of -1. To plot complex numbers on a Cartesian grid, you use a for the x-axis and b for the y-axis.

The IMCONJUGATE function creates a mirror image of a point, flipped across the x-axis. Put another way, the function changes the sign of the imaginary component. For example, $10 + 3i$ becomes $10 - 3i$, and $10 - 3i$ becomes $10 + 3i$.

Syntax:

IMCONJUGATE(*inumber*)

The IMCONJUGATE function returns the complex conjugate of a complex number in $x + yi$ or $x + yj$ text format. The argument *inumber* is a complex number for which you want the conjugate.

If *inumber* is not in the form $x + yi$ or $x + yj$, IMCONJUGATE returns a #NUM! error.

Figure 15.23 shows the results of several IMCONJUGATE formulas.

Calculating Powers, Logarithms, and Trigonometry Functions with Complex Numbers

The remaining 17 IM functions calculate powers, exponents, logs, and trig functions from complex numbers:

- **IMSQRT**—Calculates the square root of a complex number
- **IMPOWER**—Raises a complex number to a certain power

Figure 15.23
You can reverse the sign of the imaginary component of a complex number with IMCONJUGATE.

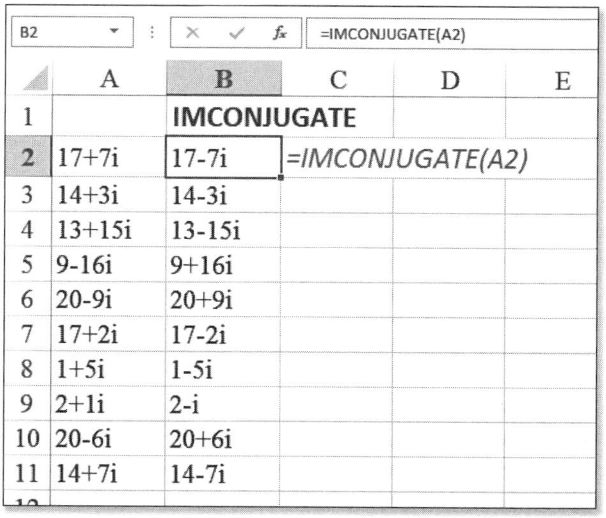

	A	B	C	D	E
B2	▼ : × ✓ *fx*	=IMCONJUGATE(A2)			
1		**IMCONJUGATE**			
2	17+7i	17-7i	*=IMCONJUGATE(A2)*		
3	14+3i	14-3i			
4	13+15i	13-15i			
5	9-16i	9+16i			
6	20-9i	20+9i			
7	17+2i	17-2i			
8	1+5i	1-5i			
9	2+1i	2-i			
10	20-6i	20+6i			
11	14+7i	14-7i			

- **IMLOG10**—Calculates the base-10 logarithm or common logarithm of a complex number

- **IMLOG2**—Calculates the base-2 logarithm of a complex number

- **IMEXP**—Raises the constant e to a complex number

    ➥ *For more information about the IMEXP function,* **see** *"Using LN and EXP to Calculate Natural Logarithms,"* **p. 572.**

- **IMLN**—Calculates the natural log of a complex number

- **IMARGUMENT**—Returns the argument q, an angle expressed in radians

- **IMSIN**—Returns the sine of a complex number

- **IMCOS**—Returns the cosine of a complex number

- **IMTAN**—Returns the tangent of a complex number

- **IMCSC**—Returns the cosecant of a complex number

- **IMSEC**—Returns the secant of a complex number

- **IMCOT**—Returns the cotangent of a complex number

- **IMSINH**—Returns the hyperbolic sin of a complex number

- **IMCOSH**—Returns the hyperbolic cosine of a complex number

- **IMCSCH**—Returns the hyperbolic cosecant of a complex number

- **IMSECH**—Returns the hyperbolic secant of a complex number

Figure 15.24 shows the results of these functions for a complex number.

	A	B	C
1		**10+3i**	
2	=IMSQRT(B1)	3.19689744196702+0.469204917339189i	
3	=IMPOWER(B1,3)	730+873i	
4	=IMLOG10(B1)	1.01871324897031+0.126578077554948i	
5	=IMLOG2(B1)	3.38409216238846+0.420483272026613i	
6	=IMEXP(B1)	-21806.035863485+3108.37503049351i	
7	=IMLN(B1)	2.34567394111457+0.291456794477867i	
8	=IMARGUMENT(B1)	0.291456794	
9	=IMSIN(B2)	-0.0614737139162052-0.485867598193283i	
10	=IMCOS(B2)	-1.11041065397891+0.0268982341131743i	
11	=IMTAN(B1)	0.00451676457829321+0.997968764785854i	
12	=IMCSC(B1)	-0.0544144574063206+0.0835111595554563i	
13	=IMSEC(B1)	-0.083587306041153-0.053926728596906i	
14	=IMCOT(B1)	0.0045350769621522-1.00201484396117i	
15	=IMSINH(B1)	-10903.0179092697+1554.18751845018i	
16	=IMCOSH(B1)	-10903.0179542153+1554.18751204334i	
17	=IMCSCH(B1)	-0.0000898911797926148-0.0000128136769851275i	
18	=IMSECH(B1)	-0.0000898911794515742-0.0000128136768308695i	

Figure 15.24
These functions calculate powers, logs, and trig functions, using text-based complex numbers.

Solving Simultaneous Linear Equations with Matrix Functions

You can use the Solver add-in to solve simultaneous equations. However, Excel also offers three matrix functions that you can use to solve these equations. Although the math involved is beyond the scope of this book, the steps to produce an answer are fairly straightforward.

The following is a problem taken from a math textbook in the Han Dynasty. The solution can be derived by using matrix functions in Excel.

There are three types of grain. Three bundles of the first, two of the second, and one of the third make 39 bushels. Two of the first, three of the second, and one of the third make 34 bushels. One of the first, two of the second, and three of the third make 26 bushels. How many bushels are in the bundles of each type of grain? To solve this problem, follow these steps:

1. Convert the problem's words into algebraic equations. Assuming that the first type of grain is *a*, the second is *b*, and the third is *c*, you have these three equations:

   $3a + 2b + 1c = 39$
   $2a + 3b + 1c = 34$
   $1a + 2b + 3c = 26$

2. In Excel, set up three columns with headings a, b, and c. In the three rows below these columns, enter the coefficients from each equation. For example, the first row contains 3, 2, and 1. The second row contains 2, 3, and 1. The third row contains 1, 2, and 3. In Figure 15.25, the range C5:E7 contains the matrix of coefficients.

3. In another range, enter a matrix of the answers for each equation. This range should be one column wide by three rows tall. The cells should contain 39, 34, and 26. In Figure 15.25, this range is in G5:G7.

Figure 15.25
Amazingly, Excel can solve simultaneous equations by using a pair of matrix functions.

| I5 | ▼ | : | × | ✓ | fx | {=MMULT(C10:E12,G5:G7)} |

	A	B	C	D	E	F	G	H	I	J	K	L	M
1	3a + 2b + 1c = 39												
2	2a + 3b + 1c = 34												
3	1a + 2b + 3c = 26												
4			a	b	c		Ans		Answers	Check:			
5			3	2	1		39	a=	9.25		39	=3*I5+2*I6+1*I7	
6			2	3	1		34	b=	4.25		34	=2*I5+3*I6+1*I7	
7			1	2	3		26	c=	2.75		26	=1*I5+2*I6+3*I7	
8													
9			MINVERSE										
10			0.583	-0.33	-0								
11			-0.42	0.67	-0								
12			0.083	-0.33	0								
13													
14			MMULT										
15			1	0	0								
16			0	1	0								
17			0	0	1								
18													

4. Select a new range that is the same size as the range in step 2. This range will hold an intermediate step with the inverse matrix. In the new range, type the formula =**MINVERSE(C5:E7)**. Do not press Enter. Instead, hold down Ctrl+Shift while you press Enter. This key combination tells Excel to calculate an array and enter the results in all the selected cells (see range C10:E12 in Figure 15.25). The inverse of an array is an array that, when multiplied by the original array, produces a *unit array*—an array with ones along the diagonal and zeros everywhere else. In Figure 15.25, the range C15:E17 contains the array formula =MMULT(C5:E7,C10:E12). The result of the

MMULT operation is indeed a matrix with a one along the diagonal and zeros everywhere else, as shown in Figure 15.25. Array formulas are special multicell formulas that are entered using Ctrl+Shift+Enter.

5. Select a range that is three cells high and one column wide. In this column, enter an MMULT function that multiplies the MINVERSE array from step 4 by the answers in step 3. In Figure 15.25, the formula in I5:I7 is =MMULT(C10:E12,G5:G7). Again, you must select all three cells before entering this formula. Next, you must hold down Ctrl+Shift+Enter to enter the formula. The results in cells I5, I6, and I7 stand for the values of a, b, and c, respectively.

6. To make sure that everything worked, set up test formulas in column K. For example, the test formula in K5 checks to see if $3a+2b+1c$ equals 39.

This entire process is fairly amazing. All the formulas are live formulas. If you change one of the input variables in any of the ranges, all the matrix functions instantly recalculate to solve the three simultaneous equations.

 **Tip**

An array can be entered in curly braces and is called an *array constant*. Each comma in the array constant indicates that Excel should move to the next column in the current row. Each semicolon indicates that Excel should move to the next row. To picture the actual shape of {1,2,3;4,5,6;7,8,9}, picture the value 1 in A1, 2 in B1, 3 in C1, 4 in A2, and so on down to 9 in C3.

Syntax:

MINVERSE(*array*)

The MINVERSE function returns the inverse matrix for the matrix stored in an array. The argument *array* is a numeric array with an equal number of rows and columns. The *array* can be given as a cell range such as A1:C3. It can also be given as an array constant such as {1,2,3;4,5,6;7,8,9}. Finally, it can be given as a name for either of these.

You must enter formulas that return arrays as array formulas. To indicate that a formula is an array formula, type the formula and then hold down Ctrl and Shift while pressing Enter.

Inverse matrices, like determinants, are generally used for solving systems of mathematical equations that involve several variables. The product of a matrix and its inverse is the identity matrix—the square array in which the diagonal values equal 1 and all other values equal 0.

As an example of how a two-row, two-column matrix is calculated, suppose that the range A1:B2 contains the letters a, b, c, and d, which represent any four numbers. Table 15.5 shows the inverse of the matrix A1:B2.

 Note

If any cells in array are empty or contain text, MINVERSE returns a #VALUE! error. MINVERSE also returns a #VALUE! error if *array* does not have an equal number of rows and columns.

Table 15.5   Inverse of the Matrix Shown in A1:B2 in Figure 15.26

	Column A	Column B
Row 1	d/(a*d–b*c)	b/(b*c–a*d)
Row 2	c/(b*c–a*d)	a/(a*d–b*c)

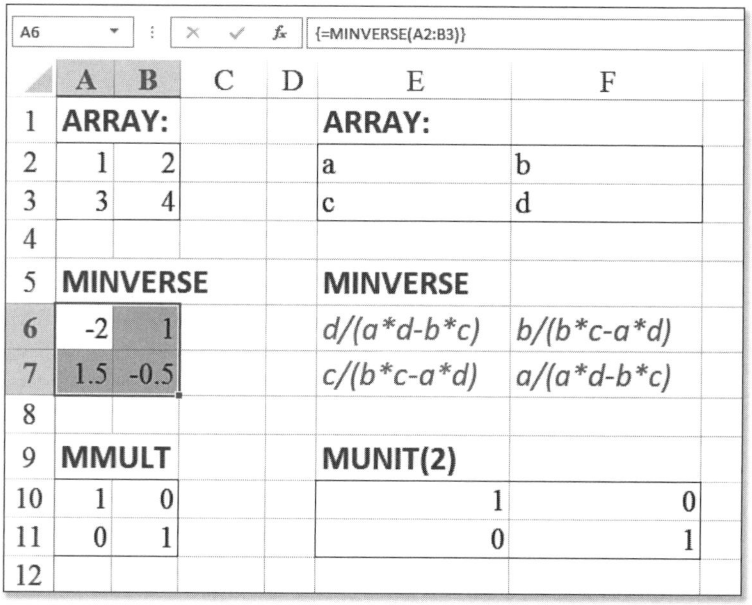

Figure 15.26
Range A6:B7 contains the
MINVERSE of the original array.
When you multiply an array
and its MINVERSE array, the
resulting array in A10:B11 contains 1's along the diagonal.

MINVERSE is calculated to an accuracy of approximately 16 digits, which might lead to a small numeric error when the cancellation is not complete. Thus, when you use MMULT on this array with the original array, you might find 0.00000000000001 instead of 0 in some cells.

Some square matrices cannot be inverted and return a #NUM! error with MINVERSE. The determinant for a noninvertible matrix is 0.

The MUNIT function is new in Excel 2013. It returns a *unit matrix* (also known as an *identity matrix*). Although Figure 15.26 shows the results of a 2×2 unit matrix in cells E10:F11, the more common use would be to use MUNIT to spawn a unit matrix as one argument of the MMULT function.

For example, to return the first column of a matrix in A2:C4, you could select a three-row-by-one-column range, type =MMULT(A2:C4,MUNIT(3)), and press Ctrl+Shift+Enter.

To return the first row of a 4×4 matrix in A2:D5, select a one-row-by-four-column range. Type =MMULT(A2:D5,MUNIT(4)) and press Ctrl+Shift+Enter.

Syntax:

MUNIT(*dimension*)

The MUNIT function returns the unit matrix (also known as identity matrix) of the size *dimension* × *dimension*.

Using =MUNIT(10) returns a 10×10 array of cells. The cells down the diagonal from top left to bottom right are 1's. All other cells are 0's.

When you enter a single MUNIT function in a range of cells, complete the formula by pressing Ctrl+Shift+Enter.

In previous versions of Excel, you might have tried to generate an identity matrix using MMULT(MINVERSE(A1:C3),A1:C3). The answer might require more precision than Excel is able to handle, and you would end up with something about 14 decimal places off from 1. Using MUNIT(3) is a far safer way to return the exact identity matrix.

The MMULT function multiplies two arrays. The basic logic is that the top-left cell of the resulting array is the sum of multiplying the first row of array 1 by the first column of array 2. Figure 15.27 shows the rest of the rules for a 2×2 matrix.

Syntax:

MMULT(*array1*,*array2*)

The MMULT function returns the matrix product of two arrays. The result is an array with the same number of rows as *array1* and the same number of columns as *array2*.

The arguments *array1* and *array2* are the arrays you want to multiply. The number of columns in *array1* must be the same as the number of rows in *array2*, and both arrays must contain only numbers. *array1* and *array2* can be given as cell ranges, array constants, or references. If any cells are empty or contain text, or if the number of columns in *array1* is different from the number of rows in *array2*, MMULT returns a #VALUE! error.

In Figure 15.27, A2:B3 contains array A. A6:B7 contains array B. The result of the MMULT formula, array M, is in A10:B11. The rules for the calculation of each cell in M are shown in D2:D5. The actual formulas are shown in D10:D13.

Using MDETERM to Determine Whether a Simultaneous Equation Has a Solution

If your matrix of simultaneous equations is square, Excel can calculate a determinant of the array by using MDETERM. The determinant returns a single number, which means this function does not need to be entered as an array. If the determinant of an array is nonzero, the simultaneous equation has a solution.

Figure 15.28 shows the calculation for the determinant of a 2×2 matrix.

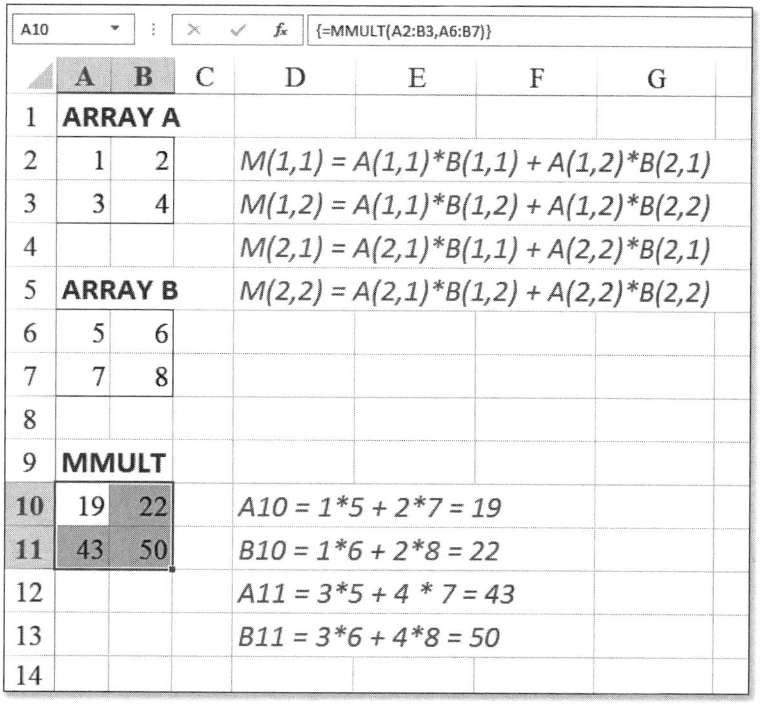

Figure 15.27
The MMULT function performs matrix multiplication.

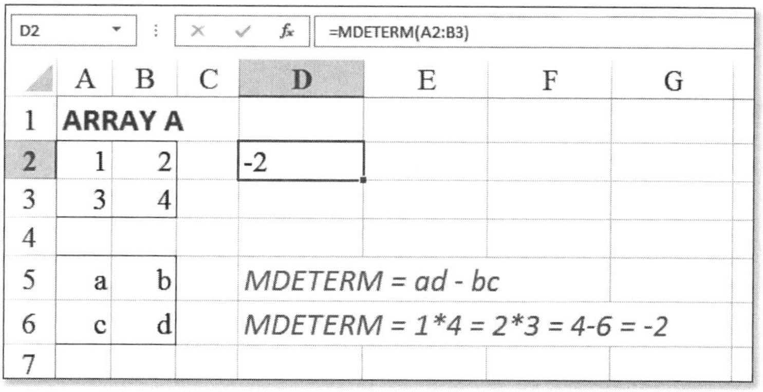

| A10 | ▾ | ⋮ | × | ✓ | *fx* | {=MMULT(A2:B3,A6:B7)} |

▲	A	B	C	D	E	F	G
1	**ARRAY A**						
2	1	2		$M(1,1) = A(1,1)*B(1,1) + A(1,2)*B(2,1)$			
3	3	4		$M(1,2) = A(1,1)*B(1,2) + A(1,2)*B(2,2)$			
4				$M(2,1) = A(2,1)*B(1,1) + A(2,2)*B(2,1)$			
5	**ARRAY B**			$M(2,2) = A(2,1)*B(1,2) + A(2,2)*B(2,2)$			
6	5	6					
7	7	8					
8							
9	**MMULT**						
10	19	22		$A10 = 1*5 + 2*7 = 19$			
11	43	50		$B10 = 1*6 + 2*8 = 22$			
12				$A11 = 3*5 + 4 * 7 = 43$			
13				$B11 = 3*6 + 4*8 = 50$			
14							

Figure 15.28
MDETERM returns the determinant of any square array. Determinants that are nonzero indicate that the simultaneous equations have a solution.

| D2 | ▾ | ⋮ | × | ✓ | *fx* | =MDETERM(A2:B3) |

▲	A	B	C	D	E	F	G
1	**ARRAY A**						
2	1	2		-2			
3	3	4					
4							
5	a	b		$MDETERM = ad - bc$			
6	c	d		$MDETERM = 1*4 = 2*3 = 4-6 = -2$			
7							

Syntax:

MDETERM(*array*)

The MDETERM function returns the matrix determinant of an array. The argument *array* is a numeric array with an equal number of rows and columns. The *array* can be given as a cell range such as A1:C3; an array constant such as {1,2,3;4,5,6;7,8,9}; or a name to either of these. If any cells in *array* are empty or contain text, MDETERM returns a #VALUE! error. MDETERM also returns #VALUE! if *array* does not have an equal number of rows and columns.

The matrix determinant is a number derived from the values in *array*. For a three-row, three-column array, A1:C3, the determinant is defined as follows:

MDETERM(A1:C3) = A1*(B2*C3-B3*C2) + A2*(B3*C1-B1*C3) + A3*(B1*C2-B2*C1)

You generally use matrix determinants for solving systems of mathematical equations that involve several variables.

MDETERM is calculated with an accuracy of approximately 16 digits, which might lead to a small numeric error when the calculation is not complete. For example, the determinant of a singular matrix might differ from zero by $1E - 16$.

Figure 15.28 shows a MDETERM calculation for a 2×2 array.

Using SERIESSUM to Approximate a Function with a Power Series

There are situations in mathematics in which a value can be approximated by summing many factors in a series. If the series gets progressively smaller, such as 1/2, 1/3, 1/4, 1/5, 1/6, 1/7, the numbers eventually become smaller than Excel's 15-digit significance limit. This is referred to as a *power series*. In a power series, the exponent of each term is progressively changed. An example of a power series is $=a_1x^\wedge 1 + a_2x^\wedge 3 + a_3x^\wedge 5 + a_4x^\wedge 7 + a_5x^\wedge 9$.

Figure 15.29 shows a long, complex calculation. The coefficients in column D are found by dividing factorials of even number digits into the number 1 and then multiplying every other value by –1. The value of x is 60 degrees, or PI() / 3. The exponents shown in column E increase from 0 to 16 by 2's. In column F, you raise B1 to the power in column E. In column G, you multiply column D by column F. Finally, you add up all the values in column G to arrive at 0.5, which is a really good approximation of the cosine of 60 degrees.

This example is rather trivial because Excel offers a COS function. However, other functions use a power series to approximate a function. For example, one SERIESSUM function in B17 replaces all the calculations in columns E, F, and G. The function needs the list of coefficients in column D. In fact, the number of coefficients tells Excel how far to extend the series.

Figure 15.29
The SERIESSUM function can calculate a power series, given a value X, a pattern for the exponents, and a list of coefficients.

B16	▼	:	×	✓	f_x	=SERIESSUM(B1,E4,E5,D4:D12)			

	A	B	C	D	E	F	G	H
1	**X:**	1.047198	=PI()/3					
2								
3	**Even #s**	**Pos/Neg**	**1/A!**	**B*C**	**Exp**	**X^E**	**D*F**	
4	0	1	1.000E+00	1.000E+00	0	1	1.000E+00	
5	2	-1	5.000E-01	-5.000E-01	2	1.09662	-5.483E-01	
6	4	1	4.167E-02	4.167E-02	4	1.20258	5.011E-02	
7	6	-1	1.389E-03	-1.389E-03	6	1.31878	-1.832E-03	
8	8	1	2.480E-05	2.480E-05	8	1.4462	3.587E-05	
9	10	-1	2.756E-07	-2.756E-07	10	1.58594	-4.370E-07	
10	12	1	2.088E-09	2.088E-09	12	1.73918	3.631E-09	
11	14	-1	1.147E-11	-1.147E-11	14	1.90722	-2.188E-11	
12	16	1	4.779E-14	4.779E-14	16	2.0915	9.996E-14	
13							0.50	
14								
15	=SeriesSum(x,n,m,a,a,a,a,a) = a1x^n + a2x^(n+m) + a3x^(n+2m)...							
16		0.5	=SERIESSUM(B1,E4,E5,D4:D12)					
17								

Syntax:

SERIESSUM(*x*,*n*,*m*,*coefficients*)

The SERIESSUM function returns the sum of a power series. Many functions can be approximated by a power series expansion. This function takes the following arguments:

- ***x***—The input value to the power series.

- ***n***—The initial power to which you want to raise **x**.

- ***m***—The step by which to increase **n** for each term in the series.

- ***coefficients***—A set of coefficients by which each successive power of **x** is multiplied. The number of values in **coefficients** determines the number of terms in the power series. For example, if there are three values in **coefficients**, there are three terms in the power series.

If any argument is nonnumeric, SERIESSUM returns a #VALUE! error.

Using `SQRTPI` to Find the Square Root of a Number Multiplied by π

The `SQRTPI` function multiplies a number by π and then takes the square root of the result. In the previous edition of this book, I was at a loss to explain a use for this function. The difficulty in finding uses for `SQRTPI` and `DOUBLEFACT` became a running joke in my Power Excel seminars. Finally, someone from Custom Metalcraft in Springfield, Missouri pointed out that `SQRTPI` is used when you need to figure out what size of a square tank is equivalent to a certain size round tank.

As a general example, Figure 15.30 shows how to use `SQRTPI` to find that a pizza that is 10.6" square contains the same area as a 12" round pizza.

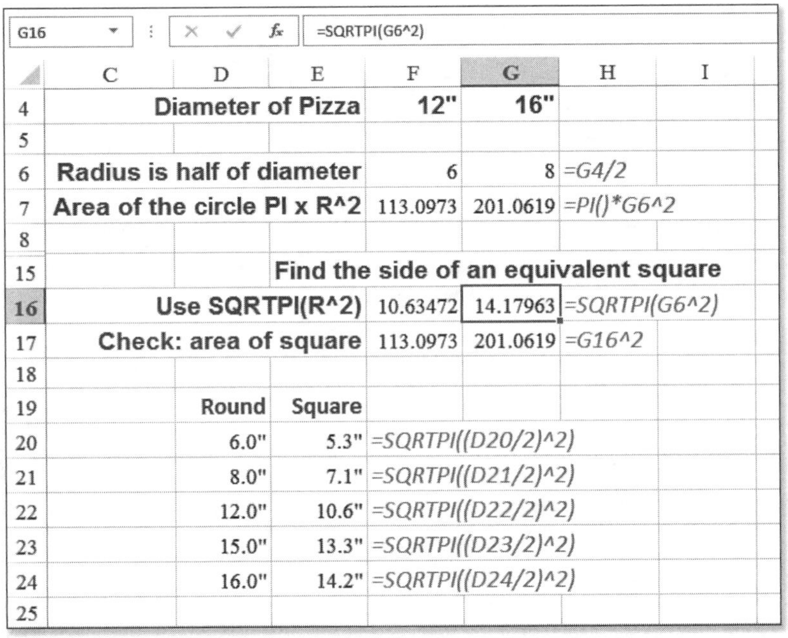

G16 =SQRTPI(G6^2)

	C	D	E	F	G	H	I
4		Diameter of Pizza		12"	16"		
5							
6	Radius is half of diameter			6	8	=G4/2	
7	Area of the circle PI x R^2			113.0973	201.0619	=PI()*G6^2	
8							
15			Find the side of an equivalent square				
16		Use SQRTPI(R^2)		10.63472	14.17963	=SQRTPI(G6^2)	
17		Check: area of square		113.0973	201.0619	=G16^2	
18							
19		Round	Square				
20		6.0"	5.3"	=SQRTPI((D20/2)^2)			
21		8.0"	7.1"	=SQRTPI((D21/2)^2)			
22		12.0"	10.6"	=SQRTPI((D22/2)^2)			
23		15.0"	13.3"	=SQRTPI((D23/2)^2)			
24		16.0"	14.2"	=SQRTPI((D24/2)^2)			
25							

Figure 15.30
`SQRTPI` is useful for converting round areas to square areas.

Syntax:

```
SQRTPI(number)
```

The `SQRTPI` function returns the square root of π. The argument *`number`* is the number by which π is multiplied. If *`number`* is less than 0, `SQRTPI` returns a `#NUM!` error.

`=SQRTPI(5)` calculates `5*PI()` as 15.7 and then takes the square root of 15.7, to return 3.96.

Using SUMPRODUCT to Sum Based on Multiple Conditions

The use of SUMPRODUCT has been dropping dramatically since Excel 2007. Until this point, SUMPRODUCT was one of the favorite methods for solving a particular limitation with SUMIF. However, because Microsoft added the SUMIFS function to Excel 2007, there is less need for SUMPRODUCT.

In case you need to share your workbooks with people using legacy versions of Excel, you can work through this example to solve the problem of conditionally summing a range based on two conditions. Suppose you are starting with the data in column A:C of Figure 15.31. This simple data set has fields for region, product, and sales.

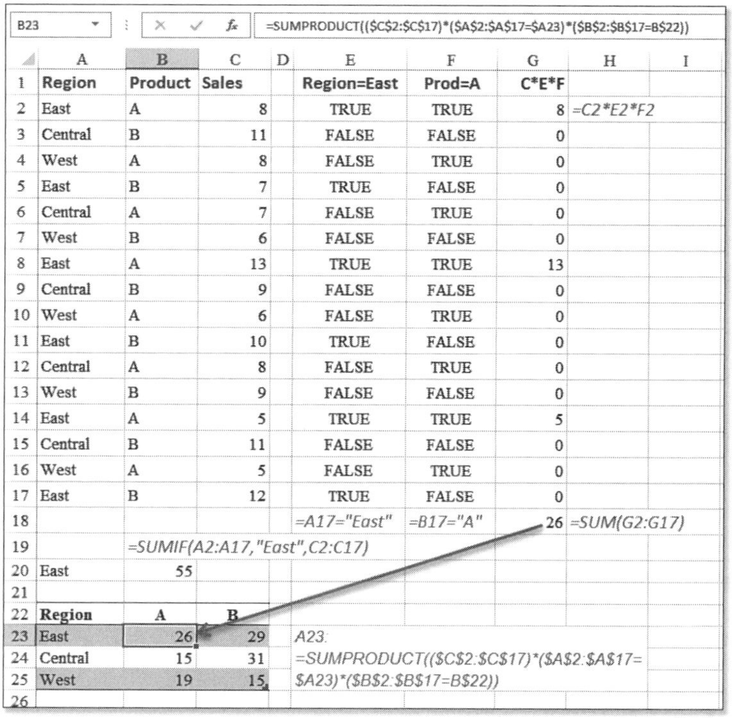

B23 =SUMPRODUCT(($C$2:$C$17)*($A$2:$A$17=$A23)*($B$2:$B$17=B$22))

	A	B	C	D	E	F	G	H	I
1	Region	Product	Sales		Region=East	Prod=A	C*E*F		
2	East	A	8		TRUE	TRUE	8	=C2*E2*F2	
3	Central	B	11		FALSE	FALSE	0		
4	West	A	8		FALSE	TRUE	0		
5	East	B	7		TRUE	FALSE	0		
6	Central	A	7		FALSE	TRUE	0		
7	West	B	6		FALSE	FALSE	0		
8	East	A	13		TRUE	TRUE	13		
9	Central	B	9		FALSE	FALSE	0		
10	West	A	6		FALSE	TRUE	0		
11	East	B	10		TRUE	FALSE	0		
12	Central	A	8		FALSE	TRUE	0		
13	West	B	9		FALSE	FALSE	0		
14	East	A	5		TRUE	TRUE	5		
15	Central	B	11		FALSE	FALSE	0		
16	West	A	5		FALSE	TRUE	0		
17	East	B	12		TRUE	FALSE	0		
18					=A17="East"	=B17="A"	26	=SUM(G2:G17)	
19		=SUMIF(A2:A17,"East",C2:C17)							
20	East	55							
21									
22	Region	A	B						
23	East	26	29		A23:				
24	Central	15	31		=SUMPRODUCT(($C$2:$C$17)*($A$2:$A$17=				
25	West	19	15		$A23)*($B$2:$B$17=B$22))				
26									

Figure 15.31
The rather long and winding calculations in E2:G18 answer how many units meet two conditions. A single formula in B23 replaces all these steps.

The SUMIF command can add all the sales that occurred in the East region: =SUMIF(A2:A17,"East",C2:C17). However, there is no way to use SUMIF to find the sum of all records that are in the East and for product A. Using SUMPRODUCT to solve this problem requires you to think about a couple virtual arrays. These arrays are entered as intermediate steps in Figure 15.31 so you can picture them.

- In column E, the formula tests whether the cell in column A is equal to East.
- In column F, the formula tests whether the cell in column B is equal to A.

- Column G contains an interesting formula. Cell G2 multiplies the sales in cell C2 by the TRUE/FALSE value in cell E2 and then multiplies that by the TRUE/FALSE value in cell G2. In Excel's treatment of TRUE/FALSE values, a TRUE is calculated as a 1, and a FALSE is calculated as a 0. Thus, in cell G2, the 8 × TRUE × TRUE is like multiplying 8 × 1 × 1, which results in 8.

- If either cell in column E or column F is FALSE, Excel treats the value as a zero. Because zero times anything is zero, the result in column G shows up as zero if the corresponding value in either column E or column F is FALSE.

- In cell G18, a SUM function totals the products from column G to answer how many sales of product A were made in the East region.

The SUMPRODUCT function does all the steps from columns E, F, and G in a single function, as shown in cell B23 in Figure 15.31.

There is a strange problem when using SUMPRODUCT to multiply arrays that contain TRUE or FALSE. Although Boolean logic says that TRUE × TRUE is TRUE, the SUMPRODUCT function cannot do this operation. Thus, you have to change the array of TRUE/FALSE values to an array of 0's and 1's. There are three generally accepted ways of doing this.

Method 1 replaces the commas indicated in the syntax with asterisks. This forces the TRUE values in the arrays to become 1s and the FALSE values to become 0s:

`=SUMPRODUCT(($C$2:$C$17)*($A$2:$A$17=$A$23)*($B$2:$B$17=$B$22))`

Method 2 surrounds the TRUE/FALSE arrays with the N() function to force a conversion to a number:

`=SUMPRODUCT($C$2:$C$17,N($A$2:$A$17=$A$23),N($B$2:$B$17=$B$22))`

Method 3 uses a double negative before each TRUE/FALSE array to change the TRUE/FALSE values to 1/0:

`=SUMPRODUCT($C$2:$C$17,--($A$2:$A$17=$A$23),--($B$2:$B$17=$B$22))\`

Syntax:

`SUMPRODUCT(array1,array2,array3,...)`

The SUMPRODUCT function multiplies corresponding components in the given arrays and returns the sum of those products. The arguments *array1, array2, array3,...* are 2 to 255 arrays whose components you want to multiply and then add together.

The *array* arguments must have the same dimensions. If they do not, SUMPRODUCT returns a #VALUE! error. SUMPRODUCT treats array entries that are not numeric as if they were zeros.

To solve a problem that has multiple conditions, you need to create three virtual arrays in the function arguments. Here's how you do it:

1. Make the first array the sales in C2:C17.

2. Make the second array a test to see whether A is equal to East: (A2:A17="East").

3. Make the third array a test to see whether B is equal to A: (B2:B17="A").

4. Multiply these three arrays to get the formula =SUMPRODUCT((C2:C17)*(A2:A17="East")* (B2:B17="A")). This provides a result of 26, just as in the previous example.

5. Make the function from step 4 more generic. In Figure 15.31, a summary table in A19:C22 has the headings East, Central, West, A, and B. The formula in B20 is =SUMPRODUCT(($C$2:$C$17)* ($A$2:$A$17=$A20)*($B$2:$B$17=B$19)). This formula adds dollar signs so that the formula can be copied. It also replaces "East" with $A20 and "A" with B$19.

6. Copy this formula to the rest of the table. You now have an efficient conditional total that sums records based on two criteria.

Examples of Engineering Functions

There are not many true engineering functions in Excel. Notice that in this book, most of the IM functions are reclassified into the previous section on imaginary numbers. All the BIT, BASE, DECIMAL, BIN2, DEC2, HEX2, and OCT2 functions are, at best, interesting to software engineers.

The CONVERT function is interesting to everyone and is truly the one engineering function that could have been included in Chapter 11, "Using Everyday Functions: Math, Date and Time, and Text Functions."

Therefore, there are just a handful of true engineering functions: The various BESSEL functions as well as the ERF, DELTA, and GESTEP functions are of use exclusively to engineers.

Using CONVERT to Convert English to Metric

The CONVERT function is an incredibly versatile function. It can convert measures in the following areas:

- Weight and mass

- Distance

- Time

- Pressure

- Force

- Energy

- Power

- Magnetism

- Temperature

- Liquid measure

Syntax:

```
CONVERT(number,from_unit,to_unit)
```

The CONVERT function converts a number from one measurement system to another. For example, CONVERT can translate a table of distances in miles to a table of distances in kilometers. This function takes the following arguments:

- **number**—This is the value in *from_unit* to convert.

- **from_unit**—This is the units for *number*. Note that this argument and the next argument are case sensitive.

- **to_unit**—This is the units for the result.

Tables 15.6 through 15.15 list the text values that CONVERT accepts for **from_unit** and **to_unit**, which can be summarized as follows:

- If the input data types are incorrect, CONVERT returns a #VALUE! error. If the unit does not exist, CONVERT returns an #N/A error.

- If the unit does not support an abbreviated unit prefix, CONVERT returns an #N/A error.

- If the units are in different groups, CONVERT returns an #N/A error.

- The unit abbreviations to use in CONVERT are case sensitive.

Table 15.6 shows conversions possible for weights.

Table 15.6   Units of Weight and Mass

Unit of Weight	Abbreviation to Use in CONVERT
Gram	g
Slug	sg
Pound mass	lbm
Atomic unit	u
Ounce mass	ozm
Exagram	Eg
Petagram	Pg
Teragram	Tg
Gigagram	Gg
Megagram	Mg
Kilogram	kg
Hectogram	hg

Unit of Weight	Abbreviation to Use in CONVERT
Dekagram	eg
Decigram	dg
Centigram	cg
Milligram	mg
Microgram	ug
Nanogram	ng
Pictogram	pg
Femtogram	Fg
Attogram	Ag

Figure 15.32 shows a conversion of weights and masses.

Table 15.7 shows conversion units for distance.

Figure 15.32
This table converts between the mass units in the left column and the various units along the top row.

	A	B	C	D	E	F	G	H	I
				fx	=CONVERT(1,"sg","u")				
3				TO---->					
4				Gram	Slug	Pound Mass	Atomic Unit	Ounce Mass	
5				g	sg	lbm	u	ozm	
6	FROM	Gram	g	1	6.85218E-05	0.002205	6.02E+23	0.035274	
7		Slug	sg	14593.9	1	32.17405	8.79E+27	514.7848	
8		Pound Mass	lbm	453.5924	0.03108095	1	2.73E+26	16	
9		Atomic Unit	u	1.66E-24	1.13783E-28	3.66E-27	1	5.86E-26	
10		Ounce Mass	ozm	28.34952	0.001942559	0.0625	1.71E+25	1	
11		exagram	Eg	1E+18	6.85218E+13	2.2E+15	6.02E+41	3.53E+16	
12		petagram	Pg	1E+15	68521765857	2.2E+12	6.02E+38	3.53E+13	
13		teragram	Tg	1E+12	68521765.86	2.2E+09	6.02E+35	3.53E+10	
14		gigagram	Gg	1E+09	68521.76586	2204623	6.02E+32	35273962	
15		megagram	Mg	1000000	68.52176586	2204.623	6.02E+29	35273.96	
16		kilogram	kg	1000	0.068521766	2.204623	6.02E+26	35.27396	
17		hectogram	hg	100	0.006852177	0.220462	6.02E+25	3.527396	
18		dekaogram	eg	10	0.000685218	0.022046	6.02E+24	0.35274	
19		decigram	dg	0.1	6.85218E-06	0.00022	6.02E+22	0.003527	
20		centigram	cg	0.01	6.85218E-07	2.2E-05	6.02E+21	0.000353	
21		milligram	mg	0.001	6.85218E-08	2.2E-06	6.02E+20	3.53E-05	
22		microgram	ug	0.000001	6.85218E-11	2.2E-09	6.02E+17	3.53E-08	
23		nanogram	ng	1E-09	6.85218E-14	2.2E-12	6.02E+14	3.53E-11	
24		picogram	pg	1E-12	6.85218E-17	2.2E-15	6.02E+11	3.53E-14	
25		femtogram	fg	1E-15	6.85218E-20	2.2E-18	6.02E+08	3.53E-17	
26		attogram	ag	1E-18	6.85218E-23	2.2E-21	602214.2	3.53E-20	
27									
28		Atomic Units in a slug?			8.78866E+27	=CONVERT(1,"sg","u")			

Table 15.7 Units of Distance

Unit of Distance	Abbreviation to Use in CONVERT
Statute mile	mi
Nautical mile	Nmi
Inch	in
Foot	ft
Yard	yd
Angstrom	ang
Pica (1/72 in.)	Pica
Meter	M
Exameter	Em
Petameter	Pm
Terameter	Tm
Gigameter	Gm
Megameter	Mm
Kilometer	Km
Hectometer	Hm
Dekameter	Em
Decimeter	Dm
Centimeter	Cm
Millimeter	Mm
Micrometer	Um
Nanometer	Nm

Figure 15.33 shows a conversion of distances.

Table 15.8 shows conversion abbreviations for measures of time.

Figure 15.33
This table converts between the distance units in the left column and the various units along the top row.

	A	B	C	D	E	F	G	H	I	J	K
D31				f_x	=CONVERT(1,"yd","Pica")						
3		Distances		TO---->							
4				Statute mile	Nautical mile	Inch	Foot	Yard	Angstrom	Pica (1/72 in.)	Meter
5				mi	Nmi	in	ft	yd	ang	Pica	m
6	FROM	Statute mile	mi	1	0.8689762	63360	5280	1760	1.60934E+13	4561920	1609.344
7		Nautical mile	Nmi	1.150779	1	72913.386	6076.1155	2025.372	1.852E+13	5249763.78	1852
8		Inch	in	1.58E-05	1.371E-05	1	0.0833333	0.027778	254000000	72	0.0254
9		Foot	ft	0.000189	0.0001646	12	1	0.333333	3048000000	864	0.3048
10		Yard	yd	0.000568	0.0004937	36	3	1	9144000000	2592	0.9144
11		Angstrom	ang	6.21E-14	5.4E-14	3.937E-09	3.281E-10	1.09E-10	1	2.83465E-07	1E-10
12		Pica (1/72 in.)	Pica	2.19E-07	1.905E-07	0.0138889	0.0011574	0.000386	3527777.778	1	0.00035278
13		Meter	m	0.000621	0.00054	39.370079	3.2808399	1.093613	10000000000	2834.645669	1
14		exameter	Em	6.21E+14	5.4E+14	3.937E+19	3.281E+18	1.09E+18	1E+28	2.83465E+21	1E+18
15		petameter	Pm	6.21E+11	5.4E+11	3.937E+16	3.281E+15	1.09E+15	1E+25	2.83465E+18	1E+15
16		terameter	Tm	6.21E+08	539956803	3.937E+13	3.281E+12	1.09E+12	1E+22	2.83465E+15	1E+12
17		gigameter	Gm	621371.2	539956.8	3.937E+10	3.281E+09	1.09E+09	1E+19	2.83465E+12	1000000000
18		megameter	Mm	621.3712	539.9568	39370079	3280839.9	1093613	1E+16	2834645669	1000000
19		kilometer	km	0.621371	0.5399568	39370.079	3280.8399	1093.613	1E+13	2834645.669	1000
20		hectometer	hm	0.062137	0.0539957	3937.0079	328.08399	109.3613	1E+12	283464.5669	100
21		dekaometer	em	0.006214	0.0053996	393.70079	32.808399	10.93613	1E+11	28346.45669	10
22		decimeter	dm	6.21E-05	5.4E-05	3.9370079	0.328084	0.109361	1000000000	283.4645669	0.1
23		centimeter	cm	6.21E-06	5.4E-06	0.3937008	0.0328084	0.010936	100000000	28.34645669	0.01
24		millimeter	mm	6.21E-07	5.4E-07	0.0393701	0.0032808	0.001094	10000000	2.834645669	0.001
25		micrometer	um	6.21E-10	5.4E-10	3.937E-05	3.281E-06	1.09E-06	10000	0.002834646	0.000001
26		nanometer	nm	6.21E-13	5.4E-13	3.937E-08	3.281E-09	1.09E-09	10	2.83465E-06	1E-09
27		picometer	pm	6.21E-16	5.4E-16	3.937E-11	3.281E-12	1.09E-12	0.01	2.83465E-09	1E-12
28		femtometer	fm	6.21E-19	5.4E-19	3.937E-14	3.281E-15	1.09E-15	0.00001	2.83465E-12	1E-15
29		attometer	am	6.21E-22	5.4E-22	3.937E-17	3.281E-18	1.09E-18	0.00000001	2.83465E-15	1E-18
30											
31		Picas in a yard?		2592	=CONVERT(1,"yd","Pica")						

Table 15.8 Units of Time

Unit of Time	Abbreviation to Use in CONVERT
Year	yr
Day	day
Hour	hr
Minute	mn
Second	sec

Figure 15.34 shows a conversion of times.

Table 15.9 shows conversion values for units of pressure.

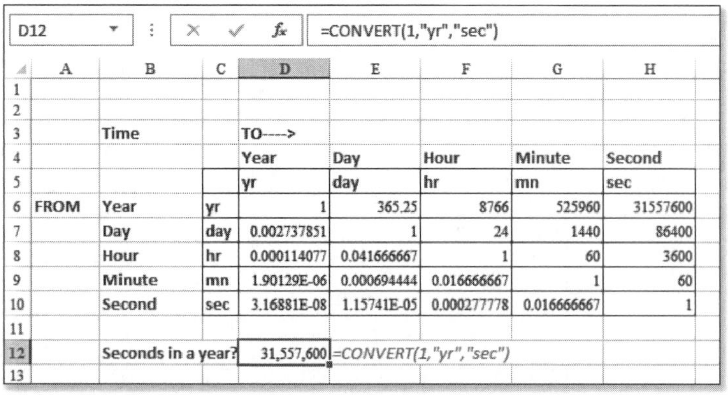

D12	▼	:	×	✓	fx	=CONVERT(1,"yr","sec")		
▲	A	B	C	D	E	F	G	H
1								
2								
3		Time		TO---->				
4				Year	Day	Hour	Minute	Second
5				yr	day	hr	mn	sec
6	FROM	Year	yr	1	365.25	8766	525960	31557600
7		Day	day	0.002737851	1	24	1440	86400
8		Hour	hr	0.000114077	0.041666667	1	60	3600
9		Minute	mn	1.90129E-06	0.000694444	0.016666667	1	60
10		Second	sec	3.16881E-08	1.15741E-05	0.000277778	0.016666667	1
11								
12		Seconds in a year?		31,557,600	=CONVERT(1,"yr","sec")			
13								

Figure 15.34
This table converts between the time units in the left column and the various units along the top row.

Table 15.9   Units of Pressure

Unit of Pressure	Abbreviation to Use in CONVERT
Pascal	Pa
Atmosphere	atm
mm of Mercury	mmHg
Exaatmosphere	Eatm
Petaatmosphere	Patm
Teraatmosphere	Tatm
Gigaatmosphere	Gatm
Megaatmosphere	Matm
Kiloatmosphere	katm
Hectoatmosphere	hatm
Dekaatmosphere	eatm
Deciatmosphere	datm
Centiatmosphere	catm
Milliatmosphere	matm
Microatmosphere	uatm
Nanoatmosphere	natm
Picoatmosphere	patm
Femtoatmosphere	fatm
Attoatmosphere	aatm

Figure 15.35 shows a conversion of pressures.

Table 15.10 shows conversion values for units of force.

Figure 15.35
This table converts between the pressure units in the left column and the various units along the top row.

	A	B	C	D	E	F
	E6	▾ : ✕ ✓ fx	=CONVERT(1,$C6,E$5)			
3		Pressure		TO---->		
4				Pascal	Atmosphere	mm of Mercury
5				Pa	atm	mmHg
6	FROM	Pascal	Pa	1	9.86923E-06	0.007500638
7		Atmosphere	atm	101325	1	760.0021002
8		mm of Mercury	mmHg	133.322	0.001315786	1
9		exaatmosphere	Eatm	1.01325E+23	1E+18	7.60002E+20
10		petaatmosphere	Patm	1.01325E+20	1E+15	7.60002E+17
11		teraatmosphere	Tatm	1.01325E+17	1E+12	7.60002E+14
12		gigaatmosphere	Gatm	1.01325E+14	1000000000	7.60002E+11
13		megaatmosphere	Matm	1.01325E+11	1000000	760002100.2
14		kiloatmosphere	katm	101325000	1000	760002.1002
15		hectoatmosphere	hatm	10132500	100	76000.21002
16		dekaoatmosphere	eatm	1013250	10	7600.021002
17		deciatmosphere	datm	10132.5	0.1	76.00021002
18		centiatmosphere	catm	1013.25	0.01	7.600021002
19		milliatmosphere	matm	101.325	0.001	0.7600021
20		microatmosphere	uatm	0.101325	0.000001	0.000760002
21		nanoatmosphere	natm	0.000101325	0.000000001	7.60002E-07
22		picoatmosphere	patm	1.01325E-07	1E-12	7.60002E-10
23		femtoatmosphere	fatm	1.01325E-10	1E-15	7.60002E-13
24		attoatmosphere	aatm	1.01325E-13	1E-18	7.60002E-16
25						

Table 15.10   Units of Force

Unit of Force	Abbreviation to Use in CONVERT
Newton	N
Dyne	dyn
Pound force	lbf
Exanewton	EN
Petanewton	PN
Teranewton	TN
Giganewton	GN
Meganewton	MN
Kilonewton	kN
Hectonewton	hN
Dekanewton	eN

Unit of Force	Abbreviation to Use in CONVERT
Decinewton	dN
Centinewton	cN
Millinewton	mN
Micronewton	uN
Nanonewton	nN
Piconewton	pN
Femtonewton	fN
Attonewton	aN
Exadyne	Edyn
Petadyne	Pdyn
Teradyne	Tdyn
Gigadyne	Gdyn
Megadyne	Mdyn
Kilodyne	kdyn
Hectodyne	hdyn
Dekadyne	edyn
Decidyne	ddyn
Centidyne	cdyn
Millidyne	mdyn
Microdyne	udyn
Nanodyne	ndyn
Picodyne	pdyn
Femtodyne	fdyn
Attodyne	adyn

Figure 15.36 shows a conversion of forces.

Table 15.11 shows conversions available for energy.

Figure 15.36
This table converts between the force units in the left column and the various units along the top row.

E6	▼	:	× ✓	fx	=CONVERT(1,$C6,E$5)	
⊿	A	B	C	D	E	F	G
3		Force		TO---->			
4				Newton	Dyne	Pound force	
5				N	dyn	lbf	
6	FROM	Newton	N	1	100000	0.2248089	
7		Dyne	dyn	0.00001	1	2.248E-06	
8		Pound force	lbf	4.4482216	444822.16	1	
9		exanewton	EN	1E+18	1E+23	2.248E+17	
10		petanewton	PN	1E+15	1E+20	2.248E+14	
11		teranewton	TN	1E+12	1E+17	2.248E+11	
12		giganewton	GN	1E+09	1E+14	224808943	
13		meganewton	MN	1000000	1E+11	224808.94	
14		kilonewton	kN	1000	100000000	224.80894	
15		hectonewton	hN	100	10000000	22.480894	
16		dekaonewton	eN	10	1000000	2.2480894	
17		decinewton	dN	0.1	10000	0.0224809	
18		centinewton	cN	0.01	1000	0.0022481	
19		millinewton	mN	0.001	100	0.0002248	
20		micronewton	uN	0.000001	0.1	2.248E-07	
21		nanonewton	nN	1E-09	0.0001	2.248E-10	
22		piconewton	pN	1E-12	0.0000001	2.248E-13	
23		femtonewton	fN	1E-15	1E-10	2.248E-16	
24		attonewton	aN	1E-18	1E-13	2.248E-19	
25		exadyne	Edyn	1E+13	1E+18	2.248E+12	
26		petadyne	Pdyn	1E+10	1E+15	2.248E+09	
27		teradyne	Tdyn	10000000	1E+12	2248089.4	
28		gigadyne	Gdyn	10000	1E+09	2248.0894	
29		megadyne	Mdyn	10	1000000	2.2480894	
30		kilodyne	kdyn	0.01	1000	0.0022481	
31		hectodyne	hdyn	0.001	100	0.0002248	
32		dekaodyne	edyn	0.0001	10	2.248E-05	
33		decidyne	ddyn	0.000001	0.1	2.248E-07	
34		centidyne	cdyn	0.0000001	0.01	2.248E-08	
35		millidyne	mdyn	1E-08	0.001	2.248E-09	
36		microdyne	udyn	1E-11	0.000001	2.248E-12	
37		nanodyne	ndyn	1E-14	1E-09	2.248E-15	
38		picodyne	pdyn	1E-17	1E-12	2.248E-18	
39		femtodyne	fdyn	1E-20	1E-15	2.248E-21	
40		attodyne	adyn	1E-23	1E-18	2.248E-24	
41							

Table 15.11   Units of Energy*

Unit of Energy	Abbreviation to Use in CONVERT
Joule	J
Erg	e
Thermodynamic calorie	c
IT calorie	cal
Electron volt	eV
Horsepower-hour	HPh
Watt-hour	Wh
Foot-pound	flb
BTU	BTU
Exajoule	EJ
Petajoule	PJ
Terajoule	TJ

Unit of Energy	Abbreviation to Use in CONVERT
Gigajoule	GJ
Megajoule	MJ
Kilojoule	kJ
Hectojoule	hJ
Dekajoule	eJ
Decijoule	dJ
Centijoule	cJ
Millijoule	mJ
Microjoule	uJ
Nanojoule	nJ
Picojoule	pJ
Femtojoule	fJ
Attojoule	aJ

This table shows the complete metric prefixes for joules. Similar metric prefixes can also be applied to ergs, thermodynamic calories, IT calories, electron volts, and Watt-hours. This adds 80 additional measurements available in the CONVERT function for energy. Figure 15.37 shows a conversion of energies.

Table 15.12 shows conversions available for power.

Table 15.12 Units of Power

Unit of Power	Abbreviation to Use in CONVERT
Horsepower	HP
Watt	W
Exawatt	EW
Petawatt	PW
Terawatt	TW
Gigawatt	GW
Megawatt	MW
Kilowatt	kW
Hectowatt	hW
Dekawatt	eW

Unit of Power	Abbreviation to Use in CONVERT
Deciwatt	dW
Centiwatt	cW
Milliwatt	mW
Microwatt	uW
Nanowatt	nW
Picowatt	pW
Femtowatt	fW
Attowatt	aW

Figure 15.37
This table converts between the energy units in the left column and the various units along the top row.

			Joule	Erg	Thermodynamic calorie	IT calorie	Electron volt	Horsepower	Watt-hour	Foot-pound	BTU
			J	e	c	cal	eV	HPh	Wh	flb	BTU
FROM	Joule	J	1	10000000	0.239005736	0.2388459	6.24E+18	3.72506E-07	0.000278	0.737562	0.000948
	Erg	e	0.0000001	1	2.39006E-08	2.3885E-08	6.24E+11	3.72506E-14	2.78E-11	7.38E-08	9.48E-11
	Thermodynamic calorie	c	4.184	41840000	1	0.99933123	2.61E+19	1.55857E-06	0.001162	3.08596	0.003966
	IT calorie	cal	4.1868	41868000	1.000669216	1	2.61E+19	1.55961E-06	0.001163	3.088025	0.003968
	Electron volt	eV	1.60218E-19	1.60218E-12	3.82929E-20	3.8267E-20	1	5.96821E-26	4.45E-23	1.18E-19	1.52E-22
	Horsepower-hour	HPh	2684519.538	2.68452E+13	641615.5683	641186.476	1.68E+25	1	745.6999	1980000	2544.434
	Watt-hour	Wh	3600	36000000000	860.4206501	859.845228	2.25E+22	0.001341022	1	2655.224	3.412142
	Foot-pound	flb	1.355817948	13558179.48	0.324048267	0.32383155	8.46E+18	5.05051E-07	0.000377	1	0.001285
	BTU	BTU	1055.055853	10550558526	252.1644007	251.995761	6.59E+21	0.000393015	0.293071	778.1693	1
	kilojoule	kJ	1000	1000000000	239.0057361	238.845897	6.24E+21	0.000372506	0.277778	737.5621	0.947817
	kiloerg	ke	0.0001	1000	2.39006E-05	2.3885E-05	6.24E+14	3.72506E-11	2.78E-08	7.38E-05	9.48E-08
	kilocalorie (Therm)	kc	4184	41840000000	1000	999.331231	2.61E+22	0.001558566	1.162222	3085.96	3.965667
	kilocalorie (IT)	kcal	4186.8	41868000000	1000.669216	1000	2.61E+22	0.001559609	1.163	3088.025	3.968321
	kiloelecton volt	keV	1.60218E-16	1.60218E-09	3.82929E-17	3.8267E-17	1000	5.96821E-23	4.45E-20	1.18E-16	1.52E-19
	kilowatt-hour	kWh	3600000	3.6E+13	860420.6501	859845.228	2.25E+25	1.34102209	1000	2655224	3412.142
	exajoule	EJ	1E+18	1E+25	2.39006E+17	2.3885E+17	6.24E+36	3.72506E+11	2.78E+14	7.38E+17	9.48E+14
	petajoule	PJ	1E+15	1E+22	2.39006E+14	2.3885E+14	6.24E+33	372506.136	2.78E+11	7.38E+14	9.48E+11
	terajoule	TJ	1E+12	1E+19	2.39006E+11	2.3885E+11	6.24E+30	372506.136	2.78E+08	7.38E+11	9.48E+08
	gigajoule	GJ	1000000000	1E+16	239005736.1	238845897	6.24E+27	372.506136	277777.8	7.38E+08	947817.1
	megajoule	MJ	1000000	1E+13	239005.7361	238845.897	6.24E+24	0.372506136	277.7778	737562.1	947.8171
	kilojoule	kJ	1000	1000000000	239.0057361	238.845897	6.24E+21	0.000372506	0.277778	737.5621	0.947817
	hectojoule	hJ	100	1000000000	23.90057361	23.8845897	6.24E+20	3.72506E-05	0.027778	73.75621	0.094782
	dekaojoule	eJ	10	100000000	2.390057361	2.38845897	6.24E+19	3.72506E-06	0.002778	7.375621	0.009478
	decijoule	dJ	0.1	1000000	0.023900574	0.02388846	6.24E+17	3.72506E-08	2.78E-05	0.073756	9.48E-05
	centijoule	cJ	0.01	100000	0.002390057	0.00238846	6.24E+16	3.72506E-09	2.78E-06	0.007376	9.48E-06
	millijoule	mJ	0.001	10000	0.000239006	0.00023885	6.24E+15	3.72506E-10	2.78E-07	0.000738	9.48E-07
	microjoule	uJ	0.000001	10	2.39006E-07	2.3885E-07	6.24E+12	3.72506E-13	2.78E-10	7.38E-07	9.48E-10
	nanojoule	nJ	0.000000001	0.01	2.39006E-10	2.3885E-10	6.24E+09	3.72506E-16	2.78E-13	7.38E-10	9.48E-13
	picojoule	pJ	1E-12	0.00001	2.39006E-13	2.3885E-13	6241510	3.72506E-19	2.78E-16	7.38E-13	9.48E-16
	femtojoule	fJ	1E-15	0.00000001	2.39006E-16	2.3885E-16	6241.51	3.72506E-22	2.78E-19	7.38E-16	9.48E-19
	attojoule	aJ	1E-18	1E-11	2.39006E-19	2.3885E-19	6.24151	3.72506E-25	2.78E-22	7.38E-19	9.48E-22

The metric prefixes also apply to e, c, cal, eV, Wh

Cell E6: =CONVERT(1,$C6,E$5)

Figure 15.38 shows a conversion of powers.

Table 15.13 shows conversions available for units of magnetism.

E6 =CONVERT(1,$C6,E$5)

	A	B	C	D	E	F	G
3		Power		TO---->			
4				Horsepower	Watt		
5				HP	W		
6	FROM	Horsepower	HP	1	745.6998716		
7		Watt	W	0.001341022	1		
8		exawatt	EW	1.34102E+15	1E+18		
9		petawatt	PW	1.34102E+12	1E+15		
10		terawatt	TW	1341022090	1E+12		
11		gigawatt	GW	1341022.09	1000000000		
12		megawatt	MW	1341.02209	1000000		
13		kilowatt	kW	1.34102209	1000		
14		hectowatt	hW	0.134102209	100		
15		dekaowatt	eW	0.013410221	10		
16		deciwatt	dW	0.000134102	0.1		
17		centiwatt	cW	1.34102E-05	0.01		
18		milliwatt	mW	1.34102E-06	0.001		
19		microwatt	uW	1.34102E-09	0.000001		
20		nanowatt	nW	1.34102E-12	0.000000001		
21		picowatt	pW	1.34102E-15	1E-12		
22		femtowatt	fW	1.34102E-18	1E-15		
23		attowatt	aW	1.34102E-21	1E-18		
24							

Figure 15.38
This table converts between the power units in the left column and the various units along the top row.

Table 15.13 Units of Magnetism

Unit of Magnetism	Abbreviation to Use in CONVERT
Tesla	T
Gauss	Ga
Exatesla	ET
Petatesla	PT
Teratesla	TT
Gigatesla	GT
Megatesla	MT
Kilotesla	kT
Hectotesla	hT
Dekatesla	eT
Decitesla	dT

Unit of Magnetism	Abbreviation to Use in CONVERT
Centitesla	cT
Millitesla	mT
Microtesla	uT
Nanotesla	nT
Picotesla	pT
Femtotesla	fT
Attotesla	aT
Exagauss	Ega
Petagauss	Pga
Teragauss	Tga
Gigagauss	Gga
Megagauss	Mga
Kilogauss	kga
Hectogauss	hga
Dekagauss	ega
Decigauss	dga
Centigauss	cga
Milligauss	mga
Microgauss	uga
Nanogauss	nga
Picogauss	pga
Femtogauss	fga
Attogauss	aga

Figure 15.39 shows a conversion of magnetisms.

Table 15.14 shows conversion factors available for temperature systems.

Table 15.14 Units of Temperature

Unit of Temperature	Abbreviation to Use in CONVERT
Degree Celsius	C
Degree Fahrenheit	F
Degree Kelvin	K

E6 =CONVERT(1,$C6,E$5)

	A	B	C	D	E
4				Tesla	Gauss
5				T	ga
6	FROM	Tesla	T	1	10000
7		Gauss	ga	0.0001	1
8		exatesla	ET	1E+18	1E+22
9		petatesla	PT	1E+15	1E+19
10		teratesla	TT	1E+12	1E+16
11		gigatesla	GT	1000000000	1E+13
12		megatesla	MT	1000000	10000000000
13		kilotesla	kT	1000	10000000
14		hectotesla	hT	100	1000000
15		dekaotesla	eT	10	100000
16		decitesla	dT	0.1	1000
17		centitesla	cT	0.01	100
18		millitesla	mT	0.001	10
19		microtesla	uT	0.000001	0.01
20		nanotesla	nT	0.000000001	0.00001
21		picotesla	pT	1E-12	0.00000001
22		femtotesla	fT	1E-15	1E-11
23		attotesla	aT	1E-18	1E-14
24		exagauss	Ega	1E+14	1E+18
25		petagauss	Pga	1E+11	1E+15
26		teragauss	Tga	100000000	1E+12
27		gigagauss	Gga	100000	1000000000
28		megagauss	Mga	100	1000000
29		kilogauss	kga	0.1	1000
30		hectogauss	hga	0.01	100
31		dekaogauss	ega	0.001	10
32		decigauss	dga	0.00001	0.1
33		centigauss	cga	0.000001	0.01
34		milligauss	mga	0.0000001	0.001
35		microgauss	uga	1E-10	0.000001
36		nanogauss	nga	1E-13	0.000000001
37		picogauss	pga	1E-16	1E-12
38		femtogauss	fga	1E-19	1E-15
39		attogauss	aga	1E-22	1E-18
40					

Figure 15.39
This table converts between the magnetism units in the left column and the various units along the top row.

Figure 15.40 shows a conversion of temperature systems.

D8 =CONVERT(1,$C8,D$5)

	A	B	C	D	E	F	G
3		Temperature		TO---->			
4				Degree Celsius	Degree Fahrenheit	Degree Kelvin	
5				C	F	K	
6	FROM	Degree Celsius	C	1	33.8	274.15	
7		Degree Fahrenheit	F	-17.2222	1	255.9277778	
8		Degree Kelvin	K	-272.15	-457.87	1	
9							
10		Fahrenheit	Celsius				
11	Cold Day	0	-17.8	=CONVERT(B11,"F","C")			
12	Frz Pt	32	0.0	=CONVERT(B12,"F","C")			
13	Room Temp	68	20.0	=CONVERT(B13,"F","C")			
14	Hot Day	95	35.0	=CONVERT(B14,"F","C")			
15	Boiling Pt	212	100.0	=CONVERT(B15,"F","C")			
16							

Figure 15.40
This table converts between the temperature scales in the left column and the various scales along the top row.

Table 15.15 shows conversion units available for liquid measurements.

Table 15.15   Units of Liquid Measure

Unit of Liquid Measure	Abbreviation to Use in CONVERT
Teaspoon	tsp
Tablespoon	tbs
Fluid ounce	oz
Cup	cup
U.S. pint	pt
U.K. pint	uk_pt
Quart	qt
Gallon	gal
Liter	l
Exaliter	El
Petaliter	Pl
Teraliter	Tl
Gigaliter	Gl
Megaliter	Ml
Kiloliter	kl
Hectoliter	hl
Dekaliter	el
Deciliter	dl
Centiliter	cl
Milliliter	ml
Microliter	ul
Nanoliter	nl
Picoliter	pl
Femtoliter	fl
Attoliter	al

Figure 15.41 shows a conversion of liquid measures.

F11 =CONVERT(1,$C11,F$5)

	A	B	C	D	E	F	G	H	I	J	K	L
4				Teaspoon	Table spoon	Fluid ounce	Cup	U.S. pint	U.K. pint	Quart	Gallon	Liter
5				tsp	tbs	oz	cup	pt	uk_pt	qt	gal	l
6	FROM	Teaspoon	tsp	1	0.3333	0.1667	0.021	0.01	0.0087	0.0052	0.0013	0.0049
7		Tablespoon	tbs	3	1	0.5	0.063	0.031	0.026	0.0156	0.00391	0.0148
8		Fluid ounce	oz	6	2	1	0.125	0.063	0.052	0.0313	0.00781	0.0296
9		Cup	cup	48	16	8	1	0.5	0.4163	0.25	0.0625	0.2366
10		U.S. pint	pt	96	32	16	2	1	0.8327	0.5	0.125	0.4732
11		U.K. pint	uk_pt	115.291193	38.43	19.215	2.402	1.201	1	0.6005	0.15012	0.5683
12		Quart	qt	192	64	32	4	2	1.6653	1	0.25	0.9464
13		Gallon	gal	768	256	128	16	8	6.6614	4	1	3.7854
14		Liter	l	202.884136	67.628	33.814	4.227	2.113	1.7598	1.0567	0.26417	1
15		exaliter	El	2.0288E+20	7E+19	3E+19	4E+18	2E+18	2E+18	1E+18	2.6E+17	1E+18
16		petaliter	Pl	2.0288E+17	7E+16	3E+16	4E+15	2E+15	2E+15	1E+15	2.6E+14	1E+15
17		teraliter	Tl	2.0288E+14	7E+13	3E+13	4E+12	2E+12	2E+12	1E+12	2.6E+11	1E+12
18		gigaliter	Gl	2.0288E+11	7E+10	3E+10	4E+09	2E+09	2E+09	1E+09	2.6E+08	1E+09
19		megaliter	Ml	202884136	7E+07	3E+07	4E+06	2E+06	2E+06	1E+06	264172	1E+06
20		kiloliter	kl	202884.136	67628	33814	4227	2113	1759.8	1056.7	264.172	1000
21		hectoliter	hl	20288.4136	6762.8	3381.4	422.7	211.3	175.98	105.67	26.4172	100
22		dekaoliter	el	2028.84136	676.28	338.14	42.27	21.13	17.598	10.567	2.64172	10
23		deciliter	dl	20.2884136	6.7628	3.3814	0.423	0.211	0.176	0.1057	0.02642	0.1
24		centiliter	cl	2.02884136	0.6763	0.3381	0.042	0.021	0.0176	0.0106	0.00264	0.01
25		milliliter	ml	0.20288414	0.0676	0.0338	0.004	0.002	0.0018	0.0011	0.00026	0.001
26		microliter	ul	0.00020288	7E-05	3E-05	4E-06	2E-06	2E-06	1E-06	2.6E-07	1E-06
27		nanoliter	nl	2.0288E-07	7E-08	3E-08	4E-09	2E-09	2E-09	1E-09	2.6E-10	1E-09
28		picoliter	pl	2.0288E-10	7E-11	3E-11	4E-12	2E-12	2E-12	1E-12	2.6E-13	1E-12
29		femtoliter	fl	2.0288E-13	7E-14	3E-14	4E-15	2E-15	2E-15	1E-15	2.6E-16	1E-15
30		attoliter	al	2.0288E-16	7E-17	3E-17	4E-18	2E-18	2E-18	1E-18	2.6E-19	1E-18
31												

Figure 15.41
If someone in the U.K. offers you a "pint," expect a bonus 3.2 fluid ounces.

Performing Bitwise Operations for Electrical Engineering

Excel 2013 adds five new functions that perform bitwise operations. Any introduction to computer engineering covers the use of AND, OR, and NAND gates in the design of microprocessors. Bitwise operations are primitive but fast. Of course, in Excel, dozens of intermediate operations happen when you use `BITAND` to simulate an AND gate.

The five functions are `BITAND`, `BITOR`, `BITXOR`, `BITRSHIFT`, and `BITLSHIFT`. Although you pass the function one or two decimal numbers, Excel converts the numbers to binary, performs the bitwise operation, and returns the result as decimal.

If you want to pass an argument that is binary, convert it to decimal using either `BIN2DEC` or `DECIMAL(,2)`, as discussed later in this chapter.

If you want to show the result in binary, you can use either `DEC2BIN` or `BASE(,2)`, as discussed later in this chapter.

The values passed to these functions must be integers in the range of 0 to (2^48)–1.

Figure 15.42 shows examples of the five functions.

Figure 15.42
Doing bit math in Excel 2013.

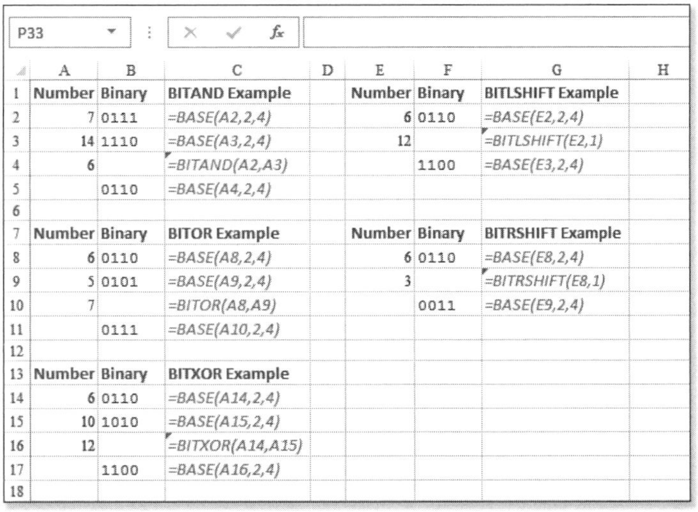

	A	B	C	D	E	F	G	H
	P33	▼	: × ✓ fx					
1	Number	Binary	BITAND Example		Number	Binary	BITLSHIFT Example	
2	7	0111	=BASE(A2,2,4)		6	0110	=BASE(E2,2,4)	
3	14	1110	=BASE(A3,2,4)		12		=BITLSHIFT(E2,1)	
4	6		=BITAND(A2,A3)			1100	=BASE(E3,2,4)	
5		0110	=BASE(A4,2,4)					
6								
7	Number	Binary	BITOR Example		Number	Binary	BITRSHIFT Example	
8	6	0110	=BASE(A8,2,4)		6	0110	=BASE(E8,2,4)	
9	5	0101	=BASE(A9,2,4)		3		=BITRSHIFT(E8,1)	
10	7		=BITOR(A8,A9)			0011	=BASE(E9,2,4)	
11		0111	=BASE(A10,2,4)					
12								
13	Number	Binary	BITXOR Example					
14	6	0110	=BASE(A14,2,4)					
15	10	1010	=BASE(A15,2,4)					
16	12		=BITXOR(A14,A15)					
17		1100	=BASE(A16,2,4)					
18								

In the first example, =BITAND(7,14) returns 6. Here is how Excel calculates that result:

- The decimal number 7 is 0111 in binary, as shown in B2.

- The decimal number 14 is 1110 in binary, as shown in B3.

- The BITAND function compares the "digits" in the binary numbers. Both numbers must have a 1 in the same position for there to be a 1 in the result. In the current example, both 7 and 14 have a 1 in the second and third positions of their binary representation. Thus, the answer of the BITAND in binary is 0110. The BITAND function returns the decimal number 6 as the result.

Syntax:

BITAND(*number1*,*number2*)

Returns a bitwise AND of two numbers. The argument accepts integers expressed in decimal and returns a decimal answer. In the course of processing, both numbers are converted to binary. The value of each bit position is counted only if both arguments' bits at that position are 1. The values returned from the bit positions progress from right to left as powers of 2. The rightmost bit returns 1 (2^0). The next bit to the left returns 2 (2^1), and so on.

The next example in Figure 15.42 is a BITOR example. When comparing the binary representations of 6 and 5, Excel returns a bit if either argument has a bit turned on in a given position. As shown in B8, 6 is 0110. As shown in B9, 5 is 0101. The result is 0111 or 7.

Syntax:

BITOR(*number1*,*number2*)

Returns a bitwise OR of two numbers. The argument accepts integers expressed in decimal and returns a decimal answer. In the course of processing, both numbers are converted to binary. The value of each bit position is counted if either arguments' bits at that position are 1. The values returned from the bit positions progress from right to left as powers of 2. The rightmost bit returns 1 (2^0). The next bit to the left returns 2 (2^1), and so on.

The next example in Figure 15.42 is the BITXOR function. XOR stands for *eXclusive OR*. XOR returns a bit only if exactly one argument has a bit at that position. In row 14, 6 is shown as 0110. In row 15, 10 is shown as 1010. As Excel evaluates the BITXOR, the result is 1100 in binary or 12. In the two left positions, exactly one bit is on, so the resultant bit is on. When both bits are on or both bits are off, the resultant bit is off.

Syntax:

BITXOR(*number1*,*number2*)

Returns a bitwise exclusive OR of two numbers. The argument accepts integers expressed in decimal and returns a decimal answer. In the course of processing, both numbers are converted to binary. The value of each bit position is counted if exactly one of the arguments' bits at that position is 1. The values returned from the bit positions progress from right to left as powers of 2. The rightmost bit returns 1 (2^0). The next bit to the left returns 2 (2^1), and so on.

The final two functions shift bits to the left or right. The 0110 in cell F2 of Figure 15.42 becomes 1100 when shifted left by one position. Because 1100 is the binary representation for 12, the formula =BITLSHIFT(6,1) returns 12. The 0110 in cell F8 becomes 0011 when shifted to the right one position. The formula =BITRSHIFT(6,1) returns 3.

Syntax:

BITLSHIFT(*number*,*shift_amount*)

Returns a number shifted right by *shift_amount* bits. This is equivalent to adding zeros to the right of the binary representation of the number. *number* should be in decimal. It should be an integer between 0 and (2^48)–1, inclusive. *shift_amount* should have an absolute value less than or equal to 53. You may use a negative number as the shift amount; this will shift bits to the right.

Syntax:

BITRSHIFT(*number*,*shift_amount*)

Returns a number shifted right by *shift_amount* bits. This is equivalent to removing digits from the rightmost side of the binary representation of the number. *number* should be in decimal. It should be an integer between 0 and (2^48)–1, inclusive. *shift_amount* should have an absolute value less than or equal to 53. You may use a negative number as the shift amount; this will shift bits to the left.

Converting to Other Number Systems

A long time ago, I held a summer internship writing COBOL programs for a company. Whenever one of my programs crashed in the middle of the night, I was supposed to read a hexadecimal printout of the computer memory to figure out what went wrong.

In the hexadecimal numbering system, there are 16 digits. In order, the digits are 0, 1, 2, 3, 4, 5, 6, 7, 8, 9, A, B, C, D, E, and F. The number that you know as 10 is written as A in hexadecimal. The number 15 is written as F in hexadecimal. After F comes the hexadecimal number 10, which is equivalent to 16 in decimal.

Before Excel 2013, Microsoft offered 12 functions that converted between binary, octal, decimal, and hexadecimal. Although these were certainly the most common number systems in the days of 16-bit computers, there are other numbering systems. Those of you of a certain age will remember when *School House Rock* sang about a base-12 numbering system.

Starting in Excel 2013, Microsoft offers `BASE` and `DECIMAL` for converting to and from all numbering systems from Base 2 to Base 36 (see Figure 15.43). These improved functions work with larger numbers than the old functions.

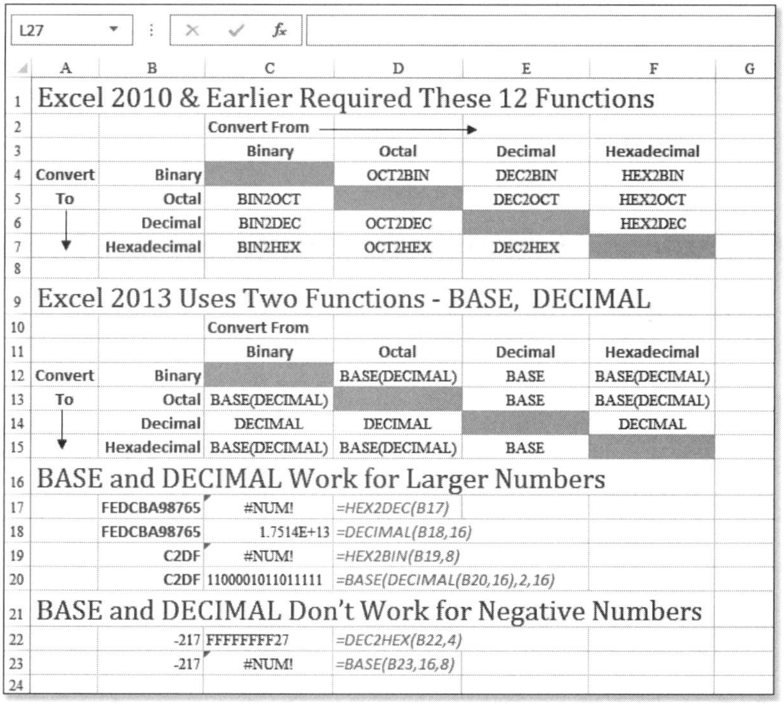

L27

	A	B	C	D	E	F	G
1	Excel 2010 & Earlier Required These 12 Functions						
2			Convert From →				
3			Binary	Octal	Decimal	Hexadecimal	
4	Convert	Binary		OCT2BIN	DEC2BIN	HEX2BIN	
5	To	Octal	BIN2OCT		DEC2OCT	HEX2OCT	
6	↓	Decimal	BIN2DEC	OCT2DEC		HEX2DEC	
7		Hexadecimal	BIN2HEX	OCT2HEX	DEC2HEX		
8							
9	Excel 2013 Uses Two Functions - BASE, DECIMAL						
10			Convert From				
11			Binary	Octal	Decimal	Hexadecimal	
12	Convert	Binary		BASE(DECIMAL)	BASE	BASE(DECIMAL)	
13	To	Octal	BASE(DECIMAL)		BASE	BASE(DECIMAL)	
14	↓	Decimal	DECIMAL	DECIMAL		DECIMAL	
15		Hexadecimal	BASE(DECIMAL)	BASE(DECIMAL)	BASE		
16	BASE and DECIMAL Work for Larger Numbers						
17		FEDCBA98765	#NUM!	=HEX2DEC(B17)			
18		FEDCBA98765	1.7514E+13	=DECIMAL(B18,16)			
19		C2DF	#NUM!	=HEX2BIN(B19,8)			
20		C2DF	1100001011011111	=BASE(DECIMAL(B20,16),2,16)			
21	BASE and DECIMAL Don't Work for Negative Numbers						
22		-217	FFFFFFFF27	=DEC2HEX(B22,4)			
23		-217	#NUM!	=BASE(B23,16,8)			
24							

Figure 15.43
`BASE` and `DECIMAL` replace 12 legacy functions, unless you need to handle negative numbers.

However, we still have to discuss the 12 old functions in case you share your workbook with someone using Excel 2010 or older. Also, the old functions handled negative numbers using the Two's Complement method. The BASE and DECIMAL functions chose to handle larger numbers instead of handling negative numbers.

There are several good reasons to start using BASE and DECIMAL:

- They work with any radix (base) from 2 to 36.

- They handle much larger numbers than legacy functions. Whereas DEC2BIN would fail with numbers higher than 255, BASE can handle decimal numbers up to $(2^{53})-1$.

- The two function names are easier to remember than the 12 function names of BIN2OCT, BIN2DEC, BIN2HEX, OCT2BIN, OCT2DEC, OCT2HEX, DEC2BIN, DEC2OCT, DEC2HEX, HEX2BIN, HEX2OCT, and HEX2DEC.

You might still need to use the legacy functions for the following reasons:

- They work natively back to Excel 2007 and work in prior versions if the user has activated the Analysis Toolpack add-in.

- They work with negative numbers using the Two's Complement system.

- A single function converts directly from binary to hexadecimal without having to create an intermediate result in decimal. Using the new functions, you would have to use =DECIMAL(Number,2) to convert from binary to decimal and then BASE(DECIMAL(Number,2),16) to convert to hexadecimal. Although, in speed tests, a formula with BASE and DECIMAL still calculates faster than a formula with just BIN2HEX.

Syntax:

BASE(*number*,*radix*,*min_length*)

Converts a number into a text representation of the number with a given radix (base). *number* must be an integer greater than or equal to 0 and be less than 2^53. *radix* is an integer between 2 and 36. If you want to ensure that the returned number has a certain length, you can specify the minimum length. This forces shorter numbers to be padded on the left with zero.

For example, to convert 252 to binary, use =BASE(252,2). To convert 252 to hexadecimal, use =BASE(252,16). To convert 252 to Base 36, use =BASE(252,36).

Cells D2:D9 of Figure 15.44 show several examples of the BASE formula with different radices.

 Note

With a radix of 9 or less, the resultant number system contains the digits from 0 to (radix–1). With a radix greater than 10, the number system uses A as the digit after 9. Base 12 uses 0 through 9 and A and B. Base 36 uses 0 through 9 and A through Z. This is why the BASE function only supports number systems up to Base 36—you run out of symbols after using digits and the 26 letters.

Figure 15.44
Use BASE to convert from decimal to any number system.

	D2	▼	:	×	✓	fx	=BASE(B2,C2)	

	A	B	C	D	E	F
1	System	Decimal	Radix	Result	Formula	
2	binary	5	2	101	=BASE(B2,C2)	
3	binary	5	2	00000101	=BASE(B3,C3,8)	
4	quaternary	1.23E+08	4	1311233031011	=BASE(B4,C4)	
5	octal	1.23E+08	8	726746425	=BASE(B5,C5)	
6	duodecimal	11	12	B	=BASE(B6,C6)	
7	hexadecimal	1.23E+08	16	75BCD15	=BASE(B7,C7)	
8	base 32	17946272	32	H3LL0	=BASE(B8,C8)	
9	base 36	1584973	36	XYZ1	=BASE(B9,C9)	
10						
11	Converting Back to Decimal					
12		Number	Radix	Decimal	Formula	
13		10101010	2	170	=DECIMAL(B13,C13)	
14		CC00FF11	16	3422617361	=DECIMAL(B14,C14)	
15		XXX0	34	1336302	=DECIMAL(B15,C15)	
16						
17	Hexadecimal to Binary and back					
18		FFCC	1111111111001100		=BASE(DECIMAL(B18,16),2)	
19		11110101	F5		=BASE(DECIMAL(B19,2),16)	
20	Works for decimals from 0 to (2^53)-1 and text up to 255 characters					

Converting from Other Number Systems to Decimal

Use the new DECIMAL function to convert from a text representation of another number system.

Syntax:

DECIMAL(*text*,*radix*)

Converts a text representation of a given base (radix) into a decimal number. *text* must be less than or equal to 255 characters. The decimal result should be less than 2^53. A text argument that resolves to a number of 2^53 or larger might result in a loss of precision.

 Note

The 255-character limitation rarely comes into play. The longest binary number that is under the 2^53 limit is 53 characters long. The longest Base 26 number that is under the 2^53 limit is 11 characters long. Unless your number has 202 leading zeros, you will never run into the 255 character limit.

This function is new in Excel 2013. In prior versions, you would use BIN2DEC, OCT2DEC, or HEX2DEC, as described in the following sections.

Refer to cells D13:D15 in Figure 15.44 for an example of DECIMAL.

> **⚠ Caution**
>
> DECIMAL cannot work with negative numbers. To convert negative numbers in the Two's Complement syntax, use BIN2DEC, OCT2DEC, or HEX2DEC.

Converting from Binary to Hexadecimal

The legacy functions of BIN2HEX or HEX2BIN would enable you to convert directly from binary to hexadecimal and back. The new BASE and DECIMAL functions can be combined. Start with DECIMAL("FF",16) to convert from hexadecimal to decimal and then wrap that function in the BASE function to convert to binary: =BASE(DECIMAL("FF",16),2). Although you are using two functions, this method calculates faster than a single BIN2HEX or HEX2BIN function.

Rows 18 and 19 of Figure 15.44 show examples of converting from binary to hexadecimal and back.

Converting Using the Legacy Functions

Excel offers 12 legacy functions that convert between binary, octal, decimal, and hexadecimal. Although these functions can be replaced in Excel 2013 with the versatile BASE and DECIMAL functions discussed earlier, the old functions remain for backward compatibility with prior versions of Excel.

The legacy functions can also deal with negative numbers stored in Two's Complement notation.

Figure 15.45 shows each of the 12 legacy functions.

Syntax:

DEC2HEX(*number*,*places*)

The DEC2HEX function converts a decimal number to hexadecimal. This function takes the following arguments:

- **number**—This is the decimal integer you want to convert. If *number* is negative, the *places* argument is ignored, and DEC2HEX returns 10 characters, which is a 40-bit hexadecimal number in which the most significant bit is the sign bit. The remaining 39 bits are magnitude bits. Negative numbers are represented using Two's Complement notation.

- **places**—This is the number of characters to use. If *places* is omitted, DEC2HEX uses the minimum number of characters necessary. *places* is useful for padding the return value with leading 0's.

If *number* is less than −549,755,813,888 or greater than 549,755,813,887, DEC2HEX returns a #NUM! error. If *number* is nonnumeric, DEC2HEX returns a #VALUE! error. If DEC2HEX requires more than *places* characters, it returns a #NUM! error.

If *places* is not an integer, it is truncated. If *places* is nonnumeric, DEC2HEX returns a #VALUE! error. If *places* is negative, DEC2HEX returns a #NUM! error.

Figure 15.45
Use BASE to convert from decimal to any number system.

	A	B	C	D	E	F
1	From	To	Number	Result	Formula	
2	Binary	Decimal	10101	21	=BIN2DEC(C2)	
3	Binary	Hexadecimal	11111011	FB	=BIN2HEX(C3)	
4	Binary	Octal	1111	17	=BIN2OCT(C4)	
5	Hexadecimal	Binary	FC	11111100	=HEX2BIN(C5)	
6	Hexadecimal	Octal	FC	374	=HEX2OCT(C6)	
7	Hexadecimal	Decimal	FC	252	=HEX2DEC(C7)	
8	Octal	Binary	71	111001	=OCT2BIN(C8)	
9	Octal	Decimal	777	511	=OCT2DEC(C9)	
10	Octal	Hexadecimal	7770	FF8	=OCT2HEX(C10)	
11	Decimal	Binary	217	11011001	=DEC2BIN(C11)	
12	Decimal	Octal	217	331	=DEC2OCT(C12)	
13	Decimal	Hexadecimal	217	D9	=DEC2HEX(C13)	
14	Decimal	Hexadecimal	-217	FFFFFFFF27	=DEC2HEX(C14)	
15						

Syntax:

HEX2DEC(*number*)

The HEX2DEC function converts a hexadecimal number to decimal. The argument *number* is the hexadecimal number you want to convert. *number* cannot contain more than 10 characters, which is 40 bits. The most significant bit of *number* is the sign bit. The remaining 39 bits are magnitude bits. Negative numbers are represented using Two's Complement notation.

If *number* is not a valid hexadecimal number, HEX2DEC returns a #NUM! error.

Figure 15.45 shows a conversion from decimal to hexadecimal and back.

Syntax:

DEC2OCT(*number*,*places*)

The DEC2OCT function converts a decimal number to octal. This function takes the following arguments:

- **number**—This is the decimal integer you want to convert. If *number* is negative, *places* is ignored and DEC2OCT returns ten characters, which is a 30-bit octal number in which the most significant bit is the sign bit. The remaining 29 bits are magnitude bits. Negative numbers are represented using Two's Complement notation.

■ *places*—This is the number of characters to use. If *places* is omitted, DEC2OCT uses the minimum number of characters necessary. *places* is useful for padding the return value with leading 0's.

If *number* is less than −536,870,912 or greater than 536,870,911, DEC2OCT returns a #NUM! error. If *number* is nonnumeric, DEC2OCT returns a #VALUE! error. If DEC2OCT requires more than *places* characters, it returns a #NUM! error. If *places* is not an integer, it is truncated. If *places* is nonnumeric, DEC2OCT returns a #VALUE! error. If *places* is negative, DEC2OCT returns a #NUM! error.

Syntax:

OCT2DEC(*number*)

The OCT2DEC function converts an octal number to decimal. The argument *number* is the octal number you want to convert. *number* cannot contain more than ten octal characters, which is 30 bits. The most significant bit of *number* is the sign bit. The remaining 29 bits are magnitude bits. Negative numbers are represented using Two's Complement notation.

If *number* is not a valid octal number, OCT2DEC returns a #NUM! error.

Syntax:

DEC2BIN(*number*,*places*)

The DEC2BIN function converts a decimal number to binary. This function takes the following arguments:

■ *number*—This is the decimal integer you want to convert. If *number* is negative, *places* is ignored, and DEC2BIN returns 10 characters, which is a 10-bit binary number in which the most significant bit is the sign bit. The remaining 9 bits are magnitude bits. Negative numbers are represented using Two's Complement notation.

■ *places*—This is the number of characters to use. If *places* is omitted, DEC2BIN uses the minimum number of characters necessary. *places* is useful for padding the return value with leading 0's.

If *number* is less than −512 or greater than 511, DEC2BIN returns a #NUM! error. If *number* is nonnumeric, DEC2BIN returns a #VALUE! error. If DEC2BIN requires more than *places* characters, it returns the #NUM! error. If *places* is not an integer, it is truncated. If *places* is nonnumeric, DEC2BIN returns a #VALUE! error. If *places* is negative, DEC2BIN returns a #NUM! error.

Syntax:

BIN2DEC(*number*)

The BIN2DEC function converts a binary number to decimal. The argument *number* is the binary number you want to convert. *number* cannot contain more than 10 characters, which is 10 bits. The most significant bit of *number* is the sign bit. The remaining 9 bits are magnitude bits. Negative numbers are represented using Two's Complement notation.

If *number* is not a valid binary number, or if *number* contains more than 10 characters, which is 10 bits, BIN2DEC returns a #NUM! error.

The formulas in Figure 15.45 convert from decimal to binary and from binary to decimal.

Excel offers six additional functions that can convert directly from octal to hexadecimal to binary. The major limitation of these functions is that Excel can represent as binary only numbers up to 511 in decimal. This is a significant limitation; anything larger than 1FF in hex or larger than 777 in octal returns an error if you try to convert it to binary.

The following are the additional conversion functions:

- **BIN2HEX**(*number,places*)—Converts a binary number to hexadecimal

- **BIN2OCT**(*number,places*)—Converts a binary number to octal

- **HEX2BIN**(*number,places*)—Converts a hexadecimal number to binary

- **HEX2OCT**(*number,places*)—Converts a hexadecimal number to octal

- **OCT2BIN**(*number,places*)—Converts an octal number to binary

- **OCT2HEX**(*number,places*)—Converts an octal number to hexadecimal

Explaining the Two's Complement for Negative Numbers

Results for DEC2BIN, DEC2OCT, and DEC2HEX look bizarre for negative numbers. This is a special notation called *Two's Complement*. In Excel, we have to agree that a negative number occupies 10 characters. For example, cell A1 in Figure 15.46 contains the number 5 in binary.

If the leftmost bit is a 1, then the number is assumed to be negative, and Excel assumes that the number is in Two's Complement notation. There are two simple steps to convert a positive number to a negative number in Two's Complement:

1. Change every 0 to a 1 and every 1 to a 0. This produces a number in One's Complement, as shown in cell A2 in Figure 15.46.

2. Add 1 to the result from step 1 to convert to Two's Complement, as shown in cell A3 in Figure 15.46.

Converting from negative to positive in Two's Complement follows exactly the same method. Cell A13 in Figure 15.46 contains –5 in Two's Complement. In cell A14, you switch all the 0s and 1s. In cell A15, you add 1 to produce the original result in binary.

 Note

The leftmost bit is always set to a 1 for a negative number. This prevents Excel from representing 512 in binary. The binary representation of 512—1000000000—has a 1 in the leftmost digit, which means no numbers greater than 511 can be represented in binary in Excel.

A1	▼	:	×	✓	*fx*	'00 0000 0101			

	A	B	C	D	E	F	G	H
1	00 0000 0101	Original Number in Binary (5)						
2	11 1111 1010	Switch 0 and 1 to move to Ones complement						
3	11 1111 1011	Add 1 to convert to two's complement (-5)						
4								
5	00 0000 0000	Zero in Binary						
6	11 1111 1111	Switch 0 and 1 to move to Ones complement						
7	00 0000 0000	Add 1 to convert to two's complement (ignoring the overflow digit)						
8								
9	00 0000 0001	One in binary						
10	11 1111 1110	Ones complement						
11	11 1111 1111	Add one to create one's complement						
12								
13	11 1111 1011	-5 in two's complement						
14	00 0000 0100	Switch 0 and 1						
15	00 0000 0101	Add 1 to produce positive five in binary						
16								

Figure 15.46
Negative numbers in Two's Complement are initially unnerving until you understand the steps for converting them.

Using DELTA or GESTEP to Filter a Set of Values

The functions DELTA and GESTEP are left over from a long-ago era. In the SUMPRODUCT function, you can see that Excel can now evaluate TRUE*100 as 100 and FALSE*100 as 0. In early spreadsheet programs, you needed to convert TRUE to 1 and FALSE to 0 explicitly. These two functions explicitly return 1 when a condition is true and 0 when a condition is false, enabling you to multiply the original number by the function in order to get conditional sums.

DELTA tests whether two values are equal. GESTEP tests whether a value is greater than or equal to a threshold value.

Syntax:

DELTA(*number1*,*number2*)

The DELTA function tests whether two values are equal. It returns 1 if *number1* equals *number2*; it returns 0 otherwise. You use this function to filter a set of values. For example, by summing several DELTA functions, you can calculate the count of equal pairs. This function is also known as the Kronecker Delta function. This function takes the following arguments:

- **number1**—This is the first number.

- **number2**—This is the second number. If omitted, number2 is assumed to be 0.

If either *number1* or *number2* is nonnumeric, DELTA returns a #VALUE! error.

Figure 15.47 shows a list of students and their test scores in columns A and B. A large matrix of DELTA functions in C:W counts how many students achieved each score. Excel has many newer, better functions, such as COUNTIF, that can also achieve this result.

Figure 15.47
The DELTA functions in C2:W24 check whether the score in column B is the same as the score in row 1. Totals in row 25 complete the analysis.

| C2 | ▼ | : | × | ✓ | *fx* | =DELTA($B2,C$1) |

	A	B	C	D	E	F	G	H	I	J	K	L	M	N	O	P	Q	R	S	T	U	V	W
1	STUDENT	SCORE	80	81	82	83	84	85	86	87	88	89	90	91	92	93	94	95	96	97	98	99	100
2	RAYMOND	81	0	1	0	0	0	0	0	0	0	0	0	0	0	0	0	0	0	0	0	0	0
3	SEAN	100	0	0	0	0	0	0	0	0	0	0	0	0	0	0	0	0	0	0	0	0	1
4	ERIN	100	0	0	0	0	0	0	0	0	0	0	0	0	0	0	0	0	0	0	0	0	1
5	JACK	90	0	0	0	0	0	0	0	0	0	0	1	0	0	0	0	0	0	0	0	0	0
6	BRYAN	90	0	0	0	0	0	0	0	0	0	0	1	0	0	0	0	0	0	0	0	0	0
7	RANDY	85	0	0	0	0	0	1	0	0	0	0	0	0	0	0	0	0	0	0	0	0	0
8	HOWARD	92	0	0	0	0	0	0	0	0	0	0	0	0	1	0	0	0	0	0	0	0	0
9	TERESA	90	0	0	0	0	0	0	0	0	0	0	1	0	0	0	0	0	0	0	0	0	0
10	ELLA	89	0	0	0	0	0	0	0	0	0	1	0	0	0	0	0	0	0	0	0	0	0
11	BETTY	83	0	0	0	1	0	0	0	0	0	0	0	0	0	0	0	0	0	0	0	0	0
12	LUZ	89	0	0	0	0	0	0	0	0	0	1	0	0	0	0	0	0	0	0	0	0	0
13	ALICIA	97	0	0	0	0	0	0	0	0	0	0	0	0	0	0	0	0	0	1	0	0	0
14	CHARLENE	100	0	0	0	0	0	0	0	0	0	0	0	0	0	0	0	0	0	0	0	0	1
15	VICTORIA	83	0	0	0	1	0	0	0	0	0	0	0	0	0	0	0	0	0	0	0	0	0
16	LAUREN	87	0	0	0	0	0	0	0	1	0	0	0	0	0	0	0	0	0	0	0	0	0
17	TRACEY	97	0	0	0	0	0	0	0	0	0	0	0	0	0	0	0	0	0	1	0	0	0
18	KYLE	83	0	0	0	1	0	0	0	0	0	0	0	0	0	0	0	0	0	0	0	0	0
19	WILMA	100	0	0	0	0	0	0	0	0	0	0	0	0	0	0	0	0	0	0	0	0	1
20	MARCIA	89	0	0	0	0	0	0	0	0	0	1	0	0	0	0	0	0	0	0	0	0	0
21	WILLIE	98	0	0	0	0	0	0	0	0	0	0	0	0	0	0	0	0	0	0	1	0	0
22	EUGENE	83	0	0	0	1	0	0	0	0	0	0	0	0	0	0	0	0	0	0	0	0	0
23	LEAH	90	0	0	0	0	0	0	0	0	0	0	1	0	0	0	0	0	0	0	0	0	0
24	LORI	86	0	0	0	0	0	0	1	0	0	0	0	0	0	0	0	0	0	0	0	0	0
25		Total	0	1	0	4	0	1	1	1	0	3	4	0	1	0	0	0	0	2	1	0	4
26																							

Syntax:

GESTEP(*number*,*step*)

The GESTEP function returns 1 if *number* is greater than or equal to *step*; it returns 0 otherwise. You can use this function to filter a set of values. For example, by summing several GESTEP functions, you can calculate the count of values that exceed a threshold. This function takes the following arguments:

- **number**—This is the value to test against *step*.

- **step**—This is the threshold value. If you omit a value for *step*, GESTEP uses 0.

If any argument is nonnumeric, GESTEP returns a #VALUE! error.

Using ERF and ERFC to Calculate the Error Function and Its Complement

An error function is designed to make it easier to represent integrals in the form $x^n \times e^{(-ax^2)}\,dx$. All such integrals can be written in terms of the integral $e^{(-u^2)}\,du$. If you integrate this from 0 to infinity, it converges to SQRT(PI)/2. The ERF function, then, is defined so that ERF converges to 1 at infinity.

The ERF function is ERF(x) = 2/SQRT(PI()) times the integral of $e^{(-u^2)}du$ integrated from 0 to x. The result of ERF is a value between 0 and 1.

Contrary to what Excel Help says, two syntax options are available in Excel for ERF:

- **ERF(*x*)**—The common use of ERF is with a single argument. In this case, the function returns the ERF function. In the preceding formula, the integral is evaluated from 0 to x. For example, ERF(0.1) is 0.112463.

- **ERF(*lower_limit,upper_limit*)**—The second syntax for ERF provides a lower and an upper limit. In this case, Excel integrates from x to y.

The ERFC function provides the complement to ERF. In all cases, ERFC(x) is equal to 1-ERF(x).

Figure 15.48 charts the ERF and ERFC functions.

 Note

Although ERF is defined for negative values, Excel does not calculate ERF for less than 0. If you need to do this, you have to turn to more comprehensive calculation engines, such as Mathematica.

Figure 15.48
ERF converges very close to 1 for values of 3 or greater. ERFC is 1 − ERF.

	A	B	C	D	E	F	G	H
1		ERF	ERFC					
2	0	0	1		0.8427	=ERF(1)		
3	0.05	0.056371978	0.94363		0.99532	=ERF(2)		
4	0.1	0.112462916	0.88754		0.15262	=ERF(1,2)		
5	0.15	0.167995971	0.832					
6	0.2	0.222702589	0.7773					
7	0.25	0.27632639	0.72367					
8	0.3	0.328626759	0.67137					
9	0.35	0.379382054	0.62062					
10	0.4	0.428392355	0.57161					
11	0.45	0.47548172	0.52452					
12	0.5	0.520499878	0.4795					
13	0.55	0.563323366	0.43668					
14	0.6	0.603856091	0.39614					
15	0.65	0.642029327	0.35797					
16	0.7	0.677801194	0.3222					
17	0.75	0.711155634	0.28884					
18	0.8	0.742100965	0.2579					
19	0.85	0.770668058	0.22933					
20	0.9	0.796908212	0.20309					

Syntax:

ERF(*x*)

In this first syntax, the ERF function returns the error function for x.

Syntax:

ERF(*lower_limit*,*upper_limit*)

In this second syntax, the ERF function returns the error function integrated between *lower_limit* and *upper_limit*. This function takes the following arguments:

- *lower_limit*—This is the lower bound for integrating ERF.

- *upper_limit*—This is the upper bound for integrating ERF. If any argument is nonnumeric, ERF returns a #VALUE! error. If any argument is negative, ERF returns a #NUM! error.

Syntax:

ERFC(*x*)

The ERFC function returns the complementary ERF function integrated between x and infinity. The argument x is the lower bound for integrating ERF. If x is nonnumeric, ERFC returns a #VALUE! error. If x is negative, ERFC returns a #NUM! error.

Calculating the BESSEL Functions

The BESSEL function is useful in many physics applications that involve solving classical partial differential equations in cylindrical coordinates. Excel offers four versions of the BESSEL function:

- **BESSELJ**—This solves the BESSEL function of the first kind. You use this function to solve BESSEL differential equations that are nonsingular at the origin.

- **BESSELY**—This solves the BESSEL functions of the second kind. You use this function to solve BESSEL differential equations that are singular at the origin. The BESSEL functions of the second kind are sometimes called Weber or Neumann functions.

- **BESSELI**—This solves the modified BESSEL differential equation. It is closely related to BESSELJ.

- **BESSELK**—This solves the modified BESSEL function of the second kind. This function is also known as the Basset function, Macdonald function, or BESSEL function of the third kind.

Each Bessel function takes two required arguments:

- *x*—This is the value at which to evaluate the function.

- *n*—This is the order of the BESSEL function. If *n* is not an integer, it is truncated.

If *x* is nonnumeric, BESSELI returns a #VALUE! error. If *n* is nonnumeric, BESSELI returns a #VALUE! error. If *n* is less than 0, BESSELI returns a #NUM! error.

Figure 15.49 shows the BESSELJ and BESSELY functions for orders of *n* from 0 through 4.

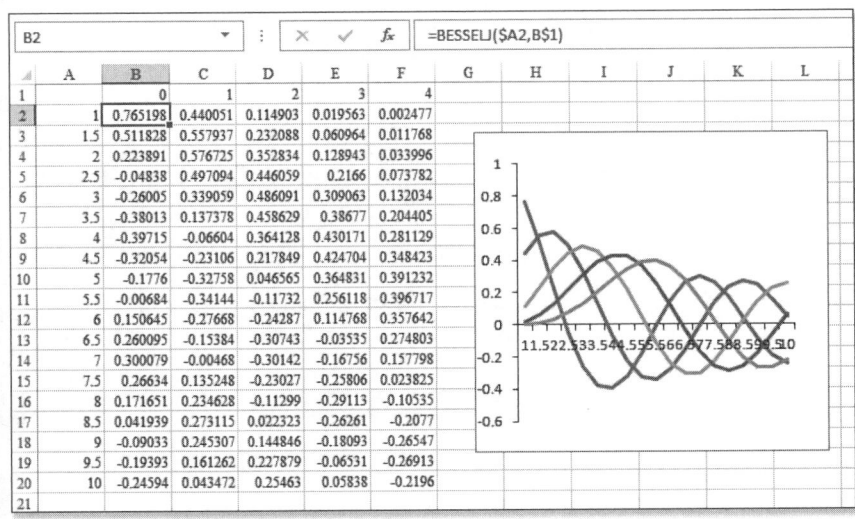

Figure 15.49
This chart shows the BESSELJ and BESSELY functions.

Using the Analysis Toolpack to Perform Fast Fourier Transforms (FFTs)

Many of the engineering functions have been promoted from the Analysis Toolpack to the regular version of Excel. However, one feature is left orphaned in the Analysis Toolpack. If you need to perform Fourier analysis, you should install the Analysis Toolpack.

➡ *See the "Installing the Analysis Toolpack in Excel 2013" section in Chapter 14, "Using Statistical Functions."*

Fourier transforms are used to evaluate the output of an analog-to-digital conversion (ADC). To perform a Fourier transform, follow these steps:

1. Import your ADC data into Excel. The ADC record should contain a specific number of records that are powers of 2, up to 4,096 (such as 2, 4, 8, 16, 32, 64, 128, 256, 512, 1,024, 2,048, or 4,096).

2. Make sure the Analysis Toolpack is installed.

3. From the Data tab, select Data Analysis.

4. Select Fourier Analysis and click OK. The Fourier Analysis dialog appears.

5. In the Fourier Analysis dialog, select your ADC data as the input range. If your input range includes a heading, select the Labels in First Row check box. In this case, your data must be $(n^2) + 1$ records long.

6. Select the top-left cell of the output range.

7. Leave the Inverse check box clear. This check box is used to convert FFT numbers in imaginary format back to the ADC format.

8. Click OK to perform the transformation.

CONNECTING WORKSHEETS, WORKBOOKS, AND EXTERNAL DATA

In Chapters 10, "Understanding Functions," and 11, "Using Everyday Functions: Math, Date and Time, and Text Functions," you find out how to set up formulas that calculate based on values within one worksheet. You can also easily connect a worksheet to several other worksheets or connect various workbooks. Excel 2013 offers easier-than-ever ways to connect a worksheet to data from the Web, data from text files, or data from databases such as Access.

In this chapter, you discover how to do the following:

- Connect two worksheets
- Connect two workbooks
- Manage links between workbooks
- Connect to Web data
- Connect to text data
- Connect to Access data
- Manage connections

Connecting Two Worksheets

Although Excel 2013 offers 17 billion cells on every worksheet, it is fairly common to separate any model onto several worksheets. You might choose to have one worksheet for each month in a year or to have one worksheet for each functional area of a business. For example, Figure 16.1 shows a workbook with worksheets for revenue and expenses. Because different departments might be responsible for the functional areas, it makes sense to separate them into different worksheets. Eventually, though, you will want to pull information from the various worksheets into a single summary worksheet.

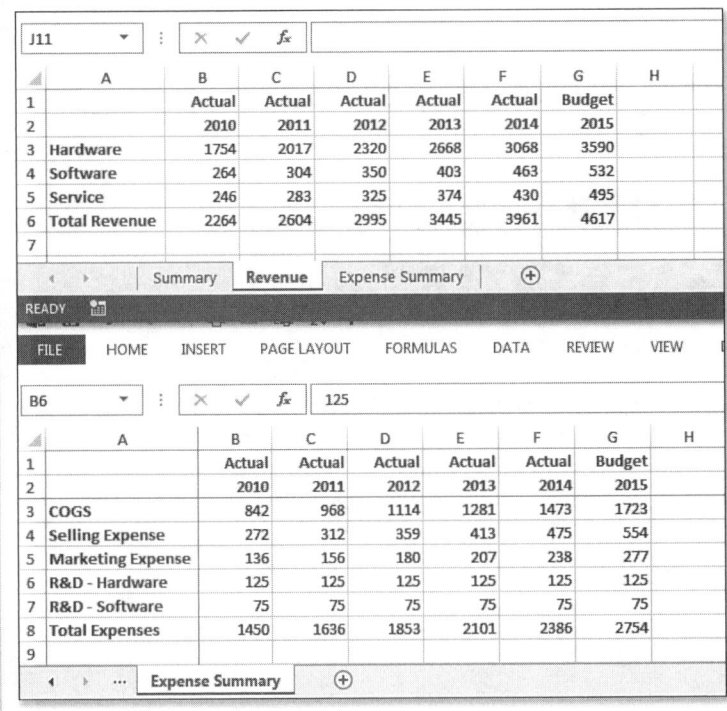

Figure 16.1
Different functional areas need to work on budgets for revenue and expenses, so revenue and expenses are kept on separate worksheets.

To return to a single window, click the Close Window icon, which is the "X" in the top-right corner of window 2.

As shown in Figure 16.2, the goal is to have the values from cells F6:G6 on the Revenue tab carry forward to cells B5:C5 on the Summary tab. There are four ways to achieve this goal:

- Type a formula, such as =Revenue!F6, in cell B5.

- Build the formula using the mouse.

- Right-drag cells F6:G6 on the Revenue tab to the proper location on the Summary tab and then select Link Here.

- Copy cells F6:G6 on the Revenue tab. Paste to cells B5:C5 and then use the paste options fly-out menu to Link Here. This is the newest method and is discussed in the next section.

 Note

Note that you have not created a second workbook. Instead, you have created a second camera looking at a different section of the same workbook. Any changes you make in the left window appear in the second window.

Figure 16.2
Set up a link to get information from the Revenue tab to appear on the Summary tab.

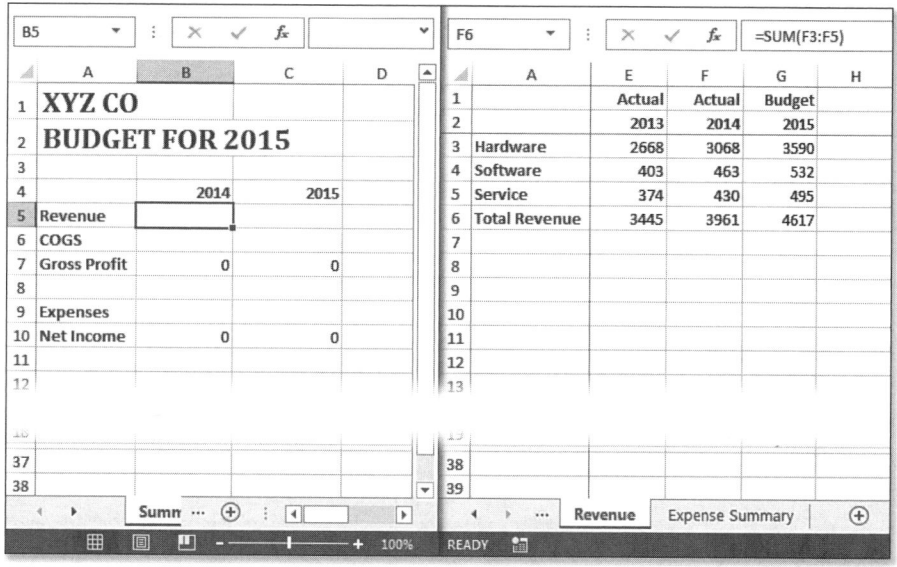

Excel in Practice: Seeing Two Worksheets of the Same Workbook Side by Side.

The workbook in Figure 16.1 illustrates a useful trick—seeing two worksheets of the same workbook side by side. Follow these steps to see two worksheets of the same workbook side by side:

1. Open the first worksheet that you want to view.

2. On the View tab, click New Window. If your workbook is in full-screen mode, it appears that nothing happened. However, when you look in the title bar, you see your workbook title has ":2" after the title.

3. On the View tab, click Arrange All and then click either Vertical or Horizontal. Click the Windows of Active Workbook check box. The arrangement in Figure 16.1 is horizontal, whereas the arrangement in Figure 16.2 is vertical.

4. In the second window, click the second worksheet tab that you want to view. You can now see both worksheets of the same workbook side by side. New in Excel 2013, each window has its own ribbon and status bar.

Creating Links Using Paste Options Menu

Follow these steps to set up a link using the new Paste Options fly-out menu:

1. Select the cells that have the figures you want to copy. For this example, select cells F6:G6 on the Revenue tab.

2. Press Ctrl+C to copy those cells.

3. Select the cells where the link should appear. For this example, select B5 on the Summary tab.

4. Press Ctrl+V to paste. As shown in Figure 16.3, the formula from the source cells is pasted in the target cells, giving the wrong answer—but do not panic. In addition, note that a new Paste Options menu appears near the pasted cell.

5. Press Ctrl to open the Paste Options menu. Select the Chain icon in the bottom row of the fly-out menu. Alternatively, you can press N to Paste Link (see Figure 16.3).

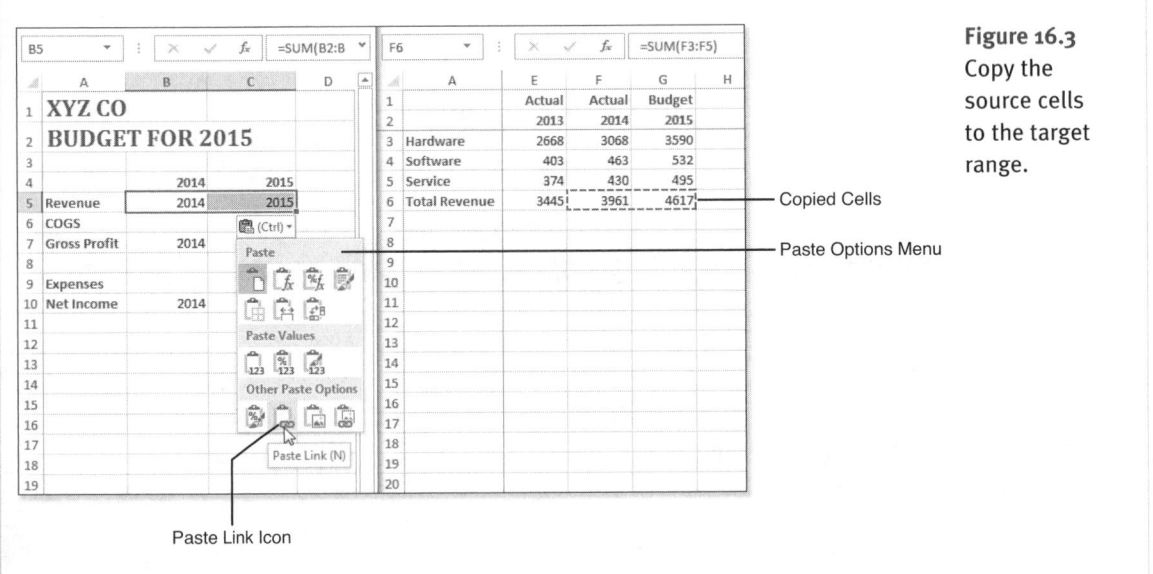

Figure 16.3
Copy the source cells to the target range.

Excel changes the formula from Figure 16.3 to have the correct syntax to point to cells F6 on the Revenue tab (see Figure 16.4). Note that if data changes on the Revenue worksheet, the new results appear on the Summary worksheet. In Figure 16.4, the hardware budget changed from 3590 to 3625, and the resulting change appears on the Summary worksheet.

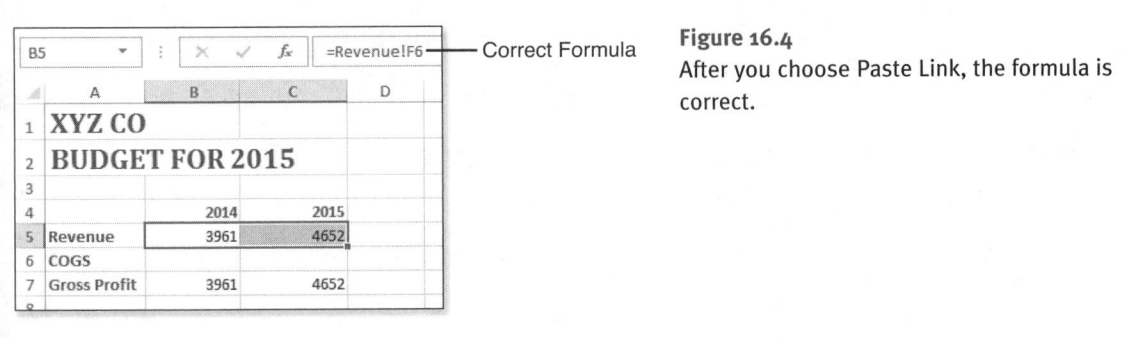

Figure 16.4
After you choose Paste Link, the formula is correct.

Creating Links Using the Right-Drag Menu

If you are adept with the mouse, there is an easier way to create links. This is particularly true if you have the two worksheets arranged side by side, which was presented previously in the Excel in Practice sidebar.

This method uses the Alternate Drag-and-Drop menu. This amazing menu, which has been hiding in Excel for several versions, offers a fast way to copy cells, link cells, change formulas to values, and more.

The Alternate Drag-and-Drop menu appears any time you right-click the border of a selection, right-drag to a new location, and then release the mouse button.

In Figure 16.5, on the Expense Summary tab, select cells F3:G3. Hover over the edge of the selection rectangle until you see the four-headed arrow. Right-click and begin to drag to the other window.

Figure 16.5
Right-click and drag the source cells.

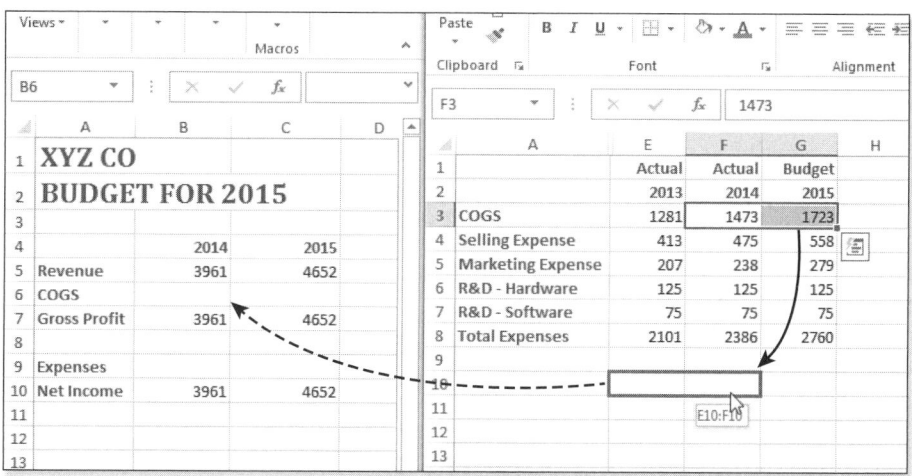

When you have arrived at the new location, release the right-mouse button and select Link Here, as shown in Figure 16.6. Excel builds a formula in the target location that has the proper syntax to link to the source cells. Note that because the worksheet name contains a space, Excel wraps the sheet name in apostrophes: ='Expense Summary'!F3 (see Figure 16.7).

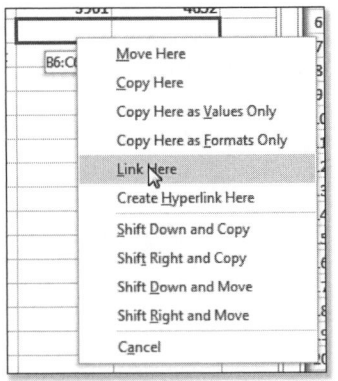

Figure 16.6
Release the mouse button to access this menu.

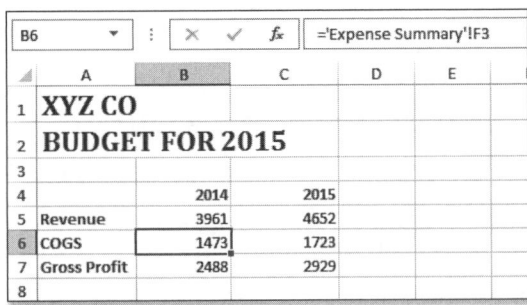

Figure 16.7
Excel builds the proper formula.

Building a Link by Using the Mouse

Another method is to build a formula by pointing to the correct cell with the mouse. Start in a target cell, such as cell B9 on the Summary tab (see Figure 16.8).

Instead of trying to remember the exact syntax, you can point to the correct cell. Type the equal sign and then click the desired worksheet tab. Using the mouse, click a cell to get the value from that cell. Excel builds the formula ='Expense Summary'!F8 in the formula bar (see Figure 16.8). Excel waits for you to either press the Enter key to accept the formula or press another operator key to add other cells to the formula.

When you press the Enter key to accept the formula, Excel jumps back to the starting worksheet. The desired figure is carried through to the worksheet.

 **Note**

The formula that Excel builds is a relative formula. You can copy B9 to B10 to retrieve the 2015 budget.

Figure 16.8
Type an equal sign, and then click the source cell.

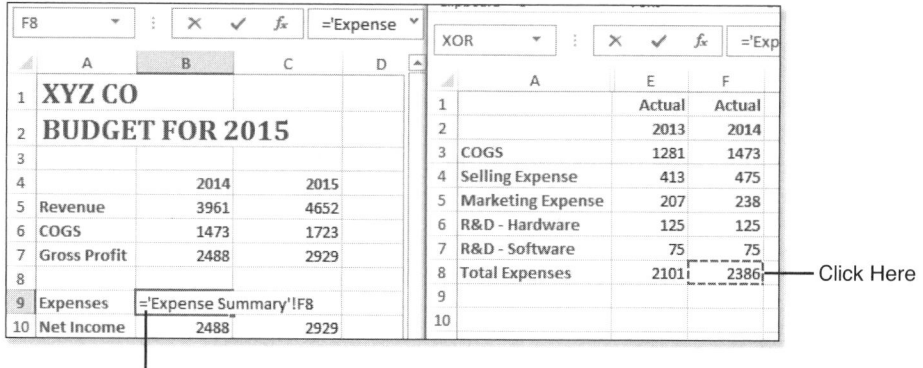

Type an Equals Sign Here

Click Here

Links to External Workbooks Default to Absolute References

You can use any of the four methods described previously for building links to other worksheets when you want to build links to external workbooks. It is easiest if you open both workbooks.

Note that if you use any of the methods illustrated previously, Excel defaults to adding dollar signs into the external reference. The dollar signs create an absolute reference that make it more difficult to copy.

Here is an example. When you use the mouse method described in Figure 16.8 to link to a worksheet in the same workbook, the cell reference is something like F8. If you use the same method to link to a worksheet in a different workbook, the cell reference created by Excel is automatically $F$8. The dollar signs make this an absolute reference, which is difficult to copy. If you need to copy this formula to other cells, you should press the F4 key three times to change from an absolute reference to a relative reference.

Building a Formula by Typing

You can always build the links by typing the formula. This is the least popular method, because you need to understand an array of syntax rules. Keep in mind that these syntax rules change depending on whether the worksheet name contains a space, whether the link is external, and whether the linked workbook is open or closed.

Here are the syntax rules:

- For an internal link where the worksheet name does not contain a space, use
  =SheetName!CellAddress. An example is =Result!B3.

- When the worksheet name contains a space or certain special characters, Excel automatically adds apostrophes around the workbook name and sheet name. An example is
  ='Result Sheet'!B3.

- For an external link, the name of the workbook is wrapped in square brackets and appears before the sheet name. An example is =[LinkToMe.xlsm]Sheet1!B3.

- If the workbook name or sheet name contains a space, add an apostrophe before the opening square bracket and after the sheet name. An example is =`'[My File.xls]Income Statement'!B3`.

- When Excel refers to a file such as [RegionTotals.xlsm], you can assume that the file is currently open. When you close the linked file, Excel updates the formula in the linking workbook to include the complete pathname. An example is =`SUM('C:\[Region Totals.xlsm]Quota'!$B$2:$E$2)`.

- Figure 16.9 illustrates examples of various formulas:

1	Link Syntax					
2						
3	Type	Spaces?	Result	Formula		
4	Internal	No	5	=Result!B3		
5	Internal	Yes	6	='Result Sheet'!B3		
6	External	No	1	=[16LinkToMe.xlsm]Sheet1!$B$3		
7	External	Yes	3	='[16-Link To Me.xlsm]Sheet3'!$B$4		
8	External	No	7	='C:\Links\[16Closed.xlsm]Sheet1'!$B$3		
9	External	No	8	='C:\Links\[16Closed.xlsm]Sheet 2'!$B$3		
10						

Figure 16.9
Syntax for various types of links.

Creating Links to Unsaved Workbooks

You can build a formula that links to a source workbook where the source workbook has not been saved. This formula might point to Book1 or Book3 or a workbook such as that. When you attempt to save the target workbook, Excel presents a dialog that asks, "Save <filename> with references to unsaved documents?" In general, you should cancel the save, switch to the unsaved source workbook, and then select File, Save As to save the file with a permanent name. Then you can come back to save the linking workbook.

Using the Links Tab on the Trust Center

By default, Excel applies security settings that frustrate your attempts to pull values from closed workbooks. Consider the following scenario using two workbooks labeled Workbook A and Workbook B:

1. Establish a link from Workbook A to Workbook B.
2. Save and close Workbook A.
3. Make changes to Workbook B. Save and close Workbook B.
4. Later, open Workbook B.
5. Open Workbook A.

In this case, the new values in Workbook B automatically flow through to Workbook A.

However, if you attempt to later open Workbook A before opening Workbook B, you see the following message: "Automatic Update of Links Has Been Disabled" (see Figure 16.10).

Figure 16.10
The link message initially appears in the info bar.

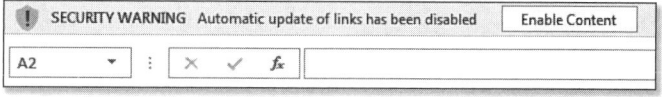

After you enable the content the first time, Excel marks the document as a trusted document. The next time you open the workbook, Excel displays a different cautionary message about links to external sources that could be unsafe, as shown in Figure 16.11.

Figure 16.11
Later, the Excel 2003–style link question appears.

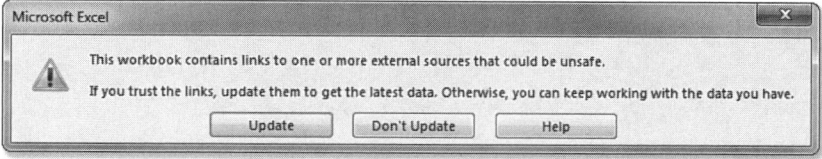

You might wonder what could be unsafe about a link. I do, too. When I asked someone at Microsoft about this, they painted an incredibly convoluted scenario that I have never seen happen. The links that are described in this section are safe. Feel free to click Update.

Opening Workbooks with Links to Closed Workbooks

Suppose that you have saved and closed the linking workbook. You update numbers in the linked workbook. You save and close the linked workbook. Later, when you open the linking workbook, Excel asks if you want to update the links to the other workbook. If you created both workbooks and you have possession of both workbooks, it is fine to allow the workbooks to update.

Dealing with Missing Linked Workbooks

If you received a linking workbook via email and do not have access to the linked workbooks, Excel alerts you that the workbook contains links that cannot be updated right now. In this case, you should click Continue in the dialog box, as shown in Figure 16.12.

Figure 16.12
This message means that the linked workbook cannot be found. It shows up most often when someone mails you only the linking workbook.

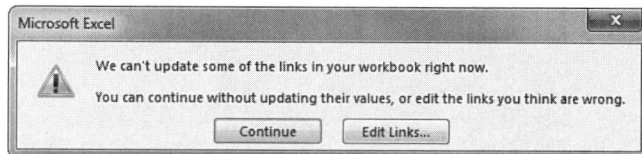

You also get this message if the linked workbook was renamed, moved, or deleted. In that case, you should click the Edit Links button to display the Edit Links dialog (see Figure 16.13). Then you should click the Change Source button to tell Excel that the linked workbook has a new name or location. Alternatively, you might need to click the Break Link button to change all linked formulas to their current values.

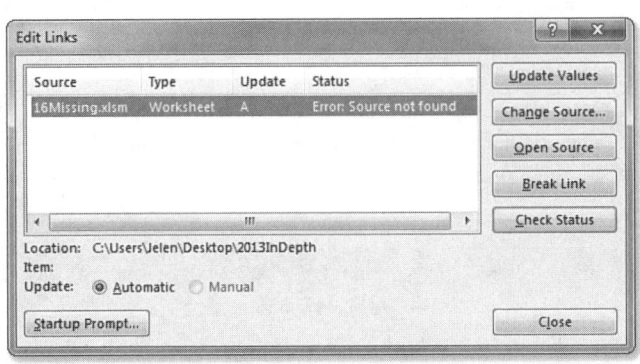

Figure 16.13
Manage or change links by using this dialog.

Preventing the Update Links Dialog from Appearing

Suppose that you need to send a linking workbook to a co-worker. You want your co-worker to see the current values of the linking formulas without having the linked workbook. In this case, you want the co-worker to click Continue in Figure 16.12. However, some newer Excel customers think that every warning box is a disaster, so you might prefer to suppress that box for your co-worker. To do so, follow these steps:

1. On the Data tab, in the Connections group, select Edit Links.

2. In the lower-left corner of the dialog that appears, click the Startup Prompt button. The Startup Prompt dialog appears.

3. Select Don't Display the Alert and Don't Update Automatic Links (see Figure 16.14).

After emailing the workbook to your co-worker, you need to redisplay the Startup Prompt dialog and change it back so that you will get the updated links.

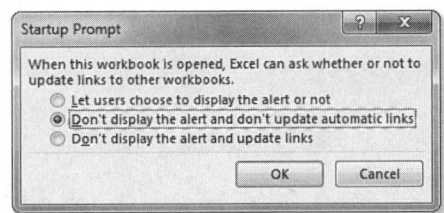

Figure 16.14
You can prevent others from seeing the Update Links message.

Connecting to Data on a Web Page

Many web pages comprise many tables of data. Any time you see columns of numbers or columns of data, it is likely that you see the results of a table. Usually, the only things not in a table are paragraphs of body copy. In addition, it is not usually necessary to update this information on a daily basis. Excel 2013 makes it even easier than past versions of Excel to link your Excel worksheet to a table on any web page.

Setting Up a Connection to a Web Page

To set up a connection between a worksheet and a web page, follow these steps:

1. Find a section of the worksheet that has several blank rows and blank columns. Depending on the size of the selected sections of the web page, you can return many rows or columns of data.

2. On the Data tab, from the Get External Data group, select From Web. Excel opens the New Web Query dialog. This dialog looks remarkably like a mini web browser, and it even opens to your default home page from Internet Explorer. However, as shown in Figure 16.15, the rendered web page includes one or more yellow boxes with black arrows. These arrows indicate the tops of various tables on the page.

Figure 16.15
Notice the arrows indicating available tables on the web page.

Arrow for Table

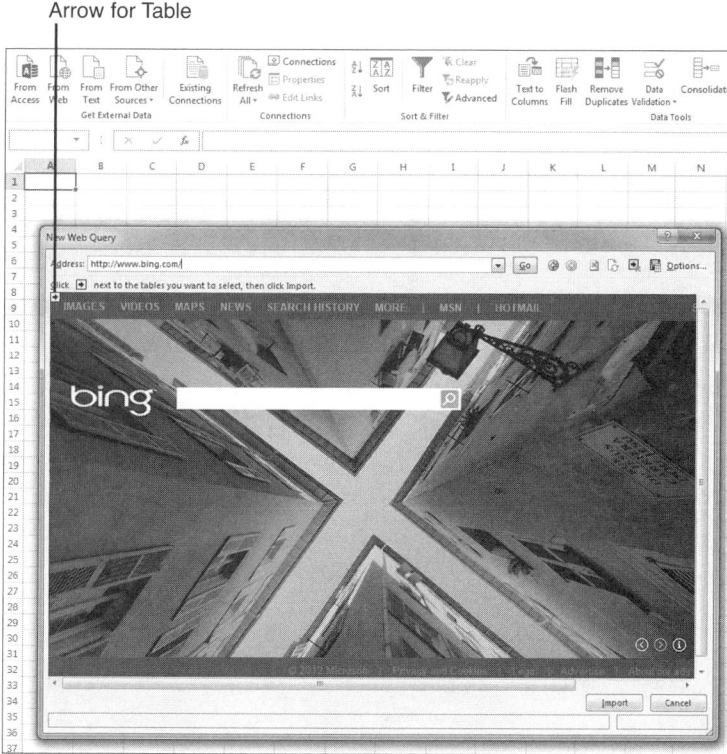

3. Using the search bar or the address bar, navigate to the selected web page. For example, to retrieve stock quotes, you might use http://bing.com/finance.

4. If the web page has a form, enter any values needed by the form. In this example, enter your desired ticker symbols into the Bing Finance Get Quotes box and then click Go. The resulting web page will probably have many tables.

5. Hover the mouse over various yellow and black arrows. Excel highlights the entire range of each table.

6. When you find the table that contains the information you want, click that arrow. The arrow changes to a green check mark, as shown in Figure 16.16.

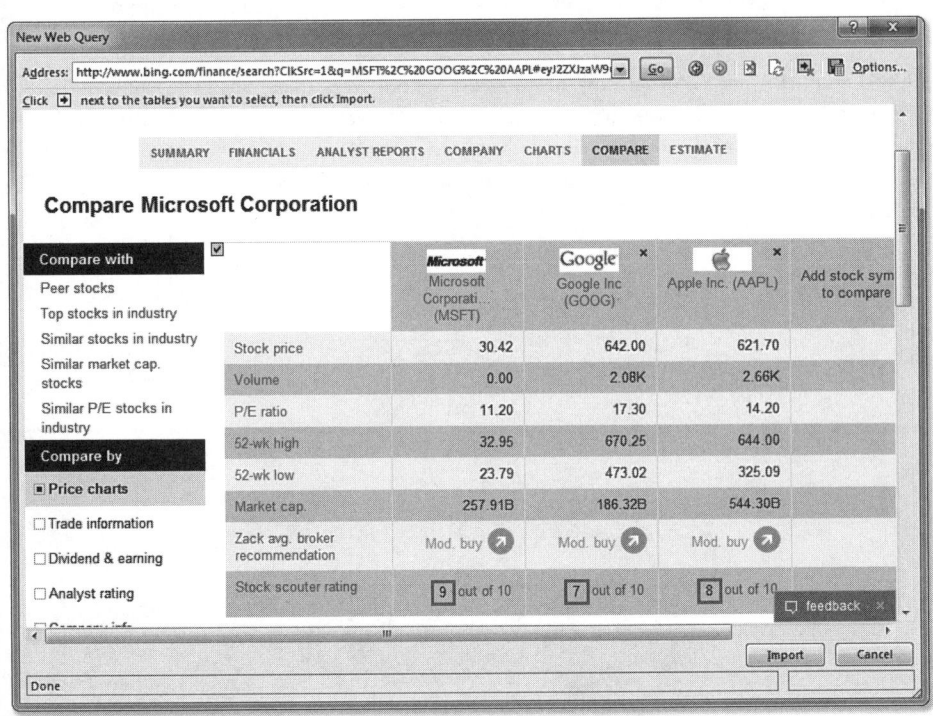

Figure 16.16
Select the table that contains the data for the worksheet.

7. In the upper-right corner of the New Web Query dialog, click the Options button. The External Data Range Properties dialog appears (see Figure 16.17).

Figure 16.17
Most of the time, you want unformatted text.

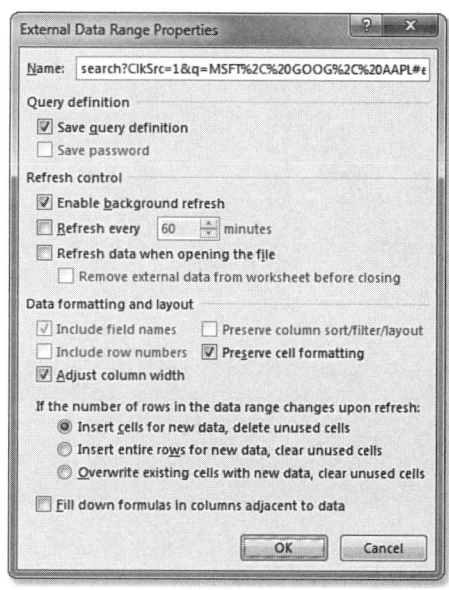

8. Select whether the data from the web page should be retrieved as text only or have full HTML formatting in the results. Then click OK.

9. Click the Import button in the lower-right corner of the New Web Query dialog. Excel displays the Import Data dialog, which enables you to confirm the output location for the data from the web query (see Figure 16.18).

Figure 16.18
Confirm where the data should be returned.

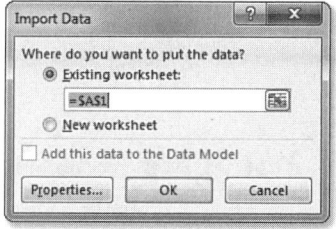

10. If desired, click the Properties button to set up automatic refreshing of the web data. The External Data Range Properties dialog appears (see Figure 16.19).

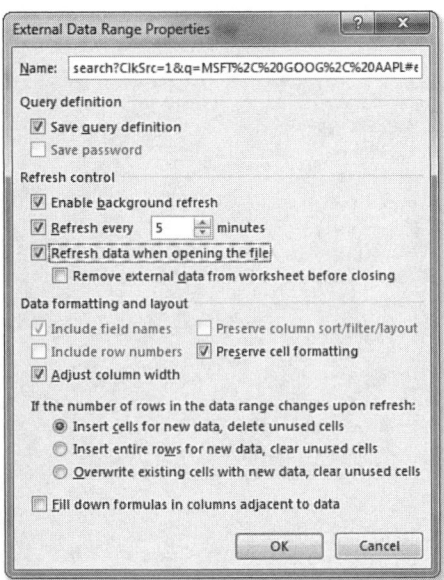

Figure 16.19
Control the refresh rate for the web query on this dialog.

11. Use the Connection Properties dialog to set refresh options. For example, you can have the web query refreshed every so many minutes, and you can also have the web data refreshed when a file opens. This way, you can retrieve new data each day when you open the file. When you are done selecting options on this dialog, click OK. You briefly see a bit of web query code appear in the worksheet at your destination location. If your Internet connection is working, this is soon replaced by the data from the web page, as shown in Figure 16.20.

 Note

When the active cell is in the range of data retrieved by a web query, all the Get External Data options in the ribbon are disabled. This happens when your cell pointer is located in external data. To set up a new web query on the same worksheet, move the cell pointer to a cell outside the retrieved data.

Managing Properties for Web Queries

After you retrieve a web query, you can select a single cell in the query and select Properties from the Connections group on the Data tab. The External Data Range Properties dialog appears, similar to the dialog shown previously in Figure 16.19. This dialog box includes additional properties for the query. In the Data Formatting and Layout section, you can choose options to preserve cell formatting and adjust column widths. Most important, you can specify that if the query returns more rows tomorrow, any formulas adjacent to the web query should be expanded.

Figure 16.20
The results of the web query are imported to your workbook.

▲	A	B	C	D	
1		MSFT	GOOG	AAPL	Add stock s
2		Microsoft Corporati... (MSFT)	Google Inc (GOOG)	Apple Inc. (AAPL)	
3	Stock price	-	-	-	
4	Volume	-	-	-	
5	P/E ratio	11.2	17.3	14.2	
6	52-wk high	32.95	670.25	644	
7	52-wk low	23.79	473.02	325.09	
8	Market cap.	257.91B	186.32B	544.30B	
9	Zack avg. broker recommendation	Mod. buy	Mod. buy	Mod. buy	
10	Stock scouter rating		9	7	8
11		out of 10	out of 10	out of 10	
12					

Setting Up a Connection to a Text File

It is possible to load data from a text file into Excel using the connection group. Consider the text file shown in Figure 16.21.

Figure 16.21
Connect to a simple text file using Excel.

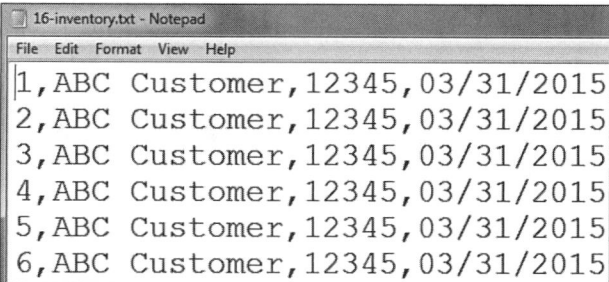

```
1,ABC Customer,12345,03/31/2015
2,ABC Customer,12345,03/31/2015
3,ABC Customer,12345,03/31/2015
4,ABC Customer,12345,03/31/2015
5,ABC Customer,12345,03/31/2015
6,ABC Customer,12345,03/31/2015
```

Follow these steps to set up a connection:

1. On the Data tab, select the From Text icon in the Get External Data group. The Import Text File dialog appears.

2. Browse to and select your text file. Excel launches the familiar Text Import Wizard – Step 1 of 3, where you can specify that the text is either delimited or fixed width.

3. Select Delimited, as shown in Figure 16.22, and then click Next.

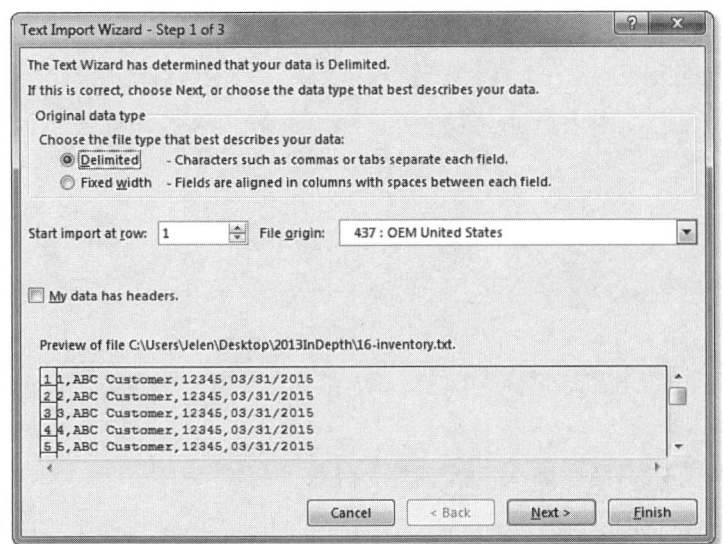

Figure 16.22
You navigate through the Text Import Wizard to set up a connection to a text file.

4. In step 2 of the wizard, change the Excel default tab character between fields to a comma, as shown in Figure 16.23.

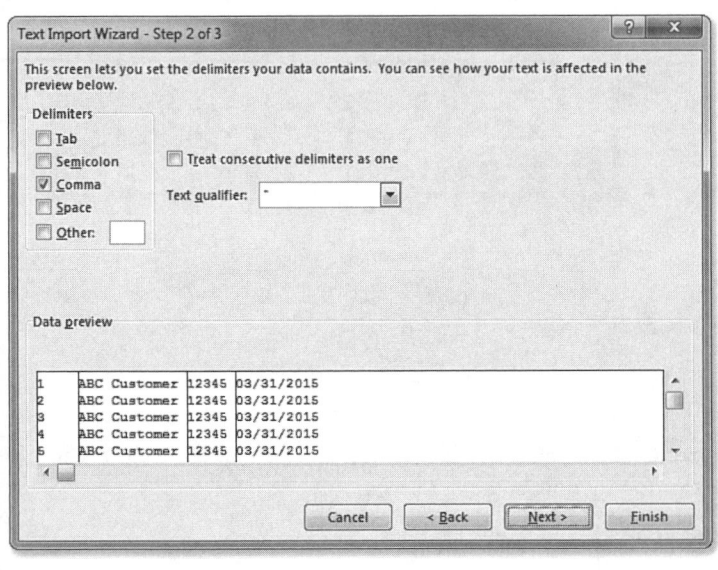

Figure 16.23
You specify the delimiter character in step 2.

5. In step 3, specify the field type for each field and whether certain fields should be skipped.

6. If you have a column of numbers where a leading zero needs to be preserved (for example, the ZIP Code of Fort Kent, Maine, needs to stay as 04743 instead of being converted to 4743), select Text as the field type for the ZIP Code field.

7. Click the Advanced button to specify the characters used for thousands and decimal separators (see Figure 16.24). You can also specify that the minus appears after the number.

> ### 🔍 Note
>
> Delimited text is text in which each column is separated by a character such as a comma or a tab. With fixed-width data, each field is neatly lined up when viewed using a monospace font such as Courier New.

Figure 16.24
You select field types in step 3.

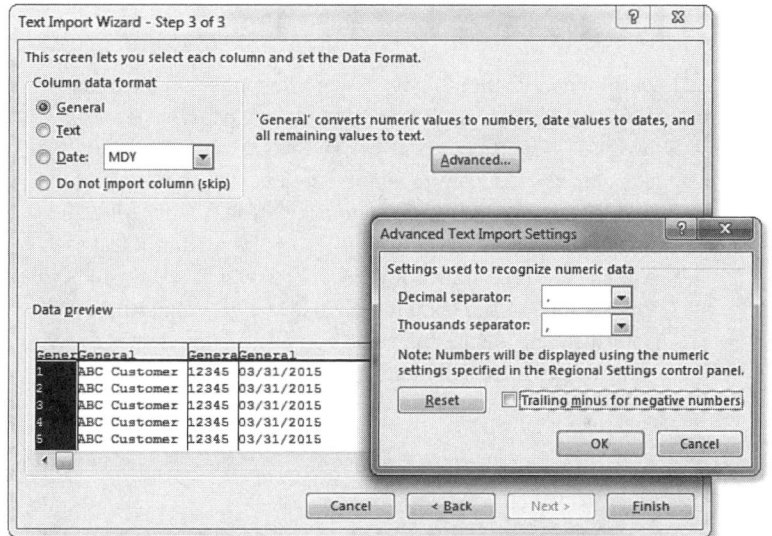

8. Click Finish. The Import Data dialog appears.

9. Specify a starting cell for the data, as shown in Figure 16.25. Excel 2013 offers new options in this dialog box. For information on creating a data model, see Chapter 25, "Mashing Up Data with PowerPivot."

10. Click the Properties button. The Properties dialog appears.

Figure 16.25
In addition to specifying a starting cell, click the Properties button.

11. Determine whether to have Excel ask you for the filename each day or if you should use the same filename each day. If your IT department puts out an inventory.txt file every day, you always want to connect to inventory.txt. Instead, your IT department might export inv20140217.txt today and inv20140218.txt tomorrow. In that case, you want Excel to ask you for a filename during every refresh. Excel defaults to Prompt for File Name on Refresh, as shown in Figure 16.26. If your filename will be the same and in the same folder every day, then clear this default setting.

 Note

You might occasionally encounter files with a delimiter such as a pipe (|) or some other character. You can specify such a delimiter by selecting the Other check box and then specifying the character.

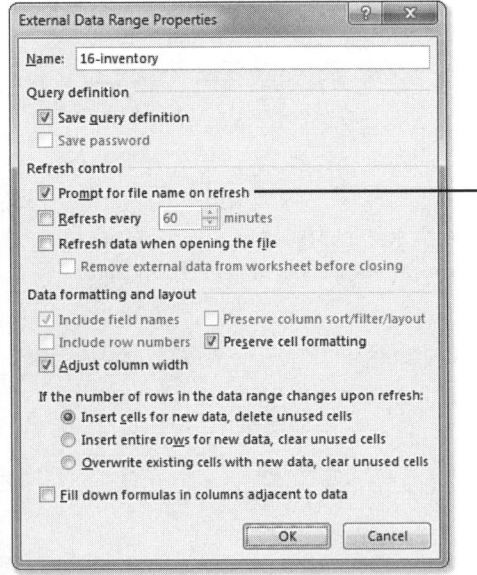

Prompt for Filename on Refresh

Figure 16.26
By default, Excel asks you for the filename during every refresh from a text connection. Turn this off if your file will be in a consistent location with the same name.

12. Accept the location for the import. Excel brings in all the records from the text file (see Figure 16.27).

Figure 16.27
Click Refresh to reload the current text file.

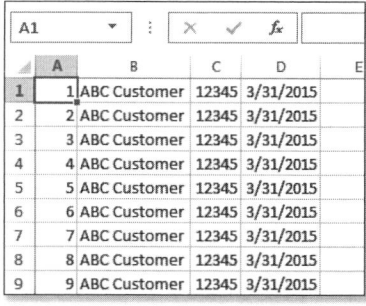

Setting Up a Connection to an Access Database

Although Excel 2013 can handle 1.1 million rows, you might encounter larger data sets that you need to store in Access. You can connect to these larger data sets. You can create a connection to any table in an Access database by following these steps:

1. On the Data tab, in the Get External Data group, select From Access.

2. Browse to select the .mdb file to which you want to link. You are then given an opportunity to choose any one table or query from the database. Each query is listed in the Type column as VIEW, as shown in Figure 16.28.

Figure 16.28
Using an Access connection, you can import a table or a predefined query.

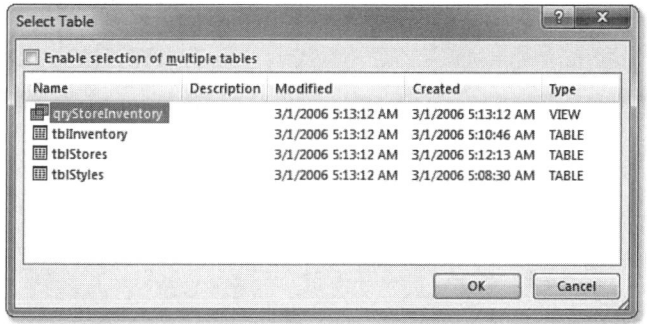

3. Choose whether your data should be imported as a table or used in a pivot table. With the Access connection, there is an additional option, as shown in Figure 16.29. You can have the table imported to a regular table or have the data used as the data source for a pivot table report. When the Access data is delivered to Excel, it is automatically set up as an Excel table with default formatting, as shown in Figure 16.30.

Note

Note that if you select a query in Access, a delay might occur as the query is calculated. Excel displays a Getting Data message in the table while the calculation is in process.

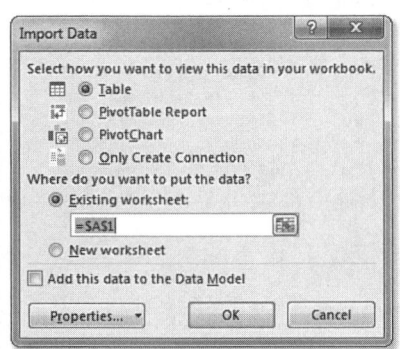

Figure 16.29
Access connections can be returned as a table or used as the source in a pivot table report.

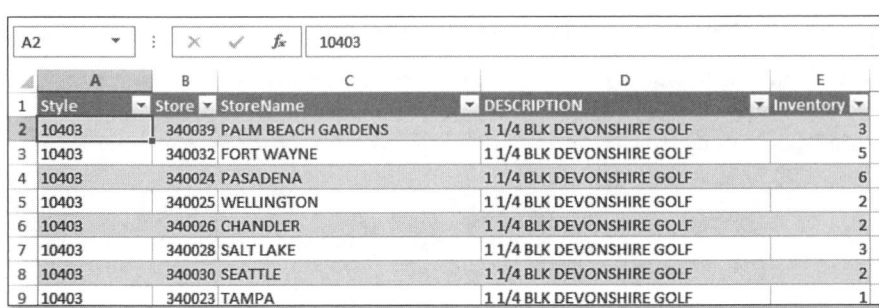

Figure 16.30
By default, Excel treats the data with Excel 2013's table formatting and features.

To learn more about pivot tables, **see** Chapter 23, "Using Pivot Tables to Analyze Data."

Setting Up SQL Server, XML, OLE DB, and ODBC Connections

Although Excel 2013 offers icons for Access, web, and text connections, you can connect to a variety of other data sources. You access all these sources by clicking the From Other Sources icon on the Data tab. When you choose this option, you are presented with seven choices, as shown in Figure 16.31.

Figure 16.31
Excel can connect to SQL Server, Analysis Services, XML, OLE DB data sources, or ODBC through Microsoft Query.

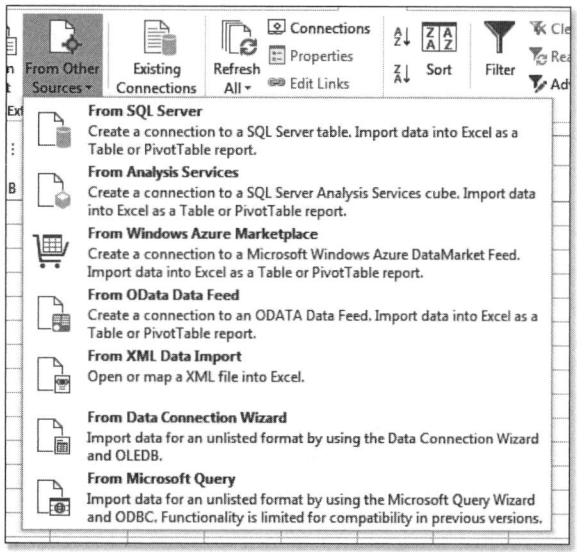

SQL Server is Microsoft's structured query language database. Typically, when applications get too big to run smoothly in Microsoft Access, they are migrated to the more robust SQL Server platform. Because SQL Server is a Microsoft product, connecting to SQL Server is a straightforward process. To connect, you need the server name, a user ID, and a password.

Analysis Services is Microsoft's cube functionality, currently marketed as SQL Server Analysis Services. A cube database represents data along three or more dimensions. To connect, you need the server name, a user ID, and a password.

Windows Azure Marketplace offers a number of third-party data sources, some free and some that require a subscription. The data varies from real estate values from Zillow to weather data.

OData is a web protocol for querying and updating data. XML stands for Extensible Markup Language. This is a simple text file that includes both data and tags used to identify the data.

Data Connection Wizard is used to connect to any Object Linking and Embedding for Databases (OLE-DB) data source. This is a Microsoft interface written in the COM environment that allows Windows-based applications to access a variety of database types. Consult your database administrator for required settings to connect through OLE-DB.

Microsoft Query is an older technology that uses Open Database Connectivity (ODBC). If your company has implemented a non-Microsoft platform, ODBC is the interface that allows other programs such as Excel to connect to the database. Typically, the administrator of the system is able to provide you with a connect string that you use to access the other system's data. Microsoft Query also provides a method for Excel to build SQL queries against Access databases.

Connecting Using Microsoft Query

The From Access icon on the Data tab enables you to retrieve all fields from any Access table or predefined query. At times, you might want to join Access tables, filter records, or select only a subset of fields from a query. Excel 2013 offers the old Microsoft Query product for building such connections.

To build a new query against a table in an Access database, follow these steps:

1. In Excel 2013, select Data, Get External Data, From Other Sources, From Microsoft Query. The Choose Data Source dialog appears.

2. Select MS Access Database, as shown in Figure 16.32. Click OK. The Select Database dialog appears.

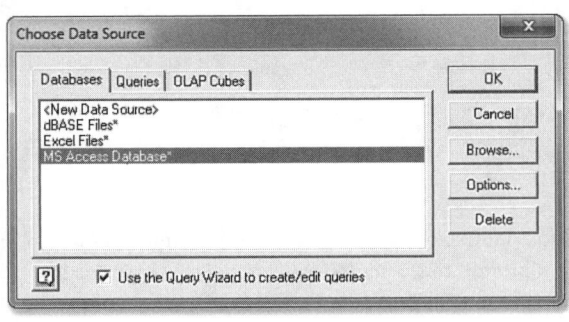

Figure 16.32
Select MS Access Database in the Choose Data Source dialog.

3. In the Select Database dialog, browse to and select the desired Access database.

4. Choose to include particular fields from any table or query in the database. You choose fields on the left side of the dialog and click the > button to move them to the right side of the dialog, as shown in Figure 16.33.

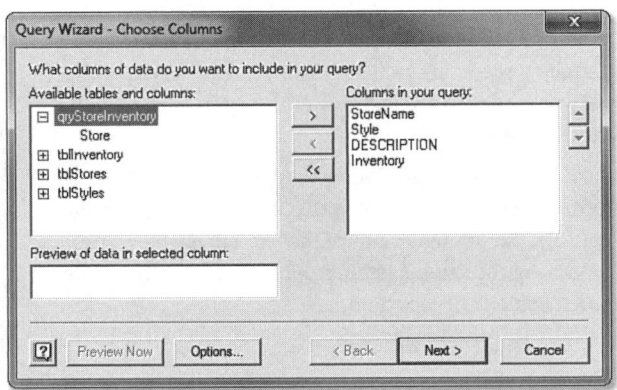

Figure 16.33
Select fields to be included in the query.

5. In the next step of the Query Wizard, set up filters for the query. In Figure 16.34, the filter is defined as only items where the inventory is greater than five.

Figure 16.34
Define filters for the query.

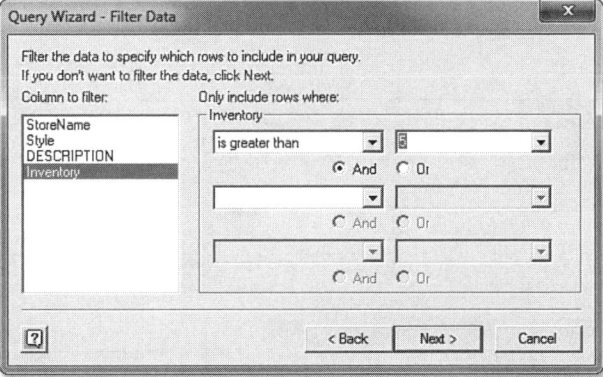

6. In the next step of the Query Wizard, specify up to three sort fields for the query, as shown in Figure 16.35.

7. In the final step of the Query Wizard, specify that you want to return the data to Microsoft Office Excel. You are presented with an Import dialog that is similar to the one shown earlier.

Figure 16.35
Specify sort criteria.

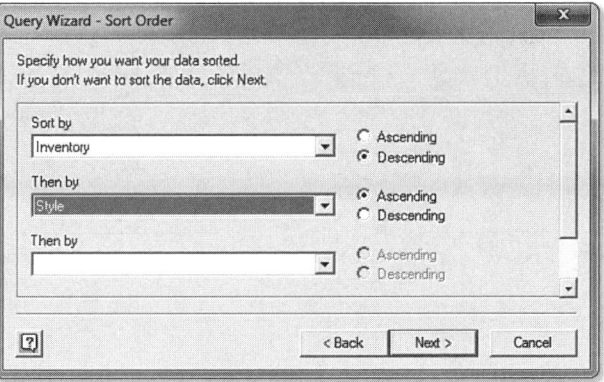

Contrast the current example with the previous example in "Setting Up a Connection to an Access Database." Although the previous example and this example use the same query from Access, the Microsoft Query option enables you to retrieve only the records with more than five items in inventory. The overhead involved in returning a few records causes the query to run significantly faster. The data is returned in a sorted manner.

Managing Connections

The Data tab includes a group called Manage Connections. As shown in Figure 16.36, this group includes an option to refresh all connections. Although the icon says Refresh All, a drop-down enables you to choose to refresh only the current query or to view properties for a connection.

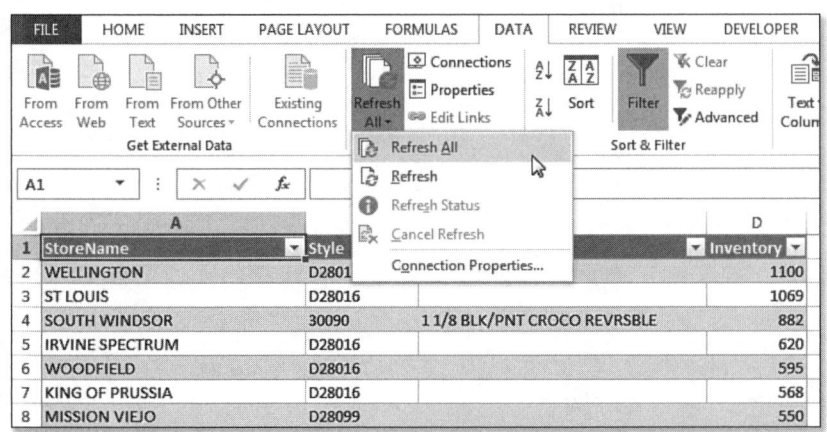

Figure 16.36
You have one-click access to refreshing all connections.

Clicking the Connections icon brings up a summary of all the web, text, Access, or ODBC connections in your workbook. This is a fantastic improvement in Excel 2013. As shown in Figure 16.36, you can click any connection in the top and then follow the hyperlink Click Here to See Where the Selected Connections Are Used to jump to the worksheet range that houses the results of the connection.

USING SUPER FORMULAS IN EXCEL

Excel offers an amazing variety of formulas. This chapter covers some of the unorthodox formulas you can build in Excel. In this chapter, you discover the following:

- Using a formula to add the same cell across many sheets

- Using a formula to reference the previous sheet

- Editing multiple formulas into one

- Assigning a formula to a name

- Letting data determine the cell reference to use with the INDIRECT function

- Using a dynamic range with an offset

- Transposing relative column references to rows

- Using ROW() or COLUMN() to return an array of numbers

- Replacing thousands of formulas with one Ctrl+Shift+Enter (CSE) array formula

- Using one formula to return a whole range of answers

- Doing conditional sums based on two or more conditions

Using 3D Formulas to Spear Through Many Worksheets

It is common to have a workbook composed of identical worksheets for each month or quarter of the year. Every worksheet needs to have the same arrangement of rows.

If you want to total a particular cell across all the worksheets, you might try to write a formula with one term for each sheet—for example, =Sheet1!A1+Sheet2!A1+Sheet3!A1.... However, Excel supports a special type of formula that spears through several worksheets to add a particular cell from each worksheet. The syntax of the formula is =SUM(Sheet1:Sheetn!A1).

As shown in Figure 17.1, Net Revenue is in row 4 on the January worksheet and is in the same row on the February worksheet. You cannot see this in Figure 17.1, but the arrangement of rows is identical on every worksheet.

	A	B	C	D		A	B	C
1	January				1	February		
2					2			
3		This Year	Prior Year		3		This Year	Prior Year
4	Net Revenue	9231	8049		4	Net Revenue	9416	8210
5	Cost of Sales	4028	3269		5	Cost of Sales	4109	3335
6					6			
7	Gross Margin	5203	4780		7	Gross Margin	5307	4875
8					8			
9	R&D	1176	1186		9	R&D	1200	1210
10	Mktg, G&A	1342	1170		10	Mktg, G&A	1369	1193
11					11			
12	Operating Expenses	2518	2356		12	Operating Expenses	2569	2403
13					13			
14	Operating Income	2685	2424		14	Operating Income	2738	2472
15					15			
16	Interest	127	47		16	Interest	130	48
17					17			
18	Income Before Taxes	2812	2471		18	Income Before Taxes	2868	2520
19					19			
20	Provision for Taxes	716	663		20	Provision for Taxes	730	676
21					21			
22	Net Income	2096	1808		22	Net Income	2138	1844
23					23			

◄ ► ··· | Jan | Feb | Mar | Aß ···   ◄ ► ··· | Jan | **Feb** | Mar | A

Figure 17.1
The 12 workbooks, Jan through Dec, contain an identical arrangement of rows and columns.

When creating a worksheet, you might be tempted to write a formula such as =Jan!B4+Feb!B4+Mar!B4+Apr!B4, but doing so would be rather tedious.

Instead, you can write a formula that totals cell B4 from each worksheet, Jan through Dec. An example of the formula is =SUM(Jan:Dec!B4). After you enter this formula in cell B4, you can easily copy it to all the other relevant cells in the worksheet, as shown in Figure 17.2.

Excel 2013 has introduced a new worksheet function called SHEETS(). You can use =SHEETS(Jan:Dec!A1) to learn that there are 12 sheets in the reference.

Figure 17.2
This formula spears through 12 worksheets to total cell B4 from each worksheet from Jan through Dec.

B4	▼	:	✗	✓	f_x	=SUM(Jan:Dec!B4)		
⊿	A	B	C	D	E	F	G	H
1	Total Year							
2								
3		This Year	Prior Year			# of Sheets in references		
4	Net Revenue	119727	104394			12	=SHEETS(Jan:Dec!B4)	
5	Cost of Sales	49911	40508					
6								
7	Gross Margin	69816	63886					
8								
9	R&D	15253	15383					
10	Mktg, G&A	17406	15176					
11								
12	Operating Expenses	32659	30559					
13								
14	Operating Income	37157	33327					
15								
16	Interest	1648	610					
17								
18	Income Before Taxes	38805	33937					
19								
20	Provision for Taxes	9286	8599					
21								
22	Net Income	29519	25338					
23								

 Tip

Sometimes you might need to sum a cell on all sheets that have a common naming convention. Perhaps you have worksheet names such as CostQ1, ExpensesQ1, CostQ2, ExpensesQ2, CostQ3, ExpensesQ3, CostQ4, and ExpensesQ4. To sum cell B4 on all of the cost sheets, type **=SUM('Cost*' !B4)**. Remarkably, Excel converts this shorthand to a formula that points to each of the cost sheets:

```
=SUM(CostQ1!B4,CostQ2!B4,CostQ3!B4,CostQ4!B4)
```

I need to give a tip of the cap to Microsoft MVP Bob Umlas for this cool trick.

Referring to the Previous Worksheet

When you have an arrangement of several sequential worksheets, you might want to keep a running total. This total would be calculated as the total on this sheet plus the running total from the previous sheet.

It is somewhat difficult to build a formula that always points to the previous sheet. Maybe you've tried this wrong approach: You build a formula on Sheet2 that points to Sheet1. When you make copies of Sheet2, to Sheet3, Sheet4, and so on, the formula continues to always point back to Sheet1. This is rarely what you want.

The solution involves a tiny user-defined function that you can write in Excel's macro editor. This specific example shows you how to build a general-purpose function that returns a value from a previous worksheet. This function can work in any situation.

Figure 17.3 shows a formula that returns the value from the previous month. On the Feb worksheet, this would refer to =Jan!B4. You could easily copy this formula to other cells within the Feb worksheet. However, if you copy the formula to Mar or Apr, the formula still points to the Jan worksheet, which is not what you want.

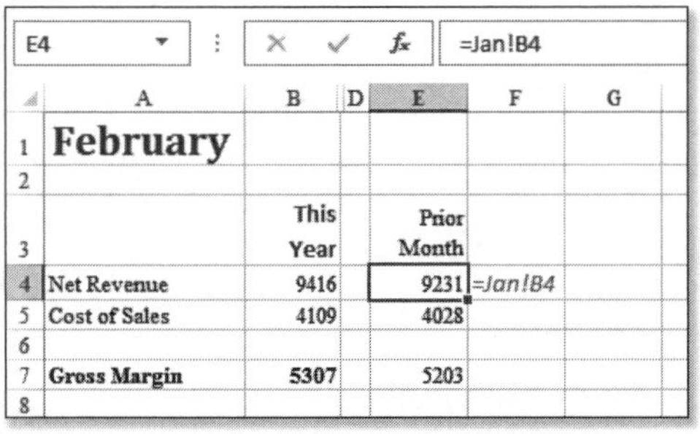

Figure 17.3
You must rewrite this formula for each of the 11 other months.

Excel offers a very cool solution to this problem. The solution requires a few lines of VBA macro code. Don't be afraid. I can get you there and back without any problems. Here's what you do:

1. Press Alt+F11 to launch the VBA editor.

2. In the VBA editor, select Insert, Module.

3. Type the following lines into the blank module:

```
Function PrevSheet(ByVal MyCell As Range)
    Application.Volatile
    On Error Resume Next
    PrevSheet = Sheets(MyCell.Parent.Index - 1).Range(MyCell.Address)
End Function
```

Your screen should look similar to Figure 17.4.

4. Select File, Close and Return to Microsoft Excel to return to Excel.

Figure 17.4
The VBA editor screen should look like this.

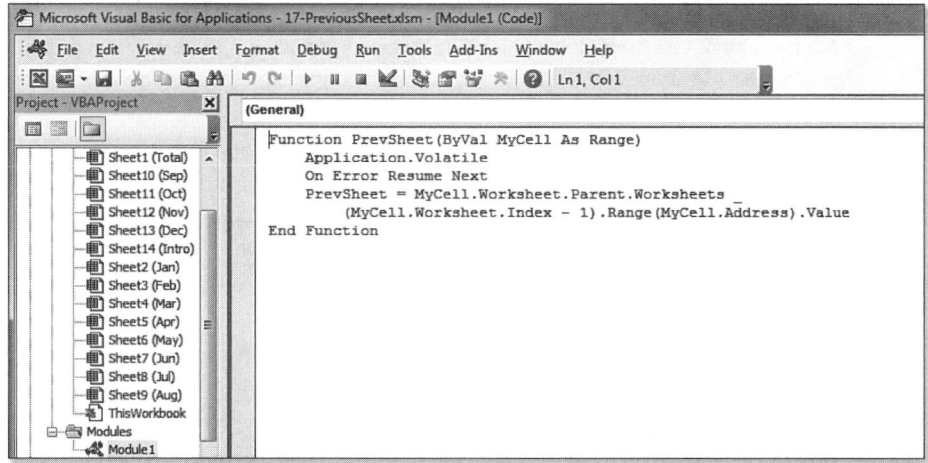

To realize the power of this function, you can put the workbook in Group mode and enter the function in 11 worksheets at once:

1. Select the Feb worksheet.

2. Hold down the Shift key while clicking the Dec worksheet tab. This highlights all 11 worksheets. Although you see the Feb worksheet, anything you do on that worksheet is also done to all 11 selected worksheets.

3. In cell E4, enter **=PrevSheet(B4)**. Press Enter to accept the formula. The Feb worksheet picks up the value from Jan, but each additional worksheet picks up the value from the previous sheet, as shown in Figure 17.5.

Figure 17.5
One formula using the custom function PrevSheet solves the prior month problem seamlessly across all the worksheets.

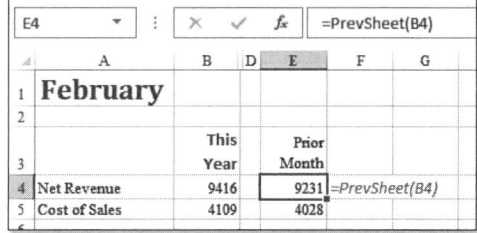

4. With the worksheets still in Group mode, copy cell B4 from the Feb worksheet to cells B5, B7, and so on.

5. Right-click any sheet tab and select Ungroup.

Combining Multiple Formulas into One Formula

With more than 460 functions available in Excel, it is possible to perform just about any calculation. Many times, however, it is easier to break the task down into many subformulas as you try to solve the problem.

For example, fellow Excel MVP and guru Bob Umlas taught me that I could use the Substitute function to locate the last space in a word. This is handy for finding the last word in a sentence or name. However, unlike Bob, I always need to build this formula over the course of several columns. It takes me seven columns to do a trick that Bob can do in one. Figure 17.6 shows all the formulas used to replicate the trick.

Figure 17.6
It takes me seven formulas to isolate the last name.

F2   × ✓ *fx*   =SUBSTITUTE(A2," ","!",E2)

	A	B	C	D	E	F	G	H
1	NAME	No Spaces	Len A	Len B	# Spaces	Replace Last Space	Find !	MID
2	ALLISON GILMORE	ALLISONGILMORE	15	14	1	ALLISON!GILMORE	8	GILMORE
3	MARY ELLEN JELEN	MARYELLENJELEN	16	14	2	MARY ELLEN!JELEN	11	JELEN
4	FANNIE PERRY	FANNIEPERRY	12	11	1	FANNIE!PERRY	7	PERRY
5	JOE BOB BRIGGS	JOEBOBBRIGGS	14	12	2	JOE BOB!BRIGGS	8	BRIGGS
16								
17	Formulas used in Row 2:							
18	B2:	=SUBSTITUTE(A2," ","")						
19	C2:	=LEN(A2)						
20	D2:	=LEN(B2)						
21	E2:	=C2-D2						
22	F2:	=SUBSTITUTE(A2," ","!",E2)						
23	G2:	=FIND("!",F2)						
24	H2:	=MID(A2,G2+1,C2-G2)						
25								

If you've ever built a formula in small steps as shown above, you can begin consolidating the formulas into one monster formula.

However, there's an easier way to combine many formulas into one formula. As an example, follow these steps:

1. Examine the final formula. It references cells that contain one or more subformulas. In Figure 17.7, cell H2 has a formula that references the value in A2 and subformulas in G2, C2, and G2. You remove the reference to G2 first.

2. Move the cell pointer to the subformula in G2.

3. Press F2 to put the formula in edit mode.

4. With the mouse, highlight the formula in the formula bar, but do not highlight the equal sign in the subformula (see Figure 17.8).

Figure 17.7
The goal is to replace G2 in this formula.

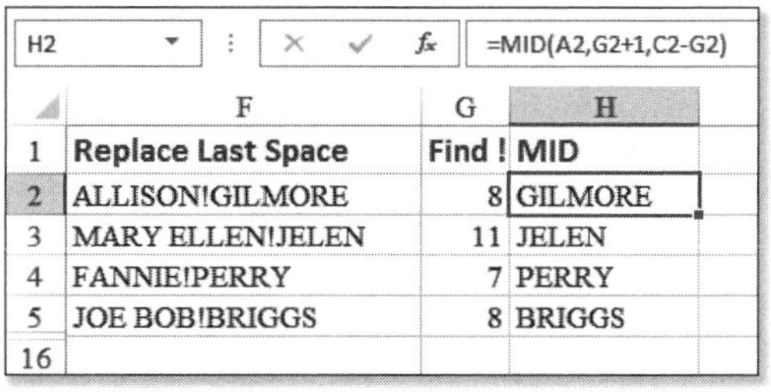

| H2 | ▾ | : | ✕ | ✓ | *fx* | =MID(A2,G2+1,C2-G2) |

◢	F	G	H
1	**Replace Last Space**	**Find !**	**MID**
2	ALLISON!GILMORE	8	GILMORE
3	MARY ELLEN!JELEN	11	JELEN
4	FANNIE!PERRY	7	PERRY
5	JOE BOB!BRIGGS	8	BRIGGS
16			

Figure 17.8
Copying characters from the formula bar is different from copying a cell.

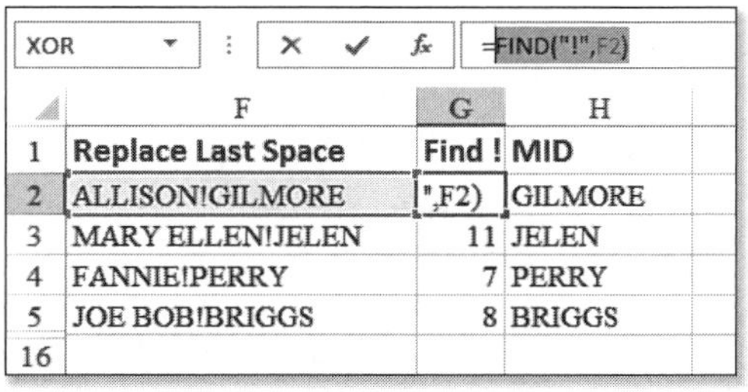

| XOR | ▾ | : | ✕ | ✓ | *fx* | =FIND("!",F2) |

◢	F	G	H
1	**Replace Last Space**	**Find !**	**MID**
2	ALLISON!GILMORE	",F2)	GILMORE
3	MARY ELLEN!JELEN	11	JELEN
4	FANNIE!PERRY	7	PERRY
5	JOE BOB!BRIGGS	8	BRIGGS
16			

5. Press Ctrl+C to copy this portion of the subformula to the Clipboard.

6. Go back to the final formula. Press F2 to put the formula in edit mode.

7. In the formula bar, using the mouse, highlight the first instance of G2, as shown in Figure 17.9.

Figure 17.9
With the formula from cell G2 on the Clipboard, you select G2 in the final formula.

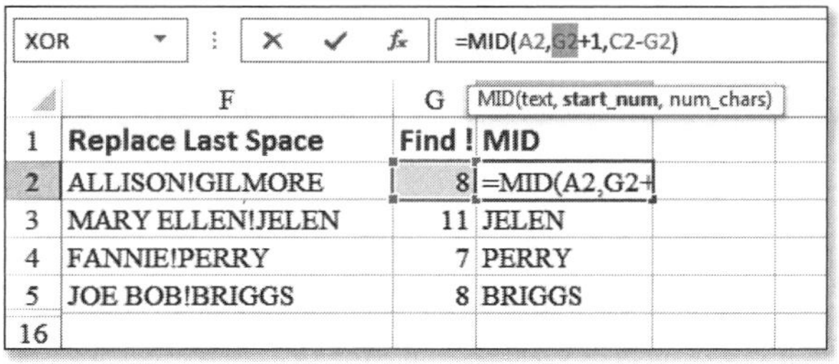

| XOR | ▾ | : | ✕ | ✓ | *fx* | =MID(A2,G2+1,C2-G2) |

◢	F	G	
1	**Replace Last Space**	**Find !**	**MID**
2	ALLISON!GILMORE	8	=MID(A2,G2+
3	MARY ELLEN!JELEN	11	JELEN
4	FANNIE!PERRY	7	PERRY
5	JOE BOB!BRIGGS	8	BRIGGS
16			

MID(text, **start_num**, num_chars)

8. Press Ctrl+V to paste the subformula from cell G2 in place of the letters G2. The formula appears as shown in Figure 17.10. Note that you just added a new reference to the F2 subformula.

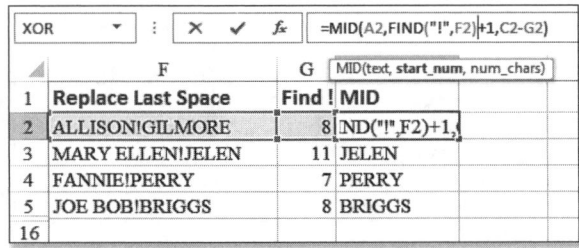

Figure 17.10
You can press Ctrl+V to paste the characters from the cell G2 formula instead of the reference to cell G2.

9. Because G2 appears again in this formula, repeat steps 7 and 8 for the second instance of G2.

10. Press Enter to accept this intermediate formula of `=MID(A2,FIND("!",F2)+1,C2-FIND("!",F2))`.

11. If there are additional references to a cell with a subformula in the new formula, repeat steps 1–10 for the next reference. In this case, you would replace the characters "F2" with `SUBSTITUTE(A2," ","!",E2)`. Continue working through the formula, replacing E2, then D2, then C2, then B2. Eventually you end up with a monster formula, as shown in Figure 17.11. Your co-workers will look at that formula and assume you must be a spreadsheet wizard like Excel MVP Bob Umlas.

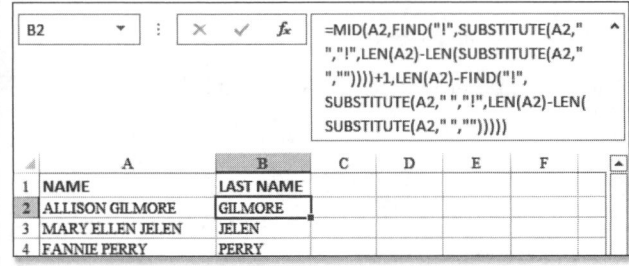

Figure 17.11
After several iterations of replacing references in the formula, you end up with one monster formula to replace the six subformulas.

Calculating a Cell Reference in the Formula by Using the INDIRECT Function

Usually, a formula points to a particular cell or range of cells. Sometimes, though, you want a formula to point to a different cell as the result of a calculation. You can do this by using the INDIRECT function.

In general, this process involves writing a text-based formula that evaluates to a cell address. Although your particular situation will certainly be different, here are some examples of formulas that evaluate to a cell address:

- `=CHAR(64+COLUMN(B275))&ROW(ZZ999)`—Evaluates to B999.

- `="Sheet"&ROW(A1)&"!C2"`—Evaluates to Sheet1!C2 in the current row, but to Sheet2!C2 when copied down one row, and to Sheet3!C2 when copied down to a third row.

- `=CHAR(65+MONTH(ROW(A1)))&"19"`—Evaluates to B19 in January, C19 in February, and so on. To use this trick, jot a sticky note that says CHAR(65)=A and hang it on your cube wall.

After you have a formula that evaluates to text that looks like a cell reference, you can use that formula as the argument to the INDIRECT() function. Excel returns the value in the cell indicated by the text formula.

Suppose that in Figure 17.12 you would like to build a table to copy the current-month totals from each worksheet to a summary table on the Total worksheet. Without the INDIRECT function, you would have to separately enter 12 different formulas in row 4—one for each month (for example, =Jan!$B4 for January, =Feb!$B4 for February, and so on).

Figure 17.12
The first of 12 different formulas required in E4:P4.

E4		▼	:	×	✓	f_x	=Jan!B4	

	A	B	C	D	E	F
1	**Total Year**					
2						
3		This Year	Prior Year		Jan	Feb
4	Net Revenue	119727	104394		9231	
5	Cost of Sales	49911	40508			
6						
7	Gross Margin	69816	63886			
8						
9	R&D	15253	15383			
10	Mktg, G&A	17406	15176			
11						
12	Operating Expenses	32659	30559			
13						
14	Operating Income	37157	33327			
15						
16	Interest	1648	610			
17						
18	Income Before Taxes	38805	33937			
19						
20	Provision for Taxes	9286	8599			
21						
22	Net Income	29519	25338			
23						

You can solve this problem with a single formula that you can copy to the entire total worksheet. Follow these steps:

1. You want to design a text formula in cell E4 to point to the correct sheet and cell.

2. The worksheet has month headings in row 3, so you can start to build a formula as =E$3&"!". Note that the $ before the 3 ensures that as the formula is copied to lower rows in the summary table; it always points to the month heading in row 3.

3. The next trick is finding a function that returns the address of column B for row 3. To do this, you can use the versatile function called CELL. The CELL function can return many bits of information about a reference, including the address of the cell. For example, =CELL("address",$B4) returns the text $B$4.

4. Figure 17.13 shows the intermediate result of entering =E$3&"!"&CELL("address",$B4) into the table.

The last step is to wrap the INDIRECT function around the formula in cell E4. This tells Excel to evaluate the function inside INDIRECT to learn that Excel should return the value from cell B4 on the Jan worksheet.

 Caution

There is an important limitation with INDIRECT functions. If you build an INDIRECT function that points to an external workbook, the formula works only when the external workbook is open. Two people have workarounds. Lorent Longre's MOREFUNC.XLL provides INDERECT.EXT. Harlan Grove's PULL code does the same thing. Search for either in your favorite search engine.

| E4 | ▼ | : | × | ✓ | f_x | =E$3&"!"&CELL("Address",$B4) |

▲	A	B	C	D	E	F	G	H	I
1	**Total Year**								
2									
3		This Year	Prior Year		Jan	Feb	Mar	Apr	
4	Net Revenue	119727	104394		Jan!$B$4	Feb!$B$4	Mar!$B$4	Apr!$B$4	May!$B
5	Cost of Sales	49911	40508		Jan!$B$5	Feb!$B$5	Mar!$B$5	Apr!$B$5	May!$B
6									
7	**Gross Margin**	**69816**	**63886**		**Jan!$B$7**	**Feb!$B$7**	**Mar!$B$7**	**Apr!$B$7**	**May!$B**
8									
9	R&D	15253	15383		Jan!$B$9	Feb!$B$9	Mar!$B$9	Apr!$B$9	May!$B
10	Mktg, G&A	17406	15176		Jan!$B$10	Feb!$B$10	Mar!$B$10	Apr!$B$10	May!$B
11									
12	**Operating Expenses**	**32659**	**30559**		**Jan!$B$12**	**Feb!$B$12**	**Mar!$B$12**	**Apr!$B$12**	**May!$B**
13									
14	**Operating Income**	**37157**	**33327**		**Jan!$B$14**	**Feb!$B$14**	**Mar!$B$14**	**Apr!$B$14**	**May!$B**
15									

Figure 17.13
All the formulas in E4:P22 are identical, but they return the reference to the cell from which the result should be copied.

Rather than change each formula to include INDIRECT, you only have to change the formula in E4 and copy it to the other formulas. The easiest way to do that is to copy E4, select All, Ctrl+G for Go To, click Special, Formulas, and click OK. Then click Paste.

The whole trick to being efficient in Excel is being able to write one formula that can be copied to an entire range. Rather than going through the tedium of entering 12 different formulas in row 4, you can use the INDIRECT function to enter just one formula everywhere in the range (see Figure 17.14).

 Note

Excel gurus will point out another benefit of the INDIRECT function. If you have a formula such as =SUM(A1:A10), and you insert a new row 5, the formula normally expands to =SUM(A1:A11). However, at times you might want to sum only the first ten records on the sheet. In this case, you can use the formula =SUM(INDIRECT("A1:A10")) to always point to rows 1 through 10, no matter what rows are inserted or deleted.

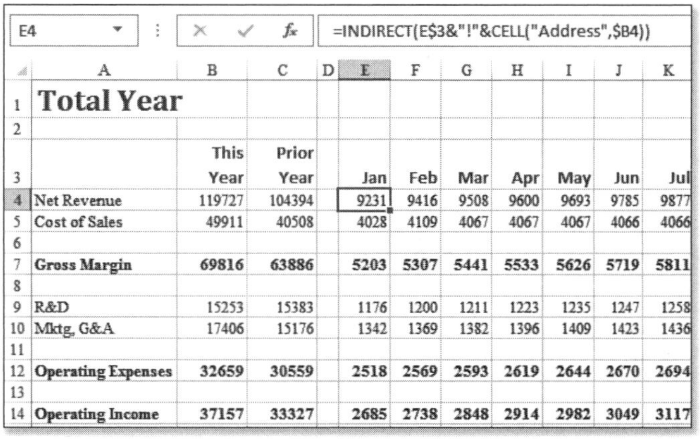

Figure 17.14
You can wrap the formulas in the
INDIRECT function to allow one for-
mula to fill the entire table.

Using OFFSET to Refer to a Range That Dynamically Resizes

When you first read the Help topic on the OFFSET function, you might wonder about the point of such a function. The OFFSET function enables you to describe a range by specifying five parameters:

- Any cell or range from which to start.

- The number of rows to move from the original cell to get to the upper-left corner of the reference. Positive numbers move down the worksheet, and negative numbers move up the worksheet.

- The number of columns to move from the original cell to get to the upper-left corner of the reference. Positive numbers move to the right from the original cell, and negative numbers move to the left.

- The number of rows in the reference.

- The number of columns in the reference.

It would be difficult to imagine why you would ever use =OFFSET(A1,2,3,4,5) to refer to the range D3:H6. However, when you consider that these arguments can be functions that calculate the size of a range, it starts to make sense.

Suppose that you start entering invoice amounts in cell B2 and proceed down column B. To write a sum formula that can expand to include any number of entries in column B, you could count the number of numeric entries in column B by using =COUNT(B:B). If you then use the COUNT function as the fourth argument in the OFFSET function, you have set up a dynamic formula that always expands as new items are entered, as shown in Figure 17.15.

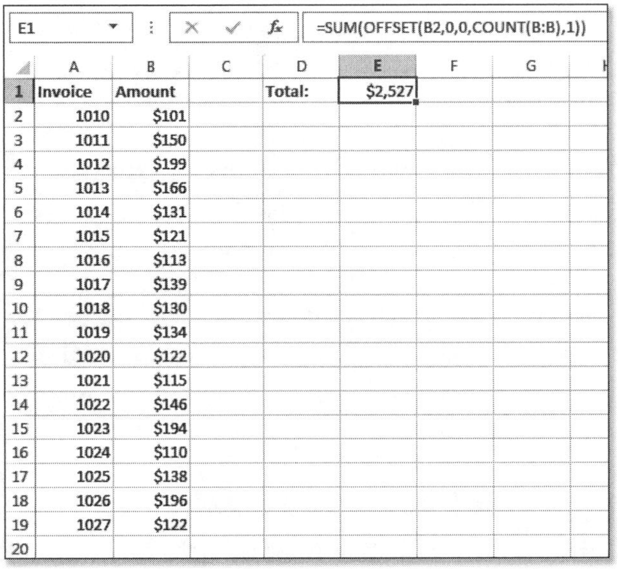

Figure 17.15
The OFFSET function enables you to describe a rectangular range that starts a calculated number of rows and columns from a starting point.

Assigning a Formula to a Name

When you set up a named range, the Names box shows that the name has a value such as =Sheet1!A1. Think about it—because this value starts with an equal sign, you know that this is a formula.

Instead of pointing to a static range, you can define a name to point to the result of a formula that generates a dynamic range on the fly. One common example is a list to be used by Data Validation.

Suppose you want to display a drop-down with a list of possible values. Do the following:

1. Begin by inserting a new Lists worksheet.

2. Type a heading in cell A1. Don't skip the formula as the formula in step 6 assumes the heading is there.

3. Type the list in column A of the Lists worksheet, starting in cell A2. Do not leave any blank cells in the list. As you add new items to the list, you would like the named range to automatically extend.

4. On the Formulas tab, choose Define Name.

5. Type a name, such as **RegionList**, in the Name field (see Figure 17.16).

6. Type =OFFSET(Lists!$A$2,0,0,COUNTA(Lists!$A:$A)-1,1) in the Refers To box. This formula tells Excel to start at cell A2 on the Lists worksheet. Move zero rows down. Move zero columns over. Return a range that is the count of items in column A minus 1. Return a range that is one column wide. Remember to include the sheet name in two places in this formula and remember to include dollar signs in each reference.

Figure 17.16
Define a name that expands as more items are entered in column A.

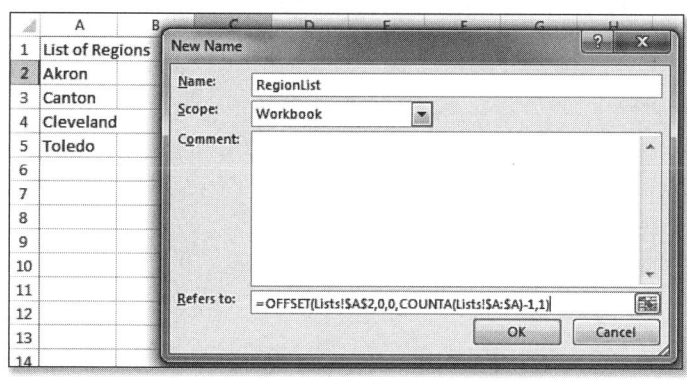

After you've defined a name for RegionList, you can set up any cell in the workbook with Data Validation. Select the cell. Choose Data Validation from the Data tab. In the Allow drop-down, choose List. In the Source box, type **=RegionList**, as shown in Figure 17.17.

Figure 17.17
Define the dynamic named range as the source of the validation.

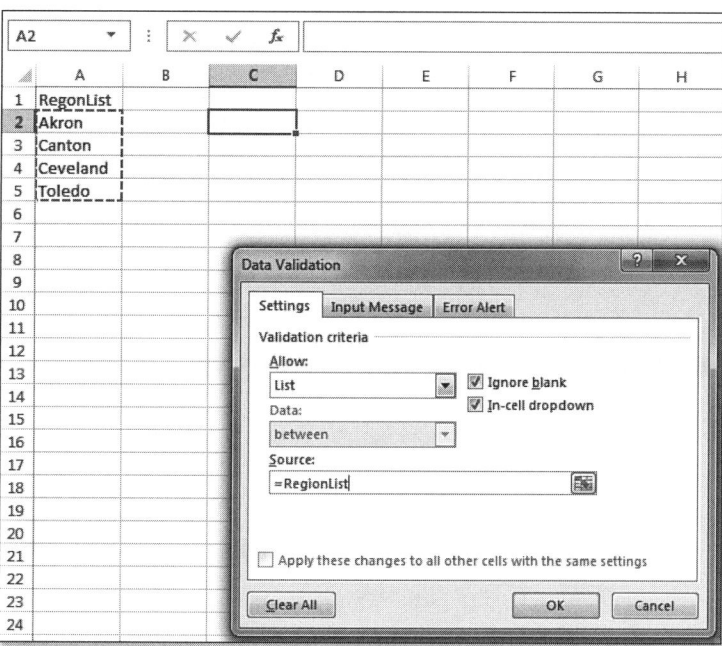

As you later add new items to the bottom of the list in column A, the list in the validation drop-down automatically expands. In Figure 17.18, Zanesville is added to column A and is automatically available in the validation drop-down.

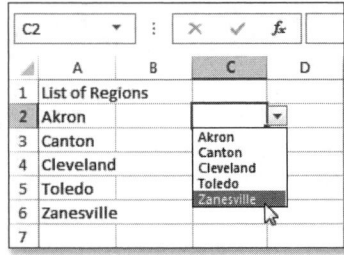

Figure 17.18
Add a new entry to A. The formula in the named range causes the validation list to expand as well.

Turning a Range of Formulas on Its Side

The Transpose option in the Paste Options dialog is great for changing values that span across several columns into values that go down a column. Here's an example:

1. In Figure 17.19, you select B1:M1 and then press Ctrl+C.

Figure 17.19
Use the Transpose option to turn B1:M1 on its side.

2. Select the top-left cell where the range should be copied. In this example, select cell A7.

3. Right-click. In the Paste Options section, select Transpose, as shown in Figure 17.19. The month names now go down the row.

However, there's no good way to copy the calculation for profit from row 4 to the new table. You normally have to enter 12 different formulas in the range B7:B17, as shown in Figure 17.20.

However, there are two ways to easily enter a single formula that turns those results on their side.

Figure 17.20
Transposing with a formula requires a different formula in each cell.

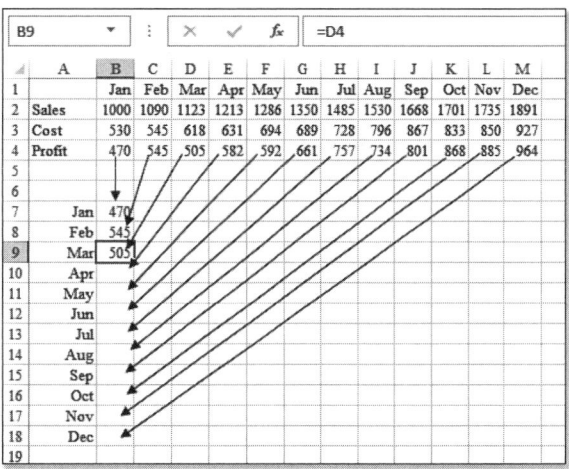

First, you can use the OFFSET function you learned about earlier in this chapter. You can set up an OFFSET function that points to $A$4 and offsets by an additional column as you copy the formula down the rows. Try it:

1. In cell B7, enter **=ROW(A1)**. The result is the number 1.

2. Copy the formula from cell B7 down to B7:B18. The result returns a string of integers from 1 through 12.

3. Use the formula =ROW(A1) as the third argument in the OFFSET function. A formula of =OFFSET($A$4,0,ROW(A1)) achieves the perfect result, as shown in Figure 17.21.

Figure 17.21
You can use the ROW(A1) trick as the Column Offset parameter in the OFFSET function to turn a range on its side.

B7	▼	:	×	✓	fx	=OFFSET($A$4,0,ROW(A1))						
	A	B	C	D	E	F	G	H	I	J	K	L	M
1		Jan	Feb	Mar	Apr	May	Jun	Jul	Aug	Sep	Oct	Nov	Dec
2	Sales	1000	1090	1123	1213	1286	1350	1485	1530	1668	1701	1735	1891
3	Cost	530	545	618	631	694	689	728	796	867	833	850	927
4	Profit	470	545	505	582	592	661	757	734	801	868	885	964
5													
6													
7	Jan	470	=OFFSET($A$4,0,ROW(A1))										
8	Feb	545	=OFFSET($A$4,0,ROW(A2))										
9	Mar	505	=OFFSET($A$4,0,ROW(A3))										
10	Apr	582	=OFFSET($A$4,0,ROW(A4))										
11	May	592	=OFFSET($A$4,0,ROW(A5))										
12	Jun	661	=OFFSET($A$4,0,ROW(A6))										
13	Jul	757	=OFFSET($A$4,0,ROW(A7))										
14	Aug	734	=OFFSET($A$4,0,ROW(A8))										
15	Sep	801	=OFFSET($A$4,0,ROW(A9))										
16	Oct	868	=OFFSET($A$4,0,ROW(A10))										
17	Nov	885	=OFFSET($A$4,0,ROW(A11))										
18	Dec	964	=OFFSET($A$4,0,ROW(A12))										
19													

One danger exists with just about every method described in this chapter: They produce results that the average person does not understand. So if you want to end up with straightforward formulas in B7:B18, you can use the following method:

1. Enter a formula, such as **=B4**, in cell B5.

2. Copy the first formula across row 5 for each month.

3. Highlight the formulas in B5:M5.

4. Use Home, Editing, Find & Select, Replace to display the Find and Replace dialog. In the Find What box, enter an equal sign. In the Replace With box, enter an exclamation point. Click Replace All to change every occurrence of = to !. This converts the formulas to text, as shown in row 5 of Figure 17.22.

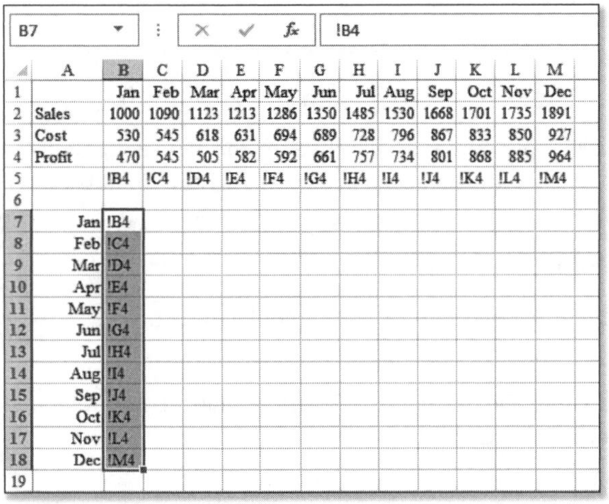

Figure 17.22
Converting the formulas to text allows them to be transposed.

5. Copy the range and highlight a new cell (in this example, cell B7).

6. Right-click and select Transpose. Because the cells are all text, they transpose perfectly, as shown in B7:B18 of Figure 17.22.

7. Use Ctrl+H or Home, Editing, Find & Select, Replace to display the Find and Replace dialog. Type an exclamation point in Find What and an equal sign in Replace With. Click Replace All to change every ! back to =. It now looks as if you actually typed all 12 formulas individually.

Replacing Multiple Formulas with One Array Formula

A wildly powerful type of formula exists that most Excel users have never experienced. This single formula can do thousands of calculations. The formula is known as an *array formula*. You must use Ctrl+Shift+Enter when entering an array formula to tell Excel to evaluate the formula as an array.

Here is an example of the power of an array formula: It is not easy to sum, count, or average based on multiple conditions using SUMIFS, COUNTIFS, or AVERAGEIFS. However, what if you need to calculate a standard deviation on records that match multiple conditions? An array formula can solve this problem.

A simple formula such as =STDEV.P(A1:A10) calculates a standard deviation, as shown in cell A12 of Figure 17.23. In this particular example, some outliers are causing the standard deviation to be large.

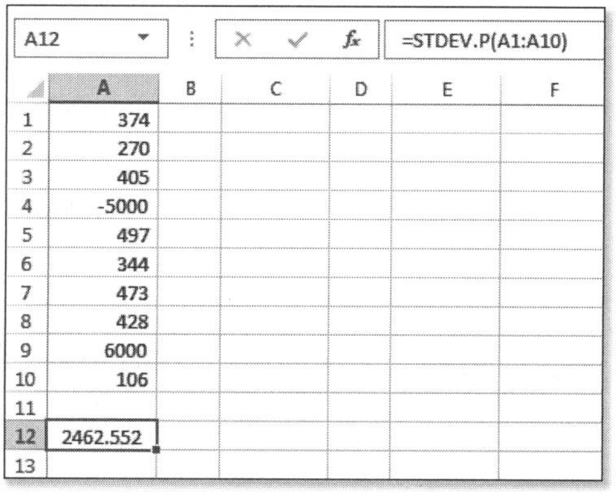

Figure 17.23
The goal is to build a model to calculate standard deviation of all but the largest and smallest values.

	A
1	374
2	270
3	405
4	-5000
5	497
6	344
7	473
8	428
9	6000
10	106
11	
12	2462.552
13	

A12 =STDEV.P(A1:A10)

Suppose that you want to calculate a standard deviation after throwing out the smallest and largest value in the data.

As shown in Figure 17.24, you could perform this calculation by adding many new formulas to the worksheet. Here's how:

1. Add a formula in D2 to calculate the minimum value in the data.

2. Add a formula in D3 to calculate the minimum value in the data.

3. For every row in the data set, add a new formula that compares the data point to the minimum and maximum values. If the data point is between the minimum or maximum value, bring the original number to column F. Otherwise, use the value FALSE. The standard deviation calculation ignores cells that contain FALSE.

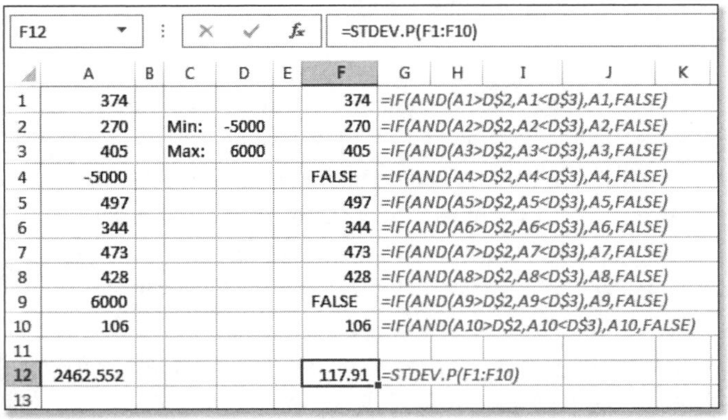

Figure 17.24

Thirteen formulas are required for this ten-row data set. If you had one million rows, you would need 1,000,003 formula cells.

| F12 | ▼ | : | × | ✓ | fx | =STDEV.P(F1:F10) |

◢	A	B	C	D	E	F	G	H	I	J	K
1	374					374	=IF(AND(A1>D$2,A1<D$3),A1,FALSE)
2	270		Min:	-5000		270	=IF(AND(A2>D$2,A2<D$3),A2,FALSE)
3	405		Max:	6000		405	=IF(AND(A3>D$2,A3<D$3),A3,FALSE)
4	-5000					FALSE	=IF(AND(A4>D$2,A4<D$3),A4,FALSE)
5	497					497	=IF(AND(A5>D$2,A5<D$3),A5,FALSE)
6	344					344	=IF(AND(A6>D$2,A6<D$3),A6,FALSE)
7	473					473	=IF(AND(A7>D$2,A7<D$3),A7,FALSE)
8	428					428	=IF(AND(A8>D$2,A8<D$3),A8,FALSE)
9	6000					FALSE	=IF(AND(A9>D$2,A9<D$3),A9,FALSE)
10	106					106	=IF(AND(A10>D$2,A10<D$3),A10,FALSE)
11							
12	2462.552					117.91	=STDEV.P(F1:F10)
13							

4. Add a formula in F12 to calculate the standard deviation of the new column.

Another approach is to replace the IF functions with SMALL functions. By asking for the smallest second through ninth values, you are removing the smallest and largest values from the data set (see Figure 17.25). Here are the steps to follow:

1. Enter the numbers 2 through 9 in C2:C9. These cells could contain constants, or they could contain a formula such as =ROW(A2).

2. Enter =SMALL(A$1:A$10,C2) in cell D2 and copy down to D9.

3. Enter a STDEV.P function in D12.

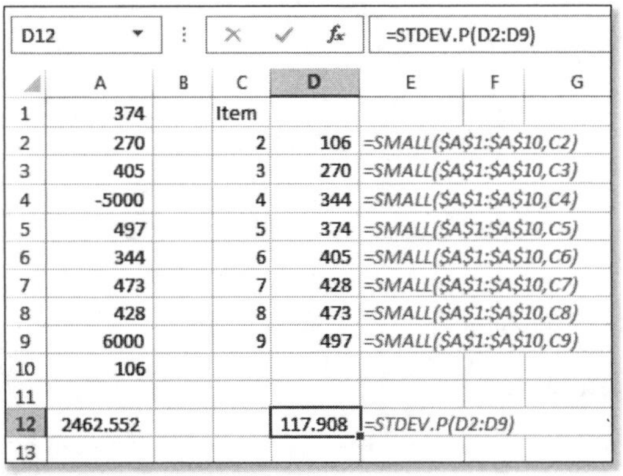

Figure 17.25

A series of SMALL functions eliminates the outliers.

| D12 | ▼ | : | × | ✓ | fx | =STDEV.P(D2:D9) |

◢	A	B	C	D	E	F	G
1	374		Item				
2	270		2	106	=SMALL($A$1:$A$10,C2)
3	405		3	270	=SMALL($A$1:$A$10,C3)
4	-5000		4	344	=SMALL($A$1:$A$10,C4)
5	497		5	374	=SMALL($A$1:$A$10,C5)
6	344		6	405	=SMALL($A$1:$A$10,C6)
7	473		7	428	=SMALL($A$1:$A$10,C7)
8	428		8	473	=SMALL($A$1:$A$10,C8)
9	6000		9	497	=SMALL($A$1:$A$10,C9)
10	106						
11							
12	2462.552			117.908	=STDEV.P(D2:D9)
13							

Setting Up an Array Formula

Both of the preceding approaches require many formulas. You can use an array formula to solve the problem with a single formula.

The SMALL function has two arguments. The first argument is usually a range containing many values. The second argument is usually a single number. Now, imagine if there were a way to ask the SMALL function to return items 2 through 9 at one time. With this small data set, you could type the following:

=SMALL(A1:A10,{2,3,4,5,6,7,8,9})

This approach would not work if your data set contains hundreds or thousands of data points. Instead of typing the position numbers 2 through 9, you could ask for ROW(A2:A9). This function returns an array of {2;3;4;5;6;7;8;9}.

Using SMALL(A1:A10,ROW(A2:A9)) returns an array of the second through ninth smallest values in A1:A10. A single cell cannot hold an array of nine values, so you want to wrap the formula in the STDEV.P function.

The formula =STDEV.P(SMALL(A1:A10,ROW(A2:A9))) is known as an array formula. To make the array formula work, you must hold down Ctrl+Shift while pressing Enter. When you press Ctrl+Shift+Enter, Excel evaluates the formula as an array. It displays the formula in the formula bar surrounded by curly braces.

> **Tip**
>
> Because a single array formula can replace thousands of intermediate formulas, I call these *Super Excel formulas*. At MrExcel.com, I have many examples of formulas I call *CSE formulas*. The CSE acronym stands for *Create Super Excel* and also stands for the keystrokes that you must hold down after typing the formula: Ctrl+Shift+Enter.

Understanding an Array Formula

The Evaluate Formula tool on the Formulas tab helps you to visualize how an array formula is being calculated. In Figure 17.26, a single array formula is shown in cell A12.

Figure 17.26
Excel starts evaluating the formula by solving ROW(A2:A9).

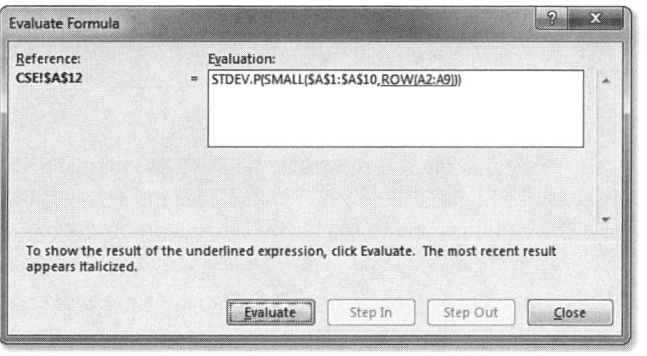

The underlined portion of the formula in the Evaluate Formula dialog shows the portion of the formula that will be solved next. In this example, Excel solves ROW(A2:A9) first.

Click Evaluate. You see that the ROW(A2:A9) is changed to {2;3;4;5;6;7;8;9}. Click Evaluate to have Excel calculate the SMALL function. The result is an array of {106;270;344;374; 405;428;473;497}. Click Evaluate to have Excel calculate the STDEV.P of that array. The result is 117.9082688.

Contrast this result to a nonarray formula. Edit the formula in A12 and press Enter instead of Ctrl+Shift+Enter. The result changes to a zero. Using Evaluate Formula, you can see that the ROW(A2:A9) function returns a single value of 2. The SMALL function then returns a single value of 106. The standard deviation of a single number is always zero.

> **Note**
>
> Pressing Ctrl+Shift+Enter allows Excel to return many intermediate values even though the function might be expecting only a single value. Excel stores all these results in memory and essentially is calculating the function repeatedly for each element in the array.

Coercing a Range of Dates Using an Array Formula

Suppose you want to find out how many Wednesdays occurred between two dates. Enter the starting and ending dates in cells in an Excel worksheet, as shown in Figure 17.27.

		:	✕	✓	f_x	{=SUM(IF(WEEKDAY(ROW(INDIRECT(C1&":"&C2)))=4,1,0))}		

	B	C	D	E	F	G	H	I
	Start Date:	6/30/2010				6/30/2010	4	1
	End Date:	9/15/2015				7/1/2010	5	0
	Wednesdays:	272				7/2/2010	6	0
						7/3/2010	7	0
						7/4/2010	1	0
						7/5/2010	2	0

Figure 17.27
This single array formula replaces hundreds of intermediate calculations.

To start, the WEEKDAY function returns a number from 1 to 7 corresponding to the day of the week. =WEEKDAY(C1) returns the number 4 if the day is a Wednesday.

To check to see whether a particular day is a Wednesday, use the IF function:

```
=IF(WEEKDAY(C1)=4,1,0)
```

Using that formula, you could build a table showing all dates from the beginning date to the ending date as rows. The second column uses the IF/WEEKDAY function to test if each date is a Wednesday. Sum that column to count the Wednesdays in the range. However, this table will contain hundreds of rows for every year in the data range.

Instead, use ROW(INDIRECT(C1&":"&C2)) to build an array in memory of all the dates. Although cell C1 is displaying 6/30/2010, it actually contains the number 40359. Similarly, cell C2 contains the number 42262. Concatenating C1 with a colon and C2 builds a text string of "40359:42262". This text is a valid reference, pointing to all the rows from 40359 to 42262. Asking for the ROW of that reference returns an array with the numbers 40359 to 42262.

To build the array formula, replace "C1" in the original IF/WEEKDAY function with the ROW/INDIRECT functions:

```
=IF(WEEKDAY(ROW(INDIRECT(C1&":"&C2)))=4,1,0)
```

That formula returns a series of zeroes and ones. Because you want to add up the ones in the resulting array, wrap the formula in a SUM function:

```
=SUM(IF(WEEKDAY(ROW(INDIRECT(C1&":"&C2)))=4,1,0))
```

After you type that formula, press Ctrl+Shift+Enter. Excel calculates hundreds of intermediate results and shows the answer in a single cell.

Excel in Practice: Copying Array Formulas

There is a difficulty when copying array formulas. In Figure 17.28, the array formula in D5 needs to be copied to D5:J35.

Normally, you copy cell D5 and then paste to cells D5:J35. With array formulas, this leads to an error. If you attempt to do this copy, you are told that you cannot move or change part of an array. The solution is to do the copy in two pieces:

1. Copy cell D5 to D6:D35.
2. Copy D5:D35 and paste it to E5:J35.

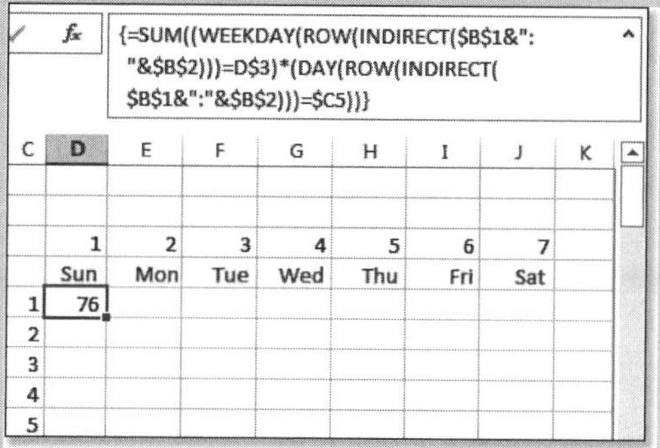

Figure 17.28
You want to copy this formula to the rest of the summary table.

18

USING NAMES IN EXCEL

Long before Microsoft introduced tables and formulas such as
=[@Revenue]-[@Cost], spreadsheets have offered the ability to assign a
name to a cell, range of cells, or formula. The theory is that using a name
for a range is easier to understand when used in a formula. For instance,
=SUM(MyExpenses) makes formulas more self-documenting than
=SUM(Sheet5!AB2:AB99). In Excel 2013, you use the Name Manager
interface to assign and use names effectively.

Advantages of Using Names

Names have a variety of uses in a workbook. A name can be applied to
any cell or range. Names are also useful for the following:

- Making formulas easier to understand and write. Defined names are
  offered in the Formula AutoComplete drop-down as you start to type
  a formula.

- Quick navigation.

- Forcing a formula reference to remain absolute, without having to use
  the dollar sign.

- Doing a two-way lookup with the intersection operator.

- Improving report results from Solver and Scenario Manager.

- Storing a value that will be used repeatedly but that might occasionally
  need to change, such as a sales tax rate.

- Storing formulas.

- Defining a dynamic range.

You have various ways to name a cell. The easiest way to define a name for a cell is to use the name box. To do so, select any cell in your worksheet. To the left of the formula bar is a box with the address of that cell. This box is known as the *name box* (see Figure 18.1). The quick way to assign a name is to click inside the name box and type the name, such as Revenue.

When you press Enter, Excel tries to assign the name. If you get no message, the name is valid. If you get the message, "You must enter a valid reference you want to go to, or type a valid name for the selection," then the name is invalid. If you are taken to a new range, that name already exists.

 **Note**
Excel offers the Table functionality, which is described in Chapter 19, "Fabulous Table Intelligence." Although the Table feature enables you to create formulas using column names, the individual column names and table name are not considered named ranges.

Name Box

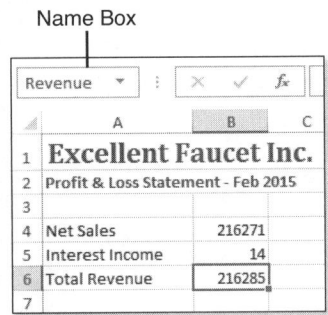

Figure 18.1
The name box is to the left of the formula bar.

The following are some basic rules for valid names:

- Names can be up to 255 characters long.

- Names can start with a letter, an underscore, or a backslash. Numbers can be used in a name, but not as the first character.

- Names cannot contain spaces. However, you can use an underscore or a period in a name. For example, the names Gross_Profit and Gross.Profit are valid.

- Names cannot look like cell addresses. ROI2015 is already a cell address. The names R, r, C, and c cannot be used because these are the shorthand for selecting an entire row or column.

- Names cannot contain operator characters such as these:

  + - * / ( ) ^ & < > = %

- Names cannot contain special characters such as these:

  ! " # $ ' , ; : @ [ ] { } ` ¦ ~

- Names cannot start with "c" or "r" followed by numbers and text. For example, r82hello or c123test are not valid. There is no longer a valid reason for this anomaly.

Table 18.1 provides some examples of valid and invalid names.

Table 18.1 Examples of Valid and Invalid Names

Valid Names	Invalid Names (Why)
SalesTax	Sales Tax (includes a space)
Sales_Tax	XFD123 (valid cell address)
Sales.Tax	Tax2015 (valid cell address)
SalesTax2014	MyResults! (invalid special character)

Naming a Cell by Using the Name Dialog

The Formulas tab contains a group called Defined Names. The following example introduces the Name dialog:

1. Select a cell that you would like to name. Click the Define Name icon from the Formulas tab. The New Name dialog box appears. In Figure 18.2, Cell B8 is being assigned a name.

Figure 18.2
Choose a cell to be named and then select Define Name from the Formulas tab.

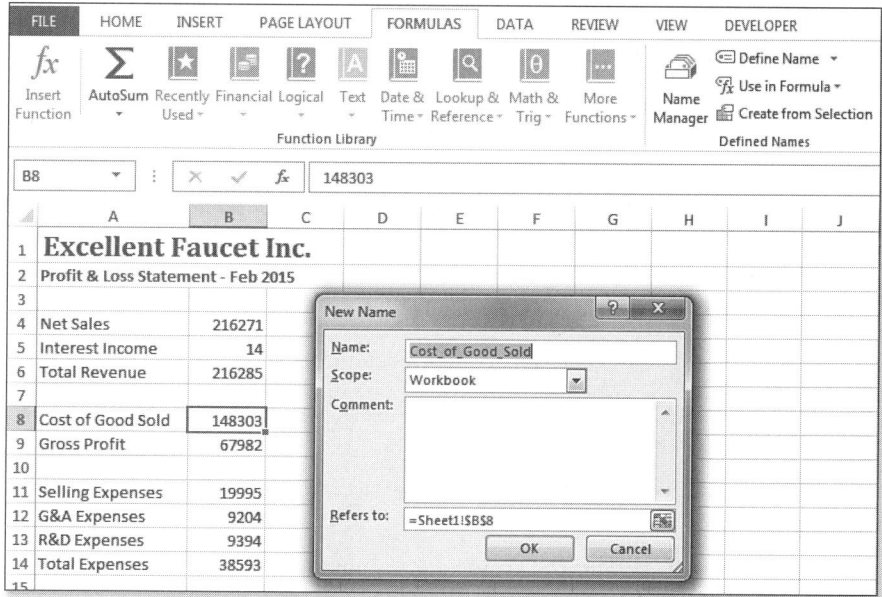

2. The New Name box uses IntelliSense to propose a name. Notice that in this particular example, Excel's IntelliSense was able to ascertain that this cell contains the text Cost of Good Sold. Because that is not a valid name, Excel instead proposed naming the cell Cost_of_Good_Sold. You can either keep that name or override it with a name you prefer. In this case, override that name with the name COGS.

3. For now, leave the scope as Workbook. For a discussion of when to use worksheet-level scope, see "Avoiding Problems by Using Worksheet-Level Scope," later in this chapter.

As you can see in Figure 18.3, the name was applied because the name box now shows COGS instead of B8.

Figure 18.3
After you assign a name, the name box reflects the new name.

Using the Name Box for Quick Navigation

One advantage of using names is that you can use the drop-down in the name box to jump to any named cell. This includes cells that might be in distant sections of the worksheet or even on other sheets in the workbook.

If you plan to use the name box for navigation, assign a name to the upper-left corner of each section of your workbook. The name box drop-down then provides a mini table of contents, and people can use the name box to jump to any section of the workbook.

To illustrate this concept, follow these steps:

1. Click the New Sheet icon (next to the right-most sheet tab) to add a new sheet to the workbook.

2. On the new sheet, go to a distant cell. Give that cell a name, such as SectionTwo. Return to the original sheet in the workbook.

3. Click the name box's drop-down arrow to access a list of all names in the workbook, as shown in Figure 18.4.

4. Choose a name from the list to navigate quickly to that cell, even if it is on another worksheet.

Figure 18.4
The Name Box drop-down contains a list of all names in the workbook.

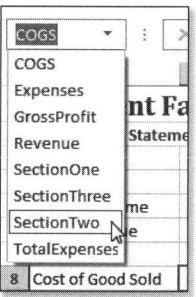

As you can see, named ranges are a great tool for quickly navigating a workbook. Note that names are presented in the name box alphabetically. If you want the names to appear sequentially, you can add names such as Section1, Section2, Section3, and so on. You can also prefix the section names with letters such as A-Income, B-Costs, C-Expense, D-Tax, E-Income. Then, you can jump to a section by choosing it from the alphabetical list in the name box. When used in this way, names in Excel are almost like bookmarks in Word.

> **Tip**
>
> If your names are too long to appear in the name box, you can widen the name box. Look for the three vertical dots between the name box and the formula bar. Drag to the right to expand the name box.

Avoiding Problems by Using Worksheet-Level Scope

Most names have workbook-level scope. There are two specific reasons why you might want to use worksheet-level scope instead:

- You have many similar worksheets in a workbook and you want to define the same names on each sheet. For example, you might want Revenue and COGS on each sheet from Jan through Dec.

- You routinely copy a worksheet from one workbook and you want to avoid phantom names with #REF! errors from appearing in the copied sheet. Note that this problem was prevalent before Excel 2013 but has now been corrected.

Defining a Worksheet-Level Name

To declare a name with worksheet-level scope, you can use one of these methods:

- Use Insert, Define Name. In the New Name dialog, choose Worksheet from the Scope drop-down.

- Click in the name box and type **Jan!Revenue**, as shown in Figure 18.5. If the sheet name contains a space, wrap the sheet name in apostrophes: **'Budget 2016'!Revenue**.

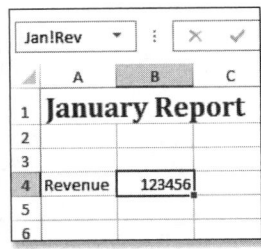

Figure 18.5
Create worksheet-level scope in the name box using this syntax.

- You will often inadvertently create a worksheet-level name by using a duplicate name. If you define Revenue on the Jan worksheet without declaring a scope, the name will have workbook-level scope. If you then define Revenue on the Feb worksheet, it will automatically have worksheet-level scope.

Referring to Worksheet-Level Names

If you want to refer to the Revenue cell on the Jan worksheet from anywhere else on the Jan worksheet, simply use =Revenue.

If you want to refer to the Revenue cell on the Jan worksheet from anywhere else in the workbook, use =Jan!Revenue.

Understanding Phantom Names in Excel 2010 and Earlier

Say that you have a report on a worksheet in Excel 2010 or earlier, and this worksheet contains 20 named ranges. Also in the workbook is a notes page with notes and assumptions. The notes page does not have any named ranges.

You have another workbook that needs a notes page. Because many of the notes are similar, you copy the Notes worksheet from the first workbook to the second workbook. Even though there are no defined names on the Notes worksheet, the copied Notes worksheet drags all 20 defined names to the new workbook and all 20 names are defined as a #REF! error. This is confusing and annoying.

Worse, if the other workbook has some names in common with your 20 phantom names, you get a bewildering error message asking you if you want to keep the current name or redefine the broken #REF! name. When you say to keep the current name, you are asked to rename the broken name to something else. Imagine having to do this once for each phantom name. I've heard horror stories from people who've had 150 phantom names, and this message kept appearing.

At the 2012 MVP Summit, I asked the Excel team how to avoid this mess. In unison, several project managers all said, "Use worksheet-level names!" If you still use Excel 2010 or earlier, and you routinely run into this problem, you can set up all 20 names

 Note

The names Print_Area and Print_ Titles are common worksheet-level names. These names are assigned by Excel after you set certain print settings.

on the Report worksheet to be worksheet-level names. Then, you can copy other worksheets without the phantom names coming along.

Now that I finally understand how to solve this problem, the Excel team made it a non-issue starting with Excel 2013. The phantom names will no longer be created.

Using Named Ranges to Simplify Formulas

As introduced at the start of this chapter, the original reason for having named ranges was to simplify formulas. In theory, it is easier to understand a formula such as =(Revenue-COGS)/Revenue.

Be sure to define the names before entering formulas that refer to those cells. When you create a formula using the mouse or arrow key method, Excel automatically uses the names in the formula.

In the following example, the worksheet in Figure 18.6 has a name of "Revenue" assigned to B6 and a name of "COGS" assigned to B8. Rather than typing =B6-B8 in cell B9, follow these steps to have Excel create a formula using names:

1. Select the cell where the formula should go. In this example, it is cell B9.

2. Type =.

3. Using the mouse, click the first cell in your formula. In this case, it is cell B6.

4. Type -.

5. Using the mouse, click the next cell in your formula. In this case, it is cell B8.

6. Press Enter.

7. Move the cell pointer back to the formula cell and look in the formula bar. You can see that Excel has built the formula =Revenues-COGS, as shown in Figure 18.6. In theory, this formula is self-documenting and easier to understand than =B6-B8.

Figure 18.6
New formulas created after names have been assigned reflect the cell names in the formula.

	A	B	C	D	E	F
	GrossPr... ▾	⋮ ✕ ✓ fx	=Revenue-COGS			
4	Net Sales	216271				
5	Interest Income	14				
6	Total Revenue	216285				
7						
8	Cost of Good Sold	148303				
9	Gross Profit	67982				
10						
11	Selling Expenses	19995				
12	G&A Expenses	9204				
13	R&D Expenses	9394				
14	Total Expenses	38593				
15						
16	Profit Before Tax	29389				
17						

If you prefer to type your formulas, named ranges can also be a timesaver. Say that you start to type =R. Excel displays a drop-down offering many functions that start with R, such as RADIANS, RAND, and RANDBETWEEN. Your defined name of Revenue will be in this list of 20 items.

Keep typing. After you type E, the list shortens to four items: RECEIVED, REPLACE, REPT, and Revenue. Keep typing. When you type V, the only item in the list is your defined name of Revenue. You can now click Tab to insert this named range in your formula.

Type the minus sign, type **COG**, and then press Tab to select COGS from the list.

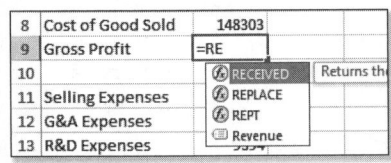

Figure 18.7
Type enough of the name to be unique, and then press Tab to insert the name in your formula.

However, a problem crops up when one of the cells in the formula contains a name—especially if that name is defined strictly for navigational purposes. In this case, Excel creates an absolute reference to that cell. When you copy a formula that contains a name, the copied formula always points to the name. This can lead to unhappy results.

Here is an example to show how easily this can happen.

Figure 18.8 shows cell A2 named SectionThree so that the name can be used as a bookmark.

	A	B	C	D	E
1	Date	Invoice	Amount	Terms	Due Date
2	2/1/2015	1270	11425	20	
3	2/3/2015	1271	18765	30	
4	2/5/2015	1272	12310	30	
5	2/8/2015	1273	20950	30	
6	2/10/2015	1274	16832	10	
7	2/17/2015	1275	16520	10	
8	2/1/2015	1276	15979	10	
9	2/3/2015	1277	12496	20	

Figure 18.8
Cell A2 is named SectionThree to aid navigation.

In cell E2 you enter a formula to calculate a due date. Using the mouse method, you type =, touch cell A2 with the mouse, type +, and then touch cell D2 with the mouse. Instead of entering the formula =A2+D2, you end up with the formula =SectionThree+D2.

Select cell E2 and double-click the fill handle to copy the formula down to all rows. Examine the formula in cell E7. As shown in Figure 18.9, although cell D2 was correctly changed to cell D7 in the copied formula, this cell and all the remaining cells in column E are incorrectly pointing to cell A2 because it was previously defined as a named range.

Figure 18.9
When you copy this formula, every cell points at cell A2 because that cell previously had a defined name.

E7		:	×	✓	fx	=SectionThree+D7	

⊿	A	B	C	D	E
1	Date	Invoice	Amount	Terms	Due Date
2	42036	1270	11425	20	=SectionThree+D2
3	42038	1271	18765	30	=SectionThree+D3
4	42040	1272	12310	30	=SectionThree+D4
5	42043	1273	20950	30	=SectionThree+D5
6	42045	1274	16832	10	=SectionThree+D6
7	42052	1275	16520	10	=SectionThree+D7
8	42036	1276	15979	10	=SectionThree+D8
9	42038	1277	12496	20	=SectionThree+D9
10	42040	1278	10188	10	=SectionThree+D10

To overcome this problem, use care when entering the original formula: Type =, type **A2+**, and then click cell D2. This overrides Excel's default behavior of automatically converting relative reference names to preexisting range names.

Retroactively Applying Names to Formulas

When you learn the trick that was discussed in the "Using Named Ranges to Simplify Formulas" section, you might start naming all the input cells in your workbook, hoping that all the preexisting formulas will take on the new names. Unfortunately, this does not work automatically.

In Figure 18.10, the formula in cell B16 was entered first. Later, cells B9 and B14 were given the names GrossProfit and TotalExpenses, respectively. However, the preexisting formula in B16 continues to reflect the cell addresses instead of the names.

Figure 18.10
The legacy formula in cell B16 does not reflect the new named ranges. Use Define Name, Apply to display this dialog.

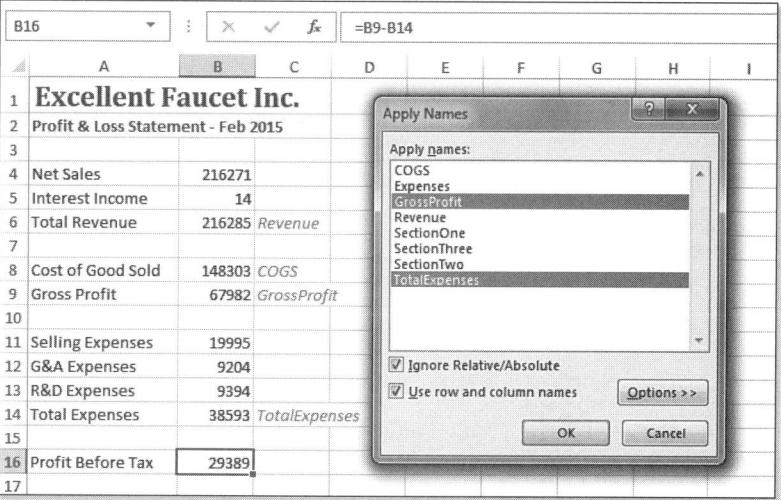

To make the names become part of existing formulas, you have to use the Apply command. To do this, follow these steps:

1. On the Formulas tab, select the drop-down next to Define Name and select Apply Names. The Apply Names dialog appears, as shown in Figure 18.10.

2. Choose as many names as you want in the Apply Names box. In this example, you should choose at least GrossProfit and TotalExpenses and then click OK. Any existing formulas that point to these named cells change to include the cell names in the formula. You see those cells animate with the slot-machine effect to indicate that they have been changed. The new formula is shown in Figure 18.11.

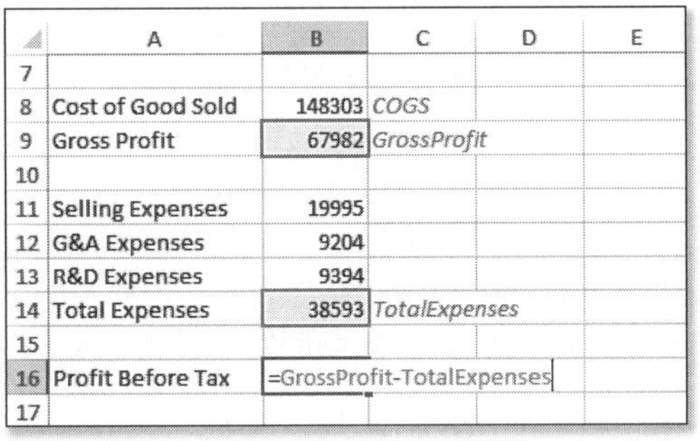

> **Tip**
>
> If you recently defined the names, those names will be preselected when you open the Apply Names dialog.

Figure 18.11
After you apply names, existing formulas are rewritten.

Using Names to Refer to Ranges

It is possible to define a name that refers to a larger range of cells. For example, you can select B11:B13 in Figure 18.12 and type a name such as **Expenses** into the name box.

If you later select Expenses from the name box, your cursor moves to cell B11, and the entire range is selected. Having a name apply to a range allows formulas such as =Sum(Expenses).

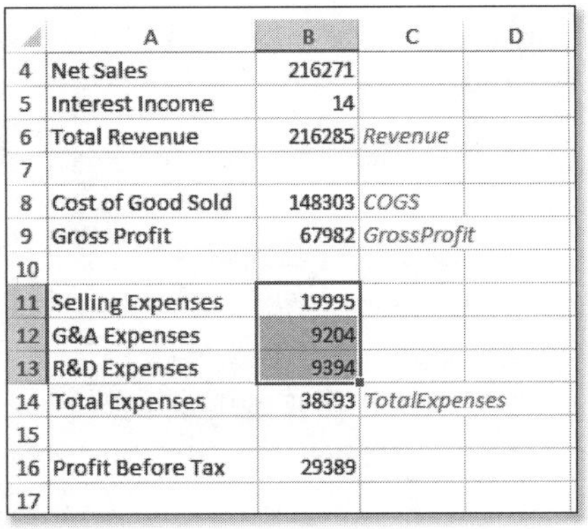

Figure 18.12
A name can refer to a rectangular range.

Dealing with Invalid Legacy Naming

To prevent confusion, a valid cell address may not be used as a name. In legacy versions of Excel, this eliminated names from A1 through IV65536.

Excel 2013 has columns named A through Z, AA through ZZ, and AAA through XFD. The same rule applied to Excel 2013 now invalidates names that start with IW through ZZ and AAA through XFD.

You can think of many three-letter names, such as Tax2007 and ROI5, that might have been common in Excel 2003. Although those are perfectly legal in Excel 2003, they are no longer valid in Excel 2013 because they duplicate existing cell addresses in Excel 2013.

Figure 18.13 shows an Excel 2003 workbook that contains names such as Tax2004, Tax2005, and so on.

Figure 18.13

In Excel 2003, a range named Tax2004 for cell B4 was perfectly legal because with only 256 columns, there was not a column called Tax.

Tax2005	▼	f_x	6.5%		
	A	B	C	D	E	F
1						
2						
3		2004	2005	2006	2007	
4	Tax Rates	7%	6.50%	6.75%	6.25%	
5						
6	Date	Amount	Tax			
7	6/19/2004	502.99	35.2093			
8	1/3/2006	312.64	21.1032			

You can open this workbook in Excel 2013. The workbook initially opens in Compatibility mode, with columns only through IV. When you attempt to save the file as an Excel 2013 workbook, Excel warns you of the first named range that must be changed. In Figure 18.14, Tax2006 is being changed to _Tax2006.

Figure 18.14

When you try to save the Excel 2003 workbook as an Excel 2013 file, the established names must be changed.

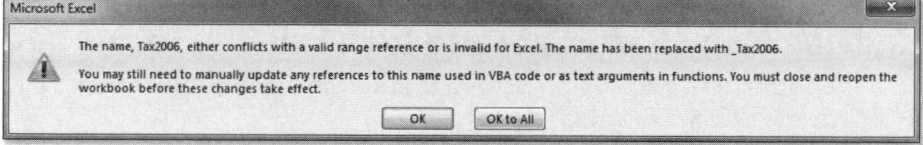

Microsoft Excel

The name, Tax2006, either conflicts with a valid range reference or is invalid for Excel. The name has been replaced with _Tax2006.

You may still need to manually update any references to this name used in VBA code or as text arguments in functions. You must close and reopen the workbook before these changes take effect.

OK | OK to All

Excel attempts to warn you about every existing name that must be changed. You can either click OK to each message or skip them by clicking OK to All. Note that after the Save As, the workbook is still in Compatibility mode. Close the workbook and then reopen it to see the new names.

Excel does a great job of updating the names and the formulas that use invalid names. Figure 18.15 shows the Excel 2003 worksheet after it is converted to Excel 2013. Each name now has an underscore at the beginning.

 Caution

Excel is not able to update some formulas. It would be efficient to rewrite the formula in Figure 18.13 as =B7*INDIRECT("TAX"&YEAR(A7)). During the conversion of names from TAX2006 to _TAX2006, Excel does not update your formula to refer to "_TAX". Formulas such as these fail after the conversion. You have to edit the formula manually.

Underscore Added

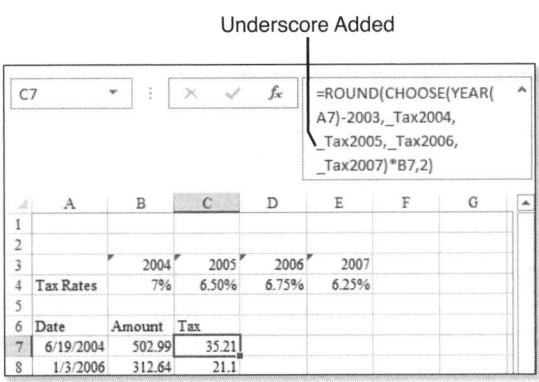

Figure 18.15
Excel correctly updated these references.

Adding Many Names at Once from Existing Labels and Headings

With Excel 2013, you can add many names in a single command, particularly if the names exist as labels or headings adjacent to the cells.

Suppose you have a worksheet with a series of labels in column A and values in column B. One example is shown in Figure 18.16. To do a wholesale assignment of names to the cells in column B, follow these steps:

1. Select the range of labels and the cells to which they refer. In this example, this would be A4:B16.

2. Select Formulas, Defined Names, Create from Selection. Excel displays the Create Names from Selected Range dialog.

3. Because the row labels are in the left column of the selected range, select Left Column and then click OK, as shown in Figure 18.16.

Figure 18.16
When you make this selection, Excel uses the text values in the left column to assign names to all the nonblank cells in column B of this range.

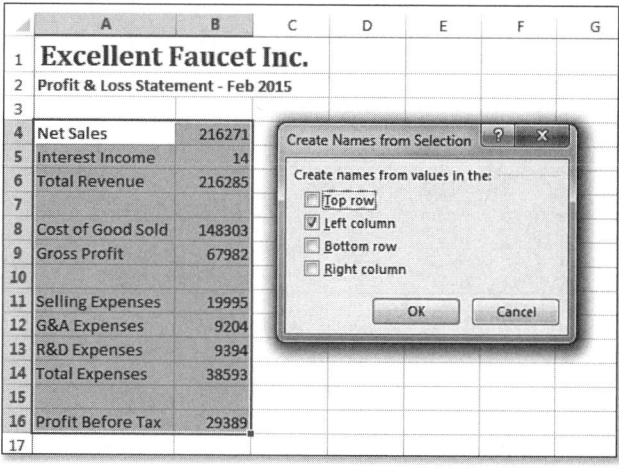

Excel does a fairly good job of assigning the names. Spaces are replaced with underscores to make the names valid. Figure 18.17 shows the names created as a result of this command. In this example, cell B4 is assigned the name Net_Sales. Cell C8 is assigned the name Cost_of_Good_Sold. In row 12, where the label contains an ampersand (&), Excel replaces the ampersand with an underscore, to form the name G_A_Expenses. Although this is not as meaningful as it could be if you wrote the name yourself, it is still pretty good.

> ▲ **Caution**
> If a cell contained G & A Expenses, Excel would replace every space and ampersand with an underscore, creating the name G___A_Expenses.

Figure 18.17
Excel replaces spaces and ampersands with underscores when creating names from a selection.

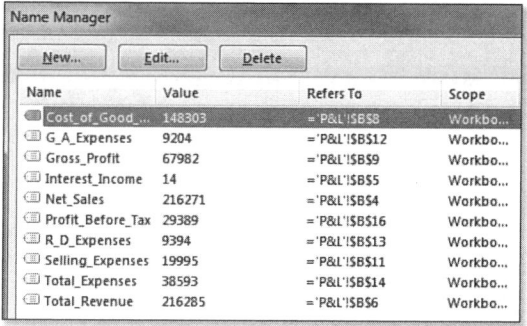

In Excel 2013, you can apply names by using both the row labels and column headings at the same time. In Figure 18.18, the selections in the Create Names from Selected Ranges dialog mean that nine new names will be added to the workbook. For example, Northeast refers to B2:F2, and Week5 refers to F2:F5.

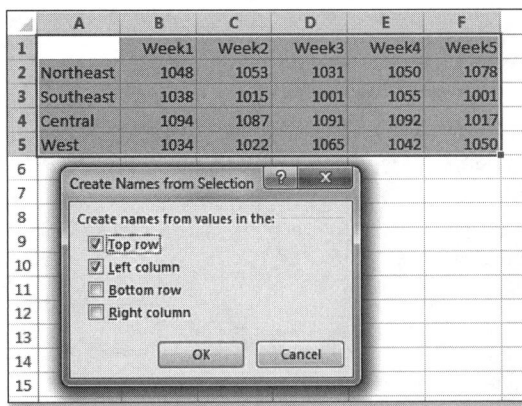

Figure 18.18
In Excel 2013, you can create names based on the row labels and column headers at the same time.

Using Intersection to Do a Two-Way Lookup

After using Create from Selection in Figure 18.18, the name Southeast applies to the range B3:F3. The name Week5 applies to F2:F5. You can do a two-way lookup by using the intersection operator within the SUM function. The intersection operator is a space. A formula such as =SUM(Week5 Southeast) looks for the intersection of the two ranges and returns the value 1001 from cell F3 (see Figure 18.19).

The formula in Figure 18.19 is significantly easier than a traditional two-way lookup with

`=INDEX(B2:F5,MATCH("Southeast",$A$2:$A$5,0),MATCH("Week5",$B$1:$F$1,0))`

 Caution
The intersection example works because you are hard-coding Southeast and Week5 into the formula. If those values were stored in other cells, you would have to use a pair of INDIRECT functions: =SUM(INDIRECT(E7) INDIRECT(E8)). Using INDIRECT makes the formula volatile, which forces that cell to recalculate more often, thus slowing down the worksheet.

▲	A	B	C	D	E	F	G	H	I
1		Week1	Week2	Week3	Week4	Week5			
2	Northeast	1048	1053	1031	1050	1078			
3	Southeast	1038	1015	1001	1055	1001			
4	Central	1094	1087	1091	1092	1017			
5	West	1034	1022	1065	1042	1050			
6									
7						=SUM(Week5 Southeast)			
8									
9									

Figure 18.19
This formula is asking for the intersection of two ranges.

Using Implicit Intersection

In Figures 18.18 through 18.20, the name "Northeast" applies to B2:F2. If you type =Northeast anywhere in columns B:F, Excel uses implicit intersection. Excel assumes that you only want to refer to the portion of the Northeast range that intersects the current column. Typing =Northeast in D7 returns 1031 because of the five values in the Northeast region: The 1031 in D2 intersects with the formula in D7. This is a cool shortcut method.

In Figure 18.20, an identical formula of =Southeast+Northeast is used in B8:F8.

Implicit intersections also work with vertical ranges. Week4 is defined as E2:E5. If you enter =Week4 anywhere in rows 2 through 5, Excel returns the value from the Week4 range that intersects with the row that contains the formula. This allows identical formulas of =Week4+Week5, as shown in H2:H5 of Figure 18.20.

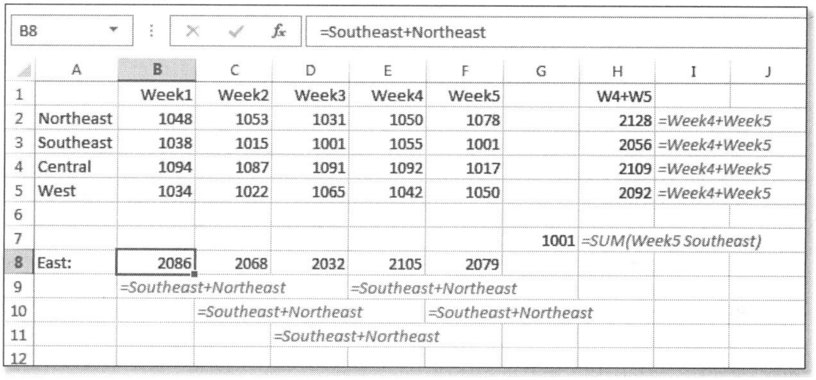

> **⚠ Caution**
>
> You cannot use implicit intersection in an array formula. If you use =Southeast outside of columns B:F, it will refer to the entire range, so you would have to wrap it in a SUM or other function.

Figure 18.20
Refer to =Northeast anywhere in columns B:F to invoke implicit intersection.

Managing Names

In Excel 2013, you can manage names using the Name Manager dialog. This dialog offers many new features to manage names.

To open the dialog, click the Name Manager icon in the Formulas tab (see Figure 18.21).

The Name Manager dialog shows the five fields for each name. Initially, certain columns might not be wide enough to show all the text in each column. You can resize the entire dialog by using the triangle in the lower-right corner. You can also resize columns by dragging the vertical bars between the column headings. You can sort by a column by clicking on a column heading in the dialog box.

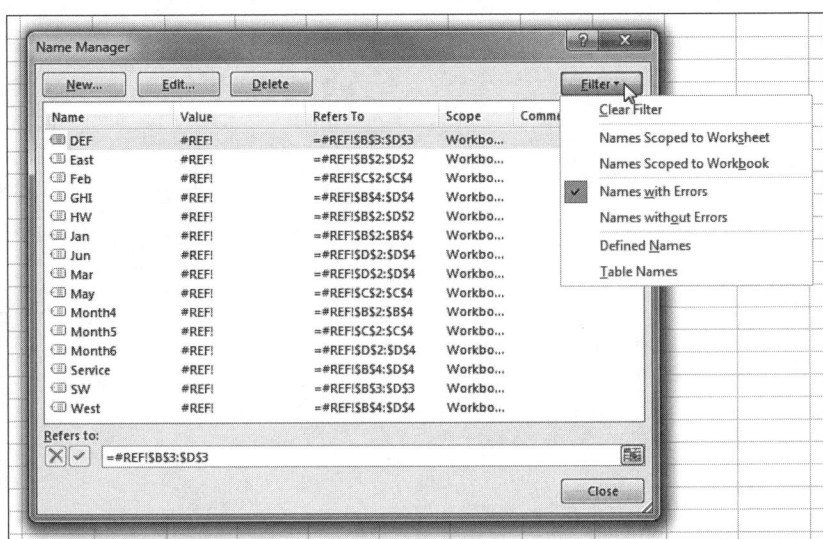

Figure 18.21
Click Name Manager to display the vastly improved Name Manager dialog.

Excel In Practice

The Filter button enables you to filter the list. For example, I just deleted two worksheets from the workbook. All of the names on those worksheets still show up in the Name Manager, but they refer to #REF! errors. To quickly delete these names, use these steps:

1. Click Name Manager to display the Name Manager dialog.
2. Open the Filter and choose Names with Errors.
3. Click the first name in the dialog.
4. Shift-click the last name in the dialog to select all names with errors.
5. Click the Delete button.
6. Confirm the deletion of the names.

The following are the columns in the Name Manager dialog:

- **Name**—Shows the current name.
- **Value**—Shows the current value. If the Name column refers to a rectangular range, each value in the range is shown in the Value column.
- **Refers To**—Shows the formula defined for the name. This might be a reference to a cell address, a constant value, or a formula.

- **Scope**—Indicates whether the name applies to the whole workbook or just to a certain worksheet.

- **Comment**—Shows any comments you might have typed when you originally defined a name.

Working with the Name Manager dialog is straightforward:

- To create a new name, click the New button.

- To delete a name, highlight the name and click Delete. However, this should be done with caution. If the name is being used, all the formulas that point to that name change to #NAME? errors.

- To view the cells represented by a certain name, select the name from the Name column of the dialog and then click at the end of the Refers To box. Excel shows you the section of the worksheet behind the dialog.

- To reassign a name to a different set of cells, choose the name from the Name column of the dialog and then click in the Refers To box. On the worksheet, point to the new location for the name. After you select a new location, click the check box to accept the new location. Click the X button to revert to the original location.

- If you click a name from the Name column of the dialog and then click Edit, you have an opportunity to add or change the comment to the name or to change the scope.

- When you modify an existing name in the Name column of the dialog, any formulas that specifically reference that name are updated to point to the new cell.

Filtering the Name Manager Dialog

In the upper-right corner of the Name Manager dialog is a button labeled Filter that can be clicked to access many powerful options. If you have defined names that have scope only to a worksheet, you can select Names Scoped to Worksheet to limit the Name Manager dialog to only those names.

Following are the options in the Filter button's drop-down list:

- **Clear Filter**—Restores the list to the complete list.

- **Names Scoped to Worksheet**—Shows all worksheet-level names for the active worksheet and other worksheets.

- **Names Scoped to Workbook**—Shows all the global names that are scoped to a workbook.

- **Names with Errors**—Finds all names where the value is a cell error. Often, stray names are left behind after a worksheet that contains names has been deleted. You can use the Names with Errors filter to find those names.

- **Names Without Errors**—Hides any invalid names.

- **Defined Names**—Specifies the names defined using the techniques described in this chapter. This option removes names defined as a result of creating pivot tables or formatting ranges as tables.

- **Table Names**—Shows only the values of table names. When you define a range as a table, the entire table is given a name such as Table1.

Using a Name to Simplify an Absolute Reference

A common scenario is when a formula such as VLOOKUP is used in a data set to look up data on another worksheet. You might enter a VLOOKUP formula in cell B2 and copy it to hundreds of records. The formula in cell B2 might be =VLOOKUP(A2,'Lookup Table'!A2:B25,2,False). As you copy this formula to row 3, the reference in the second argument will incorrectly change to 'Lookup Table'!A3:B26. When you need the reference to always point to A2:B25, you can add dollar signs to the reference: $A$2:$B$25.

If you will be frequently adding VLOOKUP formulas that will point to 'Lookup Table'!$A$2:$B$25, it can get tedious to continually use the syntax. After all, it is a confusing mix of dollar signs, apostrophes, and exclamation points.

To simplify the VLOOKUP formula, give A2:B25 a name such as ItemLookup. Then, the formula simply becomes =VLOOKUP(A2,ItemLookup,2,False). As you copy the formula down, it continues to point to A2:B25 on the Lookup Table worksheet. Figure 18.22 compares the formula without a name in B2 and the formula with a name in B3.

◢	A	B	C	D	E	F	G
1	SKU	Title					
2	B2	Don't Fear the Spreadsheet	=VLOOKUP(A2,'Lookup Table'!$A$2:$B$25,2,FALSE)				
3	C9	VBA & Macros for Microsoft Excel 2013	=VLOOKUP(A3,ItemLookup,2,FALSE)				
4	C4	Excel Gurus Gone Wild	=VLOOKUP(A4,ItemLookup,2,FALSE)				
5	A4	Slaying Excel Dragons	=VLOOKUP(A5,ItemLookup,2,FALSE)				

Figure 18.22
The formula in B3 is easier to type because it uses a named range for the lookup table.

Using a Name to Hold a Value

So far, all the names defined in this chapter have referred to a cell or a range of cells. It is possible to assign a constant value to a name by using the New Name dialog. You might do this to hold a value that could possibly change, but would likely rarely change, such as a sales tax rate.

To use a name to hold a value, follow these steps:

1. Either click the Define Name icon or the Name Manager icon and then click New. The New Name dialog appears.

2. In the Name field of the New Name dialog, type a name such as Sales_Tax.

3. In the Refers To box, remove any existing cell reference and type the new value (=6.5%, as shown in Figure 18.23).

4. Write formulas that refer to the new name, such as Sales_Tax. The formula might be something like =C2*Sales_Tax. In Figure 18.24, the range has been defined as a table. Thus, the formula of =[@MerchAmt]*Sales_Tax uses both a table field name in square brackets and the defined name Sales_Tax.

Figure 18.23
In the New Name dialog, you can assign a constant value to a name.

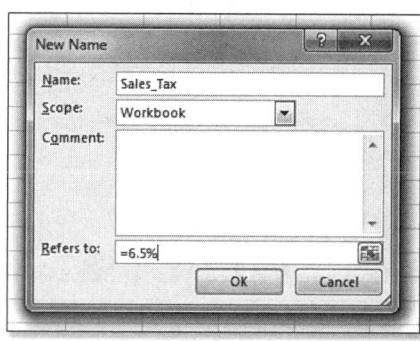

The advantage of using a name to refer to a constant is that if your tax rate changes, you can edit the value defined in the name, and all the formulas in the workbook recalculate. To edit an existing name, click the Name Manager, click the name, and then select Edit Name.

Figure 18.24
MerchAmt, in square brackets, is a field name in the table. Sales_Tax is a defined name.

	A	B	C	D	E	F
	Invoice	MerchAmt	Sales T.			
1						
2	1901	159.8	10.387			
3	1902	59.85	3.89025			
4	1903	39.9	2.5935			
5	1904	79.9	5.1935			

C2 = [@MerchAmt]*Sales_Tax

 Caution

Use care when viewing potentially ambiguous references such as Sales_Tax and [@Sales Tax], as shown in Figure 18.25. Remember, the name in square brackets is a table name assigned automatically by Excel. The @ symbol indicates that you are referring to a value from this row of the table.

Figure 18.25
With defined names and table column names floating around, ambiguous formulas like this can turn up.

E2 = [@Total]/(1+Sales_Tax)-([@Total]-[@[Sales Tax]])

	A	B	C	D	E	F
1	Invoice	MerchAmt	Sales Tax	Total	Rounding Error	
2	1901	159.8	10.387	170.19	-0.000183099	
3	1902	59.85	3.89025	63.74	1.52582E-05	
4	1903	39.9	2.5935	42.49	0.000213615	

Assigning a Formula to a Name

Although names are traditionally used to refer to cells or constant values, you can use a name to refer to a formula. Look at any name in the Name Manager. The Refers To column starts with an equal sign, which means that named ranges always contain a formula.

As described in the following sections, assigning a formula to a name can be useful in a variety of situations.

Using Basic Named Formulas

A named formula enables you to replace a complicated formula with an easy-to-remember name. In this basic case, the formula does not contain cell references. For example, suppose you have discovered a fairly complex formula that would be difficult to remember, such as the formula shown in Figure 18.26.

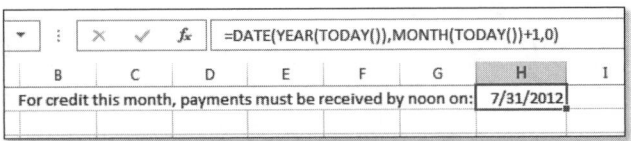

Figure 18.26
You can assign a complicated formula to a simpler name.

In this case, you could assign the formula =Date(Year(Today()),Month(Today())+1,0) to a name such as MonthEnd, as shown in Figure 18.27. You could then use =MonthEnd in any cell to calculate the end of the current month.

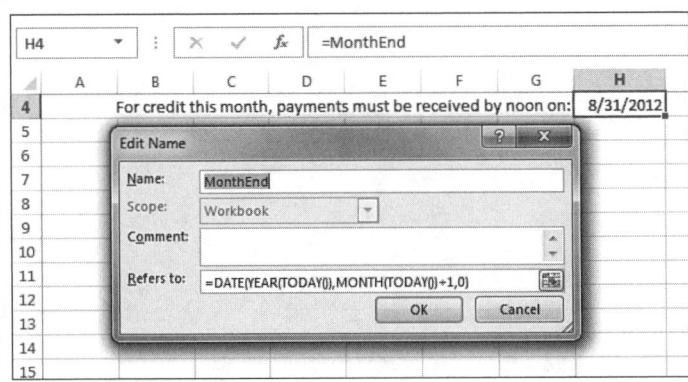

Figure 18.27
After a formula has been assigned to a name, you can use it as you would a constant.

Using Dynamic Named Formulas

An interesting example of a named formula is a reference that dynamically expands as more data is filled down a column.

Suppose that you have a list of valid sales reps on a hidden RepList to be used as the list for a data validation drop-down. The list might extend from A1:A9 today, but as new sales reps are hired, the list may expand to A10, A11, A12, and so on.

The OFFSET() function has a parameter that specifies that a range should extend for X rows. If you use COUNTA to return the number of rows, you can create a formula to dynamically expand or contract as cells are filled in or deleted. In theory, you would set up a formula to point to this range: =OFFSET(RepList!A1,0,0,COUNTA(RepList!A:A),1). However, absolute references should be used in the definition. In Figure 18.28, for example, the formula assigned to RepList is =OFFSET(RepList!$A$1,0,0,COUNTA(RepList!$A:$A),1).

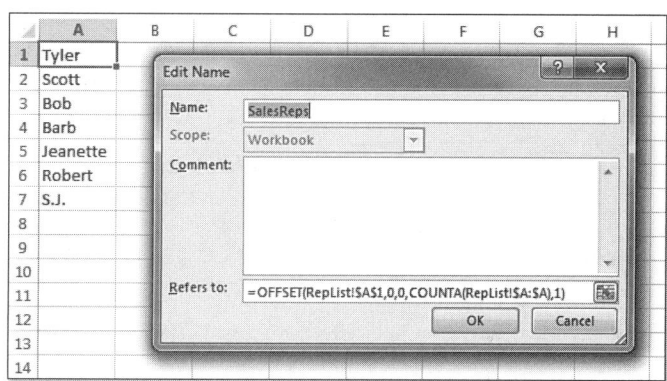

Figure 18.28
This formula can expand to include the number of entries in column A.

The name automatically expands as new entries are added. To make use of this name in an in-cell drop-down, follow these steps:

1. Select Data, Data Validation.

2. Change the Allow drop-down to List.

3. In the Source box, type =SalesReps.

4. Leave the In-Cell Dropdown box selected.

The completed dialog box is shown in Figure 18.29. Initially, the cell with validation offers a drop-down that lists the nine current reps, as shown in Figure 18.30.

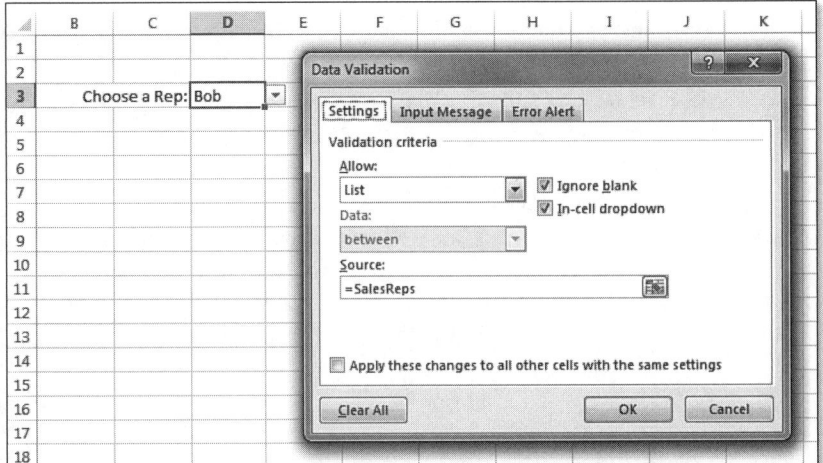

Figure 18.29
You can set up data validation to use a dynamic name.

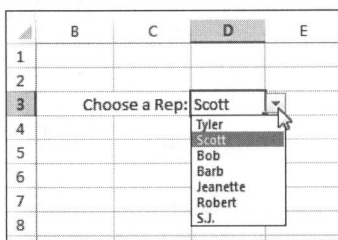

Figure 18.30
The result of adding data validation to a cell.

When the list on RepList is edited, the drop-down is automatically updated. For example, in Figure 18.31, you can see that Mario replaced Jeanette, and two new reps were added. The window on the left shows the new list on RepList, and the window on the right shows the current drop-down list.

You can use a similar technique to make a chart series expand as new months are added.

➡ *For details on charting,* **see** *Chapter 32, "Graphing Data Using Excel Charts."*

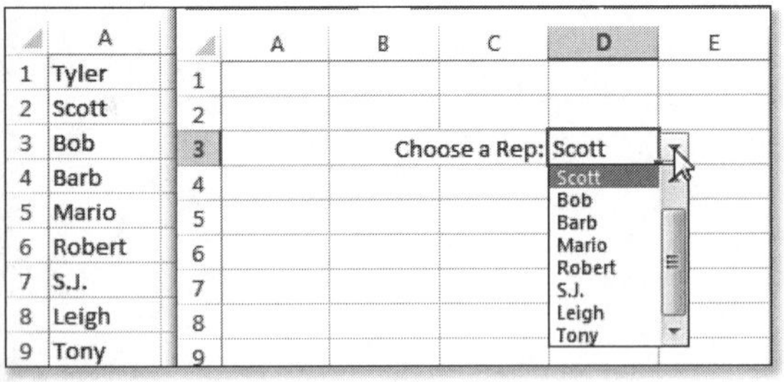

Figure 18.31
As the list on RepList changes, the dynamic formula expands to include the new cells in the list.

Using a Named Formula to Point to the Cell Above

In all the examples in this chapter, it was important to make sure that all references were absolute. Although it seems strange, it is possible to make use of a relative reference in a named formula. However, this should be done only if you understand one slightly buggy gotcha and two cautions if you use VBA or share the workbook with someone using Excel 97:

■ The gotcha happens in workbooks with multiple worksheets. A relative formula will work fine on the original worksheet, but incorrectly when used on another worksheet. A workaround that starts the reference with an ! solves this problem.

■ The first caution is that this method fails if you are using VBA macros and the macro causes the worksheet to calculate.

■ The second caution is that this method crashes Excel if the workbook is opened in Excel 97.

In Figure 18.32, the cell pointer is on the Relative worksheet in cell A3. The name AboveMe is being defined as pointing to cell A2. However, in the Refers To box, press F4 three times to remove all the dollar signs from the reference.

Figure 18.32
Defining a relative reference in a named formula.

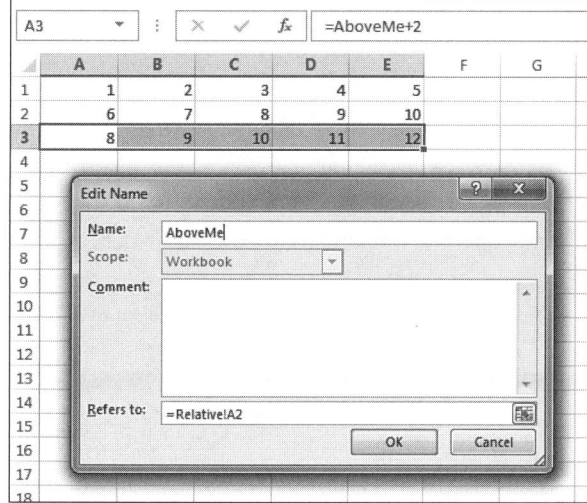

This relative formula initially appears to work perfectly. Cells A3:E3 in Figure 18.33 all contain the formula =AboveMe+2.

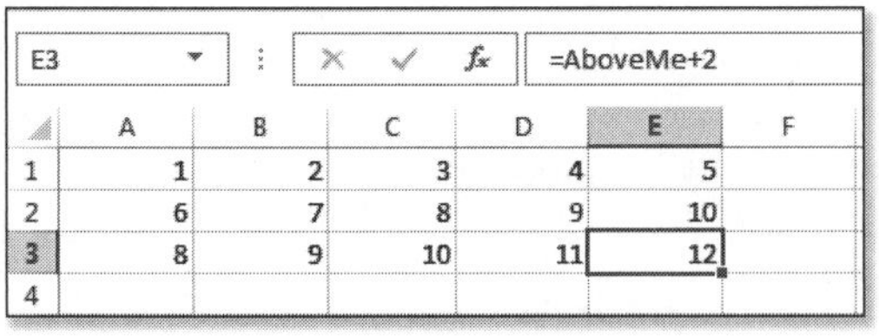

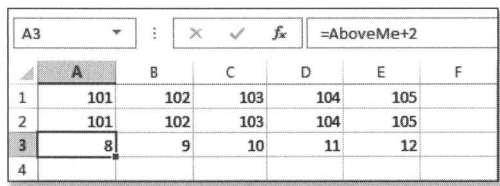

Figure 18.33
In this example, the relative reference in the named formula is working fine.

However, if you go to Sheet2 and enter the formula =AboveMe+2 in cells A3:E3, the formula returns the value from row 2, but from the Relative sheet instead of the current worksheet. Figure 18.34 shows the answer 8 when you would expect 103.

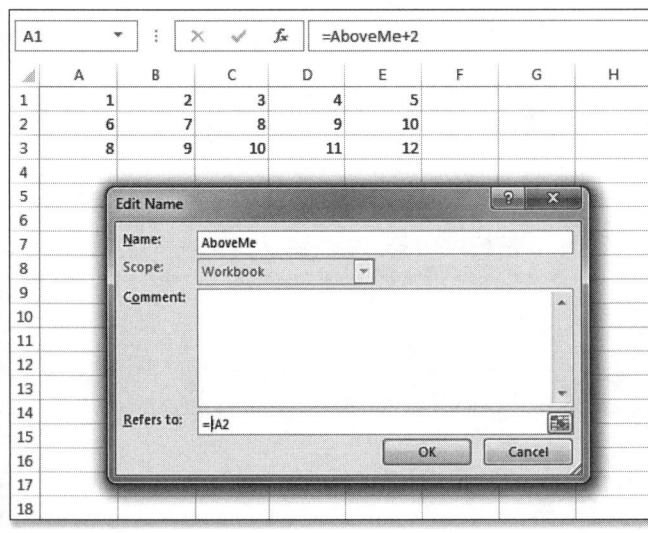

Figure 18.34
The relative reference in the named formula fails on another sheet.

The solution is to edit the name. To do so, remove the reference to Sheet1, leaving a definition of =!A2, as shown in Figure 18.35.

Figure 18.35
Edit the formula to point to =!A2.

Now, when you close the Name Manager dialog, the formulas work as expected, as shown in Figure 18.36.

Figure 18.36
The relative reference of =!A2 now works as expected.

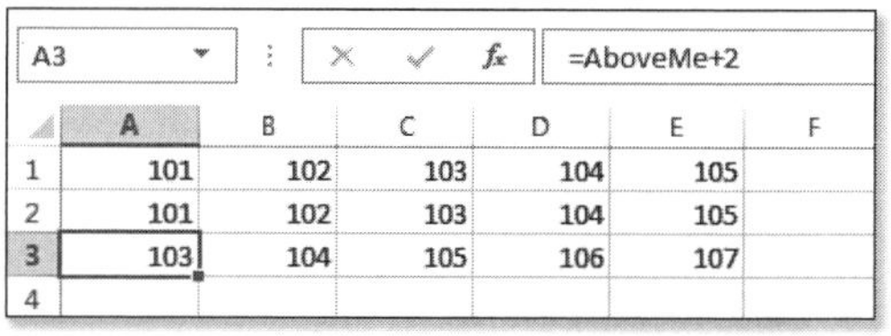

A3		⋮	×	✓	f_x	=AboveMe+2	
	A	B	C	D	E	F
1	101	102	103	104	105	
2	101	102	103	104	105	
3	103	104	105	106	107	
4						

FABULOUS TABLE INTELLIGENCE

A fundamental use of Excel is for analyzing two-dimensional tables of data. Most worksheets contain headings at the top and then rows of data. Most Excel customers spend a lot of time working with tables of data. Microsoft recognized this and added intelligent tables, beginning with Excel 2007. If you explicitly tell Excel 2013 that you are working on a table of data, it displays a custom Table tab that has a number of amazing features.

Excel's intelligent tables enable you to do the following:

- Automatically add filter drop-downs to the headings in a table.

- Have one-click access to banded rows, banded columns, and other autoformats.

- Toggle a total row on or off.

- Have one-click access to removing duplicates.

- Automatically copy new formulas to all cells in a column.

- Automatically extend a table when new data is typed below or to the right of the table. This feature also affects any charts, formulas, or pivot tables that pointed to the table, causing them to expand as well.

- Extend conditional formatting to new rows in the table.

- Automatically freeze panes to show the heading row as you scroll off the page.

- Automatically set up range names for an entire table and each column within the table.

Tables were introduced in Excel 2007. Minor refinements to the table formula syntax has occurred in Excel 2010 with the @ replacing the `ThisRow` syntax. Otherwise, Excel 2013 tables are similar to what you encountered in Excel 2007. If you are upgrading from Excel 2003, the table functionality is dramatically improved from the List functionality introduced in Excel 2003.

Defining Suitable Data for Excel Tables

Many Excel spreadsheets contain data that is suitable for Excel tables. For the purpose of this chapter, a *table* is a range of Excel data. Each row in the range is one record of data. For example, each row might describe an invoice, a customer, or an inventory item. Each column in the table creates another field for each row. Fields might include invoice number, customer name, and total sales. A table usually includes headings in the first row.

The simple range in Figure 19.1 makes a suitable table because each row in this range is a record and each column is a field.

	A	B	C	D
1				
2	Region	Customer	Revenue	Cost
3	East	Leading Camera Traders	65073	31235
4	Central	Magnificent Sandal Company	23345	12840
5	West	Special Edger Corporation	98274	51102
6	East	Cool Scooter Company	20619	10310
7	Central	Hip Calculator Corporation	71626	34380
8	West	Different Radio Inc.	45541	20949
9	East	Matchless Clipboard Company	45521	24126

Figure 19.1
This makes an ideal table in Excel.

Defining a Table

You can define a table in Excel 2013 in four ways:

- Choose a cell in the data set and then select Insert, Table.

- Select a cell in the data set and then select Home, Format as Table. Choose a Style and then click OK.

- Select a cell in the data set and press Ctrl+T.

- Select a cell in the data set and press Ctrl+L.

 Caution

For several versions, Excel has offered a feature called Custom Views. If any worksheet in your workbook contains a table, then Custom Views is grayed out for the entire workbook. Because not many people use Custom Views, this is not entirely a bad thing. However, if you use Custom Views, it can be a horrible limitation.

When you use any of these methods, Excel uses IntelliSense to determine the edge of the table. Excel looks for a completely blank row and a completely blank column to define the edges of the table.

Excel shows the suspected table range in the Create Table dialog, as shown in Figure 19.2. You need to verify that this range is correct. If your table has headers, leave the My Table Has Headers check box selected and click OK.

Figure 19.2
Excel's IntelliSense guesses the extent of the table.

As shown in Figure 19.3, Excel adds a default table format to your range. The headings gain filter drop-downs. A ribbon tab called Table Tools – Design is displayed. Excel assigns a name similar to `Table1` to the table.

Figure 19.3
The table has an interesting autoformat, but there are many more features.

	A	B	C	D
1				
2	Region	Customer	Revenu	Co
3	East	Leading Camera Traders	65073	31235
4	Central	Magnificent Sandal Company	23345	12840
5	West	Special Edger Corporation	98274	51102
6	East	Cool Scooter Company	20619	10310

Keeping Headers in View

Notice that in Figure 19.3, the headings appear in row 2 of the worksheet. As you scroll through the table, you can eventually scroll to the point where row 2 is no longer visible in the window. At this point, Excel moves the headings from row 2 and shows them where column names A, B, C, and D normally display. Figure 19.4 shows the headings as column names.

Headings Replace Column Letters

	Region	Customer	Revenue	Cost
16	Central	User-Friendly Scooter Corporation	55780	29006
17	West	Matchless Gadget Inc.	27796	12508
18	East	User-Friendly Freezer Corporation	96391	52051
19	Central	Inventive Kiln Supply	55722	25075
20	West	Unique Treadmill Corporation	76671	36035

Figure 19.4
When you do not use the Freeze Panes command, Excel automatically moves the heading values up to the column names when you scroll the headings off the window.

These heading names stay as column names as long as each factor listed here is true:

■ The cell pointer is inside the range of the table.

■ The header row is not visible in the window.

■ At least one row of the table is visible in the window. If you leave the cell pointer in the table and then use a scrollbar to scroll the table out of view, the column names revert to column letters.

When any of the preceding conditions is no longer true, the headings disappear from the column name area.

Although Microsoft introduced this feature in Excel 2007, it made one significant improvement starting in Excel 2010. The filter drop-downs are now available after the headers move up to become the column labels.

Freezing Worksheet Panes

Excel 2013's automatic heading visibility feature is very cool. With legacy versions of Excel, many users did not know there was a way to freeze panes. Regardless of whether you knew about that feature, it is a positive feature 90% of the time, although it is not perfect.

For example, it is a bit annoying that the headings disappear when you select a cell outside the table. It seems logical that if you can see part of a table in the window, Excel should keep the headings up as part of the column names. In addition, the cell pointer can be a distraction in a data set. For example, if you are showing your manager something on the screen, you might have a tendency to click outside the table so that the manager does not think you are trying to show one particular cell.

Another annoying issue is that the automatic heading visibility feature does not work with labels in the left column. For example, in Figure 19.5, a wide table has labels in column A. After you select First Column, Excel properly formats column A. However, if you scroll over to see the month of December, Excel does not make the column A values stay visible as they normally do with row numbers.

Figure 19.5
The automatic heading visibility feature does not work for the first column.

	A	B	C	D	E
1	Name ▾	Jan ▾	Feb ▾	Mar ▾	Apr ▾	May
2	A	48	19	78	46
3	B	82	82	69	70
4	C	20	14	29	54

The old-style Freeze Panes command is still available and is even a bit easier to use in Excel 2013.

In legacy versions of Excel, you had to put the cell pointer in the first cell that should not be frozen before invoking the Freeze Panes command. However, beginning with Excel 2007, Microsoft added two commands that enable you to freeze the first row or the first column from anywhere. Here's how you freeze the first row:

1. Make sure the row that you want to stay at the top of the window is the first visible row in the window.

2. Select View, Freeze Panes. The drop-down that appears is shown in Figure 19.6.

Figure 19.6
Excel 2013 offers three commands to the Freeze Panes area.

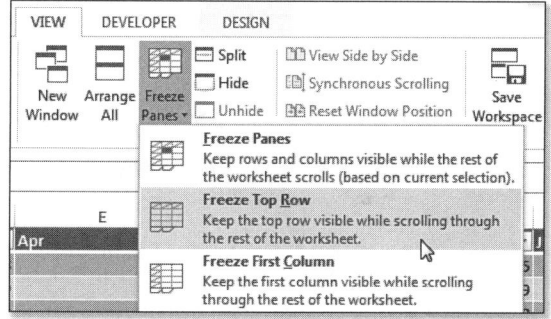

3. Select Freeze Top Row.

You can now scroll anywhere on the worksheet and always see the first row.

It is annoying, but the Freeze First Column resets the Freeze First Row icon, and vice versa. If you need to freeze both the first column and first row, you have to use the Freeze Panes command as described in the following sections.

Clearing Freeze Panes

To turn off the Freeze Panes option, select the Freeze Panes icon again in the View tab. Now the first option in the drop-down is Unfreeze Panes. Select this option to unlock the view, which enables you to scroll anywhere in the window.

Using the Old Version of Freeze Panes for Absolute Control

At times, you might want several rows or columns to remain visible. Just as in legacy versions of Excel, you can do this when you understand how Freeze Panes works.

Consider the worksheet in Figure 19.7. Suppose you always want to see the data in columns A:D at the left side of the window. Several rows of title information don't necessarily need to be visible at the top of the worksheet as you scroll, but it would be good to see rows 5 and 6 at the top of the window as you scroll.

	A	B	C	D	E	F	G	H	I
1	XYZ COMPANY								
2	SALES REPORT								
3	QUARTER 1, 2015								
4									
5					Product Line A			Product Line B	
6	Country	Region	District	Sales Rep	Sales	Profit	GP%	Sales	Profit
7	USA	East	Northeast	Giannotti	9680	4743	49.0%	4132	1694
8	USA	East	Northeast	Alfredo	6406	2819	44.0%	6544	2748
9	USA	East	Northeast	Strong	4916	2163	44.0%	20694	9105
10	USA	East	Northeast	Mosley	10103	4142	41.0%	14380	5752

Figure 19.7
This worksheet is too complex for the Freeze Top Row command to work as desired.

You can set up the headings to stay visible by following these steps:

1. Click the arrow at the bottom of the vertical scrollbar four times to make row 5 the first row visible in the window.

2. Select the first cell that will not be frozen in the window. Everything visible in the window above and to the left of this cell will be frozen. In Figure 19.8, this would be cell E7. It is critical that you select this cell before moving on to step 3.

	A	B	C	D	E	F
5					Product Line A	
6	Country	Region	District	Sales Rep	Sales	Profit
7	USA	East	Northeast	Giannotti	9680	4743
8	USA	East	Northeast	Alfredo	6406	2819

Figure 19.8
Select the first cell that will not be frozen.

3. Select View, Freeze Panes, and then select Freeze Panes from the drop-down.

The result is that you can scroll down and right. Even when you are at column V, row 62, you can still see the headings in rows 5:6 and the values in columns A:D, as shown in Figure 19.9.

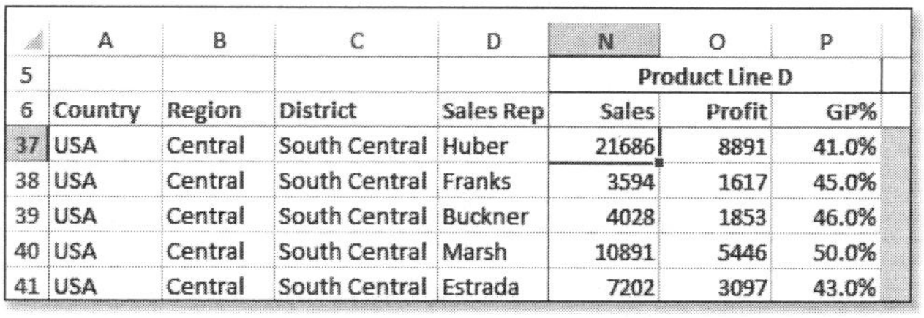

Figure 19.9
After you use the original Freeze Panes command, you can have multiple rows and columns frozen at the top and left of the worksheet.

⊿	A	B	C	D	N	O	P
5					Product Line D		
6	Country	Region	District	Sales Rep	Sales	Profit	GP%
37	USA	Central	South Central	Huber	21686	8891	41.0%
38	USA	Central	South Central	Franks	3594	1617	45.0%
39	USA	Central	South Central	Buckner	4028	1853	46.0%
40	USA	Central	South Central	Marsh	10891	5446	50.0%
41	USA	Central	South Central	Estrada	7202	3097	43.0%

The key to using the Freeze Panes command is that you must place the cell pointer before using the command. The command freezes everything that is above and to the left of the cell pointer location when the command is invoked.

To freeze only columns A:B and no rows, you would invoke the command from row 1 of column C. However, because there is nothing above the cell pointer, no rows are frozen.

Adding a Total Row to a Table

The Table Styles Options group of the Table Tools Design tab contains a Total Row check box. When you select this box, Excel automatically adds a total to the bottom of your table.

By default, Excel adds the word *Total* to the first column of the table and adds a formula to the right-most column of the table to sum the column. You can add totals to additional columns.

Figure 19.10 shows the default total row for a table. A drop-down appears when you select a cell in the Total row. To add a sum formula to column I, select the cell for column I in the Total row. When a drop-down arrow appears, open the drop-down and select Sum from the list.

When you use Total Row for a table, Excel uses the SUBTOTAL function instead of the SUM function. Excel specifies 109 as the function number argument. The SUBTOTAL function is similar to the SUM function, with two exceptions. First, the function ignores other SUBTOTAL functions in the range. Second, with a first argument in the 101–111 range, Excel ignores any values that are hidden, including rows that are hidden by the filter drop-downs.

The total cost in Figure 19.10 is $186,449. In Figure 19.11, the Region column is filtered to only the Central region. Because the SUBTOTAL function ignores hidden rows, the total cost automatically updates to show $52,000.

Total Row Checkbox

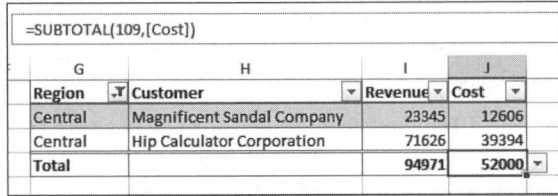

G	H	I	J
Region ▾	Customer ▾	Revenue ▾	Cost ▾
East	Leading Camera Traders	65073	35790
Central	Magnificent Sandal Company	23345	12606
West	Special Edger Corporation	98274	48154
East	Cool Scooter Company	20619	9072
Central	Hip Calculator Corporation	71626	39394
West	Different Radio Inc.	45541	20493
East	Matchless Clipboard Company	45521	20940
Total		▾	186449

None
Average
Count
Count Numbers
Max
Min
Sum
StdDev
Var
More Functions...

Figure 19.10
Clicking the Total Row check box in the ribbon adds a default Total row. Use the drop-downs to change the function or add totals to other columns.

=SUBTOTAL(109,[Cost])

G	H	I	J
Region ▾	Customer ▾	Revenue ▾	Cost ▾
Central	Magnificent Sandal Company	23345	12606
Central	Hip Calculator Corporation	71626	39394
Total		94971	52000 ▾

Figure 19.11
Choose a region from the filter drop-down, and the SUBTOTALS function reflects the total of the visible rows.

Toggling Totals

When you use tables, you can toggle the Total row on and off. Use the Total Row check box in the Table Tools Design tab to turn the totals on or off. In most cases, Excel remembers when you have customized the totals to provide totals for the last two columns. However, you might find that if you add new columns to a table, you need to add these totals to the new columns using the drop-down in the Total row.

Expanding a Table

A common feature of tables is that they tend to grow and expand. Every day, you might add new records to a table or paste new records to the bottom of a table, or you might add a new column with a new calculation.

Excel can automatically expand a table, or you can choose to expand a table manually. When you expand a table, any references to the table automatically expand.

Adding Rows to a Table Automatically

The easiest way to add rows to a table is from the last row of the table. If you are in the last column of the last row and press the Tab key, Excel adds a new row to the table and moves the cell pointer to the first column in the new row. This behavior is similar to existing functionality in tables in Microsoft Word.

However, the simplest way to add a new row to a table is to click in the blank row under the table and type new data. As soon as you enter something in a cell just below the table, Excel expands the table formatting to include the new row. Excel also displays an AutoCorrect lightning bolt icon. If you do not want Excel to expand the table automatically, you can use the drop-down next to this icon to undo the table AutoExpansion, as shown in Figure 19.12. Alternatively, you can immediately press Ctrl+Z to undo adding the row to the table.

Figure 19.12
If you type a new value below the table, Excel automatically extends the table to include the new row.

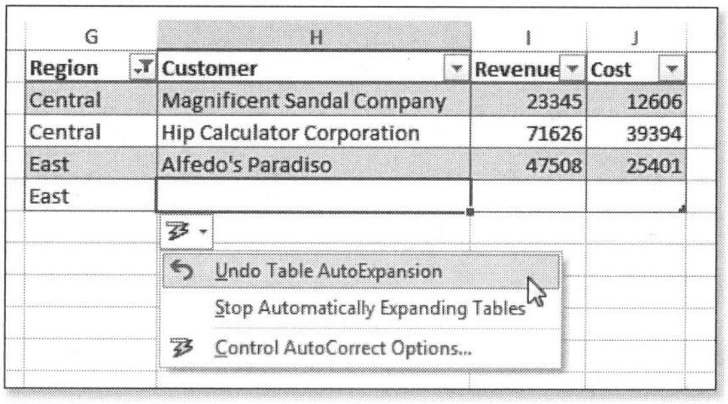

G	H	I	J
Region	Customer	Revenue	Cost
Central	Magnificent Sandal Company	23345	12606
Central	Hip Calculator Corporation	71626	39394
East	Alfedo's Paradiso	47508	25401
East			

Undo Table AutoExpansion
Stop Automatically Expanding Tables
Control AutoCorrect Options...

Manually Resizing a Table

The bottom-right cell of a table contains a small angle bracket in the lower-right corner of the cell. You can use this angle bracket to extend the table manually.

When you click the angle bracket, you can either drag down to add more rows or drag right to add more columns to the table. You cannot drag both down and right in the same operation. Drag once to add rows, and then click and drag again to add columns.

You can also select Table Tools, Design, Properties, Resize Table. The Resize Table dialog appears so you can specify the new range for the table. However, a few limitations exist; for example, you cannot change the header row during this process.

Adding New Columns to a Table

To add a new column to a table, go to the blank cell to the right of the last header and type a new header for the column. Excel automatically extends the table by another column and copies any table formatting to the new column. The AutoCorrect lightning bolt icon appears. If you do not want the new column to be part of the table, use the drop-down next to the AutoCorrect icon to undo the table AutoExpansion.

Adding New Formulas to Tables

Way back in Excel 97, Microsoft added something called Natural Language Formulas to Excel. Beginning with Excel 2007, those old formulas no longer work. Even so, the newer style table formulas are reminiscent of those formulas.

In Figure 19.13, a new column has been added to the table, with the heading Profit. To add a formula to that column, follow these steps:

1. Select cell K2.

2. Type an equal sign.

3. Using either the mouse or the arrow keys, select the first revenue cell in I2. Note that the formula is unlike any formula you have seen before. It starts out with =[@Revenue], as shown in Figure 19.13.

G	H	I	J	K	L
Region	Customer	Revenue	Cost	Profit	
East	Leading Camera Traders	65073	35790	=[@Revenue]	
Central	Magnificent Sandal Company	23345	12606		
West	Special Edger Corporation	98274	48154		
East	Cool Scooter Company	20619	9072		
Central	Hip Calculator Corporation	71626	39394		

Figure 19.13
When you start entering a formula in a table, Excel uses table nomenclature for the formula references.

4. Type a minus sign.

5. Click cell J2 for Cost. The formula now reads =[@Revenue]-[@Cost], as shown in Figure 19.14.

6. An amazing thing happens when you press the Enter key to accept the formula: Excel automatically copies the formula to all rows in the table, as shown in Figure 19.15.

I	J	K	L	M
Revenue	Cost	Profit		
65073	35790	=[@Revenue]-[@Cost]		
23345	12606			
98274	48154			
20619	9072			

Figure 19.14
Without adding any named ranges, the formula =[@Revenue]-[@Cost] is easier to understand than I2-J2.

Figure 19.15
The new formula is copied to all rows of the table automatically.

I	J	K	L	M	N	O	P
Revenue	**Cost**	**Profit**					
65073	35790	29283					
23345	12606	10739					
98274	48154	50120	Undo Calculated Column				
20619	9072	11547	Stop Automatically Creating Calculated Columns				
71626	39394	32232	Control AutoCorrect Options...				
45541	20493	25048					
45521	20940	24581					
47508	25401	22107					
54125	26445	27680					

In legacy versions of Excel, after adding a formula to a new column, you had to double-click the fill handle to copy the formula down to all rows of the table. This functionality saves you time.

If you do not want to have the formula copied to all rows, you can undo the behavior by selecting the AutoCorrect icon and then choosing the appropriate option or by immediately pressing Ctrl+Z.

Stopping the Automatic Copying of Formulas

At some point, you might have a column in a table and not want Excel to use the same formula everywhere in that column. Excel 2013 calls this a *calculated column exception*. Because any formula you enter in the column is copied automatically to the entire column, you need to use special care to set up a calculated column exception.

> **Tip**
>
> When you set up a single-cell column exception, Excel stops automatically copying formulas in that column.

Suppose that you already have a formula in a column and want to change to a different formula in just one cell. In this case, follow these steps:

1. Enter the different formula in the one cell. Excel automatically copies the formula to the entire column.

2. Immediately click the Undo button in the Quick Access Toolbar.

Excel marks this cell with a green triangle. If you hover your mouse over the green triangle, Excel tells you, "This cell is inconsistent with the column formula."

There are other ways to set up a first column exception:

- Type data other than a formula in a calculated column cell.

- Delete a single formula from one or more cells in the calculated column.

- Move or delete a cell on another worksheet area that is referenced by one of the rows in the calculated column. This changes the formula in that one cell, creating a column exception. Excel then stops copying the calculation in that column.

Formatting the Results of a New Formula

The automatic copying of formulas includes one minor annoyance. In legacy versions of Excel, you would add a new column by following these steps:

1. Type the heading.

2. Type the first formula.

3. Format the first formula.

4. Double-click the fill handle to copy the formula.

Now that Excel is essentially performing the last step for you, there is no chance to format the first cell before it is copied. In Figure 19.16, the calculation for gross profit percentage was copied before the cell could be formatted as a percentage.

	I	J	K	L	M
	Revenue	Cost	Profit	GP%	
	65073	35790	29283	0.450002	
	23345	12606	10739	0.460013	
	98274	48154	50120	0.510003	
	20619	9072	11547	0.560017	
	71626	39394	32232	0.450004	
	45541	20493	25048	0.55001	
	45521	20940	24581	0.539993	
	47508	25401	22107	0.465332	
	54125	26445	27680	0.511409	

Figure 19.16
Excel copies a formula to all rows before you have a chance to format the new column.

This requires a small change in your usual process. You can try formatting cell F3 before entering the formula. However, this is a bit tricky because you do not have a number in that cell to use to check that you clicked Increase Decimal the proper number of times. Because it is common for people to confuse the Increase Decimal and Decrease Decimal icons, hover over the icon to see the tooltip before clicking the icon three times.

Selecting Only the Data in the Column

You can use several new options when selecting data in a table. If you are going to format a table, you probably just want to format the numbers in the table and not the headings. Excel includes distinct methods for selecting the data portion of a column or selecting the entire table column with headings and totals.

Selecting by Right-Clicking

One way to select the data in a column is to right-click a cell in the table. From the context menu, choose the Select option. The fly-out menu offers three choices, as shown in Figure 19.17:

- **Table Column Data**—Choose this option to select just the data rows of that column. This skips the heading row and the total row.

- **Entire Table Column**—Choose this option to include the heading for the column and the cell in the Total row.

- **Table Row**—Choose this option to select an entire row of a table.

Figure 19.17
Right-click to select the data in the column.

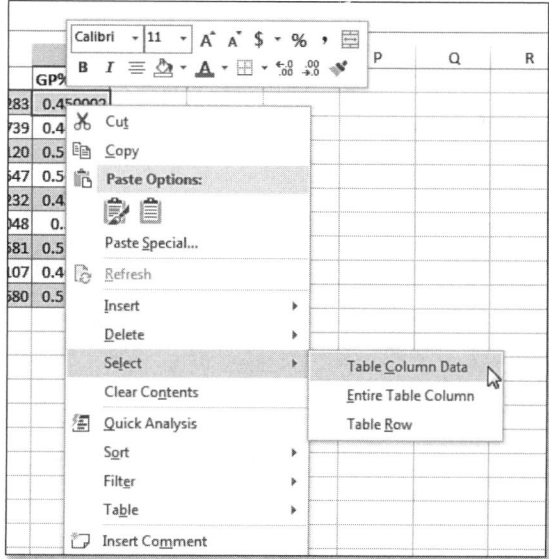

Selecting by Using Shortcuts

You can also use the tried and true Excel shortcuts to select rows or columns. Keep in mind that these shortcut keys are modified when you are in a table:

- Press Shift+spacebar once to select an entire row in a table.

- Press Shift+spacebar a second time to select the entire worksheet row.

- Press Ctrl+spacebar once to select the table data in the current column of the table. This excludes the total row and the heading row. Figure 19.18 shows the selection after Ctrl+spacebar has been pressed once from cell J6.

- Press Ctrl+spacebar again to expand the selection to include the heading and Total cell for that column, as shown in Figure 19.19.

- Press Ctrl+spacebar a third time to select the entire worksheet column.

◢	G	H	I	J	K
1	Region	Customer	Revenue	Cost	Profit
2	East	Leading Camera Traders	65073	35790	29283
3	Central	Magnificent Sandal Company	23345	12606	10739
4	West	Special Edger Corporation	98274	48154	50120
5	East	Cool Scooter Company	20619	9072	11547
6	Central	Hip Calculator Corporation	71626	39394	32232
7	West	Different Radio Inc.	45541	20493	25048
8	East	Matchless Clipboard Company	45521	20940	24581
9	East	Alfedo's Paradiso	47508	25401	22107
10	East	Cozy Corner Café	54125	26445	27680
11	Total		471632	238295	233337

Figure 19.18
Press Ctrl+spacebar once to select the data portion of the current column.

◢	G	H	I	J	K
1	Region	Customer	Revenue	Cost	Profit
2	East	Leading Camera Traders	65073	35790	292
3	Central	Magnificent Sandal Company	23345	12606	107
4	West	Special Edger Corporation	98274	48154	501
5	East	Cool Scooter Company	20619	9072	115
6	Central	Hip Calculator Corporation	71626	39394	322
7	West	Different Radio Inc.	45541	20493	250
8	East	Matchless Clipboard Company	45521	20940	245
9	East	Alfedo's Paradiso	47508	25401	221
10	East	Cozy Corner Café	54125	26445	276
11	Total		471632	238295	2333
12					

Figure 19.19
Press Ctrl+spacebar a second time to expand the selection to include the heading and total cells.

Selecting by Using the Arrow Mouse Pointers

Beginning with Excel 2007, an arrow mouse pointer was added that you can use to select table rows and table columns. However, it is a bit tricky to use this mouse pointer. The following figures provide some examples for using the mouse pointer effectively:

- In Figure 19.20, the mouse is hovering over the box containing the column H column letter. Make sure the mouse pointer does not extend below the bottom edge of the column H heading box. You are in the correct place when the background behind the letter H turns dark green. With your mouse in this position, click to select all of column H. You can click here any number of times to select the entire column.

◢	G	↓ H
1	Region	Customer
2	East	Leading Camera Traders
3	Central	Magnificent Sandal Company

Figure 19.20
The traditional select column mouse pointer causes the column letter to be highlighted.

- In Figure 19.21, the mouse is moved down slightly so that it is partially above cell G1, which is the first row of the table. The first click here selects G2:G10. The second click here selects G1:G11. Alternating clicks toggle between G2:G10 (the table data without headers and totals) and G1:G11 (the complete table column).

Figure 19.21

Move just a bit into the table header and the new (but identically appearing) mouse pointer takes over.

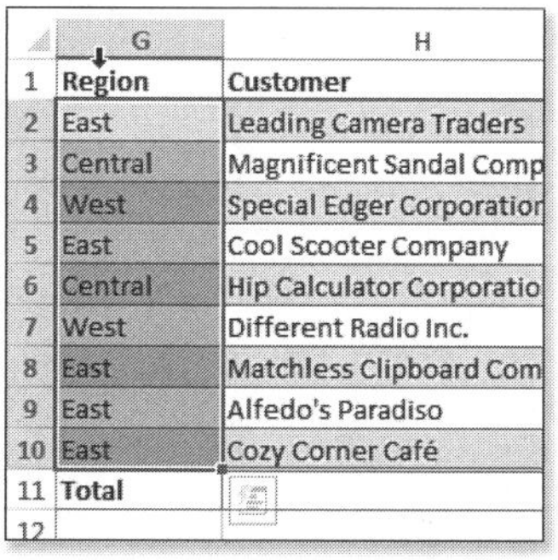

- In Figure 19.22, the mouse is hovering over the top-left corner of cell G1. The first click here selects G2:L10 (the table without headings and totals). The next click selects G1:L11 (the entire table). Additional clicks toggle between these two selections.

Figure 19.22

Move to the corner of the table to get the table selection mouse pointer.

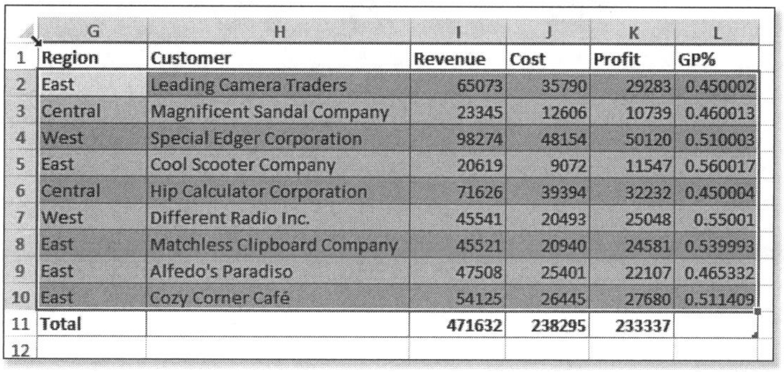

Similar logic applies for selecting rows. If you hover inside the 2 row header, the row header background turns green. Click to select the entire row: A2:XFD2. If you move to the right so the mouse pointer is on the edge of the 2 row header and slightly inside cell G2, you select G2:L2.

If you are a heavy-duty user of Excel, you will likely use these new table selection methods. The new conditional formatting options such as data bars and color scales require you to select the data in a column without the total row. Mastering the various selection methods will greatly enhance your ability to work with the formatting.

Using Table Data for Charts to Ensure Stickiness

When you define a range as a table and expand the table, any references to the table also expand. If you routinely re-create new charts every month when you receive new data, you will love this feature.

Before creating a chart, make a table out of the underlying data. For example, in Figure 19.23, the chart is based on the table in A1:E4. Currently, the chart has four months' worth of data.

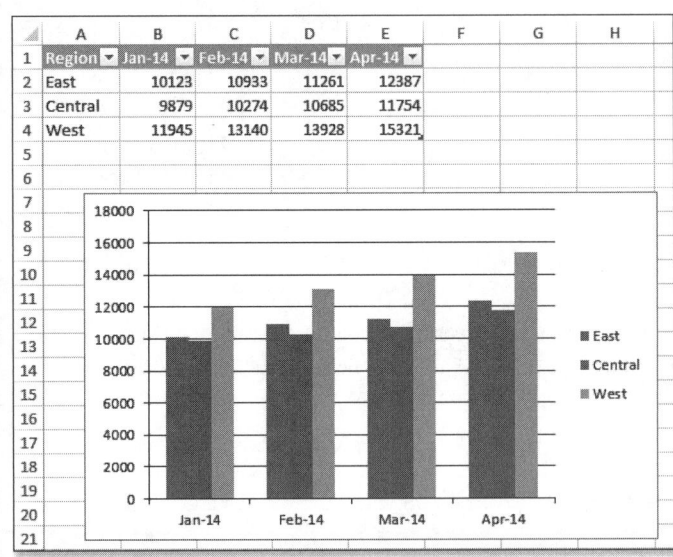

Figure 19.23
This chart is based on the table in A1:E4.

If you type a heading for the new month in cell F1, immediately the chart redraws to include data for May. After you fill in the data for the new month, you will not have to ever re-create a chart. Instead, the new data is added to the chart, preserving the old formatting, as shown in Figure 19.24.

Replacing Named Ranges with Table References

A benefit of using tables is that Excel understands a new reference style for formulas that point to data in a table. A new name is created automatically when a table is defined. The name includes the name of the table, such as `Table1`, and the name of the column.

The biggest benefit of this referencing style is that the ranges that the names refer to are expanded automatically when the table expands. This referencing style eliminates many chances for errors that exist when using named ranges.

Figure 19.24
Add new data to the table, and the chart automatically expands.

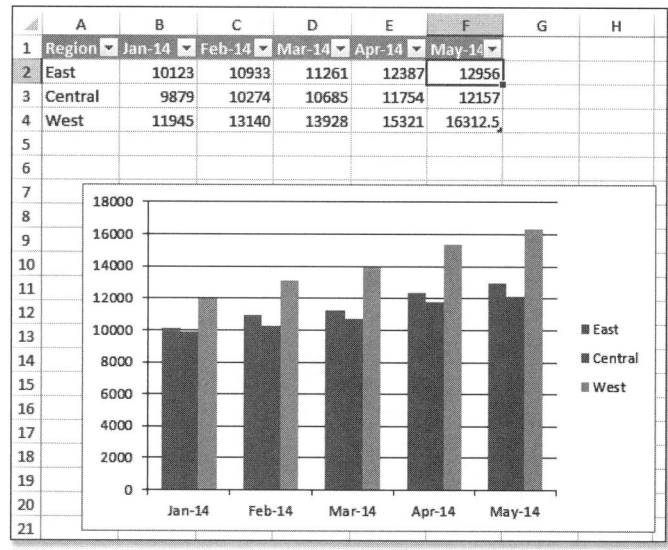

Referencing an Entire Table from Outside the Table

When a table is defined, it becomes easier to reference the table from outside the table. Figure 19.25 shows a sales rep lookup table. Because this is the first table in the workbook, Excel has assigned the name Table1 to this table. Feel free to rename the table to something meaningful, such as Reps. Click in the Table Name text box, type a new name, and press Enter.

Figure 19.25
Change the generic Table1 name to Reps.

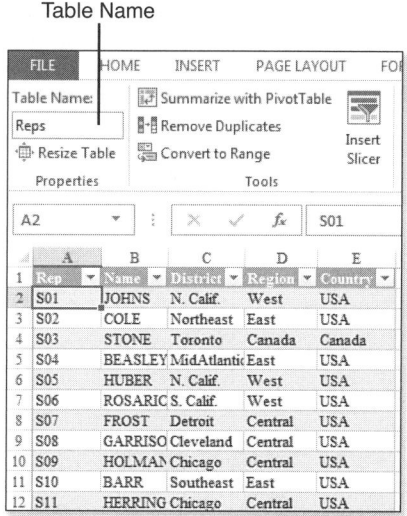

Figure 19.26 shows an invoice register located on another sheet in the workbook. Like many mainframe reports, this one includes the sales rep number, without the name and region information. To add a VLOOKUP function to Figure 19.26 that references the Reps table, follow these steps:

1. Start to type a VLOOKUP formula in column D. When you get to the second argument, type the letters **Re**, and the AutoComplete list filters to show only functions and names that start with "Re." Among the function names is an entry for Reps, as shown in Figure 19.26.

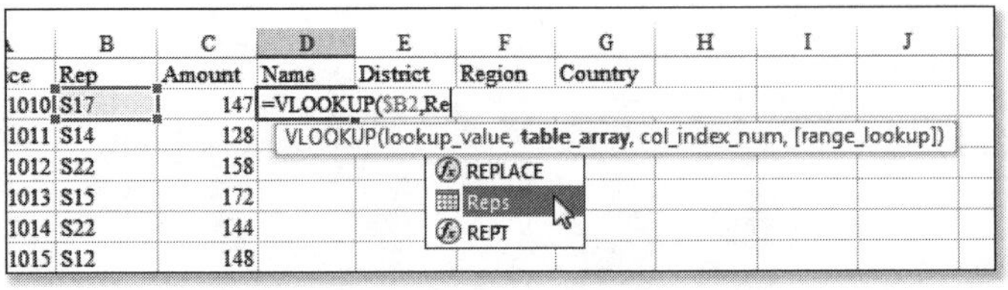

Figure 19.26
Even though there are no defined names in the workbook, Excel understands the Reps table name nomenclature.

2. Select Reps from the list and press Tab.

3. Finish the formula so that it is =VLOOKUP($B2,Reps,COLUMN(B2),False). Note that you could use 2 as the third argument, but then you would have to edit the formula as you copy it across the columns.

4. Copy the formula to the rest of the range. Like chart references, table references are sticky. In Figure 19.27, there are a couple records for a new sales rep, S26, who is not yet in the original table.

Figure 19.27
When you add the missing reps to the Reps table, the references to Reps also expand.

5. Go back to the original table and add a new row with S26 data. Notice that all the formulas that reference Table1 automatically recalculate to include the new rows.

Referencing Table Columns from Outside a Table

To reference an entire column from outside a table, use the syntax `TableName[ColumnName]`. When you do this, Excel's AutoComplete feature provides a list of column names. After you type **Table2[**, the AutoComplete list shows all the columns in the table, plus additional keywords. See the following section, "Using Structured References to Refer to Tables in Formulas," for more information about keywords. The AutoComplete list is shown in Figure 19.28.

Figure 19.28
Excel offers AutoComplete entries from which you can choose the column name when entering a formula.

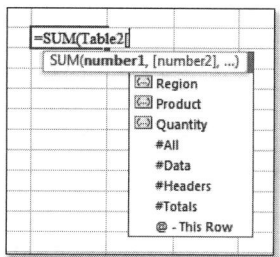

References to a table column do not include the header or Total row. Although this behavior is usually desired, there might be instances when you use an `INDEX` or `OFFSET` function that you expect Excel to include the heading as row 1 in the function.

The formula in Figure 19.29 uses three references to a table to find the sales for a particular product and a particular region. The nomenclature Quantity, Product, and Region is easier to understand than cell addresses such as D2:D87. Here is the complete formula in cell G3:

`=SUMIFS(Table2[Quantity],Table2[Product],$F3,Table2[Region],G$2)`

Figure 19.29
This formula is a fairly complex conditional sum that relies on three columns from the table.

	A	B	C	D	E	F	G	H	I	J	K	L	M
1	Invoice	Region	Product	Quantity									
2	8753	Americas	M465	50		Product	Americas	EMEA	Asia				
3	8753	Asia	H952	30		M465	=SUMIFS(Table2[Quantity],Table2[Product],$F3,Table2[Region],G$2)						
4	8753	Americas	S864	10		H952	570	500	450				
5	8753	Americas	H803	30		S864	410	500	450				
6	8753	Asia	H952	20		H803	480	380	460				
7	8753	EMEA	S864	50		U300	340	340	610				
8	8753	EMEA	H803	50									
9	8753	Americas	H803	20									

Table references are valid on any worksheet in the workbook. If you want to refer to a table that is seven worksheets away, you can still use the Table2 nomenclature, without prefixing the worksheet name.

Using Structured References to Refer to Tables in Formulas

Microsoft has created a fairly comprehensive way to refer to various parts of tables. You have seen some of the table nomenclature syntax in the previous two sections. The following are complete details for writing formulas that refer to tables:

- The reference to a table starts with the table name. If you are creating the formula within the table itself, you can omit the table name.

- If no further qualifiers are entered, the table name refers to the data rows of the table. This excludes the headings and Total rows.

- Further qualifiers should be enclosed in square brackets. If you are using one qualifier, only one set of square brackets is needed. You may specify TableName[Qualifier] or TableName[[Qualifier]].

- If you are specifying multiple qualifiers, each qualifier must be surrounded by square brackets. The qualifiers must be separated by commas. The complete set of qualifiers must be surrounded by square brackets. The syntax follows this pattern:

  TableName[[Qualifier1],[Qualifier2],[Qualifier3]]

- For a table with a header row, each column heading is automatically added to the list of qualifiers.

- For a table without a header row, the list of qualifiers includes Column1, Column2, and so on.

- Every table also has these qualifiers: #All, #Data, #Headers, #Totals, and @ (which means This Row).

- The @ qualifier must be used in conjunction with another qualifier.

> **Note**
>
> In Excel 2007, the @ qualifier was actually spelled out as #ThisRow. Formulas originally created in Excel 2007 as =Table1[[#ThisRow],[Revenue]] appear in Excel 2013 as =Table1[@ Revenue].

This system enables you to select a variety of references without having to use cell references. To get the total of sales from Table1, you can either use =SUM(Table1[Sales]) or =Table1[[#Total],[Sales]]. The second syntax returns a #REF! error if someone turns off the Totals Row check box in the Table Tools Design tab.

Figure 19.30 shows various structured references.

| H2 | ▼ | : | ✕ | ✓ | fx | =COUNTA(Table3[#All]) |

▲	A	B	C	D	E	F	G	H	I	J	K	L	M	N
1	Invoice ▼	Region ▼	Product ▼	Quantity ▼	% of Total ▼									
2	8753	Americas	M465	50	0.73%			1155	=COUNTA(Table3[#All])					
3	8753	Asia	H952	30	0.44%			1150	=COUNTA(Table3[#Data])					
4	8753	Americas	S864	10	0.15%			5	=COUNTA(Table3[#Headers])					
5	8753	Americas	H803	30	0.44%			1	=COUNTA(Table3[#Totals])					
6	8753	Asia	H952	20	0.29%			1	=COUNTA(Table3[@Quantity])					
7	8753	EMEA	S864	50	0.73%			231	=COUNTA(Table3[[#Headers],[#Data],[Region]])					
8	8753	EMEA	H803	50	0.73%			1150	=COUNTA(Table3)					
9	8753	Americas	H803	20	0.29%									
10	8753	Americas	H803	50	0.73%									
11	8753	EMEA	U300	20	0.29%									

Figure 19.30
Structured references are shown in column I.

Creating Banded Rows and Columns with Table Styles

In legacy versions of Excel, creating banded rows or columns required creative conditional formatting or tedious manual work. However, creating banded rows or columns in a table is relatively straightforward in Excel 2013.

The fourth group on the Table Tools Design tab is Table Style Options. This group includes check boxes for Banded Rows and Banded Columns. These check boxes work only if the selected table style includes rules for banded columns and/or banded rows. If you have selected the plain white table style, turning on or off banded rows and columns will have no effect.

Figure 19.31 shows five tables. The first table contains banded rows. The second table has banded columns. The third table leaves banded rows and columns off, but the first column, last column, header row, and Total row are checked. The top table in column H contains both banded rows and banded columns. The last table contains a custom format to change the banding from one stripe to two stripes. The next section provides details on how to customize the table style.

Figure 19.31 These tables exhibit various combinations of the table style options. The fifth table requires a customization of the table style.

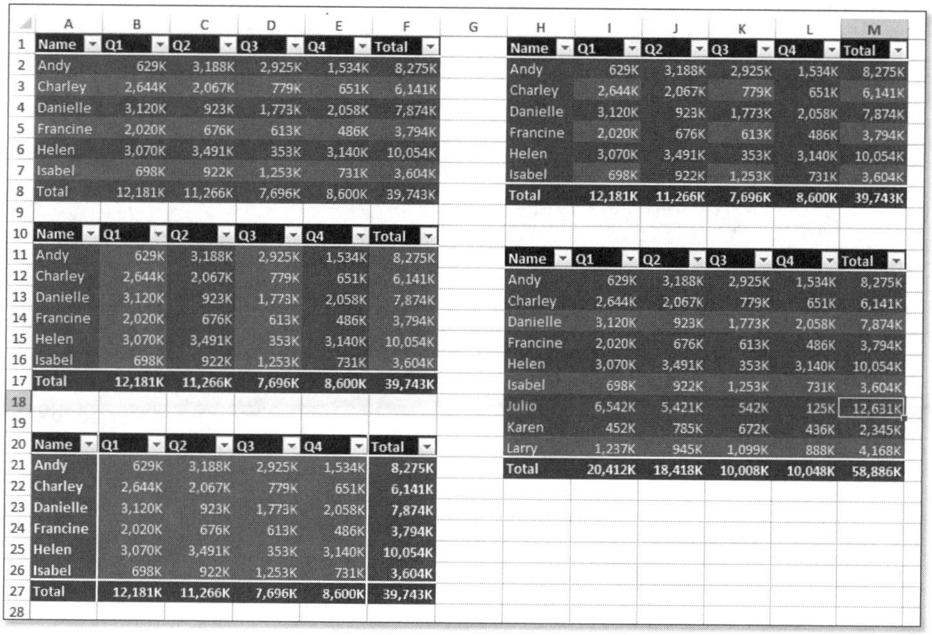

Name	Q1	Q2	Q3	Q4	Total
Andy	629K	3,188K	2,925K	1,534K	8,275K
Charley	2,644K	2,067K	779K	651K	6,141K
Danielle	3,120K	923K	1,773K	2,058K	7,874K
Francine	2,020K	676K	613K	486K	3,794K
Helen	3,070K	3,491K	353K	3,140K	10,054K
Isabel	698K	922K	1,253K	731K	3,604K
Total	12,181K	11,266K	7,696K	8,600K	39,743K

Name	Q1	Q2	Q3	Q4	Total
Andy	629K	3,188K	2,925K	1,534K	8,275K
Charley	2,644K	2,067K	779K	651K	6,141K
Danielle	3,120K	923K	1,773K	2,058K	7,874K
Francine	2,020K	676K	613K	486K	3,794K
Helen	3,070K	3,491K	353K	3,140K	10,054K
Isabel	698K	922K	1,253K	731K	3,604K
Total	12,181K	11,266K	7,696K	8,600K	39,743K

Name	Q1	Q2	Q3	Q4	Total
Andy	629K	3,188K	2,925K	1,534K	8,275K
Charley	2,644K	2,067K	779K	651K	6,141K
Danielle	3,120K	923K	1,773K	2,058K	7,874K
Francine	2,020K	676K	613K	486K	3,794K
Helen	3,070K	3,491K	353K	3,140K	10,054K
Isabel	698K	922K	1,253K	731K	3,604K
Total	12,181K	11,266K	7,696K	8,600K	39,743K

Name	Q1	Q2	Q3	Q4	Total
Andy	629K	3,188K	2,925K	1,534K	8,275K
Charley	2,644K	2,067K	779K	651K	6,141K
Danielle	3,120K	923K	1,773K	2,058K	7,874K
Francine	2,020K	676K	613K	486K	3,794K
Helen	3,070K	3,491K	353K	3,140K	10,054K
Isabel	698K	922K	1,253K	731K	3,604K
Total	12,181K	11,266K	7,696K	8,600K	39,743K

Name	Q1	Q2	Q3	Q4	Total
Andy	629K	3,188K	2,925K	1,534K	8,275K
Charley	2,644K	2,067K	779K	651K	6,141K
Danielle	3,120K	923K	1,773K	2,058K	7,874K
Francine	2,020K	676K	613K	486K	3,794K
Helen	3,070K	3,491K	353K	3,140K	10,054K
Isabel	698K	922K	1,253K	731K	3,604K
Julio	6,542K	5,421K	542K	125K	12,631K
Karen	452K	785K	672K	436K	2,345K
Larry	1,237K	945K	1,099K	888K	4,168K
Total	20,412K	18,418K	10,008K	10,048K	58,886K

Customizing a Table Style: Creating Double-Height Banded Rows

At the bottom of the Table Styles gallery is a New Table Style button. It is recommended that you not use this button! It can be rather intimidating to set up a completely new style. It is often easier to start with an existing style and modify it. To do this, right-click a style and select Duplicate, as shown in Figure 19.32.

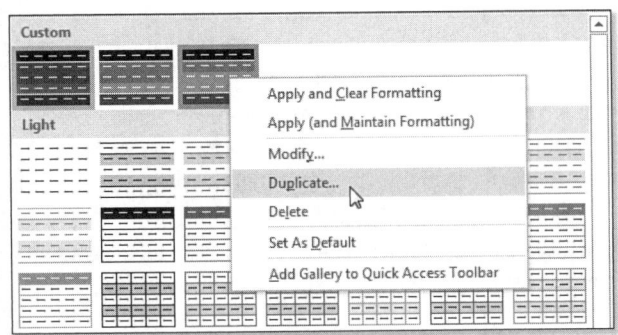

Figure 19.32
Instead of using New Table Quick Style, you can duplicate an existing style.

After you select Duplicate, Excel displays the Modify Table Quick Style dialog. Excel assigns a new name to the style, adding a 2 or 3 or 4 to the existing style name. You can rename the style if you like.

To create double-height banded rows, follow these steps:

1. Select First Row Stripe from the Table Element list. A Stripe Size drop-down appears.

2. Select 2 from the Stripe Size drop-down.

3. Select Second Row Stripe from the Table Element list. A Stripe Size drop-down appears.

4. Select 2 from the Stripe Size drop-down (see Figure 19.33).

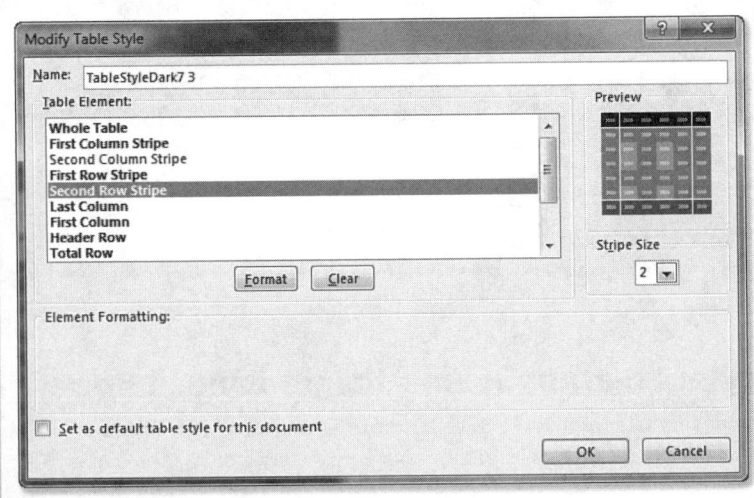

Figure 19.33
For double-height row banding, change the stripe size.

5. If you would like the modified theme to be the default style for all new tables created in this document, select the Set as Default Table Style for This Document check box in the lower-left corner of the dialog.

6. Click OK, and your custom style is saved to a new Custom section at the top of the Table Styles drop-down.

Creating Banded Rows Outside a Table

You might find some of the table behavior annoying. For example, you might want banded columns, but you do not want to use a full-fledged table. In this case, you can temporarily create a table, apply a banded row format to the table, and then convert it back to a range to have a banded row format on the range. Here's how you do it:

1. Select a cell in the range to be formatted.

2. Press Ctrl+T to make the range a table.

3. If your default table style does not include banded rows, choose a new table style from the Table Styles gallery on the Table Tools Design tab.

4. In the Table Tools Design tab, select Tools, Convert to Range. This removes the table properties but keeps the table formatting.

 Caution

A custom table style only applies to a workbook. Say that you want to use a custom style from workbook A in workbook B. Temporarily copy the table from workbook A to workbook B. Apply the custom table style to an existing table in workbook B. You can then delete the temporary table.

Dealing with the Filter Drop-Downs

A common spreadsheet style rule says that you should right-align the headings above numeric columns. If you regularly follow this convention, you will certainly be annoyed with the default choice that all tables are automatically created with the filter drop-downs applied.

In Figure 19.34, the first range contains data with the Q1 headings in the first row. If you apply a table to a range, the filter drop-downs completely cover the headings, making the table useless, as shown in rows 9:15.

One option, shown in row 17, is to begin centering your headings instead of right-justifying them.

The final option, shown in row 25, is to keep the table, but turn off the filter for the table. Uncheck Filter Button in the Table Style Options group of the Table Tools Design tab to toggle away the drop-downs.

To learn more tricks available for tables, see Chapter 20, "Sorting Data," and Chapter 21, "Removing Duplicates and Filtering."

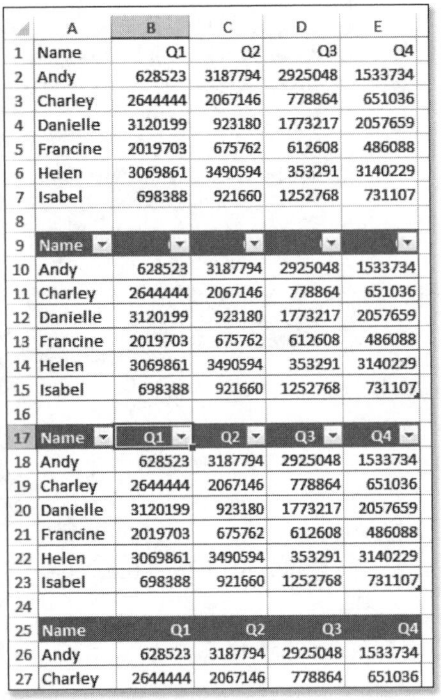

	A	B	C	D	E
1	Name	Q1	Q2	Q3	Q4
2	Andy	628523	3187794	2925048	1533734
3	Charley	2644444	2067146	778864	651036
4	Danielle	3120199	923180	1773217	2057659
5	Francine	2019703	675762	612608	486088
6	Helen	3069861	3490594	353291	3140229
7	Isabel	698388	921660	1252768	731107
8					
9	Name ▼	▼	▼	▼	▼
10	Andy	628523	3187794	2925048	1533734
11	Charley	2644444	2067146	778864	651036
12	Danielle	3120199	923180	1773217	2057659
13	Francine	2019703	675762	612608	486088
14	Helen	3069861	3490594	353291	3140229
15	Isabel	698388	921660	1252768	731107
16					
17	Name ▼	Q1 ▼	Q2 ▼	Q3 ▼	Q4 ▼
18	Andy	628523	3187794	2925048	1533734
19	Charley	2644444	2067146	778864	651036
20	Danielle	3120199	923180	1773217	2057659
21	Francine	2019703	675762	612608	486088
22	Helen	3069861	3490594	353291	3140229
23	Isabel	698388	921660	1252768	731107
24					
25	Name	Q1	Q2	Q3	Q4
26	Andy	628523	3187794	2925048	1533734
27	Charley	2644444	2067146	778864	651036

Figure 19.34
The headings in row 1 become unreadable when the range is converted to a table.

20

SORTING DATA

Sorting data is one of the key capabilities of a spreadsheet program such as Excel. With a click of the mouse, you can rearrange data so that it is presented in an alphabetical sequence or in a sequence with the largest numbers at the top or bottom of a list of data.

One of the considerations when sorting is what happens when there are ties in the column on which the sort is based. If you have a database of product sales and sort the data by the product field, you will likely have many rows with identical products. In that case, you can specify a secondary sort criteria. You might want to have Excel sort the records so that the sales date is to be used to sequence records when there is a tie in the product field. In this case, you might say you want to sort by sales date within product. Excel simplifies this task.

In legacy versions of Excel, only three key fields could be handled in a sort at any one time. You could specify that you wanted to sort by date within product within region. However, in a large company you would likely sell the same product on the same date in the same region. With only three sort levels, ties would still occur in the data.

With the powerful sorting capabilities in Excel 2013, you are not limited to three sorting levels. Options are available for case-sensitive sorting. In addition, you can sort data by color. This sounds like a silly feature, but it is handy for finding all the cells marked in red or to bring together the results of conditional formatting. Methods used in legacy versions of Excel to sort by a custom list and sort from left to right are still available in Excel 2013, and now they are a bit more accessible.

Introducing the Sort Dialog

Sorting in Excel 2013 is handled in the Sort dialog or by using the AZ and ZA buttons on the Data tab. In all, there are five entry points for sorting:

- Select the Home tab and then select Editing, Sort & Filter, Custom Sort.

- Right-click any cell and choose Sort.

- Select Sort from any filter drop-down.

- Select the Data tab and then select Sort & Filter, AZ or Sort & Filter, ZA.

- Open the Sort dialog box by selecting Sort & Filter, Sort on the Data tab.

The Sort dialog in Excel 2013 offers up to 64 different sorting levels. If you get into sorting by color, you often have to specify several rules for one column, so the theoretical number of columns you can sort by is probably fewer than 64. However, compared to the limit of three sort levels in legacy versions, this is a fantastic improvement.

For example, to sort a data set by the values in four columns, follow these steps:

1. Ensure that each column has a one-row heading above the data.

2. Select a cell within the data.

3. Select the Data tab, and then select the large Sort icon in the Sort & Filter group. Alternatively, you can select the Home tab, Sort & Filter, Custom Sort. The Sort dialog appears.

4. If your data is not in a defined table, make sure that the My Data Has Headers check box is selected (assuming your first row contains headers).

5. In the Sort By drop-down, select the Major Sort field. If you want to sort by region and then by customer with region, for example, select the Region field as the First Sort field.

6. To sort by values, leave the Sort On drop-down set to Values.

7. In the Order drop-down, choose either A to Z or Z to A. If your column contains dates, this drop-down offers Oldest to Newest and Newest to Oldest. If your column contains mostly numbers, this drop-down offers Smallest to Largest and Largest to Smallest.

8. Click the Add Level button.

9. Repeat steps 5 through 8 for each additional sort field.

10. Review your sort choices, which should look similar to the ones shown in Figure 20.1. If you see that one of the fields was added in the wrong order, you can select that field and use the up-arrow or down-arrow button at the top of the Sort dialog to reorder the fields in the sort.

11. When you are ready to perform the sort, click OK.

If you have multiple records with identical values in all four fields, the sort retains the previous sequence for the tied records. If you ever have to sort by more than 64 columns, this feature enables you to sort by the minor columns first and then by the major columns.

Figure 20.1
Performing a four-field sort based on values.

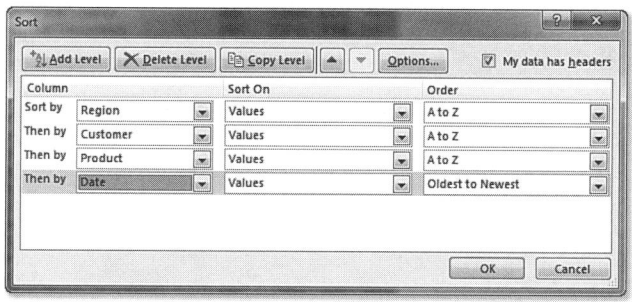

Using Specialized Sorting

Although the process shown in Figure 20.1 is the typical use for sorting, specialized options also are available. In certain cases, you might want to sort by color, uppercase or lowercase, a custom sequence, or even data in a left-to-right fashion. Excel 2013 offers methods to solve all these needs.

Sorting by Color or Icon

Excel can sort data by fill color, font color, or icon set. This also works with color applied through conditional formatting or color that you applied by using the cell format icons.

Because color is subjective, there is not a default color sequence. If one column contains 17 colors, you need to set up 17 rules in the Sort dialog just to sort by that one column.

To sort by color, follow these steps:

1. Select a cell within your data.

2. Select the Sort icon on the Data tab. The Sort dialog appears.

3. Select the desired field from the Sort By drop-down.

4. Change the Sort On drop-down to Cell Color.

5. In the Order drop-down, choose the color that should appear first.

6. In the final drop-down, select On Top.

7. To specify the next color, click the Copy Level button at the top of the Sort dialog.

8. Choose the next color in the Order drop-down for the copied rule.

9. Repeat steps 7 and 8 for each additional color. The Sort dialog should look something like Figure 20.2.

10. If you want to specify that values in another column should be used to break ties in the color column, select the Add Level button and specify the additional columns.

11. Click OK to sort the data.

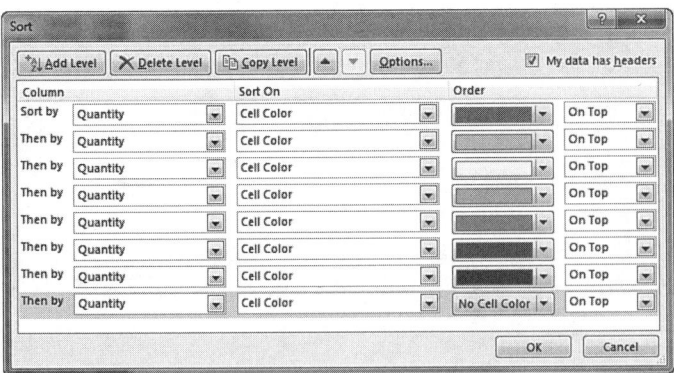

Figure 20.2
When you sort by color, explicitly specify the order of the colors.

Factoring Case into a Sort

Typically, an Excel sort ignores the case of the text. Values that are lowercase, uppercase, or any combination of the two are treated equally in a sort. For example, in Figure 20.3, all the values in A2:A9 would be considered a tie.

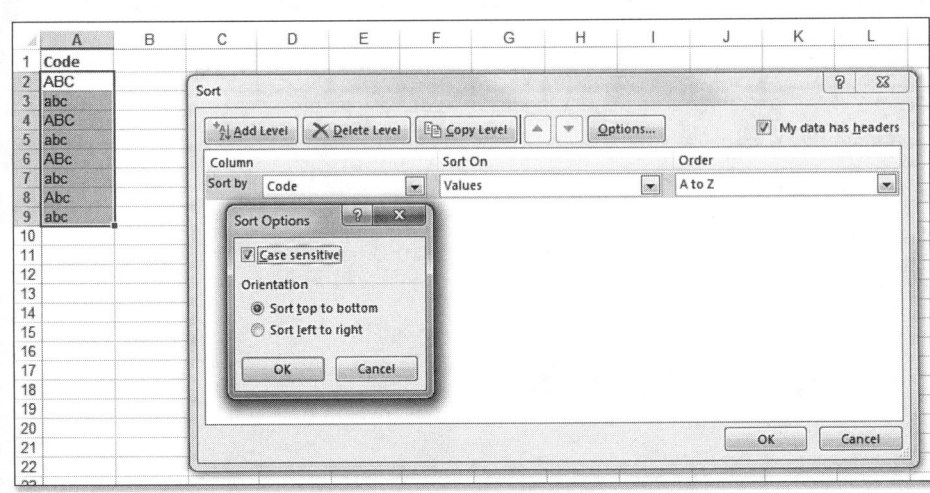

Figure 20.3
Use Sort Options when you need Excel to factor upper-case and lower-case into a sort.

In Excel 2013, a case-sensitive sort sorts lowercase values before uppercase values. For example, abc sorts before ABC. Similarly, ABc sorts before ABC.

If you want Excel to consider case when sorting, follow these steps:

1. Select a cell within your data.

2. Select the Sort icon on the Data tab. The Sort dialog appears.

3. Choose the column from the Sort By drop-down.

4. Click the Options button. The Sort Options dialog appears.

5. Select the Case Sensitive check box, as shown in Figure 20.3.

6. Click OK to close the Sort Options dialog.

7. Click OK to sort.

Reordering Columns with a Left-to-Right Sort

If you receive a data set from a colleague and the columns are in the wrong sequence, you could cut and paste them into the right sequence, or you could fix them all in one pass by using a left-to-right sort. To do this, follow these steps:

1. Insert a new blank row above the headings.

2. In the new row, type numbers corresponding to the correct sequence of the columns.

3. Make sure that one cell in the range is selected.

4. Select the Sort icon on the Data tab. The Sort dialog appears.

5. Click the Options button. The Sort Options dialog appears.

6. Select Sort Left to Right. Click OK to close the Sort Options dialog.

7. The Sort By drop-down now contains a list of row numbers. Choose the first row. The remaining drop-downs should already include Values and Smallest to Largest, as shown in Figure 20.4.

8. Click OK to perform the sort.

9. Delete your temporary extra row at the top of the data set. The columns are then resequenced into the desired order.

 Tip

Excel does not change the original column widths. Select all cells with Ctrl+A and then use Home, Format, AutoFit Column Width to resize all the columns.

Figure 20.4
Add an extra row to specify the correct sequence of the columns and then sort from left to right.

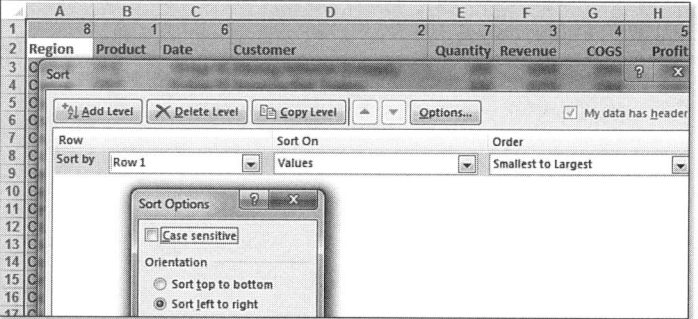

Sorting into a Unique Sequence by Using Custom Lists

Sometimes company tradition dictates that regions or products should be presented in an order that is not alphabetic. For example, the sequence East, Central, West makes more sense geographically than the alphabetic sequence Central, East, West.

It is possible to set up a custom list to tell Excel that the region sequence is East, Central, West. You can then sort your data based on this sequence. You need to set up the custom list only once per computer. Follow these steps to do so:

1. Go to a blank section of any worksheet. Type the correct sequence for the values in a column.

2. Select this range.

3. Select File, Options. The Options dialog appears.

4. Click the Advanced Group. Scroll down to the General section and then select Edit Custom Lists. The Custom Lists dialog appears.

5. In the Custom Lists dialog, the bottom section shows the range of cells you selected in step 2 (see Figure 20.5). If it is correct, click the Import button. Your new list, with the correct sequence, is added to the default custom lists.

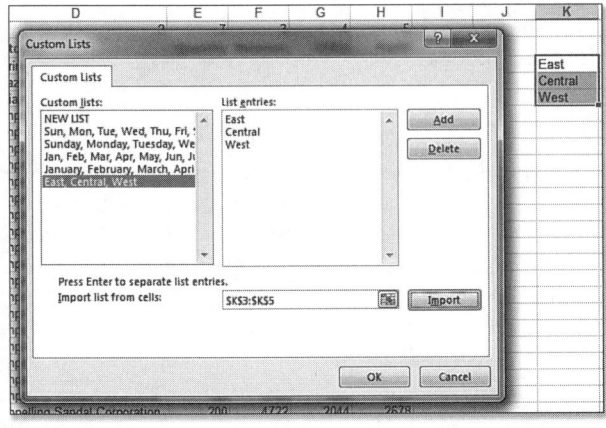

Figure 20.5
By preselecting the range with your correct list sequence, you only have to click Import and OK in this dialog.

6. Click OK to close the Custom Lists dialog. Click OK to close the Options dialog.

7. Clear your temporary data range from step 1.

After you set up a custom list, it is available for more than just custom sorting. For example, you can use the custom list when dragging the fill handle in order to extend a list. Here are the steps to use the new custom list with the fill handle:

1. Type **East** into a cell and then select the cell.

2. Drag the square dot from the lower-right corner to the right. Excel automatically types additional values from your custom list.

To use the list with custom sorting, follow these steps:

1. Select one cell in your data.

2. Select the Sort icon on the Data tab. The Sort dialog appears.

3. In the Sort By drop-down, choose the region with the custom sort sequence.

4. From the Order drop-down, select Custom List. You should now be back in the Custom Lists dialog, similar to the one shown in Figure 20.5.

5. Click your custom list and then click OK. The Sort dialog shows that the order is based on your custom list (see Figure 20.6).

6. Click OK to sort into the custom sequence.

Figure 20.6
Excel indicates that the Region field will be sorted into East, Central, West sequence.

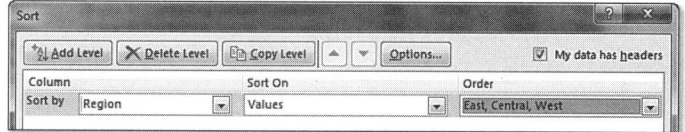

One-Click Sorting

All the examples discussed so far in this chapter have used the Sort dialog, which is required for left-to-right sorting, custom sorting, and case-sensitive sorting. It also makes color sorting easier. You can accomplish all other sorts by using the AZ buttons on the various tabs.

It is important to select a single cell in the column to be sorted. When you select a single cell, Excel extends the selection to encompass the entire current region. If you select two cells or even the whole column, Excel warns you that it is about to sort part of your data and ignore the adjacent data. This is rarely what you want.

You can find the one-click sorting options on the Home and Data tabs. On the Home tab, they are buried in the Sort & Filter drop-down. On the Data tab, they are clearly visible as AZ and ZA buttons.

You can also find sorting options by right-clicking a cell in the column you want to sort and selecting Sort. As shown in Figure 20.7, options in this menu enable you to sort in ascending or descending order. You can also put the cell color, font color, or icon on top.

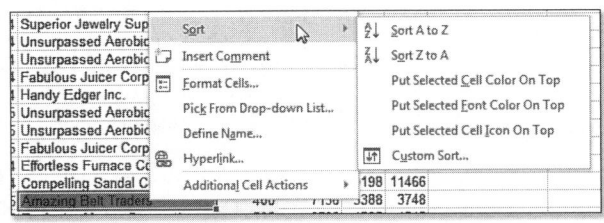

Figure 20.7
By using the context menu, you can perform rudimentary quick sorts by color.

Additional quick-sorting options are located in the Filter drop-downs. You can use these options to sort in ascending order, in descending order, and by color. For tips on setting up the filter drop-downs, see Chapter 21, "Removing Duplicates and Filtering."

Sorting by Several Columns Using One-Click Sorting

Even though the AZ button sorts by one column at a time, you can also sort a list by several columns by using the AZ button.

Remember that when Excel encounters a tie in the Sort column, the previous order remains intact. Because of this rule, you can perform quick sorts in reverse order. For example, if you want to sort by product within region, follow these steps:

1. Select one cell in the Product column.

2. Click the AZ button in the Data tab.

3. Select one cell in the Region column.

4. Click the AZ button in the Data tab.

Sorting Randomly

Suppose that you have a list of students, and you need to select the sequence in which they should present their science projects. Rather than always allowing Amber and Andy to go first, you can sort the class into a random sequence. To do so, follow these steps:

1. Add a new column to the right of your list. Give the column a heading, such as Sequence or Random.

2. In the first data cell of the new column, type **=RAND()** and then press Ctrl+Enter to keep the cell pointer in the first data cell. The formula calculates a random decimal value between 0 and 1.

3. Double-click the fill handle in the lower-right corner of this cell to copy the formula to all rows of your data.

4. Select the heading in the new column.

 Note

When you perform a random sort, it is important to note that the data is sorted into a new sequence. However, the numbers in the =RAND column do not appear to be in sequence. This is because the random numbers are recalculated after the sort is completed.

5. From the Data tab, select the AZ icon. The list is sorted into a random sequence as shown in Figure 20.8.

6. Delete the data in the temporary new column.

Figure 20.8
After you randomly sort, the RAND ( ) function recalculates, giving the appearance that the sort did not work.

	A	B	C	D	E
1	Student	Sequence			
2	Leigh	0.495512			
3	Fannie	0.50853			
4	Denise	0.296991			
5	Shelley	0.435116			
6	Tony	0.960423			
7	Cecilia	0.395568			
8	Brandi	0.083809			

(B2 — =RAND())

Fixing Sort Problems

If it appears that a sort did not work correctly, check this list of troubleshooting tips:

- If the headers were sorted into the data, it usually means that one or more columns had a blank heading. Every column should have a nonblank heading. If you want the heading to appear blank, use an underscore in a white font to fool Excel. If you cannot insert a heading, you will have to use the Sort dialog.

  Unhide rows and columns before sorting. Hidden rows are not resequenced in a sort.

- Use only one row for headings. If you need the headings to appear as if they are taking up several rows, put the headings in one row and wrap the text. To have control over where the text wraps, type the first line, press Alt+Enter, and then type the second line.

- Data in a column should be a similar type. For example, if you have a column of ZIP Codes, you might have numeric cells for ZIP Codes of 10001 through 99999 and text cells for ZIP Codes of 00001 through 09999. This is one common way to keep leading zeroes. Because text cells are sorted sequentially after numeric cells, sorting the ZIP Codes in this case will appear not to work. To fix this problem, convert the entire column to one data type to achieve the expected results.

- If your data has volatile formulas or formulas that point to cells outside the sort range, Excel calculates the range after sorting. If your sort sequence is based on this column, Excel accurately sorts the data, based on the information before the recalculation. If the values change after calculation, it will appear that the sort did not work. For an example, refer to Figure 20.8.

- If your data must have blank columns or rows, follow the steps in the sidebar "Excel in Practice: Sorting with Blank Columns."

Excel in Practice: Sorting with Blank Columns

In a perfect world, you will never have data sets with completely blank columns. However, this is not always possible. I have worked for managers who demanded a blank column between each data column in order to have a small break between the bottom cell borders in the headings. In addition, QuickBooks is notorious for exporting data to Excel with blank columns between data columns.

You cannot successfully sort a data set that contains blank columns by using the quick-sort buttons. Therefore, you need to follow these steps to sort the data by using the Sort dialog:

1.   Examine the data. Even if there are multiple rows of headings, include only the last row of headings, directly above your data row.

2.   Select a range that includes all columns and the one heading row.

3.   From the Data tab, click the Sort button. The Sort dialog appears.

4.   In the Sort dialog, select the My Data Has Headers check box.

5.   As shown in Figure 20.9, the Sort By column contains a mix of column headings and placeholders for blank headings such as (column F). Choose the proper heading from the drop-down. Click OK, and the entire data set is properly sorted.

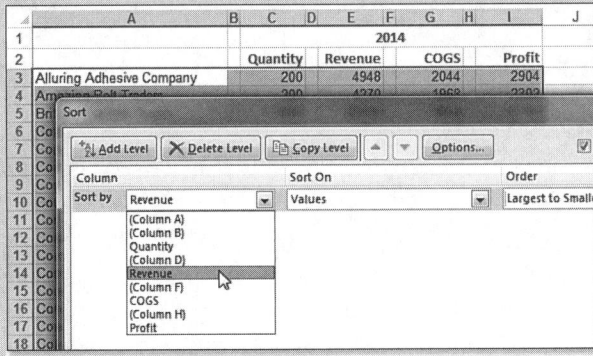

Figure 20.9
To sort data with blank columns, you must first preselect the entire range to be sorted.

Figure 21.1
The filter drop-down now features a multiselect list, as well as new special filters.

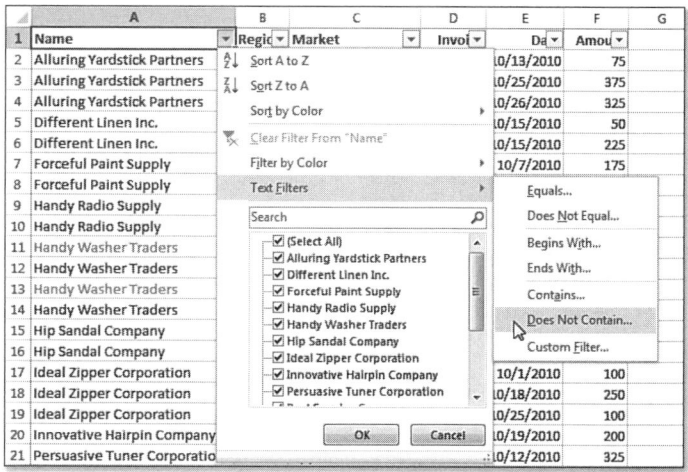

Selecting One or Multiple Items from the Filter Drop-Down

In legacy versions of Excel, the filter drop-down included a simple list of items in the column, and you selected one of the values. The multiselect nature of filters included since Excel 2007 offers far more power, but you have to exercise special care in using the drop-down.

Follow these steps to select a single item:

1. When you initially select the drop-down, all the check boxes that appear in the column are selected, as shown in Figure 21.1.

2. To select a single value, click Select All. This clears all the items in the list, as shown in Figure 21.2.

Figure 21.2
Click Select All to clear the check boxes for all items.

Select All

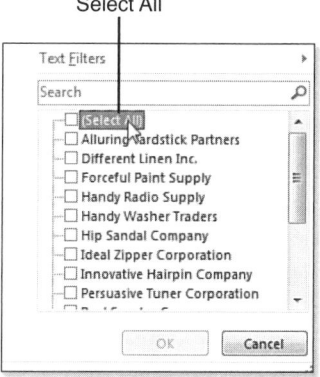

3. Click the value on which you want to filter, as shown in Figure 21.3.

4. Click OK at the bottom of the drop-down to apply the filter.

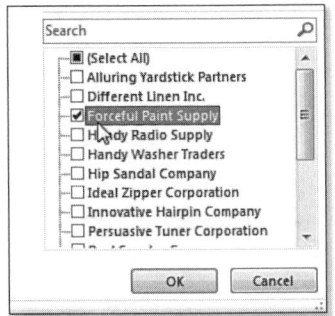

Figure 21.3
When the check boxes have been cleared, select the one value of interest and click OK.

The process you use to filter to multiple values is similar. First, click Select All to clear the check boxes for all items. You can then select the items that should be included in the filter.

The multiselection capability is a vast improvement for filtering that can be completed in four clicks. Even though the old AutoFilter in legacy versions of Excel required only two clicks, the improvements are worth this hassle. For example, when you need to select everything except one certain value, you select the drop-down, clear the undesired value, and click OK.

Identifying Which Columns Have Filters Applied

Listed here are the visual clues in Excel 2013 you can use to identify columns in which a filter has been applied to a data set:

- The row numbers in the range appear in blue to indicate that the rows have a filter applied.

- The message area of the status bar in the lower-left corner of the screen shows a message similar to "6 of 34 records found."

- The drop-down for the filtered column changes from a simple drop-down arrow to a Filter icon, as shown in Figure 21.4.

 **Tip**

With more than 1 million rows in Excel, you have the possibility for a long list of items in the Filter list—up to 10,000 items. Using the scrollbar to navigate through a list of 10,000 items will be inexact. However, there is a fast way to jump to a certain section of the list. Click any name in the list to activate the list. Then, type the first letter of your selection. Excel instantly jumps to the first item that starts with this letter. You can then use PgDn or PgUp to move quickly through the items that start with that letter.

Figure 21.4
After you apply a filter to column A, the icon on the filter drop-down changes.

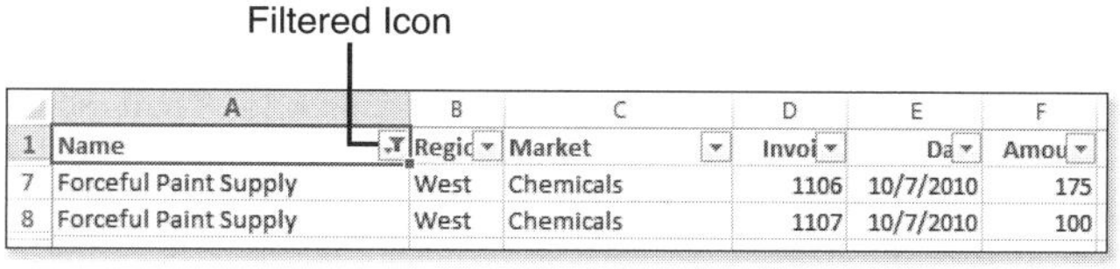

Filtered Icon

	A	B	C	D	E	F
1	Name	Regic ▾	Market ▾	Invoi ▾	Da ▾	Amou ▾
7	Forceful Paint Supply	West	Chemicals	1106	10/7/2010	175
8	Forceful Paint Supply	West	Chemicals	1107	10/7/2010	100

Combining Filters

Filters are additive, which means that after you place a filter on a column, you can apply a filter to another column to show even fewer rows. You can apply two filters to the same column, such as when you want to select all the West region cells that are red.

Clearing Filters

After you apply a filter, you have several options for clearing the filter:

- From the filter drop-down, select Clear Filter from Column. This leaves filters on in other columns.

- From the filter drop-down, choose a different filter.

- From the Data tab, select Clear from the Sort & Filter group. This clears selected filters from any column but leaves the drop-downs in place, so you can continue to select other filters.

- Select the Filter icon from the Data tab or the Home tab to clear all filters and turn off the filter feature.

Refreshing Filters

Keep in mind that when data in a range changes, the filters do not update automatically. This can happen when you add new rows or edit data. It can also happen if your data range has formulas that point to lookup tables in other parts of the workbook. In such a case, you need to have Excel calculate the filter again. Excel calls this feature *Reapply*. There are several ways you can reapply a filter:

- On the Data tab, select the Reapply icon.

- On the Home tab, select Sort & Filter, Reapply.

- Right-click a cell and then select Filter, Reapply.

Resizing the Filter Drop-Down

The filter drop-down always starts fairly small. If you have a long list of items, you might want the drop-down to be larger. To do this, hover your mouse over the three dots in the lower-right corner of the drop-down menu. When the mouse pointer changes to a two-headed diagonal arrow, click and drag down or to the right.

Filtering by Selection—Hard Way

You can filter without using the filter drop-downs. Microsoft Access has offered a Filter by Selection icon in the toolbar for more than a decade. Excel includes this functionality, but it is hidden where most people will never find it.

To access the Filter by Selection feature, right-click any cell and then select Filter from the context menu. You then have an opportunity to filter based on the cell's value, color, font color, or icon, as shown in Figure 21.5.

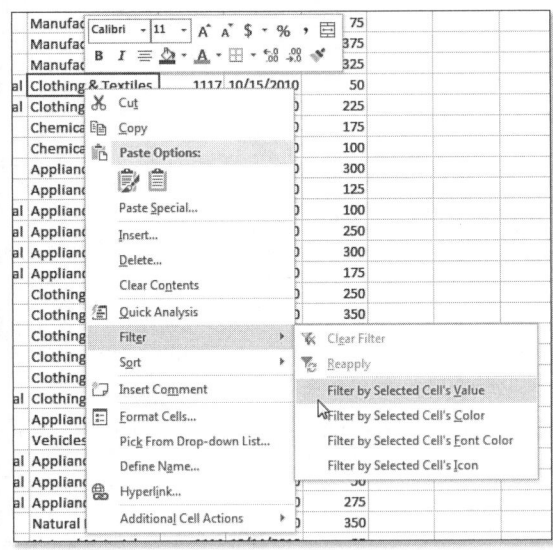

Figure 21.5
Although it is hidden, the Filter by Selection command provides a quick way to see all the other rows that match a single cell.

The Filter by Selection feature works even if the filter drop-downs have not been activated previously. Using this feature turns on the filter drop-downs for the data set.

It would be helpful if you could use this feature to select multiple values, such as selecting a cell that says East and then Ctrl-clicking a cell for West. You might think that filtering by selection would filter to both East and West, but that does not work in Excel 2013.

Filtering by Selection—Easy Way

The fast way to filter by selection is to add the AutoFilter icon to the Quick Access Toolbar.

To get one-click access to Filter by Selection, follow these steps:

1. Right-click the Quick Access Toolbar and select Customize Quick Access Toolbar.

2. In the Choose Commands From drop-down, select Commands Not in the Ribbon.

3. In the left list box, browse to and select AutoFilter, as shown in Figure 21.6. Click the Add button.

Figure 21.8
The Filter by Color fly-out menu offers to filter by icon, cell color, or font color.

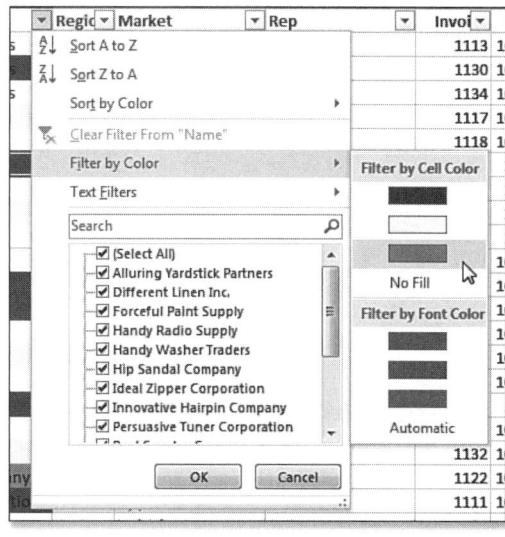

Figure 21.9
Excel automatically groups dates up to years in the filter drop-down.

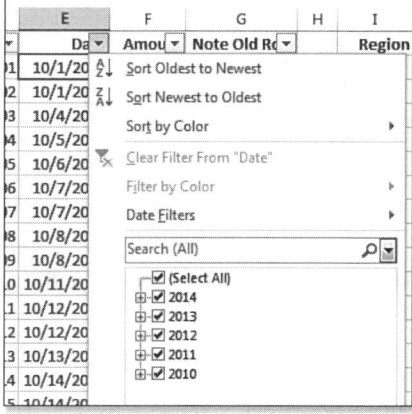

Click the plus sign next to any year to expand the list to show months within the year, as shown in Figure 21.10. You can then click the plus sign next to a month to see the days within the month.

 Tip

You can turn off the hierarchical grouping of dates in the filter drop-down. To do so, click the File menu and choose Options. In the Options dialog, choose the Advanced category. Scroll down to the section for Display for This Workbook. Next, select a workbook and then clear the check box for Group Dates in the AutoFilter Menu.

Figure 21.10
Expand the hierarchical view to see months within the years.

Using Special Filters for Dates, Text, and Numbers

Excel examines the data in a column to determine whether it contains mostly text, dates, or numeric values. Depending on which data type appears most often, Excel offers special filters designed for that data type.

For columns that contain mostly text, Excel offers the filters Begins With, Ends With, Contains, Does Not Contain, Equals, and Does Not Equal. You are allowed to use wildcard characters in these filters. For example, you can use an asterisk (*) for any number of characters or a question mark (?) to represent a single character. The Contains filter seems obsolete with the Search box in the Filter drop-down.

For columns with mostly numeric values, the special filters include Top 10, Above Average, Below Average, Between, Less Than, Greater Than, Does Not Equal, and Equals. For the Top 10 filter, you can specify the top or bottom values. You can also specify whether the results are based on the top 10 items or the top 10 percent of items. Finally, you can change the number 10 to any number. Thus, you can use this filter to show the bottom 20 percent or the top three items.

For columns with mostly dates, the special filters include Before, After, or Between a particular day, week, month, quarter, or year. The special filters also include Year to Date or All Dates in a particular period, as shown in Figure 21.11.

All the special filters offer a pathway to the legacy Custom AutoFilter dialog. This filter enables you to combine two conditions by using an AND or OR clause. This feature solves your problems some of the time, but there are still complex conditions that require you to resort to using the advanced filter.

The Custom AutoFilter dialog was nominally improved in Excel 2007. For example, a calendar control was added that can be used to select dates when you are filtering a date column. You can use the dialog shown in Figure 21.12 to select dates that are within a certain range of dates.

Figure 21.11
Excel offers myriad date filters.

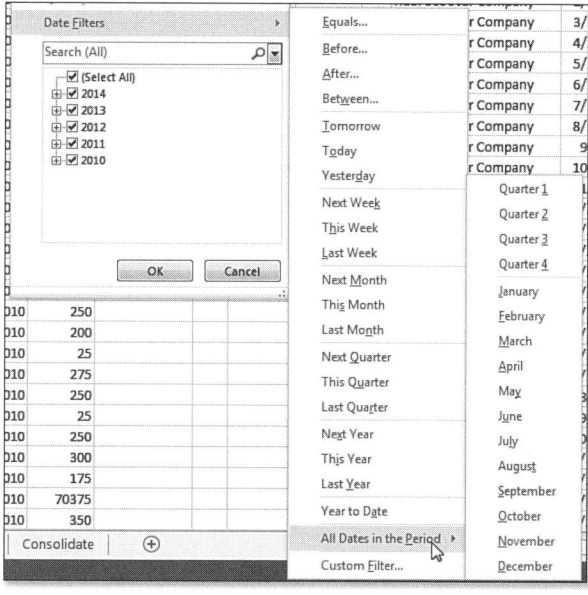

Figure 21.12
The custom filters allow you to build simple combinations of two conditions for filtering.

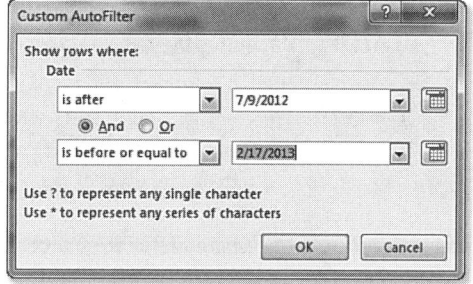

Sorting Filtered Results

The filter drop-down provides choices to sort a column. Note that if you apply a filter and then sort the results, the sort commands apply only to the visible rows. In Figure 21.13, a Top 10 filter shows the 10 largest invoices in a data set. Note that you can see rows 108, 123, 151, and so on.

If you use the Sort Largest to Smallest selection in the drop-down in cell F1, Excel sorts the 10 visible rows and leaves the hidden rows in their original location. In Figure 21.14, you can still see rows 108, 123, 151, and so on, but the $99225 from F244 moves to row 108.

⟋	A	B	C	D	E	F	G
1	Name ▼	Regio ▼	Market ▼	Invoi ▼	Da ▼	Amou ▼	Note Old R ▼
108	Alluring Yardstick Partners	East	Manufacturing	2320	7/1/2013	97375	108
123	Alluring Yardstick Partners	East	Manufacturing	2490	11/18/2013	96375	123
151	Alluring Yardstick Partners	East	Manufacturing	2800	7/29/2014	98325	151
244	Different Linen Inc.	Central	Clothing & Textiles	2410	9/13/2013	99225	244
1036	Innovative Hairpin Company	Central	Clothing & Textiles	2550	1/7/2014	97200	1036
1706	User-Friendly Juicer Company	West	Appliances	1690	1/31/2012	95350	1706
1750	User-Friendly Juicer Company	West	Appliances	2180	3/6/2013	99025	1750
1780	User-Friendly Juicer Company	West	Appliances	2520	12/11/2013	96025	1780
1826	Vibrant Vegetable Inc.	East	Natural Materials	1320	4/1/2011	96200	1826
1871	Vibrant Vegetable Inc.	East	Natural Materials	2850	9/12/2014	99200	1871

Figure 21.13
After the Top 10 filter is applied to column F, Excel shows the top 10 values, but they are unsorted.

⟋	A	B	C	D	E	F	G
1	Name ▼	Regio ▼	Market ▼	Invoi ▼	Da ▼	Amou ▼	Note Old R ▼
108	Different Linen Inc.	Central	Clothing & Textiles	2410	9/13/2013	99225	244
123	Vibrant Vegetable Inc.	East	Natural Materials	2850	9/12/2014	99200	1871
151	User-Friendly Juicer Company	West	Appliances	2180	3/6/2013	99025	1750
244	Alluring Yardstick Partners	East	Manufacturing	2800	7/29/2014	98325	151
1036	Alluring Yardstick Partners	East	Manufacturing	2320	7/1/2013	97375	108
1706	Innovative Hairpin Company	Central	Clothing & Textiles	2550	1/7/2014	97200	1036
1750	Alluring Yardstick Partners	East	Manufacturing	2490	11/18/2013	96375	123
1780	Vibrant Vegetable Inc.	East	Natural Materials	1320	4/1/2011	96200	1826
1826	User-Friendly Juicer Company	West	Appliances	2520	12/11/2013	96025	1780
1871	User-Friendly Juicer Company	West	Appliances	1690	1/31/2012	95350	1706

Figure 21.14
Use the Sort command in the filter drop-down. Excel sorts the 10 visible rows, leaving all the hidden rows in their original unsorted location.

Totaling Filtered Results

After you have applied a filter, you might want to sum the visible cells in a column. This task is straightforward in Excel 2013. Select the first visible blank cell below the column and click the AutoSum button. Instead of inserting a SUM function, Excel inserts a SUBTOTAL function. The =SUBTOTAL(9,F2:F1874) function sums the visible rows from a data set that has been filtered. You can edit the first argument in the SUBTOTAL function to find the count, average, minimum, and maximum, as well as other calculations on the visible rows.

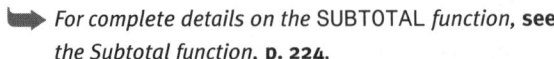 *For complete details on the* SUBTOTAL *function,* **see** *the Subtotal function,* **p. 224.**

Formatting and Copying Filtered Results

When you apply a filter, some rows are hidden and other rows are visible. The rows hidden by the filter are different from rows hidden with the Hide Rows command. Rows that are hidden using Hide Rows are often included when you copy or format a range

 Caution
When you get beyond the 11 functions offered in the SUBTOTAL function or the 19 functions offered in the AGGREGATE function, it becomes incredibly difficult to have formulas operate on the visible results of a filter. One option is to copy the filtered records to another section of the worksheet. For an example of how you can simulate the COUNTIF function on the visible rows of a filtered data set, see episode #946 of the Learn Excel from MrExcel podcast. To see this podcast, search for "Learn Excel 946" at YouTube.

that contains those rows. When you have manually hidden rows, you must use Alt+; to narrow your selection to only the visible rows. It is not necessary to use Alt+; when the rows have been hidden by the Filter command. Alt+; is the shortcut for Go To Special, Visible Cells Only.

You can use this behavior to format or copy rows matching a criteria. If you want to highlight all rows matching a criterion by changing the background color of the cell, follow these steps:

1. Select one cell in the unfiltered data set that matches the proper criterion.

2. Click the Filter by Selection icon in the Quick Access Toolbar. If you don't have this icon available, refer to Figure 21.6 and follow the instructions there.

3. Select the first visible cell below the headings.

4. Press Ctrl+Shift+Down Arrow and then Ctrl+Shift+Right Arrow to select all the cells below the heading.

5. Format the cells as desired.

6. Select Data, Filter to remove the filter and show all rows. You will find that only the rows that were visible during the filter have the new formatting.

Using the Advanced Filter Command

The Advanced Filter command is still present in Excel 2013. Microsoft should give this feature a new name because it is remarkably powerful and does much more than filtering. However, the Advanced Filter command is admittedly one of the more confusing commands in Excel. This is particularly true because you can use the Advanced Filter in eight ways, and each method requires slightly different steps.

The eight ways to use the Advanced Filter are derived by multiplying $2 \times 2 \times 2$. There are three options in the Advanced Filter dialog, and depending on your choices for those three options, you can have possible combinations:

- You can choose either Filter in Place or Copy to a New Location.

- You can choose to filter with a criteria range or without any criteria.

- You can choose to return all matching values or only the unique values.

 **Tip**

You can only copy filtered results to the active sheet, not to a new sheet. However, if you start on a blank sheet, you can specify that you want to filter data from another sheet and pull that data to the active sheet.

In reality, there are more than eight ways to use Advanced Filter. If you choose to copy records to a new location, you can either copy all the input columns in order or specify a subset of columns and/or a new sequence of columns.

You can build a simple filter for one column. You can combine any number of filters for multiple columns. You can build incredibly complex filters, using any formula imaginable. Alternatively, you can use no criteria at all. Using no criteria is common when you are using Advanced Filter to extract unique values or when you want to use Advanced Filter to reorder the sequence of columns.

To use Advanced Filter on a data set, follow these steps:

1. If you are using criteria, copy one or more headings from your data set to a blank section of the worksheet. Under each heading, list the value(s) you want to be included.

2. If you are using an output range and want to reorder the columns or include a subset of the columns, copy the headings into the appropriate order in a blank section of the worksheet. If you want all the original columns in their original sequence, the output range can be any blank cell.

3. Select a cell in your data range.

4. Select Data, Sort & Filter, Advanced.

5. Verify that the list range contains your original data set.

6. If you are using criteria, enter the criteria range.

7. If you want to copy the matching records to a new location, select Copy to Another Location. This enables the reference box for Copy To. Fill in the output range.

8. If you want the output range to contain only unique values, click Unique Records Only. If your output range contains a single field, a list of the values in that field is displayed that match the criteria. If your output range contains two or more fields, every unique combination of those two or more fields is displayed.

9. Click OK to perform the filter.

Excel in Practice: Using Formulas for Advanced Filter Criteria

Sometimes you might need to filter based on criteria that are too complex for any of Excel's built-in rules. For example, suppose you want to create an advanced filter to find all records where one of 30 customers bought one of 20 products. The necessary criteria range would cover 601 rows and would take hours to build.

There is one obscure syntax of advanced filter criteria that enables you to filter to anything for which you can build a TRUE/FALSE formula. Use the following specifics to set up a filter that contains formulas:

1. This criteria range is two cells tall by one column wide.

2. The top cell is blank or contains text not found in the data range headers.

3. The second cell contains a formula that should have relative references pointing to the first data row of the input range.

4. The formula should evaluate to TRUE or FALSE. For example, to select all the West records where the invoice is above average for the West, use this:

```
=AND(B2="West",F2>AVERAGEIF($B$2:$B$1874,"West",$F$2:$F$1874))
```

When Excel sees that the first row of the criteria range is blank, it takes the formula in the second cell and applies it to all rows in the range. Any rows that would evaluate to TRUE are returned in the filter.

Advanced Filter Criteria

Even though it is not obvious from the instructions for using Advanced Filter, you can build advanced filter criteria that can ask for a range of values. For example, if you are using an advanced filter, it is unlikely you will want to filter to the customer with exactly $7,553 in sales. However, you might want to filter to invoices that are more than $5,000 in sales. To set up this criterion, type **Sales** into cell K1. In cell K2, type the text **>5000**. When you issue the Advanced Filter, Excel returns all invoices in excess of $5,000.

In Figure 21.15, the Advanced Filter operation extracts all East region sales in the Vehicles market. Three columns from the matching records will be copied to Columns L:N.

Figure 21.15
Advanced Filter is a powerful tool that can do much more than filter.

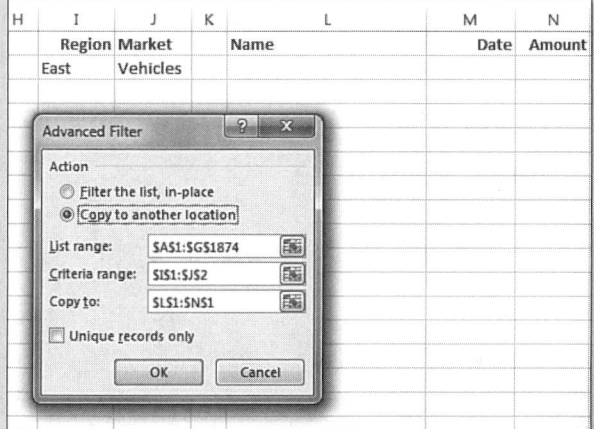

Note that criteria values that are in the same row are treated as if they were joined by AND. Because East and Vehicles are both in row 2, a record must be from the East region and have a market of vehicles to appear in the data set. If you move Vehicles from row 2 to row 3 and expand the criteria range to I1:J3, the two values are joined with an OR. All records that either are from the East region or Vehicles market appear in the results.

Using Remove Duplicates to Find Unique Values

By its nature, transactional data has a lot of detail. You end up with transactional data in Excel because it is often the easiest to obtain. As you start to analyze transactional data, you often want to find the number of customers, number of products, or number of something in the data set.

For example, transactional data can tell you that there were 34 invoices issued last month, but that doesn't mean there were 34 customers. Some of those customers might have made repeat purchases. In this case, 20 customers could account for 34 invoices.

To find the number of unique customers, you need a way to eliminate the duplicate records in a data set. In legacy versions of Excel, this usually meant using Advanced Filter, some IF functions, or possibly a pivot table. However, in Excel 2013, the Remove Duplicates data tool makes it easier to remove duplicates.

The first thing to realize is that the Remove Duplicates tool is destructive because it really removes the duplicate records. If you want to keep the original transactional data intact, you should either make a copy of the customer column in a blank section of the workbook or make a backup copy of the workbook.

To find the unique values in a data set, follow these steps:

1. Copy the data set to a blank section of the worksheet. Make sure to leave a blank column between your real data and the copy of the data.

2. Select a single cell within the data set.

3. On the Data tab, in the Data Tools group, select Remove Duplicates. Excel expands the selection to include the entire range. In the Remove Duplicates dialog, Excel predicts if your data has headers. This dialog also shows a list of all the fields in the data set.

4. Because you are interested in a unique list of customers, click the Unselect All button to clear all check boxes, and then select the Customer field, as shown in Figure 21.16.

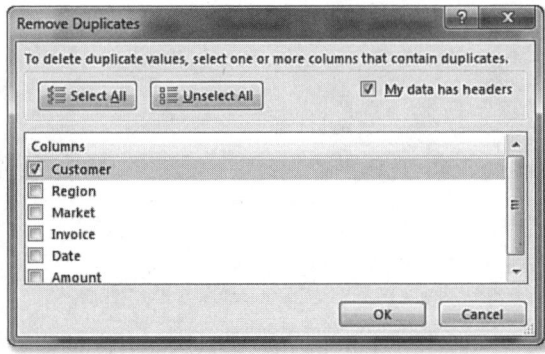

Figure 21.16
Choose which columns should be considered when analyzing duplicates.

 Tip

Remember that the Remove Duplicates command is destructive. For this reason, sometimes you might want to find the duplicates and choose which version to remove. In that case, you Select Home, Conditional Formatting, Highlight Cell Rules, Duplicate Values.

Other times, you might want to send a copy of the unique values to a new location. In this case, use the Advanced Filter command discussed earlier in this chapter.

Finally, you might want to remove duplicates, but add up the sales for all the removed records and then add them to the Customer field. Although this can be achieved with pivot tables, it can also be achieved using the Consolidate feature, which is discussed in the next section.

5. Click OK to perform the action. Excel tells you how many duplicate values were found and removed. It also tells you how many unique values remain.

Removing Duplicates Based on Several Columns

In the previous set of steps, you analyzed only a single column when looking for duplicates. However, sometimes you need to find each unique combination of two fields, such as a list of each unique combination of region and market. In this case, follow these steps:

1. Copy the data set to a blank section of the worksheet. Make sure to leave a blank column between your real data and the copy of the data.

2. Select a single cell within the data set.

3. On the Data tab, in the Data Tools group, select Remove Duplicates.

4. In the Remove Duplicates dialog, leave the check boxes for both of the fields selected.

5. Click OK to remove the duplicate values.

In this case, the result is a list of all unique combinations of market and customer.

Handling Duplicates Other Ways

The Remove Duplicates command is also available in Table Tools, Design tab. For example, you can use this option to remove duplicates from a table.

Combining Duplicates and Adding Values

In columns A:D of Figure 21.17, each customer appears one or more times in the list with a sales, cost, and profit values. In addition to finding a unique list of customers, you would like to know the total sales and profit for each customer. You can use a pivot table to find the total sales for each customer. Alternatively, you can use the data tools to consolidate the table down to one record per customer.

Figure 21.17
Start at a blank section of the workbook before invoking the Consolidate feature.

	A	B	C	D	E	F	G	H	I	J
1	Customer	Sales	COGS	Profit						
2	Handy Radio Supply	300	151.8	148.2						
3	Ideal Zipper Corporation	100	49.3	50.7						
4	Savory Edger Corporation	50	22.25	27.75						
5	Handy Radio Supply	125	55.125	69.875						
6	Real Scooter Company	50	26.35	23.65						
7	Forceful Paint Supply	175	92.575	82.425						
8	Forceful Paint Supply	100	55.9	44.1						
9	Savory Edger Corporation	50	27.95	22.05						
10	Tasty Chopstick Traders	350	166.95	183.05						
11	Handy Washer Traders	21100	9368.4	11731.6						
12	Persuasive Tuner Corporation	325	176.8	148.2						
13	User-Friendly Juicer Company	350	193.2	156.8						
14	Alluring Yardstick Partners	75	40.5	34.5						
15	Tasty Chopstick Traders	25	13.475	11.525						
16	User-Friendly Juicer Company	200	109.4	90.6						
17	Vibrant Vegetable Inc.	200	93	107						

Consolidate

Function:
Sum

Reference:
$A$1:$D$1874

All references:

Use labels in
☑ Top row
☑ Left column   ☐ Create links to source data

Add
Delete

OK   Close

To use the Consolidate feature to total sales from all the records for that customer, follow these steps:

1. Instead of preselecting the data, move the cell pointer to a blank section of the worksheet.

2. Select Data, Data Tools, Consolidate. The Consolidate dialog box appears.

3. In the Consolidate dialog box, enter the reference to your data in the Reference box. The data will be combined based on the field in the left column of the range. If you have multiple lists of customers, you can click the Add button and enter additional ranges.

4. Make sure to select the Top Row and Left Column check boxes in the Use Labels in section.

5. Click OK.

Excel creates a new table. Each customer appears in the table just once. The sales associated with all the records of the customer appear in the new total, as shown in Figure 21.18.

F	G	H	I
	Sales	COGS	Profit
Handy Radio Supply	532675	263796.6	268878.4
Ideal Zipper Corporation	946850	470308.7	476541.3
Savory Edger Corporation	1228675	629414.6	599260.5
Real Scooter Company	2750	1376.4	1373.6
Forceful Paint Supply	658125	334804.7	323320.3
Tasty Chopstick Traders	702625	337767.2	364857.9
Handy Washer Traders	1124375	559745.1	564629.9
Persuasive Tuner Corporation	17875	8945.95	8929.05
User-Friendly Juicer Company	1265625	647611.6	618013.4
Alluring Yardstick Partners	1233625	620172.9	613452.2
Vibrant Vegetable Inc.	620000	319127.8	300872.2
Different Linen Inc.	609125	309001.4	300123.6
Unsurpassed Scooter Inc.	648125	307050.8	341074.2
Innovative Hairpin Company	755000	367083.2	387916.8
Hip Sandal Company	33000	16735.3	16264.7
Trustworthy Glass Supply	17875	8984.95	8890.05

Figure 21.18
Excel consolidates all data by customer.

Two annoyances remain with this command. First, the heading for the leftmost column is never filled in. Second, the command leaves the results in the same sequence in which they originally appeared. In this example, you will probably want to add the heading above cell F2 and also sort the data.

USING AUTOMATIC SUBTOTALS

The Subtotal command was added way back in Excel 97. Not enough people realize that the command is in Excel, and those who have tried it often don't realize how powerful the command truly is. I used to have a regular gig as the Excel guy on Leo Laporte's *Call for Help* television show. During one appearance, I showed people how to use the Subtotal command. I figured it was probably the most boring 6 minutes of television in the history of the world. However, that one show generated more fan email than any other. People wrote to say that they have been spending 2 hours every day adding subtotals manually and used the trick from the show to reduce the task to a minute.

Adding Automatic Subtotals

When you have a database of detailed data, you might want to add subtotals to each group of records. If your data has one field that identifies the groups, you can use the Subtotals command to quickly add the subtotals. Figure 22.1 shows a data set that is suitable for this.

Figure 22.1
After sorting, you can quickly add subtotals to this data set.

	A	B	C	D	E	F	G	H
1	Region	Product	Date	Customer	Quantity	Revenue	COGS	Profit
2	East	XYZ	1/1/2015	Functional Eggbeater Co	1000	22810	10220	12590
3	Central	DEF	1/2/2015	Vivid Edger Co	100	2257	984	1273
4	East	DEF	1/4/2015	Powerful Edger Supply	800	18552	7872	10680
5	East	XYZ	1/4/2015	Trendy Notebook Corp	400	9152	4088	5064

C2   fx   1/1/2015

Follow these steps to add subtotals to a data set:

1. Sort the data set by your group field. Select one cell in that column and then select Data, Sort & Filter, AZ.

2. Select one cell in your data set.

3. Select Data, Outline, Subtotal. Excel displays the Subtotal dialog.

4. In the Subtotal dialog, change the At Each Change In drop-down to reflect your group field.

5. Ensure that Use Function is set to Sum.

6. For each field you want totaled, select the field in the Add Subtotal To list, as shown in Figure 22.2.

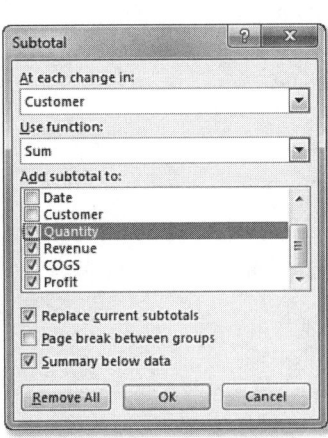

Figure 22.2
You specify the fields to be totaled in the Subtotal dialog.

7. If you want a page break after each group, select Page Break Between Groups.

8. Click OK to add subtotals. Excel adds a subtotal between each group, as shown in Figure 22.3.

At the very bottom of the data set, Excel has added a Grand Total row. This row is smart enough to ignore all the other subtotal rows in the data set (see Figure 22.4).

Adding hundreds of subtotal rows is amazing in and of itself. However, the subtotals command offers so much more. You can go on to show only the subtotals, show the largest groups at the top, or copy the subtotals.

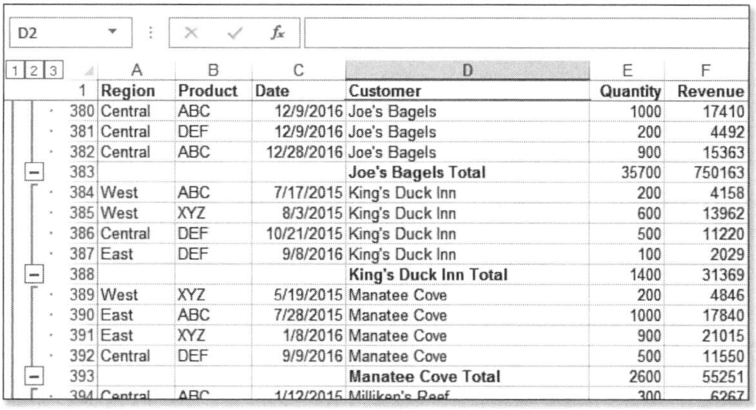

Figure 22.3
Excel inserts extra rows between groups and adds subtotals.

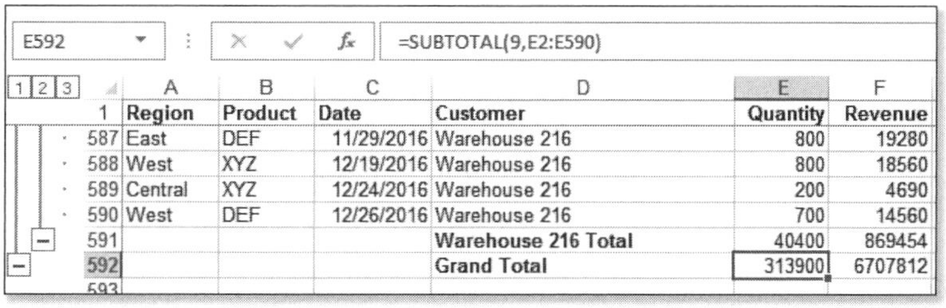

	A	B	C	D	E	F
1	Region	Product	Date	Customer	Quantity	Revenue
380	Central	ABC	12/9/2016	Joe's Bagels	1000	17410
381	Central	DEF	12/9/2016	Joe's Bagels	200	4492
382	Central	ABC	12/28/2016	Joe's Bagels	900	15363
383				**Joe's Bagels Total**	35700	750163
384	West	ABC	7/17/2015	King's Duck Inn	200	4158
385	West	XYZ	8/3/2015	King's Duck Inn	600	13962
386	Central	DEF	10/21/2016	King's Duck Inn	500	11220
387	East	DEF	9/8/2016	King's Duck Inn	100	2029
388				**King's Duck Inn Total**	1400	31369
389	West	XYZ	5/19/2015	Manatee Cove	200	4846
390	East	ABC	7/28/2015	Manatee Cove	1000	17840
391	East	XYZ	1/8/2016	Manatee Cove	900	21015
392	Central	DEF	9/9/2016	Manatee Cove	500	11550
393				**Manatee Cove Total**	2600	55251
394	Central	ABC	1/12/2015	Milliken's Reef	300	6267

Figure 22.4
At the bottom of the data set, Excel inserted a Grand Total row.

E592   =SUBTOTAL(9,E2:E590)

	A	B	C	D	E	F
1	Region	Product	Date	Customer	Quantity	Revenue
587	East	DEF	11/29/2016	Warehouse 216	800	19280
588	West	XYZ	12/19/2016	Warehouse 216	800	18560
589	Central	XYZ	12/24/2016	Warehouse 216	200	4690
590	West	DEF	12/26/2016	Warehouse 216	700	14560
591				**Warehouse 216 Total**	40400	869454
592				**Grand Total**	313900	6707812
593						

Working with the Subtotals

Take a close look at the left side of the worksheet in Figure 22.3. You see three new buttons to the left of column A labeled 1, 2, and 3. Those buttons are called Group and Outline buttons and were added automatically by the Subtotals command. They are the key to further analysis of the subtotals.

Showing a One-Page Summary with Only the Subtotals

Click the #2 button that appears to the left of and just above cell A1. Excel hides all the detail rows, leaving only the customer subtotals and the Grand Total row.

After setting the print area, you would have a one-page summary of the 500+ rows of data (see Figure 22.5).

If you click the #1 Group and Outline button, Excel hides everything except for the Grand Total. If you click the #3 button, Excel brings the detail rows back.

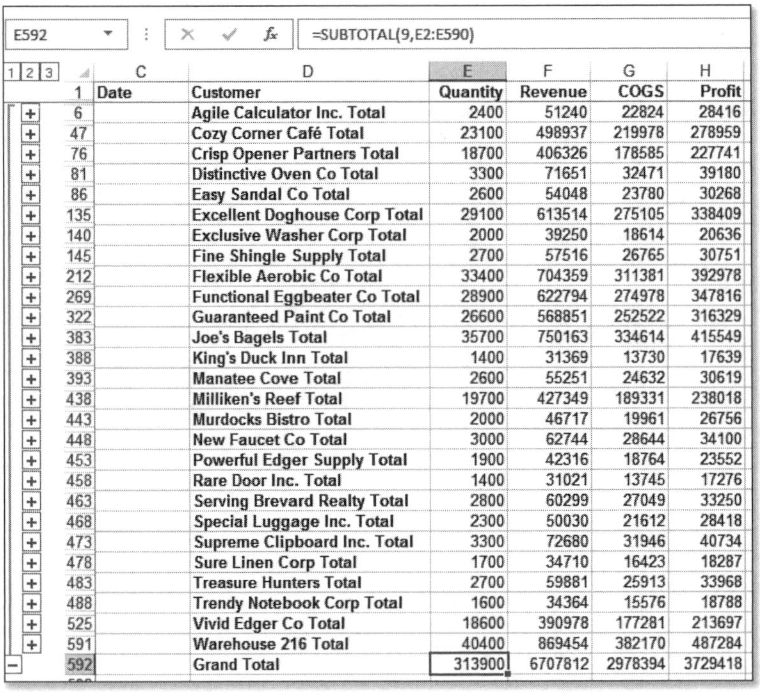

Figure 22.5
Click the #2 Group and Outline button to show a summary report.

Sorting the Collapsed Subtotal View So the Largest Customers Are on Top

In Figure 22.5, you have the customers in alphabetical sequence. However, your manager is probably going to want to see the largest customers at the top of the report.

Think about this request, though. In row 591, the subtotal for Warehouse 216 is the largest customer in the group, adding up data in rows 526 through 590. If you try to sort in descending order, and the data in row 591 comes up to row 2, the formula that looks at 64 rows of data will certainly evaluate to a #REF! error.

Amazingly, though, you can easily sort data when it is in the collapsed #2 view. Follow these steps:

1. Add subtotals as indicated previously in this chapter.

2. Collapse the subtotals by clicking the #2 Group and Outline button.

3. Select one single cell in your revenue column.

4. Sort in descending order by clicking the ZA button on the Data tab.

The result is shown in Figure 22.6. The total for Warehouse 216 comes flying to the top of the data set, but it does not come to row 2. Instead, the total comes to row 67. The total for the second largest customer is in row 128.

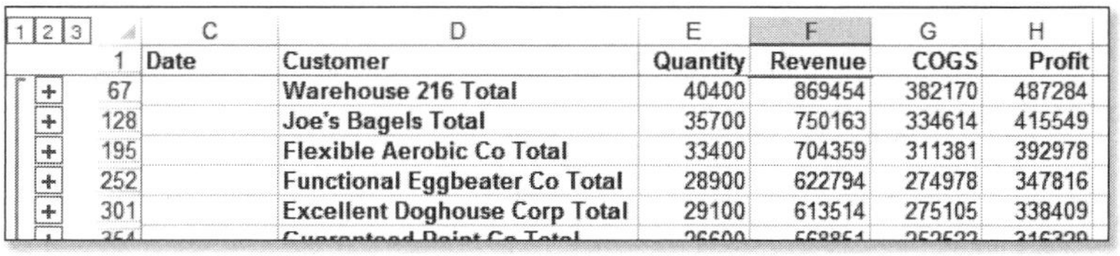

Figure 22.6
Amazingly, you can sort data when it is collapsed.

			C	D	E	F	G	H
1	2	3						
		1	Date	Customer	Quantity	Revenue	COGS	Profit
	+	67		Warehouse 216 Total	40400	869454	382170	487284
	+	128		Joe's Bagels Total	35700	750163	334614	415549
	+	195		Flexible Aerobic Co Total	33400	704359	311381	392978
	+	252		Functional Eggbeater Co Total	28900	622794	274978	347816
	+	301		Excellent Doghouse Corp Total	29100	613514	275105	338409
		354		Guaranteed Paint Co Total	26600	558861	252622	316239

Figure 22.7 shows the #3 view of Figure 22.6. You can see that Excel sorted groups of records when the data was collapsed. All the detail rows for a customer come along with the subtotal row, but the detail rows are not sorted by revenue.

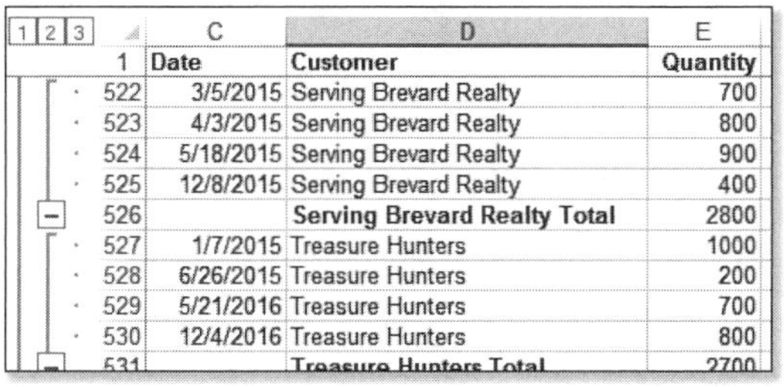

Figure 22.7
Excel brings all the collapsed detail rows along with the subtotal row during a sort.

			C	D	E
1	2	3			
		1	Date	Customer	Quantity
	·	522	3/5/2015	Serving Brevard Realty	700
	·	523	4/3/2015	Serving Brevard Realty	800
	·	524	5/18/2015	Serving Brevard Realty	900
	·	525	12/8/2015	Serving Brevard Realty	400
	−	526		Serving Brevard Realty Total	2800
	·	527	1/7/2015	Treasure Hunters	1000
	·	528	6/26/2015	Treasure Hunters	200
	·	529	5/21/2016	Treasure Hunters	700
	·	530	12/4/2016	Treasure Hunters	800
		531		Treasure Hunters Total	2700

Copying Only the Subtotal Rows

A problem occurs when you try to copy the collapsed subtotal rows from Figure 22.6. If you select D1:H592, Copy, and then Paste to a new worksheet, you discover that Excel has copied all the hidden rows as well. Worse, the pasted data no longer has the group and outline symbols, so there is no way to collapse the data again.

The key to this task is to use a trick called Go To Special, Visible Cells Only. Excel still makes it hard to find this command.

Follow these steps:

1. Add subtotals to a data set as described previously.

2. Collapse to the subtotal-only view by clicking the #2 Group and Outline button.

3. Select the entire range of collapsed subtotals.

4. Open the Find and Select drop-down from the right side of the Home tab. Select the Go To Special command. Excel displays the Go To Special dialog, as shown in Figure 22.8. This dialog enables you to narrow a selection down to only certain types of elements within your selection. This is a powerful dialog.

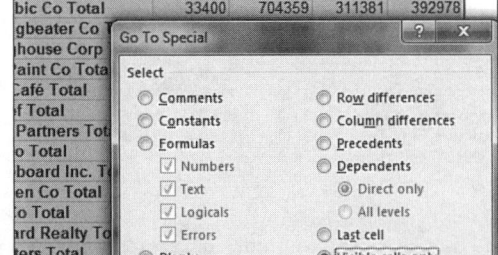

Figure 22.8
The Go To Special dialog enables you to reduce your selection to items meeting a certain criteria.

5. In the Go To Special dialog, select Visible Cells Only. Click OK. Excel deselects all the hidden rows.

 **Tip**

You can replace steps 4 and 5 with a single keystroke. Hold down the Alt key while pressing the semicolon key. It turns out that Alt+; is the equivalent of selecting Home, Find & Select, Go To Special, Visible Cells Only, OK.

6. Click Ctrl+C to copy those rows. As you can see in Figure 22.9, Excel has selected each visible row separately.

	C	D	E	F	G	H
1	Date	Customer	Quantity	Revenue	COGS	Profit
67		Warehouse 216 Total	40400	869454	382170	487284
128		Joe's Bagels Total	35700	750163	334614	415549
195		Flexible Aerobic Co Total	33400	704359	311381	392978
252		Functional Eggbeater Co Total	28900	622794	274978	347816
301		Excellent Doghouse Corp Total	29100	613514	275105	338409
354		Guaranteed Paint Co Total	26600	568851	252522	316329
395		Cozy Corner Café Total	23100	498937	219978	278959
440		Milliken's Reef Total	19700	427349	189331	238018
469		Crisp Opener Partners Total	18700	406326	178585	227741

Figure 22.9
Excel copies only the visible rows.

7. Select a blank section of the workbook. Use Ctrl+V to paste only the subtotals. The subtotal formulas are converted to values. This is the only thing that would make sense.

Formatting the Subtotal Rows

When the Subtotal command adds subtotals, it inserts a new row for each subtotal. Excel copies your key field to the new row and appends the word *Total* after the key field. This text in the key field column appears in bold font. Unfortunately, Excel does not widen this column, so frequently the word "Total" appears to be truncated because it will not fit in the column.

The other subtotal columns get a formula that uses the SUBTOTAL function. Strangely, the cells containing the formulas in each subtotal row are not bold.

When I am doing my Power Excel seminars, I'm frequently asked how to bold the subtotal rows. Many people will try selecting E67:H592 in the collapsed #2 view and pressing Ctrl+B. Although this initially looks like it works, it actually fails.

The problem becomes apparent when you go back to the #3 view to see the detail rows. The detail rows up through row 66 are fine. The problem is that all the detail rows from row 68 through the end of the data set have been bolded. For some reason, Microsoft formats the rows that are hidden as a result of the Subtotal command.

At this point, many people press Undo twice and start the process of manually formatting each individual subtotal row. There is, of course, an easier way. Follow these steps to format the subtotal rows:

1. Add subtotals to a data set as described previously.

2. Click the #2 Group and Outline button to collapse the data set to show only the subtotals.

3. Select from the first subtotal row down to the grand total row. In the current data set, select from D67 through H592.

4. Hold down Alt and press semicolon. Excel selects on the visible rows, which in this case are only the subtotal rows.

5. Apply any desired formatting. In Figure 22.10, the cells are showing a mix of Cell Styles, Heading 4, and a light red background from the Fill drop-down.

Figure 22.10

Format only the subtotal rows.

	C	D	E	F	G	H
1 Date		Customer	Quantity	Revenue	COGS	Profit
518	7/26/2015	New Faucet Co	1000	23890	10220	13670
519	7/14/2016	New Faucet Co	700	14497	6888	7609
520	10/13/2016	New Faucet Co	1000	17190	8470	8720
521		New Faucet Co Total	3000	62744	28644	34100
522	3/5/2015	Serving Brevard Realty	700	12474	5929	6545
523	4/3/2015	Serving Brevard Realty	800	20408	8176	12232
524	5/18/2015	Serving Brevard Realty	900	17757	8856	8901
525	12/8/2015	Serving Brevard Realty	400	9660	4088	5572
526		Serving Brevard Realty Total	2800	60299	27049	33250
527	1/7/2015	Treasure Hunters	1000	21730	9840	11890
528	6/26/2015	Treasure Hunters	200	4754	1968	2786
529	5/21/2016	Treasure Hunters	700	13853	5929	7924
530	12/4/2016	Treasure Hunters	800	19544	8176	11368
531		Treasure Hunters Total	2700	59881	25913	33968

6. Click the #3 Group and Outline button to show all the detail rows.

Step 4 in this process is the key step. Using Alt+; selects only the visible rows in the collapsed subtotal view.

Removing Subtotals

After you add subtotals and copy those subtotal rows to another worksheet, you might want to remove the subtotals from the original data set. Follow these steps to remove the subtotals:

1. Select one cell in the subtotaled data set.

2. Go back to the Subtotals command on the Data tab of the ribbon.

3. In the lower-left corner of the Subtotals dialog box, click the button for Remove All.

The subtotal rows are removed.

Using Specialty Subtotal Techniques

Over the years, the MrExcel podcast has covered a number of unusual questions about subtotals. The next section goes through the techniques for two of the more useful subtotal situations.

Summing Some Columns While Counting Another Column

It is easy for Excel to sum the numeric columns with the Subtotal command. Sometimes, your manager will want to see a count of how many sales were made to a particular customer.

Microsoft has a solution to this problem that yields an ugly result. Using Microsoft's solution, you add totals to the numeric columns first. Then, you go back to the Subtotals dialog, specify to Count a text column, and clear the check box for Replace Current Subtotals.

The result shown in Figure 22.11 is that the Count occurs on one row, and the totals appear on another row. This creates a horrible-looking summary view because every customer appears twice.

1 2 3 4		A	B	C	D	E
	1	Region	Product	Date	Customer	Quantity
·	398	East	XYZ	10/15/2016	Cozy Corner Café	900
·	399	East	DEF	11/28/2016	Cozy Corner Café	600
·	400	West	XYZ	12/21/2016	Cozy Corner Café	800
−	401	40			**Cozy Corner Café Count**	
−	402				Cozy Corner Café Total	23100

Figure 22.11
If you count one field and sum the others, you get two summary rows per customer.

Here is a workaround that produces a suitable-looking summary report. Follow these steps:

1. Add subtotals to a data set. In the Subtotal dialog, choose to sum all the numeric columns. Also, choose to sum one text column. The result is that the subtotals added to the text column are all zero.

2. Examine the formula in the subtotal row of one of the text columns. The formula will be something like =SUBTOTAL(9,A479:A514). The trick is to change the first argument in the formula from 9 to 3. In the help topic for the Subtotal function, you can see that 9 means Sum and 3 means CountA.

3. Select your entire text column.

4. Use Ctrl+H to display the Find and Replace dialog. In the Find and Replace dialog, choose to replace every **(9,** with a **(3,** as shown in Figure 22.12. Click Replace All. Excel responds with "All done. We made 28 replacements."

Figure 22.12
Edit the formulas in column A to convert from Sum to CountA.

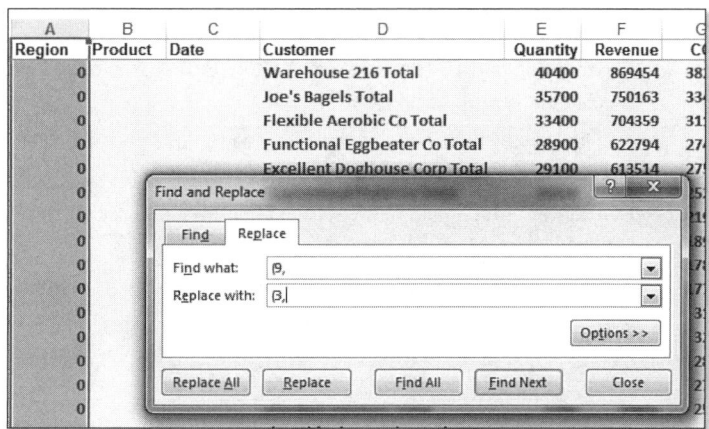

The result shown in Figure 22.13 is a Count in column A and Sums in the numeric columns. You have only one total line per customer.

Figure 22.13
The result is a Count in column A and Sums elsewhere.

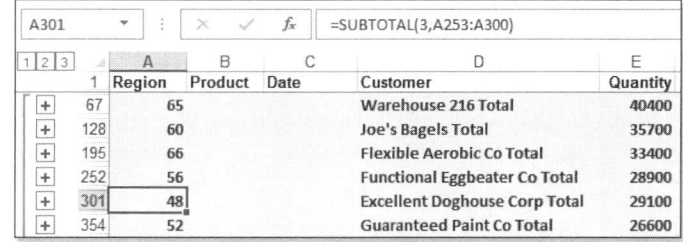

Add Subtotals by Two Fields

Suppose you want to add subtotals by region and product. You will add the subtotals twice. In the second Subtotal command, make sure you clear the Replace Current Subtotals check box.

Make sure that your data is sorted properly. You can either use the Sort dialog to sort by region and then by product, or you can follow this set of steps, which requires only four clicks:

1. Select one cell in the Product column.
2. Click the AZ button on the Data tab.
3. Select one cell in the Region column.
4. Click the AZ button on the Data tab.

Because the sort in step 4 keeps the ties in the previous sequence, this set of steps effectively sorts by product within region.

It is important that you add subtotals to the outer group first. Use the instructions earlier in this chapter to add totals to the Region field.

Run the Subtotals command again. This time, specify Each Change in Product. Clear the Replace Current Subtotals check box.

You now have four Group and Outline buttons. If you press the #3 button, you see product totals and region totals, as shown in Figure 22.14. Note that Excel supports a maximum of eight Group and Outline buttons, so you could add up to six levels of subtotals.

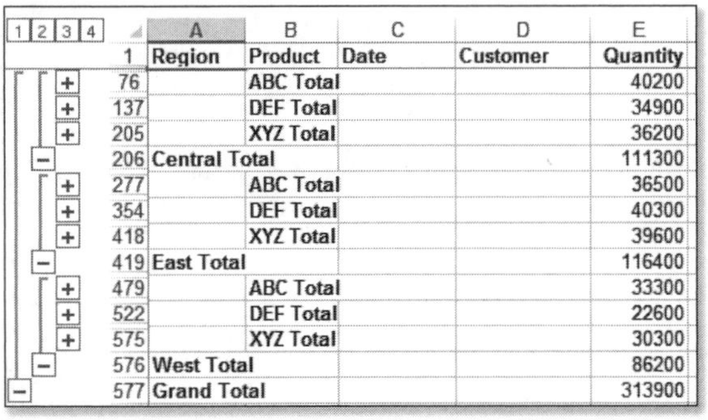

	A	B	C	D	E
1	Region	Product	Date	Customer	Quantity
76		ABC Total			40200
137		DEF Total			34900
205		XYZ Total			36200
206	Central Total				111300
277		ABC Total			36500
354		DEF Total			40300
418		XYZ Total			39600
419	East Total				116400
479		ABC Total			33300
522		DEF Total			22600
575		XYZ Total			30300
576	West Total				86200
577	Grand Total				313900

Figure 22.14
Two sets of subtotals mean four Group and Outline buttons.

USING PIVOT TABLES TO ANALYZE DATA

A pivot table enables you to summarize thousands or millions of records of data to a one-page summary in just a few clicks.

Pivot tables were introduced in Excel 95 and have been evolving ever since:

- Excel 2013 adds a new entry point for pivot tables called Recommended Pivot Tables. This feature shows you various thumbnails of pivot tables before you begin creating one.

- Excel 2013 adds the ability to create a data model from several different tables. You can create a relationship between tables without using VLOOKUPs and base pivot tables on the model.

- Timelines are a visual date filter introduced in Excel 2013. They join slicers, the visual filter introduced in Excel 2010. The best feature of timelines and slicers is the capability for them to drive multiple pivot tables built from the same data set.

- Power View, PowerPivot, and GeoFlow are powerful add-ins for Excel 2013 that enhance pivot tables. If you are using Excel 2013 Pro Plus or higher, you have access to these add-ins. PowerPivot enhances the ability to build multitable models and provides key performance indicators (KPIs) and the DAX formula language. Power View uses Silverlight to animate pivot charts over time. GeoFlow plots your geographic pivot table information on a map and creates visual tours of the data.

- Excel 2010 introduced new calculations such as Rank, Percent of Parent, and Running Percentage of Total.

- Excel 2010 introduced the option to replace blanks in the outer row fields by repeating item labels from above.

- Excel 2007 simplified the pivot table interface and added new filters.

Suppose you have 400,000 records of transactional data. It is easy for some people to look at this and figure out that it represents $x million. But to learn some things about the data, you need to do some more analysis to spot trends in the data. A pivot table enables you to analyze trends in data without having to worry about formulas.

By using a pivot table, it is possible to create a number of views of your data, including the following:

- Breakdown of sales by product

- Sales by month, this year versus last year

- Percentage of sales by customer

- Customers who bought XYZ product in the East region

- Sales by product by month

- Top five customers with products

Of course, these are just examples. You can use pivot tables to slice and dice your data in almost any imaginable way.

Creating Your First Pivot Table

Pivot tables are best created from transactional data—that is, raw data files directly from your company's IT department.

To create the best pivot tables, make sure your data follows these rules:

- Ensure each column has a one-cell heading. Keep the headings unique; don't use the same heading for two columns. If you need your headings to appear on two rows, type the first word, press Alt+Enter, and then type the second word.

- If a column should contain numeric data, don't allow blank cells in the column. Use zeros instead of blanks.

- Do not use blank rows or blank columns.

- If totals are embedded in your report, remove them.

- The workbook should not be in Compatibility mode. Many pivot table features from Excel 2007–2013 are disabled if the workbook is in Compatibility mode.

- If you add new data to the bottom of your data set each month, you should strongly consider converting your data set to a table using Ctrl+T. Pivot tables created from tables automatically pick up new rows pasted to the bottom of the tables after a refresh.

- If your data has months spread across many columns, go back to the source software program to see if a different view of the data is available with months going down the rows.

For most of this chapter, the pivot tables shown in the figures are from the data set in Figure 23.1. This data set has two years of transactional data. Text columns include Region, Product, and Customer. There is a single date column. Numeric columns include Quantity, Revenue, COGS, and Profit.

Figure 23.1

This data set follows the rules of a good pivot table source.

	A	B	C	D	E	F	G	H
1	Region ▾	Product ▾	Date ▾	Customer ▾	Quantity ▾	Revenue ▾	COGS ▾	Profit ▾
2	East	XYZ	1/1/2015	Functional Eggbeater Co	954	22810	10213	12597
3	Central	DEF	1/2/2015	Vivid Edger Co	124	2257	998	1259
4	East	XYZ	1/4/2015	Trendy Notebook Corp	425	9152	4083	5069
5	East	DEF	1/4/2015	Powerful Edger Supply	773	18552	7883	10669
6	East	ABC	1/7/2015	Improved Vegetable Inc.	401	8456	3389	5067
7	East	DEF	1/7/2015	Tremendous Thermostat Partners	1035	21730	9839	11891
8	Central	ABC	1/9/2015	Improved Vegetable Inc.	750	16416	6768	9648
9	Central	XYZ	1/10/2015	Wonderful Kettle Corp	901	21438	9209	12229
10	Central	ABC	1/12/2015	Matchless Hardware Traders	342	6267	2541	3726
11	East	XYZ	1/14/2015	Cool Bottle Co	91	2401	1031	1370
12	East	ABC	1/15/2015	Vivid Edger Co	547	9345	4239	5106
13	East	ABC	1/16/2015	Excellent Doghouse Corp	558	11628	5093	6535
14	West	DEF	1/19/2015	Vivid Edger Co	100	2042	983	1059

Browsing Four "Recommended" Pivot Tables Using the Quick Analysis Icon

The Excel team added two new entry points for pivot tables in Excel 2013. These are designed to give you inspiration and ideas of how you might want to summarize your data.

Select your entire data set by using Ctrl+*. A Quick Analysis icon displays to the right of the data, as shown in Figure 23.2.

Figure 23.2

Select the entire data set to cause the Quick Analysis icon to appear.

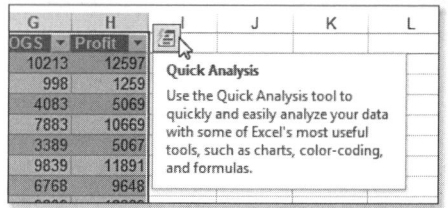

G	H		J	K	L
OGS ▾	Profit ▾				
10213	12597		**Quick Analysis**		
998	1259				
4083	5069		Use the Quick Analysis tool to		
7883	10669		quickly and easily analyze your data		
3389	5067		with some of Excel's most useful		
9839	11891		tools, such as charts, color-coding,		
6768	9648		and formulas.		

Click the Quick Analysis icon, and then choose Tables from across the top. The second through fifth icons offer four basic pivot tables. Hover over each icon to see a preview of the pivot table, as shown in Figure 23.3.

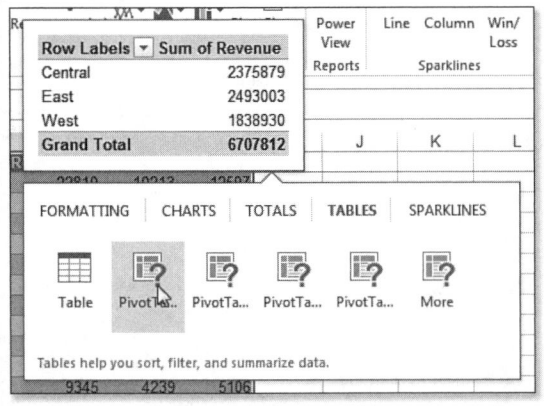

If one of those pivot tables looks correct or even close to correct, click the icon to create the pivot table on a new worksheet. Because pivot tables are easy to change, you can rearrange or reformat after the pivot table is created.

The sixth icon, called More Pivot Tables, leads to the Recommended Pivot Table dialog, discussed in the next section.

Browsing Ten "Recommended" Pivot Tables

The Quick Analysis described in the previous section is designed to allow people who have never heard of pivot tables to discover them. If you are reading this chapter, you are aware of pivot tables. You can save a few mouse clicks by starting with the Recommended Pivot Table dialog.

Select a single cell in your data. On the Insert tab, choose Recommended Pivot Tables. Excel displays a dialog with 10 pivot tables down the left side. Click each pivot table to see a preview of the pivot table in the dialog (see Figure 23.4). When you find one that is close, click OK to create that pivot table on a new worksheet.

Is it worthwhile to use the Recommended Pivot Tables dialog? The 10 suggestions are not perfect, but many near the top of the list are a great starting point. Provided that you want your pivot table to appear on a new worksheet, and provided that you are building a pivot table from a single table, then you lose nothing by using Insert, Recommended Pivot Table, OK instead of Insert, Pivot Table, OK. At the very least, you start with two common fields in your pivot table and are usually two mouse clicks closer to being finished with the pivot table.

The rules for choosing the recommended pivot tables are fairly complex. Microsoft is filing for a patent on this algorithm. Although this is great for them, it is bad for you because the Excel team is keeping quiet on the exact rules until the patent has been filed. Through some reverse engineering, I believe some of the rules for deciding on the top 10 pivot tables are as follows:

Figure 23.4
Excel uses heuristics to guess at 10 pivot tables that make sense.

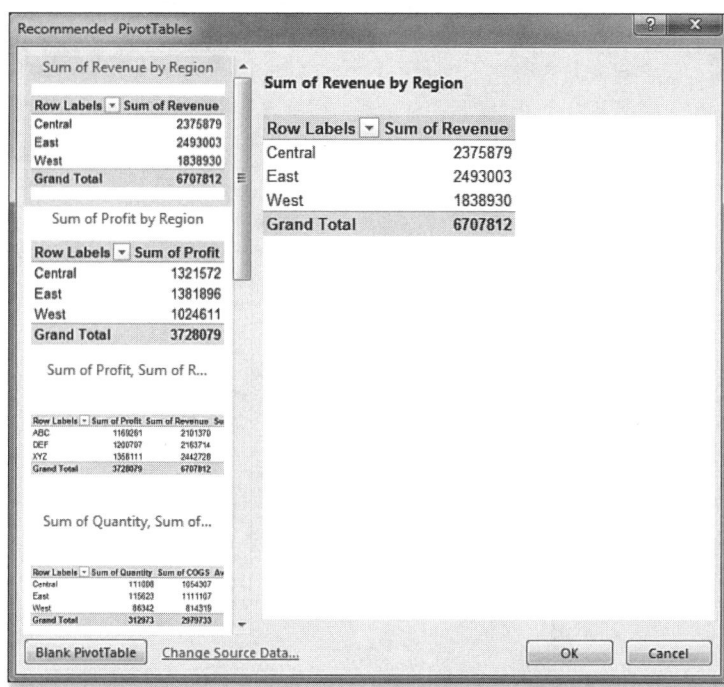

- If you have a numeric field with a label of Revenue, then that field is always given priority and appears in the first few pivot tables.

- If you use Sales instead of Revenue, then Excel looks for a field called Profit.

- If Excel does not recognize any of the numeric field headings, then it looks for the field with the largest total or the field on the right for the first few recommended pivot tables.

- Excel analyzes the text fields to determine the number of unique values for each field. The two fields with the fewest unique values are often suggested as the row fields in the first four pivot tables.

- Three of the 10 pivot tables offer multiple numeric fields going across the report. At least one of those offers a Count or Average of one field.

- The final three pivot tables might contain an attempt to offer a cross-tab report, with fields in Row and Column, or with two fields in the row field. This logic is the weakest. In 50+ experiments, the logical combinations of Customers and Products or Region and Product only appeared in 6% of the trials. Hopefully, the Excel team can refine this logic over time.

Starting with a Blank Pivot Table

The traditional method for creating a pivot table is to create a blank one. Choose one cell in your data. Select Pivot Table from the Insert tab. Excel displays the Create PivotTable dialog, as shown in Figure 23.5.

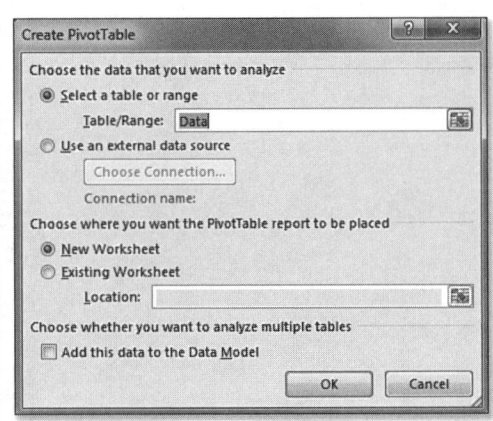

Figure 23.5
Using the Create PivotTable dialog, you can choose where to place the pivot table.

This dialog confirms the range of your data. Provided you have no blank rows or blank columns, Excel normally gets this right. In Figure 23.5, the underlying data has been made into a table using Ctrl+T and renamed as Data. You could instead choose to use an external data source.

Using the Create PivotTable dialog, you have the choice of creating the pivot table on a new blank worksheet or in an existing location. You might decide to put the pivot table in J2 on this worksheet, or next to another existing pivot table or pivot chart if you plan on building a dashboard of several pivot tables.

New in Excel 2013, you can build a pivot table from a relational model by checking the Add This Data to the Data Model check box. For details on building a pivot table from two or more tables, see Chapter 25, "Mashing Up Data with PowerPivot."

Adding Fields to Your Pivot Table Using the Field List

If you started with a blank pivot table, you see a Field Table Field panel that looks like Figure 23.6. The graphic shown in columns A:C is a placeholder to indicate where the pivot table will appear after you choose some fields. The PivotTable Fields area has a list of fields from your original data set at the top and four drop zones at the bottom. To build your report, you add fields to the drop zones at the bottom.

Figure 23.6
A blank pivot table and the PivotTable Fields list.

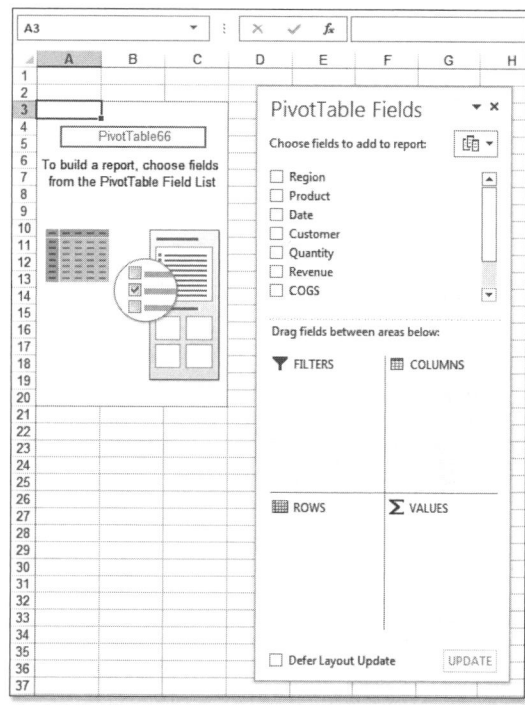

 Note

The field list is generally docked to the right side of the Excel window. The figures in this book show the field list as undocked. To undock the field list, drag the title bar away from the edge of the window. It is hard to redock the field list. You have to grab the left side of the title bar and drag the field list more than 50% off the right side of the Excel window.

If you built your pivot table using the Quick Analysis icon or the Recommended Pivot Table dialog, you already see a few fields in the drop zones and a few fields in the report. Figure 23.7 shows the initial pivot table and field list when you choose Sum of Revenue by Region.

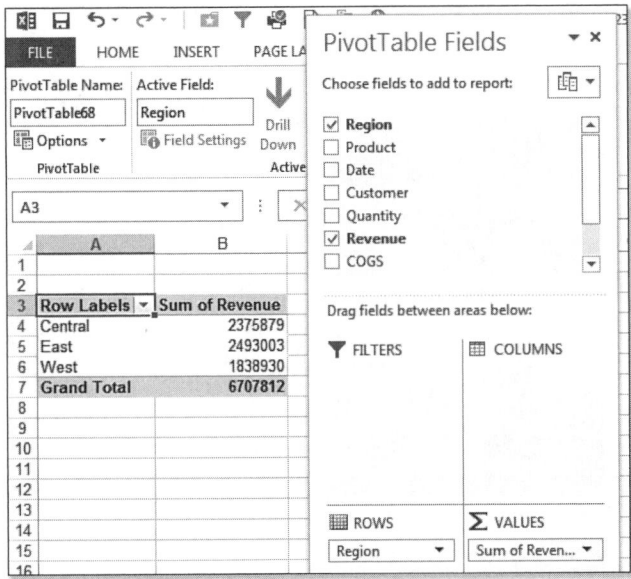

Figure 23.7
If you choose a Recommended Pivot Table, the first few fields are added to the pivot table.

Changing the Pivot Table Report by Using the Field List

If you are starting with Figure 23.6, check the Region, Product, and Revenue fields. If you are starting with Figure 23.7, check the Product field.

When you check a text or date field, that field automatically moves to the ROWS drop zone in the Pivot Table Field List. When you check a numeric field, that field moves to the VALUES drop zone and is changed to Sum of *Field*.

By choosing Region, Product, and Revenue, you see Sum of Revenue by region and product, as shown in Figure 23.8.

You can further customize the pivot table by moving fields around in the drop zones. For example, drag the Region field so it is below the Product field in the ROWS drop zone. The report updates to show Regions within Product, as shown in Figure 23.9.

Drag the Region field from the ROWS drop zone to the COLUMNS drop zone, and you have a cross-tab report, as shown in Figure 23.10.

Figure 23.8
Check fields in the top of the field list to build this report.

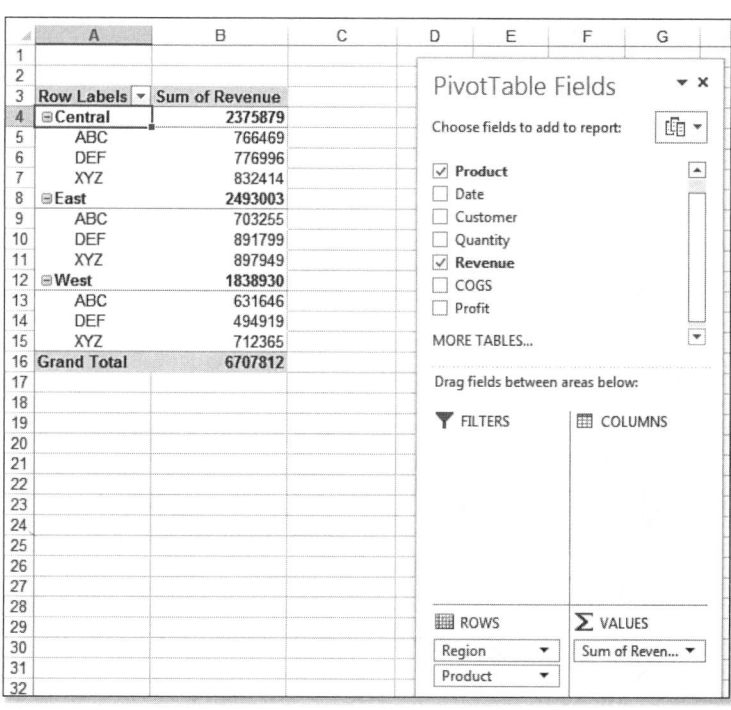

Figure 23.9
Drag the Region field to appear after the Product field in the ROWS drop zone to change the report.

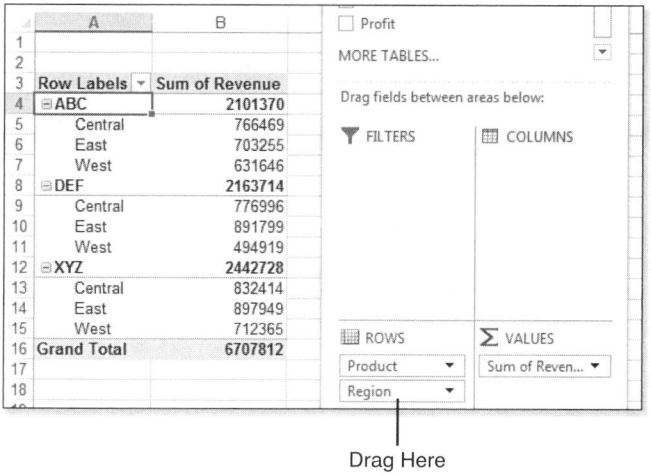

Drag Here

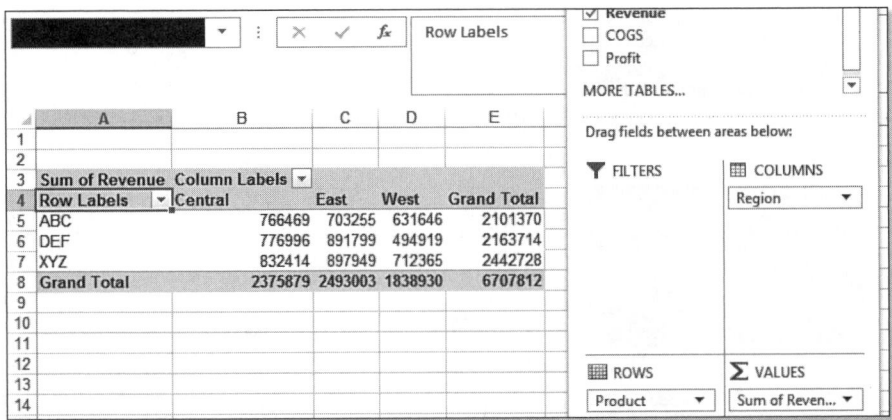

Figure 23.10
Pivot the Region field to the columns of the report.

Dealing with the Compact Layout

If you've been using pivot tables for many versions of Excel, you have to wonder about the bizarre layout of the pivot table in Figure 23.8. The totals appear at the top of each group instead of at the bottom. Two fields, Region and Product, appear in column A. Collapse buttons appear next to the regions.

This is a report layout called Compact Form. Introduced in Excel 2007, it is beautiful if you plan to present your pivot table in an interactive touch-screen kiosk complete with slicers. However, if you plan to reuse the results of the pivot table, the Compact Form is horrible. Every pivot table you create in the Excel interface starts with Compact Form. Here is how to go back to the Tabular Form layout:

1. Make sure that the active cell is inside the pivot table.

2. Go to the Design tab in the ribbon. Open the Report Layout drop-down. Select Show in Tabular Form. As shown in Figure 23.11, the totals move back to the bottom of each region. Also, Product moves to column B.

3. Open the Report Layout drop-down and select Repeat All Item Labels. This eliminates the blanks in column A of the pivot table, as shown in Figure 23.12. This is a feature that has been badly needed in Excel for 15 years. It was finally added to Excel 2010.

Figure 23.11
Change from
Compact Form to
Tabular Form to
put each field in a
new column.

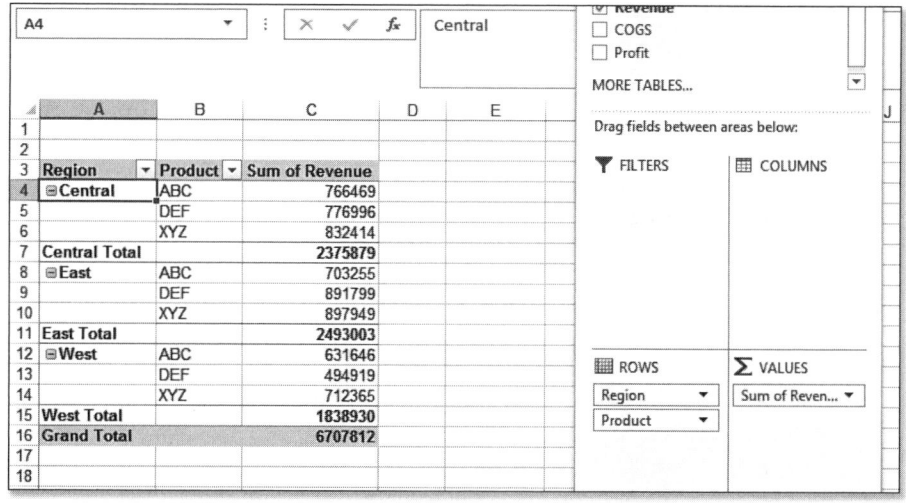

Figure 23.12
Using Repeat All Item Labels fills in blanks in the row area.

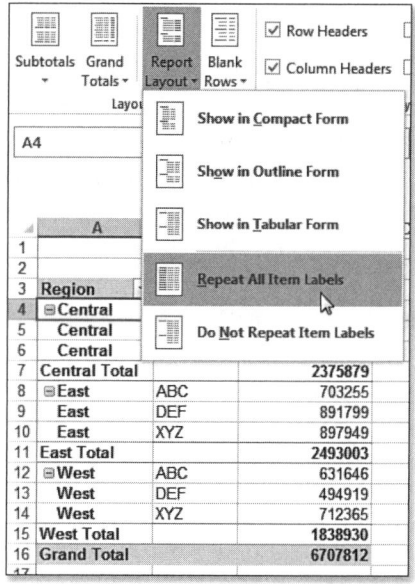

Rearranging a Pivot Table

The drop zone sections of the PivotTable Fields list box are as follows:

- **Filter**—You use this section to limit the report to only certain criteria. This section is analogous to the PageField section in the old pivot table model. It is virtually replaced by the new slicer feature.

  ➡ *To learn more about filtering pivot tables,* **see** *"Filtering Using Filter Fields,"* **p. 797.**

- **Rows**—This section is for fields that appear on the left side of the table. By default, all text fields move here when you select the check boxes in the top of the field list.

- **Columns**—This section is for fields that stretch along the top rows of columns of your table. Old database geeks refer to this as a *crosstab report.*

- **Values**—This section is for all the numeric fields that are summarized in the table. By default, most fields are automatically summed, but you can change the default calculation to an average, minimum, maximum, or other calculation.

You can add fields to a drop zone by dragging from the top of the PivotTable Fields list to a drop zone, or by dragging from one drop zone to another. To remove a field from a drop zone, drag the field from the drop zone to outside of the PivotTable Fields list.

Finishing Touches: Numeric Formatting and Removing Blanks

After you arrange your data in the report, you want to consider formatting the numeric fields. For example, the pivot table in Figure 23.13 has Customer and Product in the ROWS drop zone, Region in COLUMNS, and Revenue in VALUES. It would be helpful if the numbers were formatted with commas as thousands separators. Also, consider changing the words Sum of Revenue to something less awkward, such as Total Revenue or even Revenue.

3	Sum of Revenue		Region ▾			
4	Customer	▾ Product ▾	Central	East	West	Grand Total
5	⊟Agile Calculator Inc.	ABC			15104	15104
6	Agile Calculator Inc.	DEF	4060	14004		18064
7	Agile Calculator Inc.	XYZ			18072	18072
8	Agile Calculator Inc. Total		4060	14004	33176	51240
9	⊟Cool Bottle Co	ABC	37600	75912	28900	142412
10	Cool Bottle Co	DEF	84778	51445	46532	182755
11	Cool Bottle Co	XYZ	28932	72625	72213	173770
12	Cool Bottle Co Total		151310	199982	147645	498937
13	⊟Crisp Opener Partners	ABC	24003	89960		113963

Figure 23.13
You should add numeric formatting to this pivot table.

Follow these steps to apply a numeric format to the Revenue field:

1. Select one cell that contains a revenue amount. If you look on the Analyze tab, you see a box that reports the active field. By choosing a cell with Revenue, the Active Field box indicates that Sum of Revenue is the active field.

2. Click the Field Settings icon in the Active Field group of the Analyze tab. Excel displays the Value Field Settings dialog.

3. The label for this field appears in the Custom Name box at the top of the dialog. Change Sum of Revenue by typing a space and then the word *Revenue*. Note that the space is critical. You cannot use just the word *Revenue* without a space because this would create a duplicate field name.

4. Click the Number Format button in the bottom of the Value Field Settings dialog. Excel displays the familiar Number tab of the Format Cells dialog.

5. Select the Number category. Select 0 decimal places. Add a thousands separator. Click OK to close the Format Cells dialog. Click OK to close the Value Field Settings dialog.

Figure 23.14 shows the new number format applied to the pivot table, along with the Field Settings icon and the Value Field Settings dialog.

Figure 23.14
You should add numeric formatting to this pivot table.

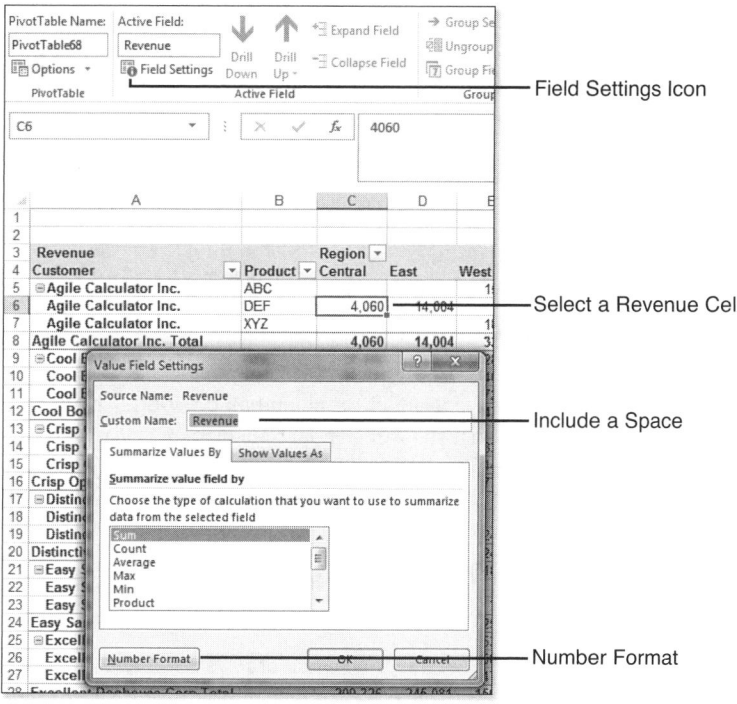

- Field Settings Icon
- Select a Revenue Cell
- Include a Space
- Number Format

Caution

Avoid the temptation to format cells B5:F113 using the formatting commands on the Home tab. This formats the current pivot table, but as you continue to add fields to the pivot table later, the shape of the pivot table will change and the Home tab formatting will not stick. When you go through the process previously described, the Revenue field will continue to have the correct format.

Notice the blank cells in the values area of the pivot table. For example, the blank cell in C5 of the pivot table means that there are no records in the data set where Agile Calculator bought product ABC in the Central region. You would probably rather have zeros in those cells instead of blanks. You will perform the following steps so often, you will wonder why Microsoft did not make this the default choice:

1. Select any one cell inside the pivot table.

2. On the Analyze tab, select the Options icon on the left side of the ribbon.

3. On the Layout & Format tab of the PivotTable Options dialog, type **0** next to For Empty Cells Show.

4. Click OK. Excel fills in the empty cells with zeros.

Four Things You Have to Know When Using Pivot Tables

Pivot tables are the greatest invention in spreadsheets. However, you have to understand the following four issues, presented in order of importance.

Your Pivot Table Is in Manual Calculation Mode Until You Click Refresh!

Most people are shocked to learn that changes to underlying data do not appear in a pivot table. After all, you change a cell in Excel, and all the formulas derived from the cell automatically change. You would think that the same should hold true for pivot tables, but it does not. Pivot tables are fast because the original data from the worksheet is loaded into a pivot cache in memory. Until you click the Refresh icon on the Analyze ribbon, Excel does not pick up the changes to the underlying data.

One Blank Cell in a Value Column Causes Excel to Count Instead of Sum

Suppose your data set has thousands of rows of data. For any reason, if one of the revenue cells happens to be blank, this completely confuses Excel. There can be 999,999 cells with numbers and one blank cell, but Excel no longer realizes that the Revenue column is a numeric column. When you add Revenue to the pivot table, Excel decides to count the number of rows instead of summing the revenue. To correct the problem, you have two choices:

- Delete the pivot table, fill the blanks in the original data with zeros, and re-create the pivot table.

- Select one cell that contains Count of Revenue. Select the Field Settings icon, and then change from Count to Sum in that dialog.

If You Click Outside the Pivot Table, All the Pivot Table Tools Disappear

If your field list disappeared and the Options and Design tabs are missing, it is likely that you clicked outside of the pivot table.

I've had the argument with Microsoft that because nothing is on the worksheet other than the pivot table, I am still looking at the pivot table even when I click outside of the pivot table. I continue to lose this argument, however. If the field list disappears and the tabs are gone, click back inside your pivot table.

You Cannot Change, Move a Part of, or Insert Cells in a Pivot Table

Many times, pivot tables get you very close to the final report you want, and you just want to insert a row or move one bit of the table. You cannot do this. If you try, you will be greeted with the ubiquitous message that you cannot change a pivot table. This is a fair limitation. After all, Excel needs to figure out how to redraw the table when you move something in the field list.

The solution is to copy the entire pivot table and then use Paste Values to convert the report to regular Excel data. You can either put this on a new worksheet or paste the entire table back over itself. If you go to a new worksheet, you can continue to modify the original pivot table. If you paste values over the original worksheet, the pivot table converts to a range, and you cannot pivot it further.

Calculating and Roll-ups with Pivot Tables

Pivot tables offer many more calculation options than those shown so far in this chapter. One of the most amazing features of pivot tables built from regular data is the capability to roll daily dates up to months, quarters, and years.

Grouping Daily Dates to Months and Years

Good pivot tables start with good transactional data. Invariably, that transactional data is stored with daily dates instead of monthly summaries. It is easy to roll a pivot table up to months, quarters, and years.

To produce a summary by month, quarter, and year, follow these steps:

1. Build a pivot table with daily dates going down the row field, Region in the columns, and Sum of Revenue in the value area.

2. Select either the Date heading or one of the cells containing a date.

3. From the Analyze tab, select Group Field.

4. In the Group Field dialog, select Months, Quarters, and Years, as shown in Figure 23.15.

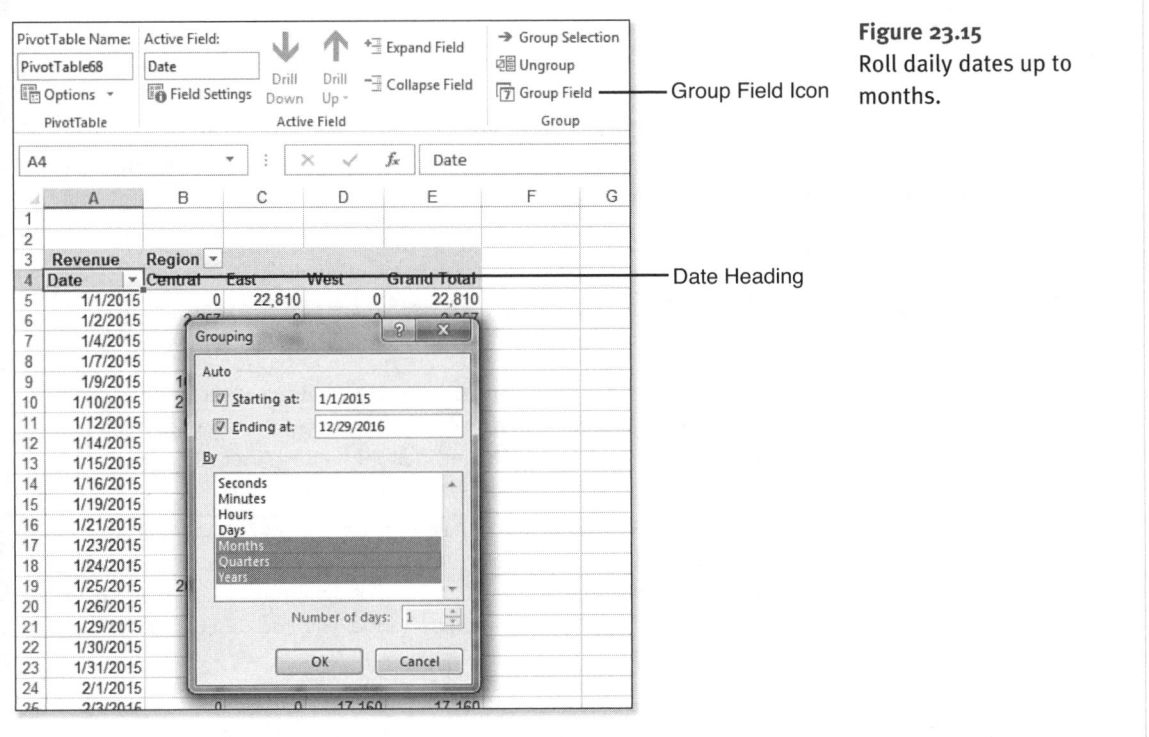

Figure 23.15
Roll daily dates up to months.

— Group Field Icon

— Date Heading

5. Click OK. Hundreds of daily dates are rolled up to 24 rows of monthly data. The resulting field has years, then quarters, and then months as row labels. Because of a strange bug, the year and quarter fields do not have subtotals (see Figure 23.16).

For an interesting alternative to the report in Figure 23.16, follow these steps:

1. Uncheck the Region field to remove Region from the report.

2. Drag the Years field from the ROWS area to the COLUMNS area.

3. Select a cell that contains a quarter. Select the Field Settings button in the Analyze tab and then select Automatic and click OK.

Figure 23.16
Excel rolls the daily date cells up to months, quarters, and years.

3	Revenue				Region ▾		
4	Years ▾	Quarter ▾	Date ▾	Central	East	West	Grand Total
5	⊟2015	⊟Qtr1	Jan	67,148	185,888	20,186	273,222
6	2015	Qtr1	Feb	125,777	107,311	68,532	301,620
7	2015	Qtr1	Mar	157,038	52,876	70,327	280,241
8	2015	⊟Qtr2	Apr	80,536	167,167	28,937	276,640
9	2015	Qtr2	May	82,869	142,275	106,932	332,076
10	2015	Qtr2	Jun	125,269	34,562	5,738	165,569
11	2015	⊟Qtr3	Jul	104,392	195,054	86,321	385,767
12	2015	Qtr3	Aug	84,506	91,362	135,877	311,745
13	2015	Qtr3	Sep	136,658	80,250	39,532	256,440
14	2015	⊟Qtr4	Oct	99,477	127,822	76,947	304,246
15	2015	Qtr4	Nov	87,735	70,427	73,710	231,872
16	2015	Qtr4	Dec	97,539	92,631	97,945	288,115
17	⊟2016	⊟Qtr1	Jan	88,926	104,726	81,284	274,936
18	2016	Qtr1	Feb	112,143	74,233	50,189	236,565
19	2016	Qtr1	Mar	48,871	71,197	96,493	216,561
20	2016	⊟Qtr2	Apr	116,859	95,456	79,688	292,003
21	2016	Qtr2	May	124,682	78,048	84,713	287,443
22	2016	Qtr2	Jun	59,892	131,188	50,803	241,883
23	2016	⊟Qtr3	Jul	105,153	109,579	81,119	295,851
24	2016	Qtr3	Aug	125,451	43,289	118,151	286,891
25	2016	Qtr3	Sep	82,744	102,477	31,855	217,076
26	2016	⊟Qtr4	Oct	105,000	136,024	67,962	308,986
27	2016	Qtr4	Nov	53,544	119,775	128,561	301,880
28	2016	Qtr4	Dec	103,670	79,386	157,128	340,184
29	Grand Total			2,375,879	2,493,003	1,838,930	6,707,812

You now have a pivot table that provides totals by month and quarter and compares years going across the report (see Figure 23.17). Notice that your pivot table field list includes three fields related to dates: The years and quarters fields are virtual fields. The original Date field includes the months. This was a brilliant design decision on Microsoft's part because it allows years and months to be pivoted to different sections of the pivot table.

Figure 23.17
Pivot years to the column area to show year over year.

3	Revenue		Years ▾		
4	Quarters ▾	Date ▾	2015	2016	Grand Total
5	⊟Qtr1	Jan	273,222	274,936	548,158
6	Qtr1	Feb	301,620	236,565	538,185
7	Qtr1	Mar	280,241	216,561	496,802
8	Qtr1 Total		855,083	728,062	1,583,145
9	⊟Qtr2	Apr	276,640	292,003	568,643
10	Qtr2	May	332,076	287,443	619,519
11	Qtr2	Jun	165,569	241,883	407,452
12	Qtr2 Total		774,285	821,329	1,595,614
13	⊟Qtr3	Jul	385,767	295,851	681,618
14	Qtr3	Aug	311,745	286,891	598,636
15	Qtr3	Sep	256,440	217,076	473,516
16	Qtr3 Total		953,952	799,818	1,753,770
17	⊟Qtr4	Oct	304,246	308,986	613,232
18	Qtr4	Nov	231,872	301,880	533,752
19	Qtr4	Dec	288,115	340,184	628,299
20	Qtr4 Total		824,233	951,050	1,775,283
21	Grand Total		3,407,553	3,300,259	6,707,812

Adding Calculations Outside the Pivot Table

Figure 23.18 shows % Growth instead of Grand Total in column E. However, after you group the dates in the pivot table, you are prevented from adding a calculated item inside the pivot table, so you have to turn back to regular Excel to provide the % Growth column.

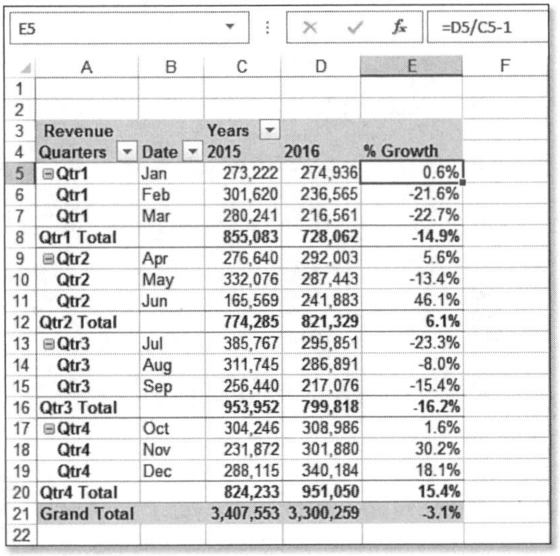

	A	B	C	D	E	F
1						
2						
3	Revenue		Years			
4	Quarters	Date	2015	2016	% Growth	
5	⊟Qtr1	Jan	273,222	274,936	0.6%	
6	Qtr1	Feb	301,620	236,565	-21.6%	
7	Qtr1	Mar	280,241	216,561	-22.7%	
8	Qtr1 Total		855,083	728,062	-14.9%	
9	⊟Qtr2	Apr	276,640	292,003	5.6%	
10	Qtr2	May	332,076	287,443	-13.4%	
11	Qtr2	Jun	165,569	241,883	46.1%	
12	Qtr2 Total		774,285	821,329	6.1%	
13	⊟Qtr3	Jul	385,767	295,851	-23.3%	
14	Qtr3	Aug	311,745	286,891	-8.0%	
15	Qtr3	Sep	256,440	217,076	-15.4%	
16	Qtr3 Total		953,952	799,818	-16.2%	
17	⊟Qtr4	Oct	304,246	308,986	1.6%	
18	Qtr4	Nov	231,872	301,880	30.2%	
19	Qtr4	Dec	288,115	340,184	18.1%	
20	Qtr4 Total		824,233	951,050	15.4%	
21	Grand Total		3,407,553	3,300,259	-3.1%	
22						

Figure 23.18
The % Growth column is a regular formula outside the pivot table, formatted to look like it is part of the pivot table.

However, it is not simple for Excel to create that column. In particular, step 3 trips up most people. Follow these steps:

1. Select one cell in the pivot table. Go to the Design tab and choose Grand Totals, On For Rows Only. This command removes the Grand Total column.
2. Copy D3:D21. Use Paste, Paste Special Formats to copy the formatting to E3.
3. In cell E5, type **=D5/C5-1**. You really have to type this formula! Do not touch the mouse or the arrow keys while you are building the formula, or you will be stung by the GetPivotData bug.
4. Format cell E5 as a percentage with one decimal place.
5. Copy cell E5.
6. Select E5:E21. Open the Paste drop-down and select the Formulas & Number Formatting icon. (It is the icon with % and fx symbols.)

Changing the Calculation of a Field

By default, a numeric column will be added to the pivot table with a default calculation of Sum. Excel offers 10 other calculations such as Average, Count, Max, and Min. Excel 2010 added several new calculations and did a great job of bringing the old calculations to the forefront by adding the Show Values As drop-down to the Pivot Table Options tab.

For this section, the figures start with a completely new pivot table. You can follow along with these steps:

1. Delete the worksheet that contains the pivot table from the previous examples. This clears the pivot cache from memory.

2. Select one cell on the Data worksheet.

3. Choose Insert, Pivot Table.

4. Add a check next to the Region, Product, and Revenue fields. Check Quantity and Profit. You end up with a default pivot table showing Sum of Revenue, Sum of Quantity, and Sum of Profit, as shown in Figure 23.19.

Figure 23.19
This new pivot table starts with three numeric columns that default to Sum.

C4				f_x	111008
	A	B	C	D	E

	Row Labels ▾	Sum of Revenue	Sum of Quantity	Sum of Profit
4	⊟Central	2375879	111008	1321572
5	ABC	766469	40319	425742
6	DEF	776996	34767	433448
7	XYZ	832414	35922	462382
8	⊟East	2493003	115623	1381896
9	ABC	703255	36229	393949
10	DEF	891799	39966	494891
11	XYZ	897949	39428	493056
12	⊟West	1838930	86342	1024611
13	ABC	631646	33473	349570
14	DEF	494919	22592	272368
15	XYZ	712365	30277	402673
16	Grand Total	6707812	312973	3728079

In column C, you would like a count of the number of records. Follow these steps to change column C from Sum of Quantity:

1. Select one cell in the C3:C16 range (that is, any cell that contains quantity or the heading above those cells).

2. On the Analyze tab, choose Field Settings. Excel displays the Value Field Settings dialog.

3. In the Value Field Settings dialog, choose Count instead of Sum.

4. In the Custom Name field, type **Count of Orders** or any other name that makes sense to you.

5. Click OK. Column C now shows a count of records instead of a sum (see Figure 23.20).

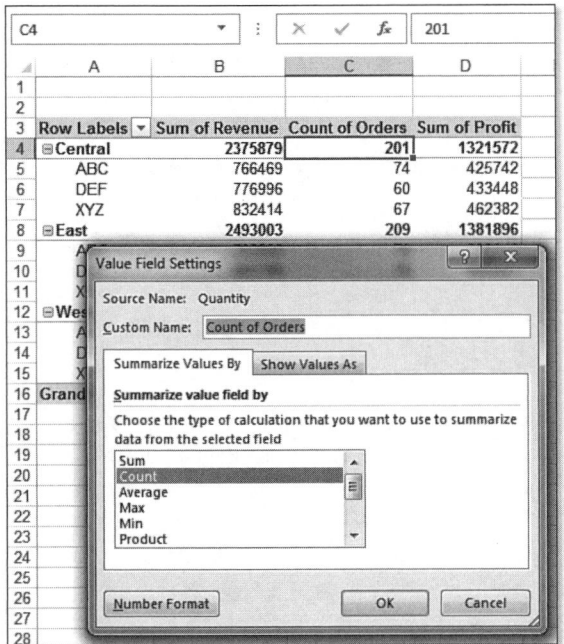

To change column D to show average profit, follow these steps:

1. Choose one cell in Sum of Profit column.

2. Click the Field Settings icon.

3. Change the calculation to Average.

4. Change the Custom Name field to **Avg Profit**.

5. Click the Number Format button.

6. Choose Currency with two decimal places.

7. Click OK twice to close the Format Cells and the Value Field Settings dialogs. Excel now shows Avg Profit in column D.

You can use a similar method to change to any of the 11 calculations offered in the Summarize Values By tab.

That's not all—there are more ways to show the values, as discussed in the next section.

Showing Percentage of Total Using Show Value As Settings

In addition to the 11 ways to summarize values, Excel 2013 offers 14 different calculation options on the second tab of the Value Field Settings dialog. These settings have undergone changes in recent versions:

- These settings had been promoted to a drop-down on the ribbon in Excel 2010 but have been banished back to the Value Field Settings dialog in Excel 2013. This is no great loss because many of the settings required additional choices that were not available in the drop-down.

- Excel 2010 introduced new calculations such as Percentage of Parent, Rank, and Running Percentage Total. These calculations are still available.

- Typically, most people consider the calculations on the two tabs in Value Field Settings to be mutually exclusive. But with some of the new calculations, it could make sense to combine a calculation. You might choose Average Revenue on the Summarize Values By tab and then choose Rank Largest to Smallest on the Show Values As tab.

To experiment with these 14 calculations, drag the Revenue field to the VALUES drop zone two more times. Follow these steps:

1. Select a cell in column E of the pivot table. This is the second revenue column. Choose the Field Settings icon in the Analyze tab. Select the second tab in the Value Field Settings dialog. Choose % of Column Total from the drop-down. Change the Custom Name to % of Total. Click OK.

2. Select a cell in column F of the pivot table. This is the third revenue column. Choose the Field Settings icon in the Analyze tab. Select the second tab in the Value Field Settings dialog. Choose % of Parent Row Total from the drop-down. Change the Custom Name to % of Parent. Click OK.

Figure 23.21 shows the result. In row 5, the $766,469 of revenue in B5 is 11.43% of the grand total revenue. E5 shows 11.43%. The calculation in F5 was added in Excel 2010. It shows that the revenue in B5 is 32.26% of the Central region revenue shown in B4.

Figure 23.21
Use Show Values As for 14 additional calculations.

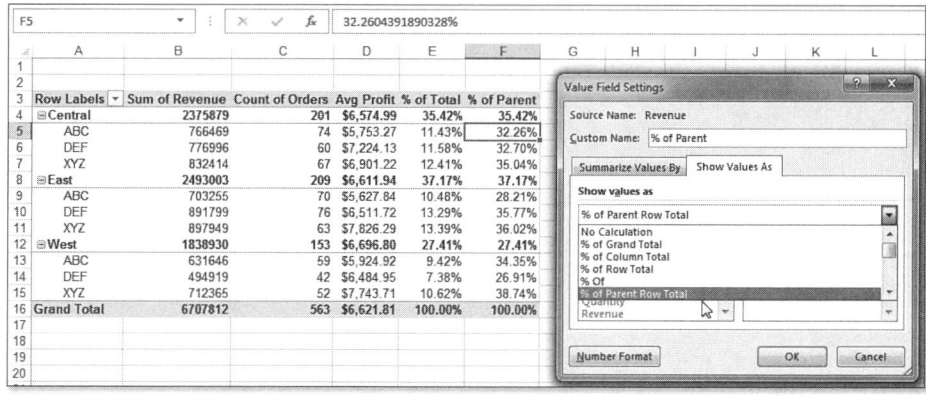

Showing Running Totals and Rank

Other options in the Show Values As drop-down include running totals and a ranking. These work best when there is only one field in the row area.

Delete the worksheet that contains the existing pivot table. Build a new pivot table with Customer in the ROWS area. Drag Revenue six times to the VALUES area.

Initially, the customers are sorted alphabetically. Open the Row Labels drop-down in cell A3. Choose More Sort Options. In the Sort (Customer) dialog, choose Descending (Z to A) By. In the drop-down, choose Sum of Revenue. Click OK. The pivot table shows the largest customers at the top.

To change the calculation in each column, follow these steps:

1. Choose cell B3. Click Field Settings. Change the Custom Name to **Revenue** with a leading space. Click Number Format. Choose Currency with 0 decimal places. Click OK twice.

2. Choose cell C3. Click Field Settings. On the Show Values As tab, choose Running Total In. In the Base Field list, choose Customer. Change the Custom Name to **Accum. Total**. Click Number Format. Choose Currency with 0 decimal places. Click OK twice.

3. Choose cell D3. Click Field Settings. On the Show Values As tab, choose % Running Total In. In the Base Field list, choose Customer. Change the Custom Name to **Accum. %**. Click Number Format. Choose Percentage with 1 decimal places. Click OK twice.

4. Choose cell E3. Click Field Settings. On the Show Values As tab, choose Rank Largest to Smallest. In the Base Field list, choose Customer. Change the Custom Name to **Rank**. Click OK.

5. Choose cell F3. Click Field Settings. On the Show Values As tab, choose % of Column Total. Change the Custom Name to **% of Total**. Click Percentage 1 decimal places. Click OK twice.

6. Choose cell G3. Click Field Settings. On the Show Values As tab, choose % Of. In the Base Field list, choose Customer. In the Base Item field, you can choose (previous), (next), or a specific customer. Because the largest customer is Wonderful Kettle Corporation, choose that customer as the Base Item setting. Change the Custom Name to **% of WKC**. Choose the Number Format button. Click Percentage 1 decimal places. Click OK twice.

The resulting pivot table in Figure 23.22 shows examples of the 14 different Show Values As options. Note that many of the options require the choice of a base field. A few also require that you select a base item.

Figure 23.22
Columns C:G are created using the Show Values As tab.

3	Row Labels	Revenue	Accum. Total	Accum. %	Rank	% of Total	% of WKC
4	Wonderful Kettle Corp	$869,454	$869,454	13.0%	1	13.0%	100.0%
5	Improved Vegetable Inc.	$750,163	$1,619,617	24.1%	2	11.2%	86.3%
6	Flexible Aerobic Co	$704,359	$2,323,976	34.6%	3	10.5%	81.0%
7	Functional Eggbeater Co	$622,794	$2,946,770	43.9%	4	9.3%	71.6%
8	Excellent Doghouse Corp	$613,514	$3,560,284	53.1%	5	9.1%	70.6%
9	Guaranteed Paint Co	$568,851	$4,129,135	61.6%	6	8.5%	65.4%
10	Cool Bottle Co	$498,937	$4,628,072	69.0%	7	7.4%	57.4%
11	Matchless Hardware Traders	$427,349	$5,055,421	75.4%	8	6.4%	49.2%
12	Crisp Opener Partners	$406,326	$5,461,747	81.4%	9	6.1%	46.7%
13	Vivid Edger Co	$390,978	$5,852,725	87.3%	10	5.8%	45.0%
14	Supreme Clipboard Inc.	$72,680	$5,925,405	88.3%	11	1.1%	8.4%
15	Distinctive Oven Co	$71,651	$5,997,056	89.4%	12	1.1%	8.2%
16	New Faucet Co	$62,744	$6,059,800	90.3%	13	0.9%	7.2%
17	Savory Opener Inc.	$60,299	$6,120,099	91.2%	14	0.9%	6.9%
18	Tremendous Thermostat Partners	$59,881	$6,179,980	92.1%	15	0.9%	6.9%
19	Fine Shingle Supply	$57,516	$6,237,496	93.0%	16	0.9%	6.6%
20	Magnificent Shingle Corp	$55,251	$6,292,747	93.8%	17	0.8%	6.4%
21	Easy Sandal Co	$54,048	$6,346,795	94.6%	18	0.8%	6.2%
22	Agile Calculator Inc.	$51,240	$6,398,035	95.4%	19	0.8%	5.9%
23	Special Luggage Inc.	$50,030	$6,448,065	96.1%	20	0.7%	5.8%
24	Mouthwatering Bicycle Corp	$46,717	$6,494,782	96.8%	21	0.7%	5.4%
25	Powerful Edger Supply	$42,316	$6,537,098	97.5%	22	0.6%	4.9%
26	Exclusive Washer Corp	$39,250	$6,576,348	98.0%	23	0.6%	4.5%
27	Sure Linen Corp	$34,710	$6,611,058	98.6%	24	0.5%	4.0%
28	Trendy Notebook Corp	$34,364	$6,645,422	99.1%	25	0.5%	4.0%
29	Inventive Door Inc.	$31,369	$6,676,791	99.5%	26	0.5%	3.6%
30	Rare Door Inc.	$31,021	$6,707,812	100.0%	27	0.5%	3.6%
31	**Grand Total**	**$6,707,812**				100.0%	

Using a Formula to Add a Field to a Pivot Table

The previous examples took an existing field and used the Show Values As setting to change how the data is presented in the pivot table. In this example, you learn how to add a brand-new calculated field to the pivot table. Follow these steps:

1. Select one of the numeric cells in the pivot table.

2. On the Analyze tab in the ribbon, choose Fields, Items, & Sets. Choose Calculated Field from the drop-down. (If this option is grayed out, choose a cell in the value area of the pivot table.) Excel displays the Insert Calculated Field dialog. The default field name of Field 1 and the default formula of =0 appear in the dialog.

3. Type a new name, such as **GP%**.

4. The Formula field starts out as an equal sign, a space, and then a zero. You have to click in this field and backspace to remove the zero.

5. Build the formula by double-clicking Profit, typing a slash, and then double-clicking Revenue. The dialog box should look like Figure 23.23. Click OK.

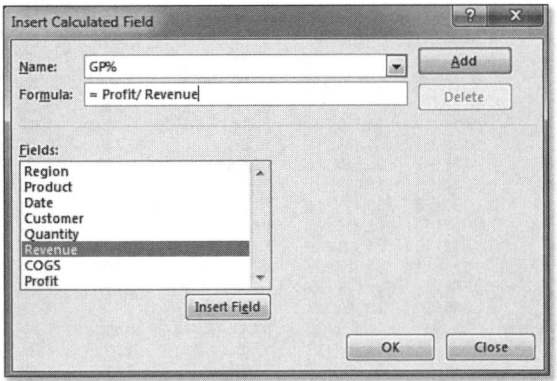

Figure 23.23
Build a calculated field.

6. The headings for calculated fields always appear strange. Select a cell in column H and choose Field Settings. Change the Custom Name from Sum of GP% to **GP%** with a leading space. Change the Number Format to Percentage with 1 decimal. Click OK twice. The final pivot table is shown in Figure 23.24.

Row Labels	Revenue	Accum. Total	Accum. %	Rank	% of Total	% of WKC	GP%
Wonderful Kettle Corp	$869,454	$869,454	13.0%	1	13.0%	100.0%	56.0%
Improved Vegetable Inc.	$750,163	$1,619,617	24.1%	2	11.2%	86.3%	55.4%
Flexible Aerobic Co	$704,359	$2,323,976	34.6%	3	10.5%	81.0%	55.8%
Functional Eggbeater Co	$622,794	$2,946,770	43.9%	4	9.3%	71.6%	55.8%
Excellent Doghouse Corp	$613,514	$3,560,284	53.1%	5	9.1%	70.6%	55.1%
Guaranteed Paint Co	$568,851	$4,129,135	61.6%	6	8.5%	65.4%	55.6%
Cool Bottle Co	$498,937	$4,628,072	69.0%	7	7.4%	57.4%	55.9%
Matchless Hardware Traders	$427,349	$5,055,421	75.4%	8	6.4%	49.2%	55.7%
Crisp Opener Partners	$406,326	$5,461,747	81.4%	9	6.1%	46.7%	56.0%
Vivid Edger Co	$390,978	$5,852,725	87.3%	10	5.8%	45.0%	54.6%
Supreme Clipboard Inc.	$72,680	$5,925,405	88.3%	11	1.1%	8.4%	56.0%
Distinctive Oven Co	$71,651	$5,997,056	89.4%	12	1.1%	8.2%	54.7%

Figure 23.24
This pivot table includes four value fields plus two calculated fields.

Formatting a Pivot Table

Excel offers a PivotTable Styles gallery on the Design tab. Instead, if you try to format individual cells in a pivot table, you will experience frustration. After you rearrange the pivot table, your manual formatting will be lost.

The PivotTable Styles gallery on the Design tab contains 73 built-in styles for a pivot table. These styles differ significantly from the hideous built-in styles available in Excel 2003. Whereas the AutoFormat styles in Excel 2003 would actually change the shape of a pivot table, the formatting styles in Excel 2013 apply a style to the table, without changing the structure.

The 73 styles are further modified by using the four check boxes for Banded Rows, Banded Columns, Row Headers, and Column Headers. Multiply that by the 49 color themes on the Page Layout tab, and you have 57,232 different styles. Multiply by the three report layouts, two options for blank rows, Grand Totals On or Off for Rows or Columns, Subtotals Above or Below, and you have more than 2.7 million styles available for your pivot table. And, unlike the formats in Excel 2003, all of these styles look good!

You can also build new styles. For example, if you would like the banded rows to be two rows tall, you can design a style for that.

To format a pivot table, select Banded Rows, Row Headers, and Column Headers from the Design tab of the ribbon. Then open the Styles gallery. Figure 23.25 shows some of the choices available in the gallery.

Figure 23.25
Select a style from the gallery on the Design tab.

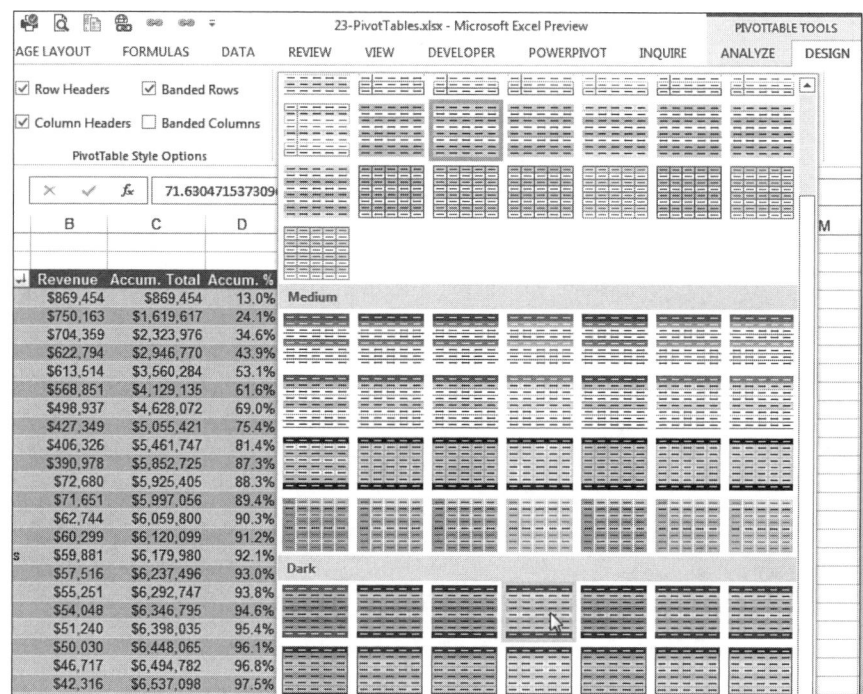

Finding More Information on Pivot Tables

Chapter 24 covers slicers and other ways to filter a pivot table.

Chapter 25, "Mashing Up Data with PowerPivot," covers creating pivot tables from multiple tables, the new PowerPivot add-in. Chapter 26 covers the Power View and GeoFlow add-ins.

For more information on pivot tables, check out my other books on the subject:

- *Excel 2013 Pivot Table Data Crunching* (Que, ISBN 978-0-7897-4875-1), coauthored with Mike Alexander

- *PowerPivot for the Excel Data Analyst* (Que, ISBN 978-0-7897-4315-2)

USING SLICERS AND FILTERING A PIVOT TABLE

Pivot table filters have been quietly evolving over the past several versions of Excel. Back in Excel 2003, you were able to select multiple items in the row labels filter. In Excel 2007, you could select multiple items in the page filter. Finally, in Excel 2010, you see the vision of where this work was leading. Excel 2010 pivot tables introduced a visual filter called a *slicer*. Slicers enable you to perform ad-hoc analysis by choosing various items from various fields in the pivot table. Excel 2013 adds a new date-centric visual filter called a *timeline*.

Filtering Using the Row Label Filter

To follow along, create a new pivot table from the 24-Slicers.xlsx file. Check the Customer, Date, Quantity, Revenue, COGS, and Profit fields. On the Design tab, open the Report Layout drop-down. Choose Tabular form and then choose Repeat All Item Labels. Choose the Banded Rows check box on the Design tab. You will end up with the pivot table shown in Figure 24.1. Drop-downs in cells A3 and B3 lead to the row filter menus.

Figure 24.1
Drop-downs in A3 and B3 lead to filters for Customer and Date.

	A	B	
1			
2			
3	Customer ▼	Date ▼	Sum c
4	⊟Agile Calculator Inc.	8/31/2015	
5	Agile Calculator Inc.	4/13/2016	
6	Agile Calculator Inc.	6/24/2016	
7	Agile Calculator Inc.	11/4/2016	
8	Agile Calculator Inc. Total		
9	⊟Cool Bottle Co	1/14/2015	

Figure 24.2 shows the Filter menu for the Customer field. This drop-down contains four separate filter mechanisms:

- The Label Filters fly-out menu appears for fields that contain text values. You can use this fly-out to select customer names that contain certain words, begin with, end with, or fall between certain letters.

- The Value Filters fly-out menu enables you to filter the customers based on values elsewhere in the pivot table. If you want only orders over $20,000, or if you want to see the Top 10 customers, use the Values Filter fly-out.

- The Search box was added in Excel 2010 and is similar to using Label Filters, but faster.

- The check boxes enable you to exclude individual customers, or you can clear or select all customers by using Select All.

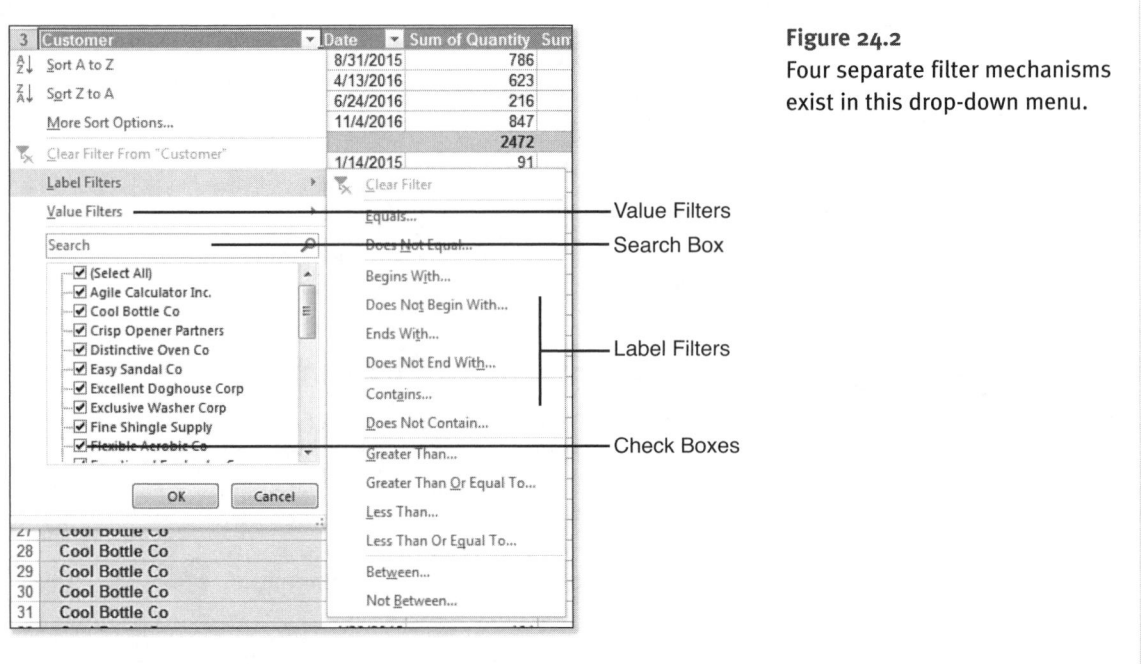

Figure 24.2
Four separate filter mechanisms exist in this drop-down menu.

Figure 24.3 shows the detail of the Value Filter fly-out. All these filters except Top 10 were new in Excel 2007.

When you access the filter drop-down for a field that contains 100% dates, the Label Filters fly-out is replaced by a Date Filters fly-out, as shown in Figure 24.4. This fly-out offers conceptual filters, such as Last Month, Next Quarter, and This Year. The All Dates in Period choice leads to a second fly-out where you can choose based on month or quarter.

Figure 24.3
Detail of the Value Filters fly-out.

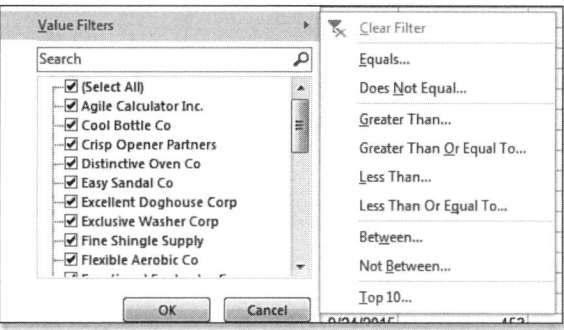

Figure 24.4
The Date Filters fly-outs appear when your field contains all date values.

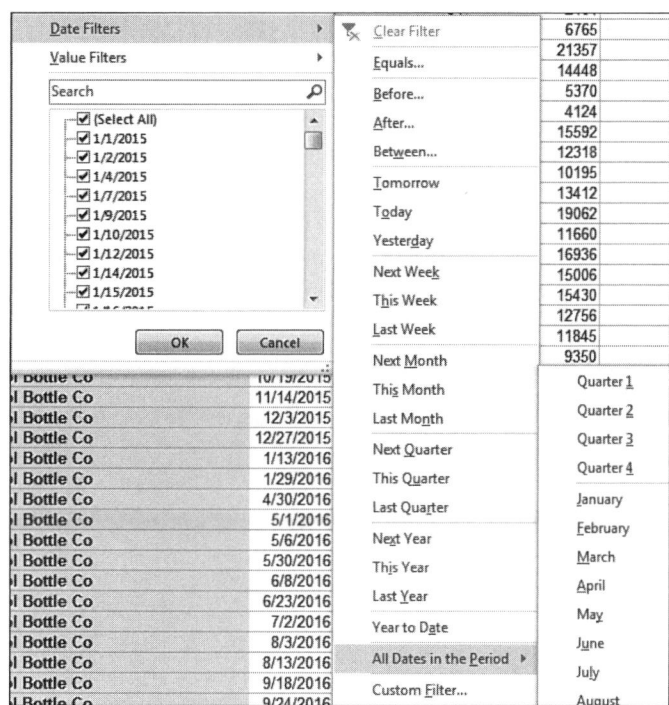

Filtering Using the Search Box

The Search box was added in Excel 2010 and works amazingly well. The Search box lets you filter to labels that include a certain word. The power of the Search box is when you go back to it a second time to search for another word. You can add the results of the second search to the results from the first search.

Here is an example:

1. Open the Customer filter drop-down. Type **Shingle** into the search box. Pause for a moment, and Excel shows the customers who contain "shingle" in their name. By default, a special check box called (Select All Search Results) is selected (see Figure 24.5). Click OK to filter the pivot table to the "shingle" customers.

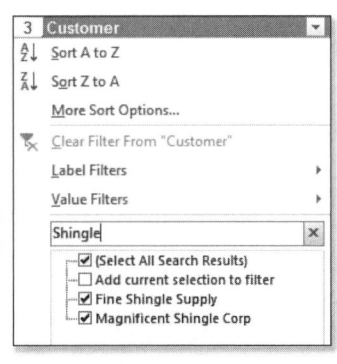

Figure 24.5
The first time you use search, it seems like an easier version of Label Contains.

2. Open the Customer filter drop-down again. Type **Door** into the search box. Pause for a moment. The "door" customers appear. This time, you want to select the check box called Add Current Selection to Filter (see Figure 24.6). Click OK.

Figure 24.6
The second time you use Search, the capability to add these results to the previous results makes the Search box powerful.

3. Repeat step 2 looking for customers with "faucet" in their name. Select Add Current Selection to Filter. Click OK.

The result shown in Figure 24.7 is a union of the customers returned by all three searches.

Figure 24.7
This pivot table contains all customers from three searches.

3	Customer	Date	Sum of Quantity	Sum of Revenue
4	⊟Fine Shingle Supply	4/28/2015	782	18264
5	Fine Shingle Supply	9/18/2015	788	16784
6	Fine Shingle Supply	10/5/2015	760	16936
7	Fine Shingle Supply	8/28/2016	337	5532
8	Fine Shingle Supply Total		2667	57516
9	⊟Inventive Door Inc.	7/17/2015	188	4158
10	Inventive Door Inc.	8/3/2015	561	13962
11	Inventive Door Inc.	10/21/2015	526	11220
12	Inventive Door Inc.	9/8/2016	137	2029
13	Inventive Door Inc. Total		1412	31369
14	⊟Magnificent Shingle Corp	5/19/2015	225	4846
15	Magnificent Shingle Corp	7/28/2015	1001	17840
16	Magnificent Shingle Corp	1/8/2016	928	21015
17	Magnificent Shingle Corp	9/9/2016	522	11550
18	Magnificent Shingle Corp Total		2676	55251
19	⊟New Faucet Co	7/2/2015	317	7167
20	New Faucet Co	7/26/2015	1046	23890
21	New Faucet Co	7/14/2016	664	14497
22	New Faucet Co	10/13/2016	1024	17190
23	New Faucet Co Total		3051	62744
24	⊟Rare Door Inc.	4/19/2015	206	4948
25	Rare Door Inc.	8/24/2015	806	17856
26	Rare Door Inc.	10/7/2015	93	2358
27	Rare Door Inc.	3/31/2016	307	5859
28	Rare Door Inc. Total		1412	31021
29	Grand Total		11218	237901

Clearing a Filter

To clear all filters in the pivot table, use the Clear icon in the Sort & Filter group of the Data tab. To clear filters from one field in the pivot table, open the filter drop-down for that field and select Clear Filter From "Field".

Filtering Using the Check Boxes

The Customer drop-down includes a list of all the customers in the database. If you need to exclude a few specific customers, you can clear their check boxes in the filter list.

The (Select All) item restores any cleared boxes. If all the boxes are already selected, clicking (Select All) clears all the boxes.

Because it is easier to select three customers than to clear 27, if you need to remove most of the items from the list of customers, you can follow these steps:

1. If any customers are cleared, select (Select All) to reselect all customers.

2. Select (Select All) to clear all customers.

3. Select the particular customers you want to view, as shown in Figure 24.8.

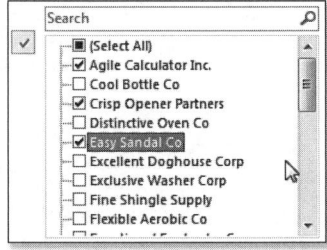

Figure 24.8
Select (Select All) to clear all customers and then select the few desired customers.

Filtering Using the Label Filter Fly-Out

All of the Label Filters choices shown previously in Figure 24.2 lead to the same dialog. Suppose that you are interested in finding all customers whose name ends in "Corp." Follow these steps:

1. Open the Customer filter drop-down.

2. Open the Label Filters fly-out.

3. Select Ends With. Excel displays the Label Filter dialog.

4. Type **Corp**, as shown in Figure 24.9. Click OK. The pivot table is filtered to customers whose name ends with "Corp."

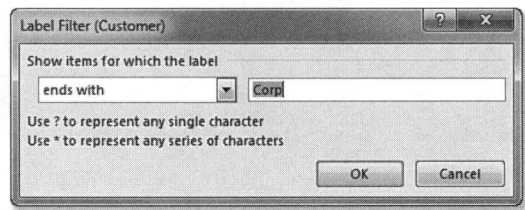

Figure 24.9
Look for customer names matching a pattern.

If you open the first drop-down in the Label Filter dialog, you see the following choices:

- equals

- does not equal

- is greater than

- is greater than or equal to

- is less than

- is less than or equal to

- begins with

- does not begin with

- ends with

- does not end with

- contains

- does not contain

- is between

- is not between

You can use the wildcards * and ?. Whereas * represents any character(s), the ? wildcard represents one single character.

Filtering Using the Date Filters

When a field in the original data set contains only values formatted as dates, Excel offers the Date Filters fly-out shown previously in Figure 24.4.

Many of the date filters contain conceptual filters. If you filter a pivot table to "Yesterday" and then refresh the data set a week later, the dates returned by the filter will change.

The list of conceptual filters feels like it was borrowed from QuickBooks, but it is not quite as complete as those from QuickBooks. It would be nice to have choices such as Last 30 Days, Month to Date, and so on.

The penultimate choice in the first fly-out is All Dates in the Period, which leads to a second fly-out. Choosing January or Quarter 1 is great when you have dates from several years and you want to compare January from each year.

The last choice in the first fly-out is Custom Filter. As shown in Figure 24.10, you can use this filter to build a custom date range. Change the first drop-down to Is Between. Then use the date icons to choose your selected dates. The Whole Days check box is new in Excel 2013. Use this to truncate times from fields that contain date and time.

Figure 24.10
The Custom Filter in a date field offers to let you build any range of dates.

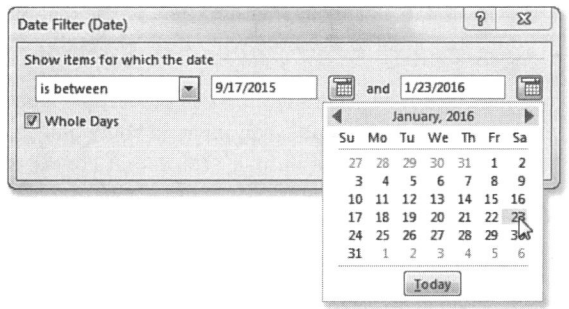

Filtering Using Value Filters

The Value Filters are fairly powerful in Excel 2013. You can choose to filter the customers based on other values in the pivot table.

Suppose you want to see all the customers who had revenue greater than $100,000. You could apply this filter to the Customer field using the Value Filters fly-out. Follow these steps:

1. Open the Customer Field drop-down.

2. Select the Values Filter fly-out.

3. Select Greater Than or Equal To. Excel displays the Value Filter dialog (see Figure 24.11).

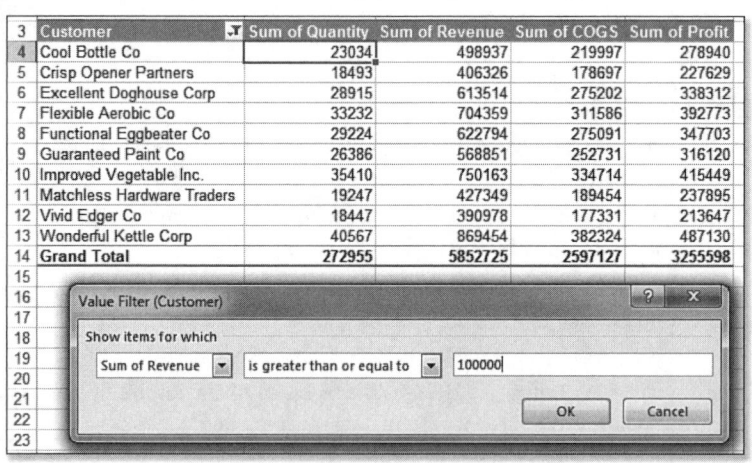

Figure 24.11
Filter the Customer field based on values in the Revenue column.

4. Open the first drop-down and choose the appropriate numeric field. Although the dialog defaults to the first numeric field in the pivot table, you can choose any of the fields in the Values area, including any calculated fields.

5. Fill in **100000** as the third field in the dialog. Click OK. Only customers with revenue greater than or equal to $100,000 will be shown in the pivot table.

Use caution when filtering one of multiple label fields. Say that you added Date as a second row field. The pivot table continues to show daily sales for Excellent Doghouse, even though those daily sales are not greater than $100,000. All of the day's sales for Excellent Doghouse make it into the filter because the total sales for the customer exceed the $100,000 limit. When you move Customer to the second row field, the filter starts working on the sales for that customer for that day. Because no customers bought $100,000 in one day, no customers appear as the result of the filter.

Here is another example: Figure 24.12 is filtered to show only days with sales greater than $30,000. January 7, 2015 makes it into the report because of the two sales that day.

Figure 24.12
Apply a filter to the outer row field.

	A	B	C	D	
2					
3	Date	Customer	Sum of Quantity	Sum of Revenue	Su
4	⊟1/7/2015	Improved Vegetable Inc.	401	8456	
5	1/7/2015	Tremendous Thermostat Partners	1035	21730	
6	1/7/2015 Total		1436	30186	
7	⊟2/20/2015	Flexible Aerobic Co	568	11124	
8	2/20/2015	Functional Eggbeater Co	296	5700	
9	2/20/2015	Wonderful Kettle Corp	1023	23810	
10	2/20/2015 Total		1887	40634	

If you then apply a filter to Customer asking to only see customers where the daily sales for that customer are greater than $20,000, the January 7 record for Improved Vegetable Inc. will be hidden. January 7 continues to be shown in the pivot table because the unfiltered total for January 7 would have been greater than the $30,000 limit (see Figure 24.13).

Figure 24.13
Further filter by an inner row field. The inner filter does not change which values are selected by the outer filter.

	A	B	C	D	
2					
3	Date	Customer	Sum of Quantity	Sum of Revenue	S
4	⊟1/7/2015	Tremendous Thermostat Partners	1035	21730	
5	1/7/2015 Total		1035	21730	
6	⊟2/20/2015	Wonderful Kettle Corp	1023	23810	
7	2/20/2015 Total		1023	23810	
8	⊟2/26/2015	Easy Sandal Co	882	20610	
9	2/26/2015	Wonderful Kettle Corp	969	25140	
10	2/26/2015 Total		1851	45750	
11	⊟3/13/2015	Excellent Doghouse Corp	1026	24430	
12	3/13/2015 Total		1026	24430	
13	⊟4/3/2015	Savory Opener Inc.	845	20408	

Filtering to the Top 10

The problem with the Value Filter is that you have to commit to a threshold value. At the beginning of a year, you might have no customers who have purchased at the $100,000 level yet.

Pivot tables offer a feature called Top 10. Despite the name, the filter is not just for finding the top 10 values. You can use the filter to find top or bottom items. You can specify 5, 7, 10, or any number of items.

The Top 10 filter has some new features since Excel 2003. To start the filter, open the Customer filter drop-down. Open the Value Filters fly-out and select Top 10. Excel displays the Top 10 Filter dialog.

In Figure 24.14, the report has been filtered to show the top five customers based on revenue.

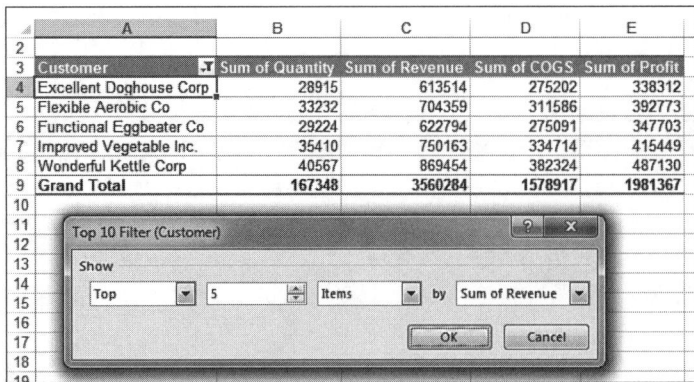

Figure 24.14
Filter to the top five customers based on revenue.

The Top 10 filter offers these options:

- The first drop-down in the dialog offers a choice between Top and Bottom.

- The second field is a spin button and a text box. You can use the spin button to change from 5 to 10. If you need to get to 1,000,000, you should type that value into the text box instead of trying to hit the spin button 999,990 times.

- The next field is a drop-down with choices Items, Percent, and Sum. These three choices are discussed in the next sections.

- The final drop-down offers all the numeric fields in the VALUES area of the pivot table.

The Items/Percent/Sum drop-down offers a lot of flexibility. If you select Percent, the pivot table shows you enough customers so that you see *n*% of the value field. For example, in Figure 24.15, the pivot table shows enough customers to represent the top 80% of profit.

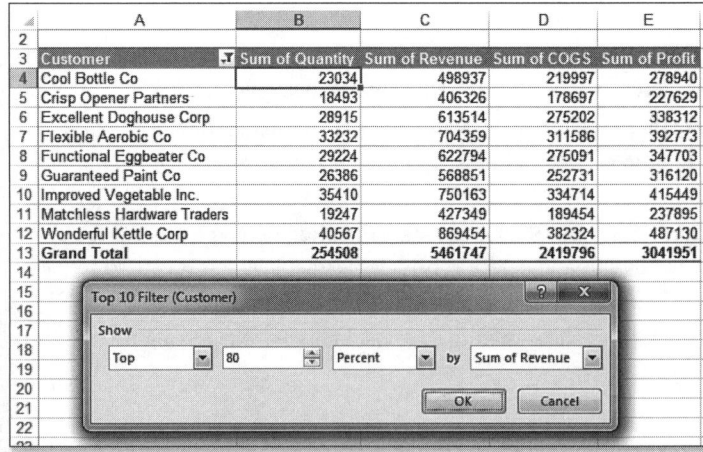

Figure 24.15
Filter to 80% of the revenue based on profit.

If you choose Sum, you can specify a large number as the second field in the dialog. In Figure 24.16, you are looking for the smallest customers, up to about $500,000 in sales.

Figure 24.16
Find the bottom $500K of customers based on revenue.

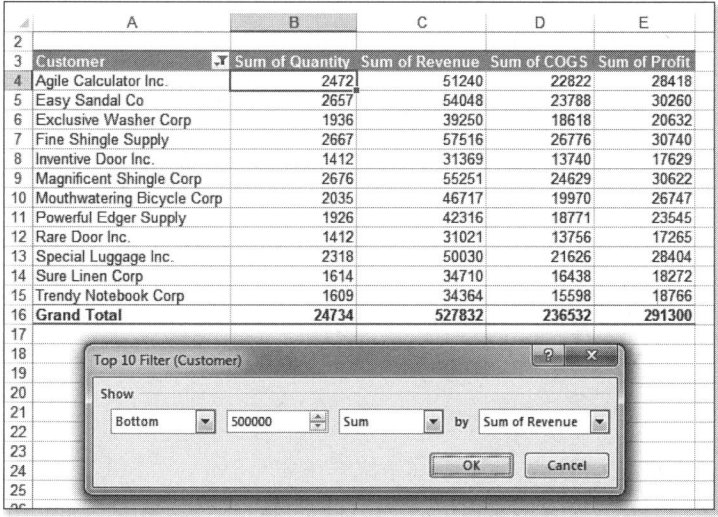

	A	B	C	D	E
2					
3	Customer	Sum of Quantity	Sum of Revenue	Sum of COGS	Sum of Profit
4	Agile Calculator Inc.	2472	51240	22822	28418
5	Easy Sandal Co	2657	54048	23788	30260
6	Exclusive Washer Corp	1936	39250	18618	20632
7	Fine Shingle Supply	2667	57516	26776	30740
8	Inventive Door Inc.	1412	31369	13740	17629
9	Magnificent Shingle Corp	2676	55251	24629	30622
10	Mouthwatering Bicycle Corp	2035	46717	19970	26747
11	Powerful Edger Supply	1926	42316	18771	23545
12	Rare Door Inc.	1412	31021	13756	17265
13	Special Luggage Inc.	2318	50030	21626	28404
14	Sure Linen Corp	1614	34710	16438	18272
15	Trendy Notebook Corp	1609	34364	15598	18766
16	Grand Total	24734	527832	236532	291300

Top 10 Filter (Customer)

Show

Bottom | 500000 | Sum | by | Sum of Revenue

OK   Cancel

Filtering Using Filter Fields

Those who are familiar with pivot tables in legacy versions of Excel know the Filter as the Page Field area of the layout. Although the new field-filtering tools described in the preceding sections offer far more powerful filtering, you can use the Filters drop zone to add filter cells to a pivot table to do basic ad-hoc analysis.

To add filter drop-downs to the top of the pivot table, you drag the fields to the Filters drop zone in the PivotTable Field List.

The Date Filters in the Report Filter of the Pivot Field are not as intelligent as a date field in the regular filter. The pivot table filter drop-down offers hundreds of daily dates without the month and year hierarchies. Before adding a date field to the Filters, follow these steps to create your own hierarchy:

1. Add the date field temporarily to the row field area of the pivot table.

2. Select the first cell containing a date in the pivot table.

3. In the Analyze tab, click Group.

4. In the Grouping dialog box, select Days, Months, Quarters, and Years. Click OK.

5. Move the Date, Months, Quarters, and Years fields to the Filters drop zone.

In Figure 24.17, six fields have been added to the Filters area. If you need to see a report of East region customers who purchased in January 2015, you would select from the drop-downs in B1, B3, and B5.

	A	B	C
1	Region	East ▼	
2	Product	(All) ▼	
3	Years	2015 ▼	
4	Quarters	(All) ▼	
5	Months	Jan ▼	
6	Date	(All) ▼	
7			
8	Customer ▼	Sum of Quantity	Sum of Revenue
9	Cool Bottle Co	91	2401
10	Excellent Doghouse Corp	558	11628
11	Functional Eggbeater Co	954	22810
12	Improved Vegetable Inc.	1819	41246
13	Matchless Hardware Traders	971	20734
14	Powerful Edger Supply	773	18552
15	Supreme Clipboard Inc.	760	14440
16	Tremendous Thermostat Partners	1035	21730
17	Trendy Notebook Corp	814	16288
18	Vivid Edger Co	547	9345
19	Wonderful Kettle Corp	338	6714
20	Grand Total	8660	185888

Figure 24.17
Fields in the Report Filter area allow for interesting ad-hoc reporting.

Arranging the Filters

When you have many fields in the Report Filter area, you might want to arrange those filters. The vertical arrangement in Figure 24.17 means that seven rows of your screen will be taken up with non-customer data.

Select one cell in your pivot table, and then click the Options icon in the left side of the Options tab.

In the PivotTable Options dialog, the Layout & Format tab offers two settings that affect the arrangement of the Report Filter. In Figure 24.18, the Display Fields in Report Filter area is set to Over, Then Down. The Report Filter Fields Per Row is set to 2. This creates a 3×2 arrangement of the six filter fields.

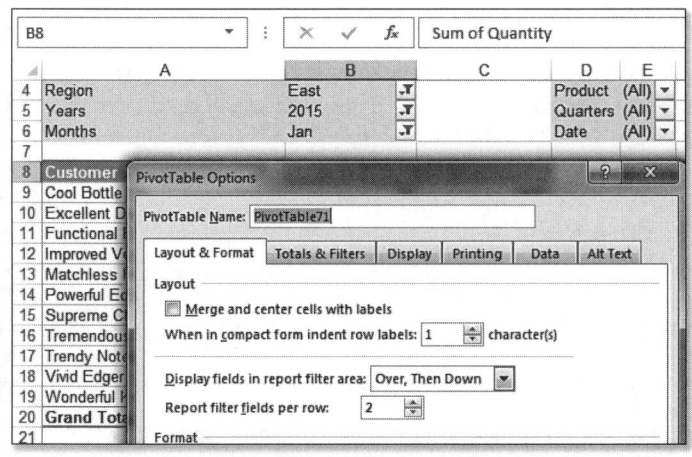

Figure 24.18
Use the PivotTable Options dialog to rearrange the Report Filter fields.

Selecting Multiple Items

Excel 2007 introduced the capability to choose multiple items from a Report Filter field. Figure 24.19 shows the initial state of the Region filter.

Figure 24.19
Initially, the filter allows you to select one item or (All).

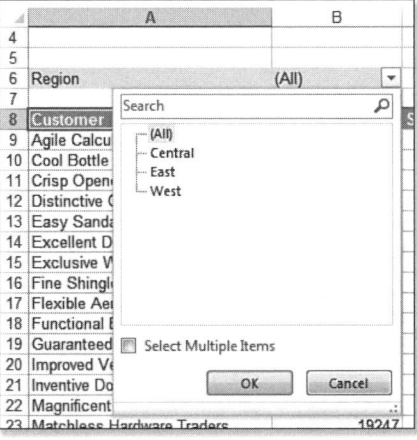

To enable the capability to select multiple items, choose Select Multiple Items in the bottom of the drop-down. Check boxes appear, and you can select multiple items from the list. Figure 24.20 shows a selection for Central and West.

Figure 24.20
You can now select multiple items from the filter drop-down.

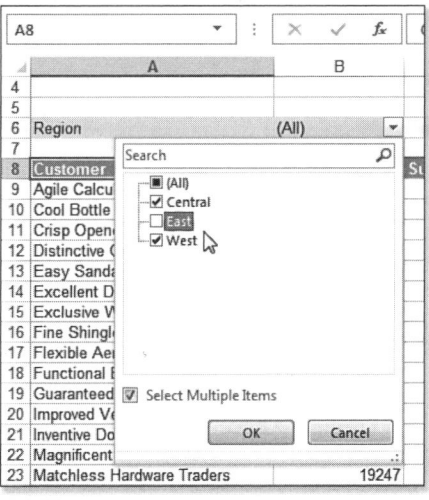

Caution

It feels like the Select Multiple Items feature wasn't quite done in Excel 2007. When you choose multiple items from the list and close the drop-down, the filter shows the not-very-useful heading of (Multiple Items), as shown in Figure 24.21. When you print this report, no one will have any idea what items are actually selected in the filter. When you see the slicers described in the next section, you will understand that Select Multiple Items was an intermediate solution added to make slicers possible.

Figure 24.21
Regions are filtered to (Multiple Items). Is this the worst title ever?

 Tip

To clear all the filters and return them to the (All) selection, click the Clear icon in the Sort & Filter section of the Data tab.

Filtering Using Slicers

Slicers are visual filters that were new in Excel 2010. They solve the problem of selecting multiple items, as shown in Figure 24.21. Although slicers take up much more space than the equivalent Report Filters, the slicer arrangement invites people to start running ad-hoc analyses by clicking the slicers.

Adding Slicers

Before you add slicers, insert some extra rows above your pivot table, insert some extra columns to the left of your pivot table, or do both. Slicers take up a lot of room.

To add default slicers, follow these steps:

1. Select one cell in your pivot table.

2. On the Analyze tab, select the Insert Slicer icon. Excel shows the Insert Slicers dialog.

3. Choose any fields that would make suitable filter fields. In Figure 24.22, Region, Product, and Years are selected. Months, Quarters, and Date would also be effective, but you see how they can be filtered using a timeline later in this chapter. Click OK.

Excel adds default filters, tiled in the center of your screen (see Figure 24.23).

Figure 24.22
Choose all fields that are suitable for visual filters.

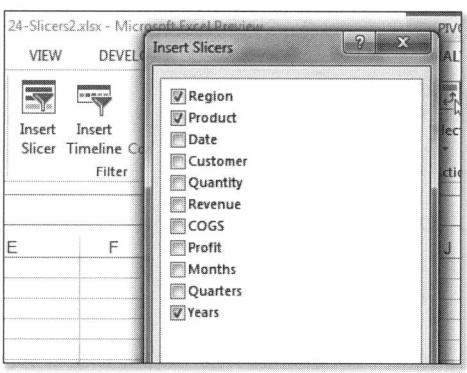

Figure 24.23
Excel tiles a bunch of one-column slicers.

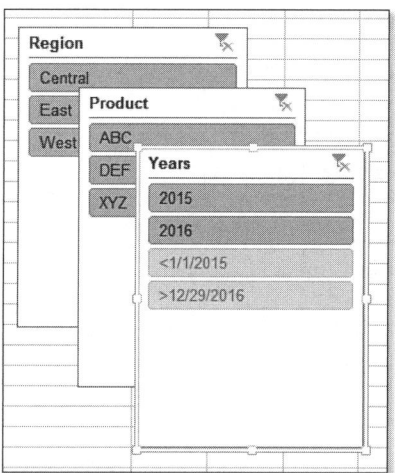

Arranging the Slicers

You can reposition and resize the slicers. Choose a logical arrangement for the slicers. Following are some examples.

The Region and Product slicers contain short entries. Make each slicer wider and then use the Columns setting in the Slicer Tools Options tab to increase each slicer to three columns. See Figure 24.24 for the setting.

The Year slicer is wider than it needs to be. There are also two extra items (<1/1/2015 and >12/31/2016) in the slicer that are remnants of the grouping operation. You can turn these off in the Slicer Settings dialog. Select the slicer and choose Slicer Settings. In Figure 24.25, you can see that "Years" has been changed to "Year." Also, Hide Items with No Data is checked.

Columns Setting

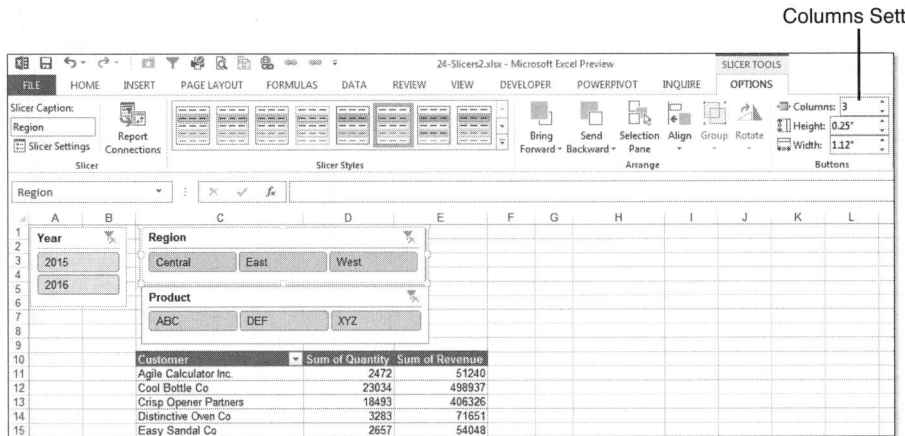

Figure 24.24
The Slicer
Tools Options
tab allows
you to control
the number of
columns in a
slicer.

Slicer Settings Icon

Caption

Style Gallery

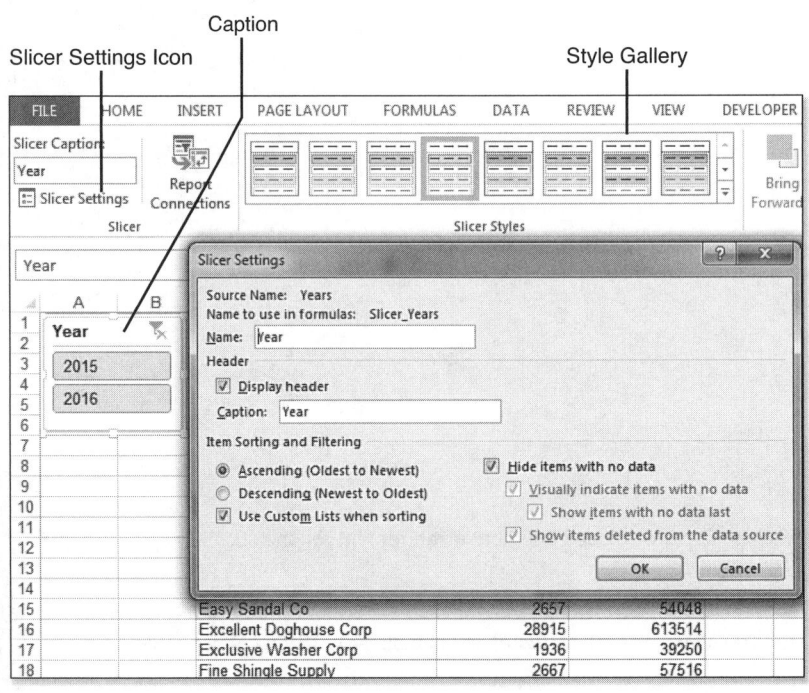

Figure 24.25
Control the slicer in the
Slicer Settings dialog.

Formatting the Slicers

A gallery on the Slicer Tools Options offers 14 slicer color themes. Click each slicer and choose a different color scheme for each one.

It is a novelty, but you can create your own slicer style. Rob Collie at PowerPivotPro.com used this technique to build a slicer with item tiles in Wingdings font. He used J, K, L in a Rating column. When displayed in Wingdings, those characters show as a happy face, sad face, and in-between face. After creating a slicer for Rating, he followed these steps:

1. Right-click a slicer style and choose Duplicate.

2. Choose Whole Slicer. Click Format. On the Font tab, choose Wingdings 22 point. Click OK.

3. Choose Header. Click Format. On the Font tab, choose a regular font such as Calibri. Click OK twice. This defines a new slicer style, but does not apply it to the slicer.

4. Select the slicer. Choose the new custom style from the Slicer Styles gallery. You end up with a unique slicer, as shown in Figure 24.26

Figure 24.26
A clever use of Wingdings font creates icons in the slicer.

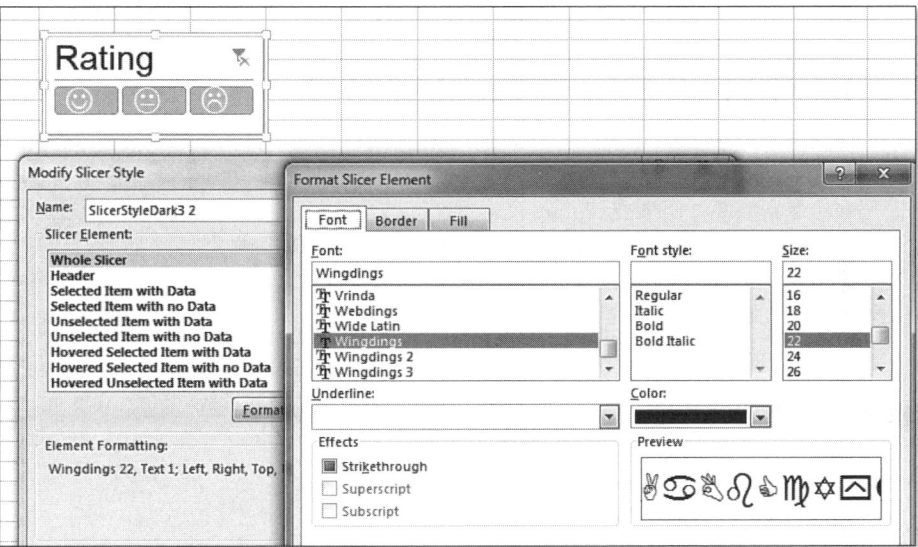

Using the Slicers

To select a single item from a slicer, choose that item. To multiselect from a single slicer, hold down the Ctrl key while selecting the multiple items. To select adjacent items, click the first item and drag to the last item to be selected. Figure 24.27 shows the formatted slicers with one year, two adjacent products, and two nonadjacent regions selected.

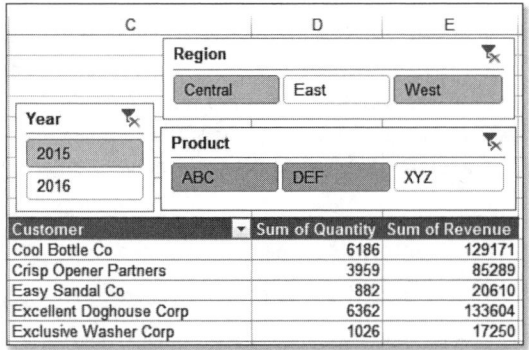

Figure 24.27
Slicers provide a visual indication of what is included in the report.

Selections in one slicer might cause items in other slicers to gray out. In this case, those items move to the end of the list. This gives you a visual indication that the item is not available based on the current filters.

To clear a filter from a slicer, click the Funnel-X icon in the top right of the slicer.

Filtering Using Timelines

Figure 24.28 shows a new timeline in Excel 2013. Each timeline control enables you to filter a pivot table using one of the date fields in the underlying data set. Even when the dates are stored as daily dates and have not been grouped, you can use a timeline to filter by year, quarter, month, or day. The timeline in Figure 24.28 has been set to filter by Quarter.

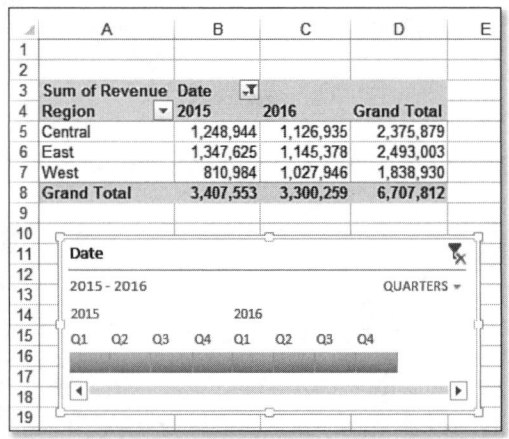

Figure 24.28
A timeline control lets you filter daily dates by month, quarter, or year without grouping.

This data set includes two years' worth of dates. When you display the timeline with quarters, you have eight quarters to choose from. You can choose one quarter or a consecutive string of quarters. To get the result shown in Figure 24.29, you click on 2015-Q4 and drag to 2016-Q2 to select a range of three quarters.

Figure 24.29
You can filter to more than one quarter, but the selection must be contiguous.

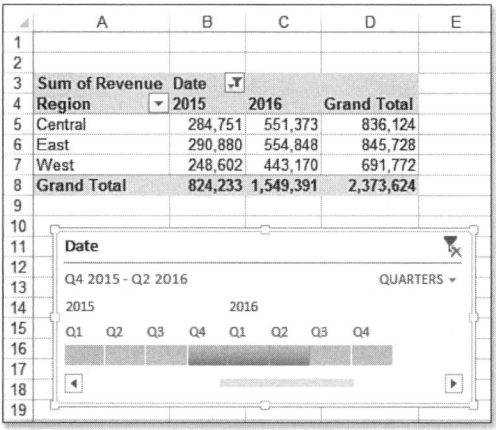

Use the drop-down in the top right of the timeline to change to a different level of filtering. When you switch to a less-granular period, the resulting timeline might show a selection that would normally be unselectable. In Figure 24.29, the selection of three quarters spanned 2015 and 2016. After you change that timeline to show years, the selected year is 25% of 2015 and 50% of 2016, as shown in Figure 24.30. Now that the timeline is showing years, you can select 2015 and/or 2016, but you cannot use the timeline to select a portion of each year.

Figure 24.30
Switch from quarters to years, and the timeline shows part of each year.

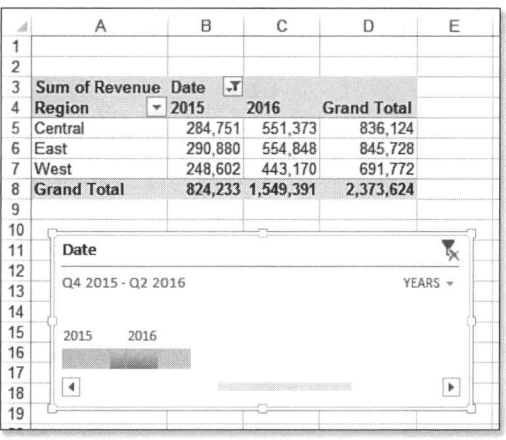

Adding a Timeline

Select one cell in your pivot table. From the Analyze tab, choose Insert Timeline. The Insert Timelines dialog offers all of the date fields in your data set.

Timelines require your data to include one or more columns that are defined as a date column. For OLAP or PowerPivot, that means that a database administrator has explicitly defined the column as a date. For regular Excel data, it means that 100% of the values in the column are dates.

Choose one of the available date fields and click OK. By default, the timeline initially appears at the Month level. In Figure 24.31, there are 24 months in the data, so you only see part of the time horizon with a horizontal scrollbar at the bottom.

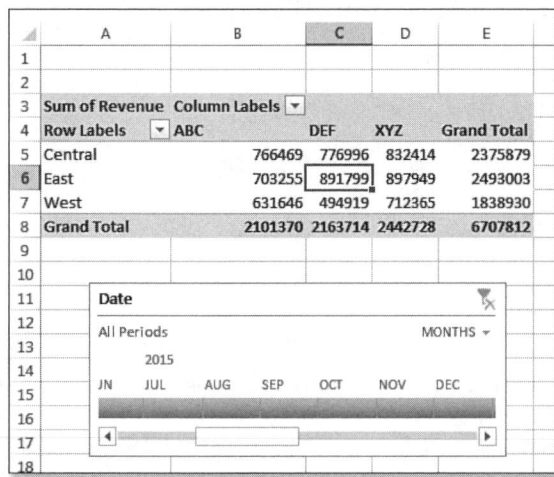

Figure 24.31
The default timeline shows the date at the month level.

Use the Months drop-down in the top right of the timeline to choose Days, Months, Quarters, or Years. In Figure 24.32, the timeline at the Days level shows only 8 days out of 700+ days in the data set.

Choosing Between Timelines or Grouped Slicers

As I was first starting to work with timelines, I tried to select non-contiguous ranges such as Q2 of this year and Q2 of last year. I quickly learned that this is not possible with timelines.

Because my pivot table came from a regular Excel data set, I used the Group Field icon in the Analyze tab to group the date field up to days, months, quarters, and years. I then created slicers from Years, Quarters, and Months fields. As shown in Figure 24.33, this is far more flexible than a timeline. You can use the pivot table to compare Q2 of 2015 to Q2 of 2016 by selecting only Q2 from the Quarters slicer.

Figure 24.32
For this data set with two years of daily dates, the Days version of the timeline shows only a narrow window of the entire timeframe.

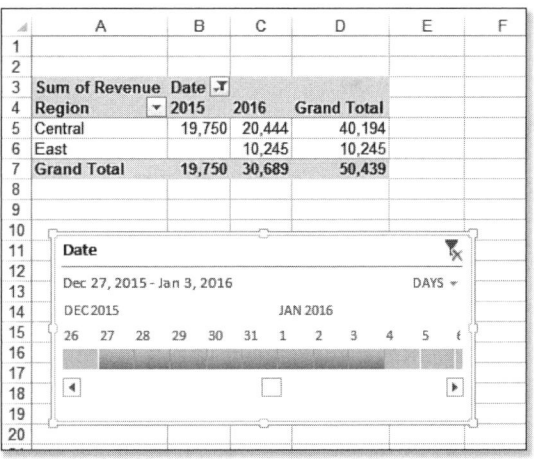

Figure 24.33
The three slicers in F:K are more versatile than the timeline.

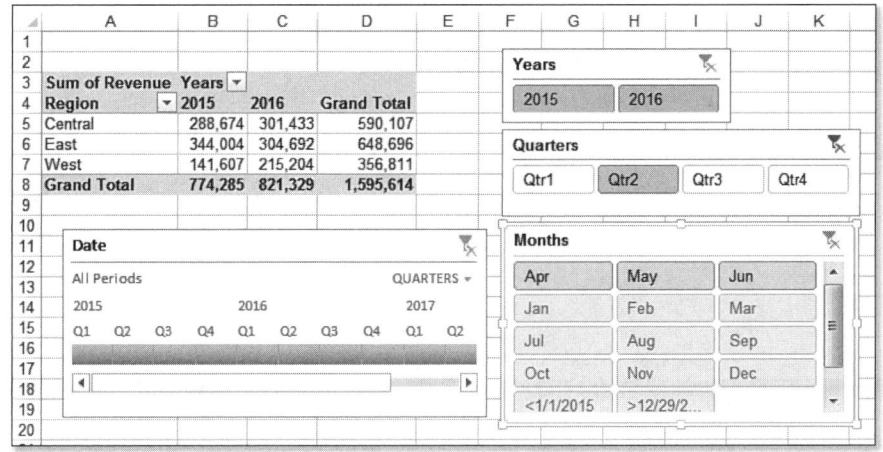

The three time slicers take up about two times as much space as the timeline, but they are more versatile.

Frankly, if you are creating a pivot table from regular Excel data, it makes sense to keep using slicers based on grouped date fields.

The difficulty lies with people who are creating pivot tables from PowerPivot or from external OLAP data sources. You cannot group dates up to months, quarters, or years in an OLAP pivot table. If you wanted to show data by month in a PowerPivot pivot table, you would have to use the DAX formula language to add a month name column to your data set. That adds many new cells to your data and slows down the model.

Thus, it seems that timelines were introduced as an alternative way of filtering OLAP or PowerPivot data sets.

If you have a regular Excel pivot table using a single data source in Excel, you have more flexibility if you avoid timelines and use slicers on grouped dates instead.

Filtering Oddities

The next sections discuss a few additional features available for filtering pivot tables.

AutoFiltering a Pivot Table

I was doing a Power Excel seminar in Philadelphia when someone in the audience asked whether it is possible to AutoFilter a pivot table. The answer is no; the Filter field is grayed out when you are inside a pivot table.

There is a surprising bug, however. If you put the cell pointer to the right of the last heading of a data set and click the Filter icon, Excel turns on the AutoFilter drop-downs. I call this cell the magic cell.

The guy at Microsoft in charge of graying out the AutoFilter icon when you are in a pivot table evidently forgot about that magic cell to the right of the headings. If you put the cell pointer in cell D1 in Figure 24.34, the Filter icon is not grayed out.

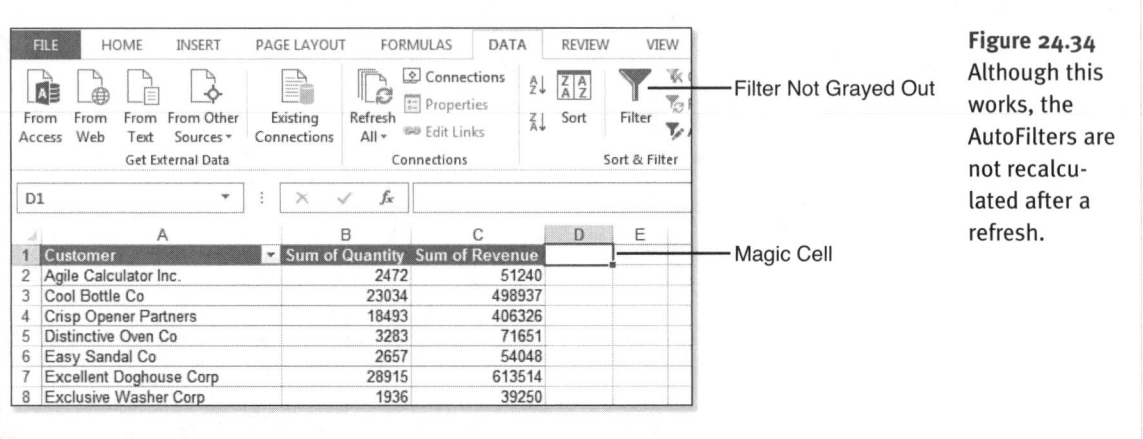

Figure 24.34 Although this works, the AutoFilters are not recalculated after a refresh.

What is the advantage of using the AutoFilters? The Top 10 AutoFilter works differently than the Top 10 PivotTable filter. In Figure 24.35, the Top 10 AutoFilter for the top six items returns the top five customers and the true grand total.

If you try this method, remember that you have to go back to the magic cell in order to toggle off the AutoFilter. Also, if you change the underlying data and refresh the pivot table, the AutoFilter is not updated. After all, the Excel team believes that you can't AutoFilter a pivot table.

Figure 24.35
The AutoFilter Top 10 works differently than the pivot table filters.

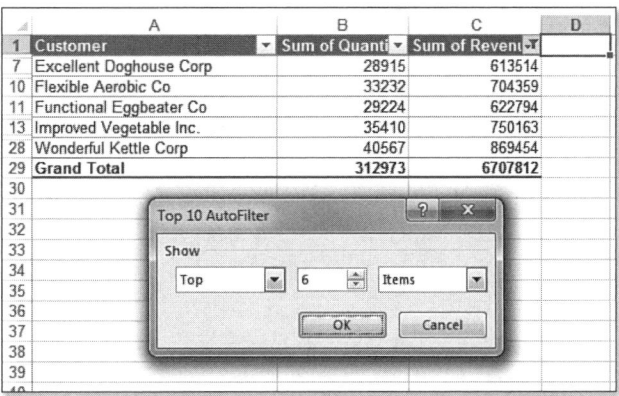

Applying Row Label Filters to Fields Not in the Pivot Table Report

You can apply a filter to a field that does not appear in the pivot table. Go to the top of the PivotTable Fields list and hover over any field. A drop-down appears on that field, as shown in Figure 24.36. Open the drop-down and you can apply a filter to the field, even though it is not in the current report.

Figure 24.36
Hover over a field in the top of the PivotTable Field list to reveal a secret drop-down.

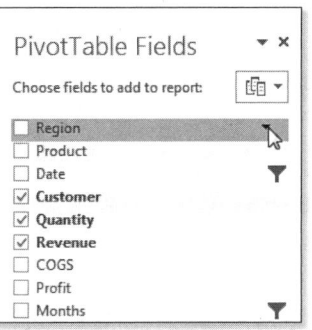

As shown in Figure 24.37, the secret drop-down leads to Label Filters, Value Filters, the Search box, and the item check boxes.

 Caution

When you use the menu shown in Figure 24.37, nothing in the pivot table indicates that these fields have been filtered. The only indication that a filter is applied is the funnel icon at the right side of the PivotTable Fields list.

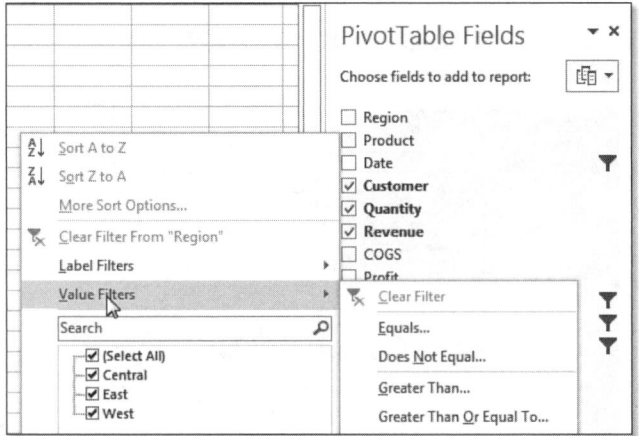

Replicating a Pivot Table for Every Customer

This technique makes many copies of the pivot table, with a different Report Filter value in each copy. If your pivot table contains at least one Report Filter field, select the Options drop-down from the Analyze tab. Select Show Report Filter Pages from the drop-down menu, as shown in Figure 24.38. Confirm which field should be used. Excel adds worksheets to your workbook. Each worksheet contains the original pivot table, with a different value chosen for the selected filter field.

> ⚠ **Caution**
> Slicers are not visible on the copied pivot tables when you use this technique.

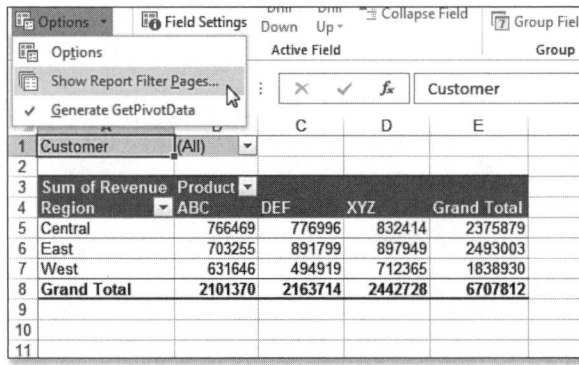

Figure 24.38
Replicate your pivot table for every value in a Report Filter field.

Sorting a Pivot Table

In all the pivot tables so far in this chapter, the customers are presented in alphabetical sequence. In each case, the report would be more interesting if it were presented sorted by revenue instead of by customer name.

The Customer drop-down offers choices to sort a field in ascending or descending order, as shown in Figure 24.39. However, you can find more powerful options by selecting More Sort Options from this drop-down.

Figure 24.39
Use More Sort Options.

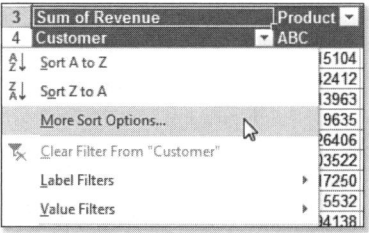

When you choose More Sort Options from the Customer drop-down, the Sort dialog appears. This dialog initially offers to sort in ascending order, based on customer. If you choose Descending and then use the drop-down, you can choose to sort the report based on sum of revenue, as shown in Figure 24.40.

Figure 24.40
Sort descending based on revenue.

One more sorting option is available in Excel 2013. Suppose you have a pivot table showing revenue with products going across the columns and customers down the rows. If you want to sort the report by one particular product, Excel 2013 allows this. Here's how:

1. Open the Customer filter drop-down.

2. Select More Sort Options.

3. Select Descending by Revenue.

4. Click More Options.

5. In the More Sort Options dialog, specify that you want to sort by Values in Selected Column. Click the column containing the desired product (see Figure 24.41).

 **Tip**

Starting in Excel 2010, if you sort using the AZ or ZA buttons icons on the Data tab, Excel replicates the changes described in this section. Prior to Excel 2010, using the Sort options on the Data tab would do a one-time sort and no rules would be set up to change the sort as the pivot table changed.

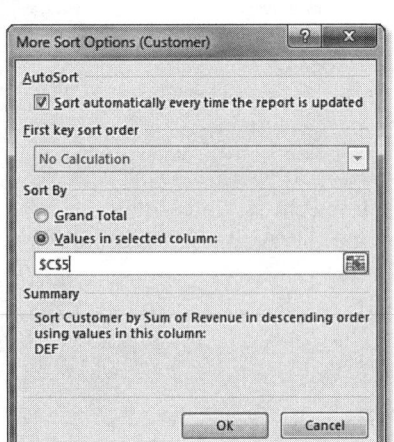

Figure 24.41
Excel offers to sort by one specific column.

25

MASHING UP DATA WITH POWERPIVOT

In Chapter 24, "Using Slicers and Filtering a Pivot Table," you learned how to build pivot tables from a single data source. A revolutionary add-in called PowerPivot debuted in Excel 2010 that enabled you to build pivot tables from multiple tables. For Excel 2013, that core functionality of PowerPivot is built directly into Excel. This chapter starts by showing you how anyone with Excel 2013 can build pivot tables from multiple tables.

Certain versions of Excel 2013 also ship with the full PowerPivot add-in. If you have one of these versions, you can activate the add-in and access additional tools such as a powerful Data Analysis Expressions (DAX) formula language. The latter part of the chapter describes the additional benefits of PowerPivot.

Joining Multiple Tables Using the Data Model in Regular Excel 2013

The Microsoft team faces a marketing dilemma. They had built the best features of PowerPivot right into Excel 2013, yet they want to get customers to spend extra money for Office Professional Plus to get PowerPivot, Power View, and Inquire.

Although the name PowerPivot sounds really awesome and powerful, the Microsoft team had to come up with a name that describes pivot tables built in regular Excel 2013 that use the PowerPivot engine. When you see the term *Data Model* in Excel 2013, that is Microsoft's way of saying you are using PowerPivot without calling it PowerPivot. Figure 25.1 shows the Create PivotTable dialog. A new check box for Add This Data to the Data Model really means that you are using the free version of the PowerPivot engine.

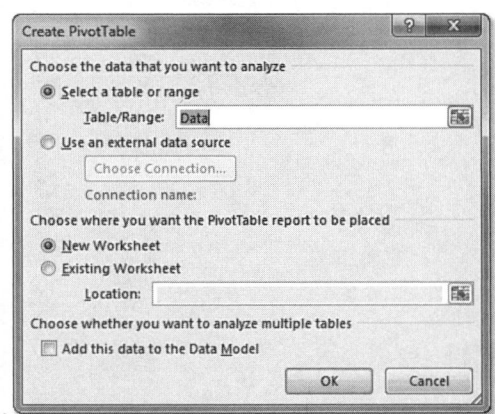

Figure 25.1
When Excel 2013 refers to the Data Model, you are using the PowerPivot engine.

Preparing Data for Use in the Data Model

When you are planning on using the Data Model to join multiple tables, you should always convert your Excel ranges to tables before you begin. You theoretically do not have to convert the ranges to tables, but it is far easier if you convert the ranges to tables and give the tables a name. If you don't convert the ranges to tables first, Excel secretly does it in the background and gives your tables meaningless names such as "Range."

Figure 25.2 shows two ranges in Excel. Columns A:H contain a transactional data set. Columns J:K contain a customer lookup table to add an industry sector for each customer. You would like to create a pivot table showing revenue by sector.

Customer	Quantity	Revenue	COGS	Profit		Customer	Sector
Functional Eggbeater Co	954	22810	10213	12597		Agile Calc	Electronics
Vivid Edger Co	124	2257	998	1259		Cool Bottle	Consumer
Trendy Notebook Corp	425	9152	4083	5069		Crisp Oper	Hardware
Powerful Edger Supply	773	18552	7883	10669		Distinctive	Electronics
Improved Vegetable Inc.	401	8456	3389	5067		Easy Sand	Apparel
Tremendous Thermostat Pa	1035	21730	9839	11891		Excellent [	Hardware
Improved Vegetable Inc.	750	16416	6768	9648		Exclusive	Electronics
Wonderful Kettle Corp	901	21438	9209	12229		Fine Shing	Hardware
Matchless Hardware Traders	342	6267	2541	3726		Flexible A	Apparel
Cool Bottle Co	91	2401	1031	1370		Functional	Consumer
Vivid Edger Co	547	9345	4239	5106		Guarantee	Chemical
Excellent Doghouse Corp	558	11628	5093	6535		Improved V	Food

Figure 25.2
You want to join these two tables together in a single pivot table.

Excel gurus are thinking, "Why don't you do a VLOOKUP to join the tables?" PowerPivot lets you avoid the VLOOKUP. In this case, the tables are small and a VLOOKUP would calculate quickly. However, imagine that you have a million records in the transactional table and 10 columns in the lookup table. The VLOOKUP solution quickly becomes unwieldy. The PowerPivot engine available in the Data Model can join the tables without the overhead of VLOOKUP.

Convert the first data set to a table by following these steps:

1. Select any one cell in the first data set.

2. Press Ctrl+T or select Home, Format as Table and then select a format.

3. The Create Table dialog suggests the address of your range, as shown in Figure 25.3. Provided you have no blank rows, the address is correct. Provided you have a heading above each column and three or more columns, the dialog preselects My Table Has Headers. Make sure to check this box if it is not already checked. Click OK to convert the range to a table.

Figure 25.3
Use Ctrl+T to convert the range to a table.

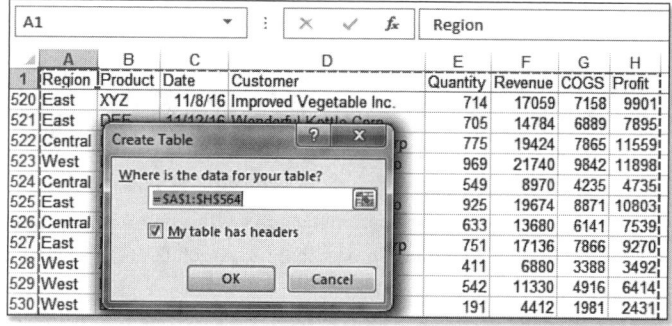

You immediately notice the AutoFilter drop-downs in each heading and that a formatting style has been applied to the first range. This is not the important part. A new Table Tools Design tab is available in the ribbon. The Table Name field in the left part of the ribbon shows a table name such as Table1 (see Figure 25.4).

Figure 25.4
Excel uses a default table name.

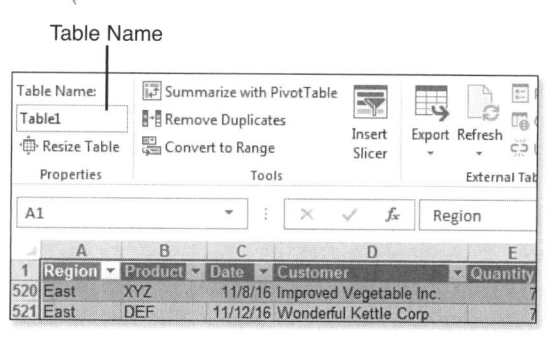

Click in the Table Name field and give the table a meaningful name. Database experts would call this the Fact table, but using a name such as Fact makes you sound like a database nerd. You might call this Data or Sales or InvoiceRegister. Whatever you choose, click in the Table Name box and type a meaningful name. The figures in this book use Sales as the table name.

Now, convert the second range to a table by following these steps:

1. Select cell J1.

2. Press Ctrl+T.

3. Because this table is only two columns, Excel doesn't select My Table Has Headers, so choose this option. Click OK.

4. Type a table name such as **Sectors** in the Table Name field in the ribbon.

You now have two tables defined in this workbook. You are ready to begin building the pivot table.

Adding the First Table to the Data Model

Choose one cell in the first data set and select Insert, PivotTable from the ribbon. You can't use the Recommended Pivot Tables or the Quick Analysis to build a Data Model pivot table.

In the Create PivotTable dialog, the table name appears. Choose the check box for Add This Data to the Data Model (see Figure 25.5). Then click OK.

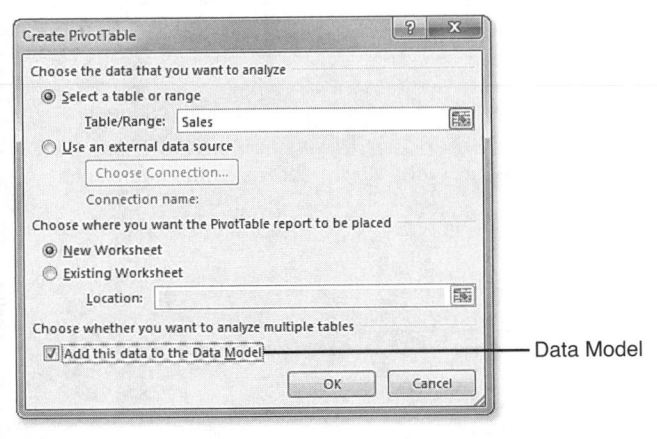

Figure 25.5
Remember "Data Model" is the boring name for "PowerPivot."

You get a new blank workbook with a PivotTable icon in A3:C20, just like with a regular pivot table. The PivotTable Fields task pane displays, but this is a slightly different version. Note the addition of the line with the choice of Active or All (see Figure 25.6).

You can arrange fields in the PivotTable field list just as with a regular pivot table. Choose Product and Revenue, and you have a pivot table report that looks just like a regular pivot table (see Figure 25.7).

Figure 25.6
The choice of Active or All indicates that you have a pivot table using the PowerPivot engine.

Figure 25.7
Add fields from the first table to the pivot table.

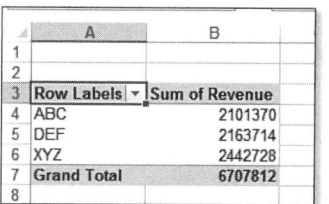

Adding the Second Table and Defining a Relationship

Focus on the PivotTable Fields task pane. In the second line of the pane, you have a choice for Active or All. Choose All. You now see a list of each defined table in the Excel workbook. There is a plus sign next to each table (see Figure 25.8).

Figure 25.8
Choose All to see a list of all available tables.

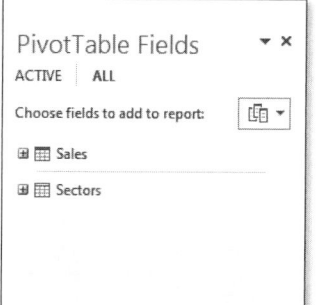

Click the plus sign next to Sectors to see a list of the available fields in the Sectors table (see Figure 25.9).

Figure 25.9
Expand the Sectors table to see a list of fields.

Drag the Sector field from the top of the PivotTable Field List to the Columns area in the bottom of the PivotTable Field List.

You will notice three things:

- The bottom of the PivotTable Field List is now showing fields from two different tables (see Figure 25.10).

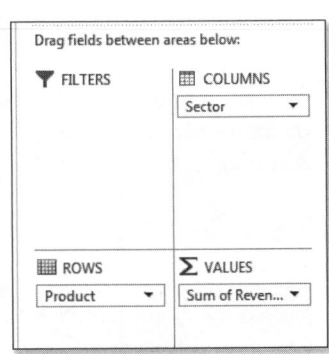

Figure 25.10
Choose one field from the lookup table.

- The pivot table is showing sectors, but the numbers are identical and clearly wrong in each column (see Figure 25.11).

- A yellow warning appears in the top of the PivotTable Field List indicating that relationships between tables may be needed and offering a Create button (see Figure 25.12).

Figure 25.11
The column labels are from the second table, but the numbers are wrong.

Sum of Revenue	Column Labels							
Row Labels	Apparel	Chemical	Consumer	Electronics	Food	Hardware	Textiles	Grand Total
ABC	2101370	2101370	2101370	2101370	2101370	2101370	2101370	2101370
DEF	2163714	2163714	2163714	2163714	2163714	2163714	2163714	2163714
XYZ	2442728	2442728	2442728	2442728	2442728	2442728	2442728	2442728
Grand Total	6707812	6707812	6707812	6707812	6707812	6707812	6707812	6707812

Figure 25.12
Excel warns you that you need to define a relationship between the two tables.

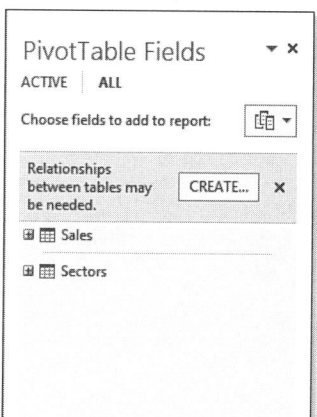

Note

 Note

It is confusing that Excel puts numbers in the report that are clearly wrong.

The attitude of the PowerPivot team is that these wrong numbers are designed to alert and remind you that you need to define a relationship. The big yellow box in the PivotTable Field List reminds you that you need to define a relationship. If I were in charge, I would force you to define the relationship before drawing a pivot table with clearly wrong numbers. If you have the full version of PowerPivot, you are allowed to define the relationship before creating the pivot table. But here, in this free "Data Model" version of PowerPivot, you are stuck with this awkward process of adding the field from the second table, getting wrong results, and then defining the relationship.

Click the Create button in the PivotTable Field List. Excel displays the Create Relationship dialog. Define the fields that are related in each table. Choose Sales as the first table and Customer as the column. Choose Sectors as the second table and Customer as the related column (see Figure 25.13).

After defining the relationship, you have successfully completed the Data Model. The pivot table updates with correct numbers, as shown in Figure 25.14.

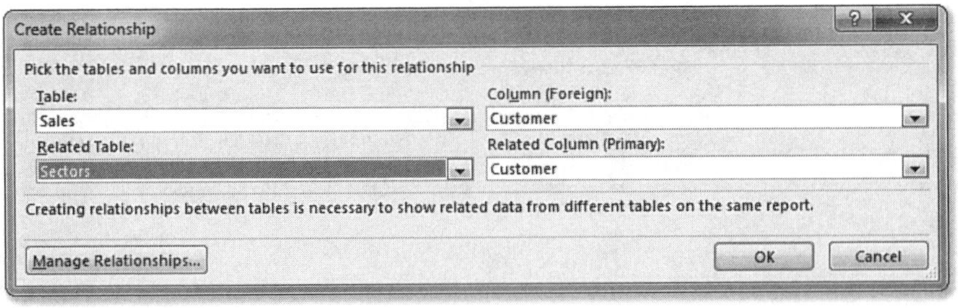

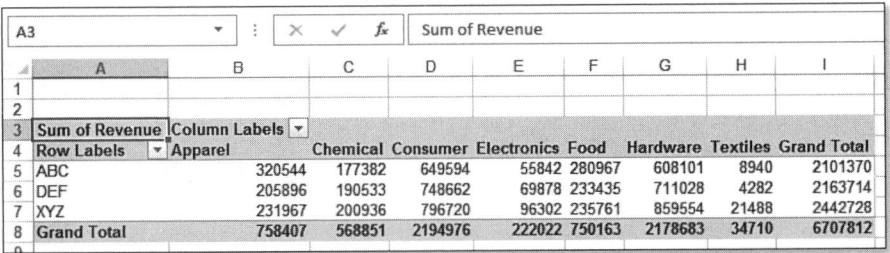

Figure 25.13
It is easy to define a relationship.

Figure 25.14
Without doing a VLOOKUP, you've successfully joined data from two tables in this report.

In the PivotTable Field List, choose Active from the second line of the task pane. You now see fields from both tables in the PivotTable Field List. You can rearrange the fields just as in a regular pivot table (see Figure 25.15).

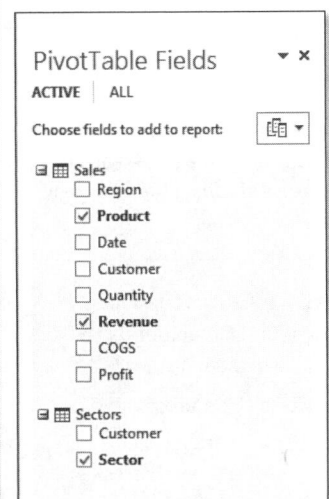

Figure 25.15
You have a choice of all fields in both tables.

Understanding the Limitations of the Data Model

On the face of it, this new Data Model pivot table feels like a regular pivot table. But they are not the same. By using the Data Model, you've just taken your regular Excel data moved it to a tabular model that is considered external to Excel. There are annoying limitations and some benefits available to pivot tables built on the Data Model. The Excel team tried to mitigate some of the limitations for Excel 2013, but many are still present.

Here are some of the benefits:

- The Value Field Settings dialog now offers a Distinct Count option for Summarize Values By. It no longer offers Product as a calculation, but I don't think anyone ever used Product, so that is fine.

- Say that you've filtered your report to show the top 10 customers but would like the total for all customers. Go to Design, Subtotals. The option for Include Filtered Items in Totals is now available to you. Choose this, and the pivot table shows only 10 customers but shows the totals from all customers. This avoids the need to use the AutoFilter hack described in the previous chapter.

- You can now use Named Sets to produce asynchronous reports. Say that you want to show Actuals for last year and Budget for next year. A Named Set lets you define a group of fields, such as [Prior Year | Actuals] and [Current Year | Budget]. Named Sets don't work with regular pivot tables. Take your data through the Data Model, and you can now define Named Sets.

- Use Analyze, OLAP Tools, Convert to Formulas to convert your entire pivot table to Cube Formulas.

These are four very specific benefits that are great in very narrow situations. If you are trying to perform a Distinct Count, you will love the benefits of the Data Model. I do not mean to belittle PowerPivot and the Data Model. The four micro-benefits just described are in addition to two enormous benefits: You can join two tables without doing a VLOOKUP and you have to use the Data Model if you want to use Power View or GeoFlow.

However, there are some big drawbacks to using the Data Model. The following features are used frequently by pivot table fans, so you are more likely to be stung by these issues:

- **No grouping**—PowerPivot cannot use the Group feature of pivot tables. You can no longer roll daily dates up to months, quarters, and years. You can work around this by adding calculations to the original data set, but this is not as simple as using the Group feature.

- **Strange drilldown**—Usually, you can double-click a cell in a pivot table and see the rows that make up that cell. This now works with the Data Model, but only for the first 1,000 rows.

- **No calculated fields or calculated items**—The Data Model does not support traditional calculated fields or calculated items. If you have PowerPivot, the DAX measures run circles around these old calculations. But if you don't have PowerPivot, you would have to learn the MDX formula language to add calculations to the pivot table.

- **Excel 2013 only**—Workbooks that use the Data Model do not work in earlier versions of Excel.

Benefits of Moving to PowerPivot

If your version of Excel 2013 includes the full PowerPivot add-in, there are several benefits:

- More ways to get data into PowerPivot. More data sources, plus linked tables, copy and paste, and feeds.

- You can view, sort, and filter data in the PowerPivot grid.

- Big data—you can import 999 billion rows into the PowerPivot grid.

- DAX formula calculations, both in the grid and as a new calculated field called a *measure*. DAX is composed of 117 functions that enable you to do two types of calculations. You can use the 81 typical Excel functions to add a calculated column to a table in the PowerPoint window. Then you can use 54 functions to create a new measure in the pivot table. These 54 functions add incredible power to pivot tables.

- More ways to create relationships, including a Diagram View to show relationships.

- You can hide or rename columns.

- You can define key performance indicators (KPIs) or hierarchies.

- You can use compression. Excel workbooks with PowerPivot data are smaller than workbooks that use traditional PivotCache pivot tables. The data is still stored inside the .xlsx workbook file, but the PowerPivot team came up with better ways to compress the data.

>  **Note**
>
> If you plan to deal with millions of records, you want to go with the 64-bit versions of Office and PowerPivot. The 64-bit version of Office can make use of memory sizes beyond the 4GB limit in 32-bit Windows.

Benefits of the Server Version of PowerPivot

If you get your IT folks to install PowerPivot Server, you get these additional benefits:

- **Automatic refresh**—In the client side, you have to open PowerPivot every day and click Refresh to have PowerPivot read the updated data sources. With the Server version, this can automatically happen overnight.

- **Publish to Report Gallery**—With the Server version, you can publish your PowerPivot pivot tables to a SharePoint server. Someone without Excel can open your workbook in a web page and use the slicers to filter the data. Those people have a nice gallery of report thumbnails from which to choose. The people in IT get to monitor which reports are actually used and by whom.

Enabling PowerPivot

PowerPivot is not a part of Office 2013 Home and Student or even Office 2013 Standard. If you have Office 365, Office 2013 Pro Plus, Office 2013 Enterprise, or a standalone boxed version of Excel 2013, you probably have PowerPivot.

To enable PowerPivot, follow these steps:

1. Open Excel 2013.

2. Click File, Options. Choose Add-Ins from the left column. At the bottom, choose Manage: COM Add-Ins. Click Go.

3. Look for Microsoft Office PowerPivot for Excel 2013 in the list of available COM add-ins (see Figure 25.16). Check the box next to this option and click OK.

> ## 🔺 Caution
> You have to use Microsoft Office PowerPivot for Excel 2013. The old "PowerPivot for Excel" is from Excel 2010 and does not work with Excel 2013.

Figure 25.16
Choose PowerPivot for Excel 2013 from the list.

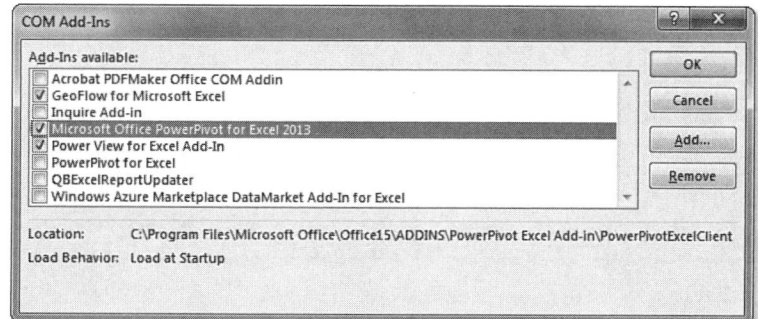

4. If the PowerPivot tab does not appear in the ribbon, close Excel 2013 and restart.

After installing the add-in, you should see a PowerPivot tab on the Excel 2013 ribbon, as shown in Figure 25.17.

Figure 25.17
After successful installation, you have a PowerPivot tab in the ribbon.

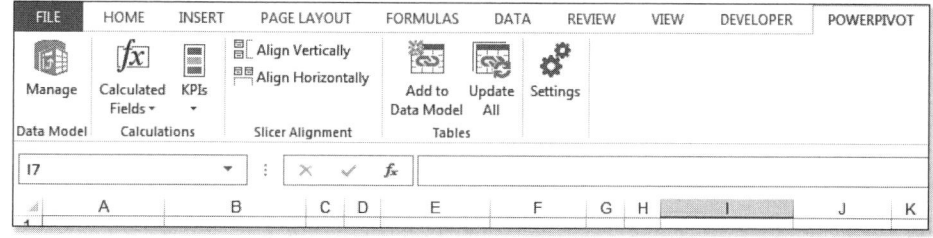

Case Study: Building a PowerPivot Report

This case study walks you through your first PowerPivot data mash-up. In this example, you create a report that merges a 1.8 million–row CSV file with a store identifying data in Excel.

Your main table is a 1.8 million–record CSV file called demo.txt. This file is shown in Notepad in Figure 25.18. It is important that you have column headings in row 1 of the CSV file. The point-of-sale vendor who provides this data usually has a "Run on mm/dd/yyyy" row at the top of the file, a blank row, and then headings in row 3. This does not work for PowerPivot. You need to get rid of those extraneous rows at the top of the data set.

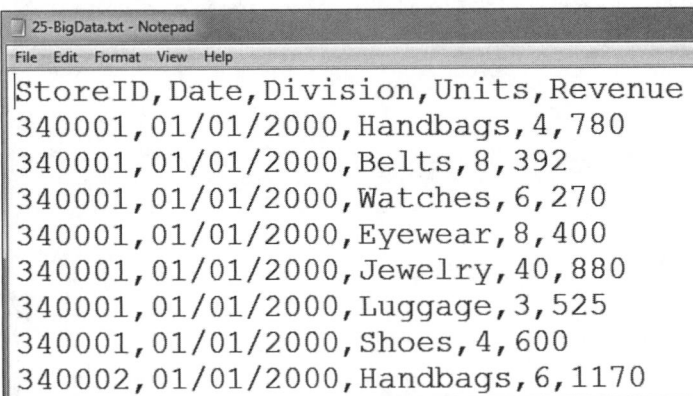

Figure 25.18
This 1.8 million–row file is too big for Excel.

Import a Text File

To import the 1.8 million–row file into PowerPivot, follow these steps:

1. Select the PowerPivot tab in Excel 2013.

2. Select the Manage icon. A new PowerPivot application window appears. This window contains a grid where you can eventually browse the data in the PowerPivot model. You can also use this window to browse data that you built using the Data Model discussed earlier in this chapter. PowerPivot offers three ribbon tabs: Home, Design, and Advanced.

3. You want to import your main table first. This is the large CSV file shown in Figure 25.17. From the Get External Data group, select From Other Sources. PowerPivot shows the Table Import Wizard.

4. Scroll to the bottom of the Table Import Wizard and select Text File. Click Next >.

5. Type a friendly connection name, such as **Sales History**.

6. Click the Browse button and locate your text file. PowerPivot detects whether your data contains headers.

7. Verify that your delimiter is a comma. The drop-down offers standard delimiters, such as comma, semicolon, vertical bar, and so on.

8. If there are any columns that you don't need to import, clear the check box next to the heading for those columns. The entire file is going to be read into memory. If you have extraneous columns, particularly columns with long text values, you can save memory by clearing them. Figure 25.19 shows the data preview with Units cleared.

Figure 25.19
Choose which columns to import.

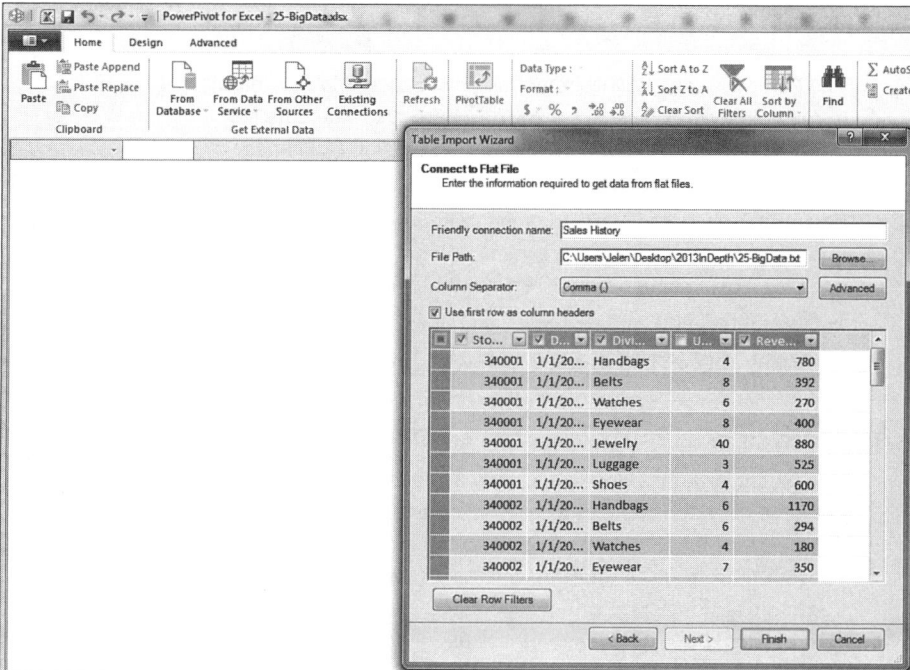

9. Note that there are filter drop-downs for each field. You can sort and filter this 1.8 million–row data set here, although it will be slower than in a few steps from now. If you open a filter field, you can choose to exclude certain values from the import.

10. Click Finish, and PowerPivot begins loading the file into memory. The wizard shows how many rows have been fetched so far (see Figure 25.20).

11. When the file is imported, the wizard confirms how many rows have been imported. Click Close to return to the PowerPivot window.

12. The 1.8 million–row data set is shown in the PowerPivot window. Go ahead and grab the vertical scrollbar and scroll through the records. You can also sort, change the number format, or filter.

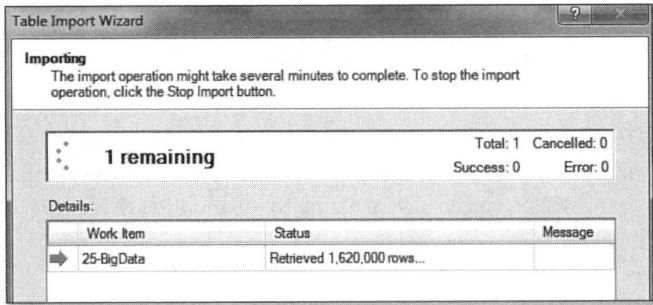

Figure 25.20
In less than a minute, PowerPivot is up to 1.6 million rows.

The Filters in PowerPivot are not as powerful as the new filters introduced way back in Excel 2007. In particular, the date columns do not show a hierarchical filter where you can choose a year or month.

If you right-click a column, a menu appears where you can rename, freeze, and copy the columns. You can also use this menu to hide a column from the pivot table field list in Excel.

The bottom line is that you have 1.8 million records you can sort, filter, and, later, pivot. This is going to be cool.

 **Note**

Note that although this feels like Excel, it is not Excel. You cannot edit an individual cell. If you add a calculation in what amounts to cell E1, that calculation is automatically copied to all rows. If you format the revenue in one cell, all the cells in that column are formatted.

You can change column widths by dragging the border between the column names, just like in Excel.

Add Excel Data by Copying and Pasting

The file imported previously has only StoreID as a field. It does not have the store name or location. However, you probably have a small Excel file that maps StoreID to the store name and other relevant data. You can add this data as a new tab in PowerPivot.

You can use Copy and Paste as described here, or you can create a linked table as described in the next section. Linked tables work better.

Follow these steps to use Copy and Paste:

1. Open a workbook containing a range that maps StoreID to Store Name in Excel.

2. Select the data with Ctrl+*.

3. Copy it with Ctrl+C.

4. Click the PowerPivot tab in Excel.

5. Click the Manage icon to open the PowerPivot window. You see your 1.8 million–row data set that you previously imported.

6. Click the Paste icon on the left side of the PowerPivot Home tab. You see a Paste Preview window.

7. Give the new table a better name than "Table"—perhaps **StoreInfo**. Click OK.

You now see the store information in a new StoreInfo tab. Notice that there are now two worksheet tabs in PowerPivot.

The data you have pasted is a static copy of the Excel data. If the original Excel data changes, you have to copy the data and do a Paste Replace in PowerPivot.

Add Excel Data by Linking

In the previous example, you added the StoreInfo table by using Copy and Paste. This creates two copies of the data. One is stored in an Excel worksheet somewhere, and the other is stored in the PowerPivot window. When the original worksheet changes, those changes do not make it through to PowerPivot. An alternative is to link the data from Excel to PowerPivot.

To link to Excel data, you must convert that data to the Table Format introduced in Excel 2007. Here's how:

1. If you start with an Excel worksheet, make sure you have single-row headings at the top as well as no blank rows or blank columns.

2. Select one cell in the worksheet and press Ctrl+T. Excel asks you to confirm the extent of your table and whether your data has headers.

3. Go to the Table Tools Design tab. On the left side of the ribbon, you see that this table is called Table1. Type a new name, such as **StoreInfo**.

4. On the PowerPivot tab, in the Tables group, find an icon that says Add to Data Model. When you hover, the tooltip says Create Linked Table. Click this icon to have a copy of the table appear in the PowerPivot grid.

Define Relationships

Normally, in regular Excel you would be creating VLOOKUPs to match the two tables. Defining a relationship is far easier in PowerPivot. Follow these steps:

1. In the PowerPivot window, go to the Home tab and choose Diagram View. PowerPivot shows your two tables, side by side.

2. Click the StoreID field in the main table and drag to the Store field in the lookup table. Excel draws arrows indicating the relationship (see Figure 25.21).

3. To return to the grid, click the Data View icon in the Home tab of the PowerPivot window.

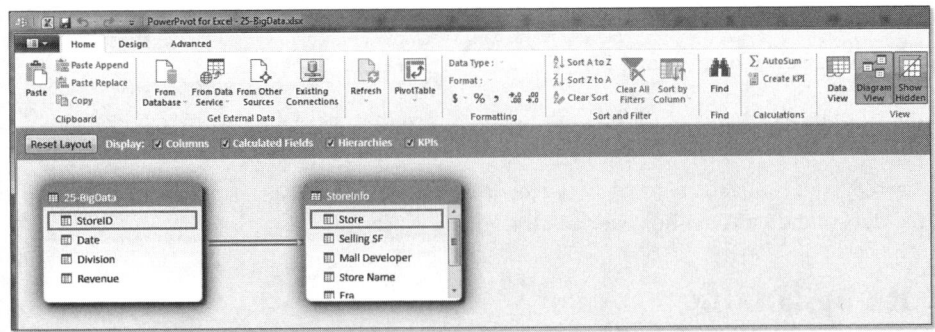

Figure 25.21
Drag from one field to another to define a relationship.

Add Calculated Columns Using DAX

One downside to pivot tables created from PowerPivot data is that they cannot automatically group daily data up to years. Before building the pivot table, let's use the DAX formula language to add a new calculated column to the data in PowerPivot.

Follow these steps to add a Year field:

1. Click the first worksheet tab at the bottom of the PowerPivot window. This is your 1.8 million–row data set.

2. The column to the right of Revenue has a heading of Add Column. Click in the first cell of this blank column.

3. Click the fx icon to the left of the formula bar. The Insert Function dialog appears with categories for All, Date & Time, Math & Trig, Statistical, Text, Logical, Filter, Information, and Parent/Child. Select Date & Time from the drop-down. You instantly notice that this is not the same list of functions in Excel. Five of the first six functions that appear in the window are exotic and new.

4. Luckily, some familiar old functions are in the list as well. Scroll down and select the YEAR function. Click OK to insert the YEAR function in the formula bar. Click the first date in the Date column. PowerPivot proposes a formula of =year(demo[Date]. Type the closing parenthesis and press Enter. Excel fills in the column with the year associated with the date, as shown in Figure 25.22.

5. Right-click the column and select Rename Column. Type a new name, such as **Year**.

You could probably think of many more columns to add, but let's move on to using the pivot table.

Figure 25.22
A new calculated column is
added. You want to rename
this.

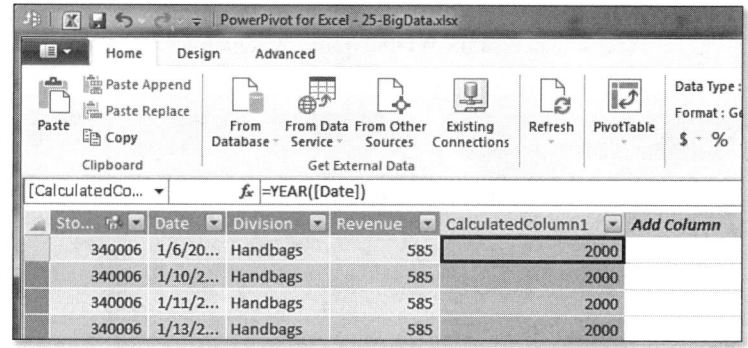

Build a Pivot Table

Open the PivotTable drop-down on the Home tab of the PowerPivot ribbon. As shown in Figure
25.23, you have choices for a single pivot table, a single chart, a chart and a table, two charts, Power
View, and so on.

Figure 25.23
You have many options beyond a single
table or chart.

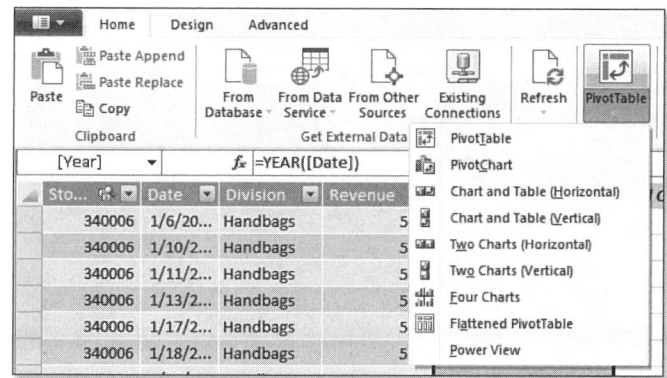

➡ *To learn how to deal with two or more pivot charts,* **see** *"Combination Layouts,"* **p. 837.**

Follow these steps:

1. Select PivotTable. You now see the PowerPivot tab back in the Excel window.

2. Select to put the pivot table on a new worksheet and click OK. You are now back in Excel. The
   PivotTable Field List shows both tables, although you must use the plus symbol next to each
   table to see the fields in the table.

3. Expand the BigData table in the PowerPivot Field List and select Revenue. Expand the StoreInfo table and select Region. Excel builds a pivot table showing sales by region (see Figure 25.24). You now have a pivot table from 1.8 million rows of data with a virtual link to a lookup table.

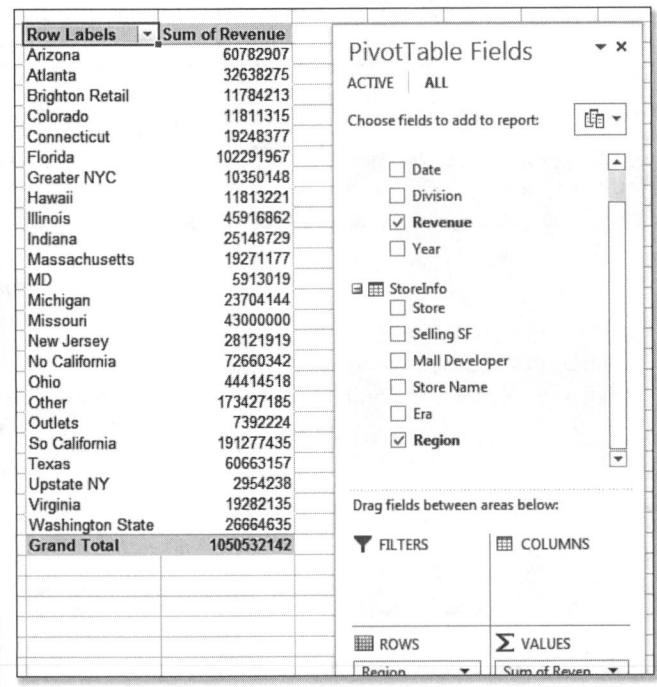

Figure 25.24
This pivot table summarizes 1.8 million rows and data from two tables.

At this point, you might want to go to the PivotTable Tools tabs to further format the pivot table. You could apply a currency format and rename the Sum of Revenue field. You could also choose a format with banded rows, and so on.

Some Things Are Different

If you have spent your whole Excel life building pivot tables out of regular Excel data, you are going to find some annoyances with these PowerPivot pivot tables. Many of these issues are not because of PowerPivot. They are because any PowerPivot pivot table automatically is an OLAP pivot table. This means that it behaves like an OLAP pivot table.

Here are some items to note:

- Days of the week do not automatically sort into the proper sequence. You have to choose More Sort Options, Ascending, More Options. Uncheck the AutoSort box. Open the First Key Sort Order drop-down and choose Sunday, Monday, Tuesday.

- There is a trick in regular Excel pivot tables that you can do instead of dragging field names to the right place. You can go to a cell that contains the word *Friday* and type **Monday** there. When you press Enter, the Monday data moves to that new column. This does not work in PowerPivot pivot tables!

- When you enter a formula in the Excel interface, you can point to a cell to include that cell in the formula. You can do this using the mouse or the arrow keys. Apparently, the PowerPivot team is made up of mouse people, because they support building a formula using the mouse in PowerPivot. Old-time Lotus 1-2-3 customers who build their formulas using arrow keys will be disappointed to find that the arrow key method doesn't work.

Two Kinds of DAX Calculations

You've already seen an example where you used a DAX function to add a calculated column to a table in the PowerPivot window. There are 81 functions that are mostly copied straight from Excel for doing these types of calculations. The RELATED function can also be used in a calculated column to grab a value from a different table.

DAX can also be used to create new measures in the pivot table. These functions do not calculate a single cell value. They are all aggregate functions that calculate a value for the filtered rows behind any cell in the pivot table. There are 54 new DAX functions to enable these calculations. The real power is in these functions.

DAX Calculations for Calculated Columns

You've already seen one example of a calculated column. The functions are remarkably similar to the same functions in Excel and mostly don't require a lot of explanation. There are, however, a few oddities where an Excel function was renamed:

- The rarely documented DATEDIF function in Excel is now renamed as YEARFRAC and is rewritten to actually work.

- The TEXT function in Excel is renamed to FORMAT.

- The SUMIFS function is replaced by CALCULATE.

- The VLOOKUP function is simplified with the RELATED function. The RELATED( ) function is described in the next section.

- DAX introduces the BLANK( ) function. Because some of the aggregation functions can base a calculation on either ALLNONBLANKROW or FIRSTNONBLANK, you can use the BLANK( ) function in an IF( ) function to exclude certain rows from measure calculations.

- The CHOOSE function is renamed as the SWITCH function. Whereas CHOOSE must work with values from 1 to 255, the SWITCH function can be programmed to work with other values.

Using RELATED() to Base a Column Calculation on Another Table

When you are building a calculation in the PowerPivot grid, you might need to refer to a value in another PowerPivot table. In normal Excel, you might do a VLOOKUP. In PowerPivot, you use RELATED.

In the current example, the BigData table has StoreID and total sales for a day. One popular metric in retail reporting is sales per square foot. The StoreInfo lookup table has Store ID and Selling Square Feet, so you have all the data you need to do the calculation.

Go to the PowerPivot grid and click in a blank cell to start a new calculation. Type the equal sign. Click a cell in the Sales column. PowerPivot shows a starting formula of `=[Revenue]`. Type the slash to indicate division.

Now, you need to grab the Selling SF field from the StoreInfo table. Rather than do a VLOOKUP, type **RELATED(**. Start to type the first few letters in the table name. After typing **STO**, you can easily see the list of fields in the StoreInfo table. Click on Selling SF. Finish the formula with a closing parenthesis and press Enter.

Using these calculated columns and relationships, you can create some interesting pivot tables. Remember that calculated columns are calculated for every row in your underlying data. The Sales Per Square Foot formula is evaluated 1.8 million times in the PowerPivot grid.

Instead, you can use DAX formulas to define a new calculated field that is only calculated once per cell in the final pivot table.

Using DAX to Create a Calculated Field in the Pivot Table

DAX calculated fields can run circles around traditional calculated fields. Before you dive in, though, you need to remember one mantra: "Filter first, then calculate." To understand this mantra, consider cell D11 in Figure 25.25.

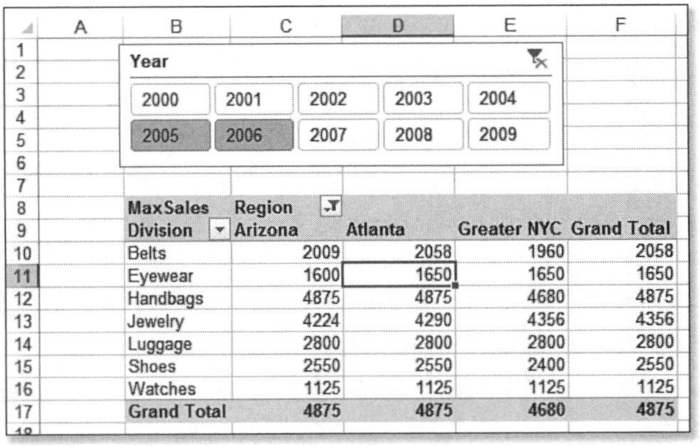

MaxSales	Region			
Division	Arizona	Atlanta	Greater NYC	Grand Total
Belts	2009	2058	1960	2058
Eyewear	1600	1650	1650	1650
Handbags	4875	4875	4680	4875
Jewelry	4224	4290	4356	4356
Luggage	2800	2800	2800	2800
Shoes	2550	2550	2400	2550
Watches	1125	1125	1125	1125
Grand Total	4875	4875	4680	4875

Figure 25.25
How many filters are on cell D11?

Think about how many filters are applied to cell D11. Would you say one? I think the answer is three.

Everyone would agree that cell D11 is filtered to show only records that fall in the year 2006. In addition, the row and column fields are really filters as well. For cell D11, you want only sales from the eyewear division. You also only want records from stores in the Atlanta region. Those are two additional filters for cell D11.

As you start to think about DAX calculated fields, remember that to figure out the value for a particular cell in the pivot table, a DAX calculated field must first filter and then calculate the result using the DAX formula.

You should realize that a DAX calculated field is only calculated once per value cell in the final pivot table. Rather than calculating once per row in the data, these formulas are only evaluated once per cell in the final pivot table. In Figure 25.25, the calculation only happens 32 times because there are only 32 value cells in the pivot table.

To define a new calculated field, go to the Excel ribbon, click the PowerPivot tab, and choose Calculated Fields, New Calculated Field. Excel displays the Calculated Field dialog.

You should specify your main table in the Table Name field. Give the field a name, such as **NumberStoresOpen**. Repeat the name in the Description field. Type your formula in the formula box. Use the fx icon to insert function names. For field names, start by typing a few characters of the table name and then use the AutoComplete list to select the field.

When you are done, click the Check Formula button to check the syntax. Note that the tooltip for the function still covers up the result of the check formula. You need to click and hold the Check Formula button to see "No Errors in Formula," as shown in Figure 25.26.

Click OK to add the new calculated field to the PivotTable Field List.

Figure 25.26
Define a new calculated field.

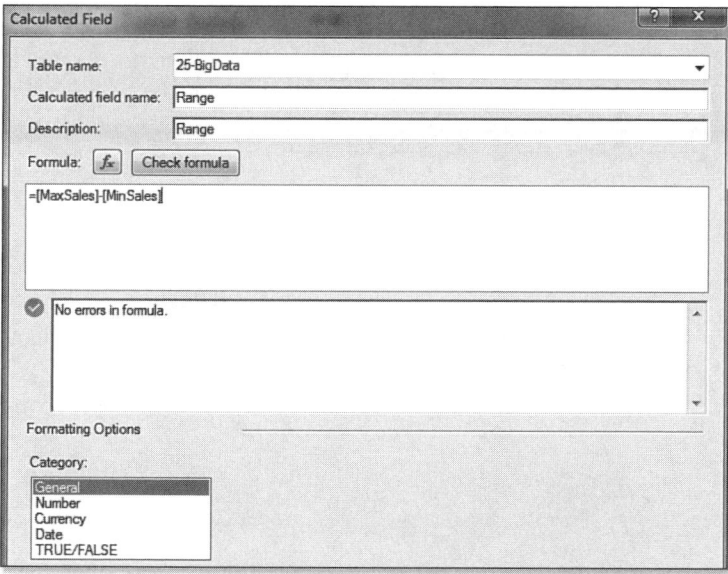

Count Distinct Using DAX

DAX lets you count how many distinct values meet the filter. Wait, that is so good, I am going to repeat it: DAX lets you count how many distinct values meet the filter! Do you understand the gravity of that statement? People who create advanced pivot tables always get tripped up because pivot tables cannot come up with a distinct count of something.

In Chapter 28, "Automating Repetitive Functions Using VBA Macros," I offer the ridiculous formula `=1/COUNTIFS(...)` to try to replicate Count Distinct. DAX now lets you count how many distinct values meet the filter.

In Figure 25.27, it looks like sales in the Arizona region doubled from 2000 to 2001, going from $2,975,025 in cell D10 to $5,951,928 in cell D12.

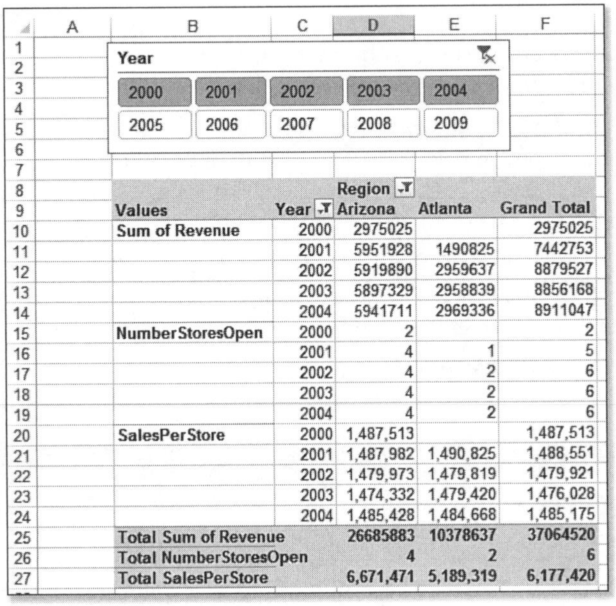

Year: 2000 | 2001 | 2002 | 2003 | 2004 | 2005 | 2006 | 2007 | 2008 | 2009

		Region		
Values	Year	Arizona	Atlanta	Grand Total
Sum of Revenue	2000	2975025		2975025
	2001	5951928	1490825	7442753
	2002	5919890	2959637	8879527
	2003	5897329	2958839	8856168
	2004	5941711	2969336	8911047
NumberStoresOpen	2000	2		2
	2001	4	1	5
	2002	4	2	6
	2003	4	2	6
	2004	4	2	6
SalesPerStore	2000	1,487,513		1,487,513
	2001	1,487,982	1,490,825	1,488,551
	2002	1,479,973	1,479,819	1,479,921
	2003	1,474,332	1,479,420	1,476,028
	2004	1,485,428	1,484,668	1,485,175
Total Sum of Revenue		26685883	10378637	37064520
Total NumberStoresOpen		4	2	6
Total SalesPerStore		6,671,471	5,189,319	6,177,420

Figure 25.27
Did Arizona sales really double from 2000 to 2001?

It turns out that the Arizona region went from two stores in 2000 to four stores in 2001. Two calculated fields in the pivot table illustrate the difference.

Rows 15:19 calculate NumberStoresOpen using the DAX formula `=DISTINCTCOUNT('25-BigData'[StoreID])`.

After you define a calculated field, you can use that field in future calculations. The `SalesPerStore` field in rows 20:24 is calculated as `=SUMX('25-BigData','25-BigData'[Revenue])/ [NumberStoresOpen]`.

You do not have to display Sum of Revenue or NumberStoresOpen in the pivot table. You could simplify the pivot table to show only SalesPerStore. PowerPivot calculates the NumberStoresOpen field for each cell in the pivot table and then displays the SalesPerStore, as shown in Figure 25.28.

Figure 25.28
SalesPerStore is calculated from a field in the data divided by a different DAX calculated field.

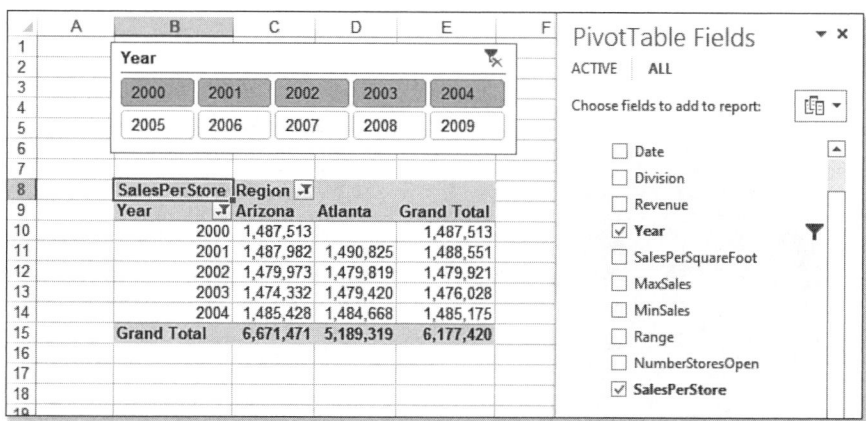

Defining KPIs with PowerPivot

KPI stands for *key performance indicator*. Starting in Excel 2013, PowerPivot offers support for KPIs. A KPI can only be created for a calculated field that has been defined using the Insert Calculated Field command.

To define a KPI, go to the PowerPivot tab in the Excel window. Choose KPIs, Create New KPI. Choose a calculated field and enter a target value. Choose an icon set and then specify ranges for each icon as shown in Figure 25.29.

Once defined, the KPI appears in the PivotTable Field List. If you expand the KPI using the plus icon, you can see three virtual fields: Value, Goal, and Status. The icon is stored in the Status field (see Figure 25.30).

In Figure 25.31, the pivot table shows the value in rows 10:12, the goal in 13:15, and the status in rows 16:18.

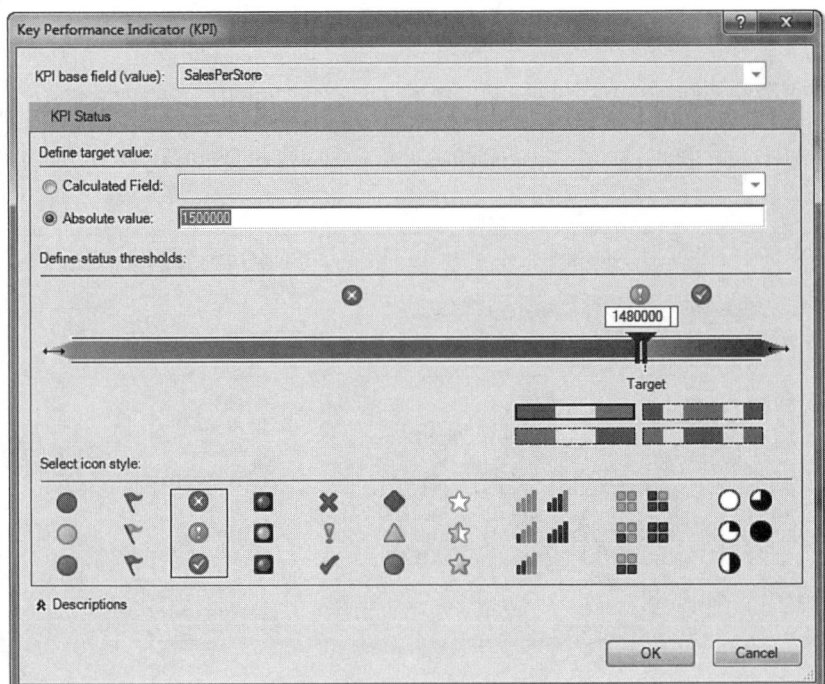

Figure 25.29
Define a KPI.

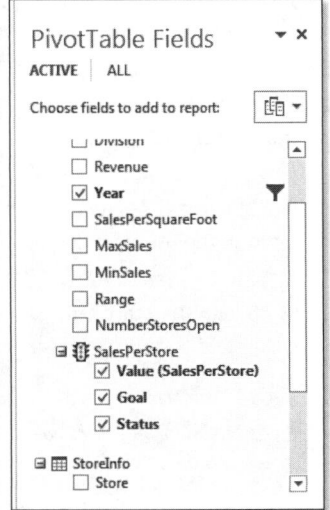

Figure 25.30
The KPI appears in the field list as three values.

Figure 25.31
You can choose to report one or all of
the three fields associated with the KPI.

Values	Year	Arizona	Atlanta	Greater NYC	Grand Total
			Region		
SalesPerStore	2005	1483774.5	1488620.667	1476420	1484672.5
	2006	1488088.75	1488284	1485551	1487844.75
	2007	1483298.8	1482060.333	1481880	1482728.333
SalesPerStore Goal	2005	1500000	1500000	1500000	1500000
	2006	1500000	1500000	1500000	1500000
	2007	1500000	1500000	1500000	1500000
SalesPerStore Status	2005	○	○	●	○
	2006	○	○	○	○
	2007	○	○	○	○
Total SalesPerStore		3860789.4	4458965	4443851	4124965.889
Total SalesPerStore Goal		1500000	1500000	1500000	1500000
Total SalesPerStore Status		●	●	●	●

Using QuickExplore

If you select a value cell in a PowerPivot pivot table, Excel displays a QuickExplore icon to the right and below the cell. Click this icon for a list of ways to drill down on the cell, as shown in Figure 25.32.

Figure 25.32
Click the Lightning-Bolt-Magnifying-
Glass icon to see various ways to
explore one cell in the pivot table.

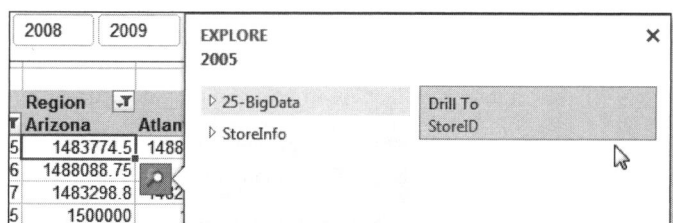

Other Notes

The topic of PowerPivot deserves a whole book. (In fact, you can find my whole book on the subject: *PowerPivot for the Excel Data Analyst*, ISBN 978-07897-4315-2 published by Que.) For learning DAX, check out Rob Collie's book, *DAX Formulas for PowerPivot* (ISBN 978-1-61547-015-0) for numerous examples and tutorials.

The next section covers a few miscellaneous topics that didn't make it elsewhere in this chapter.

Combination Layouts

The PivotTable drop-down in the PowerPivot window offers eight choices. The first choice is a single pivot table and has been used throughout this chapter. The last choice is a flattened pivot table. That is a pivot table that starts in Outline layout instead of Compact layout. The Repeat All Row Labels feature is turned on. If you plan to convert the pivot table to values to reuse it, choosing a flattened pivot table can save you a few clicks along the way.

The other six layouts include up to four pivot charts. I don't get this. Pivot charts look great in Microsoft demos, but no one actually uses them. I can see why Microsoft had to put them here, because they give Microsoft something to demo, but I cannot figure out why Microsoft gives you six different versions. If one pivot chart is bad, why would anyone ever want four of them?

However, let's assume you are actually trying to create a dashboard of four pivot charts and you found this section in the index.

When you choose a combination of multiple elements, you have multiple outlines on the worksheet. To add fields to a specific pivot table or pivot chart, put the active cell inside the outline for that pivot table and then add fields using the PivotTable Field List.

When you are ready to work on another element in the combination, click that element. The Field List resets to blank, and you can design that element. All elements share the same slicers.

Note that for each chart on your layout, Excel inserts a new worksheet to hold the actual pivot table for the chart.

Report Formatting

I am excited about PowerPivot. It lets people who cannot do VLOOKUPs mash up data and create reports that have never been imagined before. However, every Microsoft blog is busy showing the same layout for PowerPivot demos.

Because you've probably seen this layout a thousand times, let's talk about how to replicate the type of layout shown in the blogs and press:

1. Insert a new worksheet to hold the workbook.

2. Create a combo of two or four pivot charts. Choose a location rather than letting them default. Choose a spot on row 5 of the new workbook.

3. Add as many slicers as possible to the top and left of the charts.

4. Build the charts.

5. Make row 1 very tall—perhaps 270 to 300 points tall. Use Insert, Screenshot to add an interesting graphic to row 1.

6. Add an interesting graphic below the charts to balance the graphic on top of the charts.

7. Go to File, Options, Advanced, Display Options for This Worksheet. Clear the Gridlines check box. If you want to go all out, scroll up and remove the scrollbars, sheet tabs, and formula bars.

8. Minimize the ribbon.

9. Add a fill color behind the whole worksheet.

10. While the pivot table is active, click the bounding box around each slicer. Right-click the border. Select Properties. Select Move and Size with cells.

11. Click away from the pivot table. The result is shown in Figure 25.33.

Figure 25.33
This dashboard tracks how many publications have shown this style of dashboard generated by PowerPivot.

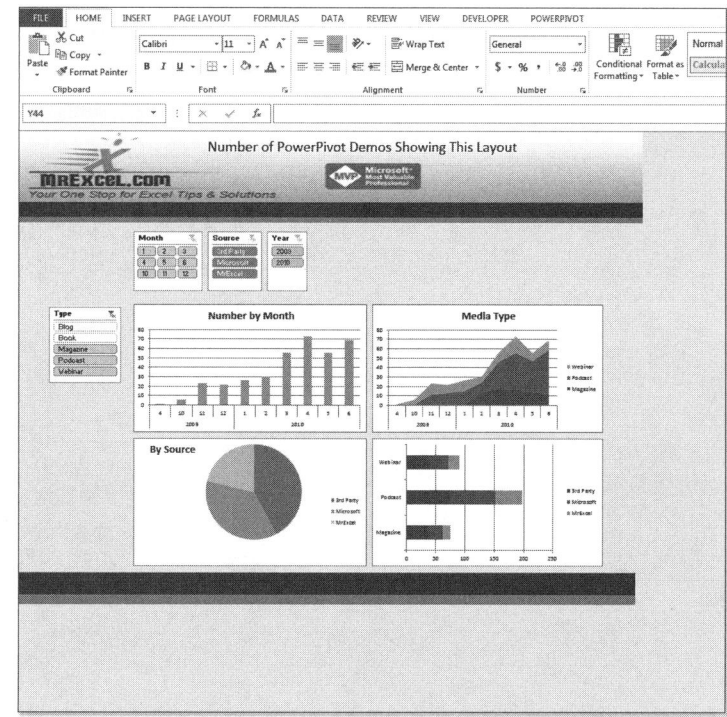

If your layout contains an actual pivot table, consider converting the pivot table to formulas. You can then insert extra rows between the pivot table rows, adding color and so on.

Refreshing the Pivot Table Refreshes PowerPivot

This is new in Excel 2013. When you click Refresh on the Analyze tab in Excel, all of the data is refreshed. This means that PowerPivot reloads the 1.8 million–row text file, even if it did not change.

Back in Excel 2010, there were two Refresh operations: one in PowerPivot and one in the Excel interface. Those have been combined now, as you will quickly realize when a refresh takes several long minutes.

Getting Your Data into PowerPivot with SQL Server

Data coming from SQL Server already has a lot of relationships defined. Find the main fact table, select that table, and then click the button for Select Related Tables. PowerPivot reads the database schema and brings in all the tables with relationships predefined. It is, of course, then possible to add in additional Excel or text data to mash up with the SQL Server data.

Other Issues

Can multiple relationships exist between two tables? No. If you need two relationships, import the lookup table twice and link to each copy separately.

Will PowerPivot ever be available for Excel 2007? No. Will models created in Excel 2013 ever be compatible with Excel 2010? No. Significant changes happened inside both Excel 2010 and Excel 2013.

CREATING INTERACTIVE DASHBOARDS WITH POWER VIEW OR GEOFLOW

Excel 2010 brought the amazing PowerPivot add-in for Excel. Excel 2013 now builds on PowerPivot, providing add-ins that let you create beautiful interactive dashboards based on data stored in the Model.

Power View, like PowerPivot, is free if you have Office 2013 Pro Plus or higher. Power View combines pivot tables, charting, mapping, product images, tables, slicers, filters, and a date animation in a single screen-sized canvas.

Preparing Your Data for Power View

Spend a little extra time up front to get your data ready for Power View. The data has to be in the Data Model, so if you have data in Excel, you have to use Ctrl+T to convert each data set to a table.

To truly test out Power View, you want to gather data that includes date, geography, and various categories that can be used as slicers. The following are some extra steps that I used for the sample data set available for download as noted in the introduction:

- I created a Date table that converts daily dates to years and quarters. Yes, I could have done this in PowerPivot with DAX, but I used a separate Date table instead. I copied a column of 411,000 dates to a new worksheet and then used Data, Remove Duplicates. The new Year column came from the =YEAR() function. The new Quarter column required a VLOOKUP from MONTH() to convert to a quarter number.

- The main table has a field for GeographyID and ProductID. In PowerPivot, I linked a Geography table that identifies City, State, and Region for each market. I did not previously have Region fields, but I looked at a map and logically grouped states into several regions. I think SQL Server people are being geeks when they call their main data table "Fact," but because I was going to be using a tool that came out of the SQL Server camp, I jumped on the geek bandwagon and called my table "Fact" instead of something like "Data."

- The product table has information such as product name, list price, and so on. I added several other fields, such as Category, Publisher, and Version of Excel. I added these fields because I thought they might potentially make interesting ad-hoc analyses.

- This step took an hour. I knew pictures of every product were on our company website, and I figured out where the web designer stored those pictures (by the way, five different folders—talk about geeks!). I downloaded the images to my hard drive and then included the path and file-name for each product image in a new column in the Product table.

- I converted each of the four data sets to tables using Ctrl+T. I visited the Table Name box on the Table Tools Design tab of the ribbon to give the tables meaningful names, such as Geography, Dates, and Products.

For each of the four tables, I visited the PowerPivot tab and chose Add to Data Model. I switched to the PowerPivot window using the Manage icon on the PowerPivot tab.

On the Design tab, you can build relationships to link the Fact table to each of the lookup tables. Several additional steps can be taken to make the Power View experience better:

1. Select the DateTable tab in PowerPivot. On the Design tab, open the Mark as Date Table drop-down and then choose the redundant Mark as Date Table command (see Figure 26.1). You have to specify which column contains a date field and contains only unique dates.

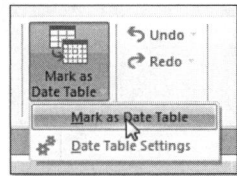

Figure 26.1
Declare the date lookup table as a date table.

2. Go to the Advanced tab in the PowerPivot window. There is a Data Category drop-down field. Mark as many columns as you can with a Data Category. In Figure 26.2, select the entire ImagePath column and choose a date category of Image URL. Note that you don't have to do any-thing fancy like FILE://MyPath/Filename.jpg. The ImagePath is simply C:\Artwork\file1.jpg.

3. Mark the City column with a category of City.

Figure 26.2
Declare the URL column to be an Image URL type.

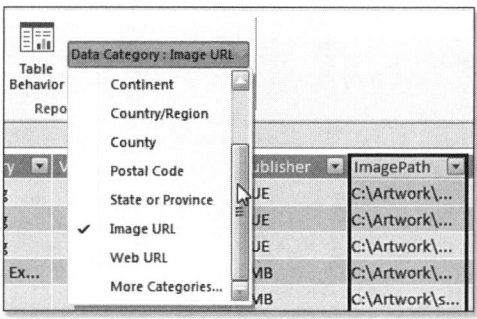

4. The data has both State and State Abbreviation columns. Mark both of these with a category of State or Province.

5. Mark the Product Name category with a category of Product. Note that Product is not in the drop-down. You have to choose More Categories, All and then choose Product.

After you are done defining the relationships and the categories, close the PowerPivot window to return to Excel.

Creating a Power View Worksheet

A Power View dashboard is just another worksheet in your workbook. Go to the Insert tab in the ribbon and choose Power View (see Figure 26.3). A new worksheet is inserted to the left of the current worksheet. The worksheet is given a name such as Power View1. You can right-click the sheet tab to delete it just like a worksheet. You can drag to move it to a new location. It is just like a worksheet.

Figure 26.3
Choose Power View from the Insert tab.

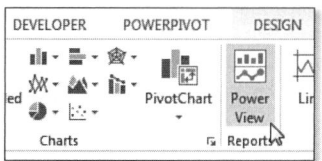

The Power View window contains a Power View Field List, sort of like the PivotTable Field List on the right side. A large blank canvas appears on the left. A collapsible Filters panel appears to the right of the canvas (see Figure 26.4). As you work with Power View, several ribbon tabs related to Power View will come and go. If you see a tab labeled Formatting, Text, or Analyze to the right of the Power View tab, it is related to Power View. These tabs are not labeled as Power View Tools Design like every other contextual tab.

Blank Canvas   Filter Pane   Field List

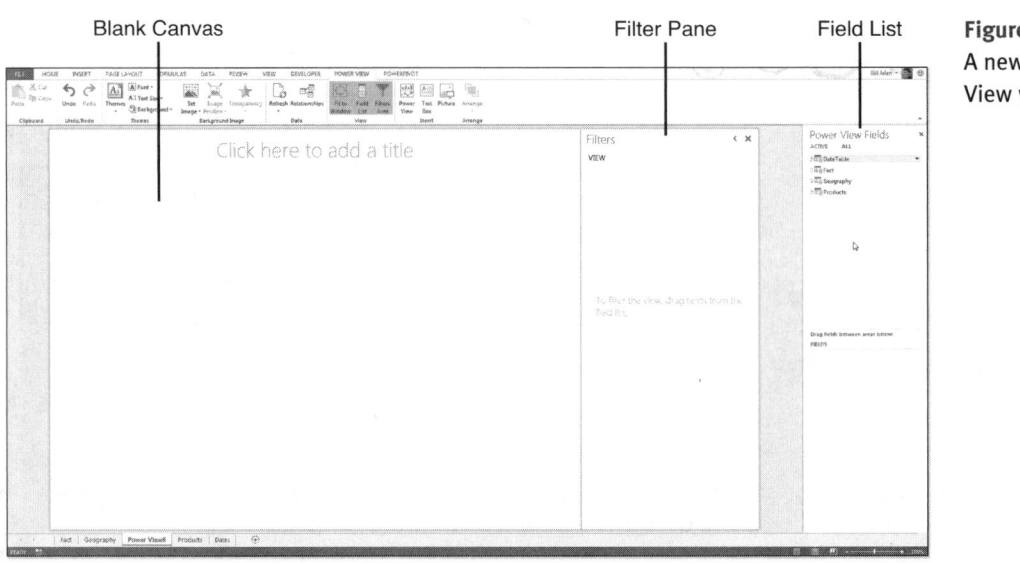

Figure 26.4
A new Power
View window.

Every New Dashboard Element Starts as a Table

Expand one of the data tables in the Field List and choose any field. That field flies over to a new element on the canvas. Every new element starts as a table. You can change an element to something else, but it starts as a table.

The active element has four L-shaped gray corners. If you choose another field from the Field List, that field is added to the active element. Figure 26.5 shows the table created by choosing Year and Revenue.

Convert the Table to a Chart

With the first table selected, you see a Design tab in the ribbon. The left group in this tab is called Switch Visualization. There are 13 choices in four drop-downs and the Map icon. The Column Chart drop-down offers Stacked, 100% Stacked, and Clustered Column charts. The Other Chart drop-down offers Line, Scatter, and Pie charts (see Figure 26.6).

Figure 26.5
The Field List shows settings for the active element.

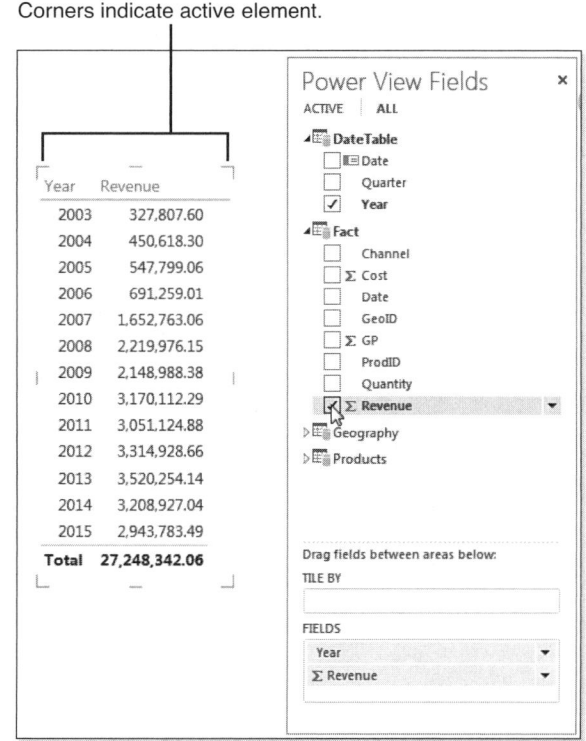

Corners indicate active element.

Figure 26.6
Convert the default table to a chart or a map.

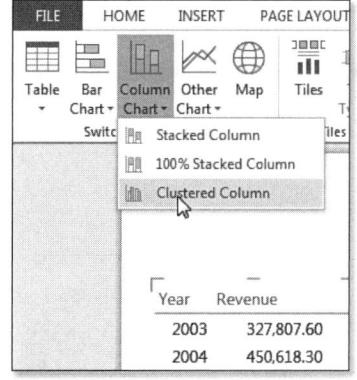

For now, choose a stacked column chart. The element stays the exact same size, and Power View tries to fit a chart in that small area. It doesn't fit, as you can see in Figure 26.7.

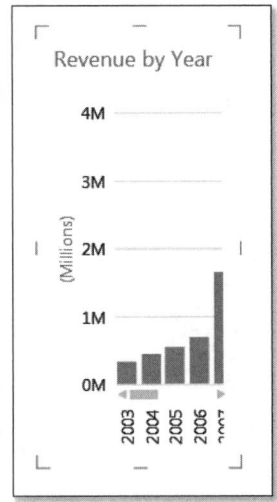

Figure 26.7
The converted chart doesn't fit in the previous space.

Click one of the eight resize handles and stretch the element frame until the chart looks good. At this view, shown in Figure 26.8, you see several interactive elements:

- A drop-down lets you choose how to sort the chart. In this case, sorting by ascending years is really the only way that makes sense, but you could sort by Revenue descending to have the highest years at the left.

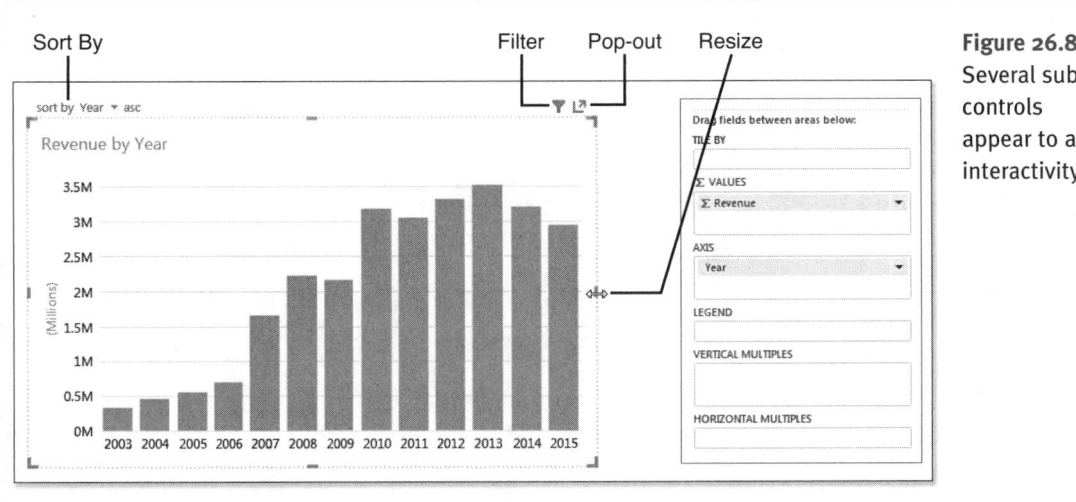

Figure 26.8
Several subtle controls appear to add interactivity.

- The Funnel icon takes you to the Filters panel. You could choose to show only years greater than $1.5 million in order to get rid of the start-up years of a product.

- The pop-out icon makes the element temporarily display at full screen. Say that you have 10 small elements on the dashboard. You can click the pop-out icon to make one of the small elements full screen. After the element is full screen, a pop-in icon returns the element to the original size.

In the Field List, drag the Channel field to the Legend area. The chart becomes a stacked chart showing book sales by Online, eBook, and Brick and Mortar stores (see Figure 26.9). Notice that the legend starts on the right, which takes up some space. Power View automatically staggers the years along the horizontal axis to get them to fit.

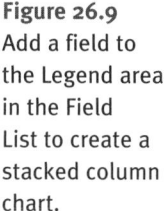

Figure 26.9
Add a field to the Legend area in the Field List to create a stacked column chart.

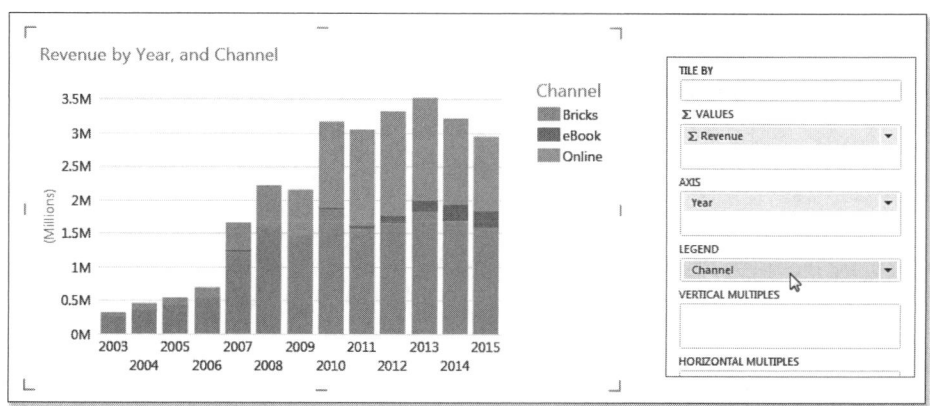

Although a chart is selected, a Layout tab appears in the ribbon. Using the Layout tab, you can move the legend to the top, add data labels, or change the type of horizontal axis.

Creating a New Element by Dragging

To add a new element to the dashboard, you drag a field from the Field List and drop it in a blank portion of the canvas. Just as with the first element, this element starts as a small table. You can switch it to a chart, resize it, and add more fields. Keep adding new elements as necessary.

You can also create a new element by copying and pasting an existing element. If you have designed one chart, right-click that chart and choose Copy. Click in a blank area of the canvas and paste. You can now change the fields in the Field List to change the chart.

The next bit is magic.

Every Chart Point Is a Slicer for Every Other Element

In Figure 26.10, three charts appear on the canvas. The top-left chart shows revenue by year by channel. The bottom-left chart shows revenue by year by version. The top-right chart is a pie chart showing total revenue by version.

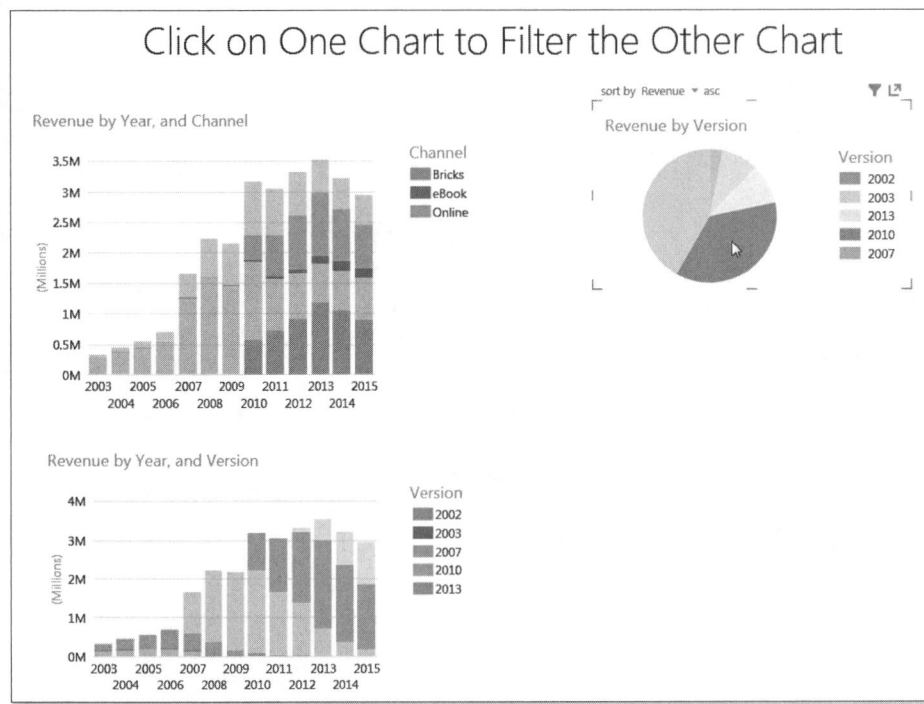

Figure 26.10
All elements are connected. Click on a pie wedge, and the other charts highlight the corresponding data.

If you click on any part of any chart, all of the other charts are filtered to the same element. The mouse pointer is clicking on the Excel 2010 version in the pie chart. The other two charts instantly update. All of the non-2010 portions of the columns are faded, leaving only the colored portions as bright.

You can select the original chart element again to turn the filter off.

Adding a Real Slicer

The slicers in Power View look different than regular slicers, but they act the same way. To create a slicer, drag a field to a blank area of the canvas. That field starts out as a new table. Go to the Design tab of the ribbon and choose Slicer. The table is converted to a Power View slicer (see Figure 26.11).

Figure 26.11
A slicer on the
canvas controls
all elements on
the canvas.

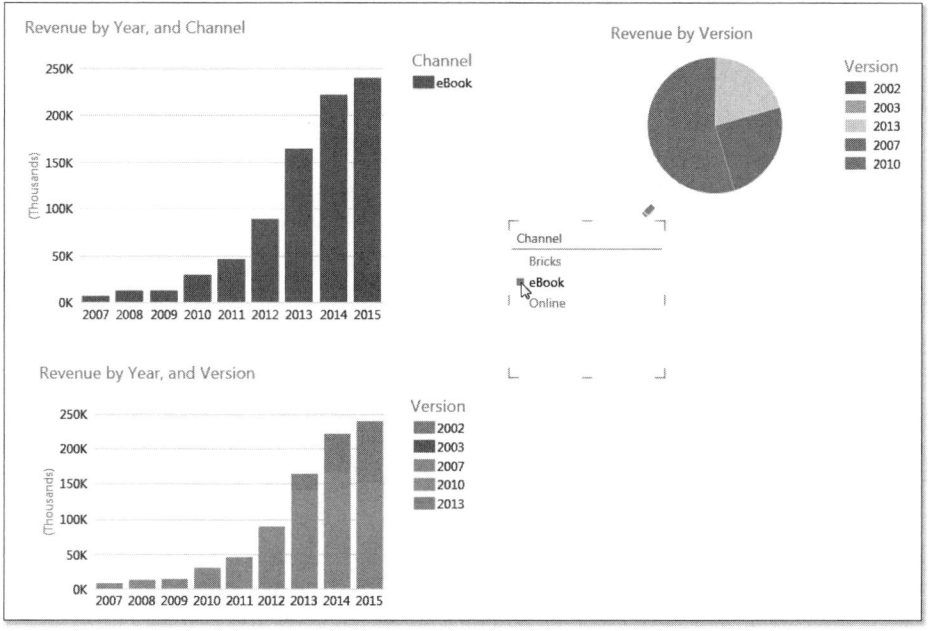

You'll notice these differences from a regular slicer:

- A colored square next to an item means the item is selected.

- You can click one item to select that one item.

- To select multiple items, you have to Ctrl+click the other items.

- The slicer is always one column. You cannot rearrange slicers in Power View as you can in a regular pivot table.

- An eraser icon appears in the top right of the slicer. This is the Clear Filter icon. It is equivalent to the Funnel with X icon in a regular slicer.

The Filter Pane Can Be Confusing

The last two sections show you how to filter the canvas. There is also a filter pane. The filter pane includes a category for View, Chart, or Table. The Chart or Table category only appears when an individual chart or table element is active.

The other distinction is not as confusing and actually makes sense. Filters applied to the view affect all elements in the view. Filters applied to a chart affect only the active chart.

> ## 📡 Caution
>
> There are two really important distinctions when working with the filter pane. The first involves how Power View calculates the filter:
>
> - When you are working with a Chart filter, you are filtering at the summary level. Ask for years greater than $1.5 million and you only get the years with a total yearly revenue over $1.5 million.
> - When you are working with the View filter, you are filtering at the detail row level. Apply a filter where Revenue is greater than $100 and Power View goes back to the original 411,000 records and only rolls up the records greater than $100.

The Filter pane for Chart or Table starts with the fields in the chart or table. The Filter pane for View is always an empty canvas. You have to drag fields from the top of the Field List to the Filter pane.

Use Tile Boxes to Filter One or a Group of Charts

The Power View Field List offers a field called Tile By that provides another way to filter an element on the dashboard.

Select a chart or table that you want to filter. In the Field List, hover over the filter field. A drop-down menu appears. Open the drop-down and choose Add as Tile By.

The filter appears as a category list across the top of the chart. Notice the thick blue lines above and below the chart. These lines tell you that only the one chart between the lines is affected by the Tile categories (see Figure 26.12).

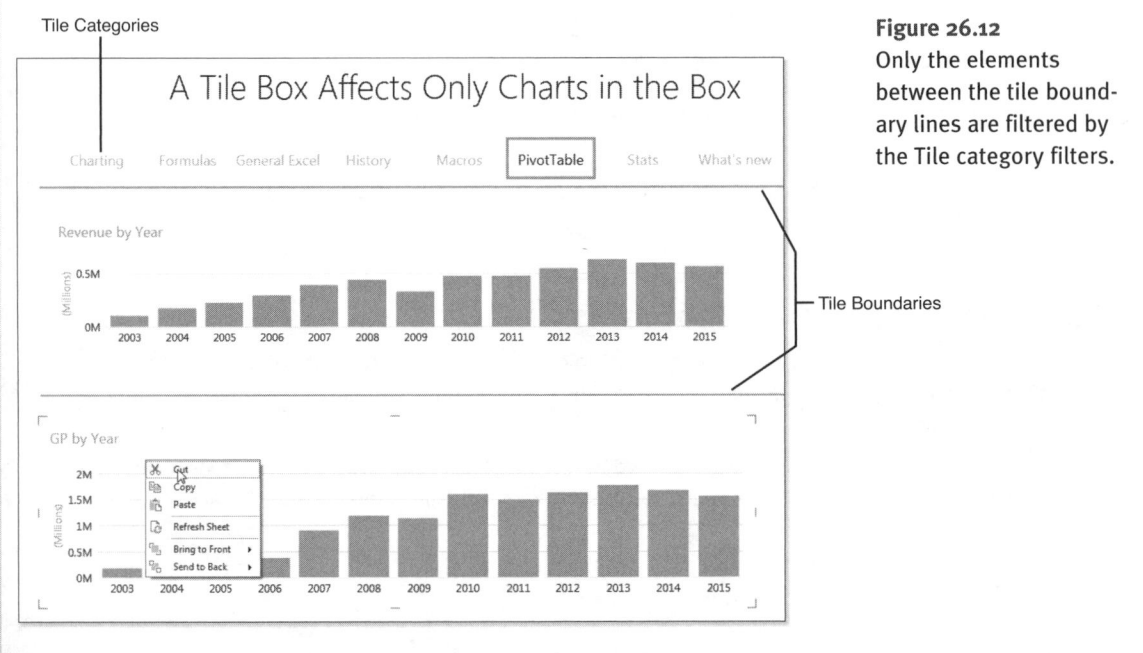

Figure 26.12
Only the elements between the tile boundary lines are filtered by the Tile category filters.

Tiles are good. They provide a way to filter one chart and not the other charts. But I can already sense that you will want to have two charts controlled by Tile 1 and another chart controlled by Tile 2. Fortunately, this can be done.

In Figure 26.12, right-click the element that is outside of the boundary and choose Cut. Click anywhere inside the Tile boundary lines, right-click, and paste. The result will inevitably be two charts right on top of each other. Drag the bottom boundary line to add some room. Then, individually move the two charts so they fit. The result is shown in Figure 26.13. Both of these charts are within the boundary lines, so they are both controlled by the category filters at the top.

Figure 26.13
Both elements are within the boundary lines and they are filtered together.

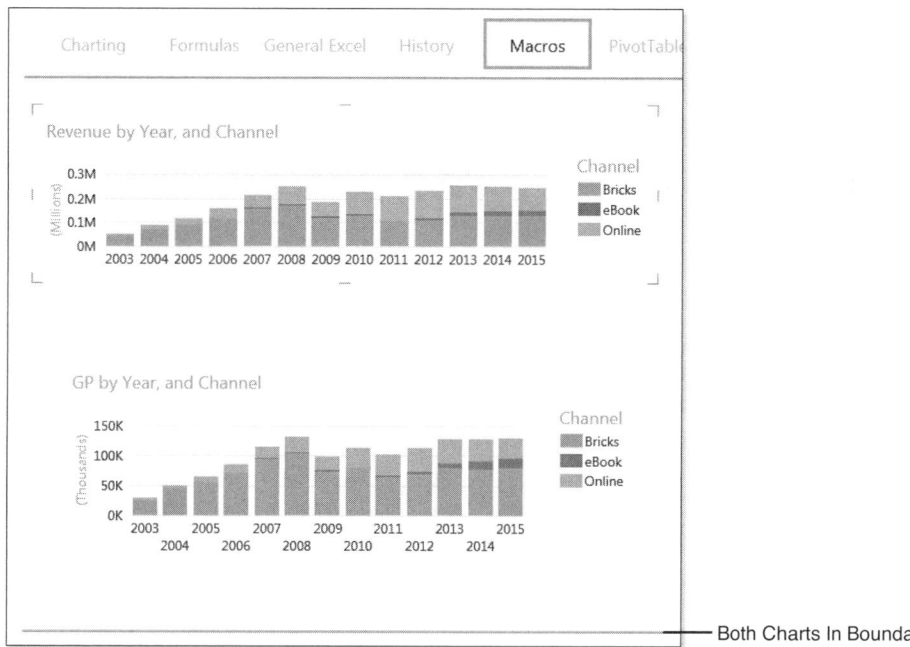

Both Charts In Boundary

Replicating Charts Using Multiples

Say that you have a chart element that shows revenue by year. You could add a new field to the Legend area in order to create a stacked or clustered column chart.

Alternatively, you can drag the new field to the Vertical Multiples or Horizontal Multiples field. This causes Power View to replicate the chart for each value in that field. In Figure 26.14, the revenue chart appears as three charts based on the Channel field dropped in the Vertical Multiples field.

 Note

It seems that in many cases, there is no difference between dropping a field in Vertical Multiples and Horizontal Multiples. Power View chooses the best arrangement to make the charts fit inside the element.

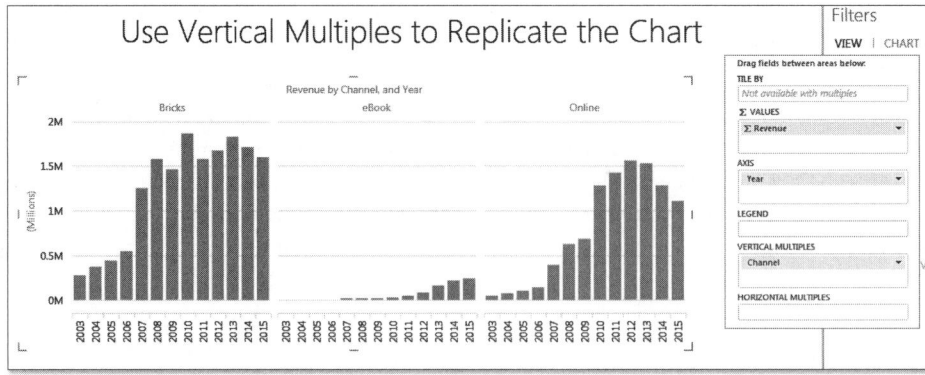

Figure 26.14
Add a field to the Vertical Multiples field to replicate the chart.

Showing Data on a Map

As you probably know, Microsoft owns Bing. Bing maps are pretty cool. Because Microsoft owns Bing, they seem to have free rein to use the Bing API as much as they want to, and it is evident with this feature.

In a blank section of the Power View canvas, build a table showing Revenue by State. With the table active, go to the Design tab in the ribbon and choose Map from the Switch Visualization category.

A warning appears that Excel has to send a list of states to Bing. I am trying to think of a case where you would care. Perhaps if you were working for a secret government agency and were mapping the location of where the Atomic Energy Commission stores remains of alien UFO crashes, and you think that some random person at Bing Maps is a UFO conspiracy theorist, then maybe you would care. But, I have to believe that Bing Maps is getting a million requests a day, and the odds of anyone figuring out that your list is UFO storage sites instead of the location of Starbucks stores is slim.

After a few seconds of geocoding, a map displays. By default, the Revenue field becomes the size of the bubble in each state (see Figure 26.15).

When you click the map, icons let you zoom in or zoom out. With apologies to my friend Brian in Maui, you can zoom to the continental United States to get a better view.

In Figure 26.16, the Channel field has been moved to the Color area. This creates a pie chart in each state showing the relative percentage of sales by channel. Apparently, eBooks are doing better in California than in Arizona and New Mexico.

 Note

Like all data sets in this book, the numbers in these screenshots are not actual figures. Fellow PowerPivot Guru Rob Collie and I often note that we both get sucked into fake data sets, trying to find meaning in them. If you really need statistics on sales of eBooks versus print books, do not use the data set that comes with this chapter.

Figure 26.15
Power View
uses the Bing
Maps API
to plot geo-
graphic data
on a map.

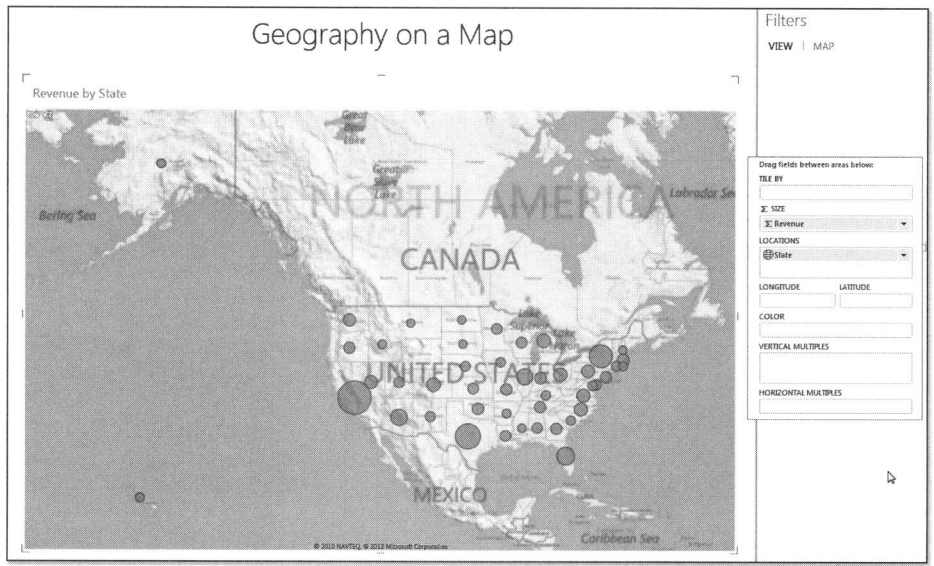

Figure 26.16
Filter by year
and add
Channel to the
Color area.

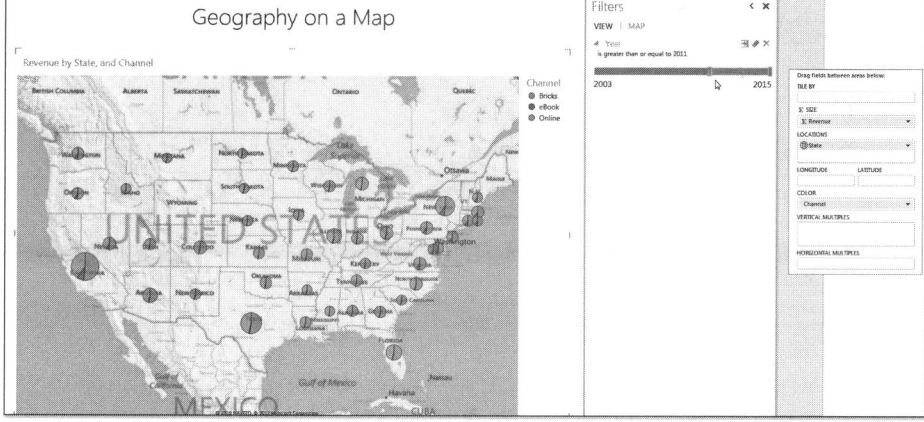

Using Table or Card View with Images

It keeps getting better. Remember that all new elements start as tables. There are three kinds of tables: Table, Matrix, and Card.

A Matrix is similar to a regular pivot table. A Table presents the fields in a boring old table. Click any heading to sort the table by that heading. But wait! Add the image URL field to your table. After a quick warning that the pictures are coming from an external source, the images show up in the table. How cool is that? In Figure 26.17, three slicers on the left control the table. Select from the slicers, and the table shows the books that match the slicers, in descending revenue, with pictures.

Figure 26.17
Add the Picture URL field to get product pictures in the report.

Pictures also work in Card view. To switch a table to Card view, go to Design, Switch Visualizations, Table, Card View. This view presents the field title for each field in every card (see Figure 26.18). It makes me wish that I would have used a different field name than ImageURL.

Figure 26.18
Card view adds heading names to every record.

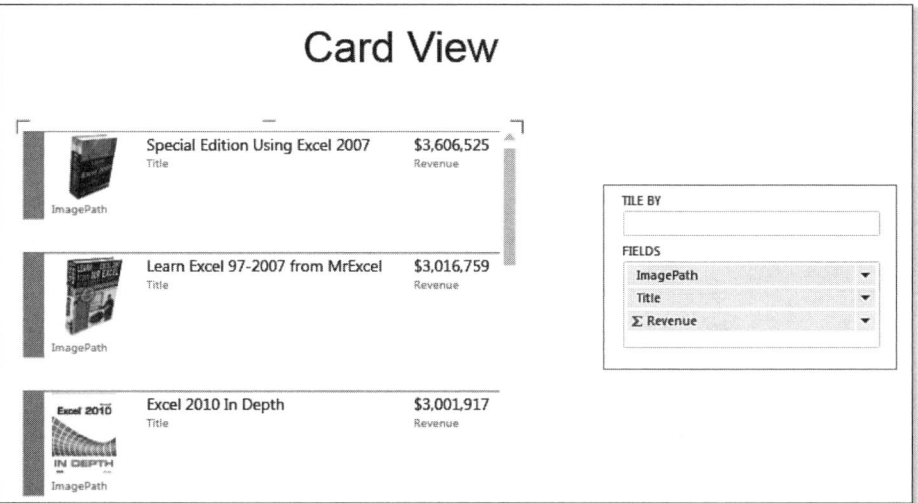

Power View enables you to do the same trick. To create a great scatter chart, you need three or four numeric fields that are related. Drag the first field to a blank section of the canvas. Choose Design, Switch Visualizations, Other Charts, Scatter. Figure 26.19 shows the detail of the choices available in the Field List when you are creating a scatter chart:

Animating a Scatter Chart Over Time

My world changed the day I saw Hans Rosling talk about religions and babies on the Internet. One of my fellow MVPs alerted me to the video. Although the 13-minute talk is interesting, it is not life changing. The life-changing feature of the video comes at the 4:46 mark in the video, when Mr. Rosling presses the Play button and his scatter chart animates to show the changes over the last 50 years. At the 5:15 mark in the video, the animation is done. Listen to the video carefully. The live studio audience applauded the chart. Check it out at http://www.ted.com/talks/hans_rosling_religions_and_babies.html.

Power View enables you to do the same trick. To create a great scatter chart, you need three or four numeric fields that are related. Drag the first field to a blank section of the canvas. Choose Design, Switch Visualizations, Other Charts, Scatter. Figure 26.19 shows the detail of the choices available in the Field List when you are creating a scatter chart:

- Any numeric field for the X axis.

- Any numeric field for the Y axis.

- Optionally, a field to control the size of the data point.

- A Details field. For every unique value in the Details field, you get one point in the scatter chart.

- Optionally, a color field. Each point will be colored according to values in this field.

- A time field for the Play axis.

Figure 26.19
The scatter chart offers the most choices for drop zones.

Note that you can change the calculation for any field after you drop it in the area. Choose the drop-down to the right of the field. Each field can use Sum, Average, Max, and Min. Also, you can choose to count the non-blanks or to provide a distinct count. In the chart shown in Figure 26.20, the Y-axis initially summed the list price for all books sold, which is not meaningful. Changing the calculation to Min, Max, Average would all present the actual list price for the title in the bubble.

A scrubber control appears along the bottom of the chart. You can drag the marker left or right to see the chart at various points in time, or you can click the Play button to watch the chart animate.

The Play dimension is the key to having the chart animate. Unfortunately, at this time, only the scatter chart offers a Play field. You cannot animate column charts, bar charts, pie charts, or tables.

By early 2013, Microsoft will release the GeoFlow add-in, which allows the animation of map data over time.

Using Drill-Down

Set up a bar or column chart with Region in the Axis field and Revenue in the VALUES area. Add the State field as the second Axis field. Nothing changes in the chart view, but you can now double-click one bar or column to drill down and see the states in that region. Add City as a third Axis field, and you can zoom in from State to City. A bent up-arrow appears at the top of the chart. Click this to zoom out.

Figure 26.20
Add a field to the Play axis, and you can animate the chart over time.

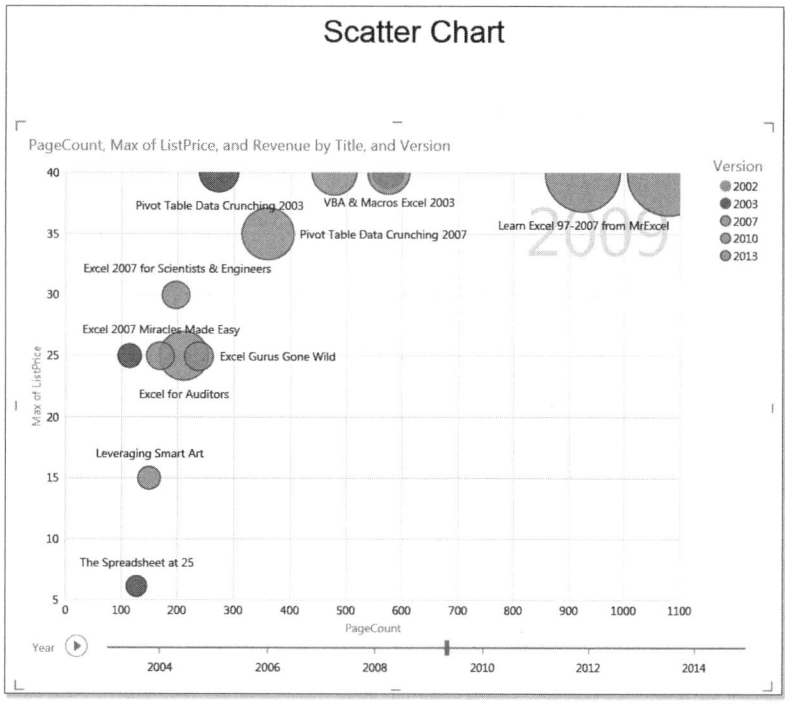

Some Closing Tips on Power View

As you experiment with Power View, keep these tips in mind:

- Be careful when clicking on charts. Click in the whitespace to select a chart. If you advertently click one of the chart columns, you've just filtered everything else on the canvas.

- The Field List has headings for Active and All. If you just created a little chart with two fields, it is likely that the Field List is now in Active mode, which means you only see the tables used in that chart. This is alarming, because all of your other tables and fields are missing. Don't be alarmed. Click All at the top of the field list, and they all come back.

- Don't be afraid to try new charts or tables. Create something. If it doesn't look good, right-click and cut it. No harm. After using Power View, I am surprised how snappy and efficient it is. I have been dealing with 411,000 records in five charts and animating over time and have not had one crash.

Creating a Map in GeoFlow

GeoFlow is an add-in from the Excel team at Microsoft. Using GeoFlow, you can explore your map in 3-D. You can watch a map populate over time, much the same way that Power View shows a scatter chart over time. You also can create a video tour where the map populates over time and then you fly from region to region in the map.

GeoFlow requires the PowerPivot and GeoFlow add-ins to be enabled in Excel 2013 Pro Plus. PowerPivot is already installed if you have the correct edition of Excel 2013. You will have to download GeoFlow from Microsoft. As of this writing, the final URL has not been published because the product will not release until January 2013. You could search for Microsoft GeoFlow to find the download site.

After installing GeoFlow, visit the COM Add-Ins section of Excel Options to ensure that the product is enabled. Go to File, Options, Add-Ins. In the bottom of the Excel options, choose Manage COM Add-Ins and click Go. In the next dialog, add a checkmark next to GeoFlow.

Add data with any geographic component, such as Address, City, State, Province, Country, or Latitude and Longitude, to the PowerPivot data model. The sample data used in this section is a list of all Dairy Queen and Starbucks locations in Florida.

From Excel, choose Data, 3D Map, Explore in 3-D.

Excel switches to the GeoFlow window (see Figure 26.21). You see a large globe in the center of the screen and a list of fields available on the right side. Choose the geographic fields, and click the Map It button at the bottom right.

The process of locating each record in the map is called *Geocoding*. A small set of roughly 600 points that contain latitude and longitude will be mapped nearly instantly. A data set of 15,000 points with street address, city, and state will take a couple of minutes to geocode.

GeoFlow maps the data. Drag the Name field to the Category drop zone to use a different color for Starbucks versus Dairy Queen (see Figure 26.22).

GeoFlow allows for more interesting panning and zooming.

- Click and drag the map to change the center position of the map.

- Roll the mouse wheel to zoom in or out.

- Use Ctrl+Wheel to change the altitude of the camera.

- Hold down Alt while dragging to rotate the map.

Figure 26.21
Choose the geography fields and click Map It.

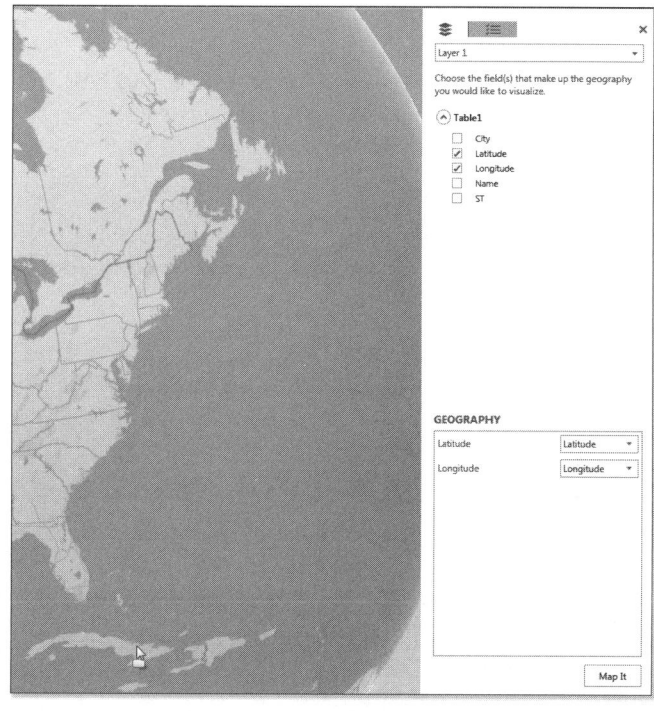

Figure 26.22
Drag the Name field to the Category. Each point will be color-coded based on Starbucks or Dairy Queen.

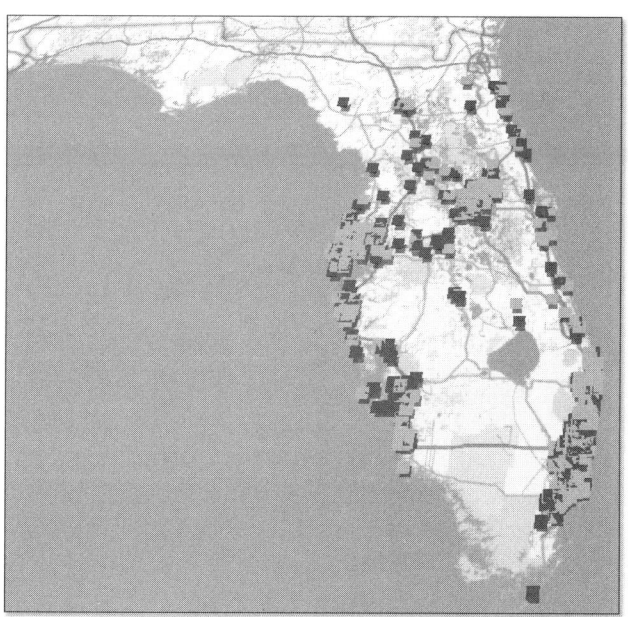

Figure 26.23 shows a GeoFlow map where median income controls the height of the marker. Using the navigation controls mentioned earlier, this map shows the Orlando and Central Florida area looking from the east. You can see Cocoa Beach in the foreground, plus Tampa and Saint Petersburg in the background. From here, you could arrange a tour that flies in for a close-up look at Orlando by neighborhood.

Figure 26.23
You can fly through the map.

You also can use GeoFlow to animate a data set over time, just as you can do with the scatter chart in Power View. Add a date field to the Time drop zone. When you add the scene to a GeoFlow tour, the data animates over time.

USING WHAT-IF, SCENARIO MANAGER, GOAL SEEK, AND SOLVER

When Dan Bricklin invented VisiCalc in 1979, he was trying to come up with a tool that would let him quickly recalculate his MBA school case studies. Thirty-five years later, spreadsheets are still used for the same functionality.

Newer spreadsheet tools such as Goal Seek and an improved Solver enable you to back directly into the assumptions that lead to a solution. This chapter discusses some of Excel 2013's features that are helpful when you are trying to find a specific answer.

Using What-If

After you have set up a model in Excel, you can make copies of the model side by side and then change the various input variables to test their impact on the final result. Because this type of analysis answers the question of what happens if a change is made, it is known generically as *what-if analyses*.

What-if analyses are the least formal method in this chapter. You copy the input variables and formulas multiple times. You can then vary the input variables until you reach a suitable solution.

For example, Figure 27.1 shows a worksheet to calculate the monthly payment on a car purchase. Cells E1, E2, and E3 are the known values: the price, term, and interest rate. Cell E4 calculates the monthly payment using the =PMT ( ) function.

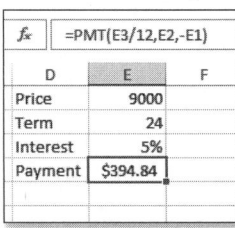

Figure 27.1
You might not like the answer in cell E4, but Excel makes the answer easy to find.

Cells E1:E4 are a self-contained minimodel. You can copy these cells several times over and perform what-if analysis on the car payment model.

Figure 27.2 shows a basic what-if worksheet that you can use to plug in different numbers manually. Columns F and G show the effects of changing the number of months. Columns H:J factor in a lower interest rate. Columns K:M show the effects of finding a lower price. Based on a number of options, column N starts to hone in on a scenario to get to the $225 target payment: Use 42 months, 5% interest, and a price of $8750.

D	E	F	G	H	I	J	K	L	M	N	O
Price	9000	9000	9000	9000	9000	9000	8500	8500	8500	8700	8500
Term	36	42	48	36	42	48	36	42	48	42	42
Interest	5.0%	5.0%	5.0%	4.5%	4.5%	4.5%	5.0%	5.0%	5.0%	5.0%	5.0%
Payment	$270	$234	$207	$268	$232	$205	$255	$221	$196	$226	$221

Figure 27.2
By making multiple copies of the table, you can create a What-If model.

There is nothing magic about this type of what-if analyses. There are no ribbon commands involved (other than applying Conditional Formatting, Color Scale to show the changing cells). You copy the model and plug in a few different numbers. This is how most Excel worksheets use what-if analyses. The remaining topics in this chapter cover the format What-If commands on the ribbon.

Creating a Two-Variable What-If Table

The analysis in Figure 27.2 is fairly ad hoc in that it basically enables you to try various combinations until you find one that is close to your target payment. If you have two variables to manipulate, you can use Excel's fairly powerful Data Table command. To use a data table, follow these steps to build the table shown in Figure 27.3:

1. Enter a formula in the upper-left corner of the table. This formula should point to at least two variable cells.

2. Along the left column of the table, enter various values for one of the input values. These values are substituted in a cell known as the Column Input Cell.

3. Along the top row of the table, enter various values for the other input variable. These values are substituted in a cell that Excel calls the *row input cell*.

Figure 27.3

Preparing for a two-variable what-if analysis.

f_x =PMT(E3/12,E2,-E1)

D	E	F	G	H	I	J	K
Price	9000						
Term	24						
Interest	5%						
Payment	$394.84	24	30	36	42	48	54
	5000						
	5250						
	5500						
	5750						
	6000						

4. Select the entire table.

5. From the Data tab, select Data Tools, What-If Analysis, Data Table.

6. In the Data Table dialog, enter a row input cell and a column input cell.

7. Click OK to complete the table.

You can use the Data Table command to negotiate the price and term of the loan by following these steps:

1. Use the formula in cell E4 as the formula in the top-left corner of your table.

2. From E5:E21, fill in various possible values for purchase price.

3. From F4:K4, fill in various possible values for the term of the loan.

4. Select the entire table, E4:K17, as shown in Figure 27.3.

5. Select Data Table from the Data tab to display the Data Table dialog, as shown in Figure 27.4. The dialog asks you for a row input cell and a column input cell. The Row Input Cell field offers to take each value from the top row of the table and plug it into a particular cell.

Figure 27.4

Setting up the Data Table dialog.

Replace the top row cells in the Row Input Cell.

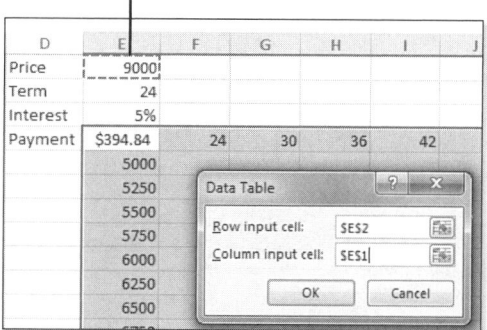

D	E	F	G	H	I	J
Price	9000					
Term	24					
Interest	5%					
Payment	$394.84	24	30	36	42	
	5000					
	5250					
	5500					
	5750					
	6000					
	6250					
	6500					

Data Table

Row input cell: $E$2

Column input cell: $E$1

OK   Cancel

6. Because the values in F4:K4 are loan terms, specify E2 for the row input cell.

7. Similarly, the Column Input Field offers to take each value from the left column and replace that value in a particular cell. Because these cells contain vehicle prices, select E1 as the column input cell.

8. Click OK. Excel fills in the intersection of each row and column with the monthly payment, based on the price in the left column combined with the loan term in the top row. Figure 27.5 shows the resulting table.

t $394.84	24	30	36	42	48	54
5000	219.357	177.647	149.854	130.015	115.146	103.592
5250	230.325	186.529	157.347	136.516	120.904	108.771
5500	241.293	195.412	164.84	143.017	126.661	113.951
5750	252.26	204.294	172.333	149.517	132.418	119.13
6000	263.228	213.176	179.825	156.018	138.176	124.31
6250	274.196	222.059	187.318	162.519	143.933	129.489
6500	285.164	230.941	194.811	169.02	149.69	134.669

Figure 27.5
Excel performs 102 what-if analyses in one command.

9. Select just the interior of the table. You can see that Excel represents the table with the TABLE() array function. Figure 27.6 shows the table after a color scale has been applied.

`{=TABLE(E2,E1)}`

D E	F	G	H	I	J	K
e 9000						
h 24						
rest 5%						
nent $394.84	24	30	36	42	48	54
5000	219.3569	177.6468	149.8545	130.0152	115.1465	103.5915
5250	230.3248	186.5292	157.3472	136.5159	120.9038	108.7711
5500	241.2926	195.4115	164.8399	143.0167	126.6611	113.9507
5750	252.2605	204.2938	172.3327	149.5174	132.4184	119.1302
6000	263.2283	213.1762	179.8254	156.0182	138.1758	124.3098
6250	274.1962	222.0585	187.3181	162.519	143.9331	129.4894
6500	285.164	230.9409	194.8108	169.0197	149.6904	134.669
6750	296.1319	239.8232	202.3036	175.5205	155.4477	139.8485
7000	307.0997	248.7056	209.7963	182.0212	161.2051	145.0281
7250	318.0676	257.5879	217.289	188.522	166.9624	150.2077
7500	329.0354	266.4702	224.7817	195.0227	172.7197	155.3873
7750	340.0033	275.3526	232.2745	201.5235	178.477	160.5668
8000	350.9711	284.2349	239.7672	208.0243	184.2343	165.7464
8250	361.939	293.1173	247.2599	214.525	189.9917	170.926
8500	372.9068	301.9996	254.7526	221.0258	195.749	176.1056
8750	383.8747	310.8819	262.2453	227.5265	201.5063	181.2851
9000	394.8425	319.7643	269.7381	234.0273	207.2636	186.4647

Figure 27.6
The values in the table are calculated by a single TABLE() array formula. Oddly, you cannot enter the TABLE formula by typing it. You must use the Data Table command.

Note

You can use the Data Table command when only a single variable is changing. Enter values for the variable down the left column and enter a single cell with 1 in the top row. In the Data Table dialog, specify any blank cell as the Row Input Cell. Alternatively, enter the changing values across the top row, and use a blank cell as the Column Input Cell.

Using Scenario Manager

The Data Table command is great for models with two variables that can change. However, sometimes you have models with far more variables that can change. In such a case, you should use the Scenario Manager, which enables you to create multiple scenarios, each changing up to 32 variables.

With up to 32 variables changing, it is best to use named ranges for all the input variables before you define your first scenario. One of the results of the Scenario Manager is a summary report. Using named ranges for all the input cells makes the report easier to understand.

➡ *To learn how to use named ranges to your advantage,* **see** *"Using Named Ranges to Simplify Formulas" on* **p. 679.**

Generally, Scenario Manager enables you to set up named scenarios such as Best Case, Worst Case, and Most Likely. In each scenario you can specify values for up to 32 variables. You would then have a model that calculates results based on the 32 input variables. For example, you might have a business plan that projects sales for the next 120 months using growth rates in the input variable section of the spreadsheet. The important distinction is that although you might only have 32 input variables, you might base millions of formulas on these 32 input variables.

Use the Scenario Manager dialog box to switch to a different set of input variables. The worksheet can be calculated using Best Case and Worst Case scenarios. For a specific example, Figure 27.7 shows a sales forecasting model. All the highlighted cells are variables that can change. The model calculates a total forecast in cell B16 and a ratio in cell B18. To set up and use scenarios, use the following steps:

1. Select Data, Data Tools, What-If Analysis, Scenario Manager to display the Scenario Manager dialog. Initially, the Scenario Manager indicates that no scenarios are defined, as shown in Figure 27.8.

2. Click the Add button to add the first scenario. The Add Scenario dialog appears.

 **Note**

It is best to add one scenario that represents your starting assumptions. Otherwise, those numbers will be lost.

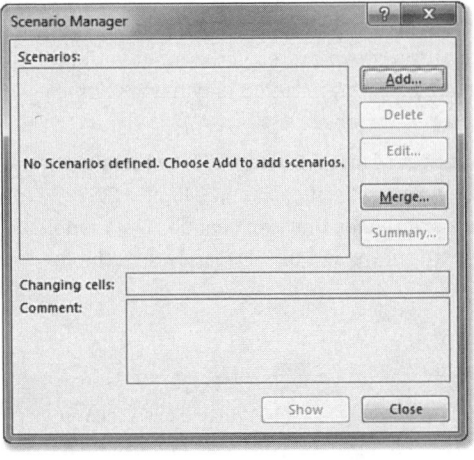

	A	B	C	D	E
1	Sales Forecasting Model				
2		Total	2012	2013	2014
3	Existing Market Size	400,000,000	750,000,000	750,000,000	750,000,000
4	% Upgrading		7%	15%	35%
5	Total Upgraders		52,500,000	112,500,000	262,500,000
6	% Upgraders buying book		4%	3%	2%
7	Upgrade Books		2,100,000	3,375,000	5,250,000
8	Market Growth	1%	7,500,000	7,500,000	7,500,000
9	% New Buying Book		10%	10%	10%
10	Growth Books		750,000	750,000	750,000
11	Total Books		2,850,000	4,125,000	6,000,000
12	OurCo Market Share	12%			
13	Competitor A	10%			
14	Competitor B	11%			
15	All Others	67%			
16	OurCo Book Sales	1,557,000	342,000	495,000	720,000
17	Office Sales	450,000,000	60,000,000	120,000,000	270,000,000
18	Conversion Rate	0.3%			

Figure 27.7
This forecast model is based on nine variable cells.

Figure 27.8
The Scenario Manager dialog before you add the first scenario.

3. In the Add Scenario dialog, enter a name for this scenario and then choose which cells will be changing. Because the variable cells are not adjacent, select the first contiguous range and then Ctrl-click to add additional ranges, as shown in Figure 27.9.

The Scenario Values dialog box appears, which can be used to edit the values for each starting cell (see Figure 27.10). Note that if you had previously named your input cells, the cell names appear in this dialog instead of addresses.

Figure 27.9
Ctrl-click to
select all the
changing cells.

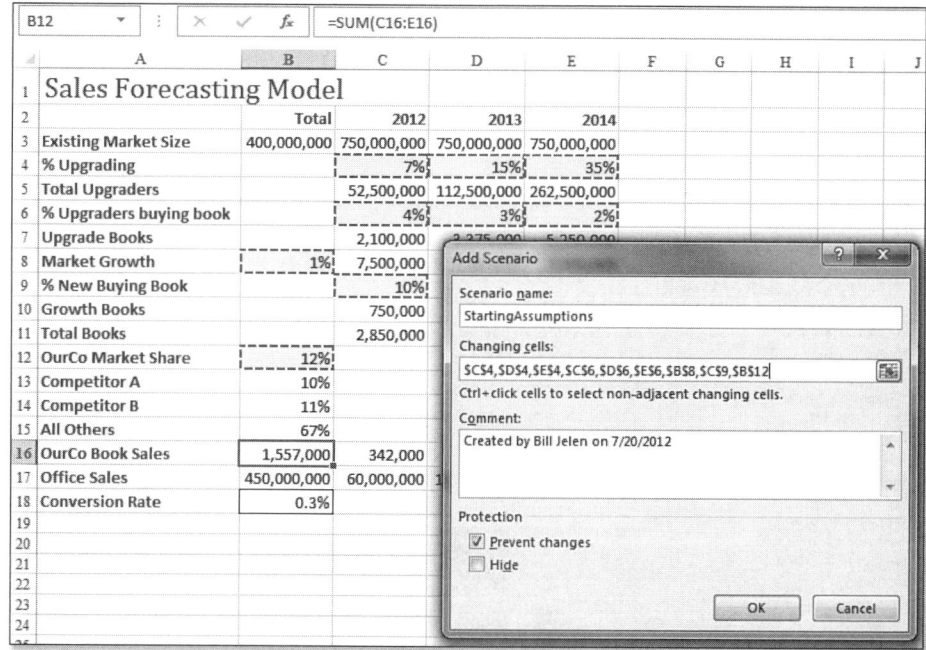

Figure 27.10
Use the Scenario Values dialog to edit values for a scenario. The
labels here show cell addresses if you do not define names for
the cells.

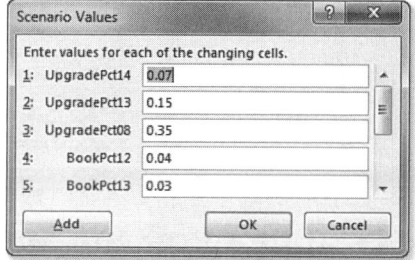

4. Edit any values in the Scenario Values dialog. If you have additional scenarios to add, click the
Add button. When you are done assigning scenarios, click OK.

5. Try switching between scenarios in the Scenario Manager by either double-clicking a scenario or
clicking the scenario and clicking Show, as shown in Figure 27.11. If you are going to add a new
scenario similar to one of the existing scenarios, show that scenario before clicking Add.

> ## 🩺 Tip
>
> It is a little annoying that the Scenario Values dialog can show only five values at a time. If your model contains the maximum of 32 values that can change, you need to scroll several times to see all the values in this dialog.

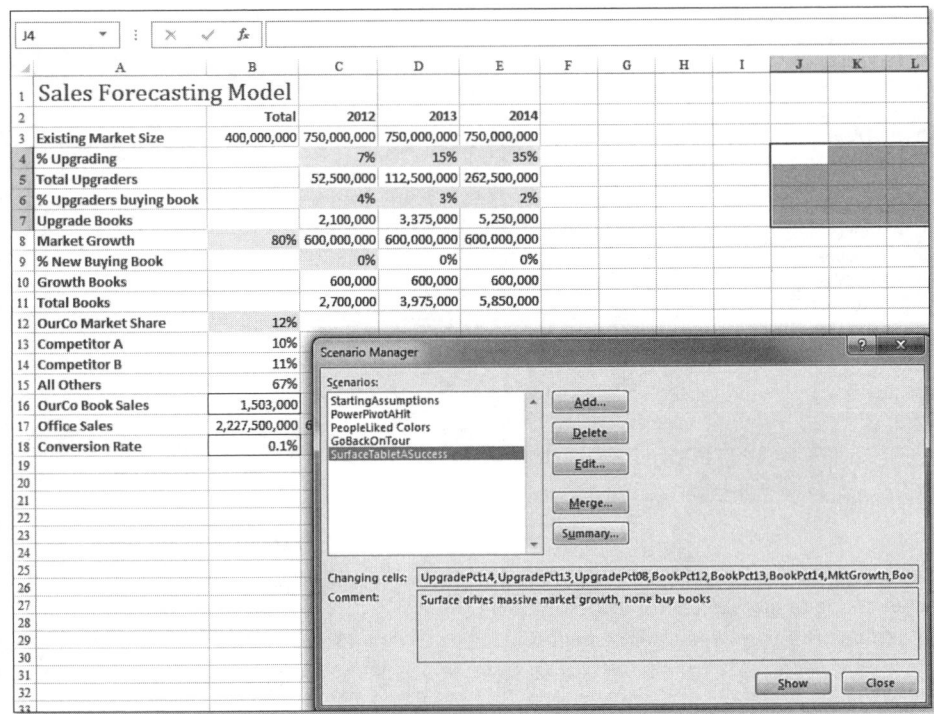

Figure 27.11
The new scenario is shown behind the dialog after you double-click a scenario name.

Creating a Scenario Summary Report

One powerful feature of Excel scenarios is the capability to create a Scenario Summary report. When you click the Summary button on the Scenario Manager dialog, Excel enables you to choose either a scenario summary report or a pivot table report. In either case, you should select one or more cells that represent the results of the model. For example, Figure 27.12 shows OurCo Book Sales and Conversion Rate selected.

After the results cells have been specified, the Scenario Summary report is added on a new worksheet in the workbook. This is a useful report that has a number of valuable features.

After the initial creation, the summary is as shown in Figure 27.13. Notice the group and outline buttons along both the rows and the columns of the report. The plus sign next to cell A3 indicates that the comments in row 4 are currently hidden.

Figure 27.12
Hold down Ctrl to select more than one result cell.

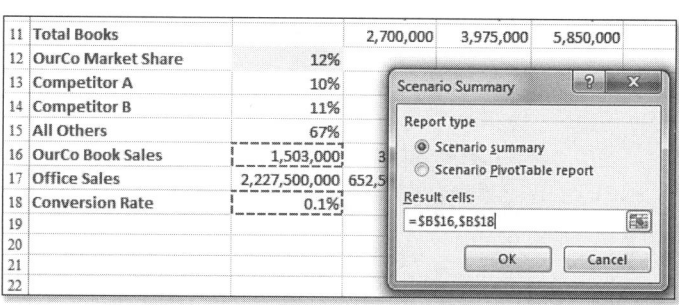

Figure 27.13
The default Scenario Summary report.

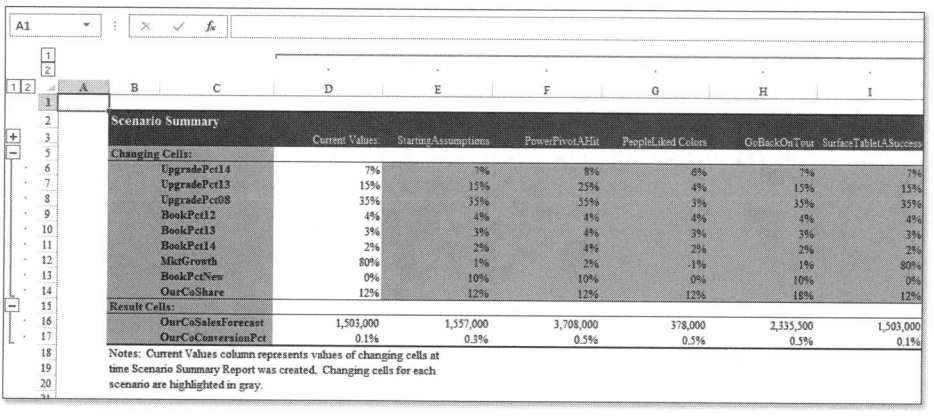

You can use word wrapping in a summary report. For example, Figure 27.14 shows that word wrapping was used to make the headings in row 3 appear on two lines and that the column widths were adjusted. The plus sign next to cell A3 is clicked to show the comments for each scenario. You will probably always have to make these adjustments to make your summary reports look better.

If you click the minus sign next to row 5, you can hide the assumption cells and just show the results, as shown in Figure 27.15.

> **Caution**
>
> The Scenario Summary report is a snapshot in time. If you later change scenarios or add new scenarios, you have to re-create and reformat the Scenario Summary report.

 **Tip**

To force word wrapping in the middle of a cell, position your cursor at the break point and press Alt+Enter.

Scenario Summary	Current Values:	Starting Assumptions	PowerPivot A Hit	People Liked Colors	Go Back On Tour	Surface Tablet ASuccess
		Created by Bill Jelen on 7/20/2012	Assumes PowerPivot Drives Massive Growth	Assumes people reject office because of lack of color	Assumes World Tour in 2013-2014	Surface drives massive market growth, none buy books
Changing Cells:						
UpgradePct14	7%	7%	8%	6%	7%	7%
UpgradePct13	15%	15%	25%	4%	15%	15%
UpgradePct08	35%	35%	55%	3%	35%	35%
BookPct12	4%	4%	4%	4%	4%	4%
BookPct13	3%	3%	4%	3%	3%	3%
BookPct14	2%	2%	4%	2%	2%	2%
MktGrowth	80%	1%	2%	-1%	1%	80%
BookPctNew	0%	10%	10%	0%	10%	0%
OurCoShare	12%	12%	12%	12%	18%	12%
Result Cells:						
OurCoSalesForecast	1,503,000	1,557,000	3,708,000	378,000	######	1,503,000
OurCoConversionPct	0.1%	0.3%	0.5%	0.5%	0.5%	0.1%

Notes: Current Values column represents values of changing cells at time Scenario Summary Report was created. Changing cells for each scenario are highlighted in gray.

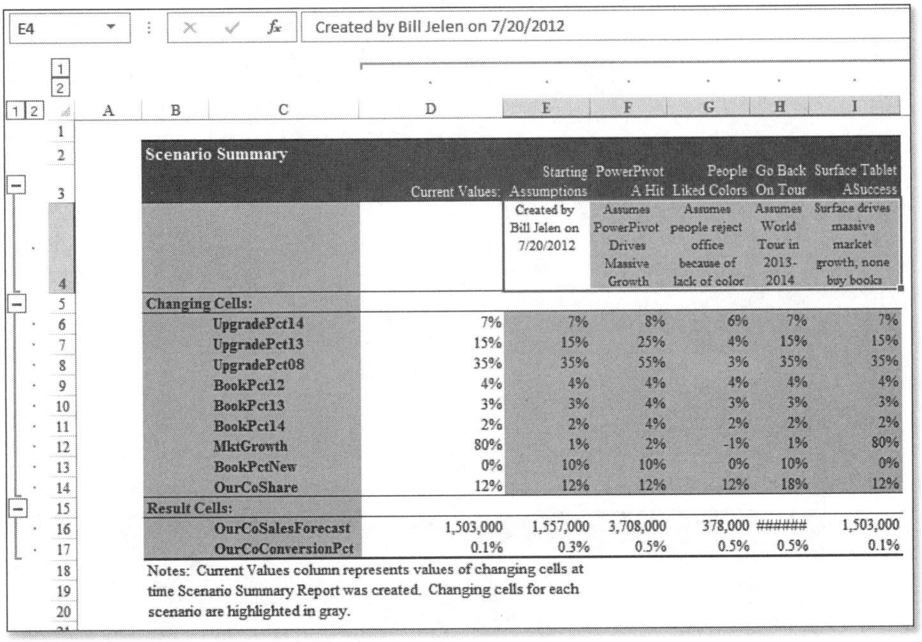

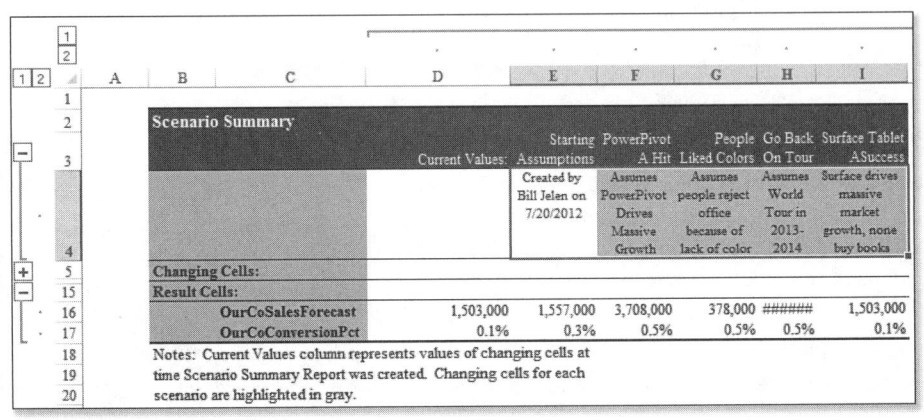

Figure 27.14 Word wrapping and column widths can be adjusted.

Scenario Summary	Current Values:	Starting Assumptions	PowerPivot A Hit	People Liked Colors	Go Back On Tour	Surface Tablet ASuccess
		Created by Bill Jelen on 7/20/2012	Assumes PowerPivot Drives Massive Growth	Assumes people reject office because of lack of color	Assumes World Tour in 2013-2014	Surface drives massive market growth, none buy books
Changing Cells:						
Result Cells:						
OurCoSalesForecast	1,503,000	1,557,000	3,708,000	378,000	######	1,503,000
OurCoConversionPct	0.1%	0.3%	0.5%	0.5%	0.5%	0.1%

Notes: Current Values column represents values of changing cells at time Scenario Summary Report was created. Changing cells for each scenario are highlighted in gray.

Figure 27.15 To make the table easier to read, you can show just the results.

Adding Multiple Scenarios

You might want to share a workbook with others and have them add their own scenarios to get opinions from people in other areas of your company, such as sales, marketing, engineering, and manufacturing. To do this, follow these steps:

1. Save the workbook with just the starting scenario.

2. Route the workbook to each person. In a hidden field, Excel keeps track of who adds each scenario.

3. When you get the routed workbook back, open both the original workbook and the routed workbook.

4. Display the Scenario Manager in the original workbook.

5. Click the Merge button to display the Merge Scenarios dialog, as shown in Figure 27.16.

Figure 27.16
Merged scenarios from a workbook routed to others.

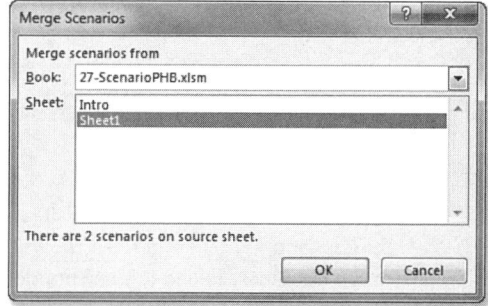

6. In the Book drop-down, select the name of the routed workbook. In Figure 27.16, the dialog shows that two scenarios are available on sheet 1.

7. Excel usually encounters identically named scenarios in the merge process. It differentiates any scenarios with identical names by adding a date or name to the incoming scenarios, as shown in Figure 27.17. If these scenarios are truly identical to the scenario that you originally sent out, delete them.

Figure 27.17
Merged scenarios are added to the bottom of the list.

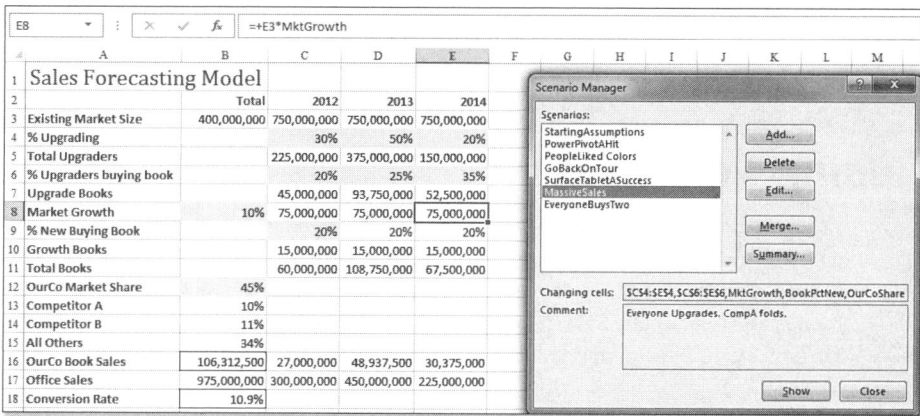

8. In the Scenario Manager, click Summary. The Scenario Summary dialog appears.

9. In the Scenario Summary dialog, click Scenario PivotTable report. The initial pivot table appears, as shown in Figure 27.18.

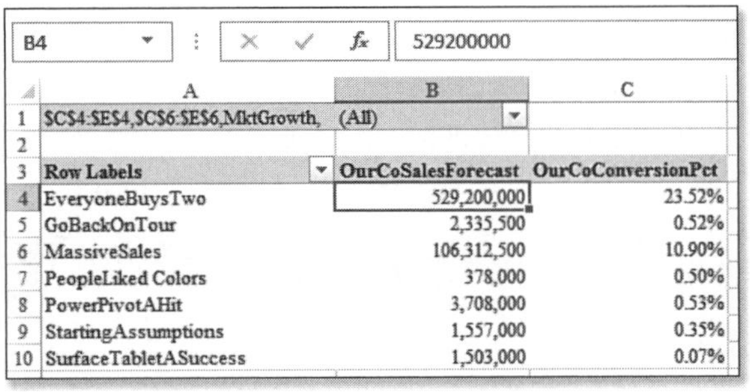

Figure 27.18
The default pivot table shows scenarios from all people on the routing list.

10. Drag the field from the Report Filter area to be the first Row Labels field. You can now see scenarios grouped by author. As shown in Figure 27.19, although this is an interesting view, there is not a good way to see the assumptions that each author used to arrive at his or her results.

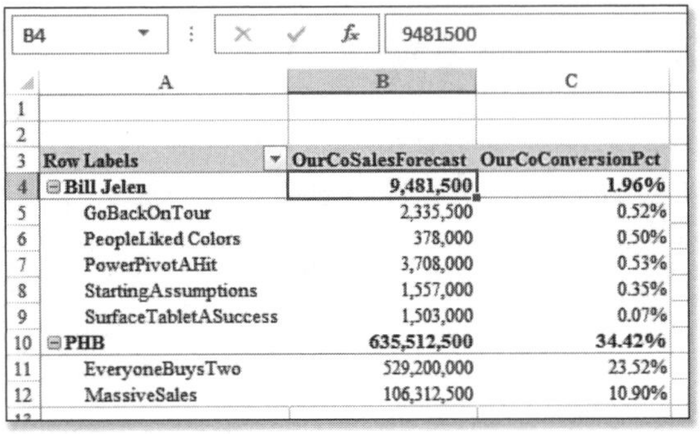

Figure 27.19
Move the field from the Report Filter to the first row label to compare scenarios by person.

Using Goal Seek

On the television show *The Price Is Right*, one of the games is the Hi-Lo game. A contestant tries to guess the price of an item, and the host tells the player that the actual price is higher or lower. The process of honing in on a price of $1.67 might involve guesses of $2, $1, $1.50, $1.75, $1.63, $1.69, $1.66, $1.68, and finally $1.67. Using the techniques described so far in this chapter, you might play this game with Excel to try to narrow in on an answer.

You might have an Excel worksheet set up that calculates a final value using several input variables. To solve the formula in reverse, you need to find input variables that generate a certain answer. There are several possible approaches:

- One difficult approach is to determine whether another Excel function reverses the calculation. For example, =ARCSIN() performs the opposite of =SIN(), and =NPER(), =RATE(), or =PV() back into a =PMT().

- Another approach is to use algebra to attempt to solve for one of the input variables.

- Most people simply play the Hi-Lo game by successively plugging in higher and lower answers to the input cell until they narrow in on an input variable that produces the desired result.

- If you play the Hi-Lo game, consider using the Goal Seek command. In effect, this command plays the Hi-Lo game at hyperspeed, arriving at an answer within a second.

Consider the car payment example at the beginning of the chapter. You want to find a price that yields a $225 monthly payment. You might find a =PV() function that can solve this. However, most people plug in successively higher or lower values for the price in cell E1 (see Figure 27.20).

Figure 27.20
Goal Seek lets you find one value by changing one other cell.

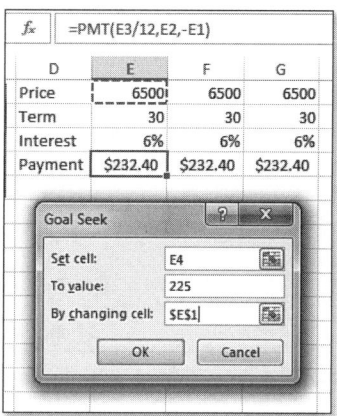

Excel's Goal Seek option, on the other hand, enables you to hone in quickly on a value. To use Goal Seek, follow these steps:

1. Select the answer cell. In this example, it would be the payment in cell E4.

2. From the Data Tools group of the Data tab, select the What-If Analysis drop-down and then select Goal Seek. The Goal Seek dialog appears, as shown in Figure 27.20.

3. In the Goal Seek dialog, indicate that you want to set the answer cell to a particular value by changing a particular input cell. In this example, set cell E4 to the value of 225 by changing cell E1. Excel begins trying to hone in on a value. When Excel gets to within a penny of the value,

the Goal Seek Status dialog appears, as shown in Figure 27.21. This dialog reports that it was trying to reach a target value of 225 and reached that value. Behind the dialog, the worksheet shows the proposed price of 6293.053 in the worksheet.

4. Either accept this value by clicking OK or revert to the original value by clicking Cancel.

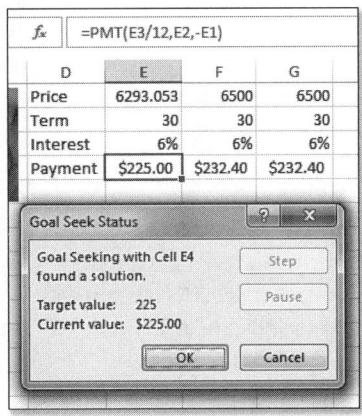

Figure 27.21
Choose to accept the proposed solution or revert to the previous numbers.

Goal Seek works well for quick calculations, such as the two additional Goal Seek operations that were done in Figure 27.22. One operation set cell F4 to $225 by changing the term in cell F2. The next operation set cell G4 to $225 by changing the interest rate in cell G3.

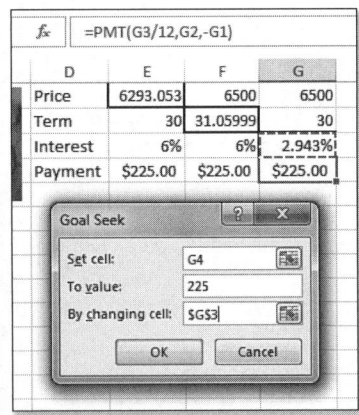

Figure 27.22
Three different Goal Seek commands find how to yield a $225 payment by changing either the price, term, or rate.

Is It Cheating to Use Brute Force to Think Less?

Most of the time when you could use Goal Seek, there is a brainier solution. If you have a complex series of formulas set up using just the +, -, *, /, and ^ operators, you could almost certainly get out a pencil and do the algebra required to derive the formula you need.

In the preceding text, Figure 27.22 shows how you can use Goal Seek to figure out how to achieve a certain monthly payment by changing three different cells. Besides Goal Seek, Excel provides the NPER() function, which can correctly find the term for a given price, interest, and payment. For example, you can use the NPER() function in cell G11 to calculate a more exact version than Goal Seek is able to discover (see Figure 27.23). Similarly, in cell E11 you can use =PV(E9/12,E8,-E10) to discover the present value (that is, the vehicle price) of a loan. In cell I11 you can use =RATE(I9,-I10,18)*12 to discover the rate needed to generate a monthly payment of $225 for a certain price and term.

Excel might have to go through 100 iterations of a lightning-fast Hi-Lo-type game to find the solution. However, the solution is usually found within a second or two. This is definitely faster than using paper and pencil to do the algebra or pulling out this book to learn about the NPER() function.

If you are a loan officer at a bank, it might be worthwhile for you to learn how to use the NPER() function. However, if you are using this worksheet once every four years to figure out your next car purchase, it is perfectly fine to let Excel sweat through the brute-force calculations with Goal Seek.

Figure 27.23
Goal Seek prevents you from having to learn functions such as NPER().

f_x	=NPER(G9/12,-G10,G8)					
	D	E	F	G	H	I
Price	6293.05294		6500		6500
Term	30		31.05999		30
Interest	6%		6%		2.943%
Payment	$225.00		$225.00		$225.00
Term	30	Price	6500	Price	6500
Interest	6%	Interest	6%	Term	30
Payment	$225.00	Payment	$225.00	Payment	$225.00
Price	$6,293.05	Term	31.05999	Rate	2.943%

When Goal Seek Won't Work

Some problems are not well suited to using Goal Seek. Goal Seek needs a clear mathematical relationship between the starting and ending cells. For example, the model in Figure 27.24 is set up to choose from among 20 different package plans. Each package offers a different number of tickets, meals, and vouchers. Cell E1 chooses a particular plan, and cell E2 uses the INDEX() function to calculate the number of tickets associated with the plan. Because there is no mathematical sequence to the number of tickets in each plan, Goal Seek has little chance of succeeding in this situation.

	A	B	C	D	E
1				Plan	2
2				Tickets	12
3				Value	695
4				Total	8340
5					
6	Plans:	Tickets	Meals	Vouchers	
7	A	4	15	6	
8	B	12	4	9	
9	C	13	11	1	
10	D	5	18	2	
11	E	6	11	8	
12	F	20	1	4	
13	G	10	6	9	
14	H	7	14	4	
15	I	8	7	10	
16	J	15	2	8	
17	K	16	6	3	
18	L	11	0	14	
19	M	18	0	7	
20	N	17	5	3	
21	O	3	15	7	
22	P	9	8	8	
23	Q	14	8	3	
24	R	19	0	6	
25	S	2	1	22	
26	T	1	8	16	

Figure 27.24
Because there is no mathematical order to the number of tickets offered in each plan, Goal Seek has little chance of finding a solution in this case.

Suppose that you want to set the Total value in cell E4 equal to 6950. A quick scan through the list of plans shows that Plan G offers 10 tickets, which would be worth exactly $6,950. However, Excel will not be able to figure this out using Goal Seek.

The following steps illustrate how you can watch the Goal Seek process in slow motion to see if Excel is getting closer:

1. Start Goal Seek. An answer is not immediately found.

2. Click the Pause button on the Goal Seek Status dialog. The Pause button changes to a Continue button. As shown in Figure 27.25, Excel is on its 93rd attempt at finding a value. In this pass, Excel is trying 32.98 billion in Cell E1. This is producing a #REF error instead of the desired value of 6950.

Figure 27.25
After pausing, you can examine how Excel is trying to solve the problem.

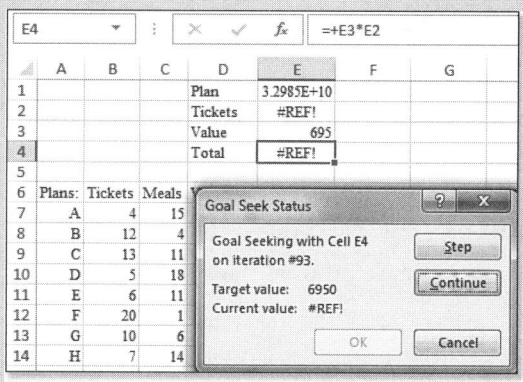

3. Click the Step button to proceed to the next guess. Excel successively tries higher and higher values. Eventually, after 100 iterations, Excel gives up and reports that it cannot find a solution, as shown in Figure 27.26.

Figure 27.26
Goal Seek gives up after 100 iterations.

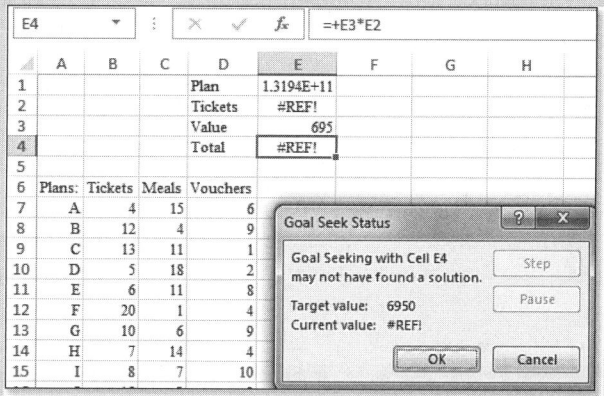

Using Solver

It is possible to design problems that are far too complex for Goal Seek. These problems might have dozens of independent variables and various constraints. In such a case, you can use the Excel Solver add-in.

With Solver, you identify an output formula cell that you want to be maximized, minimized, or set to a particular value. You specify a range of cells that can be changed. You then specify a number of constraints on input cells or other formulas in the model.

The Solver add-in, which is free with Excel, was written by Dan Fylstra and Frontline Systems. History buffs might remember than Dan Fylstra was the president of VisiCorp—the world's first spreadsheet program. Frontline Systems offers more advanced versions of Solver plus an Excel Data Miner tool at www.Solver.com.

 **Tip**

Solver was improved in Excel 2010. To get the old Solver to work, you had to have a good grasp on linear mathematics. Hence, the old Solver never worked for me. The new Solver offers advanced methodologies that find solutions to far more problems. If you had tried Solver before without success, it is time to try it again.

Installing Solver

To install Solver, follow these steps:

1. Press Alt+T and then press I to display the Add-Ins dialog.

2. In the Add-Ins dialog, make sure that Solver is checked.

Solving a Model Using Solver

To use Solver, your worksheet should contain one or more input variables. The worksheet should also contain one or more formulas that result in a solution within a single cell.

For each input variable, there might be certain constraints. For example, you might want to assume that a certain variable must be positive or that it should be in a certain range of values.

When using Solver, you identify the input range, the output cell, and the constraints. You can ask Solver to minimize or maximize the input cell. Alternatively, you can ask Solver to set the output cell to a particular value. Solver uses advanced algorithms to find input variables that meet your goal and fit within the constraints.

This might be easier to understand with a concrete example. Figure 27.27 shows a worksheet used to model the production of widgets. Cell B23 indicates that each worker in your factory can make 40 widgets per hour. Workers who work evenings, nights, or weekends are paid a shift differential. You can choose to keep your factory running for anywhere from five shifts a week (Monday through Friday, first shift) up to 21 shifts per week. You can sell as many widgets as you can produce, provided that the overall cost is less than $2 per widget. You have a skilled workforce of 100 workers available for first shift, 82 workers for second shift, and 75 workers for third shift. How many shifts should the plant be open to maximize production? Solver runs circles around Goal Seek in situations that deal with multiple constraints. To use Solver to find the answer, use the following steps:

1. Note that cells B3 through B11 define how many shifts the factory will be open. All the remaining cells in the model calculate the total number of widgets produced and the average cost per widget.

2. As with Goal Seek, start by telling Solver that you want to set a target cell equal to a maximum, minimum, or certain value by changing other cells. For example, the Solver Parameters dialog shown in Figure 27.28 indicates that the goal is to maximize widget production by altering the number of shifts.

Figure 27.27
A worksheet to model widget production.

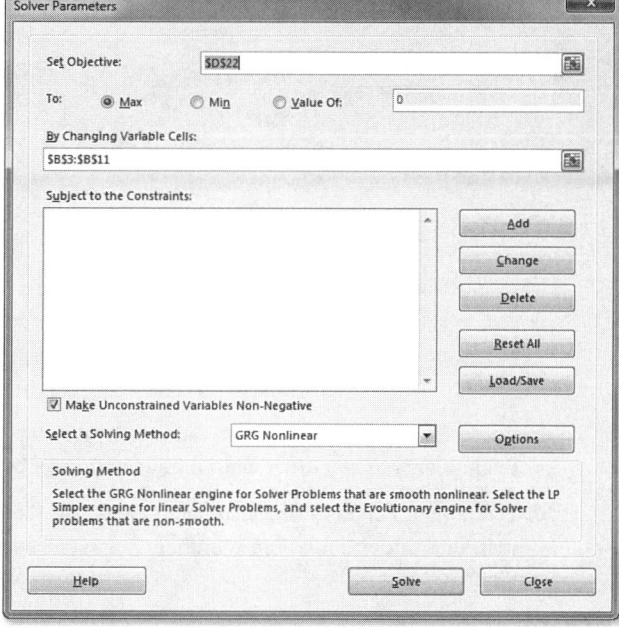

F21	▼	:	×	✓	*fx*	Per Widget

▲	A	B	C	D	E	F
1	**Manufacturing Plant Productivity**					
2						
3	Day Shift M-F	5		Goals:		
4	Evening Shift M-F	5		*Maximize widget production*		
5	Night Shift M-F	5		*Keep cost of widgets < $2.00*		
6	Day Shift Saturday	1				
7	Evening Shift Saturday	1				
8	Night Shift Saturday	1				
9	Day Shift Sun	1				
10	Evening Shift Sun	1				
11	Night Shift Sun	1				
12	Labor Cost Per Shift		Workers Avail per Shift	Total Widgets	Total Cost	
13	Day Shift M-F	8.25	100	20000	38000	
14	Evening Shift M-F	8.75	82	16400	33700	
15	Night Shift M-F	9.25	75	15000	32750	
16	Day Shift Saturday	12.38	80	3200	8923.2	
17	Evening Shift Saturday	13.13	72	2880	8562.88	
18	Night Shift Saturday	13.88	65	2600	8217.6	
19	Day Shift Sun	16.5	50	2000	7600	
20	Evening Shift Sun	17.5	36	1440	6040	
21	Night Shift Sun	18.5	30	1200	5440	Per Widget
22	Overhead per shift	1000	Total	64720	149234	2.3058356
23	Widgets Per Worker Per Shift	40				

Figure 27.28
Maximizing widget production.

Solver Parameters

Se_t Objective: $D$22

To: ● Ma_x ○ Mi_n ○ _Value Of: 0

_By Changing Variable Cells:
$B$3:$B$11

_Subject to the Constraints:

[_Add]
[_Change]
[_Delete]
[_Reset All]
[_Load/Save]

☑ Ma_ke Unconstrained Variables Non-Negative

_Select a Solving Method: GRG Nonlinear ▼   [O_ptions]

Solving Method

Select the GRG Nonlinear engine for Solver Problems that are smooth nonlinear. Select the LP Simplex engine for linear Solver Problems, and select the Evolutionary engine for Solver problems that are non-smooth.

[_Help]   [_Solve]   [Cl_ose]

3. Enter the first constraint, which is that the market will bear only a manufacturing cost of $2 per widget. To specify this constraint, click the Add button in the Solver Parameters dialog.

4. Tell Solver that the manufacturing cost must be less than or equal to $2 per widget, as shown in Figure 27.29.

Figure 27.29
Building the cost constraint.

5. Tell Solver that there cannot be a negative number of shifts. To do so, you need to add a constraint to indicate $B$3:$B$11 >= 0.

6. Specify that cells B3:B5 must be less than or equal to 5 because you can have only five of each shift during the week.

7. In this model, it is not valid to work 0.32 shifts; only integer values can be used in a given range. Therefore, select the value int for the comparison operator to tell Solver that a certain range can accept only integers (see Figure 27.30).

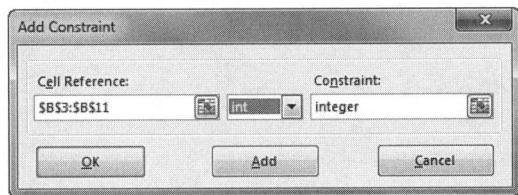

Figure 27.30
Use the integer constraint to prevent fractional answers.

8. In this case, the Saturday and Sunday shifts are a special case: The company is either open or not, which means the only two possible values for each cell are 0 or 1. This is a special constraint called a *binary constraint*. Select the bin value in the comparison operator to specify that cells B6 through B11 are limited to binary values.

9. Three Solving Methods are available. Always start with GRG Nonlinear. If that doesn't work, try Evolutionary. If you are a math genius and have built a model with pure linearity, try Simplex LP.

10. Your Solver Parameters dialog should look like Figure 27.31. Click the Solve button. Solver begins to iterate through possible solutions. If Solver finds a result, it reports success, as shown in Figure 27.32.

Figure 27.31
You are ready to solve the model.

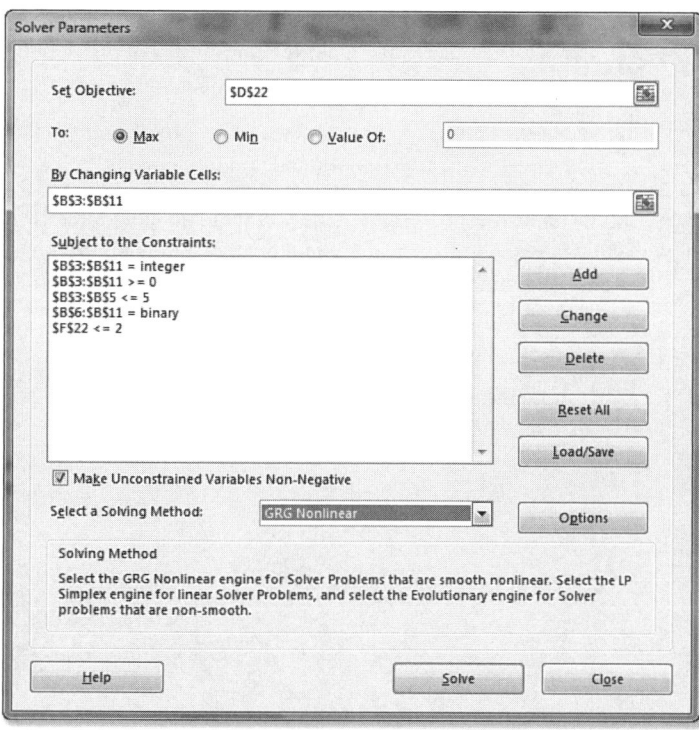

Figure 27.32
Solver reports success.

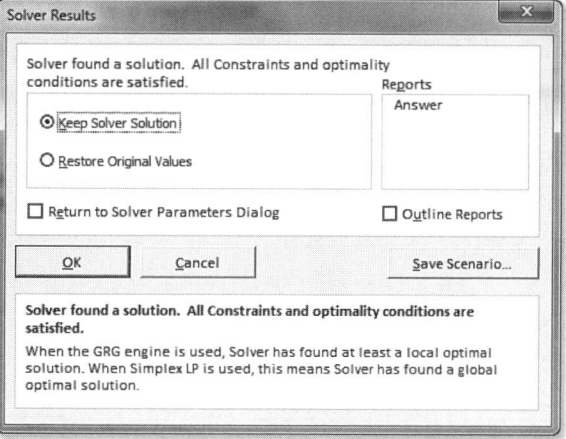

11. Click Save Scenario and give the scenario a solution such as SolverSolution. If you are going to define a scenario, after doing step 12, you can choose Restore Original Values and click OK. You can then use Data, What-If Analysis, Scenario Manager to add a scenario with your original values.

12. Select the Answer Report to have Excel provide a new worksheet that compares the original and final values.

In the answer report, Solver tells you that you can produce 42,400 widgets by operating five day and evening shifts and two night shifts. The remaining shifts are not cost-effective to keep the cost per widget in cell F22 less than $2.

With this current solution, the cost per widget is exactly $2.

The night shift workers will be losing some Saturday overtime because of Solver.

 **Note**

The GRG engine finds a solution that matches the constraints. However, it might not be the best solution. The LP Solver engine finds the best solution but only if you set up the model as a linear problem. The Evolutionary engine uses Monte Carlo to try random choices, hoping to narrow in on a better solution.

AUTOMATING REPETITIVE FUNCTIONS USING VBA MACROS

Every copy of Excel shipped since 1995 has included the powerful Visual Basic for Applications (VBA) lurking behind the grid. With VBA, you can do anything that you can do in the regular interface, and you can do it much faster. VBA shines when you have many repetitive tasks to undertake.

Learning to use macros is a good news/bad news proposition. The good news is that Microsoft Office provides a macro recorder that can write a macro as you work. The bad news is that it is not easy to record a macro that works consistently with any data set. To unleash the power of macros, you need to understand how to edit recorded macro code. You can then record a macro that is close to what you want and edit that macro to create something that runs the way you want it to work.

Checking Security Settings Before Using Macros

On March 26, 1999, a hacker named Kwyjibo launched the Melissa virus. This particular virus used VBA macros in Word to propagate itself. Microsoft took a lot of heat because macros could run without the knowledge of the person running the computer. In response, Microsoft has made it more difficult to run macros in subsequent versions of Excel. At one point, there was some concern that Microsoft would remove support for VBA macros, but Microsoft has committed to supporting VBA macros for another 15 to 20 years.

Before you can use macros, you have to take some positive steps to affirm that you want to record or run a macro.

Triple Word Score

The original Melissa virus macro spread via email as a Word document. The document would arrive with the message subject "Here is the document that you asked for." When a user opened the document in Word, the virus would attach itself to the Normal.dot file and attempt to email itself to others in the user's address book. This propagation method is what attracted the attention.

The point of the Melissa virus was to check the system clock every time the user opened a document. If the user happened to open the document when the minute, day, and month all matched, the virus would perform its dirty work. Therefore, for example, if you opened the document on October 10 at 8:10 a.m. or perhaps on June 6 at 6:06 p.m., the virus would kick in. Assuming an 8-hour workday, there are 96 minutes throughout the year when opening the Word document would trigger the virus. That works out to about a 7 in 1,000 chance that a user who opened the email attachment would be struck by the virus.

In a tip of the hat to the old board game *Scrabble*, the hacker had an insidious plan. If the user opened the document at the moment when the month, day, and minute matched on the system clock, the program would insert the following text in the Word document: "Twenty-two points, plus triple-word-score, plus fifty points for using all my letters. Game's over. I'm outta here."

Thanks to this silly virus, VBA programmers now have to jump through hoops to use macros.

Enabling VBA Security

To enable VBA security, follow these steps:

1. Select File, Options to open the Excel Options dialog.

2. Select the Customize Ribbon category. In the right-side list box, select the Developer tab check box.

3. Click OK to exit the Excel Settings dialog. You now have a Developer tab on the ribbon.

4. On the Developer tab, click Macro Security in the Code group. The Security dialog appears.

5. In the Security dialog, change the Macro Settings option to Disable All Macros with Notification. With this setting, Excel alerts you whenever you open a workbook that has macros attached.

6. When you open a document and get the warning that the document has macros attached, if this is a document that you wrote and you expect macros to be there, click Enable Content to enable the macros.

> **Note**
>
> In step 5, *with* is the operative word. You are choosing to disable macros and to display a notification to let you decide whether or not the macros should be enabled. Before choosing to enable macros, you can switch over to VBA and see what macros are in the workbook.

Recording a Macro

Plan your macro before recording it by thinking through the steps you need to perform. If you need to fix many items in a worksheet, you might want to select the first item first. This way, the macro can perform an action on cells relative to the original selection.

To record a macro, follow these steps:

1. On the Developer tab, select Record Macro.

2. In the Record Macro dialog box, type a name for the macro. The name cannot contain spaces. For example, instead of using Macro Name, you need to use MacroName.

3. Choose whether you want to store the macro in the current workbook, a new workbook, or a special Personal Macro Workbook. The personal macro workbook is a special workbook designed to hold general-purpose macros that might apply to any workbook. If you are unsure, select to store the recorded macro in the current workbook.

4. Assign a shortcut key for the macro. Ctrl+J is a safe key because nothing is currently assigned to Ctrl+J. This shortcut key enables you to run the macro again.

5. Click OK to close the Record Macro dialog.

6. Turn on relative recording by clicking the Use Relative References icon in the Code group of the Developer tab. Relative recording records the action of moving a certain number of cells from the active cell.

7. Perform the actions you want to store in the macro.

8. Click the red Stop Recording button on the left side of the status bar at the bottom of the Excel window.

9. Save the workbook before testing the macro.

10. Test the macro playback by typing the shortcut key assigned in step 4.

> **Caution**
>
> The alternative is an absolute recording. This method is extremely literal. The action of moving down three cells from A1 is recorded as "Select cell A4." That action is extremely limited—it would work only when the macro is played back with the active cell in A1.

Case Study: Macro for Formatting for a Mail Merge

Suppose that your co-worker has some names and addresses in Excel and she needs to do a mail merge in Word. Instead of teaching her how to do a mail merge, you offer to do the mail merge for her. In theory, this should take you a couple minutes. However, when the list of names arrives in the Excel worksheet, you realize the data is in the wrong format. In the Excel worksheet, the names are going down column A, as shown in Figure 28.1.

To complete a mail merge successfully, the Excel worksheet should have fields for name, street address, and city+state+ZIP Code, as shown in Figure 28.2.

Figure 28.1
A simple task, such as doing a mail merge, is incredibly difficult when the data is in the wrong format.

	A
1	Tracy Buckner
2	1292 Cedar Road
3	Greenwood, IA 35968
4	
5	Vincent Alexander
6	1282 First Avenue
7	Mill Valley, MD 54751
8	
9	Pearl Guzman
10	1919 Washington Avenue
11	Midway, TX 65197
12	
13	Matthew Rodgers

Figure 28.2
The goal is to produce data with fields in columns.

	A	B	C	D	E
1	Tracy Buckner	1292 Cedar Road	Greenwood, IA 35968		
2	Vincent Alexander	1282 First Avenue	Mill Valley, MD 54751		
3	Pearl Guzman	1919 Washington Avenue	Midway, TX 65197		
4	Matthew Rodgers	1825 Jackson Blvd.	Greenwood, AZ 75420		
5	Nancy Roach	1144 Davis Lane	Riverside, NY 89224		
6	Jeannette Ross	454 Hill Highway	Centerville, WA 82020		
7	William Hester	405 Poplar Circle	Georgetown, ME 38799		
8	Tina Morrison	551 Fourteenth Highway	Mount Pleasant, VI 29331		
9	Victor Gilliam	828 Adams Highway	Akron, NE 29598		
10	Sandy Pickett	941 Spring Blvd.	Rosemount, WY 17764		
11	Patrick Cleveland	308 River Street	Forest Lake, MT 60502		

Before you start recording a macro, you need to think about how to break the task into easily repeatable steps.

It would be good to record a macro that can fix one name in the list. Assume that you start with the cell pointer on a person's name at the beginning of the macro, as shown in Figure 28.3. The macro would need to perform these steps to fix one record and end up on the name of the second person in the list:

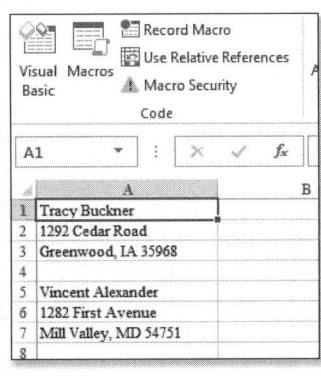

Figure 28.3
You start with a name selected.

1. Press the down-arrow key to move to the address cell.

2. Press Ctrl+X to cut the address.

3. Press the up-arrow key and then the right-arrow key to move next to the name.

4. Press Ctrl+V to paste the address, as shown in Figure 28.4.

Figure 28.4
You cut and paste the address.

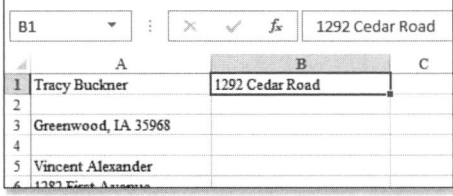

Figure 28.5
Cut the city.

5. Press the left-arrow key once and the down-arrow key twice to move to the cell for city, state, and ZIP Code.

6. Press Ctrl+X to cut the city, as shown in Figure 28.5.

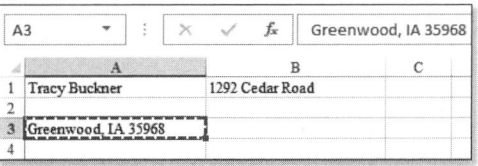

7. Press the up-arrow key twice and the right-arrow key twice to move to the right of the street cell.

8. Press Ctrl+V to paste the city.

9. Press the left-arrow key twice and the down-arrow key once to move to the now blank row just below the name.

10. Hold down the Shift key while pressing the down-arrow key twice to select the three blank rows, as shown in Figure 28.6.

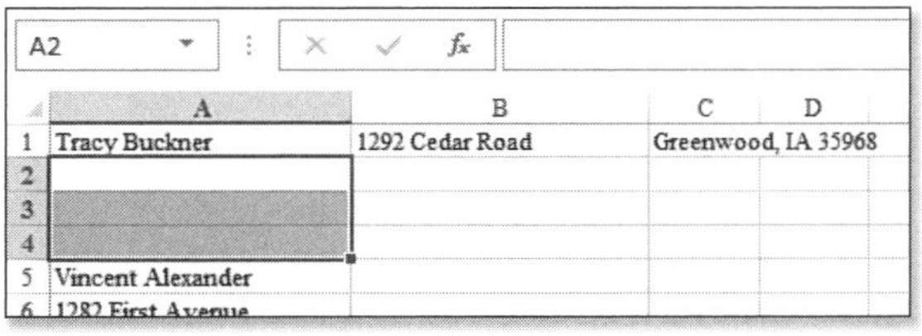

Figure 28.6
Select three blank rows prior to deleting.

11. Press Ctrl+- to invoke the Delete command. Press R and then Enter to delete the row.

When you run a macro that goes through these steps, Excel deletes the three blank rows, but the selection now contains the three cells that encompass the next record, as shown in Figure 28.7. Ideally, the macro should end with only the name selected. Press Shift+Backspace to reduce the selection to the active cell, as shown in Figure 28.8.

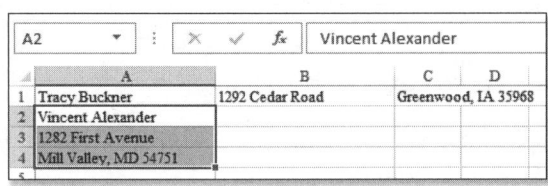

Figure 28.7
You need only one cell selected instead of three.

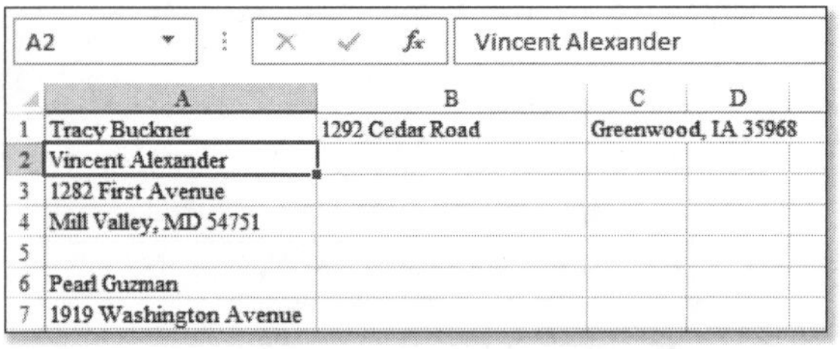

Figure 28.8
Finish the macro with the cell pointer on the next name.

If the macro correctly performs all these steps, the first name and address are properly formatted. The blank rows left between the first and second names are deleted.

By making sure that the macro starts on a name and ends up on the next name, you allow the macro to be run repeatedly. If you assign this macro to the keyboard shortcut Ctrl+J, you can then hold down Ctrl+J and quickly fix records, one after the other.

How Not to Record a Macro: The Default State of the Macro Recorder

The default state of the macro recorder is a stupid state. If you recorded the preceding steps in the macro recorder, the macro recorder would take your actions literally. The English pseudocode for recording these steps would say this:

1. Move to cell A2.

2. Cut cell A2 and paste to cell B1.

3. Move to cell A3.

4. Cut cell A3 and paste to cell C1.

5. Delete rows 2 through 4.

6. Select cell A2.

This macro works, but it works for only one record. After you've recorded this macro, your worksheet looks like the one shown in Figure 28.9.

Figure 28.9
After recording the macro in default mode, you have fixed the first record, and you might think you are ready to run the macro to fix the second record.

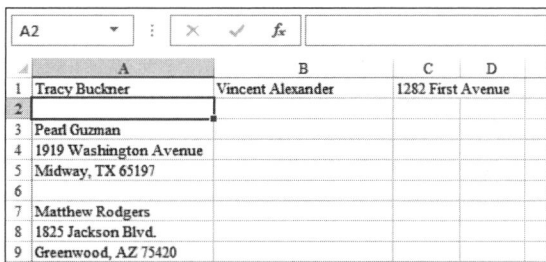

When the default macro runs, it moves the name Vincent Alexander from cell A2 and pastes it on top of the address in cell B1. It then takes the address in cell A3 and pastes it on top of the city in cell C1. It then deletes rows 2, 3, and 4, removing the city and state. As shown in Figure 28.10, the macro provides the wrong result.

Figure 28.10
When the default macro runs, it ruins two records.

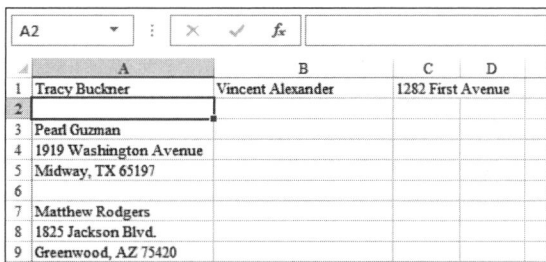

If you blindly ran this macro 100 times to convert 100 addresses, the macro would happily "eat" all 100 records, leaving you with just one record (and not even a correct record), as shown in Figure 28.11. To overcome this problem, use relative references, as discussed in the next section.

Figure 28.11
If you run the default macro 100 times, it destroys your entire data set. Fortunately, a different mode is available for recording relative macros, as described in the next section.

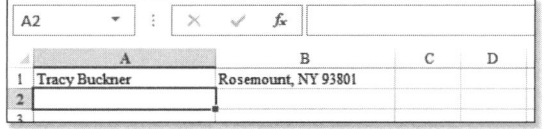

Relative References in Macro Recording

Locate the icon in the Code group on the Developer tab on the ribbon called Use Relative References. The key to recording useful macros is to be judicious in turning on and off the relative recording setting. If you performed the steps described in the preceding section in relative recording mode, Excel would write code that does this:

1. Move down one cell.

2. Cut that cell.

3. Move up and over one cell and paste.

4. Move left and down two cells.

5. Cut that cell.

6. Move up and over two cells and paste.

7. Move left two cells, move down one cell, and delete three rows.

8. Move up and down one cell to select a single cell.

These steps are far more generic than those recorded using the default state of the macro recorder. These steps work for any record, provided that you started the macro with the cell pointer on the first cell that contains a name.

For this example, you need to record the entire macro with relative recording turned on.

 **Tip**

Ninety-eight percent of the time you are recording macros, you should have Use Relative Reference turned on.

Starting the Macro Recorder

At this point, you have rehearsed the steps needed for a macro that puts data records into a format that is usable for a mail merge. After you make sure that the cell pointer is starting on the name in cell A1, you are ready to turn on the macro recorder.

You should not be nervous, but you need to perform the steps correctly. If you move the cell pointer in the wrong direction, the macro recorder happily records that for you and plays it back. It is annoying to watch the macro recorder play back your mistakes 100 times a day for the next 5 years. Therefore, follow these steps to create the macro correctly:

1. On the Developer tab, click the Record Macro icon from the Code group. The Record Macro dialog appears, as shown in Figure 28.12.

2. Excel suggests giving this macro the unimaginative name Macro1. Use any name you want, up to 64 characters and without spaces. For this example, name the macro FixOneRecord. Choose a shortcut key for the macro. The shortcut key is important. Because you have to run this macro once for each record in the present example, you might choose something like Ctrl+A, which is easy to press.

Figure 28.12
After making the needed selections,
click OK to begin recording.

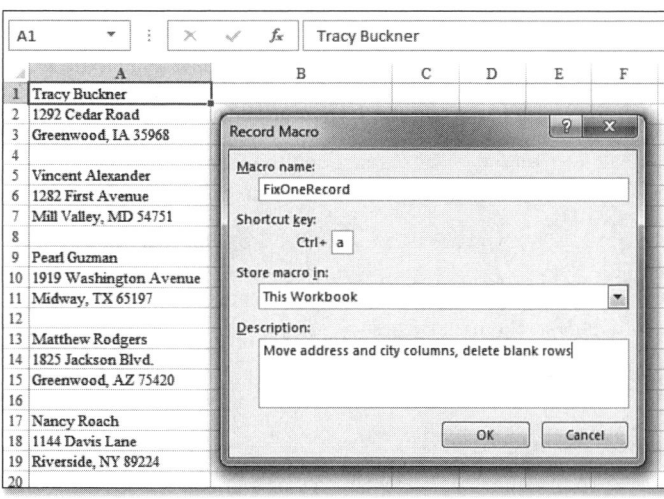

3. Make a selection from the Store Macro In drop-down. You have the option of storing the macro in this workbook, in a new workbook, or in the personal macro workbook. If this is a general-purpose macro that you will use every day on every file, it makes sense to store the macro in the personal macro workbook. However, because this macro will be used just to solve a current problem, store it in the current workbook.

4. Fill in a description if you think you will be using this macro long enough to forget what it does. When you are done making selections on the Record Macro dialog (see Figure 28.12), click OK. The Record Macro icon changes to a Stop Recording icon.

5. Click the Use Relative References icon in the Developer tab. The icon is highlighted.

6. Press the down-arrow key to move to the address cell.

7. Press Ctrl+X to cut the address.

8. Press the up-arrow key and then the right-arrow key to move next to the name.

9. Press Ctrl+V to paste the address.

10. Press the left-arrow key once and the down-arrow key twice to move to the cell for city, state, and ZIP Code.

11. Press Ctrl+X to cut the city.

12. Press the up-arrow key twice and the right-arrow key twice to move to the right of the street cell.

13. Press Ctrl+V to paste the city.

 Note

Keep in mind that assigning a macro to Ctrl+A overwrites the usual action of that keystroke (selecting all cells). If you are writing a macro that will be used all day, every day, you should use a shortcut key that is not assigned to any existing shortcuts, such as Ctrl+J. Although most of the letter keys are already assigned to a shortcut, you can always use the shifted shortcut keys. To assign a macro to Ctrl+Shift+A, press Shift+A into the shortcut field.

14. Press the left-arrow key twice and the down-arrow key once to move to the now-blank row just below the name.

15. Hold down the Shift key while pressing the down-arrow key twice to select the three blank rows.

16. Press Ctrl+- to invoke the Delete command. Press R and then Enter to delete the row.

17. Press the up-arrow key and the down-arrow key. Moving the cell pointer up a cell and then back to the name causes only a single cell to be selected.

18. When you are done, click the Stop Recording button.

This macro successfully fixes any record in the database, provided the cell pointer is on the cell containing the name when you run the macro. Try playing back the macro by pressing Ctrl+A to fix one record. To fix all records, hold down Ctrl+A until all records are fixed.

Running a Macro

To run a macro, follow these steps:

1. Click the Macros icon in the Code group of the Developer tab. The Macro dialog appears, as shown in Figure 28.13.

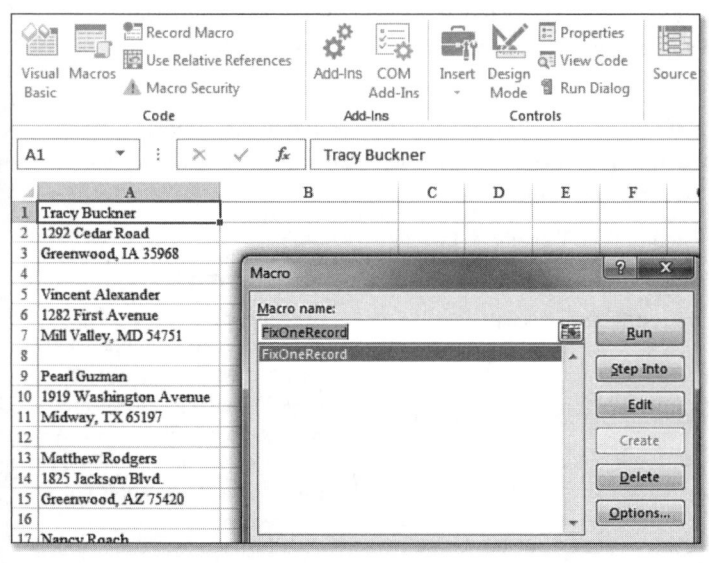

Figure 28.13
Playing back a macro by using the Macro dialog.

 **Tip**

Displaying the Macro dialog every time you want to run a macro is not efficient. Try running the macro with a shortcut key.

2. Select your macro and click the Run button. The macro fixes the first record.

3. Press Ctrl+A to run the FixOneRecord macro. As shown in Figure 28.14, the second record is fixed.

Figure 28.14
Results of a successful macro.

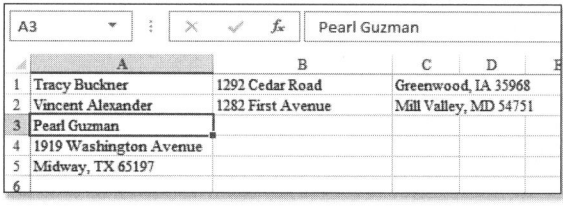

4. Hold down Ctrl+A to repeatedly run the macro. In a matter of seconds, all 100 names are in a format ready to use in a mail merge.

This example represents an ideal use of a one-time macro. The process of fixing the data someone gave you involved mindless repetition. If there had just been four records, you could have mindlessly fixed the records. However, because there were 100 records in this example, it made sense to record a macro and then run the macro repeatedly to solve the problem. You recorded the entire macro in relative mode, and you did not have to edit the macro. You probably run into a few situations a week where a quick one-time-use macro would make your job easier.

> **⚡ Caution**
> When you run a macro, there is no undo. Therefore, you should save a file before running a new macro on it. It is easy to have accidentally recorded the macro in default mode instead of relative mode. You need to save the macro so that you can easily go back to the current state in case something does not work right.

Everyday-Use Macro Example: Formatting an Invoice Register

The macro recorder does not solve all tasks perfectly, however. Many times, you need to record a macro and then edit the recorded code to make the macro a bit more general. This example demonstrates how to do that.

In this example, a system writes out a file every day. This file contains a list of invoices generated on the previous day. The file predictably contains six columns—NAME, DATE, INVOICE, REVENUE, SALES TAX, and TOTAL—as shown in Figure 28.15. The file also looks horrible: The columns are the wrong width, there is no title, and there isn't a Total row at the bottom. You would like a macro that opens this file, makes the columns wider, adds a total row, adds a title, makes the headings bold, and saves the file with a new name. The following sections describe how to create this macro.

	A	B	C	D	E	F	G	H
1	NAME	DATE	INVOICE	REVENUE	SALES TAX	TOTAL		
2	TERRI DC	2/17/2015	10217	252.11	15.13	267.24		
3	ELSIE HO	2/17/2015	10218	68.67	4.12	72.79		
4	HAROLD	2/17/2015	10219	111.4	6.68	118.08		
5	SHAWN (	2/17/2015	10220	151.47	9.09	160.56		
6	KRISTIN	2/17/2015	10221	131.71	7.9	139.61		
7	DAVID A	2/17/2015	10222	221.62	13.3	234.92		
8	ROSA PR	2/17/2015	10223	225.02	13.5	238.52		
9	NORA SH	2/17/2015	10224	261.84	15.71	277.55		
10	CRAIG BE	2/17/2015	10225	195.08	11.7	206.78		
11	BILLIE CF	2/17/2015	10226	72.31	4.34	76.65		
12	ADAM W	2/17/2015	10227	168.12	10.09	178.21		
13	ANDREW	2/17/2015	10228	79.54	4.77	84.31		
14	BRANDI :	2/17/2015	10229	258.73	15.52	274.25		
15	LAURIE F	2/17/2015	10230	248.44	14.91	263.35		
16								

Figure 28.15
Create a macro to format this file every day.

Using the Ctrl+Down Arrow Key to Handle a Variable Number of Rows

One of the inherent problems with this example is that your file will have a different number of rows every day. If you record a macro for this today to add totals in row 16, it will not work tomorrow, when you might have 22 invoices. The solution is to use the Ctrl+Down Arrow key to navigate to the last row of your data.

You use Ctrl and any arrow key to move to the edge of a contiguous range of data. In Figure 28.15, if you press Ctrl+Down Arrow, you would move to cell A15. From cell A15, press Ctrl+Up Arrow to move back to cell A1. You can press the Ctrl+Right Arrow to move to cell F1.

You can also use the Ctrl+arrow key to jump over an abyss of empty cells. If you are currently at the edge of a range (for example, cell F1) and press Ctrl+Right Arrow, Excel jumps over all the blank cells and stops either at the next nonblank cell in row 1 or at the right edge of the worksheet, cell XFD1.

Making Sure You Find the Last Record

You might be tempted to start in cell A1, press Ctrl+Down Arrow, and then press the down-arrow key again to move to the first blank row in the data. However, that is not the safest method. This data file is coming from another system. Undoubtedly, one day, a cashier will find a way to enter an order without a customer name. She will happen upon the accidental keystroke combination that causes the cash register to allow an order without a customer name. On that day, the Ctrl+Down Arrow combination will stop at the wrong row and add totals in the middle of your data set. Thus, it is safer to use the Go To dialog to move to A1048576 and use Ctrl+Up Arrow to find the last record.

Recording the Macro in a Blank Workbook

Create a blank workbook, and save it with a filename such as MacroToImportInvoices.xlsm. You can record your macro in this blank workbook and save it. Then, each day, you can open the macro workbook. The macro will handle opening the data file and formatting it. Go through these steps while the macro recorder is running:

1. Open the file.

2. Press the F5 key to display the Go To dialog.

3. Go to cell A1048576 (the last cell in column A).

4. Turn on relative recording by clicking Use Relative References in the Developer tab. You use relative recording because you want to record the action of jumping to the last row, and that row will be in a different location each day.

5. Press End+Up Arrow to move to the last row that contains data.

6. Press the down-arrow key to move to the blank row below the last row for data.

7. Type the word **Total**.

8. Move right three cells.

9. Type the formula **=SUM(D$2:D15)**. Press Ctrl+Enter to stay in the current cell. Be sure to include a single dollar sign to lock the start of the range to row 2. Do not use the AutoSum icon to add this formula!

10. Drag the fill handle to the right two cells to copy the formula from D to E and F.

11. Select all cells with Ctrl+Shift+Home.

12. Select Home, Format, AutoFit Column Width to make all of the columns wide.

13. Turn off relative recording by clicking the Use Relative References icon in the Developer tab. At this point, you always want to return to row 1 to format the headings. You don't want the recorder to record "Move up 15 rows." You always want to go to row 1.

14. Select row 1.

15. Open the Cell Styles gallery on the home tab and choose Heading 4.

16. Insert two rows using your favorite method. One method is to press Alt+I+R twice.

17. Move to Cell A1.

18. Type the formula **="Invoices for "&TEXT(B4,"mmmm d, yyyy")**. Press Ctrl+Enter to accept the formula and stay in the cell.

19. Open the Cell Styles gallery and choose Title.

20. Use Save As to save the file with a new name to reflect today's date.

21. Click the Stop Recording button.

In this macro example, you use a mix of relative and absolute recording to produce a macro that handles any number of rows of data. The macro will be somewhat useful, with two annoying limitations:

- If you saved the file as 2015-Feb-17Invoices.xls, the macro will attempt to overwrite that file every day.

- The macro will always want to open the same file. This is great if your cash register system always produces a file with the same name in the same folder. However, you might want the option to browse for a different file each day.

Both of these changes require you to edit the recorded macro. Before editing the macro, here is a look at how to open the Visual Basic Editor and at the syntax of VBA. To see the code to finish this example, refer to "Customizing the Everyday-Use Macro Example: GetOpenFileName and GetSaveAsFileName," later in this chapter.

Editing a Macro

To edit a macro, follow these steps:

1. Open the Macros dialog by pressing Alt+F8. The Macro dialog appears.

2. In the Macro dialog, select your macro and click Edit (see Figure 28.16). The Visual Basic Editor (VBE) is launched.

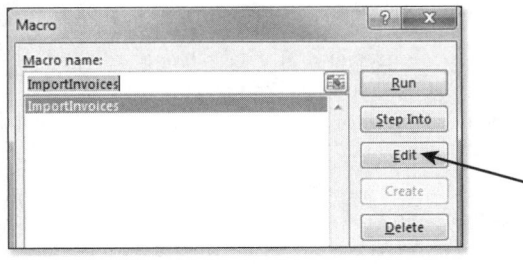

Figure 28.16
Launching the VBE through the Macro dialog is an easy way to make sure you find the proper code.

A number of panes are available in the VBE, but it is common to have three particular panes displayed, as shown in Figure 28.17:

- **Code pane**—The actual lines of the macro code are in the Code pane, which is usually on the right side of the screen.

- **Project Explorer pane**—This pane, which is in the upper left, shows every open workbook. Within the workbooks, you can see objects for each worksheet, an object for this workbook, and one or more code modules. If you cannot see the Project pane, you press Ctrl+R or select View, Project Explorer to open it.

- **Properties pane**—This pane, in the lower left, is useful if you design custom dialogs. You can Press F4 to display the Properties pane.

Figure 28.17
The VBE allows editing of recorded macro code.

Project Pane

Code Pane

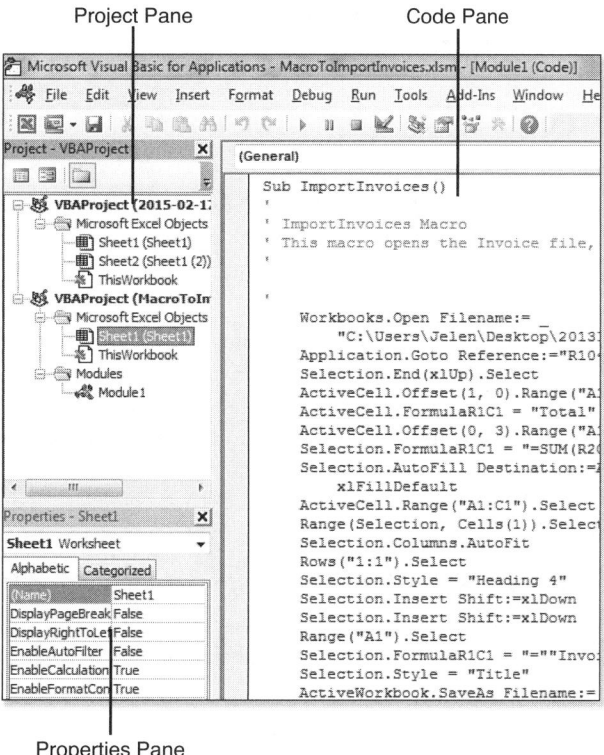

Properties Pane

Understanding VBA Code—An Analogy

In the 1980s and early 1990s, many people going through school were exposed to an introductory class in a programming language called BASIC. Although Excel macros are written in Visual Basic for Applications, the fact that both languages contain the word *basic* does not mean that BASIC and VBA are the same or even similar. BASIC is a procedural language. VBA is an object-oriented language. In VBA, the focus is on objects. This can make VBA confusing to someone who has learned to program in BASIC.

The syntax of VBA consists of objects, methods, collections, arguments, and properties. If you have never programmed in an object-oriented language, these terms, and the VBA code itself, might seem foreign to you. The following sections compare these five elements to parts of speech:

- An object is similar to a noun.

- A method is similar to a verb.

- A collection is similar to a plural noun.

- An argument is similar to an adverb.

- A property is similar to an adjective.

Each of the following sections describes the similarity between the VBA element and a part of speech. These sections also describe how to recognize the various elements when you examine VBA code.

Comparing Object.Method to Nouns and Verbs

As an object-oriented language, the objects in VBA are of primary importance. Think of an object as any noun in Excel. Examples of objects are a cell, a row, a column, a worksheet, and a workbook.

A method is any action that you can perform on an object. This is similar to a verb. You can add a worksheet. You can delete a row. You can clear a cell. In Excel VBA, words such as *Add*, *Delete*, and *Clear* are methods.

Objects and methods are joined by a period, although in VBA, people pronounce the period as *dot*. The object is first, followed by a dot, followed by the method. For example, object.method, which is pronounced "object-dot-method," indicates that the method performs on the object. This is confusing because it is backward from how English is spoken. If everyone spoke VBA instead of English, we would use sentences such as "car.drive" and "dinner.eat." When you see a period in VBA, it usually means that the word after the period is acting upon the word to the left of the period.

Comparing Collections to Plural Nouns

In an Excel workbook, there is not a single cell but rather a collection of many cells. Many workbooks contain several worksheets. Any time you have multiple instances of a certain object, VBA refers to this as a *collection*.

The *s* at the end of an object may seem subtle, but it indicates you are dealing with a collection instead of a single object. Whereas ThisWorkbook refers to a single workbook, Workbooks refers to a collection of all the open workbooks. This is an important distinction to understand.

You have two main ways to refer to a single worksheet in a collection of worksheets:

- By its number, such as `Worksheets(1)`
- By its name, such as `Worksheets("Jan")`

Comparing Parameters to Adverbs

When you invoke a command such as the Save As command, a dialog pops up, and you have the opportunity to specify several options that change how the command is carried out. If the Save As command is a method, the options for it are parameters. Just as an adverb modifies a verb, a parameter modifies a method.

Most of the time, parameters are recorded by using the syntax `ParameterName:=ParameterValue`.

One of the reasons that recorded code gets to be so long is that the macro recorder makes note of every option on the dialog, whether you select it or not.

Consider this line of code for `SaveAs`:

```
ActiveWorkbook.SaveAs Filename:="C:\Something.xlsx", _
FileFormat:=xlOpenXMLWorkbook, CreateBackup:=False
```

In this recorded macro for `SaveAs`, the recorder noted parameter values for `Filename`, `FileFormat`, and `CreateBackup`. Figure 28.18 shows the Save As dialog. `Filename` and `FileFormat` are evident on the form. However, where is the option for Create Backup?

Figure 28.18
It seems like the macro recorder is making up options that are not on the dialog.

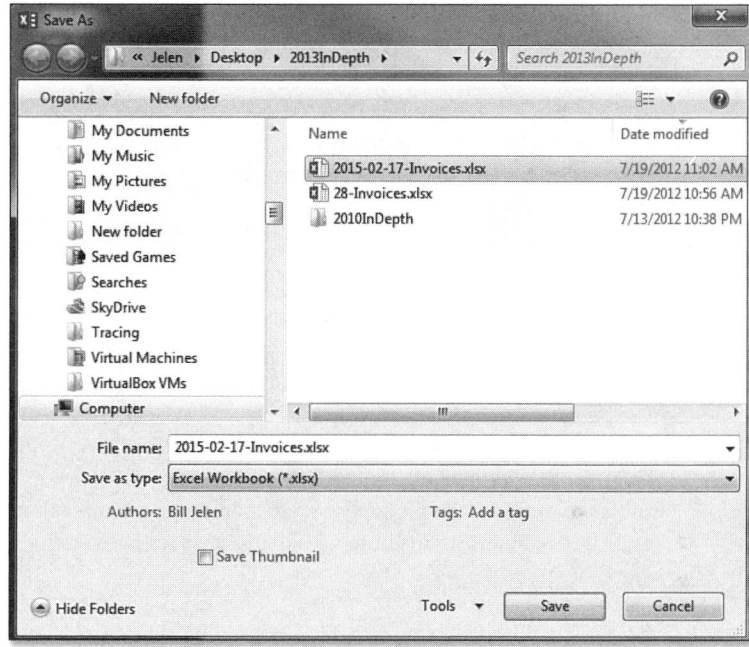

In the bottom center of the dialog is a Tools drop-down. If you select Tools, General Options, you see a dialog with four additional options, as shown in Figure 28.19. Even though you did not touch this Save Options dialog, Excel recorded the Backup value from the dialog for you.

Figure 28.19
Even though you did not touch the Save Options dialog, the macro recorder recorded the values from it.

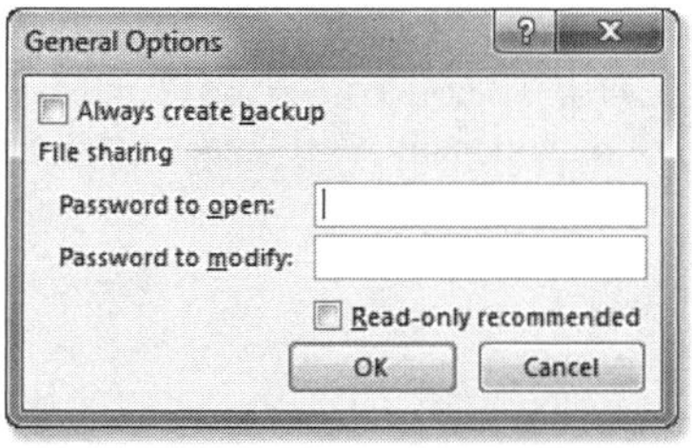

Parameters have some potentially confusing aspects. Most of the time, there is a space following the method and then a list of one or more `ParameterName:=ParameterValue` constructs, separated by a comma and a space. However, there are a few exceptions:

- If the result of the method is acted upon by another method, the list of parameters is enclosed in parentheses, and there is no space after the method name. One example is when you add a shape to a worksheet and then Excel selects the shape. The code to insert the shape uses the `AddShape` method and five named parameters:

```
ActiveSheet.Shapes.AddShape Type:=msoShapeRectangle, _
Left:=60, Top:=120, _
Width:=100, Height:=100
```

- The macro recorder will record the process of adding the shape and then selecting the shape. Because the `.Select` method is acting upon the result of the `.AddShape` method, you see the parameters for the `AddShape` method surrounded by parentheses:

```
ActiveSheet.Shapes.AddShape(Type:=msoShapeRectangle, _
    Left:=60, Top:=120, _
    Width:=100, Height:=100).Select
```

- When you use the parameter name, you can specify the parameters in any sequence you like. The Help topic for the method reveals the official default order for the parameters. If you specify the parameters in the exact sequence specified in Help, you are allowed to leave off the parameter names. However, this is a poor coding practice. Even if you have memorized the default order for the parameters, you cannot assume that everyone else reading your code will know the default order. The problem is that sometimes the macro recorder will record code in this style. For example, here is the actual line of code that was recorded when I added a shape to a worksheet:

  ```
  ActiveSheet.Shapes.AddShape(msoShapeRectangle, 60, 120, 100, 100).Select
  ```

- It would be difficult to figure out this line of code without looking at the Help topic. To access Help, click anywhere in the method of `AddShape` and then press the F1 key. The Help topic reveals that the correct parameter order is the one shown in Figure 28.20.

 Note

Keep in mind that parameters are like adverbs. They generally appear with a `Parameter Name:=Parameter Value` construct. However, there are times when the macro recorder lists the parameter values in their default order, without the parameter names or the `:=`.

Figure 28.20
The Help topic
for each method
helps decode
the default
order of the
parameters.

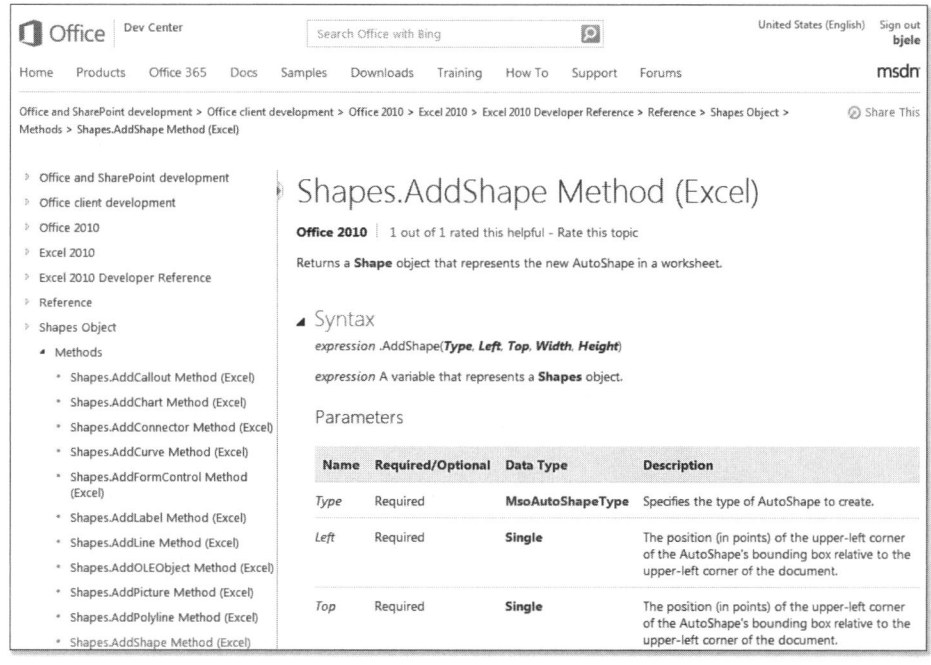

When VBA Help is installed, you can click any object, method, argument, or parameter in VBA
and press the F1 key to display a complete description of the item. The Help topic lists the valid
properties associated with the object and the valid methods that can be used on the object.
Often, the Help topic will include an example as well. To use the code in the example, you can
highlight the code, press Ctrl+C to copy, and then paste this code directly into the Code pane of
the Visual Basic Editor (also known as the VBE).

Comparing Adjectives to Properties

The final construct in VBA is the adjective used to describe an object. In VBA, adjectives are called
properties. Think about a cell in Excel with a formula in it. The cell has many properties. These are
some of the most popular properties:

- Value (the value shown in the cell)

- Formula (the formula used to calculate Value)

- Font Name

- Font Size

- Font Color

- Cell Interior Color

In VBA, you can check on the value of a property, or you can set the property to a new value. To change several cells to be bold, for example, you would change their Bold property to True:

```
Selection.Font.Bold = True
```

You can also check to see whether a property equals a certain value:

```
If Selection.Value = 100 then Selection.Font.Bold = True
```

Properties are generally used with the dot construct, and they are almost always followed by =, as contrasted with the := used with parameters (for example, PropertyName = value).

Using the Analogy While Examining Recorded Code

When you understand that a period generally separates an object from a method or a property, you can start to make sense of the recorded code.

For example, the following line performs the Open method:

```
Workbooks.Open Filename:="C:\Invoices.xls"
```

In this example, the Filename parameter is shown with := after the parameter name. This first line in the following example performs the Select method on one particular member of the Rows collection:

```
Rows("1:1").Select
Selection.Font.Bold = True
```

The second line then sets the Bold property of the Font property of the selection to True. Using these two lines of code is equivalent to selecting row 1 and clicking the Bold icon. You notice that one property such as Font can have subproperties such as Bold and Italic.

 **Tip**

In the Excel user interface, you generally have to select a cell before you can change something in it. In a macro, there is no need to select something first. For example, you can replace the two lines in the preceding example with this single line of code: Rows("1:1").Font.Bold = True.

Using Simple Variables and Object Variables

The macro recorder never records a variable, but you can add variables to a macro when you edit the code. Suppose that you need to do a number of operations to the row where the totals will be located. Instead of repeatedly going to the last row in the spreadsheet and pressing End+Up Arrow, you can assign the row number to a variable:

```
FinalRow = Range("A1048576").End(xlup).Row
TotalRow = FinalRow + 1
```

The words `FinalRow` and `TotalRow` are variables that each hold a single value. If you have data in rows 2 through 25 today, `FinalRow` will hold the value 25, and `TotalRow` will hold the value of 26. This enables you to use efficient code such as the following:

```
Range("A" & TotalRow).Value = "Total"
Range("C" & TotalRow).Formula = "=SUM(C2:C"& TotalRow & ")"
Range("D" & TotalRow).Formula = "=SUM(D2:D"& TotalRow & ")"
Range("E" & TotalRow).Formula = "=SUM(E2:E"& TotalRow & ")"
```

VBA also offers a powerful variable called an *object variable*. An object variable can be used to represent any object such as a worksheet, chart, or cell. Whereas a simple variable holds one value, an object variable holds values for every property associated with the object.

Object variables are declared using the `Dim` statement and then assigned using the `Set` statement:

```
Dim WSD as worksheet
Set WSD = Worksheets("Sheet1")
```

Using object variables offers the following advantages:

- It is easier to refer to WSD than to `ActiveWorkbook.Worksheets("Sheet1")`.

- If you define the object variable with a DIM statement at the beginning of the macro, as you type new lines of code, the VBE's AutoComplete feature shows a list of valid methods and properties for the object, as shown in Figure 28.21.

Figure 28.21
Object variables hold many properties instead of a single value.

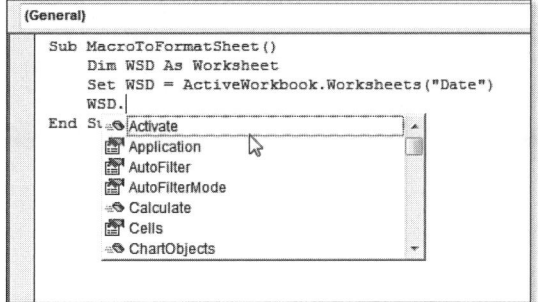

Using R1C1-Style Formulas

If you are a history buff of technology, you might know that VisiCalc was the first spreadsheet program for PCs. When Dan Bricklin and Bob Frankston invented VisiCalc, they used the A1 style for naming cells. In those early days, VisiCalc had competitors such as SuperCalc and a Microsoft program called MultiPlan. This early Microsoft spreadsheet used the notation of R1C1 to refer to cell A1. The cell that we know today as E17 would have been called R17C5, for row 17, column 5.

In 1985, Microsoft launched Excel version 1.0 for the Macintosh. Excel originally continued to use the R1C1 style of notation. During the next 10 years, Excel and Lotus 1-2-3 were locked in a bitter battle for market share. Lotus was the early leader, and it had adopted the A1 notation style familiar to VisiCalc customers. To capture more market share, Microsoft allowed Excel to use either A1-style notation or R1C1-style notation. Even today, in Excel 2013, you can turn on R1C1-style notation by selecting File, Options, Formulas, R1C1 Reference Style. In R1C1 reference style, column letters A, B, C are replaced with column numbers 1, 2, 3. Hardly anyone uses R1C1 reference style; however, the macro recorder always records formulas in R1C1 style.

Figure 28.22 shows the familiar formula =SUM(D$2:D15). When entered in cell D16, this formula adds up everything from row 2 to the row just above the current cell.

Figure 28.22
This familiar formula is in A1-style notation.

If you now turn on R1C1 style in this worksheet, the formula changes to =SUM(R2C:R[-1]C), as shown in Figure 28.23.

In R1C1 notation, the reference RC refers to the current cell. You can modify RC by adding a particular row number or column number. For example, R2C refers to the cell in row 2 of the current column. RC1 refers to the cell in this row that is in column 1.

If you put a row number or column number in square brackets, it refers to a relative number of cells from the current cell. If you have a formula in cell D16 and use the reference R[1]C[-2], you are referring to the cell one row below D16 and two columns to the left of D16, which would be cell B17.

Figure 28.23
The formula in R1C1 notation would be confusing to most spreadsheet users.

R16C4	▼	:	× ✓ *fx*	=SUM(R2C:R[-1]C)

	1	2	3	4	5	6
1	NAME	DATE	INVOICE	REVENUE	SALES TAX	TOTAL
2	TERRI DONOVAN	2/17/2015	10217	252.11	15.13	267.24
3	ELSIE HOUSTON	2/17/2015	10218	68.67	4.12	72.79
4	HAROLD HARTMAN	2/17/2015	10219	111.4	6.68	118.08
5	SHAWN GREER	2/17/2015	10220	151.47	9.09	160.56
6	KRISTIN ATKINS	2/17/2015	10221	131.71	7.9	139.61
7	DAVID ALLEN	2/17/2015	10222	221.62	13.3	234.92
8	ROSA PRATT	2/17/2015	10223	225.02	13.5	238.52
9	NORA SHEPHERD	2/17/2015	10224	261.84	15.71	277.55
10	CRAIG BERNARD	2/17/2015	10225	195.08	11.7	206.78
11	BILLIE CRAWFORD	2/17/2015	10226	72.31	4.34	76.65
12	ADAM WINTERS	2/17/2015	10227	168.12	10.09	178.21
13	ANDREW DODSON	2/17/2015	10228	79.54	4.77	84.31
14	BRANDI SHAW	2/17/2015	10229	258.73	15.52	274.25
15	LAURIE HOWARD	2/17/2015	10230	248.44	14.91	263.35
16	Total			2446.06	146.76	2592.82

You are probably wondering why the macro recorder uses this arcane notation style when recording formulas. It turns out that this style is fantastic for formulas. Whereas a column of formulas in A1 style will have a different formula in each cell, the same column of formulas in R1C1 style will be identical down the column. For example, notice that every formula in column E & F of the worksheet is a little different (see Figure 28.24). When you copy F2 to F3, Excel changes the references of E2 and D2 to be E3 and D3.

Figure 28.24
In A1 style, every formula in E2:F15 is different.

	D	E	F
1	REVENUE	SALES TAX	TOTAL
2	252.11	=ROUND(0.06*D2,2)	=E2+D2
3	68.67	=ROUND(0.06*D3,2)	=E3+D3
4	111.4	=ROUND(0.06*D4,2)	=E4+D4
5	151.47	=ROUND(0.06*D5,2)	=E5+D5
6	131.71	=ROUND(0.06*D6,2)	=E6+D6
7	221.62	=ROUND(0.06*D7,2)	=E7+D7
8	225.02	=ROUND(0.06*D8,2)	=E8+D8
9	261.84	=ROUND(0.06*D9,2)	=E9+D9
10	195.08	=ROUND(0.06*D10,2)	=E10+D10
11	72.31	=ROUND(0.06*D11,2)	=E11+D11
12	168.12	=ROUND(0.06*D12,2)	=E12+D12
13	79.54	=ROUND(0.06*D13,2)	=E13+D13
14	258.73	=ROUND(0.06*D14,2)	=E14+D14
15	248.44	=ROUND(0.06*D15,2)	=E15+D15
16	=SUM(D$2:D15)	=SUM(E$2:E15)	=SUM(F$2:F15)

Now look at these same formulas in R1C1 style, as shown in Figure 28.25. Every formula in E2:E15 is identical. This makes sense because the formula is saying, "Add the sales tax one cell to the left of me to the merchandise amount that is two cells to the left of me." Every formula in F2:F15 is identical; even the total formulas in D16:F16 are identical.

| R2C5 | ▼ | : | × | ✓ | *fx* | =ROUND(0.06*RC[-1],2) |

⊿	4	5	6
1	REVENUE	SALES TAX	TOTAL
2	252.11	=ROUND(0.06*RC[-1],2)	=RC[-1]+RC[-2]
3	68.67	=ROUND(0.06*RC[-1],2)	=RC[-1]+RC[-2]
4	111.4	=ROUND(0.06*RC[-1],2)	=RC[-1]+RC[-2]
5	151.47	=ROUND(0.06*RC[-1],2)	=RC[-1]+RC[-2]
6	131.71	=ROUND(0.06*RC[-1],2)	=RC[-1]+RC[-2]
7	221.62	=ROUND(0.06*RC[-1],2)	=RC[-1]+RC[-2]
8	225.02	=ROUND(0.06*RC[-1],2)	=RC[-1]+RC[-2]
9	261.84	=ROUND(0.06*RC[-1],2)	=RC[-1]+RC[-2]
10	195.08	=ROUND(0.06*RC[-1],2)	=RC[-1]+RC[-2]
11	72.31	=ROUND(0.06*RC[-1],2)	=RC[-1]+RC[-2]
12	168.12	=ROUND(0.06*RC[-1],2)	=RC[-1]+RC[-2]
13	79.54	=ROUND(0.06*RC[-1],2)	=RC[-1]+RC[-2]
14	258.73	=ROUND(0.06*RC[-1],2)	=RC[-1]+RC[-2]
15	248.44	=ROUND(0.06*RC[-1],2)	=RC[-1]+RC[-2]
16	=SUM(R2C:R[-1]C)	=SUM(R2C:R[-1]C)	=SUM(R2C:R[-1]C)
17			

Figure 28.25
In R1C1 style, every formula in F2:F15 is identical.

If you are forced to use A1-style formulas in a macro, you might try to enter the formula in cell F2 and then copy the formula from F2 to the remaining cells:

```
Range("F2").Formula = "=D2+E2"
Range("F2").Copy Destination:=Range("F3:F15")
```

On the other hand, you can enter all the formulas in one line of code when using R1C1-style formulas:

```
Range("F2:F15").FormulaR1C1 = "=RC[-2]+RC[-1]"
```

Tip

Although the macro recorder always records formulas in R1C1 style, you are allowed to write the macros using regular formulas. Change the FormulaR1C1 property to Formula. The following two lines of code are equivalent:

```
Range("F2:F15").FormulaR1C1 = _
    "=RC[-2]+RC[-1]"
Range("F2:F15").Formula = _
    "=D2-E2"
```

Fixing Calculation Errors in Macros

Probably the most important reason to understand R1C1 formulas is to make sure that the macro recorder recorded the proper formula. This is important because the macro recorder does not do a good job of recording the intent of the AutoSum button. If your data set has numbers in D2:D15 today, pressing AutoSum from cell D16 will record the following line of macro code:

```
Selection.FormulaR1C1 = "=SUM(R[-14]C:R[-1]C)"
```

This formula adds a range from 14 rows above the selection to the cell just above the selection. This works only on days when you have exactly 14 rows of data. This is one of the most annoying bugs in a macro.

It is annoying because this type of logic error will not cause an actual error. If you run this macro on the invoice file you receive tomorrow that contains 20 invoices, the macro will happily total only the last 14 invoices instead of all 20. This means that you could distribute this report with a wrong total for several days before someone realizes that something is amiss.

However, you can correct this formula. You know that you have headings in row 1 and that the first invoice will appear in row 2. You need the macro to sum from row 2 to the row just above the current cell. Therefore, you need to change the formula to this:

```
Selection.FormulaR1C1 = "=SUM(R2C:R[-1]C)"
```

Customizing the Everyday-Use Macro Example: GETOPENFILENAME and GETSAVEASFILENAME

The everyday-use macro you recorded earlier in this chapter for formatting an invoice register is hard-coded to always open the same file and always save with the same filename. To make the macro more general, you can allow the person running the macro to browse for the file each morning and to specify a new filename during the Save As. Excel offers a straightforward way to display the File Open or File Save As dialog. Here is the code you need to use:

```
FileToOpen = Application.GetOpenFileName( _
    FileFilter:="Excel Files,*.xl*", _
    Title:="Select Today's Invoice File")
```

Note that this code displays the File Open dialog and allows a file to be selected. When you click Open, the dialog assigns the filename to the variable. It does not actually open the file. You then need to open the file specified in the variable:

```
Workbooks.Open Filename:=FileToOpen
```

When you want to ask for the filename to use in saving the file, use this code:

```
NewFileName = Application.GetSaveAsFilename( _
    Title:="Select File Name for Today")
ActiveWorkbook.SaveAs Filename:=NewFileName, _
    FileFormat:=xlOpenXMLWorkbookMacroEnabled
```

The following macro is the final macro to use each day:

```
Sub ImportInvoicesFixed()
' ImportInvoices Macro
' With Changes
    FileToOpen = Application.GetOpenFileName( _
        FileFilter:= _
```

```
        "Excel files (*.xls;*.xlsb;*.xlsx;*.xlsm)" & _
        ",*.xls;*.xlsb;*.xlsx;*.xlsb)", _
        Title:="Select Today's Invoice File")
    Workbooks.Open Filename:=FileToOpen
    Application.Goto Reference:="R1048576C1"
    Selection.End(xlUp).Select
    ActiveCell.Offset(1, 0).Range("A1").Select
    ActiveCell.FormulaR1C1 = "Total"
    ActiveCell.Offset(0, 3).Range("A1").Select
    Selection.FormulaR1C1 = "=SUM(R2C:R[-1]C)"
    Selection.AutoFill Destination:=ActiveCell.Range("A1:C1"), Type:= _
        xlFillDefault
    ActiveCell.Range("A1:C1").Select
    Range(Selection, Cells(1)).Select
    Selection.Columns.AutoFit
    Rows("1:1").Select
    Selection.Style = "Heading 4"
    Selection.Insert Shift:=xlDown
    Selection.Insert Shift:=xlDown
    Range("A1").Select
    Selection.FormulaR1C1 = "="""Invoices for ""&TEXT(R[3]C[1],""mmmm d, yyyy"")"
    Selection.Style = "Title"
    NewFileName = Application.GetSaveAsFilename( _
        Title:="Select File Name for Today")
    ActiveWorkbook.SaveAs Filename:=NewFileName, _
        FileFormat:=xlOpenXMLWorkbookMacroEnabled
End Sub
```

Of the 19 lines in the macro, you added two lines and corrected two lines. This is typical because between 10% and 20% of a recorded macro generally needs to be adjusted.

From-Scratch Macro Example: Loops, Flow Control, and Referring to Ranges

Suppose you work for a company that sells printers and scanners to commercial accounts. When you sell a piece of hardware, you also try to sell a service plan for that hardware. Customers in your state are taxed. Your accounting software provides a daily download that looks like columns A:D in Figure 28.26.

You want to create a macro that examines each row in the data set and carries out a different action, based on the value in column C. You will probably want to write this macro from scratch. The following sections describe how to do this.

Figure 28.26
Your accounting software groups all hardware, service, and tax amounts into a single column.

	A	B	C	D	E
1	Invoice	Customer	Product	Revenue	
2	1010	Supreme Toothpick Company	Printer	262	
3	1010	Supreme Toothpick Company	Scanner	454	
4	1010	Supreme Toothpick Company	Service Plan	107	
5	1010	Supreme Toothpick Company	Sales Tax	49.38	
6	1011	Fashionable Necktie Company	Printer	127	
7	1011	Fashionable Necktie Company	Scanner	994	
8	1011	Fashionable Necktie Company	Sales Tax	67.26	
9	1012	Top-Notch Juicer Inc.	Printer	985	
10	1012	Top-Notch Juicer Inc.	Service Plan	148	
11	1012	Top-Notch Juicer Inc.	Sales Tax	67.98	

Finding the Last Row with Data

The recorded macro examples discussed earlier in this chapter suggested going to the last cell in column A and then pressing End followed by the up-arrow key to find the last row with data in column A.

In legacy versions of Excel, this would be accomplished with this code:

```
FinalRow = Range("A65536").End(xlUp).Row
```

This command became more complicated in Excel 2007. The last row in the worksheet is either 1048576 or 65536, depending on whether the workbook is in compatibility mode. The solution is to use Rows.Count, which is shorthand for Application.Rows.Count. This solution returns the total number of rows available in the current worksheet. Note that this property returns 65,536 in compatibility mode and 1,048,576 in regular mode.

The following line of code finds the last row in column A with a nonblank value:

```
FinalRow = Cells(Rows.Count, 1).End(xlUp).Row
```

Looping Through All Rows

The loop most commonly used in VBA is a For-Next loop. This is identical to the loop that you might have learned about in a BASIC class.

In this example, the loop starts with a For statement. You specify that on each pass through the loop, a certain variable will change from a low value to a high value. This simple macro will run through the loop ten times. On the first pass through the loop, the variable x will be equal to 1. The two lines inside the loop will assign the value 1 to cells A1 and B1. When the macro encounters the Next x line, it will return to the start of the loop, increment x by 1, and run through the loop again. The next time through the loop, the value of x will be 2. Cell A2 will be assigned the number 2, and cell B2 will show 4, which is the square of 2. Eventually, x will be equal to 10. At the Next x line, the macro will allow the loop to finish. The following is the code for this macro:

```
Sub WriteSquares()
    For x = 1 To 10
        Cells(x, 1).Value = x
```

```
        Cells(x, 2).Value = x * x
    Next x
End Sub
```

After you run this macro, you have a simple table that shows the numbers 1 through 10 and their squares, as shown in Figure 28.27.

	A	B	C
1	1	1	
2	2	4	
3	3	9	
4	4	16	
5	5	25	
6	6	36	
7	7	49	
8	8	64	
9	9	81	
10	10	100	
11			

Figure 28.27
This simple loop fills in ten rows.

After a loop is written, it can be adjusted easily. For example, if you want a table showing all the squares from 1 to 100, you can adjust the `For x = 1 to 10` line to be `For x = 1 to 100`.

There is an optional clause in the `For` statement called the *step value*. If no step value is shown, the program moves through the loop by incrementing the variable by one each time through the loop. If you wanted to check only the even-numbered rows, you could change the loop to be `For x = 2 to 100` in step 2.

If you are going to be optionally deleting rows from a range of data, it is important to start at the bottom and proceed to the top of the range. You would use `-1` as the step value:

```
For x = 100 to 1 step -1
```

Referring to Ranges

The macro recorder uses the `Range` property to refer to a particular range. You might see the macro recorder refer to ranges such as `Range("B3")` and `Range("W1:Z100")`.

The loop code shown in the preceding section emulates this style of referring to ranges. On the third time through the loop, this line of code would refer to cell B3:

```
Range("B" & x).value = x * x
```

However, how would you handle looping through each column? If you wanted to continue using the `Range` property, you need to jump through some hoops to figure out the letter associated with column 5:

```
For y = 1 to 26
    ThisCol = Chr(64+y)
    Range(ThisCol & 1).value = ThisCol
Next y
```

This method works fine if you are using only 26 or fewer columns. However, if you need to loop through all the columns out to column XFD, you will spend all day trying to write the logic to assign the column label WMJ to column 15896.

The solution is to use the `Cells` property instead of the `Range` property. `Cells` require that you specify a numeric row number and a numeric column number. For example, cell B3 is specified as follows:

```
Cells(3, 2)
```

If you need to refer to a rectangular range, you can use the `Resize` property. `Resize` requires you to specify the number of rows and the number of columns. For example, to refer to W1:Z100, use this:

```
Cells(1, 23).Resize(100, 4)
```

It is difficult to figure out that this refers to W1:Z100, but it enables you to loop through rows or columns.

You can use the following code to make every other column bold:

```
For y = 1 to 100 step 2
    Cells(1, y).Resize(200, 1).Font.Bold = True
Next y
```

Combining a Loop with `FinalRow`

Earlier in this chapter, you learned how to use the Ctrl+Up Arrow to find the final row in a data set. After finding the final row in the data set and assigning it to a variable, you can specify that the loop should run through `FinalRow`:

```
FinalRow = Cells(Rows.Count, 1).End(xlUp).row
For x = 2 to FinalRow
    ' Perform some action
Next x
```

Making Decisions by Using Flow Control

Flow control is the ability to make decisions within a macro. The following sections describe two commonly used flow control constructs: `If - End If` and `Select Case`.

Using the `If - End If` Construct

Say you need a macro to delete any records that say Sales Tax. You could accomplish this with a simple `If - End If` construct:

```
If Cells(x, 4).Value = "Sales Tax" Then
    Rows(x).Delete
End If
```

This construct always starts with the word If, followed by a logical test, followed by the word Then. Every line between the first line and the End If line is executed only if the logical test is True.

Now suppose that you want to enhance the macro so that any other amounts that contain service plan revenue are moved to column F. To do this, you use the ElseIf line to enter a second condition and block of lines to be used in that condition:

```
If Cells(x, 4).Value = "Sales Tax" Then
    Cells(x, 1).EntireRow.Delete
ElseIf Cells(x, 4).Value = "Service Plan" Then
    Cells(x, 5).Cut Destination:=Cells(x, 6)
End If
```

You could continue adding ElseIf statements to handle other situations. Eventually, just before the End If, you could add an Else block to handle any other condition you have not thought about.

Using the Select Case Construct

If you reach a point where you have many ElseIf statements all testing the same value, it might make sense to switch to a Select Case construct. For example, suppose you want to loop through all the records to examine the product in column C. If column C contains a printer, you want to move the amount in column D to a new column E. Scanner revenue should go to a new column F. Service plans go to a new column H. Sales tax goes to a new column I. You should also handle the situation when something is sold that contains none of those products. In that case, you would move the revenue to a new column G.

The construct begins with Select Case and then the value to check. The construct ends with End Select, which is similar to End If.

Each subblock of code starts with the word Case and one or more possible values. If you needed to check for Printer or Printers, you would enclose each in quotes and separate them with a comma.

After checking for all the possible values you can think of, you might add a Case Else subblock to handle any other stray values that might be entered in column C.

The following code checks to see what product is in column C. Depending on the product, the program copies the revenue from column D to a specific column.

```
Select Case Cells(x, 3).Value
    Case "Printer", "Printers"
        Cells(x, 4).Copy Destination:=Cells(x, 5)
    Case "Scanner", "Scanners"
        Cells(x, 4).Copy Destination:=Cells(x, 6)
    Case "Service Plan"
        Cells(x, 4).Copy Destination:=Cells(x, 8)
    Case "Sales Tax"
        Cells(x, 4).Copy Destination:=Cells(x, 9)
    Case Else
        ' Something unexpected was sold
        Cells(x, 4).Copy Destination:=Cells(x, 7)
End Select
```

Putting Together the From-Scratch Example: Testing Each Record in a Loop

Using the building blocks described in the preceding sections, you can now write the code for a macro that finds the last row, loops through the records, and copies the total revenue to the appropriate column. Now you need to add new headings for the additional columns, as shown in Figure 28.28.

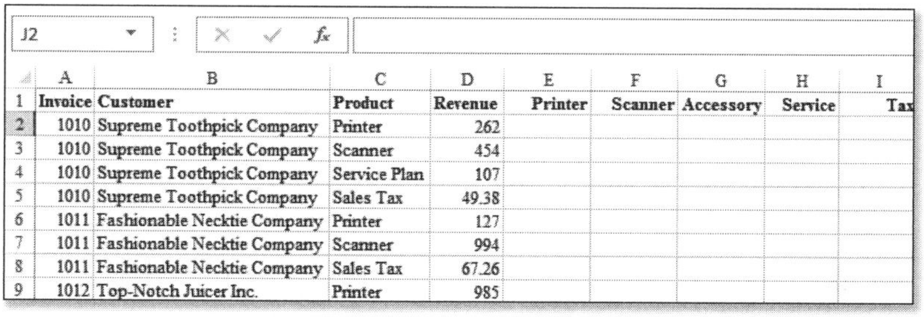

Figure 28.28
Adding new headings before running the macro.

The macro should use the End property to locate the final row and prefill columns E through I with zeros. Next, it should loop from row 2 down to the final row. For each record, the revenue column should be moved to one of the columns. At the end of the loop, the program alerts you that the program is complete, using a MsgBox command. The following is the complete code of this macro:

```
Sub MoveRevenue2()
    FinalRow = Cells(Rows.Count, 1).End(xlUp).Row
    Range("E2", Cells(FinalRow, 9)).Value = 0
    For x = 2 To FinalRow
        Select Case Cells(x, 3).Value
            Case "Printer", "Printers"

                Cells(x, 4).Copy Destination:=Cells(x, 5)
            Case "Scanner", "Scanners"
                Cells(x, 4).Copy Destination:=Cells(x, 6)
            Case "Service Plan"
                Cells(x, 4).Copy Destination:=Cells(x, 8)
            Case "Sales Tax"
                Cells(x, 4).Copy Destination:=Cells(x, 9)
            Case Else
                ' Something unexpected was sold - Accessory?
                Cells(x, 4).Copy Destination:=Cells(x, 7)
        End Select
    Next x
    MsgBox "Macro complete"
End Sub
```

 **Tip**

An alternative syntax of the Range property is to specify the top-left and bottom-right cells in the range, separated by a comma. In the macro described here, for example, you know you want to fill from cell E2 to the last row in column I. You can describe this range as follows:

```
Range("E2", Cells(FinalRow, 9))
```

This syntax is sometimes simpler than using `Cells()` and `Resize()`.

After you run this macro, you see that the revenue amounts have been copied to the appropriate columns, as shown in Figure 28.29.

	A	B	C	D	E	F	G	H	I
1	Invoice	Customer	Product	Revenue	Printer	Scanner	Accessory	Service	Tax
2	1010	Supreme Toothpick Company	Printer	262	262	0	0	0	0
3	1010	Supreme Toothpick Company	Scanner	454	0	454	0	0	0
4	1010	Supreme Toothpick Company	Service Plan	107	0	0	0	107	0
5	1010	Supreme Toothpick Company	Sales Tax	49.38	0	0	0	0	49.38
6	1011	Fashionable Necktie Company	Printer	127	127	0	0	0	0
7	1011	Fashionable Necktie Company	Scanner	994	0	994	0	0	0
8	1011	Fashionable Necktie Company	Sales Tax	67.26	0	0	0	0	67.26
9	1012	Top-Notch Juicer Inc.	Printer	985	985	0	0	0	0
10	1012	Top-Notch Juicer Inc.	Service Plan	148	0	0	0	148	0
11	1012	Top-Notch Juicer Inc.	Sales Tax	67.98	0	0	0	0	67.98
12	1013	Unusual Aquarium Traders	Printer	290	290	0	0	0	0
13	1013	Unusual Aquarium Traders	Scanner	655	0	655	0	0	0
14	1013	Unusual Aquarium Traders	Sales Tax	56.7	0	0	0	0	56.7
15	1014	Fashionable Adhesive Inc.	Printer	250	250	0	0	0	0
16	1014	Fashionable Adhesive Inc.	Scanner	679	0	679	0	0	0
17	1014	Fashionable Adhesive Inc.	Service Plan	139	0	0	0	139	0
18	1014	Fashionable Adhesive Inc.	Sales Tax	64.08	0	0	0	0	64.08
19	1015	Fashionable Sprayer Traders	Printer	800	800	0	0	0	0

Figure 28.29
After running the macro, you have a breakout of revenue by product.

A Special Case: Deleting Some Records

If a loop is conditionally deleting records, you will run into trouble if it is a typical For-Next loop. Suppose you want to delete all the sales tax records, as follows:

```
Sub ThisWontWork()
    FinalRow = Cells(Rows.Count, 1).End(xlUp).Row
    For x = 2 To FinalRow
        If Cells(x, 3).Value = "Sales Tax" Then
            Cells(x, 1).EntireRow.Delete
        Else
            Cells(x, 5).Value = "Checked"
        End If
    Next x
End Sub
```

Consider the data in Figure 28.30. The first time through the loop, x is equal to 2. Cell C2 does not contain sales tax, so cell E2 has the word checked. A similar result occurs for rows 3 and 4. The fourth time through the loop, cell C5 contains sales tax. The macro deletes the tax in row 5. However, Excel then moves the old row 6 up to row 5, as shown in Figure 28.31. The next time through the loop, the program inspects row 6, and the data that is now in row 5 will never be checked.

The macro succeeds in deleting tax. However, several rows were not checked, and several extra blank rows at the bottom were checked needlessly, as shown in Figure 28.32.

Figure 28.30
Before the macro deletes row 5, the Printer record is in row 6.

Printer in Row 6

Figure 28.31
The old row 6 data moves up to occupy the deleted row 5. However, the macro blindly moves on to check row 6 next. The printer that moved to row 5 never gets checked.

Printer Moved to Row 5

Figure 28.32
Several rows were not checked in this loop.

The solution is to have the loop run backward. You need to start at the final row and proceed up through the sheet to row 2. When the macro deletes tax in row 31, it can then proceed to checking row 30, knowing that nothing has been destroyed (yet) in row 30 and above.

To reverse the flow of the loop, you have to tell the loop to start at the final row, but you also have to tell the loop to use a step value of -1. The start of the loop would use this line of code:

```
For x = FinalRow to 2 Step -1
```

The macro you need here represents a fairly common task: looping through all the records to do something conditionally to each record.

The following macro correctly deletes all the sales tax records:

```
Sub DeleteTaxOK()
    FinalRow = Cells(Rows.Count, 1).End(xlUp).Row
    For x = FinalRow To 2 Step -1
        If Cells(x, 3).Value = "Sales Tax" Then
            Cells(x, 1).EntireRow.Delete
        Else
            Cells(x, 5).Value = "Checked"
        End If
    Next x
End Sub
```

For the example described here, the macro recorder would be almost no help. You would have to write this simple macro from scratch. However, it is a powerful macro that can simplify tasks when you have hundreds of thousands of rows of data.

Combination Macro Example: Creating a Report for Each Customer

Many real-life scenarios require you to use a combination of recorded code and code written from scratch. For example, Figure 28.33 shows a data set with all your invoices for the year. In this case, suppose you would like to produce a workbook for each customer that you can mail to the customer.

Figure 28.33
The goal is to provide a subset of this data to each customer.

	A	B	C	D	E	F
1	Customer	Invoice	Date	Purchas	Paid	Open Balance
2	Hip Lawn Corporatic	1001	1/4/15	8846	8846	0
3	Vivid Chopstick Tra	1002	1/4/15	1688	1688	0
4	Unusual Doorbell Cc	1003	1/4/15	8415	8415	0
5	Excellent Utensil Co	1004	1/4/15	2619	2619	0
6	Hip Lawn Corporatic	1005	1/5/15	11476	11476	0
7	Fascinating Oven Su	1006	1/5/15	4958	0	4958
8	Savory Glass Inc.	1007	1/5/15	11243	11243	0
9	Superior Bobsled Cc	1008	1/5/15	4419	4419	0
10	Hip Lawn Corporatic	1009	1/5/15	12562	12562	0
11	Savory Glass Inc.	1010	1/5/15	7409	7409	0
12	Fascinating Oven Su	1011	1/6/15	8141	0	8141

One way to handle this task would be to use an advanced filter to get a list of all unique customers in column A. You would then loop through these customers, applying an AutoFilter to the data set to see only the customers that match the selected customer. After the data set is filtered, you can select the visible cells only and copy them to a new workbook. Then you can save the workbook with the name of the customer and then return to the original workbook.

You can start by creating a blank procedure with comments to spell out the steps in the preceding paragraphs. Then you add code for the loop and other simple tasks such as copying the selection to a new workbook. Whenever you encounter a step for which you have never written code, you can leave a comment with question marks. This enables you to go back and record parts of the process to finish the macro.

 Note

It is common to indent each line of code with four spaces. Any lines of code inside an `If-EndIf` block or inside a `For-Next` loop are indented an additional four spaces. If you have typed a line of code that is indented eight spaces and then press Enter at the end of the line of code, the VBE automatically indents the next line to eight spaces. Each press of the Tab key indents by an additional four spaces. Pressing Shift+Tab removes four spaces of indentation. Although four is the default number of spaces for a tab, you can change this to any number of spaces using Tools, Options in the Visual Basic Editor.

Your first pass at a well-commented macro might look like this:

```
Sub ProduceReportForEachCustomer()
    ' Define object variables for new workbook
    ' Suffix of N means New
    Dim WBN As Workbook
    Dim WSN As Worksheet
    ' Define object variables for the current workbook
    ' Suffix of O means Old
    Dim WBO As Workbook
    Dim WSO As Worksheet
    Set WBO = ActiveWorkbook
    Set WSO = ActiveSheet
    ' Find the FinalRow in today's dataset
    FinalRow = Cells(Rows.Count, 1).End(xlUp).Row

    ' Use an Advanced filter to copy unique customers
    ' from column A to column H
    ' ???

    'Find the final customer in column H
    FinalCust = Cells(Rows.Count, 8).End(xlUp).Row
    ' Loop through each customer
    For x = 2 To FinalCust
```

```
    ' Turn on the AutoFilter for this customer
    ' ???

    ' Create a new workbook
    Set WBN = Workbooks.Add
    Set WSN = WBN.Worksheets(1)


    ' In the original workbook, select visible cells
    ' ???


    ' Copy the selection to the new workbook
    Selection.Copy Destination:=WSN.Cells(3, 1)

    ' AutoFit columns in the new workbook
    WSN.Columns.AutoFit

    ' Add a title to the new workbook
    WSN.Range("A1").Value = _
        "Recap of Purchases for " & WSN.Cells(4, 1).Value

    ' Save the new book
    WBN.SaveAs Filename:="C:\" & WSN.Cells(4, 1).Value & ".xlsx"
    WBN.Close SaveChanges:=False

    'Return to the original workbook
    WBO.Activate
    WSN.Select
  Next x

End Sub
```

The following sections describe that to create this macro, you need to figure out how to code the advanced filter to copy a unique list of customers to column H. You then need to figure out how to apply a filter to column A. Finally, you need to figure out how to select only the visible cells from the filter.

Using the Advanced Filter for Unique Records

You need to figure out how to use an advanced filter to finish the following section of code:

```
' Find the FinalRow in today's dataset
FinalRow = Cells(Rows.Count, 1).End(xlUp).Row

' Use an Advanced filter to copy unique customers
' from column A to column H
' ???
```

To use an advanced filter on this section of code, follow these steps:

1. Turn on the macro recorder.

2. On the Data tab, in the Sort & Filter group, click the Advanced icon to open the Advanced Filter dialog.

3. Select the option Copy to Another Location.

4. Adjust the list range to refer only to column A. The copy-to range will be cell H1.

5. Check the Unique Records Only box.

6. When the dialog looks as shown in Figure 28.34, click OK. The result is a new range of data in column H, with each customer listed just once, as shown in Figure 28.35.

Figure 28.34

Using an advanced filter to get a unique list of customers.

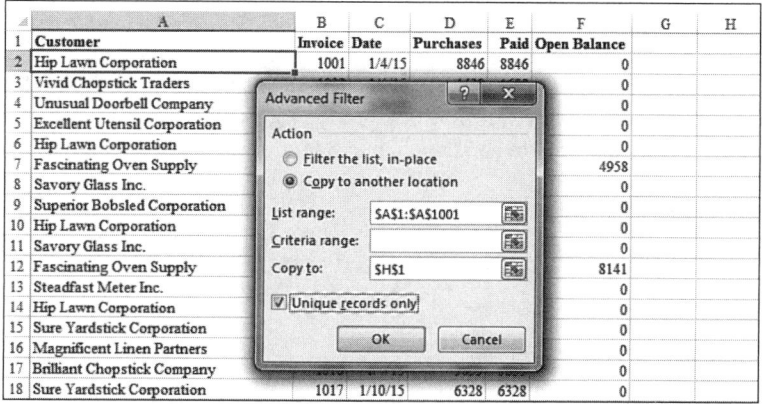

Figure 28.35

The advanced filter produces a list of customers for the macro to loop through.

Customer
Hip Lawn Corporation
Vivid Chopstick Traders
Unusual Doorbell Company
Excellent Utensil Corporation
Fascinating Oven Supply
Savory Glass Inc.
Superior Bobsled Corporation
Steadfast Meter Inc.
Sure Yardstick Corporation
Magnificent Linen Partners
Brilliant Chopstick Company
Different Scooter Supply
Mouthwatering Clipboard Corporation
New Gadget Company
Appealing Opener Partners
Trouble-Free Bottle Inc.
Wonderful Opener Supply
Modular Tuner Corporation
Magnificent Doghouse Inc.
Stunning Freezer Inc.

7. On the Developer tab, click Stop Recording.

8. Use the Macros button to select Macro1 and then select Edit.

Even though the Advanced Filter dialog is still one of the most complicated facets of Excel 2013, the recorded macro is remarkably simple:

```
Sub Macro1()
'
' Macro1 Macro
'


    Range("A1:A1001").AdvancedFilter Action:=xlFilterCopy, CopyToRange:=Range( _
        "H1"), Unique:=True
    Range("H1").Select
End Sub
```

In your macro, there is no reason to select cell H1 so delete that line of code. The remaining problem is that the macro recorder hard-coded that today's data set contains 1,001 rows. You might want to generalize this to handle any number of rows. The following code reflects these changes:

```
FinalRow = Cells(Rows.Count, 1).End(xlUp).Row
Range("A1:A" & FinalRow) .AdvancedFilter Action:=xlFilterCopy, _
    CopyToRange:=Range("H1"), Unique:=True
```

Using AutoFilter

When you have a list of customers, the macro loops through each customer. The goal is to use an AutoFilter to display only the records for each particular customer. Next, finish this section of code as follows:

```
' Loop through each customer
For x = 2 To FinalCust
    ' Turn on the AutoFilter for this customer
    ' ???
```

To apply an AutoFilter to this section of code, follow these steps:

1. On the Developer tab, select Record Macro.

2. On the Home tab, select the icon Sort & Filter – Filter. Drop-down arrows are turned on for each field.

3. In the drop-down in cell A1, clear Select All and then select Hip Lawn Corporation.

4. Back on the Developer tab, stop recording the macro.

5. Use the Macros button to locate and edit Macro2 as follows:

```
Sub Macro2()
'
' Macro2 Macro
'


    Range("A2").Select
    Application.CutCopyMode = False
    Selection.AutoFilter
    Selection.AutoFilter Field:=1, Criteria1:="Hip Lawn Corporation"
End Sub
```

The macro recorder always does too much selecting. You rarely have to select something before you can operate on it. You can theorize that the only line of this macro that matters is the `Selection.AutoFilter` line. Because you will always be looking at the AutoFilter drop-down in cell A1, you can replace `Selection` with `Range("A1")`. Rather than continually ask for one specific customer, you can replace the end of the line with a reference to a cell in column H:

Tip

Even though you have an existing Module1 with your code, Excel chooses to record the new macro into a new module. Therefore, you need to copy recorded code from Module2 and then use the Project Explorer to switch to Module1 to paste the code into your macro.

```
Range("A1").AutoFilter Field:=1, Criteria1:=Cells(x,
➡8).Value
```

Selecting Visible Cells Only

After you use the AutoFilter in the macro, you see records for only one customer. However, as you can see in Figure 28.36, the other records are still there, but they are hidden. If you copied the range to a new worksheet, all the hidden rows would come along, and you would end up with 20 copies of your entire data set.

Figure 28.36
If you copy this range to a new worksheet, the hidden rows copy as well.

	A	B	C	D	E	F
1	Customer	Invoi	Date	Purch	P	Open Balan
2	Hip Lawn Corporation	1001	1/4/15	8846	8846	0
6	Hip Lawn Corporation	1005	1/5/15	11476	11476	0
10	Hip Lawn Corporation	1009	1/5/15	12562	12562	0
14	Hip Lawn Corporation	1013	1/6/15	4876	4876	0
60	Hip Lawn Corporation	1059	1/24/15	1813	1813	0
67	Hip Lawn Corporation	1066	1/25/15	6317	6317	0
76	Hip Lawn Corporation	1075	1/31/15	5454	5454	0
89	Hip Lawn Corporation	1088	2/4/15	11234	11234	0
90	Hip Lawn Corporation	1089	2/4/15	5490	5490	0
142	Hip Lawn Corporation	1141	2/23/15	1430	1430	0
150	Hip Lawn Corporation	1149	2/28/15	1633	1633	0

The long way to select visible cells only is to press F5 to display the Go To dialog. In the Go To dialog, click the Special button and then click Visible Cells Only. However, the shortcut is to press Alt+;.

To learn how to select visible cells only in VBA, record the macro by following these steps:

1. Select the data in columns A through F.

2. Turn on the macro recorder and press Alt+;.

3. Stop the macro recorder. You should see that the recorded macro has just one line of code:

```
Sub Macro5()
'
' Macro5 Macro
'


'
    Selection.SpecialCells(xlCellTypeVisible).Select
End Sub
```

In your original outline of the macro, you had contemplated selecting visible cells only and then doing the copy in another statement, like this:

```
' In the original workbook, select visible cells
' ???

' Copy the selection to the new workbook
Selection.Copy Destination:=WSN.Cells(3, 1)
            Instead, copy the visible cells in one statement:
' In the original workbook, select visible cells
WSO.Range("A1:F" & FinalRow).SpecialCells(xlCellTypeVisible).Copy _
    Destination:=WSN.Cells(3, 1)
```

Combination Macro Example: Putting It All Together

The following macro started as a bunch of comments and a skeleton of a loop:

```
Sub ProduceReportForEachCustomerFinished()
    ' Define object variables for new workbook
    Dim WBN As Workbook
    Dim WSN As Worksheet
    ' Define object variables for the current workbook
    Dim WBO As Workbook
    Dim WSO As Worksheet
    Set WBO = ActiveWorkbook
    Set WSO = ActiveSheet
```

```
' Find the FinalRow in today's dataset
FinalRow = Cells(Rows.Count, 1).End(xlUp).Row

' Use an Advanced filter to copy unique customers
' from column A to column H
Range("A1:A" & FinalRow).AdvancedFilter Action:=xlFilterCopy, _
    CopyToRange:=Range("H1"), Unique:=True

'Find the final customer in column H
FinalCust = Range("H1").End(xlDown).Row

' Loop through each customer
For x = 2 To FinalCust
    ' Turn on the AutoFilter for this customer
    Range("A1").AutoFilter Field:=1, Criteria1:=Cells(x, 8).Value

    ' Create a new workbook

    Set WBN = Workbooks.Add
    Set WSN = WBN.Worksheets(1)

    ' In the original workbook, select visible cells
    WSO.Range("A1:F" & FinalRow).SpecialCells(xlCellTypeVisible).Copy _
        Destination:=WSN.Cells(3, 1)

    ' AutoFit columns in the new workbook
    WSN.Columns.AutoFit

    ' Add a title to the new workbook
    WSN.Range("A1").Value = "Recap of Purchases for " & WSN.Cells(4, 1).Value

    ' Save the new book
    WBN.SaveAs Filename:="C:\" & WSN.Cells(4, 1).Value & ".xls"
    WBN.Close SaveChanges:=False

    'Return to the original workbook
    WBO.Activate
    WSO.Select
Next x


End Sub
```

After doing three small tests with the macro recorder, you were able to fill in the sections to copy the customer records to a new workbook. After running this macro, you should have a new workbook for each customer on your hard drive, ready to be distributed via email.

VBA macros open up a wide possibility of automation for Excel worksheets. Any time you are faced with a daunting, mindless task, you can turn it into a challenging exercise by trying to design a macro to perform the task instead. It usually takes less time to design a macro than it does to complete the task. You should save every macro you write. Soon you will have a library of macros that handle many common tasks, and they will enable you to develop macros faster. The next time you need to perform a similar task, you can roll out the macro and perform the steps in seconds instead of hours.

29

MORE TIPS AND TRICKS FOR EXCEL 2013

The chapters in this book are full of tips and tricks. This particular chapter is a catch-all for some of the tips that did not find a home elsewhere in the book.

A few of the features discussed in this chapter, such as comparing files with the Inquire add-in, are new in Excel 2013. Other features, such as the Equation editor, were introduced in Excel 2010. Others, such as multithreaded calculation, digital signatures, translations, and protecting a worksheet, have been around for a while.

Speeding Up Calculation

Computing power has improved over the past decade, and Excel 2013 offers features to support that extra computing power. For example, 32-bit versions of Excel 2013 can use up to 3GB of system RAM. In a default install, you get the 32-bit version of Excel. However, if you do a custom install, you can install the 64-bit version of Excel 2013 and use all the available memory on the machine. As this book is being written, it is common to find machines with 8, 10, or 12GB of RAM. If you hope to load millions of records in a PowerPivot pivot table, switching to 64-bit Office allows Excel to take advantage of the extra memory on the machine.

By default, Excel now takes advantage of all cores available on the machine for calculation and several other CPU-intensive tasks. If you have a dual-core or quad-core processor, operations such as calculation, opening or saving a file, or even autofitting columns are multithreaded.

The first time you calculate a spreadsheet in Excel 2013 on a multiple-core machine, Excel has to examine the formula dependency table and then perform the calculation. The process of deciding which formulas can be calculated concurrently causes the first calculation to take as long as normal. However, the time required for the next calculation dramatically decreases. In a perfect example (a workbook with Monte Carlo simulation), the reduction is linear: The workbook calculates in half the time. In other workbooks, the reduction is significant but not linear.

When a large file is being opened, the second core works on formatting the visible portion of the worksheet while the first core continues reading the rest of the file.

To see how many cores are available on your machine, go to File, Options, Advanced, Formulas. The number shown after Use All Processors on This Computer shows the number of processors available to Excel (see Figure 29.1).

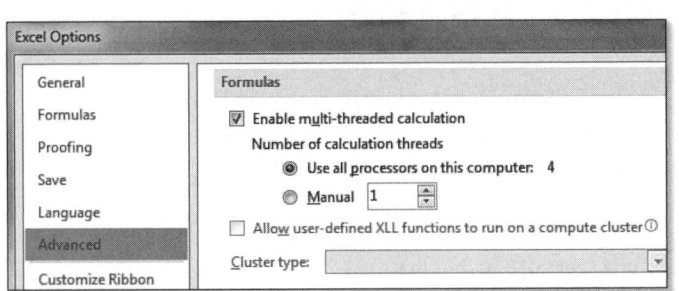

Figure 29.1
The multithreaded calculation option is buried in the Advanced category of the Excel Options dialog.

It is possible to choose Manual in Figure 29.1 and to set the calculation threads to a number higher than the number of processors. This is beneficial if your workbook is making calls to XLL user-defined functions on a server. (XLL is a special type of compiled add-in for Excel.) If each function requires 15 seconds and you have a dozen such functions, Excel must wait for each function to finish before calling the next function, thus requiring 3 minutes to calculate. If you set the number of threads to 12, Excel could call all 12 XLL functions simultaneously, reducing calculation time to less than 30 seconds.

The option for allowing XLL functions to run on a compute cluster was introduced in Excel 2010. Some applications in the insurance industry have workbooks that take 2 to 3 days to calculate. Microsoft now supports a High Performance Computing Cluster for processing of the XLL functions. If you are interested, type **HPC XLL** into a search engine to read about case studies where people have 100 desktop computers calculating their Excel workbook.

Watching the Results of a Distant Cell

Sometimes you need to keep an eye on a single result on a worksheet other than the one you're currently in. For example, you might have a workbook in which assumptions on multiple worksheets produce a final ROI. As you change the assumptions, it would be good to know the effect on ROI.

It can be time consuming to constantly switch back and forth to the results worksheet after every change. Instead, you can set up a watch to show you the current value of the distant cell(s). People developing VBA macros in Excel have had a Watch Window dialog available in VBA for more than a decade. Microsoft finally added a Watch Window dialog to Excel 2003.

To set up a watch, follow these steps:

1. Select Formulas, Watch Window to display the floating Watch Window dialog over the worksheet.

2. Click Add Watch in the Watch Window dialog.

3. In the Add Watch dialog, click the RefEdit button and then click the cells you want to watch.

4. Click Add to add the cell(s) to the Watch Window dialog.

5. Repeat steps 2–4, as necessary.

6. Position the Watch Window dialog in an out-of-the-way location above your worksheet so that you can continue to work.

Every time you make a change to the worksheet, the Watch Window dialog shows you the current value of the watched cells, as shown in Figure 29.2.

When the watch is defined, you can toggle the Watch Window dialog by using the Watch Window icon in the Formulas tab.

 **Tip**

You can double-click any entry in the Watch Window dialog to scroll to that cell.

Figure 29.2
The Watch Window dialog shows you the results of key cells that you define. These cells can be in far-off cells or on other worksheets.

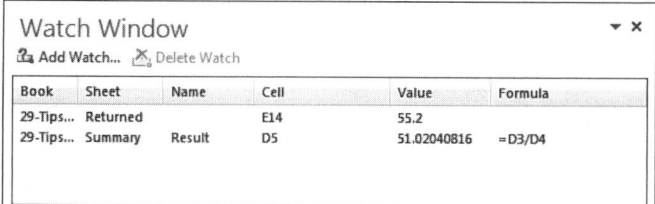

Book	Sheet	Name	Cell	Value	Formula
29-Tips...	Returned		E14	55.2	
29-Tips...	Summary	Result	D5	51.02040816	=D3/D4

Opening the Same Files Every Day

In some jobs, you might have to open the same workbooks at the same time to perform a certain recurring task. For example, perhaps you spend an hour every morning recording new accounts receivable balances while processing the morning postal mail. This task might require you to open the AR.xlsm file, the Customer.xlsm file, and the BankDeposit.xlsm file. If these three files are stored in different folders, it can be slightly tedious to open each document, one at a time.

After opening the files manually, you can specify that the files belong to a workspace. Then, when you open that workspace, Excel opens all the documents associated with the workspace.

To set up a workspace, follow these steps:

1. Close all open workbooks.

2. Open each workbook associated with the task.

3. From the View tab, select Window, Save Workspace. The Save Workspace dialog appears.

4. Browse to a location to save the workspace. Give the workspace a name. Click Save. Note that the file is saved with an .xlw extension.

The next time you need to open these files, select File, Open and select the XLW file. If you later rename one of the files or move one of them to a new location, you have to re-create and resave the workspace.

Comparing Documents Side by Side with Synchronous Scrolling

Suppose you have two documents that should be nearly identical. Perhaps you started with a workbook and then routed the workbook to a co-worker. You have your original workbook and the new workbook, and you want to compare them visually.

A feature introduced in Excel 2003 lets you scroll both windows at the same time. You can arrange the windows so that they are both visible. As you scroll the active document, the other document scrolls at the same rate. This can allow you to compare the documents visibly.

To compare two documents side by side in this manner, follow these steps:

1. Close all other documents.

2. Open the first workbook.

3. Open the second workbook.

4. Select View, Window, View Side by Side.

5. If you have more than two workbooks open, you have to choose just one of the other workbooks to be used for the comparison. The two workbooks appear together.

6. If the windows are split horizontally, one above the other, select View, Window, Arrange, Vertical to have the worksheets appear side by side.

7. Begin scrolling through the data using the scrollbar or the scroll wheel on your mouse.

Synchronous scrolling does not work well if someone has deleted or inserted extra rows in one workbook. To solve this problem, follow these steps:

1. If one worksheet has extra rows and is out of sync with the other worksheet, click View, Window, Synchronous Scrolling to temporarily turn off this feature.

2. Use the arrow keys or scrollbar to line up the worksheets. Scroll one worksheet so that both worksheets have the same record as the top row in the window.

3. Click View, Window, Synchronous Scrolling again to turn the feature back on. You can now continue scrolling the rows below the mismatched rows.

Calculating a Formula in Slow Motion

If you have a particularly complicated formula, you can watch how Excel calculates the formula in slow motion. This can help you locate any logic errors in the worksheet.

To evaluate a formula in slow motion, follow these steps:

1. Select the cell that contains the formula.

2. Select Formulas, Evaluate Formula. The Evaluate Formula dialog appears, showing the formula. One element of the formula is underlined, indicating that this element will be calculated next.

3. To see the value of the underlined element immediately, click Evaluate.

4. If you want to see how that element is calculated, instead of clicking Evaluate, click Step In. Excel shows the formula for that element.

5. Eventually, the final level is evaluated to a number. Click Step Out to return one level up the dialog.

6. Continue clicking Evaluate until you arrive at the answer shown in the cell.

Figure 29.3 shows an Evaluate Formula dialog after Evaluate was clicked a few times.

Figure 29.3
The Evaluate
Formula dialog
enables you to
watch the formula
calculation in slow
motion.

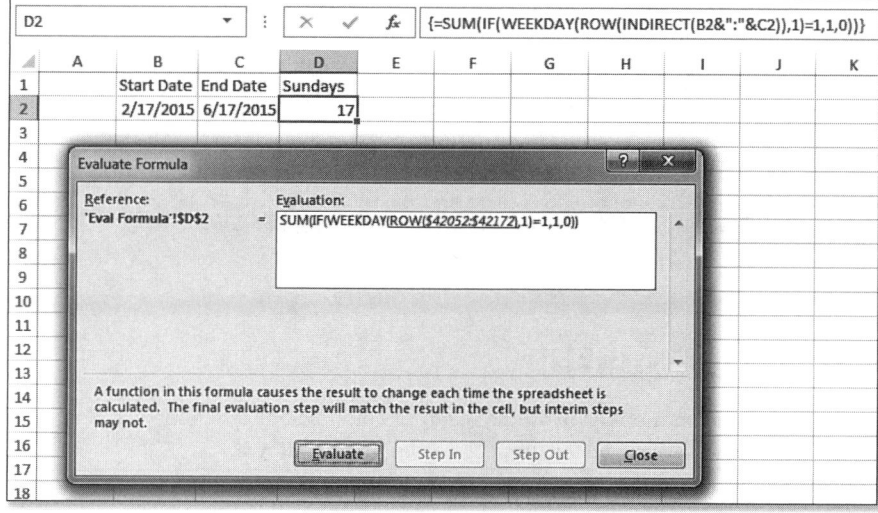

Inserting a Symbol in a Cell

Obscure key combinations are available to insert many symbols. However, you do not have to learn any of them. Instead, you can use the Symbol icon on the Insert tab to display the Symbol dialog.

In the Symbol dialog, you scroll through many subsets of the current font. When you find the desired symbol, select it and click the Insert button, as shown in Figure 29.4.

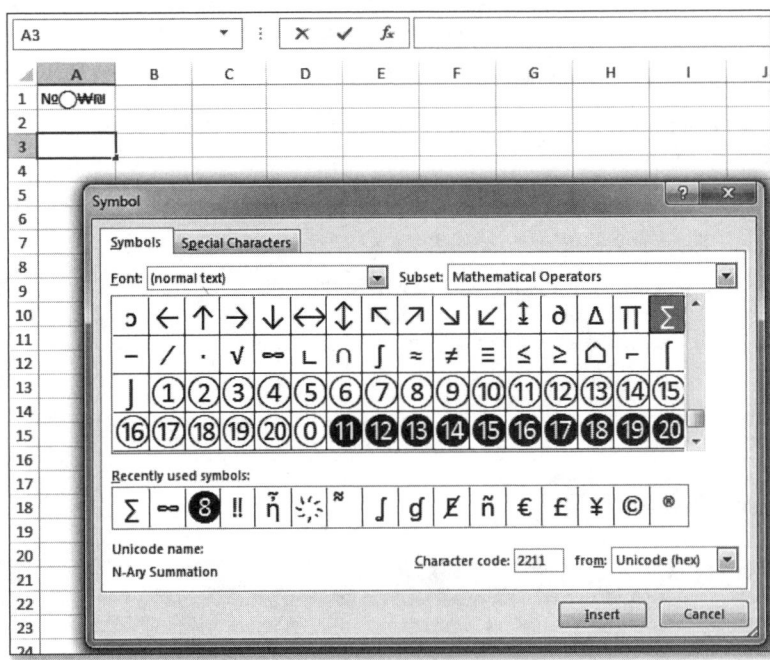

Figure 29.4
Instead of memorizing arcane key combinations, you can use Insert Symbol to add symbols to a workbook.

Edit an Equation

The Equation drop-down on the Insert tab offers eight prebuilt equations. If you happen to need one of these equations, you can select it from the drop-down.

If you need to build some other equation, insert a shape in the worksheet first. While the shape is selected, use Insert, Equation, Insert New Equation. A blank equation is added to the shape.

It seems very touchy, but you have to be inside the equation to have the Equation Tools Design tab showing. From the ribbon, you can open the various drop-downs to insert a mathematical symbol. In Figure 29.5, some symbols have three placeholders. These are tiny text boxes where you can type various values.

Figure 29.5
Most equations will be built using the drop-downs on the Equation Tools Design tab.

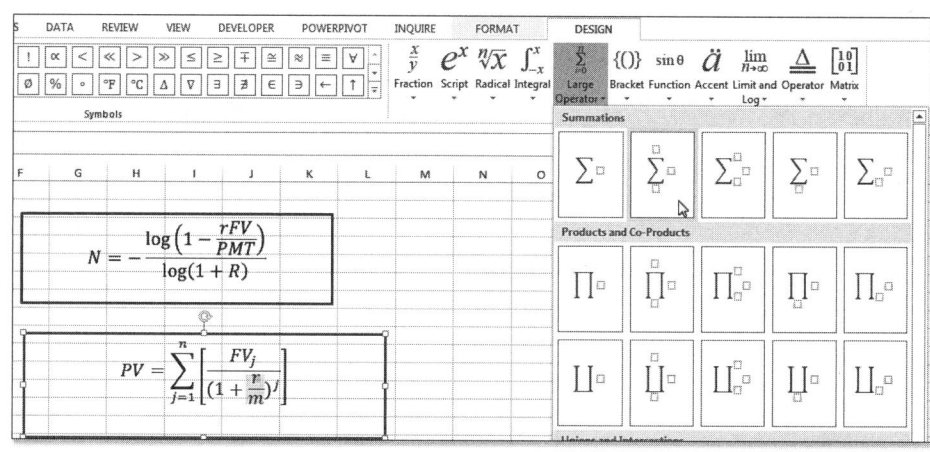

Adding a Digital Signature Line to a Workbook

You've probably encountered web pages where the authenticity of the web owner is verified with a digital certificate. Most likely, you notice this when the person's certificate has expired.

Microsoft has added a similar concept to Microsoft Excel. When you attach a digital signature to a document, you are authenticating that you are really you. This process helps to prevent others from altering your work. After you sign a document, it is converted to read-only to ensure that no one changes the document after you sign it.

Digital signatures are provided by a third-party certifying authority. There is a fee for this service. To purchase a digital signature, you select Insert, Text, Signature Line, Add Signature Services. This leads to a list of approved digital certificate providers. Choose a provider and follow the steps on the provider's website to purchase and install the signature.

To add a digital signature to a file, open the file and then select Insert, Text, Digital Signature. Then right-click the signature and select Signature Setup to access the dialog shown in Figure 29.6.

To sign a signature line, follow these steps:

1. Double-click the signature line in the document. The Sign dialog appears.

2. In the Sign dialog (see Figure 29.6), do one of the following:

   ■ Type your name in the box next to the X to add a printed version of your signature.

   ■ Click Select Image and choose a graphics file of your signature.

   ■ On a tablet PC, sign your name in the box by using the inking feature.

3. Choose your role in signing. You can indicate that you approved the document, created the document, or both.

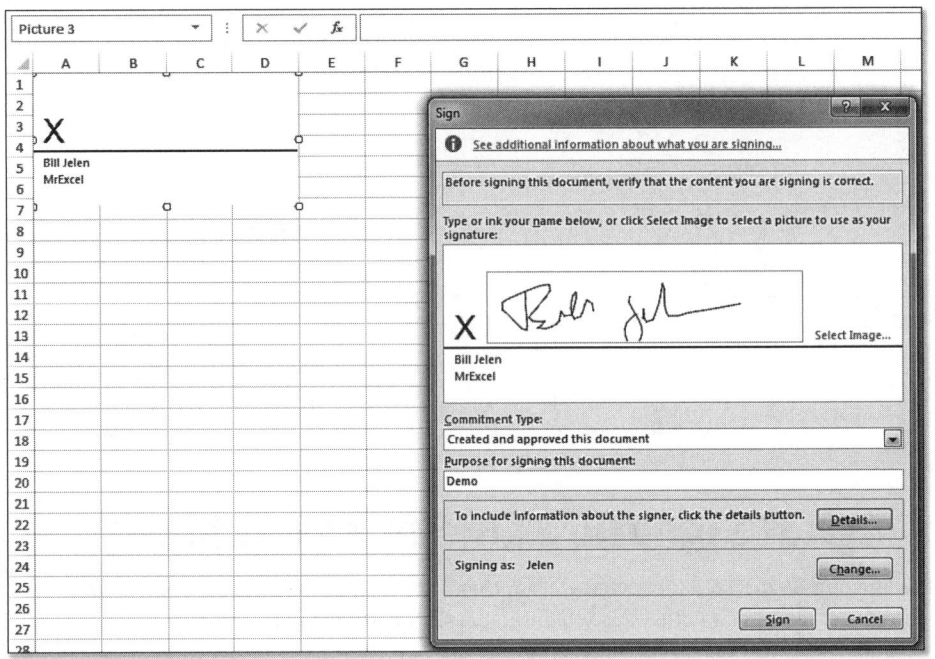

Figure 29.6
Use a touch-screen or tablet to sign the document.

4. Optionally, add your contact information and a comment.

5. Click OK.

Your document is now electronically signed. This marks the document as final, as shown in Figure 29.7.

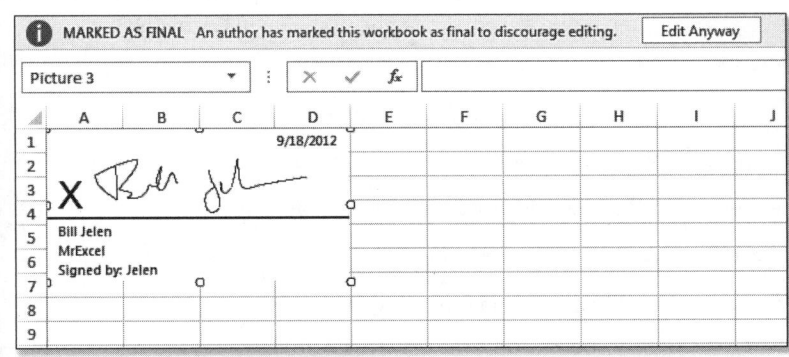

Figure 29.7
Signing a document marks it as final. If someone changes the document, the signature is marked as invalid.

Protecting a Worksheet

If you have many formulas in a worksheet, you might want to prevent others from changing them. In a typical scenario, your worksheet might have some input variables at the top. You might want to allow those items to be changed, but you might not want your formulas to be changed.

To protect a worksheet, follow these steps:

1. Select the input cells in your worksheet. These are the cells you want to allow someone to change.

2. Press Ctrl+1 or go to the Cells group of the Home tab and select Format, Format Cells. The Format Cells dialog appears.

3. On the Protection tab of the Format Cells dialog, clear the Locked check box. Click OK.

4. Select Review, Protect Sheet. The Protect Sheet dialog appears, as shown in Figure 29.8.

Figure 29.8
Do not rely on this password for security, because it can easily be broken.

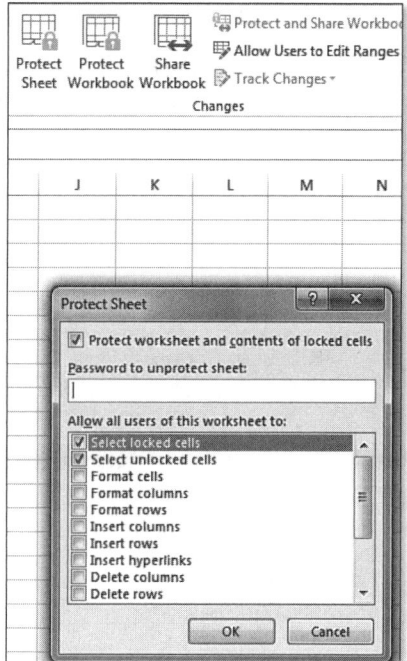

5. Optionally, change what is allowed to happen in the protected workbook.

6. Click OK to apply the protection.

Sharing a Workbook

Excel on a computer is not a collaborative program. Multiple people cannot access a workbook at the same time. Excel offers a Share Workbook icon under Review, Share Workbook. After you share a workbook, it becomes so limited that it is practically unusable.

Shared workbooks cannot have tables. You cannot insert blocks of cells in them. You cannot delete their worksheets. You cannot merge cells, add conditional formats, add validation, add charts, add pictures, add or change pivot tables, insert hyperlinks, use scenarios, use subtotals, write macros, or edit array formulas in shared workbooks. Basically, all but the simplest spreadsheets are unsharable.

However, if you upload the workbook to the SkyDrive and access it with the Excel Web App, then unlimited people can edit the workbook at the same time.

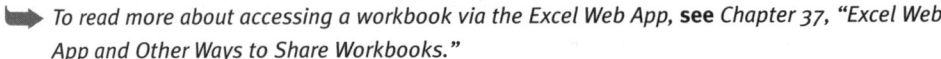 *To read more about accessing a workbook via the Excel Web App,* **see** *Chapter 37, "Excel Web App and Other Ways to Share Workbooks."*

Separating Text Based on a Delimiter

Depending on the source of your data, you might find that information is loaded into Excel with many fields in one cell. If the fields are separated by a character, you can separate the data into multiple columns. To do so, follow these steps:

1. Select the one-column range that contains multiple values in each cell.

2. Select Data, Data Tools, Convert Text to Column. Excel displays the Convert Text to Columns Wizard dialog.

3. In step 1 of the wizard, select Delimited and click Next.

4. In step 2 of the wizard, choose your delimiter. Excel offers check boxes for Tab, Semicolon, Comma, and Space. If your delimiter is something different, select the Other box and type the delimiter. Click Next.

5. In step 3 of the wizard, indicate whether any of your columns are dates. Click the column in the Data Preview section and then select Date in the Column Data Format section.

6. By default, Excel replaces the selected column and uses adjacent blank columns. To write the results to a different output area, enter a destination in step 3 of the wizard, as shown in Figure 29.9.

7. Click Finish to parse the column.

8. Excel does not automatically make the columns wide enough, so select the Cells section of the Home tab and then select Format, Width, AutoFit to make the output columns wide enough for the contents.

Figure 29.9
You specify
field types
and an output
range in step 3
of the wizard.

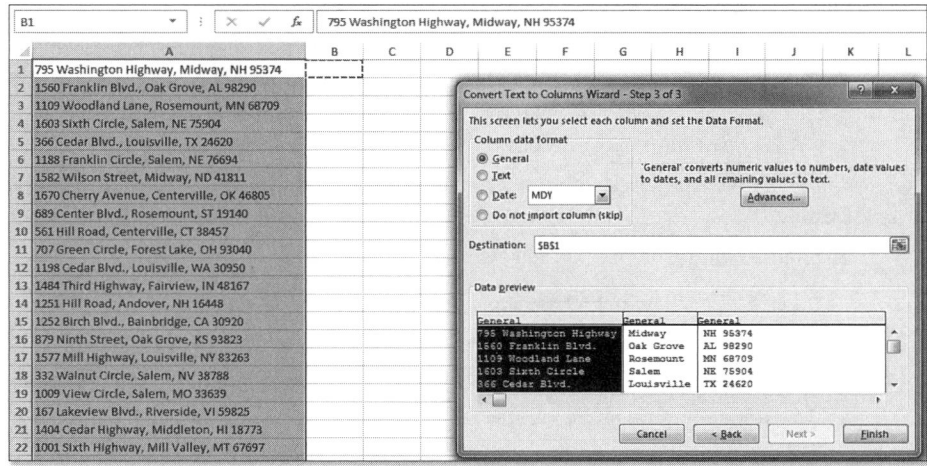

Translating Text

Bing and Google offer rudimentary translate tools in the browser. You can now access Microsoft Translator and/or WorldLingo right in Excel. These services are getting better, but they cannot replace a professional translator. The translations produced are often very rough and sometimes humorous.

However, if someone has sent you a document in a foreign language, you can convert the text from the foreign language to a form of broken English so that you can often get the basic meaning of the text.

Excel 2013 translation service offers two services for most language pairs. Microsoft Translator is the default translation engine for many language pairs. Other language pairs go back to WorldLingo, which has been providing translations since Excel 2007.

The Excel 2013 service can translate only a single cell at a time. To use the service, follow these steps:

1. Select the cell containing text you want to translate.

2. On the Review tab, click Translate.

3. In the Research task pane, choose a From and a To language.

4. If the translation was provided by Microsoft Translation, you can select a new cell and click Insert in the Research Task Pane. For WorldLingo results, select the translated text by dragging over it with the mouse. Press Ctrl+C to copy the translation to the Clipboard. Select a cell and press Ctrl+V to paste.

This feature would be far more powerful if you could translate entire blocks of cells and automatically return the translations in an adjacent column.

Auditing Worksheets Using Inquire

The Inquire add-in is new in Excel 2013. If you have Office 2013 Pro Plus or higher, you can enable the Inquire add-in. The add-in enables tools for discovering potential problems in workbooks. You can see a visual map of relationships, mark cells that contain certain potential problems, or compare two versions of the same workbook.

You won't have access to Inquire if you are using Office 2013 Home and Student or Office 2013 Standard.

To enable Inquire, do both of these steps:

1. Press Alt+T followed by I to display the Add-Ins dialog. Choose Inquire.InteractiveDiagnosticsAddIn and click OK.

2. Select File, Options, Add-Ins. At the bottom of the screen, choose Manage Com Add-Ins and click Go. Choose Inquire and click OK.

You see a new Inquire tab in the ribbon.

Analyzing a Workbook

There is an art and a science to auditing worksheets. You frequently will encounter an accounting department with thousands of workbooks. The auditor looks for workbooks that have a high number of risk situations and focuses on those workbooks.

Tools such as ActiveData from InformationActive.com scan all workbooks in a folder and build a report showing the number of cells, formulas, and so on for every workbook. Microsoft is now offering a similar but more expensive option with the Microsoft Discovery and Risk Assessment. Microsoft is offering the Workbook Analysis Report, which is the same technology, but it only scans the active workbook instead of all workbooks in the folder.

To scan the active workbook, go to Inquire Workbook Analysis Report. It takes the dialog 20 to 30 seconds to scan a large workbook. Eventually, results appear in the right side of the dialog, as shown in Figure 29.10.

The results pane identifies things that could potentially be a problem. Not everything reported is a problem. The workbook in Figure 29.10 has 28 visible sheets, which is not an area for concern. However, if there were several Very Hidden sheets, that might be a red flag.

As you read through the list of items reported, you can often figure out situations where a certain item might cause concern. One common problem is numbers stored as text. When formulas start referencing numbers stored as text, particularly if it is a SUM() formula, the results do not include those text cells.

If you find an area of concern, check that item in the left side of the dialog. Click the Excel Export button to build a brand new workbook that lists all of the offending cells (see Figure 29.11).

If you get a report of all formulas, it would actually create a nice bit of documentation for your worksheet. The report in Figure 29.11 shows that many of the formulas referencing text cells are using the CONVERT function. This function usually has text for the second and third arguments, so those are not a problem.

Figure 29.10
Initially, the right side of the report shows a count of all potentially problematic issues.

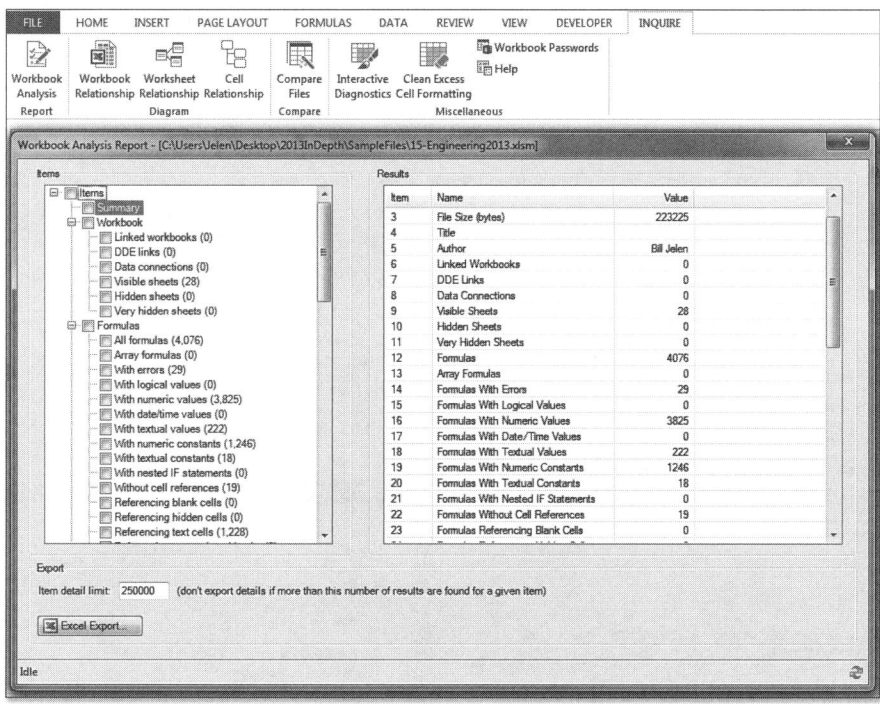

Figure 29.11
Export to Excel to get a list of where the potential problems occur.

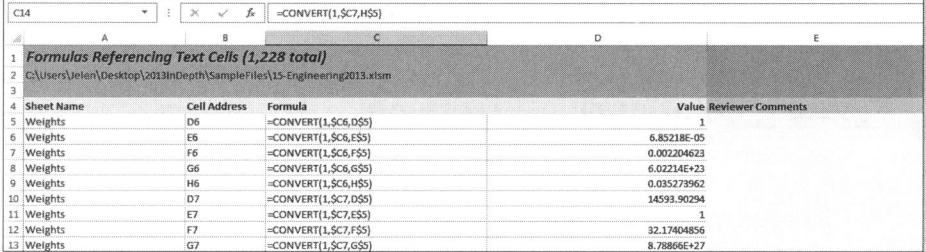

Highlighting Potential Problems Using Interactive Diagnostics

Although the report in the preceding section generates a list of the problems, sometimes you want to analyze those problems right in the worksheet. Choose Interactive Diagnostics from the Inquire tab. Excel displays a list of all the types of potential problems. When you click an item in the dialog, all those cells are formatted with a certain color. This enables you to examine each cell.

In Figure 29.12, all the cells with hard-coded numeric constants in the formula are highlighted. Even though I personally use this workbook frequently, by clicking on the various items, I was surprised to see that one of my input cells had no dependent formulas.

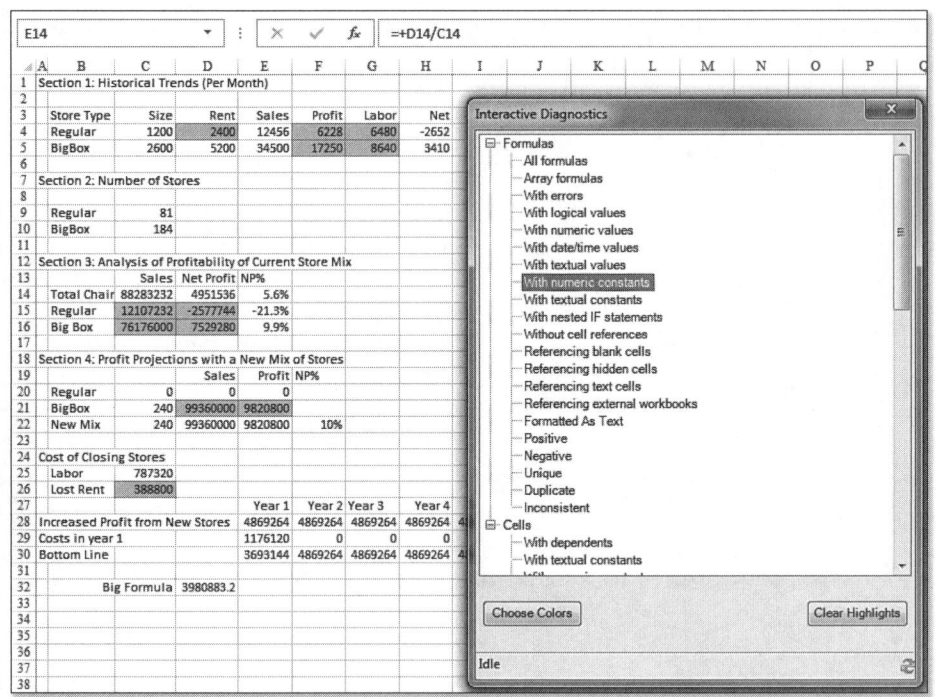

Figure 29.12
Click an item in the dialog, and the Inquire add-in temporarily highlights cells matching that condition.

Building Relationship Diagrams

The Inquire tool offers three types of relationship diagrams. You can see links between the open workbook and other workbooks. You can see links between the active worksheet and other worksheets. Or you can see links between the active cell and other cells.

To test this feature, think of your most complicated workbook and find a cell with a lot of references. Choose that cell and then click Cell Relationship on the Inquire tab. By default, the diagram shows two levels of precedents and dependents.

Figure 29.13 shows the Cell Relationship Diagram for one of my favorite complicated formula cells.

Figure 29.13
Visualize relationships between cells, worksheets, or workbooks using the Inquire diagramming tools.

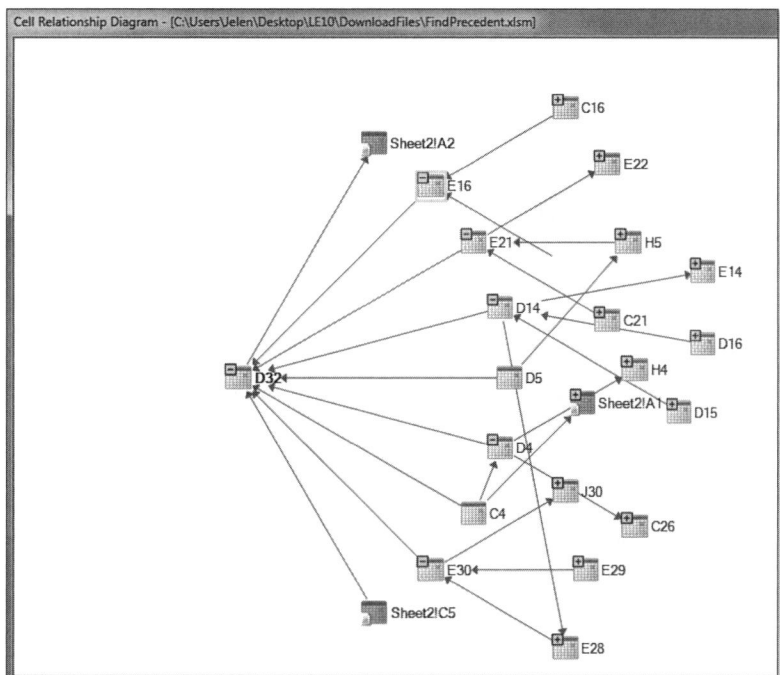

Comparing Two Versions of a Workbook

Say that you have a workbook. You send that workbook to a co-worker for review. You receive the changed version of the workbook back from the co-worker. You would like to see if any changes were made to the workbook.

Rename one or both of the workbooks so you can tell which is the original and which is the changed version.

Open both workbooks. From the Inquire tab, choose Compare Files. Specify the newer, changed version of the workbook in the Compare drop-down. Specify the original workbook in the To drop-down (see Figure 29.14). This might seem backward from the way that you would think the files should be specified.

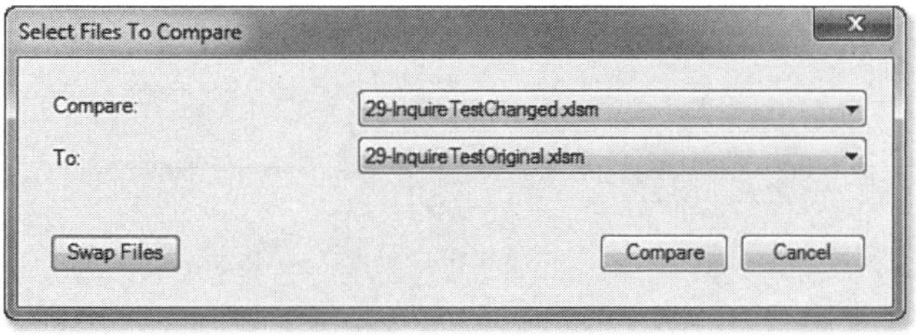

Figure 29.14
Specify the newer version of the workbook first and the older version second.

After you click Compare, the results show in the Spreadsheet Compare tool. Start with the column chart in the bottom right to see where the majority of changes happened. In Figure 29.15, a lot of values, some cell formats, and a few formulas changed.

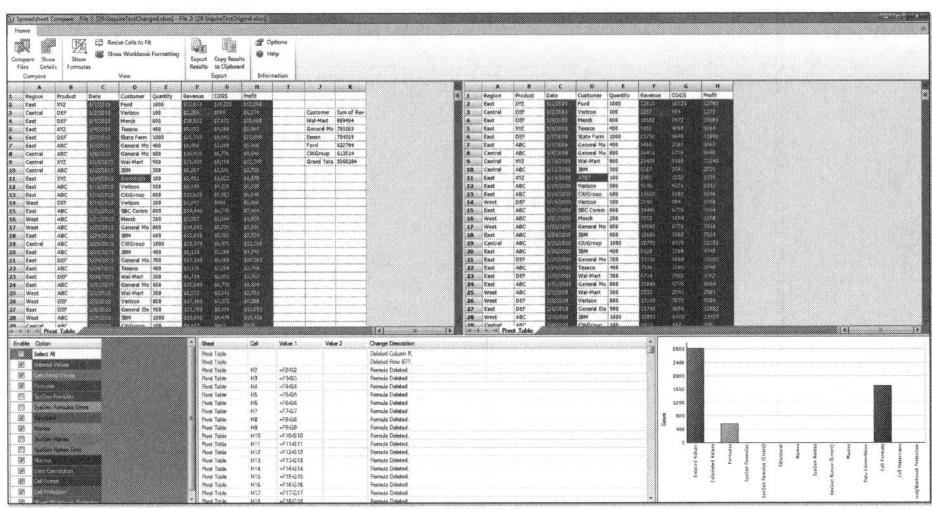

Figure 29.15
The report shows and lists all changes between the two versions of the workbook.

If you don't care about cell formatting changes, uncheck that category in the lower left of the window.

The top of the window shows a view of the two workbooks. Any changes are color-coded to match the color legend shown in the lower left.

FORMATTING WORKSHEETS

Formatting adds interest and readability to documents. If you have taken time to create a spreadsheet, you should also take the time to make sure that it is eye catching and readable.

You can format documents in Excel 2013 with any of these three methods:

- **Use tables styles**—You can use table styles to format a table with banded rows, accents for totals, and so on.

   **See** *Chapter 19, "Fabulous Table Intelligence," for more information on the use table styles method.*

- **Use cell styles**—You can use cell styles to identify titles, headings, and accent cells. The advantage of using cell styles is that you can quickly apply new themes to change the look and feel of a document.

- **Use formatting commands**—You can use traditional formatting commands to change the font, borders, fill, numeric formatting, column widths, and row heights. The usual formatting icons are now found on the Home tab as well as in the Format Cells dialog.

Why Format Worksheets?

You can open a blank worksheet and fill it with data without ever touching any of Excel's formatting commands. The result is functional, but not necessarily readable or eye catching. Figure 30.1 contains an unformatted report in Excel.

Figure 30.2 contains exactly the same data but with formatting applied. The formatted report in Figure 30.2 is more interesting and easier to read than the unformatted one for the following reasons:

- The reader can instantly focus on the totals for each line.

- Headings are aligned with the data.

- Borders break the data into sections.

- Accent colors highlight the subtotals and totals.

- The title is prominent, in a larger font, and a headline typeface is used.

- Numeric formatting has removed the extra decimal places and added thousands separators.

- Quarterly totals appear in italics.

- The column widths are adjusted properly.

- A short row adds a visual break between the product lines.

- Headings for each product line are rotated, merged, and centered.

The formatting applied to Figure 30.2 takes a few extra minutes, but it dramatically increases the readability of the report. Because you have taken the time to put the worksheet together, it is worth a couple of extra minutes to make the worksheet easier for the consumer to read.

Figure 30.2
Readability is
improved after
formatting the
report.

Larger Font Size   Headings Aligned with Data

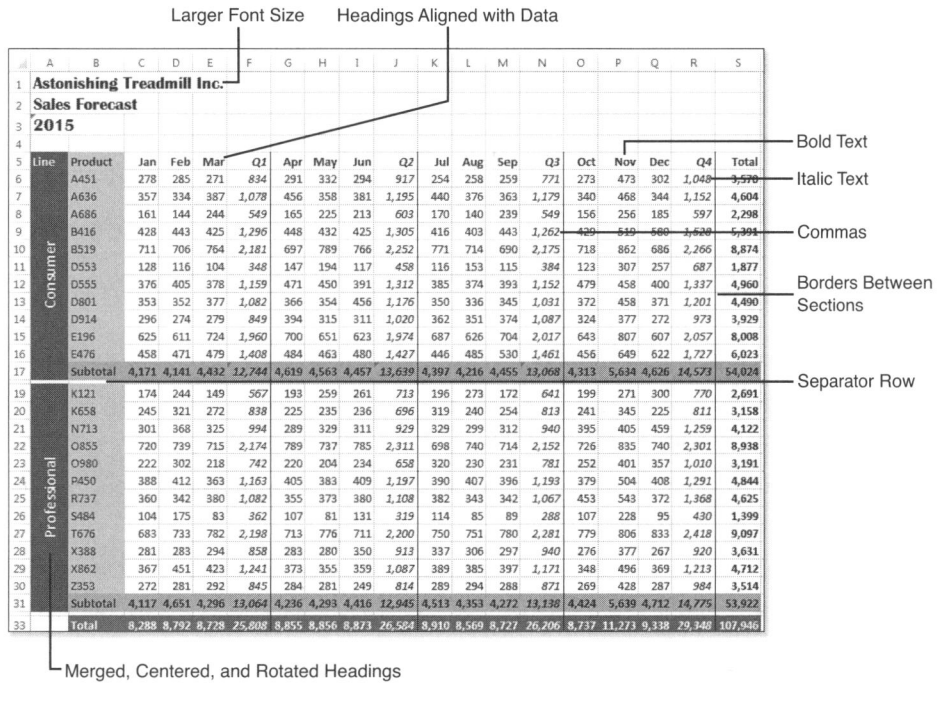

- Bold Text
- Italic Text
- Commas
- Borders Between Sections
- Separator Row

Merged, Centered, and Rotated Headings

Using Traditional Formatting

Formatting is typically carried out in the Format Cells dialog or using the formatting icons located on the Home tab.

In Excel 2013, the traditional formatting icons are in the Font, Alignment, and Number groups on the Home tab, as shown in Figure 30.3. Additional column- and row-formatting commands are available in the Format drop-down in the Cells group on the Home tab.

Figure 30.3
Most icons from the former
Formatting toolbar are in the
Font, Alignment, and Number
groups on the Home tab.

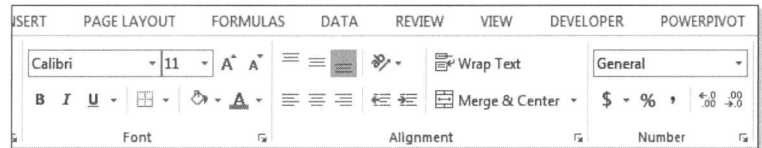

If your favorite setting is not on the Home tab, you can take one of the four entry paths to the Format Cells dialog, which provides access to additional settings, such as Shrink to Fit, Strikethrough, and more border settings:

- Press Ctrl+1, which is Ctrl and the number 1. You can press Ctrl+Shift+F to display the Font tab on the same dialog.

- Click the dialog launcher icons in the lower-right corner of the Font, Alignment, or Number groups. Each icon opens the dialog, with the focus on a different tab.

- Right-click any cell and select Format Cells.

- Select Format Cells from the Format drop-down on the Home tab.

As shown in Figure 30.4, the Format Cells dialog includes the following six tabs:

- **Number**—Gives you absolute control over numeric formatting. You can choose from 96,885 built-in formats or use the Custom category to create your own.

- **Alignment**—Offers settings for horizontal alignment, vertical alignment, rotation, wrap, merge, and shrinking to fit.

- **Font**—Controls font, size, style, underline, color, strikethrough, superscript, and subscript.

- **Border**—Controls line style and color for each of the four borders and the diagonals on each cell.

- **Fill**—Offers 16 million fill colors and patterns. Beginning with Excel 2007, cell gradients are available.

- **Protection**—Used to lock or unlock certain cells.

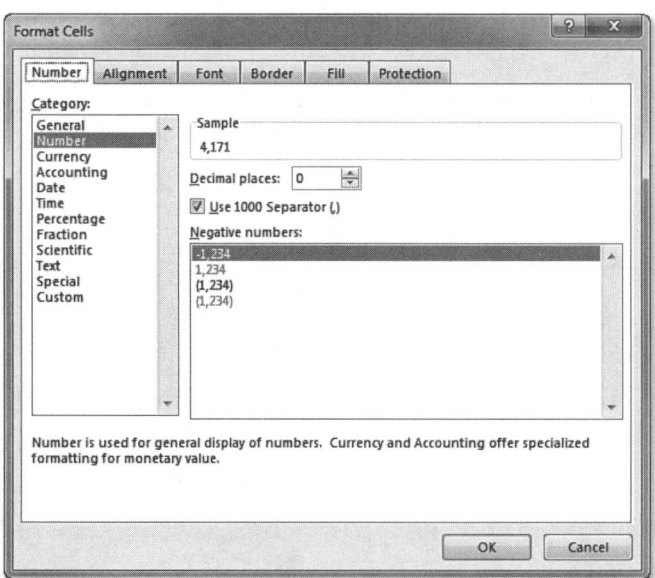

Figure 30.4
The Format Cells dialog offers complete control over cell formatting. You can visit this dialog when the icons on the ribbon do not provide enough detail.

Changing Numeric Formats by Using the Home Tab

If you ever shop for hardware at a general-purpose store, you have probably experienced how it can have almost what you need, but never exactly what you need. At this point, you probably curse your decision to stop at the general-purpose retailer and drive another mile down the road to Home Depot or Lowe's, where you can always find exactly what you need.

Using the Number group on the Home tab is like shopping at a general-purpose retailer. It has many settings for numeric formatting, but often they are not exactly what you need. When this happens, you end up visiting the Number tab on the Format Cells dialog.

To start, there are three icons—for currency, percentage, and comma style. The Percentage icon is useful. Unfortunately, the Currency and Comma icons apply an Accounting style to a cell, and the Accounting style is inappropriate for everyone except accountants. Furthermore, these three icons are not toggle buttons, which means that when you use one of them, there is not an icon to go back quickly to a general style, other than Undo.

The Increase and Decrease Decimal icons are useful. Each click of one of these buttons forces Excel to show one more or one fewer decimal place. If you have numbers showing two decimal places in all cells, two clicks on the Decrease Decimal icon solves the problem.

 **Tip**

Excel uses the value in the active cell for each of the formats inside the drop-down, and no sample if the cell is blank.

Figure 30.5 shows the Currency, Percentage, Comma, Increase Decimal, and Decrease Decimal buttons in the Number group of the Home tab.

Figure 30.5
The Currency and Comma icons both use an Accounting style. This is wonderful for accountants, but others should resist using them.

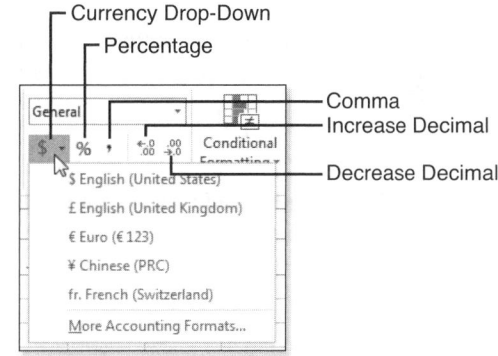

Above the five buttons in the Number group is a drop-down that has a dozen popular number styles. Figure 30.6 shows the styles in the drop-down. The range A2:F12 shows these styles applied to four different numbers.

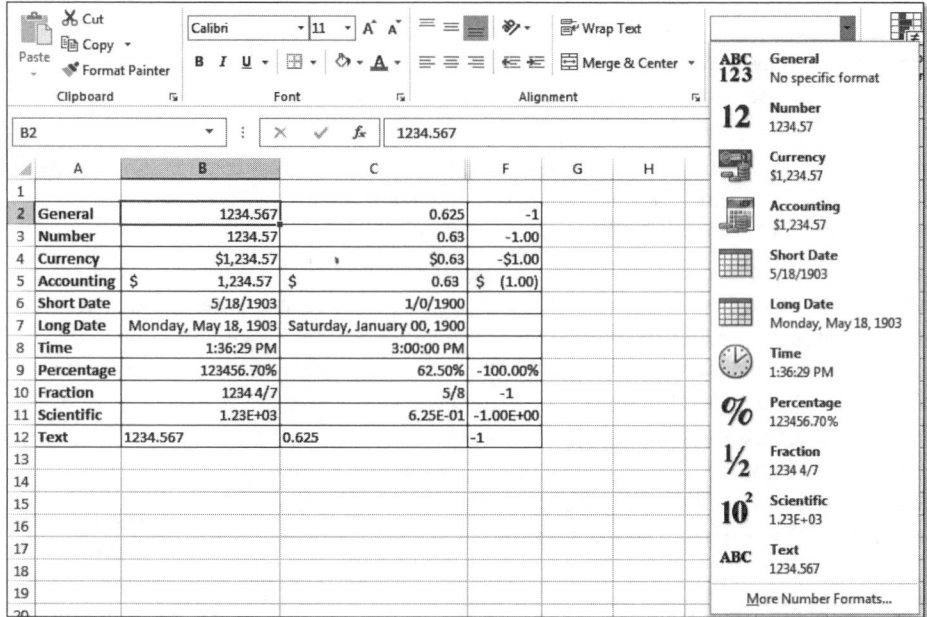

Figure 30.6
Excel 2013
offers 11 popu-
lar number
styles in this
drop-down.

The following list provides some comments and cautions about using the number styles from the drop-down in the Home tab:

- General format is a number format. Decimal places are shown if needed. No thousands separator is used. A negative number is shown with a minus sign before the number.

- Number does not use a thousands separator. It forces two decimal places, even with numbers that do not need decimal places, such as in cell F3.

- Currency is a useful format for everyone. The currency symbol is shown immediately before the number. All numbers are expressed with two decimal places. Negatives are shown with a hyphen before the number.

- Accounting is great for financial statements and annoying for everything else. Negative numbers are shown in parentheses. Currency symbols are left-aligned with the edge of the cell. Positive numbers appear one character from the right edge of the cell to allow them to line up with negative numbers.

- Percentage uses two decimal places when selected from the drop-down. This is one format for which it is actually better to use the icon on the ribbon than the Format Cells dialog.

- Fraction defaults to showing a fraction with a one-digit divisor. If you have a number such as 0.925, some Excel number formats correctly show this as 15/16. Unfortunately, the Fraction setting in this drop-down rounds it to one-digit divisors.

Changing Numeric Formats by Using Built-in Formats in the Format Cells Dialog

The Format Cells dialog offers more number formats than the Home tab. My favorite number format can be accessed only through the Format Cells dialog. I find that I avoid the buttons in the Number group in the Home tab and go directly to the Format Cells dialog.

You can display the Format Cells dialog by clicking the dialog launcher icon in the lower-right corner of the Number group of the Home tab. When you open the Format Cells dialog this way, the Number tab is the active tab.

Twelve categories appear on the left side of the Number tab. The General and Text categories each have a single setting. The Custom category allows you to use formatting codes to build any number format. The remaining nine categories each offer a collection of controls to customize the numeric format.

Using Numeric Formatting with Thousands Separators

Using numeric formatting with thousands separators is my favorite format. The thousands separators make the number easy to read. You can suppress the decimal places from the numbers. Microsoft does not offer buttons on the Home tab to select this format. The comma button is a perfect place for it, but instead Microsoft assigns that to the accounting format.

To format cells in numeric format, follow these steps:

1. Press Ctrl+1 to display the Format Cells dialog.

2. Select the Number category from the Number tab.

3. Select the Use 1000 Separator check box.

4. Optionally, adjust the Decimal Places spin button to 0.

5. Optionally, select a method for displaying negative numbers.

Figure 30.7 shows the Number category of the Format Cells dialog.

Figure 30.7
The Number category is the workhorse in Excel.

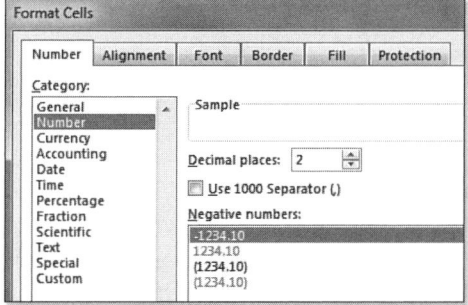

Displaying Currency

Two categories are used for currency: Currency and Accounting. The Currency category is identical to the Number category shown in Figure 30.7, with the addition of a currency symbol drop-down. This drop-down offers 409 different currencies from around the world.

The second category is Accounting. With this category, the currency symbol is always left-aligned in the cell. The last digit of positive numbers appears one character from the right edge of the cell so that positive and negative numbers line up. In addition, negative numbers are always shown in parentheses.

Displaying Dates and Times

The Date category offers 17 built-in formats for displaying dates, and the Time category offers nine built-in formats for displaying time. Each category has two formats that display both date and time.

The date formats vary from short dates such as 3/14 to long dates such as Wednesday, March 14, 2001. You should pay particular attention to the Date formats and the Sample box. Some formats show only the month and the day. Other formats show the month and the year. For example, the values in the Type box are for March 14, 2001. Other types such as March-01 display month-year. Types such as 14-Mar display day-month.

An interesting format near the bottom of the list is the M type. This displays month names in JFMAMJJASOND style, as shown in Figure 30.8. Readers of the *Wall Street Journal*'s financial charts will instantly recognize that each month is represented by the first letter of the month in this style. This style works great when used as the labels along the x-axis of a chart.

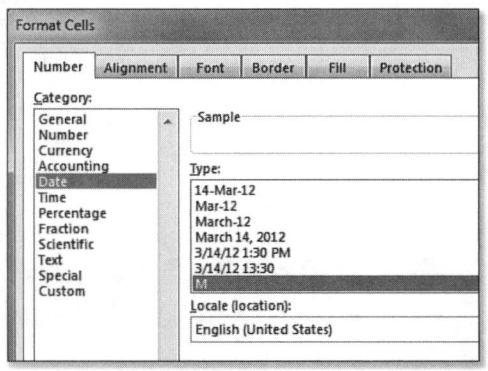

Figure 30.8
A variety of date and time formats is available.

In the Time category, pay attention to an important distinction between the 1:30 PM, 13:30, and 37:30:55 types. The first type displays times from 12:00 AM through 11:59 PM. The second type displays military time. In this system, midnight is 0:00, and 11:59 PM is 23:59. Neither of these types displays hours in excess of 24 hours. If you are working on a weekly timesheet or any application where you need to display hours that total to more than 24 hours, you need to use the 37:30:55 type in the Time category. This format is one of few that displays hours in excess of 24.

Displaying Fractions

The Fractions category rounds a decimal number to the nearest fraction. Types include fractions in halves, quarters, eighths, sixteenths, tenths, and hundredths. In addition, the first three types specify that the decimal should be reduced to the nearest fraction with up to one, two, or three digits in the denominator.

Figure 30.9 shows a variety of decimals formatted with five different fractional types. In row 14, notice that this random number can appear as 1/2, 49/92, or 473/888 when using the Up To *N* Digit types. Excel rounds the number to the closest fraction.

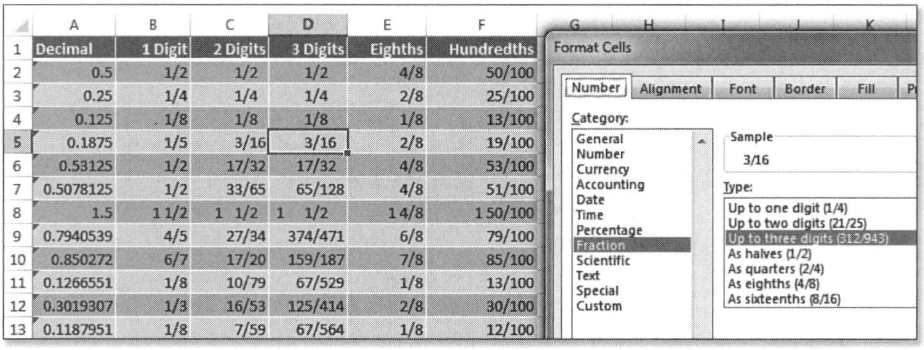

Figure 30.9
Excel can display decimals as fractions in a variety of formats.

In column E, note that if you ask Excel to show the number in eighths, Excel uses 4/8 and 2/8 instead of 1/2 or 1/4.

You probably feel as if you spent too much time in junior high math learning how to reduce fractions. The good news is that the first three fraction types of number formatting in Excel eliminate the need for manually reducing fractions.

Displaying ZIP Codes, Telephone Numbers, and Social Security Numbers

Spreadsheets were invented in Cambridge, Massachusetts. However, if you enter the ZIP code for Cambridge (02138) in a cell, Excel does not display the ZIP code correctly. It truncates the leading zero, giving you a ZIP code of 2138.

To combat this problem, Excel provides four special formatting types, all of which are U.S. centric:

- The Zip Code and Zip Code + 4 styles ensure that East Coast cities do not lose the leading zeros in their ZIP Codes.

- The Phone Number type formats a telephone number with parentheses around the area code and a hyphen after the exchange.

- The Social Security Number type groups the digits into groups of three, two, and four numbers that are separated by hyphens.

Figure 30.10 shows cells formatted with the four types available in the Special category.

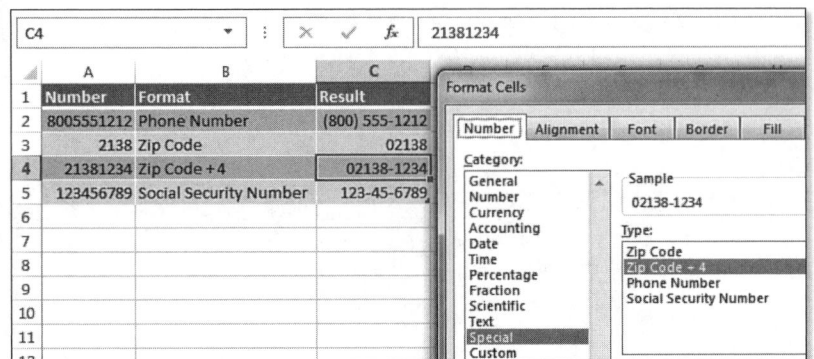

Figure 30.10
United States customers will appreciate the Special category in the Format Cells dialog.

 Note

If you happen to live in one of the 195 countries in the world besides the United States, you will undoubtedly need other formatting for your postal codes, telephone numbers, or national ID numbers. You can create number formats such as the ones shown in the Special category as well as the other formats you might need by using the Custom category, as discussed in the next section.

Changing Numeric Formats Using Custom Formats

Custom number formats provide incredible power and flexibility. Although you do not need to know the complete set of rules for them, you will probably find a couple of custom number formats that work perfectly for you and be able to make use of them.

To use a custom number format, follow these steps:

1. Select the cells to be highlighted.

2. Display the Format Cells dialog by pressing Ctrl+1.

3. Select the Number tab.

4. Select the Custom category.

5. Type the formatting codes into the Type box. Excel shows you a sample of the active cell with this format in the Sample box.

6. After you make sure this format looks correct, click OK to accept it.

 Tip

A good way to learn custom number formatting codes is to select a format and then click Custom to see the code for the selected format. For example, click Fraction and then click As Quarters (2/4). When you click Custom, you learn that the custom number code is # ?/4. Using this knowledge, you could build a new custom format code to show data in 17ths: # ?/17.

Using the Four Zones of a Custom Number Format

A custom number format can contain up to four different formats, each separated by a semicolon. The semicolons divide the format into as many as four zones. Excel allows different formatting, depending on whether a cell contains a positive number, a negative number, a zero, or text. You need to keep in mind the following:

- Separate formatting codes for zones by using semicolons.

- If you type only one number format, it applies to all numbers.

- If you type only two formats, the first format applies to positive and zero. The second format is used for negative.

- If all four formats are used, they refer to positive, negative, zero, and text values, respectively.

In Figure 30.11, a custom number format uses all four zones. The table in rows 11:14 shows how various numbers are displayed in this format. Notice that cell B12 appears in red type.

Figure 30.11
The four zones of a custom number format can cause positive, negative, zero, and text values to display differently.

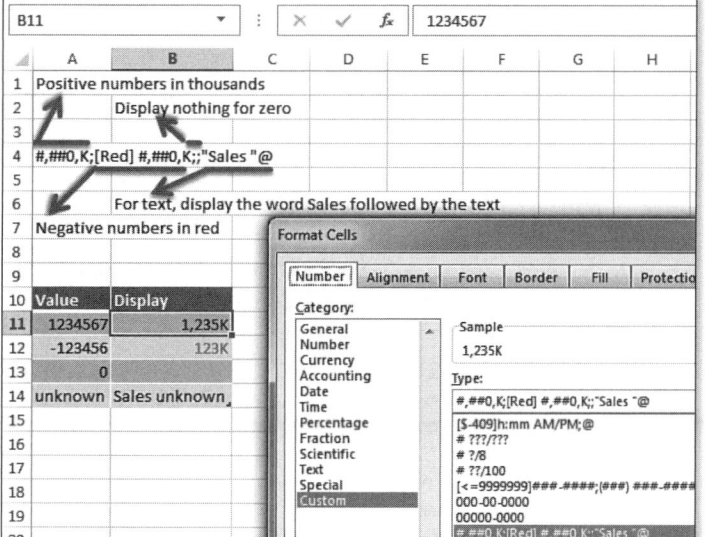

Controlling Text and Spacing in a Custom Number Format

You can display a mix of text and numbers in a numeric cell by including the text in double quotation marks. For example, `"The total is "$#,##0` precedes the number with the text shown in quotes.

If you need a single character, you can omit the quotation marks and precede the character with a backslash (\). For example, the code `$#,##0,,\M` displays numbers in millions and adds an M indicator after the number. The letters BDEGHMNSY require a backslash. The rest of the letters can be used without a backslash.

Some characters require neither a backslash nor quotation marks. These special characters are $ - + / ( ) : ! ^ & ' ~ { } = < >$ and the space character.

To add a specific amount of space to a format, you enter an underscore followed by a character. Excel then includes enough space to include that particular character. One frequent use for this is to include _) at the end of a positive number to leave enough space for a closing parenthesis. The positive numbers then line up with the negative numbers shown in parentheses.

To fill the space in a cell with a repeating character, use an asterisk followed by the character. For example, the format `**0` fills the leading space in a cell with asterisks. The format `0*-` fills the trailing space in a cell with hyphens.

If you are expecting numbers but think you might occasionally have text in the cell, you can use the fourth zone of the format. You use the @ character to represent the text in the cell. For example, `0;0;0;"Unexpected entry of "@` highlights the text cells with a note. If someone types a number, they get the number. If someone types hello, they get "Unexpected entry of hello".

Controlling Decimal Places in a Custom Number Format

Use a zero as a placeholder when you want to force the place to be included. For example, `0.000` formats all numbers with three decimal places. If the number has more than three places, it is rounded to three decimal places.

Use a pound sign (#) as a placeholder to display significant digits but not insignificant zeros. For example, `0.###` displays up to three decimal places, if needed, but can display `1.` for a whole number.

Use a question mark to replace insignificant zeros on either size of the decimal point with enough space to represent a digit in a fixed-width font. This format was designed to allow decimal points to line up, but with proportional fonts, it may not always work.

To include a thousands separator, include a comma to the left of the decimal point. For example, `#,##0` displays a thousands separator.

To scale a number by thousands, include a comma after the numeric portion of the format. Each comma divides the number by a thousand. For example, `0,` displays numbers in thousands, and `0,,` displays numbers in millions.

Using Conditions and Color in a Custom Number Format

The condition codes available in numeric formatting predate conditional formatting by a decade. You should consider the flexible conditional formatting features for any new conditions. However, in case you encounter an old worksheet with these codes, it is valid to use colors in the format: red, blue, green, yellow, cyan, black, white, magenta, Color 1, ..., Color 56. You include the color in square brackets. It should be the first element of any numeric formatting zone.

➡ **See** Chapter 31, "Using Data Visualizations and Conditional Formatting," for more information about flexible conditional formatting features.

You can include a condition in square brackets after the color but before the numeric formatting. For example, [Red][<=100];[Color 17][>100] displays numbers under 100 in red and other numbers in blue. The United States telephone special format uses this custom condition:

[<=9999999]###-####;(###) ###-####

Using Dates and Times in a Custom Number Format

Although many of these settings are arcane, I still regularly use many of the date and time formats shown in Table 30.1. The various m and d codes allow flexibility in expressing dates.

Table 30.1 Date and Time Formats

To Display This:	Use This Code:
Months as 1–12	m
Months as 01–12	mm
Months as Jan–Dec	mmm
Months as January–December	mmmm
Months as the first letter of the month	mmmmm
Days as 1–31	d
Days as 01–31	dd
Days as Sun–Sat	ddd
Days as Sunday–Saturday	dddd
Years as 00–99	yy
Years as 1900–9999	yyyy
Hours as 0–23	h
Hours as 00–23	hh
Minutes as 0–59	m
Minutes as 00–59	mm
Seconds as 0–59	s
Seconds as 00–59	ss
Hours as 4 AM	h AM/PM
Time as 4:36 PM	h:mm AM/PM
Time as 4:36:03 P	h:mm:ss A/P
Elapsed time in hours such as 25:02	[h]:mm
Elapsed time in minutes such as 63:46	[mm]:ss
Elapsed time in seconds	[ss]
Fractions of a second	h:mm:ss.00

The custom number format m/d/yy displays the month and day numbers as one digit if possible. For example, dates formatted with this code display as 1/9/08, 1/31/08, 9/9/09, and 12/31/08.

A custom number format of mm/dd/yy always uses two digits to display the month and day. Examples are 01/09/08 and 01/31/08.

The remaining date and time codes can display months as Jan, January, or J and days as 1, 01, Fri, or Friday.

 Note

Note that the letter m can be used either as a month or as a minute. If the m is preceded by an h or followed by an s, Excel assumes you are referring to minutes. Otherwise, the month is displayed instead.

Displaying Scientific Notation in Custom Number Formats

To display numbers in scientific format, you use E- or E+ exponent codes in a zone.

If a format contains a zero (0) or pound sign (#) to the right of an exponent code, Excel displays the number in scientific format and inserts an E. The number of zeros or pound signs to the right of a code determines the number of digits in the exponent. E- or e- places a minus sign by negative exponents. E+ or e+ places a minus sign by negative exponents and a plus sign by positive exponents.

Take the following, for example:

- 1450 formatted with 0.00E+00 displays as 1.45E+03.

- 1450 formatted with 0.00E-00 displays as 1.45E03.

- 0.00145 formatted with either code displays as 1.45E-03.

Aligning Cells

Worksheets look best when the headings above a column are aligned with the data in the column. Excel's default behavior is to left-align text and right-align values and dates.

In Figure 30.12, the month heading in F1 is left-aligned, and the numeric values starting in row 2 are right-aligned. This makes the worksheet look haphazard. To solve the problem, you can right-align the headings cells.

To right-align cells, select the cells and click the Right Align icon in the Alignment group of the Home tab.

 Note

The Alignment tab of the Format Cells dialog offers additional alignment choices, such as justified and distributed.

Figure 30.12
In column F, the left-aligned heading appears out of alignment with the numbers. Columns G and H show the headings after the Right Align icon is clicked.

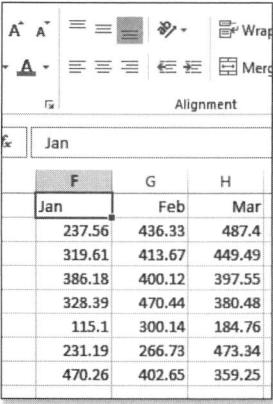

Changing Font Size

There are three icons in the Font group of the Home tab for changing font size:

- The Increase Font Size A▲ icon increases the font size in the selected cells to the next larger setting.

- The Decrease Font Size A▼ icon decreases the font size in the selected cells to the next smaller setting.

- The Font Size drop-down offers a complete list of font sizes. You can hover over any font size to see the Live Preview of that size in the selected cells of the worksheet (see Figure 30.13).

Figure 30.13
When you use the Font Size drop-down, Live Preview shows you the effect of an increased font size before you select the font.

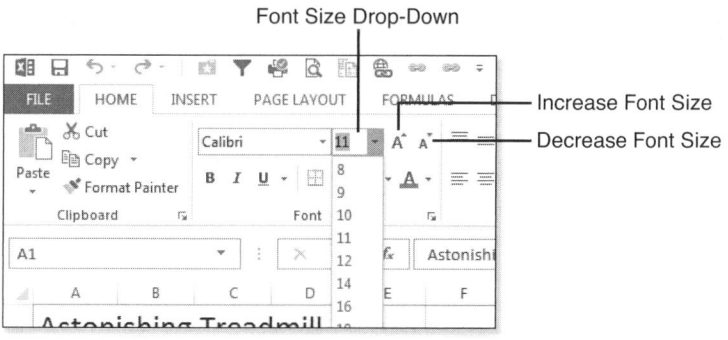

Changing Font Typeface

Beginning with Excel 2007, changing the font typeface is vastly improved. In some legacy versions of Excel, the Font drop-down showed the font names in the style of each font. However, beginning with Excel 2007, Live Preview shows how the font will look as you hover over the font in the selected cells (see Figure 30.14). Notice that the Font name drop-down is in the Font group of the Home tab.

 **Note**

By using the Font tab of the Format Cells dialog, you can also apply strikethrough, superscript, and subscript.

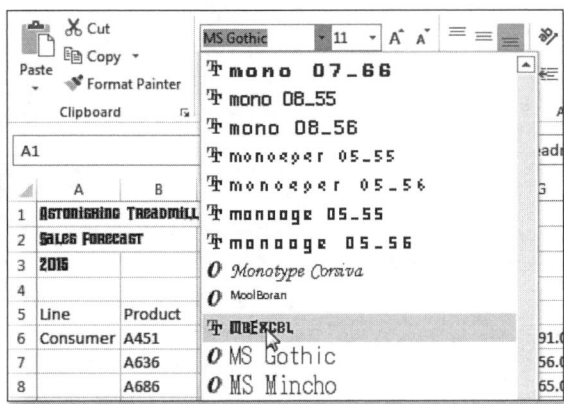

Figure 30.14
The Font drop-down in the Home tab shows the look of each font, and Live Preview shows how individual cells will look with the font applied.

Applying Bold, Italic, and Underline

Three icons in the Font group in the Home tab enable you to change the font to apply bold, italic, and underline. Unlike the icons in the Number group, these icons behave properly, toggling the property on and off. The Bold icon is a bold letter *B*. The Italic icon is an italic letter *I*. The Underline icon is either an underlined *U* or a double-underlined *D*. The Underline icon is actually a drop-down. As shown in Figure 30.15, you can select the drop-down to change from Single Underline to Double Underline.

The underline style applies to the characters in the cell. If you have a cell that contains 123, the underline is three characters wide. If you have a cell with 1,234,567.89, the underline is 12 characters wide.

The Format Cells dialog offers more choices. Settings for Single Accounting underline create an underline that extends nearly to the edges of the cell, but leaves a gap between the underline in the next cell. This often looks better than using a bottom border across the cells.

Figure 30.15
The underline drop-
down offers single or
double underlining,
but the extra choices
in the Format Cells
dialog solve some text
underlining issues.

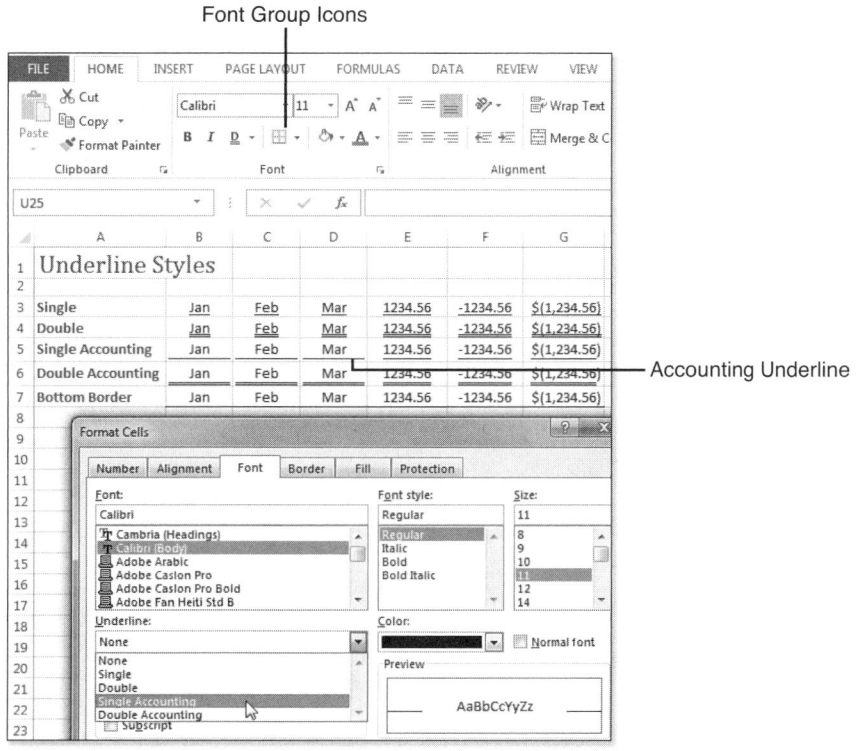

Accounting Underline

Using Borders

There are 1.7 billion unique combinations of borders for any four-cell range. The Borders drop-down in the Font group of the Home tab offers 13 popular border options plus five border tools, as shown in Figure 30.16.

Excel 2007 offered only the 13 border choices before you had to use the Border tab of the Format Cells dialog to find additional choices. However, you might find that the five tools in the Draw Border section of the drop-down are the fastest way to draw borders.

To use the Draw Border tool, follow these steps:

1. If you desire a color other than black, open the Borders drop-down, hover over Line Color, and choose a color from the fly-out menu.

2. If you desire a thickness other than a continuous hairline border, open the Borders drop-down, hover over Line Style, and choose a style from the fly-out menu.

> **Note**
>
> Performing either step 1 or step 2 automatically puts you in Draw Border mode. In this case, you can skip step 3.

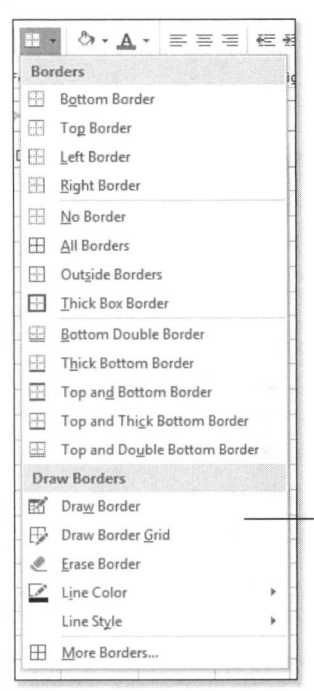

—— Border Drawing Tools

Figure 30.16
The Borders drop-down offers 13 of the most popular border choices and five border-drawing tools. The border-drawing tools might be the fastest way to create anything other than basic borders.

3. If you opted for black continuous hairline borders and skipped steps 1 and 2, open the Borders drop-down and select Draw Border. The mouse cursor changes to a pencil.

4. To draw in a single border, click one edge of a cell. In Figure 30.17, the stair-step in rows 2 through 4 was achieved in five clicks.

   ■ Click the border between B2 and B3.

   ■ Click the border between B3 and C3.

   ■ Click the border between C3 and C4.

   ■ Click the border between C4 and D4.

   ■ Click the border between D4 and D5.

5. To draw an outline around a range, click in one corner cell and drag it down to the opposite corner. The outline around B6:D9 in Figure 30.17 was achieved by clicking in B6 and dragging to D9.

6. To draw a grid in a range, hold down the Ctrl key while dragging. The grid in B11:D14 was achieved by Ctrl+dragging from B11 to D14.

Figure 30.17
The Draw Border tool was deprecated in Excel 2007 but came back after many users complained.

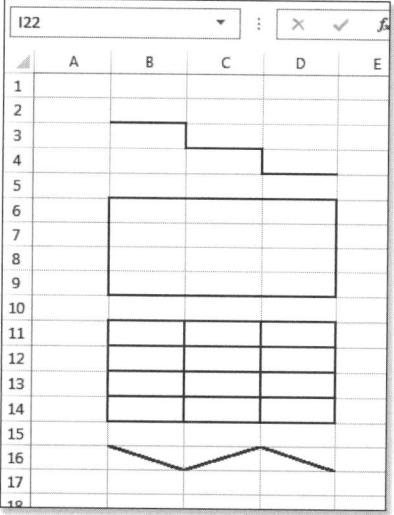

7. Drawing diagonals takes a bit of practice. Click at the top-left corner of a cell and drag to the bottom-right corner of the cell. As you are dragging, Excel starts to draw in a border around the whole cell. When you reach the bottom-right corner, the outline changes to a diagonal. Three separate diagonal borders are shown in row 16 of Figure 30.17.

8. If you make a mistake, use Undo or hold down Ctrl+Shift while dragging the mouse to erase borders.

9. When you are done drawing borders, press the Esc key to exit Draw Border mode.

> **Note**
> The Draw Border Grid icon in the drop-down draws a border around each individual cell in a range. This is equivalent to holding down the Ctrl key while using the Draw Border tool.

Drawing a Border Around a Range

You need to understand an important concept when applying borders to a range. Suppose you select 20 rows by 20 columns, such as cells A1:T20. If you apply a top border by using the drop-down, only the top row of cells A1:T1 have the border. Often, this is not what you were expecting. For example, you might have wanted a border on the top of all 400 cells.

Notice that in the Format Cells dialog, there is a representation of a 2×2 cell range. The border style drawn in the top edge of this box affects only the top edge of the range. The border style drawn in the middle horizontal line of the box affects all the horizontal borders on the inside of the selected range.

The fastest way to select all horizontal and vertical borders in the range is to click the Outline button and then the Inside button in the Presets section of the dialog.

> ## 🛜 Caution
>
> The Erase Border tool will not clear all borders in a range. By default, the tool clears only the outline border around the entire range. This is rarely what you want. You can hold down the Ctrl key while using the Erase Border tool, or instead make a habit of preselecting the range and then choosing No Border, the fifth item in the Borders drop-down. Ctrl+Shift+Minus Sign also clears all borders.

Coloring Cells

Excel 2007 added the capability to use a gradient to fill a cell. This can provide an interesting look for a title cell. Gradient formatting is available only in the Format Cells dialog.

The Font group on the Home tab offers a paint bucket drop-down and an A drop-down. The paint bucket is a color chooser for the background fill of the cell. The A drop-down is a color chooser for the font color in the cell. Both drop-downs offer six shades of the 10 theme colors, 10 standard colors, and the More Colors option. The paint bucket drop-down also offers the menu choice No Fill, as shown in Figure 30.18.

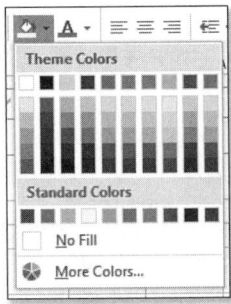

Figure 30.18
The paint bucket drop-down offers theme colors, 10 standard colors, and the link More Colors.

The More Colors link offers the two-tabbed Colors dialog. You can either choose a color from the Standard tab or enter an RGB value on the Custom tab.

The ability to use a two-color gradient in a cell was a new feature beginning with Excel 2007. To activate this feature, follow these steps:

1. Select one or more cells. If you select a range of cells, Excel repeats the gradient for each cell in the range.

2. Press Ctrl+1 to display the Format Cells dialog.

3. Select the Fill tab.

4. Click the Fill Effects button.

5. In the Color 1 and Color 2 drop-downs, choose two colors or choose one color and white.

6. In the Shading Styles section, choose a shading style.

7. In the Variants section, choose one of the three variations. A sample is shown in the Sample box.

8. Click OK to close the Fill Effects dialog.

9. Click OK to close the Format Cells dialog.

Figure 30.19 shows the Fill Effects dialog. Cell A1 contains a vertical shading, from left to right. Cell A4 shows the opposite variant of vertical shading. Cell A9 shows the from-the-center variant of the vertical shading. Cell A13 shows a diagonal-down shading style.

Figure 30.19
Since Excel 2007, you can add gradients as the fill within cells.

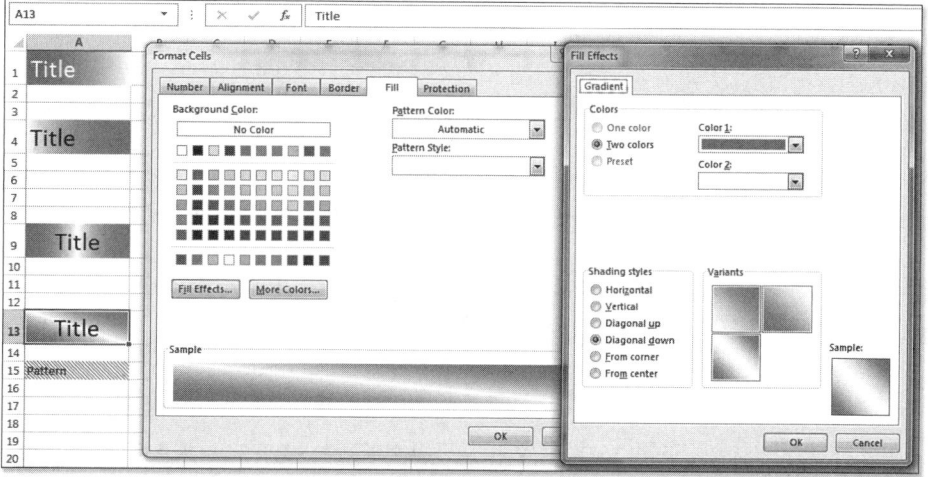

After a brief absence in Excel 2007, pattern fills are back. Use the Pattern Color and Pattern Style drop-downs in the Fill tab of the Format Cells dialog to add a pattern shading to a cell. A15 of Figure 30.19 shows a pattern.

Adjusting Column Widths and Row Heights

You can adjust the width of every column in a worksheet. In many cases, narrowing the columns to reduce wasted space can allow a report to fit on one page.

Most tasks in Excel can be accomplished in three or more ways. In most cases, I have a favorite method to perform any task and use that method exclusively. However, setting column widths and row heights is a task where I actively use many methods, depending on the circumstances.

You can use the following seven methods to adjust column width (each method applies equally well to adjusting row heights):

- **Click the border between the column headings**—As shown in Figure 30.20, you can drag to the left to make the column narrower. You can drag to the right to make the column wider. A tooltip appears, showing the width in points and pixels. The advantage of this method is that you can drag until the column feels like it is the right width. The disadvantage is that this method fixes one column at a time.

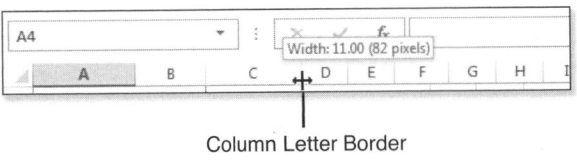

Figure 30.20
The right border between one cell letter and the next is the key to adjusting column widths.

- **Double-click the border between column headings**—Excel automatically adjusts the left column to fit the widest value in the column. The advantage of this method is that the column is exactly wide enough for the contents. The disadvantage is that a very long title in cell A1, for example, makes this method ineffective. You might have been planning to allow the title in cell A1 to spill over to B1, C1, and D1. However, the double-click method makes the column wide enough for the long title. In this case, you want to use the last method in this list.

- **Select many columns and drag the border for one column**—When you do this, the width for all columns is adjusted. The advantage of this method is that you can adjust all columns at once, and they are all a uniform width.

- **Select many columns and double-click one of the borders between column letters**—When you do this, all the columns adjust to fit their widest value.

- **Use the ribbon**—Select one or more columns. From the Cells group of the Home tab, select Format, Column Width. Then enter a width in characters and click OK.

- **Apply one column's width to other columns**—If one column is a suitable width, and you want all other columns to be the same width, you should use this method. Select the column with the correct width and then press Ctrl+C to copy. Next, select the columns to be adjusted. Select the Clipboard section of the Home tab and select Paste, Paste Special, Column Widths. Finally, click OK.

- **AutoFit a column to all the data below the title rows**—If you have a long title in the first few rows and need to AutoFit the column to all the data below the title rows, use this method. Click the first cell in the data range and then press the End key. Next, hold down the Ctrl and Shift keys while pressing the down-arrow key. This selects a contiguous range from the starting cell downward. Now select the Cells section of the Home tab and then select Format, AutoFit Selection. If you were a power user in Excel 2003 or before, you might remember this method as Alt+O+C+A. This legacy keyboard shortcut still works.

Using Merge and Center

In general, merged cells are bad. If you have a merged cell in the middle of a data table, you will be unable to sort the data. You will be unable to cut and paste data unless the same cells are merged. However, it is okay to use merged cells as a title to group several columns together.

In Figure 30.21, the Consumer and Professional headings correspond to the columns B:F and G:K, respectively. It is appropriate to center each heading above its columns.

 **Tip**

Merging cells brings some negative side effects. Say that you had merged B100:G100. You start in cell B1, hold down the Shift key, and start pressing PgDn to select cells in column B. When you reach or pass the merged cell B100, your selection size will automatically expand to be six columns wide because this is the width of the merged cell. To prevent this problem, you might use Center Across Selection, found in the Home tab. This gives the same look as the merged cell, without the problems caused by the merge.

Figure 30.21
Because the row 2 categories are not part of the data table and will never need to be sorted, it is okay to merge and center those cells.

	A	B	C	D	E	F	G	H	I	J	K
1											
2		**Consumer**					**Professional**				
3	Month	A451	A636	A686	B416	B519	K121	K658	N713	O855	O980
4	Jan	167	198	168	139	153	145	144	198	195	168
5	Feb	166	132	135	150	183	170	198	103	195	194
6	Mar	191	103	112	190	136	124	151	108	167	182
7	Apr	125	147	175	150	190	182	154	140	173	178
8	May	121	160	147	169	170	183	147	138	196	181
9	Jun	131	166	548	179	196	165	140	177	191	177
10	Jul	182	118	144	116	172	171	158	141	149	170
11	Aug	137	129	183	163	105	188	103	116	195	102
12	Sep	130	108	124	177	170	108	168	168	142	138
13	Oct	146	197	180	177	143	180	152	177	188	123
14	Nov	154	153	180	158	129	110	118	179	151	155
15	Dec	107	162	151	145	158	178	180	159	129	188

To merge and center cells, follow these steps:

1. Click in the cell that contains the value that is to be centered and then drag to select the entire range to be merged. In this example, click in cell B2 and drag to cell F2. The result is that B2 is the active cell, and B2:F2 is selected.

2. From the Home tab, select Alignment, Merge & Center, and then select Merge & Center again, as shown in Figure 30.22.

Figure 30.22
Select Merge & Center from the drop-down.

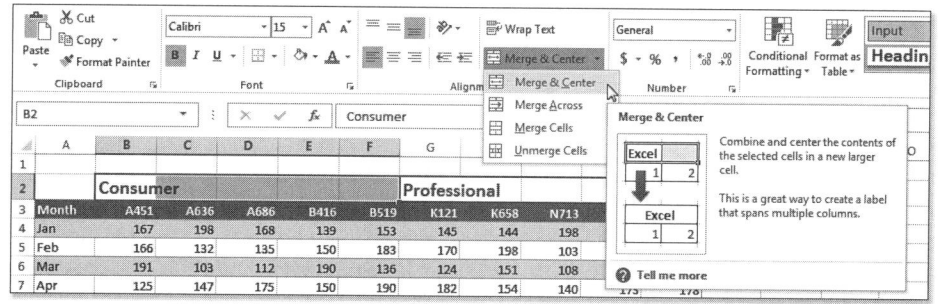

3. Repeat steps 1 and 2 for any other column headings.

4. Optionally, apply an outline border around the merged cells.

Note that after you merge the cells, the entire range becomes one cell. In Figure 30.23, the word *Consumer* is in an ultra-large cell B2. In this worksheet, cells C2, D2, E2, and F2 no longer exist. If you attempt to use the Go To dialog to move to cell C2, you will be taken to cell B2 instead.

◢	A	B	C	D	E	F	G	H	I	J	K
1											
2				Consumer					Professional		
3	Month	A451	A636	A686	B416	B519	K121	K658	N713	O855	O980
4	Jan	167	198	168	139	153	145	144	198	195	168
5	Feb	166	132	135	150	183	170	198	103	195	194
6	Mar	191	103	112	190	136	124	151	108	167	182

Figure 30.23
Columns are visually grouped into product lines by the merged cells.

Rotating Text

Vertical text is difficult to read. However, at times space considerations make it advantageous to use vertical text. In Figure 30.24, for example, the names in row 5 are much wider than the values in the rest of the table. If you use Format, AutoFit Selection, the report is too wide.

		Product	Blankenship	Cunningham	Fitzpatrick	Hamilton	Hernderson
4							
5		Product	Blankenship	Cunningham	Fitzpatrick	Hamilton	Hernderson
6		A451	339	258	293	316	252
7		A636	438	332	377	408	325
8		A686	218	166	188	203	162
9		B416	513	389	442	477	380
10		B519	844	640	727	786	626
11		D553	178	135	154	166	132
12	Consumer	D555	472	358	407	439	350
13		D801	427	324	368	397	317
14		D914	374	283	322	348	277
15		E196	761	578	656	709	564
16		E476	573	434	494	533	425
17		Subtotal	5,137	3,897	4,428	4,782	3,810

Figure 30.24
The headings are much wider than the data. Vertical text can solve the problem.

In the Alignment tab of the Home group, an Orientation drop-down offers five variations of vertical text. Figure 30.25 compares the five available options. Although the Angle options look great, they only reduce the column width by 12%. Vertical Text reduces the column width by 75% but takes far more vertical space. The option Rotate Text Up reduces the column width by 73% and takes up less than half the vertical space of the Vertical Text option.

 Note

After you rotate the text, select the Cells section of the Home tab and then select Format, AutoFit Selection again to narrow the columns.

Figure 30.25
Of the five options, the Rotate Text options take up the least space.

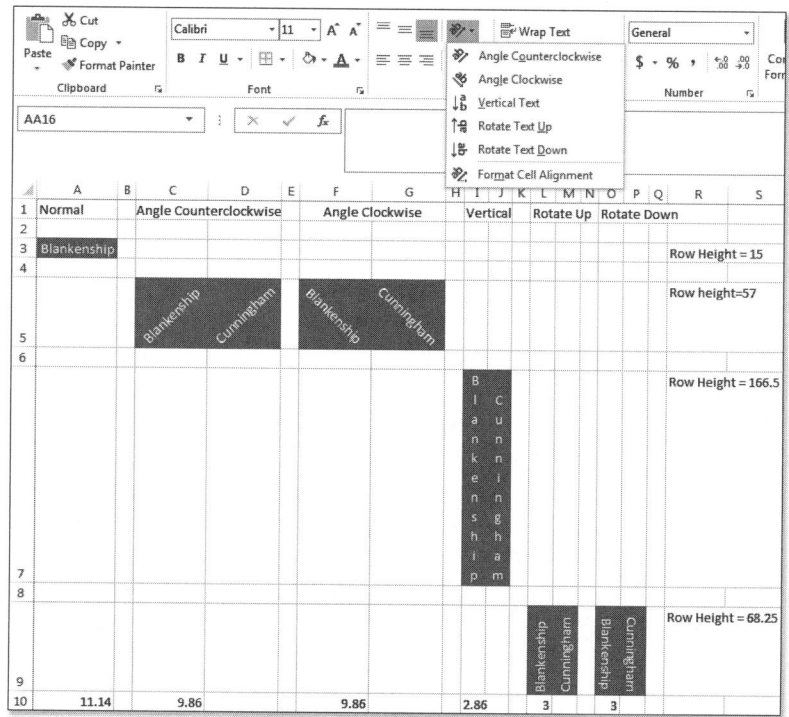

If you need more control over the text orientation, you can select the Alignment option in the drop-down to display the Alignment tab of the Format Cells dialog. This tab allows rotation from 90 degrees to −90 degrees, in 1-degree increments, as shown in Figure 30.26.

Figure 30.26
The Alignment option allows 182 different orientation settings.

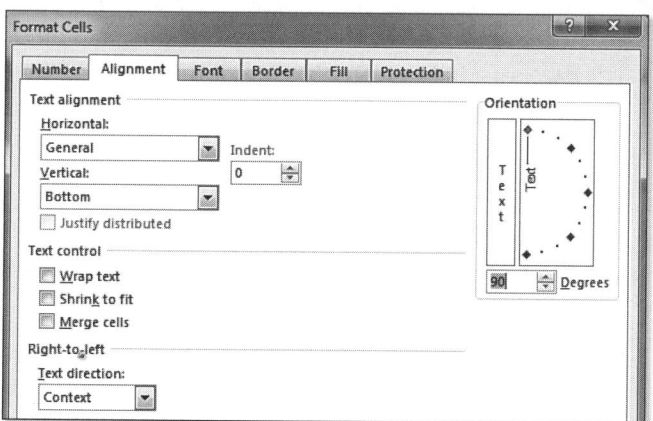

Formatting with Styles

Instead of using the settings in the Font group of the Home tab, you can format a report by using the built-in cell styles. Cell styles have been popular in Word for more than a decade. They have been available in legacy versions of Excel, but because they were not given a spot on the Formatting toolbar, few people took advantage of them.

Figure 30.27 shows the styles available when you select Styles, Cell Styles in the Home tab.

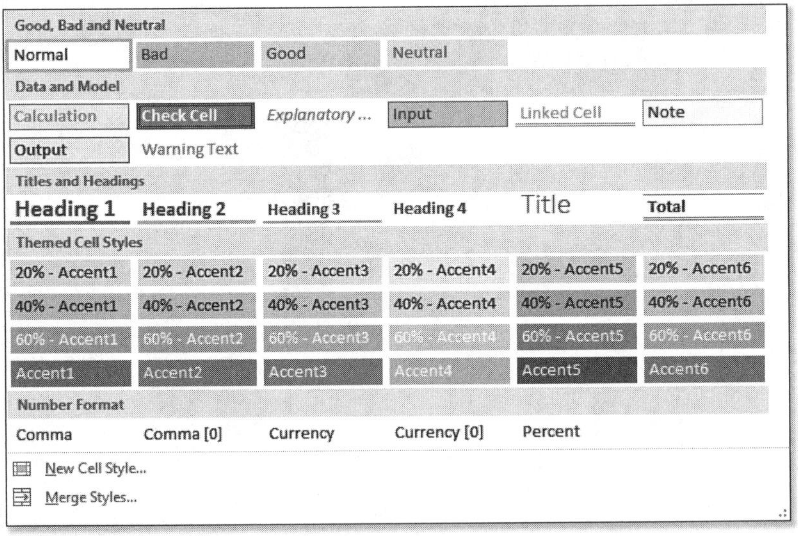

Figure 30.27
The Cell Styles gallery offers various built-in cell styles.

An advantage to using cell styles is that you can convert the look and feel of a report by choosing from the themes on the Page Layout tab. Figure 30.28 shows one of the 48 available themes applied to the report.

The Cell Styles gallery offers a menu item to add additional styles to a workbook. Using cell styles provides an interesting alternative to the traditional method of formatting.

Note

You might wonder why Excel 2013 suggests that calculated cells should be in orange font or why Notes should have a yellow background. I spent the first two years of working with Excel 2007 wondering why calculated cells should be orange. However, the better question is, "Why not orange?" When I receive worksheets from others who use this convention, it is easy to understand that they are using the built-in cell styles, which makes it easier to follow the logic of the worksheet. In Figure 30.29, the forecasting model was formatted using Cell Styles from the Data and Model section of the Cell Styles menu. If everyone in your company used these styles, it would be easier to spot the input cells in any model.

Figure 30.28
When you choose a new theme, a report formatted with cell styles takes on a new look.

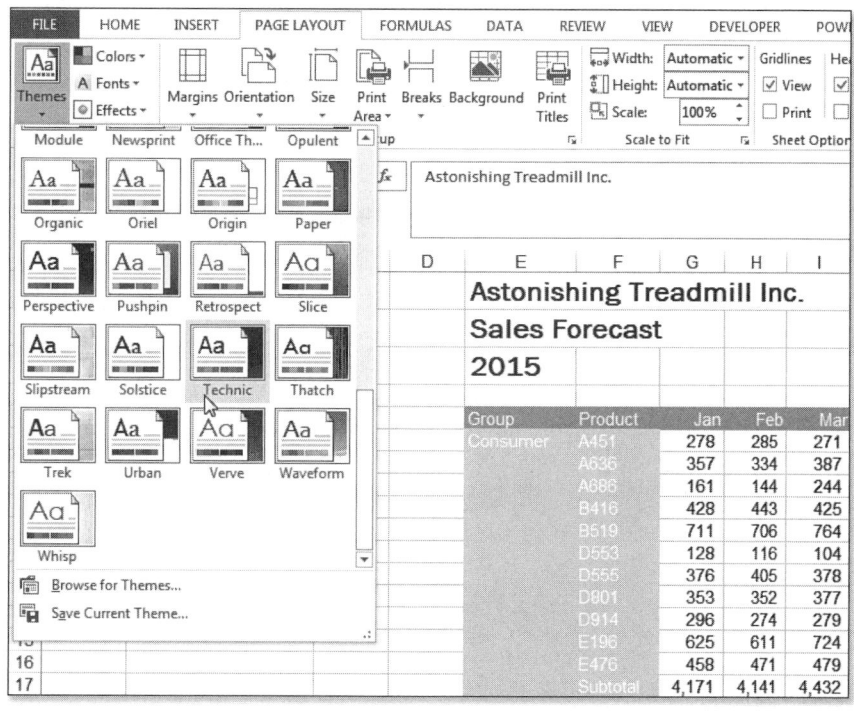

Figure 30.29
Adopt the cell styles suggestions for input cells, calculated cells, and so on to make it easier to see the logic in the model.

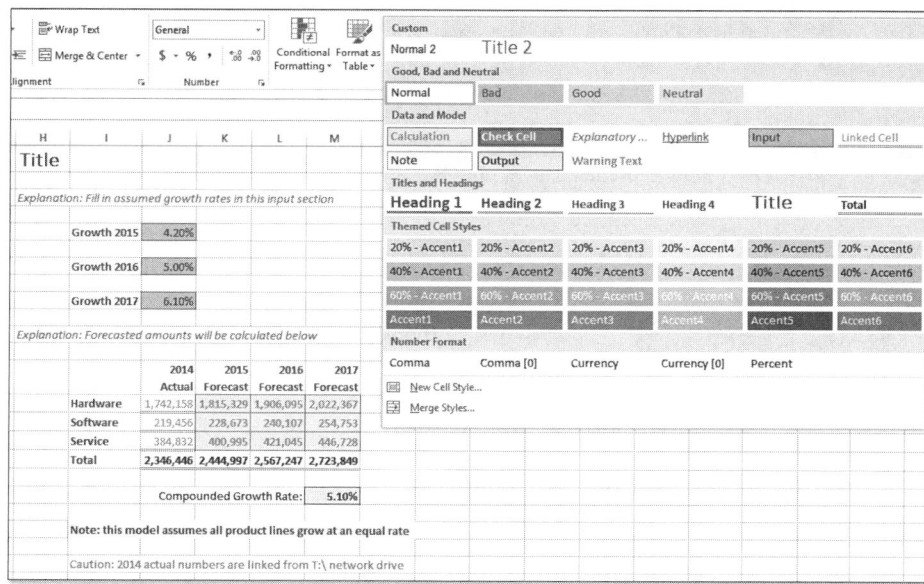

Understanding Themes

A *theme* is a collection of colors, fonts, and effects. Office 2013 has 48 built-in themes. You can also download new themes from Office Online or design your own themes.

 Tip

The Office theme is the default theme in Excel 2013. In an effort to look modern, Microsoft changed the Office theme starting in Excel 2013. If you had previously embraced themes in Excel 2007 or Excel 2010, you might have become a fan of the old Office theme. The Title cell style in the old Office theme was better than the Title cell style in the new Office theme. Worse, if you open an old document created with Excel 2007 or Excel 2010, the old Office theme will still be available. New workbooks have the new Office theme. It is annoying that they used the same name for two different themes.

Here is how to get the old Office theme back. On the Page Layout tab, open three drop-downs for color, font, and effects. In each drop-down, choose Office 2007–2010 theme. After choosing from those three drop-downs, choose Themes, Save Current Theme. Save the theme with a name such as OfficeReal or aaaOffice. Custom themes appear at the top of the Themes drop-down, so it will be relatively easy to go back to the old theme, even in new workbooks.

Themes are shared in simple XML files, which means they can be propagated throughout a company. A theme has the following components:

- **Fonts**—A theme has two fonts: one for body text and one for titles. The fonts come into play more often in PowerPoint and Word than in Excel. However, styles in Excel also use fonts.

- **Colors**—There are 12 colors: four for text and backgrounds, six accent colors that are used in charts and table accents, and two for hyperlinks. One of the two colors for hyperlinks indicates followed hyperlinks, whereas the other color indicates hyperlinks that have not been followed. You see the 10 colors besides the hyperlink colors in the first row of the color chooser, as shown in Figure 30.30. The first four colors are for text and backgrounds. The next six colors are the accent colors. In each column, you then see various shades of these 10 colors.

- **Effects**—Each theme includes a number of object effects, such as bevel and line style.

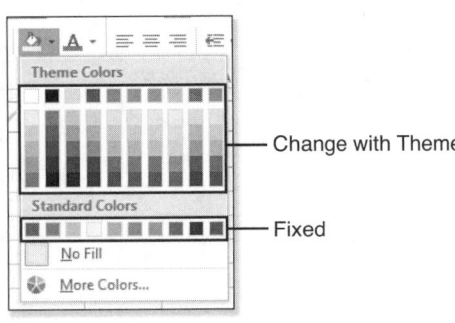

Figure 30.30
The Color Chooser shows six shades of each of the 10 theme colors.

Change with Theme

Fixed

Choosing a New Theme

Themes are managed on the Page Layout tab. Listed next are the four drop-downs available in the Themes group:

- **Themes**—Allows you to switch among the 49 built-in themes.

- **Colors**—Allows you to change the color scheme to use the colors from another theme.

- **Fonts**—Allows you to use the fonts from another theme.

- **Effects**—Allows you to use the effects from another theme.

🔍 Note

Note that you can use only one theme per workbook. If you are changing the theme on Sheet33, the same changes are made on all the other worksheets in the workbook.

Changing a theme affects charts, tables, SmartArt diagrams, and inserted objects.

To switch to another theme, follow these steps:

1. Arrange your worksheet so that you can see any themed elements, such as tables or charts, on the right side of the screen.

2. From the Page Layout tab, select the Themes drop-down from the Themes group.

3. Hover over the various themes. The worksheet updates to show the new colors, fonts, and effects.

4. When you identify a theme you like, click the theme to apply it to the workbook.

Figures 30.31 and 30.32 show the same worksheet with two different themes.

Figure 30.31
The Solstice theme features a sans-serif font and bright colors.

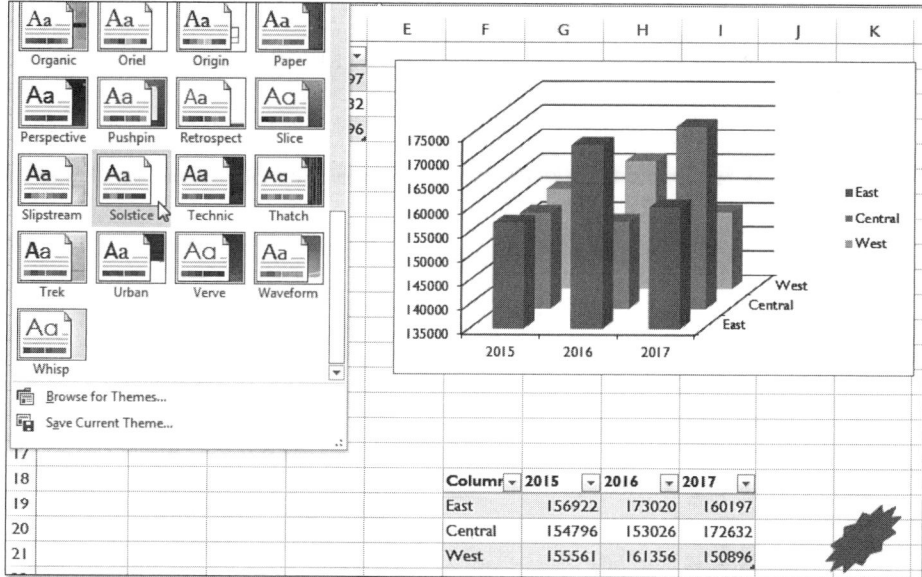

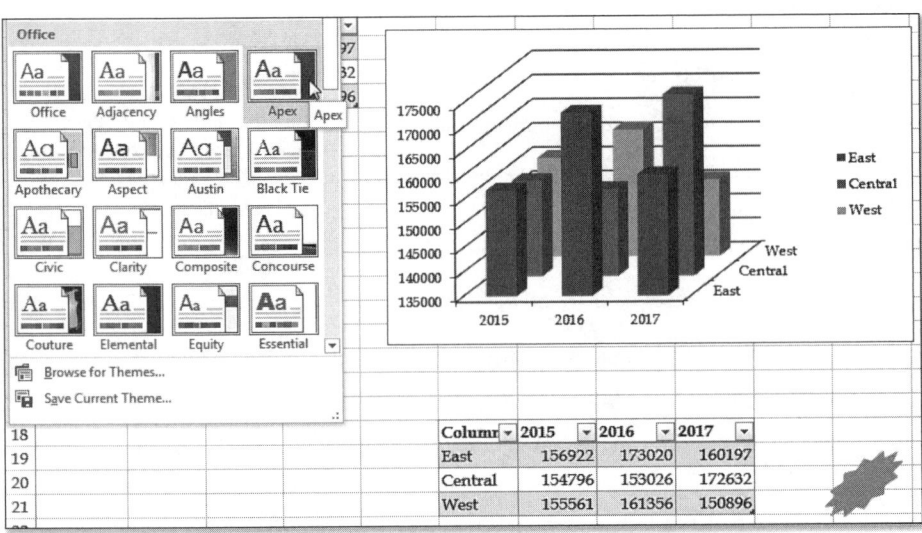

Figure 30.32
The Apex theme features a serif font, muted colors, and different effects.

If you are strictly interested in the accent colors, you can select the Colors drop-down from the Themes group to see the accent colors used in each theme. Figure 30.33 shows the options in the Colors drop-down. Note that this drop-down offers a grayscale option that is not available in the Themes drop-down.

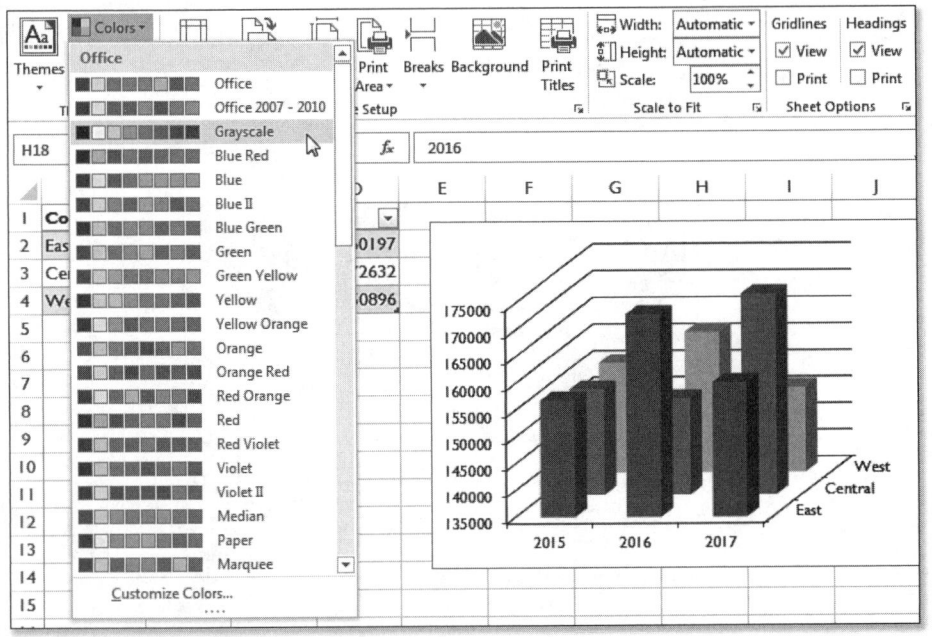

Figure 30.33
The Colors drop-down shows the accent colors for all 49 themes at once.

Creating a New Theme

You might want to develop a special theme, which is fairly easy to do. First, you need to select two fonts and six accent colors. For example, suppose you want to create a theme to match your company's color scheme. The hardest part is finding six colors to represent your company, because most company logos have two or three colors. The following sections describe how to create a new theme and suggest resources for choosing complementary colors for your company colors.

Understanding RGB Color Codes

Colors on computer monitors are described as a mix of red (R), green (G), and blue (B). Each color channel is assigned a value from 0 to 255. For example, a color of R=255, G=0, B=0 is a bright red. As you add more blue, the red shifts toward a pink or violet color. A color of R=255, G=0, B=128 is a pinkish violet color.

A color of R=0, G=0, B=0 is black. A color of R=255, G=255, B=255 is white. You can create 16.7 million different colors by using combinations of red, green, and blue.

To discover the codes for your company's color scheme, follow these steps:

1. Open your company's Home page in a browser.

2. In Internet Explorer, select View, Source. In Firefox, select View, Page Source. You now see the underlying HTML code.

3. Find the colors used in the page by searching for a pound sign (#). A web page specifies colors by using a pound sign followed by six characters, such as #4F81BD.

Even though every web page uses the #123456 notation for describing colors, Microsoft Excel's theme specification needs the RGB value for the color. Fortunately, it is fairly easy to convert between the two.

Hexadecimal is a numbering system that has digits 0 through 9 and letters A through F. Including 0, there are 16 digits in the hexadecimal numbering system. In the decimal system, a two-digit number can represent 10×10 different combinations. There are 100 numbers, from 00 to 99. In a hex system, a two-digit number can represent 16×16 different numbers—that is, 256 numbers, from 0 to 255.

In the #123456 nomenclature, the # sign indicates that the number is in hexadecimal. The first two digits are the hex representation of the red value. The next two digits are the hex representation of the green value. The next two digits are the hex representation of the blue value.

Converting from Hex to Decimal

If you do not have Photoshop or another tool that converts from a hex color to an RGB value for you automatically, you can use functions in Excel to do the conversion. For example, the worksheet in Figure 30.34 converts from a hex color in cell B1 to the RGB values in B7:B9:

- The formulas in B2:B4 use the MID function to extract each pair of numbers from the color code. The formula for cell B2 is shown in cell C2.

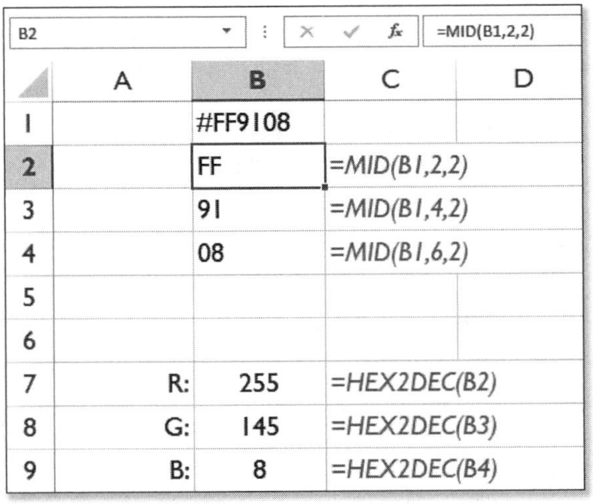

B2	▾	:	×	✓	fx	=MID(B1,2,2)

	A	B	C	D
1		#FF9108		
2		FF	=MID(B1,2,2)	
3		91	=MID(B1,4,2)	
4		08	=MID(B1,6,2)	
5				
6				
7	R:	255	=HEX2DEC(B2)	
8	G:	145	=HEX2DEC(B3)	
9	B:	8	=HEX2DEC(B4)	

Figure 30.34
This quick Excel worksheet can convert from a six-digit hex color code to a decimal RGB value.

- The formulas in B7:B9 use the HEX2DEC function to convert the two-digit hex number to decimal.

To represent the color #FF9108 in Excel, for example, use R=255, G=145, B=8.

Finding New Colors

If you look at your company's logo and website, you can probably identify two or three colors to use in the theme. You need to come up with a total of six accent colors for a theme.

 **Note**

You can use the free web-based tool at http://colorschemedesigner.com/ to find colors that look good together.

To find complementary colors, follow these steps:

1. Start with a hex representation of one of your logo colors.

2. Open http://colorschemedesigner.com in a browser (see Figure 30.35).

3. In the bottom, just left of center, click the RGB code.

4. In the window that pops up, enter the portion of the color code after the pound sign, such as FF9108.

Figure 30.35
This web page suggests colors that complement your logo colors.

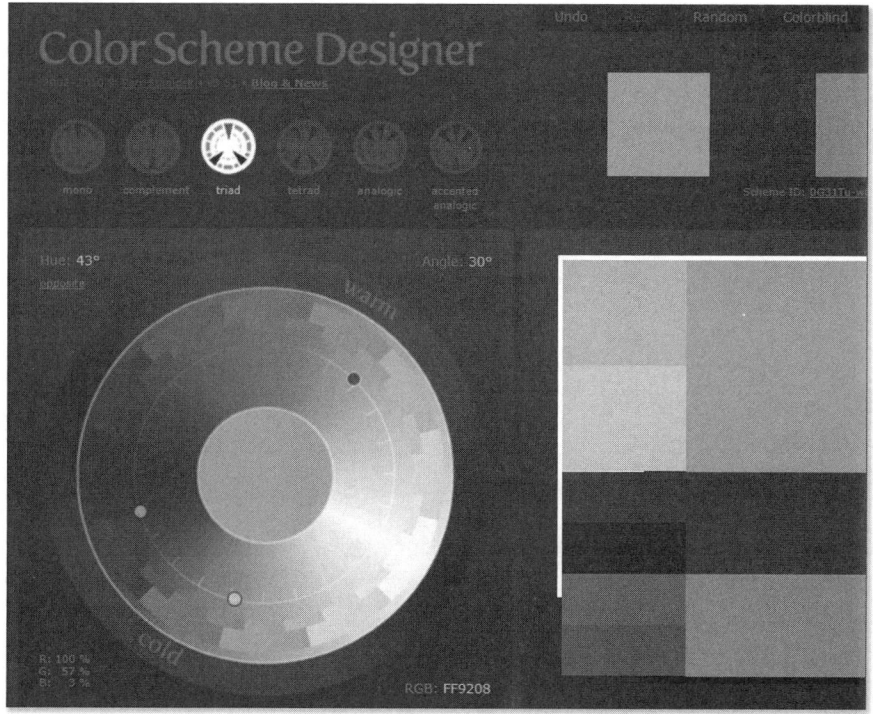

5. Click each of the six icons under the color wheel on the left. The six icons represent mono, complement, triad, tetrad, analogic, and accented analogic. In the Triad view, the website shows your original color, three others, and three variations of each.

6. In the bottom navigation, select Color List. The website shows the hex color codes for all the colors shown.

Specifying a Theme's Colors

To specify new theme colors, follow these steps:

1. Select Page Layout, Themes, Colors, Create New Theme Colors. The Create New Theme Colors dialog appears. Remember that a theme is composed of two text colors, two background colors, six accent colors, and two hyperlink colors. These 12 colors are shown in the Create New Theme Colors dialog (see Figure 30.36).

2. To change any accent color, select the drop-down next to Accent 1 through Accent 6. The Color Chooser appears.

3. From the bottom of the Color Chooser drop-down, select More Colors. The Colors dialog appears.

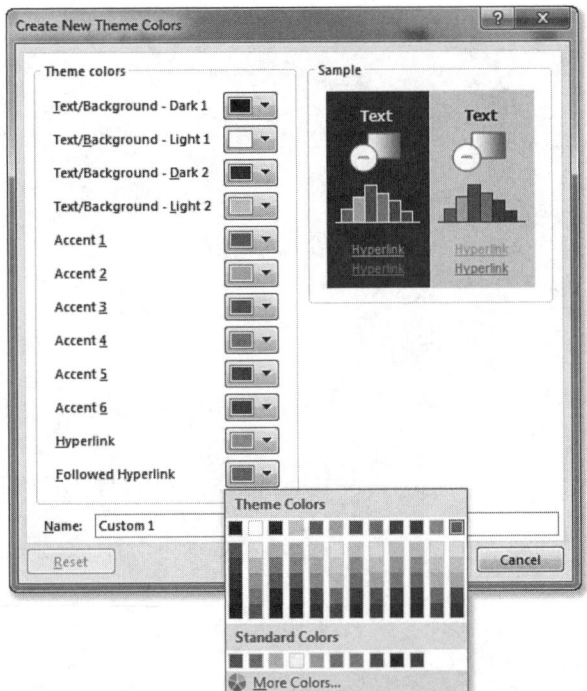

Figure 30.36
The 12 colors in the current theme are shown here.

4. In the Custom tab of the Colors dialog, enter values for red, green, and blue, as shown in Figure 30.37. The New color block shows the color. Click OK to accept the color.

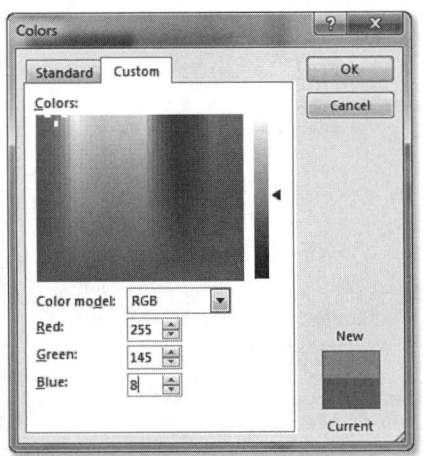

Figure 30.37
You specify the RGB values for the first color.

5. Repeat steps 2–4 for each of the accent colors.

6. If you want to change the colors for Hyperlink, Followed Hyperlink, and Text, repeat steps 2–4 for any of those.

7. In the Name box, give the theme a name, such as your company name.

8. Click Preview to see the theme applied to your workbook.

9. Click Save to accept the theme.

Specifying a Theme's Fonts

To specify new theme fonts, follow these steps:

1. Select Page Layout, Themes, Fonts, Create New Theme Fonts. The Create New Theme Fonts dialog appears, as shown in Figure 30.38. Remember that a font theme contains a heading font and a body font.

Figure 30.38
A theme is composed of two fonts.

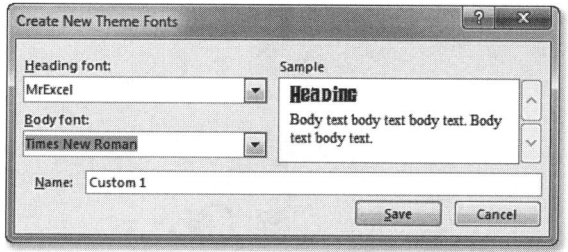

2. Select a font from the Heading Font drop-down. If a custom font is used in your company's logo, using it might be appropriate.

3. Select a font from the Body Font drop-down. This should be a font that is easy to read. Avoid stylized fonts for body copy.

4. Give the theme a name. It is okay to reuse the same name from the color theme.

5. Click Save to accept the theme changes.

 **Tip**

In June 2009, famed font designer Erik Spiekermann released the Axel font family, which he designed specifically for showing tables of numbers in Microsoft Excel.

Reusing Another Theme's Effects

There is no dialog to choose the effects associated with a theme. Other than editing the XML by hand, you are limited to using the effects from one of the built-in themes.

To select effects for a theme, from the Page Layout select Themes, Effects. Then choose one of the existing themes.

The Effects drop-down is initially vexing. There are only subtle clues about the effects used in the theme, as shown in Figure 30.39. Each effects icon consists of a circle, an arrow, and a rectangle. These shapes give you clues about the effects in the theme.

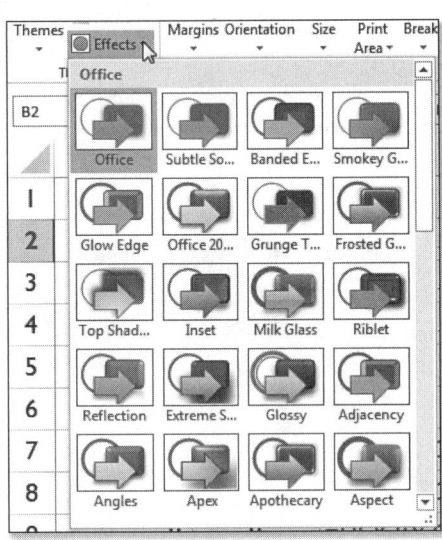

Figure 30.39
The Effects drop-down offers subtle clues about the effects in a theme.

When you insert a shape on a worksheet, six rows of Shape Styles are available in the gallery on the Drawing Tools – Format tab. These styles range from simple (row 1) to moderate (row 4) to intense (row 6):

Examine the circle in the upper left of each theme icon. Glossy uses a double line for the simple shape styles. The effect shown on the circle relates to the simple shape styles.

The arrow indicates moderate shape effects. For example, Grunge uses a faded grungy pattern for moderate styles.

The rectangle indicates the effects applied for intense styles. Even though they are barely perceptible, a bit of a reflection appears under the rectangle in Reflection and a bezel is used around Riblet.

These effects apply to various shape styles. In Figure 30.40, the Shape Effect drop-down is shown in the top-left corner. Six lines show how the effects from each of the six rows apply to six different shapes in the Grunge theme. The left-most shape is formatted using the first row and corresponds to the circle in the thumbnail from Figure 30.39.

Figure 30.40
These shapes illustrate changes introduced by the Theme Effects drop-down.

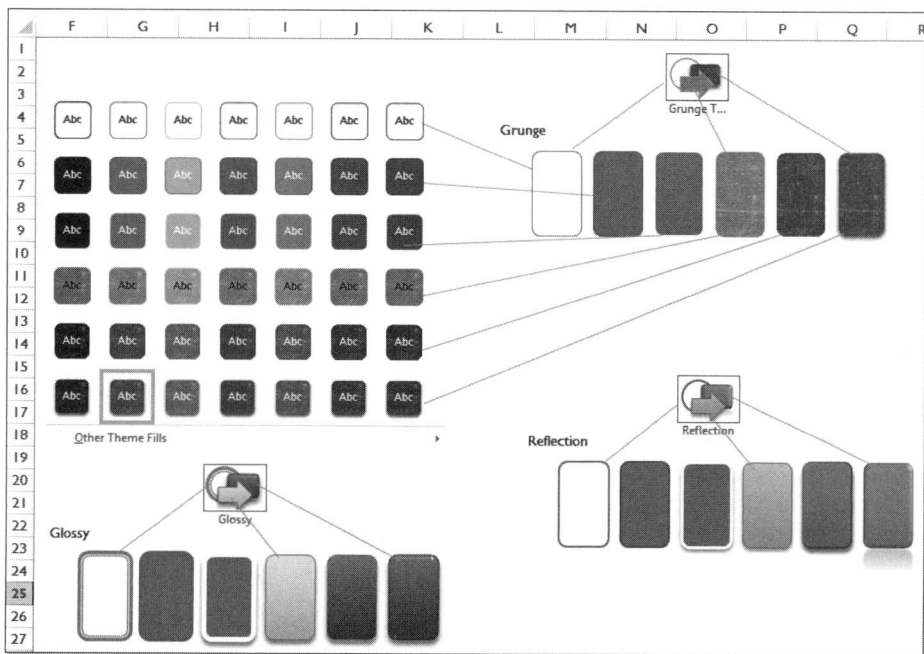

Two additional examples, Reflection and Glossy, show how the effects on the circle, arrow, and rectangle in the thumbnail correspond to rows 1, 4, and 6 in the drop-down.

Saving a Custom Theme

To reuse a theme, you must save it. To save a theme, from the Page Layout tab select Themes, Save Current Theme (see Figure 30.41).

By default, themes are stored in the Document Themes folder. In Windows Vista and Windows 7, the folder is in C:\Users\user name\AppData\Roaming\Microsoft\Templates\Document Themes.

Be sure to give your theme a useful name and then click Save.

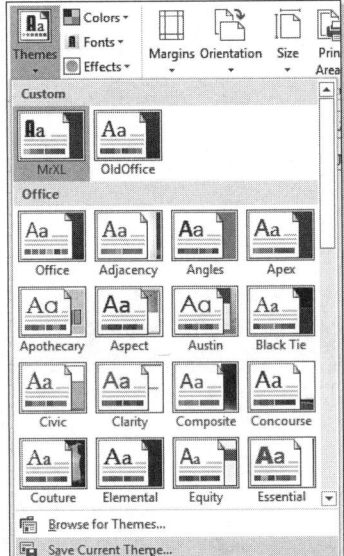

Figure 30.41
The option to save a theme is at the bottom of the Themes drop-down.

Using a Theme on a New Document

When you open a new document on the same computer, the Custom theme is in the Themes drop-down on the Page Layout tab. You can use this theme on all future documents.

Sharing a Theme with Others

If you want to share a theme with others, you need to send them the .thmx file from the theme folder.

The people you share the theme with can either copy the .thmx file to their equivalent folder or save the .thmx file to their desktop and use the Browse for Themes option, by choosing Page Layout, Themes, Browse for Themes.

Other Formatting Techniques

Now that you have the basics for formatting cells and worksheets, the rest of this chapter provides an overview of various formatting tips and tricks. These techniques discuss how to mix formatting within a single cell, wrap text in several cells, and use cell comments.

 Tip

After selecting characters in the cell, move the mouse pointer to the right and up to activate a shortened version of the mini toolbar. You can use icons on this floating toolbar to format the selected characters.

Formatting Individual Characters

Occasionally, you might find yourself entering a short memo on a worksheet. This might occur as an introduction or as instructions to a lengthy workbook. Although Excel is not a full-featured word processor, it can do a few word processing tricks.

One trick is to highlight individual characters in a cell in order to add emphasis or to make them stand out. You can do this to any cell that does not contain a formula. In Figure 30.42, for example, text has been typed in column A and allowed to extend over the edge of the column into columns A:J. One word in row 4 is in a bold, underlined, red font.

Figure 30.42
Formatting for individual characters in a cell can be changed by selecting those characters while in edit mode.

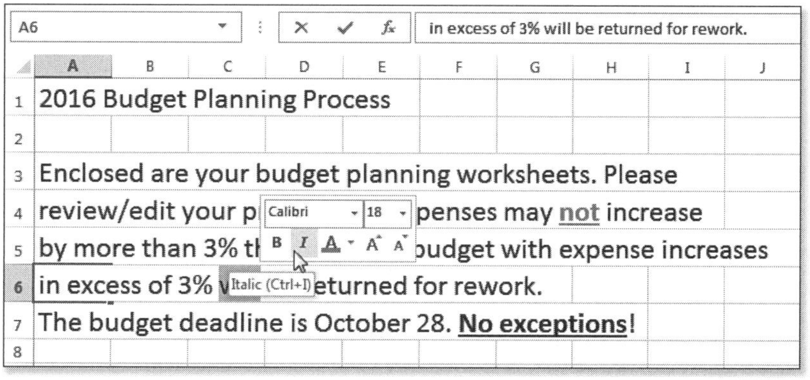

To format individual characters, follow these steps:

1. Display the Home tab.

2. Select the cell that contains the characters to be formatted.

3. Press the F2 key to edit the cell.

4. Using the mouse, highlight the characters in the cell. Move up and to the right to display the mini toolbar.

5. Although most of the ribbon is grayed out, the options for font size, color, underline, bold, italic, and font name are available in the Font group of the Home tab. Apply any formatting, as desired, from this group.

6. If the changes are not visible in the formula bar, press Enter to accept the changes in order to preview them.

Changing the Default Font

Excel offers a default font setting to be used for all new workbooks. With the Excel 2013 paradigm of themes, the default font for new workbooks is initially the generic value of BODY FONT. However, this is not an actual font; instead, it refers to the main font used by the current theme.

To change your default font for all new workbooks, follow these steps:

1. The menu for changing the default font does not offer Live Preview of the fonts. Therefore, go to the Font section of the Home tab and select the Font drop-down to inspect the available fonts in their actual styles. Find the name of the font you want to use.

2. From the File menu, select Excel Options. The Excel Options dialog appears.

3. Click the Popular category in the left margin.

4. In the second section, When Creating New Workbooks, select the Use This Font drop-down. Select the font name you chose in step 1.

5. Click OK to close the Excel Options dialog.

6. Close and restart Microsoft Excel for the changes to take effect.

The default font setting has an effect only in new workbooks. It does not affect workbooks previously created.

> **Note**
>
> If you like the concept of using themes to change the look and feel of a document, you should leave the default font setting as BODY FONT and change the font used in the theme.

Wrapping Text in a Cell

You might have one column in a table that contains long, descriptive text. If the text contains several sentences, it would be impractical to make the column wide enough to include the longest value in the column. Excel offers the capability to wrap text on a cell-by-cell basis to solve this problem.

When you wrap text, one annoying feature of Excel becomes evident. All cells in Excel are initially set to have their contents aligned with the bottom of the cell. You probably do not notice this because most cells in Excel are the same height. However, when you wrap text, the cell heights double or more. When this occurs, it becomes evident that the bottom alignment looks strange. To correct this problem, follow these steps:

1. Decide on a reasonable column width for the column that contains the descriptive text. If you try to wrap text in a column that is only 8 points wide, you will be lucky to fit one word per line. If you have the space, a width of at least 24 allows suitable results for the text wrapping.

> **Note**
>
> If the rows are too tall, you will have a tendency to grab the right edge of the column and drag it outward to make the description column wider. A long-standing bug causes Excel not to resize the row heights automatically after this step. Instead, you need to select the Cells section of the Home tab and then select Format, AutoFit Row Height to resize the row height after adjusting the column width.

2. From the Cells section of the Home tab, select Format, Column Width. Choose a width of 24 or greater.

3. Choose the cells in the column to be wrapped.

4. From the Home tab, select Alignment, Wrap Text.

5. Select all cells in the range.

6. From the Home tab, select Alignment, Top Align. The values in the other columns now align with the top of the descriptive text.

Figure 30.43 shows a table where the descriptions in column B have had their text wrapped and all the cells are top-aligned.

Figure 30.43
After wrapping text in a column, you should top-align all columns.

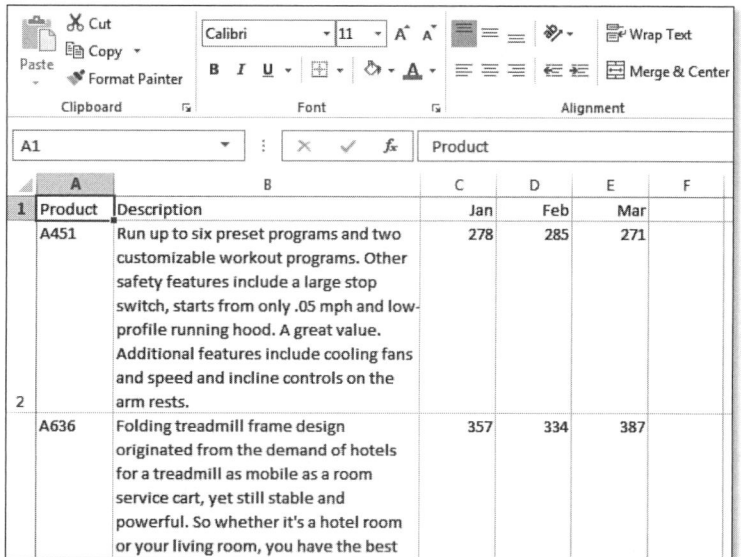

Justifying Text in a Range

When using Excel as a word processor to include a paragraph of explanatory body copy in a worksheet, you usually have to decide where to break each line manually. Otherwise, Excel offers a command that reflows the text in a paragraph to fit a certain number of columns.

For this reason, you should to do some careful preselection work before invoking the command by following these steps:

1. Ensure that your text is composed of one column of cells that contain body copy. It is fine if the sentences extend beyond one column, but the text should be arranged so that the left column contains text and the remaining columns are blank.

2. Ensure that the upper-left cell of your selection starts with the first line of text.

3. Ensure that the selection range is as wide as you want the finished text to be.

4. If your sentences currently extend beyond the desired width, Excel requires more rows in order to wrap the text. Include several extra rows in the selection rectangle. Figure 30.44 shows a suitable-sized selection range.

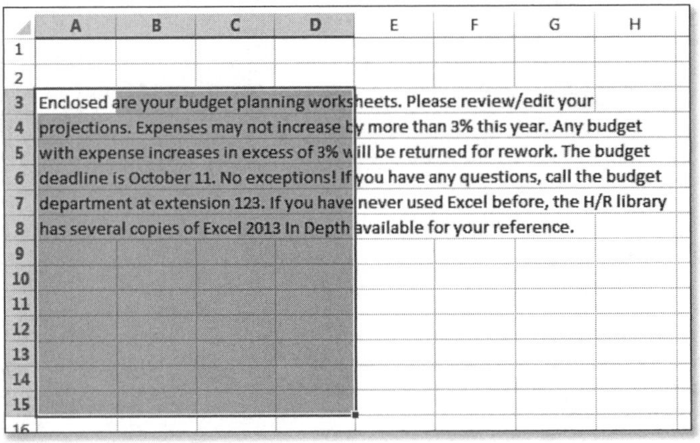

Figure 30.44
You need to select more rows than necessary. The number of columns selected determines the width of the final text.

5. From the Home tab, select Editing, Fill, Justify. Excel flows the text so that each line is shorter than the selection range. Figure 30.45 shows the result.

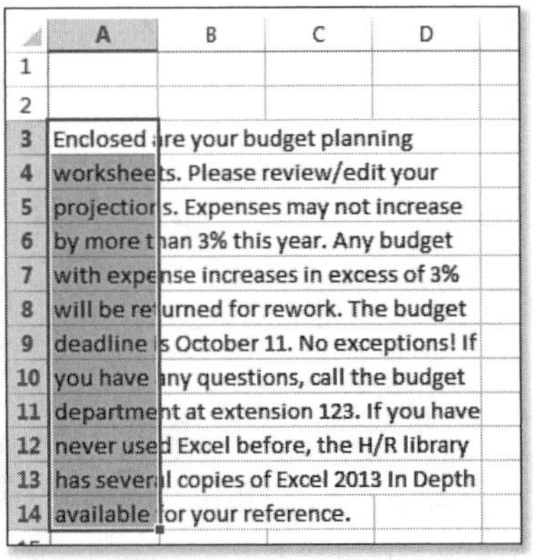

Figure 30.45
Excel flows the text to fit the width of the original selection.

Adding Cell Comments

Cell comments can contain a few sentences or paragraphs to explain a cell. Although the default is for all comments to use a yellow sticky-note format, you can customize comments with colors, fonts, or even pictures.

In the default case, a comment causes a red triangle to appear in a cell. If you hover over the triangle, the comment appears. Alternatively, you can request that comments be displayed all the time. This creates an easy way to add instructions to a worksheet.

Follow these steps to insert a comment, format it, and cause it to be displayed continuously:

1. Select a cell to which you want to add a comment.

2. Select Review, Comments, New Comment, or right-click the cell and select New Comment, or press Shift+F2.

3. The default comment starts with your name in bold on line 1 and the insertion point on line 2. To remove your name from the comment, backspace through your name and then press Ctrl+B to turn off the bold.

 **Note**

Keep in mind that a comment can contain more than 2,000 words of body copy.

4. Type instructions to the person using the worksheet. You can make the instructions longer than the initial size of the comment.

5. After entering the text, click the resize handle in the lower-right corner of the comment. Drag to allow the comment to fit the text.

6. The selection border around the comment can be made of either diagonal lines or dots. If your selection border is diagonal lines, click the selection border to change it to dots.

7. Right-click the selection border and select Format Comment. The Format Comment dialog appears.

8. In the Format Comment dialog, change the font, alignment, colors, and so on, as desired. The Transparency setting on the Colors and Lines tab allows the underlying spreadsheet to show through the comment. If you choose the Fill Color drop-down, you can select Fill Effects and insert a picture as the background in the comment.

9. Click OK to return to the comment.

10. Right-click in the cell and select Show/Hide Comments. This causes the comment to be permanently displayed on the worksheet.

11. To reposition the comment, click the comment. Drag the selection border to a new location.

Figure 30.46 shows a comment that has been formatted, resized, and set to be displayed.

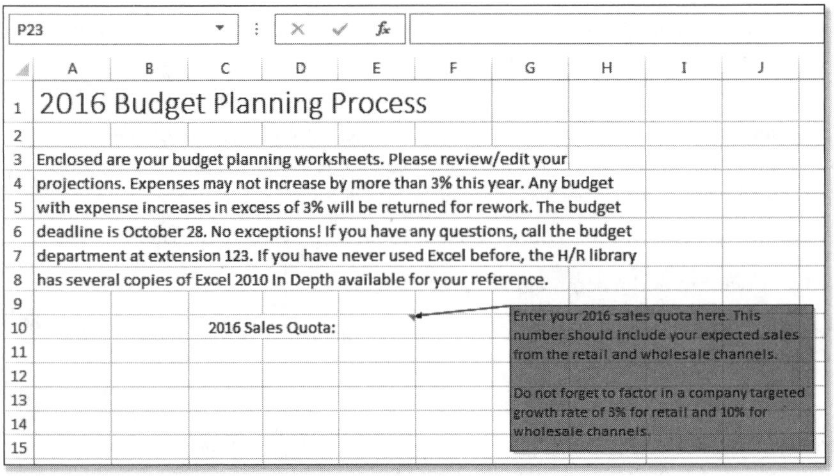

Figure 30.46
Cell comments can provide instructions or tips for people who use your spreadsheet.

Copying Formats

Excel worksheets tend to have many similar sections of data. After you have taken the time to format the first section, it would be great to be able to copy the formats from one section to another section. The next sections in this chapter discuss the two methods offered in Excel 2013 for doing this: pasting formats and using the Format Painter icon.

Pasting Formats

An option on the Paste Options menu allows you to paste only the formats from the Clipboard. The rules for copying and pasting formats are as follows:

- If your original selection is one cell, you can paste the formats to as many cells as you want.

- If your original selection is one row tall and multiple cells wide, you can paste the formats to multiple rows, and the final paste area will be as wide as the original copied range.

- If your original selection is one column wide and multiple cells tall, you can paste the formats to multiple columns, and the final paste area will be as tall as the original copied range.

Follow these steps to copy formats:

1. Select a formatted section of a report. This might be one cell, one row of cells, or a rectangular range of cells.

2. Press Ctrl+C to copy the selected section to the Clipboard.

3. Select an unformatted section of your worksheet. If your selection in step 1 is a rectangular range, you can select just the top-left cell of the destination range.

4. Press Ctrl+V to paste. Press Ctrl again to open the Paste Options menu, as shown in Figure 30.47. Press R to paste only the formats. The formats from the original selection are copied to the new range. Although the amounts initially changed after you pressed Ctrl+C, the original amounts are restored after you press R.

Figure 30.47
Format from the Paste Options menu copies cell formatting without affecting values or formulas.

	A	B	C	D	E	F	G	H
1								
2								
3								
4		Product	Jan	Feb	Mar	Q1		Product
5		A451	278	285	271	834		A451
6		A636	357	334	387	1,078		A636
7		A686	161	144	244	549		A686
8		B416	428	443	425	1,296		B416
9		B519	711	706	764	2,181		B519
10		D553	128	116	104	348		D553
11		D555	376	405	378	1,159		D555
12		D801	353	352	377	1,082		D801
13		D914	296	274	279	849		D914
14		E196	625	611	724	1,960		E196
15		E476	458	471	479	1,408		E476
16		Total	4,171	4,141	4,432	12,744		Total
17								
18								
19		Product	Jul	Aug	Sep	Q3		Product
20		A451	254	258	259	771		A451
21		A636	440	376	363	1,179		A636
22		A686	170	140	239	549		A686
23		B416	416	403	443	1,262		
24		B519	771	714	690	2,175		
25		D553	116	153	115	384		
26		D555	385	374	393	1,152		
27		D801	350	336	345	1,031		
28		D914	362	351	374	1,087		
29		E196	687	626	704	2,017		
30		E476	446	485	530	1,461		
31		Total	4,397	4,216	4,455	13,068		
32								
33								

5. If you have multiple target destinations to format, repeat step 4 as needed.

The disadvantage of using the Paste Formats method is that it does not change column widths. To copy column widths without pasting values, on the Home tab, click the Paste drop-down and then select Paste Special, Column Widths, OK, as shown in Figure 30.48.

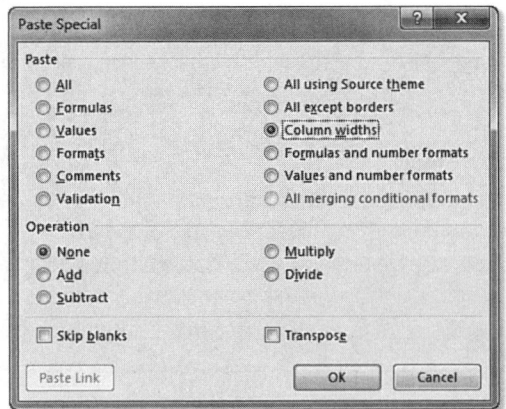

Figure 30.48
Use Paste Special to paste column widths.

Pasting Conditional Formats

Starting in Excel 2010, the rules changed when you paste a range with one conditional formatting onto another range with a different conditional formatting. The copied conditional format replaces the existing conditional formatting. There might be times when you want to merge the existing icon set in the source range with the existing color scale in the target range. In this case, choose All Merging Conditional Formats from the Paste Special dialog, or the elusive icon in the second row, fourth column of the Paste Options menu. Note that this pastes formats, formulas, and borders as well as merges the conditional formats.

Using the Format Painter

The Format Painter icon appears in the Clipboard group of the Home tab. The prominent location of the icon might encourage you to attempt to use this feature. The Format Painter is still tricky to use.

To copy a format from a source range to a destination range, follow these steps:

1. Select the source range. If you want to copy column widths, the source range must include complete columns.

2. Click the Format Painter icon once in the Clipboard group of the Home tab. The mouse icon changes to a plus and a paintbrush.

3. Immediately use the mouse to click and drag to select a destination range. If the source range was five columns wide, the destination range should also be five columns wide.

4. If you accidentally click somewhere else or click the wrong size range, undo and start over.

The tooltip for the Format Painter icon advertises a little-known feature. This feature enables you to copy a format to many different ranges. To do this, follow these steps:

1. Select the source range.

2. Double-click the Format Painter icon.

3. Click a new destination range. The format is copied. Alternatively, you can drag to paint a different size range.

4. Repeat step 3 as many times as you want.

5. When you are done formatting ranges, press Esc or single-click the Format Painter icon to turn off the feature.

Copying Formats to a New Worksheet

You can use a straightforward way to make a copy of a worksheet. This method is better than creating a new worksheet and copying formats from the original sheet to the new sheet. Among its advantages is the fact that column widths and row heights are copied and page setup settings are copied.

To copy a worksheet within the current workbook, follow these steps:

1. Activate the worksheet to be copied.

2. Hold down the Ctrl key. Click the worksheet tab and drag it to a new location. A new sheet is created with a strange name, such as Sheet3 (2).

3. Right-click the sheet tab and select Rename. The cursor moves to the tab, which is now editable.

4. Type a new name and press Enter. The tab has a new name.

To copy a worksheet to a new workbook, follow these steps:

1. Activate the worksheet to be copied.

2. Right-click the sheet tab. Select Move or Copy to display the Move or Copy dialog.

3. In the To Book drop-down, select (new book).

4. Click Create a Copy.

5. Click OK. The single worksheet is copied to a new workbook. Note that all cell styles defined in the original workbook are copied to the new workbook.

Excel in Practice: Elbow Formatting

A slick effect for the upper-left corner of a table is to include two headings: a heading for the column labels and a heading for the row labels. Figure 30.49 shows an example. Although it might require a little trial and error, you can achieve this effect by using these steps:

1. Select the top-left cell in a table.
2. Press the spacebar four or five times.
3. Type the heading for the column labels.
4. Press Alt+Enter twice.
5. Type the heading for the row labels.
6. Press Ctrl+Enter to finish entering the cell and to keep the cell pointer in the top-left cell.
7. From the Home tab, select Font, Borders, More Borders.
8. In the Format Cells dialog, on the Border tab, click the lower-right icon in the Border section. This icon is for a diagonal that goes from the top left to the bottom right.
9. Click OK to close the Format Cells dialog.
10. If the top word hits the diagonal line in the cell, edit the cell and add a space or two before the top word.

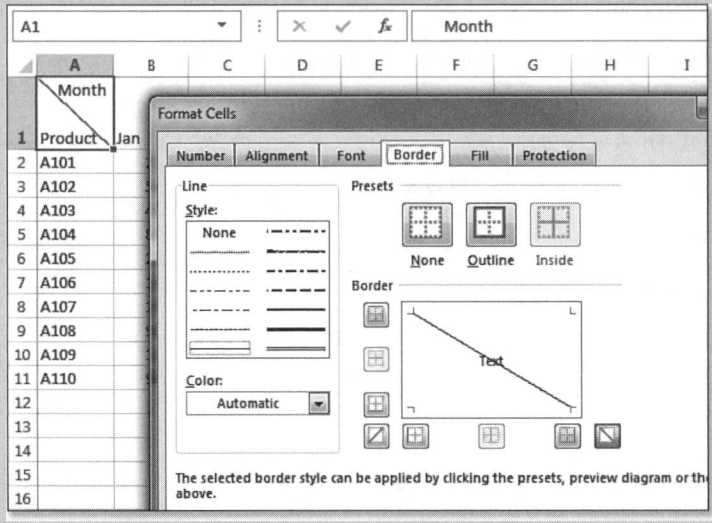

Figure 30.49
The elbow effect is used in cell A1.

Unmerging Cells in Data Pasted from the Web

Web designers use invisible tables as the underlying structure for almost every web page. In an obsessive attempt to control spacing, the author of the HTML for a page often defines that certain values should span two columns or multiple rows. Unfortunately, when you copy and paste this data from the Web to Excel, the spanning of columns or rows causes Microsoft to turn on merged cells in the data. Although merged cells are fine for headings, they should not be used in the middle of data.

To turn off merged cells in data pasted from a web page, follow these steps:

1. Select the pasted data.

2. Display the Format Cells dialog by pressing Ctrl+1.

3. Select the Alignment tab.

4. The Merge Cell icon has a square in the check box to indicate that the selection has a mixture of merged and unmerged cells. Click the box once to select the box. Click the box a second time to clear the Merge Cells check box.

5. Click OK. The merged cells are converted to individual cells. You can now sort and copy the data as usual.

USING DATA VISUALIZATIONS
AND CONDITIONAL FORMATTING

Many people feel their eyes glaze over when they encounter a screen full of numbers. Fortunately, Microsoft has added terrific new data-visualization features to Excel that make those screens full of numbers a little easier on the eyes.

As mentioned in Chapter 2, "Introducing Flash Fill and Quick Analysis," the Quick Analysis icon that pops up on the grid offers six types of data visualizations when you select a range of contiguous data. This usually includes one example of an icon set, one data bar, one color scale, greater than, top 10%, and clear. The Quick Analysis feature is a great way for people to learn that these features exist, but it offers no flexibility in the options presented. If you discovered icon sets through the Quick Analysis feature, this chapter shows you how to use the full-featured data visualizations available on the Home tab.

Excel has had a weak conditional formatting feature since Excel 97 through Excel 2003. It was limited and tricky to use. Excel tipsters often showed the incredibly hard way to make conditional formatting just a bit more powerful.

Beginning with Excel 2007, Microsoft made data visualization easy to use. You are just a few clicks away from features that would have required a Ph.D. in legacy versions of Excel. The following are some of the possibilities in data visualization:

- Adding data bars (that is, tiny, in-cell bar charts) to cells based on the cell value. In Excel 2013, data bars can be negative, include an axis, and have new scaling options.

- Adding color scales to cells based on the cell value. This is often called a *heat map*. Whereas the old conditional formatting would allow you to apply one color if a value exceeds a certain amount, a color scale applies a range from a gradient based on how high the value is.

- Adding icon sets (think traffic lights) to cells based on the cell value. Excel 2013 adds three new icon sets.

- Adding color, bold, italic, strikethrough, number formatting, and so on to cells based on the cell values.

- Quickly identifying cells that are above average.

- Quickly identifying the top *n* or bottom *n*% of cells.

- Quickly identifying duplicate values.

- Quickly identifying dates that are today or yesterday or last week.

- Sorting by color or by icon (after you've added icons or color). This is a huge improvement.

The following are some of the improved conditional formatting features that were added to Excel 2007:

- A cell can meet more than one condition. If you have one rule that makes the cell bold and another rule that makes the cell red, for example, you can have some cells that are red, some that are red bold, some that are bold, and some that are normal.

- There is no longer a limit of only three rules per cell.

- You can easily manage rules. If you want to change the order in which rules are applied, it is easy to reorder the rules.

- It is now obvious that a cell's format can be based on other cell values. This was always the case in legacy versions of Excel, but most people using conditional formatting never discovered the secret. Further, a big improvement is that a formula can now refer to a cell on another worksheet in the current workbook.

Although it is easy to set up basic conditional formatting, you need to know a few tricks, which you discover later in this chapter, for creating better conditional formatting than most people will figure out on their own.

Using Data Bars to Create In-Cell Bar Charts

A *data bar* is a swath of color that starts at the side of a cell and extends into the cell based on the value of the cell. Small numbers get less color. The largest numbers might be 100% filled with color. This creates a visual effect that enables you to visually pick out the larger and smaller values. Figure 31.1 shows many examples of data bars.

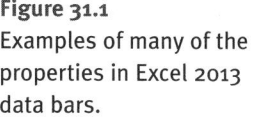

Figure 31.1
Examples of many of the properties in Excel 2013 data bars.

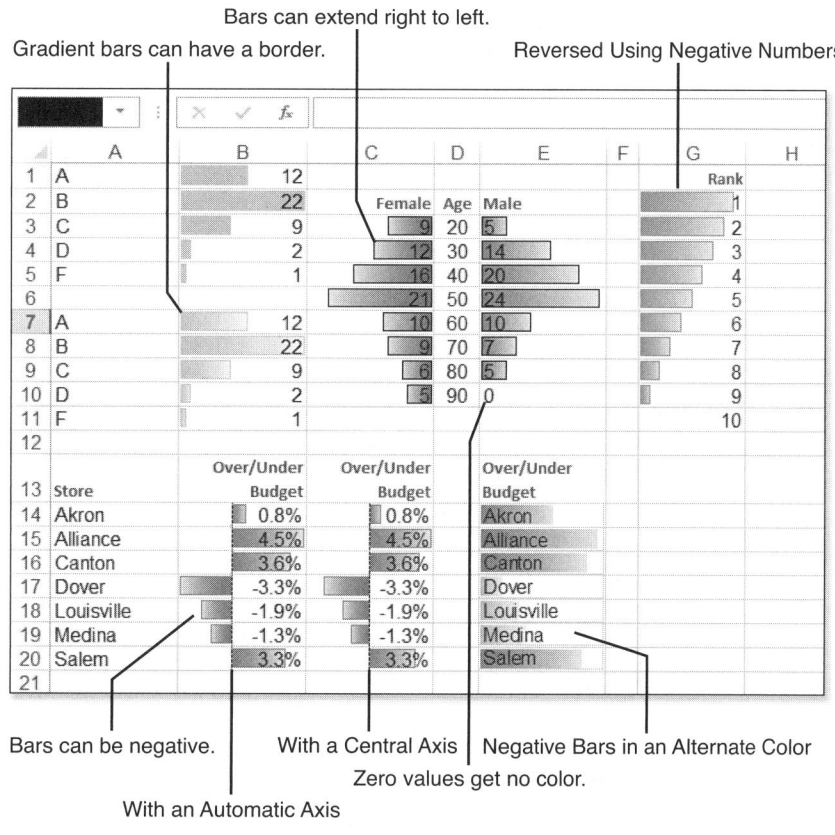

Gradient bars can have a border.

Bars can extend right to left.

Reversed Using Negative Numbers

Bars can be negative.

With an Automatic Axis

With a Central Axis

Negative Bars in an Alternate Color

Zero values get no color.

Many options are available in Excel 2013 data bars:

- Data bars can be solid or a gradient. Data bars with a gradient have a border, so there is no doubt where the data bar ends.

- Values of zero get no data bar, as shown in cell E10.

- Data bars can be negative. Negative bars are shown in a different color and usually extend to the left of a central axis. You have three choices in where to place the zero axis. In cells B14:B20, the setting is Automatic. Because the largest positive number is further from zero than the smallest negative number, the axis appears slightly to the left of center. This allows the bar for 4.5% in B15 to appear larger than the bar for –3.3% in B17. You can also force the axis to appear in the center, as in cells C14:C20. Or, in a bizarre setting, you can force the negative bars to extend in the same direction as the positive values, but with a different color. There are two philosophical ways to show the negative bars. You can assign –3.3% the most color because it is farthest from zero, or you could assign –1.3% the most color because it is the mathematically the largest of the negative numbers (–1.3% > –3.3%). Excel 2013 uses the latter method.

- To "reverse" a data bar—to show the most color for the largest number, multiply the numbers by −1 to make them negative. Use a custom number format of "0;0;0;" to display the negative numbers as positive. Make the negative bars extend in the same direction as positive. You end up with the surprising results shown in G1:G11.

- You can control the color of the positive bar, the positive bar border, the negative bar, the negative bar border, and the axis color.

- Bars can now extend right to left, as shown in cells C3:C10. This allows comparative histograms as in C2:E10.

- You can specify the scale of the data bars. Although the scale is initially set to automatic, you can specify that the min and/or max is set to a certain number or to the lowest value, a percentage, a percentile, or a formula.

- You can choose to show only the data bar and to hide the number in the cell. This is how I managed to get words in cells E14:E20. The numbers are hidden by the conditional formatting dialog, and then a linked picture of the words is pasted over the cells. Because the data bars are on a drawing layer above the regular drawing layer, this works.

- All data bars in a group have the same scale. This is unlike sparklines, where the scale is allowed to change from graphic to graphic.

 Note

If you don't like the six basic colors Excel offers for data bars, you can choose any other color, as described in the next section.

Creating Data Bars

Creating data bars requires just a few clicks. Follow these steps:

1. Select a range of numeric data. Do not include the total in this selection. If the data is in noncontiguous ranges, hold down the Ctrl key while selecting additional areas. This range should be composed of numbers of similar scale. For example, you can select a column of sales data or a column of profit data.

2. From the Home tab, select Conditional Formatting, Data Bars. You see six built-in colors for the data bars: blue, green, red, orange, bright blue, and pink. The colors appear both in solid and gradient forms. Select one of them. The result is a swath of color in each cell in the selection, as shown in Figure 31.2.

 Caution

In step 1, if you attempt to select a range that contains both units sold and revenue dollars, the size of the revenue numbers overpowers the units sold numbers, and no color appears in the units sold cells.

Figure 31.2
After applying a data bar, you can easily see that California is a leading exporter of agriculture products.

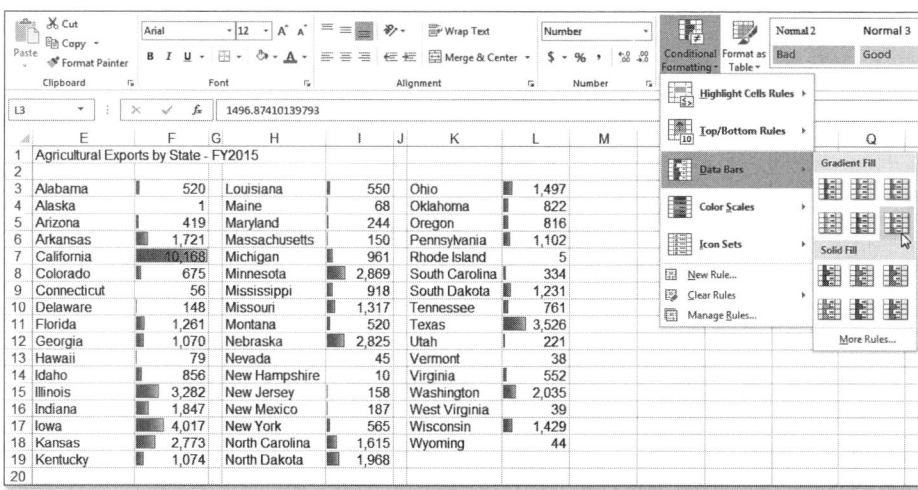

Customizing Data Bars

By default, Excel assigns the largest data bar to the cell with the largest value and the smallest data bar to the cell with the smallest value. You can customize this behavior by following these steps:

1. From the Conditional Formatting drop-down on the Home tab, select Manage Rules.

2. From the Show Formatting Rules drop-down, select This Worksheet. You now see a list of all rules applied to the sheet.

3. Click the Data Bar rule.

4. Click the Edit Rule button. Alternatively, you could simply double-click the rule in step 3. You see the Edit Formatting Rule dialog, as shown in Figure 31.3.

A number of customizations are available in this dialog, as detailed next.

- Select the Show Bar Only setting to hide the numbers in the cells and to show only the data bar.

- For the Minimum and Maximum values, you can choose from Automatic, Number, Percent, Percentile, Formula, and Smallest/Largest Number. If you select Automatic, Excel chooses a minimum and maximum value. You can override this by setting one value to a specific number.

- In the Bar Appearance section, you can specify gradient or solid fill for the bar. You can specify a solid border or no border. Two color chooser drop-downs enable you to change the color of the bar and the border.

- The Bar Direction drop-down enables you to select Context, Left to Right, or Right to Left. The default choice of Context is always left to right, unless you are in an international edition of Excel in which the language reading order is right to left.

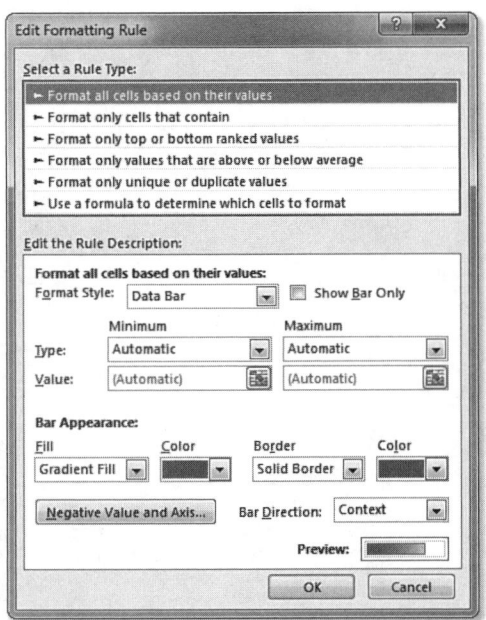

Figure 31.3
You customize data bars by using the Edit Formatting Rule dialog.

When you choose Negative Values and Axis, you have new settings to adjust the color of the bar and the border for negative bars. You can also control whether the zero axis is shown at the cell midpoint or at an automatic location based on the relative size of the negative and positive numbers. If the axis is shown, you can adjust the color as well.

Showing Data Bars for a Subset of Cells

In the data bars examples given in the previous sections, every cell in the range receives a data bar. But what if you just want some of the values (for example, the top 20% or the top 10) to have data bars? The process for making this happen isn't intuitive, but it is possible. You apply the data bar to the entire range. Then you add a new conditional format (a very plain format) to all the cells that you don't want to have data bars. For example, you might tell Excel to use a white background on all cells with values outside of the top 10.

The final important step is to manage the rules and tell Excel to stop processing more rules if the white background rule is met. This requires clever thinking. If you want to apply data bars to cells in the top 10, you first tell Excel to make all the cells in the bottom 40 look like every other cell in Excel. Turning on Stop If True (in the Conditional Formatting Rules Manager dialog) is the key to getting Excel to not apply the data bar to cells with values outside of the top 10.

Figure 31.4 shows data bars applied to only the top 10 states.

Figure 31.4
Using Stop If True after formatting the lower 21 with no special formatting allows the data bars to appear only for the top states.

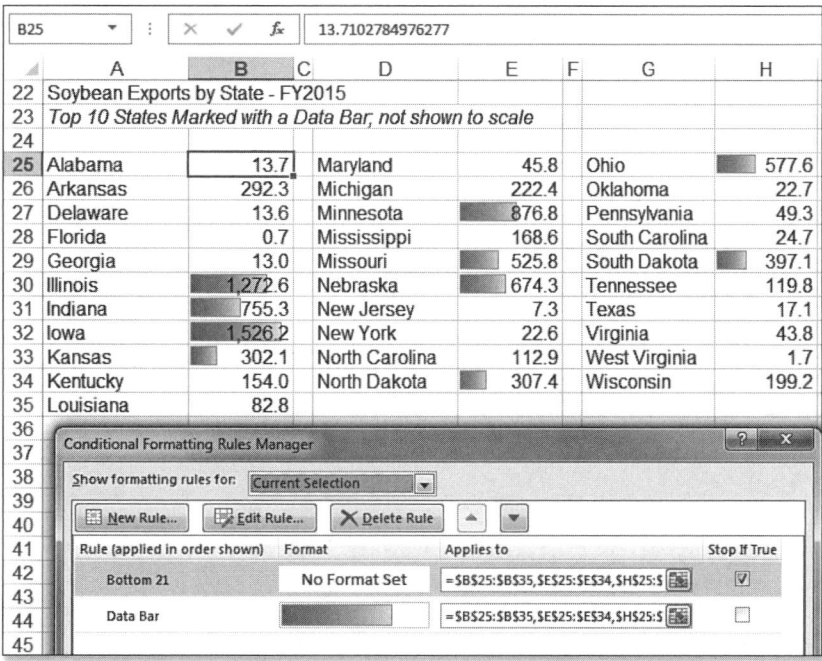

Using Color Scales to Highlight Extremes

Color scales are similar to data bars. Instead of having a variable-size bar in each cell, however, color scales use gradients of two or three different colors to communicate the relative size of each cell. Here's how you apply color scales:

1. Select a range that contains numbers. Be sure not to include headings or total cells in the selection.

2. Select Conditional Formatting, Color Scales from the Home tab.

3. From the Color Scales fly-out menu, select one of the 12 styles to apply the color scale to the range. (Note that this fly-out menu offers subtle differences that you should pay attention to. The first six options are scales that use three colors. These are great onscreen or with color printers. The last six options are scales that use two colors. These are better with monochrome printers.)

In a two-color red/white color scale, the largest number is formatted with a dark red fill. The smallest number has a white fill. All the numbers in between receive a lighter or darker shade of pink based on their position within the range (see Figure 31.5).

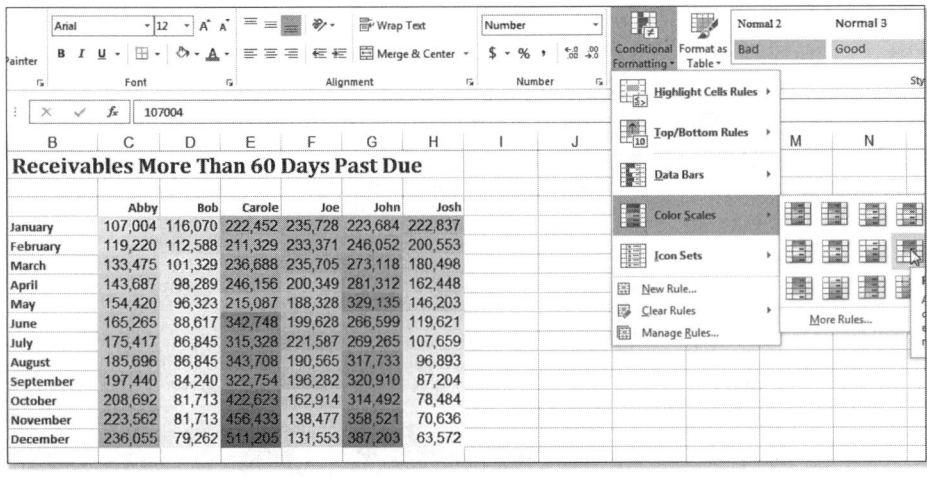

Figure 31.5
Excel provides a range of shading, depending on the value. You can see that Carole's and John's receivables have been increasing throughout the year.

Customizing Color Scales

You are not limited to the color scales shown in the fly-out menu. If you select Home, Conditional Formatting, Manage Rules, Edit Rule, you can choose any two or three colors for the color scale.

You also can choose where to assign the smallest, largest, and midpoint values (see Figure 31.6). Column E and the Edit Formatting Rule show how to highlight central values. Using a three-color scale, the minimum and maximum are set to white whereas the middle numbers are assigned a color.

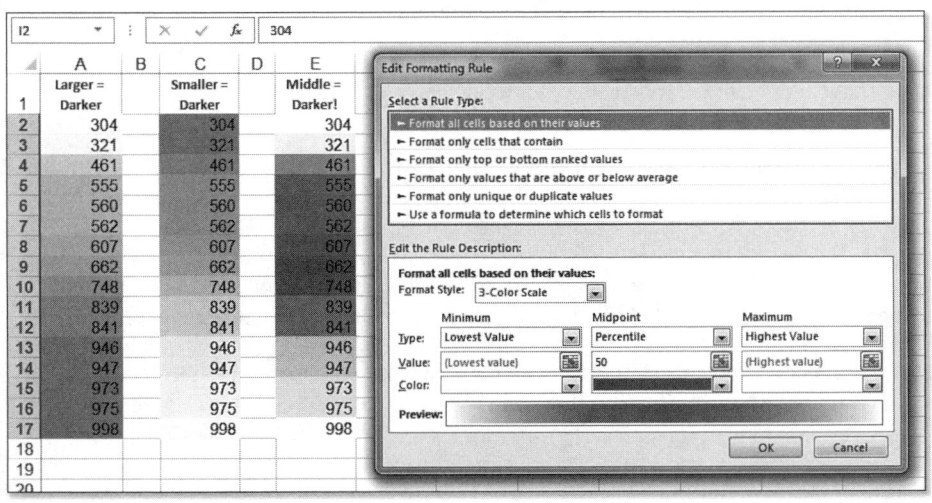

Figure 31.6
You can choose any colors to use in the color scale.

You should be aware of one strange situation: Normally, Excel lets you mix conditional formatting in the same range. You might apply both a color scale and an icon set.

If you have a three-color scale applied to some cells and choose a different three-color scale from the fly-out menu, the latter choice overwrites the first choice.

However, Excel treats two-color scales as a different visualization than three-color scales. If you have a three-color scale applied and you then try to switch it to a two-color scale using the fly-out menu, Excel creates two rules for those cells. The latter two-color scale is the only one to appear in Excel 2013, but you might be confused when you go to the Manage Rules dialog to see two different rules applied to the cells.

Using Icon Sets to Segregate Data

Icon sets, which were popular with expensive management reporting software in the late 1990s, have now been added to Excel. An icon set might include green, yellow, and red traffic lights or another set of icons to show positive, neutral, and negative meanings. With icon sets, Excel automatically applies an icon to a cell, based on the relative size of the value in the cell compared to other values in the range.

Excel 2013 ships with 20 icon sets that contain three, four, or five different icons. The icons are always left-aligned in the cell. Excel applies rules to add an icon to every cell in the range:

- **Three-icon sets**—For the three-icon sets, you have a choice between arrows, flags, two varieties of traffic lights, signs, stars, triangles, and two varieties of what Excel calls 3 Symbols. This last group consists of a green check mark for the good cells, a yellow exclamation point for the middle cells, and a red X for the bad cells. You can either get the symbols in a circle—that is, 3 Symbols (Circled)—or alone on a white background (that is, 3 Symbols). One version of the arrows is available in gray. All the other icon sets use red, yellow, and green.

- **Four-icon sets**—For the four-icon sets, there are two varieties of arrows, a black-to-red circle set, a set of cell phone power bars, and a set of four traffic lights. In the traffic light option, a black light indicates an option that is even worse than the red light. The power bars icons seem to work well on both color displays and monochromatic printouts.

- **Five-icon sets**—For the five-icon sets, there are two varieties of arrows, boxes, a five-power bar set, and an interesting set called 5 Quarters. This last set is a monochromatic circle that is completely empty for the lowest values, 25% filled, 50% filled, 75% filled, and completely filled for the highest values.

 Tip

After creating several reports with icon sets, I have started to favor the cell phone power bars, which look good in both color and black and white.

Setting Up an Icon Set

Icon sets require a bit more thought than the other data visualization offerings. Before you use icon sets, you should consider whether they will be printed in monochrome or displayed in color. Several of the 20 icon sets rely on color for differentiation and look horrible in a black-and-white report.

To set up an icon set, follow these steps:

1. Select a range of numeric data of a similar scale. Do not include the headers or total rows in this selection.

2. From the Home tab, select Conditional Formatting, Icon Sets. Select one of the 20 icon sets. Figure 31.7 shows the 3 Triangles choice selected.

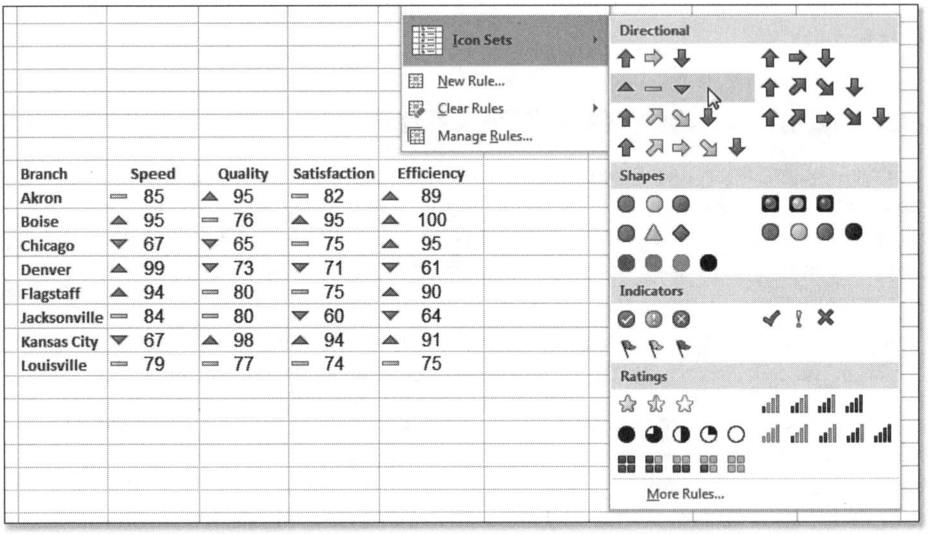

Figure 31.7
You can choose from the 20 icon sets.

Branch	Speed	Quality	Satisfaction	Efficiency
Akron	═ 85	▲ 95	═ 82	▲ 89
Boise	▲ 95	═ 76	▲ 95	▲ 100
Chicago	▼ 67	▼ 65	═ 75	▲ 95
Denver	▲ 99	▼ 73	▼ 71	▼ 61
Flagstaff	▲ 94	═ 80	═ 75	▲ 90
Jacksonville	═ 84	═ 80	▼ 60	▼ 64
Kansas City	▼ 67	▲ 98	▲ 94	▲ 91
Louisville	═ 79	═ 77	═ 74	═ 75

Moving Numbers Closer to Icons

In the top rows of Figure 31.8, the icon set has been applied to a rectangular range of data. The icons are always left-aligned. Numbers are typically right-aligned. This can be problematic. Someone might think that the icon at the left side of cell G3 is really referring to the right-aligned number in F3, for example.

You might try centering the numbers to get the numbers closer to the icons in rows 7–9. This drives purists crazy because the final digit of the 100 in cell H8 doesn't line up with the final digits of cells H7 and H9.

A better solution is to use the Alignment tab of the Format Cells dialog. Select Right (Indent) for the horizontal alignment. Bump the indent figure up to move the numbers closer to the icon. In rows 12–14, the indent is set at four characters.

If you don't want to show numbers at all, you can edit the conditional formatting rule and select Show Icon Only. Rows 17–19 show this solution. Ironically, when the numbers are no longer displayed, you can position the icons by using the Left Align, Center Align, and Right Align icons.

The over-the-top solution in rows 22–24 involve using Show Icon Only and then pasting a linked picture of the numbers from other cells.

Figure 31.8
Changing the alignment of the numbers moves them closer to the icon.

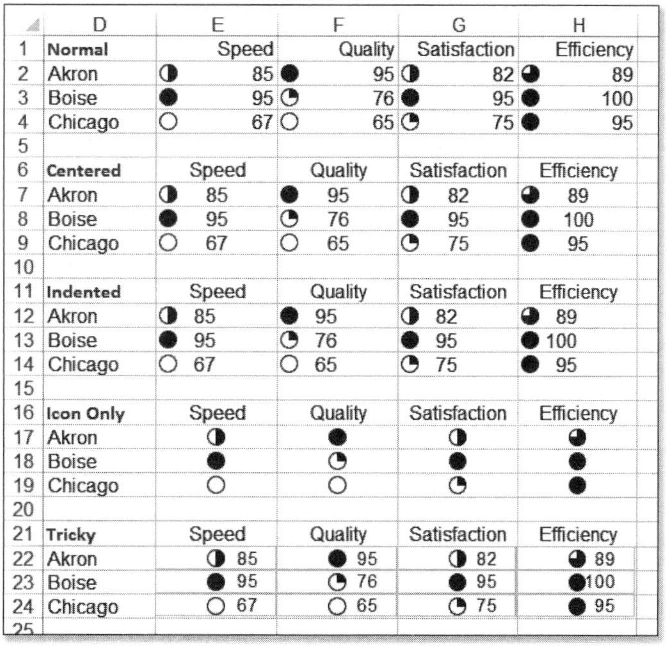

	D	E	F	G	H
1	Normal	Speed	Quality	Satisfaction	Efficiency
2	Akron	◑ 85	● 95	◑ 82	◕ 89
3	Boise	● 95	◔ 76	● 95	● 100
4	Chicago	○ 67	○ 65	◔ 75	● 95
5					
6	Centered	Speed	Quality	Satisfaction	Efficiency
7	Akron	◑ 85	● 95	◑ 82	◕ 89
8	Boise	● 95	◔ 76	● 95	● 100
9	Chicago	○ 67	○ 65	◔ 75	● 95
10					
11	Indented	Speed	Quality	Satisfaction	Efficiency
12	Akron	◑ 85	● 95	◑ 82	◕ 89
13	Boise	● 95	◔ 76	● 95	● 100
14	Chicago	○ 67	○ 65	◔ 75	● 95
15					
16	Icon Only	Speed	Quality	Satisfaction	Efficiency
17	Akron	◑	●	◑	◕
18	Boise	●	◔	●	●
19	Chicago	○	○	◔	●
20					
21	Tricky	Speed	Quality	Satisfaction	Efficiency
22	Akron	◑ 85	● 95	◑ 82	◕ 89
23	Boise	● 95	◔ 76	● 95	●100
24	Chicago	○ 67	○ 65	◔ 75	● 95
25					

Here are the steps to create rows 22 through 24:

1. Select one of the cells with the icon set formatting.

2. From the Home tab, select Conditional Formatting, Manage Rules.

3. In the Conditional Formatting Rules Manager dialog, click the Icon Set rule and then click Edit Rule.

4. In the middle of the Edit Formatting Rule dialog, select Show Icon Only. Click OK twice to close the two dialog boxes.

5. Select all the cells that contain icons and click the Align Center button on the Home tab.

6. Page down so that you are outside of the printed range. Stay in the same column. Set up a formula to point to the number in the top-left corner of the icon set range. Copy this formula down and over to be the same size as your icon set range. This gives you a range of just the numbers.

7. Format this range of numbers to be right-aligned with an indent of 1.

8. Copy this range of numbers.

9. Go back to the original set of icons and select Paste, Picture Link. A picture of the original numbers appears behind the icons.

Mixing Icons or Hiding Icons

As of Excel 2010, it is possible to mix icons from different sets. In Figure 31.9, A2:C7 is a five-icon set with a mix of icons—gold star, green flag, yellow caution sign, and so on. You start with any five-icon set. Edit the rule and change the icon for each position.

In A11:D17, scores of 95 and higher receive a gold star, and all other scores get no icon. The open dialog box shows how this is done; the lower two rules show No Cell Icon.

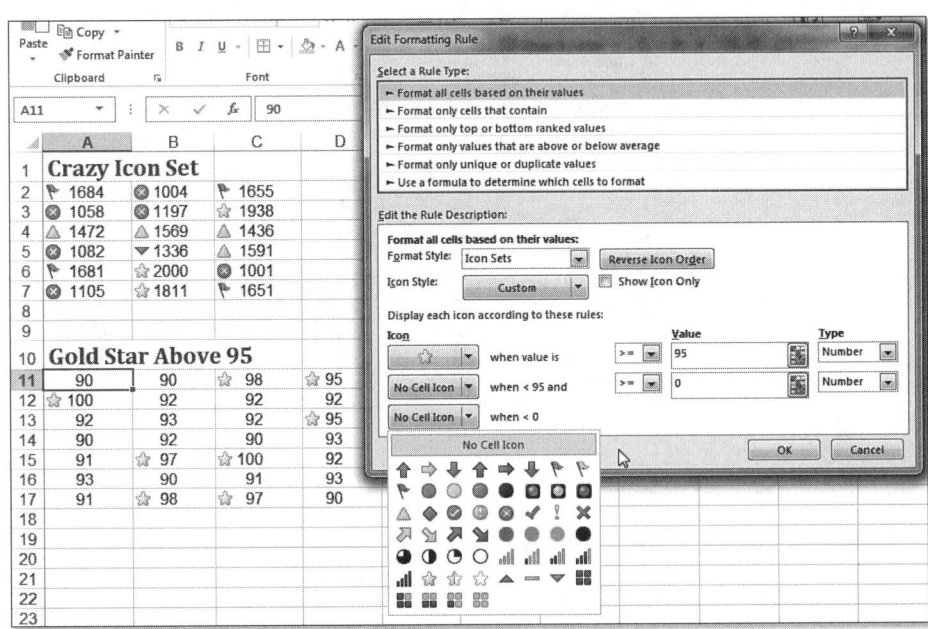

Figure 31.9
Mix icons to create unusual sets.

Using the Top/Bottom Rules

The top/bottom rules are a mix of the old- and new-style conditional formatting. They are similar to the old conditional formatting because you must select one formatting scheme to apply to all the cells that meet the rule. However, they are new because rather than specifying a particular number limit, you can ask for any of these conditions:

- **Top 10 Items**—You can ask for the top 10, top 20, or any number of items.

- **Top 10%**—If 20% of your records account for 80% of your revenue, you can highlight the top 20% or any other percentage.

- **Bottom 10 Items**—To highlight the lowest-performing records, select Bottom 10.

- **Bottom 10%**—To highlight the records in the lowest 5%, select Bottom 10%.

- **Above Average**—You can highlight the records that are above the average. As with all the other rules, the average is recalculated as the numbers in the range change.

- **Below Average**—You can highlight the records that are below the average.

Setting Up Conditional Formatting Rules

To set up any of these conditional formatting rules, follow these steps:

1. From the Home tab, select Conditional Formatting, Top/Bottom Rules, and then choose one of the six rule types shown in Figure 31.10.

Figure 31.10
You can choose one of these six rule types.

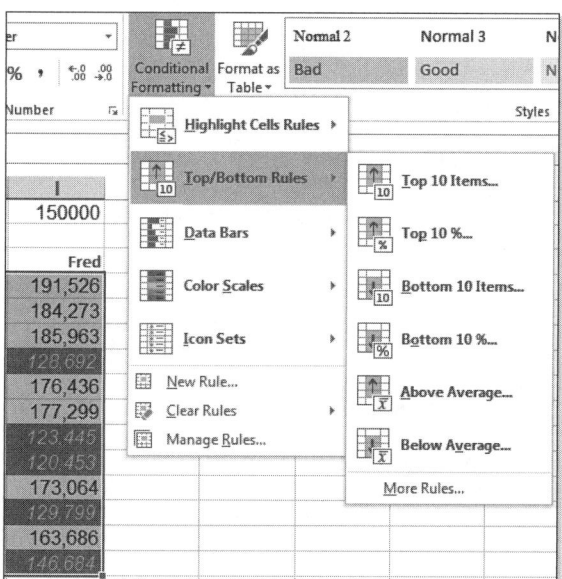

2. The dialog for above/below average does not require you to select a threshold value, but for the other four rule types Excel asks you to enter the value for N. As you change the spin button, the Live Preview feature keeps updating the selection with the appropriate number of highlighted cells.

3. The drop-down portion of the dialog initially shows Light Red Fill with Dark Red Text. When you select the drop-down, you have six default styles and the powerful Custom Format option. If one of the six styles is suitable, choose it. Otherwise, proceed to step 4.

4. If you choose Custom Format, you are taken to a special version of the Format Cells dialog box. This version has Number, Font, Border, and Fill tabs. You can choose settings on one or more of these tabs. Click OK to close the Format Cells dialog.

5. Click OK to close the dialog box for your particular rule.

Excel adds the rule to the list of rules. By default, rules added most recently are applied first.

Using the Highlight Cells Rules

The traditional conditional formatting rules appear in the Highlight Cells Rules menu item of the Conditional Formatting drop-down, along with several new rules. The traditional rules include Greater Than, Less Than, Between, and Equal To. Note that slightly obscure rules such as Greater Than or Equal To are hidden behind the More Rules option. The following are the traditional rules:

- **Text That Contains**—This rule enables you to highlight cells that contain certain text.

- **A Date Occurring**—With this rule, you can define conceptual rules such as yesterday, today, tomorrow, last week, this week, next week, last month, this month, next month, or in the last seven days.

- **Duplicate Values**—With this rule, you can highlight both records of a duplicate or highlight all the records that are not duplicated.

The options for Highlight Cell Rules are shown in Figure 31.11.

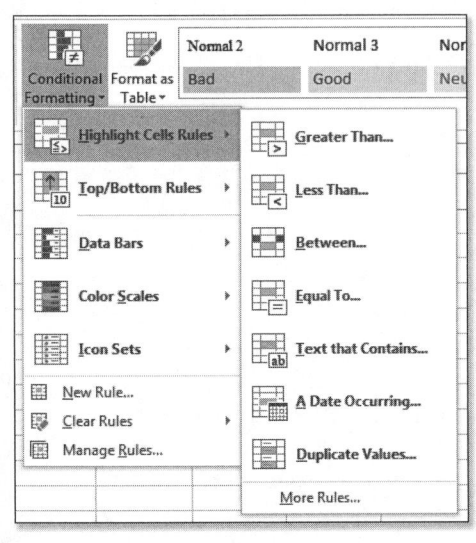

Figure 31.11
Many powerful and easy conditions are available in the Highlight Cell Rules menu.

Highlighting Cells by Using Greater Than and Similar Rules

You might think that Greater Than and the similar rules for Less Than, Equal To, and Not Equal To are some of the less powerful conditional formatting rules. In fact, these are the first rules described in this chapter that you can use to base the conditional format threshold on a particular cell or cells.

This enables you to build some fairly complex rules without having to resort to the formula option of conditional formatting.

To set up a rule to highlight values greater than a threshold, follow these steps:

1. Select a range of data. Unlike with the other rules, you might choose to include totals in this selection.

2. Select Home, Styles, Conditional Formatting, Highlight Cell Rules, Greater Than to display the Greater Than dialog box.

3. Enter a threshold value in the Greater Than dialog.

4. Choose one of the six formats from the With drop-down. Or choose Custom Format from the With drop-down to have complete control over the number format, font, borders, and fill.

5. Click OK to apply the format.

By way of example, let's look at several options for filling in the threshold value in the Greater Than dialog box. Figure 31.12 shows the conditional formatting rule for all cells greater than 200,000. This is a simple threshold value.

Figure 31.12

You can format all cells greater than a certain value, such as 200,000.

	C	D	E	F	G	H	I
	Monthly Quota:	150000	150000	79000	225000	175000	150000
		Adam	Bill	Chris	Donna	Ed	Fred
January		131,369	155,769	58,421	255,092	183,467	191,526
February		199,094	152,907	64,380	226,175	183,736	184,273
March		176,510	135,689	61,378	228,949	231,998	185,963
April		124,482	137,682	60,432	208,101	186,445	128,692
May							
June							
July							
August							
September							
October							
November		171,101	152,490	52,431	231,417	200,500	103,000
December		120,209	168,683	51,394	295,438	195,420	146,684

Greater Than

Format cells that are GREATER THAN:

200000   with   Custom Format...

OK   Cancel

You can specify a cell as the threshold value. You can either use the reference icon at the right side of the box or type an equal sign and the cell reference. In Figure 31.13, the formula highlights any cell that does not exceed the quota in row 1 above the current cell using =D$1.

The formula in Figure 31.13 has to be written for the active cell. Although D4:I15 is the selected range, the name box shows that D4 is the active cell. The formula of =D$1 is compared to the active cell of D4. The threshold cell then becomes the cell in row 1 that is in the same column as each cell in the selection.

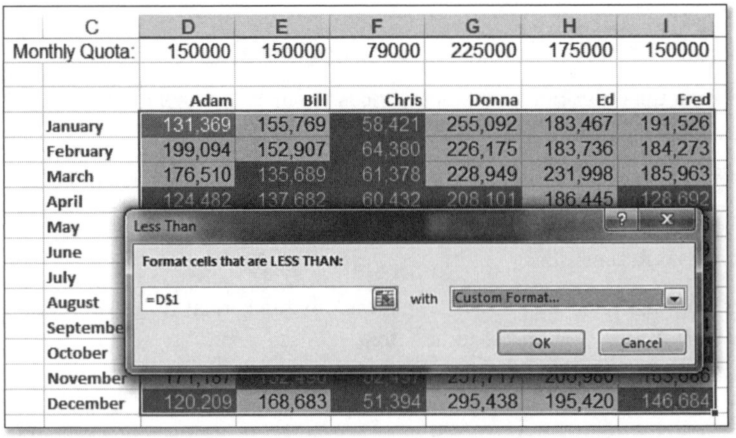

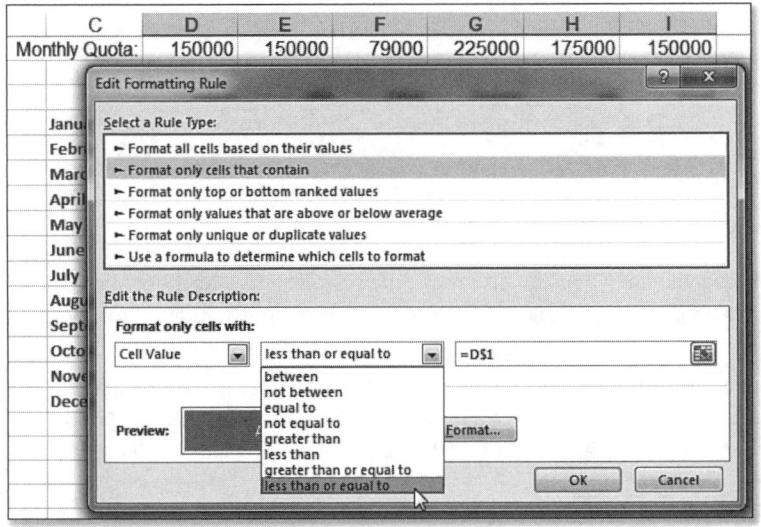

Figure 31.13
You can format all cells less than a certain cell. Prefix the cell reference with an equal sign.

The Greater Than concepts discussed here apply equally well to the Less Than, Equal To, and Between rules. If you need to access other rules, such as Less Than or Equal To, you can follow these steps:

1. Set up the rule by using Less Than.

2. From the Conditional Formatting icon, select Manage Rules.

3. Select the Less Than rule and click Edit Rule.

4. Use the drop-down shown in Figure 31.14 to select Less Than or Equal To.

Figure 31.14
After using a quick format with Less Than, you can go to the Manage Rules option to access Less Than or Equal To.

Comparing Dates by Using Conditional Formatting

The date feature was added in Excel 2007. If you are familiar with the reporting engine in Quicken or QuickBooks, the list of available dates will seem similar. A nice feature is that Excel understands the dates conceptually. If you define a feature to highlight dates from last week, the rule automatically updates based on the system clock. If you open the workbook a month from now, new dates are formatted, based on the conditional formatting.

Some of the date selections are self-explanatory, such as Yesterday, Today, and Tomorrow. Other items need some explanation:

- A week is defined as the seven days from Sunday through Saturday. Choosing This Week highlights all days from Sunday through Saturday, including the current date.

- In the Last 7 Days includes today and the six days before today.

- This Month corresponds to all days in this calendar month. Last Month is all days in the previous calendar month. For example, if today is May 1 or May 31, the period Last Month applies to April 1 through April 30.

Figure 31.15 shows the various formatting options, with a system date of July 26, 2012.

The date formatting option would be particularly good for highlighting the items in a to-do list that are due, overdue, or about to be due.

Figure 31.15
In the Last 7 days is the odd option among the date formatting options.

	A	B	C	D	E	F	G
1	Today is Thursday, Jul 26, 2012						
2	**This Week**		**Last Week**		**Next Week**		**Last 7 Days**
3	Tue 7/24		Wed 7/18		Tue 7/31		Wed 7/18
4	Wed 7/25		Thu 7/19		Wed 8/1		Thu 7/19
5	Thu 7/26		Fri 7/20		Thu 8/2		Fri 7/20
6	Fri 7/27		Sat 7/21		Fri 8/3		Sat 7/21
7	Sat 7/28		Sun 7/22		Sat 8/4		Sun 7/22
8	Sun 7/29		Mon 7/23		Sun 8/5		Mon 7/23
9	Mon 7/30		Tue 7/24		Mon 8/6		Tue 7/24
10	Tue 7/31		Wed 7/25		Tue 8/7		Wed 7/25
11	Wed 8/1		Thu 7/26		Wed 8/8		Thu 7/26
12	Thu 8/2		Fri 7/27		Thu 8/9		Fri 7/27
14	**Today**		**Yesterday**		**Tomorrow**		
15	Tue 7/24		Tue 7/24		Tue 7/24		
16	Wed 7/25		Wed 7/25		Wed 7/25		
17	Thu 7/26		Thu 7/26		Thu 7/26		
18	Fri 7/27		Fri 7/27		Fri 7/27		
19	Sat 7/28		Sat 7/28		Sat 7/28		
21	**This Month**		**Last Month**		**Next Month**		
22	Sat 5/26		Sat 5/26		Sat 5/26		
23	Tue 6/26		Tue 6/26		Tue 6/26		
24	Thu 7/26		Thu 7/26		Thu 7/26		
25	Sun 8/26		Sun 8/26		Sun 8/26		
26	Wed 9/26		Wed 9/26		Wed 9/26		
27							

Identifying Duplicate or Unique Values by Using Conditional Formatting

Conditional formatting claims that it can mark either duplicate or unique values in a list of values. It seems that Microsoft missed an opportunity to include a different version of unique values than the one that it included. It would be very useful if Microsoft had included an option to mark only the first occurrence of each unique item.

In column A of Figure 31.16, Excel has marked the duplicate values. Both Adam and Bill appear twice in the list, and Excel has marked both occurrences of the values. You might be tempted to sort by color to bring the red cells to the top, but you still have to carefully go through to delete one of each pair.

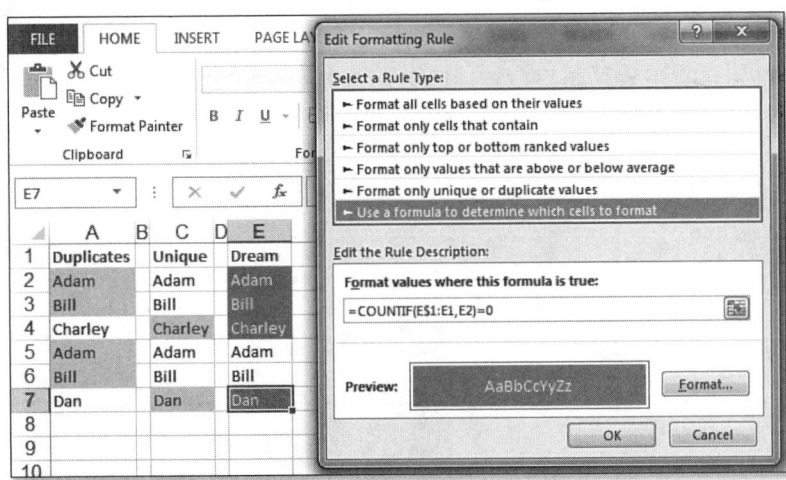

Figure 31.16
Marking duplicates or unique values with the built-in conditional formatting choices requires additional work to decide which of the duplicates to keep in order to produce a unique list.

In column C of Figure 31.16, Excel has applied a conditional format to the unique values in the list. In Excel parlance, this means that Excel marks the items that appear only once in a list. If you would keep just the marked cells as a list of the unique names in the list, you would effectively miss any name that was duplicated.

In a perfect world, this feature would have the logic to include one of each name in the conditional format. The conditional formatting in column E resorts to using the fairly complex formula of =COUNTIF(E$1:E1,E2)=0 to highlight the unique values.

➡ *To learn more about using formulas to mark cells,* **see** *"Using a Formula for Rules,"* **p. 1011.**

Using Conditional Formatting for Text Containing a Value

The Text That Contains formatting rule is designed to search text cells for cells that contain a certain value.

Figure 31.17 contains a column of cells. Each cell in the column contains a complete address, with street, city, state, and ZIP. It would normally be fairly difficult to find all the records for a particular state. However, this is easy to do with conditional formatting. Follow these steps:

1. Select a range of cells that contains text.

2. From the Home tab, select Conditional Formatting, Highlight Cell Rules, Text That Contains.

3. In the Refers To box, enter a comma, a space, and the state you want to find. Note that this test is not case sensitive (for example, searching for ", pa" is the same as searching for ", PA").

4. Choose an appropriate color from the drop-down.

5. Click OK to apply the format.

Figure 31.17
Without having to use a wildcard character, you can use the new Text That Contains dialog to mark cells based on a partial value.

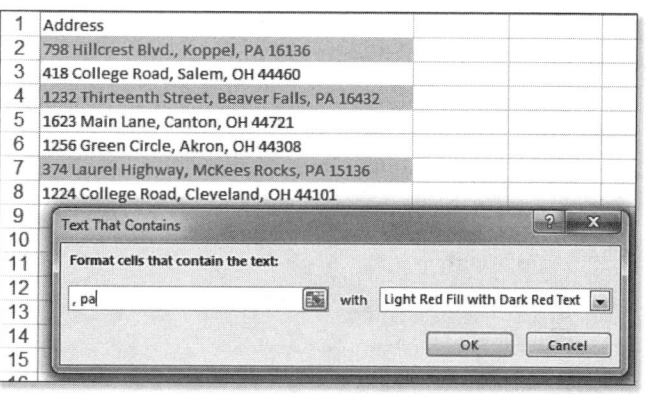

As with the Find dialog box, you are allowed to use wildcard characters. You can use an asterisk (*) to indicate any number of characters and a question mark (?) to indicate a single character.

Tweaking Rules with Advanced Formatting

All the formats available from icons on the Conditional Formatting group are referred to as *quick formatting*. According to legend, the Excel team bought and read a number of Excel books, and if the author spent a page trying to explain a convoluted way to format something using formulas in conditional formatting, then that option became a quick formatting icon.

Every quick formatting item has an option at the bottom called More Rules. When you click this option and get to the New Formatting Rule dialog, you find options that didn't make it as quick formatting icons.

The next section of this chapter discusses using the formula option for conditional formatting. Almost anything is possible by using the formula option, but it is harder to use than the quick formatting icons. If Excel offers a built-in, advanced option, you should certainly use it instead of trying to build a formula to do the same thing.

The lists shown in Tables 31.1 and 31.2 are organized to show all the options for specific rule types. The six rule types are in the top of the New Formatting Rule dialog. Items listed in the right column are advanced options that are available only by clicking More Rules.

Table 31.1 Options for Formatting Cells Based on Content

Option	Advanced Options Available Using More Rules
Cell value between x and y	Cell value not between x and y
Cell value equal to x	Cell value not equal to x
Cell value greater than x	Cell value less than x
Cell value greater than or equal to x	Cell value less than or equal to x
Specific text containing x	Specific text not containing x
	Specific text beginning with x
	Specific text ending with x
Dates occurring yesterday	
Dates occurring today	
Dates occurring tomorrow	
Dates occurring in the last 7 days	
Dates occurring last week	
Dates occurring next week	
Dates occurring last month	
Dates occurring this month	
Dates occurring next month	
More Rules	Blanks
	No Blanks
	Errors
	No Errors

Table 31.2   Options for Formatting Values That Are Above or Below Average

Option	Advanced Options Available Using More Rules
Above the average for the selected range	One standard deviation above the average for the selected range
	Two standard deviations above the average for the selected range
	Three standard deviations above the average for the selected range
Below the average for the selected range	One standard deviation below the average for the selected range
	Two standard deviations below the average for the selected range
	Three standard deviations below the average for the selected range

Using a Formula for Rules

Excel has three dozen quick conditional formatting rules and twice as many advanced conditional formatting rules. What if you need to build a conditional format that is not covered in the quick or advanced rules? As long as you can build a logical formula to describe the condition, you can build your own conditional formatting rule based on a formula.

Some basic tips can help you successfully use formulas in conditional formatting rules. When you understand these rules, you can build just about any rule you can imagine.

One feature introduced in Excel 2007 is that a formula is allowed to refer to cells on another worksheet. This enables you to compare cells on one worksheet to a worksheet from a previous month or to use a VLOOKUP table on another worksheet.

Getting to the Formula Box

To set up a conditional format based on a rule, follow these steps:

1. Select a range of cells.

2. In the Style group of the Home tab, select Conditional Formatting, Add New Rule.

3. In the New Formatting Rule dialog, choose the rule type Use a Formula to Determine Which Cells to Format. You now see the New Formatting Rule dialog.

The following sections give you some tips for building a successful formula.

Working with the Formula Box

Following are the key concepts involved in writing a successful formula:

- The formula must start with an equal sign.

- The formula must evaluate to a logical value of TRUE or FALSE. The numeric equivalents of 1 and 0 are also acceptable results.

- When you use the mouse to select a cell or cells on a worksheet, Excel inserts an absolute reference to the cell. This is rarely what you need for a successful conditional formatting rule. You can immediately press the F4 key three times to toggle away the dollar signs in the formula.

- You probably have many cells selected before starting the conditional formatting rule. You need to look at the left of the formula bar to see which cell in the selection is the active cell. If you write a relative formula, you should write the formula that will appear in the active cell. Excel applies the formula appropriately to all cells. This is a key point.

- If the dialog box is in the way of cells you need to select, you can drag the dialog out of the way by dragging the title bar. If you absolutely need to get the dialog out of the way, you can use the Collapse Dialog button at the right side of the formula box. This collapses the dialog to a tiny area. To return it to full size, you click the Expand Dialog button at the right side of the collapsed dialog.

- The formula box is one of the evil set of controls that have three possible statuses: Enter, Point, and Edit. Look in the lower-left corner of the Excel screen. The status initially says that you are in Enter mode. This means that Excel is expecting you to type characters such as the equal sign. If, instead, you use the mouse to select a cell, Excel changes to Point mode. In Point mode, the selected cell's address is added to the formula box.

 Caution

The annoying thing about the formula box is that you always start in something called Enter mode. When you are in Enter mode, if you use any of the navigation keys (that is, Page Down, Page Up, left arrow, right arrow, down arrow, up arrow), Excel changes to Point mode and starts inserting random cell addresses at inappropriate places in your formula. Press F2 until you see Edit in the lower-left corner of the Excel window. You can now use the left and right arrows to move through the formula.

The following sections describe several useful conditional formatting rules. This list only scratches the surface of the possible rules you can build. It is designed to generate ideas of what you can accomplish by using conditional formatting.

Finding Cells Within Three Days of Today

The quick formatting feature offers to highlight yesterday or today or tomorrow, but what if you need to find any cells within three days of today, either plus or minus? If the active cell is B2, use a formula of =ABS(TODAY()-B2)<4.

Finding Cells Containing Data from the Past 30 Days

The Excel quick formatting option offers to highlight this month or last month. However, highlighting this month or last month can mean a number of vastly different things. Highlighting this month on the second of the month shows a lot of the future and only one day of the past. The same rule on the 29th of the month highlights a lot of the past and only a few days of the future. It would be more predictable to write a rule that shows the past 30 days.

You create this rule similarly to the way you created the Next Seven Days rule in the preceding section. You first compare the date in the cell by using TODAY() to make sure the date in the cell is less than today. If the active cell is F4, you use the following formula:

```
=AND(F4<TODAY(),(TODAY()-F4)<=30)
```

To generalize this formula for other periods, such as the past 15 days or the past 45 days, you change the 30 to a different number.

Highlighting Data from Specific Days of the Week

The WEEKDAY() function converts a date to a number from 1 through 7. When used without any additional arguments, the value of WEEKDAY(date) for a Sunday is 0 and Saturday is 7.

Say the active cell is H4. If you needed to highlight all the Wednesdays, for example, you could check to see whether WEEKDAY(H4)=4. To find all the Fridays, you would check to see whether WEEKDAY(H4)=6. To find either date, you would use =OR(WEEKDAY(H4)=4,WEEKDAY(H4)=6).

To generalize this formula, you could substitute any number from 1 through 7 to highlight Sundays, Mondays, and so on.

Highlighting an Entire Row

Most conditional formatting highlights a cell based on the value in that cell. In this case, you would like to highlight the entire row for the row with the largest product sale.

In Figure 31.18, cell A2 is the active cell. You need to select the entire range of A2:G14. Your goal is to write a rule for all of those cells that will look at column D for the same row as the cell. In this case and in any case in which you want to highlight the entire row based on one column, you use the mixed reference with a dollar sign before the column letter. You want to see whether =$D2 is equal to the largest value in the range.

To find the largest value in column D, you use an absolute reference to D2:D14—that is, =MAX($D$2:$D$14). The conditional formatting formula for this specific case is =$D2=MAX($D$2:$D$14).

To change this rule to highlight the smallest value in column D, you change MAX to MIN. To base the test on another column, change D to the other column in three places in the formula.

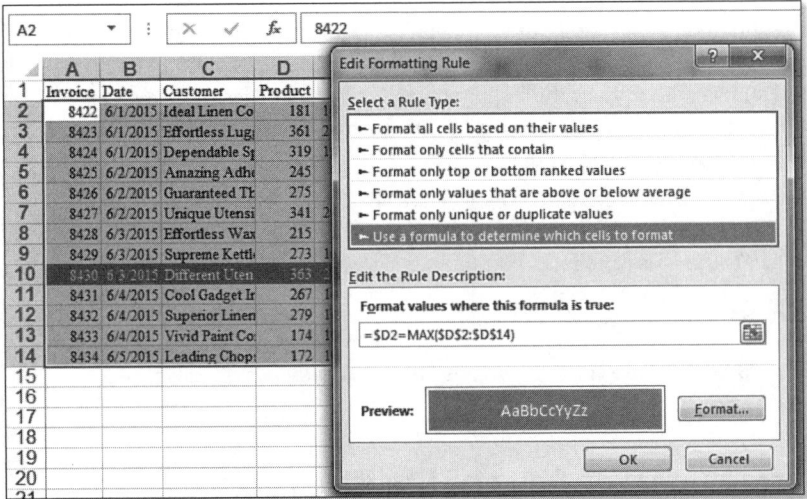

Figure 31.18
The combination of a mixed reference and the absolute reference enables you to highlight an entire row.

Highlighting Every Other Row Without Using a Table

You might find yourself using the Format as Table feature only to add alternating bands of color to a table. If you don't need the other table features, using a conditional format can achieve the same effect.

Do you remember when you were first learning to do division? You would express the quotient as an integer and then a remainder. For example, 9 divided by 2 is 4 with a remainder of 1, sometimes written as 4R1.

The trick to formatting every other row is to check the remainder of the row number after dividing by 2. Excel has functions that make this easy. First, =ROW() returns the row number of the given cell. Next, =MOD(ROW(),2) divides the row number by 2 and tells you the remainder. The task is then simply to highlight the rows where the remainder is equal to 1 or equal to zero.

In Figure 31.19, the active cell is A2. The formula to achieve the banding effect is =MOD(ROW(),2)=0.

To generalize this formula for your particular data set, you could change A2 to be the active cell's address.

 Note

The Excel table formatting enables you to create alternate formatting where every other two rows are formatted. To duplicate this with conditional formatting, you have to divide the row number by 4 and examine the remainder. There are four possible remainders: 0, 1, 2, and 3. You can either look for results greater than 1 or less than 2 to be formatted. To do this, you change the preceding formula to =MOD(ROW(),4)<2.

Figure 31.19
It is possible to create a row-banding effect without using the Excel table formatting.

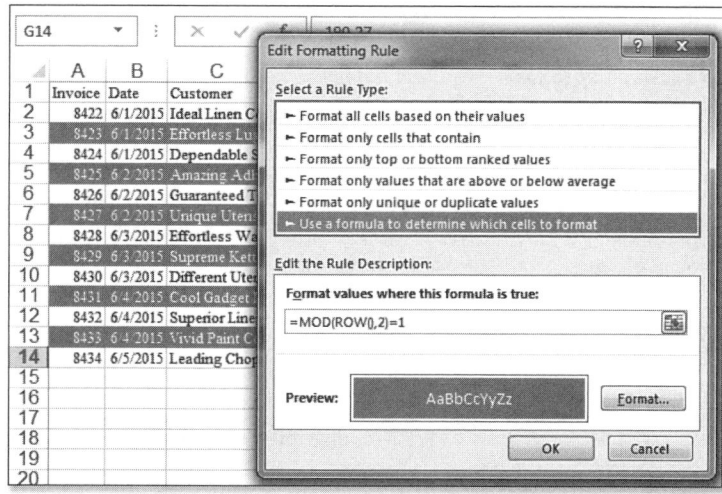

Combining Rules

Excel now allows multiple conditions to evaluate to TRUE. In legacy versions of Excel, when a condition was met, Excel quit evaluating additional conditions. For each rule in Excel 2013, you can decide whether Excel should stop evaluating additional rules or whether Excel can continue evaluating rules.

For example, one rule might set the font color to blue. Another rule might set the font style to bold. Cells meeting both rules can be formatted in blue bold. Cells meeting one rule can be either blue or bold. Cells meeting neither rule will be in normal font style.

If two rules attempt to create conflicting formatting, Excel uses the first rule in the list. For example, if Rule 1 turns the font red and Rule 7 turns the font blue, the font is red.

Ten types of formatting can be changed in each cell. Naturally, each type conflicts with others of the same type. Only the first rule that evaluates to TRUE can change the fill color.

Very few formatting styles conflict with each other. Only the cell fill and the color scale are mutually exclusive. Otherwise, you can have up to nine rules evaluate to TRUE for any given cell. Table 31.3 illustrates the interplay between the ten formatting styles.

Table 31.3   Cell Formatting Styles

Style	Effect
Font color	Changes the font color for cells meeting a condition.
Font style	Applies normal, bold, italic, or bold italic to cells meeting a condition.
Underline	Adds or removes single or double underlining for cells meeting a condition.

Style	Effect
Strikethrough	Applies strikethrough for cells meeting a condition.
Number format	Changes the number format for cells meeting a condition.
Border	Alters the borders for cells meeting a condition. You might think that you could combine two rules that both affect the border. For example, you might want to make the top border blue for cells that meet Rule 1 and the right border red for cells that meet Rule 2. Even though this conceptually makes sense, Excel allows only the first true rule to change the borders.
Cell fill	Changes the cell background for cells meeting a condition. Amazingly, this works fine in combination with data bars. (The cell fill appears to the right of the data bar.) It also works fine with icon sets, and it works fine with all the preceding options. However, cell fill and color scales cannot coexist. Only the first true rule appears in the cell.
Color scale	Changes the cell background for all cells in the range, with the color being determined by the value of one cell in relation to the other cells in the range. This rule can coexist with everything but itself and the cell fill formatting.
Data bar	Adds an in-cell bar chart in each cell. This rule can coexist with any other type of rule.
Icon set	Adds an icon in the left side of the cell. This rule can coexist with any other type of rule.

Clearing Conditional Formats

You can use a number of ways to clear conditional formats. A few quick options are available from the ribbon:

- You can highlight the entire range with conditional formatting and then use Home, Styles, Conditional Formatting, Clear, Selected Cells. This removes all conditions from the current selection.

- To clear all the conditional formats from the current worksheet, you can use Home, Styles, Conditional Formatting, Clear, Entire Sheet. This is handy if you have only one set of rules set up on the sheet. You can delete all the rules without having to select the entire range.

- If you have rules assigned to a pivot table or a table, you can select one cell in the pivot table or table. This enables new options for Home, Styles, Conditional Formatting, Clear, This Table or Home, Styles, Conditional Formatting, Clear, This PivotTable.

 Note

Deleting columns or rows deletes the rules associated with those columns or rows. Selecting Home, Editing, Clear, All or Home, Editing, Clear, Formats removes the rules.

If you have multiple rules assigned to a range and you need to delete just a portion of those rules, you can use Home, Styles, Conditional Formatting, Manage Rules. In the Conditional Formatting Rules Manager dialog, you should use the top drop-down to display rules in the current selection, this worksheet, or any other worksheet. You can then highlight a specific rule and click the Delete Rule button.

Extending the Reach of Conditional Formats

In every example in this chapter you have been advised to highlight the entire range before setting up the conditional format. It is also possible to assign a conditional format to one cell and then extend the rule to other cells. There are three ways to copy a conditional format:

- You can select a cell with the appropriate rule and then press Ctrl+C to copy it. Then you select the new range and select Home, Clipboard, Paste, Paste Special, Formats, OK to copy the conditional formatting from the one cell to the entire range.

- Select a cell with the appropriate rule. Click the Format Painter icon in the Home tab. Select a new range to paste the conditional format to the new range.

- You can select Home, Styles, Conditional Formatting, Manage Rules. Then you select a rule. In the Applies To column you see the list of cells that have this rule. You can type a new range there or use the collapse button to make the dialog smaller so that you can highlight the new range.

When you are using conditional formats that compare one cell to the entire range, using the second method is safer to ensure that Excel understands your intention.

Special Considerations for Pivot Tables

This section talks about the special conditional formatting options that are available for pivot tables.

➡ **See** Chapter 23, "Using Pivot Tables to Analyze Data," to review the detailed discussion of pivot tables.

A typical pivot table might contain two or more levels of summary data. In the pivot table in Figure 31.20, for example, cells H4:J16 contain sales data. However, if you tried to create a data bar for this entire range, the subtotal values in rows 9 and 15 would make the data bars in the other rows look too small.

To set up a data bar for the detail items in a pivot table, follow these steps:

1. Select a detail cell in the pivot table. In Figure 31.20, a cell such as H4 will do.

2. Choose any visualization from the Conditional Formatting drop-down. In Figure 31.20, the 3-stars icons set is shown.

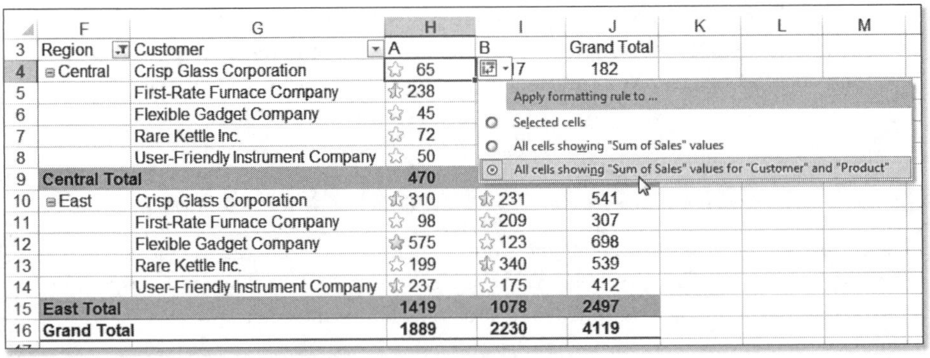

PART

IV

Figure 31.20
The trick to a successful conditional format in a pivot table is to apply the format only to items at the same detail level.

3. A tiny pivot icon appears to the right of the cell. Click this drop-down to access three conditional formatting settings for pivot tables. The choices are

   ■ **Selected Cells**—You can apply the rule to just the one cell. This is not what you want in this case.

   ■ **All cells showing "Sum of Sales" values**—You can apply the rule to cells including the total column, grand total row, and all the subtotal rows. Remember that the size of the grand total causes all the detail items to have data bars that are too small.

   ■ **All cells showing "Sum of Sales" values for "Customer" and "Product"**—This is the option you use most of the time. The meaning of this option is dependent on careful selection of a detail cell in step 1. If you selected a subtotal row instead, this option would apply the data bars only to the subtotal rows.

   Your actual words in the second and third options vary, depending on the fields displayed in your pivot table. For successful pivot table formatting, select the third option.

Excel in Practice: Showing Data Bars in Two Colors

This obscure trick has been posted in the Microsoft Excel team blog. It turns out that every conditional formatting rule has a formula value that determines whether the rule is shown. Microsoft exposed this rule in the user interface for some conditional formatting rules but not for the data bars. You can, however, access it in the VBA editor!

Suppose that your goal is to add a data bar to a range of cells. If the value is 90 or greater, you would like the bars to be green. If the value is 89 or less, you would like the bars to be red. Here's how you accomplish this:

1. Select the range of cells to be formatted.

2. Use the conditional formatting quick options to add to the range of a data bar that is red.

3. Select Conditional Formatting, Add New Rule to add a second rule that applies a green data bar. You see only the most recent rule, so all the data bars are green.

4. Note in the Name box which cell is the active cell. You need this information in step 7.

5. Press Alt+F11 to switch to the VBA editor.

6. Press Ctrl+G to display the Immediate pane.

7. Type `Selection.FormatConditions(1).Formula = "=if(A2>89, TRUE, FALSE)"` and then press Enter. Cell A2 should be changed to the name of the active cell from step 4.

The result is that the green bars are visible only when the value is 90 or greater. In all other cases, the bars appear red.

GRAPHING DATA USING EXCEL CHARTS

Scott Ruble is paying attention. Scott and his team are in charge of charting on the Microsoft Excel team. They have watched people try to create charts in Excel. With 93 different chart types and millions of possible variations, people were not getting the right chart. The charting focus for Excel 2013 is to significantly lower the bar for creating and customizing charts.

Starting in Excel 2013, the Recommended Charts feature analyzes your data and suggests charts that might look good. The rules behind the chart recommendations are surprisingly good. You will create good-looking charts in most cases by going with one of the recommendations. Excel never suggests a 3-D chart because they misrepresent the data.

After you have the chart, a paintbrush icon offers 10 to 15 different ways to style the chart. Styles range from minimalist to intense. If you are a disciple of Professor Edward R. Tufte and you believe every bit of ink on the chart has to have a meaning, you will find minimalist styles. If you are a reader of *Vogue* or *GQ*, you will find designer-quality chart styles. Although I previously dismissed the Chart Layouts drop-down introduced in Excel 2007, the chart styles in Excel 2013 offer combinations that would have been possible but very difficult before.

Here are the highlights of the charting improvements in Excel 2013:

- Excel suggests recommended charts.

- No legend for charts with only a single series.

- New data labels can appear in a balloon, getting data from other cells.

- Easy-to-Label XY charts.

- Remarkable error correction, even if you accidentally include grand totals.

- If Excel sees repeating groups in your data, it might recommend a pivot chart to summarize and chart the data. (Unfortunately, the pivot chart still puts a legend for a single series.)

Charting is covered in a few other places in this book. Chapter 26, "Creating Interactive Dashboards with Power View or GeoFlow," covers Power View, a new tool that animates pivot charts over time. Chapter 33, "Using Sparklines," covers sparklines, which are tiny, word-sized charts introduced in Excel 2010.

Choosing from Recommended Charts

The data in Figure 32.1 is a simple trend of monthly sales. Headings for the months appear in B1:M1. Sales appear in B2:M2. A label of "Sales" appears in A2. The label in A1 is optional. To create a chart, follow these steps:

1. Select A1:M2.

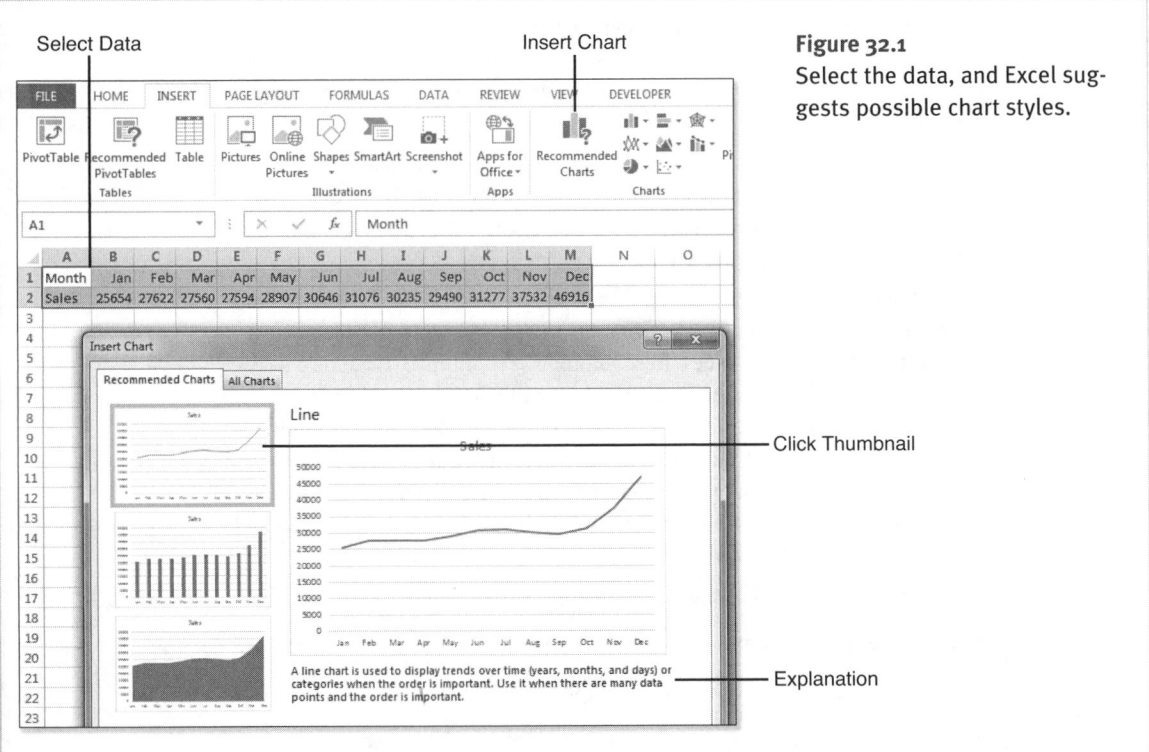

Figure 32.1
Select the data, and Excel suggests possible chart styles.

2. On the Insert tab, choose Recommended Charts. Excel displays the new Insert Chart dialog. The Recommended Charts tab shows three thumbnails on the left side. Click each thumbnail to see a larger chart on the right side. A description below the chart explains why this chart is appropriate. In Figure 32.2, the dialog explains that a line chart is used to show data over time.

Figure 32.2
You have the right chart type, but you aren't done yet.

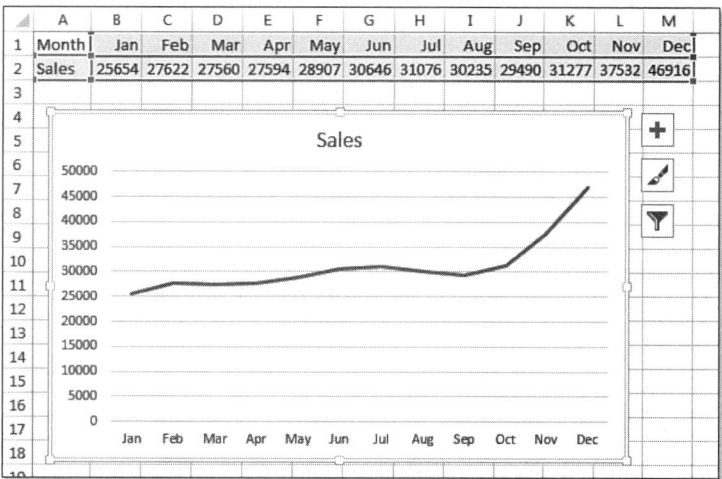

3. Optionally, click the other recommended charts thumbnails on the left to see them and read the description on the right. From the three charts suggested, choose the one that looks best to you.

4. Click OK to insert the chart in the center of the visible window.

5. Grab the border of the chart and drag to the appropriate place. (See the following tip if you have to move the chart more than a screenful of data away.)

6. Notice the three icons to the right of the chart and the two contextual ribbon tabs that appear while the chart is selected. The following sections show you how to use those tools to polish the chart.

 **Tip**

If your chart appears in row 500 and you want it to appear in row 5, you should consider changing how you select a data set. Say that you have data in A1:C500 that should appear on a chart. You would probably start in A1, press Ctrl+Shift+Down Arrow and Ctrl+Shift+Right Arrow. You end up with rows 490 through 520 visible on your screen. When you insert a chart, it appears at the bottom of your data instead of the top of your data.

After the chart appears in row 500, it is very difficult to drag it back to the top. Instead, select the chart, press Ctrl+X to cut, press Ctrl+Home to move to the top, and press Ctrl+V to get the chart at the top of the data. You can now move it to the correct position.

It is simpler to move the focus back to the top of the worksheet before you insert the chart. When you have A1:C500 selected, press Ctrl+Period once or twice to move to the next corner of the selection. When you can see the top of the data set, insert the chart.

The simplest choice is to change how you select the data in the first place. If you start in A1 and press Ctrl+*, Excel selects the current region of data without moving the window to show the bottom of the data set. Insert the chart, and it appears near the top of the data set.

Using Paintbrush Icon for Styles

In prior versions of Excel, I would complain about how ugly the choices were in the Quick Layout drop-down in the ribbon. In Excel 2013, you can ignore that drop-down in the ribbon and head straight for the paintbrush icon to the right of the chart.

Click the paintbrush icon to reveal a fly-out menu with 12 to 15 different professionally designed chart styles for the selected chart (see Figure 32.3).

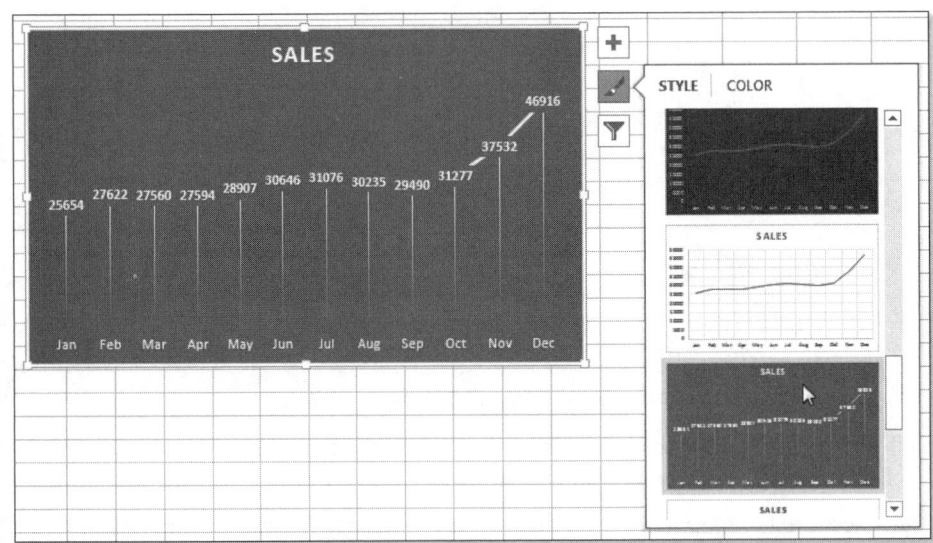

Figure 32.3
New in Excel 2013 are these professionally designed chart styles.

The chart styles in this menu look new and stylish. Consider the style shown in Figure 32.3. You have fading drop lines extending from a data label down toward the baseline of the chart. The chart area and plot area are dark blue and all chart elements are white. The marker is really the data label. The actual line only appears between October and December because of the jump in sales. I went back to Excel 2010 to see whether it's possible to create the identical chart. You can. It takes 26 separate steps, most of which require at least two mouse clicks. And that is 26 steps when you are trying to mimic an existing chart. If you were to try to come up with those steps without having a pattern to follow, it would be very time consuming. Excel 2013 makes this chart style a few clicks away.

The chart styles rely on rarely used settings that were available in previous versions of Excel. Replicating the chart style above would require more than 50 clicks in Excel 2010.

Note

I am not suggesting that you try these steps in Excel 2010. They are listed here to show you all of the settings that happen automatically when you choose the chart style in Figure 32.3: Insert, Line, Line without Markers. Delete legend. Chart area fill color to dark blue. Plot area fill color to dark blue. Series line color to white. Horizontal Axis labels to white. Title to white. Delete gridlines. Delete left axis. Layout, Data Labels, Center. Change data label font color to white. Add drop lines. Select drop lines and press Ctrl+1. Choose Gradient Line. Open the Direction drop-down and choose Linear Down. Click on first Gradient Stop. Open the Color drop-down and choose White. Click on the third Gradient stop. Open the Color drop-down and choose Blue. While the Format dialog is open, click on month names. Change Major Tick Mark Type to None. Click Line color category and choose No Line. While the Format dialog is open, click on data label in the chart. Click the Fill Category. Choose a Solid Fill. Fill Color is Blue. Click Close.

It is not just that one of the chart styles looks great. Most of them look interesting and would have required a lot of steps back in Excel 2010. Figure 32.4 shows nine of the chart layouts.

Figure 32.4
Nine of the 15 chart styles available for line charts.

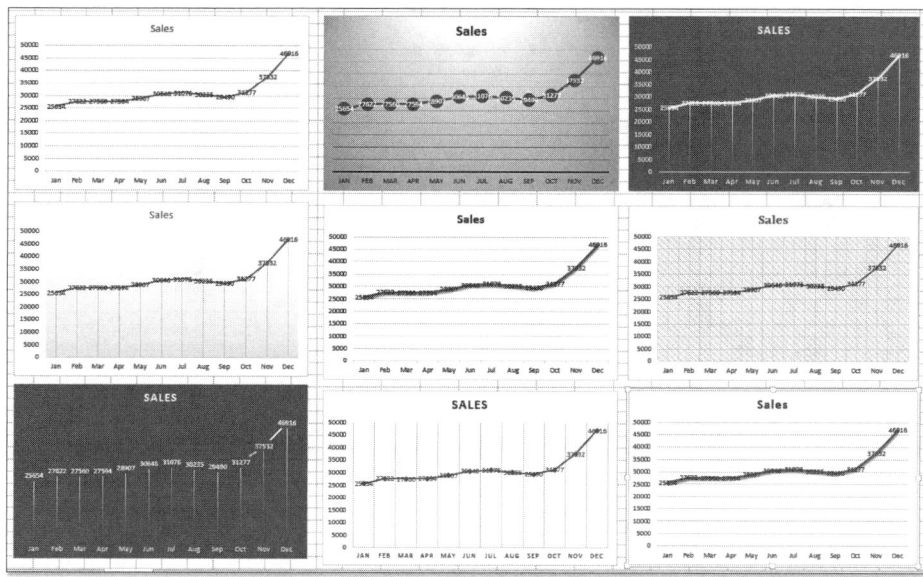

Deleting Extraneous Data Using the Funnel

The data in Figure 32.5 includes a Total formula in column N. Accidentally including this data in the chart is a common mistake. The size of the Total column (12 times an average month) makes the final column in the chart way too tall and makes all of the other columns indistinguishable from each other.

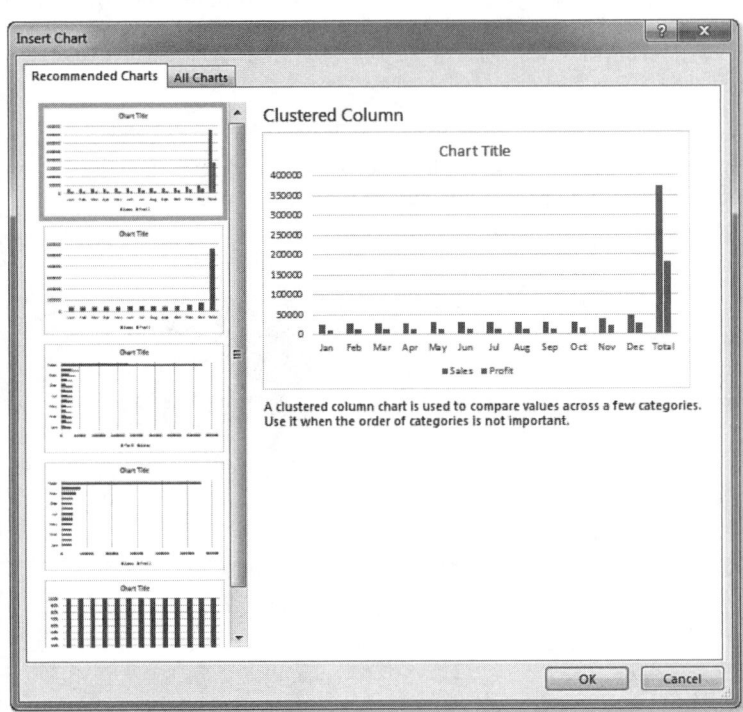

Figure 32.5
This chart is doomed because the selected data includes the Total column.

The funnel icon to the right of the chart makes it easy to remove unwanted series or points from the chart. Click on the Funnel. The top of the fly-out menu (which has scrolled out of view in Figure 32.6) provides check boxes where you can turn off either Revenue or Profit. Scroll to the bottom of the list and uncheck the choice for Total. Click Apply, and the scale of the chart goes back to a size that lets you see the growth from January to December (see Figure 32.6).

Figure 32.6
Use the funnel icon to remove unwanted points from the chart.

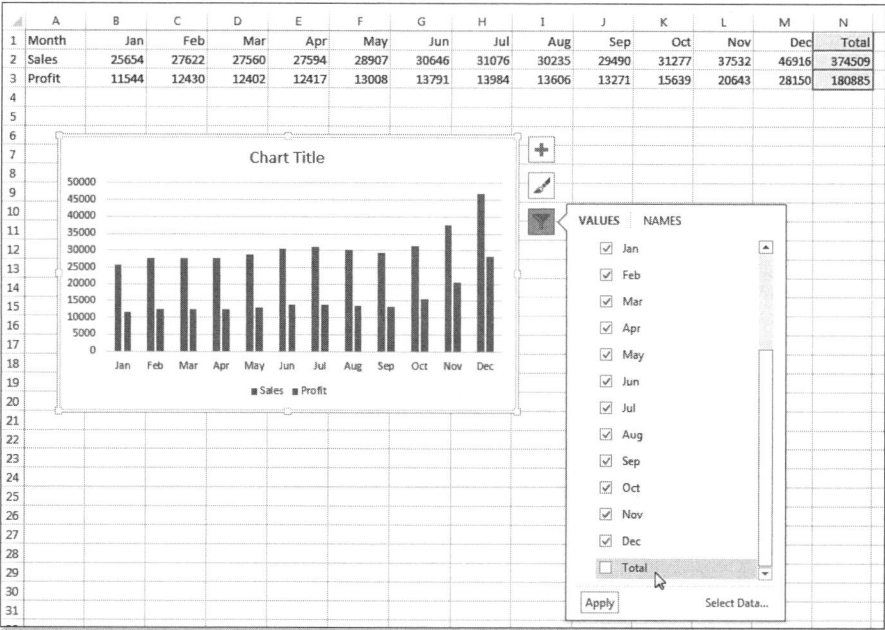

Changing Chart Options Using the Plus Icon

I am starting to think that Scott Ruble's team is doing their best to do away with the ribbon. In Excel 2010, three charting tabs appeared in the ribbon. Nearly the entire Excel 2010 Layout tab is now housed in the plus icon that appears to the right of the chart. This new icon offers Live Preview of the choices, all in a very compact area.

As shown in Figure 32.7, click the plus icon. Hover over Chart Title to have a fly-out appear to the right with choices of Above Chart and Centered Overlay. If you decide you don't need a chart title, simply uncheck the option from the initial menu.

Figure 32.7
Use the plus icon to reach settings for major chart elements.

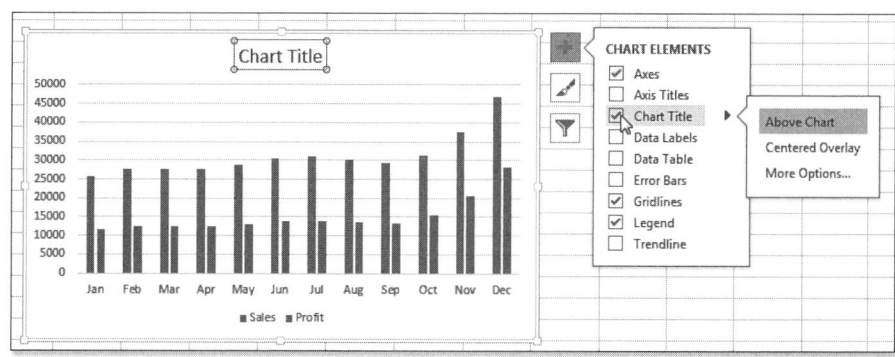

Good charting style says that the legend should be at the top of the chart. Click the plus icon, hover over Legend, and choose Top.

In Figure 32.8, you can see the Live Preview showing what would happen if you tried the new Data Callout option for Data Labels. This looks so bad, you can easily choose something else before committing the change to the chart.

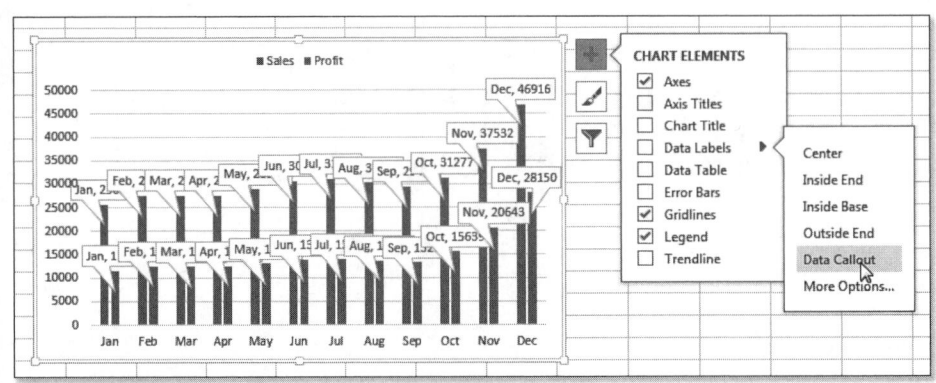

Figure 32.8
Live Preview enables you to realize something is a bad decision before adding it to the chart.

Changes that you make in the plus icon persist in the paintbrush icon. After adding data labels using the plus icon, you can visit the paintbrush icon to arrive at the chart shown in Figure 32.9, with the chart labels rotated to allow them to fit.

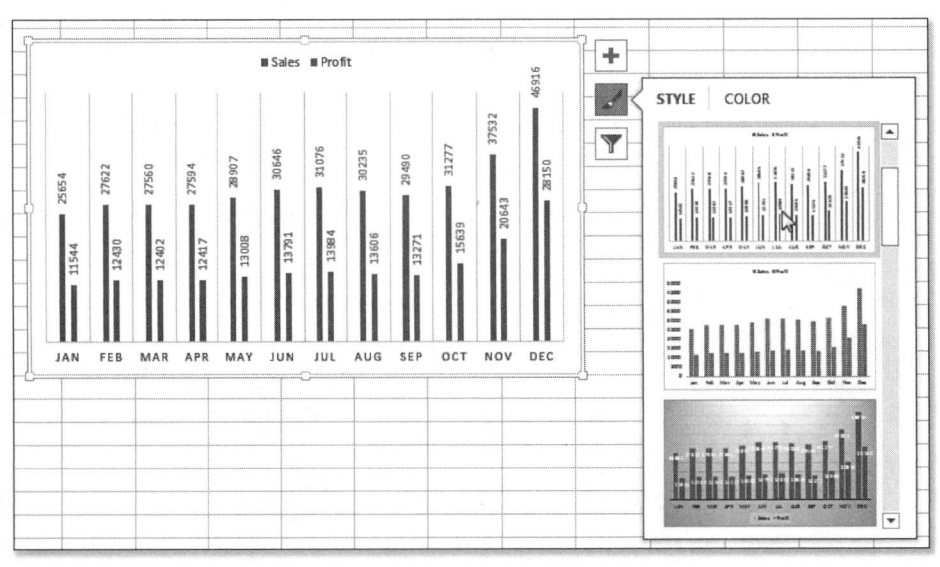

Figure 32.9
A chart style that rotates the data labels so they fit.

Showing Two Orders of Magnitude Using a Combo Chart

Combo charts are easier to create in Excel 2013. These charts are great when you have two different orders of magnitude in the same chart. Combo charts appeared in the Excel 2003 Chart Wizard.
They were hidden on a back tab in the wizard, but at least they were there. In Excel 2007, they
were out of the wizard, but charting gurus could figure out how to create them. Now, in Excel 2013,
you have an incredibly flexible interface for creating combo charts.

Figure 32.10 shows a perfect example of data needing a combo chart. Row 2 shows monthly sales.
Row 3 shows the YTD number and accumulates all of the monthly sales. The problem, once again, is
that the height of the December YTD number forces the monthly sales line to be too small for you to
actually notice any variability.

Figure 32.10
The YTD number is too
large compared to the
monthly numbers.

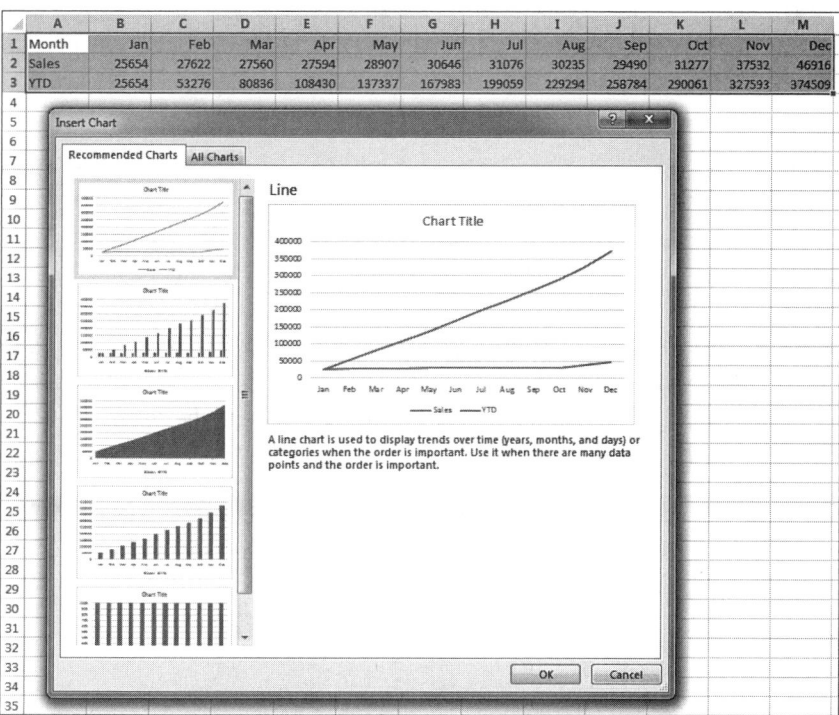

This is the first chart in this chapter for which the Recommended Charts feature does not solve the
problem. Click the All Charts tab. Immediately, you should notice some improvements in All Charts.
Column is chosen along the left side. Seven drawings across the top illustrate Clustered Columns,
Stacked Columns, 100% Stacked Columns, and then some hideous 3-D charts. Below that, two

full-color samples show how the data would look if each row is a series or if each column is a series. This prevents you from having to use Switch Row/Column after the chart is created. These two samples, shown in Figure 32.11, don't solve the current problem, though.

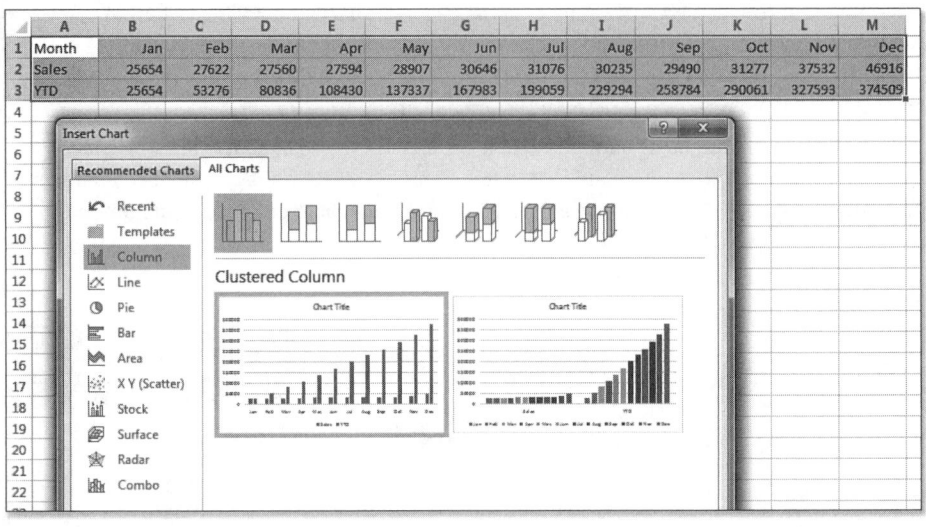

Figure 32.11
The chart previews under All Charts let you see what the chart will look like with either rows or columns representing each series.

A new category along the left side is called Combo. Click this category. Four thumbnails across the top hint that multiple combo charts are available. The first thumbnail converts the YTD to a line chart, but the months still are too small. Notice, at the bottom of the dialog, that the thumbnail uses a Clustered Column for Sales, a Line for YTD, and neither series is on the secondary axis (see Figure 32.12).

Choose the second thumbnail at the top of the dialog in Figure 32.13. This chart solves the problem perfectly. The one change is that the YTD numbers are moved to the secondary axis. The month numbers use the left vertical axis, which runs from $0 to $50,000. The YTD numbers on the line use the right axis, which goes from $0 to $400,000.

Counting the mouse clicks, you had to select Insert, Recommended Charts, All Charts, Combo, the second icon, and then OK to create this fairly complicated chart. That's six clicks. It is not as easy as accepting the first recommended chart, but it is far easier than the dozens of clicks required to create the same chart in Excel 2010.

 Tip

Any time you know you will be creating a combo chart, skip the Recommended Charts icon and go straight for the Combo Chart drop-down in the Insert tab. You could create the chart from Figure 32.13 in three clicks. Also, you might have many series and need series 1, 3, 4, and 6 as columns and series 2 and 5 as lines on the secondary axis. You can use the drop-downs and check boxes at the bottom of Figure 32.13 to create any custom combination of two chart types.

Figure 32.12
The first combo chart does not solve
the scale problem.

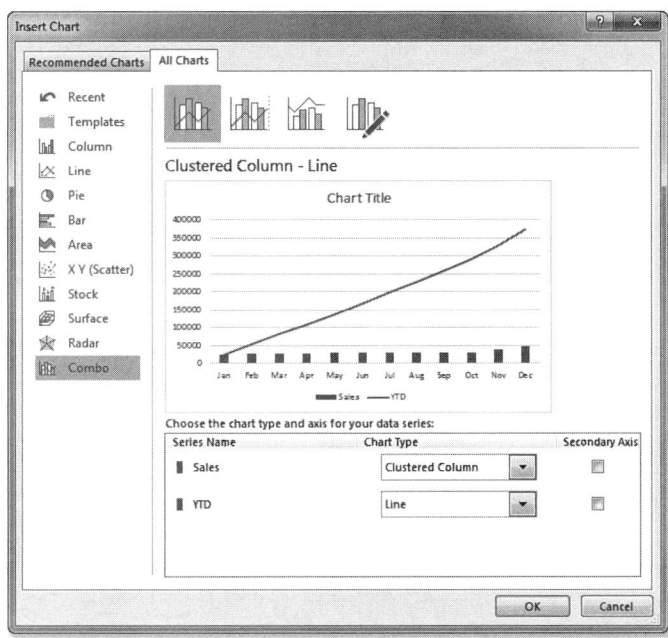

Figure 32.13
It took just six clicks to get to this
acceptable chart.

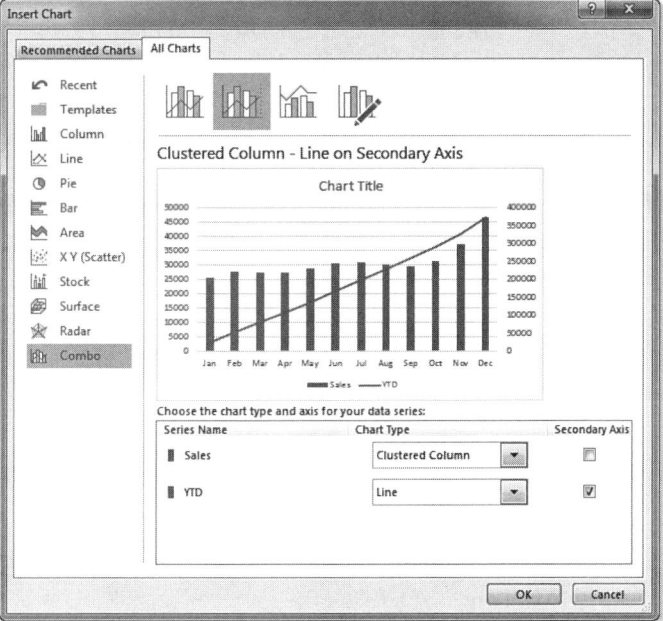

After you have the combo chart, you can use the paintbrush icon to apply interesting effects to the combo chart. Figure 32.14 shows an all-caps CHART TITLE and a pattern for the revenue columns.

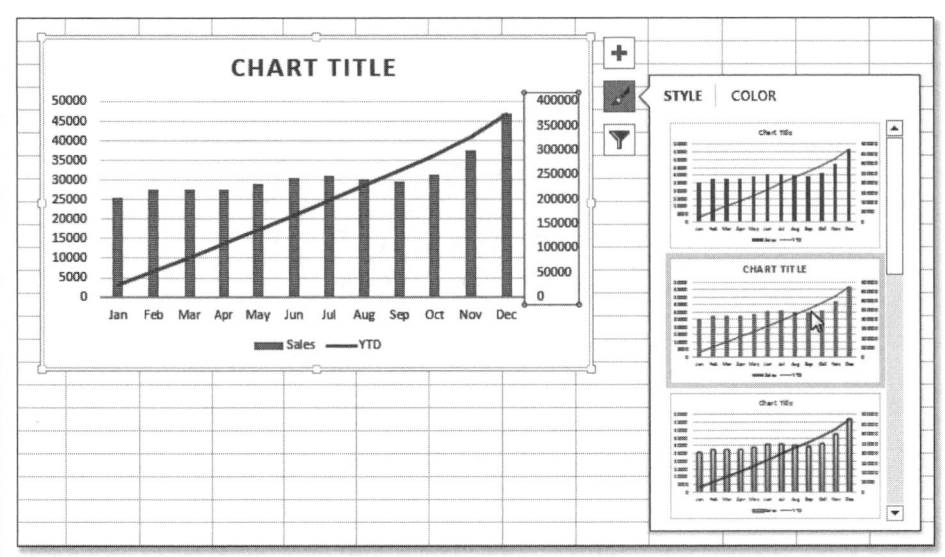

Figure 32.14
The paintbrush icon offers chart styles for combo charts.

Using Ctrl+1 to Format Any Chart Element

The plus icon helps you in some cases, but not all cases. The previous chart now has two vertical axes. The plus icon won't get you to fly-out menus to control the number format in the right axis. To format the right axis, it is best to go straight to the task pane.

Click the right axis and press Ctrl+1 or double-click on the right axis to display the Format task pane.

Task panes were popular in Excel 2003 but were mostly abandoned in Excel 2007. They are back in Excel 2013. This task pane replaces the Format dialog from Excel 2010. Here are some tips for working with task panes:

- Three levels of menus usually appear within the task pane. The first level is Axis Options or Text Options at the top of the task pane. The second level is the icons. Figure 32.15 shows four icons. For each icon, there are several categories of settings. By default, the categories are collapsed. Click the triangle to the left of a category to expand the category. In the figure, the Number category is expanded, but more settings are available in Axis Options, Tick Marks, and Labels. There are even more options under the three other Icons. And even more icons are available if you choose Text Options.

- If you click on another chart element, the choices in the task pane change. You might get different first-level words, second-level icons, and third-level categories.

Figure 32.15
The task pane packs hundreds of settings into a narrow strip of the Excel screen by using three levels of menuing.

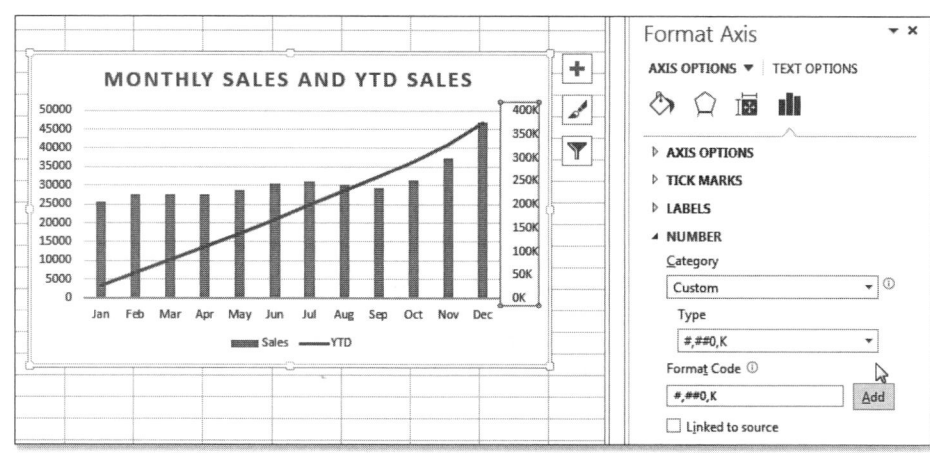

- You can float the task pane by dragging the words in the title of the task pane into the work-sheet. To re-dock the task pane, drag the words more than halfway off the right or left side of the screen.

- If anything, the Format task pane hangs around too long. You can be done with the chart and the Format task pane hangs around until you dismiss it using the X at the top of the pane. I actually appreciate seeing the task pane hang around too long. For many years, decisions about Excel were made by the Excel team. In 2005–2006, certain people in charge of Office stepped in and made all sorts of edicts: "All commands must be at the top," "No more floating pallets," "No ribbon customizations." The fact that you now have some floating elements that hang around too long tell me that those certain people have moved on and no longer have their fingers in our beloved Excel.

>  **Tip**
>
> By default, all axis labels are now Linked to Source for the numeric formatting. Although I actually went to the task pane in Figure 32.15 to apply a custom number format, I could have achieved the same effect in the chart by applying a numeric format to the values in the worksheet.

Labeling Charts

Many of your data label frustrations are over: Excel 2013 now allows data labels to have a balloon shape and allows you to specify a cell range that can contain labels. Even XY charts can support labels. Take a look at Figure 32.16; because all but two of the cells in the label range are blank, the label bubbles only appear on two of the columns.

To set up the labels shown in Figure 32.16, follow these steps:

1. Create a label range. Type labels only for the columns that should have one.

2. Click on one column in the chart to select the series.

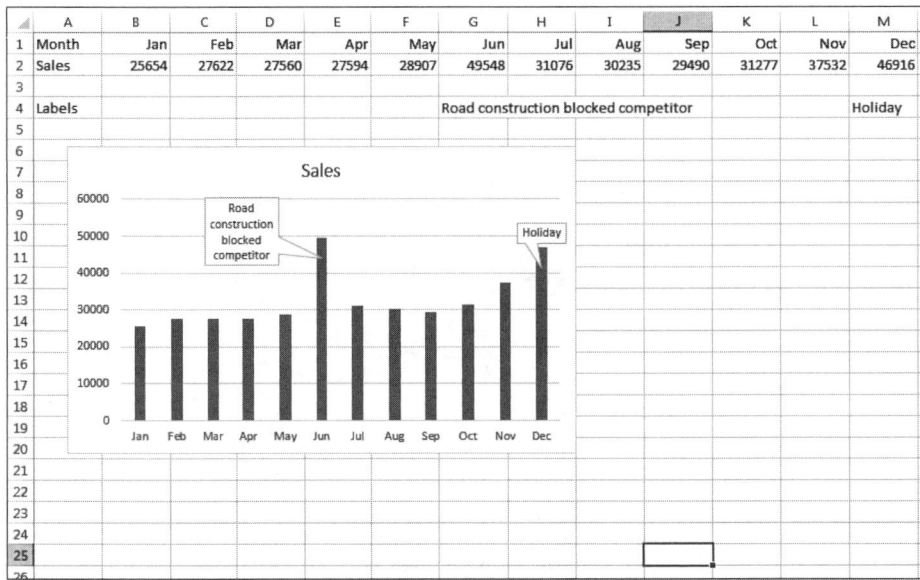

Figure 32.16
Range B4:M4 is the source for the data labels.

3. Open the plus icon. Hover over Data Labels until the fly-out menu appears. Choose Data Callout. Initially, you see the ugly labels such as "Dec, 47K" on each column.

4. Click one of the data label balloons and press Ctrl+1. The Format Data Labels task pane appears.

5. Near the top of the task pane, choose the icon with three columns.

6. Below the line in the task pane, unselect Category Name. Unselect Values.

7. Choose Value from Cells (see Figure 32.17).

Figure 32.17
Value from Cells is new in Excel 2013.

8. Click the Select Range button.

9. Specify a label range that is the same size as the data series. Even though you only have two labels in Figure 32.16, specify the entire B4:M4 range, as shown in Figure 32.18. Click OK.

Figure 32.18
Specify a range for the labels.

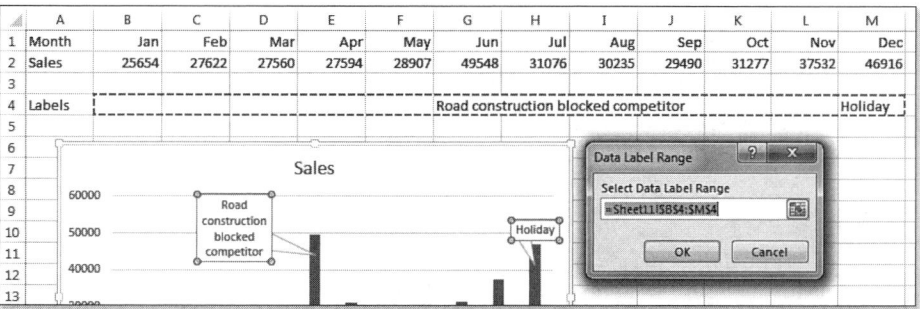

With the labels selected, you can visit the Chart Tools Format tab and select Change Shape to alter the shape of the balloon.

 Caution

The new data labels look great in Excel 2013 but change to ugly [CELLRANGE] labels if you open the workbook in Excel 2010. Make sure that you are only going to be sharing the workbook with people who have Excel 2013, or convert the workbook to PDF before sending it to them.

Controlling the Axis Range

Figure 32.19 shows another example of a combo chart. This chart tracks monthly sales in dollars and also sales of high-end leather jackets. After using the paintbrush icon to choose this chart layout, you might be surprised to see that the values for the secondary axis appear to the left of the values for the primary axis. This is an interesting view that was possible in Excel 2010, but it was never the default. To move the secondary axis values to the right of the chart, double-click the axis values. Choose the Axis Labels drop-down and change from Low to Next to Axis. The labels for the secondary axis move back to the right side of the chart.

You should also be aware of one possibly annoying behavior with Excel charts. The sales columns in Figure 32.19 look like they've doubled in size from January to July. In fact, the sales have been almost constant, in the range of $42,000 to $49,000.

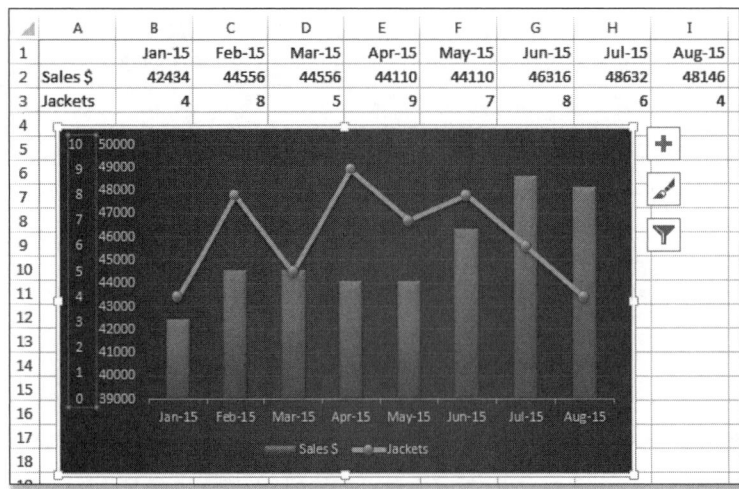

▲	A	B	C	D	E	F	G	H	I
1		Jan-15	Feb-15	Mar-15	Apr-15	May-15	Jun-15	Jul-15	Aug-15
2	Sales $	42434	44556	44556	44110	44110	46316	48632	48146
3	Jackets	4	8	5	9	7	8	6	4

Figure 32.19
Based on the height difference in the columns, it looks like sales doubled from January to July.

This is what some chart gurus call a "Wow Chart." It is achieved by having the horizontal axis appear at $39,000 instead of at $0. What you are really seeing is just the top of each column.

If you intend to create a chart designed to lie, you are more than welcome to consciously change the lower axis to exaggerate the difference between the high and low points. However, you should be aware that Excel will do this for you in certain situations.

Whenever the range of numbers in the series is smaller than 16.67% of the max of the series, Excel adopts a scale that does not start at zero. For example, in Figure 32.19, the max is 48,632. The min of the series is 42,434. The range is the max − min, or 6,198. When you divide the range by the max, you get 12.7%. Thus, Excel automatically zooms in to show a scale from 39,000 to 50,000. This behavior is automatic. If you were to change the sales in one cell to $51,000, Excel recalculates the range to be 8,566. Because 8,566/5,100 is 16.7961%, the axis automatically changes to start at zero.

Deciding to lie with a chart is a pretty important step. You wouldn't want to leave it up to Excel to decide on the fly to change from a regular chart to a lying chart, or vice versa.

To take control of the axis, double-click the sales numbers along the axis. The settings appear in the task pane. You want to focus on Bounds and Units. Initially, all four settings say "Auto" to the right of the setting. This means that Excel calculates the values every time the worksheet recalculates.

Initially for this chart, this minimum is 39,000, the maximum is 50,000, and the Major Unit is 1,000. This causes a gridline and a number to appear every 1,000 units along the axis.

At the very minimum, you should click in the box for minimum and change the minimum to zero. However, when you make this change, Excel automatically calculates a new maximum of 60,000 and a major unit of 10,000. This causes the axis of the chart to show values and gridlines at 10,000, 20,000, ..., 60,000. Feel free to change the maximum to 50,000, as shown in Figure 32.20. However, if sales later extend beyond $50,000, you have to revisit the task pane to change the Maximum value.

Figure 32.20
Override the automatic settings for Minimum, Maximum, and Major Units.

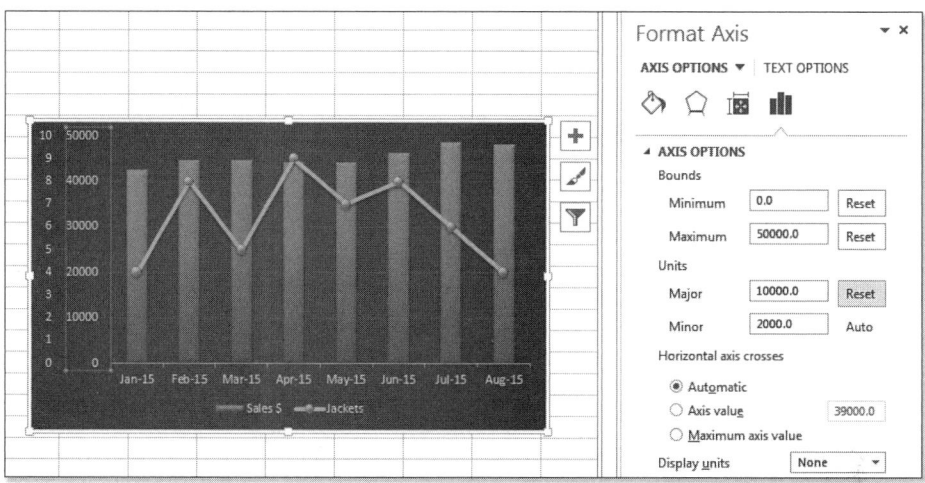

Seeing the Relationship Between Two Variables in a Scatter Chart

Scatter charts (XY charts) are a useful tool for comparing two numeric variables. They are designed to show if there is a dependent relationship between the variables.

The data set in Figure 32.21 represents the price for several used cars for sale. They are all the same model. Column A shows the mileage of the used car. Column B shows the price in thousands. Theoretically, the higher the mileage, the lower the price.

Figure 32.21
Excel correctly suggests a scatter chart.

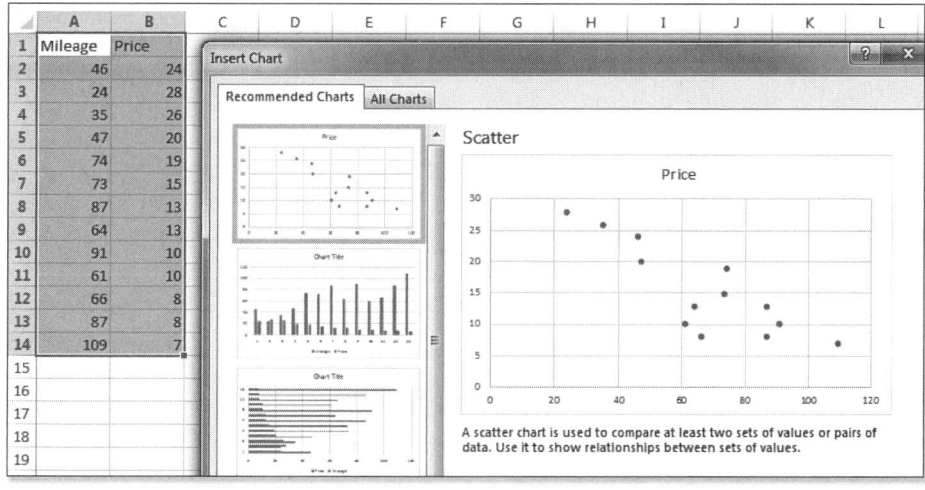

When you have two, four, or six series that are completely numeric with no category labels, Excel recommends a scatter chart. This is great because a scatter chart is a good way to show the relationship. However, there are certain tricks to dealing with scatter charts.

By default, the title of the scatter chart is the label for the second column of data. Thus, you end up with a chart with a title of "Price" and no explanation that you are comparing price to mileage (see Figure 32.22).

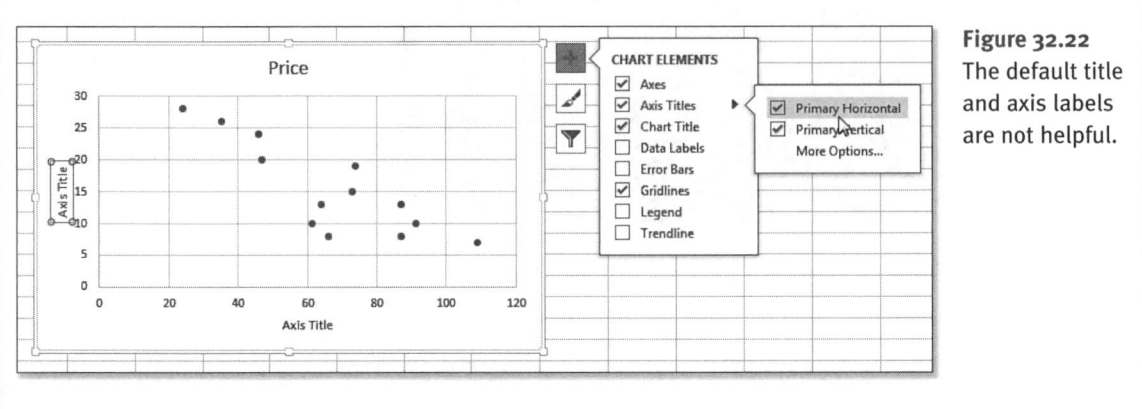

Figure 32.22
The default title and axis labels are not helpful.

To fix the default scatter chart, follow these steps:

1. Click the plus icon to the right of the chart.

2. Hover over Axis Titles until the fly-out menu appears.

3. Choose both Primary Horizontal and Primary Vertical in the fly-out menus. This adds the words *Axis Title* to each axis.

4. Triple-click the axis title for the vertical axis. Type a useful title, such as **Price ($000)**.

5. Triple-click the axis title for the horizontal axis. Type a useful title, such as **Mileage (k)**.

6. Triple-click the chart title and type a useful title such as **Price versus Mileage**.

Note that in steps 4–6, you can single-click the title and then watch the letters you type appear in the formula bar. I prefer to triple-click and edit the titles directly in the chart.

In the past, applying labels to scatter charts was difficult. Kudos should go to Excel MVP Rob Bovey. Rob has freely given his Chart Labeler add-in to anyone who asked for the last 10 years to enable labeling of scatter charts. Finally, Excel 2013 has a way to deal with labels in scatter charts.

When you initially add data labels, Excel 2013 shows the X and Y value to the right of each label, as shown in Figure 32.23. I don't agree that this is particularly useful. After all, you should be able to roughly figure out the position of the point by following an imaginary line back to each axis.

Figure 32.23
Initially, the labels for a scatter chart show only the X and Y value.

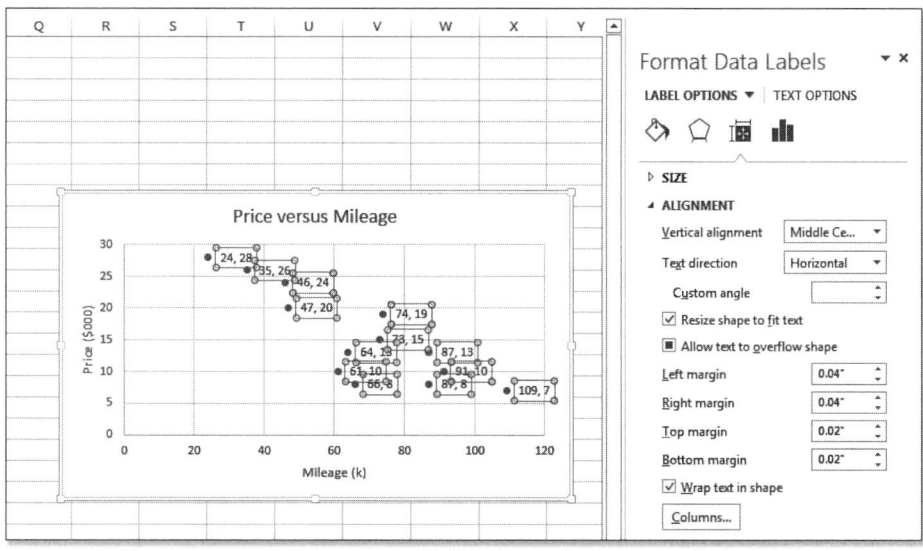

You can add a useful label to the scatter chart by using the Value from Cells setting. Follow the steps between Figure 32.16 and Figure 32.17 to tie the labels to some label cells near your data. Figure 32.24 applies a simple A, B, C identifying label next to each data point.

Figure 32.24
Specify a range of labels for each point.

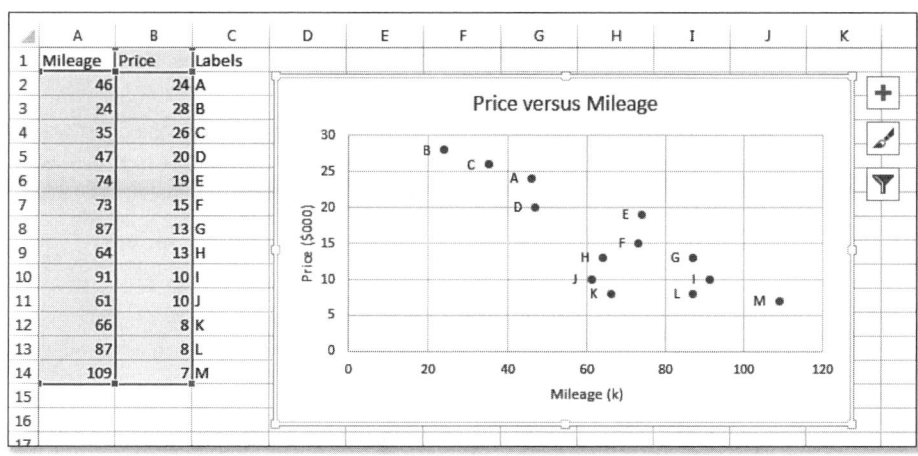

Adding a Third Variable with a Bubble Chart

Think about buying a used vehicle. The primary drivers of price are going to be the age of the car and the mileage. The previous charts show a relationship between miles on the car and the price. A better analysis would compare miles, age, and price. You can show this relationship in a bubble chart.

To set up a bubble chart, create three columns of numeric data. The values for the horizontal axis should appear in the first column. The values for the vertical axis should appear in the second column. The values for the size of the bubble should appear in the third column.

Even if you set up the data correctly, Excel does not suggest a bubble chart as the first recommended chart. However, if you scroll down through the various chart suggestions, a bubble chart should appear near the end of the list (see Figure 32.25).

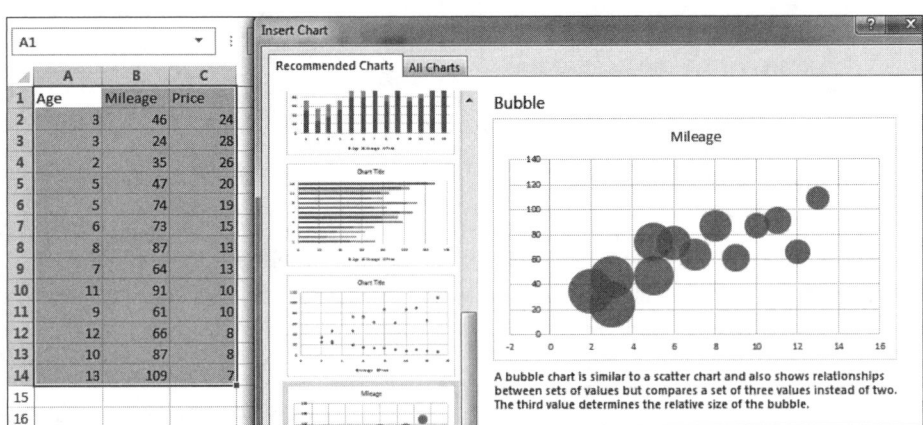

Figure 32.25
Set up data for a bubble chart.

Just as with a scatter chart, you want to add axis titles and adjust the chart title. Figure 32.26 shows the final bubble chart after applying a chart style from the paintbrush icon. The relative size of each circle represents the price of the vehicle. As you would expect, newer cars with fewer miles are priced higher.

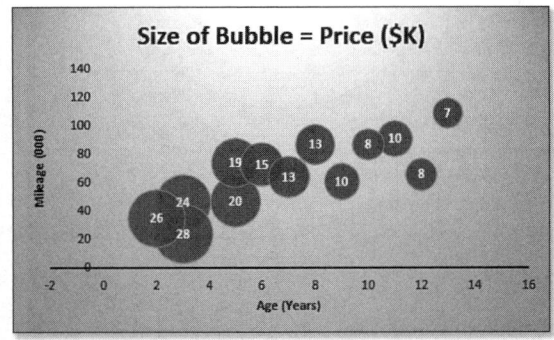

Figure 32.26
Each data point in a bubble chart communicates three values.

Plotting Two Populations on One Scatter Chart

Another way to create a scatter chart is to compare two different populations on the same chart. The data in Figure 32.27 shows the relationship between tenure and salary. The data in A1:B19 shows salary and years of service for several managers in a company. The data in C1:D41 shows similar data for several hourly workers on the factory floor.

Figure 32.27
Create a scatter chart from two different sets of XY data.

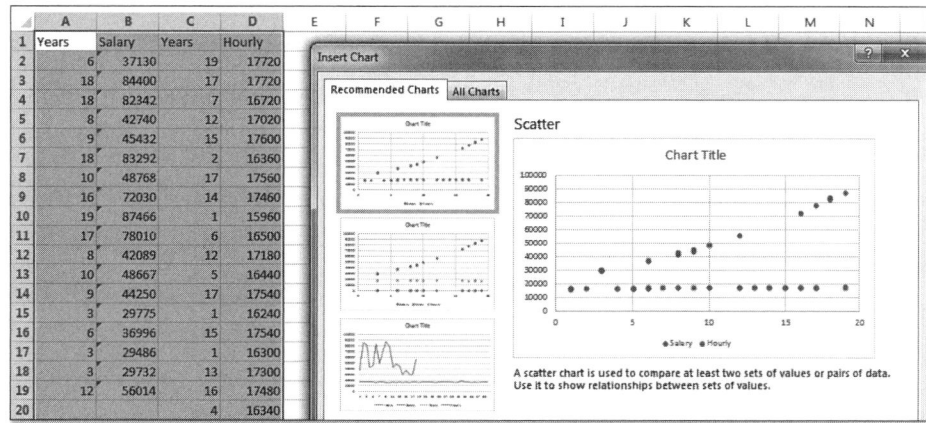

For the first time, Excel 2013 actually allows you to create this scatter chart from A1:D41. If you have an even number of numeric columns, Excel 2013 assumes that you have X1, Y1, X2, Y2, and so on. This never worked in Excel 2010.

In prior versions of Excel, you would have to add the additional pairs of data using the Paste Special dialog. This is still a cool trick. In Figure 32.28, the initial scatter chart includes data from A1:B19. To add a second data series, follow these steps:

1. Select the data for the second population. For example, select C1:D41.

2. Copy that data to the Clipboard using Ctrl+C.

3. Click the chart to select the chart.

4. On the Home tab, open the Paste drop-down and choose Paste Special (see Figure 32.28).

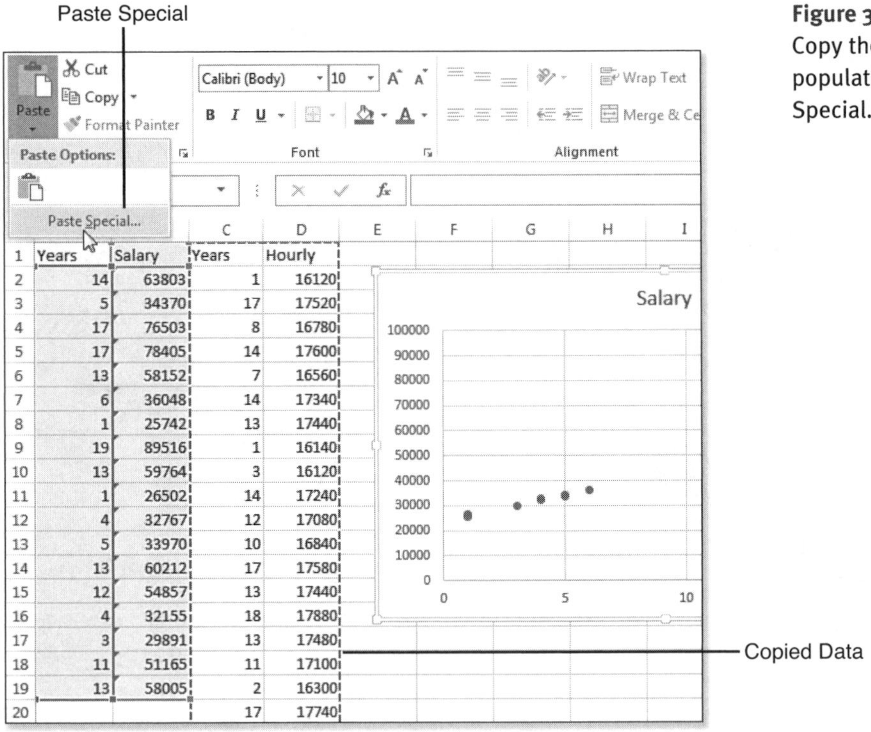

Paste Special

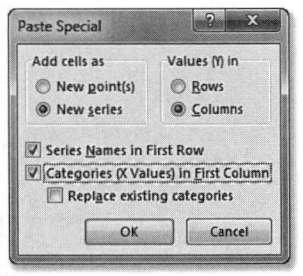

1	Years	Salary	Years	Hourly
2	14	63803	1	16120
3	5	34370	17	17520
4	17	76503	8	16780
5	17	78405	14	17600
6	13	58152	7	16560
7	6	36048	14	17340
8	1	25742	13	17440
9	19	89516	1	16140
10	13	59764	3	16120
11	1	26502	14	17240
12	4	32767	12	17080
13	5	33970	10	16840
14	13	60212	17	17580
15	12	54857	13	17440
16	4	32155	18	17880
17	3	29891	13	17480
18	11	51165	11	17100
19	13	58005	2	16300
20			17	17740

Copied Data

Figure 32.28
Copy the data for the second population and choose Paste Special.

5. In the Paste Special dialog, the default shows New Series instead of New Points. However, you need to override the defaults and choose Categories (X Values) in First Column (see Figure 32.29).

Figure 32.29
Choose Categories in First Column.

6. Click OK. Excel adds the second series to the chart.

7. Adjust the axis titles and chart titles as in the previous examples.

The final chart is shown in Figure 32.30.

Figure 32.30
After adjusting the axis titles, you have this chart.

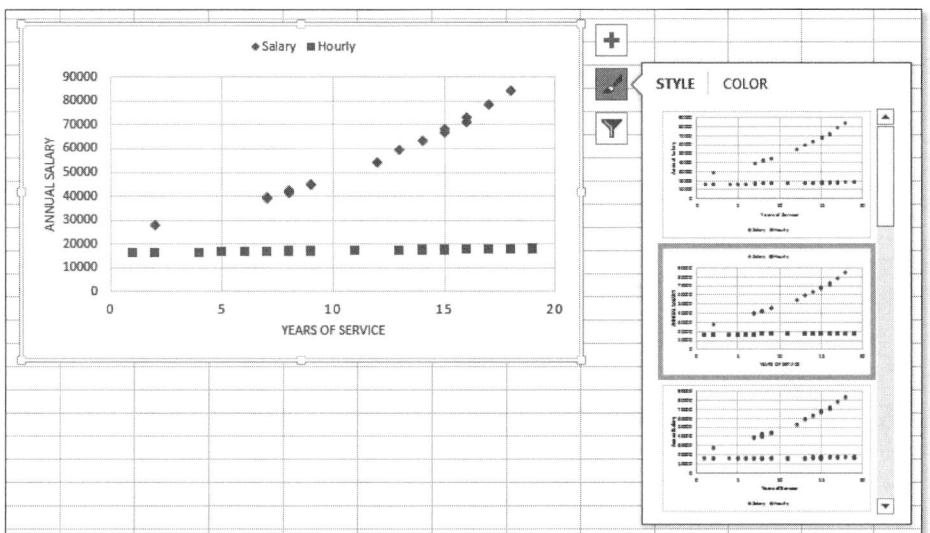

Summarizing Data Using the Quick Analysis Icon

As mentioned at the beginning of this chapter, the focus for charting in Excel 2013 was to lower the bar for creating charts. This example is an extreme example of lowering the bar.

Say that you have a 500-row data set with columns for Region, Product, Date, Customer, Quantity, Revenue, COGS, and Profit. Normally, this would not be a data set that you could chart. To create a chart, you would normally create a pivot table, or add subtotals and then chart that data.

However, the Quick Analysis icon makes it easy to chart this data in Excel 2013. Follow these steps:

1. Select the entire data set by selecting cell A1 and pressing Ctrl+*. A new Quick Analysis icon appears to the right of the last visible row in the window.

2. Click the Quick Analysis icon.

3. Across the top of the pop-up menu, choose Charts.

4. Hover over the first Clustered Column thumbnail. The preview offers to chart revenue by region (see Figure 32.31).

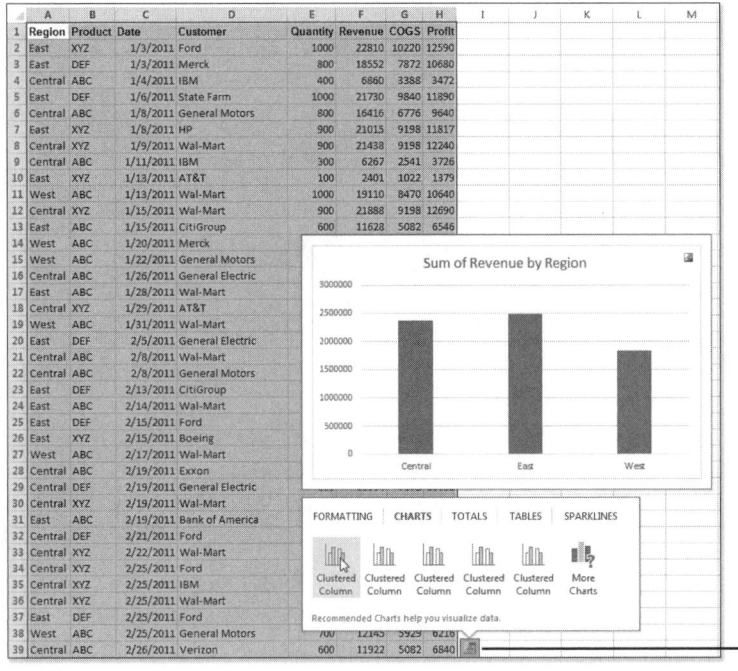

Figure 32.31
Miraculously, Excel 2013 is offering to convert hundreds of rows of detail data into a summary chart.

Quick Analysis Icon

5. Hover over the second Clustered Column thumbnail. The preview shows profit by product (see Figure 32.32).

As you continue previewing the suggested charts, you see that Excel offers various combinations of Region, Product, Revenue, Profit, and Cost. Excel sees that the Region column contains three values that frequently repeat. Similarly, the Product column contains three distinct values that appear over and over.

Say that you wanted to show revenue by customer. Because there are 27 different customer values, Excel never offers to create a chart with Customer. However, you can easily modify the chart to show data by customer.

Figure 32.32
Revenue by Region, Profit by Product. Will Excel offer Revenue by Customer?

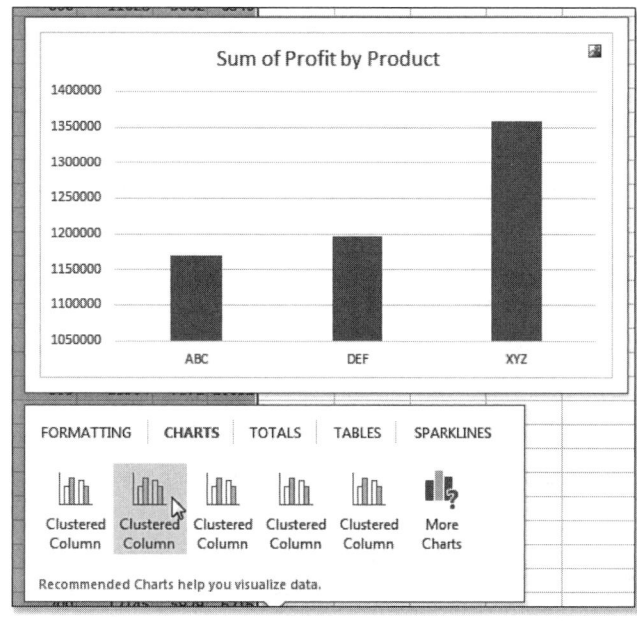

Follow these steps to create the Revenue by Customer chart shown in Figure 32.33:

1. Select cell A1.

2. Press Ctrl+* to select the entire data set.

3. Click the Quick Analysis icon.

Figure 32.33
The Quick Analysis makes creating this chart much easier than starting from scratch.

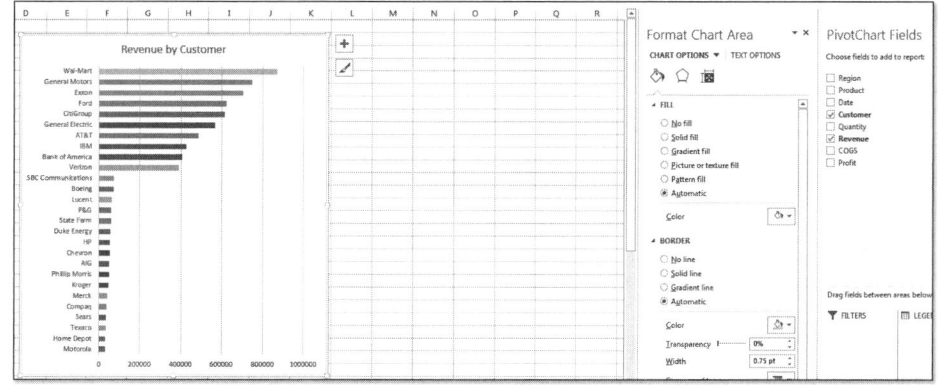

4. From the Quick Analysis menu, click Charts.

5. Choose the first chart thumbnail to get Revenue by Region. The chart appears on a brand-new worksheet. A PivotTable Fields task pane appears on the right side. A summary by customer appears on the left.

6. In the task pane, unselect Region and select Customer.

7. In the ribbon, choose the Design tab. Choose Change Chart Type. Convert the chart to a bar chart.

8. Bar charts look better when the data is sorted. Click in cell B2 and use Data, AZ to sort the data by revenue.

9. Make the chart taller. Click the chart. Use the resize handle at the top or bottom to resize the chart.

10. In the ribbon, go to the Analyze tab and toggle off the field buttons.

11. Double-click a bar in the chart. In the Format Data Series task pane, open the paint bucket icon and then the Fill category. Choose Vary Colors by Point.

12. In the same task pane, click the Chart icon. In the Series Options category, drag the Gap Width from 219% down to about 50%. This makes the bars taller and the gaps narrower.

Saving Time with Charting Tricks

The rest of this chapter details some charting techniques that have been in Excel for several versions.

Adding New Data to a Chart by Pasting

Even though this next trick has existed in Excel since 1997, not many people know about it—you can add new data to a chart by pasting. Suppose you have a chart showing data for several months. You have nicely formatted and customized the chart. You now have new data available. Instead of re-creating the chart, you can paste the new data to the existing chart.

Follow these steps to expand the chart by pasting new data on it:

1. Make sure the new data has a heading consistent with the old data. Note that if you accidentally enter the heading as Text instead of Date, or vice versa, the trick has unexpected results.

2. Select the new data, including the heading.

3. Press Ctrl+C to copy the new data.

4. Select the chart.

5. Press Ctrl+V to paste the new data on the chart.

Adding New Data to a Chart by Using a Table

If you use Excel's new table functionality, charts are automatically updated when new data is added. This method works even if the chart is based on data that is not currently in a table. Follow these steps to make the data into a table and extend the chart:

1. Select a cell in the source data for the chart.

2. Press Ctrl+T to make the range into a table.

3. Confirm the location for the table. Excel applies a default table format to the table, as shown in Figure 32.34.

Figure 32.34
Converting the source data into a table.

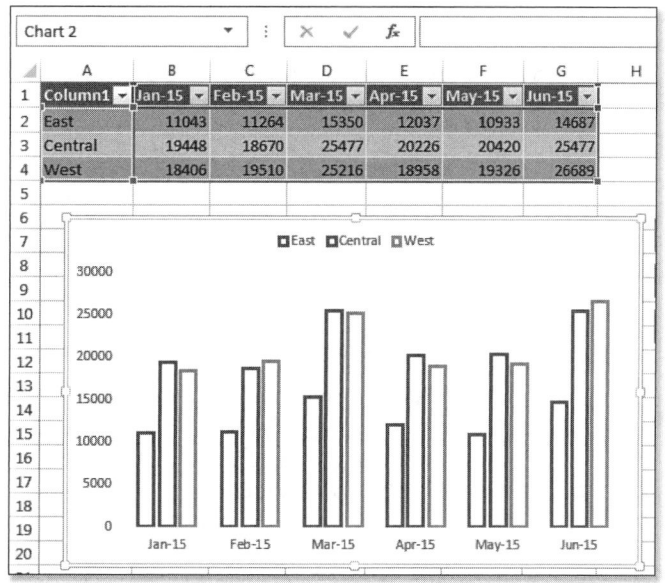

4. In the blank column next to the table, type the heading for the next month. Excel automatically extends the table and adds the new month to the chart, as shown in Figure 32.35.

5. Type the values for the new column. Excel extends both the table and the chart.

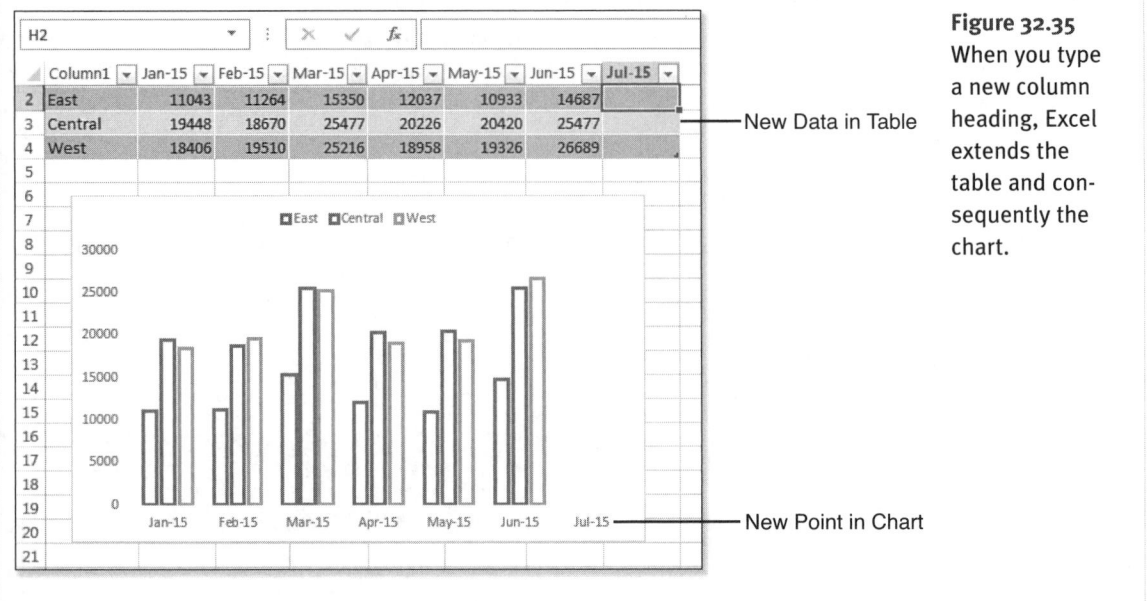

New Data in Table

New Point in Chart

Figure 32.35
When you type a new column heading, Excel extends the table and consequently the chart.

Adding Drop Lines to a Surface Chart

Surface charts can be hard to read. Excel draws a smooth line between adjacent data points. It is difficult for your eye to follow the label on the X-axis up to the point on the surface chart. Although drop lines are available in some Chart Styles, for some reason, they are not available from the plus icon in Excel 2013. To manually add drop lines, select the chart. In the Design tab of the ribbon, choose Add Chart Element, Lines, Drop Lines (see Figure 32.36).

Predicting the Future by Using a Trendline

As you might recall, Chapter 15, "Using Trig, Matrix, and Engineering Functions," presented some fairly complicated functions for calculating linear regression lines. Instead of using those functions, it is simpler to plot the data on a chart and ask Excel to add a trendline.

A line chart shows progress toward a goal for the first eight days of a month, as shown in Figure 32.37. Excel can add a trendline to the chart and extend the trendline to predict the final goal. You can consider the trendline to be a predictor of what will happen if things continue to progress at the same pace. If the trendline after 30 days does not meet the goal, you need to start working harder.

Follow these steps to add a trendline to a chart:

1. Select a chart that contains data of past actuals.

2. On the Design tab in the ribbon, choose Add Chart Element, Trendline, More Trendline Options. Excel displays the Format Trendline task pane.

Figure 32.36
Vertical drop lines make
it easier to figure out
where each data point
crosses the chart.

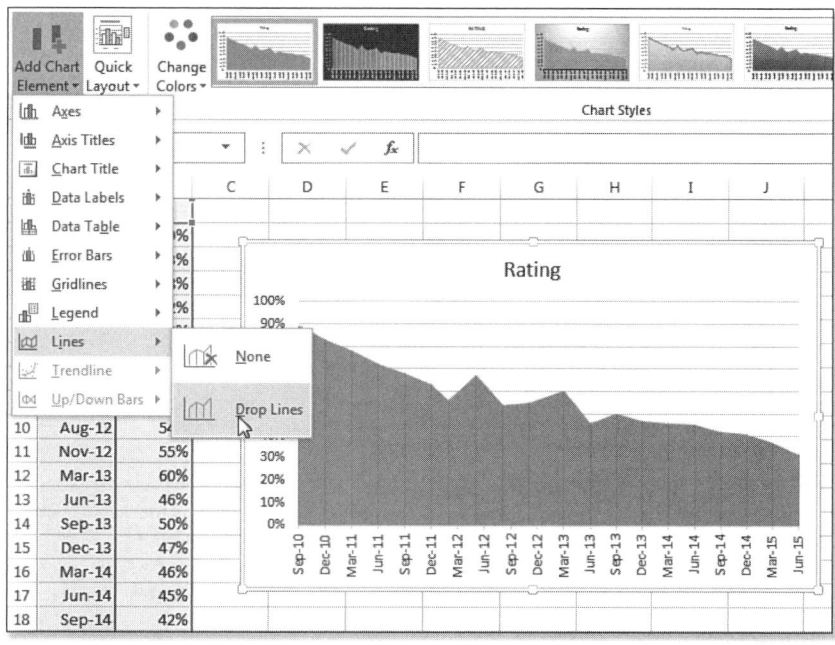

Figure 32.37
This simple chart plots
historical data.

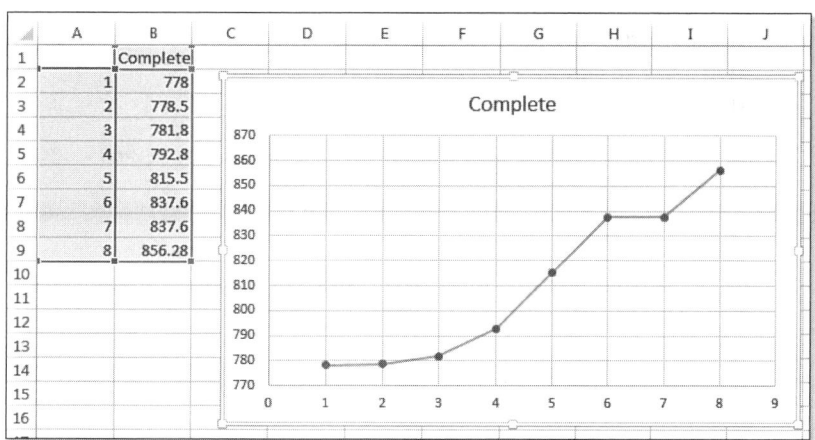

3. In the Format Trendline task pane, choose a Linear trendline. Type a name such as **Prediction**.
   In the Forecast section, enter a positive value in the Forward section. For this example, assume
   21 days is appropriate. Choose Display Equation on Chart and Display R-Squared Value on Chart
   (see Figure 32.38).

The result is a graphical prediction of the future.

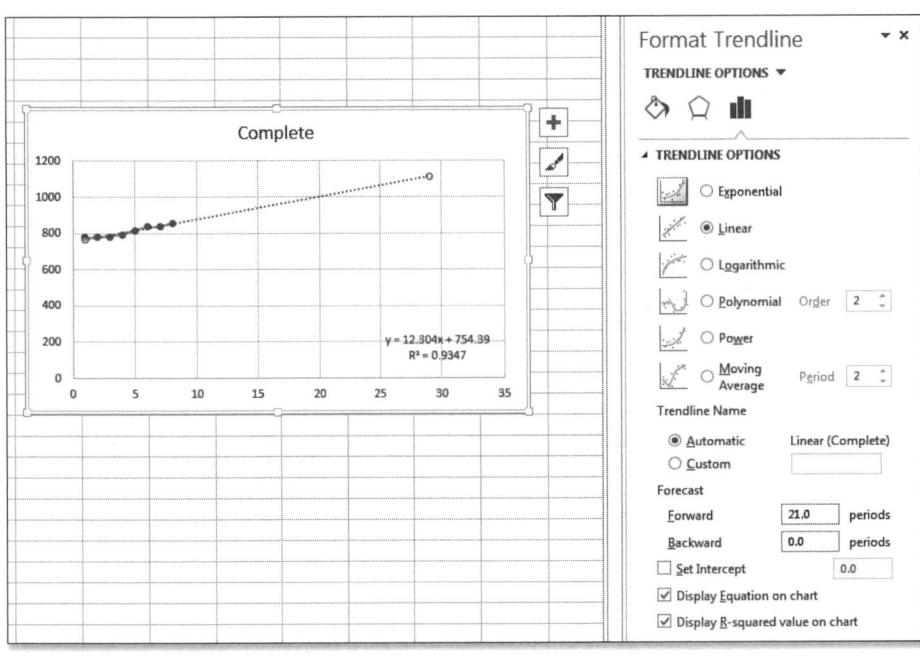

Figure 32.38
The trendline
does a straight
line regression.

Creating Stock Charts

Excel offers four varieties of stock market charts to track historical stock performance. Each variety requires a slightly different organization for the data. The order of the data must match the following requirements exactly:

- **High-Low-Close**—These charts require four columns of data: date, high, low, and close.

- **Open-High-Low-Close**—These charts require five columns of data: date, open, high, low, and close.

- **Volume-High-Low-Close**—These charts require five columns of data: date, volume, high, low, and close.

- **Volume-Open-High-Low-Close**—These charts require six columns of data: date, volume, open, high, low, and close.

To create a stock chart, follow these steps:

1. Import your data from http://finance.yahoo.com or another data source.

2. If necessary, cut and paste the columns into the proper sequence to match your desired chart type.

3. Sort the data by date, oldest to newest.

4. Select the data, including the headings.

5. From the Insert tab, open the Radar chart icon. At the top of the menu are four stock charts. Select the appropriate chart type to match your data.

6. If you prefer the volume columns to occupy the bottom half of the chart, format the left scale. Specify a maximum value about two times larger than the largest value. This keeps the volume data near the bottom of the chart.

The result, shown in Figure 32.39, is a chart similar to those published in the financial websites.

 Tip

Stock traders use far more complex charts for their analyses. Add-ins are available to produce box-and-whisker charts, point-and-figure charts, and so on. Perform a Google search for the word *Excel* combined with the particular chart type to locate these add-ins.

Figure 32.39
Excel creates this stock chart.

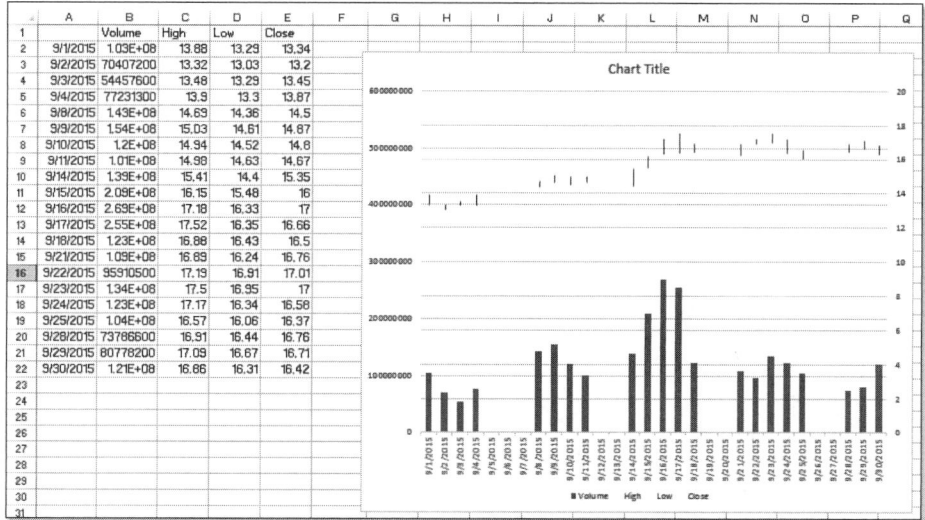

Dealing with Small Pie Slices

In many data series, a few pie slices take up 80% of the pie, and many tiny slices account for the rest of the pie. Typically, the last pie slices end up at the back of the pie, where it is impossible to fit the labels, so no one can make out what they are.

When you have several small data points at the end of a pie chart series, and you need to see all the smaller segments, you can change the chart type to a special type called *bar of pie*. In this type, the smallest few categories are exploded out and shown as a bar chart next to the pie.

To change an existing pie chart to a bar of pie chart, follow these steps:

1. Select the chart.

2. From the Type group of the Design tab, select Change Chart Type. The Change Chart Type dialog appears.

3. In the Change Chart Type dialog, select the last option for pie charts: Bar of Pie.

4. Click OK to close the dialog.

5. Double-click the bar chart. The Format Data Series task pane appears. Choose the chart icon.

6. In the Format Data Series task pane, you have control over the number of values in the bar chart. You can indicate to Split Series by Percentage Value and say that any items less than 10% should end up in the bar portion of the chart. The result is shown in Figure 32.40.

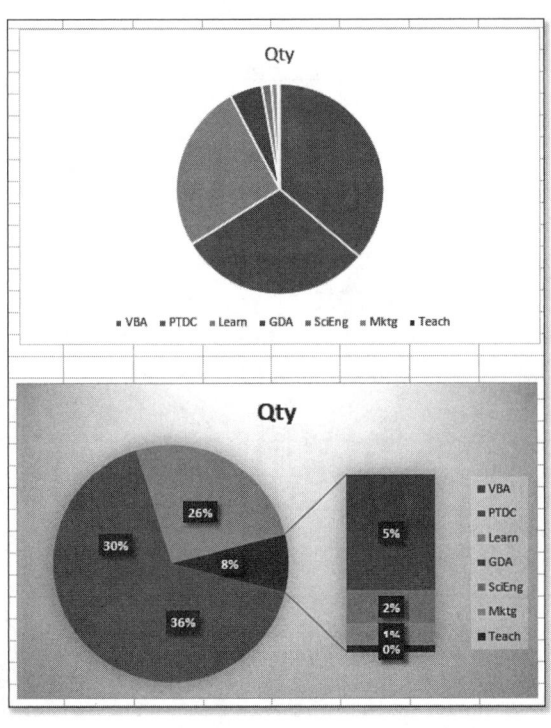

Figure 32.40
In a bar of pie chart, the tiny slices are exploded so it is easy to see the details.

Saving a Favorite Chart Style As a Template

Although Microsoft has provided great-looking built-in charts, you will likely design some great-looking charts of your own. After you have designed a chart, you can save it as a template. When you build new charts based on that template, all the settings for colors, fonts, effects, and chart elements are applied to the new data.

For all the power and glitz of Excel's built-in chart styles, the chart templates feature can save you massive amounts of time, such as if you routinely customize your charts to meet company standards.

Follow these steps to create a template:

1. Build a chart and customize it as necessary.

2. Right-click the chart. Choose Save as Template. Give the chart template a name. Excel saves the template with a .crtx file extension.

To create a chart by using your template, follow these steps:

1. Select the data you want to chart.

2. From the Insert tab, choose any of the Chart drop-downs and then select All Chart Types. The Create Chart dialog appears.

3. In the Create Chart dialog, select the Templates category.

4. Click the desired template, if there is more than one.

5. Click OK. Excel creates the chart with all the custom formatting from the saved template.

If you like your template so much that you want all future charts to be based on the template, follow these steps to make the template your default style:

1. Select a chart based on the desired template.

2. From the Design tab, select Change Chart Type. The Create Chart dialog appears.

3. In the Create Chart dialog, select the Templates category.

4. Select the desired template.

5. In the lower-left corner of the Change Chart Type dialog, select Set as Default Chart.

In the future, you can create a chart that uses this template by following these steps:

1. Select the data you want to chart.

2. Press Alt+F1 to apply your default template.

USING SPARKLINES

Edward Tufte wrote about small, intense, simple datawords in his 2006 book, *Beautiful Evidence*. Tufte called them *sparklines* and produced several examples where you could fit dozens of points of data in the space of a word. Six months later, the Excel team began planning for Excel 2010, and Tufte's concepts made it into that version.

Fitting a Chart into the Size of a Cell with Sparklines

Excel's implementation of sparklines offers line charts, column charts, and a win/loss chart. Figure 33.1 shows an example of each:

- **Win/Loss**—The 1951 Pennant Race (in rows 7 and 8) shows two examples of a Win/Loss chart. Each event (in this case, a baseball game) is represented by either an upward-facing marker (to indicate a win) or a downward-facing marker (to indicate a loss). This type of chart shows winning streaks. The final three games were the playoffs between the Dodgers and the Giants, with the Giants winning two games to one.

- **Line**—The sparkline in row 12 shows 120 monthly points of the Dow Jones Industrial Index, indicating the closing price for each month in one decade.

- **Column**—Rows 16 through 21 compare monthly high temperatures for various cities using sparkcolumns. The minimum and maximum values for each city are marked in a contrasting color. Curitiba, in the southern hemisphere, has its warmest month in February.

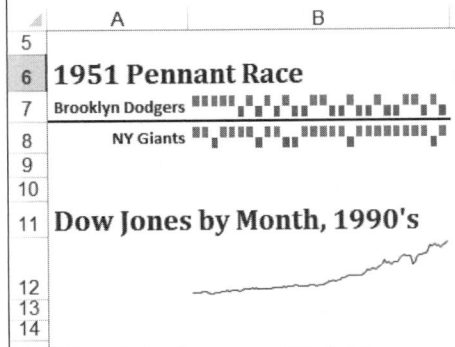

Figure 33.1
Excel 2013 offers three types of sparklines.

Sparklines can exist as a single cell (the Dow Jones example) or as a group of sparklines (the temperature example). When sparklines are created as a group, you can specify that all the sparklines should have the same scale or that they should be independent. There are times where each is appropriate.

The Sparkline feature offers the capability to mark the high point, the low point, the first point, the last point, and/or all negative points.

There is no built-in way to label sparklines. However, sparklines are drawn on a special drawing layer that was added to Excel 2007 to accommodate the data visualizations discussed in Chapter 31, "Using Data Visualizations and Conditional Formatting." This layer is transparent, so with some clever formatting, you can add some label information in the cell behind the sparkline.

Understanding How Excel Maps Data to Sparklines

Contrary to most examples that you see in the Microsoft demos, sparklines do not have to be created adjacent to the original data set.

Suppose that you have the 4-row-by-12-column data set shown in Figure 33.2. This data shows four series of economic data. It can be used to create four sparklines.

Figure 33.2
Four series
of economic
indicators for a
duodecennial.

	2000	2001	2002	2003	2004	2005	2006	2007	2008	2009	2010	2011
Unemployment	4	4.7	5.8	6	5.5	5.1	4.6	4.6	5.8	9.3	9.6	8.9
GDP	9952	10286	10642	11142	11853	12623	13377	14029	14292	13939	14527	15094
New Construction	1569	1603	1705	1848	1956	2068	1801	1355	906	554	586.9	608.8
Consumer Credit	1717	1867	1972	2077	2192	2290	2385	2528	2548	2439	2411	2508

You can create the sparklines in a four-row-by-one-column range, as shown in D3:D6 of Figure 33.3, or in a one-row-by-four-column range, as shown in A1:D1 of the same figure. When you specify a sparkline, you specify the source data and the target range. Given a 4×12 cell source data and a 1×4 or 4×1 target range, Excel figures out that it should create four sparklines.

Figure 33.3
The sparklines can be plotted in a row or a column, regardless of whether the original data was in rows or columns.

	A	B	C	D
1	........▄▂▆	....▄▄▆▆▆	▆▅▄▂▂..	....▄▄▆▆▆
2				
3				
4				
5				
6				
7				
8				

What if your original data set is perfectly square? This occurs when you have four rows by four columns, as shown in Figure 33.4.

You then have the chance that Excel will choose to create the sparklines along the wrong axis (see Figure 33.5).

Figure 33.4
The original data set has the same number of rows and columns.

	2008	2009	2010	2011
Unemployment	5.8	9.3	9.6	8.9
GDP	14292	13939	14527	15094
New Construction	906	554	586.9	608.8
Consumer Credit	2548	2439	2411	2508

Figure 33.5
Excel might choose the wrong way to draw the sparklines.

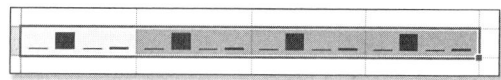

While those sparklines are selected, go to the Sparkline Tools Design tab of the ribbon, open the Edit Data drop-down, and select Switch Row & Column (see Figure 33.6).

The sparkline is reversed, as shown in Figure 33.7.

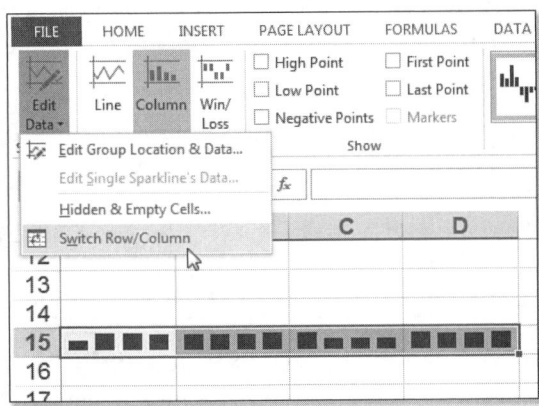

Figure 33.6
Excel offers a way to reverse the row and column.

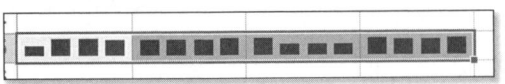

Figure 33.7
Excel now plots like values in each sparkline.

Creating a Group of Sparklines

The worksheet in Figure 33.8 includes more than a decade of leading economic indicators. Use the following steps to add sparklines to the table:

	A	B	C
3	Economic Indicators 2000-2011		
4			2000
5	Unemployment		4
6	GDP		9952
7	New Construction		1569
8	Consumer Credit		1717
9			

Figure 33.8
Add space in your table for the sparklines.

1. Insert a blank column between columns A and B. This provides room for the sparklines to appear next to the labels in column A.

2. Select the data in C4:N8. Note that you should not include any headings in this selection.

3. On the Insert tab, select Column from the Sparkline Group. Excel displays the Create Sparklines dialog. This dialog is the same for all three types of sparklines. You have to specify the location of the data and the location where you want the sparklines. Because your data is 4 rows by 12 columns, the Location Range must be a four-cell vector. You can either specify one row by four columns or four rows by one column.

4. Select B5:B8 as the location range, as shown in Figure 33.9.

5. Click OK to create the default sparklines.

> **Tip**
> In step 1, you might find that you don't need to print the table of numbers; just the labels and sparklines will suffice.

Figure 33.9
Preselect the data range and then specify the location range.

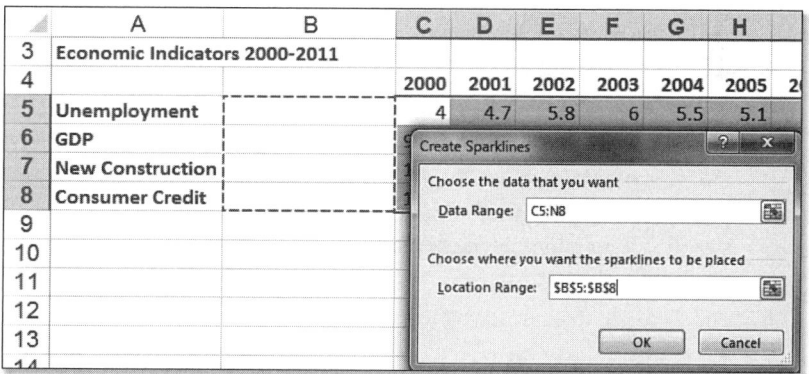

As shown in Figure 33.10, the sparklines have no markers. They are scaled independently of each other. The unemployment max of 9.6 reaches nearly to the top of cell B5, indicating the maximum for Unemployment is probably about 10. By contrast, the maximum for GDP in B6 is closer to 15,250.

Figure 33.10
Default sparklines have no markers and are autoscaled to fit the cell.

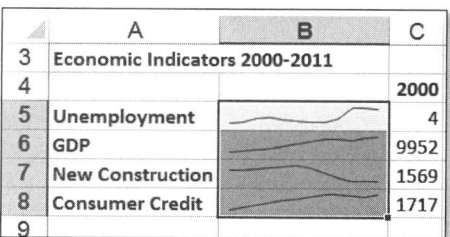

The Show group of the Sparkline toolbar enables you to mark certain points on the line. In Figure 33.11, the high point is marked with a dot. This one change adds a lot of information to the sparklines. New Construction peaked in 2005. Unemployment peaked in 2010, and GDP hit a new high in 2011.

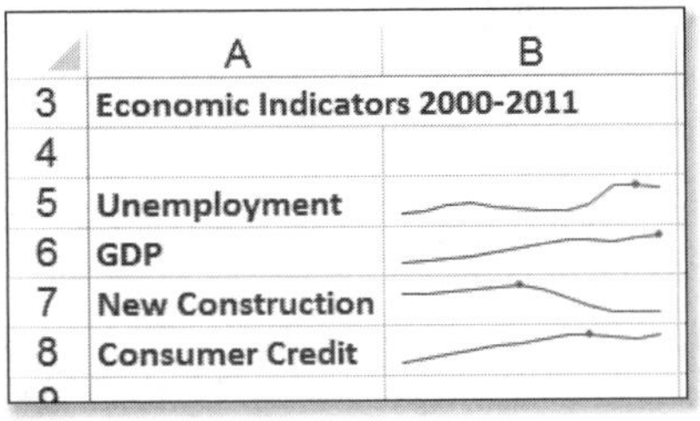

⬛	A	B
3	Economic Indicators 2000-2011	
4		
5	Unemployment	
6	GDP	
7	New Construction	
8	Consumer Credit	

Figure 33.11
Placing a marker at the high point adds key information to the sparkline.

Built-in Choices for Customizing Sparklines

The Sparkline Tools Design tab offers five groups of choices for customizing sparklines: Edit Data, Type, Show, Style, and Group. Each is discussed below.

The Edit Data drop-down enables you to redefine the data range for the source data and the location. If you have to add new data to existing sparklines, you can do so here. Generally, you would edit the location for the whole group, but the drop-down menu enables you to edit data for a single sparkline.

The Type group enables you to switch between Line, Column, and Win/Loss charts.

The Show group offers the second-most useful settings in the tab. The six check boxes here control which points should display markers in the sparkline:

- High Point

- Low Point

- First Point

- Last Point

- Negative Points

- All Points

Here, you can choose to highlight the high point, low point, first point, or last point. Note that if there is a tie for high or low point, both points in the tie are marked. You can also choose to highlight all points and/or the negative points.

For sparklines, any item you choose in the Show Group is drawn as a marker on the line. You can control the color for each of the six options using the Marker Color drop-down, discussed next.

For sparkcolumns, the markers are always shown for All Points, so the All Points check box is grayed out. Choosing any of the five other check boxes in the Show group causes those particular columns to be drawn in a different color.

For Win/Loss, you'll generally choose Markers and Negative. This is how the losses show in a contrasting color from the wins.

In Figure 33.12, examples of the various options are shown:

- In cell B3, the high, low, first, and last points are shown.

- In cell B5, all markers are shown in the same color.

- When you choose Markers and Negative, all points appear, but you can change the negative points to another color, as shown in cell B7.

- In cells B11 and B13, the chosen markers are shown in a contrasting color.

- Cells B9 and B15 are examples where the horizontal axis is shown. This helps to differentiate positive from negative. Note that the axis always appears at a zero location.

Figure 33.12
Use the Show Group to highlight certain points.

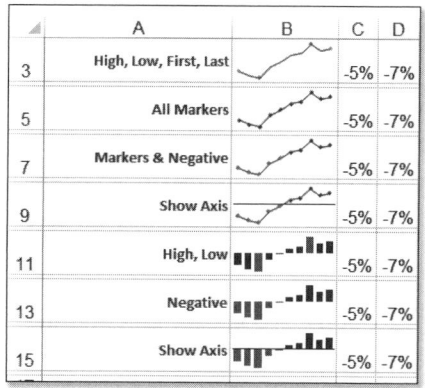

The Style gallery seems to be a huge waste of real estate. In the Office theme, it offers 36 ugly alternatives for sparkline color. This group also offers the Sparkline Color drop-down, which is the standard Excel 2013 color chooser. The color chosen here controls the line in a sparkline. You use the Marker Color drop-down to control the color of the high, low, first, last, negative points, as well as the default color for regular markers. Figure 33.13 shows the Marker Color drop-down.

You use the Group group to ungroup a group of sparklines. Any changes that you make on the Design tab apply to all the sparklines in the group. This is usually a desired outcome. However, if you needed to mark the high point in one line and the low point in another line, you would ungroup the sparklines.

 Note

For sparklines, the sparkline color controls the color of the line. For sparkcolumns or the win/loss chart, the sparkline color controls the color of the columns.

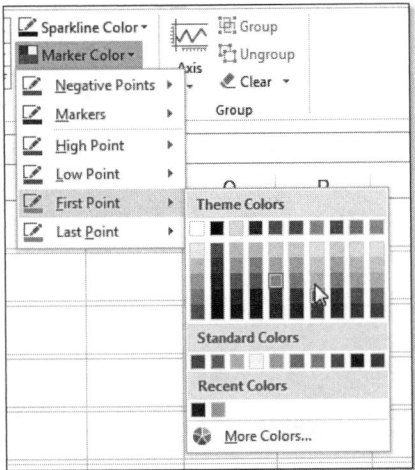

Figure 33.13
Control the color of the chosen markers in this drop-down.

You can also group sparklines or clear sparklines using icons in the Group group. The Axis drop-down appears in this group and contains the most important settings for sparklines. You learn how to use the Axis drop-down in the next example.

Controlling Axis Values for Sparklines

Figure 33.14 presents a group of sparkcolumns showing the average high temperatures for several cities. These cities are a mix of tropical and frigid locales.

The default behavior is that each sparkline in the group gets its own scale. This worked for the varying economic indicators in Figure 33.8. However, it does not work here.

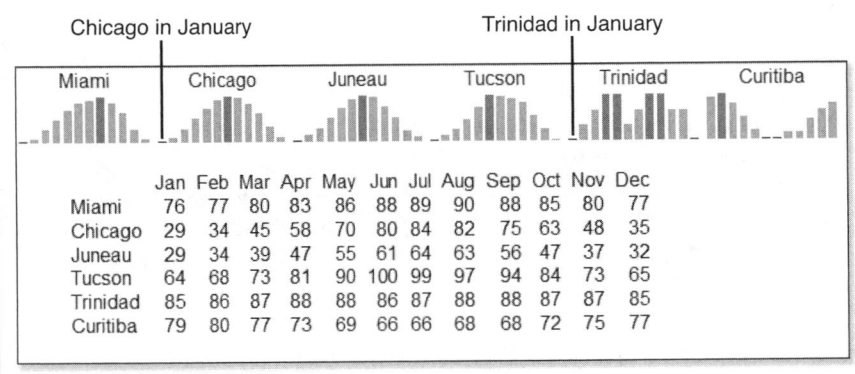

Figure 33.14
The automatic vertical scale assigned to each sparkline doesn't work in this example.

Chicago in January   Trinidad in January

	Jan	Feb	Mar	Apr	May	Jun	Jul	Aug	Sep	Oct	Nov	Dec
Miami	76	77	80	83	86	88	89	90	88	85	80	77
Chicago	29	34	45	58	70	80	84	82	75	63	48	35
Juneau	29	34	39	47	55	61	64	63	56	47	37	32
Tucson	64	68	73	81	90	100	99	97	94	84	73	65
Trinidad	85	86	87	88	88	86	87	88	88	87	87	85
Curitiba	79	80	77	73	69	66	66	68	68	72	75	77

When the vertical axis scale is set to Automatic, you can never really know the high and low of the scale in use. If you study the data and the sparkline for Trinidad, it appears as if Excel has chosen a min point of 84.8 and a max point of 89. Without any scale, you might think that Trinidad in January is as cold as Chicago in January.

Figure 33.15 shows the options available in the Axis drop-down on the right end of the Sparkline Tools Design tab. The important settings here are the options for the minimum value and maximum value.

Figure 33.15
Control the vertical axis using this drop-down.

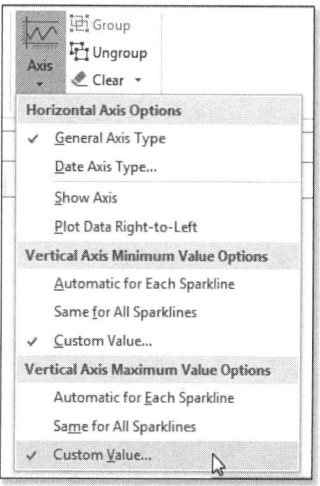

If you change the minimum and maximum values to the setting Same for All Sparklines, then all six sparklines in this group have the same min and max scale. The sparklines in Figure 33.16 initially look better. Juneau is never as warm as Tucson, but you still do not know what the max and min values are.

Figure 33.16
Force all sparklines to have the same vertical scale.

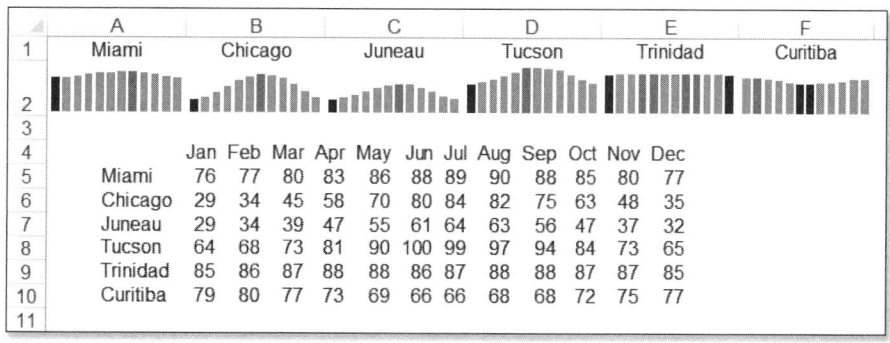

	A	B	C	D	E	F
1	Miami	Chicago	Juneau	Tucson	Trinidad	Curitiba
2						

		Jan	Feb	Mar	Apr	May	Jun	Jul	Aug	Sep	Oct	Nov	Dec
5	Miami	76	77	80	83	86	88	89	90	88	85	80	77
6	Chicago	29	34	45	58	70	80	84	82	75	63	48	35
7	Juneau	29	34	39	47	55	61	64	63	56	47	37	32
8	Tucson	64	68	73	81	90	100	99	97	94	84	73	65
9	Trinidad	85	86	87	88	88	86	87	88	88	87	87	85
10	Curitiba	79	80	77	73	69	66	66	68	68	72	75	77

Take a close look at Chicago. It appears that the January high temperature is about zero, but the data table shows that the average high temperature in January is 29. You can estimate that these columns run from a minimum of 28 to a maximum of 101, based on looking through the data.

My suggestion is to always visit the Axis drop-down and set custom min and max values. For example, in the temperature example, you would set a minimum of 0 and a maximum of 100.

Setting Up Win/Loss Sparklines

The data for a Win/Loss sparkline is simple: Put a 1 (or any positive number) for a win and put a –1 (or any negative number) for a loss. Put a zero to have no marker.

In Figure 33.17, you can see the data for a pair of Win/Loss sparklines. The 2 in cell F3 does not cause the marker to appear any taller than any of the 1's in the other cells. However, it does cause that marker to be shown as the max point.

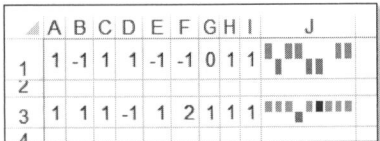

Figure 33.17
Data sets for wins and losses are composed of 1's and –1's.

The data for the Win/Loss sparkcolumn chart does not have to be composed of 1's and –1's. Any positive and negative numbers will work.

In Figure 33.18, the data shows the closing price for the Dow for a period of a few months. Column D calculates the daily change. The Win/Loss chart in rows 4 and 5 does not show the magnitude of the change, but instead focuses on how many days in a row had market gains versus market losses.

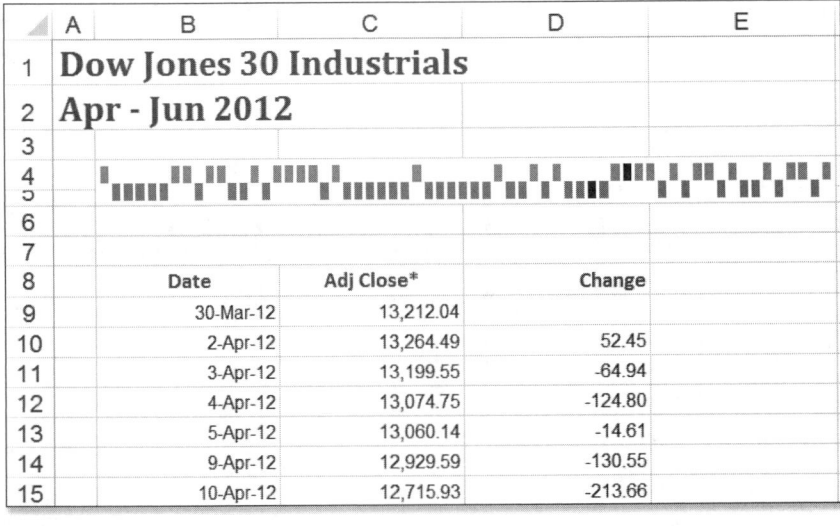

Figure 33.18
This chart focuses on how many days in a row were gains or losses. The magnitude of the change is not factored in.

The following are some notes about the chart in Figure 33.18:

- Cells B4:E5 are merged in order to show a larger sparkline.

- If you stretch a sparkcolumn or a win/loss chart out wide enough, gaps eventually show up between the columns. This helps to quantify the number of events in a streak.

- Two markers near the right side of column D are a darker color. These represent the largest negative change and largest positive change.

Showing Detail by Enlarging the Sparkline and Adding Labels

The examples of sparklines created by Tufte in *Beautiful Evidence* almost always label the final point. Some examples include min and max values or a gray box to indicate the normal range of values.

Professor Tufte's definition of sparklines includes the word *small*. If you are going to be showing sparklines on a computer screen, there is no reason they have to stay small.

When you increase the height and width of a cell, the sparkline automatically grows to fill the cell. If you merge cells, the sparkline fills the complete range of merged cells.

In Figure 33.19, the height of row 2 is set to 56.25. This height allows for five rows of 8-point Calibri text to appear in the cell. To determine the optimum height for your font, type **1** and press Alt+Enter, type **2** and press Alt+Enter, type **3** and press Alt+Enter, type **4** and press Alt+Enter, and then type **5** in a cell. Then select Home, Format, AutoFit Row Height.

The sparkline in cell B2 is set to have a custom minimum and a custom maximum that match the minimum and maximum of the data set.

Figure 33.19
This sparkline has many labels, but they are all manually added outside of the sparkline.

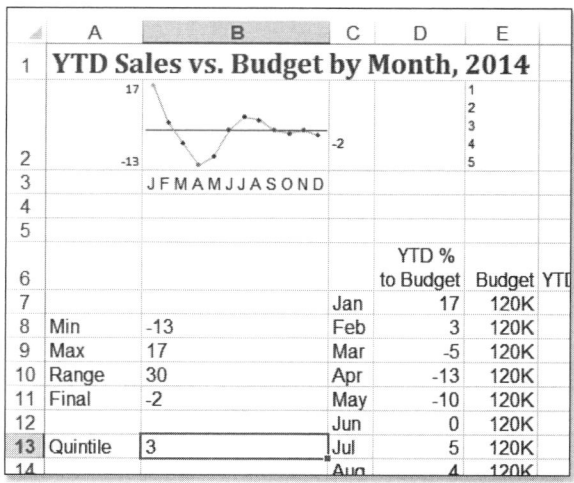

The label in cell A2 is right-justified 8-point Calibri font. The formula in A2 is
=B9&REPT(CHAR(10),4)&B8. This formula concatenates the maximum value, four line feeds, and
the minimum value. Ensure the Wrap Text icon is selected on the Home tab.

The labels in B3 are 10-point Calibri. Type **J F M A M J J A S O N D** in cell B3 and adjust the
column width to fit the text.

Formulas in B10 and B13 calculate the range from min to max as well as the quintile where the final
value falls. The formula in C2 uses =REPT(CHAR(10),B13-1)&B11 to put the final label at about the
right height to match the final point.

In Figure 33.20, the city labels are values typed in the same cell as the sparkcolumns. The max scale
is set to 120 to make sure there is room for the city name to appear. The Month abbreviations below
the charts are "J F M A M J J A S O N D" in 6.5-point Courier New font.

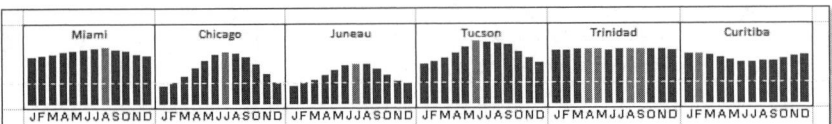

Figure 33.20
Labels are created by
typing in a small font in
the cell.

If you set a row height equal to 110, you can fit 10 lines of text in
the cell using Alt+Enter. Even with a height of 55, you can fit five
lines of text. This enables the label for the final point to get near
to the final point.

In Figure 33.21, a semitransparent gray box indicates the acceptable limits for a measurement. In this case, anything outside of
95% to 105% is sent for review. These gray boxes are Shapes
from the Insert tab.

Use the following tips when setting up the box:

 **Tip**

After trying both 6-point and
7-point font and not having the
labels line up with the bars, I
ended up using 6.5-point font
and adjusting the column widths
until the columns lined up with
the labels.

1. Temporarily change the first two points in the first cell to be at the min and max for the box.

2. Increase the zoom to 400%.

3. Draw a rectangle in the cell.

4. Use the Drawing Tools Format tab to set the outline to None.

5. Under Shape Fill, select More Fill Colors. Choose a shade of gray. Because shapes are drawn on
   top of the sparkline layer, drag the transparency slider up to about 70% transparent.

6. Use the resize handles to make sure the top and bottom of the box go through the first and
   second points of the line.

Figure 33.21
A gray box shows the acceptable range to help the reader locate items outside of this range.

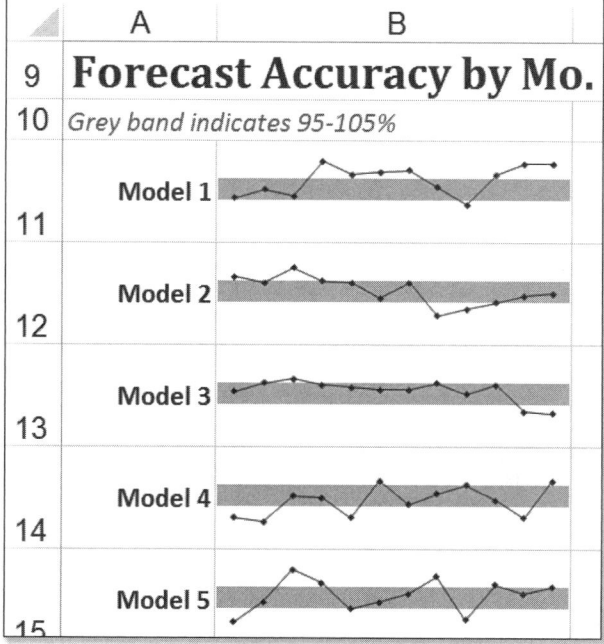

7. After getting the box sized appropriately, reset the first two data points back to their original values.

8. Copy the cell that contains the first box. Paste onto the other sparkline cells. Because the sparklines are not copied, only the box is pasted.

 **Tip**

It is possible to copy sparklines. You have to copy both the sparkline and the data source in a single copy. If your copy range includes both elements, the sparkline is pasted.

Other Sparkline Options

You can choose how to deal with gaps in the data. Select Sparkline Tools Design, Edit Data, Hidden and Empty Cells to display the Hidden and Empty Cell Settings dialog, shown in Figure 33.22.

By default, any missing data in the source range is plotted as a gap, as shown in the top chart in Figure 33.22. Alternatively, you can choose to plot the missing values as zero (center chart) or have Excel connect the data points with a straight line (bottom chart). Also, by default, any data in hidden rows or columns is removed from the sparkline. To keep the hidden data in the chart, select the Show Data in Hidden Rows and Columns check box in Figure 33.22.

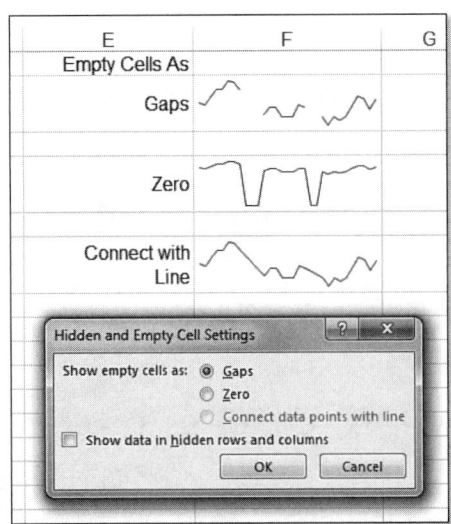

Figure 33.22
Choose how to deal with missing points.

USING SMARTART, SHAPES, WORDART, AND TEXT BOXES

Images and artwork provide an interesting visual break from tables of numbers in Excel 2013. Office 2013 provides four elements that you can use to illustrate a workbook:

- **SmartArt**—SmartArt is a collection of similar shapes, arranged to imply a process, groups, or a hierarchy. You can add new shapes, reverse the order of shapes, and change the color of shapes. SmartArt includes a text editor that allows for Level 1 and Level 2 text for each shape in a diagram. Many styles of SmartArt include the capability to add a small picture or logo to each shape.

- **Shapes**—You can add interesting shapes to a document. Shapes can contain words. In fact, shapes are the only art objects in which the words can come from a cell on the worksheet. You can add glow, bevel, and 3D effects to shapes.

- **WordArt**—WordArt enables you to present ordinary text in a stylized manner. You can use WordArt to bend, rotate, and twist the characters in text.

- **Text boxes**—With text boxes, you can flow text in a defined area. The text box feature is excellent if you need to include paragraphs of body copy in a worksheet. Text boxes support multiple columns of text.

Using SmartArt

You use SmartArt to show a series of similar shapes, where each shape represents a related step, concept, idea, or grouping. You build SmartArt by typing Level 1 text and Level 2 text in a text pane. Excel automatically updates the diagram, adding shapes as you add new entries in the text pane.

The goal of SmartArt is to enable you to create a great-looking graphic with a minimum of effort. After you define a SmartArt image, you can change to any of the other 180 layouts by choosing the desired layout from the gallery. Text is carried from one layout to the next. Figure 34.1 shows four SmartArt styles:

- **Basic Process**—In this layout, all text is typed as Level 1.

- **Accent Process**—This layout puts the Level 1 text in the background and highlights the Level 2 text in the foreground boxes.

- **Picture Accent Process**—This layout gives equal weight to the Level 1 and Level 2 text. Pictures are added behind each shape.

- **Picture Accent List**—Unlike the process charts, a list chart does not include arrows to indicate a process.

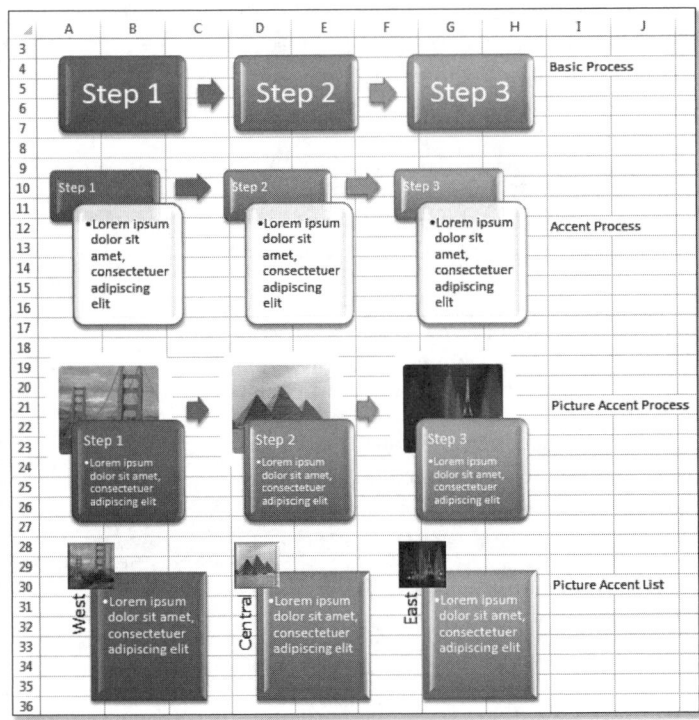

Figure 34.1
Subtle differences in four of the 180 possible SmartArt layouts give more weight to either Level 1 or Level 2 text.

Elements Common in Most SmartArt

A SmartArt style is a collection of two or more related shapes. In most styles, you can add additional shapes to illustrate a longer process. However, a few styles are limited to only a certain number of items.

Each shape can contain a headline (Level 1 text). Most shapes allow for body copy (Level 2 text). A few shapes allow for a picture. Some of the 180 layouts show only Level 1 text. If you switch to a style that does not display Level 2 text and then back, the shape remembers the Level 2 text it originally included. After you save and close the file, the hidden text is removed.

While you are editing SmartArt, a text pane that is slightly reminiscent of PowerPoint appears. You can type some bullet points into the text pane. If you demote a bullet point, the text changes from Level 1 text to Level 2 text. If you add a new Level 1 bullet point, Excel adds a new shape to the SmartArt.

Tour of the SmartArt Categories

The SmartArt gallery groups the 129 SmartArt layouts into the following eight broad categories:

- **List**—Designed to show a nonsequential list of information. Variations include horizontal, vertical, and bending lists. Some lists include chevrons, and some include pictures. In general, these styles do not include arrows between shapes.

- **Process**—Designed to show a sequential list of steps. Variations include horizontal, vertical, bending, equations, funnels, gears, and several varieties of arrows. Some process charts allow the inclusion of images. Most styles include arrows or other connectors in order to convey a sequence.

- **Cycle**—Designed to show a series of steps that repeat. It includes cycle charts, radial charts, a gear chart, and a pie chart.

- **Hierarchy**—Designed to show organization charts, decision trees, and other hierarchical relationships. Variations include horizontal, vertical, and with and without connecting lines.

- **Relationship**—Designed to show a relationship between items. Many of the layouts in this category are duplicated from the other seven categories.

- **Matrix**—Designed to show four quadrants of a list. The Titled Matrix layout offers a fifth block for an overall title. New in Excel 2013 is the Cycle Matrix that allows for Level 2 text outside the main blocks.

- **Pyramid**—Designed to show containment, overlapping, proportional, or interconnected relationships.

- **Picture**—All the layouts that contain pictures are repeated in this category. In Excel 2013, Microsoft added 16 new picture layouts that appear only in this category. Some of these picture layouts are appropriate only for pictures with little or no text.

 **Note**

Thirty of the SmartArt layouts can include pictures.

Figure 34.2 shows one version of each of the eight categories.

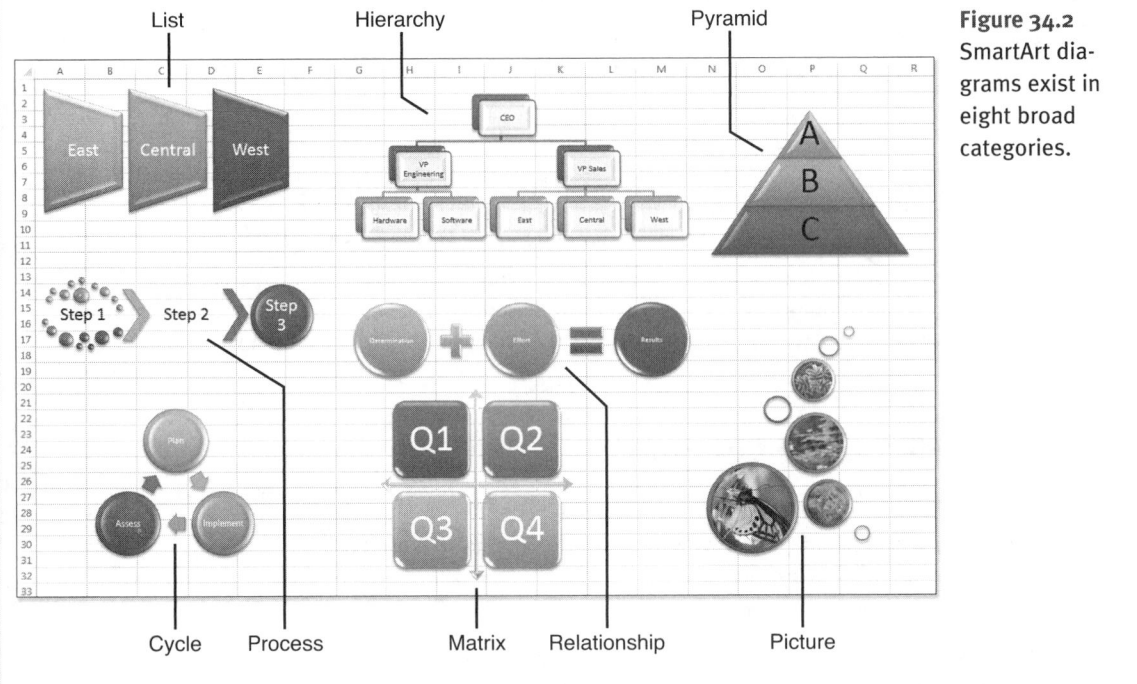

Figure 34.2
SmartArt diagrams exist in eight broad categories.

Inserting SmartArt

Although there are 180 different layouts of SmartArt, you follow the same basic steps to insert any SmartArt layout:

1. Select a cell in a blank section of the workbook.

2. From the Insert tab, select SmartArt from the Illustrations group. The Choose a SmartArt Graphic dialog appears.

3. Choose a category in the left side of the Choose a SmartArt Graphic dialog.

4. Click a SmartArt type in the center of the Choose a SmartArt Graphic dialog.

5. Read the description on the right side. This description tells you if the layout is good for Level 1 text, Level 2 text, or both. In Figure 34.3, the Vertical Chevron List layout is good for large amounts of Level 2 text.

6. Repeat steps 4 and 5 until you find a style suitable for your content. Click OK. Figure 34.4 shows an outline of the SmartArt drawn on the worksheet. The flashing insertion cursor is in the first item of the text pane. One element of the SmartArt is selected. When you type text at the flashing insertion point, it is added to the selected shape.

Figure 34.3
The description for each style tells you whether a particular style is appropriate for Level 1 or Level 2 text.

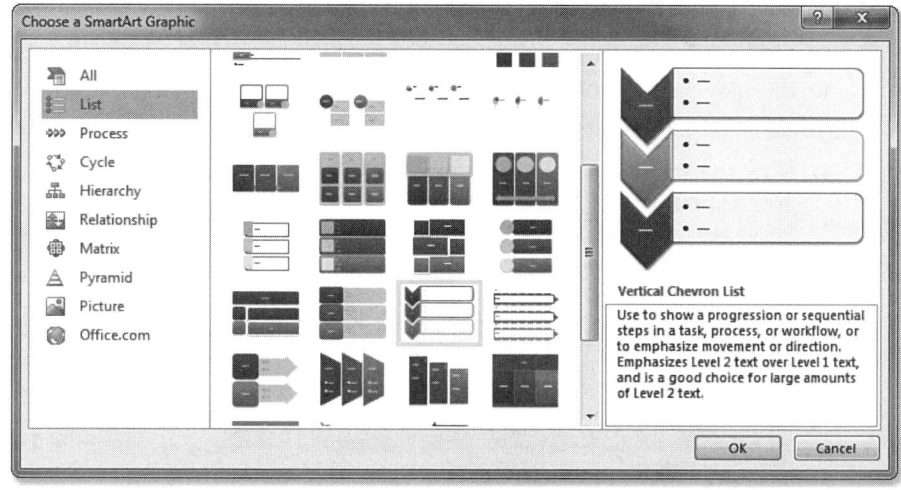

Figure 34.4
When you type in the text pane, the text is added to the selected element of the SmartArt.

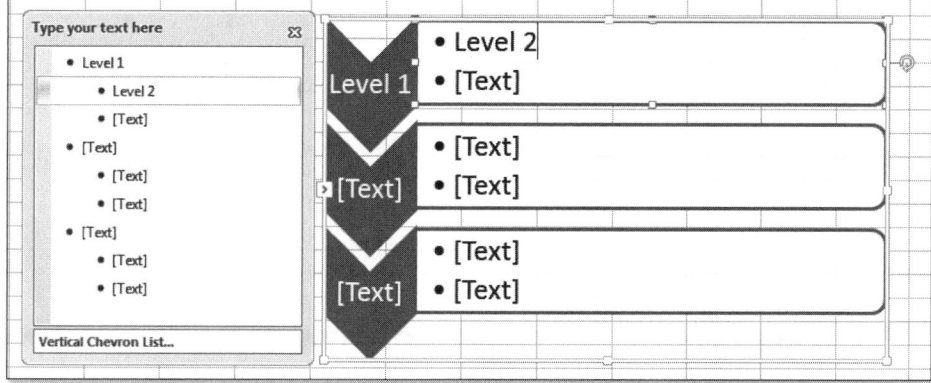

7. Fill in the text pane with text for your SmartArt. You can add, delete, promote, or demote items by using icons in the SmartArt Tools Design tab. The SmartArt updates as you type more text. In most cases, adding a new Level 1 item adds a new shape element to the SmartArt.

8. Add longer text to the SmartArt, and Excel shrinks the font size of all the elements to make the text fit. You can make the entire SmartArt graphic larger at any time by grabbing the resize handles in the corners of the SmartArt and dragging to a new size. After you resize the graphic, Excel resizes the text to make it fit in the SmartArt at the largest size possible.

9. The color scheme of the SmartArt initially appears in one color. To change the color scheme, use the Change Colors drop-down in the SmartArt Tools Design tab. Excel offers several versions of monochrome styles and five styles of color variations for each diagram.

10. Choose a basic or 3D style from the SmartArt Styles gallery. The first three 3D styles (Polished, Inset, or Cartoon) have a suitable mix of effects but are still readable.

11. Move the SmartArt to the proper location. Position the mouse over the border of the SmartArt, avoiding the eight Resize handles. The cursor changes to a four-headed arrow. Click and drag the SmartArt to a new location. If you drag the SmartArt to the left side of the worksheet, the text pane moves to the right of the SmartArt.

12. Click outside the SmartArt. Excel embeds the SmartArt graphic in the worksheet and hides the SmartArt tabs, as shown in Figure 34.5.

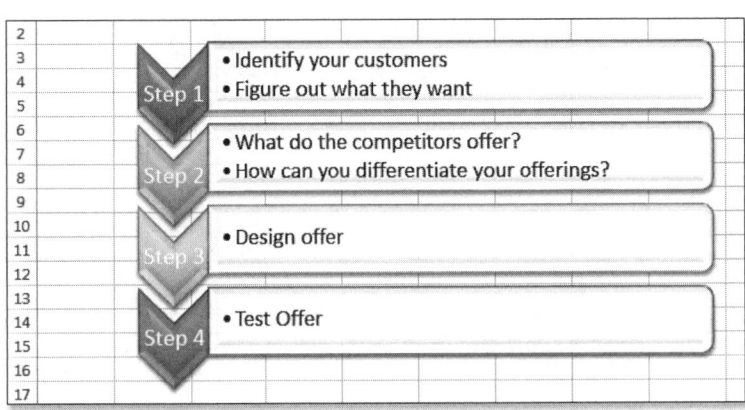

Figure 34.5
Click outside the SmartArt boundary to embed the completed SmartArt.

Changing Existing SmartArt to a New Style

You can change SmartArt to a new style in a couple ways:

- Left-click the SmartArt and then select SmartArt Tools, Layouts from the Design tab to choose a new layout. The Layouts drop-down initially shows only the styles that Excel thinks are a close fit to the current style. If you want to access the complete list of styles, you have to select More Layouts. Hover over layouts to preview how the message will appear in the new layout. Figure 34.6 shows the same message from Figure 34.5 in four different layouts.

- A faster way to access the complete list of styles is to right-click between two shapes in the SmartArt and select Change Layout from the context menu. This step is a little tricky because you cannot click an existing shape. Instead, you must click inside the SmartArt border, but on a portion of the SmartArt that is empty.

Figure 34.6
The same words in four different layouts.

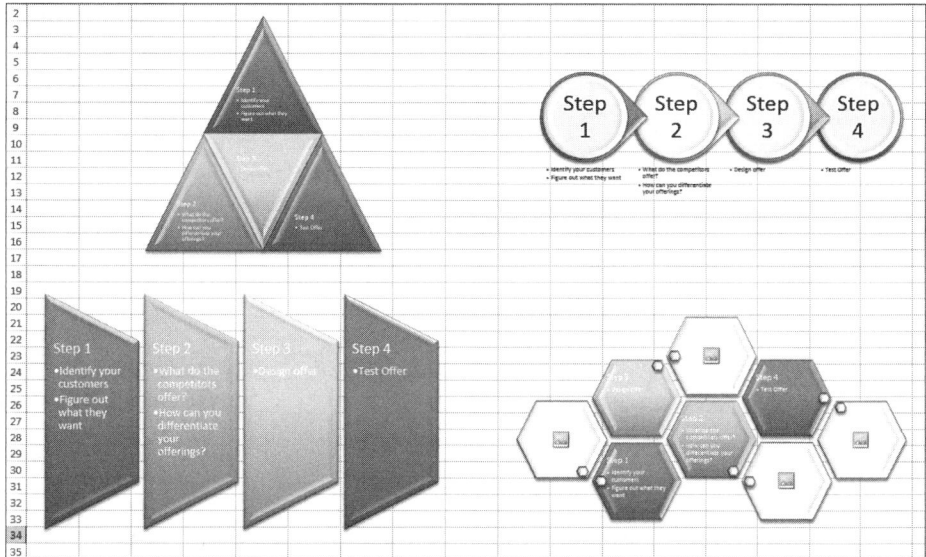

Micromanaging SmartArt Elements

The two tabs for SmartArt tools enable you to manage the SmartArt elements—the Design tab and the Format tab.

The Design tab enables you to change the overall design of the SmartArt. If you stay on the Design tab, Microsoft makes sure that your SmartArt looks good because it keeps the font for all Level 2 text consistent for all shapes and all the shapes proportional.

However, if you need to override some aspect of one shape, you can do so on the Format tab.

 Caution

If you want to fine-tune the text in a particular box, select the SmartArt Tools from the Format tab to micromanage any element in the SmartArt. However, use caution because adjusting the built-in properties is a great way to ruin the look of the SmartArt.

Changing Text Formatting in One Element

In Automatic mode, Excel chooses a font size that is small enough to show the longest text completely. This can cause problems if you have one shape with long text and short text everywhere else. In this case, Excel chooses a small font size for the long text and then forces all the other items to have tiny text as well. In such a situation, you might want to override the text size for the shape that has the longest text. Excel then automatically resizes the font size in the remaining automatic shapes to be larger.

The mini toolbar is useful for making these changes. You select the text either directly in the shape or in the text pane. Immediately after you complete the selection, you should watch for an almost-transparent formatting box to appear. Then you immediately move the mouse to the box to prevent it from disappearing. You can change the font size by using the drop-down in the mini toolbar. If you allow the mini toolbar to disappear, you can use the formatting tools on the Home tab to change the font size.

As shown in Figure 34.7, the long Level 2 text in step 4 was resized. Excel then calculated the proper text size for steps 1 through 3, resulting in the text in the top three shapes automatically growing to a larger font size.

Caution

When you change any setting on the Format tab, Microsoft turns off the automatic formatting for the other elements. For this reason, changing a setting on the Format tab is a great way to make horrible-looking SmartArt. If you absolutely have to use the Format tab, you should first get your SmartArt as close as possible to the final version by using the Design tab.

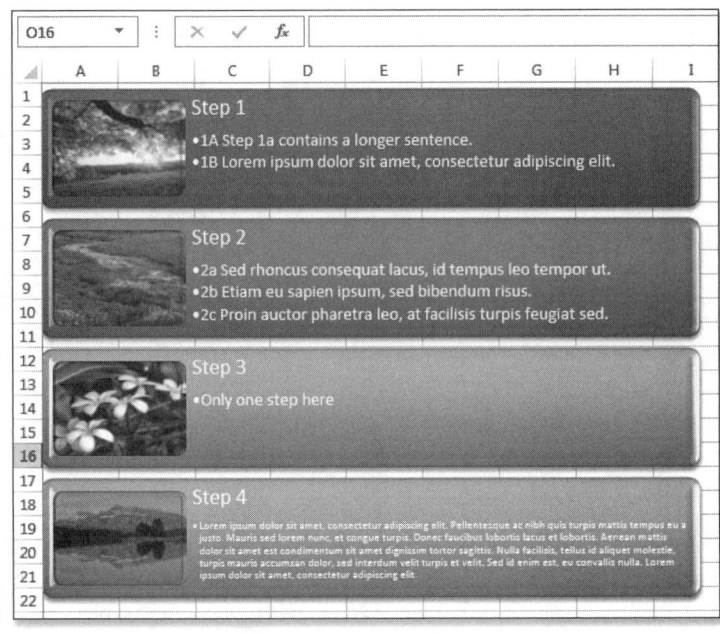

Figure 34.7
When you manually override the font size in the fourth shape, the text in the remaining three shapes automatically becomes larger.

Changing One Shape

You can edit many items for a SmartArt shape. To see how this works, click any shape in the SmartArt and then try the following:

- Use the green handle to rotate the shape.

- Use the resize handles to resize the shape.

- Use the move handle to nudge the shape.

- Select Shapes, Change Shape from the SmartArt Tools Format tab to change the shape completely.

- Select settings from the Shape Styles group to change fill, outline, and effects for the shape.

- Choose settings from the WordArt Styles group to change the text inside the shape.

- Right-click the shape and select Format Shape to have complete control over the shape.

In general, SmartArt created on the Design tab looks uniform and neat. When you move to the Format tab, the possibility for chaos arises. For example, the SmartArt in Figure 34.8, which was created in the Format tab, contains mixed effects, font sizes, and rotation.

Figure 34.8
After experimenting with the Format tab, select Reset Graphic on the Design tab to make the SmartArt uniform.

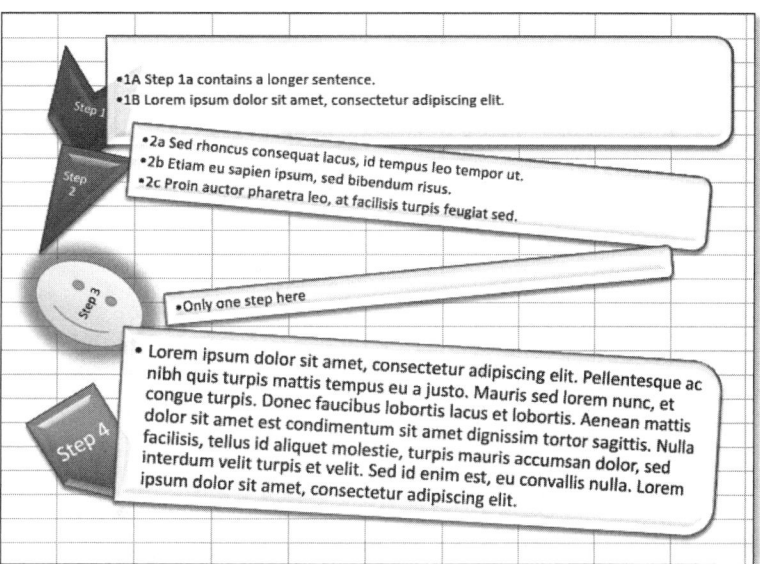

Controlling SmartArt Shapes from the Text Pane

The text pane represents a fantastic improvement over business diagrams in legacy versions of Excel. By using only the keyboard, you can add or delete shapes and promote or demote items. Furthermore, the text pane has proofing tools such as spell check. Using the text pane is similar to creating bullet points in a PowerPoint slide.

Figure 34.9 shows a newly inserted pyramid SmartArt in Excel. By default, most new SmartArt diagrams have three shapes, but you can change that number by using the text pane.

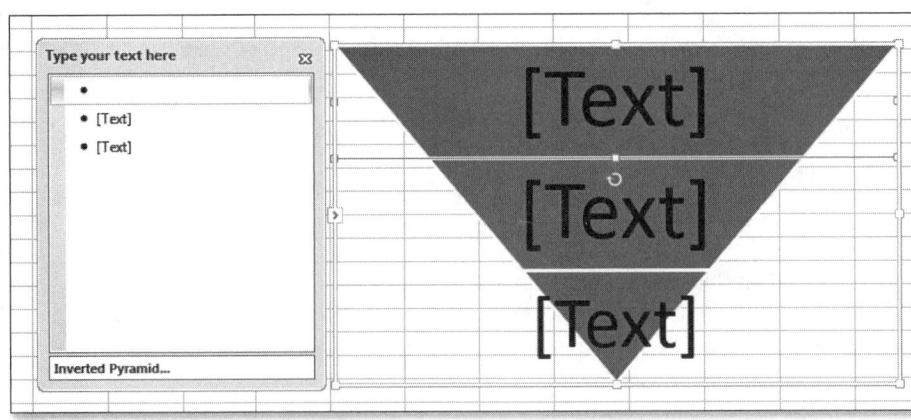

Figure 34.9
A default SmartArt includes three shapes. You can edit the number of shapes by using the text pane.

The following rules apply to the text pane for SmartArt:

- Press the up-arrow and down-arrow keys to move from one line to another.

- Press the Enter key to insert a new line below the current line. The new line is at the same level as the current line. Adding a new Level 1 line inserts a new shape in the SmartArt.

- Press the Tab key to demote Level 1 text to Level 2 text.

- Press Shift+Tab to promote Level 2 text to Level 1 text.

- Press the Backspace key on an empty line to delete the line.

- Press Delete at the end of any line to combine text from the next line with this line.

- Press End to move to the end of the current line.

- Press Home to move to the beginning of the current line.

As you add shapes, Excel continues to attempt to squeeze them into the default size. You can resize an entire piece of SmartArt by using the resize handles around the SmartArt.

Strictly as an example of how the text pane works, you can use the following steps to customize Figure 34.9 into Figure 34.10. This example illustrates how quickly you can change from the default SmartArt with three shapes to any number of shapes:

1. Type **Item 1** and press Enter.

2. Type **1SubA** and then press Tab to demote the item. Next, press the down-arrow key to move to Text 2.

3. Type **Item 2** and press Enter.

4. Type **2a** and press Tab and Enter.

5. Type **2b** and press Tab and the down-arrow key.

6. Type **Item 3** and press Enter.

7. Type **3a** and press Tab and Enter.

8. Because Excel assumes the next item will be Level 2 text, press Shift+Tab to promote this item to Level 1.

9. Type **Item 4** and press Enter. Type **Item 5** and press Enter. Type **Item 6** and press Enter.

10. Using the mouse, resize the SmartArt so it is larger.

11. From the Quick Styles gallery on the Design tab, choose a color scheme.

The result is shown in Figure 34.10. As this example shows, by using only the keyboard and the text pane, you can quickly expand SmartArt and add Level 2 subpoints.

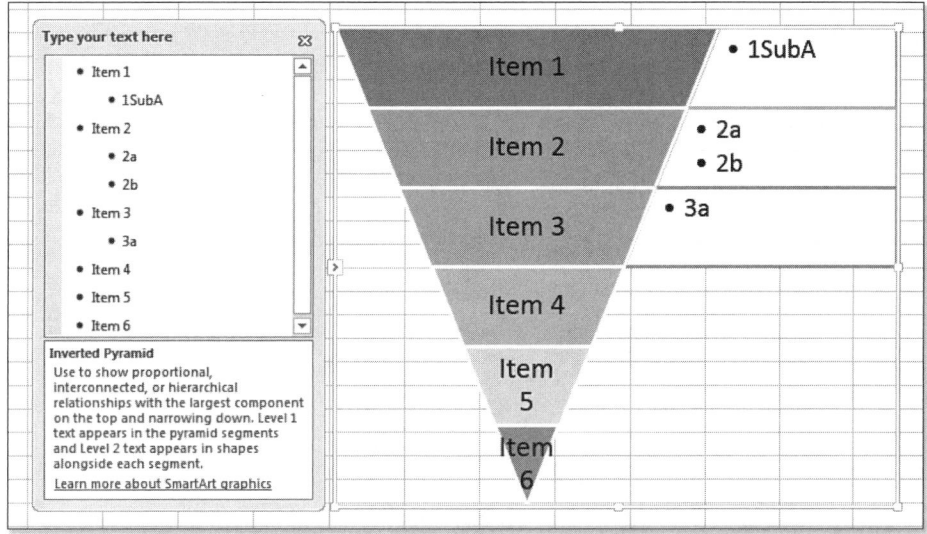

Figure 34.10
Add additional shapes and subpoints by using the text pane.

Adding Images to SmartArt

Thirty SmartArt layouts in the Picture category are designed to hold small images in addition to the text. In some of these styles, the picture is emphasized. However, in other pictures, the focus is on the text, and the picture is an accent.

When you select one of these styles, you can add text using the text pane and then specify pictures by clicking the picture icon inside each Level 1 shape. The SmartArt shows a picture icon next to bullet points in the text pane and in each shape, as shown in Figure 34.11.

Clickable Picture Icons

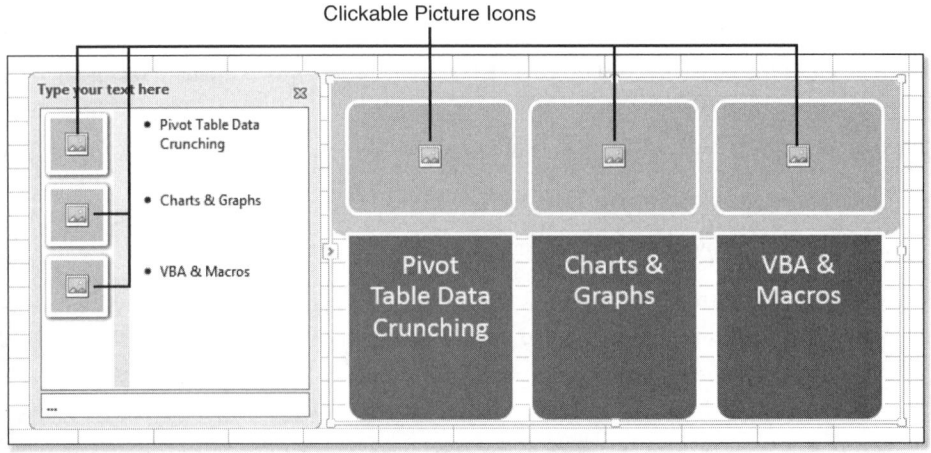

Figure 34.11
Each Level 1
bullet includes
a picture
placeholder.

You can click a picture icon to display the Insert Picture dialog. Then you can choose a picture and click Insert. Repeat this process to add each additional picture. The pictures are cropped automatically to fit the allotted area, as shown in Figure 34.12.

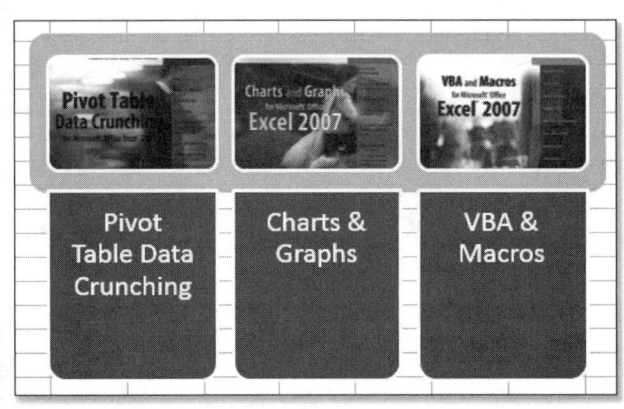

Figure 34.12
Pictures have been added to each shape.

After adding pictures, you can use all the formatting tools on the Picture Tools Format tab.

➡ *For details on the picture formatting tools,* **see** *Chapter 35, "Using Pictures and Clip Art."*

Special Considerations for Organizational Charts and Hierarchical SmartArt

Hierarchical SmartArt can contain more than two text levels. As you add more levels to the SmartArt, Excel continues to intelligently add boxes and resize them to fit.

Figure 34.13 shows a diagram created in the Hierarchy layout. In this layout, each level is assigned a different color.

Figure 34.13
Hierarchical SmartArt can contain more than two levels.

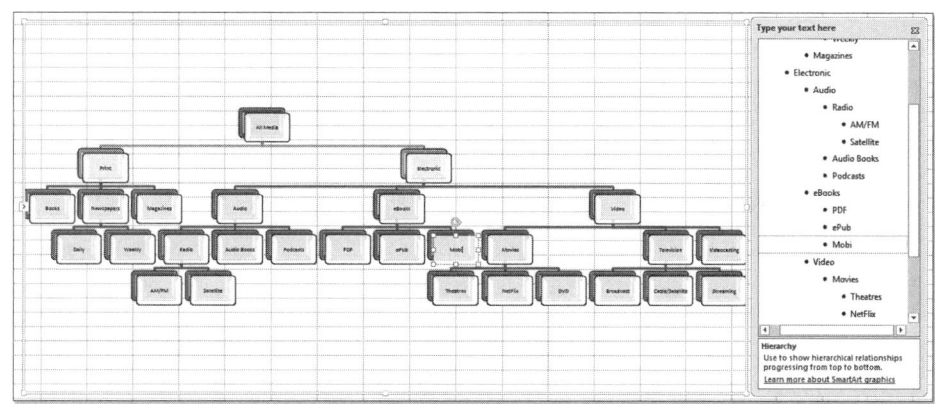

Four styles in the Hierarchical category are organization charts. These layouts are used to describe reporting relationships in an organization. There are a few extra options in the ribbon for organization charts. For example, if you select the SmartArt Tools Design tab, the Add Shape drop-down includes the option Add Assistant, as shown in Figure 34.14. You can select this option to add an extra shape immediately below the selected level.

In the Create Graphic group of the Design tab, the Org Chart drop-down offers four options for showing the boxes within a group. First, you select the manager for the group. Then you select the appropriate type from the drop-down to affect all direct reports for the manager. Figure 34.15 illustrates the four options for Org Chart:

- **VP of Sales**—Shows a standard organization chart. The regions are arranged side by side.

- **VP of Manufacturing**—Includes a Right Hanging group that enables departments to be arranged vertically to the right of the line.

- **VP of Engineering**—Includes a Left Hanging group that enables departments to be arranged vertically to the left of the line.

- **CFO**—Includes a Both group that lists direct reports in two columns under the manager on both sides of the vertical line.

In each group, the assistant box is set off from the other boxes.

Add Assistant

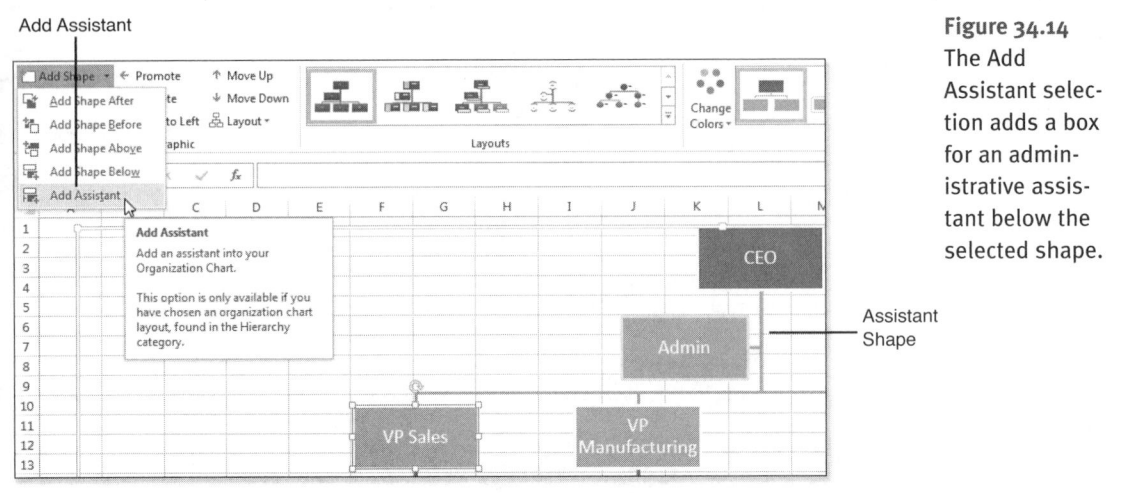

Assistant
Shape

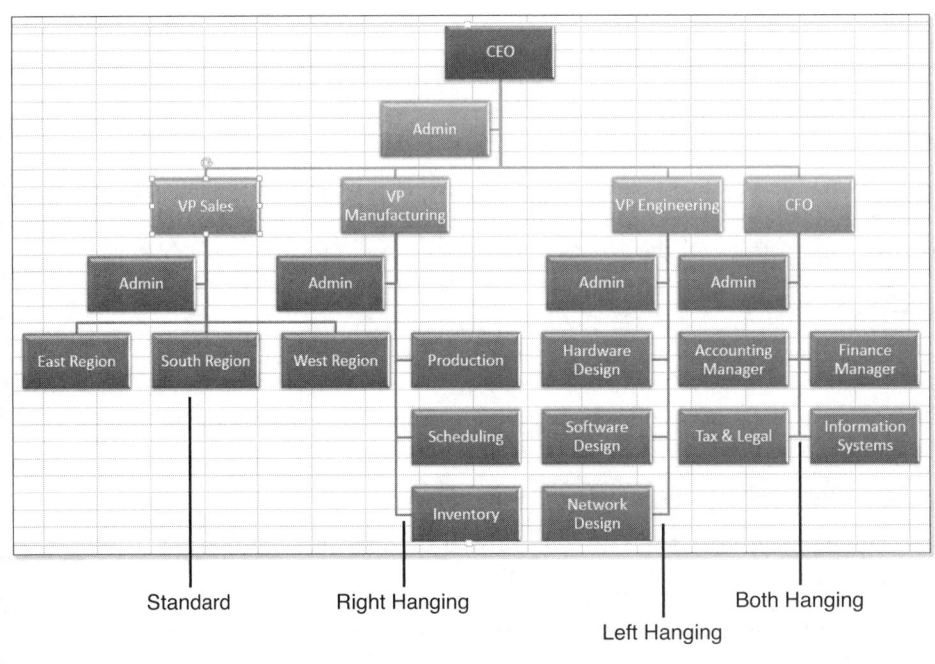

Standard   Right Hanging   Both Hanging

Left Hanging

Using Limited SmartArt

Most of the SmartArt examples in the previous section are expandable, which means that new shapes are added to the SmartArt as you add Level 1 text. However, the following SmartArt styles cannot be expanded:

- The top-left image in Figure 34.16 shows a gear chart. Both the gear and funnel charts are limited to three items. If you add additional items to the text pane, each appears with a red X. These items do not display in the SmartArt, but they are stored temporarily in case you change to another SmartArt layout. When you save the workbook, the text associated with the fourth and subsequent shapes is deleted. This prevents you from inadvertently leaving hidden bullet points before sending the workbook to a client.

- Many of the arrow layouts in the Relationship category are limited to two shapes.

- The Matrix layouts are limited to four quadrants. Grid Matrix offers four quadrants plus a title, as shown in the center of Figure 34.16.

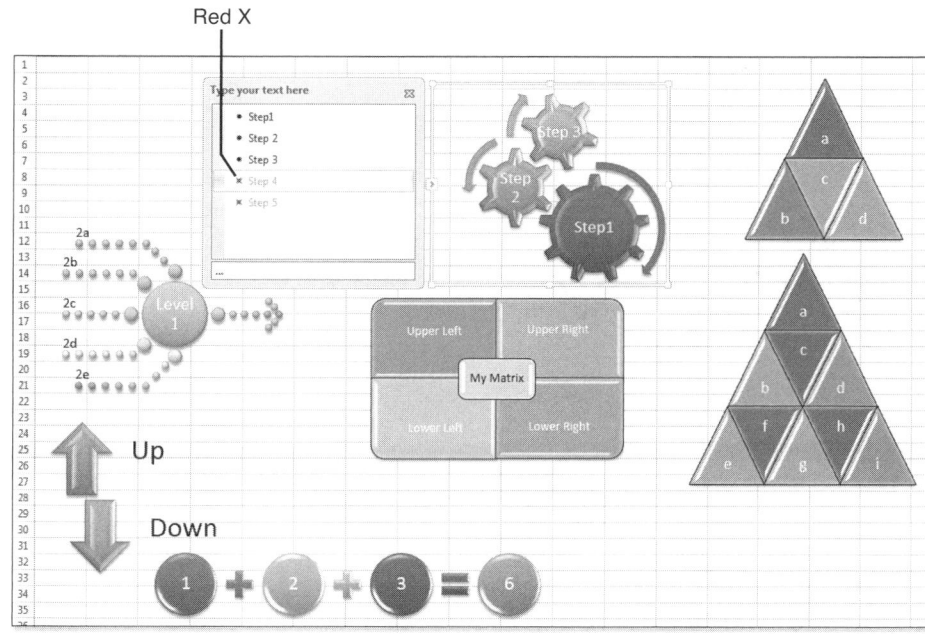

Figure 34.16
Arrows, gears, funnels, and matrix shapes have certain limitations on the number of shapes they can contain.

- The Segmented Pyramid style can be expanded, but it must contain 1, 4, 9, or 16 shapes. As soon as you add a fifth shape to the four-shape triangle in the upper-right corner of Figure 34.16, an entire row is added to the bottom of the pyramid, whether you specify five, six, seven, eight, or nine shapes.

- The Equation style can be expanded, but the answer is always the last Level 1 item in the text pane.

Deciphering the Labeled Hierarchy Layouts

A few of the SmartArt layouts in Excel 2013 are somewhat confusing. For example, Figure 34.17 shows a Labeled Hierarchy Chart. In this layout, the first Level 1 text is shown in a box at the beginning of the diagram. All the sub-items should be typed as Level 2 items below the first shape. After building all the boxes in the hierarchy, you should add an additional Level 1 item for each level in the diagram. These final Level 1 items will be used for the labels at the left side of the diagram.

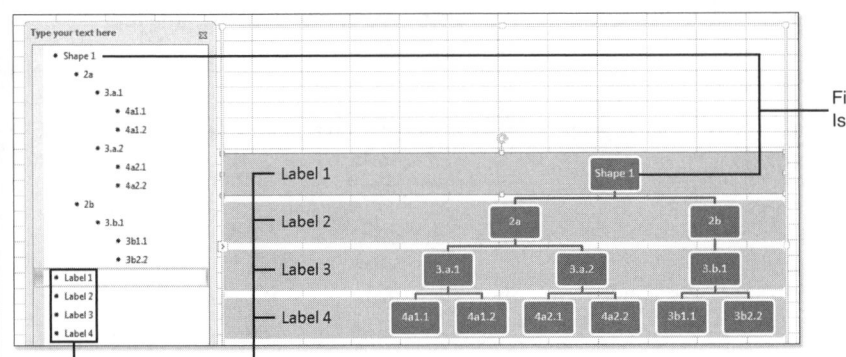

Figure 34.17
The Labeled Hierarchy layouts require extra Level 1 elements after the main part of the diagram to label each level.

First Level 1 Is Top Shape

Add Additional Level 1 Shape for Level Labels

Overall, SmartArt is a great addition to the Office family. The one real drawback related to using SmartArt in Excel is its inability to create dynamic SmartArt where the text for a shape is the result of a calculation.

The following section details how a regular shape can contain calculated text. The solution to creating dynamic SmartArt is to build SmartArt and then use the Convert to Shapes icon in the SmartArt Tools Design tab. You can then link the individual shapes to formula cells.

Using Shapes to Display Cell Contents

In legacy versions of Excel, shapes were known as AutoShapes. Excel 2013 shapes have some new formatting options, such as shadow, glow, and bevel.

Perhaps the best part of shapes is that you can tie the text on a shape to a worksheet cell. For example, in Figure 34.18, the shape is set to display the current value of cell B2. Every time the worksheet is calculated, the text on the shape is updated.

Follow these steps to insert a shape into a worksheet:

1. Select a blank area of the worksheet.

2. From the Insert tab, open the Shapes drop-down.

3. Select one of the 160 basic shapes, as shown in Figure 34.19.

Figure 34.18
You can set shapes to display the current value of a cell.

Figure 34.19
Choose from these shapes.

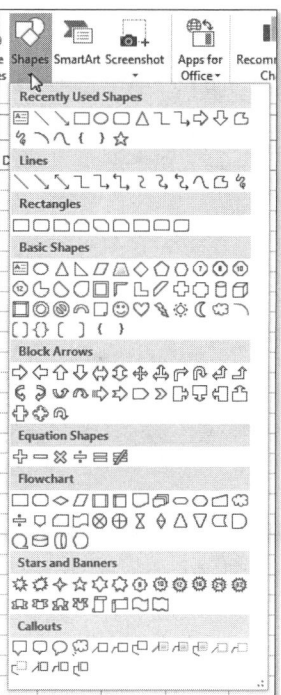

4. The mouse pointer changes to a small crosshair. Click and drag in the worksheet to draw the shape.

5. Choose a color scheme from the Shapes Styles drop-down.

6. Select Shape Effects, Preset, and select an effect.

7. Look for a yellow handle on the shape, which enables you to change the inflection point for the shape. For example, on the rounded rectangle, sliding the yellow handle controls how wide the rounded corners are.

8. Look for a gray circle on the outside of the shape. If necessary, drag this circle to rotate the shape.

9. To include static text in the shape, click in the middle of the shape and type the text. You can control the style by using the WordArt Styles drop-down. You can control text size and color by using the formatting buttons on the Home tab. The shape can include text from any cell, but it cannot perform a calculation.

 Note

If you want the shape to include a calculated value, skip step 9 and follow steps 10 through 12.

10. If desired, add a new cell that formats a message for the shape. As shown in Figure 34.20, add the formula `="We are at "&TEXT(B13,"0%")&" of our goal!"` to an empty cell to convert the calculation in cell B13 to a suitable message.

11. Click in the middle of the text box as you would if text was being added.

12. Click in the formula bar, type `=B14`, and then press Enter. As shown in Figure 34.20, the shape displays the results from the selected cell.

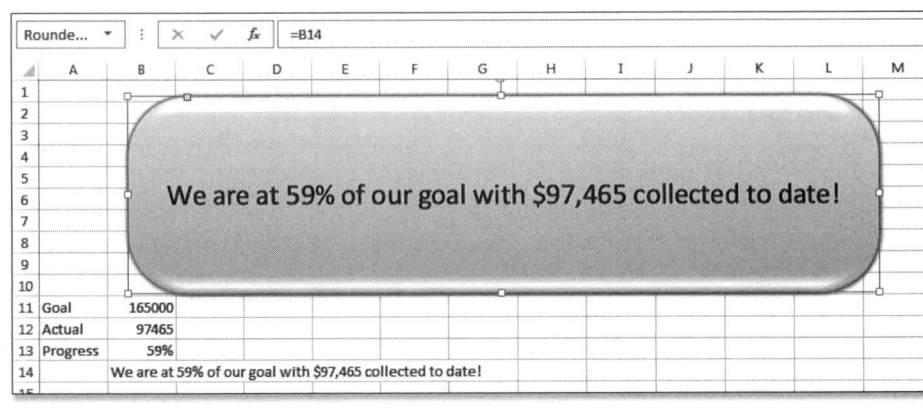

Figure 34.20
This shape picks up the formula from cell B14 to show how a message changes with the worksheet.

Working with Shapes

The Drawing Tools section of the Format tab contains sections to change the shape style, fill, outline, effects, and WordArt effects.

In the Insert Shapes dialog, use the Edit Shape, Change Shape command to choose another shape style.

If you right-click a shape and select Format Shape, Excel displays the Format Shape dialog, with the fine-tuning settings Fill, Line, Line Style, Shadow, 3D Format, 3D Rotation, and Text Placement.

Using the Freeform Shape to Create a Custom Shape

Despite my friendly relationship with Microsoft, I have not convinced them to add the MrExcel logo to the Shapes gallery—yet. However, you can build any shape by using the Freeform line tools in the Shapes gallery.

After you create a shape, you can add 3D effects, glow, and so on. For example, you can enhance your company logo, as shown in Figure 34.21.

Figure 34.21
After I created this shape with the Freeform shape tool, I enhanced it using the Drawing Tools section of the Format tab.

To create a custom shape, follow these steps:

1. Insert a picture of the shape that you can use as a guide to trace.

2. From the Insert tab, select the Shapes drop-down. In the Lines section, the last two shapes are Freeform and Scribble. Select the Freeform shape.

3. Click one corner of your logo.

4. Move the mouse to the adjacent corner of the logo and click again.

5. Repeat step 4 for each corner. If your logo has a curve, click several times around the perimeter of the curve. The more often you click, the better the curve will be.

6. When you arrive back at the original corner, click one final time to close the shape and complete the drawing.

7. Use the effect and fill settings to color and stylize the logo.

Using WordArt for Interesting Titles and Headlines

Even though WordArt was redesigned in Excel 2007, it is still best to use it sparingly, such as for a headline or title at the top of a page. It is best to use it for impressive display fonts to add interest to a report. However, you would not want to create an entire 20-page document in WordArt.

To use WordArt, follow these steps:

1. Select a blank section of the worksheet.

2. From the Insert tab, select the WordArt drop-down.

3. As shown in Figure 34.22, choose from the 20 WordArt presets in the drop-down. Do not worry that these presets seem less exciting than the WordArt in legacy versions of Excel. You can customize the WordArt later.

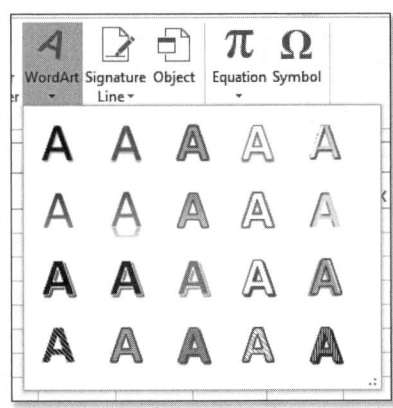

Figure 34.22
Excel 2013 offers 20 WordArt presets, including the Pattern fill.

4. Excel adds the generic text "Your Text Here" in the preset WordArt you chose. Select this default text and then type your own text.

5. Select the text. Choose a new font style by using either the mini toolbar that appears or the Home tab.

6. Use the WordArt Styles group on the Drawing Tools Format tab to color the WordArt. To the right of the Styles drop-down are icons for text color and line color and a drop-down for effects. The Effects drop-down includes the fly-out menus Shadow, Reflection, Glow, Soft Edges, Bevel, and 3D Rotation.

7. To achieve the old-style WordArt effects, from the Format tab select Drawing Tools, WordArt Styles, Text Effects, Transform, and then select a shape for the text. Figure 34.23 shows the WordArt with a Curve Down transformation.

Figure 34.23
WordArt
includes the
Transform menu
to bend and
twist type.

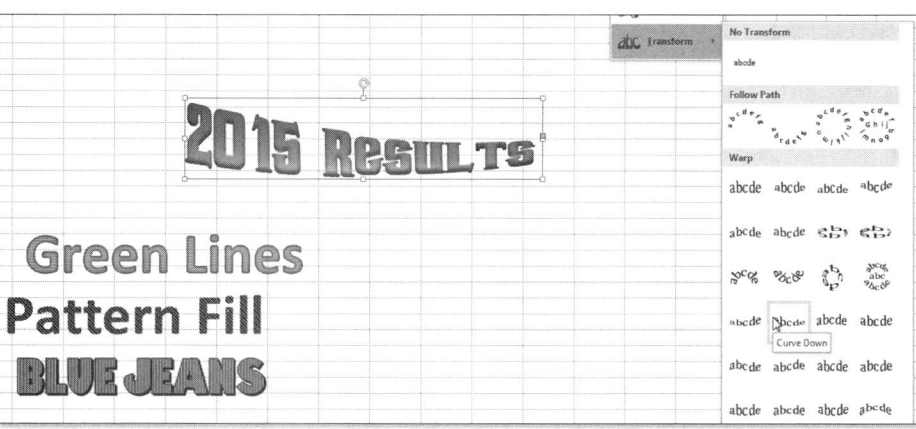

Using Text Boxes to Flow Long Text Passages

WordArt is perfect for short titles. However, it is not suitable for long text passages that you want to fit in a range. Figure 34.24 shows a series of sentences in a column that are of different lengths. You would like to have these sentences fit in a range from column A through column D.

Figure 34.24
At times, you need Excel to act like a word processor.

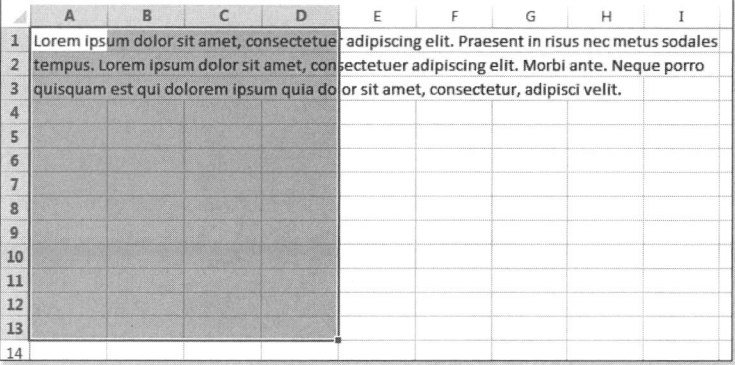

You can solve this particular problem by following these steps:

1. Select a range to include the sentences and extend the range out to column D.

2. Select the Home tab and then select Editing, Fill, Justify as shown in Figure 34.25. Excel word wraps the sentences to fit the current widths of Columns A:D, as shown in Figure 34.26.

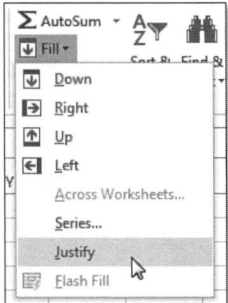

Figure 34.25
Select Justify from the Fill drop-down.

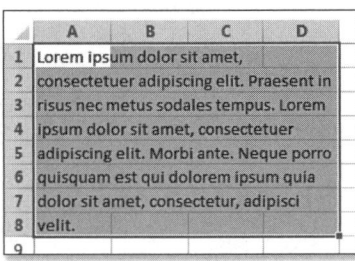

Figure 34.26
The Justify command wraps the text to the width of the range that was selected before the command was invoked.

If you subsequently resize column A, the text does not reflow. You have to use the Justify command again. In addition, if you change the font size of the text in column A, you have to use the Justify command again.

If any cell in the input range contains more than 255 characters, the cell is truncated. This fatal flaw causes Justify to fail most often. To solve this problem, you use a Text Box object. Text boxes allow multiple columns.

To use a Text Box object to create two columns of text, follow these steps:

1. Select a blank section of the worksheet.

2. From the Insert tab, select Text, Text Box.

3. Drag in your document to draw a large text box on the worksheet.

4. Either type your text here or switch to Word, copy the text, and then switch back to Excel and paste the text.

5. Right-click the text box and select Exit Edit Mode.

6. Use the Font group on the Home tab to adjust the font size and face.

> **Caution**
>
> Using Justify is not perfect, because it was written more than a decade ago when a cell could not contain more than 255 characters. For example, if you attempt to use the Justify command on a cell that contains more than 255 characters, the extra characters are truncated without any warning.

7. Right-click the text box and select Format Shape. The Format Shape task pane appears.

8. In the headline of the task pane, choose Text Options.

9. Choose the third icon below the headline to display the Text Box options.

10. Adjust the margins and alignment, if desired.

11. Click the Columns button. The Columns dialog appears.

12. Choose two columns with nonzero spacing between them, as shown in Figure 34.27.

Figure 34.27
You can change the number of columns.

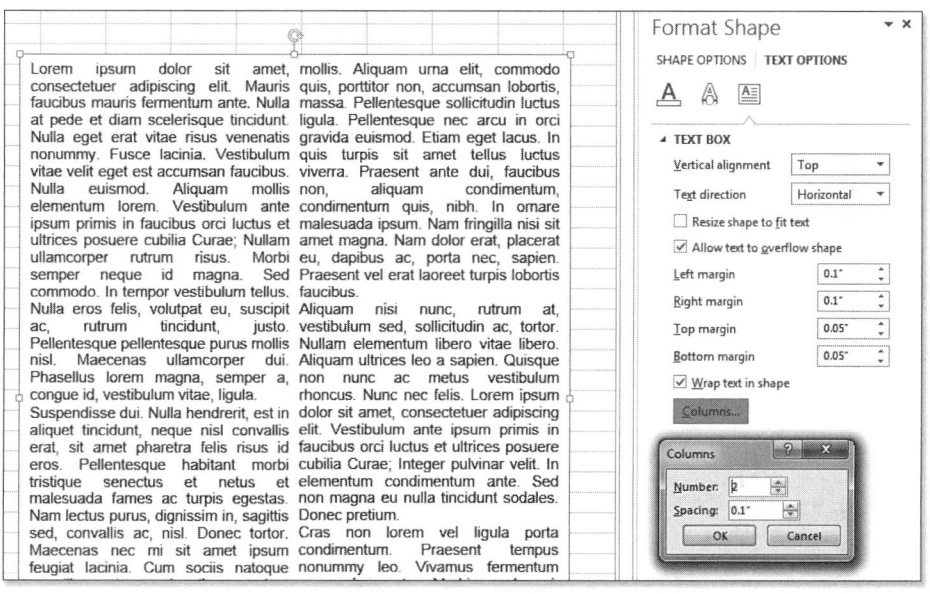

13. Click the X at the top right of the task pane to close the task pane. The result is a text box that has two columns of text. As you change the size of the text, it automatically reflows to fit the desired columns.

Eliminating Stray Drawing Objects

As you add multiple objects to one screen in an Excel workbook, you might find stray ghost objects left behind. It seems that when the selection box for the second shape overwrites the first shape, part of the shape is lost.

To solve this problem, scroll down the worksheet so that the shapes are not visible. When you scroll back up, Excel redraws the shapes correctly.

USING PICTURES AND CLIP ART

Excel worksheets have a tendency to be dominated by numbers. A picture can liven up a spreadsheet and add interest. The picture functionality in Excel 2013 is vastly improved over that in legacy versions of Excel.

Excel 2013 offers 28 quick picture styles and the tools to create thousands of additional effects.

When the spreadsheet was invented in 1979, accountants were amazed and thrilled with the simple black-and-white, numbers-only spreadsheets. The image processing tools available in Excel 2013 elevate spreadsheets from simple tables of numbers to beautiful marketing showpieces.

Getting Your Picture into Excel

For reasons unknown, you cannot simply drag and drop photographs into Excel. Drag and Drop works in Word, PowerPoint, and even OneNote, but not Excel. In Excel, you have to use the Insert tab and choose either Pictures or Pictures Online.

Use the Pictures icon for pictures stored on your PC or network.

Use Online Pictures for pictures stored in your SkyDrive, on your Flickr account, in the Office Online clip art collection, or to do a Bing Image search.

Use Screenshot to capture a picture already displayed in a browser or other application on your computer.

Inserting a Picture from Your Computer

When you choose the Picture icon, you can browse to any folder on your computer or network, as shown in Figure 35.1. Use the Views drop-down to display thumbnails so you can browse by picture instead of picture name.

Excel inserts the picture so the top-left corner of the picture is aligned with the active cell. The picture usually extends and covers hundreds of cells.

Inserting Multiple Pictures at Once

If you multiselect pictures using the Ctrl key while browsing, Excel inserts all of the pictures, overlaps them, and selects all of the pictures. If the size of the entire stack of pictures seems too large, you can resize them all by using the Height and Width settings in the ribbon. But soon, you have to rearrange the pictures so you can actually see them. Follow these steps:

1. Click outside the picture stack, on the Excel grid, to deselect the pictures.

2. Click the top photo in the stack to select that one single photo.

3. Drag the photo to a new location on the worksheet.

4. Repeat steps 2 and 3 for the remaining pictures in the stack.

Inserting a Picture or Clip Art from Online

When you choose the Online Pictures icon, you can load pictures from your SkyDrive, Flickr, Office Online, or you can search Bing Images for pictures with a Creative Commons license (see Figure 35.2).

If options for SkyDrive or Flickr are not showing, as is the case in Figure 35.2, you need to add a connection to those services. Open the File menu and choose Account from the left navigation area. Your connected services appear in the center portion of the screen. Click the Add Service button to connect to an existing Flickr or SkyDrive account (see Figure 35.3).

Figure 35.2
Choose a picture stored in an online account or browse Bing Images.

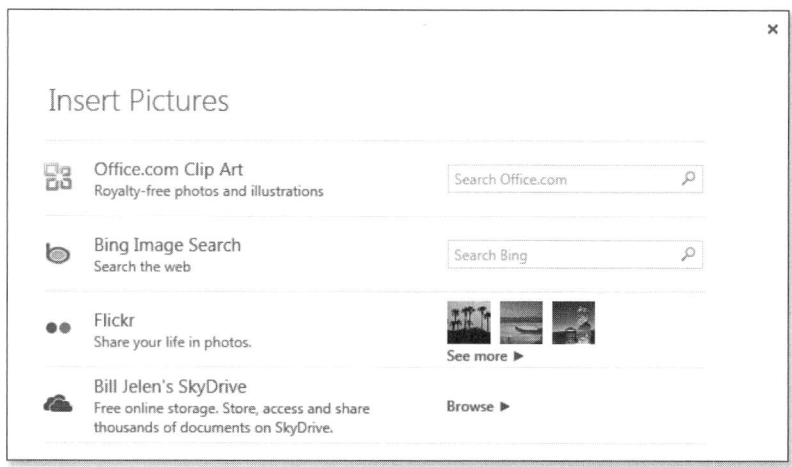

Figure 35.3
To connect to your Flickr or SkyDrive account, click Add a Service.

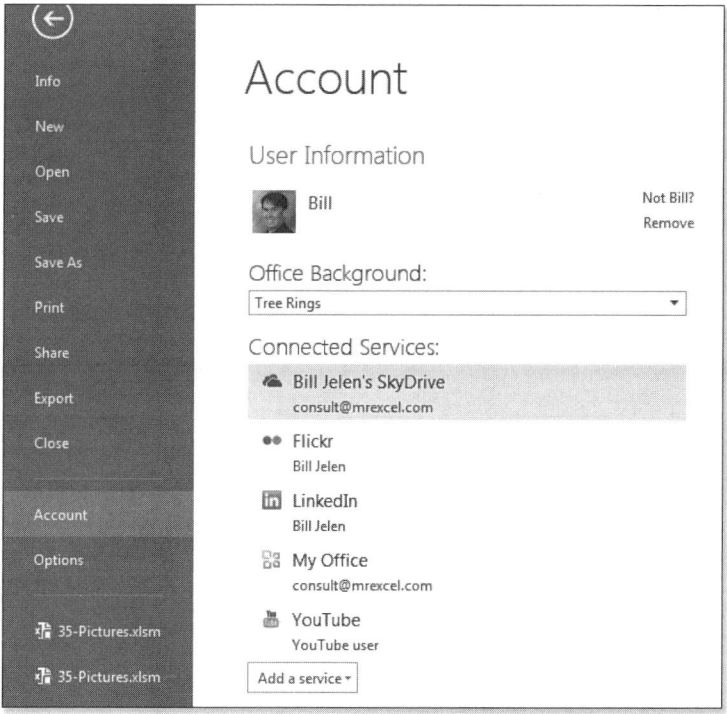

Even if you don't have a lot of photos stored online, you can access the royalty-free images and clip art at Office Online. Follow these steps:

1. Select a cell where you want the picture to start.

2. Choose Insert, Online Pictures.

3. In the Insert Pictures dialog, type a keyword next to Office.com Clip Art, as shown in Figure 35.4.

Figure 35.4
Enter a keyword to search.

4. Click the magnifying glass icon to search. In a few moments, a wide variety of choices are presented in a gallery (see Figure 35.5).

5. Choose an image and click Insert. Excel pauses briefly while the image is downloaded and then inserts the image in the worksheet.

You can also search Bing Images. Initially, the results will only show images that Bing believes to be licensed under Creative Commons. This clearly is not a perfect system. In my first search, the first set of results included a trademarked Pizza Hut logo from some random website. Just because that webmaster stole the image and slapped a Creative Commons license on his website does not protect you from using the image illegally. Therefore, use caution when distributing worksheets that contain images sourced from Bing (and even more so if you click the Show All Web Results button to broaden the Bing search to include copyrighted images).

Figure 35.5
Browse the royalty-free images.

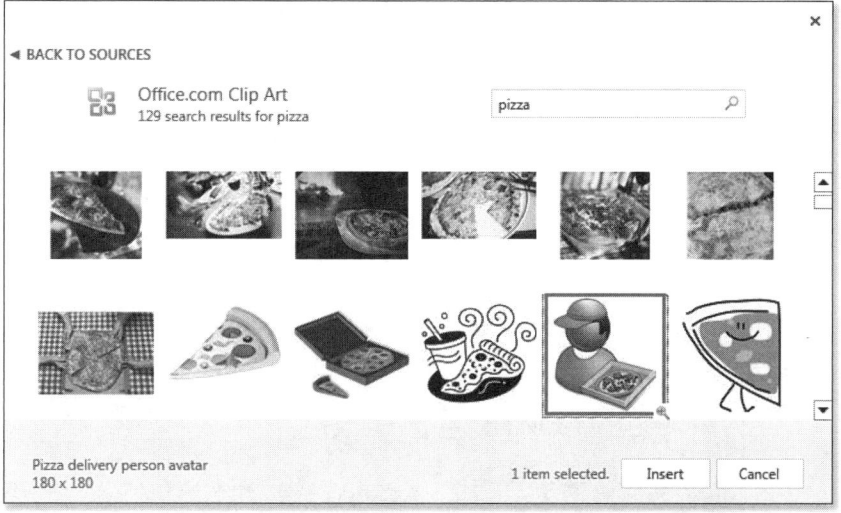

Adjusting the Picture Using the Ribbon Tab

When a picture is selected, the Picture Tools Format tab of the ribbon is available. The choices on this ribbon tab offer a number of presets that will save you time in adjusting the picture. For example, a single click in the Picture Styles gallery can replace 16 micro-adjustments in the Format Picture task pane. To save time, always try using the presets on the ribbon. If you can't quite get the right setting, you can press Ctrl+1 to display the Format Picture task pane to reach additional adjustment settings.

Resizing the Picture to Fit

One problem you might have when using a picture on a worksheet is that the image may be too large. As digital cameras improve, it is becoming increasingly common for digital images to be 9, 10, 11, or more megapixels. These images are very large. For example, an image from a 3-megapixel camera occupies the area from A1 through Q41. You would have to zoom out before you can even see the whole photo. Your first step is usually to reduce the picture size so it fits on your cover page or report.

If you frequently use the mouse, your first inclination would be to drag the lower-right corner of the picture up and to the left to reduce the picture size. If the picture is too large for the window, you can zoom out to 10%. Instead, use the spin buttons for Height and Width located in the Size group of the Picture Tools Format tab of the ribbon. Reduce the height or width, and the other setting reduces proportionally. Click and hold the "down" icon next to height until you can see the entire image in the Excel window.

When the entire picture is visible in the window, you can use the resize handle in any corner to change the picture size.

> ### 🔍 Note
>
> When you use the mouse or the ribbon tools to resize a photo, Excel ensures that the picture stays proportional. If you actually want to change a landscape picture to portrait, you can either use the Crop tool or turn off the Lock Aspect Ratio setting. Figure 35.6 compares these methods. The original picture is too large. A proportional resize keeps everything from the original picture while changing the size. If you need the picture to be taller than wide, you can unlock the aspect ratio and change the width. This creates a funny-looking picture, such as trees that are skinny and too tall. A better choice might be using the Crop tool to remove unnecessary parts of the photograph.

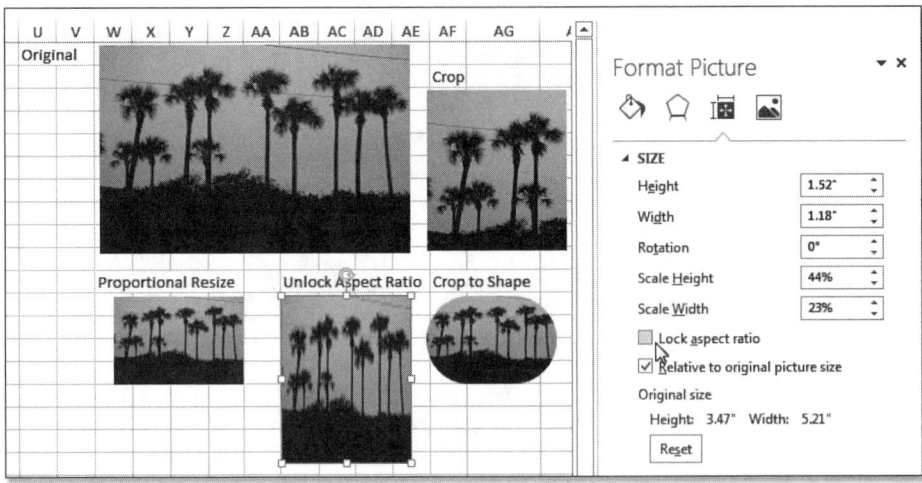

Figure 35.6
Resize proportionally or use the cropping tool to avoid distortion in the photograph.

To unlock the aspect ratio for a photograph, follow these steps:

1. Select the photograph by clicking it.

2. Press Ctrl+1 to display the Format Picture task pane.

3. Four icons appear at the top of the task pane. Click the third icon to display the Size, Properties, Text Box, and Alt Text categories.

4. Click the Size heading to open the size choices.

5. Uncheck the Lock Aspect Ratio check box. You can now stretch or compress the height or width alone.

Cropping a picture involves removing extraneous parts of the picture while in Crop mode. To crop a picture, follow these steps:

1. Select a picture.

2. Click the top half of the Crop icon in the Size group of the Picture Tools section of the Format tab. Eight crop handles appear on the edges and corners of the picture. Use the handles as follows:

   ■ To crop out one side of a picture, drag the center handle on that side inward toward the middle of the picture.

   ■ To crop both sides equally, hold down Ctrl while you drag the center handle on either side inward.

   ■ To crop equally on all four sides, hold down Ctrl while dragging one of the corner handles inward.

3. When the picture is cropped appropriately, click the Crop icon in the Picture Tools Format tab to exit Crop mode.

The rounded corners of the bottom-right photo in Figure 35.6 are achieved by cropping the photo to a shape. Open the Crop drop-down and choose Crop to Shape. You can choose from the 135 built-in shapes and then further change the shape using the yellow inflection handles on the shape.

Adjusting the Brightness and Contrast

You might capture a photograph in less than optimal lighting conditions. I went out one evening to capture photos of the latest rocket launch from Cape Canaveral when an osprey came flying by with his freshly caught dinner. The photograph was a cool action shot, but was too dark because I did not have time to adjust the camera settings. Excel offers 201 choices each for Brightness, Contrast, and Sharpness. With 201 choices each, you have 8.1 million ways to adjust a photo. This is overwhelming.

Starting in Excel 2010, Microsoft began offering 25 thumbnails in the Corrections drop-down (see Figure 35.7). Select the picture, open the drop-down, and choose the thumbnail that gives the best light to the picture. You can also choose from the five thumbnails at the top to soften or sharpen the image. Most users will be able to tell which of these 25 thumbnails makes the picture look the best. If you are a professional photographer, you can access the Format Picture task pane to micromanage the settings.

For more adjustments, the Color drop-down offers Sepia, Black and White, and various other settings.

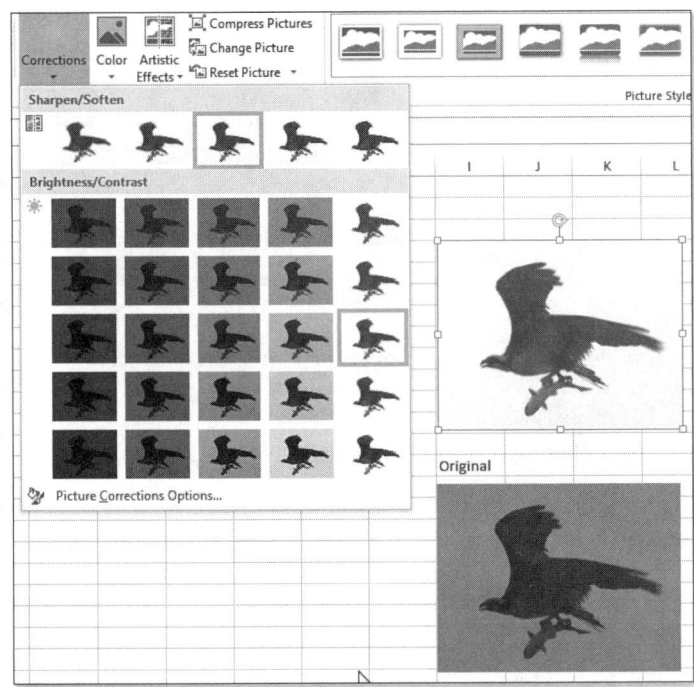

Figure 35.7
One of the presets rescued this photograph.

Adding Interesting Effects Using the Picture Styles Gallery

For a quick way to make a picture look interesting, you can use one of the 28 presets in the Picture Styles gallery. These presets include various combinations of rotation, bevel, lighting, surface, shadow, frame, and shape. Here's how you use them:

1. Select a picture. The Picture Tools Format tab appears.

2. To the right of the Picture Styles icon, select the drop-down arrow.

3. Hover over the 28 built-in styles until you find one that is suitable.

4. To apply the style, click the style in the gallery.

Figure 35.8 shows the gallery and several varieties of built-in picture styles.

The 28 styles in the Picture Styles gallery were professionally chosen by graphic design experts. There is nothing in here that you could not do using the settings in the Format Picture task pane. However, choosing a style is much faster and requires less experimentation. To illustrate, two similar pictures appear in Figure 35.9. The top picture was formatted in two clicks using the Picture Styles gallery. The bottom picture was formatted by adjusting 16 different settings in the Format Picture task pane. The list of settings is shown in column L.

Figure 35.8
The Picture Styles gallery offers many quick alternatives for formatting pictures.

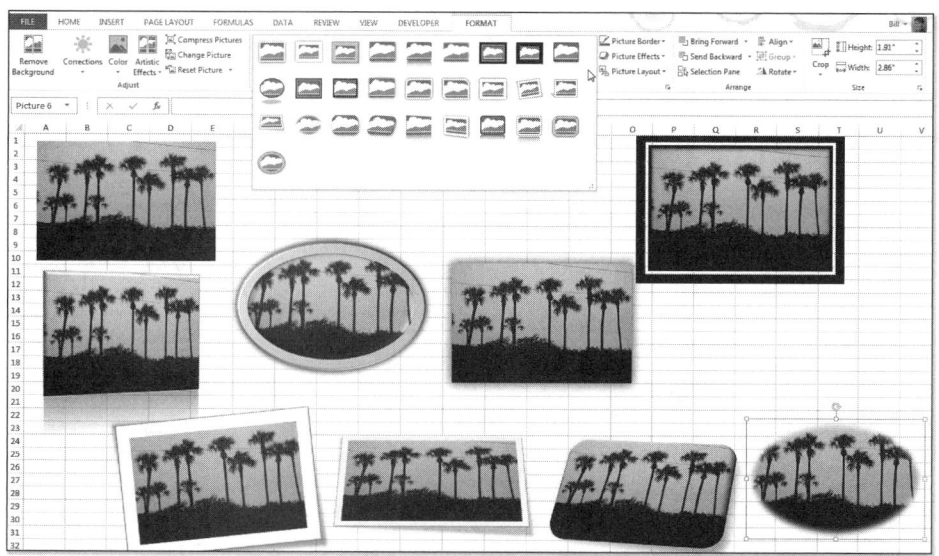

Figure 35.9
You can replicate the styles in the gallery by combining 16 different settings.

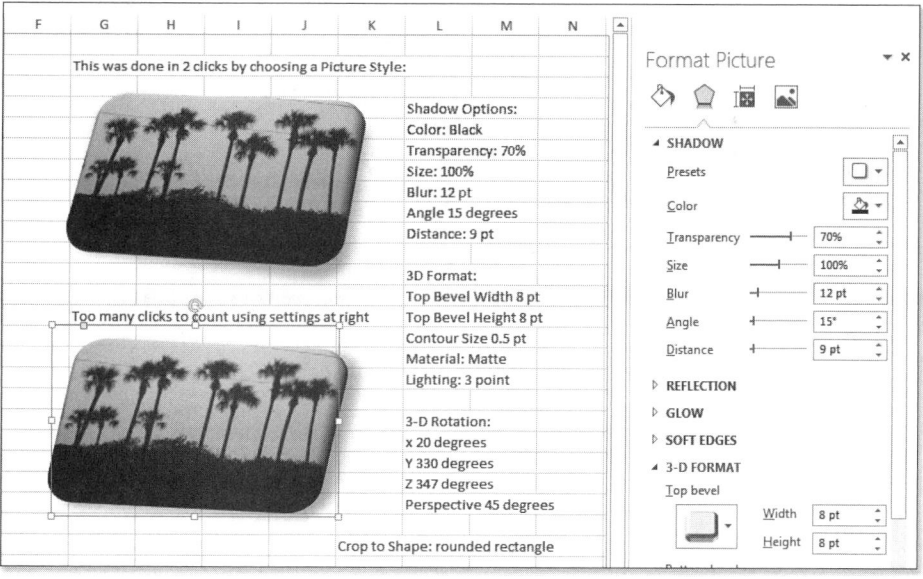

By using the Format Picture task pane, you could expand the 28 styles to millions of styles. However, it takes much longer to find the right combination of shadow, reflection, and so on when you opt to use the task pane instead of the Picture Styles gallery.

Applying Artistic Effects

Figure 35.10 shows the Artistic Effects fly-out menu. All these effects were new in Excel 2010. You can make your photo look like a pencil sketch, a mosaic, a photocopy, and more. Figure 35.10 shows some of the more interesting artistic effects.

The original photo is in the top left. Artistic effects make the photo look like an illustration.

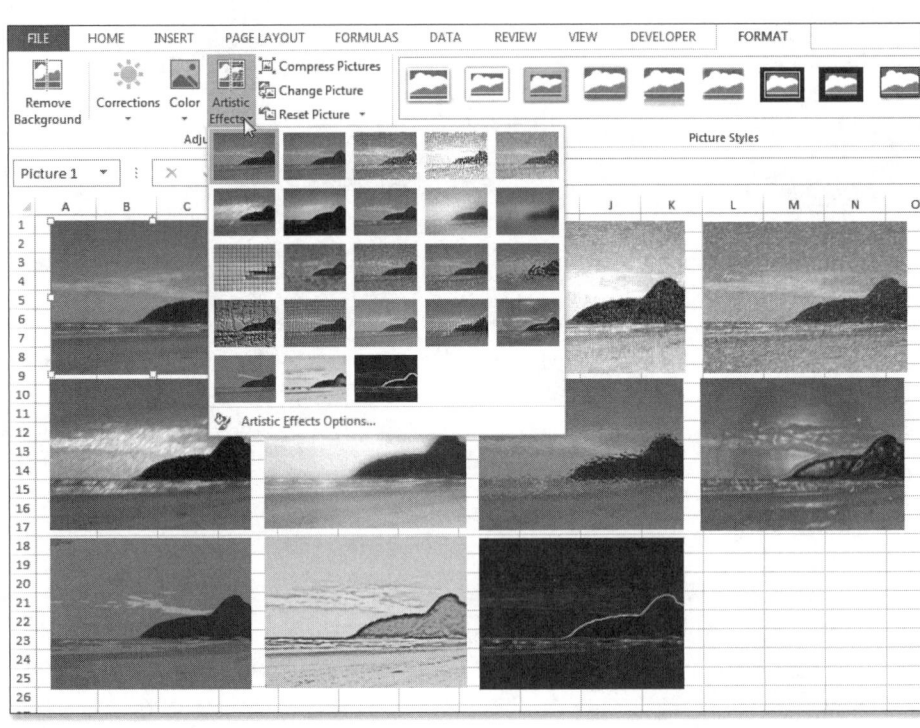

Figure 35.10
These artistic effects were added in Excel 2010.

Removing the Background

Legacy versions of Excel offered a Set Transparent Color setting that would never work. However, Microsoft added impressive logic to Excel 2010 to help you remove the background from a picture. A few simple tweaks will make the tool even better. Follow these steps:

1. Select the photo.

2. Click the Remove Background icon. A new Background Removal tab appears in the ribbon. Excel also takes a first pass at guessing which portions of the photo are background. You can improve this guess dramatically in step 3.

3. Excel draws a bounding box around the area it believes is the subject of the photograph. It often misses a corner of the subject; for example, a foot or an arm is outside of the box. When you resize the bounding box to exactly include 100% of the subject, Excel recalculates which portions of the photograph are background. Anything deemed to be background is shown in purple. I usually find that the first guess in step 2 is 50% correct and that the second guess after step 3 is 95% correct.

4. If there are tiny areas of background that Excel did not "purple out," use the Areas to Remove Icon and click in those areas. If there are tiny areas of the subject that are erroneously purpled out, click the Areas to Keep icon and click those areas (see Figure 35.11).

Figure 35.11
Adjust the bounding box to improve Excel's prediction of the background.

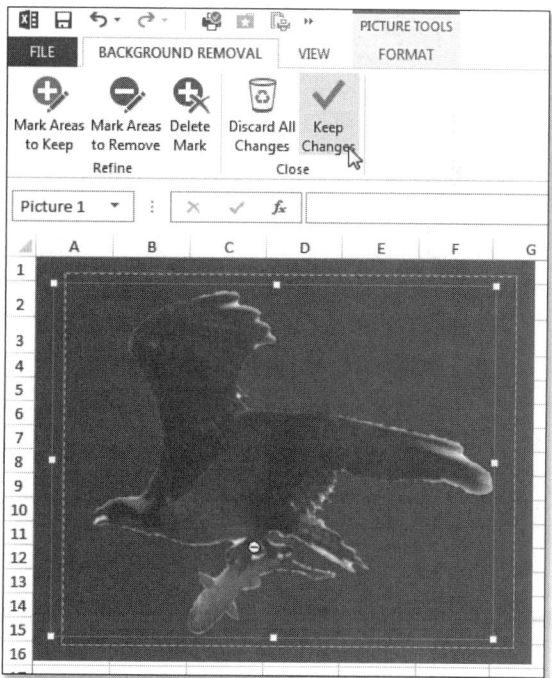

5. When the image looks correct, click Keep Changes. The grid now shows through the background of the photograph.

6. To edit cells behind the photograph, you cannot click on the cells. Click outside of the photograph and use the arrow keys to move underneath the photograph. You can then add text or titles (see Figure 35.12).

Figure 35.12
Use the arrow keys to reach cells behind the photograph.

Reducing a Picture's File Size

When you import a picture into a workbook, the file size of the workbook can increase dramatically. If you plan to view the image onscreen only, you can reduce the size of the picture to reduce the size of the workbook. Here's how you do it:

1. Select the picture.

2. In the Picture Tools Format tab, select Compress Pictures from the Adjust group. Excel displays the Compress Pictures dialog, as shown in Figure 35.13. Based on your choices here, Excel reduces the file size and removes the cropped areas of the photo.

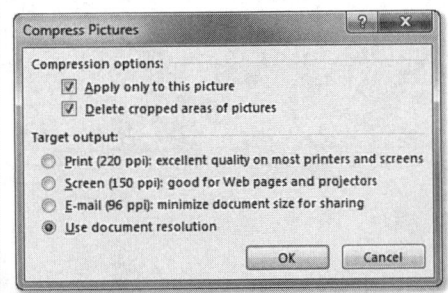

Figure 35.13
You use the Compress Pictures dialog to reduce file size.

Adding Captions to Images

As described in Chapter 34, "Using SmartArt, Shapes, WordArt, and Text Boxes," the SmartArt feature enables you to create professional-looking business diagrams. SmartArt mixes words, shapes, and images together. The new Picture Layout menu on the Picture Tools Format tab enables you to embed a single selected photograph into a SmartArt diagram. This effectively allows you to add a caption to an image.

To create the SmartArt, follow these steps:

1. Select a single image on the worksheet.

2. From the Picture Tools Format tab, open the Picture Layout tab (see Figure 35.14). Use Live Preview as you hover over various thumbnails. The various SmartArt layouts offer variations, such as emphasizing text and emphasizing pictures.

Figure 35.14
Add a caption to an image by converting the image to SmartArt.

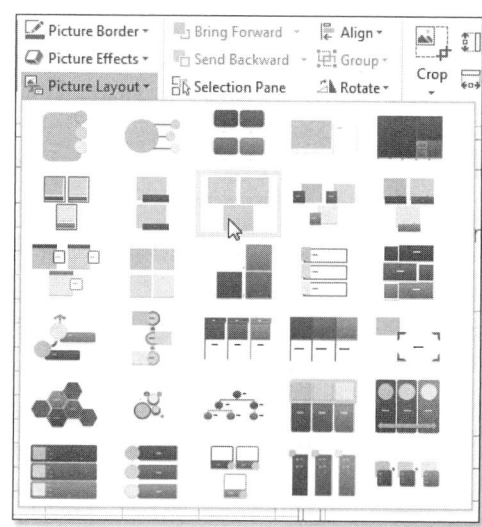

3. Click the desired layout.

4. Follow the instructions in Chapter 34 for finishing the SmartArt diagram. In Figure 35.15, a simple caption is added to the photograph.

Figure 35.15
Type text in the SmartArt pane to add a caption to the photograph.

Using the Format Picture Task Pane

In Excel 2013, the old Format dialog box has been replaced with a task pane. The task pane starts out docked to the right side of the screen. You can tear off the task pane and float it above your worksheet. To dock the task pane again, drag it more than half way off the screen.

Typically, the ribbon offers the popular subset of commands and the task pane offers the complete set of commands. However, this is not true with pictures. Some important settings, such as Crop to Shape, appear in the ribbon and not in the task pane.

You can display the Picture Task pane by selecting a picture and pressing Ctrl+1. Alternatively, right-click any picture and choose Format Picture, or choose any of the More options from the drop-downs in the Picture Tools Format tab of the ribbon.

Four icons appear at the top of the task pane, each one leading to a new section of the task pane:

- The paint bucket leads to Fill and Line.

- The pentagon leads to Shadow, Reflection, Glow, Soft Edges, 3-D Format, 3-D Rotation, and Artistic Effects.

- The resize icon leads to Size, Properties, Text Box, and Alt Text.

- The picture icon leads to Picture Corrections, Picture Color, and Crop.

 **Caution**

The task pane never closes itself. Even if you click away from the picture, the task pane remains. You can use the X in the top right of the task pane to close the task pane.

When you click one of the four icons, the categories appear as lines below the icons. Click one or more categories to reveal the choices in that category. In Figure 35.16, the Crop category has been opened. You can see additional settings under Picture Corrections and Picture Color when you click those entries.

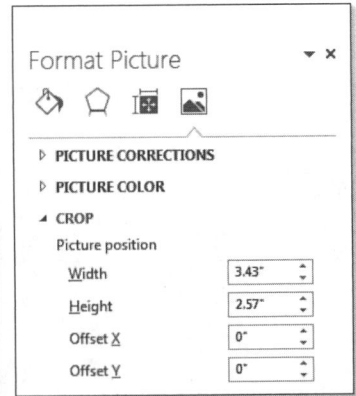

Figure 35.16
The task pane offers four icons and several categories under each icon.

Rotating a Shape over a Picture

Excel offers 139 closed shapes. This sounds like a lot of shapes, but many shapes are missing. For example, it offers a right triangle with the hypotenuse running from top left to bottom right. It doesn't offer the other three right triangles, though, because it is simple enough to use the rotation handle to rotate a shape.

However, if you are trying to crop to a rotated shape, the settings in the Format Picture task pane don't seem to work. In Figure 35.17, the left triangle is a picture that was cropped to a triangle and then rotated. The picture always rotates with the shape.

Figure 35.17
Getting a shape to rotate while the picture remains fixed is tricky.

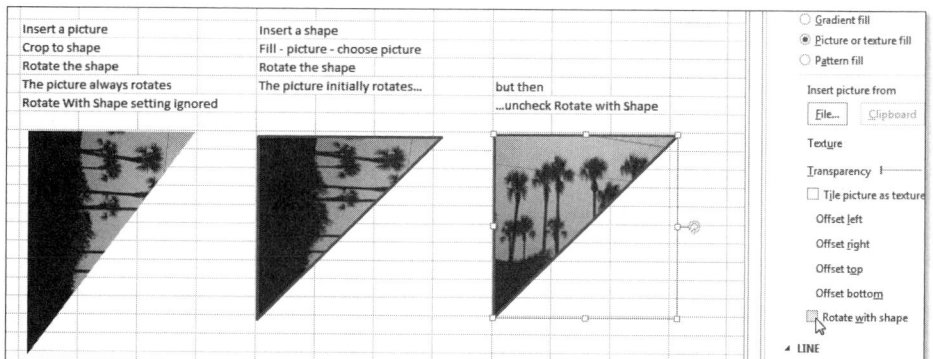

Instead, insert a triangle shape first. Then, in the Drawing Tools format, choose Fill, Picture Fill and specify the picture. When you rotate the triangle, the picture initially rotates. Click F1 to access a slightly different version of the Format Picture task pane. Choose Shape Options, Fill. Uncheck the box that says Rotate with Shape. The picture now stays unrotated.

Inserting Screen Clippings

If you need to grab an image of a web page, a PDF file, or a PowerPoint slide, you can grab a screen capture of the entire window or a portion of the window. I use this feature frequently and find the technique for inserting a portion of a window is more useful most of the time.

1. In Excel, position the cell pointer at the point where you want to insert the screen clipping.

2. If you have two monitors, get the other application visible in the other monitor. If you have a single monitor, switch to the other application and then immediately back to Excel. The screen clipping tool is going to hide the current Excel window, revealing the previously active application. Thanks to the new Excel 2013 Single Document Interface, you can now use this trick to capture a picture of another Excel workbook.

3. Select Insert, Screenshot. You see a thumbnail of each open window. Skip all of those big icons and go to the words Screen Clipping at the bottom of the menu (see Figure 35.18). The current Excel screen disappears, and the remaining window's screen stays visible but dims.

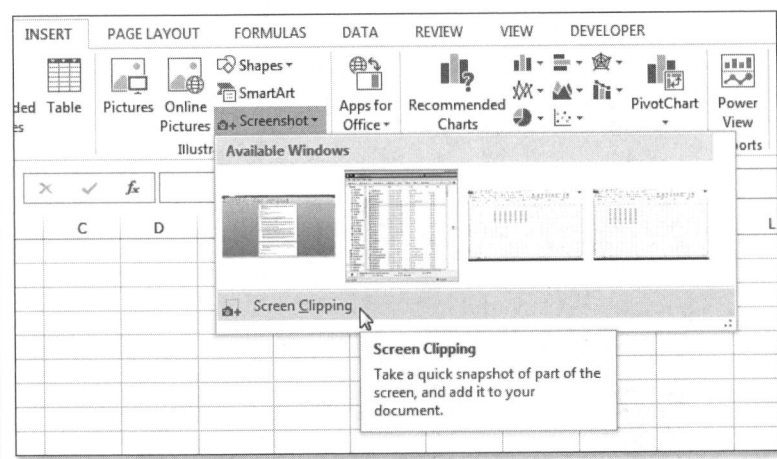

Figure 35.18
Choose Screen Clipping to copy a portion of another window.

4. Using the mouse, draw a rectangle around the portion of the application window that you want to capture. As you drag, that portion of the screen brightens.

5. Release the mouse. The original Excel window will reappear and a picture of the clipped screen will be inserted in the workbook.

Selecting and Arranging Pictures

You will sometimes have two pictures that overlap. Excel maintains an order for the pictures. Typically, the picture inserted most recently is shown on top of earlier pictures. You can haphazardly resequence the pictures using the Send Backward or Send Forward command on the Picture Tools Format tab. Say that you've inserted 12 pictures. Picture 1 and Picture 12 are overlapping and you want Picture 1 to be on top of Picture 12. You would have to choose Send Backward 11 times before they appear correctly. Next to Send Backward is a drop-down with a choice called Send to Back. This moves the selected picture to the back of the stack.

Even easier is the Selection pane. Use Home, Find & Select, Selection Pane to list all shapes and pictures in the sheet. You can drag a picture to a new location in the list as shown in Figure 35.19. Pictures at the top of the list appear on top of pictures at the bottom of the list. You can also choose to hide a picture by clicking the Eye icon.

If you need to select many pictures at once, choose Home, Find & Select, Select Objects. Draw a large rectangle around many objects, and they all will be selected.

Figure 35.19
Picture 7 has been hidden, and Picture 3 is in the process of being moved within the stack.

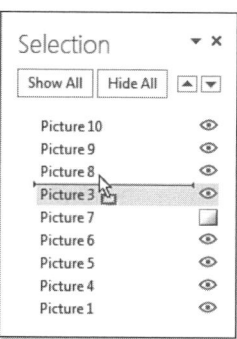

The Align option enables you to make sure that several images line up. To make Picture 3 and Picture 2 line up with Picture 1, you would follow these steps:

1. Select Picture 3.

2. Ctrl-click Picture 2 and then Ctrl-click Picture 1.

3. Select Align, Align Left. The left edges of Picture 2 and Picture 3 move so they line up with the left edge of Picture 1.

> **⚠ Caution**
> After you use Select Objects, the mouse pointer remains a white arrow and you will be unable to select cells. Press the Escape key to exit this mode.

If you select multiple images and group them together by using the Group drop-down, you can then move the images, and their location relative to each other remains the same.

PRINTING

The Excel team has attempted to streamline the printing process in Excel. Starting with Excel 2010, they consolidated settings from several different dialogs plus Print Preview into the new Print panel on the File menu.

I remain unconvinced. Here's why:

- The Print panel does bring together many print settings that were formerly spread across several dialogs, but it does not bring them all in one place. You now have nine different places where you can control page setup and print settings.

- Ctrl+P used to be a one-key method for doing a quick print using the default settings, and now it takes you to the Print panel instead. If you miss this functionality, you should consider adding Quick Print to the Quick Access Toolbar.

Printing in One Click

If you're a keyboard enthusiast, you might be upset that in Excel 2013 Ctrl+P takes you to the Print panel instead of performing a quick print. In a few steps, you can bring Quick Print back to Excel 2013.

The Quick Access Toolbar is the row of small icons that appears just above or just below the ribbon. At the right edge of this toolbar is a drop-down menu. Open the drop-down at the right edge of the Quick Access Toolbar to display a short list of popular commands. Choose Quick Print, as shown in Figure 36.1.

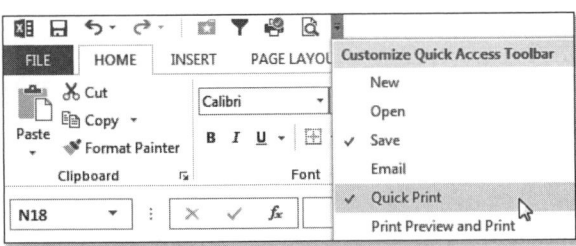

Figure 36.1
Add Quick Print to the Quick Access Toolbar.

When you click the Quick Print icon, one copy of the current worksheet is sent to the last printer you used in Excel. If you have not previously printed in this Excel session, the worksheet is sent to the default printer.

Although this brings the Quick Print back as a mouse click, it still isn't great for keyboard-centric people. If you press and release the Alt key in Excel, you see a row of shortcuts for the first nine items in the Quick Access Toolbar. Because Quick Print is the sixth icon in Figure 36.1, Alt+6 does a Quick Print.

Finding Print Settings

There are at least nine places in Excel where you can change the print settings and/or page setup. The most common tasks are found in multiple places. For example, you can change margins in five of the nine places. You can change paper size and orientation in four of the nine places.

As you move down to the obscure settings, you might be able to find them in only one or two places. Figure 36.2 shows a cross reference. For any given task, you can locate where you might be able to change the setting.

Nine places are listed across the top of Figure 36.2. Here is where to find each place:

- **File, Print**—Open the File menu and choose Print to display the Print panel. This panel has a mix of Printer and Page Setup settings in the center and a large Print Preview on the right. Introduced in Excel 2010, it aims to be a one-stop place for getting your printout to look right (see Figure 36.3).

- **Page Layout Tab of the Ribbon**—Click the Page Layout tab in the ribbon. You find three groups related to printing: Page Setup, Scale to Fit, and Sheet Options (see Figure 36.4).

- **Page Setup Dialog**—Click the diagonal arrow icon in the lower-right corner of the three groups in the Page Layout ribbon tab to launch the legacy Page Setup dialog. This dialog contains four tabs. The superscript next to each bullet in Figure 36.2 identifies the tab: 1 for Page, 2 for Margins, 3 for Header/Footer, 4 for Sheet. You can also reach this dialog by clicking the Print Titles icon in the Page Layout tab of the ribbon (see Figure 36.4).

Figure 36.2
Various printing tasks are spread throughout the Excel interface. The superscript in the Page Setup Dialog column refers to the tab within the dialog.

Task	File, Print	Page Layout Tab	Page Setup Dialog	Page Layout View	Header & Footer Tab	Page Break Preview View	Printer Properties Dialog	Excel Options	Print Preview Full Screen
Get the Report to Fit On the Page									
Set the Paper Size	•	•	•[1]				•		
Select Portrait or Landscape Orientation	•	•	•[1]				•		
Adjust the Margins on the Printed Page	•	•	•[2]	•					•
Repeat titles and headings on each printed page			•[4]						
Add a page number and other header/footer items			•[3]	•	•				
Exclude part of your worksheet from the print range		•	•[4]						
Add manual page breaks to the document		•				•			
Display page breaks	•							•	•
Hide page breaks								•	
Force more data to fit on a page	•	•	•[1]			•			
Preview the printed page	•			•	•	•			•
Print the Report									
Choose which printer to use	•								
Control settings specific to that printer	•						•		
Print multiple worksheets at once	•								
Other Print Settings									
Center the report on the page			•[2]						
Collate multiple printed sets	•						•		
Control the first page number			•[1]						
Print the Excel gridlines		•	•[4]						
Print the A, B, C column headings and row numbers		•	•[4]						
Print comments			•[4]						
Replace error values when printing			•[4]						
Print on both sides of the page	•						•		
Control the order in which pages print			•[4]						
Adjust the print quality			•[1]						
Force the printout to greyscale			•[4]				•		
Print in draft quality			•[4]				•		

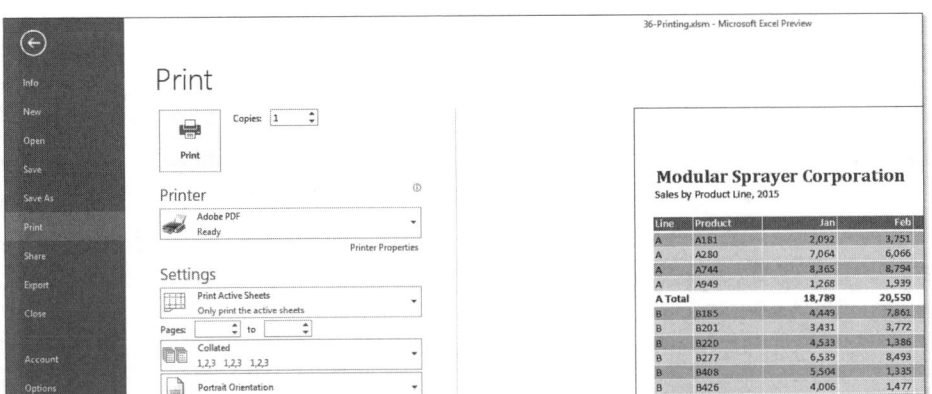

Figure 36.3
The new Print panel on the File menu consolidates Print Preview and common print settings.

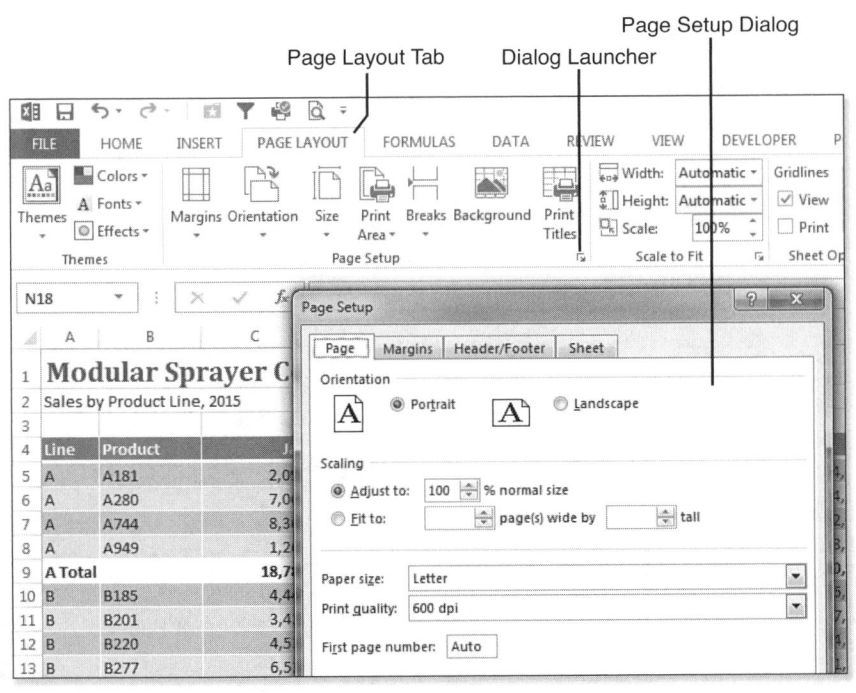

Figure 36.4
Reach the full Page Setup dialog by clicking the Dialog Launcher or the large Print Titles icon.

- **Page Layout View**—Choose Page Layout on the View tab. This icon also appears in the lower right of the Excel screen.

- **Header & Footer Tools Design Tab**—When you are in Page Layout view, click one of the three header or three footer zones on any page to have the Header & Footer Tools Design tab appear in the ribbon. Note that you have to click away from the header or footer zone to exit Page Layout view. Although this tab is the most hidden, it offers an easier way to control headers and footers (see Figure 36.5).

Figure 36.5
After you click into a header in Page Layout view, you can access the Header & Footer tools tab in the ribbon.

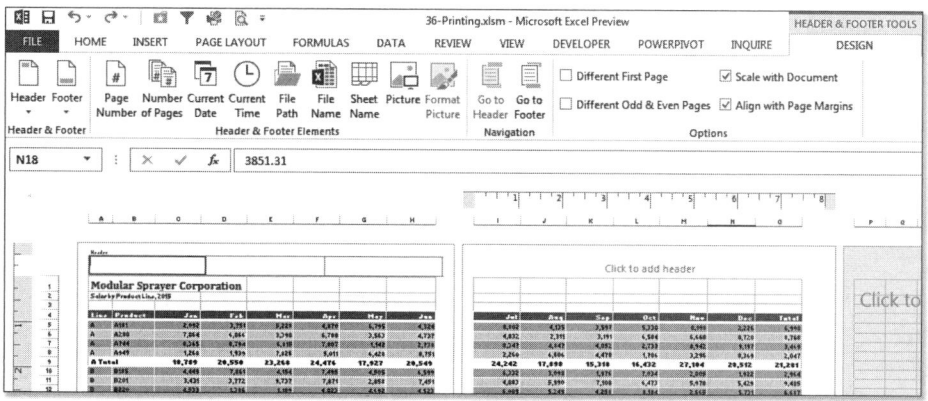

- **Page Break Preview View**—Click Page Break Preview on the View tab. This icon also appears at the bottom right of the Excel window.

- **Printer Properties Dialog**—Use Ctrl+P to display the Print panel. A Printer Properties link appears just below the printer name.

- **Excel Options**—Open the File menu and then choose Options, Advanced. This is the only place to turn off the display of automatic page breaks after you've done a Print Preview.

- **Print Preview Full Screen**—Add this icon to the Quick Access Toolbar to reach a full-screen version of Print Preview similar to older versions of Excel.

The rest of this chapter covers most of the tasks along the left side of Figure 36.2.

Previewing the Printed Report

Before you start adjusting the page settings, you can take a quick look at how the worksheet currently will print.

Using the Print Preview on the Print Panel

One method to view the printed document is to use File, Print or Ctrl+P. For now, ignore the settings in the middle panel and look at the Print Preview pane on the right.

If your document is larger than one page, you have a vertical scrollbar to the right of the print preview. Use this scrollbar to move to other pages.

If you've chosen to display more recent files than fit on your screen, you have an outer vertical scrollbar. This means you can't see the important icons at the bottom of the Print Preview. Change the number of recent files displayed using File, Options, Advanced, Display. Lower the settings for Quickly Access This Number of Recent Workbooks.

Four icons are available at the bottom of the Print Preview window (see Figure 36.6):

- To navigate to a new page, use the left-arrow or right-arrow icon in the lower left. You can also type a new page number in the page number text box and press Enter or Tab. The PgDn and PgUp controls still work, but only when you click the preview first.

- The Zoom check box feels like it is reversed. If you clear this check box, Excel zooms in to a smaller section of your printout.

- Select the Show Margins check box to have Excel draw drag-able margins in the page. Drag any of the margin lines to change the page margins. Drag any of the column handles to resize columns.

When you first look at the print preview, check for these obvious problems:

- Does one column or a few rows spill over to a second page when you want everything to fit on one page? See "Making the Report Fit on the Page" later in this chapter.

- On a multi-page report, go to page 2—are the titles and headings appearing on pages after the first page? If not, see "Adding Print Titles," later in this chapter.

- Are page numbers appearing where you want them? If not, see the "Adding Headers or Footers to the Printed Report" section.

To close the File menu and return to your document, click the large left-pointing arrow in the top-left corner of the File menu.

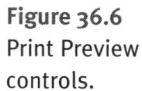

Figure 36.6
Print Preview
controls.

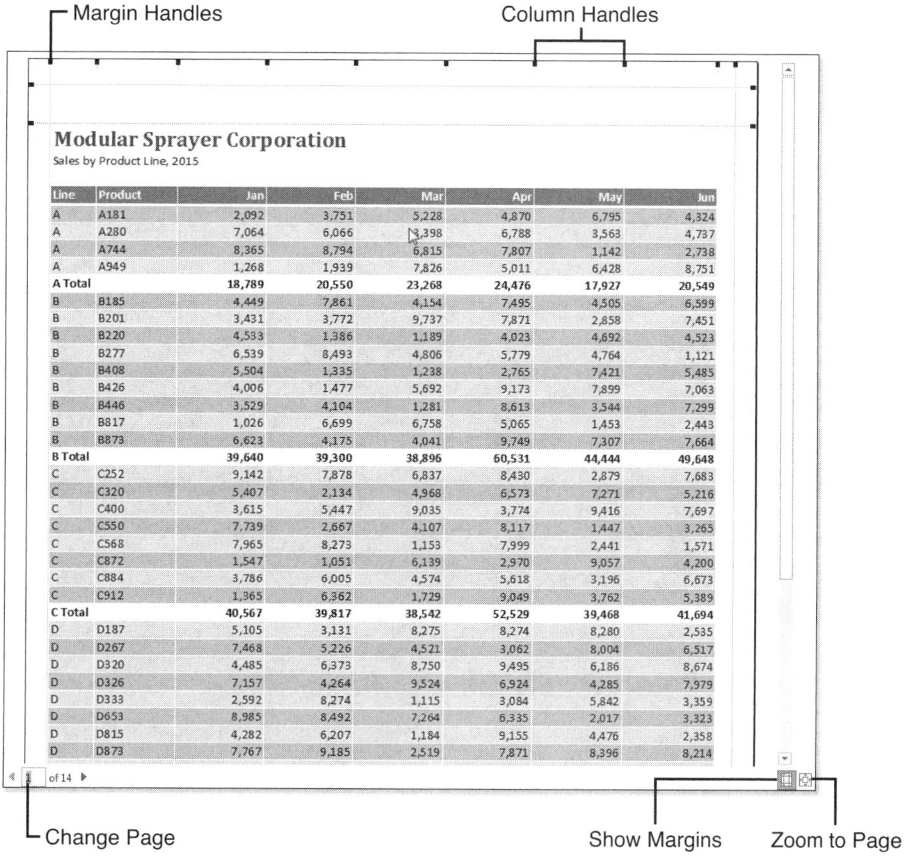

┌─ Margin Handles   Column Handles

Modular Sprayer Corporation
Sales by Product Line, 2015

Line	Product	Jan	Feb	Mar	Apr	May	Jun
A	A181	2,092	3,751	5,228	4,870	6,795	4,324
A	A280	7,064	6,066	3,398	6,788	3,563	4,737
A	A744	8,365	8,794	6,815	7,807	1,142	2,738
A	A949	1,268	1,939	7,826	5,011	6,428	8,751
A Total		18,789	20,550	23,268	24,476	17,927	20,549
B	B185	4,449	7,861	4,154	7,495	4,505	6,599
B	B201	3,431	3,772	9,737	7,871	2,858	7,451
B	B220	4,533	1,386	1,189	4,023	4,692	4,523
B	B277	6,539	8,493	4,806	5,779	4,764	1,121
B	B408	5,504	1,335	1,238	2,765	7,421	5,485
B	B426	4,006	1,477	5,692	9,173	7,899	7,063
B	B446	3,529	4,104	1,281	8,613	3,544	7,299
B	B817	1,026	6,699	6,758	5,065	1,453	2,443
B	B873	6,623	4,175	4,041	9,749	7,307	7,664
B Total		39,640	39,300	38,896	60,531	44,444	49,648
C	C252	9,142	7,878	6,837	8,430	2,879	7,683
C	C320	5,407	2,134	4,968	6,573	7,271	5,216
C	C400	3,615	5,447	9,035	3,774	9,416	7,697
C	C550	7,739	2,667	4,107	8,117	1,447	3,265
C	C568	7,965	8,273	1,153	7,999	2,441	1,571
C	C872	1,547	1,051	6,139	2,970	9,057	4,200
C	C884	3,786	6,005	4,574	5,618	3,196	6,673
C	C912	1,365	6,362	1,729	9,049	3,762	5,389
C Total		40,567	39,817	38,542	52,529	39,468	41,694
D	D187	5,105	3,131	8,275	8,274	8,280	2,535
D	D267	7,468	5,226	4,521	3,062	8,004	6,517
D	D320	4,485	6,373	8,750	9,495	6,186	8,674
D	D326	7,157	4,264	9,524	6,924	4,285	7,979
D	D333	2,592	8,274	1,115	3,084	5,842	3,359
D	D653	8,985	8,492	7,264	6,335	2,017	3,323
D	D815	4,282	6,207	1,184	9,155	4,476	2,358
D	D873	7,767	9,185	2,519	7,871	8,396	8,214

◄ of 14 ►

└─ Change Page   Show Margins   Zoom to Page

Using Full Screen Print Preview

Some people develop macros in Excel where they want someone to preview a report in Print Preview. The new Print Preview on the Print panel doesn't work with these macros, so the Excel team added a command that gets you to a full-screen Print Preview.

The full screen Print Preview works particularly well with wide reports in a landscape orientation.

You must add the Print Preview Full Screen to your ribbon or Quick Access Toolbar. For instructions, see Chapter 4, "Customizing Excel." Figure 36.7 shows the ribbon in the full-screen Print Preview.

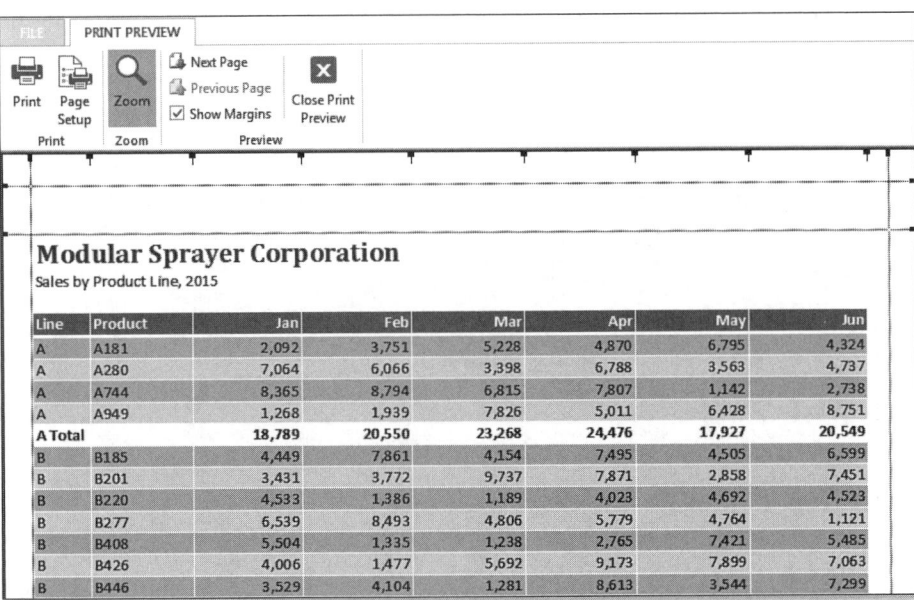

Figure 36.7
For landscape documents, consider using the full-screen print preview.

Making the Report Fit On the Page

Before you print, you want to make sure your data is going to fit on the page. You can control the paper size, orientation, and margins. You can make a few heading rows print at the top of each page. You can add information such as page number, file location, date, and time in the header or footer.

Setting Worksheet Paper Size

You can choose from a variety of paper size options in the Size drop-down in the Page Layout tab, as shown in Figure 36.8. When you encounter a report that is too wide for a regular sheet of paper, you can switch to a larger page size, such as Legal paper. You can choose one paper size or select More Paper Sizes from the bottom of the list to specify a new size.

 **Tip**

Some paper sizes, such as 11"x17", are available only if your selected printer offers that size. If your default printer cannot print large-format paper, you should change the printer selection in the Print panel and then return to the Page Setup dialog to select the larger-format paper.

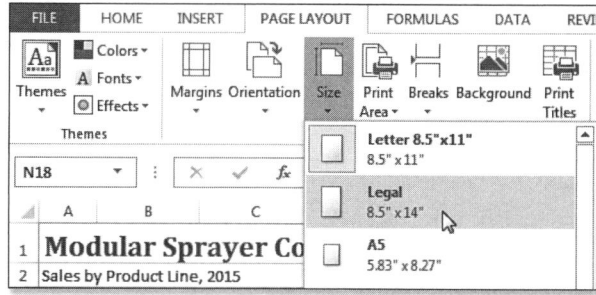

Figure 36.8
Choose a paper size.

Adjusting Worksheet Orientation

Changing a report to print sideways, which is also referred to as *landscape*, takes just a couple of mouse clicks. From the Page Layout tab, select Page Setup to see the Orientation drop-down, which offers Portrait and Landscape options, as shown in Figure 36.9.

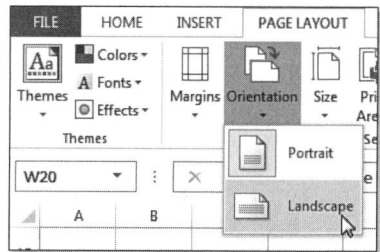

Figure 36.9
Print the report sideways by selecting the Landscape printing option.

Adjusting Worksheet Margins

When you are trying to squeeze an extra column into a report, you can tweak the report to have smaller margins. Figure 36.2 shows that there are five different places you can adjust the margins for your worksheet. Here are my favorite three methods.

- **Choose Page Layout, Margins**—This drop-down offers three settings: Normal, Wide, and Narrow. If you have previously used custom margins, another setting appears with the last custom margins you used. To apply one of these standard setups, choose the setup you want to use from the Margins drop-down, as shown in Figure 36.10. To apply a different custom margin, select Custom Margins from the bottom of this menu. Selecting Custom Margins takes you to the legacy Page Setup dialog, discussed next.

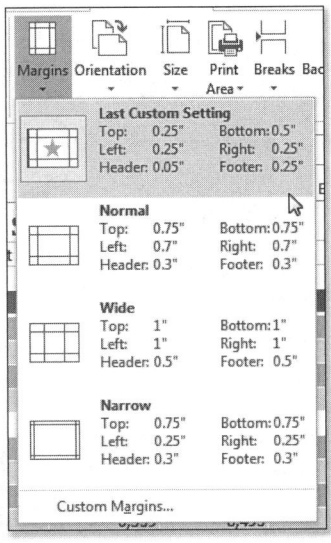

Figure 36.10
You can choose a quick setting for margins.

■ **Use the legacy Page Setup dialog**—When you click the dialog launcher icon in the bottom right of the Page Setup group, Excel displays the Page Setup dialog. As shown in Figure 36.11, use the Margins tab to adjust the margins at the top, left, right, and bottom, as well as the margins for the footer and header. This dialog offers precise control of the six margin settings.

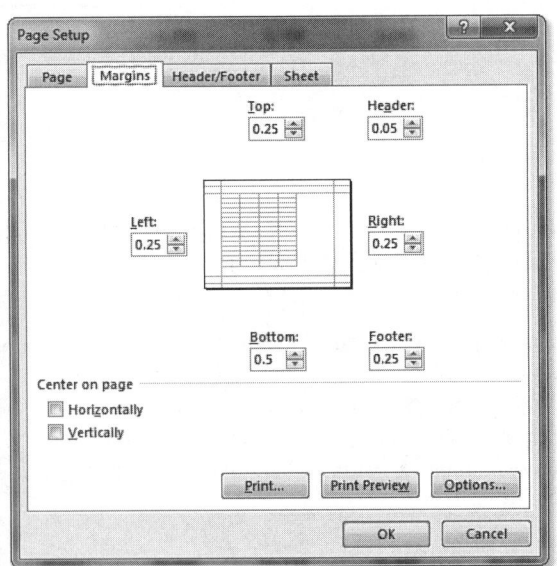

Figure 36.11
For control over each margin, use the Margins tab of the Page Setup dialog.

■ **Choose View, Page Layout View**—When you use this option, gray margins appear on each edge of the ruler. You can drag the gray margins in or out to decrease/increase the margin.

Either version of the Print Preview window has a Show Margins setting. After you've displayed the margins in Print Preview, you can move the margins in or out.

Adding Print Titles

For reports that span more than one page, you might want the headings from the report to print at the top of each page. Although the Print Titles icon was promoted to a large icon on the Page Layout tab in the ribbon, this command leads back to the somewhat confusing Page Setup dialog, as shown in Figure 36.12. Suppose that you have a report that is two pages wide and several pages long. However, you notice that the printed page 2 of the printed report does not include title or column headings. If you want to have the titles and column headings repeat at the top of each row, you need to select 1:4 in the Rows to Repeat at Top option and A:B in the Columns to Repeat at Left option. When you return to the Page Setup dialog later, Excel will have added dollar signs to these settings. You don't need to type the dollar signs; Excel will add them.

 **Note**

To specify rows to repeat at the top, you can indicate either a single row using 1:1 or a range of rows using 1:4. Similarly, columns to repeat at left might be a single column (A:A) or a range of columns (A:B).

Figure 36.12
Use the Page Setup dialog to specify print titles to repeat on each page.

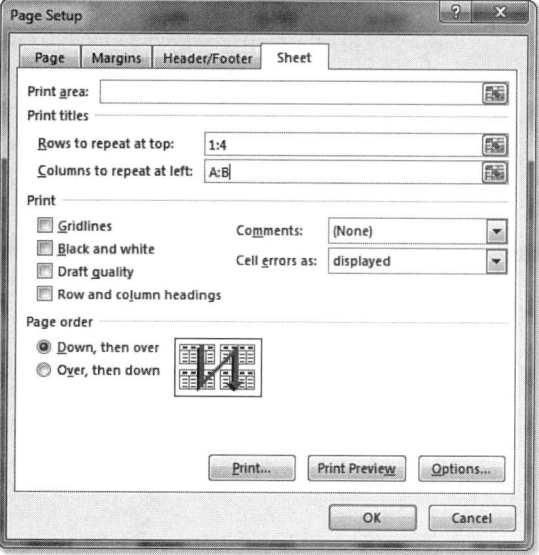

Excluding Part of Your Worksheet from the Print Range

By default, Excel prints all the nonblank cells on a worksheet. Sometimes, you have a nicely format-ted table of data to print but the spreadsheet also includes some work cells in an out-of-the way location that you do not want to print. To prevent the work cells from being printed, follow these steps:

1. Select the range of cells to be included in the print range, such as cells A1:Z99. Alternatively, you can print everything in certain columns. For example, you might select columns C:X to be printed.

2. From the Page Layout tab, select Page Setup, Print Area, Set Print Area.

To clear the print area and to print everything on the worksheet, you can use the Clear Print Area option from the Set Print Area drop-down.

Occasionally, you will want to ignore the print areas and print everything on the worksheet. As described in the "Choosing What to Print" section later in this chapter, you can use the Ignore Print Areas setting to temporarily override the print area. Alternatively, you can print a certain range by selecting the range and then using Selection in the Print panel.

Forcing More Data to Fit on a Page

You will often have worksheets in Excel that are a few columns too wide or a few rows too long to fit on a page. Legacy versions of Excel have included scaling options; however, it is not clear on the Page Layout tab how the scaling options work.

The Scale to Fit group on the Page Layout tab provides options for width, height, and a percentage scale. In most cases, you change the height, width, or both to achieve the desired effect.

If your worksheet is a few columns too wide, change the Width drop-down to specify that the work-sheet should fit on one page. If you have a report that is too tall, change the Height drop-down to specify that the worksheet should be one page tall. As shown in Figure 36.13, when you select either of these options, the Scale option is grayed out, but it still shows the scaling percentage used to make the report fit.

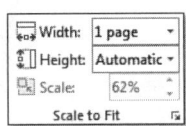

Figure 36.13
After you select the 1 Page setting for Width, the Scale option is grayed out but shows the actual percentage scaling used.

Sometimes, a report cannot fit into one page and still be readable. This is when you can make intel-ligent decisions about the best location for page breaks.

Working with Page Breaks

The two varieties of page breaks are automatic and manual. An *automatic page break* occurs when Excel reaches the bottom or right margin of a physical page. These page breaks change automatically as you adjust margins, add rows, delete rows, or even change the height of certain rows on the page.

Initially, automatic page breaks are not shown in the worksheet. However, after you go to Print Preview and return to Normal view, automatic page breaks are shown in the document using a thin dashed line. Automatic page breaks are also evident in Page Layout view and Page Break Preview mode. To turn off the page breaks, use File, Options, Advanced, Display Options for This Worksheet to find a check box for Show Page Breaks.

You can manually insert page breaks at rows or columns where you want to start a new page. For example, you might want to insert a manual page break at the start of a new section in a report. A manual page break does not automatically change in response to changes in the worksheet rows.

Manually Adding Page Breaks

To add a page break manually at a certain row, follow these steps:

1. Select an entire row by clicking the row number that should be the first row on the new page. Alternatively, select the cell in column A in that row.

2. From the Page Layout tab, select Page Setup, Breaks, Insert Page Break.

To add a page break manually at a certain column, follow these steps:

1. Select an entire column by clicking the number above the column that should be the first column on the new page. Alternatively, select row 1 in that column.

2. From the Page Layout tab, select Page Setup, Breaks, Insert Page Break.

> **Caution**
>
> If you insert a page break while the cell pointer is outside row 1 or column A, Excel simultaneously inserts a row page break and a column page break. This is rarely what you want. Make sure to select a cell in column A to insert a row break or to select a cell in row 1 to insert a column break.

Manual Versus Automatic Page Breaks

In Normal view, a subtle visual difference exists between manual and automatic page breaks. The dashed line used to indicate a manual page break is more pronounced than the line used to indicate an automatic page break.

To see a better view of page breaks, you can select View, Page Break Preview to switch to Page Break Preview mode. In this mode, automatic page breaks are shown as dotted blue lines. Manual page breaks are shown as solid lines.

Using Page Break Preview to Make Changes

An advantage of Page Break Preview mode is that while you are in this mode, you can move a page break by dragging the line associated with the page break. If you drag an automatic page break to expand the number of rows or columns on a page, Excel automatically changes the Scale percentage for all pages.

Removing Manual Page Breaks

To remove a manual page break for a row, follow these steps:

1. Position the cursor in the row below the page break.

2. From the Page Layout tab, select Page Setup, Breaks, Remove Page Break.

To remove a manual page break for a column, follow these steps:

1. Position the cursor in the column to the right of the page break.

2. From the Page Layout tab, select Page Setup, Breaks, Remove Page Break.

To remove all manual page breaks, from the Page Layout tab select Page Setup, Breaks, Reset All Page Breaks. Note that clearing the page breaks also resets the scaling back to 100%.

Adding Headers or Footers to the Printed Report

Although you might describe the row of labels that appear at the top of the report as "headings," in this section "headers" are elements that are not in the cells of the worksheet but print at the top of the page. Excel offers three header areas: left, center, and right. Similarly, there are three footer areas.

You can build headers and footers using the third tab of the legacy Page Setup dialog, but Excel now offers a graphical method for building your headers.

The only entry point for the new Header & Footer Tools Design tab of the ribbon is in Page Layout view. From the View tab, select Page Layout View. Excel displays the worksheet with white space for margins.

At the top of each page, you see gray "Click to Add Header" text. Hover the mouse in this area and you see that there are three header zones. Click in the Left, Center, or Right header to display the Header & Footer Tools Design tab in the ribbon.

You can either type a static header in the box or use the icons on the ribbon tab to add text that will change at print time. For example, if you insert the code for Date or Time, the printed header reflects the date or time that the report was printed. You can use the formatting tools on the Home tab to format the text in the header.

To exit Header/Footer mode, click in any cell of the worksheet.

Adding an Automatic Header

For a quick header or footer, you can click the Header or Footer drop-down in the Header & Footer Tools Design tab. The drop-down offers 16 different automatic headers, including various page-numbering styles, the system date, your name, your company name, the sheet name, and the file path and filename.

As shown in Figure 36.14, some of the Header entries include values separated by commas. These entries put header values into the left, center, and right header sections.

> ## Tip
> Although you cannot add to the automatic Header list, you can select an automatic header that is close to what you want and then customize it.

Figure 36.14
To add a pre-built header, you can choose from the Header list.

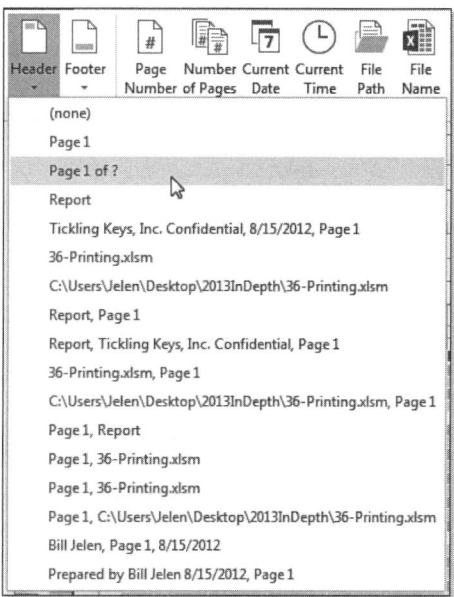

Note
The process for adding footers is identical to the process for adding headers. Throughout the rest of this chapter, several sections include additional information about headers. Keep in mind that the identical instructions apply to footers as well.

Adding a Custom Header

You can type any text you want in the three header areas. One of the automatic headers reads "Confidential," but you can customize this in any way dictated by your company. No matter what type of header you need, you can add it by clicking in any header area and then typing the desired text. To start a new line, press Enter.

Icons for dynamic fields are located in the Header & Footer Tools Design tab. To add an element, click in a header or footer area, position the cursor in the proper place, and click the appropriate icon in the ribbon. As long as the insertion cursor is in the header area, the screen displays the code for that field, such as &[Date] or &[Time].

You can mix static text and dynamic text. For example, you could type "**Page** ", and then click the Page Number icon. Type " **of** " and then click the Number of Pages icon. Type " **of the** " then click the Sheet Name icon. Type " **Worksheet**". The resulting text shows Page &[Page] of &[Pages] of the &[Tab] Worksheet. When you print, the actual text might be Page 3 of 5 of the Sales 2015 Worksheet.

 **Tip**

To include an ampersand in the header or footer, you must use the code &&. For example, to add the header Profit & Loss, type **Profit && Loss**.

Inserting a Picture or a Watermark in a Header

You can add a picture to a header or footer. It can be either a small picture that prints in the header area or a large picture that extends below the header area and acts as a watermark behind the worksheet.

To add a picture to a header, follow these steps:

1. Select View, Page Layout View.

2. Click in the header area of the document.

3. From the Header & Footer Tools Design tab, select Header & Footer Elements, Picture. Excel displays the Insert Online Picture dialog.

4. Select the picture to include in the header. Select a picture and click Insert. Excel adds the text &[Picture] to the header. You cannot tell how large the picture will print at this point.

5. Click in the spreadsheet to see the size of the picture.

6. If you discover that the picture is too large, click in the header area.

7. From the Header & Footer Tools Design tab, select Header & Footer Elements, Format Picture. The Format Picture dialog appears.

8. In the Format Picture dialog, use the Size section to reduce the scale of the picture.

9. If you want your picture to appear as a watermark behind the spreadsheet, you need to lighten the picture. To do so, click the Picture tab of the Format Picture dialog. Change the Color drop-down to Washout.

 Tip

Keep in mind that you won't actually see how large the picture will be until you click outside the header.

 Note

If you use the spin button to change the height in the Scale section, the width is automatically changed as well, in order to keep the scale proportional.

10. None of the picture items in the header features Live Preview. To preview your picture, close the dialog and then click outside the header. If the picture is not the way you want it, repeat steps 6 through 9 as necessary.

Using Different Headers and Footers in the Same Document

Excel 2013 allows the following four header and footer scenarios:

- The same header/footer on all pages

- One header/footer on page 1 and a different header/footer on all other pages

- One header/footer on all odd pages and a different header/footer on all even pages

- One header/footer on page 1, a second header/footer on even pages, and a third header/footer on all odd pages from 3 on

Excel manages these scenarios by storing three headers for each worksheet. The first header is variously called the *odd page header* or just the *header*. As you select and clear the options' check boxes, the contents of each header remain constant, even though they might be used on different pages. Table 36.1 shows the details of each header option.

Table 36.1   Header Options

Different First Page	Different Odd and Even Pages	Odd Page Header	Even Page Header	First Page Header
Cleared	Cleared	Called the header and used on all pages	Not used	Not used
Cleared	Selected	Called the odd page header and used for pages 1, 3, 5, and so on	Called the even page header and used for pages 2, 4, 6, and so on	Not used
Selected	Cleared	Called the header and used on pages 2, 3, 4, and so on	Not used	Called the first page header and used for page 1
Selected	Selected	Called the odd page header and used for pages 3, 5, 7, and so on	Called the even page header and used for pages 2, 4, 6, and so on	Called the first page header and used for page 1

If you add a header in Page Layout view, it is known as the odd page header. In the default configuration, Excel displays the odd page header on all pages of the printout.

Excel has two other sets of headers that are initially hidden. One set is called the *first page header*. The other set is called the *Different First Page*, which you can select from the Options group on the Header & Footer Tools Design tab. When this option is used, Excel displays the first page header above page 1 and uses the odd page header everywhere else.

 **Tip**

To minimize confusion, it is best to select the Options section check boxes Different First Page and Different Odd & Even before entering headers.

Scaling Headers and Footers

Settings in the Page Layout tab allow you to force a worksheet to fit a certain number of pages. If the scaling options require a 75% scale on Sheet1 and a 95% scale on Sheet2, your headings are scaled as well. This causes your page numbers to appear at a different point size in various sections of the report.

Excel offers an option to force all headers and footers to print at 100% scale, regardless of the zoom for the sheet. To select this option, from the Header & Footer Tools Design tab, select Options and clear the Scale with Document check box.

Printing from the File Menu

To access the Print panel, you can either select File, Print or press Ctrl+P. The panel merges settings from the Print and Page Setup dialogs in the middle of the screen and the Print Preview on the right side of the screen. As you update settings in the middle of the screen, the Print Preview updates, which enables you always to see the current preview (see Figure 36.15).

The left side of the screen starts with a very large Print button. Click this button to print the document. The spin button next to the Print button enables you to control the number of copies to print (see Figure 36.16).

The rest of the left panel contains a new kind of gallery. You can see the current choice of the gallery without opening the gallery. If the correct printer is already selected, there is no need to open the drop-down.

Figure 36.15
Print Preview and Print settings are combined in a single screen.

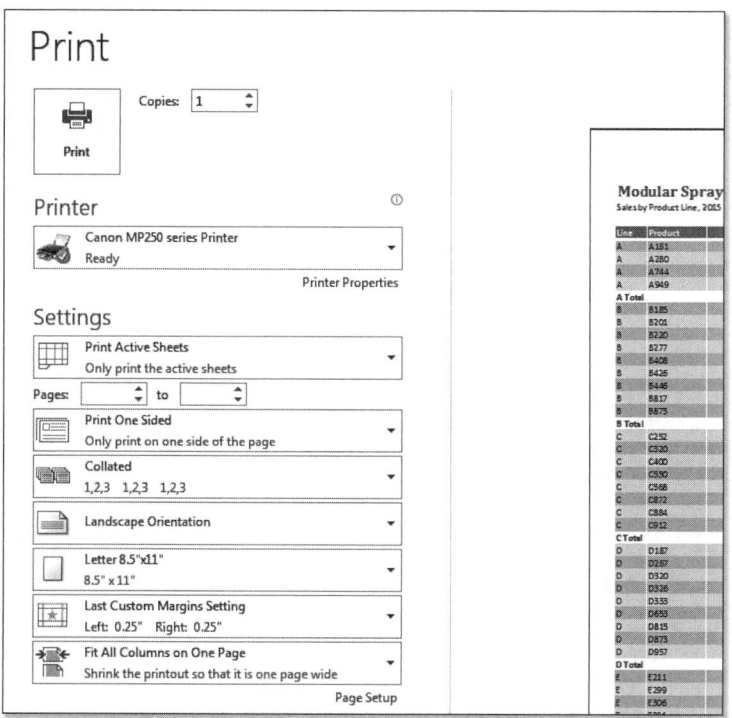

Figure 36.16
To print this document, click the Print button.

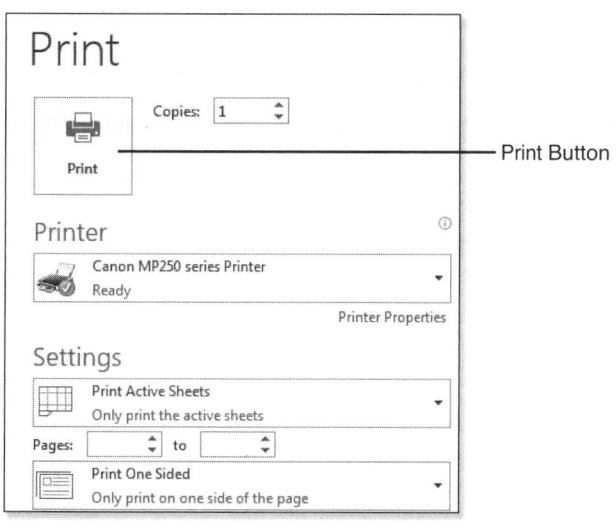

Choosing a Printer

When you open the Printer drop-down, Excel displays all the current printers and indicates if the printer is currently online and/or available. This handy improvement enables you to detect if the department printer is in a Paper Jam condition so you can print to a different printer (see Figure 36.17).

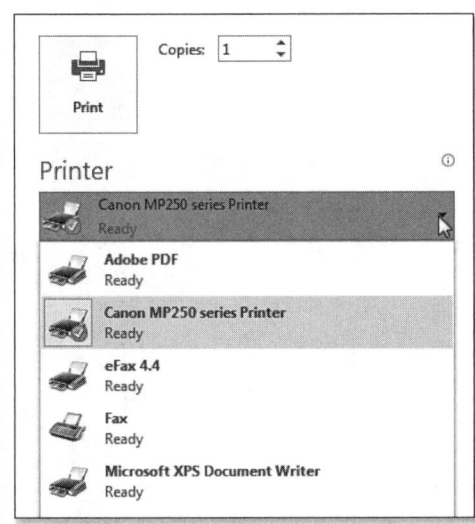

Figure 36.17
The Printers gallery shows the status of each printer.

Choosing What to Print

As shown in Figure 36.18, the Print What gallery offers Active Sheets, Entire Workbook, and Selection settings. You can further modify these settings by choosing Ignore Print Area.

If you choose the Active Sheets option, the currently selected sheet prints. If you have specified a print area, only that range prints; otherwise, Excel prints the entire used range of the document. However, if you select multiple sheets in Group mode, all the selected sheets print.

If you choose the Entire Workbook option, all the nonhidden worksheets in the workbook print. One advantage to this option is that the pages are numbered consecutively as the printout moves from Sheet1 to Sheet2.

Choosing the Selection option enables you to override the print area temporarily. However, if you need to print one small range of a large report, select that range and then choose the Selection option in the Print What gallery. This prevents you from having to change the Print Area twice.

The Ignore Print Area option causes Excel to ignore any print areas specified previously. This causes the entire used area of the worksheet to be printed.

You can select specific pages to print using the Pages spin buttons. To print a single page, enter that page number in both the Pages and To boxes.

Figure 36.18
Choosing what to print.

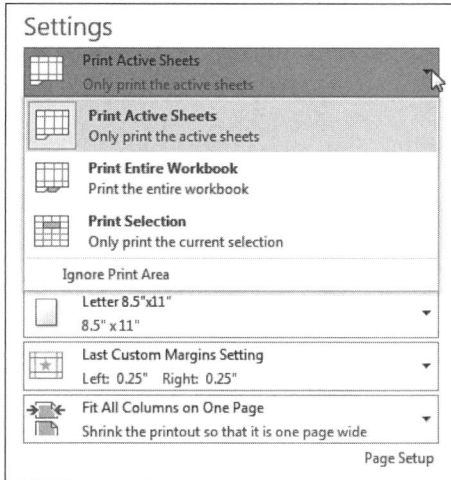

Changing Printer Properties

After you choose a printer, the remaining galleries on the left side of the Print panel are redrawn. If you are printing to an office printer that supports collating and stapling, use the galleries to select each of these options. If you are printing to a home printer that does not have these options, Excel does not show those galleries.

 **Tip**

If a specific property does not appear, you can click the Printer Properties hyperlink at the bottom of the left panel to access the vendor-supplied Printer Property dialog box.

Changing Some of the Page Setup Settings

Even though it might seem like they are out of place, the last settings on the left side of the Print panel are used to control portrait versus landscape, paper size, and margins. If you change a setting here, it will also change in the Page Setup dialog.

If your initial reaction is to wonder why these settings are repeated here, you might also wonder why your favorite Page Setup settings are not also repeated. Even though it is nice to switch from portrait to landscape here, it would also be nice to be able to change the Page Scaling or Rows to Repeat at Top settings here. However, this cannot be done because those settings require you to close the Print panel and to use the Page Layout tab of the ribbon.

Using Page Layout View

When you open Excel, the default view is called Normal view. In legacy versions of Excel, your only choices were Normal view and Page Break Preview mode. However, beginning with Excel 2007, Microsoft added the Page Layout view, which works well when you are preparing a document for printing.

In Excel 2013, the three views are available either in the View tab or on the right side of the status bar.

In Page Layout view, you have a fully functioning worksheet. For example, the formula bar works and you can scroll around the worksheet. However, listed next are the differences between Page Layout and the Normal view:

- White space appears to show the margins on each page. This is usually an advantage because you have a clear view of any page breaks between columns or rows. If you want to hide the white space, you can click the white space and choose Hide White Space.

- A ruler appears below the formula bar that you can use to change margins by dragging the gray areas of the ruler.

- Areas are marked Click to Add Header and Click to Add Footer. Whereas headers and footers are buried in legacy versions of Excel, in the Page Layout view of Excel 2013 it is obvious that headers and footers are available.

- Areas outside the data area of a worksheet are marked with Click to Add Data. One of the problems with Page Break Preview mode is that areas outside the data area were grayed out. However, the Click to Add Data labels option invites you to continue adding pages to your worksheet.

- The only disadvantage to Page Layout view is that Excel turns off your Freeze Panes settings in Page Layout view. Excel warns you that this is happening. Excel does this to emphasize that Print Titles are different from Freeze Panes.

> **Tip**
>
> Keep in mind that Excel does not restore the Freeze Panes settings when you return to Normal view.

Exploring Other Page Setup Options

Other page setup options are scattered throughout the various interface areas. Although some of these are fairly obscure, you might have a need to use them in certain situations.

Printing Gridlines and Headings

To print the gridlines on a worksheet, from the Page Layout tab select Sheet Options, Gridlines, Print.

You can also print the A-B-C column headings and 1-2-3 row headings. To do this, from the Page Layout tab, select Sheet Options, Headings, Print. This option is helpful when you are printing formulas using the FORMULATEXT function and you need to see the cell address of each cell.

Centering a Small Report on a Page

Small reports can look out of place printed in the upper-left corner of a page. Rather than increasing margins, you can choose to center the report horizontally or vertically on a page.

Select Page Layout, Margins, Custom Margins to display the Page Setup dialog. Two check boxes at the bottom of the dialog center the report on the page.

Replacing Error Values When Printing

Excel calculations sometimes result in various errors such as #N/A! or DIV/0. Although these error values help you determine how to fix the errors, they look out of place on a printed page. You can choose to replace any error cells with a blank or two hyphens.

Choose View, Print Titles to open the Sheet tab of the Page Setup dialog. Open the Cell Errors As drop-down and choose <blank> or -- (see Figure 36.19).

Figure 36.19
Replace error cells when printing.

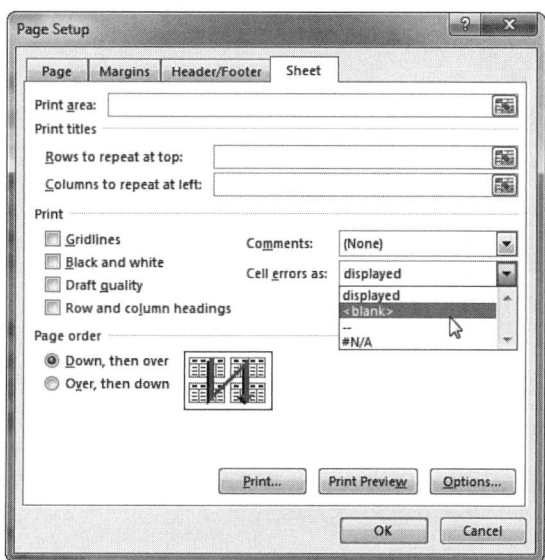

Printing Comments

Cell comments often appear as a tiny red triangle in a cell. You can print a table of all the comments at the bottom of your report. Use the Comments drop-down shown in Figure 36.19 and choose At End of Sheet.

Excel prints your report and then starts a new page listing each comment. The new page shows the cell and the comment content.

The other option for printing comments is to print any visible comments where they are currently displayed. To show all comments, choose Review, Show All Comments. When comments are displayed, you can drag them to a new location so they are not covering up important cells.

Controlling the First Page Number

You might be inserting a printed Excel worksheet in the middle of a printed Word document. If the Excel worksheet is appearing as the tenth page in the Word report, for example, you would want the Excel page numbers to start at 10 instead of 1.

From the Page Layout tab, choose the dialog launcher at the bottom right of the Page Setup group. Excel displays the Page tab of the Page Setup dialog. The last setting is First Page Number and is initially set to Auto. Type **10** in this box, and Excel prints the Excel worksheet using page numbers 10, 11, 12, and so on.

37

EXCEL WEB APP AND OTHER WAYS TO SHARE WORKBOOKS

When the precursor to the Excel Web App debuted, there was a long list of things that the Excel client could do and the Excel Web App could not do. Over time, that list has gotten shorter. And now, there are things the Excel Web App can do that the Excel client will never do.

In the original Excel Services, there was a long laundry list of things that would not work in the browser. Excel in the web was just trying to catch up with things that regular Excel could do (see Figure 37.1).

Figure 37.1
Originally, Excel in a browser offered a fraction of the client version of Excel.

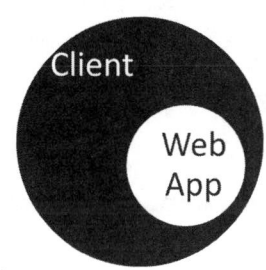

Here's what I've noticed: The Excel client is updated once every three years. The code base for Excel is nearing 30 years old. That means if you want to tweak a feature on one side of Excel, you need to make sure it doesn't break anything anywhere else in Excel. The Excel Web App does not have 30 years of history and code. The Excel Web App team is putting out new features every four months. That means in the time between Excel 2010 and Excel 2013, the Excel Web App has had close to nine iterations. Every new version brings new features. The Excel Web App is crossing differences off the laundry list of things it cannot do.

In 2011, I noticed another change: The Excel Web App team is no longer trying to play catch-up with the Excel client. The Excel Web App team is starting to put out features that will never be in the Excel client. There is now a significant slice of the Venn diagram where the Excel Web App is making things possible that the Excel client can't do (see Figure 37.2).

Figure 37.2
Now, the Excel Web App enables some features that the Excel client cannot do.

Here are a few things you can do with the Excel Web App:

- View and edit your Excel workbooks from any browser, even if the computer does not have Excel installed.

- Have two people—no, an entire team—editing the same Excel worksheet from different computers, at the same time.

- Share a range of your workbook over the Web, with interactivity, yet protect all of your formulas and intellectual property. Others can't hack in and unhide your hidden worksheets, because as far as the browser knows, the hidden worksheets aren't even there.

- Create a quickie web calculator. People reading your blog or web page can enter some input cells, and then your Excel formulas and charts update.

- Post a worksheet to Facebook, LinkedIn, or Twitter.

- Build a survey in Excel and publish the survey page. All of the results are posted into your workbook on SkyDrive.

- Turn any static table in your web page into an interactive table that can be sorted, filtered, or charted.

In addition, the Excel Web App has become the entry-level spreadsheet. Microsoft is no longer producing Microsoft Works or Excel Starter.

Viewing Your SkyDrive Workbooks from Anywhere

If you save a workbook to your SkyDrive or Office 365 SharePoint site, you can later access that file from any modern browser. Say that you take a weekend trip to your parents' house 300 miles away, and your boss calls on Saturday to say that you need to add a section to the workbook right away. Your parents have a computer but no Excel. Before you head out to the Rent-a-PC kiosk at the local FedEx Office, you can easily open and edit your file from any modern browser.

Either sign in to Live.com or to your Office 365 site, find the file on SkyDrive, and click it. Initially, the file is rendered in the browser (see Figure 37.3). At this point, you can view the data but not change anything. You see how to allow others to make changes in the next section.

Figure 37.3
You can view and scroll through the workbook from a browser.

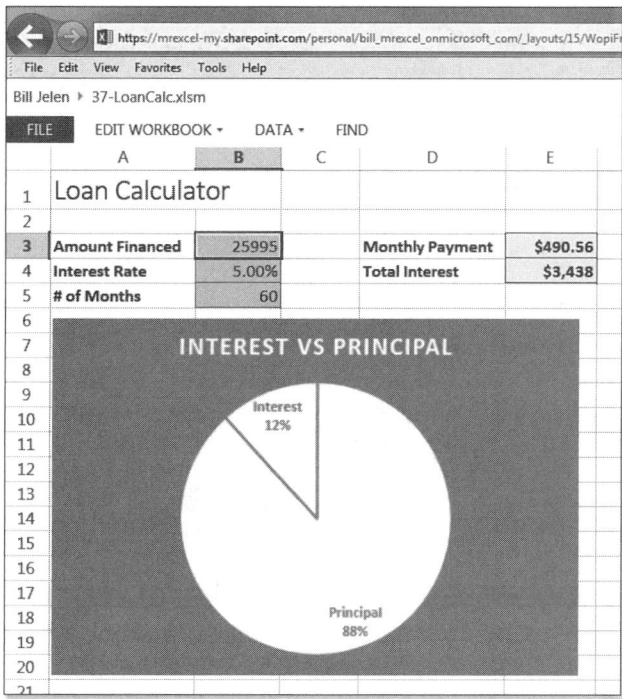

If you discover that you need to edit the workbook, you can either download a copy to edit in Excel on that computer or you can make changes right in the browser. Open the Edit Workbook menu and choose Edit in Excel Web App (see Figure 37.4).

When you choose to edit in the browser, a subset of the Excel ribbon appears. You have tabs for File, Home, Insert, and View. Working in the browser is remarkably similar to working in Excel. You can navigate the cells just as you do in Excel. The fill handle works. Formulas work, and even referring to cells in a formula with either the mouse or arrow keys works.

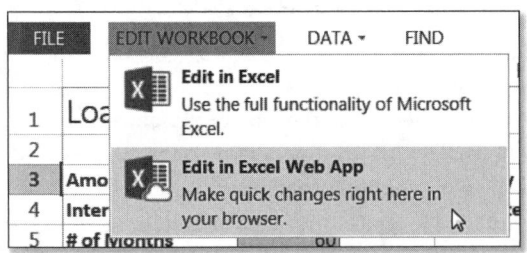

Figure 37.4
Choose to edit in the browser to unleash the Excel Web App.

In Figure 37.5, cell B23 is in the process of being edited. The IPMT function is one you might use occasionally, but most won't necessarily remember the order of the arguments. The tooltip appears to remind you that it goes rate, per, nper, pv.

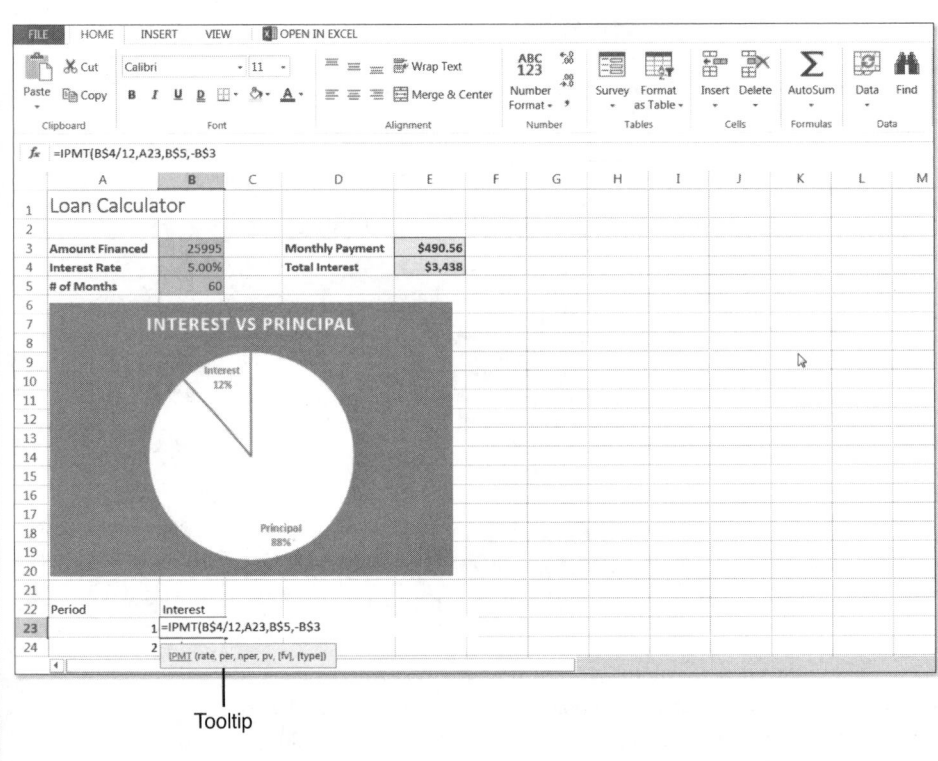

Tooltip

Figure 37.5
Build new formulas in the browser.

When you finish the formula, just double-click the fill handle to copy the formula down. Use the AutoSum at the bottom of the 12 formulas to get a total for the year. Type **First Year Interest** in D5 and build a formula in E5 to pull the total up. All of these steps feel just like Excel.

Now it is time to format D5 and E5. The Cell Styles gallery is not in the subset of commands. The other cells in this area were formatted using the Heading4 and Output styles. Although the Excel Web App does not let you apply styles, you can use the Paste drop-down to choose Paste Formatting.

Go to cell D4 and press Ctrl+C to copy. Stop. Here is the first interruption. You've just performed a Copy operation, and the browser stops you to ask whether the web page can have access to your Clipboard. Click OK. This is still impressive. You've added 28 cells to the worksheet, several formulas, used the fill handle and AutoSum—five minutes of editing and so far everything feels just like Excel. The first Ctrl+C is your only reminder that you aren't in the real Excel.

 Note

One other noticeable difference with the Excel Web App is the lack of support for the F4 key to mark a reference as absolute. F4 already has a meaning in the browser. You have to type the dollar signs in your formula manually.

Copy D4 and then select D5. Open the Paste drop-down and choose Paste Formatting. Repeat for E4 and E5 (see Figure 37.6). Note that the browser now lets you copy without nagging you about granting access to the Clipboard.

Figure 37.6
No cell styles gallery? Use Paste Formatting instead.

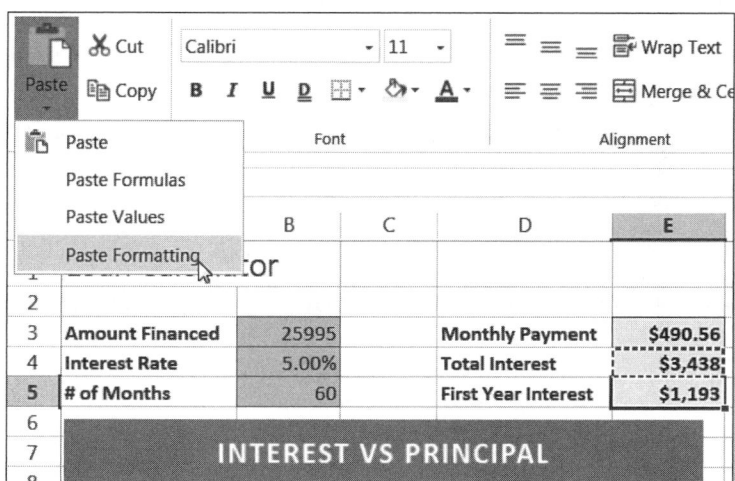

Time to save the workbook so your manager can download it. Go to the File menu and choose Save As. Notice there is no Save button (see Figure 37.7).

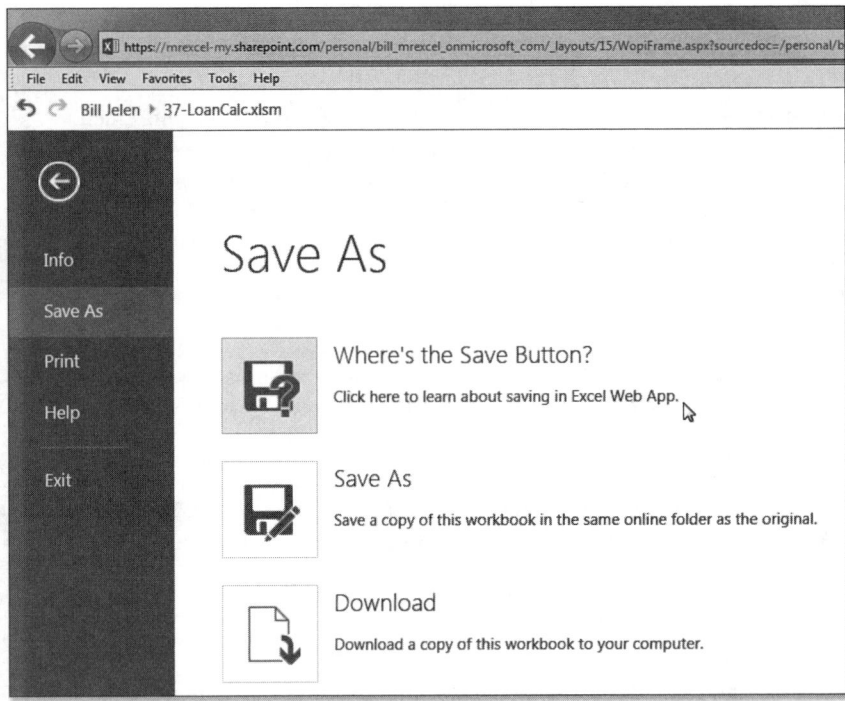

Figure 37.7
No button for Save?

It turns out that every edit you make in the browser is automatically saved every two minutes to your SkyDrive. This way, if the Internet connection goes down, your changes are always saved (see Figure 37.8).

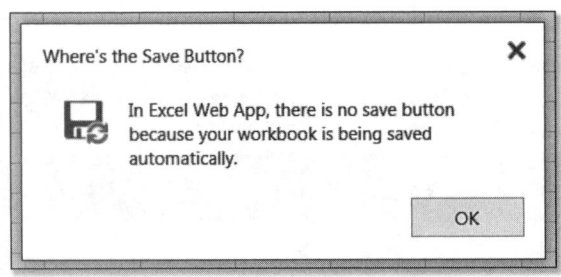

Figure 37.8
Every change is automatically saved.

Click File, Exit to close the file.

When you get back to work on Monday morning. Open Excel, and then open the file from your recent documents. All the changes you made while editing in the browser are there in the Excel client.

Editing Excel on the iPad

Greetings from September, 2012. Yes, I am writing this chapter in the past—before the debut of the Microsoft Surface tablet. Back here in the past, the leading tablet is known as the Apple iPad. Say that you need to edit your Excel workbook on the SkyDrive and all that you have is the iPad. It can be done—with one secret hitch.

After you sign in to Windows Live on the iPad, scroll to the bottom of the screen. Windows Live has detected that you are accessing the site from a mobile device and shows you the mobile version of Windows Live. At the bottom of the screen is a link to show the site as if you were using a PC. Click the link for PC site (see Figure 37.9).

Figure 37.9
Switch to viewing the PC instead of Mobile version of Windows Live.

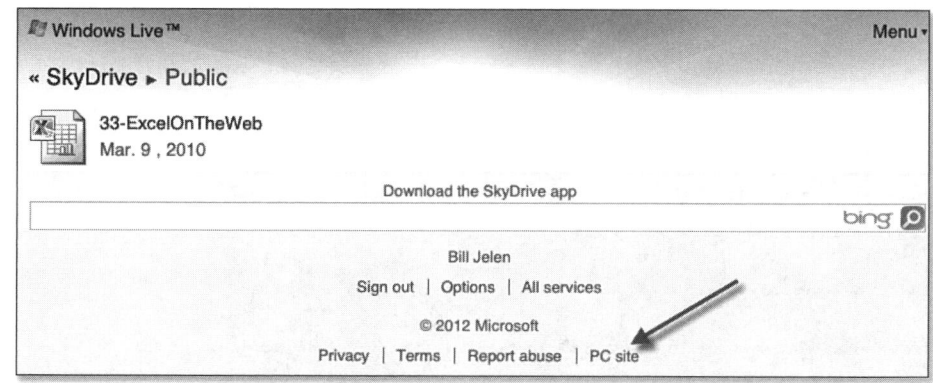

You now have access to the Edit in Browser button (see Figure 37.10).

Figure 37.10
Edit in Browser on the iPad.

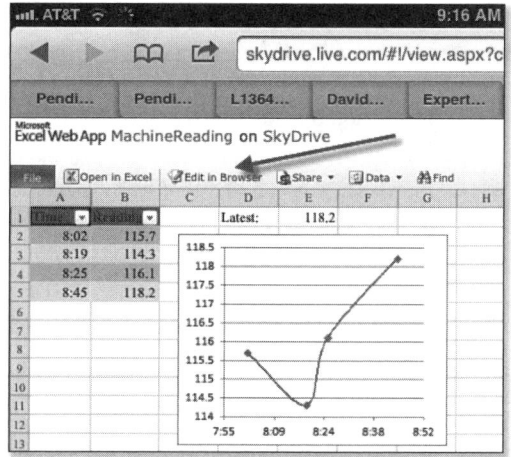

You must click a cell, and then click in the formula bar to open the keyboard (see Figure 37.11).

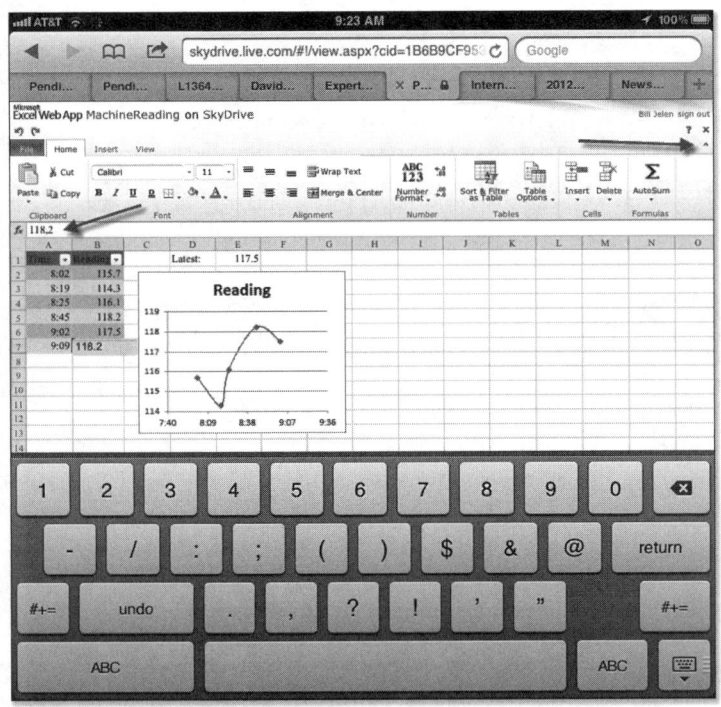

Figure 37.11
Remember that all changes are automatically saved.

Editing Excel on the Surface RT Tablet

If you have a Microsoft Surface RT tablet, you are able to edit your SkyDrive workbooks using Excel RT. This version is very similar to Excel 2013 Home and Student, which is Microsoft-speak to mean that you do not have access to PowerPivot, the Data Model, or Power View. You cannot run VBA macros on the Surface, although it preserves any code that is in the file.

With the Surface tablet, you can use the optional keyboard, the on-screen keyboard, or the touch interface. You will find that even if you use the keyboard, you will start reaching for the touch screen to scroll, zoom, or choose icons from the ribbon. If you are using the touch screen, enable Touch mode. This mode adds extra white space between the icons to give you a better chance of touching the correct icon.

To turn on Touch mode, open the drop-down at the right side of the Quick Access toolbar and add the Touch mode icon to the Quick Access Toolbar.

Selecting a Range with Touch

Selecting a range using touch is not like selecting a range using the mouse. First, touch a cell in the top-left corner of the range. Two circular handles appear in the top-left and bottom-right corners of the selection. Drag the handle to extend the range.

Using the Mini Toolbar with Touch

If you touch-and-hold a cell in Excel, a special version of the Mini toolbar appears. This toolbar has large icons for Paste, Cut, Copy, and Clear. It includes two drop-down color choosers for Fill and Font color. There is a Fill icon (discussed below), and then a drop-down menu offering choices such as Filter, Sort, Pick from Drop-down List.

The drop-down menu at the right side of the Mini toolbar is as close as you get to a right-click menu using touch. The choices are larger, but there are fewer of them. If you want access to the full right-click menu, you need the optional keyboard for the Surface.

Using the Fill Handle with Touch

The Fill Handle is frustratingly small with the Surface. Even if you use the stretch gesture to zoom in, the cells become large but the Fill Handle remains tiny. If you can't get the hang of using the Fill Handle with touch, you can use this alternative method.

1. Select cell B1 by touching the cell.

2. Type January and press Enter.

3. Click and hold cell B1. When a box animates, let go of the screen and the touch version of the Mini toolbar appears.

4. Click the AutoFill icon.

5. You should see a large down-arrow icon appear just below the active cell. If it does not appear, click the cell again.

6. Touch the arrow icon and drag either down or right to fill the series.

7. When you finish dragging, the typical on-grid drop-down appears allowing you to change from Fill Series to Copy Cells.

Using Ink Tools

While the ink features have been around since Excel 2003, you probably never encountered them if you did not have a touch screen.

Ink is really just a free-form drawing object. Excel offers a pen and a highlighter in various thicknesses and colors.

To add ink to a worksheet, go to the Review tab and choose Start Inking from the icon on the right side of the ribbon.

Choose either the Pen or Highlighter from the left side of the Ink Tools Pens tab in the ribbon. Choose a color or thickness from the Pens gallery. Use a stylus or your finger to draw on the worksheet. You can circle a cell, draw an arrow, or highlight a value. After you finish applying ink, you need to press Escape before you try to select a cell.

Group-Editing Using the Excel Web App

The client version of Microsoft Excel has a bunch of icons on the Review tab that make it sound like you can share a workbook. In particular, I am talking about the large icon that says "Share Workbook." What that icon doesn't say is that after you've shared the workbook, you can no longer add conditional formatting, data validation, charts, pictures, drawing objects, hyperlinks, scenarios, outlines, subtotals, data tables, tables, pivot tables, or protection. This is a terrible set of limitations.

If you save your workbook to the SkyDrive and then share the file in the SkyDrive, you can have any number of people editing the workbook at the same time.

Understanding the Limitations of the Excel Web App

The Excel Web App still has a list of limitations. In many cases, though, the Web App renders a feature, but it doesn't let you create that feature on the Web. For example, the Excel Web App calculates array formulas created on the client, but you cannot build a new array formula in the Excel Web App. Thus, it is best to create your workbook in Excel and then upload to the SkyDrive. The following list describes some limitations of the Web App:

- You cannot create new pivot tables on the Web, but these elements that you create in the Excel 2013 client render on the Web. You can add or remove fields from existing pivot tables.

- You do not have the full range of chart editing on the Web. You can create simple charts. Charts created in the client will render on the Web.

- Generate GetPivotData is not functional on the Web, but =GetPivotData functions that you create in the Excel client work on the Web.

- You cannot enter array formulas on the Web, but array formulas that you enter in the Excel client work.

Some features do not work on the Web:

- Data Validation does not work on the Web.

- Links to external workbooks do not work on the Web.

- VBA macros do not run in the Excel Web App.

- Worksheet protection does not work on the Web.

Hiding columns is now possible in the Excel Web App, but the process is different. Drag the column width to zero to hide a column.

Using the Excel Web App Instead of Excel Starter

You might remember the free Microsoft Works spreadsheet in Windows XP or the Excel Starter program in Windows Vista and Windows 7. These programs typically shipped with new PCs that did not include the full version of Office.

Support for Excel Starter and Word Starter has been discontinued. New PCs are not shipped with the free spreadsheet programs anymore. Instead, Microsoft suggests that you can create your small workbooks using the Excel Web App.

It is possible to create a new workbook completely within the Excel Web App. Sign in to Live.com. Navigate to the SkyDrive Documents folder. Open the Create menu and choose Excel Workbook (see Figure 37.12). You are prompted to give the workbook a name.

Figure 37.12
Create a new workbook from the SkyDrive.

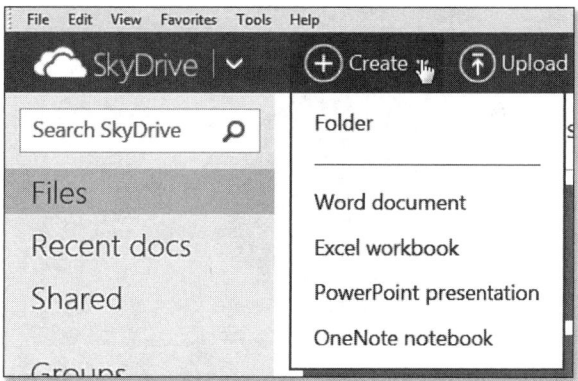

The workbook shown in Figure 37.13 was created entirely in the browser. It includes formulas, absolute references, an AutoSum, a pie chart, cell formatting, borders, fill, bold, italic, and font size changes. As a replacement for Excel Starter, this works fairly well.

There were a few issues when creating the workbook in the browser:

- Pressing F4 to mark a formula reference as absolute does not work. It seems to open the recent URL drop-down in the browser instead.

- You will find it tough to create a chart from noncontiguous ranges such as C6:C9 and F6:F9. The workbook shown in Figure 37.13 has extra formulas in the range behind the pie chart to copy those two ranges into a contiguous range, and the chart is created from that data.

- There is no option to show the category name in the chart data labels as you can do in the client. Normally, I would remove the legend and change the data labels, but this is not currently an option in the Excel Web App. However, recall that new versions of the Excel Web App come out three times a year. I would not be surprised if this functionality is eventually added.

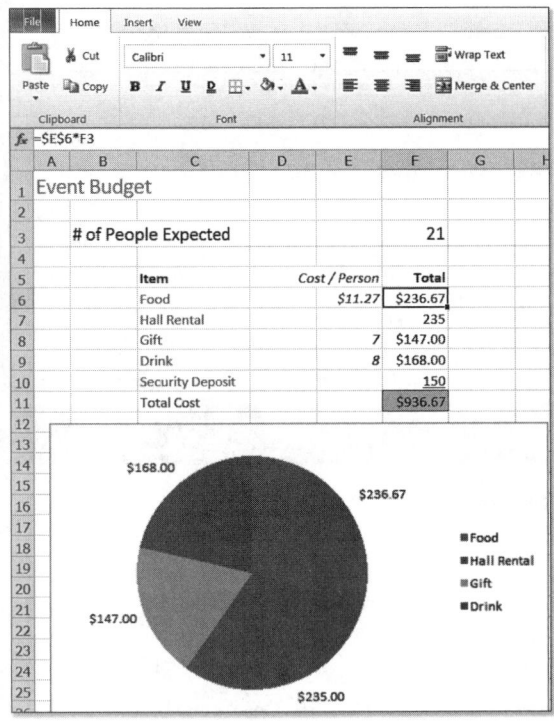

Figure 37.13
All of these elements were created in the browser.

Designing a Workbook as an Interactive Web Page

You can use the Excel client to design a workbook for use as a web page. You can build a web page that accepts input values, does calculations, presents results, and shows charts. The person who visits your workbook in a browser can interact with slicers, enter numbers for input cells, and see the results.

Here is the best part: You can protect your intellectual property. You can choose to publish Sheet1 in the browser and not show other worksheets. The formulas on Sheet1 reach back to use information on Sheet2, but no one is able to hack in and unhide Sheet2. They aren't able to see your formulas.

To adapt the earlier Loan Calculator workbook to create a web page, you can do these tasks:

- Add a new worksheet. I called the worksheet Hidden just to help me remember which worksheet won't be seen.

- Cut anything that does not need to be seen from the first worksheet and paste it to the Hidden worksheet. In this example, you could cut the formulas for first year interest and put it on the Hidden worksheet.

- Consider whether any input cells can be changed to a slicer. Slicers are excellent for selecting values in a web page. The Apply Interest Rate slicer in Figure 37.14 is tied to a simple six-row data set and pivot table on the Hidden worksheet. The Interest Rate cell is now a formula that pulls the first value from the pivot table. When someone chooses from the slicer, the interest rate tied to that type of loan is fed into the interest rate field.

- Take a few steps to make your worksheet not look like Excel. On the View tab, uncheck Formula Bar, Gridlines, and Headings.

Figure 37.14 shows the workbook in the Excel client. This is the first worksheet. Most of the data is on the Hidden worksheet.

Figure 37.14
Make a worksheet that does not look like Excel.

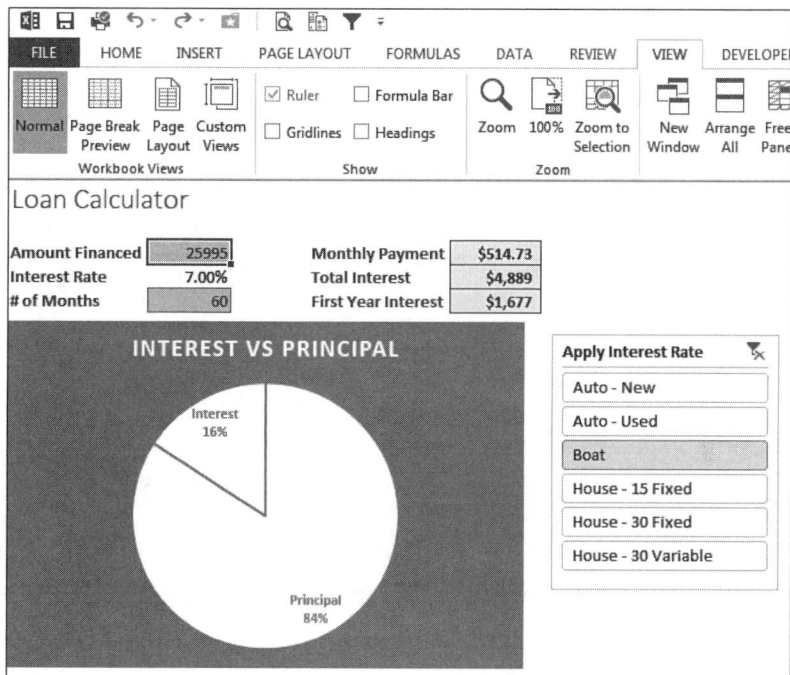

To allow certain fields to be entered on the web page, you have to define a named range for each individual cell. Click on the Amount Financed entry cell. Click in the Name box to the left of the formula bar. Type a name without spaces, such as **AmountFinanced** or **Amount_Financed**. Repeat for the # of Months field.

You need to control what is shown in the browser. Open the File menu and choose Info from the left navigation area. Click on Browser View Options in the center pane to cause the Browser View icon to appear and then click that icon.

In the Show tab, open the drop-down. Change Entire Workbook to Sheets. You can then uncheck the Hidden worksheet (see Figure 37.15).

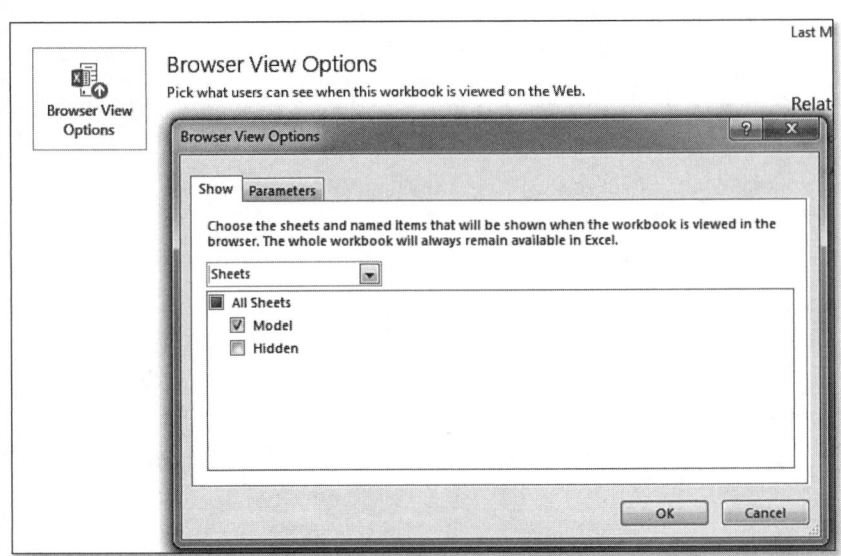

Figure 37.15
Choose which worksheet will be visible and which will be hidden.

In the Parameters tab, click the Add button. Excel shows you a list of all single-cell names in the workbook. Choose the names and the slicer (see Figure 37.16).

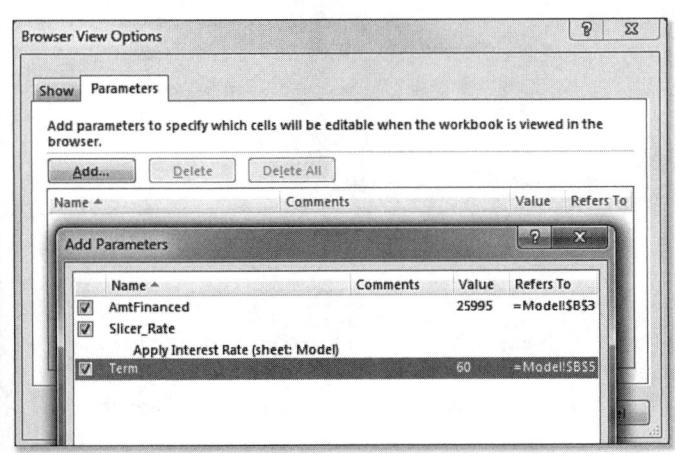

Figure 37.16
Choose which named cells should be parameters.

Save the workbook to your SkyDrive account. You should test the workbook before sharing it. Make sure that the parameters work and that everything looks correct. When you are signed in to the SkyDrive and open your own workbook, it might automatically open in Edit mode. Go to the View tab and choose Reading View.

Figure 37.17 shows the workbook in the browser. If you click on a slicer, the interest rate changes, all the formulas on the hidden worksheet update, the calculated cells in the browser update, and the chart updates.

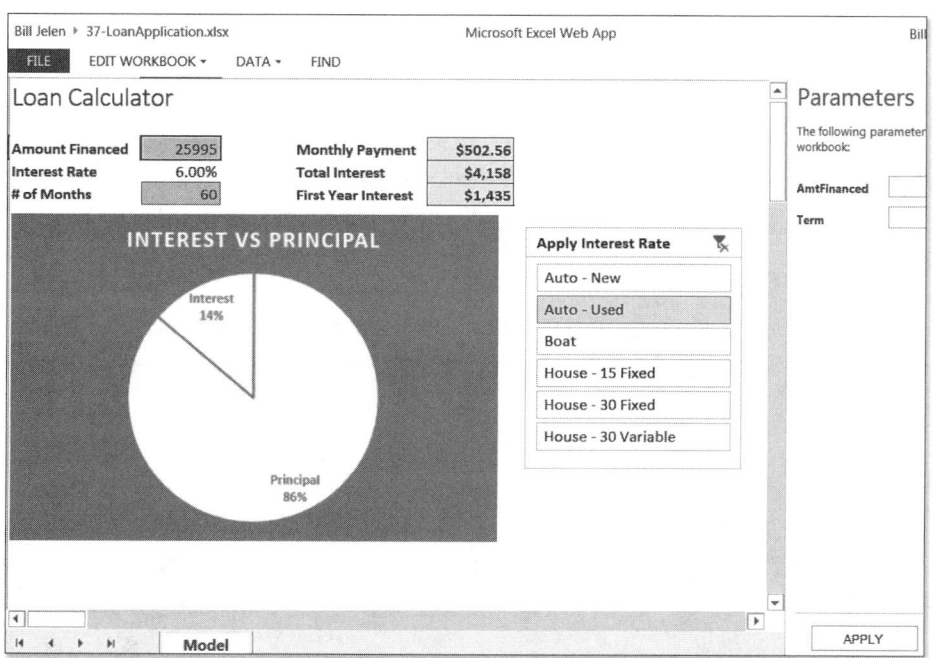

Figure 37.17
This is a cool interactive web page, all created using your Excel skills.

To edit one of the input cells, the user types new values in the Parameters pane and clicks Apply at the bottom of the pane. Again, the cells update, all the formulas calculate, the results display, and the chart changes.

Because you are reading this book, I bet you know a lot about Microsoft Excel. You can probably knock out amazing formulas that do all sorts of calculations. Now, with just knowledge you've gained in this chapter, you can create amazing interactive web pages.

Sharing a Link to Your Web Workbook

The easiest way to share your web workbook is to use the Share with People command in the SkyDrive. This enables other people to interact with your workbook, but it also lets them download the whole workbook to their computer.

While you are viewing the workbook, use Share, Share with People, as shown in Figure 37.18.

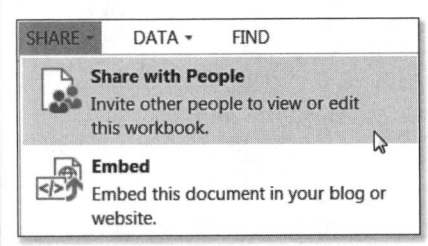

Figure 37.18
While viewing the workbook in the SkyDrive, click Share, Share with People.

The share dialog offers three categories:

- You can send an email inviting others to use the workbook.

- You can post to Facebook, Twitter, or LinkedIn.

- You can get a link that you can distribute.

In Figure 37.19, I am posting to my Facebook, Twitter, and LinkedIn accounts. Remember the limit for Twitter is 140 characters, less the 15 characters for the link. Keep the message short and to the point.

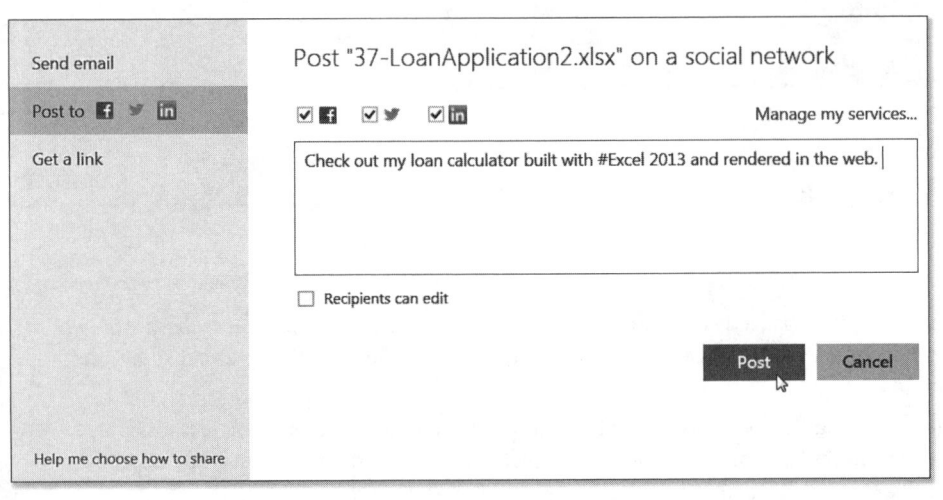

Figure 37.19
Post to your social media accounts.

A few seconds later, the tweet appears in your Twitter feed (see Figure 37.20).

It also appears in LinkedIn and Facebook (see Figure 37.21).

Figure 37.20
Excel shortens the URL to 14 characters and a space.

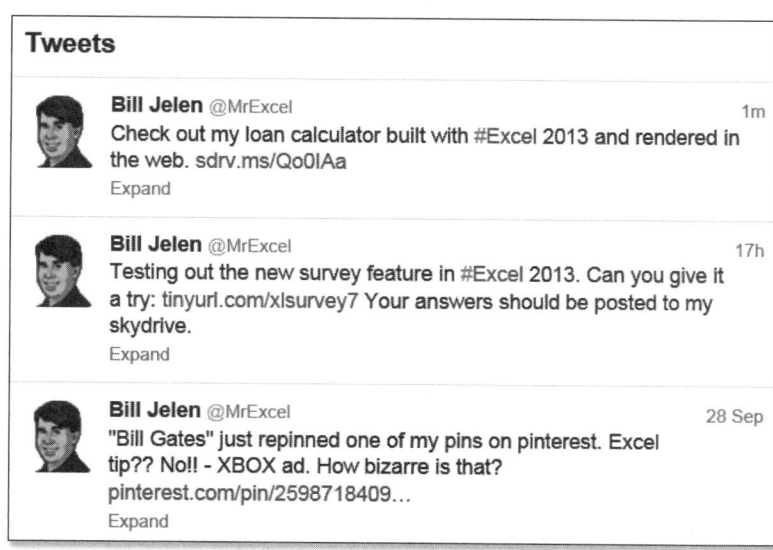

Figure 37.21
The posts simultaneously appear in LinkedIn and Facebook.

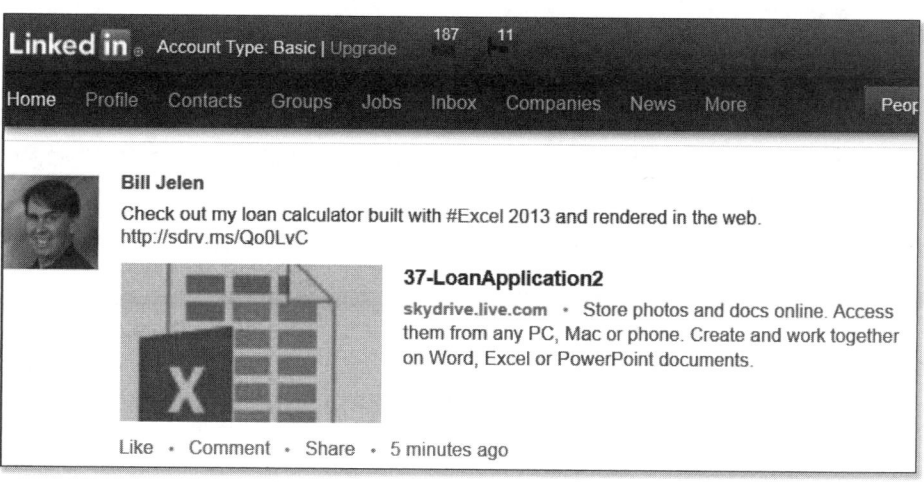

When someone sees this post and follows the link, he arrives at a read-only copy of the application shown previously in Figure 37.17. Any changes that he makes to the slicer or the parameters are not saved to the workbook. The next person gets a fresh copy of the workbook.

Embedding Your Workbook in a Blog Post or Your Web Page

If you have a blog or a web page, you can embed the workbook there. Before you proceed, though, consider saving a version of the workbook to the SkyDrive without the parameters. Go back to the dialog shown in Figure 37.16 and uncheck the parameters. Better settings in the embed process enable people to type directly into your input cells.

Then go back to the Share menu in Figure 37.18 and choose the Embed option. Excel shows a warning screen stating that people without your password are able to interact with the web page (see Figure 37.22).

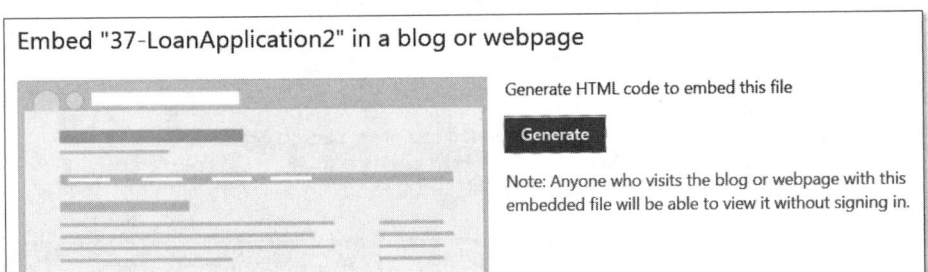

Embed "37-LoanApplication2" in a blog or webpage

Generate HTML code to embed this file

Generate

Note: Anyone who visits the blog or webpage with this embedded file will be able to view it without signing in.

Figure 37.22
Click Generate to acknowledge the message.

You can customize many things in the next screen:

- Rather than seeing the whole workbook, you can limit people to only seeing Model!A1:M20 or any other range.

- If you didn't previously hide the gridlines, you can do so.

- By default, the setting Include a Download Link is checked. If you are trying to protect the data on the hidden worksheet, you should uncheck this setting.

- Choose all three items under Interaction. The first check box allows the slicers to filter the underlying pivot table. The second check box lets people type directly into your worksheet. Note that this means they can type in your input cells as well as anywhere else. For example, they could go to cell A1 and type "Bill Jelen is a big idiot!" However, their changes will not be visible to anyone else. You can specify that the active cell starts in the first input cell.

- You can adjust the height and width of the embedded frame.

After you have answered all of the questions, the embed code appears at the bottom of the screen. You might have to scroll down to see the embed code. Click the Copy link to copy the embed code to your Clipboard (see Figure 37.23).

Figure 37.23
Copy the
embed code.

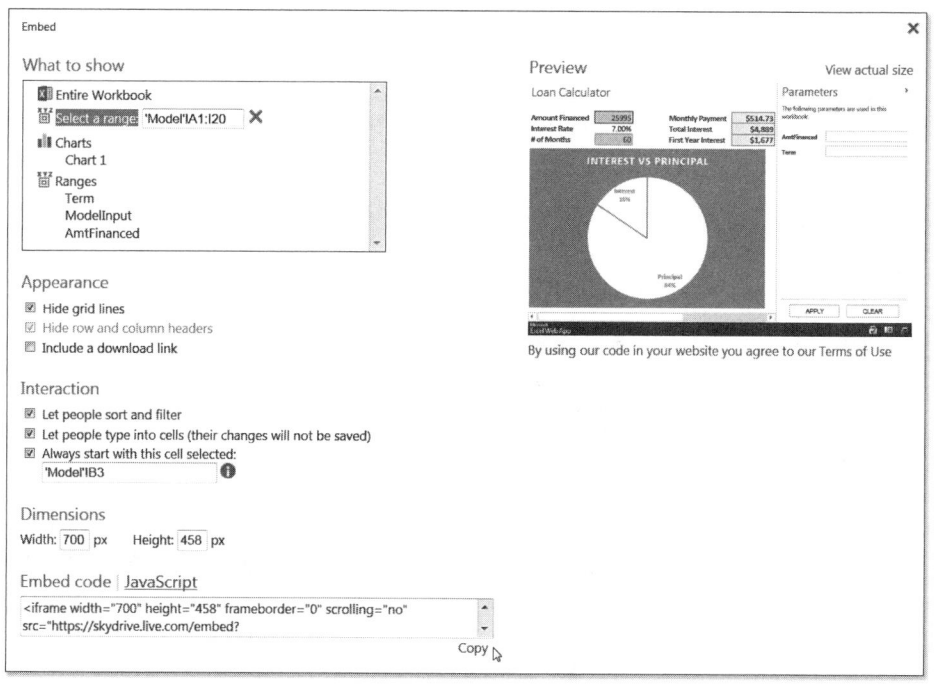

Create a new web page or blog post. Paste the embed code at the proper place (see Figure 37.24).

Figure 37.24
MrExcel.com—
creating web
pages with
Notepad since
1998.

```
<H1>Excel 2013 In Depth, Chapter 37 Demo</H1><br>
This workbook was generated in Excel 2013, saved to the SkyDrive, and then
embedded in this web page.</p>

<iframe width="700" height="458" frameborder="0" scrolling="no" src="https://sky

<b><center>MrExcel.com <a href="consult.shtml"><b>Consulting</a> can be hired to
```

The result is a web page that uses your formulas and data without revealing any of the tables on the back worksheets (see Figure 37.25). Be aware that someone with a knowledge of the Excel Web App and HTML could edit the source of the web page and bring the Download button back and access your workbook.

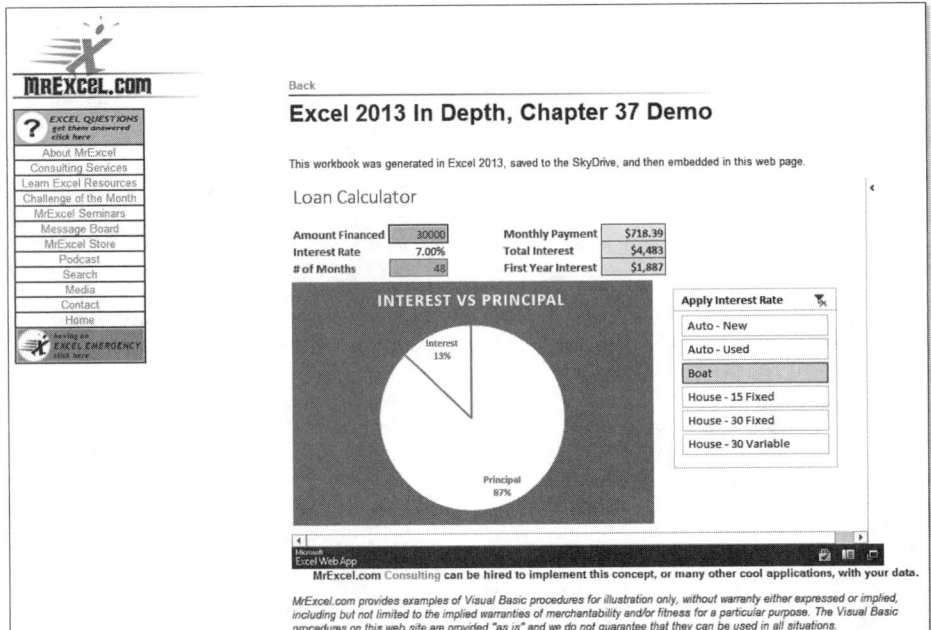

Figure 37.25
This web page
was created
with Excel.

Collecting Survey Data in the Excel Web App

You can find plenty of survey tools out on the Web. You type in some questions, send people the survey link, and they collect your data. At the end of the survey, you export the results to Excel and hope everything works alright. Starting with the latest version of the Excel Web App, you can collect the survey data directly into a blank Excel workbook on the Web.

To start, go to the SkyDrive and create a new Excel workbook. Open the Survey icon and choose New Survey (see Figure 37.26).

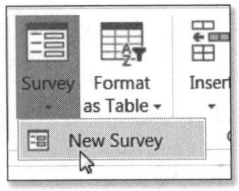

Figure 37.26
Start with a blank workbook and choose New Survey.

A survey contains a title, a description, and then several question fields. Each question field has a question, a subtitle, and a data type. As you enter the information in the fields on the right, you can see a preview of the question on the left (see Figure 37.27).

Figure 37.27
Build the survey, one question at a time.

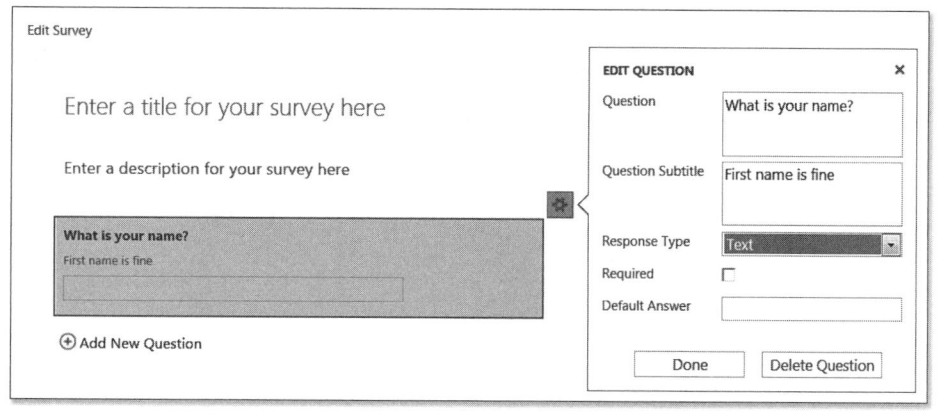

The question data types include Text, Paragraph Text, Number, Date, Time, Yes/No, and Choice (see Figure 37.28). The paragraph text choice provides a taller text box to allow more information to be typed.

Figure 37.28
Select a data type for the question.

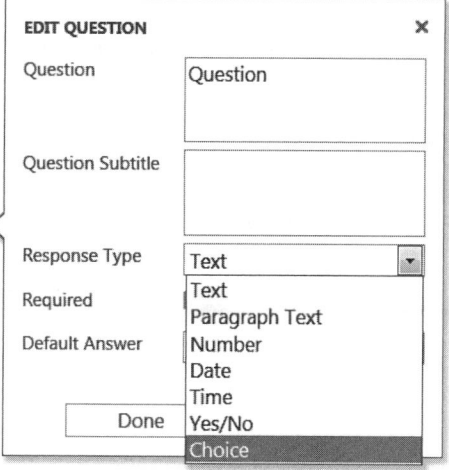

If you choose a data type of Choice, then you can type values in the Choices box. The question appears with a drop-down menu (see Figure 37.29).

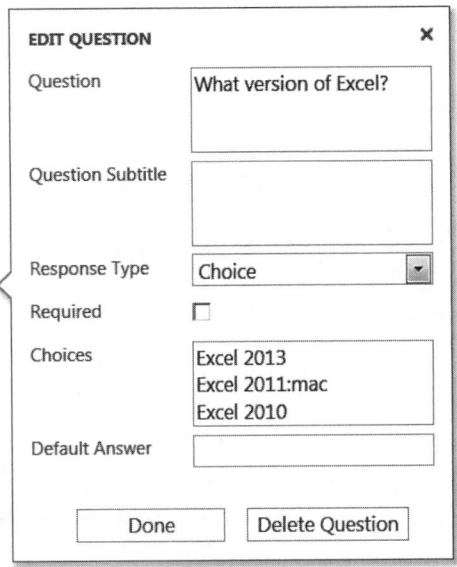

Figure 37.29
Create a drop-down list by entering items in the Choices box.

When you are done, click the Share Survey link at the bottom of the screen. The Excel Web App generates a survey link that is a mile long (see Figure 37.30).

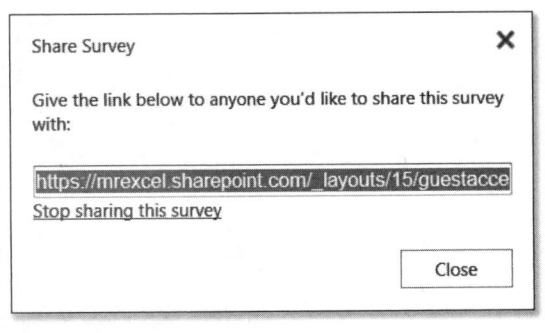

Figure 37.30
Copy this URL.

Frankly, no one will ever be able to type this entire link. Go to any URL shortener, such as www.TinyURL.com, and convert the long URL to a short URL (see Figure 37.31).

Figure 37.31
Create a shorter URL using any TinyURL
or any similar service.

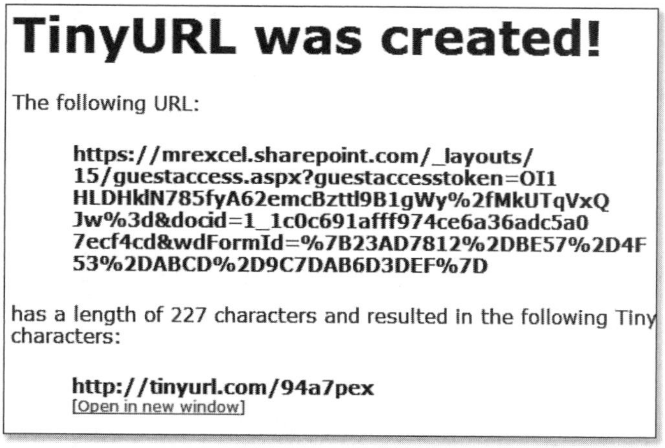

TinyURL was created!

The following URL:

> **https://mrexcel.sharepoint.com/_layouts/**
> **15/guestaccess.aspx?guestaccesstoken=OI1**
> **HLDHklN785fyA62emcBzttl9B1gWy%2fMkUTqVxQ**
> **Jw%3d&docid=1_1c0c691afff974ce6a36adc5a0**
> **7ecf4cd&wdFormId=%7B23AD7812%2DBE57%2D4F**
> **53%2DABCD%2D9C7DAB6D3DEF%7D**

has a length of 227 characters and resulted in the following Tiny
characters:

> **http://tinyurl.com/94a7pex**
> [Open in new window]

Distribute the link to others. I posted my link to Twitter on a Friday afternoon. Anyone who follows the link will see a web page like the one shown in Figure 37.32.

Figure 37.32
People who follow the link will see this
survey.

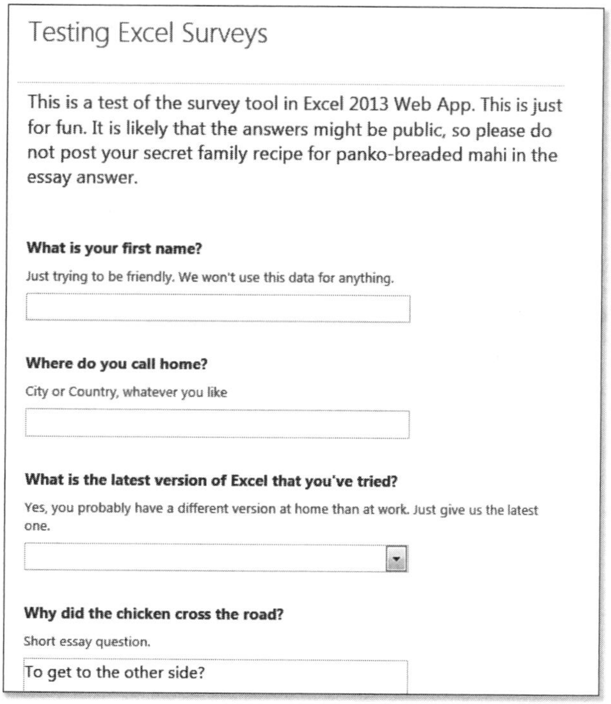

Testing Excel Surveys

This is a test of the survey tool in Excel 2013 Web App. This is just
for fun. It is likely that the answers might be public, so please do
not post your secret family recipe for panko-breaded mahi in the
essay answer.

What is your first name?
Just trying to be friendly. We won't use this data for anything.

Where do you call home?
City or Country, whatever you like

What is the latest version of Excel that you've tried?
Yes, you probably have a different version at home than at work. Just give us the latest
one.

Why did the chicken cross the road?
Short essay question.

To get to the other side?

Here is the amazing thing: When someone fills in the survey web page, his or her answers are written to the next page in your SkyDrive workbook! Go back to your SkyDrive, open the workbook, and the answers are all there (see Figure 37.33). You can sort and filter right in the Excel Web App or download to Excel to perform further analysis.

	A	B	C	D	E	F
1	What is your first name?	Where do you call home?	What is the latest version of Excel that you've tried?	Why did the chicken cross the road?	Yes? or No?	
2	Matt	Birmingham, AL	Excel 2007	Because because because because because.... Because of the wonderful things he does.	Yes	
3	Ken	Canada	Excel 2010	To show the hedgehog it could be done.	No	
4	Dan	Seattle	Excel 2013	Did the chicken really ever cross the road?	Yes	
5	Kris	Budapest	Excel 2010	To be. Or not to be?	Yes	
6	Scott	Earth; North American United States of America; Florida; Flagler County	Excel 2011:mac	We should leave the chicken alone and stop wasting so much time theorizing as to why that chicken crossed the road; we need to simply accept that it did.	Yes	
7	Isaac	United States	Excel 2013	To visit his friends in Kauai!	Yes	
8	Scott	Troon, Scotland	Excel 2010	There is no spoon.	Yes	
9	John	Los Angeles	Excel 2013	To get to the other... No, to create more location data points with which Excel will create a sparkline.	Yes	
10	Mr. Pixel	Spreadsheet	Excel 2013	To learn excel.	Yes	
11	Bart	Burmingham	Excel 2010	Too presumptious. Me thinks the road flanked said chicken.	No	

Figure 37.33
Survey results get fed directly into your Excel workbook.

Make Any Web Table Interactive with Excel Everywhere

Webmasters everywhere should take a few minutes to enhance their web pages using this trick. Say that you have a boring HTML Table in your web page with rows and columns of data, like the one shown in Figure 37.34. (You can check out the file at http://www.mrexcel.com/excelboring.html.)

You can turn that boring table into a table that can be sorted, filtered, and charted with just three lines of code. To start, go to www.ExcelMashup.com and click Get Code. Optionally, choose the button style, type a title, type a company name, and then click Generate Code (see Figure 37.35).

Figure 37.34
This is a boring
static table in a
web page.

Figure 37.35
Fill out a few
fields and click
Generate Code.

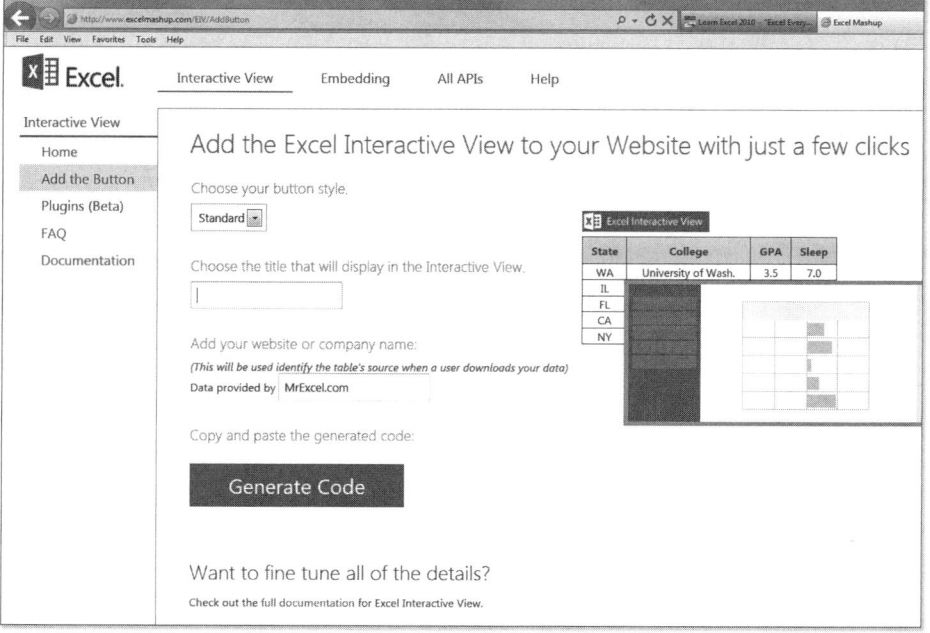

You are given two small bits of HTML code. Paste the top part just above the table in your web page. Paste the bottom part at the bottom, just before the closing </body> tag in the page (see Figure 37.36).

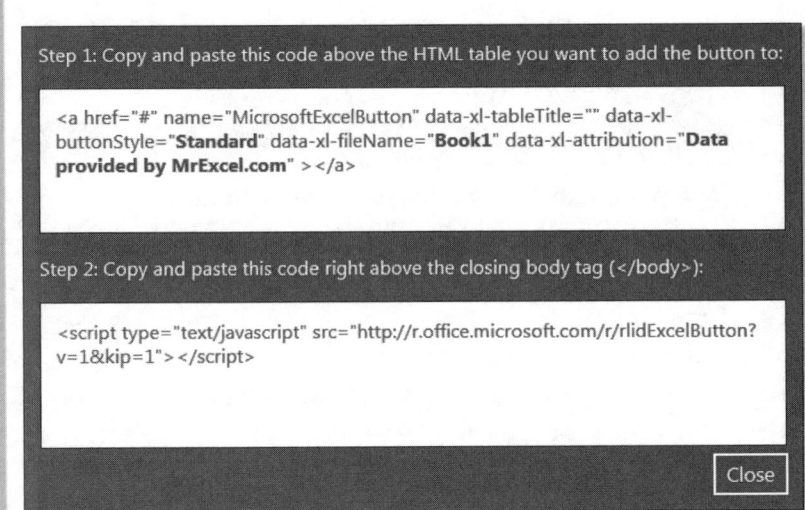

Step 1: Copy and paste this code above the HTML table you want to add the button to:

```
<a href="#" name="MicrosoftExcelButton" data-xl-tableTitle="" data-xl-
buttonStyle="Standard" data-xl-fileName="Book1" data-xl-attribution="Data
provided by MrExcel.com" ></a>
```

Step 2: Copy and paste this code right above the closing body tag (</body>):

```
<script type="text/javascript" src="http://r.office.microsoft.com/r/rlidExcelButton?
v=1&kip=1"></script>
```

Close

Figure 37.36
Copy this code and paste it in your HTML page.

Reload the web page, and a new Excel Interactive View button appears above the table (see Figure 37.37).

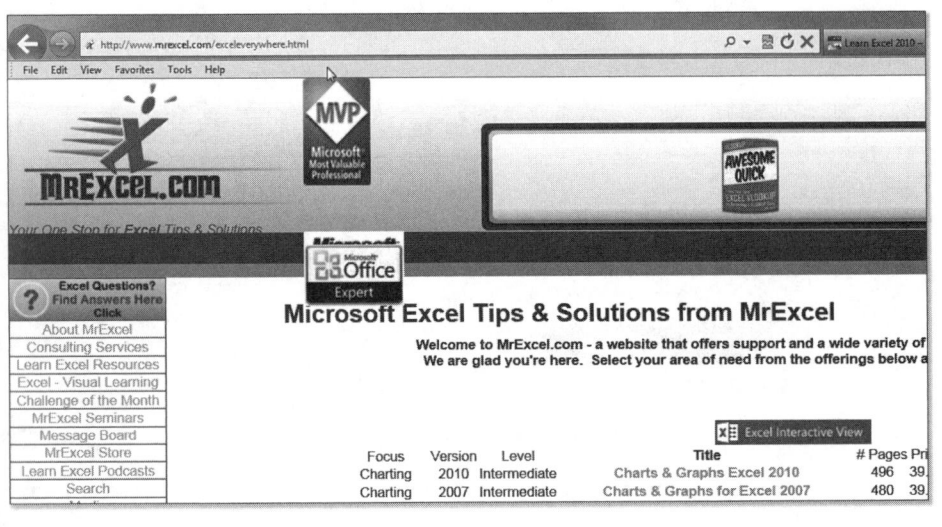

Figure 37.37
A new Excel Interactive View button appears.

The Excel Web App takes your HTML table and creates an Excel workbook on the fly. The interface lets people filter using the panel on the left. They can sort by clicking any heading (see Figure 37.38).

Figure 37.38
Filter or sort
right in the
web page.

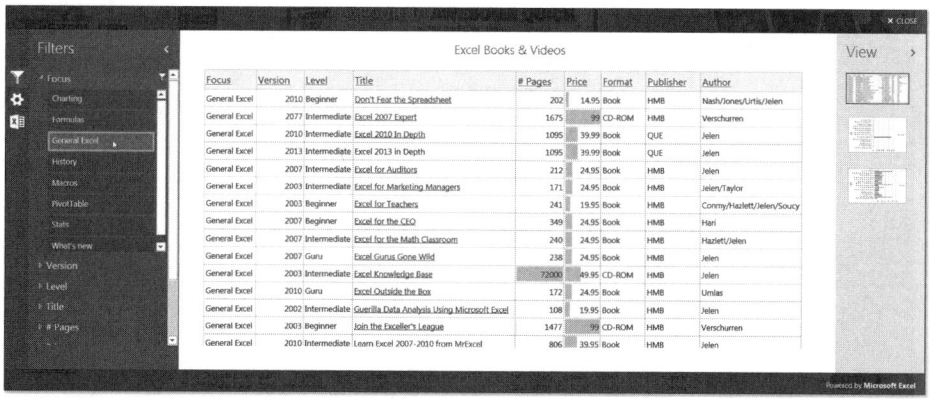

Filters are additive. After choosing General Excel as the focus, you can choose to filter to Excel 2010 or Excel 2013 by clicking on Excel 2010 and dragging to Excel 2013 (see Figure 37.39).

Figure 37.39
Numeric col-
umns have
a data bar
visualization
applied.

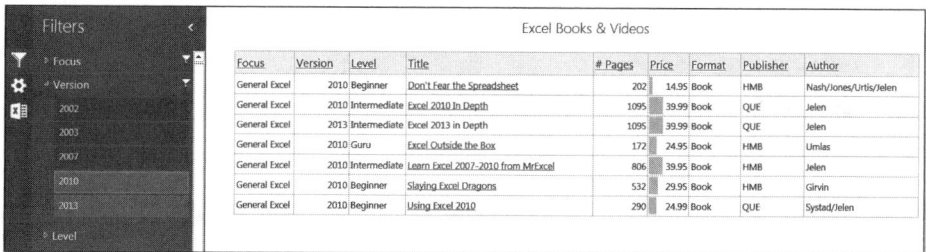

In the right panel, click on one of the chart thumbnails and the web page displays a chart of the filtered items (see Figure 37.40).

All of this happens as the result of adding three lines of code to your web page. It is simply amazing.

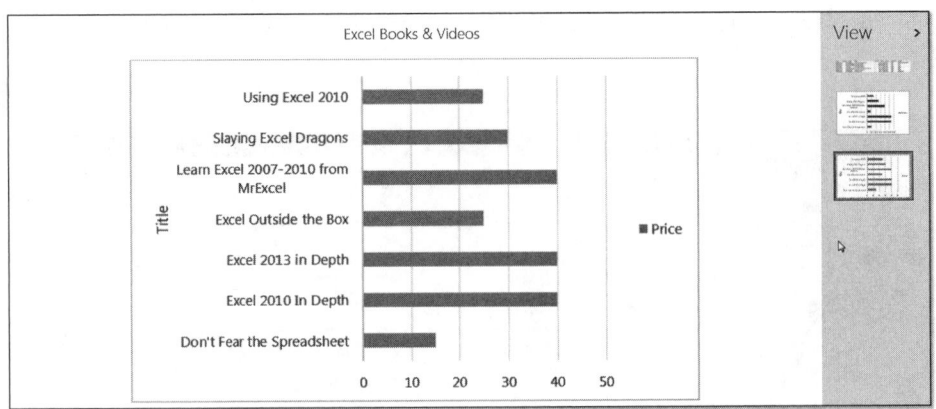

Figure 37.40
Even show the data in a chart.

Creating a PDF from a Worksheet

You can create a PDF from any workbook in Excel 2013. Think of creating a PDF as if you are "printing" to a special printer that makes PDF files. Thus, it is important that you set the print ranges before you begin. If you want multiple worksheets in your PDF, select those worksheets in Group mode before creating the PDF. (For example, select Sheet1 and then Ctrl+click the tabs for Sheet3 and Sheet7 to put those three sheets in Group mode.)

To save a worksheet as a PDF file, select File, Export, Create PDF/XPS (see Figure 37.41).

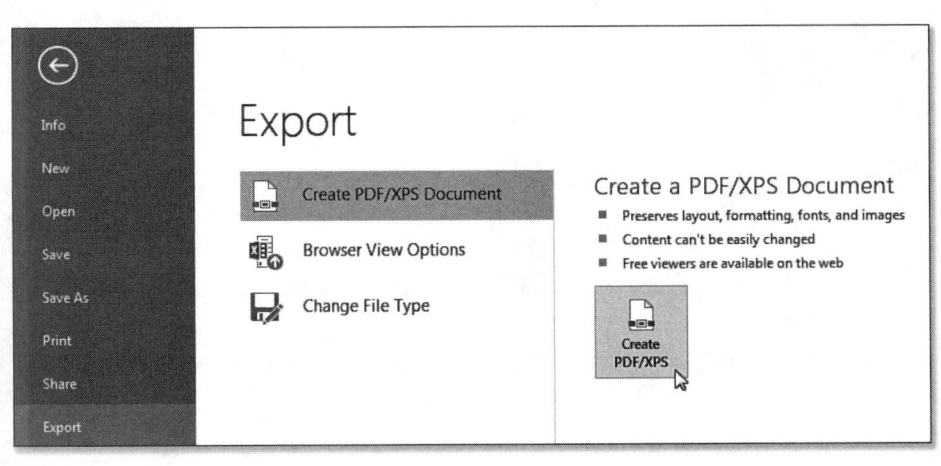

Figure 37.41
Select to create a PDF/XPS document.

You have the option to save the file in a high-resolution format suitable for printing or a low-resolution format that is suitable for viewing onscreen.

If you frequently work with PDF files, you might have noticed that some PDFs contain data that can be selected, copied, and pasted to Excel. Other PDFs contain strange formatting that causes the paste back to Excel to render horribly. You would think that a PDF file created by the Excel team would have the capability to paste back into Excel, but this is not the case. In Figure 37.42, the top left is the original data in Excel. The top right is the data in the PDF file created by Excel. The data in the bottom left is how that data was pasted back to Excel.

 Tip

If you need to convert PDF data to Excel, check out my review of Able2Extract at http://www.mrexcel.com/tip107.shtml.

Figure 37.42
Don't try to copy the PDF data and paste it back to Excel.

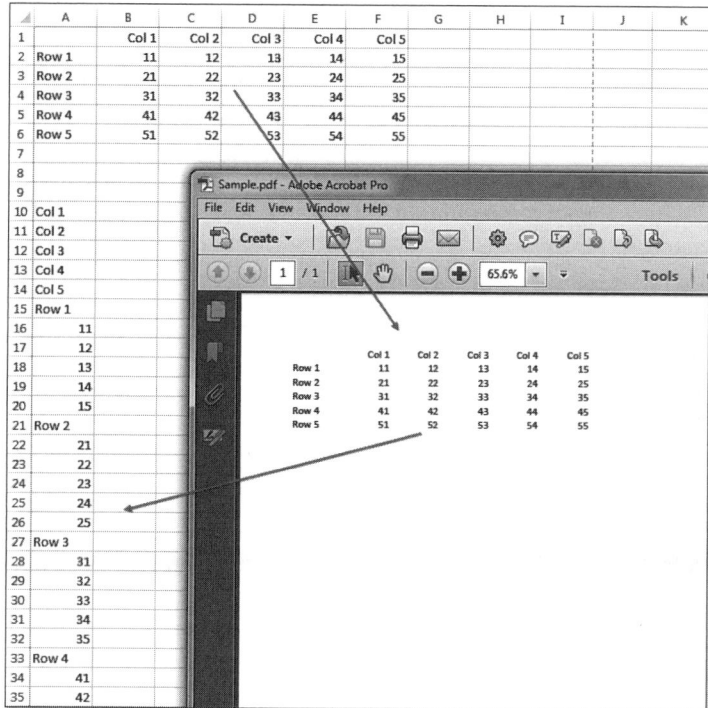

Interacting with Other Office Applications

After authoring a worksheet in Excel, you might need to include its information in a PowerPoint presentation or a Word document. Or you might want to add portions of your spreadsheet in your OneNote notebook. The collaborative nature of Office 2013 applications enable you to do this with ease.

In certain cases, you can utilize Excel data without ever opening the Excel file. If you have a list of addresses in Excel, you can access that list when doing a mail merge in Microsoft Word 2013. Excel can receive data from other Office applications. For example, you might author body copy in Word and then copy it to a text box in Excel. Data from Access can also be used as the source data for an external query in Excel or even for a pivot table.

Sending a Workbook via Outlook

The fastest way to send a workbook via email is to send it directly from Excel. If Outlook is your default email client, this is easy to do. Follow these steps:

1. Open the workbook you want to send.

2. Arrange the window so it appears as you would like it to appear for your email recipient. This might mean scrolling explanatory notes into view or making some other adjustments.

3. From the File menu, select Share, Email, Send as Attachment, as shown in Figure 37.43.

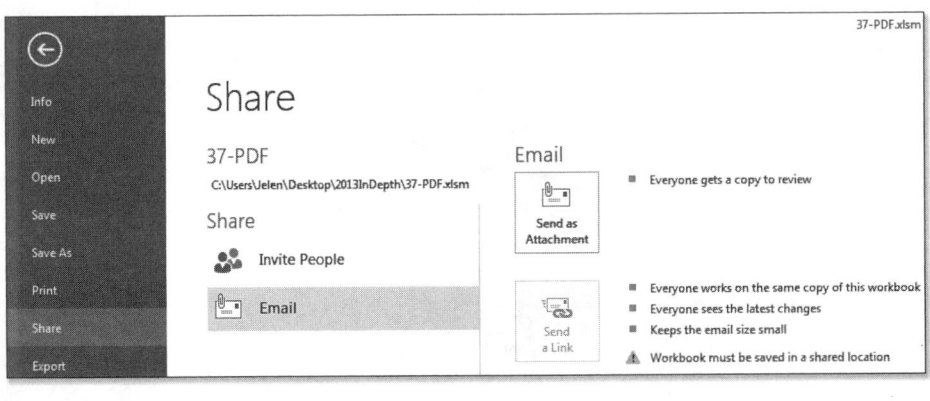

Figure 37.43
Select the Send as Attachment option.

4. Outlook opens a window that looks identical to the Outlook Send Mail window.

5. Click in the To box and type an email address or select email recipients.

6. If desired, change the subject line to something different from the filename.

7. Type any message.

8. Click the Send button to send the message and return to Microsoft Excel.

 Caution

Although the Excel Message dialog appears identical to the Outlook dialog, it is actually a modal dialog in Excel. This means that you cannot return to Excel until you have finished sending the email. If you need to look back to the Excel file to get information for the text of the email, you can try one of these two methods:

■ Drag the Message dialog out of the way by dragging the title bar. This works if the information you need is in the visible portion of the Excel window.

■ Click the Save button in the Message window to save the unsent message to the Outlook Inbox. Click the X in the upper-right corner of the Message window to return to Excel. You can now switch back and forth between Excel and Outlook to refer to specific values in any worksheet of the workbook.

Pasting Excel Data to Microsoft OneNote

In the initial release of OneNote 2003, the capability to present tabular data was dismal. OneNote 2013 now renders Excel worksheets in a tabular grid. A Table Tools tab in the OneNote ribbon enables you to do simple sorting. Figure 37.44 shows the original worksheet in Excel.

Figure 37.44
Copy the table and the chart separately.

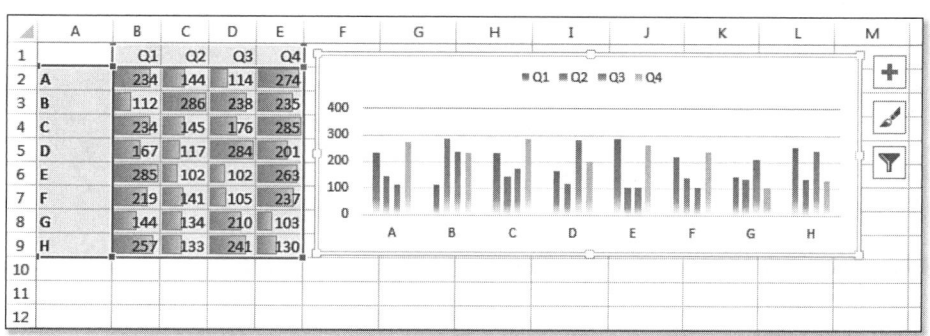

When you paste to OneNote, the chart becomes a static picture of the chart. The range of Excel cells gets pasted as a table in OneNote. In Figure 37.45, the rudimentary Sort command was used to sort by Q4 descending.

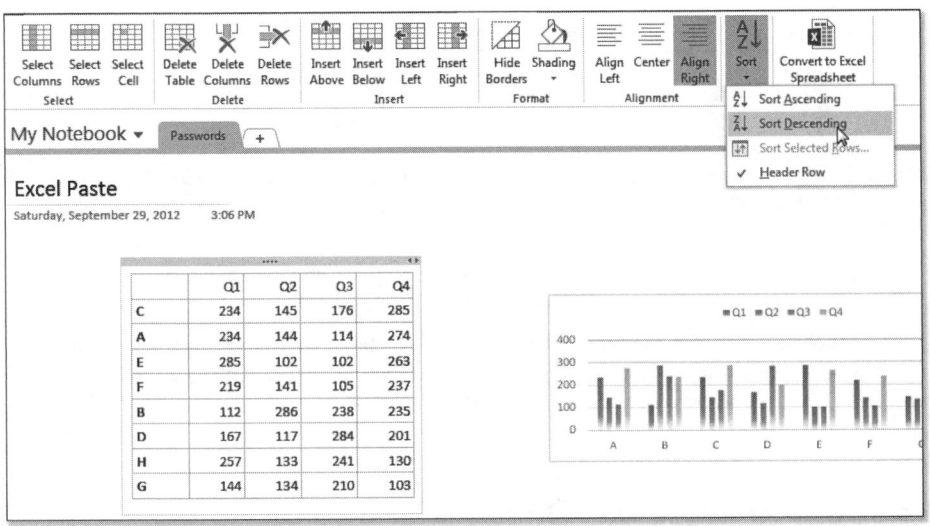

Figure 37.45
OneNote
pastes the
Excel range
as a table and
allows sorting.

Using Excel Charts in PowerPoint

The process of copying charts from Excel to PowerPoint works well in Office 2013. The resulting chart is completely editable in PowerPoint. In addition, changes to the slide theme alter the look and feel of the chart.

To copy a chart to PowerPoint, follow these steps:

1. Prepare a blank slide in PowerPoint that is ready to accept the data from Excel.

2. Open the desired Excel workbook.

3. Select the chart to be copied.

4. Press Ctrl+C to copy the selected chart.

5. Switch back to PowerPoint.

6. From the Home tab, select Paste.

The chart is pasted to the slide. You can resize the chart to fill the area on the slide. When the chart is selected in PowerPoint, three icons to the right of the chart (plus, paintbrush, and funnel) offer the same chart functionality as in Excel 2013. Three contextual ribbon tabs appear just as in Excel (see Figure 37.46). For details on using the charting tools, see Chapter 32, "Graphing Data Using Excel Charts."

Figure 37.46
All of the Excel charting tools are available after pasting to PowerPoint.

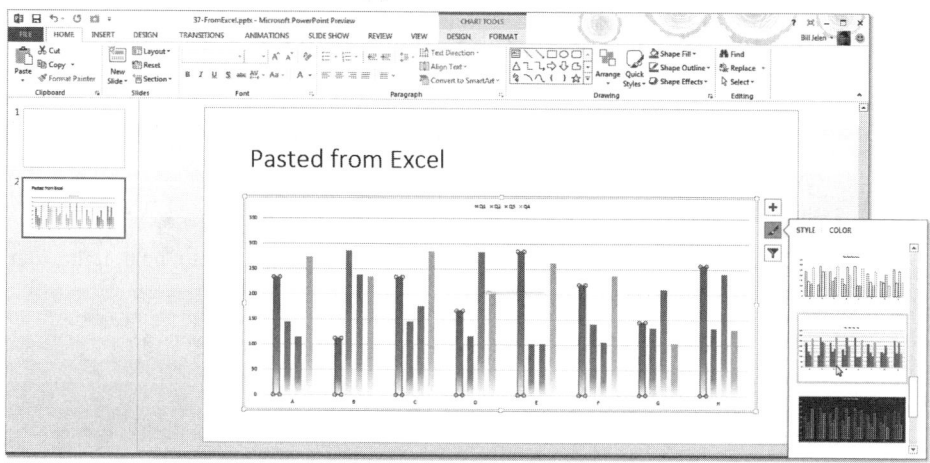

Creating Tables in Excel and Pasting to Word

Microsoft Word is excellent for typing body text. When you need to start creating tables in Word, however, the program is a bit confusing. If you are more comfortable with Excel than Word, it makes sense to switch to Excel, create and format a table, and then paste the table back to the Word document. This gives you better control over column widths, plus the possibility to provide formulas for calculating some of the content of the table.

To create a table for Word, using Excel, follow these steps:

1. Position the insertion cursor in Word at a point where the table should go.

2. Switch to Excel and create a blank workbook.

3. Type the data in columns in Excel.

4. If you use formulas to build rows of the table, it is best to convert the formulas to values before copying to Word. To do so, select the formulas and press Ctrl+C to copy. Then select Home, Paste, Paste Values.

5. If you have chosen a theme in Word, choose the identical theme in Excel.

6. Select the table and then select the Cells section of the Home tab and select Format, Width, AutoFit Selection.

7. Optionally, apply a table format.

> ➡ *To review how to apply a table format,* **see** *Chapter 19, "Fabulous Table Intelligence."*

Select the table in Excel, and then press Ctrl+C to copy. Switch to Word. From the Home tab, select Paste. An HTML representation of the table is pasted into Word. The column widths, alignment, font, font color, and fill copy perfectly from Excel.

Pasting Word Data to an Excel Text Box

Although Excel is great at handling tables of numbers, it does not have the editing tools needed to make it easy to handle body copy as well as in Word. If you want to be able to type paragraphs of text without needing to judge the length of each line, you should use Word to prepare the text and then paste it to a text box in Excel. You can follow these steps to build a section of body copy for use in Excel:

1. Switch to Microsoft Word and create a blank document.

2. Type the text. Use any formatting you like, such as underlining, bold, italic, font size, font changes, and so on.

3. Select the text in Word.

4. Press Ctrl+C to copy the selected text.

5. Switch to Excel.

6. On the Insert tab, select Shapes, Text Box.

7. Drag in the worksheet to define the shape of the text box.

8. When you release the mouse, the insertion point is at the start of the text box. Press Ctrl+V to paste.

9. By default, text boxes have a visible border. To remove the border, select Drawing Tools Format, Shape Styles, Shape Outline, No Outline.

10. If you need to resize or further format the text, select the text in the text box. The mini toolbar appears. If desired, change font size, style, and so on.

If you need to fine-tune the text box, follow these steps:

1. Click outside the text box.

2. Right-click the text box and select Format Shape. The Format Shape task pane appears.

3. In the Format Shape task pane, click Shape Options at the top. Click the third icon for Size and Properties. Expand the Text Box category. You can adjust margins or add columns in this panel.

In Figure 37.47, the text box has been adjusted to have two columns.

Figure 37.47
After copying Word text to a text box, you can use the formatting tools to fine-tune the text box.

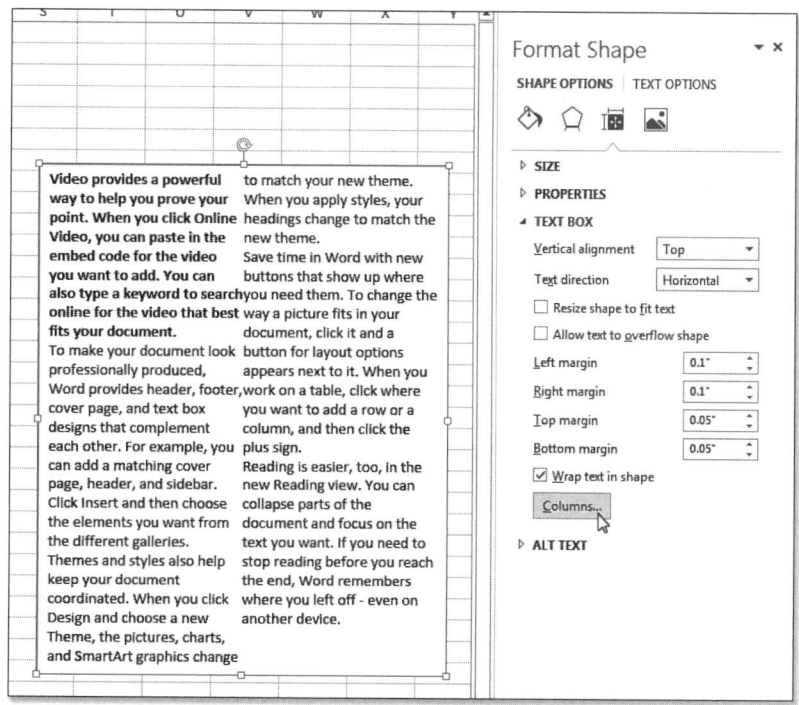

Creating Labels in Word from Excel Data

Word's mail merge tools allow you to create a form letter or labels using Excel data. Follow these steps to perform a mail merge in Word using Excel data:

1. Prepare your data in Excel. Include headings for each column. Do not include any blank columns or entirely blank rows (see Figure 37.48).

Figure 37.48
Start with a table in Excel.

	A	B	C
1	Library Name	Address	City St Zip
2	Cty Of L.A. Public Library	7400 E. Imperial Highway	Downey, CA 90241
3	Los Angeles Public Library	630 W. Fifth St.	Los Angeles, CA 90071
4	Chicago Public Library	400 South State Street	Chicago, IL 60605
5	Maricopa Cty Library	2700 N Central Ave Ste 700	Phoenix, AZ 85004
6	San Diego Public Library	820 E St.	San Diego, CA 92101
7	Orange County Public Library	1501 E. St. Andrew Place	Santa Ana, CA 92705
8	Brooklyn Public Library	10 Grand Army Plaza	Brooklyn, NY 11238
9	Miami-Dade Public Library Sys	101 West Flagler Street	Miami, FL 33130
10	Queens Borough Public Library	89-11 Merrick Boulevard	Jamaica, NY 11432
11	Riverside Public Library	3581 Mission Inn Ave.	Riverside, CA 92501
12	San Bernardino Public Library	555 W. Sixth St.	San Bernardino, CA 92410

2. To simplify the mail merge, select the range and press Ctrl+T to convert the range to a table. Be sure to specify that the table has headers.

3. Save and close the Excel workbook.

4. Open Microsoft Word.

5. Select Mailings, Start Mail Merge, Labels (see Figure 37.49).

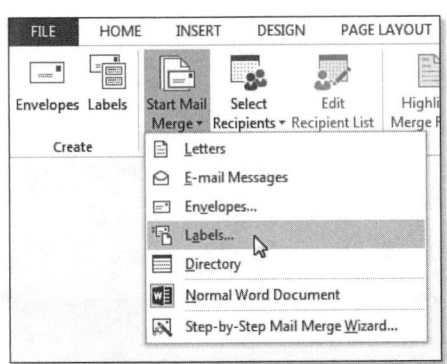

Figure 37.49
Mail merge to create labels.

6. In the Label Options dialog, choose your label vendor (such as Avery). Find the right label based on product number. Even if your labels are not made by Avery, the package probably says that the labels are compatible with Avery *NNNN* (see Figure 37.50).

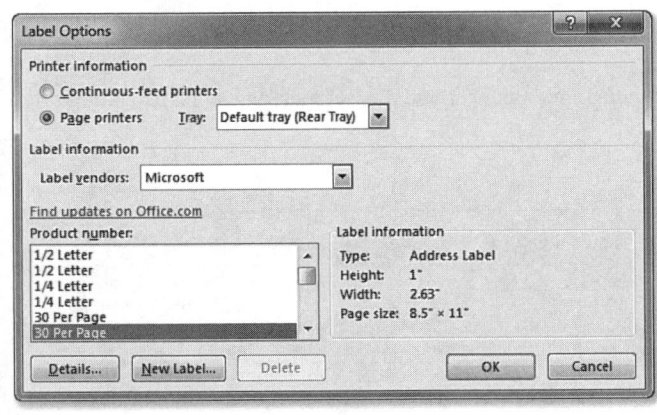

Figure 37.50
Choose the correct label size.

7. In step 2 of the task pane, select to use the current document. Click Next: Select Recipients.

8. Open the Select Recipients drop-down. Choose Use an Existing List (see Figure 37.51). The Select Data Source dialog appears.

Figure 37.51
Type a new list? Of course not, you have data in Excel!

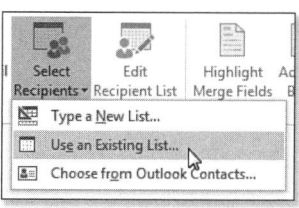

9. Browse to the right folder and select your Excel file. The Select Table dialog appears, as shown in Figure 37.52.

Figure 37.52
Choose the table you set up in step 2.

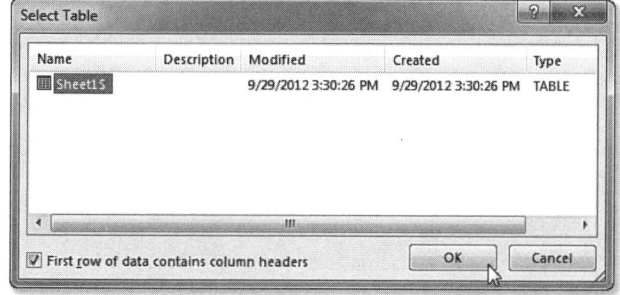

10. In the Select Table dialog, Word selects the table in your document. Click OK to confirm.

11. Open the Insert Merge Field drop-down and choose each field, one at a time. Press Shift+Enter after inserting the fields to go to a new line. At this point, you are only building the first label. You want to get that label looking correct first (see Figure 37.53).

Figure 37.53
Insert each merge field, one at a time.

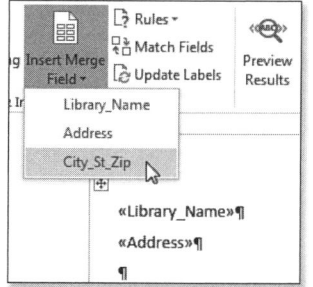

12. If you failed to use Shift+Enter instead of Enter in step 11, you end up with too much space between each line. Select those three lines. On the Home tab, open the Line Spacing drop-down and choose Remove Space Before Paragraph (see Figure 37.54).

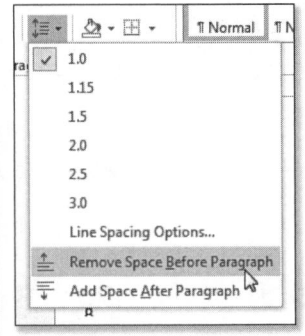

Figure 37.54
Remove space after paragraphs.

13. Do any formatting on that first label. Change the font, italic, bold, size, or anything else. Do this before going to step 14.

14. When the first label is perfect, click the Update Labels icon. Excel copies your fields to all of the labels on the page (see Figure 37.55).

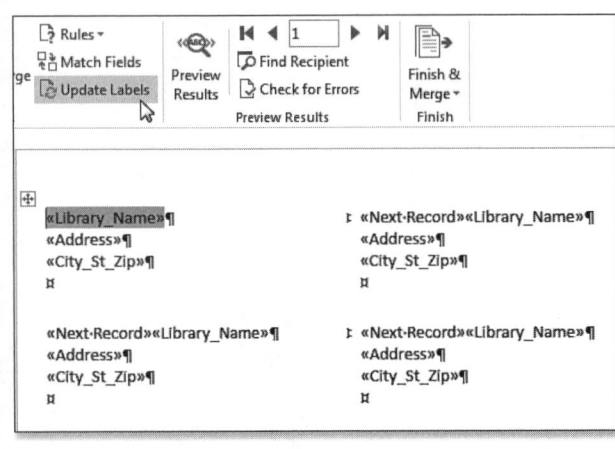

Figure 37.55
This step is the one that people seem to miss and is critical to success.

15. Open the Finish & Merge drop-down and choose Edit Individual Documents (see Figure 37.56).

Figure 37.56
This command actually does the mail merge.

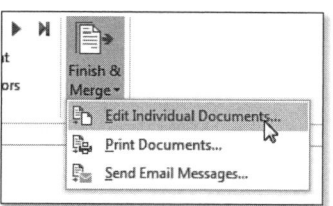

The result is multiple pages of Excel data formatted in Word, ready for you to print to your labels (see Figure 37.57).

Figure 37.57
Labels, ready to print.

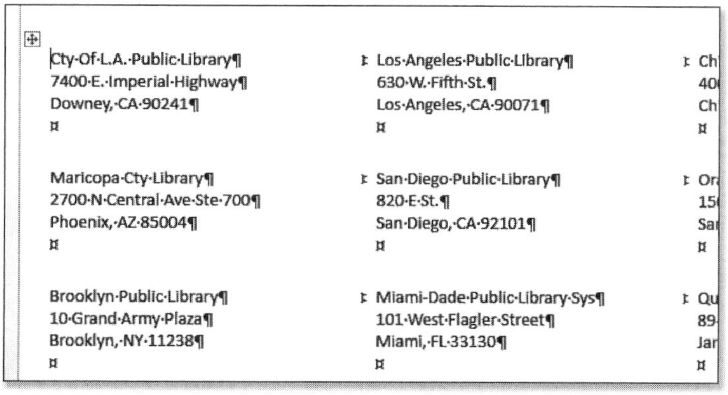

Cty·Of·L.A.·Public·Library¶	Los·Angeles·Public·Library¶	Ch
7400·E.·Imperial·Highway¶	630·W.·Fifth·St.¶	40
Downey,·CA·90241¶	Los·Angeles,·CA·90071¶	Ch
¤	¤	¤
Maricopa·Cty·Library¶	San·Diego·Public·Library¶	Or
2700·N·Central·Ave·Ste·700¶	820·E·St.¶	15
Phoenix,·AZ·85004¶	San·Diego,·CA·92101¶	Sa
¤	¤	¤
Brooklyn·Public·Library¶	Miami-Dade·Public·Library·Sys¶	Qu
10·Grand·Army·Plaza¶	101·West·Flagler·Street¶	89
Brooklyn,·NY·11238¶	Miami,·FL·33130¶	Jar
¤	¤	¤

38

SAVING TIME USING THE EASY-XL PROGRAM

My Easy-XL utility is designed to make complex data analysis tasks easy for anyone using Excel. Easy-XL adds 50 new commands to the Excel 2013 ribbon. These commands are focused on letting even a casual Exceller summarize, join, pivot, merge, match, query, categorize, combine, split, and slice and dice data like an Excel guru.

If you are already an Excel guru, you might be thinking that you can already knock out VLOOKUP and SUMPRODUCT formulas with Advanced Filter queries to do many of the tasks in this chapter. Although this is true, why would you go through all that hassle when Easy-XL can do the task in a few clicks?

As a reader of this book, you receive a 90-day license to use Easy-XL. This should be enough time for you to get through your next big data emergency. Go through an annual budget cycle using Easy-XL to split workbooks, merge data, and summarize data, and you will wonder how you ever lived without it.

If you find that Easy-XL is for you, you can buy a full license at 25% off the normal price.

Downloading and Installing Easy-XL

Easy-XL works with all 32-bit and 64-bit versions of Excel for Windows from Excel 2000 up through Excel 2013. Easy-XL runs under Windows XP, Vista, Windows 7, and Windows 8. It does not run on the Macintosh platform. To get started, visit this secret URL to download the software: www.easy-xl.com/excel2013indepth/.

After Easy-XL.exe downloads, make sure that Excel is closed. Double-click the installation file to install Easy-XL. When you load Excel, you should see a new Easy-XL tab in the Excel 2013 ribbon (see Figure 38.1).

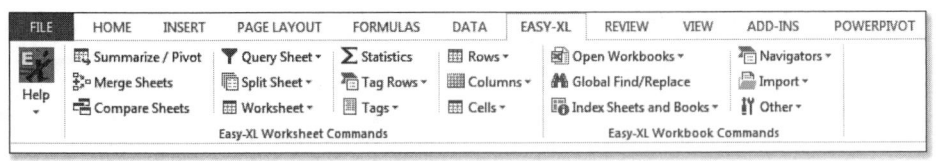

Figure 38.1
After installing Easy-XL, you should have this ribbon tab.

Easy-XL Works Best with Tabular Data

Many of Easy-XL's powerful data analytics commands are looking for tabular data. This means field headings in row 1, no blank rows, and no blank columns.

To experiment with Easy-XL, you can load up the sample workbook that ships with Easy-XL. Select Easy-XL, Other, Open Easy-XL Sample Workbook (see Figure 38.2). You get a workbook with six data worksheets. The data worksheets contain databases of invoices, products, customers, and salespeople.

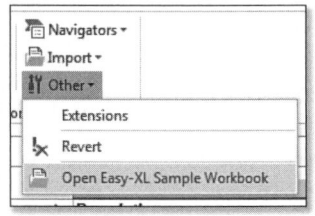

Figure 38.2
Opening the Easy-XL sample workbook. Easy-XL includes a sample data set you can use for learning the powerful Easy-XL features.

Doing Away with VLOOKUP

I love VLOOKUP. I don't know how anyone can live without knowing how to knock out VLOOKUPs with their eyes closed. However, Easy-XL enables someone who knows nothing about VLOOKUP to run circles around someone who regularly solves problems with VLOOKUP.

The Invoices 2015 worksheet in the sample data set includes a customer number column. It does not contain customer name or any other customer information. The sample workbook has a worksheet called Customer. This worksheet shows the customer name, address, city, and state for each customer number.

You want to merge data on these two sheets so that the customer name and state is included on the Invoices 2015 worksheet.

Follow these steps:

1. Start on the Invoices 2015 worksheet. Select Easy-XL, Merge Sheets. Excel displays a Select a Sheet to Merge with Invoices 2015 dialog.

2. Select Customers and click Select. Excel displays the Merge Sheets dialog.

3. In the Merge Sheets dialog, indicate that you want to group by the Customer Number field. In the right list box, select Contact Name and State. In the Merge Options section, select that you want rows in Sheet1 that match a row in Sheet2 and also rows in Sheet1 that don't match a row in Sheet2. The Merge Sheets dialog should look like the one shown in Figure 38.3. Click OK.

Figure 38.3
Combine two fields from the Customers worksheet into the Invoices worksheet.

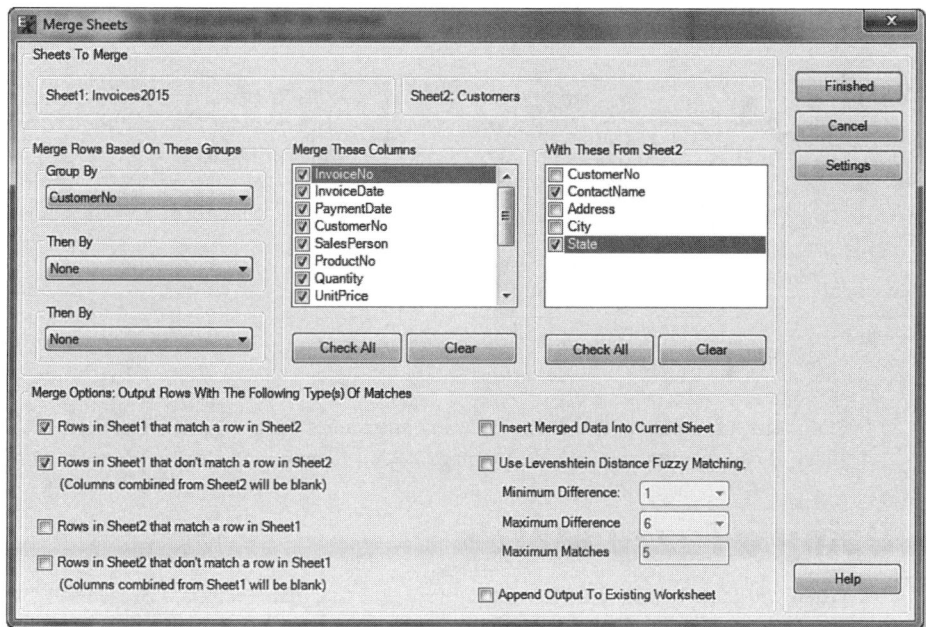

Easy-XL does several things. First, you have a brand-new worksheet called MergedInvoices2015. Second, a comment in cell A1 indicates how this sheet was created. This provides an audit trail of which worksheets were merged and how (see Figure 38.4). You never get that level of detail with the VLOOKUP method.

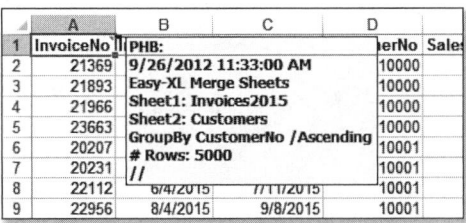

Figure 38.4
Easy-XL provides an audit trail via cell comments.

If you scroll right, you see that the data from the Customers worksheet is added to new columns. The headings indicate that the data came from the Customers worksheet (see Figure 38.5). The results are no longer formulas; you don't have to worry about using Paste Special to convert the formulas to values.

	K	L	M
	Quarter	Customers.ContactName	Customers.State
	2	Kennedy Merrill	NS
	2	Kennedy Merrill	NS
e Assurance	2	Kennedy Merrill	NS
	3	Kennedy Merrill	NS
	1	Kevon Cote De Neige	ON
	1	Kevon Cote De Neige	ON
	2	Kevon Cote De Neige	ON
	3	Kevon Cote De Neige	ON
	4	Kevon Cote De Neige	ON
	1	Annette Shields	MB

Figure 38.5
The new data is appended to the right side of the new worksheet.

Check the final rows in the data set. If any customers did not have a match in the Customers worksheet, those records appear with blank customer names at the end of the worksheet.

Using a Fuzzy Match

When you match up data from two different sources, misspellings between the lists commonly occur. This might happen if you are matching actual orders compared to a sales rep forecast. The sales reps tend to type abbreviations and have misspellings. The data from the company system tends to be spelled correctly because someone in accounts receivables is setting up the customer data.

The Easy-XL Merge dialog offers to perform something called Levenshtein Distance Fuzzy Matching. Suppose that you have two sheets: Forecast and Orders. Both sheets have a customer name and a sales amount. The names don't match well enough; they have the usual amount of errors between them.

To perform a fuzzy match, follow these steps:

1. Start on the Sales sheet.

2. Select Easy-XL, Merge Sheets.

3. Select that you want to merge with the Forecast sheet.

4. In the Merge Sheets dialog, select Use Levenshtein Distance Fuzzy Matching. In that section, you should change the default settings. You want to allow a minimum difference of zero. If you leave the Minimum Difference setting at 1, exact matches are not reported. Use a Maximum Difference setting of 6. Set Maximum Matches to 2 or 3. By using a high Maximum Difference setting, you run the risk of completely different names being reported as a fuzzy match. By limiting the match to two or three, you get only the best two or three matches.

5. In the Merge Sheets dialog, select to group by Customer. Use Check All to select all columns in both worksheets. Select both of the Rows in Sheet1 check boxes in the lower left. Your dialog box should look like Figure 38.6. Click OK.

Figure 38.6
Select a fuzzy
match.

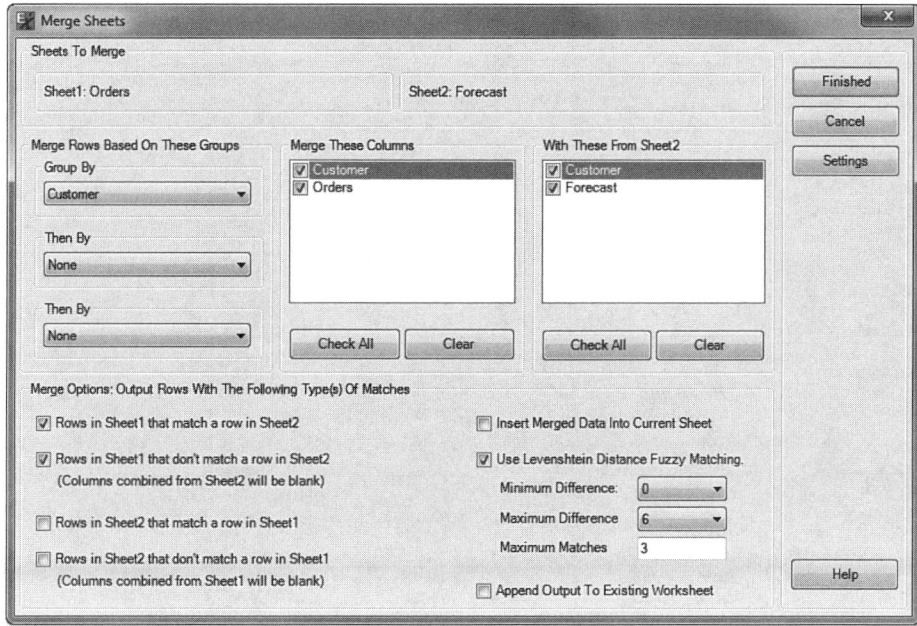

The initial results shown in Figure 38.7 are sorted by Difference. All the records at the top with a difference of zero are exact matches. When you do a fuzzy match, you need to carefully go through the results to find the best result of each pair. Here is one way to go:

1. Select all the rows that have a match of zero and apply a green fill color to those rows so that you know that they are likely the best match.

2. Sort all the rows by Tags in column F.

▲	A	B	C	D	E	F
1	Customer	Forecast.Customer	Difference	Orders	Forecast.Forecast	Tags
2	Birds Eye	Birdseye	0	14095	13000	2
3	Cooper Tire	Cooper Tire	0	20870	22000	3
4	FarmFresh	Farm Fresh	0	20987	22000	4
5	Hersheys Ice Cream	Hershey's Ice Cream	0	10860	9000	5
6	JayCo	JayCo	0	37300	36000	6
7	King Sooper	King Sooper	0	41574	43000	7
8	Matrix	Matrix	0	30582	32000	8
9	Natl Semiconductor	Natl Semiconductor	0	38563	40000	9

Figure 38.7
The best matches are shown at the top.

3. Manually go through the list, keeping only one match for each customer in column A. You need to be careful while doing this. Consider Figure 38.8.

1	Customer	Forecast.Customer	Difference	Orders	Forecast.Forecast	Tags
2	Birds Eye	Birdseye	0	14095	13000	2
3	Cooper Tire	Cooper Tire	0	20870	22000	3
4	FarmFresh	Farm Fresh	0	20987	22000	4
5	Hersheys Ice Cream	Hershey's Ice Cream	0	10860	9000	5
6	JayCo	JayCo	0	37300	36000	6
7	JayCo	Matrix	5	37300	32000	6
8	JayCo	Redbook	6	37300	35000	6
9	King Sooper	King Sooper	0	41574	43000	7
10	Matrix	Matrix	0	30582	32000	8
11	Matrix	JayCo	5	30582	36000	8
12	Matrix	Sunoco	6	30582	44000	8
13	Natl Semiconductor	Natl Semiconductor	0	38563	40000	9
14	Quaker Oats	Quaker Oats	0	35003	37000	10
15	Redbook	Redbook	0	33748	35000	11
16	Redbook	JayCo	6	33748	36000	11
17	Redbook	Sunoco	6	33748	44000	11
18	Target Stores	Target Stores	0	32414	33000	12
19	Vaseline	Vaseline	0	25086	23000	13
20	Vaseline	Matrix	6	25086	32000	13
21	Winnebago	Winnebago	0	29751	28000	14
22	Allen Bradley	Allen Bradley	0	29665	29000	15
23	Delta Airline	Delta Airlines	1	39901	41000	16
24	Sun Oil Co	Sunoco	2	43513	44000	17
25	Sun Oil Co	JayCo	6	43513	36000	17
26	Goodyear Tire	Cooper Tire	4	24091	22000	18
27	Goodyear Tire	Goodyear Tire & Rubber	6	24091	24000	18
28	Umbro	JayCo	4	24203	36000	19
29	Umbro	Matrix	5	24203	32000	19
30	Umbro	Redbook	5	24203	35000	19

Figure 38.8
After a fuzzy match, you need to carefully look through the possible matches to find the best.

- In rows 26 and 27, the fuzzy match selected Cooper Tire as the best match for Goodyear Tire. Strictly from a blind data analysis point of view, both of those strings have "_oo_er Tire" in sequence and matches closer than Goodyear Tire and Rubber. In this case, you would keep row 27 and delete row 26.

- Rows 6 through 8 are interesting. You already have an exact match in row 6, so you will obviously keep that one. In row 7, though, the program is saying that "JayCo" and "Matrix" are only off by five letters. Given that they both have an "a" in common and the second word has a stray "Mtrix," the fuzzy match is reporting this as a possible match. This could easily happen with any company name that is five or six characters long.

- In rows 28 through 30, the program comes up with possible matches for Umbro, but none of them are correct.

Go through the recordset, deleting the nonmatches. When you are done, take a look through the Tags column. The tag is the original row number on the first worksheet. You should have no gaps in that range. If a gap exists, you need to get that value from the first worksheet and add it as a possible match.

Also, you are not sure that you have a complete list from the second worksheet. You should find any records on the Forecast worksheet that don't have a match on the FuzzyMatched Sales worksheet. Follow these steps to do the Fuzzy Match in reverse:

1. Select the FuzzyMatchedSales worksheet.

2. On the Easy-XL tab, choose Merge Sheets.

3. Choose that you want to compare to the Forecast worksheet.

4. In the Merge Sheets dialog, group by Customer.

5. In the Merge Options section of the dialog, uncheck the default choices and choose Rows in Sheet2 that Don't Match a Row in Sheet1 (see Figure 38.9).

Figure 38.9
To be thorough, see if any forecast records exist that didn't match the sales.

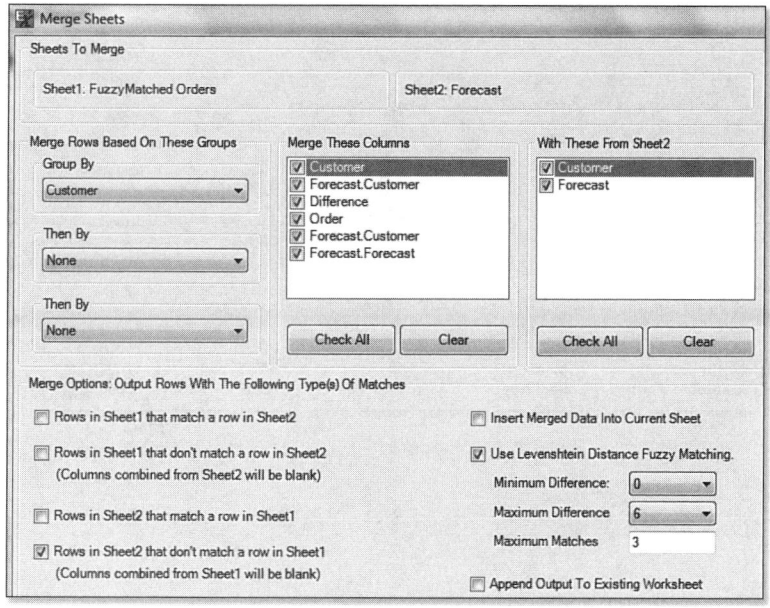

6. Click OK.

Undoubtedly, the process of manually finding the best match for the fuzzy matches is tedious. However, without Easy-XL, it would have been nearly impossible to even come up with the fuzzy matched list.

Text to Columns on Steroids

Excel has had a text-to-columns feature for two decades, so how could anyone improve on it? Here are a few ways that Easy-XL has done so:

■ When you are splitting a column into words, you can limit the maximum number of words that result. A very common problem when splitting "FirstName LastName" into words involves people with three names. "Mary Ellen Jelen," for example, always ends up spilling into three columns instead of the expected two. By limiting the result to two words, everything after Mary will be forced into the second column.

■ The delimiter drop-down offers the usual delimiters, plus all 255 ASCII characters. If you have a data set with a strange delimiter, you can break the data, even if it is a delimiter that you can't type.

■ If you need to grab the rightmost *N* characters from a column, you can do so with the Split from Right-hand Side check box.

■ Easy-XL is very smart with date columns. You can choose to produce a year, month, day, and day of the week from a single date column.

In Figure 38.10, the invoice date column is being split into years, months, days, and days of the week.

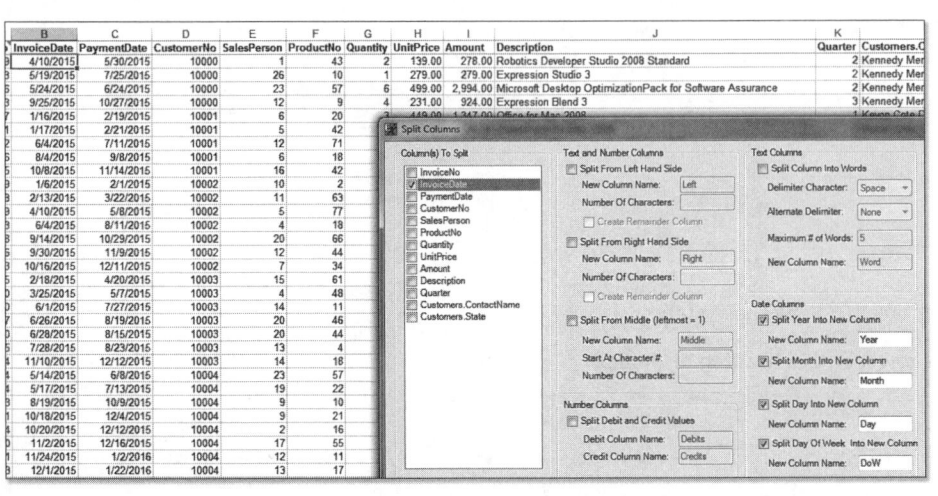

Figure 38.10
Easy-XL can split a date into columns for year, month, and day.

The result is shown in Figure 38.11. Four new columns are added to the data set.

Figure 38.11

Easy-XL adds four new columns showing Year, Month, Day, and Day of Week.

	B	C	D	E	F	
1	InvoiceDate	InvoiceDate.DoW	InvoiceDate.Day	InvoiceDate.Month	InvoiceDate.Year	Paym
2	4/10/2015	Friday	10	4	2015	5
3	5/19/2015	Tuesday	19	5	2015	7
4	5/24/2015	Sunday	24	5	2015	6
5	9/25/2015	Friday	25	9	2015	10
6	1/16/2015	Friday	16	1	2015	2
7	1/17/2015	Saturday	17	1	2015	2
8	6/4/2015	Thursday	4	6	2015	7
9	8/4/2015	Tuesday	4	8	2015	
10	10/8/2015	Thursday	8	10	2015	11
11	1/6/2015	Tuesday	6	1	2015	

Another common but difficult problem is people who have learned how to use Alt+Enter to move to a new line in a cell. Armed with this information, people start storing name, address, city, and state all in one cell. Figure 38.12 shows a list of names and addresses stored in this way. When you type Alt+Enter, you are putting a character 10 in the cell. Using the regular Text to Columns Wizard is tough because you cannot type an ASCII character 10 into the Other delimiter field in step 2. Excel MVP Bob Umlas discovered typing Ctrl+J into the Other Delimiter field in regular text to columns wizard works, but this trick is difficult to remember.

Figure 38.12

You need to break this data into columns.

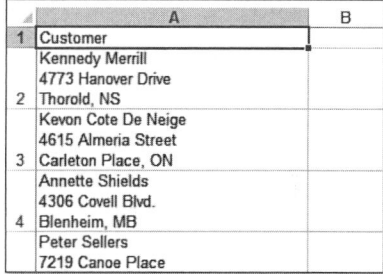

	A	B
1	Customer	
2	Kennedy Merrill 4773 Hanover Drive Thorold, NS	
3	Kevon Cote De Neige 4615 Almeria Street Carleton Place, ON	
4	Annette Shields 4306 Covell Blvd. Blenheim, MB	
	Peter Sellers 7219 Canoe Place	

To solve this problem, follow these steps:

1. Add a new row 1 with a heading of Name.

2. Select Easy-XL, Columns, Split Columns.

3. In the left list box, select Name.

4. In the top right, select Split Columns into Words.

5. Open the Delimiter drop-down. Scroll down to CHR(10). This is the code that gets typed when you press Alt+Enter.

6. Click OK.

The result is that each line of column A is split into a new column (see Figure 38.13).

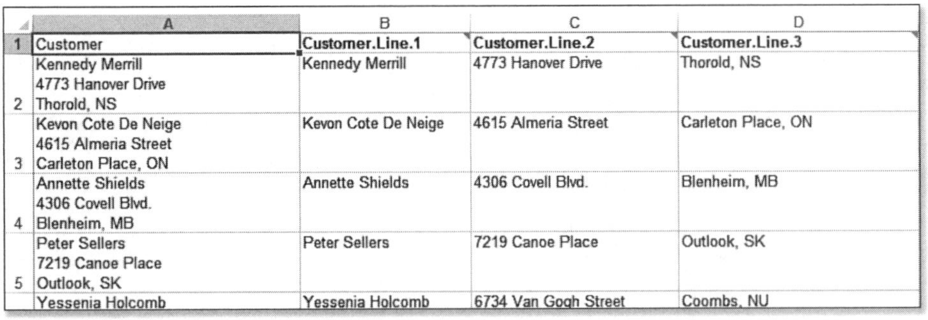

	A	B	C	D
1	Customer	Customer.Line.1	Customer.Line.2	Customer.Line.3
2	Kennedy Merrill 4773 Hanover Drive Thorold, NS	Kennedy Merrill	4773 Hanover Drive	Thorold, NS
3	Kevon Cote De Neige 4615 Almeria Street Carleton Place, ON	Kevon Cote De Neige	4615 Almeria Street	Carleton Place, ON
4	Annette Shields 4306 Covell Blvd. Blenheim, MB	Annette Shields	4306 Covell Blvd.	Blenheim, MB
5	Peter Sellers 7219 Canoe Place Outlook, SK	Peter Sellers	7219 Canoe Place	Outlook, SK
	Yessenia Holcomb	Yessenia Holcomb	6734 Van Gogh Street	Coombs, NU

Figure 38.13
Easy-XL splits each line to a new column.

Sorting Columns Left to Right

After merging sheets, you might have columns in the wrong sequence. Easy-XL offers a utility for rearranging columns. Follow these steps:

1. Select Easy-XL, Columns, Rearrange Columns. Easy-XL displays the Arrange Columns dialog with a complete list of columns.

2. Choose one column in the list and repeatedly click Move Up or Move Down to move the column.

3. Use the Rename button to create a new heading for the column.

4. Use the Format button to apply any formatting to the column.

5. Click OK.

Easy-XL rearranges the columns as you indicated.

Summarizing Data

Easy-XL offers several options for summarizing data. Suppose that you want to see total sales by state. You've already added the state field in the merge data command. Follow these steps:

1. Select Easy-XL, Summarize/Pivot.

2. Select to Group by State.

3. Select to Include Grand Totals.

4. Select to Summarize Quantity and Amount.

5. Click OK.

Easy-XL inserts a new worksheet titled Summary of Merged Invoices2015. This worksheet summarizes the 4,999 rows on the original worksheet into a tight 16-row summary. For each state, the worksheet reports the number of records, the total quantity, and the total amount.

Adding Statistics to the Report

One of the options in the Summarize/Pivot dialog is to add statistics. When you choose Select Fields, you are given a list of 30 statistics that you can add to the summary report. You can add up to 30 columns of statistics to each row in the summary table.

Getting Quick Statistics

Select any range of cells. Right-click and select Easy-XL Quick Stats. A fly-out menu appears that shows the total, min, max, median, number of positive values, number of negative values, number of errors, and so on.

Cleansing Data Without Using TRIM(), PROPER(), or CLEAN()

Data cleansing is a task that many people run into frequently. VLOOKUPs don't work because of trailing spaces. Data from websites comes in with unprintable nonbreaking spaces. Names are in uppercase instead of proper case.

You can always add a new column, enter a =PROPER() function, copy down, copy, paste values, and then cut and paste over the original data. Or you can select the cells and use the Easy-XL fly-out menu shown in Figure 38.14.

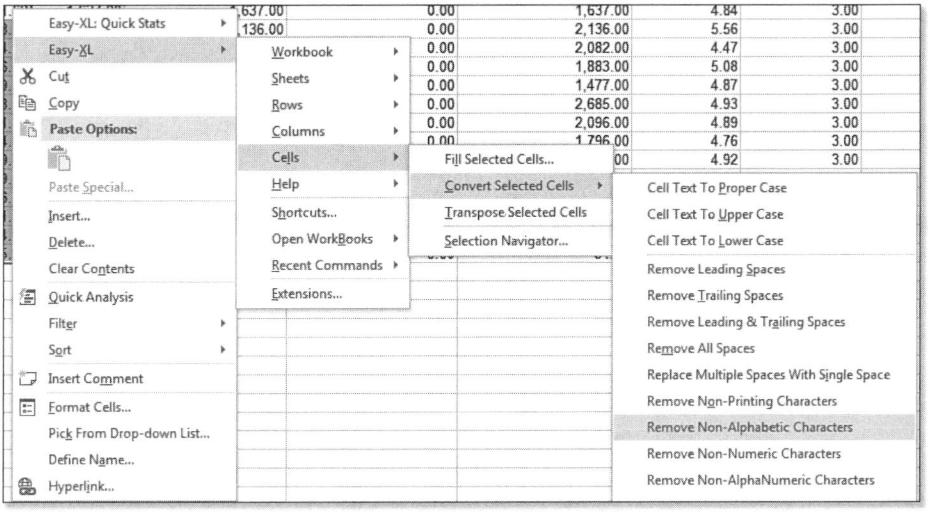

Figure 38.14 Convert case, remove spaces, and remove garbage characters.

Adding Text to Cells

This book is now nearly complete, and here is a task I have been dealing with for the 37 previous chapters: I have to produce a list of files used for the figures in the book. It is easy enough for me to use the fill handle to produce the list of filenames, as shown in Figure 38.15.

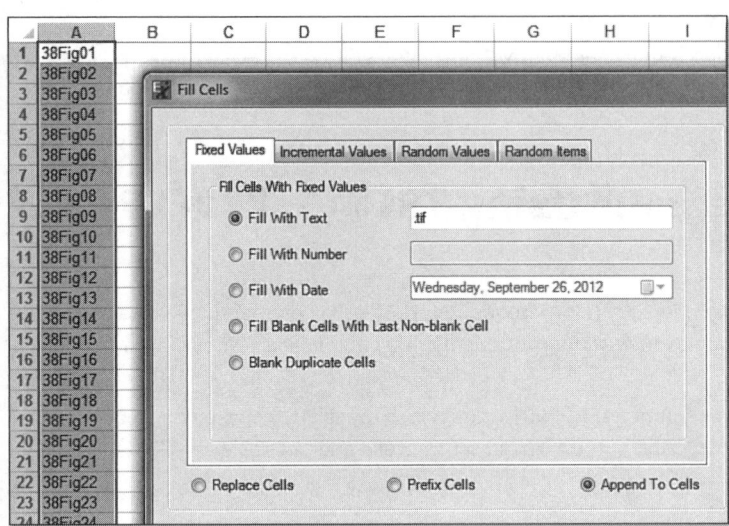

Figure 38.15
Use the fill handle, and then append .tif to each cell.

After I generate this list, I need to add ".tif" to each of those cells. Yes, I could use =A2& '.tif ', copy down, convert to values, cut, and paste. But it is so much easier to use Easy-XL, Cells, Fill Selected Cells, Fill with Text .tif, and then click Append to Cells, as shown in Figure 38.15.

After the command completes, the Fill Cells dialog stays open so that I can issue other commands. I simply click Finish when I am done.

I've been appending .tif to cells for several days in a row. Fortunately, Easy-XL remembers the last settings I used in this dialog. As soon as I select Fill Cells, the .tif is already filled in, as well as the Append to Cells setting.

Have you noticed the Settings button in every dialog? If you have a particularly complex dialog, you can save your settings and recall them later. The Settings button leads to a dialog where you can save settings for future use or load previous settings.

Filling in the Annoying Outline View

Create a pivot table with two column fields, and the default presentation leaves a lot of blanks in the outer column field. Thankfully, you can override this in Excel 2013, but a lot of people are still using old versions of Excel and can't figure out how to fill in those blanks. Use Easy-XL, Cells, Fill Selected Cells, Fill Blank Cells with Last Non-Blank Cell to fill in the Outline view.

There's More

There is still much more that can be done with Easy-XL:

- Split a worksheet out by group. Use Easy-XL, Split Sheet, By Group, and Easy-XL puts records from each state on a different worksheet.

- When Easy-XL offers Global Find and Replace, it really means *global*. I had a series of 81 Excel files out on a network drive and I knew that one of those files had the record that I was looking for. I used Global Find, and Easy-XL looked through all the records in the folder until it found the data I was looking for.

- Use Import, File and Folder Listings to bring a list of files in a folder into Excel. You can sort, filter, and so on.

- Select to Index Worksheets, and Easy-XL adds a new Index worksheet with hyperlinks to all of the worksheets in the workbook, plus a list of all cell comments in the workbook (see Figure 38.16).

Figure 38.16
Get a list of worksheets in the current workbook.

	A	B	C	D	E
1	Sheet	Type	nRows	nCols	nCells
2	Invoices2015	Sheet	5,000	13	65,000
3	Merged Invoices2015	Easy-XL Merge Sheets	5,000	17	85,000
4	Summary Of Merged Invoices2015	Easy-XL Group Summary	15	58	870
5	Sheet6	Sheet	28	1	28
6	Invoices2014	Sheet	4,263	14	59,682
7	Products	Sheet	77	9	693
8	Sheet3	Sheet	1,001	4	4,004
9	Customers	Sheet	1,001	6	6,006
10	SalesPeople2015	Sheet	27	8	216
11	SalesPeople2014	Sheet	25	8	200
12					
13		Total	16,437	138	221,699
14		Average	1,643	13	22,169
15		Max	5,000	58	85,000
16		Min	15	1	28
17					
18	Comments				
	Merged Invoices2015 (A1)	PHB: 9/26/2012 11:33:00 AM Easy-XL Merge Sheets Sheet1: Invoices2015 Sheet2: Customers GroupBy CustomerNo /Ascending # Rows: 5000			

Deal with Fiscal Years

Easy-XL adds many new functions to Excel, including `adFiscalQuarter`, `adFiscalYear`, and more (see Figure 38.17).

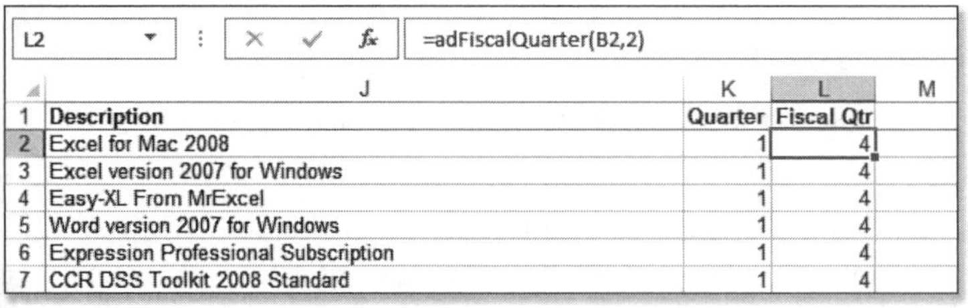

	J	K	L	M
1	Description	Quarter	Fiscal Qtr	
2	Excel for Mac 2008	1	4	
3	Excel version 2007 for Windows	1	4	
4	Easy-XL From MrExcel	1	4	
5	Word version 2007 for Windows	1	4	
6	Expression Professional Subscription	1	4	
7	CCR DSS Toolkit 2008 Standard	1	4	

Figure 38.17
Easy-XL adds some new functions to Excel.

Record Easy-XL Commands into VBA Macros

At MrExcel.com, we have an active community of Excel enthusiasts. About one-third of the questions asked at the MrExcel message board deal with VBA macros. Easy-XL is the only Excel add-in that detects whether the macro recorder is on and writes VBA code as you perform Easy-XL actions. This means that you can incorporate calls to Easy-XL into your VBA macros.

INDEX

double-declining balance depreciation, calculating, 396-397
salvage value, 393
sum-of-years'-digits, calculating, 397
useful life, 393

descriptive statistics
generating, 529
statistical functions, 439-459

Developer tab, 59

DEVSQ function, 456-459

DGET function, 371-373

dialog launchers, 52-53

dialogs
Add Watch, 182
Compress Pictures, 1104
Conditional Formatting Rules Manager, 1001
Create Pivot Table, 766
Data Table, 863
Edit Formatting Rule, 996
Evaluate Formula, 183-184
Excel Message, 1165
Excel Options, 63, 81, 85-90
External Data Range Properties, 640
File Open, 907
Find and Replace, 758-759
Format Cells, 52, 944
Format Comment, 983
Format Picture, 1126
Function Arguments, 190-192
Go To, 132, 179
Greater Than, 1004-1006
Insert Function, 189-190
legacy, selecting commands, 106-107
Name, 675-676
Name Manager, 687-689
New Formatting Rule, 52, 1009
Page Setup, 1112, 1121, 1124, 1134
Paste Options, 664
Printer Properties, 1115
Rank and Predictable, 530

Recommended Pivot Tables, 764-765
Record Macro, 884
Rename, 82
Sampling, 538
Scenario Manager, 865-872
Sort, 724
Startup Prompt, 636
Summarize/Pivot, 1184
Top 10 Filter, 795-797
Update Links, 636
Zoom, 77

digital signature lines, workbooks, adding, 931-932

DISC function, 377, 414-415

discount argument, RECEIVED function, 412

discount bonds, calculating, 417

displaying workbooks, two in two monitors, 5-9

distance, unit conversion, 596-598

distance from origin, complex numbers, finding, 581

Document Inspector, 70

documents
choosing to print, 1130-1131
comparing side by side, synchronous scrolling, 928

DOLLAR function, 206, 289-291

dollar sign entry, simplifying, F4 key, 149-153

dollar signs, references, adding to, 117

DOLLARDE function, 377, 422

DOLLARFR function, 377, 422

double-declining balance depreciation, calculating, 396-397

downloading Easy-XL utility, 1175-1176

drawing objects, eliminating, 1091

drill-down, Power View, 856

drop lines, surface charts, adding to, 1048-1049

drop-down lists, navigating, 106

DSUM function, 367-371

duplicate entries, removing, 733, 748-750

duplicate values, identifying, conditional formatting, 1008

DURATION function, 377, 420-421

dynamic named formulas, 693-694

E

Easy-XL utility, 1175, 1187-1188
cleansing data, 1185-1186
columns
sorting left to right, 1184
text-to-columns feature, 1182-1184
downloading and installing, 1175-1176
fiscal years, 1187-1188
fuzzy matches, 1178-1181
recording commands into VBA macros, 1188
summarizing data, 1184-1185
tabular data, 1176
versus VLOOKUP, 1176-1178

EDATE function, 204, 266

Edit Formatting Rule dialog, 996

editing
equations, 930-931
formulas, showing direct precedents, 180
macros, 896-897
workbooks
iPad, 1141-1142
Surface RT tablet, 1142-1144

EFFECT function, 377, 392-393

How can we make this index more useful? Email us at indexes@quepublishing.com

How can we make this index more useful? Email us at indexes@quepublishing.com

How can we make this index more useful? Email us at indexes@quepublishing.com

X-Y-Z

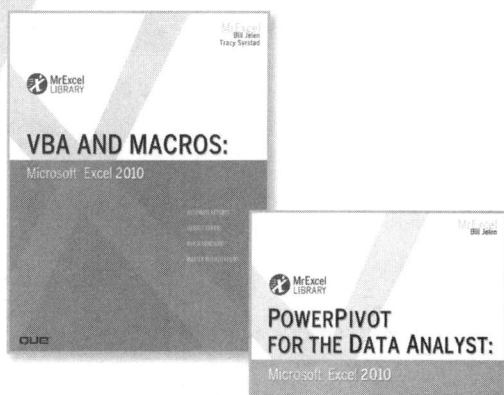

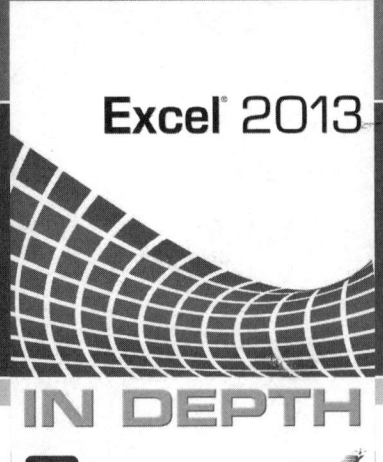

Excel® 2013

IN DEPTH

que   Bill Jalen

FREE
Online Edition

Safari
Books Online

Your purchase of *Excel 2013 In Depth* includes access to a free online edition for 45 days through the **Safari Books Online** subscription service. Nearly every Que book is available online through **Safari Books Online**, along with thousands of books and videos from publishers such as Addison-Wesley Professional, Cisco Press, Exam Cram, IBM Press, O'Reilly Media, Prentice Hall, Sams, and VMware Press.

Safari Books Online is a digital library providing searchable, on-demand access to thousands of technology, digital media, and professional development books and videos from leading publishers. With one monthly or yearly subscription price, you get unlimited access to learning tools and information on topics including mobile app and software development, tips and tricks on using your favorite gadgets, networking, project management, graphic design, and much more.

Activate your FREE Online Edition at
informit.com/safarifree

STEP 1:   Enter the coupon code: GVULPEH.

STEP 2:   New Safari users, complete the brief registration form.
            Safari subscribers, just log in.

If you have difficulty registering on Safari or accessing the online edition,
please e-mail customer-service@safaribooksonline.com

 Addison Wesley  AdobePress ALPHA  Cisco Press FT Press IBM Press. Microsoft Press  New Riders  O'REILLY

 Peachpit Press PRENTICE HALL que Redbooks SAMS SAS Publishing  vmware PRESS  WILEY wrox